THAI-ENGLISH
ENGLISH-THAI
DICTIONARY

(FOURTH REVISION)

Benjawan Poomsan Becker

เบญจวรรณ ภูมิแสน เบคเกอร์

PAIBOON

425.-

THAI-ENGLISH/ENGLISH-THAI DICTIONARY

Copyright ©2002 by Paiboon Publishing

(สำนักพิมพ์ไพบูลย์ภูมิแสน)

Printed in Thailand   All rights reserved

Paiboon Poomsan Publishing
582 Amarinniwate Village 2
Sukhapiban Road 1, Bungkum
Bangkok 10230
THAILAND
☎ 662-509-8632
Fax 662-519-5437

Paiboon Publishing
PMB 192,
1442A Walnut Street
Berkeley, California
USA 94709
☎ 1-510-848-7086
Fax 1-510-848-4521

email: paiboon@thailao.com
www.thailao.com

Cover and graphic design by Randy Kincaid
Edited by Craig Becker, Adissapong Praphantanathorn,
Kamontip Topanya, Jerapa Schaub, Preeyaporn
Chareonbutra

Printed by Chulalongkorn University Printing House
Tel. 0-2218-3563, 0-2215-3612 December, 2005 [4902-299/3,000(2)]
http://www.cuprint.chula.ac.th

PREFACE

This practical dictionary is designed to help English speakers communicate in Thai. It is equally useful for those who can read the Thai alphabet and those who can't. Whether you are visiting Thailand for a short while or living there permanently, you will find most of the vocabulary used in everyday life, including basic medical, cultural, political and scientific terms.

We suggest that you start using this book by spending some time studying the guide to pronunciation. Since every Thai word is shown in both Thai script and phonetic transliteration, it is not necessary to learn the Thai alphabet in order to use the dictionary. After a little practice you will be able to pronounce and look up Thai words using the English phonetic alphabet.

For those who are serious about studying Thai, we recommend that you learn the Thai alphabet as early as possible. To that end we have included a comprehensive guide to the Thai system of writing. The dictionary is divided into three sections: Section One [English-Phonetic-Thai], Section Two [Phonetic-Thai-English], Section Three [Thai- Phonetic-English]

Section one is for looking up words in English to find the Thai translations. Some English words have multiple meanings (e.g. 'nail' could be a fingernail or carpentry nail). In that case we often clarify in parenthesis the exact meaning of the Thai translation.

In the second section you can look up Thai words using the phonetic alphabet. For clarity and convenience, the transliteration system in the dictionary breaks up multi-syllabic words by separating syllables with a dash. Otherwise, it is the same phonetic system that is used in other Paiboon Publishing books, including *Thai for Beginners, Thai for Intermediate Learners, Thai for Advanced Readers, Thai for Lovers* and *Thai for Gay Tourists*. It accurately indicates tone, vowel length and other aspects of Thai pronunciation that may be unfamiliar to English speakers.

Section three is for looking up Thai words in the Thai alphabet. This is very useful when you are having trouble understanding a Thai friend. He/she can look up the word in your dictionary and show it to you! If you are a student of written Thai, you will soon find yourself able to use this section yourself.

Thai people are among the friendliest in the world and greatly appreciate any efforts made by foreigners to learn their language. This book has been designed to be easy to carry and to use so that you will be encouraged to keep it close at hand. We hope it will help you create new friendships and will enhance your stay in Thailand!

TABLE OF CONTENTS

4

GUIDE TO PRONUNCIATION

CHARACTERISTICS OF THE THAI LANGUAGE

Listed below are some common elements and features of
the Thai language that are different from English.

· Thai is a tonal language. Incorrect tones can
  cause the Thai speaker to be easily missunder-
  stood, even if the pronunciation is otherwise
  perfect.

· There are no variant or plural forms for adjectives
  and nouns.

· Adjectives appear after the noun.
    The Thai grammatical structure would be *'car red'* (rót
    dɛɛng) instead of the English grammatical structure *'red car'*.

· There are no verb conjugations in Thai. Tenses
  are understood from the context or from the use
  of adverbs-of-time.

· Thai has no articles (a, an, the)

· There is no verb 'to be' used with adjectives.
    'He is cute' would be *'he cute'* (káo nâa-rák).

· Thai speakers usually omit the subject of a sentence when it is understood from the context.

TRANSLITERATION

Every attempt was made to keep the transliteration in this dictionary simple and consistent. If you notice a few differences between the transliterated tones in this book compared to other Paiboon Publishing Thai language books, it is because we have tried to mimic modern colloquial use here as opposed to the "correct" tones of written Thai.

For example:

University is transliterated as 'má-hǎa-wít-ta-yaa-lai' instead of 'má-hǎa-wít-tá-yaa-lai'. Television is transliterated as 'too-ra-tát' intead of 'too-rá-tát'.

Some words borrowed from Western languages are commonly pronounced in more than one way. Young Thai people may like to pronounce the 's' sound at the end of a word, although there is no 's' ending sound in Thai.

For example:

The word 'celcius' can be pronounced as seo-sîat, sen-sîas, seo-sîat or sen-sîas.
The word 'Christmas' can be pronounced as krít-sa-mâat, krít-sa-mát or krít-sa-más.

CONSONANTS

b	as in baby	bin - fly
ch	as in chin	chûu - name
d	as in doll	duu - look
f	as in fun	fai - fire
g	as in gold	gin - eat
h	as in honey	hâa - five
j	as in jet	jèt - seven
k	as in kiss	kon - person
l	as in love	ling - monkey
m	as in money	mii - have
n	as in need	naa - rice field
p	as in pretty	pan - thousand
r	rolled like the Scottish r	rian - study
s	as in sex	sìi - four
t	as in tender	tam - do
w	as in woman	wan - day
y	as in you	yaa - medicine
kw	as in queen	kwaai - buffalo
gw	as in Guam	gwaang - deer
ng	as in ringing	ngaan - work
dt	as in stop	dtaa - eye
bp	as in spot	bpai - go

The /dt/ sound lies between the /d/ and the /t/. Similarly, the /bp/ is between /b/ and /p/ (in linguistic terms, they are both unvoiced and unaspirated). Unlike English, /ng/ frequently occurs at the beginning of words in Thai. Thai people often do not pronounce the /r/, replacing it with /l/ ('rian' will sound like 'lian'). When the /r/ is part of a consonant cluster, it is often dropped completely ('kráp' will sound like 'káp').

For final consonants of each syllable :

k is used for ก, ข, ค and ฆ.

t is used for ด, ต, จ, ช, ซ, ท, ธ, ฑ, ฒ, ถ, ฐ, ส, ศ, ษ, ฎ and ฏ.

p is used for บ, ป, พ, ฟ and ภ.

n is used for น, ณ, ร, ล, ฬ and ญ.

ng is used for ง

m is used for ม

əi, iəi is used for เ-ย

aao is used for -าว

VOWELS

Most Thai vowels have two versions, short and long. Short vowels are clipped and cut off at the end. Long ones are drawn out. This book shows short vowels with a single letter and long vowels with double letters ('a' for short; 'aa' for long).

The 'ʉ' has no comparable sound in English. Try saying 'u' while spreading your lips in as wide a smile as possible. If the sound you are making is similar to one you might have uttered after stepping on something disgusting, you are probably close!

Short & Long Vowels

a	like <u>a</u> in <u>A</u>laska	fan - teeth
aa	like <u>a</u> in f<u>a</u>ther	maa - come
i	like <u>i</u> in t<u>i</u>p	sìp - ten
ii	like <u>ee</u> in s<u>ee</u>	sìi - four
u	like <u>oo</u> in b<u>oo</u>t	kun - you
uu	like <u>u</u> in r<u>u</u>ler	sǔun - zero
ʉ	like u in ruler, but with a smile	nʉ̀ng - one
ʉʉ	like ʉ but longer	mʉʉ - hand
e	like <u>e</u> in p<u>e</u>t	sèt - finish
ee	like <u>a</u> in p<u>a</u>le	pleeng - song

ɛ	like <u>a</u> in c<u>a</u>t	lɛ́ - and
ɛɛ	like <u>a</u> in s<u>a</u>d	dɛɛng - red
ə	like <u>er</u> in teach<u>er</u> without the "r" sound	lə́ - dirty
əə	like <u>ə</u> but longer	jəə - meet
o	like <u>o</u> in n<u>o</u>te	jon - poor
oo	like <u>o</u> in g<u>o</u>	joon - robber
ɔ	like <u>au</u> in c<u>au</u>ght	gɔ́ - island
ɔɔ	like <u>aw</u> in l<u>aw</u>	nɔɔn - sleep

Complex Vowels

The following dipthongs are combinations of the above vowels.

ai	mâi - not	aai	saai - sand
ao	mao - drunk	aao	kâao - rice
ia	bia - beer	iao	nǐao - sticky
ua	dtua- body	uai	ruai - rich
ɯa	rɯa - boat	ɯai	nɯ̀ai - tired
ɔi	nɔ̀i - little	ɔɔi	kɔɔi - wait
ooi	dooi - by	əəi	nəəi - butter
ui	kui - chat	iu	hǐu - hungry
eo	reo - fast	eeo	eeo - waist
ɛo	tɛ̌o - row	ɛɛo	lɛ́ɛo - already

SHORT AND LONG VOWELS COMPARED

Short Vowel			Long Vowel		
kǎo	(เขา)	- horn	kǎao	(ขาว)	- white
kâo	(เข้า)	- to enter	kâao	(ข้าว)	- rice
jan	(จันทร์)	- moon	jaan	(จาน)	- plate
yang	(ยัง)	- yet	yaang	(ยาง)	- rubber
kun	(คุณ)	- you	kuun	(คูณ)	- to multiply
sǎi	(ใส)	- clear	sǎai	(สาย)	- late
mâi	(ไม่)	- no	mâai	(ม่าย)	- widower
jàk	(จักร)	- sewing	jàak	(จาก)	- from machine
nai	(ใน)	- in	naai	(นาย)	- Mr. (Mister)
rao	(เรา)	- we	raao	(ราว)	- about

TONE MARKS

Because Thai is a tonal language, its pronunciation presents new challenges for English speakers. If the tone is wrong, you will not be easily understood even if everything else is correct. Thai uses five tones. For example, to pronounce a rising tone your voice starts at a low pitch and goes up (much like asking a question in English). The phonetic transliteration in this book uses tone marks over the vowels to show the tone for each word. Note that the tone marks used for transliteration are different from those used in Thai script.

Tone Marks (Transliteration)

Tone	Tone Symbol	Example
mid	None	maa
low	`	màa
falling	^	mâa
high	´	máa
rising	ˇ	mǎa

TONES

Samples of the Five Tones

Words with **mid** tone:

dii	(ดี)	- good
kon	(คน)	- person
jai	(ใจ)	- heart
aai	(อาย)	- to be shy
kruu	(ครู)	- teacher

Words with **low** tone:

nùng	(หนึ่ง)	- one
sìi	(สี่)	- four
jèt	(เจ็ด)	- seven
jà	(จะ)	- will
sèt	(เสร็จ)	- to finish

Words with **falling** tone:

hâa	(ห้า)	- five
gâao	(เก้า)	- nine
nîi	(นี่)	- this
châi	(ใช่)	- correct
mâi	(ไม่)	- not, no

Words with **high** tone:

fáa	(ฟ้า)	- blue
náam	(น้ำ)	- water
chái	(ใช้)	- to use
rúu	(รู้)	- to know
rák	(รัก)	- to love

Words with **rising** tone:

mǎa	(หมา)	- dog
sǔung	(สูง)	- tall
nǎngsǔu	(หนังสือ)	- book
mǔu	(หมู)	- pig
kǎao	(ขาว)	- white

Tones, Short-Long Vowels, Similar Consonants and Vowel Sounds

When you are not understood, often you are saying the tone wrong. However, the length of the vowel is also very important. Try to get the vowel length correct. This will help you to be understood better while you are still learning to master the tones.

Here are some examples of words with different tones and their meanings.

maa	(มา)	- to come
máa	(ม้า)	- horse
mǎa	(หมา)	- dog

mai	(ไมล์)	- mile
mài	(ใหม่)	- new
mâi	(ไม่, ไหม้)	- no, to burn
mái	(มั้ย)	- ....., right?
mǎi	(ไหม)	- silk

kaao (คาว)   - fishy

kàao (ข่าว)   - news

kâao (ข้าว)   - rice

kǎao (ขาว)   - white

kào (เข่า)   - knee

kâo (เข้า)   - to enter

káo (เค้า)   - he/she

kǎo (เขา)   - animal horn

sii (ซี)   - "a particle"

sìi (สี่)   - four

sîi (ซี่)   - the classifier for "tooth"

sǐi (สี)   - color

sùa (เสื่อ)   - mat

sûa (เสื้อ)   - shirt

sǔa (เสือ)   - tiger

IRREGULAR TONES

The tone pronunciation of some common Thai words has evolved and is different from the way they are written in Thai script.

For example:

ดิฉัน (dì-chǎn) is usually pronounced ดิชั้น (dì-chán).

เขา (kǎo) is usually pronounced เค้า (káo).

ไหม (mǎi) the question particle–is usually pronounced มั้ย (mái).

The transliteration system in this book mimics the pronunciation most commonly used by modern Thai speakers. In normal speech, the tone of many initial syllables in poly-syllabic words tends to be pronounced as a mid tone, regardless of how it is written in Thai script.

For example:

à-rai sounds like a-rai in normal speech.

sà-wàt-dii sounds like sa-wàt-dii in normal speech.

COMPARISONS OF SIMILAR SOUNDS

dii	(ดี)	- good	dtii	(ตี)	- to hit
bai	(ใบ)	- leaf	bpai	(ไป)	- to go
nǔu	(หนู)	- mouse	nguu	(งู)	- snake
pèt	(เผ็ด)	- spicy	bpèt	(เป็ด)	- duck
tǔng	(ถุง)	- bag	tǔng	(ถึง)	- to
krûang	(เครื่อง)	- machine	krûng	(ครึ่ง)	- half
dao	(เดา)	- to guess	dtao	(เตา)	- stove
ùut	(อูฐ)	- camel	ùut	(อืด)	- swollen
glua	(กลัว)	- to be afraid	glua	(เกลือ)	- salt

LISTENING

When You Have Difficulty Locating a Thai Word You
Hear

PROBLEM: You may not be getting the correct first consonant or
are looking up the wrong character.
    'k' intead of 'g',
    't' intead of 'dt',
    's' intead of 'ch'.

SOLUTION: Try looking up the word under a different character.

PROBLEM: The Thai speaker may be dropping the second consonant of a cluster.
    'pom' intead of 'prom' (carpet).

SOLUTION: Check words with cluster 'r' or 'l' after the initial consonant.

PROBLEM: The Thai speaker may be using an irregular pronunciation.
    'r' often becomes 'l' in common speech ('roong-rian'-
school, bocomes 'loong-lian').

SOLUTION: Look up the word under a different character.

PROBLEM: The word may be uncommon or new slang.

SOLUTION: That word may not be listed in this dictionary. Ask a
Thai speaker to clarify it or explain it to you.

THAI WRITING SYSTEM

CONSONANT CLASSES

Thai consonants are divided into three classes — high, middle and low. Since it is one of the critical factors in determining a syllable's tone, you must know the consonant class in order to correctly pronounce what you have read. The classes are as follows:

high, middle and low

The names of the consonant classes are completely arbitrary. A low consonant may generate a high tone and a high consonant can generate a low tone, etc.

NAMES OF THE 44 THAI CONSONANTS IN ALPHABETICAL ORDER

Every Thai consonant has a name which distinguishes it from other consonants with the same sound. Since these names are standardized and universal, you can always tell Thai people how to spell a word without having to actually show them.

Consonant		Consonant Name	Sound
ก	ก ไก่	gɔɔ gài - chicken	/g/
ข	ข ไข่	kɔ̌ɔ kài - egg	/k/
ฃ	ฃ ขวด	kɔ̌ɔ kùat - bottle	/k/
ค	ค ควาย	kɔɔ kwaai - buffalo	/k/
ฅ	ฅ คน	kɔɔ kon - person	/k/
ฆ	ฆ ระฆัง	kɔɔ rá-kang - bell	/k/
ง	ง งู	ngɔɔ nguu - snake	/ng/
จ	จ จาน	jɔɔ jaan - plate	/j/
ฉ	ฉ ฉิ่ง	chɔ̌ɔ chìng - small cymbal	/ch/

ช	ช ช้าง	chɔɔ cháang - elephant	/ch/
ซ	ซ โซ่	sɔɔ sôo - chain	/s/
ฌ	ฌ เฌอ	chɔɔ chəə - a kind of tree	/ch/
ญ	ญ หญิง	yɔɔ yǐng - woman	/y/
ฎ	ฎ ชะฎา	dɔɔ chá-daa - type of crown	/d/
ฏ	ฏ ปะฏัก	dtɔɔ bpà-dtàk - type of spear	/dt/
ฐ	ฐ ฐาน	tɔɔ tǎan - base	/t/
ฑ	มณโฑ	tɔɔ mon-too - Montho the Queen	/t/
ฒ	ฒ ผู้เฒ่า	tɔɔ pûu-tâo - old man	/t/

THAI WRITING SYSTEM

ณ $^\triangle$ ณ เณร   nɔɔ neen - young monk   /n/

ด $^\circ$ ด เด็ก   dɔɔ dèk - child   /d/

ต $^\circ$ ต เต่า   dtɔɔ dtào - turtle   /dt/

ถ $^\bullet$ ถ ถุง   tɔɔ tǔng - bag   /t/

ท $^\triangle$ ท ทหาร   tɔɔ tá-hǎan - soldier   /t/

ธ $^\triangle$ ธ ธง   tɔɔ tong - flag   /t/

น $^\triangle$ น หนู   nɔɔ nǔu - mouse   /n/

บ $^\circ$ บ ใบไม้   bɔɔ bai-máai - leaf   /b/

ป $^\circ$ ป ปลา   bpɔɔ bplaa - fish   /bp/

ผ̇ ผ ผึ้ง pɔ̌ɔ pʉ̂ng - bee /p/

ฝ̇ ฝ ฝา fɔ̌ɔ fǎa - lid /f/

พ[△] พ พาน pɔɔ paan - tray /p/

ฟ[△] ฟ ฟัน fɔɔ fan - tooth /f/

ภ[△] ภ สำเภา pɔɔ sǎm-pao - a kind of ship /p/

ม[△] ม ม้า mɔɔ máa - horse /m/

ย[△] ย ยักษ์ yɔɔ yák - giant /y/

ร[△] ร เรือ rɔɔ rʉa - boat /r/

ล[△] ล ลิง lɔɔ ling - monkey /l/

ว ^Δ	ว แหวน	wɔɔ wɛ̌ɛn - ring	/w/
ศ [•]	ศ ศาลา	sɔ̌ɔ sǎa-laa - pavilion	/s/
ษ [•]	ษ ฤๅษี	sɔ̌ɔ rɯɯ-sǐi - hermit	/s/
ส [•]	ส เสือ	sɔ̌ɔ sǔa - tiger	/s/
ห [•]	ห หีบ	hɔ̌ɔ hìip - a kind of box	/h/
ฬ ^Δ	ฬ จุฬา	lɔɔ jù-laa - a kind of kite	/l/
อ [◇]	อ อ่าง	ɔɔ àang - basin	/ɔ/
ฮ ^Δ	ฮ นกฮูก	hɔɔ nók-hûuk - owl	/h/

•11 High consonants
◇9 Mid consonants
Δ24 Low consonants

44 THAI CONSONANTS IN ALPHABETICAL ORDER

ก   ข   ฃ   ค   ฅ

ฆ   ง   จ   ฉ   ช

ซ   ฌ   ญ   ฎ   ฏ

ฐ   ฑ   ฒ   ณ   ด

ต   ถ   ท   ธ   น

บ   ป   ผ   ฝ   พ

ฟ   ภ   ม   ย   ร

ล   ว   ศ   ษ   ส

ห   ฬ   อ   ฮ

ฃ and ฅ are obsolete, 11 High consonants, 9 Mid consonants, 24 Low consonants

FINAL CONSONANTS

There are eight basic final consonant sounds:

> 3 stop and
> 5 sonorant finals.

The difference is that sonorants are voiced and stops are not. If you touch your throat at the voice box, you will feel a vibration when pronouncing a sonorant, but nothing when pronouncing a stop consonant. This distinction is important for determining the tone of the syllable.

Sonorant Finals

ง	ง งู	ngɔɔ nguu - snake	/ng/
น	น หนู	nɔɔ nŭu - mouse	/n/
ม	ม ม้า	mɔɔ máa - horse	/m/
ย	ย ยักษ์	yɔɔ yák - giant	/y/
ว	ว แหวน	wɔɔ wɛ̌ɛn - ring	/w/

Stop Finals

ก	ก ไก่	gɔɔ gài - chicken[*]	/k/
ด	ด เด็ก	dɔɔ dèk - child[*]	/t/
บ	บ ใบไม้	bɔɔ bai-máai - leaf[*]	/p/

[*] Notes:

1. When ก, ด, บ and ย are initial consonants, they are transcribed as /g-/, /d-/, /b-/ and /y-/ respectively. However, when they are final consonants, they are transcribed as /-k/, /-t/, /-p/ and /-i/.

2. ว forms part of the vowels ◌ัวะ and ◌ัว, which are transcribed as /ùa/ and /ua/ respectively. ◌ิว is transcribed as /iu/ and เ◌ียว is transcribed as /iao/.

32 THAI VOWELS

อะ	อา	อิ	อี
อึ	อื	อุ	อู
เอะ	เอ	แอะ	แอ
โอะ	โอ	เอาะ	ออ
เออะ	เออ	เอียะ	เอีย
เอือะ	เอือ	อัวะ	อัว
อำ	ใอ	ไอ	เอา
ฤ	ฤๅ	ฦ*	ฦๅ*

Obsolete vowels*

THAI VOWELS PAIRED WITH SHORT AND LONG COUNTERPARTS

Short vowels are displayed in the left column and their counterparts (long vowels) are on the right.

Short Vowel		Long Vowel	
อะ	/à/	อา	/aa/
อิ	/ì/	อี	/ii/
อึ	/ù/	อือ	/ɯɯ/
อุ	/ù/	อู	/uu/
เอะ	/è/	เอ	/ee/
แอะ	/ɛ̀/	แอ	/ɛɛ/
โอะ	/ò/	โอ	/oo/

เอาะ	/ɔ́/	ออ	/ɔɔ/
อัวะ	/ùa/	อัว	/ua/
เอียะ	/ìa/	เอีย	/ia/
เอือะ	/ɯ̀a/	เอือ	/ɯa/
เออะ	/ə́/	เออ	/əə/

The following vowels may sound either short or long, but they are categorized as long vowels for tone rule purposes.

| อำ | /am/ | เอา | /ao/ |
| ใอ | /ai mái-múan/ | ไอ | /ai mái-má-lai/ |

SEVEN VOWELS THAT CHANGE THEIR FORMS

The following seven vowels change their forms when they appear in medial position.

Vowels	Final Position	Medial Position
อะ	กะ /gà/	กัด /gàt/
อือ	คือ /dtɯɯ/	คืน /dtɯɯn/
เอะ	ปะ /bpè/	เป็น /bpen/
แอะ	แตะ /dὲ/	แต็ก /dtὲk/
โอะ	โจะ /jò/	จบ /jòp/
อัว	อัว /ua/	อวน /uan/
เออ	เบอ /bəə/	เบิก /bə̀ək/

WHAT DETERMINES THE TONE

Thai incorporates a phonetic system for tones. Unless a word is irregular you can determine the tone from the way it is written. There are four elements that help determine the tone of a syllable:

Consonant Class: Whether the initial consonant is high, middle or low.

Vowel Length: Whether the vowel is short or long.

Tone Mark: Whether there is a tone mark placed above the initial consonant of a syllable. If the consonant has a superscript vowel, the tone mark is placed above that vowel.

Final Consonant: Whether there is a final consonant and, if so, whether it is a sonorant final or stop final.

LIVE AND DEAD SYLLABLES

A syllable that ends with a short vowel or a stop final consonant is called a *dead syllable*. A syllable that ends with a long vowel or a sonorant final consonant is called a *live syllable*. Rising tone and its corresponding tone mark + never occur with a *dead syllable*.

TONE RULES (IN THE ABSENCE OF TONE MARKS)

Rule 1
middle consonant with live syllable = mid tone.
For example:

กา	gaa	mid tone
กาน	gaan	mid tone

Rule 2
middle consonant with dead syllable = low tone.
For example:

กะ	gà	low tone
กาบ	gàap	low tone

Rule 3
high consonant with live syllable = rising tone.
For example:

ขา	kǎa	rising tone
ขาน	kǎan	rising tone

Rule 4

high consonant with dead syllable = low tone.
For example:

| ขะ | kà | low tone |
| ขาบ | kàap | low tone |

Rule 5

low consonant with live syllable = mid tone.
For example:

| คา | kaa | mid tone |
| คาน | kaan | mid tone |

Rule 6

low consonant with short vowel and dead syllable = high tone.
For example:

| คะ | ká | high tone |
| คับ | káp | high tone |

Rule 7

low consonant with long vowel and dead syllable = falling tone.
For example:

| คาบ | kâap | falling tone |

TONE MARKS

Thai has four tone marks. They are listed below.

Tone Mark		Name
่	(ไม้เอก)	mái èek
้	(ไม้โท)	mái too
๊	(ไม้ตรี)	mái dtrii
๋	(ไม้จัตวา)	mái jàt-dtà-waa

'mái' (ไม้) refers to the tone mark, not to the tone sound of the syllable in which it occurs. 'mái dtrii' and 'mái jàt-dtà-waa' can be used with middle consonants only.

TONE NAMES

Many Thai syllables have no tone mark at all. However, every syllable in Thai is pronounced with one of the following five tones:

Tone	Tone Name	
Mid Tone	sǐang sǎa-man	(เสียงสามัญ)
Low Tone	sǐang èek	(เสียงเอก)
Falling Tone	sǐang too	(เสียงโท)
High Tone	sǐang dtrii	(เสียงตรี)
Rising	sǐang jàt-dtà-waa	(เสียงจัตวา)

'sǐang' (เสียง) refers to the actual tone sound, not to the tone marks or tone rules that may be used in the syllable. While the tone names are similar to the tone mark names, they do not refer to the same thing. For example, the tone mark 'mái èek' (ไม้เอก) may generate the tone sound 'sǐang too' (เสียงโท) depending on the consonant class.

TONE MARKS LISTED BY CONSONANT CLASS

Middle Consonants

Mark	Tone Name	Tone		Examples
่	sĭang èek	low	ก่า	gàa
้	sĭang too	falling	ก้า	gâa
๊	sĭang dtrii	high	ก๊า	gáa
๋	sĭang jàt-dtà-waa	rising	ก๋า	gǎa

High Consonants

Mark	Tone Name	Tone		Examples
่	sĭang èek	low	ข่า	kàa
้	sĭang too	falling	ข้า	kâa

Low Consonants

Mark	Tone Name	Tone		Examples
่	sĭang too	falling	ค่า	kâa
้	sĭang dtrii	high	ค้า	káa

IRREGULAR SPELLINGS

Written Thai is quite phonetic. However, there are still many exceptions— words that are pronounced differently from the way they are spelled. Some words are borrowed from other languages such as Pali, Sanskrit and English. Others have evolved over time so that the common pronunciation today uses a different tone or vowel length from the one that the word had previously. Sometimes there is more than one correct pronunciation. Because all of these words are exceptions to the standard rules of spelling, they must be memorized. Here are some common examples of words with irregular spelling:

แฟกซ์	fèk	fax
ท่าน	tân	you, he, she
อีเมล์	ii-meo	email
ญาติ	yâat	relative
เช้า	cháao	morning
ศีรษะ	sǐi-sà	head
บอสตัน	bɔ̀t-sa-dtân	Boston
บิล	bin, biu	Bill (a man's name)
อีวาแอร์	ii-wâa-ɛɛ	Eva Airlines

เลเซอร์	lee-sôo	laser
เน็คไท	nék-tái	necktie
เก้า	gâao	nine
ไหว้	wâai	to "wai"
ไม้	máai	wood
น้ำ	náam	water
เจ้า	jâao	prince, lord
เจ้าหน้าที่	jâo-nâa-tîi	official
เท้า	táao	foot
ช่าง	châng	mechanic
จริง	jing	real
ศรัทธา	sàt-taa	have faith

OTHER SYMBOLS

Word or Phrase Repetition

ๆ (ไม้ยมก) mái yá-mók indicates the word or phrase is repeated for emphasis.

For example:

ดีๆ dii-dii - really good

Alternate Short Vowel Forms

ั (ไม้หันอากาศ) mái hăn-aa-gàat is the short vowel อะ /à/. It is written in this form when the syllable has a final consonant.

For example:

กะ gà   กัน   gan

ุ๊๊

(ไม้ไต่คู้) mái-dtài-kúu is used to change the long vowels เ (ee) and แ (εε) into the short vowels เ-ะ (è) and แ-ะ (ὲ) when the syllable has a final consonant. It also has one common irregular use; above the letter ก to create the word ก็ .

For example:

    เพน peen   เพ็น pen

Silent Syllable

ั๊

(การันต์) gaa-ran goes over a character to make that syllable silent.

For example:

    ไพบูลย์   paiboon

    จันทร์   jan

Abbreviations

ฯ (ไปยาลน้อย) bpai-yaan-nɔ́ɔi is used to show
that the word or phrase is abbreviated.

For example:

กรุงเทพฯ grung-têep - Bangkok is short for
กรุงเทพมหานคร grung-têep-ma-hǎa-ná-kɔɔn.

ฯลฯ (ไปยาลใหญ่) bpai-yaan-yài is similar to 'etc.'
in English.

Others

! (อัศเจรีย์) àt-sà-jee-rii is the exclamation
mark— a western introduction used only occasionally.

? (ปรัศนีย์) bpràt-sà-nii is the question mark—
also a western introduction used occasionally.

THAI NUMBERS

๐	ศูนย์	sǔun	0
๑	หนึ่ง	nùng	1
๒	สอง	sɔ̌ɔng	2
๓	สาม	sǎam	3
๔	สี่	sìi	4
๕	ห้า	hâa	5
๖	หก	hòk	6
๗	เจ็ด	jèt	7
๘	แปด	bpɛ̀ɛt	8
๙	เก้า	gâao	9

ALPHABET GUIDE

As you have probably noticed, the Thai language is con-
siderably different from English, and this is certainly true
with respect to the two written alphabets. Thai borrows
words from Pali, Sanskrit, English etc., but is a unique
language spoken by over 65 million people.

With some determination and effort you can master the
written Thai language yourself. A helpful way to begin
familiarizing yourself with written Thai is to seek out the
many written forms of Thai you may come across in your
travels. Signs, billboards, magazines, books and many
other written forms of Thai can be found in abundance
both in Thailand and abroad. You will notice a wide variety of font styles, some of which may take a little practice
to read and recognize.

The following character diagrams represent a cross-sec-
tion of Thai fonts and can be used as a guide to help you
in recognizing the many stylized letterforms you may
encounter.

Consonants

g [gɔɔ gài]	ก ก ก ก ก ก ก ก ก ก ก
k [kɔɔ kwaai]	ข ข ข ข ข ข ข ข ข ข ข
k [kɔɔ rá-kang]	ฆ ฆ ฆ ฆ ฆ ฆ ฆ ฆ ฆ ฆ ฆ
ng [ngɔɔ nguu]	ง ง ง ง ง ง ง ง ง ง ง
j [jɔɔ jaan]	จ จ จ จ จ จ จ จ จ จ จ
c [chɔɔ chìng]	ฉ ฉ ฉ ฉ ฉ ฉ ฉ ฉ ฉ ฉ ฉ
ch [chɔɔ cháang]	ช ช ช ช ช ช ช ช ช ช ช
s	ซ ซ ซ ซ ซ ซ ซ ซ ซ ซ ซ

ch [chɔɔ chəə]	ฌ	ฌ	ฌ	ฌ	ฌ	ฌ	ฌ	ฌ	ฌ	ฌ	ฌ	ฌ
y [yɔɔ yĭng]	ญ	ญ	ญ	ญ	ญ	ญ	ญ	ญ	ญ	ญ	ญ	ญ
d [dɔɔ chá-daa]	ฎ	ฎ	ฎ	ฎ	ฎ	ฎ	ฎ	ฎ	ฎ	ฎ	ฎ	ฎ
dt [dtɔɔ bpà-dtàk]	ฏ	ฏ	ฏ	ฏ	ฏ	ฏ	ฏ	ฏ	ฏ	ฏ	ฏ	ฏ
t [tɔ̌ɔ-tǎan]	ฐ	ฐ	ฐ	ฐ	ฐ	ฐ	ฐ	ฐ	ฐ	ฐ	ฐ	ฐ
t [tɔɔ mon-too]	ฑ	ฑ	ฑ	ฑ	ฑ	ฑ	ฑ	ฑ	ฑ	ฑ	ฑ	ฑ
t [tɔɔ pûu-tâo]	ฒ	ฒ	ฒ	ฒ	ฒ	ฒ	ฒ	ฒ	ฒ	ฒ	ฒ	ฒ
n [nɔɔ neen]	ณ	ณ	ณ	ณ	ณ	ณ	ณ	ณ	ณ	ณ	ณ	ณ
d [dɔɔ dèk]	ด	ด	ด	ด	ด	ด	ด	ด	ด	ด	ด	ด
dt [dtɔɔ dtào]	ต	ต	ต	ต	ต	ต	ต	ต	ต	ต	ต	ต

THAI WRITING SYSTEM

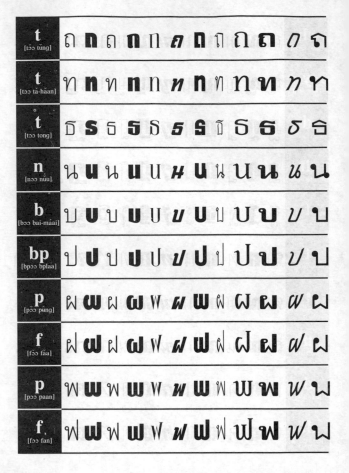

THAI WRITING SYSTEM

p [pɔɔ sǎm-pao]	ภ	ภ	ภ	ภ	ภ	*ภ*	ภ	ภ	ภ	ภ	*ภ*	ภ
m [mɔɔ ccm]	ม	ม	ม	ม	ม	*ม*	ม	ม	ม	ม	*ม*	ม
y [yɔɔ yák]	ย	ย	ย	ย	ย	*ย*	ย	ย	ย	ย	*ย*	ย
r [rɔɔ rɯa]	ร	ร	ร	ร	ร	*ร*	ร	ร	ร	ร	*ร*	ร
l [lɔɔ liŋ]	ล	ล	ล	ล	ล	*ล*	ล	ล	ล	ล	*ล*	ล
w [wɔɔ wɛɛn]	ว	ว	ว	ว	ว	*ว*	ว	ว	ว	ว	*ว*	ว
s [sɔɔ sǎa-laa]	ศ	ศ	ศ	ศ	ศ	*ศ*	ศ	ศ	ศ	ศ	*ศ*	ศ
s [sɔɔ rɯɯ-sǐi]	ษ	ษ	ษ	ษ	ษ	*ษ*	ษ	ษ	ษ	ษ	*ษ*	ษ
s [sɔɔ sɯa]	ส	ส	ส	ส	ส	*ส*	ส	ส	ส	ส	*ส*	ส
h [hɔɔ hìip]	ห	ห	ห	ห	ห	*ห*	ห	ห	ห	ห	*ห*	ห

THAI WRITING SYSTEM

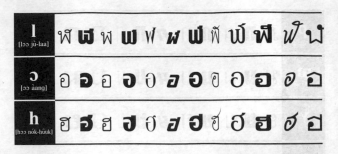

Vowels

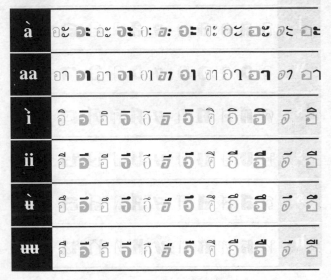

ù	อุ	อุ	อุ	อุ	อุ	อุ	อุ	อุ	อุ	อุ	อุ	อุ
uu	อู	อู	อู	อู	อู	อู	อู	อู	อู	อู	อู	อู
è	เอะ	เอะ	เอะ	เอะ	เอะ	เอะ	เอะ	เอะ	เอะ	เอะ	เอะ	เอะ
ee	เอ	เอ	เอ	เอ	เอ	เอ	เอ	เอ	เอ	เอ	เอ	เอ
ɛ̀	แอะ	แอะ	แอะ	แอะ	แอะ	แอะ	แอะ	แอะ	แอะ	แอะ	แอะ	แอะ
ɛɛ	แอ	แอ	แอ	แอ	แอ	แอ	แอ	แอ	แอ	แอ	แอ	แอ
ò	โอะ	โอะ	โอะ	โอะ	โอะ	โอะ	โอะ	โอะ	โอะ	โอะ	โอะ	โอะ
oo	โอ	โอ	โอ	โอ	โอ	โอ	โอ	โอ	โอ	โอ	โอ	โอ
ɔ̀	เอาะ	เอาะ	เอาะ	เอาะ	เอาะ	เอาะ	เอาะ	เอาะ	เอาะ	เอาะ	เอาะ	เอาะ
ɔɔ	ออ	ออ	ออ	ออ	ออ	ออ	ออ	ออ	ออ	ออ	ออ	ออ

THAI WRITING SYSTEM

ùa	อัวะ อัวะ อัวะ อัวะ อัวะ *อัวะ* อัวะ อัวะ อัวะ **อัวะ** *อัวะ* อัวะ
ua	อัว **อัว** อัว **อัว** อัว *อัว* **อัว** อัว **อัว** **อัว** *อัว* อัว
ìa	เอียะ **เอียะ** เอียะ **เอียะ** เอียะ *เอียะ* **เอียะ** เอียะ เอียะ **เอียะ** *เอียะ* เอียะ
ia	เอีย **เอีย** เอีย **เอีย** เอีย *เอีย* **เอีย** เอีย เอีย **เอีย** *เอีย* เอีย
ùa	เอือะ **เอือะ** เอือะ **เอือะ** เอือะ *เอือะ* **เอือะ** เอือะ เอือะ **เอือะ** *เอือะ* เอือะ
ua	เอือ **เอือ** เอือ **เอือ** เอือ *เอือ* **เอือ** เอือ เอือ **เอือ** *เอือ* เอือ
ə̀	เออะ **เออะ** เออะ **เออะ** เออะ *เออะ* **เออะ** เออะ เออะ **เออะ** *เออะ* เออะ
əə	เออ **เออ** เออ **เออ** เออ *เออ* **เออ** เออ เออ **เออ** *เออ* เออ
am	อำ **อำ** อำ **อำ** อำ *อำ* **อำ** อำ อำ **อำ** *อำ* อำ
ai	ใอ **ใอ** ใอ **ใอ** ใอ *ใอ* **ใอ** ใอ ใอ **ใอ** *ใอ* ใอ

ai	ไอ **โอ** ใอ **ใอ** ไอ **ไอ** ไอ ไอ ไอ **ไอ** ใอ ใอ
ao	เอา **เอา** เอา **เอา** เอา *เอา* เอา เอา เอา **เอา** *เอา* เอา
əi	เอย **เอย** เอย **เอย** เอย *เอย* เอย เอย เอย **เอย** *เอย* เอย

DICTIONARY ABBREVIATIONS

abbre.	abbreviation
adj.	adjective
adv.	adverb
art.	article
aux.	auxiliary
clf.	classifier
collq.	colloqialism
conj.	conjunction
excl.	exclamation
interj.	interjection
n.	noun
nm.	number
part.	particle
pfx.	prefix
prep.	preposition
pron.	pronoun
sfx.	suffix
v.	verb
vulg.	vulgarism

SECTION 1 ENGLISH-PHONETIC-THAI

ENGLISH • PHONETIC • THAI

A

a, *art.*, *nm.*, nùng หนึ่ง

abacus, *n.* lûuk-kít ลูกคิด

abandon, *v.* tɔ̀ɔt-tíng ทอดทิ้ง

abbreviate, *v.* yɔ̂ɔ ย่อ

abbreviation, *n.* gaan-yɔ̂ɔ การย่อ

abdomen, *n.* chɔ̂ng-tɔ́ɔng ช่องท้อง; tɔ́ɔng ท้อง

abduct, *v.* lák-paa ลักพา

abduction, *n.* gaan-lák-paa การลักพา

abet, *v.* chûai-lɛ̌a ช่วยเหลือ

abide, *v.* aa-sǎi อาศัย (live); bpà-dtì-bàt-dtaam ปฏิบัติตาม (follow)

abiding, *adj.* yút-tɛ̀a ยึดถือ (conform, comply); ton ทน (tolerate)

ability, *n.* kwaam-sǎa-mâat ความสามารถ

able, *adj.* sǎa-mâat สามารถ; gèng เก่ง

abnormal, *adj.* pìt-bpà-ga-dtì ผิดปกติ

aboard, *adv.* bon-rɯa บนเรือ (boat); bon-rót บนรถ (motor vehicle); bon-krɯ̂ang-bin บนเครื่องบิน (airplane)

abolish, *v.* lɔ̂ək-lóm เลิกล้ม (destroy or do away with); yók lɔ̂ək ยกเลิก (annul)

aborigine, *n.* kon tìn dɔɔm คนถิ่นเดิม; kon-pɯ́ɯn-mɯang คนพื้นเมือง

abort, *v.* téng แท้ง; tam-téng ทำแท้ง

abortion, *n.* tam-téng ทำแท้ง; gaan-tam-téng การทำแท้ง

about, *adv.* gìao-gàp เกี่ยวกับ (pertaining to); bprà-maan ประมาณ (approx.)

above, *adv.* nɯ̌a เหนือ; bɯ̂ang-bon เบื้องบน

abrasion, *n.* rɔɔi-sɯ̀k รอยสึก; gaan-tà-lɔ̀ɔk การถลอก

abrasive, *adj.* gàt-grɔ̀n กัดกร่อน

abroad, *adv.* dtàang-bprà-têet ต่างประเทศ

absence, *n.* gaan-mâi-yùu การไม่อยู่, gaan-kàat การขาด

absent, *adj.* mâi-yùu ไม่อยู่, kàat ขาด, mâi-maa ไม่มา

absent-minded, *adj.* jai-lɔɔi ใจลอย

absolute, *adj.* sǒm-buun สมบูรณ์ (perfect, complete); dèt-kàat เด็ดขาด (e.g. power, ruler); mâi-mii-ngɯ̂an-kǎi ไม่มีเงื่อนไข (unconditional)

absolutely, *adv.* nɛ̂ɛ-nɔɔn แน่นอน; dooi-sǒm-buun โดยสมบูรณ์

absorb, *v.* dùut ดูด; sɯm ซึม; dùut-sɯm ดูดซึม

absorption, *n.* gaan-dùut-sɯm การดูดซึม

abstain, *v.* lá-wén ละเว้น; òt อด

abstinence, *n.* gaan-lá-wén

การละเว้น

abstract, *n.* naam-ma-tam
นามธรรม

absurd, *adj.* lĕeo-lăi เหลวไหล; rái-
săa-rá ไร้สาระ

abundance, *n.* kwaam-ù-dom-sŏm-
buun ความอุดมสมบูรณ์

abundant, *adj.* ù-dom-sŏm-buun
อุดมสมบูรณ์

abuse, *v.* chái-nai-taang-tîi-pìt ใช้ใน
ทางที่ผิด (use wrongly); cham-rao
ชำเรา (rape or molest); kòm-hĕeng
ข่มเหง (physically or psychologically)

abyss, *n.* tá-lee-lúk ทะเลลึก

academic, *adj.* gìao-gàp-wi-chaa-
gaan เกี่ยวกับวิชาการ

academy, *n.* roong-rian โรงเรียน
(school); sà-tăa-ban-gaan-sùk-săa
สถาบันการศึกษา (academic institution)

accelerate, *v.* rêng เร่ง (speed up);
pôom-kûn เพิ่มขึ้น (increase)

accelerator, *n.* kan-rêng คันเร่ง
(gas pedal); dtua-rêng ตัวเร่ง (substance that increases the speed of a
reaction)

accent, *n.* sĭang-nàk เสียงหนัก
(stress); săm-niang-bplèng
สำเนียงเปล่ง (e.g. a foreign accent)

accept, *v.* yɔɔm-ráp ยอมรับ

acceptable, *adj.* yɔɔm-ráp-dâai
ยอมรับได้

acceptance, *n.* gaan-yɔɔm-ráp

การยอมรับ

access, *n.* gaan-kâo-tŭng การเข้าถึง

access, *v.* kâo-tŭng เข้าถึง

accessible, *adj.* kâo-tŭng-dâai-
ngâai เข้าถึงได้ง่าย; chái-ngaai
ใช้ง่าย

accessory, *n.* ùp-bpà-gɔɔn อุปกรณ์
(adjunct); kɔ̌ɔng-bprà-gɔ̀ɔp
ของประกอบ (supplementary item);
krûang-bprà-dàp เครื่องประดับ
(jewelry)

accident, *n.* ù-bàt-dtì-hèet อุบัติเหตุ

accidental, *adj.* bang-əən บังเอิญ

acclaim, *v.* hôo-rɔ́ɔng-yin-dii
โห่ร้องยินดี

acclimate, *v.* bpràp-dtua ปรับตัว
(adjust oneself); bpràp-dtua-hâi-
chin-gàp-aa-gàat ปรับตัวให้ชิน
กับอากาศ (adjust oneself to the
weather)

accommodate, *v.* jàt-tîi-hâi-yùu
จัดที่ให้อยู่ (provide lodging); dtɔ̂ɔn-
ráp ต้อนรับ (welcome)

accommodation, *n.* gaan-dtɔ̂ɔn-
ráp การต้อนรับ; aa-hăan-lé-tîi-pák
อาหารและที่พัก (food and lodging)

accompany, *v.* bpen-pûan
เป็นเพื่อน (be with as a companion);
maa-gàp มากับ (come with)

accomplice, *n.* pûu-sŏm-kóp
ผู้สมคบ; pûu-sŏm-rúu-rûam-kìt
ผู้สมรู้ร่วมคิด

accomplish, *v.* tam-săm-rèt

ทำสำเร็จ; ban-lú-pǒn บรรลุผล

accomplishment, *n.* kwaam-sǎm-rèt ความสำเร็จ

accord, *v.* sɔ̀ɔt-klɔ́ɔng สอดคล้อง (conform, bring into harmony); yɔɔm-dtaam ยอมตาม (acquiesce, conform); dtòk-long ตกลง (agree)

according to, *prep.* dtaam-tîi ตามที่

accordingly, *adv.* dtaam ตาม; sɔ̀ɔt-klɔ́ɔng สอดคล้อง

accordion, *n.* hìip-pleeng หีบเพลง

account, *n.* ban-chii บัญชี; rûang-raao เรื่องราว

accountable, *v.* dtɔ̂ng-ráp-pìt-chɔ̂ɔp ต้องรับผิดชอบ (responsible); dtɔ̂ng-à-tí-baai-dâai ต้องอธิบายได้ (expected to give an explanation)

accountant, *n.* nák-ban-chii นักบัญชี

accounting, *n.* wí-chaa-gaan-ban-chii วิชาการบัญชี

accumulate, *v.* sà-sǒm สะสม; pɔ̂ɔm-puun เพิ่มพูน

accuracy, *n.* kwaam-mɛ̂n-yam ความแม่นยำ

accurate, *adj.* mɛ̂n-yam แม่นยำ; tùuk-dtɔ̂ng ถูกต้อง

accuse, *v.* glàao-hǎa กล่าวหา; dtɔ̀ɔ-wâa ต่อว่า

accustom, *v.* chin ชิน; kún-kəəi คุ้นเคย

ace, *n.* dtua-yong ตัวยง (an expert); èet, èes เอซ (in playing cards)

ache, *n.* kwaam-bpùat ความปวด

achieve, *v.* tam-sǎm-rèt ทำสำเร็จ; ban-lú-pǒn บรรลุผล

achievement, *n.* kwaam-sǎm-rèt ความสำเร็จ

acid, *n.* gròt กรด

acknowledge, *v.* ráp-rɔɔng รับรอง (recognize); yɔɔm-ráp ยอมรับ (admit the existence of); sà-dɛɛng-kwaam-kɔ̀ɔp-kun แสดงความ ขอบคุณ (express thanks)

acknowledgement, *n.* gaan-yɔɔm-ráp การยอมรับ; gaan-sà-dɛɛng-kwaam-kɔ̀ɔp-kun การแสดงความ ขอบคุณ

acorn, *n.* pǒn-dtôn-óok ผลต้นโอ๊ก

acquaint, *v.* kún-kəəi คุ้นเคย (make familiar); tam-kwaam-rúu-jàk ทำความรู้จัก (cause to come to know personally)

acquaintance, *n.* kon-rúu-jàk คนรู้จัก

acquire, *v.* dâai-maa ได้มา (something); dâai-rian-rúu ได้เรียนรู้ (knowledge)

acquisition, *n.* gaan-dâai-maa การได้มา; sìng-tîi-dâai-maa สิ่งที่ ได้มา

acrobat, *n.* nák-gaai-ya-gam นักกายกรรม

across, *prep., adv.* kâam ข้าม (from one side of to the other);

dtaam-kwǎang ตามขวาง (cross-wise); yùu-lìk-kâang-nùng อยู่อีกข้างหนึ่ง (the opposite side)

act, *v.* grà-tam กระทำ; bpà-dtì-bàt ปฏิบัติ

act, *n.* chàak ฉาก (scene); lá-koon ละคร (a play)

acting, *adj.* rák-sǎa-gaan รักษาการ; gaan-sà-dɛɛng การแสดง

action, *n.* gaan-grà-tam การกระทำ; gaan-dam-nəən-gaan การดำเนินการ

activate, *v.* grà-dtûn กระตุ้น (arouse); hâi-tam-ngaan ให้ทำงาน (implement) tam-hâi-gə̀ət-paa-wá-gam-man-dtà-pâap-rang-sǐi ทำให้เกิดภาวะกัมมันตภาพรังสี (radioac-tivity)

active, *adj.* klɔ̂ɔng-klɛ̂o คล่องแคล่ว; grà-dtuu-ruu-rón กระตือรือร้น

activity, *n.* gìt-jà-gam กิจกรรม

actor, *n.* daa-raa-chaai ดาราชาย; nák-sà-dɛɛng-chaai นักแสดงชาย

actress, *n.* daa-raa-yǐng ดาราหญิง; nák-sà-dɛɛng-yǐng นักแสดงหญิง

actual, *adj.* jing จริง

actually, *adv.* dtaam-kwaam-bpen-jing ตามความเป็นจริง

acupuncture, *n.* gaan-fǎng-kěm การฝังเข็ม

adapt, *v.* bpràp-dtua ปรับตัว; bpràp-hâi-mɔ̀ ปรับให้เหมาะ

add, *v.* pɔ̂əm เพิ่ม; dtəəm เติม; pɔ̂əm-dtəəm เพิ่มเติม

addict, *v.* dtìt ติด; dtìt-yaa ติดยา

addict, *n.* kon-dtìt-yaa-sèep-dtìt คนติดยาเสพติด

addiction, *n.* gaan-dtìt-yaa-sèep-dtìt การติดยาเสพติด

addition, *n.* gaan-pɔ̂əm การเพิ่ม (the act of adding); sìng-tîi-pɔ̂əm สิ่งที่เพิ่ม (something added)

additional, *adj.* tîi-pɔ̂əm-dtəəm ที่เพิ่มเติม

address, *v.* ták-taai ทักทาย (greet)

address, *n.* tîi-yùu ที่อยู่ (for mail-ing); kam-ták-taai คำทักทาย (greeting)

addressee, *n.* pûu-ráp-jòt-mǎai ผู้รับจดหมาย

adhesive, *adj.* sǔng-yút-dtìt ซึ่งยึดติด; nǐao-dtìt เหนียวติด

adhesive tape, *n.* téep-nǐao เทปเหนียว

adjust, *v.* bpràp ปรับ; bpràp-dtua ปรับตัว (oneself); jàt จัด (manage); dàt ดัด (make fit)

adjustment, *n.* gaan-bpràp-dtua การปรับตัว; gaan-jàt การจัด

administer, *v.* jàt-gaan จัดการ; bɔɔ-rí-hǎan บริหาร

administration, *n.* gaan-bɔɔ-rí-hǎan การบริหาร; gaan-jàt-gaan การจัดการ

administrative, *adj.* gìao-gàp-gaan-bɔɔ-rí-hǎan/gaan-jàt-gaan เกี่ยวกับการบริหาร/การจัดการ

administrator, *n.* pûu-bɔɔ-ri-hăan
ผู้บริหาร

admirable, *adj.* nâa-chom-chəəi
น่าชมเชย; nâa-sàt-taa น่าศรัทธา

admiral, *n.* naai-pon-rɯa นายพล
เรือ; pon-rɯa-èek พลเรือเอก

admiration, *n.* gaan-chɯ̂un-chom
การชื่นชม

admire, *v.* chɯ̂un-chom ชื่นชม; ní-
yom นิยม

admirer, *n.* pûu-chɯ̂un-chom
ผู้ชื่นชม

admission, *n.* gaan-ráp-kâo การรับ
เข้า; gaan-yɔɔm-ráp การยอมรับ

admit, *v.* ráp-kâo รับเข้า (permit to
enter); yɔɔm-ráp ยอมรับ (accept)

admittance, *n.* gaan-à-nú-yâat-hâi-
kâo การอนุญาตให้เข้า

adolescence, *n.* wai-nùm-săao
วัยหนุ่มสาว

adolescent, *n.* wai-rûn วัยรุ่น

adopt, *v.* nam-maa-chái นำมาใช้
(to apply); líang-bpen-lûuk
เลี้ยงเป็นลูก (a child); ráp-bpen-
bùt-bun-tam รับเป็นบุตรบุญธรรม (a
child - legally)

adoption, *n.* gaan-ráp-líang-bpen-
lûuk การรับเลี้ยงเป็นลูก

adorable, *adj.* nâa-chɯ̂un-chom
น่าชื่นชม; nâa-rák น่ารัก

adore, *v.* buu-chaa บูชา; náp-tɯ̌ɯ
นับถือ

adult, *n.* pûu-yài ผู้ใหญ่

adultery, *n.* gaan-bpen-chúu
การเป็นชู้

advance, *v.* gâao-nâa ก้าวหน้า

advance, *n.* ngən-lûang-nâa
เงินล่วงหน้า

advanced, *adj.* gâao-nâa ก้าวหน้า

advancement, *n.* kwaam-gâao-nâa
ความก้าวหน้า

advantage, *n.* pŏn-bprà-yòot
ผลประโยชน์; kwaam-dâai-bprìap
ความได้เปรียบ

advantageous, *adj.* dâai-bprà-yòot
ได้ประโยชน์

adventure, *n.* gaan-pà-jon-pai
การผจญภัย

adventurer, *n.* pûu-sìang-chôok
ผู้เสี่ยงโชค; nák-pà-jon-pai
นักผจญภัย

adventurous, *adj.* chɔ̂ɔp-pà-jon-pai
ชอบผจญภัย

adverb, *n.* gà-rí-yaa-wí-sèet
กริยาวิเศษณ์

advertise, *v.* koo-sà-naa โฆษณา;
bprà-gàat ประกาศ

advertisement, *n.* gaan-koo-sà-naa
การโฆษณา

advertiser, *n.* pûu-koo-sà-naa
ผู้โฆษณา

advertising agency, *n.* bɔɔ-ri-sàt-
koo-sà-naa บริษัทโฆษณา

advice, *n.* kam-né-nam คำแนะนำ;
kam-bprùk-săa คำปรึกษา

advise, *v.* né-nam แนะนำ

adviser, advisor, *n.* tîi-bprùk-săa

ที่ปรึกษา
affair, n. rûang-sùan-dtua
เรื่องส่วนตัว (personal matter);
hèet-gaan เหตุการณ์ (event); rûang
เรื่อง (matter); rûang-chúu-sǎao
เรื่องชู้สาว (illicit romantic liaison)
affect, v. sòng-pǒn-dtɔ̀ɔ ส่งผลต่อ;
mii-pǒn-grà-tóp มีผลกระทบ
affectation, n. gaan-sêe-sɛ̂ɛng
การเสแสร้ง
affected, adj. dâai-ráp-pǒn ได้รับผล
affection, n. kwaam-chɔ̂ɔp
ความชอบ; kwaam-mêet-dtaa
ความเมตตา
affectionate, adj. mii-kwaam-rák
มีความรัก
affirm, v. ráp-rɔɔng รับรอง
afford, v. sǎa-mâat-mii-dâai
สามารถมีได้ (provide); súu-dâai
ซื้อได้ (be able to pay)
Afghanistan, n. áp-fa-gaa-nít-sà-
tǎan อัฟกานิสถาน
afraid, adj. glua กลัว
after, adv. paai-lǎng ภายหลัง
afternoon, n. dtɔɔn-bàai ตอนบ่าย
afterward, adv. paai-lǎng ภายหลัง
again, adv. ìik อีก
against, prep. dtɔ̀ɔ-dtâan ต่อต้าน
(contrary to); dtrong-gan-kâam
ตรงกันข้าม (opposite)
age, n. aa-yú อายุ (duration of life);
sà-mǎi สมัย (era, period)
aged, adj. mii-aa-yú มีอายุ

ageless, adj. mâi-yɔɔm-gɛ̀ɛ
ไม่ยอมแก่; mâi-láa-sà-mǎi ไม่ล้าสมัย
agency, n. bɔɔ-ri-sàt บริษัท (company); dtua-tɛɛn ตัวแทน (representative, agent)
agenda, n. wa-rá-gaan-bprà-chum
วาระการประชุม; raai-gaan รายการ
agent, n. dtua-tɛɛn ตัวแทน; sǎai-
láp สายลับ
aggression, n. gaan-bùk-rúk การ
บุกรุก; gaan-rúk-raan การรุกราน
aggressive, adj. gâao-ráao ก้าวร้าว
aggressor, n. kon-gâao-ráao
คนก้าวร้าว
agile, adj. wɔ̂ng-wai ว่องไว; klɔ̂ng-
klɛ̂o คล่องแคล่ว
agility, n. kwaam-wɔ̂ng-wai
ความว่องไว; kwaam-klɔ̂ng-klɛ̂o
ความคล่องแคล่ว
ago, adv. dtèe-gɔ̀ɔn แต่ก่อน; gɔ̀ɔn
ก่อน; maa-léɛo มาแล้ว
agony, n. kwaam-bpùat-ráao
ความปวดร้าว
agree, v. hěn-dûai เห็นด้วย; dtòk-
long ตกลง
agreeable, adj. nâa-pɔɔ-jai น่าพอใจ
agreement, n. gaan-dtòk-long
การตกลง
agricultural, adj. taang-gaan-gà-
sèet ทางการเกษตร
agriculture, n. gaan-gà-sèet
การเกษตร
ahead, adv. lûang-nâa ล่วงหน้า
(advance); lám-nâa ล้ำหน้า

(onward)

aid, v. chûai-lǔa ช่วยเหลือ

aid, n. kwaam-chûai-lǔa
ความช่วยเหลือ

AIDS, n. rôok-èet โรคเอดส์

ail, v. bpùai ป่วย; mâi-sà-baai
ไม่สบาย

ailing, adj. mâi-sà-baai ไม่สบาย

ailment, n. rôok-pai-kâi-jèp
โรคภัยไข้เจ็บ

aim, n. jùt-bprà-sǒng จุดประสงค์;
bpâo-mǎai เป้าหมาย

aimless, adj. rái-jùt-mǎai
ไร้จุดหมาย

air, n. aa-gàat อากาศ; lom ลม

air base, n. tǎan-táp-aa-gàat
ฐานทัพอากาศ

air-conditioned, adj. bpràp-aa-gàat
ปรับอากาศ

air-conditioner, n. krûang-bpràp-
aa-gàat เครื่องปรับอากาศ

air-conditioning, n. rá-bòp-bpràp-
aa-gàat ระบบปรับอากาศ

aircraft, n. krûang-bin เครื่องบิน

aircraft carrier, n. rua-ban-túk-
krûang-bin เรือบรรทุกเครื่องบิน

air force, n. gɔɔng-tap-aa-gàat
กองทัพอากาศ

airline, n. sǎai-gaan-bin สายการบิน

airmail, n. bprai-sà-nii-aa-gàat
ไปรษณีย์อากาศ

airplane, n. krûang-bin เครื่องบิน

airport, n. sà-nǎam-bin สนามบิน;

tâa-aa-gàat-sà-yaan ท่าอากาศยาน

airsick, adj. mao-krûang-bin
เมาเครื่องบิน

aisle, n. taang-dəən-rá-wàang-tîi-
nâng ทางเดินระหว่างที่นั่ง

Akha, n. ii-gɔ̂ɔ อีก้อ (a hill tribe)

alarm, n. sǎn-yaan สัญญาณ

alarm clock, n. naa-lí-gaa-bplùk
นาฬิกาปลุก

album, n. sà-mùt-gèp-pâap
สมุดเก็บภาพ

alchemy, n. gaan-lên-rɛ̂ɛ-bprɛɛ-
tâat การเล่นแร่แปรธาตุ

alcohol, n. ɛɛn-gɔɔ-hɔɔ แอลกอฮอล์

alcoholic, adj. dtìt-sù-raa ติดสุรา

alert, adj. dtriam-prɔ́ɔm เตรียมพร้อม

algebra, n. pii-chá-ka-nít พีชคณิต

alias, n. naam-fɛɛng นามแฝง

alien, adj., n. dtàang-dâao ต่างด้าว

alienate, v. tam-hâi-hɔ̌ɔn-hàang
ทำให้เหินห่าง

alike, adj. mǔan-gan เหมือนกัน

alimony, n. kâa-liang-duu-pan-ra-
yaa ค่าเลี้ยงดูภรรยา

alive, adj. mii-chii-wít มีชีวิต

all, pron. táng-mòt ทั้งหมด

all-around, adj. tûa-túk-hèng
ทั่วทุกแห่ง

allegiance, n. kwaam-jong-rák-pàk-
dii ความจงรักภักดี; gaan-bpà-dtì-
yaan-dton การปฏิญาณตน

allegory, n. gaan-bprìap-tiap
การเปรียบเทียบ

allergic, *adj.* bpen-rôok-puum-péɛ เป็นโรคภูมิแพ้; péɛ แพ้

allergy, *n.* rôok-puum-péɛ โรคภูมิแพ้

alley, *n.* dtrɔ̀ɔk ตรอก; taang-kɛ̂ɛp ทางแคบ; sɔɔi ซอย

alliance, *n.* pan-ta-mít พันธมิตร; sà-hà-pan สหพันธ์

alligator, *n.* jɔɔ-ra-kêe จระเข้

all-out, *adj.* dtem-tii เต็มที่

allow, *v.* à-nú-yâat อนุญาต; yɔɔm-hâi ยอมให้

allowance, *n.* gaan-à-nú-yâat การอนุญาต; ngən-chái-sɔ̌i เงินใช้สอย

alloy, *n.* loo-hà-pà-sǒm โลหะผสม

all right, *adj.* bplɔ̀ɔt-pai ปลอดภัย; châi ใช่; sà-baai-dii สบายดี

ally, *n.* fàai-pan-tá-mít ฝ่ายพันธมิตร

almanac, *n.* bpà-dtì-tin-bprà-jam-bpii ปฏิทินประจำปี

almond, *n.* má-lét-an-môn เมล็ดอัลมอนด์

almost, *adv.* gùap เกือบ

alms, *n.* taan ทาน; kɔ̌ɔng-bɔɔ-ri-jàak ของบริจาค

alone, *adj.* kon-diao คนเดียว; dooi-lam-pang โดยลำพัง

along, *adv.* dtaam ตาม (the road); dûai-gan ด้วยกัน (together with)

alongside, *adv.* yùu-kâang อยู่ข้าง; dìt-gàp ติดกับ

aloud, *adv.* dang-dang ดังๆ

alphabet, *n.* àk-sɔ̌ɔn- อักษร; pá-yan-cha-ná พยัญชนะ

alphabetical, *adj.* riang-dtaam-àk-sɔ̌ɔn เรียงตามอักษร

already, *adv.* lɛ́ɛo แล้ว; rîap-rɔ́ɔi-lɛ́ɛo เรียบร้อยแล้ว

also, *adv.* ìik-dûai อีกด้วย; chên-diao-gàp เช่นเดียวกับ

altar, *n.* tên-buu-chaa แท่นบูชา

alter, *v.* bplìan เปลี่ยน

alternate, *v.* sà-làp-gan สลับกัน

alternative, *adj.* ìik-taang-nùng อีกทางหนึ่ง

although, *conj.* tǔng-méɛ-wâa ถึงแม้ว่า

altitude, *n.* kwaam-sǔung-nǔa-rá-dàp-náam-ta-lee ความสูงเหนือระดับน้ำทะเล

altogether, *adv.* prɔ́ɔm-gan พร้อมกัน (at the same time); ruam-táng-sîn รวมทั้งสิ้น (total)

aluminum, *n.* à-luu-mi-nîam อลูมิเนียม

alumna, *n.* sìt-gào-yǐng ศิษย์เก่าหญิง

alumni, *n.* sìt-gào ศิษย์เก่า

alumnus, *n.* sìt-gào-chaai ศิษย์เก่าชาย

always, *adv.* sà-mǝ̌ǝ เสมอ; dtà-lɔ̀ɔt-wee-laa ตลอดเวลา

a.m., *abbre.* gɔ̀ɔn-tîang ก่อนเที่ยง

amateur, *n.* muu-sà-màk-lên มือสมัครเล่น

amaze, v. tam-hâi-bprà-làat-jai
ทำให้ประหลาดใจ

amazement, n. kwaam-bprà-làat-jai ความประหลาดใจ

amazing, adj. nâa-bprà-làat-jai น่าประหลาดใจ

ambassador, n. èek-àk-ka-râat-chá-tûut เอกอัครราชทูต

amber, adj. sǐi-am-pan สีอำพัน

amber, n. am-pan อำพัน

ambidextrous, adj. tà-nàt-táng-sɔ̌ɔng-muu ถนัดทั้งสองมือ

ambulance, n. rót-pa-yaa-baan รถพยาบาล

ambush, n. gaan-sûm-joom-dtii การซุ่มโจมตี

America, n. sà-hà-rát-a-mee-ri-gaa สหรัฐอเมริกา

American, n. kon-a-mee-ri-gan คนอเมริกัน (people); gìao-gàp-à-mee-ri-gaa เกี่ยวกับอเมริกา (related to America)

amnesia, n. gaan-sǔun-sǐa-kwaam-song-jam การสูญเสียความทรงจำ

amnesty, n. gɔɔn-à-pai-ya-tôot การอภัยโทษ

among, prep. nai-mùu ในหมู่; rá-wàng ระหว่าง

amorous, adj. jâo-chúu เจ้าชู้; sà-dɛɛng-kwaam-rák แสดงความรัก

amortize, v. pòn-cham-rá-nîi ผ่อนชำระหนี้

amount, n. jam-nuan จำนวน

amp, ampere, n. gam-lang-grà-

sɛ̌ɛ-fai-fáa กำลังกระแสไฟฟ้า

ample, adj. pɔɔ-piang พอเพียง

amplify, v. kà-yǎai-kwaam-tìi-sǐang ขยายความถี่เสียง

amputate, v. dtàt-ɔɔk ตัดออก

amulet, n. krûang-raang เครื่องราง

amuse, v. tam-hâi-plɔ̂ɔt-plɔɔn ทำให้เพลิดเพลิน; tam-hâi-kòp-kǎn ทำให้ขบขัน

amusement, n. kwaam-kòp-kǎn ความขบขัน

amusement park, n. sǔan-sà-nùk สวนสนุก

amusing, adj. kòp-kǎn ขบขัน

an, art., nm., nùng หนึ่ง

anal, adj. gìao-gàp-tá-waan-nàk เกี่ยวกับทวารหนัก

analyst, n. nák-wí-krɔ́ นักวิเคราะห์

analytical, adj. gìao-gàp-gaan-wí-krɔ́ เกี่ยวกับการวิเคราะห์

analyze, v. wí-krɔ́ วิเคราะห์

anarchism, n. à-naa-típ-bpà-dtai อนาธิปไตย

anatomy, n. gaai-ya-wí-pâak-sàat กายวิภาคศาสตร์

ancestor, n. ban-pá-bù-rùt บรรพบุรุษ

ancestry, n. wong-dtrà-guun วงศ์ตระกูล

anchor, n. sà-mɔ̌ɔ-rua สมอเรือ

ancient, n. boo-raan โบราณ

and, conj. lɛ́ และ; gàp กับ

anemia, n. loo-hìt-jaang โลหิตจาง

English • Phonetic • Thai

anesthetic, *n.* yaa-sà-lòp ยาสลบ
angel, *n.* tee-wa-daa เทวดา
(male); têep-tí-daa เทพธิดา
(female)
anger, *n.* kwaam-gròot ความโกรธ
angle, *n.* mum มุม
angry, *adj.* gròot โกรธ
anguish, *n.* kwaam-glàt-glûm
ความกลัดกลุ้ม
anguished, *adj.* glàt-glûm
กลัดกลุ้ม; jèp-bpùat เจ็บปวด
animal, *n.* sàt สัตว์
ankle, *n.* kɔ̂ɔ-táao ข้อเท้า
announce, *v.* bprà-gàat ประกาศ
announcement, *n.* gaan-bprà-gàat
การประกาศ
announcer, *n.* pûu-bprà-gàat
ผู้ประกาศ
annoy, *v.* róp-guan รบกวน; tam-
hâi-ram-kaan ทำให้รำคาญ
annoyance, *n.* kwaam-nâa-ram-
kaan ความน่ารำคาญ
annoying, *adj.* nâa-ram-kaan
น่ารำคาญ
annual, *adj.* bprà-jam-bpii ประจำปี;
túk-bpii ทุกปี
annuity, *n.* ngɤn-raai-dâai-bpen-
raai-bpii เงินรายได้เป็นรายปี
annul, *v.* yók-lɤ̂ɤk ยกเลิก
anonymity, *n.* gaan-bpìt-bang-chʉ̂ʉ
การปิดบังชื่อ
anonymous, *adj.* mâi-rá-bù-chʉ̂ʉ
ไม่ระบุชื่อ; ní-ra-naam นิรนาม

another, *adj.* ìik อีก; yàang-nʉ̀ng
อย่างหนึ่ง
answer, *n.* kam-dtɔ̀ɔp คำตอบ
ant, *n.* mót มด
antagonism, *n.* gaan-dtɔ̀ɔ-dtâan
การต่อต้าน (resistance); kwaam-
bpen-bpɔɔ-ra-bpàk ความเป็นปรปักษ์
(hostility, being an enemy)
antagonist, *n.* pûu-dtɔ̀ɔ-dtâan
ผู้ต่อต้าน
antagonize, *v.* dtɔ̀ɔ-dtâan ต่อต้าน;
bpen-sàt-dtruu เป็นศัตรู
Antarctica, *n.* tá-wîip-ɛɛn-dtáak-
dtì-gâa ทวีปแอนตาร์คติกา
antenna, *n.* sǎo-aa-gàat เสาอากาศ
anthem, *n.* pleeng-châat เพลงชาติ
anthropologist, *n.* nák-maa-nút-
sa-yá-wít-ta-yaa นักมานุษยวิทยา
anthropology, *n.* maa-nút-sa-yá-
wít-ta-yaa มานุษยวิทยา
anti-, *v.* dtɔ̀ɔ-dtâan ต่อต้าน
antibiotic, *n.* yaa-bpà-dtì-chii-wa-
ná ยาปฏิชีวนะ
anticipate, *v.* kâat-wǎng คาดหวัง
antidote, *n.* yaa-gɛ̂ɛ-pít ยาแก้พิษ
antique, *n.* kɔ̌ɔng-gào ของเก่า
antler, *n.* kǎo-gwaang เขากวาง
anus, *n.* tá-waan-nàk ทวารหนัก
anxiety, *n.* kwaam-gang-won
ความกังวล
anxious, *adj.* gang-won กังวล
any, *adj.* baang บ้าง; nǎi ไหน; dai
ใด

English · Phonetic · Thai

anybody, anyone, *pron.* krai-krai
ใครๆ; krai-gɔ̂ɔ-dâai ใครก็ได้

anyhow, *adv.* yàang-rai-gɔ̂ɔ-dtaam
อย่างไรก็ตาม; yang-gai-gɔ̂ɔ-dtaam
ยังไงก็ตาม

anything, *pron.* à-rai-gɔ̂ɔ-dtaam
อะไรก็ตาม; à-rai-gɔ̂ɔ-dâai อะไรก็ได้

anyway, *pron.* yàang-rai-gɔ̂ɔ-dtaam
อย่างไรก็ตาม

anywhere, *adv.* tîi-nǎi-gɔ̂ɔ-dtaam
ที่ไหนก็ตาม; tîi-nǎi-gɔ̂ɔ-dâai
ที่ไหนก็ได้

apart, *adv.* dtàang-hàak ต่างหาก

apartment, *n.* aa-páat-mént
อาพาร์ตเมนท์

ape, *n.* ling ลิง

apologize, *v.* kɔ̌ɔ-tôot ขอโทษ

apology, *n.* kam-kɔ̌ɔ-tôot คำขอโทษ

apparent, *adj.* chát-jeen ชัดเจน;
paai-nɔ̂ɔk ภายนอก

appeal, *v.* ùt-tɔɔn อุทธรณ์ (request
for a new hearing); dʉng-dùut-jai
ดึงดูดใจ (attract)

appear, *v.* bpraa-gòt ปรากฏ; sà-
dɛɛng-dtua แสดงตัว

appearance, *n.* gaan-bpraa-got-
dtua การปรากฏตัว; lák-sà-nà-paai-
nɔ̂ɔk ลักษณะภายนอก

appendectomy, *n* gaan-pàa-dtàt-
sâi-dtìng การผ่าตัดไส้ติ่ง

appendicitis, *n.* sâi-dtìng-àk-sèep
ไส้ติ่งอักเสบ

appendix, *n.* pâak-pa-nùak
ภาคผนวก

appetite, *n.* kwaam-yàak-aa-hǎan
ความอยากอาหาร

appetizer, *n.* aa-hǎan-rîak-náam-
yɔ̂i อาหารเรียกน้ำย่อย

appetizing, *adj.* jà-rəən-aa-hǎan
เจริญอาหาร

applaud, *v.* bpròp-mʉʉ ปรบมือ

applause, *n.* sǐang-bpròp-mʉʉ
เสียงปรบมือ

apple, *n.* ép-bpən แอปเปิล

appliance, *n.* krʉ̂ang-mʉʉ
เครื่องมือ; ùp-bpà-gɔɔn อุปกรณ์

applicant, *n.* pûu-sà-màk ผู้สมัคร

application, *n.* bai-sà-màk ใบสมัคร
(form); gaan-nam-bpai-chái-ngaan
การนำไปใช้งาน (putting into use)

applied, *adj.* tîi-bprà-yúk-chái
ที่ประยุกต์ใช้; tîi-bpen-bprà-yòot
ที่เป็นประโยชน์

apply, *v.* bprà-yúk ประยุกต์ (put
into action); taa ทา (put on); sà-
màk สมัคร (for employment)

appoint, *v.* dtɛŋ-dtâŋ แต่งตั้ง;
gam-nòt กำหนด

appointment, *n.* gaan-dtɛŋ-dtâŋ
การแต่งตั้ง (act of appointing); nát
นัด (a date)

appraisal, *n.* gaan-bprà-məən
การประเมิน; gaan-dtii-raa-kaa
การตีราคา

appraise, *v,* bprà-məən ประเมิน
(evaluate); dtii-raa-kaa ตีราคา
(estimate the amount of)

apprehend, *v.* jàp-kǎng จับขัง

(arrest); kâo-jai เข้าใจ (understand)

approach, v. kâo-glâi เข้าใกล้

approach, n. gaan-kâo-glâi
การเข้าใกล้ (act of approaching);
wí-tii-gaan วิธีการ (means)

appropriate, adj. mɔ̀-sǒm เหมาะสม

approval, n. gaan-hěn-dûai
การเห็นด้วย; gaan-à-nú-mát
การอนุมัติ

approve, v. hěn-dûai เห็นด้วย
(agree with); pɔɔ-jai พอใจ (be satisfied); à-nú-mát อนุมัติ (give consent)

approximate, adj. dooi-bprà-maan
โดยประมาณ (about; almost exact)

approximate, v., adj. glâi-kiang
ใกล้เคียง (come close to)

April, n. dʉan-mee-sǎa-yon
เดือนเมษายน

apron, n. pâa-gan-bpʉ̂an
ผ้ากันเปื้อน

aptitude, n. kwaam-tà-nàt
ความถนัด (ability); wǎi-prip
ไหวพริบ (intelligence)

aquarium, n. pí-pít-ta-pan-sàt-náam
พิพิธภัณฑ์สัตว์น้ำ

aquatic, adj. yùu-dtâai-náam
อยู่ใต้น้ำ; taang-náam ทางน้ำ

Arab, n. chaao-aa-ràp ชาวอาหรับ

Arabia, n. aa-ra-bia อาระเบีย

Arabian, adj. gìao-gàp-aa-ràp
เกี่ยวกับอาหรับ (related to Arab)

Arabic, n. ǎa-sǎa-aa-ràp

ภาษาอาหรับ (language); lêek-aa-
ra-bìk เลขอาระบิค (number)

arbitrary, adj. dtaam-am-pəə-jai
ตามอำเภอใจ

arbor, n. súm-dtôn-máai ซุ้มต้นไม้

arc, n. sùan-kóong ส่วนโค้ง;
kwaam-kóong ความโค้ง

arcade, n. yâan-kǎai-kɔ̌ong
ย่านขายของ (a commercial area);
aa-kèet อาร์เคด

arch, n. sên-kóong เส้นโค้ง (line);
bprà-dtuu-kóong ประตูโค้ง (gate)

archeologist, n. nák-boo-raan-na-
ka-dii นักโบราณคดี

archeology, n. boo-raan-na-ka-dii
โบราณคดี

archer, n. nák-ying-ta-nuu นักยิงธนู

architect, n. sà-tǎa-bpà-ník
สถาปนิก

architectural, adj. gìao-gàp-sà-tǎa-
bpàt-dtà-ya-gam เกี่ยวกับสถาปัตย
กรรม

architecture, n. sà-tǎa-bpàt-dtà-ya-
gam สถาปัตยกรรม

arctic, n. áak-dtìk อาร์กติก

area, n. pʉ́ʉn-tîi พื้นที่; bɔɔ-ri-ween
บริเวณ; sǎa-kǎa-wí-chaa สาขาวิชา

area code, n. rá-hàt-too-ra-sàp
รหัสโทรศัพท์

arena, n. sà-nǎam-gii-laa สนามกีฬา

argue, v. tiang เถียง; à-pí-bpraai
อภิปราย

argument, n. gaan-dtôo-tiang

English · Phonetic · Thai

การโต้เถียง; kɔ̂ɔ-pí-sùut ข้อพิสูจน์

arise, *v.* gòɔt-kûn เกิดขึ้น (happen); lúk-kûn ลุกขึ้น (get up)

arithmetic, *n.* lêek-ka-nít เลขคณิต

arm, *n.* kɛ̌ɛn แขน (body part); aa-wút อาวุธ (weapon)

armed, *adj.* mii-aa-wút มีอาวุธ

armed forces, *n.* gɔɔng-táp-kɔ̌ɔng-bprà-têet กองทัพของประเทศ

armful, *n.* mâak มาก; dtem-muu เต็มมือ

armpit, *n.* rák-rée รักแร้

army, *n.* gɔɔng-táp-bòk กองทัพบก

aroma, *n.* glìn-hɔ̌ɔm กลิ่นหอม

around, *adv.* rɔ̂ɔp รอบ (with a circular motion; in circumference; from all directions); nai-bɔɔ-ri-ween ในบริเวณ (a specific place)

arouse, *v.* grà-dtûn กระตุ้น; bplùk ปลุก

arrange, *v.* jàt จัด; dtriam เตรียม

arrangement, *n.* gaan-jàt-dtriam การจัดเตรียม

arrest, *v.* jàp-gum จับกุม

arrival, *n.* gaan-maa-tǔng การมาถึง

arrive, *v.* maa-tǔng มาถึง; bpai-tǔng ไปถึง

arrogance, *n.* kwaam-yìng-yá-sǒo ความหยิ่งยโส

arrogant, *adj.* yìng หยิ่ง; jɔɔng-hɔ̌ɔng จองหอง

arrow, *n.* lûuk-ta-nuu ลูกธนู; lûuk-sɔ̌ɔn ลูกศร

arson, *n.* gaan-lɔ́ɔp-waang-plɤɤng การลอบวางเพลิง

art, *n.* sǐn-la-bpà ศิลปะ; ngaan-fǐi-muu งานฝีมือ

artery, *n.* sên-lûat-dɛɛng เส้นเลือดแดง

arthritis, *n.* kɔ̂ɔ-dtɔ̀ɔ-àk-sèep ข้อต่ออักเสบ

article, *n.* bòt-kwaam บทความ (e.g. newspaper); raai-gaan รายการ (object or item); kam-nam-nâa-naam คำนำหน้านาม (part of speech)

articulate, *v.* pûut-chát-jeen พูดชัดเจน

artificial, *adj.* bplɔɔm ปลอม; tiam เทียม

artillery, *n.* bpuun-yài ปืนใหญ่

artisan, *n.* châng-fǐi-muu ช่างฝีมือ

artist, *n.* sǐn-la-bpin ศิลปิน

artistic, *adj.* gìao-gàp-sǐn-la-bpà เกี่ยวกับศิลปะ; mii-rót-sà-ní-yom มีรสนิยม

artistry, *n.* lák-sà-nà-taang-sǐn-la-bpà ลักษณะทางศิลปะ

as, *adv.* dtaam-tîi ตามที่; chên-diao-gàp เช่นเดียวกับ

ash, *n.* tâo เถ้า (fire residue); àt-tì อัฐิ (remains after cremation)

ashamed, *adj.* àp-aai อับอาย; lá-aai-jai ละอายใจ

ashore, *adv.* gɤɤi-fàng เกยฝั่ง

ashtray, *n.* tîi-kìa-bù-rìi ที่เขี่ยบุหรี่

Asia, *n.* ee-chia เอเชีย

Asian, *n.* gìao-gàp-ee-chia เกี่ยวกับเอเชีย; kon-ee-chia คนเอเชีย

aside, *adv.* bpai-taang-kâang ไปทางข้าง (toward the side); nɔ̂ɔk-nǔa-jàak นอกเหนือจาก (besides)

ask, *v.* tǎam ถาม

asleep, *adj.* làp หลับ

aspect, *n.* lák-sà-nà ลักษณะ (appearance); ngɛ̂ɛ-mum แง่มุม (a mental perspective)

ass, *n.* gôn ก้น (bottom); laa ลา (donkey)

assassin, *n.* pûu-lɔ̂ɔp-kâa ผู้ลอบฆ่า

assassinate, *v.* lɔ̂ɔp-kâa ลอบฆ่า

assassination, *n.* gaan-lɔ̂ɔp-kâa การลอบฆ่า

assault, *v.* joom-dtii โจมตี (raid); tam-ráai ทำร้าย (hurt, injure)

assault, *n.* gaan-joom-dtii การโจมตี; gaan-tam-ráai การทำร้าย

assemble, *v.* rûap-ruam รวบรวม (gather); bprà-chum ประชุม (have a meeting); bprà-gɔ̀ɔp-chín-sùan ประกอบชิ้นส่วน (put together)

assembly, *n.* gaan-chum-num การชุมนุม; sà-mát-chaa สมัชชา

assembly line, *n.* nɛɛo-bprà-gɔ̀ɔp-chín-sùan แนวประกอบชิ้นส่วน

assess, *v.* bprà-mɜɜn ประเมิน (estimate); gam-nòt-gann-jàai-paa-sǐi กำหนดการจ่ายภาษี (impose a tax)

assessment, *n.* gaan-bprà-mɜɜn การประเมิน

asset, *n.* sáp-sǐn ทรัพย์สิน (valuable item that is owned); kɔ̌ɔng-mii-kâa ของมีค่า (valuable item)

assign, *v.* gam-nòt กำหนด (set apart for a particular purpose); mɔ̂ɔp-mǎai มอบหมาย (designate, appoint)

assignment, *n.* nâa-tîi หน้าที่ (duty); gaan-bâan การบ้าน (homework)

assimilate, *v.* ao-yàang เอาอย่าง; tam-hâi-mǔan ทำให้เหมือน

assist, *v.* chûai ช่วย

assistance, *n.* gaan-chûai-lǔa การช่วยเหลือ

assistant, *n.* pûu-chûai ผู้ช่วย

associate, *v.* kóp-hǎa คบหา

association, *n.* sà-maa-kom สมาคม

assort, *v.* lɯ̂ak เลือก (choose); bɛ̀ng-bprà-pêet แบ่งประเภท (sort)

assorted, *adj.* lɯ̂ak เลือก; bɛ̀ng-bprà-pêet แบ่งประเภท

assortment, *n.* gaan-lɯ̂ak-sǎn การเลือกสรร; gaan-mii-làak-lǎai การมีหลากหลาย

assume, *v.* sǎn-ní-tǎan สันนิษฐาน; núk-ao นึกเอา

assumption, *n.* gaan-sǎn-ní-tǎan การสันนิษฐาน; kɔ̂ɔ-sǒm-mút ข้อสมมุติ

assurance, *n.* gaan-ráp-rɔɔng

การรับรอง; kwaam-chûa-mân
ความเชื่อมั่น

assure, v. tam-hâi-mân-jai
ทำให้มั่นใจ; tam-hâi-nɛ̂ɛ-nɔɔn
ทำให้แน่นอน

asthma, n. rôok-hɔ̀ɔp-hùut
โรคหอบหืด

astonish, v. tam-hâi-ngong
ทำให้งง; tam-hâi-dtòk-jai
ทำให้ตกใจ

astonishment, n. gaan-tam-hâi-
ngong-nguai การทำให้งงงวย

astray, adv. lǒng-taang หลงทาง;
lǒng-pìt หลงผิด

astrology, n. hǒo-raa-sàat
โหราศาสตร์

astronaut, n. ma-nút-ao-wa-gàat
มนุษย์อวกาศ

astronomy, n. daa-raa-sàat
ดาราศาสตร์

asylum, n. roong-pa-yaa-baan-kon-
bâa โรงพยาบาลคนบ้า (mental hospital); sà-tǎan-tîi-lîi-pai สถานที่ลี้ภัย
(sanctuary)

at, prep. tîi ที่; bon บน; ná ณ

atheist, n. pûu-tîi-mâi-chûa-wâa-
mii-prá-jâao ผู้ที่ไม่เชื่อว่ามีพระเจ้า

athlete, n. nák-gii-laa นักกีฬา;
nák-grii-taa นักกรีฑา

athletic, adj. mii-râang-guai kɛ̌ng-
rɛɛng มีร่างกายแข็งแรง

athletics, n. gaan-gii-laa การกีฬา

atlas, n. sà-mùt-pɛ̌ɛn-tîi สมุดแผนที่

atmosphere, n. ban-yaa-gàat
บรรยากาศ

atom, n. à-dtom อะตอม

atomic bomb, n. ra-bɛ̀ɛt-bpà-ra-
maa-nuu ระเบิดปรมาณู

attach, v. dùt ติด; nɛ̂ɛp แนบ;
bprà-gɔ̀ɔp ประกอบ

attaché, n. pûu-chûai-tûut ผู้ช่วยทูต

attachment, n. gaan-dùt การติด;
sìng-tîi-nɛ̂ɛp-maa สิ่งที่แนบมา;
gaan-yút-sáp การยึดทรัพย์

attack, v. joom-dtii โจมตี (raid);
tam-ráai ทำร้าย (hurt, injure)

attack, n. gaan-joom-dtii การโจมตี;
gaan-tam-ráai การทำร้าย

attempt, v. pá-yaa-yaam พยายาม
(try); tót-lɔɔng ทดลอง (test)

attend, v. ráp-chái รับใช้ (e.g. waiter); duu-lɛɛ ดูแล (take care of);
kâo-rûam เข้าร่วม (participate)

attendance, n. gaan-duu-lɛɛ-rák-
sǎa การดูแลรักษา; gaan-kâo-rûam
การเข้าร่วม

attendant, n. pûu-ráp-chái ผู้รับใช้;
pûu-kâo-rûam-bprà-chum
ผู้เข้าร่วมประชุม

attention, n. gaan-ao-jai-sài
การเอาใจใส่; gaan-duu-lɛɛ การดูแล

attentive, adj. ao- òk-ao-jai
เอาอกเอาใจ (giving care or attention); mii-kwaam-sǒn-jai มีความ
สนใจ (interested); rá-mát-rá-wang
ระมัดระวัง (mindful)

attic, n. hɔ̂ng-dtâai-lǎng-kaa

English • Phonetic • Thai

ห้องใต้หลังคา

attire, *n.*, *v.* chút ชุด (apparel);
dtὲng-dtua แต่งตัว (to dress)

attitude, *n.* gì-rí-yaa-tâa-taang
กิริยาท่าทาง (manner); tát-sà-ná-
ká-dtì ทัศนคติ (of mind or a feeling)

attorney, *n.* tá-naai-kwaam
ทนายความ

attract, *v.* dung-dùut ดึงดูด

attraction, *n.* gaan-dung-dùut-
kwaam-sŏn-jai การดึงดูดความสนใจ

attractive, *adj.* mii-sà-nὲe มีเสน่ห์

auction, *n.* gaan-bprà-muun
การประมูล

audible, *adj.* sǎa-mâat-dâi-yin
สามารถได้ยิน

audience, *n.* pûu-chom ผู้ชม; pûu-
fang ผู้ฟัง; pûu-àan ผู้อ่าน

audit, *v.* dtrùat-sɔ̀ɔp ตรวจสอบ;
rian-wí-chaa-tîi-mâi-ao-ká-nεεn
เรียนวิชาที่ไม่เอาคะแนน (non-credit
subject)

audit, *n.* gaan-dtrùat-sɔ̀ɔp-ban-chii
การตรวจสอบบัญชี (in accounting)

audition, *n.* gaan-dâi-yin การได้ยิน
(act of hearing); gaan-tót-lɔɔng-sà-
dεεng การทดลองแสดง (a trial performance)

auditor, *n.* pûu-dtrùat-sɔ̀ɔp-ban-chii
ผู้ตรวจสอบบัญชี; pûu-fang ผู้ฟัง

auditorium, *n.* hɔ̂ng-ban-yaai
ห้องบรรยาย; hɔ̂ng-bprà-chum
ห้องประชุม

augment, *v.* pɔ̂ɔm เพิ่ม; kà-yǎai
ขยาย

August, *n.* dʉan-sǐng-hǎa-kom
เดือนสิงหาคม

aunt, *n.* bpâa ป้า (father or mother's older sister); náa น้า (mother's
younger sister); aa อา (father's
younger sister)

auspicious, *adj.* dâai-lὲek ได้ฤกษ์;
bpen-mong-kon เป็นมงคล

Australia, *n.* bprà-têet-ɔ̀ɔt-sa-dtree-
lia ประเทศออสเตรเลีย

Australian, *n.* kon-ɔ̀ɔt-sa-dtree-lia
คนออสเตรเลีย (people); gìao-gàp-
ɔ̀ɔt-sa-dtree-lia เกี่ยวกับออสเตรเลีย
(related to Australia)

Austria, *n.* bprà-têet-ɔ̀ɔt-sa-dtria
ประเทศออสเตรีย

authentic, *adj.* tέε แท้; jing จริง

author, *n.* pûu-dtὲng ผู้แต่ง; nák-
kǐan นักเขียน

authority, *n.* jâo-nâa-tîi เจ้าหน้าที่
(authorized person); am-nâat อำนาจ
(power)

authorize, *v.* mɔ̂ɔp-am-nâat
มอบอำนาจ (give authority); dtὲng-
dtâng แต่งตั้ง (appoint)

authorship, *v.* kwaam-bpen-nák-
kǐan ความเป็นนักเขียน

autography, *n.* laai-sen-kɔ̌ɔng-
dtua-eeng ลายเซ็นของตัวเอง

autograph, *v.* sen-chʉ̂ʉ เซ็นชื่อ

autograph, *n.* laai-sen ลายเซ็น

automatic, *adj.* àt-dtà-noo-mát อัตโนมัติ

automobile, *n.* rót-yon รถยนต์

automotive, *adj.* gìao-gàp-rót-yon เกี่ยวกับรถยนต์

autonomy, *n.* èek-gà-râat เอกราช

autopsy, *n.* gaan-chan-na-sùut-sòp การชันสูตรศพ

autumn, *n.* rú-duu-bai-máai-rûang ฤดูใบไม้ร่วง

avail, *v.* mii-bprà-yòot มีประโยชน์ (be of use); chûai-dâai ช่วยได้ (help)

available, *adj.* hǎa-dâai หาได้ (obtainable); cháai-bpen-bprà-yòot-dâai ใช้เป็นประโยชน์ได้ (willing to be of service); mii-yùu มีอยู่ (present)

avalanche, *n.* hì-má-tà-lòm หิมะถล่ม (as of snow); jam-nuan-má-hù-maa จำนวนมหึมา (massive amount)

avant-garde, *n.* gɔɔng-nâa กองหน้า

avenue, *n.* tà-nǒn ถนน

average, *v.* chà-lìa เฉลี่ย

average, *n.* kâa-chà-lìa ค่าเฉลี่ย

avert, *v.* bìang-been เบี่ยงเบน (turn away); been-sǎai-dtaa เบนสายตา (the eyes); lìik-lîang หลีกเลี่ยง (avoid)

aviation, *n.* wí-chaa-gaan-bin วิชาการบิน

avid, *adj.* klâng-klái คลั่งไคล้; chɔɔp-mâak ชอบมาก

avoid, *v.* lìik-lîang หลีกเลี่ยง

await, *v.* kɔɔi คอย; fâo-rɔɔ เฝ้ารอ

awake, *adj.* dtùun ตื่น (not sleeping); rúu-sùk-dtua รู้สึกตัว (gain consciousness)

awaken, *v.* bplùk ปลุก

award, *n.* raang-wan รางวัล

aware, *adj.* rúu-dtua รู้ตัว (conscious); sâap ทราบ (knowing)

awareness, *n.* gaan-rúu-dtua การรู้ตัว; kwaam-dtrà-nàk-tǔng ความตระหนักถึง

away, *adv.* bpai ไป; jàak-bpai จากไป

awesome, *adj.* nâa-glua น่ากลัว (scary); lêet เลิศ (wonderful)

awful, *adj.* nâa-glua น่ากลัว (scary); leeo-mâak เลวมาก (very bad)

awhile, *adv.* chûa-krúu ชั่วครู่

awkward, *adj.* ngûm-ngâam งุ่มง่าม (clumsy); gêeng-gâang เก้งก้าง (not graceful); ùt-àt-jai อึดอัดใจ (uncomfortable)

ax, axe, *n.* kwǎan ขวาน

axiom, *n.* kwaam-bpen-jing ความเป็นจริง (universally recognized truth); làk-gaan หลักการ (principle)

axis, *n.* geen แกน

axle, *n.* geen-lɔ́ɔ แกนล้อ (an axis of wheels); mùt หมุด (spindle)

B

babble, *v.* pûut-plâam พูดพล่าม

babble, *n.* gaan-pûut-plâam
การพูดพล่าม

baby, *n.* taa-rók ทารก; dèk-ɔ̀ɔn
เด็กอ่อน

babysitter, *n.* kon-líang-dèk
คนเลี้ยงเด็ก

bachelor, *n.* chaai-sòot ชายโสด (a
single man); pûu-dâai-ráp-bpà-rin-
yaa ผู้ได้รับปริญญา (a graduate)

back, *n.* lǎng หลัง

back, *v.* sà-nàp-sà-nǔn สนับสนุน

backbone, *n.* grà-dùuk-sǎn-lǎng
กระดูกสันหลัง

background, *n.* kwaam-bpen-maa
ความเป็นมา (history); sùan-tîi-yùu-
lǎng ส่วนที่อยู่หลัง (scene); puum-
lǎng ภูมิหลัง (history)

backing, *n.* kwaam-chûai-lǔa
ความช่วยเหลือ; gaan-sà-nàp-sà-nǔn
การสนับสนุน

backpack, *n.* bpêe เป้

backtrack, *v.* glàp-taang-dəəm
กลับทางเดิม

backup, *v.* sà-nàp-sà-nǔn สนับสนุน
(support); sǎm-rɔɔng สำรอง
(reserve or substitute)

backward, *adj.* yɔ́ɔn-glàp ย้อนกลับ
(toward the back); láa-lǎng ล้าหลัง
(behind in progress or d--evelopment)

backyard, *n.* sà-nǎam-lǎng-bâan

สนามหลังบ้าน

bacon, *n.* bee-kôn เบคอน

bad, *adj.* mâi-dii ไม่ดี; leeo เลว

badge, *n.* krûang-mǎai เครื่องหมาย
(a characteristic mark); rǐan-bprà-
dàp เหรียญประดับ (an emblem
given as an award or honor)

badger, *n.* dtua-bέεt-jɔɔ
ตัวแบดเจอร์

badly, *adv.* mâi-dii ไม่ดี

bag, *n.* grà-bpǎo กระเป๋า (a piece
of hand luggage); tǔng ถุง (a container of flexible material, such as
paper or plastic)

baggage, *n.* grà-bpǎo กระเป๋า

baggy, *adj.* kláai-tǔng คล้ายถุง;
bpen-tǔng เป็นถุง

bail, *v.* bprà-gan-dtua ประกันตัว

bail, *n.* ngən-bprà-gan เงินประกัน
(as security); gaan-bprà-gan-dtua
การประกันตัว (act of bailing);
tǎng-náam ถังน้ำ (bucket)

bait, *n.* yùa เหยื่อ; sìng-lɔ́ɔ-jai
สิ่งล่อใจ

bake, *v.* òp อบ

baker, *n.* kon-tam-kà-nǒm
คนทำขนม

bakery, *n.* ráan-kà-nǒm-bpang
ร้านขนมปัง

balance, *n.* kwaam-sǒm-dun
ความสมดุลย์

balcony, *n.* rá-biang ระเบียง

bald, *adj.* láan ล้าน; dtian-lôong

เดียงโล่ง

ball, *n.* lûuk-bɔn ลูกบอล (i.e. for playing sports); ngaan-dtên-ram งานเต้นรำ (dance)

ballerina, *n.* nák-dtên-ban-lêe นักเต้นบัลเล่ต์

ballet, *n.* gaan-dtên-ban-lêe การเต้นบัลเล่ต์

balloon, *n.* lûuk-bpòong ลูกโป่ง

ballot, *n.* bàt-lʉ̂ak-dtâng บัตรเลือกตั้ง

bamboo, *n.* máai-pài ไม้ไผ่

bamboo shoot, *n.* nɔ̀ɔ-mái หน่อไม้

ban, *v.* hâam ห้าม

banana, *n.* glûai กล้วย

band, *n.* sǎai-kâat สายคาด (strip); sǎai-rát สายรัด (fastener); wong-don-dtrii วงดนตรี (music)

bandage, *n.* pâa-pan-plɛ̌ɛ ผ้าพันแผล

bang, *n.* pǒm-nâa-máa ผมหน้าม้า (hair); sǐang-dang เสียงดัง (loud noise)

bank, *n.* tá-naa-kaan ธนาคาร (money institution); fàng ฝั่ง (e.g. of a river)

banner, *n.* tong ธง (flag); kɔ̂ɔ-kwaam-tii-jɛɛng-hâi-sâap ข้อความที่แจ้งให้ทราบ (for message)

bar, *v.* tɔ̂ɔn ท่อน (piece of solid material); máai-raao ไม้ราว (long, narrow piece of wood); baa บาร์ (where drinks are served)

barbecue, *v., n.* yâang ย่าง; baa-bii-kiu บาร์บีคิว

barber, *n.* châng-dtàt-pǒm ช่างตัดผม

barbershop, *n.* ráan-dtàt-pǒm ร้านตัดผม

bare, *adj.* bplʉai เปลือย (naked); bplàao เปล่า (without cover; empty); mâi-mii-à-rai ไม่มีอะไร (nothing)

barefoot, *adj., adv.* táao-bplàao เท้าเปล่า

barely, *adv.* tɛ̂ɛp-jà-mâi แทบจะไม่

bargain, *v.* dtɔ̀ɔ-raa-kaa ต่อราคา

bargain, *n.* gaan-dtɔ̀ɔ-rɔɔng-raa-kaa การต่อรองราคา (act of bargaining); sǐn-káa-raa-kaa-tùuk สินค้าราคาถูก (a good buy)

barge, *n.* rʉa-ban-túk เรือบรรทุก

bark, *v.* hào เห่า

bark, *n.* bplʉ̀ak-máai เปลือกไม้ (of a tree)

barn, *n.* roong-naa โรงนา; yúng-kâao ยุ้งข้าว

barrel, *n.* tǎng ถัง; sǎam-sìp-èt-jùt-hâa-gen-lɔn 31.5 แกลลอน

barren, *adj.* hɛ̂ng-lɛ́ɛng แห้งแล้ง (dry); bpen-mǎn เป็นหมัน (unable to bear fruit or children)

barrier, *n.* sìng-gìit-kwǎang สิ่งกีดขวาง; ùp-bpà-sàk อุปสรรค

bartender, *n.* baa-ten-dɤ̂ɤ บาร์เทนเดอร์

barter, v. lɛ̂ɛk-bplìan-sĭn-káa แลกเปลี่ยนสินค้า

barter, n. gaan-lɛ̂ɛk-bplìan-sĭn-káa การแลกเปลี่ยนสินค้า

base, n. púun-tǎan พื้นฐาน (fundamental principle, etc.); tǎan ฐาน (foundation); jùt-rɔ̂ɔm จุดเริ่ม (starting point)

basement, n. hɔ̂ng-dtâai-din ห้องใต้ดิน

basic, adj. gìao-gàp-púun-tǎan เกี่ยวกับพื้นฐาน

basis, n. púun-tǎan พื้นฐาน (fundamental principle, etc.); sùan-sǎm-kan ส่วนสำคัญ (important part)

basket, n. dtà-glâa ตะกร้า; grà-jàat กระจาด

basketball, n. báat-sa-gèt-bɔɔn บาสเก็ตบอล

bass, n. bplaa-gà-pong ปลากะพง (fish); sĭang-dtàm เสียงต่ำ (sound)

bastard, n. âi-chûa ไอ้ชั่ว

bat, n. káang-kaao ค้างคาว (animal); máai-dtii ไม้ตี (racket)

bath, n. gaan-àap-náam การอาบน้ำ (act of bathing); hɔ̂ng-àap-náam ห้องอาบน้ำ (bathroom)

bathe, v. àap-náam อาบน้ำ

bathing suit, n. chút-àap-náam ชุดอาบน้ำ; chút-wâai-náam ชุดว่ายน้ำ

bathrobe, n. sûa-klum-àap-náam เสื้อคลุมอาบน้ำ

bathroom, n. hɔ̂ng-náam ห้องน้ำ

bathtub, n. àang-àap-náam อ่างอาบน้ำ

batter, v. dtii ตี; dtòp-dtii ตบตี

batter, n. bpɛ̂ɛng-pà-sǒm แป้งผสม (flour mix); mɯɯ-dtii-béet-bɔɔn มือตีเบสบอล (in baseball)

battery, n. bèt-dtɔɔ-rîi แบตเตอรี่

battle, n. sǒng-kraam สงคราม; dtɔ̀ɔ-sûu ต่อสู้

battlefield, n. sà-nǎam-róp สนามรบ

battleship, n. rɯa-róp เรือรบ

bay, n. àao อ่าว

bazzar, n. dtà-làat ตลาด

be, v. bpen เป็น (to be something); yùu อยู่ (to be somewhere); kɯɯ คือ (to be as follows)

beach, n. chaai-hàat ชายหาด

beacon, n. grà-joom-fai กระโจมไฟ; sǎn-yaan-fai สัญญาณไฟ

bead, n. lûuk-bpàt ลูกปัด

beak, n. bpàak-nók ปากนก

beam, n. kaan คาน (long piece of wood); lam-sɛ̌ɛng ลำแสง (light)

bean, n. tùa ถั่ว

bear, v. ɔ̀ɔk-lûuk ออกลูก (a child); ɔ̀ɔk-pǒn ออกผล (fruit); òt-ton อดทน (be patient)

bear, n. mǐi หมี

bearable, adj. ton-dâi ทนได้ (tolerable); ɔ̀ɔk-pǒn-dâai ออกผลได้ (able to produce offspring)

beard, n. nùat-krao หนวดเครา

bearer, n. pûu-bɛ̀ɛk ผู้แบก (one that carries); pûu-tɯ̌ɯ-chék ผู้ถือเช็ค

English • Phonetic • Thai

(one that holds a check)

bearing, *n.* kwaam-òt-ton ความอดทน; gaan-ɔ̀ɔk-pǒn การออกผล

beast, *n.* sàt สัตว์

beastly, *adj.* yîang-sàt เยี่ยงสัตว์ (bestial); hòot-ráai โหดร้าย (brutal)

beat, *v.* dtii ตี (hit); dtên เต้น (e.g. heart)

beat, *n.* jang-wà จังหวะ (rhythm)

beating, *n.* gaan-dtii การตี; gaan-dtên การเต้น

beautiful, *adj.* sǔai สวย (pretty); dii ดี (nice, good); pai-rɔ́ ไพเราะ (i.e. music)

beauty, *n.* kwaam-ngaam ความงาม (being beautiful); kon-ngaam คนงาม (beautiful woman); sìng-dii-ngaam สิ่งดีงาม (of good quality or virtue)

because, *conj.* prɔ́ เพราะ; prɔ́-wâa เพราะว่า

become, *v.* glaai-bpen กลายเป็น

becoming, *adj.* tîi-mɔ̀-sǒm ที่เหมาะสม

bed, *n.* dtiang เตียง

bedroom, *n.* hɔ̂ng-nɔɔn ห้องนอน

bee, *n.* pûng ผึ้ง

beef, *n.* núa-wua เนื้อวัว

beefsteak, *n.* sà-dtéek-núa สเต็กเนื้อ

beehive, *n.* ruang-pûng รวงผึ้ง

beer, *n.* bia เบียร์

beet, *n.* dtôn-bìit ต้นบีท

beetle, *n.* má-lɛɛng-bpìik-kěng แมลงปีกแข็ง

before, *adv.* gɔ̀ɔn ก่อน

beg, *v.* kɔ̌ɔ-taan ขอทาน (e.g. for food or money); ɔ̂ɔn-wɔɔn อ้อนวอน (implore, request)

beggar, *n.* kon-kɔ̌ɔ-taan คนขอทาน

begin, *v.* rɔ̂əm เริ่ม

beginner, *n.* pûu-rɔ̂əm-rian ผู้เริ่มเรียน

beginning, *n.* gaan-rɔ̂əm การเริ่ม; jùt-rɔ̂əm จุดเริ่ม

behalf, *n.* bprà-yòot ประโยชน์ (benefit); dtua-tɛɛn ตัวแทน (as the agent of); nai-naam ในนาม (on behalf of, on account of)

behave, *v.* bprà-prút ประพฤติ; bpà-dtì-bàt ปฏิบัติ

behavior, *n.* kwaam-bprà-prút ความประพฤติ (action); tâa-tii ท่าที (manner)

behead, *v.* dtàt-hǔa ตัดหัว

behind, *adv.* kâang-lǎng ข้างหลัง

behold, *v.* hěn เห็น; duu ดู

being, *n.* gaan-bpen-yùu การเป็นอยู่; gaan-dam-rong-yùu การดำรงอยู่

belated, *adj.* lâa-cháa ล่าช้า

belch, *v.* rəə เรอ; pôn-ɔ̀ɔk พ่นออก

Belgium, *n.* ben-yîam เบลเยียม

Belgian, *n.* kon-ben-yîam เบลเยียม (people); gìao-gàp-ben-yîam

เกี่ยวกับเบลเยี่ยม (relating to Belgium)

belief, *n.* kwaam-chûa ความเชื่อ (mental act, condition, or habit of); sàt-taa ศรัทธา (faith)

believable, *adj.* nâa-chûa น่าเชื่อ

believe, *v.* chûa เชื่อ (in something); náp-tǔu นับถือ (i.e. religion); sàt-taa ศรัทธา (have faith)

believer, *n.* pûu-chûa ผู้เชื่อ; pûu-sàt-taa ผู้ศรัทธา

bell, *n.* rá-kang ระฆัง; grà-dìng กระดิ่ง (doorbell)

bellboy, *n.* kon-kǒn-grà-bpǎo คนขนกระเป๋า; pá-nák-ngaan-nai-roong-rɛɛm พนักงานในโรงแรม

belly, *n:* tɔ́ɔng ท้อง; pung พุง

belong to, *v.* bpen-kɔ̌ɔng เป็นของ; yùu-nai อยู่ใน; sǎng-gàt สังกัด

belongings, *n.* sìng-kɔ̌ɔng สิ่งของ; sáp-sǒm-bàt ทรัพย์สมบัติ

beloved, *adj.* bpen-tîi-rák เป็นที่รัก

below, *adv.* kâang-lâang ข้างล่าง; dtàm-gwàa ต่ำกว่า

belt, *n.* kěm-kàt เข็มขัด (any belts); sǎai สาย (e.g. black belt)

bench, *n.* máa-nâng ม้านั่ง (seat); ban-lang-nai-sǎan บัลลังก์ในศาล (of a judge)

bend, *v.* ngɔɔ งอ; kɔ́ɔng โค้ง

beneath, *prep.* kâang-dtâai ข้างใต้; dtàm-gwàa ต่ำกว่า

benefactor, -tress, *n.* pûu-tam-kwaam-dii ผู้ทำความดี (good doer); pûu-bɔɔ-ri-jàak ผู้บริจาค (donator)

beneficial, *adj.* mii-bprà-yòot มีประโยชน์

beneficiary, *n.* pûu-ráp-pǒn-bprà-yòot ผู้รับผลประโยชน์

benefit, *v.* hâi-bprà-yòot ให้ประโยชน์

benefit, *n.* pǒn-bprà-yòot ผลประโยชน์

betray, *v.* tɔɔ-ra-yót ทรยศ; hàk-lǎng หักหลัง

betrayal, *n.* gaan-tɔɔ-ra-yót การทรยศ

better, *adj.* dii-gwàa ดีกว่า; dii-kûn ดีขึ้น

between, *adv.* rá-wàang ระหว่าง

beverage, *n.* krûang-dùum เครื่องดื่ม

beware, *v.* rá-wang ระวัง; rá-wang-dtua ระวังตัว

beyond, *n.* pón พ้น; glai ไกล; mâak-gwàa มากกว่า

bias, *n.* à-ka-dtì อคติ

bicycle, *n.* jàk-grà-yaan จักรยาน

bid, *v.* bprà-muun ประมูล

bid, *n.* gaan-bprà-muun-raa-kaa การประมูลราคา; gaan-chúa-chəən การเชื้อเชิญ

big, *adj.* yài ใหญ่

bigger, *adj.* yài-gwàa ใหญ่กว่า

biggest, *adj.* yài-tîi-sùt ใหญ่ที่สุด

bikini, *n.* bì-gi-nîi บิกินี

bill, *n.* bai-gèp-ngən ใบเก็บเงิน (invoice); ta-na-bàt ธนบัตร (money note); prá-râat-cha-ban-yàt พระราชบัญญัติ (legislative act); bpàak-nók ปากนก (bird beak)

billiards, *n.* bin-lîat บิลเลียด

billion, *n.* nùng-pan-láan หนึ่งพันล้าน

bind, *v.* pùuk-mát ผูกมัด (tie); pan พัน (wrap); kâo-lêm เข้าเล่ม (e.g. a book)

binding, *n.* gaan-mát การมัด (knotting or bandaging); gaan-kâo-lêm การเข้าเล่ม (book)

binoculars, *n.* glông-sŏɔng-dtaa กล้องสองตา; glông-sòng-taang-glai กล้องส่องทางไกล

biodegradable, *adj.* yɔ̂i-sà-lǎai-dooi-tam-ma-châat ย่อยสลายโดยธรรมชาติ

biography, *n.* chii-wá-bprà-wàt ชีวประวัติ

biologist, *n.* nák-chii-wá-wít-ta-yaa นักชีววิทยา

biology, *n.* chii-wá-wít-ta-yaa ชีววิทยา

bird, *n.* nók นก, lûuk-kòn gài ลูกขนไก่

birth, *n.* gaan-gə̀ət การเกิด

birth certificate, *n.* sǔu-dtì-bàt สูติบัตร

birth control, *n.* gaan-kum-gam-nə̀ət การคุมกำเนิด

birthday, *n.* wan-gə̀ət วันเกิด

birthplace, *n.* sà-tǎan-tîi-gə̀ət สถานที่เกิด

bishop, *n.* prá-bít-chɔ̀p พระบิชอป

bit, *n.* lék-nɔ́ɔi เล็กน้อย

bitch, *n.* sù-nák-dtua-mia สุนัขตัวเมีย (female dog); yǐng-leeo หญิงเลว (lewd woman)

bite, *v.* gàt กัด; dtɔ̀i ต่อย (bee)

bitter, *adj.* kǒm ขม (taste); sǎa-hàt สาหัส (grief or anguish); nǎao-jàt หนาวจัด (extremely cold)

black, *adj.* sǐi-dam สีดำ

blackberry, *n.* pǒn-blék-bəə-rîi ผลแบล็กเบอรี่

blackboard, *n.* grà-daan-dam กระดานดำ

blacken, *v.* tam-hâi-dam ทำให้ดำ

black eye, *n.* dtaa-fók-chám ตาฟกช้ำ

blackmail, *n.* gaan-kùu-ao-ngən การขู่เอาเงิน

black market, *n.* dtà-làat-mûut ตลาดมืด

blackout, *n.* kwaam-mûut-mon ความมืดมน (darkness); gaan-bpìt-kàao การปิดข่าว (concealment); fai-dàp ไฟดับ (power failure)

blacksmith, *n.* châng-dtii-lèk ช่างตีเหล็ก

bladder, *n.* grà-pɔ́-bpàt-sa-wá กระเพาะปัสสาวะ

blade, *n.* bai-mîit ใบมีด

blame, v. glàao-tôot กล่าวโทษ;
dtam-nì ตำหนิ

bland, adj. jùut-chùut จืดชืด (dull or
not much flavor); ɔ̀ɔn-yoon อ่อนโยน
(pleasant in manner)

blank, adj. wâang ว่าง; wâang-
bplàao ว่างเปล่า

blanket, n. pâa-hòm ผ้าห่ม

blast, v. rá-bɔ̀ɔt ระเบิด

blast, n. gaan-rá-bɔ̀ɔt การระเบิด;
lom-pát-grà-chôok ลมพัดกระโชก

bleach, v. fɔ̀ɔk-kǎao ฟอกขาว;

bleach, n. gaan-fɔ̀ɔk-kǎao
การฟอกขาว (act of bleaching);
náam-yaa-fɔ̀ɔk-kǎao น้ำยาฟอกขาว
(agent)

bleak, adj. bplàao-bplìao
เปล่าเปลี่ยว (gloomy and somber);
nǎao-yen หนาวเย็น (cold)

bleed, v. lûat-ɔ̀ɔk เลือดออก

blend, v. pà-sǒm ผสม

blend, n. gaan-pà-sǒm การผสม;
sìng-jʉa-bpon สิ่งเจือปน

bless, v. uai-pɔɔn อวยพร

blind, adj. dtaa-bɔ̀ɔt ตาบอด

blind (window shade), n. mâan-
bang-sɛ̌ɛng ม่านบังแสง; mûu-lìi มู่ลี่

blindfold, n. pâa-bpìt-dtaa ผ้าปิดตา

blink, v. gà-prìp-dtaa กะพริบตา;
hâi-sǎn-yaan ให้สัญญาณ

block, n. tɔ̂n-máai ท่อนไม้ (piece of
wood); gɔ̂ɔn-hǐn ก้อนหิน; blɔ́k
บล็อก (of a city or town)

block, v. gân กั้น

blond, adj. sǐi-blɔɔn สีบลอนด์

blood, n. lûat เลือด

bloodless, adj. sìit ซีด (pale);
mâi-mii-lûat ไม่มีเลือด (no blood)

blood pressure, n. kwaam-dan-
loo-hìt ความดันโลหิต

blood type, n. glùm-lûat กลุ่มเลือด

blood vessel, n. sên-lûat เส้นเลือด

bloom, v. baan บาน

bloom, n. kwaam-bplèng-bplàng
ความเปล่งปลั่ง

blossom, n. chûang-dɔ̀ɔk-máai-
baan ช่วงดอกไม้บาน

blouse, n. sʉ̂a เสื้อ

blow, v. bpào เป่า

blow, n. lom-rɛɛng ลมแรง (hard
wind); gaan-bpào การเป่า

blue, adj. sǐi-náam-ngən สีน้ำเงิน
(color); sâo เศร้า (sad)

blunt, adj. tʉ̂ʉ ทื่อ (not sharp);
tɛ̌ɛn-dtrong แทนตรง (speech)

blur, v. mua มัว

blush, v. nâa-dɛɛng หน้าแดง
(become red in the face); aai อาย
(shy, embarrassed)

board, v. kʉ̂n-rót ขึ้นรถ (a vehicle)

board, n. máai-grà-daan ไม้กระดาน
(flat piece of wood); ka-ná-gam-ma-
gaan คณะกรรมการ (committee)

boarder, n. nák-rian-gin-nɔɔn
นักเรียนกินนอน

boarding house, n. hɔ̌ɔ-pák หอพัก

English · Phonetic · Thai

English • Phonetic • Thai

boarding pass, *n.* bàt-kûn-krûang บัตรขึ้นเครื่อง

boarding school, *n.* roong-rian-gin-nɔɔn โรงเรียนกินนอน

boast, *v.* kui-móo คุยโม้; ôo-ùat โอ้อวด

boat, *n.* rɯa เรือ

bodily, *adj.* gìao-gàp-râang-gaai เกี่ยวกับร่างกาย

body, *n.* râang-gaai ร่างกาย; dtua-dtua ตัว; sòp ศพ (corpse); nɯa-hǎa-sǎm-kan เนื้อหาสำคัญ (substance)

boil, *v.* dtôm ต้ม; dùat เดือด

boiler, *n.* mɔ̂ɔ-náam หม้อน้ำ; dtao-dtôm-náam เตาต้มน้ำ

bold, *adj.* jai-glâa ใจกล้า (brave); dèn เด่น (standout); chát-jeen ชัดเจน (clear)

bolt, *n.* lûuk-gloon ลูกกลอน (e.g. deadbolt); lûuk-sɔ̂ɔn ลูกศร (arrow); gai-bpɯɯn ไกปืน (of a gun)

bomb, *n.* rá-bɤ̀ɤt ระเบิด

bomber, *n.* krûang-bin-tíng-rá-bɤ̀ɤt เครื่องบินทิ้งระเบิด

bombing, *n.* gaan-rá-bɤ̀ɤt การระเบิด

bombshell, *n.* lûuk-rá-bɤ̀ɤt ลูกระเบิด

bond, *n.* kɔ̂ɔ-pùuk-mát ข้อผูกมัด (obligation); bai-gûu-yɯɯm ใบกู้ยืม (certificate of debt), gaan bprà-gan-dtua การประกันตัว (place a guaranteed bond on)

bone, *n.* grà-dùuk กระดูก; gâang

ก้าง (fish)

bonus, *n.* boo-nát โบนัส

bony, *adj.* dtem-bpai-dûai-grà-dùuk เต็มไปด้วยกระดูก (full of bones); mii-grà-dùuk-yài มีกระดูกใหญ่ (having big bones)

book, *n.* nǎng-sɯ̌ɯ หนังสือ

bookkeeper, *n.* kon-tam-ban-chii คนทำบัญชี

booklet, *n.* nǎng-sɯ̌ɯ-lêm-lék หนังสือเล่มเล็ก

boom, *v.* mii- sǐang-dang มีเสียงดัง (noise); dtɔ̀ɔp-dtoo-yàang-rûat-reo เติบโตอย่างรวดเร็ว (grow fast)

boom, *n.* sǐang-sà-nàn-wàn-wǎi เสียงสนั่นหวั่นไหว (noise); gaan-dtɔ̀ɔp-dtoo-yàang-rûat-reo การเติบโตอย่างรวดเร็ว (fast growth)

boon, *n.* pǒn-bprà-yòot ผลประโยชน์; bun-kun บุญคุณ

boost, *v.* yók-kɯ̂n ยกขึ้น; pɤ̂ɤm-kɯ̂n เพิ่มขึ้น

boot, *n.* rɔɔng-táao-búut รองเท้าบู๊ท;

boot, *v.* sà-dtáat-krûang สตาร์ทเครื่อง (the computer)

booth, *n.* pɤɤng แผง (for selling merchandise); nùai-lûak-dtâng หน่วยเลือกตั้ง (for election)

border, *n.* chaai-dɛɛn ชายแดน

bore, *v.* tam-hâi-bɯa ทำให้เบื่อ

bore, *n.* kwaam-nâa-bɯa ความน่าเบื่อ

English · Phonetic · Thai

bored, *adj.* bùa เบื่อ .

boredom, *n.* kwaam-bùa-nàai ความเบื่อหน่าย

boring, *adj.* nâa-bùa น่าเบื่อ

born, *adj.* gə̀ət เกิด; gam-nə̀ət กำเนิด (formal)

borrow, *v.* yuum ยืม; kɔ̌ɔ-yuum ขอยืม

boss, *n.* jâo-naai เจ้านาย

bossy, *adj.* jâo-bong-gaan เจ้าบงการ

botanical, *adj.* gìao-gàp-plúk-sa-sàat เกี่ยวกับพฤกษศาสตร์

botany, *n.* plúk-sa-sàat พฤกษศาสตร์

both, *pron., adj.* táng-sɔ̌ɔng ทั้งสอง; táng-kûu ทั้งคู่

bother, *v.* róp-guan รบกวน; yûng ยุ่ง

bothersome, *adj.* yûng ยุ่ง; nâa-ram-kaan น่ารำคาญ

bottle, *n.* kùat ขวด

bottom, *n.* gôn ก้น (of anything); púun-lâang พื้นล่าง (lower floor); lâang-sùt ล่างสุด (lowest part)

boulevard, *n.* tà-nǒn-gwâang ถนนกว้าง

bounce, *v.* grà-dòot กระโดด; dêng-glàp เด้งกลับ

boundary, *n.* kèet-dɛɛn เขตแดน

bouquet, *n.* chɔ̂ɔ-dɔ̀ɔk-máai ช่อดอกไม้

bow, *v.* kóong โค้ง; kam-náp คำนับ

bow, *n.* gaan-kóong-kam-náp การโค้งคำนับ; kan-tá-nuu คันธนู (for arrows)

bowl, *n.* chaam ชาม (dish)

bowl, *v.* yoon-boo-lîng โยนโบว์ลิ่ง

bowling, *n.* gaan-lên-boo-lîng การเล่นโบว์ลิ่ง; lûuk-boo-lîng ลูกโบว์ลิ่ง (bowling ball)

bow tie, *n.* hǔu-grà-dtàai หูกระต่าย

box, *n.* glòng กล่อง

box, *v.* chók ชก; dtòi ต่อย

boxer, *n.* nák-muai นักมวย

boxing, *n.* gaan-chók-muai การชกมวย

box office, *n.* hɔ̂ng-kǎai-dtǔa ห้องขายตั๋ว

boy, *n.* dèk-pûu-chaai เด็กผู้ชาย

boyfriend, *n.* fɛɛn-chaai แฟนชาย

bracelet, *n.* gam-lai-muu กำไลมือ

brag, *v.* kui-woo คุยโว; móo โม้

braid, *v.* tàk ถัก

braid, *n.* laai-tàk ลายถัก (braided segment); pǒm-bpia ผมเปีย (hair)

brain, *n.* sà-mɔ̌ɔng สมอง

brainwash, *v.* láang-sà-mɔ̌ɔng ล้างสมอง

brake, *v.* yùt หยุด

brake, *n.* brèek เบรก; gaan-yùt การหยุด

branch, *n.* sǎa-kǎa สาขา (e.g. of a bank or restaurant); gìng-gâan กิ่งก้าน (e.g. of a tree)

brand, *n.* dtraa ตรา (trademark); cha-nít ชนิด (a particular kind)

brandy, *n.* bá-ràn-dii บรั่นดี

brass, *n.* tɔɔng-lŭang ทองเหลือง

brassiere, *n.* yók-song ยกทรง

brat, *n.* dèk-lŭa-kɔ̌ɔ เด็กเหลือขอ

brave, *adj.* glâa-hăan กล้าหาญ

bravery, *n.* kwaam-glâa-hăan
ความกล้าหาญ

Brazil, *n.* bprà-têet-braa-sin
ประเทศบราซิล

Brazilian, *n.* chaao-braa-sin
ชาวบราซิล (people); gìao-gàp-
braa-sin เกี่ยวกับบราซิล (relating to
Brazil)

bread, *n.* kà-nŏm-bpang ขนมปัง

break, *v.* dtèɛk แตก (smash);
yùt-pák หยุดพัก (stop or rest)

break, *n.* gaan-dtèɛk-ɔ̀ɔk การแตก
ออก; gaan-yùt-pák การหยุดพัก;
chá-ngák ชะงัก

breakable, *adj.* dtèɛk-dâai แตกได้

breakdown, *n.* kwaam-lóm-lĕeo
ความล้มเหลว (failure); sùk-kà-
pâap-yâm-yɛ̂ɛ สุขภาพย่ำแย่ (health)

breakfast, *n.* aa-hăan-cháao
อาหารเช้า

breakup, *n.* gaan-lɛ̂ɛk-kóp-gan
การเลิกคบกัน (e.g. relationship);
gaan-dtèɛk yɛ̂ɛk การแตกแยก (dis-
integration)

breast, *n.* nâa-òk หน้าอก

breast-feed, *v.* hâi-nom-dèk
ให้นมเด็ก

breath, *n.* lom-hăai-jai ลมหายใจ

breathe, *v.* hăai-jai หายใจ

breathing, *n.* gaan-hăai-jai
การหายใจ

breed, *v.* ɔ̀ɔk-lûuk ออกลูก (give
birth to); prêɛ-pan แพร่พันธุ์ (produce offspring)

breeder, *n.* kon-pà-sŏm-pan
คนผสมพันธุ์ (person who breeds animals); mêɛ-pan แม่พันธุ์ (animal
kept to produce offspring)

breeding, *n.* gaan-pó-pan
การเพาะพันธุ์; gaan-ɔ̀ɔk-lûuk
การออกลูก

breeze, *n.* lom ลม; aa-gàat อากาศ

brevity, *n.* ra-yá-wee-laa-sân
ระยะเวลาสั้น (short time); kwaam-
grà-tát-rát ความกะทัดรัด

brew, *v.* màk-bia หมักเบียร์

brewer, *n.* krûang-glàn-bia
เครื่องกลั่นเบียร์

brewery, *n.* roong-glàn-bia
โรงกลั่นเบียร์

bribe, *n.* sĭn-bon สินบน

brick, *n.* ìt อิฐ; kon-jai-dii คนใจดี

bride, *n.* jâao-săao เจ้าสาว

bridegroom, *n.* jâao-bàao เจ้าบ่าว

bridge, *n.* sà-paan สะพาน

brief, *adj.* gà-tát-rát กะทัดรัด (suc-
cinct); sân สั้น (short)

briefcase, *n.* grà-bpăo-èɛk-gà-săan
กระเป๋าเอกสาร

briefing, *n.* kɔ̂ɔ-sà-rùp ข้อสรุป

bright, *adj.* sà-wàang สว่าง (light);

chà-làat ฉลาด (intelligent)

brighten, v. tam-hâi-sà-wàang
ทำให้สว่าง

brilliance, n. kwaam-wɛɛo-waao
ความแวววาว; kwaam-chôot-chûang ความโชติช่วง

brilliant, adj. chôot-chûang โชติช่วง;
sùk-sǎi สุกใส

bring, v. nam-maa-hâi นำมาให้;
gɔ̀ɔ-hâi-gə̀ət ก่อให้เกิด

brink, n. rim ริม; kɔ̀ɔp ขอบ

brisk, adj. rûat-reo รวดเร็ว (fast);
yen เย็น (cool)

broad, adj. gwâang กว้าง

broadcast, v. grà-jaai-kàao
กระจายข่าว (the news); pə̀əi-prɛ̂ɛ
เผยแพร่ (make known)

broaden, v. tam-hâi-gwâang
ทำให้กว้าง

broadminded, adj. jai-gwâang
ใจกว้าง

broccoli, n. pàk-brók-ka-lîi
ผักบร็อคคะลี; pàk-ka-náa ผักคะน้า

brochure, n. broo-chua โบรชัวร์

broil, v. yâang ย่าง; bpîng ปิ้ง; pǎo
เผา

broken, adj. dtɛ̀ɛk แตก; hàk หัก

broken-hearted, adj. òk-hàk อกหัก

broker, n. naai-nâa นายหน้า

bronze, n. tɔɔng-sǎm-rít
ทองสัมฤทธิ์; tɔɔng-lǔang ทองเหลือง

brooch, n. kěm-glàt เข็มกลัด (pin)

broom, n. máai-gwàat ไม้กวาด

brother, n. pîi-chaai พี่ชาย (older);
nɔ́ɔng-chaai น้องชาย (younger)

brother-in-law, n. pîi-kə̌əi พี่เขย
(older); nɔ́ɔng-kə̌əi น้องเขย
(younger)

brow, n. kíu คิ้ว; nâa-pàak
หน้าผาก

brown, adj. sǐi-náam-dtaan สีน้ำตาล

bruise, n. rɔɔi-chám รอยช้ำ; plɛ̂ɛ-tà-lɔ̀ɔk แผลถลอก; plɛ̂ɛ-fók-chám
แผลฟกช้ำ

brush, n. bprɛɛng แปรง (any
brush); pûu-gan พู่กัน (for painting)

bubble, n. fɔɔng ฟอง

bucket, n. tǎng-náam ถังน้ำ

buckle, n. hǔa-kěm-kàt หัวเข็มขัด

bud, n. nɔ̀ɔ หน่อ; chɔ̂ɔ-dɔ̀ɔk
ช่อดอก

Buddhism, n. sàat-sà-nǎa-pút
ศาสนาพุทธ

Buddhist, n. chaao-pút ชาวพุทธ

buddy, n. pûan-sà-nìt เพื่อนสนิท

budget, n. ngóp-bprà-maan
งบประมาณ

buffet, n. búp-fêe บุฟเฟต์

bug, n. má-lɛɛng แมลง; krûang-dàk-fang เครื่องดักฟัง

bugle, n. dtrɛɛ-sǎn-yaan
แตรสัญญาณ

build, v. gɔ̀ɔ-sâang ก่อสร้าง; sâang
สร้าง

build, n. gaan-gɔ̀ɔ-sâang
การก่อสร้าง

builder, n. châng-gɔ̀ɔ-sâang
ช่างก่อสร้าง; kon-sâang คนสร้าง

building, n. dtùk ตึก; sìng-gɔ̀ɔ-
sâang สิ่งก่อสร้าง

built-in, adj. maa-gàp-krûang
มากับเครื่อง (including in the
machine)

bulb, n. hǔa หัว (shoot, root); lɔ̀ɔt
หลอด (e.g. light bulb)

bulk, n. kà-nàat-yàt ขนาดใหญ่

bulky, adj. tə́-tá เทอะทะ

bull, n. wua-dtua-pûu วัวตัวผู้; wua-
grà-ting วัวกระทิง

bulldozer, n. rót-trék-dtɔ̂ɔ
รถแทรกเตอร์

bullet, n. grà-sǔn กระสุน; lûuk-
bpʉʉn ลูกปืน

bulletin, n. bprà-gàat ประกาศ
(announcement); raai-ngaan-kàao
รายงานข่าว (brief report)

bulletin board, n. grà-daan-kàao
กระดานข่าว

bulletproof, adj. gan-grà-sǔn
กันกระสุน

bully, v. kùu ขู่ (threat)

bully, n. kon-paan คนพาล; nák-
leeng นักเลง

bump, v. chon ชน; grà-têek
กระแทก

bump, n. gaan-chon การชน; gaan-
grà-têek การกระแทก

bumper, n. gan-chon กันชน

bun, n. kà-nǒm-bpang ขนมปัง

bunch, n. glùm กลุ่ม; chɔ̂ɔ ช่อ;

puang พวง

bundle, n. hɔ̀ɔ ห่อ (package); jam-
nuan-mâak จำนวนมาก (large
amount)

burden, n. paa-rá ภาระ (responsibility or duty); kwaam-yâak-lam-
bàak ความยากลำบาก (difficulty)

burdensome, adj. bpen-paa-rá
เป็นภาระ; yâak-lam-bàak
ยากลำบาก

bureaucracy, n. bɔɔ-ri-hǎan-bɛ̀ɛp-
kâa-râat-cha-gaan บริหารแบบ
ข้าราชการ (administration of government officials)

bureaucrat, n. jâo-kǔn-muun-naai
เจ้าขุนมูลนาย

bureaucratic, adj. mii-pí-tii-rii-
dtɔɔng-mâak มีพิธีรีตองมาก

burglar, n. kà-mooi ขโมย

burglary, n. gaan-yɔ̂ng-bao
การย่องเบา

burial, n. pí-tii-fǎng-sòp พิธีฝังศพ

burn, v. pǎo เผา; lúk ลุก; mâi ไหม้

burp, v. rəə เรอ

burst, v. rá-bə̀ət ระเบิด; bprà-tú
ปะทุ

burst, n. gaan-rá-bə̀ət การระเบิด;
gaan-bprà-tú การปะทุ

bury, v. fǎng ฝัง

bus, n. rót-bát รถบัส

bush, n. pùm-máai พุ่มไม้

business, n. tú-rá-gìt ธุรกิจ (commercial dealings); gaan-káa การค้า

English • Phonetic • Thai

(trading);

businessman, *n.* nák-tú-rá-gìt นักธุรกิจ

businesswoman, *n.* nák-tú-rá-gìt-yǐng นักธุรกิจหญิง

bust, *n.* òk อก

busy, *adj.* yûng ยุ่ง; mii-tú-rá มีธุระ

busybody, *n.* kon-chɔ̂ɔp-yûng-rûang-kon-ùun คนชอบยุ่งเรื่องคนอื่น

but, *prep.* dtɛ̀ɛ แต่

butt, *n.* gôn ก้น (e.g. cigarette butt, bottom)

butter, *n.* nəəi เนย

butterfly, *n.* pǐi-sûa ผีเสื้อ

buttocks, *n.* gôn ก้น

button, *n.* grà-dum กระดุม; bpùm ปุ่ม

buy, *v.* súu ซื้อ

buyer, *n.* kon-súu คนซื้อ

buzz, *n.* sǐang-hùng-hùng เสียงหึ่งๆ

by, *prep.* dooi โดย (indicating a means of transportation); dûai ด้วย (with the action of); taang ทาง (on; along; in traversing); kâang ข้าง (next to); pàan-bpai ผ่านไป (past)

bye-bye, *interj.* laa-gɔ̀ɔn ลาก่อน; sà-wàt-dii สวัสดี

bypass, *n.* tà-nǒn-baai-pâat ถนนบายพาส; taang-ɔ̂ɔm ทางย้อม

bystander, *n.* kon-mung-duu คนมุงดู

byte, *n.* bái ไบท์

C

cab, *n.* rót-ték-sǐi รถแท็กซี่

cabbage, *n.* gà-làm-bplii กะหล่ำปลี

cabin, *n.* grà-tɔ̂m กระท่อม (cottage); hɔ̂ng-lék ห้องเล็ก

cabinet, *n.* dtûu ตู้ (cupboard)

cable, *n.* kee-bôn เคเบิล

cable television, *n.* kee-bôn-tii-wii เคเบิลทีวี

cactus, *n.* dtà-bɔɔng-pét ตะบองเพชร

café, *n.* kaa-fee คาเฟ่

cafeteria, *n.* roong-aa-hǎan โรงอาหาร

caffeine, *n.* kaa-fee-iin คาเฟอีน

cage, *n.* grong กรง; kúk คุก

cake, *n.* kà-nǒm-kéek ขนมเค้ก

calamity, *n.* krɔ́-ráai เคราะห์ร้าย

calcium, *n.* ken-sîam แคลเซี่ยม

calculate, *v.* kam-nuan คำนวณ

calculation, *n.* gaan-kam-nuan การคำนวณ

calculator, *n.* krûang-kít-lêek เครื่องคิดเลข

calendar, *n.* bpà-dtì-tin ปฏิทิน; ban-túk บันทึก

calf, *n.* lûuk-wua ลูกวัว (baby cow); nɔ̂ng น่อง (body part)

call, *v.* rîak เรียก; too-ra-sàp โทรศัพท์ (to telephone)

caller, *n.* pûu-rîak ผู้เรียก; pûu-too-rá-sàp ผู้โทรศัพท์

calling, *n.* gaan-rîak-róong การเรียกร้อง (demanding); gaan-bprà-chum การประชุม (meeting); gaan-yîam การเยี่ยม (a visit)

calm, *adj.* sà-ngòp สงบ (quiet); jai-yen ใจเย็น (mind)

calorie, *n.* kɛɛ-lɔɔ-rîi แคลอรี่

camel, *n.* ùut อูฐ

camera, *n.* glɔ̂ng-tàai-rûup กล้องถ่ายรูป

camp, *v.* kâo-kâai เข้าค่าย; dtâng-kém ตั้งแคมป์

camp, *n.* kâai ค่าย; kém แคมป์

campaign, *v.* ron-ná-rong รณรงค์

campaign, *n.* gaan-ron-ná-rong การรณรงค์

camping, *n.* gaan-kâo-kâai การเข้าค่าย

campus, *n.* wít-ta-yaa-kèet วิทยาเขต; bɔɔ-ri-ween-má-hǎa-wít-tá-yaa-lai บริเวณมหาวิทยาลัย

can, *aux. v.* sǎa-mâat สามารถ (be able); *v.* sài-grà-bpɔ̌ng ใส่กระป๋อง (put into a can)

can, *n.* grà-bpɔ̌ng กระป๋อง

Canada, *n.* bprà-têet-kɛɛ-naa-daa ประเทศแคนาดา

Canadian, *n.* chaao-kɛɛ-naa-daa ชาวแคนาดา (people); gìao-gàp-kɛɛ-naa-daa เกี่ยวกับแคนาดา (relating to Canada)

canal, *n.* klɔɔng คลอง; chɔ̂ng-taang ช่องทาง

cancel, *v.* yók-lôok ยกเลิก

cancellation, *n.* gaan-yók-lôok การยกเลิก

cancer, *n.* má-reng มะเร็ง (disease); raa-sǐi-gɔɔ-rá-gòt ราศีกรกฎ (zodiac)

candid, *adj.* bpòot-pǒoi เปิดเผย; jing-jai จริงใจ

candidate, *n.* pûu-sà-màk ผู้สมัคร

candle, *n.* tian เทียน

candy, *n.* lûuk-om ลูกอม; kà-nǒm ขนม

cane, *n.* máai-táao ไม้เท้า; máai-riao ไม้เรียว

canine, *n.* sù-nák สุนัข

cannibal, *n.* má-nút-gin-kon มนุษย์กินคน

cannon, *n.* bpuun-yài ปืนใหญ่

cannot, *v.* mâi-sǎa-mâat ไม่สามารถ; mâi-dâai ไม่ได้

canoe, *n.* rua-kɛɛ-nuu เรือแคนู

cantaloupe, *n.* kɛɛn-dtaa-lúup แคนตาลูป

canvas, *n.* pâa-bai ผ้าใบ

canyon, *n.* hùp-kǎo หุบเขา

cap, *n.* mùak หมวก (hat); fǎa-krɔ̂op ฝาครอบ (cover, lid)

capability, *n.* kwaam-sǎa-mâat ความสามารถ; bprà-sìt-ti-pâap ประสิทธิภาพ

capable, *adj.* mii-kwaam-sǎa-mâat มีความสามารถ; mii-fii-muu มีฝีมือ

capacity, *n.* bpà-ri-maan-kwaam-jù ปริมาณความจุ; kwaam-sǎa-mâat ความสามารถ (ability)

cape, n. lɛ̌ɛm แหลม (point or peninsula); pâa-klum-lài ผ้าคลุมไหล่ (shawl)

capital, n. mʉang-lʉ̌ang เมืองหลวง (city); tun ทุน (investment); dtua-kǐan-yài ตัวเขียนใหญ่ (uppercase letter)

capitalism, n. tun-ní-yom ทุนนิยม

capitalist, n. naai-tun นายทุน; nák-tun-ní-yom นักทุนนิยม

capitalize, v. long-tun ลงทุน (invest); kǐan-dûai-dtua-àk-sɔ̌ɔn-yài เขียนด้วยตัว อักษรใหญ่ (write in upper case letters)

capsule, n. kép-suun แคปซูล

captain, n. gàp-dtan กัปตัน

caption, n. kam-ban-yaai-pâap คำบรรยายภาพ

captivate, v. tam-hâi-chɔ̂ɔp ทำให้ชอบ; jàp-jai จับใจ

captive, n. chá-lɚɚi เชลย

captivity, n. gaan-kum-kǎng การคุมขัง

capture, v. jàp จับ; jàp-kum จับคุม

car, n. rót รถ; rót-yon รถยนต์

carat, n. gà-ràt กะรัต

caravan, n. kaa-raa-waan คาราวาน; kà-buan-nák-dɚɚn-taang ขบวนนักเดินทาง

carbohydrate, n. kaa-boo-hai-drèet คาร์โบไฮเดรต

carbon, n. tàan ถ่าน; tâat-kaa-bôn ธาตุคาร์บอน

carbonated, adj. mii-kaa-bôn-dai-ɔ́k-saai มีคาร์บอนไดออกไซด์; mii-gáat มีกาซ

carbon dioxide, n. kaa-bôn-dai-ɔ́k-saai คาร์บอนไดออกไซด์

card, n. gáat การ์ด (e.g. for greeting); bàt บัตร (e.g. invitation); naam-bàt นามบัตร (business card); pèn แผ่น (sheet); pâi ไพ่ (playing)

cardboard, n. grà-dàat-kǎng กระดาษแข็ง

care, v. ao-jai-sài เอาใจใส่; bpen-hùang เป็นห่วง

care, n. gaan-ao-jai-sài การเอาใจใส่; kwaam-bpen-hùang ความเป็นห่วง

career, n. aa-chîip อาชีพ (profession); ngaan งาน (work, job)

carefree, adj. rái-gang-won ไร้กังวล

careful, adj. rá-mát-rá-wang ระมัดระวัง; rɔ̂ɔp-kɔ̂ɔp รอบคอบ

careless, adj. sà-prâo สะเพร่า

carelessness, n. kwaam-sà-prâo ความสะเพร่า; kwaam-mâi-rá-wang ความไม่ระวัง

caress, v. ta-nú-tà-tɔ̌ɔm ทะนุถนอม; láo-loom เล้าโลม

caretaker, n. pûu-duu-lɛɛ ผู้ดูแล

cargo, n. klang-sǐn-káa คลังสินค้า

carnation, n. dɔ̀ɔk-kaa-nee-chân ดอกคาร์เนชั่น

carnival, n. têet-sà-gaan เทศกาล

carpenter, n. châng-máai ช่างไม้

carpentry, n. ngaan-máai งานไม้

carpet, *n.* prom พรม

carrier, *n.* pûu-kǒn-sòng ผู้ขนส่ง (one that transports); krûang-bin-kǒn-sòng เครื่องบินขนส่ง (cargo airplane); paa-hà-nam-rôok พาหะนำโรค (disease)

carrot, *n.* kee-ròt แครอท

carry, *v.* tʉ̌ʉ ถือ (hold); ûm อุ้ม (hold a person in the arms); kǒn-sòng ขนส่ง (transport)

cart, *n.* rót-kěn รถเข็น (e.g. for shopping); gwian เกวียน (drawn by animals)

cartilage, *n.* grà-dùuk-ɔ̀ɔn กระดูกอ่อน

carton, *n.* glɔ̀ng-grà-dàat กล่องกระดาษ

cartoon, *n.* gaa-dtuun การ์ตูน

cartridge, *n.* grà-sǔn-bpʉʉn กระสุนปืน

carve, *v.* gèɛ แกะ; sà-làk สลัก

carving, *n.* gaan-gè-sà-làk การแกะสลัก

case, *n.* rʉ̂ang เรื่อง (matter); gɔɔ-rá-nii กรณี (in law or medicine); glɔ̀ng กล่อง (box); bplɔ̀ɔk ปลอก (cover or sheath)

cash, *n.* ngən-sòt เงินสด

cashew, *n.* má-mûang-hǐm-ma-paan มะม่วงหิมพานต์

cashier, *n.* két-chia แคชเชียร์; kon-gèp-ngən คนเก็บเงิน

cassette, *n.* káat-sèt คาสเซ็ท; dtà-

làp-téep ตลับเทป

cast, *v.* kwâang ขว้าง (throw); tíng ทิ้ง (discard, drop); hâi-hâi ให้ให้ (give away); lɔ̀ɔ หล่อ (shape in a mold); lʉ̂ak-nák-sà-deeng เลือกนักแสดง (choose actors/actresses)

cast, *n.* fʉ̀ak เฝือก (for a broken leg, etc.); kɔ̌ɔng-lɔ̀ɔ ของหล่อ (molded object)

castrate, *v.* dtɔɔn ตอน (remove the testicles)

casual, *adj.* bang-əən บังเอิญ (occurring by chance); mâi-bpen-taang-gaan ไม่เป็นทางการ (informal); mâi-mii-pí-tii-rii-dtrɔɔng ไม่มีพิธีรีตรอง (informal)

cat, *n.* meeo แมว

catalog, *n.* két-dtaa-lɔ́k แคตตาล็อก

cataract, *n.* náam-dtòk น้ำตก (waterfall); dtɔ̂ɔ-grà-jòk ต้อกระจก (of the eye)

catch, *v.* jàp จับ (capture or seize; take hold of); dùt-chʉ́a ติดเชื้อ (a disease)

category, *n.* bprà-pêet ประเภท

cater, *v.* jàt-aa-hǎan จัดอาหาร

caterpillar, *n.* nɔ̌ɔn-pîi-sʉ̂a หนอนผีเสื้อ (wormlike larva)

catfish, *n.* bplaa-dùk ปลาดุก

cathedral, *n.* bòot-yài โบสถ์ใหญ่

Catholic, *n.* kaa-tɔɔ-lìk คาธอลิก

Catholicism, *n.* ní-gaai-kaa-tɔɔ-lìk นิกายคาธอลิก

cattle, *n.* wua-kwaai วัวควาย

cauliflower, *n.* gà-làm-dɔ̀ɔk
กะหล่ำดอก

cause, *n.* sǎa-hèet สาเหตุ; gìt-jà-
gaan กิจการ

caution, *n.* kam-dtuan คำเตือน
(warning); kwaam-rá-mát-rá-wang
ความระมัดระวัง (careful fore-
thought)

cautious, *adj.* rá-wang ระวัง; rɔ̂ɔp-
kɔ̂ɔp รอบคอบ; lá-ìat ละเอียด

cave, cavern, *n.* tâm ถ้ำ

cavity, *n.* proong โพรง; lǔm หลุม
(hole); tâm ถ้ำ (cave); fan-pù
ฟันผุ (dental)

cease, *v.* yùt หยุด (stop); wén เว้น
(abstain); dtaai ตาย (die)

ceasefire, *n.* gaan-yùt-ying
การหยุดยิง; gaan-yùt-rɔ́p
การหยุดรบ

cedar, *n.* dtôn-sǒn-sii-dâa
ต้นสนซีดาร์

ceiling, *n.* pee-daan เพดาน

Celsius, *n.* seo-sîat, sen-sîas, sen-
sìat, seo-sîas เซลเซียส

celebrate, *v.* chà-lɔɔng ฉลอง;
bprà-gɔ̀ɔp-pí-tii ประกอบพิธี

celebration, *n.* gaan-chà-lɔɔng
การฉลอง

celebrity, *n.* kon-dang คนดัง; kon-
mii-chûu-sǐang คนมีชื่อเสียง;
kwaam-dòong-dang ความโด่งดัง

celibacy, *n.* chii-wít-sòot ชีวิตโสด

celibate, *n.* pûu-ngót-rûang-gaam-
ma-rom ผู้งดเรื่องกามารมณ์

cell, *v.* seo เซลล์ (body cell); hɔ̂ng-
kǎng ห้องขัง (confining room)

cellar, *n.* hɔ̂ng-dtâai-din ห้องใต้ดิน

cello, *n.* chen-lôo เชลโล

cement, *n.* sii-men ซีเมนต์

cemetery, *n.* bpà-cháa ป่าช้า; sù-
sǎan สุสาน

censor, *v.* sen-sɔ̀ɔ เซ็นเซอร์;
dtrùat-sɔ̀ɔp ตรวจสอบ

censorship, *n.* gaan-sen-sɔ̀ɔ
การเซ็นเซอร์; gaan-dtrùat-sɔ̀ɔp
การตรวจสอบ

census, *n.* gaan-sǎm-rùat-sǎm-má-
noo-krua การสำรวจสำมะโนครัว

cent, *n.* sen เซ็นต์

centennial, *n.* mii-aa-yú-dâai-rɔ́ɔi-
bpii มีอายุได้ร้อยปี

center, *n.* sǔun-glaang ศูนย์กลาง;
jai-glaang ใจกลาง

centigrade, *n.* sen-dtì-grèet
เซนติเกรด

centimeter, *n.* sen-dtì-méet
เซ็นติเมตร

central, *adj.* sùan-glaang ส่วนกลาง;
sǎm-kan สำคัญ

centralize, *v.* tam-hâi-bpen-sǔun-
glaang ทำให้เป็นศูนย์กลาง; ruam-
kâo รวมเข้า

century, *n.* sàt-dtà-wát ศตวรรษ;
nùng-rɔ́ɔi-bpii หนึ่งร้อยปี

ceramic, *adj.* see-raa-mìk เซรามิก

cereal, *n.* sii-rîao ซีเรียล; tan-yapùut ธัญพืช

ceremony, n. pí-tii พิธี; bèɛp-pɛ̌ɛn แบบแผน

certain, adj. nɛ̂ɛ-jai แน่ใจ (sure); nɛ̂ɛ-nɔɔn แน่นอน (definite; inevitable); baang-yàang บางอย่าง (some)

certainly, adv. yàang-nɛ̂ɛ-nɔɔn อย่างแน่นอน; châi ใช่

certificate, n. bai-ráp-rɔɔng ใบรับรอง; bprà-gàat-sà-nii-yá-bàt ประกาศนียบัตร (for graduation)

certify, v. ráp-rɔɔng รับรอง;

chain, v. lâam-sôo ล่ามโซ่ (constrain; bind with chains)

chain, n. sôo โซ่ (shackles); lûuk-sôo ลูกโซ่ (series of links); sǎai-sɔ̂i สายสร้อย (necklace)

chain reaction, n. bpà-dtì-gì-rí-yaa-lûuk-sôo ปฏิกิริยาลูกโซ่

chair, n. gâo-îi เก้าอี้ (to sit on); bprà-taan ประธาน (president)

chalk, n. chɔ́k ชอล์ก

challenge, v. táa-taai ท้าทาย

challenge, n. kwaam-táa-taai ความท้าทาย

challenger, n. pûu-taa-taai ผู้ท้าทาย

challenging, adj. táa-taai ท้าทาย

chamber of commerce, n. hɔ̌ɔ-gaan-káa หอการค้า

chameleon, n. gîng-gàa-bplìan-sǐi กิ้งก่าเปลี่ยนสี

champion, n. chɛm แชมป์

championship, n. dtam-nɛ̀ng-chá-ná-lɔ̂ɛt ตำแหน่งชนะเลิศ

chance, n. oo-gàat โอกาส (opportunity); chôok โชค (luck)

change, v. bplìan เปลี่ยน; bplìan-bplɛɛng เปลี่ยนแปลง

change, n. gaan-bplìan-bplɛɛng การเปลี่ยนแปลง

changeable, adj. bplìan-bplɛɛng-dâai เปลี่ยนแปลงได้

channel, n. chɔ̂ng ช่อง (e.g. T.V.); taang ทาง (way)

chant, v. rɔ́ɔng-pleeng ร้องเพลง (a song); sùat-mon สวดมนต์ (a prayer)

chaos, n. kwaam-wûn-waai ความวุ่นวาย

chapter, n. bòt บท; dtɔɔn ตอน

character, n. dtua-àk-sɔ̌ɔn ตัวอักษร (letter of the alphabet); lák-sà-nà-pí-sèet ลักษณะพิเศษ (special characteristics); ní-sǎi นิสัย (true nature); dtua-lá-kɔɔn ตัวละคร (in a play)

characteristic, adj. mii-lák-sà-nà-pí-sèet มีลักษณะพิเศษ (distinctive)

charcoal, n. tàan ถ่าน

charge, v. chaat-fai ชาร์จไฟ (electricity); gèp-ngən เก็บเงิน (money, e.g. in restaurant); kít-raa-kaa คิดราคา (the price of something)

charge, n. gaan-duu-lɛɛ การดูแล (care taking); gaan-chaat-fai

English · Phonetic · Thai

การชาร์จไฟ (electricity)

charge account, *n.* ban-chii-kǎai-chûa บัญชีขายเชื่อ

charisma, *n.* pɔɔn-sà-wǎn พรสวรรค์ (extraordinary power); kwaam-sǎa-mâat-pí-sèt-kɔ̌ɔng-pûu-nam ความสามารถพิเศษของผู้นำ (of a leader); kwaam-mii-sà-nèe ความมีเสน่ห์ (attraction, charm)

charity, *n.* gaan-gù-sǒn การกุศล

charm, *n.* sà-nèe เสน่ห์

charming, *adj.* mii-sà-nèe มีเสน่ห์

chart, *n.* pɛ̌ɛn-puum แผนภูมิ; pɛ̌ɛn-pâap แผนภาพ; pǎng ผัง

charter, *n.* gòt-bàt กฎบัตร (a document issued by an authority); sǎn-yaa-châo สัญญาเช่า (rental contract)

chase, *v.* lâi ไล่ (follow rapidly; trying to catch); sà-wɛ̌ɛng-hǎa แสวงหา (search); dtìt-dtaam ติดตาม (follow)

chase, *n.* gaan-lâi การไล่; gaan-sà-wɛ̌ɛng-hǎa การแสวงหา; gaan-dtìt-dtaam การติดตาม

chaste, *adj.* bɔɔ-ri-sùt บริสุทธิ์ (pure); rîap-ngâai เรียบง่าย (simple in style)

chastity, *n.* kwaam-dii-ngaam ความดีงาม

chat, *v.* pûut พูด; kui คุย

chat, *n.* gaan-pûut-kui การพูดคุย

chauffeur, *n.* kon-kàp-tɛ́k-sîi คนขับแท็กซี่

cheap, *adj.* raa-kaa-tùuk ราคาถูก (price); tùuk ถูก (price); kîi-nìao ขี้เหนียว (stingy)

cheapen, *v.* lót-raa-kaa ลดราคา (reduce price); lót-kun-ná-pâap ลดคุณภาพ (degrade)

cheat, *v.* goong โกง (deceive); nɔ̂ɔk-jai นอกใจ (between lovers)

check, *v.* dtrùat ตรวจ

check, *n.* chék เช็ค (bank draft)

checking account, *n.* ban-chii-tîi-kîan-chék-dâai บัญชีที่เขียนเช็คได้

checkup, *n.* gaan-dtrùat-chék การตรวจเช็ค; gaan-dtrùat-râang-gaai การตรวจร่างกาย (physical)

cheek, *n.* gɛ̂ɛm แก้ม

cheer, *v.* chia เชียร์; hâi-gam-lang-jai ให้กำลังใจ

cheer, *n.* gaan-chia การเชียร์; gaan-hâi-gam-lang-jai การให้กำลังใจ

cheerful, *adj.* râa-rəəng ร่าเริง

Cheers!, *interj.* chai-yoo ไชโย

cheese, *n.* nəəi-kɛ̌ng เนยแข็ง

chef, *n.* chép เชฟ; hǔa-nâa-krua หัวหน้าครัว

chemical, *n.* sǎan-kee-mii สารเคมี

chemistry, *n.* kee-mii-wít-ta-yaa เคมีวิทยา

chemotherapy, *n.* kee-mii-bam-bàt เคมีบำบัด

cherry, *n.* chəə-rîi เชอร์รี่

chess, *n.* màak-rúk หมากรุก

chest, *v.* òk อก (breast); glɔ̂ng-yài

กล่องใหญ่ (big box or case)

chew, *v.* kíao เคี้ยว

chewing gum, *n.* màak-fà-ràng หมากฝรั่ง

chicken, *n.* gài ไก่; núa-gài เนื้อไก่

chief, *n.* hǔa-nâa หัวหน้า (head or boss); naai นาย (boss or master)

child, *n.* dèk เด็ก; lûuk ลูก (son or daughter)

childbirth, *n.* gaan-klôot-lûuk การคลอดลูก; gaan-klôot-bùt การคลอดบุตร

childhood, *n.* wai-dèk วัยเด็ก

childish, *adj.* mǔan-dèk เหมือนเด็ก

chili pepper, *n.* prík พริก

chill, *n.* kwaam-nǎao ความหนาว

chilly, *adj.* nǎao หนาว

chimney, *n.* bplòng-fai ปล่องไฟ

chimpanzee, *n.* chim-bpɛɛn-sii ชิมแปนซี

chin, *n.* kaang คาง

china, *n.* krûang-laai-kraam เครื่องลายคราม

China, *n.* bprà-têet-jiin ประเทศจีน

Chinese, *n.* kon-jiin คนจีน (person); paa-sǎa-jiin ภาษาจีน (language); gìao-gàp-jiin เกี่ยวกับจีน (relating to China)

chip, *n.* sèet เศษ (small piece); chíp ชิพ (e.g. computer)

chirp, *v.* rɔɔng-jíp-jíp ร้องจิ๊บๆ

chirp, *n.* sǐang-nók เสียงนก

chisel, *n.* sìu สิ่ว

chlorine, *n.* klɔɔ-riin คลอรีน

chocolate, *n.* chɔ́k-goo-lét ช็อกโกแล็ต

choice, *n.* gaan-lûak การเลือก; taang-lûak ทางเลือก

choir, *n.* ká-ná-rɔ́ɔng-pleeng คณะร้องเพลง

choke, *v.* sǎm-lák สำลัก (interfere with the respiration); jùk-nên จุกแน่น (jam, become obstructed)

cholera, *n.* à-hì-waa อหิวาต์

cholesterol, *n.* kɔɔ-léet-dtəə-rɔn, kɔɔ-lées-dtəə-rɔ̂n คอเลสเตอรอล

choose, *v.* lûak เลือก

chop, *v.* dtàt ตัด; pàa ผ่า; sàp สับ

chopsticks, *n.* dtà-gìap ตะเกียบ

chord, *n.* sǎai-krûang-don-dtrii สายเครื่องดนตรี (musical)

chore, *n.* ngaan-bâan งานบ้าน; ngaan-lék-lék-nɔ́ɔi-nɔ́ɔi งานเล็กๆน้อยๆ

chorus, *n.* kɔɔ-rát, kɔɔ-rás คอรัส; nák-rɔ́ɔng-mùu นักร้องหมู่

Christ, *n.* prá-yee-suu-krít, prá-yee-suu-krís พระเยซูคริสต์; prá-yee-suu พระเยซู

Christian, *n.* chaao-krít-sà-dtian ชาวคริสเตียน (person); gìao-gàp-sàat-sà-nǎa-krít เกี่ยวกับศาสนาคริสต์ (relating to Christianity)

Christianity, *n.* sàat-sà-nǎa-krít ศาสนาคริสต์

Christmas, *n.* krít-sa-mâat, krít-sa-

English · Phonetic · Thai

mát, krít-sa-más คริสต์มาส

chromosome, *n.* kroo-moo-soom
โครโมโซม

chronic, *adj.* rúa-rang เรื้อรัง

chronological, *adj.* dtaam-lam-
dàp-wee-laa ตามลำดับเวลา;
dtaam-lam-dàp-hèet-gaan
ตามลำดับเหตุการณ์

chuckle, *n.* húa-rɔ́-bao-bao
หัวเราะเบาๆ; ɛ̀ep-húa-rɔ́
แอบหัวเราะ

church, *n.* bòot โบสถ์

cicada, *n.* ják-gà-jàn จั๊กจั่น

cider, *n.* náam-ɛ́p-bpɔ̀n น้ำแอปเปิ้ล;
náam-sai-dɔ̂ɔ น้ำไซเดอร์

cigar, *n.* sí-gâa ซิก้า

cigarette, *n.* bù-rìi บุหรี่

cinder, *n.* tàan ถ่าน (charcoal);
gàak-rɛ̂ɛ กากแร่ (mineral leftover)

cinema, *n.* nǎng หนัง (movie);
roong-pâap-pa-yon โรงภาพยนตร์
(movie theater); roong-nǎng
โรงหนัง (movie theater - collq.)

cinnamon, *n.* òp-chəəi อบเชย

circle, *n.* wong-glom วงกลม (ring,
round object, etc.); wong-gaan
วงการ (sphere of interest; domain)

circuit, *n.* wong-jɔɔn วงจร

circular, *adj.* glom กลม (of or relating to a circle); bpen-wong-glom
เป็นวงกลม

circulate, *v.* mǔn-wian หมุนเวียน

circulation, *n.* gaan-mǔn-wian
การหมุนเวียน

circumcise, *v.* klìp ขลิบ

circumcision, *n.* gaan-klìp
การขลิบ

circumference, *n.* sên-rɔ̂ɔp-wong
เส้นรอบวง

circumstance, *n.* sà-tǎa-ná-gaan
สถานการณ์ (situation); sà-pâap-
wɛ̂ɛt-lɔ́ɔm สภาพแวดล้อม (condition)

circus, *n.* lá-kɔɔn-sàt ละครสัตว์

cistern, *n.* tîi-gèp-náam ที่เก็บน้ำ

citizen, *n.* pon-lá-muang พลเมือง

citizenship, *n.* sǎn-châat สัญชาติ

city, *n.* muang เมือง

city council, *n.* sà-paa-têet-sà-
baan-muang สภาเทศบาลเมือง

city hall, *n.* sǎa-laa-glaang
ศาลากลาง

civic, *adj.* gìao-gàp-muang
เกี่ยวกับเมือง

civil, *adj.* gìao-gàp-pon-la-ruan
เกี่ยวกับพลเรือน (relating to citizens); gìao-gàp-ká-dii-pɛɛng
เกี่ยวกับคดีแพ่ง (legal; concerning
individuals); mii-aa-ra-yá-tam
มีอารยธรรม (civilized)

civilian, *n.* pon-la-ruan พลเรือน

civilization, *n.* aa-ra-yá-tam
อารยธรรม

civilize, *v.* tam-hâi-jà-rəən
ทำให้เจริญ

claim, *v.* rîak-rɔ́ɔng เรียกร้อง

(demand, require); âang อ้าง (state to be true; assert)

clam, *n.* hɔ̌i-gàap หอยกาบ

clamp, *n.* kiim คีม

clap, *v.* dtòp-mɯɯ ตบมือ

clarify, *v.* tam-hâi-chát-jeen ทำให้ชัดเจน

clarinet, *n.* klaa-ri-nèt คลาริเน็ท

clarity, *n.* kwaam-chát-jeen ความชัดเจน

clasp, *n.* kěm-glàt เข็มกลัด (pin); dtua-chɯ̂am-dtɔ̀ɔ ตัวเชื่อมต่อ (a fastening, such as a hook or buckle)

class, *n.* chán ชั้น (grade, rank, class in school); rá-dàp ระดับ (level); bprà-pêet ประเภท (group)

classic, *n.* sìng-dii-yìam สิ่งดีเยี่ยม (something superior); wan-ná-ka-dii-boo-raan วรรณคดีโบราณ (ancient literary work)

classical, *adj.* chán-nùng ชั้นหนึ่ง; klάat-sìk คลาสสิก

classification, *n.* gaan-bèng-bprà-pêet การแบ่งประเภท

classifier, *n.* lák-sà-nà-naam ลักษณนาม (Thai part of speech)

classify, *v.* bèng-bprà-pêet แบ่งประเภท

classmate, *n.* pɯ̂an-rûam-chán เพื่อนร่วมชั้น

classroom, *n.* hɔ̂ng rian ห้องเรียน

claw, *n.* ûng-lép อุ้งเล็บ (of animals with toes); gâam-gûng ก้ามกุ้ง (of

shrimp); gâam-bpuu ก้ามปู (of crab)

clay, *n.* din-nǐao ดินเหนียว

clean, *adj.* sà-àat สะอาด

cleaner, *n.* kon-tam-kwaam-sà-àat คนทำความสะอาด

cleaning, *n.* gaan-tam-kwaam-sà-àat การทำความสะอาด

clear, *v.* yáai-ɔ̀ɔk ย้ายออก (remove); klia เคลียร์ (get rid of objects); jàt-gaan-ban-chǐi จัดการบัญชี (in accounting)

clear, *adj.* sǎi ใส (free from clouds, dust, etc); chát ชัด (bright; easily seen); sà-wàang สว่าง (not dark)

clear-cut, *adj.* bpen-kroong-râang-chát-jeen เป็นโครงร่างชัดเจน; nɛ̂ɛ-chát แน่ชัด

clergyman, *n.* prá พระ; prá-sɔ̌ɔn-sàat-sà-nǎa พระสอนศาสนา

clerical, *adj.* gìao-gàp-sà-mǐan เกี่ยวกับเสมียน; yàang-prá อย่างพระ

clerk, *n.* sà-mǐan เสมียน (in an office); kon-kǎai-kɔ̌ɔng คนขายของ (in a store)

clever, *adj.* chà-làat ฉลาด; gèng เก่ง

cliché, *n.* sǎm-nuan-sám-sâak สำนวนซ้ำซาก

click, *n.* sǐang-dang-klík เสียงดังคลิก

client, *n.* lûuk-káa ลูกค้า (customer); lûuk-kwaam ลูกความ

(of a lawyer); kon-kâi คนไข้ (patient)
clientele, *n.* lûuk-káa ลูกค้า; lûuk-kwaam ลูกความ
cliff, *n.* nâa-pǎa หน้าผา
climate, *n.* aa-gàat อากาศ
climax, *n.* jùt-sùt-yɔ̂ɔt จุดสุดยอด; jùt-sǎm-kan จุดสำคัญ
climb, *v.* bpiin ปีน; dtài ไต่
cling, *v.* yʉ́t ยึด; gɔ̀ เกาะ
clinic, *n.* klii-nìk คลีนิก
clip, *v.* nìip หนีบ; dtàt-ɔ̀ɔk ตัดออก
clip, *n.* tîi-nìip ที่หนีบ
cloak, *n.* sʉ̂a-klum เสื้อคลุม
clock, *n.* naa-lí-gaa นาฬิกา
clockwise, *adv.* dtaam-kěm-naa-li-gaa ตามเข็มนาฬิกา
clog, *v.* kàt-kwǎang ขัดขวาง; ùt-dtan อุดตัน
close, *v.* bpìt ปิด (shut); kâo-glâi เข้าใกล้ (get close)
close, *n.* gaan-bpìt การปิด
close, *adj.* glâi ใกล้
closed, *adj.* bpìt ปิด
closet, *n.* dûu-fǎa-pà-nǎng ตู้ฝาผนัง; hɔ̂ng-lék ห้องเล็ก
clot, *n.* gɔ̂ɔn-lʉ̂at ก้อนเลือด (blood); gɔ̂ɔn-lék-lék ก้อนเล็กๆ (small pieces)
cloth, *n.* sʉ̂a-pâa เสื้อผ้า
clothes, clothing, *n.* sʉ̂a-pâa เสื้อผ้า; krʉ̂ang-dtèng-gaai เครื่องแต่งกาย
cloud, *n.* mêek เมฆ; ngao-mʉ̂ut เงามืด (dark shadow)
cloudy, *adj.* mii-mêek มีเมฆ; mâi-chát ไม่ชัด (unclear)
clove, *n.* gâan-pluu ก้านพลู (a plant); glìip-grà-tiam กลีบกระเทียม (of garlic)
clown, *n.* dtua-dtà-lòk ตัวตลก
club, *n.* nái-klàp ไนท์คลับ (night-club); grà-bɔɔng กระบอง (stout heavy stick); chom-rom ชมรม (association)
clue, *n.* rɔ̂ng-rɔɔi ร่องรอย; bɔ̀-sɛ̌ɛ เบาะแส; bpom ปม
clumsy, *adj.* ngûm-ngâam งุ่มง่าม; sɔ̂ɔ-sâa เซ่อซ่า
clutch, *v.* kwáa คว้า (grasp); gam กำ (put in the hand); fák-kài ฟักไข่ (of eggs)
clutter, *v.* rîa-râat เรี่ยราด; wîng-wûn วิ่งวุ่น; yûng-yɔ̌ɔng ยุ่งเหยิง
coach, *n.* rót-dooi-sǎan รถโดยสาร (bus); kruu-fʉ̀k ครูฝึก (trainer)
coal, *n.* tàan-hǐn ถ่านหิน; tàan ถ่าน
coast, *n.* fàng-tá-lee ฝั่งทะเล
coast guard, *n.* nùai-lâat-dtrà-ween-chaai-fàng หน่วยลาดตระเวณชายฝั่ง
coat, *n.* sʉ̂a-nɔ̂ɔk เสื้อนอก (outer garment); bplʉ̀ak เปลือก (crust)
coax, *v.* glîa-glɔ̀m เกลี้ยกล่อม; lɔ̀ɔk หลอก
cobweb, *n.* yai-mɛɛng-mum

English • Phonetic • Thai

ใยแมงมุม

cocaine, *n.* koo-keen โคเคน

cock, *n.* gài-dtua-pûu ไก่ตัวผู้

cockpit, *n.* hông-kon-kàp-krûang-bin ห้องคนขับเครื่องบิน (for pilot); sà-nǎam-chon-gài สนามชนไก่ (for cock fight)

cockroach, *n.* má-lɛɛng-sàap แมลงสาบ

cocktail, *n.* kók-teo ค็อกเทล; lâo เหล้า

cocky, *adj.* yîng หยิ่ง; ùat-dii อวดดี

cocoa, *n.* goo-gôo โกโก้

coconut, *n.* má-práao มะพร้าว

cocoon, *n.* rang-mǎi รังไหม

cod, *n.* bplaa-kɔ́t ปลาคอด

code, *n.* rá-hàt รหัส

coffee, *n.* gaa-fɛɛ กาแฟ

coffee pot, *n.* mɔ̂ɔ-gaa-fɛɛ หม้อกาแฟ

coffin, *n.* loong-sòp โลงศพ

coil, *n.* kòt-lûat ขดลวด (wire); kòt-chûak ขดเชือก (rope)

coin, *n.* rǐan เหรียญ

coincidental, *adj.* bang-əən บังเอิญ

coincidence, *n.* hèet-bang-əən เหตุบังเอิญ

coitus, *n.* gaan-rûam-bprà-wee-nii การร่วมประเวณี

cold, *adj.* nǎao หนาว (feeling cold); yen เย็น (something cold)

cold, *n.* kâi-wàt ไข้หวัด (disease)

cold-blooded, *adj.* lûat-yen เลือดเย็น

collapse, *v.* lóm-long ล้มลง; pang-long พังลง

collar, *n.* bplɔ̀ɔk-kɔɔ ปลอกคอ; kɔɔ-sûa คอเสื้อ

collarbone, *n.* grà-dùuk-hǎi-bplaa-ráa กระดูกไหปลาร้า

colleague, *n.* pûan-rûam-ngaan เพื่อนร่วมงาน

collect, *v.* gèp เก็บ; rûap-ruam รวบรวม; sà-sǒm สะสม

collect call, *n.* too-gèp-ngən-bplaai-taang โทรเก็บเงินปลายทาง

collection, *n.* gaan-rûap-ruam การรวบรวม; gaan-jàt-gèp การจัดเก็บ

collector, *n.* pûu-gèp ผู้เก็บ; pûu-sà-sǒm ผู้สะสม

college, *n.* koo-loon โคโลญจ์

cologne, *n.* koo-loon โคโลญจ์

colon, *n.* krûang-mǎai-koo-lôn เครื่องหมายโคลอน (punctuation mark); lam-sâi-yài ลำไส้ใหญ่ (large intestine)

colonel, *n.* naai-pan นายพัน; pan-èek พันเอก

colonial, *adj.* gìao-gàp-aa-naa-ní-kom เกี่ยวกับอาณานิคม

colonize, *v.* lâa-aa-naa-ní-kom ล่าอาณานิคม

colony, *n.* aa-naa-ní-kom อาณานิคม

color, *n.* sǐi สี

English · Phonetic · Thai

English · Phonetic · Thai

colorblind, *adj.* dtaa-bòot-sǐi ตาบอดสี

colorful, *adj.* mii-sǐi-sǎn-mâak มีสีสันมาก; sǐi-sòt-sǎi สีสดใส

colt, *n.* lûuk-máa-dtua-pûu ลูกม้าตัวผู้

column, *n.* kɔɔ-lâm คอลัมน์

columnist, *n.* kɔɔ-lâm-nít คอลัมนิสต์; nák-kǐan-kɔɔ-lâm นักเขียนคอลัมน์

coma, *n.* koo-mâa โคม่า

comb, *v.* wǐi-pǒm หวีผม

comb, *n.* wǐi หวี (for the hair); ruang-pûng รวงผึ้ง (honeycomb); ngɔ̌ɔn-gài หงอนไก่ (of a cock)

combat, *v.* dtɔ̀ɔ-sûu ต่อสู้

combination, *n.* gaan-ruam-gan การรวมกัน

combine, *v.* ruam-gan รวมกัน; bprà-gɔ̀ɔp-gan ประกอบกัน

come, *v.* maa มา

comeback, *n.* gaan-glàp-maa การกลับมา

comedy, *n.* lá-kɔɔn-dtà-lòk ละครตลก (humorous play); kwaam-kòp-kǎn ความขบขัน (humorous occurrence)

comet, *n.* daao-hǎang ดาวหาง

comfort, *v.* bplɔ̀ɔp-yoon ปลอบโยน (soothe in time of distress); ban-tao บรรเทา (relieve)

comfort, *n.* gaan-bplɔ̀ɔp-yoon การปลอบโยน; gaan-ban-tao การบรรเทา

comfortable, *adj.* sà-baai สบาย

comic, *n.* rûang-kòp-kǎn เรื่องขบขัน

comic strip, *n.* gaa-dtuun การ์ตูน

comma, *n.* jun-la-pâak จุลภาค

command, *v.* sàng สั่ง

command, *n.* kam-sàng คำสั่ง

commander, *n.* pûu-sàng-gaan ผู้สั่งการ

comment, *n.* kɔ̂ɔ-kít-hěn ข้อคิดเห็น (opinion); kam-wí-jaan คำวิจารณ์ (criticism)

commentary, *n.* kam-wí-jaan คำวิจารณ์ (criticism); bòt-kwaam บทความ (article)

commerce, *n.* gaan-káa การค้า

commercial, *adj.* gìao-gàp-gaan-káa เกี่ยวกับการค้า

commercialize, *v.* tam-hâi-bpen-gaan-káa ทำให้เป็นการค้า

commission, *n.* gaan-mɔ̂ɔp-mǎai การมอบหมาย (assignment); kâa-kɔm-mít-chân ค่าคอมมิสชัน (fee or percentage)

commissioner, *n.* pûu-dtrùat-gaan ผู้ตรวจการ (a person authorized by a commission to perform certain duties); à-típ-bɔɔ-dii อธิบดี (governmental official)

commit, *v.* mɔ̂ɔp-mǎai มอบหมาย; tam-pìt ทำผิด

commitment, *n.* gaan-mɔ̂ɔp การมอบ; gaan-hâi-sǎn-yaa การให้สัญญา

English · Phonetic · Thai

committee, *n.* ká-ná-gam-ma-gaan คณะกรรมการ

commodity, *n.* sĭn-káa สินค้า; pà-lìt-dtà-pan ผลิตภัณฑ์

common, *adj.* tam-ma-daa ธรรมดา; mŭan-gan เหมือนกัน

commoner, *n.* săa-man-chon สามัญชน

commonplace, *adj.* tam-ma-daa ธรรมดา

common sense, *n.* săa-man-sǎm-núk สามัญสำนึก

commotion, *n.* kwaam-wûn-waai ความวุ่นวาย; jà-raa-jon จราจล

communal, *adj.* gìao-gàp-chum-chon เกี่ยวกับชุมชน

commune, *n.* bprà-chaa-kom ประชาคม; gaan-lêɛk-bplìan-kwaam-kìt-hěn การแลกเปลี่ยนความคิดเห็น

communicable, *adj.* dtìt-dtɔ̀ɔ-gan-dâai ติดต่อกันได้

communicate, *v.* dtìt-dtɔ̀ɔ ติดต่อ; sùu-sǎan สื่อสาร

communication, *n.* gaan-dtìt-dtɔ̀ɔ การติดต่อ; gaan-sùu-sǎan การสื่อสาร

communism, *n.* lát-tí-kom miu-nít ลัทธิคอมมิวนิสต์

communist, *n.* kom-miu-nít คอมมิวนิสต์

community, *n.* chum-chon ชุมชน; sǎng-kom สังคม

commute, *v.* bplìan-bpen-yàang-

ùun เปลี่ยนเป็นอย่างอื่น (transform); dɔɔn-taang-pai-bpai-maa-maa เดินทางไปๆมาๆ (travel back and forth)

commuter, *n.* kon-dɔɔn-taang-bpai-bpai-maa-maa คนเดินทางไปๆมาๆ

compact, *n.* dtà-làp-bpɛ̂ɛng ตลับแป้ง (for powder); rót-kà-nàat-yɔ̂m รถขนาดย่อม (small car); kɔ̂ɔ-dtòk-long ข้อตกลง (agreement)

companion, *n.* pûan เพื่อน (friend); kon-tîi-bpai-dûai คนที่ไปด้วย (one that goes with another)

companionship, *n.* kwaam-bpen-pûan ความเป็นเพื่อน

company, *n.* pûan-fûung เพื่อนฝูง (friends); bɔɔ-ri-sàt บริษัท (firm); ká-ná คณะ (group of persons)

compare, *v.* bprìap-tîap เปรียบเทียบ

comparison, *n.* gaan-bprìap-tîap การเปรียบเทียบ

compartment, *n.* chɔ̂ng ช่อง (slot, small room or space)

compass, *n.* kěm-tít เข็มทิศ (a device); aa-naa-kèet อาณาเขต (range or scope)

compassion, *n.* kwaam-wêet-ta-naa ความเวทนา; kwaam-hěn-jai ความเห็นใจ

compassionate, *adj.* mii-kwaam-wêet-ta-naa มีความเวทนา

compensate, *v.* chót-chəəi ชดเชย;
dtɔ̀ɔp-tɛɛn ตอบแทน

compensation, *n.* gaan-chót-chəəi
การชดเชย; sìng-dtɔ̀ɔp-tɛɛn
สิ่งตอบแทน

compete, *v.* kɛ̀ng-kǎn แข่งขัน

competence, *n.* kwaam-sǎa-mâat
ความสามารถ

competent, *adj.* mii-kwaam-sǎa-
mâat มีความสามารถ (capable);
mii-kun-ná-sǒm-bàt มีคุณสมบัติ
(qualified)

competition, *n.* gaan-kɛ̀ng-kǎn
การแข่งขัน

competitor, *n.* pûu-kɛ̀ng-kǎn
ผู้แข่งขัน

complacency, *n.* kwaam-ìm-jai
ความอิ่มใจ; kwaam-pʉng-pɔɔ-jai
ความพึงพอใจ

complacent, *adj.* ìm-òk-ìm-jai
อิ่มอกอิ่มใจ; pʉng-pɔɔ-jai พึงพอใจ

complain, *v.* bòn บ่น (express negative feelings); fɔ́ɔng ฟ้อง (bring a
formal charge)

complaint, *n.* gaan-bòn การบ่น;
gaan-rɔ́ɔng-túk การร้องทุกข์

complement, *n.* gaan-tam-hâi-sèt-
sǐn การทำให้เสร็จสิ้น (bringing to
completion); sùan-bprà-gɔ̀ɔp
ส่วนประกอบ (parts)

complete, *adj.* sǒm-buun สมบูรณ์
(entire); sèt เสร็จ (done, finished)

complete, *v.* tam-hâi-sǒm-buun

tam-hâi-sǒm-buun (make complete);
tam-hâi-sèt ทำให้เสร็จ (make finished)

completion, *n.* gaan-tam-hâi-sǒm-
buun การทำให้สมบูรณ์; gaan-sǎm-
rèt การสำเร็จ

complex, *n.* kwaam-sáp-sɔ́ɔn
ความซับซ้อน

complexion, *n.* sǐi-pǐu สีผิว (skin
color); kwaam-kít-hěn ความคิดเห็น
(viewpoint)

complexity, *n.* kwaam-sáp-sɔ́ɔn
ความซับซ้อน

compliance, *n.* gaan-yin-yɔɔm
การยินยอม; gaan-rûam-mʉʉ
การร่วมมือ

complicate, *v.* tam-hâi-sáp-sɔ́ɔn
ทำให้ซับซ้อน

complicated, *adj.* sáp-sɔ́ɔn ซับซ้อน

complication, *n.* kwaam-sáp-sɔ́ɔn
ความซับซ้อน

complicity, *n.* gaan-rûam-ngaan
การร่วมงาน; gaan-sǒm-kóp
การสมคบ

compliment, *v.* chom-chəəi ชมเชย

compliment, *n.* kam-chom-chəəi
คำชมเชย

complimentary, *adj.*, *n.* chom-
chəəi ชมเชย (using a compliment);
à-pí-nan-ta-naa-gaan อภินันทนาการ
(given free)

comply, *v.* tam-dtaam ทำตาม; yin-
yɔɔm ยินยอม

component, *n.* sùan-bprà-gòɔp ส่วนประกอบ

compose, *v.* bprà-gòɔp ประกอบ (consist); dtɛ̀ng แต่ง (e.g. music)

composer, *n.* nák-dtɛ̀ng-pleeng นักแต่งเพลง

composure, *n.* kwaam-sà-ngòp ความสงบ; aa-rom-sà-ngòp อารมณ์สงบ

compromise, *n.* bprà-nii-bprà-nɔɔm ประนีประนอม

compute, *v.* kam-nuan คำนวณ

computer, *n.* kom-piu-dtə̂ə คอมพิวเตอร์

concave, *adj.* wáo เว้า; wòo โหว่

conceal, *v.* sɔ̂n ซ่อน; bpìt-bang ปิดบัง

concede, *v.* yɔɔm-ráp ยอมรับ; yɔɔm-hâi ยอมให้

conceit, *n.* kwaam-yìng ความหยิ่ง; kwaam-tʉ̌ʉ-dii ความถือดี

conceive, *v.* nʉ́k นึก (think); kít คิด (think); kâo-jai เข้าใจ (understand); dtâng-tɔ́ɔng ตั้งท้อง (become pregnant)

concentrate, *v.* jòt-jɔ̀ɔ จดจ่อ (focus one's attention), pʉng เพ่ง (focus), dtâng-jai ตั้งใจ (direct one's thoughts or attention)

concentrated, *adj.* kêm-kôn เข้มข้น

concentration, *n.* kwaam-kêm-kôn ความเข้มข้น (density); kwaam-dtâng-òk-dtâng-jai ความตั้งอกตั้งใจ (paying attention)

concept, *n.* kɔ̂ɔ-kít-hĕn ข้อคิดเห็น; kɔn-sèp คอนเซ็ป

conception, *n.* gaan-kít การคิด

concern, *v.* gìao-kɔ̂ng เกี่ยวข้อง

concern, *n.* kwaam-gìao-pan ความเกี่ยวพัน (related affair); kwaam-hùang-yai ความห่วงใย (worrisome)

concerned, *adj.* sŏn-jai สนใจ (interested); bpen-hùang เป็นห่วง (worried)

concerning, *prep.* gìao-gàp เกี่ยวกับ

concert, *n.* kɔn-sə̀ɔt คอนเสิร์ต

concerto, *n.* pleeng-bprà-sǎan-sǐang เพลงประสานเสียง

concession, *n.* gaan-yin-yɔɔm การยินยอม; sam-bpà-taan สัมปทาน

conciliate, *v.* glài-glìa ไกล่เกลี่ย (reconcile); chá-ná-jai ชนะใจ (overcome the distrust)

concise, *adj.* gà-tát-rát กะทัดรัด; sân สั้น

conclude, *v.* sà-rùp สรุป (summarize); sîn-sùt สิ้นสุด (end)

conclusion, *n.* gaan-sà-rùp การสรุป; qaan-sîn-sùt การสิ้นสุด

concord, *n.* kwaam-sɔ̀ɔt-klɔɔng-gan ความสอดคล้องกัน (harmony); mít-dtà-pâap มิตรภาพ (friendship)

concrete, *n.* rûup-bpà-tam รูปธรรม (not abstract); kwaam-chát-jeen ความชัดเจน (clarity); kɔn-grìit

คอนกรีต (cement)

concubine, *n.* naang-bam-rəə
นางบำเรอ

concur, *v.* hěn-dûai เห็นด้วย

concurrent, *adj.* prɔ́ɔm-priang
พร้อมเพรียง; hěn-dûai เห็นด้วย

concussion, *n.* gaan-sàn-sà-tuan
การสันสะเทือน; gaan-tùuk-grà-
têɛk-yàang-rɛɛng การถูกกระแทก
อย่างแรง

condemn, *v.* dtam-nì ตำหนิ

condemnation, *n.* gaan-dtam-nì
การตำหนิ

condense, *v.* lót-bpɔɔ-ri-mâan
ลดปริมาณ (reduce the volume);
yɔ̂ɔ ย่อ (make concise)

condescend, *v.* tɔ̀m-dtua ถ่อมตัว
(lower oneself)

condiment, *n.* krûang-bprung-rót
เครื่องปรุงรส

condition, *n.* ngûan-kǎi เงื่อนไข
(provision, stipulation); sà-pâap
สภาพ (existing circumstances)

conditional, *adj.* mii-ngûan-kǎi
มีเงื่อนไข; kûn-yùu-gàp ขึ้นอยู่กับ

condole, *v.* bplɔ̀ɔp-yoon ปลอบโยน

condolence, *n.* gaan-bplɔ̀ɔp-yoon
การปลอบโยน

condom, *n.* tǔng-yaang-à-naa-mai
ถุงยางอนามัย

condominium, *n.* kɔn-doo-mii-
nîam คอนโดมิเนียม

condone, *v.* à-pai อภัย; mâi-ao-

tôot ไม่เอาโทษ

conduct, *v.* bprà-prút ประพฤติ;
chíi-nam ชี้นำ

conduct, *n.* gaan-bprà-prút
การประพฤติ; gaan-chíi-nam
การชี้นำ

conductor, *n.* pûu-nam-wong-don-
dtrii ผู้นำวงดนตรี (orchestra); grà-
bpǎo-rót กระเป๋ารถ (e.g. bus)

cone, *n.* gruai กรวย

confederate, *n.* sà-hà-pan สหพันธ์;
sǎn-ní-bàat สันนิบาต

confer, *v.* bprùk-sǎa ปรึกษา (discuss); bprà-chum ประชุม (have a
meeting)

conference, *n.* gaan-bprà-chum
การประชุม

confess, *v.* sǎa-ra-pâap สารภาพ;
yɔɔm-ráp ยอมรับ

confession, *n.* gaan-sǎa-ra-pâap
การสารภาพ

confidant, *n.* kûu-kít คู่คิด

confide, *v.* mɔ̂ɔp มอบ; wái-waang-
jai ไว้วางใจ

confidence, *n.* kwaam-mân-jai
ความมั่นใจ; kwaam-chûa-tǔu
ความเชื่อถือ

confident, *adj.* mân-jai มั่นใจ

confidential, *adj.* láp ลับ; bpen-
kwaam-láp เป็นความลับ

confine, *v.* gàk-gan กักกัน; gàk-
kǎng กักขัง; gàk-dtua กักตัว

confinement, *n.* gaan-gàk-kǎng

การกักขัง; gaan-gàk-gan การกักกัน

confines, *n.* kɔ̀ɔp-kèet ขอบเขต

confirm, *v.* ráp-rɔɔng รับรอง;
yʉʉn-yan ยืนยัน

confirmation, *n.* gaan-ráp-rɔɔng
การรับรอง; gaan-yʉʉn-yan
การยืนยัน

confiscate, *v.* yút ยึด; ríp ริบ

conflict, *v.* kàt-yέɛng ขัดแย้ง; tá-lɔ́
ทะเลาะ

conflict, *n.* gaan-kàt-yέɛng
การขัดแย้ง; gaan-tá-lɔ́ การทะเลาะ

conform, *v.* tam-dtaam ทำตาม

confound, *v.* tam-hâi-sàp-sŏn
ทำให้สับสน; tam-laai ทำลาย

confront, *v.* pà-chəən เผชิญ

confrontation, *n.* gaan-pà-chəən-
nâa การเผชิญหน้า

confuse, *v.* tam-hâi-sàp-sŏn
ทำให้สับสน; tam-hâi-yûng ทำให้ยุ่ง

confusion, *n.* kwaam-sàp-sŏn
ความสับสน

congenial, *adj.* kâo-gan-dâai
เข้ากันได้; bpen-tîi-tùuk-jai
เป็นที่ถูกใจ

congenital, *adj.* mii-maa-dtɛ̀ɛ-gam-
nə̀ət มีมาแต่กำเนิด

congested, *adj.* ɛɛ-àt แออัด
(packed or crowded); mii-lʉ̂at-kâng
มีเลือดคั่ง (lungs, respiratory)

congestion, *n.* kwaam-ɛɛ-àt
ความแออัด; gaan-kâng การคั่ง

congratulate, *v.* sà-dɛɛng-kwaam-

yin-dii แสดงความยินดี

congratulation, *n.* gaan-sà-dɛɛng-
kwaam-yin-dii การแสดงความยินดี

Congratulations!, *excl.* yin-dii-
dûai ยินดีด้วย; kɔ̌ɔ-sà-dɛɛng-
kwaam-yin-dii ขอแสดงความยินดี

congregate, *v.* rûap-ruam รวบรวม;
jàp-glùm จับกลุ่ม

congregation, *n.* gaan-chum-num
การชุมนุม; glùm-kon กลุ่มคน

congress, *n.* sà-paa-ní-dtì-ban-yàt
สภานิติบัญญัติ

congressional, *adj.* gìao-gàp-sà-
paa เกี่ยวกับสภา

congressman, -woman, *n.* sà-
maa-chík-rát-ta-sà-paa
สมาชิกรัฐสภา

conjugate, *v.* ruam รวม (join);
bprà-sǎan-gan ประสานกัน (put
together); pǎn-gà-ri-yaa ผันกริยา
(a verb)

conjugation, *n.* gaan-ruam-gan
การรวมกัน; gaan-bpen-kûu
การเป็นคู่; gaan-pǎn-gà-ri-yaa
การผันกริยา

conjunction, *n.* sǎn-taan สันธาน
(grammar); gaan-chum-num-gan
การชุมนุมกัน (state of being joined,
getting together); gaan-chûam-dtɔ̀
การเชื่อมต่อ (act of joining)

con man, *n* nák-dtôm-dtǔn
นักต้มตุ๋น

connect, *v.* chûam เชื่อม (join);

gìao-kôɔng เกี่ยวข้อง (associate or consider as related); dtìt ติด (join to or by means of a communications circuit)

connected, *adj.* chûam-gan เชื่อมกัน; dtìt-gan ติดกัน

connection, *n.* kwaam-gìao-pan ความเกี่ยวพัน; gaan-chûam-dtɔ̀ɔ การเชื่อมต่อ

connive, *v.* yin-yɔɔm-láp-láp ยินยอมลับๆ

connoisseur, *n.* pûu-chîao-chaan-sǐn-lá-bpà-wát-tù ผู้เชี่ยวชาญศิลปะวัตถุ

connotation, *n.* kwaam-mǎai-fɛ̌ɛng ความหมายแฝง

connote, *v.* mii-kwaam-mǎai-fɛ̌ɛng มีความหมายแฝง

conquer, *v.* bpràap ปราบ; cha-ná ชนะ

conqueror, *n.* pûu-cha-ná ผู้ชนะ

conquest, *n.* gaan-dâai-chai-cha-ná การได้ชัยชนะ

conscience, *n.* sà-dtì สติ

conscientious, *adj.* mii-sà-dtì มีสติ

conscious, *adj.* mii-sà-dtì มีสติ; rúu-sùk-dtua รู้สึกตัว

consciousness, *n.* kwaam-mii-sà-dtì ความมีสติ

consensus, *n.* kwaam-sɔ̀ɔt-klɔ́ɔng ความสอดคล้อง; kwaam-long-rɔɔi ความลงรอย

consent, *v.* à-nú-yâat อนุญาต; yin-

yɔɔm ยินยอม

consent, *n.* gaan-à-nú-yâat การอนุญาต; gaan-yin-yɔɔm การยินยอม

consequence, *n.* pǒn-láp ผลลัพธ์

consequently, *adv.* pǒn-tîi-sùt ผลที่สุด; prɔ́-chà-nán เพราะฉะนั้น

conservation, *n.* gaan-sà-ngǔan การสงวน

conservative, *adj.* à-nú-rák-ní-yom อนุรักษ์นิยม

conservatory, *n.* hɔ̂ng-grà-jòk-gèp-pan-máai ห้องกระจกเก็บพันธุ์ไม้

conserve, *v.* sà-ngǔan สงวน; gèp-rák-sǎa เก็บรักษา

consider, *v.* pí-jaa-ra-naa พิจารณา

considerable, *adj.* kɔ̂n-kâang-mâak ค่อนข้างมาก (large in amount); sǎm-kan สำคัญ (significant)

considerate, *adj.* hěn-jai-kon-ùun เห็นใจคนอื่น (thoughtful); greeng-jai เกรงใจ (not wanting to impose on others); pí-jaa-ra-naa พิจารณา (deliberate)

consideration, *n.* gaan-pí-jaa-ra-naa การพิจารณา (deliberation); kwaam-hěn-jai-kon-ùun ความเห็นใจคนอื่น (thoughtfulness); gaan-jàai-kâa-dtɔ̀ɔp-tɛɛn การจ่ายค่าตอบแทน (payment for goods or services)

considering, *prep.* gìao-gàp เกี่ยวกับ; mûa-pí-jaa-ra-naa-tǔng เมื่อพิจารณาถึง

consign, v. sòng-mɔ̂ɔp ส่งมอบ

consignment, n. gaan-sòng-kɔ̆ɔng การส่งของ

consist, v. bprà-gɔ̀ɔp-dûai ประกอบด้วย

consistency, n. kwaam-mân-kong ความมั่นคง (firmness); kwaam-sà-mɔ̆ɔ-dtôn-sà-mɔ̆ɔ-bplaai ความเสมอต้นเสมอปลาย (coherence)

consistent, adj. sɔ̀ɔt-klɔ́ɔng สอดคล้อง (coherent); mân-kong มั่นคง (firm); mâi-bplìan-bplɛɛng ไม่เปลี่ยนแปลง (not changing)

consolation, v. gaan-bplɔ̀ɔp-yoon การปลอบโยน

console, v. bplɔ̀ɔp-yoon ปลอบโยน

consolidate, v. tam-hâi-kĕng-rɛɛng ทำให้แข็งแรง (strengthen); ruam-gan-kâo รวมกันเข้า (combine)

consonant, n. pá-yan-cha-ná พยัญชนะ

conspicuous, adj. dèn-chát เด่นชัด

conspiracy, n. gaan-sŏm-rúu-rûam-kít การสมรู้ร่วมคิด

conspirator, n. pûu-sŏm-rúu-rûam-kít ผู้สมรู้ร่วมคิด

conspire, v. sŏm-rúu-rûam-kít สมรู้ร่วมคิด

constant, adj. dtɔ̀ɔ-nûang ต่อเนื่อง

constellation, n. glùm-daao กลุ่มดาว

constipation, n. aa-gaan-tɔ́ɔng-pùuk อาการท้องผูก

constituency, n. pûu-mii-sìt-lûak-dtâng ผู้มีสิทธิ์เลือกตั้ง; kèet-lûak-dtâng เขตเลือกตั้ง

constituent, n. sùan-bprà-gɔ̀ɔp ส่วนประกอบ (component); pûu-mii-sìt-lûak-dtâng ผู้มีสิทธิ์เลือกตั้ง (voter)

constitute, v. bprà-gɔ̀ɔp-dûai ประกอบด้วย (consist of)

constitution, n. rát-tà-tam-ma-nuun รัฐธรรมนูญ

constitutional, adj. dtaam-rát-tà-tam-ma-nuun ตามรัฐธรรมนูญ (of a constitution); bpen-râak-tǎan เป็นรากฐาน (the basic structure)

constrict, v. tam-hâi-lék-long ทำให้เล็กลง

constricted, adj. lék-long เล็กลง

construct, v. sâang สร้าง

construction, n. gaan-gɔ̀ɔ-sâang การก่อสร้าง

constructive, adj. gìao-gàp-gaan-gɔ̀ɔ-sâang เกี่ยวกับการก่อสร้าง

construe, v. à-tí-baai อธิบาย (explain); dtii-kwaam ตีความ (interpret)

consul, n. gong-sŭn กงสุล

consulate, n. sà-tǎan-gong-sŭn สถานกงสุล

consult, v. bprùk-sǎa ปรึกษา

consultant, n. pûu-hâi-kam-bprùk-sǎa ผู้ให้คำปรึกษา

consultation, n. gaan-bprùk-sǎa การปรึกษา

consume, *v.* bɔɔ-ri-pôok บริโภค

consumer, *n.* pûu-bɔɔ-ri-pôok
ผู้บริโภค

consumption, *n.* gaan-bɔɔ-ri-pôok
การบริโภค

contact, *v.* sǎm-pàt สัมผัส; dtìt-
dtɔ̀ɔ ติดต่อ

contact lens, *n.* kɔn-tèk-leen
คอนแท็คเลนส์

contagious, *adj.* dtìt-dtɔ̀ɔ ติดต่อ
(carrying a disease; communicable);
prɛ̂ɛ-dâai-ngâai แพร่ได้ง่าย (easy to
transmit)

contain, *v.* ban-jù บรรจุ

container, *n.* paa-cha-ná ภาชนะ

contaminate, *v.* jʉa-bpon เจือปน
(mix); tam-hâi-mâi-bɔɔ-ri-sùt
ทำให้ไม่บริสุทธิ์ (make impure)

contemplate, *v.* krâi-kruan
ใคร่ครวญ

contemporary, *n.* rûam-sà-mǎi
ร่วมสมัย

contempt, *v.* duu-tùuk ดูถูก; duu-
mǐn ดูหมิ่น

contempt, *n.* gaan-duu-tùuk
การดูถูก; gaan-duu-mǐn การดูหมิ่น

content, *n.* nʉ́a-hǎa เนื้อหา (e.g. of
a book); sǎa-ra-ban สารบัญ (table
of content); sùan-bprà-gɔ̀ɔp
ส่วนประกอบ (something contained)

content, *v.* pɔɔ-jai พอใจ

contented, *adj.* bpen-tîi-pɔɔ-jai
เป็นที่พอใจ

contentment, *n.* kwaam-pɔɔ-jai
ความพอใจ (satisfactory)

contest, *v.* bprà-gùat ประกวด

contest, *n.* gaan-bprà-gùat
การประกวด

contestant, *n.* pûu-kâo-kèng
ผู้เข้าแข่ง; pûu-kâo-bprà-gùat
ผู้เข้าประกวด

context, *n.* bɔɔ-ri-bòt บริบท (part
of a text or statement); sìng-wɛ̂ɛt-
lɔ́ɔm สิ่งแวดล้อม (circumstances)

continent, *n.* tá-wîip ทวีป

continental, *adj.* gìao-gàp-tá-wîip
เกี่ยวกับทวีป

contingency, *n.* kwaam-bang-əən
ความบังเอิญ

contingent, *adj.* bang-əən บังเอิญ

continual, *adj.* dtɔ̀ɔ-nʉ̂ang ต่อเนื่อง
(not interrupted); bprà-jam ประจำ
(recurring regularly)

continuation, *n.* gaan-dtɔ̀ɔ-nʉ̂ang
การต่อเนื่อง

continue, *v.* tam-dtɔ̀ɔ-bpai ทำต่อไป

continuity, *n.* kwaam-dtɔ̀ɔ-nʉ̂ang
ความต่อเนื่อง

continuous, *adj.* dtɔ̀ɔ-nʉ̂ang
ต่อเนื่อง

contorted, *adj.* bùut-bîao บูดเบี้ยว
(bent severely out of shape); kót-
ngɔɔ คดงอ (twisted)

contortion, *n.* gaan-kót-ngɔɔ
การคดงอ (act of contorting); sìng-
tîi-bìt-bîao สิ่งที่บิดเบี้ยว (something
contorted)

contour, *n.* kroong-râang โครงร่าง

contraception, *n.* gaan-kum-gam-nòət การคุมกำเนิด

contraceptive, *n.* yaa-kum-gam-nòət ยาคุมกำเนิด

contract, *n.* săn-yaa สัญญา

contract, *v.* hòt หด; yôo ย่อ

contraction, *n.* gaan-hòt-dtua การหดตัว (shrinking); gaan-yôo การย่อ (shortening)

contractor, *n.* pûu-tam-săn-yaa ผู้ทำสัญญา; pûu-ráp-mǎo ผู้รับเหมา

contradict, *v.* dtôo-yéɛng โต้แย้ง

contradiction, *n.* gaan-dtôo-yéɛng การโต้แย้ง

contradictory, *adj.* kàt-yéɛng ขัดแย้ง

contrary, *n.* sìng-dtrong-gan-kâam สิ่งตรงกันข้าม

contrast, *n.* kwaam-dtɛ̀ɛk-dtàang ความแตกต่าง

contribute, *v.* sà-nàp-sà-nǔn สนับสนุน; hâi ให้

contribution, *n.* gaan-chûai-lǔa การช่วยเหลือ; sìng-tîi-mɔ̂ɔp-hâi สิ่งที่มอบให้

contrite, *adj.* sǎm-núk-pìt สำนึกผิด

contrition, *n.* kwaam-sǎm-núk-pìt ความสำนึกผิด

contrive, *v.* bprà-dìt ประดิษฐ์ (invent); waang-pɛ̌ɛn วางแผน (plan)

contrived, *adj.* waang-pɛ̌ɛn-wái วางแผนไว้

control, *v.* kûap-kum ควบคุม (hold in restraint; regulate; prevent); bang-káp บังคับ (force)

control, *n.* gaan-kûap-kum การควบคุม; gaan-bang-káp การบังคับ

controversial, *adj.* kàt-yéɛng ขัดแย้ง

controversy, *n.* gaan-kàt-yéɛng การขัดแย้ง

convene, *v.* maa-ruam-gan มารวมกัน (gather); bprà-chum ประชุม (confer); póp-bpà พบปะ (meet)

convenience, *n.* kwaam-sà-dùak ความสะดวก

convenient, *adj.* sà-dùak สะดวก

convention, *n.* gaan-bprà-chum การประชุม (meeting); bprà-pee-nii ประเพณี (custom)

conventional, *adj.* bpen-tam-niam เป็นธรรมเนียม

conversant, *adj.* kún-kəəi คุ้นเคย (familiar with); chîao-chaan เชี่ยวชาญ (experienced)

conversation, *n.* bòt-sǒn-ta-naa บทสนทนา

converse, *adj.* dtrong-gan-kâam ตรงกันข้าม

conversion, *n.* gaan-bplìan-bplɛɛng การเปลี่ยนแปลง

convert, *v.* bplìan เปลี่ยน

converter, *n.* pûu-bplìan-sàat-sà-năa ผู้เปลี่ยนศาสนา (religious); krûang-bpleeng-fai เครื่องแปลงไฟ (electrical)

convertible, *n.* rót-bpəət-bpràtun รถเปิดประทุน

convex, *adj.* nuun นูน

convey, *v.* nam นำ; tàai-tee ถ่ายเท

convict, *v.* hĕn-wâa-pìt เห็นว่าผิด (pronounce guilty); long-tôot ลงโทษ (punish)

convict, *n.* nák-tôot นักโทษ

conviction, *n.* gaan-long-tôot การลงโทษ

convince, *v.* tam-hâi-chûa ทำให้เชื่อ

convincing, *adj.* nâa-chûa น่าเชื่อ

convoluted, *adj.* kót-ngɔɔ คดงอ

convulsion, *n.* gaan-hòt-greng-kɔ̌ɔng-glâam-núa การหดเกร็งของกล้ามเนื้อ

coo, *v.* kan ขัน; rɔ́ɔng-gùu ร้องกู

cook, *n.* kon-krua คนครัว; gúk กุ๊ก

cookbook, *n.* dtam-raa-aa-hǎan ตำราอาหาร

cookie, *n.* kúk-gîi คุกกี้

cooking, *n.* gaan-tam-aa-hǎan การทำอาหาร

cool, *adj.* yen เย็น

coop, *n.* sùm สุ่ม (for poultry); láo เล้า (for small animals); grong กรง (cage)

co-op, *n.* sà-hà-gɔɔn สหกรณ์

cooperate, *v.* rûam-mɯɯ ร่วมมือ

cooperation, *n.* gaan-rûam-mɯɯ การร่วมมือ

cooperative, *n.* sà-hà-gɔɔn สหกรณ์

coordinate, *v.* bprà-sǎan-gan ประสานกัน

coordination, *n.* gaan-bprà-sǎan-gan การประสานกัน

coordinator, *n.* pûu-bprà-sǎan-ngaan ผู้ประสานงาน

cop, *n.* dtam-rùat ตำรวจ

cope, *v.* ráp-mɯɯ รับมือ (fight or cope with something); pà-chəən เผชิญ (confront; deal with)

copier, *n.* pûu-lian-bèep ผู้เลียนแบบ (one that copies or imitates); krûang-tàai-sǎm-nao เครื่องถ่ายสำเนา (copy machine)

copious, *adj.* mâak-maai มากมาย

copper, *n.* tɔɔng-dɛɛng ทองแดง

copulate, *v.* rûam-bprà-wee-nii ร่วมประเวณี (engage in sexual intercourse)

copy, *v.* tam-sǎm-nao ทำสำเนา (make copies); lian-bèep เลียนแบบ (imitate)

copy, *n.* sǎm-nao สำเนา; lêm เล่ม (clf. for books)

copyright, *n.* lí-kà-sìt ลิขสิทธิ์

coral, *n.* bpà-gaa-rang ปะการัง

cord, *n.* chûak เชือก; sǎai สาย

core, *n.* sâi-pǒn-lá-máai ไส้ผลไม้ (fruit); gɛɛn แกน (central part)

cork, *n.* jùk-máai-gɔ́k จุกไม้ก๊อก (e.g. for bottle closures); bplùakdtôn-óok เปลือกต้นโอ๊ค (bark of the oak tree)

corkscrew, *n.* sà-wàan-bpèot-jùk-kùat สว่านเปิดจุกขวด

corn, *n.* kâao-pôot ข้าวโพด

corner, *n.* mum มุม

cornet, *n.* dtrɛɛ-tɔɔng-lŭang แตรทองเหลือง

cornflakes, *n.* kɔɔn-flèek คอร์นเฟลค; kâao-pôot-grɔ̀ɔp ข้าวโพดกรอบ

cornstarch, *n.* bpɛɛng-kâao-pôot แป้งข้าวโพด

coronation, *n.* gaan-sŭam-mong-gùt การสวมมงกุฎ

corporal, *adj.* gìao-gàp-râang-gaai เกี่ยวกับร่างกาย

corporate, *adj.* nì-dtì-bùk-kon นิติบุคคล

corporation, *n.* bɔɔ-ri-sàt บริษัท; sà-moo-sɔɔn สโมสร

corps, *n.* nùai-tá-hǎan หน่วยทหาร (unit of ground combat forces)

corpse, *n.* sòp ศพ

corpulent, *adj.* ûan อ้วน; pung-plúi พุงพลุ้ย

corpuscle, *n.* mét-lûat เม็ดเลือด

corral, *n.* kɔɔk คอก; grong กรง

correct, *adj.* tùuk-dtông ถูกต้อง

correct, *v.* gɛ̂ɛ-kǎi แก้ไข

correction, *n.* gaan-gɛ̂ɛ-kǎi การแก้ไข (act or process of correcting); gaan-long-tôot การลงโทษ (punishment)

correctness, *n.* kwaam-tùuk-dtông ความถูกต้อง

correlation, *n.* kwaam-sǎm-pan-gan ความสัมพันธ์กัน

correspond, *v.* dtrong-gan ตรงกัน (be in agreement); dùt-dtɔ̀ɔ-gan-taang-jòt-mǎai ติดต่อกันทางจดหมาย (communicate by letters)

correspondence, *n.* gaan-dùt-dtɔ̀ɔ-taang-jòt-mǎai การติดต่อทาง จดหมาย

corridor, *n.* rá-biang ระเบียง

corroborate, *v.* yʉʉn-yan ยืนยัน; tam-hâi-nɛ̂ɛ-jai ทำให้แน่ใจ

corrupt, *v.* tú-jà-rìt ทุจริต; chɔ̂ɔ-goong ฉ้อโกง

corruption, *n.* gaan-tú-jà-rìt การทุจริต

cosmetic, *n.* krʉ̂ang-sǎm-aang เครื่องสำอาง

cosmic, *adj.* gìao-gàp-jàk-grà-waan เกี่ยวกับจักรวาล

cosmopolitan, *adj.* sǎa-gon-ní-yom สากลนิยม

cosmos, *n.* jàk-grà-waan จักรวาล

cost, *n.* kâa-chái-jàai ค่าใช้จ่าย (expense); raa-kaa ราคา (price)

costly, *adj.* raa kaa-pɛɛng ราคาแพง

costume, *n.* krʉ̂ang-dtɛ̀ng-gaai เครื่องแต่งกาย

cot, *n.* bplee เปล (hammock), dtiang-dèk เตียงเด็ก (baby bed); dtiang-páp เตียงพับ (folding bed)

cottage, n. grà-tɔ̂m กระท่อม
cotton, n. fâai ฝ้าย
couch, n. gâo-ʔîi-soo-faa เก้าอี้โซฟา
cough, v. ai ไอ
cough, n. ai ไอ
council, n. sà-paa สภา; ká-ná-gam-ma-gaan คณะกรรมการ
counsel, n. kam-né-nam คำแนะนำ (advice); tá-naai-kwaam ทนายความ (lawyer)
counselor, n. tîi-bprùk-sǎa ที่ปรึกษา
countdown, n. gaan-náp-tɔ̌ɔi-lǎng การนับถอยหลัง
counter, n. káo-dtɔ̀ɔ เคาน์เตอร์
counterfeit, n. kɔ̌ɔng-bplɔɔm ของปลอม (fraudulent imitation); nák-dtùn นักต้ม (con man)
counterpart, n. kɔ̌ɔng-kûu-gan ของคู่กัน (things that come together); sìng-mǔan-gan สิ่งเหมือนกัน (one that closely resembles another); sǎm-nao สำเนา (a copy of a legal paper)
country, n. bprà-têet ประเทศ (e.g. Thailand); chon-na-bòt ชนบท (rural area)
countryman, -woman, n. kon-púun-muang คนพื้นเมือง
countryside, n. chon-na-bòt ชนบท
county, n. kèet เขต; kwǎeng แขวง
coup, coup d'état, n. rát-tà-bprà-hǎan รัฐประหาร

couple, n. kûu คู่ (pair); sǎa-mii-pan-ra-yaa สามีภรรยา (husband and wife)
coupon, n. kuu-bpɔɔng คูปอง
courage, n. kwaam-glâa-hǎan ความกล้าหาญ
courageous, adj. glâa กล้า
courier, n. kon-dəən-nǎng-sʉ̌ʉ คนเดินหนังสือ
course, n. wí-tii-taang วิถีทาง (direction); wí-chaa วิชา (subject); bpen-chút เป็นชุด (e.g. a part of a meal served as a unit at one time)
court, v. gìao-paa-raa-sǐi เกี่ยวพาราสี (court, woo); jìip จีบ (collq.)
court, n. sà-nǎam สนาม (playground); sǎan ศาล (of law); gaan-gìao-paa-raa-sǐi การเกี่ยวพาราสี (courtship, wooing)
courthouse, n. sǎan ศาล
courtyard, n. laan ลาน
cousin, n. lûuk-pîi-lûuk-nɔ́ɔng ลูกพี่ลูกน้อง
cover, v. bpòk ปก; klum คลุม
cover, n. fǎa ฝา (e.g. for jars); bpòk ปก (e.g. for books)
coverage, n. ngən-bprà-gan เงินประกัน (amount of insurance coverage); ngən-kúm-krɔɔng เงินคุ้มครอง (amount of coverage); gaan-raai-ngaan-kàao การรายงานข่าว (news)

cover charge, *n.* kâa-bɔɔ-ri-gaan ค่าบริการ

covering, *n.* gaan-bpìt การปิด; gaan-bpìt-bang การปิดบัง

cow, *n.* wua-dtua-mia วัวตัวเมีย

coward, *n.* kon-kîi-klàat คนขี้ขลาด

cowboy, *n.* kaao-bɔɔi คาวบอย

cozy, *adj.* òp-ùn อบอุ่น; sà-baai สบาย

crab, *n.* bpuu ปู

crack, *v.* dtèek แตก

crack, *n.* sĭang-dtèek เสียงแตก; rɔɔi-dtèek รอยแตก

cracker, *n.* kà-nǒm-bpang-grɔ̀ɔp ขนมปังกรอบ

cradle, *n.* bplee-dèk เปลเด็ก

craft, *n.* kwaam-cham-naan ความชำนาญ (skill); yaan ยาน (vehicle)

craftsman, *n.* châng-fǐi-mʉʉ ช่างฝีมือ

craftsmanship, *n.* kwaam-bprà-nîit ความประณีต

cramp, *n.* dtà-kriu ตะคริว (spasmodic muscular contraction)

crane, *n.* bpân-jàn ปั้นจั่น (machine); nók-grà-rian นกกระเรียน (bird)

crank, *n.* dâam-mùt ด้ามหมุน (handle for transmitting rotary motion); kon-kîi-moo hǒo คนขี้โมโห (cranky person)

cranky, *n.* aa-rom-sĭa อารมณ์เสีย

crash, *v.* chon ชน; bpà-tá ปะทะ

crash, *n.* sĭang-dang เสียงดัง (loud noise); gaan-chon-gan การชนกัน (collision)

crater, *n.* bpàak-bplɔ̀ng-puu-kǎo-fai ปากปล่องภูเขาไฟ

crave, *v.* grà-hǎai กระหาย; yàak-dâai-mâak อยากได้มาก

craving, *n.* kwaam-yàak-dâai-mâak ความอยากได้มาก

crawl, *v.* klaan คลาน; kʉ̂ʉp-klaan คืบคลาน

crayfish, *n.* gûng-naang กุ้งนาง

crayon, *n.* kree-yong เครยอง; din-sɔ̌ɔ-sǐi ดินสอสี

craziness, *n.* kwaam-bâa-klâng ความบ้าคลั่ง

crazy, *adj.* bâa บ้า; klâng-klái คลั่งไคล้

creak, *n., v.* sĭang-dang-íat เสียงดังเอี๊ยด

cream, *n.* kriim ครีม

creamy, *adj.* mii-kriim-mâak มีครีมมาก; bpen-kriim เป็นครีม

crease, *n.* rɔɔi-páp รอยพับ; rɔɔi-yáp รอยยับ

create, *v.* sâang-sǎn สร้างสรรค์ (bring into being); bprà-dìt ประดิษฐ์ (invent)

creation, *n.* gaan-sâang การสร้าง

creative, *adj.* sâang-sǎn สร้างสรรค์

creativity, *n.* gaan-kít-sâang-sǎn การคิดสร้างสรรค์

creator, *n.* pûu-sâang ผู้สร้าง

creature, *n.* sàt sàtwɔ̂ (animal); kon kon คน (human being)

credentials, *n.* kun-na-sŏm-bàt คุณสมบัติ (qualifications); nǎng-sǔu-né-nam หนังสือแนะนำ (letter of recommendation)

credit, *n.* kree-dìt เครดิต; kwaam-chûa-tǔu ความเชื่อถือ

credit card, *n.* bàt-kree-dìt บัตรเครดิต

creditor, *n.* jâo-nîi เจ้าหนี้

creek, *n.* lam-taan ลำธาร

cremate, *v.* pǎo-sòp เผาศพ

crescent, *n.* jan-sìao จันทร์เสี้ยว

crest, *n.* ngɔ̌ɔn หงอน (e.g. of a cock or bird); yɔ̂ɔt-kǎo ยอดเขา (of a mountain)

crew, *n.* lûuk-rua ลูกเรือ

crib, *n.* dtiang-kɔ̂ɔk เตียงคอก; kɔ̂ɔk-wua คอกวัว; hɔ̂ng-lék ห้องเล็ก

cricket, *n.* jîng-rìit จิ้งหรีด (animal); gii-laa-krík-gèt กีฬาคริกเก็ต (sport)

crime, *n.* àat-chá-yaa-gam อาชญากรรม

criminal, *n.* àat-chá-yaa-gɔɔn อาชญากร

cringe, *v.* ngɔɔ งอ; kòt ขด; kóong โค้ง

cripple, *n.* kon-pí-gaan คนพิการ

crisis, *n.* wí-grìt-dtà-gaan วิกฤตการณ์

crisp, *adj.* bprɔ̀ เปราะ; grɔ̀ɔp

กรอบ; yìk หยิก

criterion, *n.* geen เกณฑ์; ban-tát-tǎan บรรทัดฐาน

critic, *n.* nák-wí-jaan นักวิจารณ์

critical, *adj.* wí-jaan วิจารณ์; sǎm-kan สำคัญ; kân-an-dtà-raai ขั้นอันตราย

criticism, *n.* gaan-wí-jaan การวิจารณ์

criticize, *v.* wí-jaan วิจารณ์; wí-krɔ́ วิเคราะห์

croak, *v.* rɔ́ɔng-sǐang-hèep-hêeng ร้องเสียงแหบแห้ง

crocodile, *n.* jɔɔ-ra-kêe จระเข้

crook, *n.* sìng-tîi-ngɔɔ สิ่งที่งอ (a curve or bend); nák-tôot นักโทษ (criminal)

crooked, *adj.* ngɔɔ งอ (bent); tú-jà-rìt ทุจริต (dishonest)

crop, *n.* pùut-pŏn พืชผล

cross, *v.* kâam ข้าม

cross, *n.* gaa-gà-bàat กากบาท (the cross design or drawing); máai-gaang-kěen ไม้กางเขน (in Christianity)

crossbreed, *n.* gaan-pà-sŏm-kâam-pan การผสมข้ามพันธ์

cross-examine, *v.* sàk-tǎam-fàai-dtrong-kâam ซักถามฝ่ายตรงข้าม

cross-eyed, *adj.* dtaa-kěe ตาเข

crossing, *n.* gaan-kâam การข้าม

crossroads, *n.* taang-yêek ทางแยก

cross section, *n.* sùan-tîi-dtàtdtaam-kwǎang ส่วนที่ตัดตามขวาง

crosswalk, *n.* taang-kâam-tà-nǒn ทางข้ามถนน

crossword puzzle, *n.* bprìt-sà-nǎa-àk-sɔ̌ɔn-kwǎi ปริศนาอักษรไขว้

crotch, *n.* ngâam ง่าม (the fork of a pole); wâang-kǎa หว่างขา (between the legs)

crouch, *v.* mɔ̂ɔp หมอบ; yɔ̂ɔ-dtua-long ย่อตัวลง

crow, *n.* gaa กา

crowbar, *n.* chá-lɛɛng ชะแลง

crowd, *n.* fǔung-chon ฝูงชน

crowded, *adj.* ɛɛ-àt แออัด

crown, *n.* mong-gùt มงกุฎ

crucial, *adj.* dèt-kàat เด็ดขาด (decisive); run-rɛɛng รุนแรง (serious); kân-wí-grìt ขั้นวิกฤต (of a crisis)

crucify, *v.* dtrung-bon-máai-gaang-kěen ตรึงบนไม้กางเขน

crude, *adj.* yàap หยาบ (rough); sòk-gà-bpròk สกปรก (dirty)

crudeness, *n.* kwaam-yàap ความหยาบ; kwaam-sòk-gà-bpròk ความสกปรก

crude oil, *n.* náam-man-dìp น้ำมันดิบ

crudity, *n.* kwaam-yàap ความหยาบ; gì-rí-yaa-tîi-yàap-kaai กิริยาที่หยาบคาย

cruel, *adj.* hòot-ráai โหดร้าย

cruelty, *n.* kwaam-hòot-ráai ความโหดร้าย

cruise, *v.* lɛ̂n-rʉa แล่นเรือ

cruise, *n.* gaan-lɛ̂n-rʉa การแล่นเรือ

crumb, *n.* sèet-kà-nǒm-bpang เศษขนมปัง; kon-rái-kâa คนไร้ค่า

crumble, *v.* tam-hâi-bpen-sèet-lék-lék ทำให้เป็นเศษเล็กๆ (fall into small fragments); sà-lǎai-dtua สลายตัว (become disintegrated)

crumple, *v.* tam-hâi-yôn ทำให้ย่น (crush together); hòt หด (contract); yôn ย่น (become wrinkled)

crunch, *v.* kíao-sǐang-dang เคี้ยวเสียงดัง

crush, *v.* bòt บด (pound or grind); tam-laai ทำลาย (destroy)

crust, *n.* bplʉ̀ak เปลือก (hard outer portion); grà-dɔɔng กระดอง (hard shell)

crutch, *n.* máai-yan-rák-rɛ́ɛ ไม้ยันรักแร้

cry, *v.* rɔ́ɔng ร้อง; rɔ́ɔng-hâi ร้องไห้

cry, *n.* sǐang-rɔ́ɔng เสียงร้อง

crystal, *n.* plùk ผลึก

cub, *n.* lûuk-sàt ลูกสัตว์

cube, *n.* lûuk-bàat ลูกบาศก์

cubic, *adj.* bpen-lûuk-bàat เป็นลูกบาศก์

cucumber, *n.* dtɛɛng-gwaa แตงกวา

cuddle, *v.* gɔ̀ɔt กอด

cuff, *n.* kɔ̂ɔ-mʉʉ-sʉ̂a ข้อมือเสื้อ; gun-jɛɛ-mʉʉ กุญแจมือ (handcuff)

cuff link, *n.* grà-dum-kɔ̂ɔ-mʉʉ-sʉ̂a กระดุมข้อมือเสื้อ

English • Phonetic • Thai

cuisine, *n.* gaan-tam-aa-hǎan การทำอาหาร; aa-hǎan อาหาร

culinary, *adj.* gìao-gàp-gaan-krua เกี่ยวกับการครัว

culpable, *adj.* nâa-dtam-nì น่าตำหนิ

culprit, *n.* nák-tôot นักโทษ (one guilty of a fault or crime); pûu-ráai ผู้ร้าย (one charged with a crime)

cult, *n.* lát-tì ลัทธิ (doctrine, sect); kwaam-bâa-klâng ความบ้าคลั่ง (devotion to or veneration for something)

cultivate, *v.* pɔ́-bplùuk เพาะปลูก (plant); pát-ta-naa พัฒนา (develop)

cultural, *adj.* taang-wát-ta-ná-tam ทางวัฒนธรรม

culture, *n.* wát-ta-ná-tam วัฒนธรรม

cultured, *adj.* bplùuk-wái ปลูกไว้; mii-wát-ta-ná-tam มีวัฒนธรรม; dâai-rian-rúu ได้เรียนรู้

cultured pearl, *n.* hɔ̌i-múk-líang หอยมุกเลี้ยง

cup, *n.* tûai ถ้วย

cupboard, *n.* dtûu ตู้

cure, *n.* gaan-rák-sǎa การรักษา

curfew, *n.* kəə-fiu เคอร์ฟิว; gaan-hâam-ɔ̀ɔk-nɔ̂ɔk-bâan การห้ามออกนอกบ้าน

curio, *n.* kɔ̌ɔng-bplὲεk ของแปลก

curiosity, *n.* kwaam-yàak-rúu-yàak-hěn ความอยากรู้อยากเห็น

curious, *adj.* yàak-rúu-yàak-hěn อยากรู้อยากเห็น

curl, *n.* pǒm-yìk ผมหยิก; pǒm-lon ผมลอน

curler, *n.* tîi-múan-pǒm ที่ม้วนผม

curly, *adj.* ngɔɔ งอ; yìk หยิก

currency, *n.* ngən-dtraa เงินตรา; grà-sɛ̌ɛ-lom กระแสลม

current, *n.* grà-sɛ̌ɛ-náam กระแสน้ำ (water); grà-sɛ̌ɛ-fai กระแสไฟ (electrical)

curriculum, *n.* làk-sùut หลักสูตร

curriculum vitae, *n.* bprà-wàt-yɔ̂ɔ ประวัติย่อ

curry, *n.* gɛɛng แกง

curse, *v.* sàap สาป; chêng แช่ง

curse, *n.* kam-sàap คำสาป; gaan-sàap-chêng การสาปแช่ง

cursed, *adj.* tùuk-sàap-chêng ถูกสาปแช่ง

curtain, *n.* mâan ม่าน

curve, *v.* lέεo-kóong เลี้ยวโค้ง

curve, *n.* sên-kóong เส้นโค้ง; taang-kóong ทางโค้ง

cushion, *n.* bɔ̀ เบาะ; nûa-sà-pôok เนื้อสะโพก

custard, *n.* kát-sà-dtàat คัสตาร์ด

custody, *n.* gaan-aa-rák-sǎa การอารักขา (protection); gaan-tùuk-jàp-kum การถูกจับคุม (as a prisoner); gaan-dâai-sìt-nai-dtua-lûuk การได้สิทธิในตัวลูก (of a child)

custom, *n.* bprà-pee-nii ประเพณี (tradition); gìt-jà-wát กิจวัตร (habitual practice)

D

customary, *adj.* gìao-gàp-bprà-pee-nii เกี่ยวกับประเพณี; bpen-gìt-jà-wát เป็นกิจวัตร

customer, *n.* lûuk-káa ลูกค้า

customize, *v.* tam-hâi-mɔ̀-sǒm-gàp-dtɛ̀ɛ-lá-bùk-kom ทำให้เหมาะสมกับแต่ละบุคคล (for each individual)

customs, *n.* sǔn-lá-gaa-gɔɔn ศุลกากร

cut, *v.* dtàt ตัด

cut, *n.* gaan-dtàt การตัด (act of cutting); bàat-plɛ̆ɛ บาดแผล (wound)

cutback, *n.* gaan-glàp-sùu-hèet-gaan การกลับสู่เหตุการณ์

cute, *adj.* nâa-rák น่ารัก

cycle, *n.* wong-jɔɔn วงจร (circle, circuit); rɔ̂ɔp รอบ (round)

cyclical, *adj.* mǔm-rɔ̂ɔp หมุนรอบ

cycling, *n.* gaan-kìi-jàk-grà-yaan การขี่จักรยาน

cyclist, *n.* nák-kìi-jàk-grà-yaan นักขี่จักรยาน

cyclone, *n.* sai-kloon ไซโคลน; paa-yú-mǔn พายุหมุน

cylinder, *n.* grà-bɔ̀ɔk กระบอก

cymbal, *n.* chàap ฉาบ (large); chìng ฉิ่ง (small)

cynical, *adj.* chɔ̂ɔp-duu-tùuk-kon-ùn ชอบดูถูกคนอื่น; chɔ̂ɔp-yɔ́-yɛ́ɛi ชอบเยาะเย้ย

cynicism, *n.* làt-tí-glìat-chang-má-nút ลัทธิการเกลียดชังมนุษย์

cypress, *n.* pâa-tam-chút-wái-túk ผ้าทำชุดไว้ทุกข์

dad, *n.* pɔ̂ɔ พ่อ

daily, *adj, adv.* bprà-jam-wan ประจำวัน; túk-wan ทุกวัน

daily, *n.* nǎng-sǔu-pim-raai-wan หนังสือพิมพ์รายวัน

dairy, *n.* faam-rîit-nom ฟาร์มรีดนม

daisy, *n.* dɔ̀ɔk-dee-sîi ดอกเดซี่

dam, *n.* kùan เขื่อน

damage, *v.* tam-hâi-sǐa-hǎai ทำให้เสียหาย

damage, *n.* kwaam-sǐa-hǎai ความเสียหาย

damp, *adj.* chúun ชื้น; màat หมาด

dampen, *v.* tam-hâi-chúun ทำให้ชื้น; tam-hâi-màat ทำให้หมาด

dance, *v.* dtên เต้น (modern); ram รำ (traditional); dtên-ram เต้นรำ (ballroom)

dance, *n.* gaan-dtên-ram การเต้นรำ (dancing); ngaan-dtên-ram งานเต้นรำ (dance party)

dancer, *n.* nák-dtên-ram นักเต้นรำ

dandelion, *n.* dɔ̀ɔk-dɛɛn-dii-lai-ɔ̂n ดอกแดนดีไลออน

dandruff, *n.* rang-kɛɛ รังแค

danger, *n.* an-dtà-raai อันตราย

dangerous, *adj.* bpen-an-dtà-raai เป็นอันตราย

dangle, *v.* hɔ̂i ห้อย; kwɛɛn แขวน

dare, *v.* glâa กล้า

daring, *adj.* glâa กล้า

dark, *adj.* mûut มืด

darken, *v.* tam-hâi-mûut ทำให้มืด

darkroom, *n.* hôŋ-mûut ห้องมืด

darling, *n.* tîi-rák ที่รัก

dart, *n.* lûuk-dɔ̀ɔk ลูกดอก

dash, *v.* splash สาด

dash, *n.* gaan-sàat การสาด; sên-kìit-yaao เส้นขีดยาว (punctuation mark)

dashboard, *n.* pɛ̀n-waaŋ-kɔ̌ɔŋ แผ่นวางของ

data, *n.* kɔ̂ɔ-muun ข้อมูล

date, *n.* wan-tîi วันที่ (calendar day); gaan-nát การนัด (appointment)

daughter, *n.* lûuk-sǎao ลูกสาว

daughter-in-law, *n.* lûuk-sà-pái ลูกสะใภ้

dawn, *n.* rûŋ-cháao รุ่งเช้า; cháao-dtrùu เช้าตรู่

day, *n.* wan วัน; glaaŋ-wan กลางวัน

daybreak, *n.* rûŋ-cháao รุ่งเช้า

day-care center, *n.* sà-tǎan-ráp-líaŋ-dèk สถานรับเลี้ยงเด็ก

daydream, *n., v.* fǎn-glaaŋ-wan ฝันกลางวัน

daylight, *n.* dɛ̀ɛt แดด; sɛ̌ɛŋ-dɛ̀ɛt แสงแดด

daylight saving time, *n.* wee-laa-tîi-cháa-gwàa-mâat-dtrà-tǎan เวลาที่ช้ากว่ามาตรฐาน

daytime, *n.* wee-laa-glaaŋ-wan

เวลากลางวัน

dead, *adj.* dtaai ตาย (no longer alive); mâi-klûan-wǎi ไม่เคลื่อนไหว (no movement; inactive); yùt-tam-ŋaan หยุดทำงาน (not working)

deaden, *v.* tam-hâi-chaa ทำให้ชา; tam-hâi-ɔ̀ɔn-ɛɛ ทำให้อ่อนแอ

dead end, *n.* taaŋ-dtan ทางตัน

deadline, *n.* gam-nòt-wee-laa กำหนดเวลา

deadly, *adj.* bpen-an-dtà-raai เป็นอันตราย

deaf, *adj.* hǔu-nùaak หูหนวก

deal, *v.* dtìt-dtɔ̀ɔ-tú-rá-gìt ติดต่อธุรกิจ (business); jɛ̀ɛk-pâi แจกไพ่ (cards)

deal, *n.* gaan-dtìt-dtɔ̀ɔ-tú-rá-gìt การติดต่อธุรกิจ; gaan-jɛ̀ɛk-pâi การแจกไพ่; sǎn-yaa สัญญา

dealer, *n.* pɔ̂ɔ-káa พ่อค้า (merchant); kon-jɛ̀ɛk-pâi คนแจกไพ่ (card)

dear, *n.* tîi-rák ที่รัก (loved one)

dear, *adj.* mii-raa-kaa-sǔuŋ มีราคาสูง (expensive)

death, *n.* kwaam-dtaai ความตาย

debate, *v.* dtôo-waa-tii โต้วาที; dtɔ̂ɔ-tiaŋ โต้เถียง

debate, *n.* gaan-dtôo-waa-tii การโต้วาที; rûaŋ-dtôo-tiaŋ เรื่องโต้เถียง

debit, *n.* gaan-loŋ-ban-chii-lûuk-nîi การลงบัญชีลูกหนี้

debt, *n.* nîi หนี้

debtor, *n.* lûuk-nîi ลูกหนี้

decade, *n.* tòt-sà-wát ทศวรรษ

decaffeinated, *adj.* mâi-mii-kaa-fee-iin ไม่มีคาเฟอีน

decay, *v.* sùam เสื่อม (deteriorate); nâo-bpùai เน่าเปื่อย (rot)

decay, *n.* kwaam-sùam ความเสื่อม; gaan-nâo-bpùai การเน่าเปื่อย

deceive, *v.* lòok-luang หลอกลวง

December, *n.* duan-tan-waa-kom เดือนธันวาคม

decentralize, *v.* grà-jaai-am-nâat-bɔɔ-rí-hăan กระจายอำนาจบริหาร

deception, *n.* gaan-lòok-luang การหลอกลวง

deceptive, *adj.* lòok-luang หลอกลวง

decide, *v.* dtàt-sĭn-jai ตัดสินใจ

decimal, *adj.* gìao-gàp-tót-sà-ní-yom เกี่ยวกับทศนิยม

decipher, *v.* bplɛɛ-kwaam-măai แปลความหมาย (interpret); tòot-rá-hàt ถอดรหัส (decode)

decision, *n.* gaan-dtàt-sĭn-jai การตัดสินใจ

decisive, *adj.* nɛ̂o-nɛ̂ɛ แน่วแน่

deck, *n.* dàat-fáa ดาดฟ้า (e.g. ship); chút-pâi ชุดไพ่ (of cards); chán ชั้น (roofless, floored structure)

declaration, *n.* gaan-bprà-gàat การประกาศ

declare, *v.* bprà-gàat ประกาศ (pro-

claim); rîak-pâi เรียกไพ่ (in a card game)

decompose, *v.* yôi-sà-lăai ย่อยสลาย; nâo-bpùai เน่าเปื่อย

decorate, *v.* bprà-dàp ประดับ; dtòk-dtèng ตกแต่ง

decoration, *n.* gaan-dtòk-dtèng การตกแต่ง

decoy, *n.* nók-dtɔ̀ɔ นกต่อ; bpao-lɔ̀ɔk เป้าหลอก

decrease, *v.* lót-long ลดลง

decrease, *n.* gaan-lót-long การลดลง

decree, *n.* kam-sàng คำสั่ง (order); kam-pí-pâak-săa คำพิพากษา (judgment)

dedicate, *v.* ù-tít อุทิศ

dedication, *n.* gaan-ù-tít การอุทิศ; kam-ù-tít คำอุทิศ

deduce, *v.* à-nú-maan-jàak อนุมานจาก

deduct, *v.* hàk หัก (subtract); à-nú-maan อนุมาน (derive by deduction)

deduction, *n.* gaan-hàk-ɔ̀ɔk การหักออก; gaan-à-nú-maan การอนุมาน

deed, *n.* gaan-grà-tam การกระทำ (action); chà-nòot โฉนด (e.g. land)

deem, *v.* kâo-jai-wâa เข้าใจว่า

deep, *adj.* lúk ลึก

deepen, *v.* tam-hâi-lúk ทำให้ลึก

deer, *n.* gwaang กวาง

default, *v.* lá-lɔ̂əi ละเลย (neglect);

mâi-tam-dtaam-săn-yaa ไม่ทำตาม
สัญญา (of a contract)

defeat, *v.* ao-cha-ná เอาชนะ

defeat, *n.* gaan-bpraa-chai
การปราชัย

defect, *n.* kɔ̂ɔ-sĭa ข้อเสีย; bpom-dɔ̂i
ปมด้อย

defective, *adj.* mii-kɔ̂ɔ-sĭa มีข้อเสีย;
kàat ขาด

defend, *v.* bpɔ̂ng-gan ป้องกัน

defendant, *n.* jam-ləəi จำเลย

defense, *n.* gaan-bpɔ̂ng-gan
การป้องกัน

defenseless, *adj.* bpɔ̂ng-gan-mâi-
dâai ป้องกันไม่ได้

defensive, *adj.* gìao-gàp-gaan-
bpɔ̂ng-gan เกี่ยวกับการป้องกัน

defer, *v.* chûa-dtaam เชื่อตาม (yield
to the wishes or opinion of another);
yûut-wee-laa ยืดเวลา (postpone)

deference, *n.* gaan-à-nú-loom
การอนุโลม

defiant, *adj.* dtɔ̀ɔ-dtâan ต่อต้าน
(resistant); táa-taai ท้าทาย (challenging); duu-mìn ดูหมิ่น (contemptuous)

deficiency, *n.* paa-wá-tîi-kàat-
klɛɛn ภาวะที่ขาดแคลน (shortage);
bòk-prɔ̂ng บกพร่อง (inadequacy)

deficient (in), *adj.* kàat-klɛɛn
ขาดแคลน

deficit, *n.* kwaam-kàat-klɛɛn
ความขาดแคลน (insufficiency);

gaan-kàat-dun การขาดดุล (business
loss)

define, *v.* hâi-kwaam-mǎai
ให้ความหมาย (give meaning); à-tí-
baai อธิบาย (explain)

definite, *adj.* nɛ̂ɛ-nɔɔn แน่นอน

definition, *n.* kam-jam-gàt-kwaam
คำจำกัดความ; gaan-à-tí-baai
การอธิบาย

deflect, *v.* bàai-been บ่ายเบน

deform, *v.* tam-hâi-bplìan-rûup
ทำให้เปลี่ยนรูป

deformity, *n.* kwaam-pí-gaan
ความพิการ

defraud, *v.* goong โกง

defray, *v.* ɔ̀ɔk-kâa-chái-jàai-hâi
ออกค่าใช้จ่ายให้

defrost, *v.* tam-hâi-náam-kěng-lá-
laai ทำให้น้ำแข็งละลาย

defunct, *adj.* dtaai ตาย (die); dàp
ดับ (become extinct); mòt-aa-yú
หมดอายุ (expire)

defy, *v.* táa-taai ท้าทาย
(challenge); dtɔ̀ɔ-dtâan ต่อต้าน
(resist)

degrade, *v.* lót ลด (lower); lót-
dtam-nɛ̀ng ลดตำแหน่ง (demote)

degrading, *adj.* leeo เลว (bad);
nâa-aai น่าอาย (shameful)

degree, *n.* bpà-rin-yaa ปริญญา
(e.g. B.A., M.A.); rá-dàp ระดับ
(stage, level); ong-sǎa องศา (temperature scale)

dehydrate, v. sǔun-sǐa-náam
สูญเสียน้ำ (lose water or bodily flu-
ids); kà-jàt-náam-ɔ̀ɔk ขจัดน้ำออก
(remove water from)

delay, v. lâa-cháa ล่าช้า

delay, n. kwaam-lâa-cháa
ความล่าช้า

delegate, n. dtua-tɛɛn ตัวแทน

delegation, n. gaan-dtɛ̀ng-dtâng-
dtua-tɛɛn การแต่งตั้งตัวแทน

delete, v. lóp-ɔ̀ɔk ลบออก; dtàt-ɔ̀ɔk
ตัดออก

deliberate, v. kít-yàang-rɔ̂ɔp-kɔ̂ɔp
คิดอย่างรอบคอบ

deliberate, adj. dooi-jèet--dtà-naa
โดยเจตนา (intentional)

deliberation, n. gaan-pí-jaa-ra-naa-
yàang-rɔ̂ɔp-kɔ̂ɔp การพิจารณาอย่าง
รอบคอบ

delicate, adj. lá-ìat-ɔ̀ɔn ละเอียดอ่อน
(pleasing to the senses, especially in a
subtle way); ɔ̀ɔn-ɛɛ อ่อนแอ (weak)

delicatessen, n. aa-hǎan-sǎm-sèt-
rûup อาหารสำเร็จรูป

delicious, adj. à-rɔ̀i อร่อย

delight, n. kwaam-yin-dii ความยินดี

delightful, adj. sùk jai สุขใจ

delinquent, adj. pìt-gòt-mǎai
ผิดกฎหมาย

delirious, adj. pɔ́ɔ เพ้อ; klâng คลั่ง

deliver, v. sòng ส่ง (e.g. mail); hâi-
gam-nòət ให้กำเนิด (e.g. a baby)

delivery, n. gaan-sòng การส่ง;
gaan-klɔ̂ɔt-bùt การคลอดบุตร

delta, n. sǎam-lìam สามเหลี่ยม (triangle); sǎn-dɔɔn-mɛ̂ɛ-náam
สันดอนแม่น้ำ (of a river)

deluxe, adj. rǔu-rǎa หรูหรา

demand, v. dtɔ̂ng-gaan ต้องการ
(want); jam-bpen จำเป็น (need);
rîak-rɔ́ɔng เรียกร้อง (claim)

demand, n. ùp-bpà-sǒng อุปสงค์
(in economics)

demanding, adj. dtɔ̂ng-gaan-mâak
ต้องการมาก

democracy, adj. bprà-chaa-típ-bpà-
dtai ประชาธิปไตย

democratic, adj. gìao-gàp-bprà-
chaa-típ-bpà-dtai
เกี่ยวกับประชาธิปไตย

demon, n. bpii-sàat ปีศาจ

demonstrate, v. sà-dɛɛng แสดง;
sǎa-tít สาธิต

demonstration, n. gaan-sǎa-tít
การสาธิต

demote, v. lót-rá-dàp ลดระดับ

den, n. tâm-sàt ถ้ำสัตว์ (animal);
hɔ̂ng-lék ห้องเล็ก (small room)

denial, n. gaan-bpà-dtì-sèet
การปฏิเสธ

denim, n. pâa-fàai-yàap
ผ้าฝ้ายหยาบ

Denmark, n. bprà-têet-den-mâak
ประเทศเดนมาร์ก

dense, adj. nǎa-nɛ̂n หนาแน่น
(compact); túp ทึบ (thick, opaque)

density, n. kwaam-nǎa-nɛ̂n

ความหนาแน่น; kwaam-túp ความที่ทึบ

dent, *n.* èng แอ่ง (small notch or hollow); rɔɔi รอย (on a surface)

dental, *adj.* gìao-gàp-fan เกี่ยวกับฟัน

dentist, *n.* tan-dtà-pêɛt ทันตแพทย์; mɔ̌ɔ-fan หมอฟัน

dentistry, *n.* tan-dtà-gam ทันตกรรม

denture, *n.* fan-bplɔɔm ฟันปลอม

deny, *v.* bpà-dtì-sèet ปฏิเสธ

deodorant, *n.* yaa-dàp-glìn ยาดับกลิ่น

depart, *v.* ɔ̀ɔk-jàak ออกจาก

department, *n.* pà-nèek แผนก (in a company); pâak ภาค (in a faculty); grom กรม (in a ministry)

department store, *n.* hâang-sàp-pa-sǐn-káa ห้างสรรพสินค้า

departure, *n.* gaan-ɔ̀ɔk-dəən-taang การออกเดินทาง (taking a trip; taking off); gaan-jàak-bpai การจากไป (act of leaving)

depend, *v.* kʉ̂n-yùu-gàp ขึ้นอยู่กับ

dependable, *adj.* wái-waang-jai-dâai ไว้วางใจได้

dependence, *n.* gaan-pʉ̂ng-paa การพึ่งพา (for support); gaan-dtìt-yaa การติดยา (drug addition)

dependent, *adj.* pʉ̂ng-paa พึ่งพา; mâi-bpen-ìt-sà-rà ไม่เป็นอิสระ

deport, *v.* nee-rá-têet เนรเทศ (expel); sòng-glàp-bprà-têet ส่งกลับประเทศ (send back to one's own country)

deposit, *v.* fàak ฝาก

depositor, *n.* pûu-fàak ผู้ฝาก

depot, *n.* klang-pát-sà-dù คลังพัสดุ

depress, *v.* lot-long ลดลง (sink, lower); gòt-dtàm กดต่ำ (press down); tam-hâi-hòt-hùu ทำให้หดหู่ (lower in spirits; deject)

depressed, *adj.* hòt-hùu หดหู่; sâo เศร้า (sad)

depression, *n.* paa-wá-sèet-dtà-gìt-dtòk-dtàm ภาวะเศรษฐกิจตกต่ำ (economic); kwaam-gòt-aa-gàat-dtàm ความกดอากาศต่ำ (weather)

deprive, *v.* mâi-hâi-bpen-jâo-kɔ̌ɔng ไม่ให้เป็นเจ้าของ (keep from possessing); ao-ɔ̀ɔk-jàak เอาออกจาก (take something away from); bpà-dtì-sèet ปฏิเสธ (deny)

depth, *n.* kwaam-lʉ́k ความลึก

deputy, *n.* pûu-rák-sǎa ผู้รักษาการ

descend, *v.* dtòk-long-maa ตกลงมา (come or go down); sʉ̌ʉp-long-maa สืบลงมา (pass down by inheritance); lót-gìat ลดเกียรติ (progress downward)

descendant, *n.* taa-yâat ทายาท

descent, *n.* gaan-dtòk-long-maa การตกลงมา (act or an instance of descending); taang-lâat-long ทางลาดลง (downward slope)

describe, *v.* ban-yaai บรรยาย (depict); bɔ̀ɔk บอก (tell); à-tí-baai อธิบาย (explain)

description, *n.* gaan-ban-yaai
การบรรยาย; gaan-à-tí-baai
การอธิบาย

desert, *n.* tá-lee-saai ทะเลทราย

desert, *v.* lá-tíng ละทิ้ง

deserter, *n.* pûu-lá-tíng ผู้ละทิ้ง

deserve, *v.* sŏm-kuan-dâai-ráp
สมควรได้รับ

design, *v.* ɔ̀ɔk-bɛ̀ɛp ออกแบบ

designer, *n.* nák-ɔ̀ɔk-bɛ̀ɛp
นักออกแบบ

desirable, *adj.* tùuk-jai ถูกใจ
(pleasing); nâa-bpràat-ta-năa
น่าปรารถนา (arousing desire)

desire, *v.* dtɔ̂ng-gaan ต้องการ
(need); yàak-dâai อยากได้ (want);
bpràat-ta-năa ปรารถนา (wish, want
or need - polite form)

desire, *n.* kwaam-bpràat-ta-năa
ความปรารถนา

desk, *n.* dtó-tam-ngaan โต๊ะทำงาน

desperate, *adj.* mòt-hŏn-taang
หมดหนทาง; kâo-dtaa-jon เข้าตาจน

desperation, *n.* kwaam-sîn-wăng
ความสิ้นหวัง (despair)

despite, *prep.* yàang-rai-gɔ̂ɔ-dtaam
ยังไงก็ตาม (notwithstanding);
dooi-mâi kam-nɯng-tŭng
โดยไม่คำนึงถึง (in spite of)

dessert, *n.* kɔ̌ɔng-wăan ของหวาน

destination, *n.* jùt-măai จุดหมาย;
bplaai-taang ปลายทาง

destined, *adj.* mii-jùt-mûng-măai
มีจุดมุ่งหมาย

destiny, *n.* chôok-chá-dtaa
โชคชะตา

destroy, *v.* tam-laai ทำลาย

destruction, *n.* gaan-tam-laai
การทำลาย

destructive, *adj.* chɔ̂ɔp-tam-laai
ชอบทำลาย; bpen-gaan-tam-laai
เป็นการทำลาย

detach, *v.* yɛ̂ɛk-ɔ̀ɔk แยกออก; bplòt
ปลด

detail, *n.* raai-lá-ìat รายละเอียด

detain, *v.* gàk-dtua กักตัว (confine);
yáp-yáng ยับยั้ง (delay or retard)

detect, *v.* sùup-hăa สืบหา (discern;
learn something hidden); kón-póp
ค้นพบ (discover)

detective, *n.* nák-sùup นักสืบ

detention, *n.* gaan-kum-dtua
การคุมตัว

detergent, *n.* pŏng-sák-fɔ̂ɔk
ผงซักฟอก

deteriorate, *v.* tam-hâi-leeo-long
ทำให้เลวลง (diminish or impair in
quality); leeo-long เลวลง (grow
worse)

determination, *n.* gaan-dtòk-long-
jai การตกลงใจ

determine, *v.* gam-nòt กำหนด
(settle, establish); dtàt-sĭn-jai
ตัดสินใจ (decide)

detour, *n.* taang-ɔ̂ɔm ทางอ้อม

devalue, *v.* lót-kâa ลดคา

devastate, *v.* tam-laai ทำลาย

devastating, *adj.* tam-laai ทำลาย

develop, v. pát-ta-naa พัฒนา (improve); láang-rûup ล้างรูป (pictures)

development, n. gaan-pát-ta-naa การพัฒนา

deviate, v. hǎn-hěe หันเห (turn aside from a course or way); ɔ̀ɔk-nɔ̂ɔk-rûang ออกนอกเรื่อง (digress)

deviation, n. gaan-hǎn-hěe การหันเห

device, n. ùp-bpà-gɔɔn อุปกรณ์ (equipment); sìng-bprà-dìt สิ่งประดิษฐ์ (invention)

devil, n. bpì-sàat ปีศาจ (demon); waai-ráai วายร้าย (wicked person)

devilish, adj. hìam-hòot เหี้ยมโหด

devious, adj. kót-kíao คดเคี้ยว

devoid, adj. kàat-kleen ขาดแคลน

devote, v. ù-tít อุทิศ

devotee, n. pûu-ù-tít ผู้อุทิศ

devotion, n. gaan-ù-tít การอุทิศ

devout, adj. mii-sàt-taa มีศรัทธา (devoted to religion)

dew, n. náam-káang น้ำค้าง

dexterity, n. kwaam-cham-naan ความชำนาญ

diabetes, n. rôok-bao-wǎan โรคเบาหวาน

diagnose, v. wí-nít-chǎi-rôok วินิจฉัยโรค

diagnosis, n. gaan-wí-nít-chǎi การวินิจฉัย

diagonal, adj. tá-yɛɛng ทแยง

diagram, n. pěɛn-pâap แผนภาพ

dial, v. mǔn หมุน (e.g. telephone)

dial, n. nâa-bpàt หน้าปัด; naa-lí-gaa-dèɛt นาฬิกาแดด (sundial)

dialect, n. paa-sǎa-tìn ภาษาถิ่น

dialogue, n. gaan-sǒn-ta-naa การสนทนา

diameter, n. sên-pàa-sǔun-glaang เส้นผ่าศูนย์กลาง

diamond, n. pét เพชร

diaper, n. pâa-ɔ̂ɔm ผ้าอ้อม

diaphragm, n. gà-bang-lom กะบังลม (body part); pên-yaang-kum-gam-nɔ̀ɔt แผ่นยางคุมกำเนิด (contraceptive device)

diarrhea, n. rôok-tɔ́ɔng-sǐa โรคท้องเสีย

diary, n. dai-aa-rìi ไดอารี่; sà-mùt-ban-tʉ́k สมุดบันทึก

dice, n. lûuk-dtǎo ลูกเต๋า

dictate, v. sàng สั่ง

dictation, n. gaan-bong-gaan การบงการ (command or order); gaan-kǐan-dtaam-kam-bɔ̀ɔk-lâo การเขียนตามคำบอก (e.g. a transcription)

dictator, n. pûu-bong-gaan ผู้บงการ; jɔɔm-pà-dèt-gaan จอมเผด็จการ

dictatorship, n. rá-bòp-pà-dèt-gaan ระบบเผด็จการ

dictionary, n. pót-jà-naa-nú-grom พจนานุกรม

English • Phonetic • Thai

die, *v.* dtaai ตาย

diet, *n.* aa-hǎan อาหาร (food or drink); gaan-kûap-kum-aa-hǎan การควบคุมอาหาร (weight control)

differ, *v.* dtèek-dtàang แตกต่างจาก

difference, *n.* kwaam-dtèek-dtàang ความแตกต่าง

different, *adj.* dtèek-dtàang แตกต่าง

differentiate, *v.* tam-hâi-dtèek-dtàang ทำให้แตกต่าง

difficult, *adj.* yâak ยาก

difficulty, *n.* kwaam-yâak-lam-bàak ความยากลำบาก

diffuse, *adj.* grà-jaai กระจาย; pəəi-prêe เผยแพร่

dig, *v.* kùt ขุด

digest, *v.* yôi ย่อย (food); jam-nêek จำแนก (classify)

digestion, *n.* gaan-yôi-aa-hǎan การย่อยอาหาร (food); gaan-dtrài-dtrɔɔng การไตร่ตรอง (thought)

digit, *n.* níu นิ้ว; dtua-lêek-dòot ตัวเลขโดด (numbers); làk หลัก (in a system of numeration)

digital, *adj.* gìao-gàp-dtua-lêek เกี่ยวกับตัวเลข

dignified, *adj.* sà-ngàa สง่า

dignity, *n.* gìat เกียรติ (honor); dtam-nèng-sǔung ตำแหน่งสูง (high office or rank)

digress, *v.* wók-won วกวน; ɔ̀ɔk nɔ̂ɔk-rûang ออกนอกเรื่อง

dike, *n.* kùan เขื่อน (dam)

diligent, *adj.* kà-yǎn ขยัน

dilute, *v.* jua-jaang เจือจาง

dim, *adj.* sà-lua สลัว; tɔ̂o-tɛ́ɛ ท้อแท้; mua มัว

dimension, *n.* mì-dtì มิติ

diminish, *v.* lót-long ลดลง

dimple, *n.* lák-yím ลักยิ้ม

dine, *v.* gin-kâao กินข้าว

diner, *n.* pûu-ráp-bprà-taan-aa-hǎan ผู้รับประทานอาหาร (one that dines); ráan-aa-hǎan ร้านอาหาร (restaurant)

dining room, *n.* hɔ̂ng-ráp-bprà-taan-aa-hǎan ห้องรับประทานอาหาร; hɔ̂ng-gin-kâao ห้องกินข้าว

dinner, *n.* aa-hǎan-yen อาหารเย็น

dinosaur, *n.* dai-noo-sǎo ไดโนเสาร์

dip, *v.* jùm จุ่ม

dip, *n.* gaan-jùm การจุ่ม

diphtheria, *n.* rôok-kɔɔ-dtìip โรคคอตีบ

diploma, *n.* bprà-gàat-sà-nii-yá-bàt ประกาศนียบัตร

diplomacy, *n.* gaan-tûut การทูต

diplomat, *n.* nák-gaan-tûut นักการทูต

diplomatic, *adj.* gìao-gàp-gaan-tûut เกี่ยวกับการทูต

direct, *adj.* dooi-dtrong โดยตรง

direction, *n.* tít-taang ทิศทาง; kam-à-tí-baai คำอธิบาย; gaan-mûng-mǎai การมุ่งหมาย

director, *n.* pûu-am-nuai-gaan

ผู้อำนวยการ; puu-gam-gàp ผู้กำกับ
(e.g. movie)

directory, n. năng-sŭu-ruam-chûu-
lé-tîi-yùu หนังสือรวมชื่อและที่อยู่

dirt, n. din ดิน (soil); sìng-sòk-ga-
bpròk สิ่งสกปรก (filthy object)

dirty, adj. sòk-ga-bpròk สกปรก;
laa-mók ลามก (obscene)

disability, n. gaan-rái-kwaam-săa-
mâat การไร้ความสามารถ; kwaam-
pí-gaan ความพิการ

disable, v. tam-hâi-rái-kwaam-săa-
mâat ทำให้ไร้ความสามารถ

disabled, n. pí-gaan พิการ

disadvantage, n. kwaam-sĭa-
bprìap ความเสียเปรียบ

disagree, v. mâi-hĕn-dûai
ไม่เห็นด้วย

disagreeable, adj. mâi-tùuk-jai
ไม่ถูกใจ; mâi-long-rɔɔi ไม่ลงรอย

disagreement, n. kwaam-mâi-hĕn-
dûai ความไม่เห็นด้วย (refusal to
agree); gaan-dtôo-yéeng การโต้แย้ง
(quarrel)

disappear, v. hăai-bpai หายไป
(something disappears); hăai-dtua
หายตัว (e.g. by kidnapping or murder; vanish; used mainly with people)

disappearance, n. gaan-hăai-bpai
การหายไป; gaan-hăai-dtua
การหายตัว

disappoint, v. tam-hâi-pìt-wăng
ทำให้ผิดหวัง

disappointed, adj. sĭa-jai เสียใจ;
pìt-wăng ผิดหวัง

disappointment, n. kwaam-pìt-
wăng ความผิดหวัง

disapproval, n. gaan-mâi-à-nú-yâat
การไม่อนุญาต; gaan-mâi-hĕn-dûai
การไม่เห็นด้วย

disapprove, v. mâi-hĕn-dûai
ไม่เห็นด้วย (disagree); mâi-à-nú-
yâat ไม่อนุญาต (refuse to approve)

disarm, v. bplòt-aa-wút ปลดอาวุธ

disarmament, n. gaan-bplòt-aa-wút
การปลดอาวุธ

disaster, n. kwaam-hăa-ya-ná
ความหายนะ

disastrous, adj. gòət-hăa-ya-ná
เกิดหายนะ

discard, v. tíng ทิ้ง

discharge, v. bplòi ปล่อย (release;
let go); rá-baai-ɔ̀ɔk ระบายออก
(pour forth; emit)

discharge, n. kɔ̌ɔng-tîi-lăi-ɔ̀ɔk
ของที่ไหลออก (something that is dis-
charged)

discipline, n. rá-bìap ระเบียบ; wí-
nai วินัย

disclaim, v. sà-là-sìt สละสิทธิ์
(renounce one's right); lá-tíng ละทิ้ง
(renounce, disown)

disclose, v. bpòət-pŏəi เปิดเผย

disclosure, n. gaan-bpòət-pŏəi
การเปิดเผย

discomfort, n. kwaam-mâi-sà-dùak

ความไม่สะดวก (annoyance);
kwaam-ùt-àt ความอึดอัด (mental or
bodily distress)

disconnect, v. dtàt ตัด; yêɛk แยก

discontent, n. kwaam-mâi-pɔɔ-jai
ความไม่พอใจ

discontinue, v. yùt หยุด (stop);
yók-lôɔk ยกเลิก (cancel)

discord, n. kwaam-bàat-mǎang
ความบาดหมาง; kwaam-kàt-yéeng
ความขัดแย้ง

discordant, adj. kàt-yéeng-gan
ขัดแย้งกัน

discotheque, n. dìt-sà-gôo-tèk
ดิสโก้เธค

discount, n. sùan-lót ส่วนลด

discourage, v. tam-hâi-tɔɔ-jai
ทำให้ท้อใจ

discourse, n. gaan-ban-yaai
การบรรยาย; kam-bpraa-sǎi
การปราศรัย

discover, v. kón-póp ค้นพบ

discoverer, n. pûu-kón-póp
ผู้ค้นพบ

discovery, n. gaan-kón-póp
การค้นพบ

discredit, v. tam-hâi-sǐa-chûu-sǐang
ทำให้เสียชื่อเสียง

discreet, adj. dtrài-dtrɔɔng
ไตร่ตรอง; sù-kùm สุขุม

discrepancy, n. kwaam-kàt-yéeng
ความขัดแย้งกัน

discretion, n. kwaam-sù-kǔm
ความสุขุม

discriminate, v. bèng-yêɛk
แบ่งแยก; lûak-tîi-rák-mák-tîi-chang
เลือกที่รักมักที่ชัง

discrimination, n. gaan-bèng-yêɛk
การแบ่งแยก

discuss, v. à-pí-bpraai อภิปราย

discussion, n. gaan-à-pí-bpraai
การอภิปราย

disease, n. chúa-rôok เชื้อโรค;
rôok โรค

disembark, v. kûn-fàng ขึ้นฝั่ง

disfigure, v. tam-hâi-pìt-rûup-râang
ทำให้ผิดรูปร่าง

disgrace, n. kwaam-sùam-sǐa
ความเสื่อมเสีย

disgraceful, adj. sùam-sǐa เสื่อมเสีย

disguise, v. sɔ̂n-rén ซ่อนเร้น (conceal); bplɔɔm-bplɛɛng ปลอมแปลง
(misrepresent; make fake)

disguise, n. gaan-sɔ̂n-rén
การซ่อนเร้น; gaan-bplɔɔm-bplɛɛng
การปลอมแปลง

disgust, n. kwaam-nâa-rang-gìat
ความน่ารังเกียจ

disgusting, adj. nâa-rang-gìat
น่ารังเกียจ

dish, n. jaan จาน

dishonest, adj. mâi-sûu-sàt
ไม่ซื่อสัตย์

dishonesty, n. kwaam-mâi-sûu-sàt
ความไม่ซื่อสัตย์

dishwasher, n. krûang-láang-jaan

เครื่องล้างจาน

disinfect, v. kâa-chúa-rôok ฆ่าเชื้อโรค

disinfectant, n. yaa-kâa-chúa-rôok ยาฆ่าเชื้อโรค

disk, n. pèn-dít แผ่นดิสก์ (for computer); pèn-glom แผ่นกลม (thin, flat, circular object or plate); jaan-sǐang จานเสียง (for music)

dislike, v. mâi-chɔ̂ɔp ไม่ชอบ

dislocate, v. klûan-jàak-tîi เคลื่อนจากที่ (move); yáai ย้าย (displace)

dismiss, v. lâi-ɔ̀ɔk ไล่ออก (expel); yók-fɔ́ɔng ยกฟ้อง (dismiss a case)

disobey, v. mâi-chûa-fang ไม่เชื่อฟัง

disorganized, adj. mâi-bpen-rá-bìap ไม่เป็นระเบียบ

disoriented, adj. mâi-mii-rá-bòp-nὲɛ-nɔɔn ไม่มีระบบแน่นอน; lǒng-taang หลงทาง

dispatch, v. sòng ส่ง (send); rîip-tam รีบทำ (complete promptly)

displace, v. klûan-tîi เคลื่อนที่ (move or shift); lâi-ɔ̀ɔk ไล่ออก (discharge from an office or position)

display, v. sà-dɛɛng แสดง

disposable, adj. tíng-dâai ทิ้งได้ (can be disposed); chái-kráng-diao-tíng ใช้ครั้งเดียวทิ้ง (designed to be disposed of after one use)

dispose, v. jàt-gaan จัดการ; dam-nɔɔn-gaan ดำเนินการ

disposition, n. gaan-dtòk-long-nai-kân-sùt-táai การตกลงในขั้นสุดท้าย (final settlement)

disprove, v. pí-sùut-hàk-láang พิสูจน์หักล้าง; pí-sùut-wâa-pìt พิสูจน์ว่าผิด

dispute, v. tǐang เถียง (argue); dtɔ̀ɔ-dtâan ต่อต้าน (resist)

disqualify, v. dtàt-sìt ตัดสิทธิ์

disrespect, n. gaan-mâi-kao-róp การไม่เคารพ

disrespectful, adj. mâi-mii-kwaam-kao-róp ไม่มีความเคารพ

dissatisfaction, n. kwaam-mâi-pɔɔ-jai ความไม่พอใจ

dissatisfied, adj. mâi-pɔɔ-jai ไม่พอใจ

dissertation, n. dùt-sà-dii-ní-pon ดุษฎีนิพนธ์ (for Ph.D.); gaan-kǐan-bòt-kwaam การเขียนบทความ (research writing)

dissident, n. pûu-mâi-hěn-dûai ผู้ไม่เห็นด้วย

dissolve, v. lá-laai ละลาย; lɔ̌ɔm-lěeo หลอมเหลว

distance, n. rá-yá-taang ระยะทาง (intervening space); taang-glai ทางไกล (remoteness)

distant, adj. glai ไกล

distill, v. glàn กลั่น

distinct, adj. chát-jeen ชัดเจน

distinction, n. kwaam-dtὲɛk-dtàang ความแตกต่าง; kwaam-mii-lák-sà-nà-pí-sèet ความมีลักษณะพิเศษ

English · Phonetic · Thai

distort, v. bìt-bɯan บิดเบือน

distortion, n. gaan-bìt-bɯan
การบิดเบือน

distract, v. tam-hâi-wɔ̂k-wɛ̂ɛk
ทำให้วอกแวก (divert); guan-jai
กวนใจ (bother)

distracted, adj. wɔ̂k-wɛ̂ɛk วอกแวก

distraction, n. sìng-lɔ́ɔ-jai สิ่งล่อใจ;
kwaam-wɔ̂k-wɛ̂ɛk ความวอกแวก

distress, n. kwaam-sǐa-jai
ความเสียใจ; kwaam-yâak-lam-bàak
ความยากลำบาก

distribute, v. jɛ̀ɛk แจก; grà-jaai
กระจาย

distribution, n. gaan-jɛ̀ɛk-jàai
การแจกจ่าย; gaan-bɛ̀ng-sǎn
การแบ่งสรร

district, n. kèet เขต (in Bangkok;
division of an area); am-pəə อำเภอ
(in other provinces)

district attorney, n. ai-ya-gaan-
tɔ̀ɔng-tìn ยัยการท้องถิ่น

disturb, v. róp-guan รบกวน

disturbance, n. gaan-róp-guan
การรบกวน

ditch, v. kùt-tɔ̂ɔ ขุดท่อ

ditch, n. tɔ̂ɔ ท่อ; kuu คู

dive, v. dam-náam ดำน้ำ

dive, n. gaan-dam-náam การดำน้ำ

diver, n. nák-dam-náam นักดำน้ำ

diverse, adj. làak-lǎai หลากหลาย

diversify, v. tam-hâi-làak-lǎai
ทำให้หลากหลาย

diversion, n. gaan-tam-hâi-dtɛ̀ɛk-
dtàang การทำให้แตกต่าง

diversity, n. kwaam-làak-lǎai
ความหลากหลาย

divide, v. bɛ̀ng แบ่ง

dividend, n. ngən-bpan-pǒn
เงินปันผล

divine, adj. gìao-gàp-prá-jâao
เกี่ยวกับพระเจ้า (of or being a deity;
godlike); sàk-sìt ศักดิ์สิทธิ์ (sacred);
nɯ̌a-má-nút เหนือมนุษย์ (superhu-
man)

diving board, n. tɛ̂n-grà-dòot-náam
แท่นกระโดดน้ำ

division, n. gaan-bɛ̀ng การแบ่ง;
pà-nɛ̀ɛk แผนก (department)

divorce, v. yàa หย่า

divorce, n. gaan-yàa-ráang
การหย่าร้าง

dizziness, n. aa-gaan-wing-wian-
sǐi-sà อาการวิงเวียนศีรษะ

dizzy, adj. wing-wian วิงเวียน

do, v. tam ทำ; jàt-gaan จัดการ;
bpà-dtì-bàt ปฏิบัติ

dock, n. tâa-rɯa ท่าเรือ

doctor, n. pɛ̂ɛt แพทย์; mɔ̌ɔ หมอ;
dók-dtɤ̂ɤ ด็อกเตอร์

doctrine, n. làk หลัก; lát-tí ลัทธิ

document, n. èek-gà-sǎan เอกสาร

documentary, adj. gìao-gàp-èek-
gà-sǎan เกี่ยวกับเอกสาร (based on
documents)

documentary, n. pâap-pá-yon-sǎa-
rá-ká-dii ภาพยนตร์สารคดี (movie)

dodge, v. lòp หลบ

doe, n. gwaang-dtua-mia กวางตัว
เมีย

dog, n. sù-nák สุนัข; măa หมา

dogma, n. lát-tí ลัทธิ; kwaam-chûa
ความเชื่อ

dogmatic, adj. taang-kwaam-chûa
ทางความเชื่อ; dtaam-lát-tí ตามลัทธิ

doll, n. dtúk-gà-dtaa ตุ๊กตา

dollar, n. don-lâa ดอลล่าร์; rĭan
เหรียญ

dolphin, n. bplaa-loo-maa ปลาโลมา

domain, n. aa-naa-kèet อาณาเขต

dome, n. doom โดม; yɔ̂ɔt-glom
ยอดกลม

domestic, adj. nai-bâan ในบ้าน
(household); nai-bprà-têet
ในประเทศ (within the country)

domesticate, v. tam-hâi-yùu-nai-
bâan ทำให้อยู่ในบ้าน (make domestic); tam-hâi-chûang ทำให้เชื่อง
(tame)

dominant, adj. mii-ìt-tí-pon
มีอิทธิพล; mii-am-nâat-nŭa
มีอำนาจเหนือ

dominate, v. krɔ̂ɔp-ngam ครอบงำ;
yùu-nŭa อยู่เหนือ

domineering, adj. chái-am-nâat
ใช้อำนาจ

donate, v. bɔɔ-ri-jàak บริจาค

donation, n. gaan-bɔɔ-ri-jàak
การบริจาค

done, adj. sèt-léɛo เสร็จแล้ว (fin-

ished); sùk สุก (cooked, well done)

donkey, n. laa ลา

donor, n. pûu-bɔɔ-ri-jàak ผู้บริจาค

doom, n. krɔ́-ráai เคราะห์ร้าย

doomed, adj. tùuk-gam-nòt-chá-
dtaa ถูกกำหนดชะตา (predestined);
krɔ́-ráai เคราะห์ร้าย (unlucky)

door, n. bprà-dtuu ประตู

doorbell, n. grà-dĭng-bprà-dtuu
กระดิ่งประตู

doorman, n. kon-fâo-bprà-dtuu
คนเฝ้าประตู

doormat, n. prom-nâa-bprà-dtuu
พรมหน้าประตู

doorway, n. taang-kâo-bprà-dtuu
ทางเข้าประตู

dormitory, n. hɔ̌ɔ-pák หอพัก

dosage, n. bpà-ri-maan-gaan-chái-
yaa ปริมาณการใช้ยา; kà-năan
ขนาน

dose, n. bpà-ri-maan-yaa-dtɔ̀ɔ-
kráng ปริมาณยาต่อครั้ง; kà-năan
ขนาน

dot, n. jùt จุด

dotted line, n. sên-bprà เส้นประ

double, v. pə̂əm-bpen-sɔ̌ɔng-tâo
เพิ่มเป็นสองเท่า

double, adj. sɔ̌ɔng-tâo สองเท่า;
sɔ̌ɔng-kráng สองครั้ง

double bed, n. dtiang-kûu เตียงคู่

double-cross, v. tɔɔ-ra-yót ทรยศ

doubt, v. sŏng-săi สงสัย

doubt, n. kwaam-sŏng-săi

ความสงสัย

doubtful, *adj.* sŏng-sǎi สงสัย; mâi-nɛ̂ɛ-jai ไม่แน่ใจ

dough, *n.* bpɛ̂ɛng-nûat แป้งนวด (for bread)

doughnut, *n.* doo-nát โดนัท

dove, *n.* nók-pì-râap นกพิราบ

down, *adv.* long ลง; lâang ล่าง; kâang-lâang ข้างล่าง; dtòk ตก

down, *n.* gaan-klʉ̂an-long การเคลื่อนลง

downfall, *n.* kwaam-dtòk-dtàm ความตกต่ำ

downhill, *adv.* long-kǎo ลงเขา; dtòk-dtàm ตกต่ำ

downpour, *n.* fǒn-dtòk-nàk ฝนตกหนัก

downstairs, *adv.* chán-lâang ชั้นล่าง

downtown, *n.* yâan-gaan-káa-nai-mʉang ย่านการค้าในเมือง; jai-glaang-mʉang ใจกลางเมือง

downward, *adj.* long-dtàm ลงต่ำ

dozen, *n.* nʉ̀ng-lŏo หนึ่งโหล; jam-nuan-mâak จำนวนมาก

draft, *v.* râang ร่าง (e.g. letter); geen-tá-hǎan เกณฑ์ทหาร (soldier)

draft, *n.* chà-bàp-raang ฉบับร่าง, gaan-geen-tá-hǎan การเกณฑ์ทหาร

draftsman, *n.* kon-râang-bὲɛp คนร่างแบบ

drag, *v.* lâak ลาก (pull); tam-hâi-láa-cháa ทำให้ล่าช้า (slow something down)

dragon, *n.* mang-gɔɔn มังกร

dragonfly, *n.* má-lɛɛng-bpɔɔ แมลงปอ

drain, *v.* rá-baai ระบาย

drain, *n.* gaan-rá-baai การระบาย

drainage, *n.* gaan-rá-baai การระบาย

drain pipe, *n.* tɔ̂ɔ-rá-baai ท่อระบาย

drama, *n.* lá-kɔɔn ละคร

dramatic, *adj.* gìao-gàp-lá-kɔɔn เกี่ยวกับละคร (relating to drama); ráo-jai เร้าใจ (in appearance or effect)

drapes, *n.* mâan-bprà-dàp ม่านประดับ

draw, *v.* wâat วาด (a picture); dʉng ดึง (pull); lâak ลาก (pull)

draw, *n.* gaan-dʉng การดึง (pulling); gaan-lâak การลาก (pulling); sìng-tîi-dʉng-dùut-jai สิ่งที่ดึงดูดใจ (attraction); gaan-sà-mǒɔ-gan การเสมอกัน (a tie)

drawer, *n.* lín-chák ลิ้นชัก; kon-wâat คนวาด

drawing, *n.* gaan-wâat การวาด (act of drawing); pâap-wâat ภาพวาด (picture)

dream, *v.* fǎn ฝัน

dream, *n.* kwaam-fǎn ความฝัน

dreamer, *n.* kon-châng-fǎn คนช่างฝัน

dreary, *adj.* nâa-bʉ̀a น่าเบื่อ (boring); sâo เศร้า (sad)

dress, *v.* dtὲng-dtua แต่งตัว; dtὲng

แต่ง
dress, *n.* chút ชุด

dresser, *n.* dtó-krûeang-bpêeng
โต๊ะเครื่องแป้ง (furniture); kon-
dtèng-dtua คนแต่งตัว (one that
dresses)

dressing, *n.* náam-sɔ́ɔt น้ำซอส
(sauce)

dressing gown, *n.* sûa-klum
เสื้อคลุม

dressing table, *n.* dtó-krûeang-
bpêeng โต๊ะเครื่องแป้ง

drift, *v.* lûean-lɔɔi เลื่อนลอย

drift, *n.* gaan-lûean-lɔɔi การเลื่อนลอย

drifter, *n.* kon-pá-nee-jɔɔn
คนพเนจร

drill, *v.* fùk-fǒn ฝึกฝน

drill, *n.* sà-wàan สว่าน (tool);
gaan-fùk-fǒn การฝึกฝน (training)

drink, *v.* dùum ดื่ม; gin กิน; dùum-
lâo ดื่มเหล้า (drink alcohol)

drink, *n.* krûeang-dùum เครื่องดื่ม

drip, *v.* yòt หยด; dtòk-long ตกลง

drip, *n.* yòt หยด; gaan-hâi-náam-
glua การให้น้ำเกลือ (medical)

drive, *v.* kàp ขับ; kìi ขี่

drive, *n.* gaan-kàp-kìi การขับขี่;
rɛɛng-grà-dtûn แรงกระตุ้น

driver, *n.* kon-kàp คนขับ

driveway, *n.* taang-rót ทางรถ

drop, *v.* yòt หยด; dtòk-long ตกลง

drop, *n.* yòt หยด (e.g. drop of
water); gaan-tîng-long การทิ้งลง

(act of dropping); gaan-bplòi-sà-
biang การปล่อยเสบียง (drop of supplies)

dropper, *n.* krûeang-yòɔt
เครื่องหยอด; tîi-yòt-yaa ที่หยดยา

drought, *n.* rú-duu-lɛ́ɛng ฤดูแล้ง

drown, *v.* tûang-náam ถ่วงน้ำ (kill
by submerging and suffocating in
water)

drowned, *adj.* jom-náam-dtaai
จมน้ำตาย

drug, *n.* yaa ยา (medicine); yaa-
sèep-dtìt ยาเสพติด (addictive)

drug addict, *n.* gaan-dtìt-yaa-sèep-
dtìt การติดยาเสพติด (act of addict-
ing); kon-dtìt-yaa คนติดยา (person)

druggist, *n.* pee-sàt-cha-gɔɔn
เภสัชกร

drugstore, *n.* ráan-kǎai-yaa
ร้านขายยา

drum, *n.* glɔɔng กลอง

drummer, *n.* kon-dtii-glɔɔng
คนตีกลอง

drumstick, *n.* kǎa-gài ขาไก่ (chick-
en); máai-dtii-glɔɔng ไม้ตีกลอง

drunk, *adj.* mao-lâo เมาเหล้า

drunkard, *n.* kon-kîi-mao คนขี้เมา

drunkenness, *n.* aa-gaan-mao
อาการเมา

dry, *v.* tam-hâi-hɛ̂ng ทำให้แห้ง

dry, *adj.* hɛ̂ng แห้ง

dry-cleaning, *n.*, *v.* sák-hɛ̂ng

ชักแห้ง

dryer, *n.* krนิang-òp-pâa เครื่องอบผ้า (clothes dryer); krนิang-bpào เครื่องเป่า (machine dryer)

dryness, *n.* kwaam-hêng ความแห้ง

dual, *adj.* kûu คู่; sɔ̌ɔng สอง

dub, *v.* ban-túk-táp บันทึกทับ (record over)

duck, *n.* bpèt เป็ด

duck, *v.* lòp หลบ (avoid from getting hit); mút มุด (lower the head or body)

duct, *n.* tɔ̂ɔ ท่อ (pipe); lɔ̀ɔt หลอด (tube); proong โพรง (canal)

due, *adj.* tǔng-gam-nòt ถึงกำหนด

due, *n.* nǐi หนี้ (debt)

duel, *n.* gaan-duan-gan การดวลกัน

dues, *n.* kâa-sà-maa-chík ค่าสมาชิก

duet, *n.* pleeng-kûu เพลงคู่

dull, *adj.* tนิm ทื่อ (not sharp); mâi-mii-chii-wít-chii-waa ไม่มีชีวิตชีวา (lifeless)

dumb, *adj.* ngôo โง่ (stupid); bpen-bâi เป็นใบ้

dummy, *n.* kon-ngôo คนโง่ (stupid person); hùn-lian-bὲεp หุ่นเลียนแบบ (imitation)

dump, *v.* tîng ทิ้ง

dump, *n.* gɔɔng-kà-yà กองขยะ

dung, *n.* muun-sàt มูลสัตว์

duplicate, *v.* tam-sǎm-nao ทำสำเนา; tam-sám ทำซ้ำ

duplicate, *n.* sǎm-nao สำเนา;

gaan-tam-sám การทำซ้ำ

durable, *adj.* ton-taan ทนทาน; chái-ton ใช้ทน

during, *prep.* rá-wàang ระหว่าง

dusk, *n.* yaam-kâm ยามค่ำ; kwaam-sà-lǔa ความสลัว

dust, *v.* bpàt-fùn ปัดฝุ่น

dust, *n.* fùn ฝุ่น (dry particles); din ดิน (soil); pǒng ผง (powder)

dusty, *adj.* bpen-fùn เป็นฝุ่น; mii-fùn มีฝุ่น

Dutch, *n.* chaao-nee-tɔ̂ɔ-lɛɛn/chaao-dát ชาวเนเธอร์แลนด์/ชาวดัช (people); gìao-gàp-nee-tɔ̂ɔ-lɛɛn เกี่ยวกับเนเธอร์แลนด์ (related to the Netherlands)

duty, *n.* nâa-tîi หน้าที่ (responsibility); paa-sǐi ภาษี (tax)

duty-free, *adj.* bplɔɔt-paa-sǐi ปลอดภาษี

dwarf, *n.* kon-krέ คนแคระ

dwell, *v.* aa-sǎi อาศัย

dwelling, *n.* tîi-yùu ที่อยู่

dye, *v.* yɔ́ɔm ย้อม

dye, *n.* sǐi-yɔ́ɔm สีย้อม

dying, *adj.* glâi-dtaai ใกล้ตาย

dynamic, *adj.* gìao gàp pá-lang-ngaan เกี่ยวกับพลังงาน

dynamite, *n.* rá-bὲɔt rεεng-sǔung ระเบิดแรงสูง

dynasty, *n.* râat cha-wong ราชวงศ์

dysentery, *n.* rôok-bìt โรคบิด

English · Phonetic · Thai

E

each, *pron., adj., adv.* dtèɛ-lá แต่ละ; túk ทุก (every)

eager, *adj.* grà-hǎai กระหาย (having intense desire); tá-yəɛ-tá-yaan ทะเยอทะยาน (ambitious)

eagerness, *n.* kwaam-grà-hǎai ความกระหาย; kwaam-grà-dtɯɯ-rɯɯ-rón ความกระตือรือร้น

eagle, *n.* nók-in-sii นกอินทรี

ear, *n.* hǔu หู

eardrum, *n.* gɛ̂ɛo-hǔu แก้วหู

early, *adj.* cháao เช้า (in the morning); reo เร็ว (soon, fast)

earn, *v.* hǎa-dâai หาได้

earnest, *adj.* jing-jang จริงจัง (serious); jing-jai จริงใจ (sincere)

earnings, *n.* raai-dâai รายได้

earphone, *n.* hǔu-fang หูฟัง

earplugs, *n.* tîi-ùt-hǔu ที่อุดหู

earring, *n.* dtûm-hǔu ตุ้มหู

earth, *n.* lôok โลก

earthquake, *n.* pèn-din-wǎi แผ่นดินไหว

earthworm, *n.* sâi-dɯan ไส้เดือน

ease, *v.* ban-tao บรรเทา

ease, *n.* kwaam-sà-dùak ความสะดวก; kwaam-ngâai ความง่าย

easel, *n.* kǎa-dtâng-pâap ขาตั้งภาพ

east, *n.* tít-dtà-wan-ɔ̀ɔk ทิศตะวันออก

eastern, *adj.* taang-dtà-wan-ɔ̀ɔk ทางตะวันออก

easy, *adj.* ngâai ง่าย; mâi-kêm-ngûat ไม่เข้มงวด

easygoing, *adj.* dtaam-sà-baai ตามสบาย; bpai-rûai-rûai ไปเรื่อยๆ

eat, *v.* gin กิน (collq.); taan ทาน (polite); ráp-bprà-taan รับประทาน (formal)

eaves, *n.* chaai-kaa ชายคา

ebb, *v.* lǎai-glàp ไหลกลับ (flow back); sùam เสื่อม (deteriorate)

ebb, *n.* náam-lót น้ำลด; jùt-sùam จุดเสื่อม

eccentric, *adj.* bprà-làat ประหลาด

echo, *v.* sà-tɔ́ɔn สะท้อน; sám ซ้ำ

echo, *n.* sǐang-sà-tɔ́ɔn เสียงสะท้อน

eclipse, *n.* sù-rí-yá-kâat สุริยคราส (of the sun); jan-trá-kâat จันทรคราส (of the moon)

ecology, *n.* ní-wêet-wít-tá-yaa นิเวศน์วิทยา

economic, *adj.* gìao-gàp-sèet-tà-sàat เกี่ยวกับเศรษฐศาสตร์

economical, *adj.* bprà-yàt ประหยัด

economics, *n.* sèet-tà-sàat เศรษฐศาสตร์

economist, *n.* nák-sèet-tà-sàat นักเศรษฐศาสตร์

economize, *v.* bprà-yàt ประหยัด

edge, *n.* kɔ̀ɔp ขอบ (rim or brink); rim ริม (margin); kom-mîit คมมีด (of a knife)

edible, *adj.* gin-dâai กินได้

edit, v. gɛ̂ɛ-kǎi แก้ไข; ñap-riang เรียบเรียง

edition, n. chà-bàp-pim ฉบับพิมพ์ (of a publication; the form in which a publication is issued)

editor, n. ban-naa-tí-gaan บรรณาธิการ

editorial, n. bòt-ban-naa-tí-gaan บทบรรณาธิการ

educate, v. hâi-gaan-sùk-sǎa ให้การศึกษา

education, n. gaan-sùk-sǎa การศึกษา

educational, adj. gìao-gàp-gaan-sùk-sǎa เกี่ยวกับการศึกษา

eel, n. bplaa-lǎi ปลาไหล

effect, v. mii-pǒn-grà-tóp-dtɔ̀ɔ มีผลกระทบต่อ (impact); tam-hâi-gɤ̀ɤt ทำให้เกิด (cause to happen)

effect, n. pǒn ผล (result); pǒn-grà-tóp-dtɔ̀ɔ ผลกระทบ (influence)

effective, adj. mii-pǒn มีผล; dâai-pǒn ได้ผล

efficiency, n. bprà-sìt-tí-pâap ประสิทธิภาพ

efficient, adj. mii-bprà-sìt-tí-pâap มีประสิทธิภาพ; mɯɯ-kwaam-sǎa-mâat มีความสามารถ

effort, n. kwaam-pá-yaa-yaam ความพยายาม

egg, n. kài ไข่

eggplant, n. má-kʉ̌a มะเขือ

ego, n. àt-dtaa อัตตา

egotism, n. kwaam-hěn-gɛ̀ɛ-dtua ความเห็นแก่ตัว

Egypt, n. bprà-têet-ii-yìp ประเทศอียิปต์

eight, nm. bpɛ̀ɛt แปด

eighteen, nm. sìp-bpɛ̀ɛt สิบแปด

eighteenth, adj. tîi-sìp-bpɛ̀ɛt ที่สิบแปด

eighth, adj. tîi-bpɛ̀ɛt ที่แปด

eightieth, adj. tîi-bpɛ̀ɛt-sìp ที่แปดสิบ

eighty, nm. bpɛ̀ɛt-sìp แปดสิบ

either, pron. dtɛ̀ɛ-lá แต่ละ; an-dai-an-nùng อันใดอันหนึ่ง

ejaculate, v. rɔ́ɔng ร้อง (exclaim); làng-à-sù-jì หลั่งอสุจิ (eject semen)

eject, v. kàp-ɔ̀ɔk ขับออก; dìit-ɔ̀ɔk ดีดออก

elaborate, adj. bprà-nìit ประณีต

elastic, n. yaang-yʉ̂ʉt ยางยืด

elate, v. tam-hâi-mii-kwaam-sùk ทำให้มีความสุข

elbow, n. sɔ̀ɔk ศอก

elder, adj. aa-yú-mâak-gwàa อายุมากกว่า

elderly, adj. gɛ̀ɛ แก่

eldest, adj. aa-yú-mâak-tîi-sùt อายุมากที่สุด

elect, v. lʉ̂ak เลือก

election, n. gaan-lʉ̂ak-dtâng การเลือกตั้ง

electric, electrical, adj. gìao-gàp-fai-fáa เกี่ยวกับไฟฟ้า

electrician, n. châng-fai-fáa

ช่างไฟฟ้า

electricity, *n.* fai-fáa ไฟฟ้า

electrify, *v.* àt-fai-fáa อัดไฟฟ้า

electrocute, *v.* bprà-hǎan-dooi-gâo-îi-fai-fáa ประหารโดยเก้าอี้ไฟฟ้า

electronic, *adj.* gìao-gàp-ì-lék-trɔɔ-nìk เกี่ยวกับอิเล็กทรอนิกส์

electronics, *n.* ì-lék-trɔɔ-nìk อิเล็กทรอนิกส์

elegance, *n.* kwaam-ngót-ngaam ความงดงาม

elegant, *adj.* ngót-ngaam งดงาม

element, *n.* tâat ธาตุ (substance); bpàt-jai-sǎm-kan ปัจจัยสำคัญ (essential constituent)

elementary, *adj.* bûang-dtôn เบื้องต้น; bprà-tǒm ประถม

elephant, *n.* cháang ช้าง

elevate, *v.* yók-kûn ยกขึ้น (raise, lift); lûan-dtam-nèng เลื่อนตำแหน่ง (promote to a higher rank)

elevation, *n.* gaan-yók-hâi-sǔung-kûn การยกให้สูงขึ้น; gaan-lûan การเลื่อน

elevator, *n.* líp ลิฟต์

eleven, *nm.* sìp-èt สิบเอ็ด

eleventh, *adj.* tîi-sìp-èt ที่สิบเอ็ด

eligible, *adj.* mɔ̀-sǒm เหมาะสม (suitable); kâo-geen เข้าเกณฑ์ (qualified); mii-sìt มีสิทธิ์ (have a right, e.g. to vote)

eliminate, *v.* dtàt-ɔ̀ɔk ตัดออก; tam-laai ทำลาย

elite, *n.* hǔa-gà-tì หัวกะทิ; kon-tîi-yɔ̂ɔt-yîam คนที่ยอดเยี่ยม

elope, *v.* nǐi-dtaam หนีตาม

eloquence, *n.* sǎm-nuan-kom-kaai สำนวนคมคาย

eloquent, *adj.* mii-kaa-rom มีคารม

else, *adv.* ùun อื่น

elsewhere, *adv.* tîi-ùun ที่อื่น

embargo, *n.* gaan-hâam-káa-kǎai-rá-wàang-bprà-têet การห้ามค้าขายระหว่างประเทศ

embarrass, *v.* tam-hâi-aai ทำให้อาย

embarrassing, *adj.* nâa-aai น่าอาย

embarrassment, *n.* kwaam-kǔai-kǒən ความขวยเขิน

embassy, *n.* sà-tǎan-tûut สถานทูต

ember, *n.* tàat-tîi-kú-yùu ถ่านที่คุอยู่

embezzle, *v.* yák-yɔ̂ɔk ยักยอก

embezzlement, *n.* gaan-yák-yɔ̂ɔk การยักยอก

emblem, *n.* sǎn-ya-làk สัญลักษณ์ (symbol); krûang-mǎai เครื่องหมาย (mark)

embrace, *v.* sǔam-gɔ̀ɔt สวมกอด (hug); lɔ́ɔm ล้อม (surround)

embroider, *v.* tàk tàk; bpàk ปัก

embroidery, *n.* gaan-yép-bpàk-tàk-rɔ́ɔi การเย็บปักถักร้อย

embryo, *n.* dtua-ɔ̀ɔn ตัวอ่อน

emerald, *n.* mɔɔ-ra-gòt มรกต

emergency, *n.* hèet-gaan-chùk-chǝ̌ən เหตุการณ์ฉุกเฉิน

emigrant, *n.* pûu-òp-pa-yóp ผู้อพยพ

emigrate, *v.* òp-pa-yóp อพยพ

émigré, *n.* pûu-òp-pa-yóp ผู้อพยพ

emission, *n.* gaan-bplòi-òok-maa การปล่อยออกมา; gaan-prêɛ การแพร่

emit, *v.* bplòi-òok-maa ปล่อยออกมา; prêɛ แพร่

emotion, *n.* aa-rom อารมณ์; kwaam-rúu-sùk ความรู้สึก

emotional, *adj.* sà-tɯan-aa-rom สะเทือนอารมณ์; gìao-gàp-kwaam-rúu-sùk เกี่ยวกับความรู้สึก

empathy, *n.* kwaam-hěn-jai-pûu-ɯɯn ความเห็นใจผู้อื่น; gaan-sài-jai การใส่ใจ

emperor, *n.* jàk-gà-pát จักรพรรดิ

emphasis, *n.* gaan-nén-nàk การเน้นหนัก; kwaam-sǎm-kan ความสำคัญ

emphasize, *v.* nén เน้น; hâi-kwaam-sǎm-kan ให้ความสำคัญ

emphatic, *adj.* dèn-chát เด่นชัด; sǎm-kan สำคัญ

empire, *n.* aa-naa-jàk อาณาจักร; jàk-grà-wàt จักรวรรดิ

employ, *v.* jaang จ้าง; chái-sɔ̌ɔi ใช้สอย

employee, *n.* lûuk-jâang ลูกจ้าง; pá-nák-ngaan พนักงาน

employer, *n.* naai-jâang นายจ้าง

employment, *n.* gaan-jâang การจ้าง; gaan-ngaan การงาน

empower, *v.* hâi-am-nâat ให้อำนาจ

empress, *n.* jàk-grà-pát-dì-nii จักรพรรดินี

emptiness, *n.* kwaam-wâang-bplàao ความว่างเปล่า

empty, *adj.* wâang-bplàao ว่างเปล่า; wâang ว่าง; bplàao เปล่า

enamel, *n.* krûang-klûap เครื่องเคลือบ

enchant, *v.* tam-hâi-lûm-lǒng ทำให้ลุ่มหลง

enchanted, *adj.* mii-sà-nèe มีเสน่ห์

enchantment, *n.* sà-nèe เสน่ห์; gaan-tam-hâi-lǒng-lǎi การทำให้หลงใหล

enclose, *v.* bpìt ปิด (close in); nêɛp-wái-nai แนบไว้ใน (insert into); mii-yùu-nai มีอยู่ใน (contain)

enclosure, *n.* gaan-bpìt การปิด; gaan-lɔ́ɔm การล้อม; sìng-tîi-nêɛp-maa สิ่งที่แนบมา

encore, *n.* gaan-rîak-rɔ́ɔng-hâi-sà-dɛɛng-ìik การเรียกร้องให้แสดงอีก

encounter, *v.* pà-chəən-nâa เผชิญหน้า (meet); bpà-tá ปะทะ (clash)

encourage, *v.* hâi-gam-lang-jai ให้กำลังใจ; sà-nàp-sà-nǔn สนับสนุน

encouragement, *n.* gaan-hâi-gam-lang-jai การให้กำลังใจ; gaan-sà-nàp-sà-nǔn การสนับสนุน

encroach, *v.* bùk-rúk บุกรุก

encyclopedia, *n.* sǎa-raa-nú-grom

สารานุกรม

end, *n.* bplaai ปลาย; dtɔɔn-jòp ตอนจบ; kân-sùt-táai ขั้นสุดท้าย

endanger, *v.* tam-an-dtà-raai ทำอันตราย

ending, *n.* gaan-yú-dtì การยุติ (point in time when an action is completed); dtɔɔn-jòp ตอนจบ (the ending part); gaan-sà-rùp การสรุป (the conclusion)

endless, *adj.* mâi-jòp-sîn ไม่จบสิ้น; mâi-mii-kɔ́ɔ-sà-rùp ไม่มีข้อสรุป

endorse, *v.* sà-làk-lǎng สลักหลัง (sign); à-nú-mát อนุมัติ (approve)

endorsement, *n.* gaan-long-naam การลงนาม; gaan-á-nú-mát การอนุมัติ

endurance, *n.* kwaam-òt-ton ความอดทน; kwaam-òt-glân ความอดกลั้น

endure, *v.* òt-ton อดทน; òt-glân อดกลั้น

enema, *n.* yaa-sǔan-tá-waan ยาสวนทวาร

enemy, *n.* sàt-dtruu ศัตรู

energetic, *adj.* mii-gam-lang มีกำลัง; chɔ̂ɔp-tam-ngaan ชอบทำงาน

energy, *n.* gam-lang-ngaan กำลังงาน; gam-lang กำลัง; pá-lang พลัง; pá-lang-ngaan พลังงาน

enforce, *v.* chái-bang-káp ใช้บังคับ

engage, *v.* mân หมั้น (to be married); pua-pan พัวพัน (interact with)

engaged, *adj.* mii-kûu-mân-lɛ́ɛo มีคู่หมั้นแล้ว; pua-pan-yùu-gàp พัวพันอยู่กับ

engagement, *n.* gaan-mân การหมั้น; gaan-pua-pan การพัวพัน

engine, *n.* krûang-yon เครื่องยนต์; krûang-jàk เครื่องจักร

engineer, *n.* wít-sà-wá-gɔɔn วิศวกร

engineering, *n.* wít-sà-wá-gam-má-sàat วิศวกรรมศาสตร์

England, *n.* bprà-têet-ang-grìt ประเทศอังกฤษ

English, *n.* paa-sǎa-ang-grìt ภาษาอังกฤษ (language); chaao-ang-grìt ชาวอังกฤษ (person); gìao-gàp-ang-grìt เกี่ยวกับอังกฤษ (related to England)

Englishman, -woman, *n.* chaao-ang-grìt ชาวอังกฤษ

engrave, *v.* gè แกะ (carve); tam-plàat ทำเพลท (make a plate); dtrɯng-jai ตรึงใจ (impress)

engraving, *n.* gaan-gè-sà-làk-jaa-rɯ́k การแกะสลักจารึก

enjoy, *v.* sà-nùk สนุก; plɤ̂ɤt-plɤɤn เพลิดเพลิน

enjoyment, *n.* kwaam-sà-nùk-sà-nǎan ความสนุกสนาน

enlarge, *v.* kà-yǎai ขยาย

enlighten, *v.* sɔ̌ɔn สอน (teach); hâi-kwaam-grà-jàang

ให้ความกระจ่าง (make clear); dtàt-sà-rúu ตรัสรู้ (e.g. Lord Buddha)

enlightenment, *n.* gaan-hâi-kwaam-rúu การให้ความรู้; gaan-rúu-jeeng-hên-jing การรู้แจ้งเห็นจริง; gaan-dtàt-sà-rúu การตรัสรู้ (e.g. Lord Buddha)

enormous, *adj.* má-hù-maa มหึมา; chûa-ráai ชั่วร้าย

enough, *adj.* pɔɔ พอ; piang-pɔɔ เพียงพอ

enroll, *v.* long-tá-bian ลงทะเบียน (register); hɔɔ ห่อ (wrap)

enrollment, *n.* gaan-long-tá-bian การลงทะเบียน

enter, *v.* kâo เข้า; kâo-bpai เข้าไป; kâo-maa เข้ามา

enterprise, *n.* gìt-jà-gaan กิจการ; ùt-sǎa-hà-gìt อุตสาหกิจ

enterprising, *adj.* mii-kwaam-rí-rɔ̂ɔm มีความริเริ่ม; glâa-dâai-glâa-sǐa กล้าได้กล้าเสีย

entertain, *v.* tam-hâi-sà-nùk-sà-nǎan ทำให้สนุกสนาน (provide entertainment); ráp-rɔɔng-kɛ̀ɛk รับรองแขก (e.g. guests)

entertainer, *n.* pûu-sà-dɛɛng ผู้แสดง (actor); kon-tam-hâi-plɔ̀ɔt-pləən คนทำให้เพลิดเพลิน (one that entertains)

entertainment, *n.* gaan-ban-təəng การบันเทิง (the art of entertaining); gaan-dtɔɔn-ráp-kɛ̀ɛk การต้อนรับแขก (for guests)

enthusiasm, *n.* kwaam-grà-dtuu-ruu-rón ความกระตือรือร้น

enthusiastic, *adj.* grà-dtuu-ruu-rón กระตือรือร้น

entire, *adj.* táng-mòt ทั้งหมด (all); krób-tûan ครบถ้วน (complete)

entirely, *adv.* táng-sîn ทั้งสิ้น

entirety, *n.* kwaam-sŏm-buun ความสมบูรณ์

entity, *n.* èek-gà-lák เอกลักษณ์

entrails, *n.* krûang-nai เครื่องใน; sâi-pung ไส้พุง

entrance, *n.* taang-kâo ทางเข้า; gaan-kâo การเข้า

entrée, *n.* gaan-kâo การเข้า (entering); aa-hǎan-làk อาหารหลัก (meal)

entrepreneur, *n.* pûu-bɔɔ-rí-hǎan-gìt-jà-gaan ผู้บริหารกิจการ (person who organizes a business venture); naai-tun นายทุน (capitalist); nák-tú-rá-gìt นักธุรกิจ (business person)

entrust, *v.* wái-waang-jai ไว้วางใจ

entry, *n.* gaan-kâo การเข้า (act of entering); pûu-kâo-kèng-kǎn ผู้เข้าแข่งขัน (one entered in a competition)

entomology, *n.* gaan-sùk-sǎa-gìao-gàp-má-leeng การศึกษาเกี่ยวกับแมลง

envelop, *v.* hùm หุ้ม; hɔɔ ห่อ; bpìt ปิด

English • Phonetic • Thai

envelope, *n.* sɔɔng-jòt-mǎai ซองจดหมาย (for mailing)

envious, *adj.* ìt-chǎa อิจฉา

environment, *n.* sìng-wêet-lɔ́ɔm สิ่งแวดล้อม

environmental, *adj.* dâan-sìng-wêet-lɔ́ɔm ด้านสิ่งแวดล้อม

envy, *n.* kwaam-ìt-chǎa ความอิจฉา

enzyme, *n.* en-saai เอนไซม์; dtua-màk ตัวหมัก (for fermentation)

epic, *n.* má-hǎa-gàap มหากาพย์

epidemic, *n.* rôok-rá-bàat โรคระบาด

epilepsy, *n.* rôok-lom-bâa-mǔu โรคลมบ้าหมู

episode, *n.* dtɔɔn ตอน (e.g. in a novel or play); gɔɔ-ra-nii กรณี (incident)

epitaph, *v.* kam-jaa-rúk คำจารึก

equal, *adj.* tâo-tiam เท่าเทียม

equal, *v.* tâo-gan เท่ากัน; tâo-gap เท่ากับ

equality, *n.* kwaam-tâo-tiam-gan ความเท่าเทียมกัน

equalize, *v.* tam-hâi-tâo-gan ทำให้เท่ากัน; bèng-chà-lìa แบ่งเฉลี่ย

equally, *adv.* yàang-tâo-tiam อย่างเท่าเทียม

equate, *v.* tam-hâi-tâo-gan ทำให้เท่ากัน

equation, *v.* sà-ma-gaan สมการ (in mathematics); kwaam-sǒm-dun ความสมดุล (balance)

equator, *n.* sên-sǔun-sùut เส้นศูนย์สูตร

equip, *v.* jàt-hǎa-maa-hâi จัดหามาให้; dtìt-dtâng ติดตั้ง

equipment, *n.* ùp-bpà-gɔɔn อุปกรณ์; krûang-mʉʉ เครื่องมือ

equivalent, *n.* tâo-gan เท่ากัน

era, *n.* sà-mǎi สมัย; yúk ยุค

erase, *v.* lóp-ɔ̀ɔk ลบออก

eraser, *n.* yaang-lóp ยางลบ; krûang-lóp เครื่องลบ

erect, *adj.* dtâng-dtrong ตั้งตรง

erect, *v.* chuu ชู (raise); sâang สร้าง (build); kěng-dtua แข็งตัว (get hard)

erection, *n.* gaan-dtâng-dtrong การตั้งตรง (structure); gaan-kěng-dtua การแข็งตัว (e.g. male sexual erection)

erode, *v.* gàt-grɔ̀n กัดกร่อน; sùk-grɔ̀n สึกกร่อน

erosion, *n.* gaan-gàt-grɔ̀n การกัดกร่อน

erotic, *adj.* gìao-gàp-kwaam-krâi เกี่ยวกับความใคร่

err, *v.* tam-pìt ทำผิด

errand, *n.* tú-rá ธุระ

erratic, *adj.* ao-nɛ̂ɛ-mâi-dâai เอาแน่ไม่ได้; mâi-mân-kong ไม่มั่นคง

error, *n.* kwaam-pìt-plâat ความผิดพลาด

erupt, *v.* rá-bə̀ət ระเบิด; bpà-tú ปะทุ

eruption, *n.* gaan-rá-bə̀ət

การระเบิด; gaan-bpà-tú การปะทุ

escalator, *n.* ban-dai-lûan บันไดเลื่อน

escape, *n.* gaan-lòp-nii การหลบหนี

escort, *v.* bpai-bpen-pûan ไปเป็นเพื่อน

escort, *n.* pûu-tîi-bpai-bpen-pûan ผู้ที่ไปเป็นเพื่อน (person accompanying another); pûu-kúm-gan ผู้คุ้มกัน (protective guard)

especially, *adv.* dooi-chà-pó-yàang-yîng โดยเฉพาะอย่างยิ่ง

espionage, *n.* jaa-ra-gam จารกรรม

essay, *n.* riang-kwaam เรียงความ

essence, *n.* jùt-sǎm-kan จุดสำคัญ (crucial element); sǎa-rá สาระ

essential, *adj.* jam-bpen จำเป็น; sǎm-kan สำคัญ

establish, *v.* gòo-dtâng ก่อตั้ง; sà-tǎa-bpà-naa สถาปนา

establishment, *n.* gaan-gòo-dtâng การก่อตั้ง

estate, *n.* tîi-din ที่ดิน (land); goong-moo-ra-dòk กองมรดก (property left by one at death)

esteem, *n.* kwaam-náp-tǔu ความนับถือ; kwaam-ní-yom ความนิยม

estimate, *v.* bprà-məən ประเมิน (evaluate); bprà-maan ประมาณ (calculate approximately)

estimation, *n.* gaan-bprà-məən การประเมิน; gaan-bprà-maan

การประมาณ

etch, *v.* gè แกะ; sà-làk สลัก

etching, *n.* gaan-gè การแกะ; gaan-sà-làk การสลัก

eternal, *adj.* chûa-ní-ran ชั่วนิรันดร์

eternity, *n.* ní-ran-doon นิรันดร

ether, *n.* aa-gàat-tâat อากาศธาตุ

ethic, *n.* jà-rí-yá-tam จริยธรรม

ethical, *adj.* taang-jà-rí-yá-tam ทางจริยธรรม

ethnic, *adj.* gìao-gàp-chon-glùm-nóoi เกี่ยวกับชนกลุ่มน้อย

etiquette, *n.* maa-ra-yâat มารยาท; tam-nian-bpà-dtì-bàt ธรรมเนียมปฏิบัติ

etymology, *n.* ní-rúk-dtì-sàat นิรุกติศาสตร์

eulogy, *v.* gaan-sǎn-sǒon การสรรเสริญ

eunuch, *n.* kǎn-tii ขันที

Europe, *n.* yú-ròop ยุโรป

European, *n.* chaao-yú-ròop ชาวยุโรป

European, *adj.* gìao-gàp-yú-ròop เกี่ยวกับยุโรป

evacuate, *v.* òp-pa-yóp อพยพ; yôok-yáai โยกย้าย

evaluate, *v.* bprà-məən-kâa ประเมินค่า; dtii-raa-kaa ตีราคา

evaluation, *n.* gaan-bprà-məən-kâa การประเมินค่า

evaporate, *v.* rá-hǒoi ระเหย; hǎai-bpai หายไป

English • Phonetic • Thai

evasive, *adj.* lòp-lìik หลบหลีก; bɔ̀ɔk-bpàt บอกปัด

eve, *n.* wee-laa-yen เวลาเย็น

even, *adj.* rîap เรียบ (flat); sà-mɔ̌ɔ เสมอ (equal); lêek-kûu เลขคู่ (number)

evening, *n.* dtɔɔn-yen ตอนเย็น; dtɔɔn-glaang-kuun ตอนกลางคืน

event, *n.* hèet-gaan เหตุการณ์ (situation, circumstance); gaan-kèng-kǎn การแข่งขัน (tournament)

eventful, *adj.* mii-rûang-mâak มีเรื่องมาก (full of events); sǎm-kan สำคัญ (important)

eventually, *adv.* nai-tîi-sùt ในที่สุด

ever, *adv.* dtà-lɔ̀ɔt-bpai ตลอดไป; rûai-bpai เรื่อยไป

every, *adj., adv.*, túk ทุก (each); táng-mòt ทั้งหมด (all)

everybody, everyone, *pron.* túk-kon ทุกคน

everyday, *adv.* túk-wan ทุกวัน

everything, *pron.* túk-sìng ทุกสิ่ง; túk-yàang ทุกอย่าง

everywhere, *adv.* túk-tîi ทุกที่; túk-hèng ทุกแห่ง

evict, *v.* kàp-ɔ̀ɔk ขับออก; kàp-lâi ขับไล่

eviction, *n.* gaan-kàp-lâi การขับไล่

evidence, *n.* làk-tǎan หลักฐาน

evil, *n.* sìng-chûa-ráai สิ่งชั่วร้าย

evolution, *n.* wí-wát-ta-naa-gaan วิวัฒนาการ (in nature); kwaam-

gâao-nâa ความก้าวหน้า (development)

evolve, *v.* pát-ta-naa พัฒนา; wí-wát-ta-naa วิวัฒนา

exact, *adj.* nɛ̂ɛ-nɔɔn แน่นอน (certain); tùuk-dtɔ̂ng ถูกต้อง (correct)

exaggerate, *v.* pûut-gəən-kwaam-jing พูดเกินความจริง

exaggeration, *n.* gaan-pûut-gəən-jing การพูดเกินจริง

examination, *n.* gaan-sɔ̀ɔp การสอบ (test); gaan-dtrùat-sɔ̀ɔp การตรวจสอบ (act of examining)

examine, *v.* dtrùat ตรวจ (check, review); dtài-tǎam ไต่ถาม (interrogate)

example, *n.* dtua-yàang ตัวอย่าง

excavate, *v.* jɔ̀ เจาะ; kùt ขุด

excavation, *n.* gaan-jɔ̀ การเจาะ; gaan-kùt การขุด

exceed, *v.* gəən-gwàa เกินกว่า; mâak-gwàa มากกว่า

excel, *v.* tam-dâai-dii ทำได้ดี

excellence, *n.* kwaam-yɔ̂ɔt-yîam ความยอดเยี่ยม

excellent, *adj.* yɔ̂ɔt-yîam ยอดเยี่ยม

except, *v.* yók-wén ยกเว้น; mâi-ruam ไม่รวม

exception, *n.* gaan-yók-wén การยกเว้น

excess, *n.* sùan-gəən ส่วนเกิน

excessive, *adj.* mâak-gəən-kwaam-jam-bpen มากเกินความจำเป็น

exchange, v. lɛ̂ɛk-bplìan
แลกเปลี่ยน

exchange, n. gaan-lɛ̂ɛk-bplìan
การแลกเปลี่ยน

excite, v. grà-dtûn กระตุ้น (stir to
activity); bplùk-ráo ปลุกเร้า (arouse
feeling)

excitement, n. kwaam-dtùɯn-dtên
ความตื่นเต้น

exciting, adj. nâa-dtùɯn-dtên
น่าตื่นเต้น

exclaim, v. ù-taan อุทาน; rɔ́ɔng
ร้อง

exclamation, n. gaan-rɔ́ɔng-ù-taan
การร้องอุทาน

exclamation mark, n. krûang-
mǎai-ù-taan เครื่องหมายอุทาน

exclusive, adj. chà-pɔ́-dtua
เฉพาะตัว (single or sole); dtɛ̀ɛ-
pûu-diao แต่ผู้เดียว (e.g. exclusive
rights)

excrement, n. kɔ̌ɔng-sǐa ของเสีย
(waste material); ùt-jaa-rá อุจจาระ
(feces)

excuse, v. gɛ̂ɛ-dtua แก้ตัว (explain
a fault or an offense); kɔ̌ɔ-tôot
ขอโทษ (apologize); kɔ̌ɔ-dtua ขอตัว
(take leave)

excuse, n. kam-gɛ̂ɛ-dtua คำแก้ตัว;
kam-kɔ̌ɔ-tôot คำขอโทษ

execute, v. bprà-hǎan-chii-wít
ประหารชีวิต

execution, n. gaan-bprà-hǎan-chii-
wít การประหารชีวิต

executive, n. pûu-bɔɔ-ri-hǎan
ผู้บริหาร

exemplary, adj. bpen-bɛ̀ɛp-yàang
เป็นแบบอย่าง

exempt, adj. tùuk-yók-wén
ถูกยกเว้น

exemption, n. gaan-yók-wén
การยกเว้น

exercise, v. ɔ̀ɔk-gam-lang-gaai
ออกกำลังกาย

exercise, n. gaan-ɔ̀ɔk-gam-lang-
gaai การออกกำลังกาย (the body);
gaan-fùk-fǒn การฝึกฝน (training);
bɛ̀ɛp-fùk-hàt แบบฝึกหัด (e.g. homework)

exhale, v. hǎai-jai-ɔ̀ɔk หายใจออก

exhaust, n. ai-sǐa ไอเสีย (e.g. car)

exhaust, v. chái-mòt ใช้หมด (use
up); tam-hâi-mòt-gam-lang
ทำให้หมดกำลัง (wear out)

exhausted, adj. nùai เหนื่อย

exhibit, v. sà-dɛɛng แสดง; ɔ̀ɔk-ní-
tát-sà-gaan ออกนิทรรศการ

exhibition, n. ní-tát-sà-gaan
นิทรรศการ; ngaan-má-hà-gam
งานมหกรรม

exile, v. nee-ra-têet เนรเทศ

exile, n. gaan-nee-ra-têet
การเนรเทศ

exist, v. mii-yùu มีอยู่; mii-chii-wít-
yùu มีชีวิตอยู่

existence, n. gaan-dam-rong-yùu
การดำรงอยู่

existent, adj. mii-yùu มีอยู่; nai-kà-nà-níi ในขณะนี้

exit, *n.* taang-ɔ̀ɔk ทางออก

expand, *v.* kà-yǎai ขยาย

expansion, *n.* gaan-kà-yǎai
การขยาย

expatriate, *n.* pûu-pák-yùu-dtàang-
bprà-tɛ̂et ผู้พักอยู่ต่างประเทศ

expect, *v.* kâat-mǎai คาดหมาย;
kâat-wǎng คาดหวัง

expectation, *n.* kwaam-kâat-mǎai
ความคาดหมาย; sìng-tîi-kâat-wǎng
สิ่งที่คาดหวัง

expel, *v.* lâi-ɔ̀ɔk ไล่ออก

expense, *n.* kâa-chái-jàai ค่าใช้จ่าย

expensive, *adj.* raa-kaa-pɛɛng
ราคาแพง

experience, *v.* bprà-sòp ประสบ

experience, *n.* bprà-sòp-gaan
ประสบการณ์

experienced, *adj.* mii-bprà-sòp-
gaan มีประสบการณ์

experiment, *n.* gaan-tót-lɔɔng
การทดลอง

experimental, *adj.* gìao-gàp-gaan-
tót-lɔɔng เกี่ยวกับการทดลอง

expert, *n.* pûu-chîao-chaan
ผู้เชี่ยวชาญ

expertise, *n.* kwaam-cham-naan
ความชำนาญ

expiration, *n.* gaan-hǎai-jai
การหายใจ (breathing); gaan-mòt-
aa-yú การหมดอายุ (expiry)

expire, *v.* mòt-aa-yú หมดอายุ

explain, *v.* à-tí-baai อธิบาย

explanation, *n.* gaan-à-tí-baai
การอธิบาย; kam-à-tí-baai คำอธิบาย

explanatory, *adj.* bpen-gaan-à-tí-
baai เป็นการอธิบาย

explode, *v.* rá-bɤ̀ɤt ระเบิด

exploit, *n.* chái-bprà-yòot-hâi-
mâak-tîi-sùt ใช้ประโยชน์ให้มากที่สุด
(employ to the greatest possible
advantage); ao-bpriap เอาเปรียบ
(make use of selfishly)

exploitation, *n.* gaan-hǎa-bprà-yòot
การหาประโยชน์; gaan-ao-bpriap-
pûu-ùɤn การเอาเปรียบผู้อื่น

explore, *v.* sǎm-rùat สำรวจ

explorer, *n.* nák-sǎm-rùat นักสำรวจ

explosion, *n.* gaan-rá-bɤ̀ɤt
การระเบิด

explosive, *adj.* rá-bɤ̀ɤt-dâai
ระเบิดได้

export, *v.* sòng-ɔ̀ɔk ส่งออก

export, *n.* gaan-sòng-ɔ̀ɔk การส่งออก

exporter, *n.* pûu-sòng-ɔ̀ɔk ผู้ส่งออก

expose, *v.* sǎm-pàt-gàp สัมผัสกับ
(have contact with); tam-hâi-rúu-jàk
ทำให้รู้จัก (make known)

exposition, *n.* ní-tát-sà-gaan
นิทรรศการ (public show)

exposure, *n.* gaan-bpɤ̀ɤt-pɤ̌ɤi
การเปิดเผย (appearance in public;
revelation); gaan-dâai-sǎm-pàt
การได้สัมผัส (contact)

express, *adj.* dùan ด่วน (fast, e.g.

train, letter)

express, v. sà-dɛɛng-ɔ̀ɔk แสดงออก (oneself); sà-dɛɛng-kwaam-kìt-hěn แสดงความคิดเห็น (opinion)

expression, n. gaan-sà-dɛɛng-kwaam-kìt-hěn การแสดงความคิดเห็น (showing one's opinion); gaan-sà-dɛɛng-kwaam-rúu-sùk การแสดงความรู้สึก (showing feeling); sǎm-nuan สำนวน (a cliché)

express mail, n. jòt-mǎai-dùan จดหมายด่วน

expulsion, n. gaan-kàp-ɔ̀ɔk การขับออก

extend, v. kà-yǎai ขยาย

extension, n. gaan-kà-yǎai การขยาย (act of extending); sùan-tîi-kà-yǎai-ɔ̀ɔk ส่วนที่ขยายออก (extended part); sǎai-pûang สายพ่วง (extended line); dtɔ̀ɔ ต่อ (telephone line)

extensive, adj. gwâang กว้าง (broad); mâak มาก (large in extent)

exterior, n. paai-nɔ̂ɔk ภายนอก

external, adj. dâan-nɔ̂ɔk ด้านนอก (outside); paai-nɔ̂ɔk ภายนอก (exterior)

extinct, adj. sǔun-pan สูญพันธุ์ (no longer existing or living); dàp ดับ (no longer burning or active)

extinction, n. gaan-sǔun-pan การสูญพันธุ์

extinguish, v. dàp ดับ

extinguisher, n. krûang-dàp-pləəng เครื่องดับเพลิง

extort, v. kùu-kěn ขู่เข็ญ; bang-káp บังคับ

extortion, n. gaan-kùu-gan-chôok การขู่กรรโชก; gaan-bang-káp การบังคับ

extra, n. sìng-tîi-pɔ̂əm-dtəəm สิ่งที่เพิ่มเติม

extract, v. sà-gàt สกัด

extract, n. sìng-tîi-sà-gàt-ɔ̀ɔk สิ่งที่สกัดออก

extradite, v. sòng-pûu-ráai-kâam-dɛɛn ส่งผู้ร้ายข้ามแดน

extreme, adj. sùt-kìit สุดขีด (very intense); run-rɛɛng-gəən-bpai รุนแรงเกินไป (far beyond the norm)

extremely, adv. yîng ยิ่ง; sùt-kìit สุดขีด; yàang-mâak อย่างมาก

extremist, n. pûank-hǔa-rún-rɛɛng พวกหัวรุนแรง

extrovert, n. kon-chɔ̂ɔp-sǎng-kom คนชอบสังคม (outgoing person; one that likes to socialize)

eye, n. dtaa ตา

eyeball, n. lûuk-dtaa ลูกตา

eyebrow, n. kíu คิ้ว

eyeglasses, n. wɛ̂n-dtaa แว่นตา

eyelash, n. kǒn-dtaa ขนตา

eyelid, n. bplùak-dtaa เปลือกตา

eye shadow, n. aai-chaa-dôo อายชาโดว์

eyesight, n. sǎai-dtaa สายตา

eyewitness, n. pá-yaan พยาน

F

fable, *n.* ní-taan นิทาน

fabric, *n.* pâa ผ้า (cloth); ong-bprà-gɔ̀ɔp องค์ประกอบ (structure)

fabricate, *v.* sâang สร้าง (build); tɔɔ ทอ (weave)

fabrication, *n.* gaan-sâang-kûn การสร้างขึ้น

face, *n.* bai-nâa ใบหน้า; nâa หน้า

facelift, *n.* gaan-dung-nâa การดึงหน้า

facet, *n.* dâan ด้าน; lìam เหลี่ยม

fact, *n.* kɔ̂ɔ-tét-jing ข้อเท็จจริง

factor, *n.* bpàt-jai ปัจจัย; dtua-bprà-gɔ̀ɔp ตัวประกอบ

factory, *n.* roong-ngaan โรงงาน

factual, *adj.* gìao-gàp-kɔ̂ɔ-tét-jing เกี่ยวกับข้อเท็จจริง

faculty, *n.* ká-ná คณะ (e.g. in a university); kwaam-sǎa-mâat ความสามารถ (ability)

fad, *n.* kwaam-ní-yom-chûa-kraao ความนิยมชั่วคราว

fade, *v.* luan เลือน (lose brightness); jaang-long จางลง (dim); kɔ̂i-kɔ̂i-hǎai-bpai ค่อยๆ หายไป (disappear gradually)

fail, *v.* lóm-lěeo ล้มเหลว

fail, *n.* kwaam-lóm-lěeo ความล้มเหลว

failure, *n.* kwaam-lóm-lěeo ความล้มเหลว

faint, *v.* bpen-lom เป็นลม

faint, *adj.* sà-lǔa สลัว; luan-laang เลือนลาง

fair, *n.* ngaan-sà-dɛɛng-sǐn-káa งานแสดงสินค้า (exhibition); dtà-làat-nát ตลาดนัด (flea market)

fair, *adj.* nâa-duu น่าดู (pleasing appearance); yú-dtì-tam ยุติธรรม (just)

fairly, *adv.* yàang-dtrong-bpai-dtrong-maa อย่างตรงไปตรงมา

fairy, *n.* naang-fáa นางฟ้า

faith, *n.* kwaam-chûa ความเชื่อ; kwaam-sàt-taa ความศรัทธา

faithful, *adj.* sʉ̂ʉ-sàt ซื่อสัตย์

fake, *adj.* bplɔɔm ปลอม

fake, *n.* kɔ̌ɔng-bplɔɔm ของปลอม

falcon, *n.* yìao เหยี่ยว

fall, *v.* dtòk ตก (e.g. rain); lóm ล้ม (drop oneself; stumble)

fall, *n.* gaan-dtòk การตก (act of falling); rʉ́-duu-bai-máai-rûang ฤดูใบไม้ร่วง (autumn)

false, *adj.* pìt ผิด

falsehood, *n.* gaan-lɔ̀ɔk-luang การหลอกลวง

falsify, *v.* bplɔɔm-bplɛɛng ปลอมแปลง

fame, *n.* chʉ̂ʉ-sìang ชื่อเสียง

familiar, *adj.* kún คุ้น; chin ชิน; kún-kəəi คุ้นเคย

family, *n.* krɔ̂ɔp-krua ครอบครัว

family name, *n.* naam-sà-gun

นามสกุล

famine, *n.* kâao-yâak-màak-pεεng
ข้าวยากหมากแพง; kwaam-òt-yàak
ความอดอยาก

famous, *adj.* mii-chûu-sĭang
มีชื่อเสียง

fan, *n.* pát พัด (a device); fεεn
แฟน (e.g. in sports)

fanatic, *n.* kon-tûi-klâng-klái
คนที่คลั่งไคล้

fancy, *n.* kwaam-núk-fǎn
ความนึกฝัน

fang, *n.* kîao เขี้ยว

fantasize, *v.* jin-dtà-naa-gaan
จินตนาการ

fantastic, *adj.* nâa-àt-sà-jan
น่าอัศจรรย์; dii-lə̂ət ดีเลิศ

fantasy, *n.* gaan-jin-dtà-naa-gaan
การจินตนาการ; gaan-núk-fǎn
การนึกฝัน

far, *adj.* glai ไกล

fare, *n.* kâa-dooi-sǎan ค่าโดยสาร

Far East, *n.* dtà-wan-ɔ̀ɔk-glai
ตะวันออกไกล

farewell, *n.* gaan-am-laa การอำลา

farfetched, *adj.* mâi-nâa-bpen-bpai-
daai ไม่น่าเป็นไปได้

farm, *n.* faam ฟาร์ม; râi-naa ไร่นา

farmer, *n.* chaao-naa ชาวนา;
chaao-râi ชาวไร่; gà-sèet-dtà-gɔɔn
เกษตรกร

farmhouse, *n.* bâan-râi บ้านไร่

farming, *n.* gaan-tam-râi การทำไร่;

gaan-tam-faam การทำฟาร์ม

Farsi, *n.* paa-sǎa-kɔ̌ɔng-chaao-ì-
râan ภาษาของชาวอิหร่าน

fascinate, *v.* tam-hâi-lŏng-sà-nèe
ทำให้หลงสเน่ห์; dtrung-jai ตรึงใจ;
tam-hâi-dtà-lung ทำให้ตะลึง

fascinating, *adj.* mii-sà-nèe
มีสเน่ห์; nâa-dtà-lung น่าตะลึง

fascination, *n.* sà-nèe สเน่ห์; am-
nâat-dung-dùut-jai อำนาจดึงดูดใจ

fascism, *n.* lát-tì-pà-dèt-gaan
ลัทธิเผด็จการ

fascist, *n.* pûu-tǔu-lát-tì-pà-dèt-
gaan ผู้ถือลัทธิเผด็จการ

fashion, *n.* fεε-chân แฟชั่น;
kwaam-ní-yom ความนิยม

fashionable, *adj.* dtaam-sà-mǎi-ní-
yom ตามสมัยนิยม; tan-sà-mǎi
ทันสมัย

fast, *v.* òt-aa-hǎan อดอาหาร

fast, *adj.* reo เร็ว

fasten, *v.* rát รัด; dtrung ตรึง

fastener, *n.* tîi-glàt ที่กลัด; tîi-yút
ที่ยึด

fast food, *v.* aa-hǎan-fáat-fúut
อาหารฟาสต์ฟู้ด

fat, *n.* kǎi-man ไขมัน

fat, *adj.* ûan อ้วน

fatal, *adj.* bpen-an-dtà-raai
เป็นอันตราย; tǔng-chii-wít ถึงชีวิต

fate, *n.* chôok-cha-dtaa โชคชะตา;
prom-lí-kìt พรหมลิขิต

father, *n.* pɔ̂ɔ พ่อ; bì-daa บิดา

fatten, v. tam-hâi-ûan ทำให้อ้วน

faucet, n. gɔ́k-náam ก๊อกน้ำ

fault, n. kwaam-pìt-plâat ความผิดพลาด (mistake); fàai-pìt ฝ่ายผิด (the party to blame); kɔ̂ɔ-bòk-prɔ̂ng ข้อบกพร่อง (character weakness; a defect); chán-hǐn-tîi-dtɛ̀ɛk-hàk ชั้นหินที่แตกหัก (geological)

faulty, adj. mii-kɔ̂ɔ-pìt-plâat มีข้อผิดพลาด

favor, n. kwaam-gà-rú-naa ความกรุณา

favorable, adj. bpen-tîi-bpròot-bpraan เป็นที่โปรดปราน; bpen-tîi-chɔ̂ɔp เป็นที่ชอบ

favorite, adj. tîi-chɔ̂ɔp ที่ชอบ; chɔ̂ɔp-tîi-sùt ชอบที่สุด

favorite, n. kɔ̌ɔng-tîi-chɔ̂ɔp-tîi-sùt ของที่ชอบที่สุด

favoritism, n. kwaam-lam-iang ความลำเอียง

fawn, n. lûuk-gwaang ลูกกวาง (baby deer); sǐi-lǔang-om-náam-dtaan สีเหลืองอมน้ำตาล (color)

fax, n. fɛ̀k แฟกซ์; too-ra-sǎan โทรสาร

fear, n. kwaam-glua ความกลัว

fearless, adj. mâi-glua ไม่กลัว

feast, n. ngaan-líang งานเลี้ยง

feather, n. kǒn-nók ขนนก (bird); kǒn-gài ขนไก่ (chicken)

feature, n. nâa-dtaa หน้าตา (look);

lák-sà-nà-chà-pɔ́ ลักษณะเฉพาะ (special feature)

February, n. duan-gum-paa-pan เดือนกุมภาพันธ์

feces, n. ùt-jaa-rá อุจจาระ; kîi ขี้

federal, adj. sà-hà-pan สหพันธ์ (relating to, or being a form of government in which there is a union of states); glaang กลาง (e.g. federal government)

federation, n. sà-hà-pan สหพันธ์

fee, n. kâa-tam-niam ค่าธรรมเนียม; kâa-bɔɔ-ri-gaan ค่าบริการ

feed, v. bpɔ̂ɔn ป้อน; hâi-aa-hǎan ให้อาหาร

feedback, n. gaan-dtɔ̂ɔp-glàp การตอบกลับ

feel, v. rúu-sùk รู้สึก (perceive); sǎm-pàt สัมผัส (touch)

feeling, n. kwaam-rúu-sùk ความรู้สึก (sensation); aa-rom อารมณ์ (mood)

felony, n. kwaam-pìt-aa-yaa-kân-run-rɛɛng ความผิดอาญาขั้นรุนแรง

felt, n. sàk-gà-làat สักหลาด (cloth)

female, n. pûu-yǐng ผู้หญิง (woman); pêet-yǐng เพศหญิง (female gender); dtua-mia ตัวเมีย (used with animals)

feminine, adj. mii-kwaam-bpen-yǐng มีความเป็นหญิง

feminism, n. lát-tí-hâi-kwaam-sà-mǒɔ-pâak-gèɛ-pûu-yǐng ลัทธิให้ความ

เสมอภาคแก่ผู้หญิง; lát-ti-fee-mí-nít ลัทธิเฟมินิสต์

feminist, *n.* pûu-rîak-rɔ́ɔng-sìt-tí-sà-dtrii ผู้เรียกร้องสิทธิสตรี

fence, *n.* rúa รั้ว; krûang-gân เครื่องกั้น (any barriers)

fencing, *n.* gaan-fan-dàap การฟันดาบ (sports)

fender, *n.* sìng-bpɔ̂ɔng-gan สิ่งป้องกัน

ferment, *v.* màk หมัก

ferment, *n.* chúa-màk เชื้อหมัก (e.g. yeast)

fermentation, *n.* gaan-màk การหมัก

fern, *n.* dtôn-fəən ต้นเฟิร์น

ferocious, *adj.* dù-ráai ดุร้าย; run-rɛɛng รุนแรง

ferry, ferryboat, *n.* rua-kâam-fâak เรือข้ามฟาก

fertile, *adj.* ù-dom-sɔ̌m-buun อุดมสมบูรณ์ (fruitful); hâi-lûuk-dâai ให้ลูกได้ (capable of reproduction)

fertility, *n.* kwaam-ù-dom-sɔ̌m-buun ความอุดมสมบูรณ์

fertilizer, *n.* bpǔi ปุ๋ย

festival, *n.* ngaan-chà-lɔ̌ɔm-chà-lɔ̌ɔng งานเฉลิมฉลอง

festive, *adj.* rûun-rəəng รื่นเริง; chà-lɔ̌ɔm-chà-lɔ̌ɔng เฉลิมฉลอง

fetch, *v.* bpai-yìp-maa ไปหยิบมา; ao-maa เอามา

fetus, *n.* taa-rók-nai-kan ทารกในครรภ์

feudal, *adj.* gìao-gàp-rá-bòp-sàk-dì-naa เกี่ยวกับระบบศักดินา

fever, *n.* kâi ไข้

feverish, *adj.* mii-kâi มีไข้

few, *n.* nɔ́ɔi น้อย

fiancé, -ée, *n.* kûu-mân คู่หมั้น

fiber, *n.* sên-yai เส้นใย

fickle, *adj.* lɔ̂-lɛ̀ เหลาะแหละ

fiction, *n.* ní-taan นิทาน; ní-yaai นิยาย

fictitious, *adj.* sâang-kûn สร้างขึ้น; sǒm-mút สมมุติ

fiddle, *n.* sɔɔ ซอ

fiddle, *v.* sàai-muu-bpai-maa ส่ายมือไปมา

fidelity, *n.* kwaam-sûu-sàt ความซื่อสัตย์

fidget, *v.* ngùt-ngìt หงุดหงิด; aa-rom-sǐa อารมณ์เสีย

field, *n.* sà-nǎam สนาม; tûng ทุ่ง

fierce, *adj.* dù-ráai ดุร้าย

fifteen, *nm.* sìp-hâa สิบห้า

fifteenth, *adj.* tîi-sìp-hâa ที่สิบห้า

fifth, *adj.* tîi-hâa ที่ห้า

fifty, *nm.* hâa-sìp ห้าสิบ

fig, *n.* lûuk-fík ลูกฟิก

fight, *v.* dtɔ̀ɔ-sûu ต่อสู้; róp รบ

fight, *n.* gaan-dtɔ̀ɔ-sûu การต่อสู้; gaan-róp การรบ

fighter, *n.* nák-sûu นักสู้; nák-róp นักรบ

figure, *n.* rûup-râang รูปร่าง; dtua-

English · Phonetic · Thai

lêek ตัวเลข

filament, n. sên-yai เส้นใย

file, v. jàt-kâo-fém จัดเข้าแฟ้ม (put in a folder); dtà-bai ตะไบ (smooth or remove with a file)

file, n. èek-gà-sǎan เอกสาร (document); gaan-jàt-kâo-fém การจัดเข้าแฟ้ม (act of filing); fém แฟ้ม (folder); dtà-bai-lép ตะไบเล็บ (nail file)

fill, v. dtəəm เติม (add); ban-jù บรรจุ (contain); grɔ̀ɔk กรอก (e.g. with water)

fillet, n. sǎai-kâat-pǒm สายคาดผม (hair band); chín-núa ชิ้นเนื้อ (piece of meat)

filling, n. sâi-kà-nǒm ไส้ขนม (of sweets or desserts); sìng-tîi-sài-kâang-nai สิ่งที่ใส่ข้างใน (what is put inside); sìng-tîi-ùt-fan สิ่งที่อุดฟัน (for tooth)

film, n. pâap-pa-yon ภาพยนตร์ (movie); nǎng หนัง (movie); fiim ฟิล์ม (for camera)

filter, n. tîi-grɔɔng ที่กรอง; krûang-grɔɔng เครื่องกรอง

fin, n. krîip-bplaa ครีบปลา; krîip ครีบ

final, n. rɔ̂ɔp-sùt-táai รอบสุดท้าย; dtɔɔn-jòp ตอนจบ

finalist, n. pûu-kâo-rɔ̂ɔp-sùt-táai ผู้เข้ารอบสุดท้าย

finally, adv. nai-tîi-sùt ในที่สุด;

dooi-sà-rùp โดยสรุป

finance, n. gaan-ngən การเงิน

financial, adj. taang-gaan-ngən ทางการเงิน

financier, n. pûu-chîao-chaan-taang-gaan-ngən ผู้เชี่ยวชาญทางการเงิน

financing, n. gaan-jàt-ngən-tun การจัดเงินทุน

find, v. hǎa หา; póp พบ

fine, adj. dii ดี (good, superior quality, etc.); sà-baai-dii สบายดี (feeling well); lá-ìat-ɔ̀ɔn ละเอียดอ่อน (delicate); baang บาง (thin, e.g. hair)

fine, v. bpràp ปรับ

fine, n. kâa-bpràp ค่าปรับ

finger, n. níu-muu นิ้วมือ

fingernail, n. lép-muu เล็บมือ

fingerprint, n. laai-níu-muu ลายนิ้วมือ

finish, v. sèt เสร็จ; jòp จบ

finish, n. sùt-táai สุดท้าย (final); gaan-tam-hâi-sèt การทำให้เสร็จ (getting something done); kwaam-glîang-glao ความเกลี้ยงเกลา (e.g. matt, glossy); yaa-kàt-ngao ยาขัดเงา (polishing agent)

fire, v. ying ยิง (e.g. a gun)

fire, n. fai ไฟ; gaan-ying การยิง (shooting)

firearm, n. aa-wút-bpuun อาวุธปืน

firecracker, n. bpà-tát ประทัด

firefighter, n. pá-nák-ngaan-dàpplɔɔng พนักงานดับเพลิง

firefly, *n.* hìng-hɔ̂i หิ่งห้อย

fireplace, *n.* dtao-pìng เตาผิง

fireproof, *adj.* ton-fai ทนไฟ

firewood, *n.* fuun ฟืน

fireworks, *n.* dɔ̀ɔk-máai-fai
ดอกไม้ไฟ

firm, *n.* bɔɔ-ri-sàt บริษัท
(company); kwaam-mân-kong
ความมั่นคง (stability)

firm, *adj.* mân-kong มั่นคง (stable);
nɛ̂n แน่น (tight)

first, *adj.* tîi-nùng ที่หนึ่ง; kráng-
rɛ̂ɛk ครั้งแรก

first aid, *n.* gaan-bpà-tom-pá-yaa-
baan การปฐมพยาบาล

first-class, *adj.* chán-nùng ชั้นหนึ่ง

fish, *n.* bplaa ปลา

fish ball, *n.* lûuk-chín-bplaa
ลูกชิ้นปลา

fisherman, *n.* chaao-bprà-mong
ชาวประมง

fishhook, *n.* bèt-dtòk-bplaa
เบ็ดตกปลา

fishing, *n.* gaan-dtòk-bplaa
การตกปลา

fish market, *n.* dtà-làat-kăai-bplaa
ตลาดขายปลา

fishmonger, *n.* kon-kăai-bplaa
คนขายปลา

fishy, *adj.* kaao-bplaa คาวปลา;
nâa-sŏng-săi น่าสงสัย (suspicious)

fist, *n.* màt หมัด; gam-bpân กำปั้น

fit, *v.* sài-pɔɔ-dii ใส่พอดี

fit, *adj.* mɔ̀-sŏm เหมาะสม (proper);
pɔɔ-dii พอดี (suited); kɛ̌ng-rɛɛng
แข็งแรง (strong)

fitness, *n.* kwaam-pɔɔ-dii ความพอดี

five, *nm.* hâa ห้า

five hundred, *nm.* hâa-rɔ́ɔi ห้าร้อย

fix, *v.* sôm ซ่อม (repair); gam-nòt
กำหนด (establish)

fixed, *adj.* gam-nòt-wái กำหนดไว้
(established); nɛ̂ɛ-nɔɔn แน่นอน
(certain); sôm-lɛ́ɛo ซ่อมแล้ว
(repaired)

fixture, *n.* kwaam-nɛ̂n-nǎa ความ
แน่นหนา (firmness)

flag, *n.* tong ธง

flake, *n.* pèn-baang-baang
แผ่นบางๆ (thin slices); chín-lék-
lék ชิ้นเล็กๆ (small pieces); kon-tîi-
chûa-tǔu-mâi-dâai คนที่เชื่อถือไม่ได้
(unreliable person)

flame, *n.* bpleeo-fai เปลวไฟ;
kwaam-chôot-chûang ความโชติช่วง

flamingo, *n.* nók-grà-rian
นกกระเรียน

flannel, *n.* pâa-sàk-gà-làat-ɔɔn
ผ้าสักหลาดอ่อน

flap, *v.* grà-puu กระพือ (e.g.
wings); bòok-sà-bàt โบกสะบัด (e.g.
a flag)

flare, *n.* gaan-lúk-mâi การลุกไหม้
(flaming up); sɛ̌ɛng-sà-wàang-
wɛɛo-wáp แสงสว่างแวววับ (blaze

of light); fai-dtʉan-pai ไฟเตือนภัย (emergency light)

flash, *n.* sɛ̌ɛng-wâap แสงวาบ (brief, intense display of light); flɛ̀t แฟลช (from camera)

flash bulb, *n.* lɔ̀ɔt-fai-tîi-chái-tàai-rûup หลอดไฟที่ใช้ถ่ายจุป

flashlight, *n.* fai-flɛ̀t ไฟแฟลช

flat, *n.* flɛ̀t แฟลต

flatten, *v.* tam-hâi-bɛɛn ทำให้แบน

flatter, *v.* bprà-jòp ประจบ; yók-yɔɔ ยกยอ

flattery, *n.* gaan-yók-yɔɔ การยกยอ; gaan-sɔ̌ɔ-plɔɔ การสอพลอ

flavor, *n.* rót รส

flaw, *n.* kɔ̂ɔ-sǐa ข้อเสีย; dtam-nì ตำหนิ

flawless, *adj.* mâi-mii-tîi-dtì ไม่มีที่ติ

flea, *n.* màt หมัด

flea market, *n.* dtà-làat-kǎai-kɔ̌ɔng-gào ตลาดขายของเก่า

fledgling, *adj.* hàt-bin หัดบิน (e.g. bird); kon-mâi-mii-bprà-sòp-gaan คนไม่มีประสบการณ์ (inexperienced)

flee, *v.* nǐi หนี

fleet, *n.* gɔɔng-rʉa-róp กองเรือรบ

flesh, *n.* nʉ́a เนื้อ; lûuk-nai-sâi ลูกในไส้

flexible, *adj.* yʉ̂ʉt-yùn ยึดหยุ่น; yʉ̂ʉt-dâai ยึดได้

flier, *n.* nák-bin นักบิน (pilot); bai-bpliu ใบปลิว (pamphlet)

flight, *n.* gaan-bin การบิน (act of

flying); tîao-bin เที่ยวบิน (of an airline); gaan-nǐi การหนี (escape)

flimsy, *adj.* bɔ̀ɔp-baang บอบบาง (thin); ɔ̀ɔn-ɛɛ อ่อนแอ (weak)

flinch, *v.* tɔ̌ɔi ถอย; pà-ngà ผงะ

flint, *n.* hìn-fai หินไฟ

flirt, *v.* pûut-jaa-gîao พูดจาเกี้ยว; hâi-tâa ให้ท่า; yûa-yuan ยั่วยวน

float, *v.* lɔɔi ลอย; lɔɔi-náam ลอยน้ำ

float, *n.* gaan-lɔɔi การลอย; gaan-lɔɔi-náam การลอยน้ำ

flock, *n.* fǔung ฝูง

flock, *v.* jàp-gan-bpen-fǔung จับกันเป็นฝูง

flood, *n.* náam-tûam น้ำท่วม

floor, *n.* pʉ́ʉn พื้น; gôn (tá-lee) ก้น (ทะเล) (e.g. the bottom of the sea)

floppy disk, *n.* pɛ̀n-dít แผ่นดิสก์

floral, *adj.* bprà-gɔ̀ɔp-dûai-dɔ̀ɔk-máai ประกอบด้วยดอกไม้

florist, *n.* kon-kǎai-dɔ̀ɔk-máai คนขายดอกไม้

flounder, *v.* dtà-gìak-dtà-gaai ตะเกียกตะกาย

flounder, *n.* bplaa-flao-dɤ̂ɤ ปลาเฟลาเดอร์ (fish)

flour, *n.* bpɛ̂ɛng แป้ง

flow, *v.* lǎi ไหล

flow, *n.* gaan-lǎi การไหล (act of flowing); grà-sɛ̌ɛ-náam กระแสน้ำ (water current)

flower, *n.* dɔ̀ɔk-máai ดอกไม้

flowerbed, *n.* bpleeng-dɔɔk-máai แปลงดอกไม้

flowerpot, *n.* grà-tăang-dɔɔk-máai กระถางดอกไม้

flu, *n.* kâi-wàt-yài ไข้หวัดใหญ่

fluent, *adj.* chái-dâai-klɔ̂ɔng ใช้ได้คล่อง; klɔ̂ɔng คล่อง

fluid, *n.* kɔ̌ɔng-lɛ̌eo ของเหลว; kɔ̌ɔng-lǎi ของไหล

fluke, *n.* chôok-dii โชคดี (good luck); flúk ฟลุก; hǎang-bplaa-waan หางปลาวาฬ (whale tail)

flunk, *v.* lóm-lɛ̌eo ล้มเหลว (fail); sɔ̀ɔp-dtòk สอบตก (a test)

fluorescent, *adj.* ruang-sɛ̌eng เรืองแสง

flush, *v.* lǎi ไหล (flow); pûng พุ่ง (flow suddenly); nâa-dɛɛng หน้าแดง (blush); bplɔ̀i-náam-láang-sûam ปล่อยน้ำล้างส้วม (flush a toilet)

flush, *n.* gaan-lǎi การไหล; gaan-pûng การพุ่ง

flute, *n.* klùi ขลุ่ย

fly, *v.* bin บิน

fly, *n.* má-lɛɛng-wan แมลงวัน

foam, *n.* fɔɔng ฟอง

focus, *v.* foo-gát โฟกัส; jùt-sŏn-jai จุดสนใจ

foe, *n.* sàt-dtruu ศัตรู

fog, *n.* mɔ̀ɔk หมอก

foggy, *adj.* mii-mɔ̀ɔk มีหมอก (having fog); mâi-chát ไม่ชัด (not clear)

foil, *n.* grà-dàat-à-luu-mí-niam กระดาษอลูมิเนียม

fold, *v.* páp พับ; hɔ̀ɔ ห่อ

folder, *n.* fɛ́m-gèp-èek-gà-sǎan แฟ้มเก็บเอกสาร

folk, *n.* chaao-bâan ชาวบ้าน; kon-tûa-bpai คนทั่วไป

folklore, *n.* ká-dtì-chaao-bâan คติชาวบ้าน

follow, *v.* dtaam ตาม; dìt-dtaam ติดตาม; tam-dtaam ทำตาม

follower, *n.* pûu-dtaam ผู้ตาม (one that follows); sǎa-wók สาวก (disciple)

fond, *adj.* chɔ̂ɔp ชอบ

food, *n.* aa-hǎan อาหาร

fool, *n.* kon-ngôo คนโง่ (dumb person); dtua-dtà-lòk ตัวตลก (joker)

foolish, *adj.* ngôo โง่

foot, *n.* táao เท้า; dtiin ตีน (colloquial); fút ฟุต (measurement)

football, *n.* fút-bɔn ฟุตบอล

foothold, *n.* dtam-nɛ̀ng-tîi-mân-kong ตำแหน่งที่มั่นคง

footnote, *n.* fút-nóot ฟุตโน้ต; mǎai-hèet-kâang-táai หมายเหตุข้างท้าย

footprint, *n.* rɔɔi-táao รอยเท้า

footstep, *n.* gaan-gâao-táao การก้าวเท้า (a step with the foot)

for, *prep.* pʉ̂a เพื่อ; sǎm-ràp สำหรับ

forbid, *v.* hâam ห้าม

force, *v.* bang-káp บังคับ

force, *n.* gam-lang กำลัง (power,

energy); gaan-bang-káp การบังคับ
(act of forcing)

forceful, *adj.* mii-am-nâat มีอำนาจ

forcible, *adj.* chái-gam-lang ใช้กำลัง

forecast, *v.* pá-yaa-gɔɔn
พยากรณ์

forecast, *n.* gaan-pá-yaa-gɔɔn
การพยากรณ์

forehead, *n.* nâa-pàak หน้าผาก

foreign, *adj.* dtàang-bprà-têet
ต่างประเทศ

foreigner, *n.* kon-dtàang-châat
คนต่างชาติ

foreman, *n.* hǔa-nâa-kon-ngaan
หัวหน้าคนงาน

forest, *n.* bpàa ป่า

forever, *adv.* dtà-lɔ̀ɔt-bpai ตลอดไป

foreword, *n.* kam-nam คำนำ

forget, *v.* luum ลืม

forgetful, *adj.* kîi-luum ขี้ลืม

fork, *n.* sɔ̂m ส้อม (utensil); taang-
yɛ̂ɛk ทางแยก (intersected road)

form, *v.* mii-rûup-bɛ̀ɛp มีรูปแบบ
(become formed); gɔ̀ɔ-dtâng ก่อตั้ง
(establish)

form, *n.* rûup-bɛ̀ɛp รูปแบบ; bɛ̀ɛp-
fɔɔm แบบฟอร์ม; bɛ̀ɛp-pɛ̌ɛn
แบบแผน

formal, *adj.* dtaam-tam-niam
ตามธรรมเนียม (following or being
in accord with conventions); bpen-
pí-tii-gaan เป็นพิธีการ (executed,
carried out, or done in proper or regu-

lar form)

formality, *n.* rá-bìap ระเบียบ
(rules, regulations); pí-tii-gaan
พิธีการ (an established form or rule)

format, *n.* rûup-bɛ̀ɛp รูปแบบ

formation, *n.* gaan-gɔ̀ɔ-rûup
การก่อรูป; gaan-gɔ̀ɔ-sâang
การสร้าง

former, *adj.* gɔ̀ɔn ก่อน (previous);
à-dìit อดีต (taking place in the past)

formerly, *adv.* mûa-gɔ̀ɔn เมื่อก่อน

formula, *n.* sùut สูตร

fort, *n.* bpɔ̂m ป้อม

fortieth, *adj.* tîi-sìi-sìp ที่สี่สิบ

fortify, *v.* sɔ̌ɔm-gam-lang เสริมกำลัง

fortunate, *adj.* chôok-dii โชคดี

fortune, *n.* sáp-sǒm-bàt ทรัพย์สมบัติ
(financial wealth; treasure); chôok-
lâap โชคลาภ (luck); chá-dtaa
ชะตา (fate, destiny)

fortuneteller, *n.* mɔ̌ɔ-duu หมอดู

forty, *nm.* sìi-sìp สี่สิบ

forward, *adj.* bpai-kâang-nâa
ไปข้างหน้า; gâao-nâa ก้าวหน้า

fossil, *n.* fɔ́ɔt-sǐn ฟอสซิล

foster, *adj.* líang-duu เลี้ยงดู

foster parents, *n.* pɔ̂ɔ-mɛ̂ɛ-ùp-
bpà-tǎm พ่อแม่อุปถัมภ์

foul, *n.* gaan-pìt-gà-dtì-gaa
การผิดกติกา

foul, *adj.* chûa-ráai ชั่วร้าย
(wicked); měn-nâo เหม็นเน่า
(smelly)

found, *v.* gɔ̀ɔ-dtâng ก่อตั้ง (establish)

found, *v.* dâai-póp ได้พบ; jəə เจอ (past tense of "to find")

foundation, *n.* râak-tǎan รากฐาน (base); muun-lá-ní-tì มูลนิธิ (an institute); kriim-rɔɔng-púʉn ครีมรองพื้น (cosmetic base)

founder, *n.* pûu-gɔ̀ɔ-dtâng ผู้ก่อตั้ง

fountain, *n.* náam-pú น้ำพุ

four, *nm.* sìi สี่

four hundred, *nm.* sìi-rɔ́ɔi สี่ร้อย

fourteen, *nm.* sìp-sìi สิบสี่

fourteenth, *adj.* tîi-sìp-sìi ที่สิบสี่

fourth, *adj.* tîi-sìi ที่สี่

fox, *n.* sù-nák-jîng-jɔ̀ɔk สุนัขจิ้งจอก

foyer, *n.* hɔ̂ng-tóong ห้องโถง

fraction, *n.* sèet-sùan เศษส่วน; jam-nuan-lék-nɔ́ɔi จำนวนเล็กน้อย

fracture, *n.* gaan-dtɛ̀ɛk-hàk การแตกหัก

fragile, *adj.* dtɛ̀ɛk-ngâai แตกง่าย; bɔ̀ɔp-baang บอบบาง

fragment, *n.* chín-lék ชิ้นเล็ก; sùan-lék-lék ส่วนเล็กๆ

fragrance, *n.* kwaam-hɔ̌ɔm ความหอม; glìn-hɔ̌ɔm กลิ่นหอม

fragrant, *adj.* hɔ̌ɔm หอม

frail, *adj.* ɔ̀ɔn-ɛɛ อ่อนแอ; cham-rút-ngâai ชำรุดง่าย

frame, *v.* sài-grɔ̀ɔp ใส่กรอบ (putting a frame together); sài-ráai ใส่ร้าย (falsify someone)

frame, *n.* grɔ̀ɔp กรอบ (e.g. picture, window); kroong-râang โครงร่าง (structure that gives shape or support)

France, *n.* bprà-têet-fa-ràng-sèet ประเทศฝรั่งเศส

franchise, *n.* sǎa-kǎa สาขา

fraternal, *adj.* mǔan-pîi-nɔ́ɔng เหมือนพี่น้อง

fraternity, *n.* kwaam-bpen-pîi-nɔ́ɔng ความเป็นพี่น้อง; pá-raa-dɔɔn-pâap ภราดรภาพ

fraud, *n.* gaan-chɔ̂ɔ-goong การฉ้อโกง

fraudulent, *adj.* lɔ̀ɔk-luang หลอกลวง; goong โกง

freak, *n.* kon-bprà-làat คนประหลาด

freckle, *n.* grà กระ (on the face); jùt-dàang จุดด่าง

free, *adj.* bpen-ìt-sà-rà เป็นอิสระ (liberal); mâi-kít-ngən ไม่คิดเงิน (no charge); bpràt-sà-jàak ปราศจาก (without)

freedom, *n.* ìt-sà-ra-pâap อิสรภาพ

freeway, *n.* tà-nǒn-frii-wee ถนนฟรีเวย์; taang-dùan ทางด่วน

free will, *n.* kwaam-sà-màk-jai ความสมัครใจ

freeze, *v.* glaai-bpen-náam-kɛ̌ng กลายเป็นน้ำแข็ง; klûan-mâi-dâai เคลื่อนไม่ได้

freezer, *n.* chɔ̂ng-chɛ̂ɛ-kɛ̌ng ช่องแช่แข็ง

freight, n. kâa-kǒn-sòng ค่าขนส่ง

freighter, n. rɯa-ban-túk-sǐn-káa
เรือบรรทุกสินค้า (ship)

French, n. chaao-fa-ràng-sèet
ชาวฝรั่งเศส (people); paa-sǎa-fa-
ràng-sèet ภาษาฝรั่งเศส (language);
gìao-gàp-fa-ràng-sèet เกี่ยวกับ
ฝรั่งเศส (relating to France)

French fries, n. man-fa-ràng-tɔ̂ɔt
มันฝรั่งทอด

Frenchman, -woman, n. kon-fa-
ràng-sèet คนฝรั่งเศส

frequency, n. kwaam-tìi ความถี่

fresh, adj. sòt สด (pure, novel,
new); mài ใหม่ (new); sòt-sǎi
สดใส (clear, glowing)

friction, n. gaan-sìat-sǐi การเสียดสี;
gaan-kàt-yɛ́ɛng การขัดแย้ง

Friday, n. wan-sùk วันศุกร์

fried, adj. tɔ̂ɔt ทอด

friend, n. pɯ̂an เพื่อน

friendly, adj. bpen-mít เป็นมิตร

friendship, n. mít-dtà-pâap
มิตรภาพ

frighten, v. tam-hâi-glua ทำให้กลัว;
kùu ขู่

frightened, v. dtòk-jai-glua
ตกใจกลัว

frightful, adj. nâa-glua น่ากลัว

frill, n. jèep จีบ; fɔ̌i ฝอย

fringe, n. dtà-kèp ตะเข็บ (edging of
hanging threads, etc.); kɔ̀ɔp ขอบ
(marginal, peripheral)

frivolous, adj. lên-lên เล่นๆ; mâi-
jing-jang ไม่จริงจัง

frog, n. gòp กบ

frogman, n. má-nút-gòp มนุษย์กบ

front, n. dâan-nâa ด้านหน้า; nɛɛɔ-
nâa แนวหน้า

frontier, n. chaai-dɛɛn ชายแดน

frost, n. kwaam-yen-jàt ความเย็นจัด

frostbite, n. plɛ̌e-jàak-náam-kɛ̌ng
แผลจากน้ำแข็ง

frosty, adj. yen-jàt เย็นจัด; jàp-
bpen-náam-kɛ̌ng จับเป็นน้ำแข็ง

frown, v. kà-mùat-kíu ขมวดคิ้ว

frown, n. kíu-kà-mùat คิ้วขมวด;
kwaam-mâi-pɔɔ-jai ความไม่พอใจ

frugal, adj. bprà-yàt ประหยัด

fruit, n. pǒn ผล; pǒn-lá-máai ผลไม้

fruitful, adj. mii-pǒn-mâak มีผลมาก
(yielding a lot of fruit); mii-gam-rai
มีกำไร (profitable)

frustrate, v. tam-hâi-ngùt-ngìt
ทำให้หงุดหงิด

frustrated, adj. ngùt-ngìt หงุดหงิด

frustration, n. kwaam-ngùt-ngìt
ความหงุดหงิด

fry, v. tɔ̂ɔt ทอด

frying pan, n. grà-tá กระทะ

fuel, n. chúa-plɔɔng เชื้อเพลิง

fugitive, n. pûu-lòp-nǐi ผู้หลบหนี

fulcrum, v. jùt-ráp-náam-nàk
จุดรับน้ำหนัก

fulfill, v. tam-hâi-pɔɔ-jai
ทำให้พอใจ; tam-hâi-sǒm-buun

ทำให้สมบูรณ์

fulfillment, *n.* gaan-tam-hâi-pɔɔ-jai การทำให้พอใจ; gaan-tam-hâi-sǒm-buun การทำให้สมบูรณ์

full, *adj.* ìm อิ่ม (stomach); dtem เต็ม

full moon, *n.* prá-jan-dtem-duang พระจันทร์เต็มดวง

full-time, *adj.* dtem-wee-laa เต็มเวลา

fumble, *v.* klam-hǎa คลำหา

fun, *n.* kwaam-sà-nùk-sà-nǎan ความสนุกสนาน; rûang-sà-nùk เรื่องสนุก

function, *v.* tam-nâa-tîi ทำหน้าที่

function, *n.* nâa-tîi หน้าที่; gaan-bpà-dtì-bàt-ngaan การปฏิบัติงาน

functional, *adj.* gìao-gàp-nâa-tîi เกี่ยวกับหน้าที่

fund, *n.* ngən-tun เงินทุน; gɔɔng-tun กองทุน

fundamental, *adj.* púun-tǎan พื้นฐาน (basic); sǎm-kan สำคัญ (important)

funeral, *n.* ngaan-sòp งานศพ

fungus, *n.* chúa-raa เชื้อรา (fungi); hèt เห็ด (mushroom)

funnel, *n.* gruai กรวย

funny, *adj.* dtà-lòk ตลก

fur, *n.* kǒn-sàt ขนสัตว์

furnace, *n.* dtao-lɔ̌ɔm เตาหลอม

furnish, *v.* dtìt-dtâng-hâi ติดตั้งให้

furniture, *n.* fəə-ní-jɔ̀ɔ เฟอร์นิเจอร์

furry, *adj.* tam-jàak-kǒn-sàt ทำจากขนสัตว์ (made from fur); mii-kǒn มีขน (having fur)

further, *adj.* dtɔ̀ɔ-bpai ต่อไป (next); glai-ɔ̀ɔk-bpai ไกลออกไป (away)

furthermore, *adv.* nɔ̂ɔk-jàak-níi นอกจากนี้

fuse, *n.* fiu ฟิวส์

fuse, *v.* lɔ̌ɔm หลอม

fusion, *n.* gaan-lɔ̌ɔm-lá-laai การหลอมละลาย

fuss, *n.* kwaam-jûu-jîi ความจู้จี้; gaan-bòn การบ่น

fussy, *adj.* jûu-jîi จู้จี้

futile, *adj.* rái-pǒn ไร้ผล (fruitless); mâi-sǎm-kan ไม่สำคัญ (unimportant)

future, *n.* à-naa-kót อนาคต

fuzz, *n.* fɔ̌i ฝอย; kǒn-bpui ขนปุย

fuzzy, *adj.* bpen-fɔ̌i เป็นฝอย (of or resembling fuzz); bpen-kǒn-bpui เป็นขนปุย (fluffy); mâi-chát ไม่ชัด (not clear); mʉn-mao มึนเมา (drunk)

G

gain, *v.* dâai-maa ได้มา (acquire); dâai-bprà-yòot ได้ประโยชน์ (have benefits); daai-gam-rai ได้กำไร (profit)

gain, *n.* pǒn-bprà-yòot ผลประโยชน์; kɔ̌ɔng-tîi-dâai-maa ของที่ได้มา

gait, *n.* tâa-taang-gaan-dəən ท่าทางการเดิน

galaxy, *n.* gaa-lék-sîi กาแลกซี

gall bladder, *n.* tǔng-náam-dii ถุงน้ำดี

gallery, *n.* hông-sà-dɛɛng-ngaan ห้องแสดงงาน; chà-lĭang เฉลียง

galley, *n.* rua-jɛɛo เรือแจว (boat propelled by oars); hông-krua-bon-rua ห้องครัวบนเรือ (kitchen of a ship)

gallon, *n.* gɛn-lɔn แกลลอน

gallop, *v.* kûap-máa ควบม้า

gallows, *n.* tîi-bprà-hǎan ที่ประหาร

gamble, *v.* pá-nan พนัน

gambler, *n.* nák-pá-nan นักพนัน

gambling, *n.* gaan-pá-nan การพนัน

game, *n.* geem เกม (e.g. chess); gaan-lá-lên การละเล่น (e.g. children's game); gaan-kèng-kǎn การแข่งขัน (competition, tournament)

gang, *n.* géng แก๊ง; pûak พวก

gangster, *n.* nák-leeng นักเลง

gap, *n.* chɔ̂ng-wɔ̀o ช่องโหว่ (an opening in a solid structure or surface); kwaam-dtàang-gan ความต่างกัน (difference)

garage, *n.* roong-rót โรงรถ; ùu-rót อู่รถ

garbage, *n.* kà-yà ขยะ

garden, *n.* sǔan สวน

gardener, *n.* kon-sǔan คนสวน

gardening, *n.* gaan-tam-sǔan การทำสวน

gargle, *v.* bûan-bpàak บ้วนปาก

garland, *n.* puang-maa-lai พวงมาลัย

garlic, *n.* grà-tiam กระเทียม

garment, *n.* sûa-pâa เสื้อผ้า

garnish, *n.* sìng-bprà-dàp สิ่งประดับ (ornamentation); krûang-bprung-dtɛng เครื่องปรุงแต่ง (an embellishment for decoration or added flavor)

gas, *n.* géet แก๊ส (natural); náam-man น้ำมัน (petroleum, gasoline); aa-gàat อากาศ (air)

gasp, *v.* hɔ̀ɔp หอบ

gate, *n.* bprà-dtuu ประตู

gather, *v.* chum-num ชุมนุม; ruam-gan รวมกัน

gathering, *n.* gaan-ruam การรวม; gaan-chum-num การชุมนุม

gaudy, *adj.* rǔu-rǎa หรูหรา; bàat-dtaa บาดตา

gauze, *n.* pâa-pan-plɛ̌ɛ ผ้าพันแผล

gay, *n.* gee เกย์

gay, *adj.* râa-rəəng ร่าเริง

gear, *n.* gia เกียร์ (in a motor vehicle); fuang เฟือง (a toothed machine part, such as a wheel or cylinder)

gelatin, *n.* jee-la-dtin เจลาติน

gem, *n.* pét-plɔɔi เพชรพลอย

gender, *n.* pêet เพศ

gene, *n.* yiin ยีน

genealogy, *n.* wong-dtrà-guun-wít-tá-yaa วงศ์ตระกูลวิทยา

general, *adj.* tûa-bpai ทั่วไป

general, *n.* naai-pon นายพล (officer)

generalization, *n.* lák-sà-nà-tûa-bpai ลักษณะทั่วไป; làk-gaan หลักการ; gaan-glàao-bὲεp-gwâang-gwâang การกล่าวแบบกว้างๆ

generalize, *v.* waang-làk วางหลัก (reduce to a general form); long-kwaam-hěn ลงความเห็น (form general conclusions); glàao-bὲεp-gwâang-gwâang กล่าวแบบกว้างๆ (make universally applicable)

generally, *adv.* dooi-tûa-bpai โดยทั่วไป

generation, *n.* rûn รุ่น; yúk ยุค

generator, *n.* dai-naa-moo ไดนาโม (dynamo); sìng-tîi-hâi-gam-nὲət สิ่งที่ให้กำเนิด (something that generates)

generosity, *n.* kwaam-jai-dii ความใจดี; kwaam-jai-gwâang ความใจกว้าง

generous, *adj.* jai-gwâang ใจกว้าง; mii-náam-jai มีน้ำใจ

genetic, *adj.* gìao-gàp-pan-tú-sàat เกี่ยวกับพันธุศาสตร์

genetics, *n.* pan-tú-sàat พันธุศาสตร์

genital, *adj.* gìao-gàp-gaan-sùup-pan เกี่ยวกับการสืบพันธุ์

genius, *n.* àt-cha-ri-yá อัจฉริยะ

genocide, *n.* gaan-láang-chon-châat การล้างชนชาติ

gentle, *adj.* ɔ̀ɔn-yoon อ่อนโยน (soft in manners); sù-pâap สุภาพ (polite); jai-dii ใจดี (kind)

gentleman, *n.* sù-pâap-bù-rùt สุภาพบุรุษ

gentleness, *n.* kwaam-sù-pâap-ɔ̀ɔn-yoon ความสุภาพอ่อนโยน

genuine, *adj.* tέε แท้; jing-jai จริงใจ

genus, *n.* bprà-pêet ประเภท (kind, type); pan พันธุ์ (breed)

geography, *n.* puu-mí-sàat ภูมิศาสตร์

geological, *adj.* gìao-gàp-puu-mí-sàat เกี่ยวกับภูมิศาสตร์

geology, *n.* tɔɔ-ra-nii-wít-ta-yaa ธรณีวิทยา

geometry, *n.* ree-kǎa-ka-nít เรขาคณิต

germ, *n.* chúa-rôok เชื้อโรค

German, *n.* chaao-yəə-ra-man ชาวเยอรมัน (people); paa-sǎa-yəə-ra-man ภาษาเยอรมัน (language); gìao-gàp-yəə-ra-man เกี่ยวกับเยอรมัน (relating to Germany)

Germany, *n.* bprà-têet-yəə-ra-man ประเทศเยอรมัน

germinate, *v.* pɔ́-dtua เพาะตัว (begin to develop, as a germ); dtὲεk-nɔ̀ɔ แตกหน่อ (sprout, bud)

gestation, *n.* gaan-dtâng-kan การตั้งครรภ์

gesture, *n.* tâa-taang ท่าทาง;

gaan-hâi-sǎn-yaan การให้สัญญาณ

get, *v.* dâai ได้ (have, take, receive); ao เอา (take); kâo-jai เข้าใจ (understand); hǎa-maa หามา (acquire, find)

get about, *v.* bpai-maa ไปมา; dəən-tîao เดินเที่ยว

get along, *v.* kâo-gan-dâai เข้ากันได้

getaway, *n.* gaan-jàak-bpai การจากไป; gaan-lòp-nǐi การหลบหนี

get back, *v.* glàp-maa กลับมา (return); glàp-bâan กลับบ้าน (return home); gɛ̂ɛ-kɛ́ɛn แก้แค้น (revenge)

get dressed, *v.* dtɛ̀ng-dtua แต่งตัว

get off, *v.* long ลง; long-rót ลงรถ

get on, *v.* kûn ขึ้น; kûn-rót ขึ้นรถ

get out, *v.* ɔ̀ɔk-bpai ออกไป

get together, *v.* póp-bpà-sǎng-sǎn พบปะสังสรรค์

get up, *v.* lúk ลุก; dtɯ̀n-nɔɔn ตื่นนอน

ghastly, *adj.* nâa-glua น่ากลัว

ghetto, *n.* sà-lam สลัม

ghost, *n.* pǐi ผี; win-yaan วิญญาณ

giant, *adj.* má-hɯ̌-maa มหึมา

giant, *n.* yák ยักษ์

gift, *n.* kɔ̌ɔng-kwǎn ของขวัญ (present); pɔɔn-sà-wǎn พรสวรรค์ (special ability)

gifted, *adj.* mii-pɔɔn-sà-wǎn

มีพรสวรรค์; mii-kwaam-sǎa-mâat-pí-sèet มีความสามารถพิเศษ

giggle, *v.* hǔa-rɔ́-kík-kák หัวเราะคิกคัก

gild, *v.* chúp-tɔɔng ชุบทอง

gill, *n.* ngɯ̀ak-bplaa เหงือกปลา (fish); lam-taan ลำธาร (creek)

gimmick, *n.* krɯ̂ang-lɔ̀ɔk เครื่องหลอก (device employed to cheat); kɔ̌ɔng-lên ของเล่น (toy)

gin, *n.* lâo-glàn-jàak-kâao เหล้ากลั่นจากข้าว (alcoholic beverage)

ginger, *n.* kǐng ขิง

giraffe, *n.* yii-ráap ยีราฟ

girdle, *n.* sǎai-kâat สายคาด

girl, *n.* dèk-pûu-yǐng เด็กผู้หญิง; yǐng-sǎao หญิงสาว

girlfriend, *n.* fɛɛn แฟน; fɛɛn-sǎao แฟนสาว; kon-rák คนรัก

give, *v.* hâi ให้

glacier, *n.* taan-náam-kɛ̌ng ธารน้ำแข็ง

glad, *adj.* dii-jai ดีใจ; yin-dii ยินดี

gladly, *adv.* yàang-dii-jai อย่างดีใจ; dûai-kwaam-bə̀ək-baan ด้วยความเบิกบาน

glamour, *n.* sà-nèe สเน่ห์; kwaam-dɯng-dùut-jai ความดึงดูดใจ

glamorous, *adj.* mii-sà-nèe มีสเน่ห์

glance, *v.* cham-lɯang-mɔɔng ชำเลืองมอง; mɔɔng-pàan มองผ่าน

gland, n. dtɔ̀m ต่อม

glare, v. sòng-sɛ̌ɛng-jâa ส่องแสงจ้า; jɔ̂ng-kà-mǒng จ้องเขม็ง

glare, n. sɛ̌ɛng-jâa แสงจ้า; gaan-jɔ̂ng-kà-mǒng การจ้องเขม็ง

glaring, adj. jɛ̀ɛt-jâa เจิดจ้า; bàat-dtaa บาดตา

glass, n. gɛ̂ɛo แก้ว; grà-jòk กระจก (mirror)

glasses, n. wɛ̂n-dtaa แว่นตา

glaze, v. klʉ̀ap เคลือบ

glaze, n. wát-tù-klʉ̀ap วัตถุเคลือบ; sǐi-klʉ̀ap สีเคลือบ; pɛ̀n-náam-kɛ̌ng แผ่นน้ำแข็ง

gleam, n. sɛ̌ɛng-ɔ̀ɔn-ɔ̀ɔn แสงอ่อนๆ

glitter, n. sɛ̌ɛng-wɛɛo-wáp แสงแวววับ

gloat, v. grà-yìm-jai กระหยิ่มใจ; yìng-pà-yɔ̌ɔng หยิ่งผยอง

global, adj. táng-lôok ทั้งโลก; tûa-lôok ทั่วโลก

globe, n. lûuk-lôok ลูกโลก (a representation of the earth in the form of a ball); lôok โลก (the earth)

gloom, n. kwaam-mʉ̂ʉt-krʉ́m ความมืดครึ้ม; kwaam-mɔ̌ɔng-sâo ความหมองเศร้า

gloomy, adj. mʉ̂ʉt-krʉ́m มืดครึ้ม (weather); mɔ̌ɔng-sâo หมองเศร้า (feeling)

glorify, v. sǎn-sɔ̌ɔn สรรเสริญ; sà-dù-dii สดุดี

glorious, adj. rûng-rôot รุ่งโรจน์; song-gìat ทรงเกียรติ

glory, n. gìat-dtì-yót เกียรติยศ; kwaam-rûng-rôot ความรุ่งโรจน์

glossary, n. kam-à-tí-baai-sàp คำอธิบายศัพท์

glove, n. tǔng-mʉʉ ถุงมือ

glow, v. mii-sɛ̌ɛng-rʉang มีแสงเรือง

glue, n. gaao กาว

glutton, n. kon-dtà-glà คนตะกละ

gluttony, n. kwaam-dtà-glà ความตะกละ

gnat, n. má-lɛɛng-dtua-lék-lék แมลงตัวเล็กๆ

gnaw, v. tɛ́ แทะ; gàt กัด

go, v. bpai ไป

go after, v. lâi-dtaam ไล่ตาม

go around, v. bpai-rɔ̂ɔp-rɔ̂ɔp ไปรอบๆ

go ahead, v. bpai-kâang-nâa ไปข้างหน้า

go away, v. jàak-bpai จากไป

go back, v. glàp-bpai กลับไป; yɔ́ɔn-bpai ย้อนไป

go by, v. dəən-pàan เดินผ่าน

go down, v. dtòk ตก; sùam เสื่อม

go on, v. tam-dtɔ̀ɔ-bpai ทำต่อไป

go out, v. ɔ̀ɔk-bpai ออกไป

go over, v. tóp-tuan ทบทวน; dtrùat-taan ตรวจทาน; tam-mài ทำใหม่

go through, v. pàan ผ่าน; pí-jaa-ra-naa พิจารณา

go up, v. kʉ̂n ขึ้น

goal, n. bpâo-mǎai เป้าหมาย (aim); bprà-dtuu-fút-bon ประตู ฟุตบอล (football goal)

goat, n. pé แพะ

God, god, n. prá-jâao พระเจ้า; têep เทพ

goddess, n. têep-tí-daa เทพธิดา

godfather, n. pɔ̂ɔ-ùp-bpà-tǎm พ่ออุปถัมภ์

godmother, n. mêɛ-up-bpà-tǎm แม่อุปถัมภ์

going, n. gaan-bpai การไป

gold, n. tɔɔng-kam ทองคำ; tɔɔng ทอง

golden, adj. bpen-tɔɔng เป็นทอง (of gold); sǐi-tɔɔng สีทอง (color)

goldfish, n. bplaa-tɔɔng ปลาทอง

goldsmith, n. châng-tɔɔng ช่างทอง

golf, n. gɔ́ɔp กอล์ฟ

gong, n. kɔ́ɔng ฆ้อง

gonorrhea, n. rôok-nɔ̌ɔng-nai โรคหนองใน

good, adj. dii ดี

good afternoon, interj. sà-wàt-dii สวัสดี

good-bye, interj. laa-gɔ̀ɔn ลาก่อน; sà-wàt-dii สวัสดี

good evening, interj. sà-wàt-dii สวัสดี

good-hearted, adj. mii-mêet-dtaa-gà-ru-naa มีเมตตากรุณา; jai-dii ใจดี

good morning, interj. à-run-sà-wàt อรุณสวัสดิ์

good night, interj. raa-dtrii-sà-wàt ราตรีสวัสดิ์

good-looking, adj. nâa-dtaa-dii หน้าตาดี

goodness, n. kwaam-dii ความดี

goodwill, n. mai-dtrii-jìt ไมตรีจิต

goose, n. hàan ห่าน

gorilla, n. ling-gɔɔ-rîn-lâa ลิงกอริลลา

gossip, v. nin-taa นินทา

gossip, n. gaan-nin-taa การนินทา

Gothic, adj. gìao-gàp-sà-mǎi-gɔɔ-tìk เกี่ยวกับสมัยกอธิก

gourd, n. náam-dtâo น้ำเต้า

gourmet, n. nák-chim นักชิม

govern, v. bpòk-krɔɔng ปกครอง

governess, n. kruu-yǐng-tîi-sɔ̌ɔn-dtaam-bâan ครูหญิงที่สอนตามบ้าน

government, n. rát-tà-baan รัฐบาล

governor, n. pûu-wâa-râat-cha-gaan ผู้ว่าราชการ (of a province); pûu-wâa-gaan ผู้ว่าการ (of a state)

gown, n. sûa-klum เสื้อคลุม; sûa-krui เสื้อครุย

grab, v. kwáa คว้า; jàp จับ

grace, n. kwaam-ngót-ngaam ความงดงาม; kun-na-tam คุณธรรม

graceful, adj. sǔai-ngaam สวยงาม; sà-ngàa สง่า

grade, v. hâi-ka-nɛɛn ให้คะแนน (score a test); bpràp-hâi-sà-mǝ̌ǝ/bpràp-rá-dàp ปรับให้เสมอ/ปรับระดับ (level, smooth, e.g. the road)

grade, *n.* chán ชั้น (class); rá-dàp
ระดับ (level); chá-nít ชนิด (type);
kun-na-pâap คุณภาพ (quality)

gradual, *adj.* kôi-kôi ค่อยๆ; tii-la-
nɔ́ɔi ทีละน้อย

gradually, *adv.* kôi-kôi ค่อยๆ; tii-
la-nɔ́ɔi ทีละน้อย

graduate, *v.* rian-jòp เรียนจบ

graduate school, *n.* ban-dìt-wít-ta-
yaa-lai บัณฑิตวิทยาลัย

graduation, *n.* gaan-sǎm-rèt-gaan-
sùk-sǎa การสำเร็จการศึกษา

graft, *v.* dtɔɔn-gìng ตอนกิ่ง

graft, *n.* gìng-dtɔɔn กิ่งตอน

grain, *n.* ma-lét เมล็ด

gram, *n.* gram กรัม

grammar, *n.* wai-yaa-gɔɔn
ไวยากรณ์

grammatical, *adj.* taang-wai-yaa-
gɔɔn ทางไวยากรณ์

grand, *adj.* yài ใหญ่ (large); chán-
sǔung ชั้นสูง (having higher rank)

granddaughter, *n.* lǎan-sǎao
หลานสาว

grandfather, *n.* bpùu ปู่ (paternal);
dtaa ตา (maternal)

grandmother, *n.* yâa ย่า
(paternal); yaai ยาย (maternal)

grandparents, *n.* bpùu-yâa ปู่ย่า
(paternal); dtaa-yaai ตายาย (maternal)

grandson, *n.* lǎan-chaai หลานชาย

granite, *n.* hǐn-grɛɛ-nìt หินแกรนิต

grant, *v.* hâi ให้ (give); à-nú-yâat
อนุญาต (consent)

grant, *n.* gaan-hâi การให้ (act of
granting); tun ทุน (scholarship,
fund)

grape, *n.* à-ngùn องุ่น

grapefruit, *n.* pǒn-la-máai-kláai-
sôm-oo ผลไม้คล้ายส้มโอ; lûuk-
gréep-frúut ลูกเกรพฟรุต

graph, *n.* gráap กราฟ

graphic, *adj.* gráap-fìk กราฟฟิก

grasp, *v.* yút ยึด (clasp firmly); jàp
จับ (catch); jàp-jai จับใจ (take
hold of intellectually)

grass, *n.* yâa หญ้า

grasshopper, *n.* dták-gà-dtɛɛn
ตั๊กแตน

grate, *v.* kùut ขูด; krûut ครูด

grateful, *adj.* kɔ̀ɔp-kun ขอบคุณ

gratitude, *n.* kwaam-gà-dtan-yuu
ความกตัญญู

grave, *n.* sù-sǎan สุสาน; bpàa-cháa
ป่าช้า

gravel, *n.* grùat กรวด; lûuk-rang
ลูกรัง

gravestone, *n.* pèn-jaa-rúk-nǔa-
lǔm-fǎng-sòp แผ่นจารึกเหนือหลุม
ฝังศพ

graveyard, *n.* sù-sǎan สุสาน; bpàa-
cháa ป่าช้า

gravity, *n.* rɛɛng-dung-dùut
แรงดึงดูด (physics)

English • Phonetic • Thai

gravy, *n.* sɔ́ɔt-râat-aa-hǎan ซ้อสราดอาหาร

gray, *adj.* sǐi-tao สีเทา

gray hair, *n.* pǒm-ngɔ̀ɔk ผมหงอก

graze, *v.* hâi-yâa ให้หญ้า (feed on growing grasses); kàt-tǔu ขัดถู (scrape); tàak-bpai ถากไป (abrade)

grease, *n.* kǎi-man ไขมัน

greasy, *adj.* man-mâak มันมาก; mii-kǎi-man มีไขมัน

great, *adj.* dii-mâak ดีมาก (remarkable); yîng-yài ยิ่งใหญ่ (large)

Great Britain, *n.* sà-hà-râat-cha-aa-naa-jàk สหราชอาณาจักร

great-grandchild, *n.* lěen เหลน

great-grandfather, *n.* bpùu-tûat ปู่ทวด (paternal); dtaa-tûat ตาทวด (maternal)

great-grandmother, *n.* yâa-tûat ย่าทวด (paternal); yaai-tûat ยายทวด (maternal)

Greece, *n.* bprà-têet-grìik ประเทศกรีก

greed, *n.* kwaam-lôop ความโลภ

greedy, *adj.* lôop โลภ; lá-môop ละโมบ

Greek, *n.* paa-sǎa-grìik ภาษากรีก (language); chaao-grìik ชาวกรีก (people)

green, *adj.* sǐi-kǐao สีเขียว (color); yang-mâi-sùk ยังไม่สุก (unripe)

greenhouse, *n.* ruan-grà-jòk เรือนกระจก

greet, *v.* ták-taai ทักทาย (salute);

dtɔɔn-ráp ต้อนรับ (welcome)

greeting, *n.* gaan-ták-taai การทักทาย; kam-ták-taai คำทักทาย

grenade, *n.* lûuk-rá-bə̀ət-muu ลูกระเบิดมือ

grief, *n.* kwaam-sâo-sòok ความเศร้าโศก

grill, *v.* yâang ย่าง

grill, *n.* dtà-grɛɛng-lèk-yâang ตะแกรงเหล็กย่าง (gridiron); aa-hǎan-yâang อาหารย่าง (food cooked by grilling)

grin, *v.* yím-gwâang ยิ้มกว้าง

grind, *v.* bòt บด; fǒn ฝน

grip, *n.* gaan-jàp การจับ; gaan-yʉ́t การยึด; gaan-kâo-jai การเข้าใจ

groan, *v.* kruan-kraang ครวญคราง

groan, *n.* sǐang-kruan-kraang เสียงครวญคราง (as of pain or grief)

grocer, *n.* kon-kǎai-kɔ̌ɔng-cham คนขายของชำ

grocery, *n.* kɔ̌ɔng-cham ของชำ; kruang-ùp-bpà-pôok-bɔɔ-ri-pôok เครื่องอุปโภคบริโภค

groggy, *adj.* suan-see ซวนเซ (shaky); wian-hǔa เวียนหัว (having a headache); mao-yaa เมายา (from using drug)

groin, *n.* kǎa-nìip ขาหนีบ

groom, *n.* jâo-bàao เจ้าบ่าว

groove, *n.* rɔ̂ng ร่อง; raang ราง

gross, *n.* jam-nuan-ruam จำนวนรวม; raai-dâai-táng-mòt

รายได้ทั้งหมด

ground, *n.* púun พื้น (floor); bɔɔ-ri-ween บริเวณ (area); làk-tǎan หลักฐาน (evidence)

groundless, *adj.* mâi-mii-muun-hêet ไม่มีมูลเหตุ (in law)

group, *n.* glùm กลุ่ม; mùu หมู่; pûak พวก

grove, *n.* bpàa-lék ป่าเล็ก (small forest or woods); sǔan-pǒn-la-máai สวนผลไม้ (e.g. orange grove)

grow, *v.* dtòɔp-dtoo เติบโต (increase in size by a natural process); jà-rəən เจริญ (develop); bplùuk ปลูก (e.g. a tree)

grower, *n.* pûu-bplùuk ผู้ปลูก

growl, *v.* kam-raam คำราม

grownup, *n.* pûu-yài ผู้ใหญ่

growth, *n.* gaan-jà-rəən-dtòɔp-dtoo การเจริญเติบโต

grudge, *n.* kwaam-kùn-kéen ความขุ่นแค้น; kwaam-rít-sà-yǎa ความริษยา

gruesome, *adj.* nâa-glua น่ากลัว

grumble, *v.* bòn บ่น (complain); kam-raam คำราม (rumble or growl)

grumpy, *adj.* aa-rom-mâi-dii อารมณ์ไม่ดี

grunt, *v.* hút-hát ฮึดฮัด

guarantee, *v.* bplà-gan ประกัน (e.g. products); ráp-rɔɔng รับรอง (make certain)

guard, *n.* pûu-duu-lɛɛ-kwaam-

bplɔɔt-pai ผู้ดูแลความปลอดภัย

guardian, *n.* pûu-bpòk-krɔɔng ผู้ปกครอง

guerilla, *n.* gɔɔng-joon กองโจร

guess, *v.* dao เดา; taai ทาย

guest, *n.* kɛ̀ɛk แขก; pûu-maa-yuan ผู้มาเยือน

guidance, *n.* gaan-né-nɛɛo การแนะแนว; krûang-nam-taang เครื่องนำทาง

guide, *v.* nam นำ; nam-taang นำทาง; chii-né ชี้แนะ

guide, *n.* gái ไกด์; mák-ku-têet มัคคุเทศก์

guidebook, *n.* nǎng-sǔu-nam-tîao หนังสือนำเที่ยว

guided missile, *n.* jà-rùat-nam-wí-tii จรวดนำวิถี

guild, *n.* ong-gaan-aa-chîip องค์การอาชีพ

guilt, *n.* kwaam-pìt ความผิด; kwaam-lá-aai-jai ความละอายใจ

guilty, *adj.* mii-kwaam-pìt มีความผิด; lá-aai-jai ละอายใจ

guinea pig, *n.* nǔu-tót-lɔɔng หนูทดลอง; nǔu-dtà-pao หนูตะเภา

guitar, *n.* gii-dtâa กีตาร์

guitarist, *n.* nák-lên-gii-dtâa นักเล่นกีตาร์

gulf, *n.* àao อ่าว; lǔm-lúk หลุมลึก

gull, *n.* nók-bpèt ta-lee นกเป็ดทะเล

gullible, *adj.* tùuk-lɔ̀ɔk-ngâai ถูกหลอกง่าย

A B C D E F **G** H I J K L M N O P Q R S T U V W X Y Z

gulp, *v.* kà-mùap เขมือบ

gum, *n.* ngùak เหงือก (body part); màak-fa-làng หมากฝรั่ง (chewing)

gun, *n.* bpʉʉn ปืน

gunman, *n.* mʉʉ-bpʉʉn มือปืน

gunpowder, *n.* din-bpʉʉn ดินปืน

gunshot, *n.* sĭang-bpʉʉn เสียงปืน

gurgle, *v.* glûa-kɔɔ กลั้วคอ

gush, *v.* tá-lák ทะลัก

gust, *n.*, *v.* lom-rɛɛng ลมแรง

gusty, *adj.* lom-rɛɛng ลมแรง

gut, *n.* sâi-pung ไส้พุง (the bowels, entrails); kwaam-glâa-hăan ความกล้าหาญ (courage)

gutter, *n.* raang-náam รางน้ำ; kèet-sà-lam เขตสลัม

guttural, *adj.* gìao-gàp-lam-kɔɔ เกี่ยวกับลำคอ

guy, *n.* pûu-chaai ผู้ชาย; chûak เชือก

gym, *n.* roong-yim โรงยิม

gymnast, *n.* nák-gaai-bɔɔ-ri-hăan นักกายบริหาร

gymnastic, *adj.* gìao-gàp-gaai-bɔɔ-ri-hăan เกี่ยวกับกายบริหาร

gymnastics, *n.* gaai-bɔɔ-ri-hăan กายบริหาร

gynecology, *n.* ná-rii-wêet-wít-ta-yaa นรีเวชวิทยา

Gypsy, *n.* chaao-yíp-sii ชาวยิปซี (people); paa-săa-yíp-sii ภาษายิปซี (language)

H

habit, *n.* ní-săi นิสัย (characteristic); kwaam-kəəi-chin ความเคยชิน (routine)

habitable, *adj.* sŭng-aa-săi-dâai ซึ่งอาศัยได้

habitat, *n.* tîi-pák-aa-săi ที่พักอาศัย

habitation, *n.* gaan-yùu-aa-săi การอยู่อาศัย

habitual, *adj.* bpen-ní-săi เป็นนิสัย

hacker, *n.* pûu-jɔ́-rá-bòp-kom-piu-dtəə ผู้เจาะระบบคอมพิวเตอร์; hék-gəə แฮคเกอร์

hag, *n.* mɛ̂ɛ-mót แม่มด (witch); nɔ̌ɔng-bʉng หนองบึง (marsh)

haggle, *v.* tá-lɔ́ ทะเลาะ (argue); dtɔ̀ɔ-rɔɔng-raa-kaa ต่อรองราคา (bargain)

hail, *n.* fŏn-lûuk-hèp ฝนลูกเห็บ

hailstone, *n.* lûuk-hèp ลูกเห็บ

hair, *n.* pŏm ผม; kŏn ขน

haircut, *n.* gaan-dtàt-pŏm การตัดผม

hairdo, *n.* song-pŏm ทรงผม

hairdresser, *n.* châng-dtàt-pŏm ช่างตัดผม

hairpin, *n.* gíp-dtìt-pŏm กิ๊ปติดผม

hair spray, *n.* sà-bpree-dtɛ̀ng-pŏm สเปรย์แต่งผม

hairy, *adj.* mii-kŏn-mâak มีขนมาก

half, *n.* krʉ̂ng ครึ่ง

half brother/ sister, *n.* pîi-nɔ́ɔng-rûam-bì-daa-rʉ̌u-maan-daa-diao-gan

พี่น้องร่วมบิดาหรือมารดาเดียวกัน

half-hearted, *adj.* mâi-dtem-jai
ไม่เต็มใจ

half-price, *adj.* krûng-raa-kaa
ครึ่งราคา

halfway, *adv.* krûng-taang ครึ่งทาง

hall, *n.* hɔ̂ng-tǒong ห้องโถง

hallucinate, *v.* pɔ́ɔ-klâng เพ้อคลั่ง

hallucination, *n.* kwaam-pɔ́ɔ-klâng
ความเพ้อคลั่ง

hallway, *n.* rá-biang ระเบียง

halve, *v.* bɛ̀ng-krûng แบ่งครึ่ง

ham, *n.* mǔu-hɛm หมูแฮม

hamburger, *n.* hɛm-bəə-gɔ̂ɔ
แฮมเบอร์เกอร์

hammer, *n.* kɔ́ɔn ฆ้อน

hand, *n.* muu มือ (body part);
kěm-naa-lí-gaa เข็มนาฬิกา (of a
clock)

handbag, *n.* grà-bpǎo-tǔu
กระเป๋าถือ

handball, *n.* hɛɛn-bɔn แฮนด์บอล

handbook, *n.* kûu-muu คู่มือ

handcuffs, *n.* gun-jɛɛ-muu
กุญแจมือ

handful, *adj* hpɔɔ-ri-maan-dtem-
muu ปริมาณเต็มมือ (amount that a
hand can hold); jam-nuan-nɔ́ɔi
จำนวนน้อย (small amount)

handicap, *n,* kwaam-pí-gaan
ความพิการ (disability); gaan-dtɔ̀ɔ-
hâi การต่อให้ (e.g. in golf, bowling)

handicapped, *adj.* pí-gaan พิการ

handicraft, *n.* gaan-fǐi-muu
การฝีมือ

handkerchief, *n.* pâa-chét-nâa
ผ้าเช็ดหน้า

handle, *n.* dâam-jàp ด้ามจับ

handle, *v.* sǎm-pàt-dûai-muu
สัมผัสด้วยมือ (touch with the hands);
ráp-pìt-chɔ̂ɔp รับผิดชอบ (have
responsibility); jàt-gaan จัดการ
(cope with; deal or trade)

handlebar, *n.* tîi-bang-káp-jàk-grà-
yaan ที่บังคับจักรยาน

handmade, *adj.* tam-dûai-muu
ทำด้วยมือ

handshake, *n.* gaan-jàp-muu
การจับมือ

handsome, *adj.* lɔ̀ɔ หล่อ (used
with men); ngaam งาม (pleasing
and dignified)

handwriting, *n.* laai-muu ลายมือ

hang, *v.* hɔ̂i ห้อย; kwɛ̌ɛn แขวน

hanger, *n.* máai-kwɛ̌ɛn-sûa
ไม้แขวนเสื้อ

hanging, *n.* gaan-hɔ̂i การห้อย;
sìng-tîi-hɔ̂i สิ่งที่ห้อย

hangover, *n.* mao-káang เมาค้าง

happen, *v.* gɔ̀ɔt-kûn เกิดขึ้น

happening, *n.* hèet-gaan เหตุการณ์
(event, occurrence)

happiness, *n.* kwaam-sùk ความสุข

happy, *adj.* mii-kwaam-sùk
มีความสุข

happy-go-lucky, *adj.* mâi-túk-rɔ́ɔn
ไม่ทุกข์ร้อน

harass, v. róp-guan รบกวน; rang-kwaan รังควาญ

harassment, n. gaan-rang-kwaan การรังควาญ

harbor, n. tâa-rʉa ท่าเรือ

hard, adj. yâak ยาก (not easy); kĕng แข็ง (not soft); lam-bàak ลำบาก (with difficulty); kêm-ngûat เข้มงวด (strict)

hard disk, n. háat-dìt, háat-dís ฮาร์ดดิสก์

harden, v. tam-hâi-kĕng ทำให้แข็ง; sɔ̌ɔm-gam-lang เสริมกำลัง

hardly, adv. tɛ̂ɛp-jà-mâi แทบจะไม่ (almost not; barely); mâi-kɔ̂i ไม่ค่อย (not so ...)

hardness, n. kwaam-kĕng ความแข็ง

hardship, n. kwaam-yâak-lam-bàak ความยากลำบาก

hardware, n. háat-wɛɛ ฮาร์ดแวร์

hare, n. grà-dtàai-bpàa กระต่ายป่า

harem, n. haa-rem ฮาเร็ม

harm, n. an-dtà-raai อันตราย

harmful, adj. bpen-an-dtà-raai เป็นอันตราย

harmless, adj. mâi-mii-an-dtà-raai ไม่มีอันตราย

harmonica, n. hìip-pleeng-bpàak หีบเพลงปาก

harmonious, adj. bprà-sǎan-gan ประสานกัน; glom-gluun กลมกลืน

harmonize, v. tam-hâi-glom-gluun ทำให้กลมกลืน

harmony, n. kwaam-bprà-sǎan-gan ความประสานกัน; kwaam-glom-gluun ความกลมกลืน

harness, n. bang-hĭan บังเหียน

harp, n. pin-dtâng พิณตั้ง

harsh, adj. yàap หยาบ (rough); sɛ̀ɛp-gɛɛo-hŭu แสบแก้วหู (disagree-able to the ear); hòot โหด (cruel)

harshness, n. kwaam-yàap ความหยาบ

harvest, v. gèp-gìao เก็บเกี่ยว

harvest, n. rʉ́-duu-gèp-gìao ฤดูเก็บเกี่ยว (season); dɔ̀ɔk-pǒn ดอกผล (crop)

haste, n. kwaam-rêng-rîip ความเร่งรีบ; kwaam-rûat-reo ความรวดเร็ว

hasty, adj. rêng-rîip เร่งรีบ; reo เร็ว

hat, n. mùak หมวก

hatch, v. fák-kài ฟักไข่; gòk-kài กกไข่

hatchet, n. kwǎan-dàam-lék ขวานด้ามเล็ก

hate, v. glìat เกลียด

hateful, adj. mii-jai-pa-yaa-bàat มีใจพยาบาท; mii-jai-glìat-chang มีใจเกลียดชัง

hatred, n. kwaam-glìat ความเกลียด; kwaam-aa-kâat-kɛ́ɛn ความอาฆาตแค้น

haul, v. dʉng ดึง; lâak ลาก

haunt, v. sĭng-sùu สิงสู่; sĭng สิง

haunted, *adj.* pii-sìng ผีสิง

have, *v.* mii มี; dâai-ráp ได้รับ

havoc, *n.* hǎa-ya-ná หายนะ; kwaam-chìp-hǎai ความฉิบหาย

hawk, *n.* yìao เหยี่ยว

hay, *n.* faang ฟาง; yâa-hêng หญ้าแห้ง

hay fever, *n.* kâi-lá-ɔɔng-faang ไข้ละอองฟาง

haystack, *n.* gɔɔng-faang กองฟาง

he, *pron.* kǎo เขา

head, *n.* hǔa หัว; sǐi-sà ศีรษะ; hǔa-nâa หัวหน้า; hǔa-kàao หัวข่าว

headache, *n.* aa-gaan-bpùat-sǐi-sà อาการปวดศีรษะ; aa-gaan-bpùat-hǔa อาการปวดหัว

heading, *n.* hǔa-kɔ̂ɔ-rʉ̂ang หัวข้อเรื่อง (headline, topic); sùan-nâa ส่วนหน้า (foremost or leading position or part)

headlight, *n.* fai-nâa ไฟหน้า

headline, *n.* hǔa-kàao หัวข่าว

head-on, *adj.* bpra-sǎan-ngaa ประสานงา

headquarters, *n.* sǎm-nák-ngaan-yài สำนักงานใหญ่

headstone, *n.* sì-laa-rɛ̂ɛk ศิลาฤกษ์

heal, *v.* rák-sǎa รักษา

health, *n.* sùk-kà-pâap สุขภาพ

healthful, *adj.* bpen-bpra-yòot-dtɔ̀ɔ-râang-gaai เป็นประโยชน์ต่อร่างกาย

healthy, *adj.* sùk-kà-pâap-dii สุขภาพดี; kɛ̌ng-rɛɛng แข็งแรง

hear, *v.* dâai-yin ได้ยิน

hearing, *n.* gaan-dâai-yin การได้ยิน

hearsay, *n.* kàao-lʉʉ ข่าวลือ

hearse, *n.* rót-sòp รถศพ

heart, *n.* hǔa-jai หัวใจ (mind; the organ); jai ใจ (mind, spirit); gèn แก่น (core, the middle of); jùt-sǎm-kan จุดสำคัญ (important point)

heartache, *n.* kwaam-sâo-sǐa-jai ความเศร้าเสียใจ; kwaam-bpùat-ráao-jai ความปวดร้าวใจ

heartbreak, *n.* kwaam-bpùat-jai ความปวดใจ

heartbreaking, *adj.* tam-hâi-sâo ทำให้เศร้า

heartbroken, *adj.* òk-hàk อกหัก

heartburn, *n.* aa-gaan-sìat-tɔ́ɔng อาการเสียดท้อง

hearth, *n.* pʉ́ʉn-dtao พื้นเตา

heat, *v.* tam-hâi-ùn ทำให้อุ่น; tam-hâi-rɔ́ɔn ทำให้ร้อน

heat, *n.* kwaam-rɔ́ɔn ความร้อน

heater, *n.* krʉ̂ang-tam-kwaam-ùn เครื่องทำความอุ่น

heating, *n.* gaan-hâi-kwaam-rɔ́ɔn การให้ความร้อน

heatstroke, *n.* gaan-lóm-fúp-prɔ́-kwaam-rɔ́ɔn การล้มฟุบเพราะความร้อน

heaven, *n.* sà-wǎn สวรรค์; tɔ́ɔng-fáa ท้องฟ้า (sky)

heavenly, *adj.* hɛ̀ng-sà-wǎn แห่งสวรรค์ (celestial); lám-lɔ̂ɔt

ล้ำเลิศ (sublime)

heavy, *adj.* nàk หนัก (weight); run-rɛɛng รุนแรง (serious)

heckle, *v.* róp-guan รบกวน; kàt-kɔɔ ขัดคอ

hectic, *adj.* wûn-waai วุ่นวาย (filled with confusion); yûng-mâak ยุ่งมาก (very busy)

hedge, *n.* nɛɛo-pûm-máai แนวพุ่มไม้

heed, *v.* ao-jai-sài เอาใจใส่

heed, *n.* gaan-ao-jai-sài การเอาใจใส่

heel, *n.* sôn-táao ส้นเท้า

height, *n.* kwaam-sǔung ความสูง

heighten, *v.* tam-hâi-sǔung-kûn ทำให้สูงขึ้น

heir, heiress, *n.* taa-yâat ทายาท

helicopter, *n.* hee-li-kóp-dtɔɔ เฮลิคอปเตอร์

helium, *n.* géet-hii-lîam แก๊สฮีเลียม

hell, *n.* ná-rók นรก

hello, *interj.* sà-wàt-dii สวัสดี

helmet, *n.* mùak-gan-nɔ́k หมวกกันน็อก

helmsman, *n.* kon-tǔu-hǎang-sǔa คนถือหางเสือ

help, *v.* chûai-lǔa ช่วยเหลือ

help, *n.* kwaam-chûai-lǔa ความช่วยเหลือ

helper, *n.* pûu-chûai ผู้ช่วย; pûu-chûai-lǔa ผู้ช่วยเหลือ

helpful, *adj.* hâi-kwaam-chûai-lǔa ให้ความช่วยเหลือ

helpless, *adj.* chûai-mâi-dâai ช่วยไม่ได้

hem, *n.* kɔɔp ขอบ; rim ริม

hemisphere, *n.* krûng-wong-glom ครึ่งทรงกลม

hemorrhage, *n.* gaan-dtòk-lûat การตกเลือด

hemorrhoids, *n.* rît-sǐi-duang-ta-waan ริดสีดวงทวาร

hemp, *n.* bpàan ป่าน; bpɔɔ ปอ

hen, *n.* mɛ̂ɛ-gài แม่ไก่

henceforth, *adv.* dtɔ̀ɔ-bpai ต่อไป (next; from now on); náp-dtɛ̀ɛ-níi-bpai นับแต่นี้ไป (from now on)

henchman, *n.* kon-dùit-dtaam-tîi-wái-jai คนติดตามที่ไว้ใจ (trusted follower)

hepatitis, *n.* rôok-dtàp-àk-sèep โรคตับอักเสบ

her, *adj.* tɤɤ เธอ

herb, *n.* sà-mǔn-prai สมุนไพร

herbivorous, *adj.* gin-pùut กินพืช

herd, *n.* fǔung ฝูง

here, *adv.* tîi-níi ที่นี่

hereafter, *adv.* dtɔ̀ɔ-jàak-níi ต่อจากนี้

hereby, *adv.* ná-tîi-níi ณ ที่นี้

hereditary, *adj.* taang-gam-ma-pan ทางกรรมพันธุ์

heredity, *n.* gam-ma-pan กรรมพันธุ์

heresy, *n.* sàat-sà-nǎa-nɔ̂ɔk-rîit ศาสนานอกรีต

heretic, *n.* pûak-nɔ̂ɔk-rîit พวกนอกรีต

heritage, *n.* mɔɔ-ra-dòk มรดก

hermit, *n.* rɯɯ-sǐi ฤาษี

hernia, *n.* sâi-lɯ̂an ไส้เลื่อน

hero, *n.* prá-èek พระเอก (e.g. in movies); wii-rá-bù-rùt วีรบุรุษ (e.g. firefighters or other brave people)

heroic, *adj.* glâa-hǎan กล้าหาญ

heroin, *n.* hee-roo-iin เฮโรอีน

heroine, *n.* naang-èek นางเอก; wii-rá-sà-dtrii วีรสตรี

heron, *n.* nók-grà-sǎa นกกระสา

herring, *n.* bplaa-hɘɘ-rîng ปลาเฮอริง

hers, *pron.* kɔ̌ɔng-tɘɘ ของเธอ

herself, *pron.* dtua-tɘɘ-eeng ตัวเธอเอง

hesitant, *adj.* lang-lee ลังเล

hesitate, *v.* lang-lee ลังเล

hesitation, *n.* kwaam-lang-lee ความลังเล

heterosexual, *adj.* sǒn-jai-pêet-dtrong-kâam สนใจเพศตรงข้าม

hibernate, *v.* jam-sǐin จำศีล

hiccup, *v.* sà-ùk สะอึก

hidden, *adj.* sɔ̂ɔn-yùu ซ่อนอยู่; ɛ̀ɛp-fɛɛng แอบแฝง

hide, *v.* sɔ̂ɔn ซ่อน; ɛ̀ɛp แอบ

hide, *n.* nǎng-sàt หนังสัตว์ (leather)

hideout, hiding place, *n.* tîi-sɔ̂ɔn ที่ซ่อน

hierarchy, *n.* gaan-bɛ̀ng-chán การแบ่งชั้น (categorization of a group of people according to ability

or status); rá-bòp-sǒm-ma-ná-sàk ระบบสมณศักดิ์ (e.g. in religion or feudal system)

hieroglyphic, *n.* àk-sɔ̌ɔn-ii-yìp-boo-raan อักษรอียิปต์โบราณ

high, *adj.* sǔung สูง (tall); pɛɛng แพง (expensive); mao เมา (by alcohol or a drug)

high-class, *adj.* chán-sǔung ชั้นสูง

high fidelity, *n.* klɯɯn-sǐang-tîi-chát-jeen คลื่นเสียงที่ชัดเจน

highland, *n.* bɔɔ-ri-ween-tîi-sǔung บริเวณที่สูง

highlight, *v.* nén เน้น (emphasize)

highlight, *n.* hèet-gaan-sǎm-kan เหตุการณ์สำคัญ (important event)

highly, *adv.* yàang-mâak อย่างมาก

high school, *n.* roong-rian-mát-tá-yom-bplaai โรงเรียนมัธยมปลาย

highway, *n.* hai-wee ไฮเวย์

hijack, *v.* bplôn-glaang-taang ปล้นกลางทาง

hijacker, *n.* joon-bplôn-glaang-taang โจรปล้นกลางทาง; sà-làt-aa-gàat สลัดอากาศ (of an airplane)

hike, *v.* dɘɘn-kǎo เดินเขา; dɘɘn-taang-glai เดินทางไกล

hike, *n.* gaan-dɘɘn-taang-glai การเดินทางไกล

hill, *n.* nɘɘn-kǎo เนินเขา; kǎo-dîa-dtîa เขาเตี้ยๆ

hilt, *n.* dâam-aa-wút ด้ามอาวุธ

him, *pron.* kǎo เขา

himself, *pron.* dtua-kǎo-eeng ตัวเขาเอง

hind, *adj.* kâang-lǎng ข้างหลัง

hinder, *v.* gìit-kwǎang กีดขวาง

Hindi, *n.* pǎa-sǎa-hin-duu ภาษาฮินดู

hindrance, *n.* gaan-gìit-kwǎang การกีดขวาง; gaan-bpɔ̂ng-gan การป้องกัน

Hindu, *n.* hin-duu ฮินดู

hinge, *n.* baan-páp บานพับ

hint, *v.* bɔ̀ɔk-bpen-nai บอกเป็นนัย

hip, *n.* sà-pôok สะโพก

hippopotamus, *n.* híp-bpoo ฮิปโป

hire, *v.* jâang จ้าง

hire, *n.* gaan-jâang การจ้าง (act of hiring); kâa-jâang ค่าจ้าง (wages)

his, *pron.* kɔ̌ɔng-kǎo ของเขา

hiss, *v.* tam-sǐang-fûu ทำเสียงฟู่

hiss, *n.* sǐang-fûu เสียงฟู่; sǐang-fɔ̂ɔ เสียงฟ่อ

historian, *n.* nák-bprà-wàt-(dtì)-sàat นักประวัติศาสตร์

historical, historic, *adj.* taang-bprà-wàt-(dtì)-sàat ทางประวัติศาสตร์

history, *n.* bprà-wàt-(dtì)-sàat ประวัติศาสตร์

hit, *v.* dtii ตี; chon ชน (crash); hít ฮิต (e.g. song)

hit, *n.* gaan-dtii การตี; gaan-chon การชน; sìng-nîi-ní-yom-gan สิ่งที่นิยมกัน (e.g. song)

hit-and-run, *adj.* chon-lɛ́ɛo-nǐi ชนแล้วหนี

hitch, *v.* pùuk-chûak ผูกเชือก

hitchhike, *v.* bɔ̀ɔk-rót โบกรถ

hive, *n.* rang-pûng รังผึ้ง

hives, *n.* rôok-lom-pít โรคลมพิษ

Hmong, *n.* méɛo แม้ว (a hill tribe)

hoard, *n.* gaan-gèp-sà-sǒm การเก็บสะสม

hoarse, *adj.* sǐang-hèɛp เสียงแหบ; sǐang-hâao เสียงห้าว

hobby, *n.* ngaan-à-dì-rèek งานอดิเรก

hobbyhorse, *n.* máa-máai ม้าไม้

hockey, *n.* gii-laa-hɔ́k-gîi กีฬาฮอกกี้

hoe, *n.* jɔɔp จอบ

hog, *n.* mǔu-dtɔɔn หมูตอน

hold, *v.* jàp จับ; tǔu ถือ

hold, *n.* gaa-jàp การจับ; gaan-tǔu การถือ

holdings, *n.* sáp-sǐn ทรัพย์สิน

hole, *n.* lǔm หลุม; ruu รู

holiday, *n.* wan-yùt วันหยุด

Holland, *n.* bprà-têet-hɔɔ-lan-daa ประเทศฮอลันดา

hollow, *adj.* bpen-proong เป็นโพรง; gluang กลวง

holocaust, *n.* hǎa-ya-ná หายนะ

holy, *adj.* sàk-sìt ศักดิ์สิทธิ์; kuan-buu-chaa ควรบูชา

home, *n.* bâan บ้าน; sǔun-glaang ศูนย์กลาง

homebody, *n.* kon-chɔ̂ɔp-yùu-bâan คนชอบอยู่บ้าน

homeland, *n.* bâan-gəət บ้านเกิด

homeless, *adj.* rái-bâan ไร้บ้าน;

English · Phonetic · Thai

rɔ̂n-rée ร้อนเร่

homely, *adj.* tam-ma-daa ธรรมดา; mâi-dung-dùut-jai ไม่ดึงดูดใจ

homemade, *adj.* tam-tîi-bâan ทำที่บ้าน; pà-lìt-nai-krua-ruan ผลิตในครัวเรือน

homemaker, *n.* mɛ̂ɛ-bâan แม่บ้าน (house wife); pûu-duu-lɛɛ-bâan ผู้ดูแลบ้าน (one who manages a household)

home office, *n.* sǎm-nák-ngaan-yài-(kɔ̌ɔng-bɔɔ-ri-sàt) สำนักงานใหญ่ (ของบริษัท)

homesick, *adj.* kít-tǔng-bâan คิดถึงบ้าน

hometown, *n.* bâan-gɜ̀ɜt บ้านเกิด

homeward, *adv.* bpai-sùu-bâan ไปสู่บ้าน

homework, *n.* gaan-bâan การบ้าน

homicide, *n.* gaan-kâa-kon การฆ่าคน; gaan-kâat-dtà-gam การฆาตกรรม

homogeneous, *adj.* mǔan-gan เหมือนกัน

homogenize, *v.* tam-hâi-mǔan-gan ทำให้เหมือนกัน; tam-hâi-bpen-núa-dìao-gan ทำให้เป็นเนื้อเดียวกัน

homosexual, *adj.* rák-rûam-pêet รักร่วมเพศ

homosexuality, *n.* gaan-rák-rûam-pêet การรักร่วมเพศ

honest, *adj.* sûu-sàt ซื่อสัตย์ (loyal); bpɜ̀ɜt-pɜ̌ɜi เปิดเผย (sincere, open);

jing-jai จริงใจ (upright, genuine)

honey, *n.* náam-pûng น้ำผึ้ง (bee nectar); tîi-rák ที่รัก (darling)

honeycomb, *n.* ruang-pûng รวงผึ้ง

honeymoon, *n.* gaan-dùum-náam-pûng-prá-jan การดื่มน้ำผึ้งพระจันทร์

honk, *v.* bìip-dtrɛɛ บีบแตร

honk, *n.* sǐang-dtrɛɛ เสียงแตร

honor, *v.* hâi-gìat ให้เกียรติ

honor, *n.* gìat เกียรติ (high respect; esteem); gìat-ní-yom เกียรตินิยม (for academic achievement)

honorable, *adj.* nâa-kao-róp-náp-tǔu น่าเคารพนับถือ

honorary, *adj.* bpen-gìat เป็นเกียรติ

hood, *n.* mùak-klum หมวกคลุม (over the head); grà-bproong-rót กระโปรงรถ (of a car)

hoof, *n.* gìip-sàt กีบสัตว์

hook, *n.* dtà-kɔ̌ɔ ตะขอ (curved bent device); bèt เบ็ด (fishhook)

hoop, *n.* hùang ห่วง; wong-wɛ̌ɛn วงแหวน

hoot, *v.* nók-káo-mɛɛo-rɔ́ɔng นกเค้าแมวร้อง

hoot, *n.* sǐang-nók-káo-mɛɛo เสียงนกเค้าแมว

hop, *v.* grà-dòot กระโดด

hope, *v.* wǎng หวัง

hope, *n.* kwaam-wǎng ความหวัง

hopeful, *adj.* mii-kwaam-wǎng มีความหวัง

hopefully, *adv.* yàang-mii-kwaam-wǎng อย่างมีความหวัง

hopeless, *adj.* mâi-mii-kwaam-wǎng ไม่มีความหวัง

horizon, *n.* sên-kɔ̀ɔp-fáa เส้นขอบฟ้า (sky line); rá-dàp ระดับ (level)

horizontal, *adj.* bpen-nɛɛo-nɔɔn เป็นแนวนอน

hormone, *n.* hɔɔ-moon ฮอร์โมน

horn, *n.* dtrɛɛ แตร (musical instrument); kǎo-sàt เขาสัตว์ (animal)

hornet, *n.* dták-gà-dtɛɛn-yák ต๊กแตนยักษ์

horoscope, *n.* gaan-tam-naai-chôok-chá-dtaa การทำนายโชคชะตา

horrible, *adj.* nâa-glua น่ากลัว; yɛ̂ɛ-mâak แย่มาก

horrify, *v.* tam-hâi-glua ทำให้กลัว

horror, *n.* kwaam-nâa-glua ความน่ากลัว

horse, *n.* máa ม้า

horseback, *adv.* lǎng-máa หลังม้า

horseman, *n.* kon-kìi-máa คนขี่ม้า

horsepower, *n.* rɛɛng-máa แรงม้า

horseshoe, *v.* gùak-máa เกือกม้า

hose, *n.* tǔng-táao-yaao ถุงเท้ายาว (long socks); sǎai-yaang-chìit-náam สายยางฉีดน้ำ (watering)

hospital, *n.* roong-pa-yaa-baan โรงพยาบาล

hospitality, *n.* kwaam-mii-jai-mêet-dtaa-gà-ru-naa ความมีใจเมตตากรุณา

hospitalize, *v.* rák-sǎa-dtua-nai-

roong-pa-yaa-baan รักษาตัวในโรงพยาบาล

host, *n.* jâo-bâan เจ้าบ้าน (of a house); jâo-pâap เจ้าภาพ (e.g. of a party, ceremony, event); pûu-jàt-gaan ผู้จัดการ (who manages)

hostage, *n.* dtua-bprà-gan ตัวประกัน

hostess, *n.* jâo-bâan-yǐng เจ้าบ้านหญิง; pa-nák-ngaan-dtɔ̂ɔn-ráp-yǐng พนักงานต้อนรับหญิง

hostile, *adj.* mâi-bpen-mít ไม่เป็นมิตร

hostility, *n.* kwaam-bpen-bpɔɔ-rá-bpàk ความเป็นปรปักษ์; kwaam-mâi-bpen-mít ความไม่เป็นมิตร

hot, *adj.* rɔ́ɔn ร้อน (temperature); pèt เผ็ด (spicy); ráo-rɔ́ɔn เร่าร้อน (sexy)

hot-blooded, *adj.* lûat-rɔ́ɔn เลือดร้อน

hot cakes, *n.* kǎai-dii ขายดี

hot dog, *n.* hɔ́t-dɔ̀ɔk ฮ็อทด็อก

hotel, *n.* roong-rɛɛm โรงแรม

hound, *n.* sù-nák-lâa-núa สุนัขล่าเนื้อ; mǎa-lâa-núa หมาล่าเนื้อ

hour, *n.* chûa-moong ชั่วโมง

hourglass, *n.* naa-li-gaa-saai นาฬิกาทราย

hourly, *adv.* dtɛ̀ɛ-lá-chûa-moong แต่ละชั่วโมง; túk-chûa-moong ทุกชั่วโมง

house, *n.* bâan บ้าน

household, *n.* krua-rɯan ครัวเรือน

housekeeper, *n.* kon-duu-lɛɛ-bâan คนดูแลบ้าน

housekeeping, *n.* gaan-duu-lɛɛ-bâan การดูแลบ้าน

housemaid, *n.* mɛ̂ɛ-bâan แม่บ้าน

housewarming, *n.* ngaan-kɯ̂n-bâan-mài งานขึ้นบ้านใหม่

housewife, *n.* mɛ̂ɛ-bâan แม่บ้าน

housework, *n.* ngaan-bâan งานบ้าน

housing, *n.* bâan-pák บ้านพัก

housing project, *n.* gaan-kee-hà การเคหะ

hover, *v.* bin-rɔ̂n บินร่อน; bin-glâi บินใกล้

how, *adv.* yàang-rai อย่างไร; yang-ngai ยังไง

however, *adv.* yàang-rai-gɔ̂ɔ dtaam อย่างไรก็ตาม

howl, *v.* hɔ̌ɔn หอน

hub, *n.* dum-lɔ́ɔ ดุมล้อ (of a wheel); sǔun-glaang ศูนย์กลาง (center)

huddle, *v.* ruam-bpen-glùm-gɔ̂ɔn รวมเป็นกลุ่มก้อน

huddle, *n.* glùm-gɔ̂ɔn กลุ่มก้อน (packed group); gaan-bprà-chum-sùan-dtua การประชุมส่วนตัว (private meeting)

hug, *v.* gɔɔt กอด

hug, *n.* gaan-gɔ̀ɔt การกอด; gaan-rát การรัด

huge, *adj.* yài-mâak ใหญ่มาก

hull, *n.* lam-rɯa ลำเรือ (frame of a ship); bplɯ̀ak เปลือก (husk)

hum, *v.* ham-pleeng ฮัมเพลง

hum, *n.* gaan-ham-pleeng การฮัมเพลง (act of humming); sǐang-hùng-hùng เสียงหึ่งๆ (sound)

human, *adj.* bpen-ma-nút เป็นมนุษย์

human being, *n.* ma-nút มนุษย์

humane, *adj.* mii-ma-nút-sà-ya-tam มีมนุษยธรรม

humanitarian, *adj.* jai-bun ใจบุญ

humanities, *n.* ma-nút-sà-ya-sàat มนุษยศาสตร์

humanity, *n.* ma-nút-sà-ya-châat มนุษยชาติ

humankind, *n.* ma-nút มนุษย์

humble, *adj.* nɔ́ɔp-nɔ́ɔm-tɔ̀m-dton นอบน้อมถ่อมตน

humid, *adj.* chɯ́ɯn ชื้น

humidify, *v.* tam hâi-chɯ́ɯn ทำให้ชื้น

humidity, *n.* kwaam-chɯ́ɯn ความชื้น

humiliate, *v.* tam-hâi-kǎai-nâa ทำให้ขายหน้า

humiliation, *n.* gaan-tam-hâi-kǎai-nâa การทำให้ขายหน้า

humility, *n.* kwaam-tɔ̀m-dtua ความถ่อมตัว

humor, *n.* kwaam-kòp-kǎn ความขบขัน; aa-rom-kǎn อารมณ์ขัน

humorous, *adj.* dtà-lòk ตลก; kòp-kǎn ขบขัน

hump, *n.* nɔ̀ɔk หนอก; bpùm ปุ่ม

humpback, hunchback, *n.* kon-lǎng-kôm คนหลังค่อม

hunch, *n.* nòok โหนก

hundred, *nm.* nùng-rɔ́ɔi หนึ่งร้อย

hundredth, *adj.* tîi-nùng-rɔ́ɔi ที่หนึ่งร้อย

Hungary, *n.* bprà-tɛ̂et-hang-gaa-rii ประเทศฮังการี

hunger, *n.* kwaam-hǐu ความหิว

hungry, *adj.* hǐu หิว

hunt, *v.* lâa ล่า

hunt, *n.* gaan-lâa การล่า

hunter, -tress, *n.* nák-lâa นักล่า; naai-praan นายพราน

hunting, *n.* gaan-lâa การล่า

hurdle, *n.* rúa รั้ว (fence); krûang-gìit-kwǎang เครื่องกีดขวาง (barrier, e.g. for racing)

hurricane, *n.* paa-yú-hɤɤ-ri-keen พายุเฮอริเคน

hurried, *adj.* rîip-rêng รีบเร่ง; dùan ด่วน

hurry, *v.* rîip รีบ; rêng เร่ง

hurry, *n.* kwaam-rêng-rîip ความเร่งรีบ

hurt, *v.* tam-hâi-jèp-bpùat ทำให้เจ็บปวด

hurt, *n.* kwaam-jèp-bpùat ความเจ็บปวด; kwaam-sǐa-hǎai ความเสียหาย

husband, *n.* sǎa-mii สามี; pǔa ผัว (colloquial)

husk, *n.* bplùak เปลือก; glèɛp แกลบ

hut, *n.* grà-tɔ̂m กระท่อม

hyacinth, *n.* dɔ̀ɔk-hai-yaa-sin ดอกไฮยาซิน

hybrid, *adj.* pan-pà-sǒm พันธุ์ผสม

hydrangea, *n.* dɔ̀ɔk-hai-dren-jia ดอกไฮเดรนเจีย

hydrant, *n.* hǔa-gɔ́ɔk-náam หัวก๊อกน้ำ

hydroelectric, *adj.* gìao-gàp-fai-fáa-pá-lang-náam เกี่ยวกับไฟฟ้าพลังน้ำ

hydrogen, *n.* gáat-hai-droo-jên ก๊าสไฮโดรเจน

hyena, *n.* mǎa-nai หมาใน

hygiene, *n.* kwaam-sà-àat ความสะอาด; sùk-kà-lák-sà-nà สุขลักษณะ

hygienic, *adj.* gìao-gàp-sùk-kà-pâap เกี่ยวกับสุขภาพ

hymn, *n.* pleeng-sùat เพลงสวด

hyperbole, *n.* gaan-pûut-gɤɤn-jing การพูดเกินจริง

hypertension, *n.* rôok-kwaam-dan-loo-hìt-sǔung โรคความดันโลหิตสูง

hypertensive, *adj.* mii-kwaam-dan-loo-hìt-sǔung มีความดันโลหิตสูง

hyphen, *n.* krûang-mǎai-kìit เครื่องหมายขีด

hyphenate, *v.* kǐan-krûang-mǎai-kìit เขียนเครื่องหมายขีด

hypnosis, *n.* gaan-sà-gòt-jìt การสะกดจิต

hypnotism, *n.* wí-chaa-gaan-sà-gòt-jìt วิชาการสะกดจิต

hypnotize, *v.* sà-gòt-jìt สะกดจิต

hypochondriac, *n.* wí-dtòk-jà-rìt วิตกจริต

hypocrisy, *n.* gaan-sɛ̌e-sɛ̂eng การเสแสร้ง

hypocrite, *n.* kon-sɛ̌e-sɛ̂eng คนเสแสร้ง

hypocritical, *adj.* lɔ̀ɔk-luang หลอกลวง; sɛ̌e-sɛ̂eng เสแสร้ง

hypodermic, *adj.* gìap-gàp-dtáai-piu-nǎng เกี่ยวกับใต้ผิวหนัง

hypothesis, *n.* sǒm-mút-dtì-tǎan สมมติฐาน

hypothetical, *adj.* bpen-kɔ̂ɔ-sǒm-mút เป็นข้อสมมติ

hysteria, *n.* rôok-hít-sa-tii-ria โรคฮิสทีเรีย

hysterical, *adj.* gìao-gàp-rôok-hít-sa-tii ria เกี่ยวกับโรคฮิสทีเรีย

I

I, *pron.* chǎn ฉัน (female); dì-chǎn ดีฉัน (female - formal); pǒm ผม (male); kâa-pà-jâao ข้าพเจ้า (male or female - very formal)

ice, *n.* náam-kɛ̌ng น้ำแข็ง

iceberg, *n.* puu-kǎo-náam-kɛ̌ng ภูเขาน้ำแข็ง

ice cream, *n.* ai-sa-kriim ไอศกรีม; ai-dtim ไอติม

iced, *adj.* yen-bpen-náam-kɛ̌ng

เย็นเป็นน้ำแข็ง; sài-náam-kɛ̌ng ใส่น้ำแข็ง

icicle, *n.* sǎo-náam-kɛ̌ng เสาน้ำแข็ง

icy, *adj.* yen-mâak เย็นมาก; bpen-náam-kɛ̌ng เป็นน้ำแข็ง

idea, *n.* kwaam-kít-hěn ความคิดเห็น

ideal, *adj.* dii-lɔ̂ət ดีเลิศ; bpen-bɛ̀ɛp-yàang เป็นแบบอย่าง; nai-ù-dom-ká-dtì ในอุดมคติ

idealism, *n.* ù-dom-ká-dtì อุดมคติ; ù-dom-gaan อุดมการณ์

idealist, *n.* nák-ù-dom-ká-dtì นักอุดมคติ

identical, *adj.* mʉ̌an-gan เหมือนกัน

identification, *n.* gaan-hǎa-èek-gà-lák การหาเอกลักษณ์ (act of identifying); bàt-bprà-jam-dtua บัตรประจำตัว (I.D. card)

identify, *v.* bɔ̀ɔk-lák-sà-nà บอกลักษณะ (establish the identity of); chíi-dtua ชี้ตัว (ascertain the characteristics of; point at)

identity, *n.* èek-gà-lák เอกลักษณ์ (characteristics); làk-tǎan หลักฐาน (proof)

idiom, *n.* sǎm-nuan สำนวน

idle, *adj.* mâi-tam-ngaan ไม่ทำงาน (not working); kîi-gìat ขี้เกียจ (lazy)

idol, *n.* rûup-buu-chaa รูปบูชา (image used for worship); pûu-tii-mii-kon-klâng-klái ผู้ที่มีคนหลั่งไคล้ (one that is adored excessively)

if, *conj.* tâa ถ้า; tâa-hàak ถ้าหาก;

hàak หาก

ignite, v. tam-hâi-lúk-mâi
ทำให้ลุกไหม้ (cause to burn); dùt-
fai ติดไฟ (begin to burn)

ignition, n. gaan-dùt-fai การติดไฟ

ignorance, n. kwaam-mâi-rúu
ความไม่รู้ (condition of being unedu-
cated); gaan-pòok-chəəi การเพิกเฉย
(condition of disregarding)

ignorant, adj. mâi-rúu ไม่รู้

ignore, v. mâi-sŏn-jai ไม่สนใจ
(uninterested); lá-ləəi ละเลย (disregard)

ill, adj. mâi-sà-baai ไม่สบาย (sick);
bpùai ป่วย (very sick); leeo เลว
(bad)

illegal, adj. pìt-gòt-mǎai ผิดกฎหมาย

illegible, adj. àan-mâi-ɔ̀ɔk
อ่านไม่ออก

illiterate, adj. mâi-rúu-nǎng-sǔu
ไม่รู้หนังสือ

illness, n. gaan-jèp-kâi การเจ็บไข้;
gaan-jèp-bpùai การเจ็บป่วย

illogical, adj. mâi-mii-hèet-pŏn
ไม่มีเหตุผล

illusion, n. maa-yaa มายา (erroneous concept or belief); sìng-luang-
dtaa สิ่งลวงตา (something causing
false perception)

illustrate, v. sà-dɛɛng แสดง
(show); à-tí-baai อธิบาย (explain)

illustration, n. pâap ภาพ (figure,
picture); dtua-yàang ตัวอย่าง

(example); gaan-à-tí-baai
การอธิบาย (explanation)

illustrator, n. pûu-wâat-pâap-bprà-
gɔ̀ɔp ผู้วาดภาพประกอบ

image, n. rûup-jam-lɔɔng รูปจำลอง
(reproduction of an object); pâap
ภาพ (picture); má-noo-pâap
มโนภาพ (mental picture)

imagery, n. pâap-nai-jai ภาพในใจ
(mental picture); kwaam-núk-kít
ความนึกคิด (thought, idea)

imagination, n. jin-dtà-naa-gaan
จินตนาการ

imaginative, adj. châng-jin-dtà-
naa-gaan ช่างจินตนาการ

imagine, v. jin-dtà-naa-gaan
จินตนาการ

imbalance, n. mâi-sŏm-dun
ไม่สมดุลย์

imitate, v. lian-bὲεp เลียนแบบ

imitation, n. gaan-lɔ̂ɔk-lian-bὲεp
การลอกเลียนแบบ

imitator, n. kon-lɔ̂ɔk-lian-bὲεp
คนลอกเลียนแบบ

immaterial, adj. mâi-mii-dtua-dton
ไม่มีตัวตน (having no material
body); rái-gὲn-sǎan ไร้แก่นสาร (of
no importance or relevance)

immature, adj. yang-yao-wai
ยังเยาว์วัย (still young); yang-dtoo-
mâi-dtem-tîi ยังโตไม่เต็มที่ (not fully
grown)

immediate, adj. tan-tii ทันที

(instant); dtooi-dtrong โดยตรง
(direct); glâi-chít ใกล้ชิด (close,
e.g. family)

immediately, *adv.* yàang-mâi-rɔɔ-
cháa อย่างไม่รอช้า (without delay);
tan-tii ทันที (instantly); dooi-dtrong
โดยตรง (directly)

immense, *adj.* má-hù-maa มหึมา;
yîng-yài ยิ่งใหญ่

immigrant, *n.* pûu-òp-pa-yóp-kâo-
bprà-têet ผู้อพยพเข้าประเทศ; pûu-
òp-pa-yóp ผู้อพยพ

immigrate, *v.* òp-pa-yóp-kâo
อพยพเข้า

immoral, *adj.* pìt-sǐin-tam
ผิดศีลธรรม

immortal, *adj.* am-má-dtà อมตะ;
dtà-lɔ̀ɔt-gaan ตลอดกาล

Immortality, *n.* kwaam-bpen-am-
má-dtà ความเป็นอมตะ

immune, *adj.* mii-puum-kúm-gan-
rôok มีภูมิคุ้มกันโรค

immunity, *n.* puum-kúm-gan-rôok
ภูมิคุ้มกันโรค

immunize, *v.* hâi-puum-kúm-gan-
rôok ให้ภูมิคุ้มกันโรค

impact, *v.* grà-tóp กระทบ (effect),
bpà-tá ปะทะ (strike forcefully)

impact, *n.* gaan-grà-tóp การกระทบ
(collision; act of impacting); rɛɛng-
bpà-tá แรงปะทะ (force)

impartial, *adj.* bpen-tam เป็นธรรม;
mâi-mii-àk-ka-dti ไม่มีอคติ

impatient, *adj.* jai-rɔ́ɔn ใจร้อน

impeach, *v.* fɔ́ɔng-rɔ́ɔng ฟ้องร้อง
(charge); glàao-hǎa กล่าวหา (make
an accusation); pá-yaa-yaam-tam-
hâi-sǐa-chûu พยายามทำให้เสียชื่อ
(try to discredit)

impeachment, *n.* gaan-glàao-hǎa
การกล่าวหา; gaan-fɔ́ɔng-rɔ́ɔng
การฟ้องร้อง

imperative, *n.* kam-sàng คำสั่ง
(order); gòt-geen กฎเกณฑ์ (rule)

imperial, *adj.* hɛ̀ng-jàk-grà-pát
แห่งจักรพรรดิ (of an emperor);
yîng-yài ยิ่งใหญ่ (grand)

imperialism, *n.* lát-tí-jàk-gà-wàt-
ní-yom ลัทธิจักรวรรดินิยม

impersonal, *adj.* mâi-châi-sùan-
dtua ไม่ใช่ส่วนตัว

impersonate, *v.* lian-bɛ̀ɛp
เลียนแบบ (mimic); bplɔɔm-
bplɛɛng ปลอมแปลง (fake)

impetuous, *adj.* bùm-bàam
บุ่มบ่าม; jai-rɔ́ɔn ใจร้อน

implant, *v.* sài ใส่; fǎng ฝัง

imply, *v.* bɔ̀ɔk-bpen-nai บอกเป็นนัย

impolite, *adj.* mâi-sù-pâap ไม่สุภาพ

import, *v.* nam-kâo นำเข้า

import, *n.* gaan-nam-kao การนำเข้า

importance, *n.* kwaam-sǎm-kan
ความสำคัญ

important, *adj.* sǎm-kan สำคัญ

impose, *v.* jàt-gèp-paa-sǐi
จัดเก็บภาษี (a tax); bang-káp

English • Phonetic • Thai

บังคับ (force)

impossible, *adj.* bpen-bpai-mâi-dâai เป็นไปไม่ได้

impotent, *adj.* ɔɔn-εε อ่อนแอ (weak); rái-sà-màt-tà-pâap ไร้สมรรถภาพ (lacking physical strength or vigor; e.g. incapable of sexual intercourse)

impound, *v.* kǎng ขัง (confine); yút ยึด (seize); ríp ริบ (retain in legal custody)

impoverish, *v.* tam-hâi-yâak-jon ทำให้ยากจน (make poor); tam-hâi-ɔɔn-gam-lang ทำให้อ่อนกำลัง (make weak)

impress, *v.* bprà-táp-jai ประทับใจ

impression, *n.* kwaam-bprà-táp-jai ความประทับใจ

Impressionism, *n.* lát-tí-im-préet-chân-nít ลัทธิอิมเพรสชันนิสต์

impressive, *adj.* nâa-bprà-táp-jai น่าประทับใจ

imprison, *v.* jam-kúk จำคุก

imprisonment, *n.* gaan-jam-kúk การจำคุก; gaan-gàk-kǎng การกักขัง

improbable, *adj.* mâi-nâa-bpen-bpai-dâai ไม่น่าเป็นไปได้

impromptu, *adj.* mâi-dâai-dtriam-dtua-maa-gɔɔn ไม่ได้เตรียมตัวมาก่อน

improper, *adj.* mâi-mɔ̀-sǒm ไม่เหมาะสม

improve, *v.* bpràp-bprung ปรับปรุง

improvement, *n.* gaan-bpràp-

bprung การปรับปรุง

improvise, *v.* mâi-dâai-dtriam ไม่ได้เตรียม (perform with no preparation); jàt-dtriam-dtaam-tîi-mii จัดเตรียมตามที่มี (provide from available materials)

impulsive, *adj.* jai-reo ใจเร็ว

in, *prep.* nai ใน; kâang-nai ข้างใน

inaccessible, *adj.* kâo-mâi-tǔng เข้าไม่ถึง; kâo-bpai-mâi-dâai เข้าไปไม่ได้

inaccurate, *adj.* mâi-mên-yam ไม่แม่นยำ

inaugurate, *v.* kâo-ráp-dtam-nèng-bpen-taang-gaan เข้ารับตำแหน่งเป็นทางการ

inauguration, *n.* gaan-kâo-ráp-dtam-nèng การเข้ารับตำแหน่ง

inborn, *adj.* mii-maa-dtâng-dtèε-gɔ̀ɔt มีมาตั้งแต่เกิด (possessed at birth)

incarcerate, *v.* jam-kúk จำคุก

incarnate, *adj.* gɔ̀ɔt-mài เกิดใหม่

incarnation, *v.* gaan-gɔ̀ɔt-mài การเกิดใหม่

incense, *n.* krûang-hɔ̌ɔm เครื่องหอม (aromatic substance); tûup ธูป (joss stick)

incentive, *n.* sìng-grà-dtûn สิ่งกระตุ้น; krûang-juung-jai เครื่องจูงใจ

incest, *n.* gaan-rûam-bprà-wee-nii-rá-wàang-sǎai-lûat การร่วมประเวณี

ระหว่างสายเลือด

inch, *n.* นิ้ว นิ้ว

incidence, *n.* hèet-gaan เหตุการณ์

incident, *n.* hèet-gaan เหตุการณ์

incidental, *adj.* bang-əən บังเอิญ

incision, *n.* rɔɔi-pàa รอยผ่า; rɔɔi-chûat รอยเชือด

inclination, *n.* kwaam-nóom-iang ความโน้มเอียง; kwaam-biang-been ความเบียงเบน

incline, *v.* biang-been เบียงเบน (have a tendency towards something); iang เอียง (slant); ping พิง (lean)

include, *v.* bprà-gɔ̀ɔp-dûai ประกอบด้วย; ruam-yùu รวมอยู่

including, *prep.* ruam-táng รวมทั้ง

inclusion, *n.* gaan-ruam-kâo การรวมเข้า

income, *n.* raai-dâai รายได้; raai-ráp รายรับ

inconvenience, *n.* kwaam-mâi-sà-dùak ความไม่สะดวก

inconvenient, *adj.* mâi-sà-dùak ไม่สะดวก

incorporate, *v.* ruam-kâo-dûai-gan รวมเข้าด้วยกัน

increase, *v.* pə̂əm เพิ่ม; pə̂əm-puun เพิ่มพูน

incredible, *adj.* mâi-nâa-chûa ไม่น่าเชื่อ; lʉ̌a-chûa เหลือเชื่อ

increment, *n.* gaan-pə̂əm การเพิ่ม (process of increasing); sìng-tîi-

pə̂əm-kʉ̂n สิ่งที่เพิ่มขึ้น (something added)

incriminate, *v.* glàao-tôot กล่าวโทษ

incubator, *n.* krʉ̂ang-bpràp-sà-pâap-aa-gàat เครื่องปรับสภาพอากาศ (apparatus for creating environmental conditions); krʉ̂ang-fák-kài เครื่องฟักไข่ (for hatching eggs)

incumbent, *n.* pûu-dam-rong-dtam-nèng ผู้ดำรงตำแหน่ง

incur, *v.* gɔ̀ɔ-hâi-gə̀ət ก่อให้เกิด

indebted, *adj.* bpen-nîi เป็นหนี้

indeed, *adv.* jing-jing-lέεo จริงๆแล้ว; tέε-tîi-jing แท้ที่จริง

indefinite, *adj.* mâi-gam-nòt-nέε-nɔɔn ไม่กำหนดแน่นอน (undecided, uncertain); mâi-dtaai-dtua ไม่ตายตัว (not fixed)

indemnify, *v.* chót-chái-kâa-sǐa-hǎai ชดใช้ค่าเสียหาย

indemnity, *n.* sìng-chót-chəəi สิ่งชดเชย (something compensated); gaan-chót-chəəi-kwaam-sǐa-hǎai การชดเชยความเสียหาย (act of compensation)

indent, *v.* yɔ̂ɔ-nâa ย่อหน้า (set the first line of a paragraph); jɔ̀-ruu เจาะรู (make hole)

independence, *n.* ìt-sà-ra-pâap อิสรภาพ (freedom); èek-gà-râat เอกราช (of a country)

independent, *adj.* bpen-ìt-sà-ra-pâap เป็นอิสรภาพ

index, *n.* dàt-cha-nii ดรรชนี

India, *n.* bprà-têet-in-dia ประเทศอินเดีย

Indian, *n.* chaao-in-dia ชาวอินเดีย (people); gìao-gàp-in-dia เกี่ยวกับ อินเดีย (relating to India)

indicate, *v.* sà-dɛɛng แสดง (show); chíi-né ชี้แนะ (point out); bɔ̀ɔk บอก (suggest; state or express briefly)

indication, *n.* gaan-chíi-bɔ̀ɔk การชี้บอก; sìng-sà-dɛɛng สิ่งแสดง

indicator, *n.* dtua-bɔ̀ɔk ตัวบอก; krûang-chíi-nam เครื่องชี้นำ

indict, *v.* fɔ́ɔng-rɔ́ɔng ฟ้องร้อง (charge); glàao-hǎa-yàang-bpen-taang-gaan กล่าวหาอย่างเป็นทาง การ (make a formal accusation)

indictment, *n.* gaan-fɔ́ɔng-rɔ́ɔng การฟ้องร้อง; kɔ̂ɔ-glàao-hǎa ข้อกล่าวหา

indifferent, *adj.* mâi-sǒn-jai ไม่สนใจ (having no interest); bpen-glaang เป็นกลาง (moderate, neutral)

indigenous, *adj.* tɔ́ɔng-tìn ท้องถิ่น; púun-mʉang พื้นเมือง

indigestion, *n.* aa-hǎan-mâi-yɔ̂i อาหารไม่ย่อย

indigo, *n.* sǐi-kraam สีคราม

indirect, *adj.* taang-ɔ̂ɔm ทางอ้อม; mâi-dtrong ไม่ตรง

indiscreet, *adj.* mâi-rɔ̂ɔp-kɔ̂ɔp ไม่รอบคอบ; lɤn-lɤ̂ɤ เลินเล่อ

individual, *n.* bùk-kon บุคคล; bpàt-jèek-chon ปัจเจกชน

indivisible, *adj.* bɛ̀ng-yɛ̂ɛk-mâi-dâai แบ่งแยกไม่ได้

indoctrinate, *v.* bplùuk-fǎng-kwaam-chʉ̂a ปลูกฝังความเชื่อ

indoor, *adj.* nai-rôm ในร่ม

induct, *v.* geen-maa เกณฑ์มา

indulge, *v.* yɔɔm-pɛ́ɛ ยอมแพ้ (yield to); òt-jai-mâi-dâai อดใจไม่ได้ (can't control oneself)

indulgence, *n.* gaan-lǒng-pìt การหลงผิด

indulgent, *adj.* mòk-mûn หมกมุ่น (given in to); dtaam-jai-dtua ตามใจตัว (allow oneself); òt-ton อดทน (tolerant)

industrial, *adj.* gìao-gàp-ùt-sǎa-hà-gam เกี่ยวกับอุตสาหกรรม

industrialize, *v.* tam-bpen-ùt-sǎa-hà-gam ทำเป็นอุตสาหกรรม

industrious, *adj.* ùt-sǎa-hà อุตสาหะ; kà-yǎn ขยัน

industry, *n.* ùt-sǎa-hà-gam อุตสาหกรรม

inert, *adj.* chʉ̂ai-chaa เฉื่อยชา

inertia, *n.* kwaam-chʉ̂ai ความเฉื่อย

inevitable, *adj.* lìik-lîang-mâi-dâai หลีกเลี่ยงไม่ได้

inexpensive, *adj.* mâi-pɛɛng ไม่แพง

inexperienced, *adj.* mâi-mii-bprà-sòp-gaan ไม่มีประสบการณ์

English · Phonetic · Thai

infamous, *adj.* mii-chûu-sǐang-nai-taang-mâi-dii มีชื่อเสียงในทางไม่ดี

infancy, *n.* wai-taa-rók วัยทารก

infant, *n.* taa-rók ทารก

infantry, *n.* tá-hǎan-râap ทหารราบ

infect, *v.* tam-hâi-dùt-chúa ทำให้ติดเชื้อ

infection, *n.* gaan-dùt-chúa การติดเชื้อ; gaan-dùt-rôok การติดโรค

infectious, *adj.* dùt-chúa ติดเชื้อ; dùt-dtòɔ ติดต่อ

infer, *v.* à-nú-maan อนุมาน (conclude from evidence or premises.); pûut-bpen-nai พูดเป็นนัย (hint)

inference, *n.* gaan-à-nú-maan การอนุมาน; gaan-sà-rùp การสรุป

inferior, *adj.* dɔ̀i-gwàa ด้อยกว่า; leeo-gwàa เลวกว่า

inferiority complex, *n.* bpom-dɔ̀i ปมด้อย

infest, *v.* rang-kwaan รังควาญ; róp-guan รบกวน

infidel, *n.* kon-nɔ̂ɔk-sàat-sà-nǎa คนนอกศาสนา

infidelity, *n.* gaan-nɔ̂ɔk-jai การนอกใจ (to a sexual partner); kwaam-mâi-sûu-sàt ความไม่ซื่อสัตย์ (lack of loyalty)

infiltrate, *v.* sɛ̂ɛk-sum แทรกซึม; sum-pàan ซึมผ่าน

infinite, *adj.* mâi-mii-tîi-sîn-sùt ไม่มีที่สิ้นสุด; mâi-mii-kɔ̀ɔp-kèet ไม่มีขอบเขต

infinity, *n.* kwaam-mâi-mii-tîi-sîn-sùt ความไม่มีที่สิ้นสุด

infirm, *adj.* ɔ̀ɔn-ɛɛ อ่อนแอ (weak); mâi-mân-kong ไม่มันคง (not stable)

inflammation, *n.* gaan-àk-sèep การอักเสบ (infection); gaan-dùt-fai การติดไฟ (state of being inflamed)

inflate, *v.* kà-yǎai ขยาย; tam-hâi-ngən-fɔ́ɔ ทำให้เงินเฟ้อ

inflation, *n.* gaan-kà-yǎai-dtua การขยายตัว (swelling); gaan-pɔɔng-lom การพองลม (filling with air); ngən-fɔ́ɔ เงินเฟ้อ (economics)

inflect, *v.* tam-hâi-ngɔɔ ทำให้งอ (bend); bplìan-sǐng เปลี่ยนเสียง

inflection, *n.* gaan-tam-hâi-ngɔɔ การทำให้งอ; gaan-bplìan-sǐang การเปลี่ยนเสียง (alteration in tone of the voice)

inflict, *v.* long-tôot ลงโทษ

influence, *n.* ìt-tí-pon อิทธิพล

influential, *adj.* mii-ìt-tí-pon-dtɔ̀ɔ มีอิทธิพลต่อ; mii-pǒn-sà-tɔ́ɔn มีผลสะท้อน

influenza, *n.* rôok-kâi-wàt-yài โรคไข้หวัดใหญ่

influx, *n.* gaan-lǎi-kâo การไหลเข้า; gaan-lǎi-ta-lák การไหลทะลัก

inform, *v.* jɛ̂ɛng แจ้ง; bɔ̀ɔk บอก

informal, *adj.* mâi-bpen-taang-gaan ไม่เป็นทางการ; gan-eeng กันเอง

informant, *n.* puu-bɔ̀ɔk ผู้บอก; pûu-jɛ̂ɛng ผู้แจ้ง

information, *n.* kàao-sǎan ข่าวสาร

(news); kɔ̂ɔ-muun ข้อมูล (data);
kwaam-rúu ความรู้ (knowledge)

informative, *adj.* hâi-kɔ̂ɔ-muun
ให้ข้อมูล

infraction, *n.* gaan-tam-hâi-dtɛ̀ɛk
การทำให้แตก (breaking); gaan-lá-
mɔ̂ɔt การละเมิด (violation)

infrared rays, *n.* rang-sǐi-in-fraa-
rèet รังสีอินฟราเรด

infringe, *v.* lá-mɔ̂ɔt ละเมิด; fàa-
fǔun ฝ่าฝืน

infringement, *n.* gaan-lá-mɔ̂ɔt
การละเมิด; gaan-fàa-fǔun
การฝ่าฝืน

infuse, *v.* tee-long เทลง (pour);
chɛ̂ɛ แช่ (soak)

infusion, *n.* gaan-chong การชง;
gaan-chɛ̂ɛ การแช่

ingenious, *adj.* châng-bprà-dìt
ช่างประดิษฐ์ (having an inventive
mind); klɔ̂ng-klɛ̂o คล่องแคล่ว
(clever, adroit)

ingenuity, *n.* kon-châng-kít
คนช่างคิด; sìng-bprà-dìt สิ่งประดิษฐ์

ingenuous, *adj.* dtrong-bpai-dtrong-
maa ตรงไปตรงมา

ingrained, *adj.* fǎng-nɛ̂n ฝังแน่น

ingredient, *n.* sùan-pà-sǒm
ส่วนผสม; sùan-bprà-gɔ̀ɔp
ส่วนประกอบ

inhabit, *v.* aa-sǎi-nai อาศัยใน; yùu-
nai อยู่ใน

inhabitant, *n.* pûu-aa-sǎi ผู้อาศัย;

pon-lá-mɯang พลเมือง

inhale, *v.* hǎai-jai-kâo หายใจเข้า

inherent, *adj.* mii-dtɛ̀ɛ-gam-nə̀ət
มีแต่กำเนิด

inherit, *v.* ráp-chûang รับช่วง (receive
a title); ráp-mɔɔ-ra-dòk รับมรดก
(receive property); sùup-dtɔ̀ɔ สืบต่อ
(receive or take over from a predecessor)

inheritance, *n.* sìng-tîi-sùup-tɔ̂ɔt-
maa สิ่งที่สืบทอดมา

inhibit, *v.* kàt-kwǎang ขัดขวาง;
hâam ห้าม

initial, *n.* àk-sɔ̌ɔn-rɛ̂ɛk-kɔ̌ɔng-chûu
อักษรแรกของชื่อ (first letter of a
proper name)

initiate, *v.* rə̂əm เริ่ม; rí-rə̂əm ริเริ่ม

initiation, *n.* gaan-rí-rə̂əm การริเริ่ม

initiative, *n.* gaan-rí-rə̂əm การริเริ่ม

inject, *v.* chìit-yaa ฉีดยา
(medicine); sɔ̀ɔt-kâo-bpai
สอดเข้าไป (insert)

injection, *n.* gaan-chìit-yaa
การฉีดยา; gaan-sài-kâo-bpai
การใส่เข้าไป

injure, *v.* tam-hâi-bàat-jèp
ทำให้บาดเจ็บ

injured, *v.* bàat-jèp บาดเจ็บ

injury, *n.* gaan-dâai-ráp-bàat-jèp
การได้รับบาดเจ็บ

ink, *n.* mùk หมึก

inkwell, *n.* kùat-mùk ขวดหมึก

inland, *adj.* paai-nai-din-dɛɛn
ภายในดินแดน

inlet, *n.* wɔ́ɔng wɛ́ɛ́ng (narrow passage of water); bpàak-taang ปากทาง (an opening)

inmate, *n.* nák-tôot นักโทษ

inn, *n.* roong-rɛɛm โรงแรม

innate, *adj.* dooi-gam-nə̀ət โดยกำเนิด

inner, *adj.* kâang-nai ข้างใน

inner tube, *n.* yaang-nai-rót-yon ยางในรถยนต์

innocence, *n.* kwaam-rái-diang-sǎa ความไร้เดียงสา; kwaam-bɔɔ-ri-sùt ความบริสุทธิ์

innocent, *adj.* bɔɔ-ri-sùt บริสุทธิ์ (uncorrupted by evil, malice, or wrongdoing; pure); rái-diang-sǎa ไร้เดียงสา (naive, e.g. of a child); mâi-pìt ไม่ผิด (not guilty)

innovate, *v.* tam-sìng-mài ทำสิ่งใหม่; bpràp-bprung ปรับปรุง

innovation, *n.* sìng-bprà-dìt-mài สิ่งประดิษฐ์ใหม่

inoculate, *v.* bplùuk-fǐi ปลูกฝี

input, *v.* bpɔɔn-kɔ̂ɔ-muun ป้อนข้อมูล (data); sài-kâo-bpai ใส่เข้าไป (put something in)

input, *n.* sìng-tîi-bpɔɔn kâo bpai สิ่งที่ป้อนเข้าไป; gaan-bpɔɔn-kɔ̂ɔ-muun การป้อนข้อมูล

inquest, *n.* gaan-sɔ̀ɔp-suan การสอบสวน

inquire, *v.* tǎam ถาม; dtài-tǎam ไต่ถาม

inquiry, *n.* gaan-kɔ̌ɔ การขอ

insane, *adj.* bâa บ้า (crazy); sà-dtì-mâi-dii สติไม่ดี (afflicted with insanity)

insanity, *n.* kwaam-wí-gon-jà-rìt ความวิกลจริต

insect, *n.* má-lɛɛng แมลง

insecticide, *n.* yaa-kâa-má-lɛɛng ยาฆ่าแมลง

insemination, *n.* gaan-tam-hâi-mii-lûuk การทำให้มีลูก

insensitive, *adj.* mâi-rúu-sùk ไม่รู้สึก; dtaai-dâan ตายด้าน

insert, *v.* sài ใส่ (put into); sɔ̀ɔt สอด (put into; e.g. the body); sɛ̂ɛk แทรก (put in between)

insertion, *n.* gaan-sɔ̀ɔt-sài การสอดใส่; gaan-sɔ̀ɔt-sɛ̂ɛk การสอดแทรก

inside, *n.* kâang-nai ข้างใน

insidious, *adj.* lɔ̀ɔk-luang หลอกลวง (treacherous, deceiving); ɛ̀ɛp-fɛɛng แอบแฝง (hidden)

insight, *n.* gaan-kâo-jai-lúk-súng การเข้าใจลึกซึ้ง

insignificant, *adj.* mâi-sǎm-kan ไม่สำคัญ

insincere, *adj.* mâi-jing-jai ไม่จริงใจ

insist, *v.* yuun-graan ยืนกราน (stand one's ground); rîak-rɔ́ɔng เรียกร้อง (demand)

insistence, *n.* gaan-yuun-graan การยืนกราน

insistent, *adj.* hǔa-rán หัวรั้น

insomnia, *n.* rôok-nɔɔn-mâi-làp โรคนอนไม่หลับ

inspect, *v.* dtrùat-sɔ̀ɔp ตรวจสอบ

inspection, *n.* gaan-dtrùat-sɔ̀ɔp การตรวจสอบ

inspector, *n.* pûu-dtrùat ผู้ตรวจ

inspiration, *n.* rɛɛng-ban-daan-jai แรงบันดาลใจ

inspire, *v.* ban-daan-jai บันดาลใจ

instability, *n.* kwaam-mâi-mân-kong ความไม่มั่นคง

install, *v.* dtìt-dtâng ติดตั้ง

instance, *n.* gɔɔ-ra-nii กรณี (case); dtua-yàang ตัวอย่าง (example)

instant, *n.* tan-tii ทันที

instead, *adv.* tɛɛn แทน; tɛɛn-tîi แทนที่

instinct, *n.* sǎn-châat-(dtà)-yaan สัญชาตญาณ

instinctive, *adj.* gìao-gàp-sǎn-châat-(dtà)-yaan เกี่ยวกับสัญชาตญาณ

institute, *n.* sà-tǎa-ban สถาบัน

institution, *n.* sà-tǎa-ban สถาบัน; nùai-ngaan หน่วยงาน

instruct, *v.* sɔ̌ɔn สอน; né-nam แนะนำ

instruction, *n.* gaan-sɔ̌ɔn การสอน; gaan-né-nam การแนะนำ

instructor, *n.* pûu-sɔ̌ɔn ผู้สอน

instrument, *n.* ùp-bpà-gɔɔn อุปกรณ์ (device); krûang-muu เครื่องมือ (tool); krûang-don-dtrii เครื่องดนตรี (musical)

insulation, *n.* wat-sà-dù-tam-chà-nǔan วัสดุทำฉนวน (material); gaan-tam-chà-nǔan การทำฉนวน (act of insulating)

insulator, *n.* chà-nǔan ฉนวน

insulin, *n.* in-suu-lin อินซูลิน

insult, *v.* duu-tùuk ดูถูก (look down); yìat-yǎam เหยียดหยาม (contempt)

insult, *n.* gaan-duu-tùuk การดูถูก; gaan-yìat-yǎam การเหยียดหยาม

insurance, *n.* gaan-bprà-gan-pai การประกันภัย

insure, *v.* bprà-gan ประกัน

intact, *adj.* mâi-bplìan-bplɛɛng ไม่เปลี่ยนแปลง; mâi-sùam ไม่เสื่อม

integral, *adj.* táng-mòt ทั้งหมด; sǒm-buun สมบูรณ์

integrate, *v.* rûap-ruam รวบรวม

integrity, *n.* gaan-yút-làk-kun-na-tam การยึดหลักคุณธรรม (adherence to a moral or ethical code); kwaam-bpen-nùng-diao ความเป็นหนึ่งเดียว (condition of being whole)

intellect, *n.* sà-dtì-bpan-yaa สติปัญญา (ability to learn and reason); pûu-mii-bpan-yaa-sǔung ผู้มีปัญญาสูง (person of great intellectual ability)

intellectual, *n.* gaan-chái-bpan-yaa การใช้ปัญญา; pûu-mii-bpan-yaa ผู้มีปัญญา

intelligence, *n.* kwaam-chà-lǐao-chà-làat ความเฉลียวฉลาด

intelligent, *adj.* chà-lǐao-chà-làat เฉลียวฉลาด

intelligible, *adj.* kâo-jai-dâai เข้าใจได้

intend, *v.* dtâng-jai ตั้งใจ; mii-jèet-dtà-naa มีเจตนา

intense, *adj.* kêm-kôn เข้มข้น (extreme in degree, strength); lúk-súng ลึกซึ้ง (profound)

intensify, *v.* tam-hâi-run-rɛɛng-kûn ทำให้รุนแรงขึ้น

intensity, *n.* kwaam-kêm-kôn ความเข้มข้น; kwaam-run-rɛɛng ความรุนแรง

intensive, *adj.* kêm-kôn เข้มข้น

intent, *n.* jèet-dtà-naa เจตนา; kwaam-dtâng-jai ความตั้งใจ

intention, *n.* jèet-dtà-naa เจตนา; kwaam-dtâng-jai ความตั้งใจ

intentional, *adj.* dooi-jèet-dtà-naa โดยเจตนา; sûng-dtâng-jai ซึ่งตั้งใจ

interchange, *v.* lɛ̂ɛk-bplìan-gan แลกเปลี่ยนกัน

interchange, *n.* jùt-dtàt-gan จุดตัดกัน

interchangeable, *adj.* lɛ̂ɛk-bplìan-gan-dâai แลกเปลี่ยนกันได้

intercourse, *n.* gaan-dtìt-dtɔ̀ɔ-gan การติดต่อกัน (communications); gaan-rûam-bprà-wee-nii การร่วมประเวณี (sexual)

interest, *n.* kwaam-sǒn-jai ความสนใจ (a state of curiosity); dɔ̀ɔk-bîa ดอกเบี้ย (a charge for a loan)

interesting, *adj.* nâa-sǒn-jai น่าสนใจ

interface, *n.* jùt-chûam-dtɔ̀ɔ จุดเชื่อมต่อ; sùan-dtôo-dtɔ̀ɔp ส่วนโค้ตอบ

interfere, *v.* sɛ̂ɛk-sɛɛng แทรกแซง (intervene); yûng ยุ่ง (meddle)

interference, *n.* gaan-sɛ̂ɛk-sɛɛng การแทรกแซง; gaan-róp-guan การรบกวน

interim, *n.* chûang-wee-laa-yùt-pák ช่วงเวลาหยุดพัก; rà-wàang-wee-laa ระหว่างเวลา

interior, *n.* sùan-nai ส่วนใน

interior, *adj.* paai-nai ภายใน

interjection, *n.* gaan-pûut-sɔ̀ɔt-kûn การพูดสอดขึ้น (sudden, short utterance); kam-ù-taan คำอุทาน (part of speech)

intermediary, *n.* kon-glaang คนกลาง (mediator); sùu-nam สื่อนำ (an agent between persons or things)

intermediate, *adj.* bpaan-glaang ปานกลาง; yùu-rá-dàp-glaang อยู่ระดับกลาง

intermission, *n.* gaan-yùt-pák การหยุดพัก

intern, *n.* nák-sùk-sàa-fùk-hàt นักศึกษาฝึกหัด

internal, *adj.* paai-nai ภายใน

international, *adj.* rá-wàang-bprà-têet ระหว่างประเทศ

interpret, *v.* bplɛɛ แปล; dtii-kwaam ตีความ

interpretation, *n.* gaan-bplɛɛ การแปล

interpreter, *n.* lâam ล่าม

interrogate, *v.* sɔ̀ɔp-tǎam สอบถาม; sák-tǎam ซักถาม

interrogation, *n.* gaan-sɔ̀ɔp-tǎam การสอบถาม

interrupt, *v.* kàt-jang-wà ขัดจังหวะ (break the continuity); yùt หยุด (hinder or stop)

interruption, *n.* gaan-yùt-chá-ngák การหยุดชะงัก; gaan-kàt-jang-wà การขัดจังหวะ

intersect, *v.* dtàt-gan ตัดกัน

intersection, *n.* chum-taang ชุมทาง (place where things intersect); sìi-yɛ̂ɛk สี่แยก (four-way intersection)

intertwine, *v.* tam-hâi-pan-gan ทำให้พันกัน; pan-gan พันกัน

interval, *n.* rá-yá-wee-laa ระยะเวลา (amount of time); chûang-hàang ช่วงห่าง (space between two objects)

intervene, *v.* sɛ̂ɛk-sɛɛng แทรกแซง; gâao-gàai ก้าวก่าย

intervention, *n.* gaan-sɛ̂ɛk-sɛɛng การแทรกแซง; gaan-gâao-gàai การก้าวก่าย

interview, *n.* gaan-sǎm-pâat การสัมภาษณ์

intestine, *n.* lam-sâi ลำไส้

intimacy, *n.* kwaam-kún-kəəi ความคุ้นเคย; kwaam-sà-nìt-sà-nǒm ความสนิทสนม

intimate, *n.* pûan-sà-nìt เพื่อนสนิท

intimidate, *v.* tam-hâi-glua ทำให้กลัว (make timid); kùu ขู่ (threaten); kúk-kaam คุกคาม (coerce)

into, *prep.* kâo-bpai เข้าไป; sùu สู่; bpai-yang ไปยัง

intolerable, *adj.* sùt-tîi-jà-ton-dâai สุดที่จะทนได้

intolerant, *adj.* ton-mâi-dâai ทนไม่ได้

intonation, *n.* sǐang-sǔung-dtàm เสียงสูงต่ำ

intoxicate, *v.* tam-hâi-mʉn-mao ทำให้มึนเมา

intoxication, *n.* kwaam-mʉn-mao ความมึนเมา

intravenous, *adj.* paai-nai-lɔ̀ɔt-lûat-dam ภายในหลอดเลือดดำ

intrepid, *adj.* mâi-glua ไม่กลัว; glâa กล้า

intricate, *adj.* sàp-sɔ̌n สับสน; yâak-tîi-jà-kâo-jai ยากที่จะเข้าใจ

intrigue, *v.* waang-ù-baai วางอุบาย (engage in secret plots)

intriguing, *adj.* ráo-kwaam-sǒn-jai เร้าความสนใจ

intrinsic, *adj.* paai-nai ภายใน (within); dooi-tam-ma-châat

โดยธรรมชาติ (of essential nature)

introduce, v. né-nam แนะนำ

introduction, n. gaan-né-nam
การแนะนำ; bòt-nam บทนำ

introvert, n. pûu-mâi-chɔ̂ɔp-kâo-
sǎng-kom ผู้ไม่ชอบเข้าสังคม

intrude, v. bùk-rúk บุกรุก; lûang-
lám ล่วงล้ำ

intruder, n. pûu-bùk-rúk ผู้บุกรุก;
pûu-lûang-lám ผู้ล่วงล้ำ

intuition, n. sǎn-châat-(dtà)-yaan
สัญชาตญาณ

invade, v. bùk-rúk บุกรุก; rúk-raan
รุกราน

invader, n. pûu-bùk-rúk ผู้บุกรุก;
pûu-rúk-raan ผู้รุกราน

invalid, adj. chái-gaan-mâi-dâai
ใช้การไม่ได้; mâi-mii-pǒn-bang-káp
ไม่มีผลบังคับ

invalid, n. kon-pí-gaan คนพิการ
(one who is incapacitated); kon-
bpùiai คนป่วย (bedridden person)

invariable, adj. mâi-bplìan-bplɛɛng
ไม่เปลี่ยนแปลง; kong-tîi คงที่

invasion, n. gaan-rúk-raan
การรุกราน

invent, v. bprà-dìt ประดิษฐ์; sâang-
sǎn สร้างสรรค์

invention, n. sìng-bprà-dìt
สิ่งประดิษฐ์; gaan-sâang-sǎn
การสร้างสรรค์

inventor, n. nák-bprà-dìt
นักประดิษฐ์

inventory, n. raai-gaan-sìng-kɔ̌ɔng
รายการสิ่งของ; raai-gaan-sǐn-káa
รายการสินค้า

inverse, adj. glàp-gan กลับกัน;
dtrong-gan-kâam ตรงกันข้าม

invert, v. glàp กลับ; plík-glàp
พลิกกลับ; sàp-bplìan สับเปลี่ยน

invest, v. long-tun ลงทุน

investigate, v. sùep-sǔan สืบสวน;
sɔ̀ɔp-sǔan สอบสวน

investigation, n. gaan-sùep-sǔan
การสืบสวน

investigator, n. pûu-sùep-sǔan
ผู้สืบสวน

investment, n. gaan-long-tun
การลงทุน

investor, n. nák-long-tun นักลงทุน

invincible, adj. ao-chá-ná-mâi-dâai
เอาชนะไม่ได้

invisible, adj. mɔɔng-mâi-hěn
มองไม่เห็น

invitation, n. gaan-chúa-chəən
การเชื้อเชิญ (act of inviting); bàt-
chəən บัตรเชิญ (card)

invite, v. chəən เชิญ

invoice, n. bai-sòng-kɔ̌ɔng
ใบส่งของ (detailed list of goods);
bai-gèp-ngən ใบเก็บเงิน (bill)

invoke, v. rîak เรียก (call on);
bplùk ปลุก (wake); kɔ̌ɔ-kwaam-
yú-dtì-tam ขอความยุติธรรม (call
for earnestly)

involve, v. ruam-táng ร่วมทั้ง
(include); pua-pan พัวพัน (con-

nect)

involvement, *n.* gaan-gìao-pan
การเกี่ยวพัน

iodine, *n.* săan-ai-oo-diin
สารไอโอดีน

I.O.U., *n.* làk-tăan-gaan-yuum-ngən
หลักฐานการยืมเงิน

I.Q., *n.* ai-kiu ไอคิว

Iran, *n.* bprà-têet-ì-ràan
ประเทศอิหร่าน

Iraq, *n.* bprà-têet-ì-rák ประเทศอิรัก

irate, *adj.* gròot โกรธ; dùat-daan
เดือดดาล

ire, *n.* kwaam-gròot ความโกรธ

Ireland, *n.* bprà-têet-ai-lɛɛn
ประเทศไอร์แลนด์

iridescent, *adj.* mii-sɛ̌ɛng-wâap
มีแสงวาบ

iris, *n.* mâan-dtaa ม่านตา (of the
eye); dɔ̀ɔk-ai-rít ดอกไอริส (flower)

irk, *v.* róp-guan รบกวน; tam-hâi-rá-
kaai-kuang ทำให้ระคายเคือง

iron, *v.* rîit-pâa รีดผ้า

iron, *n.* lèk เหล็ก; tâat-lèk
ธาตุเหล็ก

ironic, *adj.* bprà-chót ประชด (using
words to express something different
from their literal meaning); dtrong-
kâam-gàp-tîi-kâat-wái ตรงข้ามกับ
ที่คาดไว้ (contrary to what was
expected)

irony, *n.* gaan-bprà-chót การประชด

irrational, *adj.* rái-hèet-pŏn
ไร้เหตุผล

irreconcilable, *adj.* kuun-dii-gan-
mâi-dâai คืนดีกันไม่ได้ (impossible
to reconcile)

irregular, *adj.* mâi-sà-màm-sà-mǝ̌ǝ
ไม่สม่ำเสมอ

irrelevant, *adj.* mâi-săm-pan
ไม่สัมพันธ์; mâi-sɔ̀ɔt-klɔ́ɔng
ไม่สอดคล้อง

irreparable, *adj.* gɛ̂ɛ-kăi-mâi-dâai
แก้ไขไม่ได้; sɔ̂m-mâi-dâai ซ่อมไม่ได้

irresistible, *adj.* dtâan-taan-mâi-
dâai ต้านทานไม่ได้

irresponsible, *adj.* mâi-mii-
kwaam-ráp-pìt-chɔ̂ɔp
ไม่มีความรับผิดชอบ

irrigation, *n.* gaan-chon-la-bprà-
taan การชลประทาน

irritate, *v.* tam-hâi-gròot-kuang
ทำให้โกรธเคือง (provoke anger);
róp-guan รบกวน (bother, annoy)

Islam, *n.* sàat-sà-năa-ìt-sà-laam
ศาสนาอิสลาม

island, *n.* gɔ̀ เกาะ

islander, *n.* chaao-gɔ̀ ชาวเกาะ

isolate, *v.* yɛ̂ɛk-ɔ̀ɔk แยกออก;
bplìik-dtua ปลีกตัว

isolation, *n.* gaan-yɛ̂ɛk-ɔ̀ɔk
การแยกออก; gaan-bplìik-dtua
การปลีกตัว

Israel, *n.* bprà-têet-ìt-sà-raa-eeo
ประเทศอิสราเอล

Israeli, *n.* gìao-gàp-bprà-têet-ìt-sà-
raa-eeo เกี่ยวกับประเทศอิสราเอล
(relating to Israel)

issuance, *n.* gaan-ɔ̀ɔk-kam-sàng
การออกคำสั่ง

issue, *v.* ɔ̀ɔk ออก (go out or come
out); jàt-pim จัดพิมพ์ (publish)

issue, *n.* chà-bàp ฉบับ (of printed
matter); bpan-hǎa ปัญหา (problem); rûang เรื่อง (matter)

it, *pron.* man มัน

Italian, *n.* chaao-ì-dtaa-lîi ชาวอิตาลี
(people); paa-sǎa-ì-dtaa-lîi
ภาษาอิตาลี (language)

italic, *n.* dtua-iang ตัวเอียง

italicize, *v.* pim-dtua-iang
พิมพ์ตัวเอียง

Italy, *n.* bprà-têet-ì-dtaa-lîi
ประเทศอิตาลี

itch, *n.* aa-gaan-kan อาการคัน

itchy, *adj.* kan คัน

item, *n.* sìng สิ่ง (thing); an อัน
(single article or unit); raai-gaan
รายการ (entry in an account)

itemize, *v.* long-raai-gaam
ลงรายการ

itinerary, *n.* raai-lá-ìat-sên-taang
รายละเอียดเส้นทาง

its, *adj.* kɔ̌ɔng-man ของมัน

itself, *pron.* dtua-man-eeng
ตัวมันเอง

ivory, *n.* ngaa-cháang งาช้าง (elephant tusk); sǐi-ngaa-cháang
สีงาช้าง (color)

ivy, *n.* dtôn-kláai-dtam-lung
ต้นคล้ายตำลึง (climbing or trailing
evergreen plants)

J

jab, *v.* tɛɛng แทง; tîm ทิ่ม

jab, *n.* gaan-tɛɛng การแทง; gaan-
tîm การทิ่ม

jabber, *v.* pûut-rua พูดรัว (talk rapidly); pûut-mâi-mii-sǎa-rá
พูดไม่มีสาระ (utter unintelligibly)

jack, *n.* mɛ̂ɛ-rɛɛng แม่แรง; bpân-
jàn ปั้นจั่น (device for raising heavy
objects); bplák ปลั๊ก (socket)

jackass, *n.* kon-ngôo คนโง่; kon-
tîm คนทิ่ม

jacket, *n.* sûa-nɔ̂ɔk เสื้อนอก; sûa-
jék-gêt เสื้อแจ็คเก็ต

jackknife, *n.* mîit-páp-kà-nàat-yài
มีดพับขนาดใหญ่

jade, *n.* yòk หยก

jagged, *adj.* bpen-lìam-lɛ̌ɛm
เป็นเหลี่ยมแหลม

jail, *n.* kúk คุก

jam, *v.* àt อัด (fill to overflowing);
bìat เบียด (pack to excess)

jam, *n.* gaan-àt การอัด; gaan-bìat
การเบียด; yɛɛm แยม (a preserve
made from whole fruit); jà-raa-jɔɔn-
dtìt-kàt จราจรติดขัด (traffic jam);
jùt-tîi-bìat-gan-nɛ̂n จุดที่เบียดกันแน่น
(a tight spot)

janitor, *n.* paan-roong ภารโรง

January, *n.* duan-mók-gà-raa-kom
เดือนมกราคม

Japan, *n.* bprà-têet-yîi-bpùn

ประเทศญี่ปุ่น

Japanese, *n.* chaao-yîi-bpùn ชาวญี่ปุ่น (people); paa-sǎa-yîi-bpùn ภาษาญี่ปุ่น (language); gìao-gàp-yîi-bpùn เกี่ยวกับญี่ปุ่น (relating to Japan)

jar, *n.* grà-bpùk กระปุก (e.g. cookie); òong โอ่ง (large water container)

jargon, *n.* paa-sǎa-chà-pó-glùm ภาษาเฉพาะกลุ่ม

jaundice, *n.* rôok-dii-sâan โรคดีซ่าน

jaunt, *n.* gaan-dəən-taang-nai-ra-yá-sân การเดินทางในระยะสั้น

jaw, *n.* graam กราม; kǎa-gan-grai ขากรรไกร

jealous, *adj.* hǔng หึง (between lovers); ìt-chǎa อิจฉา (envious)

jealousy, *n.* kwaam-ìt-chǎa ความอิจฉา; kwaam-hǔng-hǔang ความหึงหวง

jeans, *n.* gaang-geeng-yiin กางเกงยีนส์ (pants); pâa-yiin ผ้ายีนส์ (denim cloth)

jeep, *n.* rót-jíip รถจี๊ป

jeer, *v.* hǔa-ró-yó หัวเราะเยาะ

jelly, *n.* wún วุ้น

jellyfish, *n.* mɛɛng-gà-prun แมงกะพรุน

jeopardize, *v.* tam-ráai ทำร้าย; tam-an-dtà-raai ทำอันตราย

jeopardy, *n.* an-dtà-raai อันตราย; pai ภัย

jerk, *v.* grà-dtùk กระตุก (twitch); grà-châak กระชาก (sudden pull)

jerk, *n.* gaan-grà-dtùk การกระตุก; gaan-grà-châak การกระชาก; âi-sôo ไอ้เซ่อ (a dumb person)

jest, *n.* kam-pûut-lóo-lên คำพูดล้อเล่น (teasing remark); rûang-kòp-kǎn เรื่องขบขัน (joke)

jester, *n.* dtua-dtà-lòk ตัวตลก; kon-pûut-dtà-lòk คนพูดตลก

jet, *n.* krûang-yon-jét เครื่องยนต์เจ็ท

jetty, *n.* tâa-rua ท่าเรือ (pier)

Jew, *n.* chaao-yiu ชาวยิว

jewel, *n.* pét-plooi เพชรพลอย (gem); kǒong-mii-kâa ของมีค่า (precious thing)

jeweler, *n.* pôo-káa-plooi พ่อค้าพลอย; châng-tam-plooi ช่างทำพลอย

jewelry, *n.* pét-plooi เพชรพลอย

Jewish, *adj.* gìao-gàp-yiu เกี่ยวกับยิว

jigsaw puzzle, *n.* geem-dtòo-chín-sùan-pâap เกมต่อชิ้นส่วนภาพ

jilt, *v.* tíng ทิ้ง; sà-làt สลัด

jingle, *n.* sǐang-grúng-grìng เสียงกรุ๊งกริ๊ง

job, *n.* ngaan งาน

jockey, *n.* nák-kèng-máa นักแข่งม้า

jog, *v.* wîng-yó-yó วิ่งเหยาะๆ; wîng วิ่ง

join, *v.* chûam เชื่อม (connect); dtòo ต่อ (make continuous; bring together); kâo-rûam เข้าร่วม (participate); ruam รวม (merge)

joint, *n.* kɔ̂ɔ-dtɔ̀ɔ ข้อต่อ

joke, *v.* lɔ́ɔ-lên ล้อเล่น (tease); pûut-dtà-lòk พูดตลก (speak in fun)

joke, *n.* dtà-lòk ตลก

jolly, *adj.* rûun-rəəng รื่นเริง; sà-nùk-sà-nǎan สนุกสนาน

jolt, *n.* gaan-sàn-wǎi การสั่นไหว (shakiness); kwaam-pâai-pɛ́ɛ ความพ่ายแพ้ (defeat)

jostle, *v.* grà-têɛk กระแทก (push and shove); plàk-dan ผลักดัน (push hard)

jot down, *v.* jòt-ban-tʉ́k จดบันทึก

journal, *n.* waa-ra-sǎan วารสาร (e.g. magazine); ban-tʉ́k-raai-wan บันทึกรายวัน (diary)

journalism, *n.* waa-ra-sǎan-sàat วารสารศาสตร์

journalist, *n.* nák-nǎng-sʉ̌ʉ-pim นักหนังสือพิมพ์

journey, *v.* gaan-dəən-taang การเดินทาง

jovial, *adj.* bə̀ək-baan เบิกบาน; rɑ̂a-rəəng ร่าเริง

jowl, *n.* nʉ́ang เหนียง

joy, *n.* kwaam-yin-dii ความยินดี; kwaam-dii-jai ความดีใจ

joyful, *adj.* yin-dii ยินดี; dii-òk-dii-jai ดีอกดีใจ

jubilant, *adj.* bplʉ́ʉm-bpì-dtì ปลื้มปีติ; rɑ̂a-rəəng ร่าเริง

jubilee, *n.* gaan-chà-lɔ̌ɔng-króp-rɔ̂ɔp-hâa-sìp-bpii การฉลองครบรอบ ๕๐ ปี (celebration for a 50th anniversary); gaan-chà-lɔ̌ɔng-rʉ̂ʉn-rəəng การฉลองรื่นเริง (festival)

Judaism, *n.* sàat-sà-nǎa-yiu ศาสนายิว

judge, *v.* pí-pâak-sǎa พิพากษา; dtàt-sǐn ตัดสิน

judge, *n.* gam-ma-gaan กรรมการ (in a contest); pûu-pí-pâak-sǎa ผู้พิพากษา (in court)

judgment, *n.* gaan-dtàt-sǐn การตัดสิน (in a contest); kam-pí-pâak-sǎa คำพิพากษา (in court)

judicial, *adj.* gìao-gàp-sǎan-yút-dtì-tam เกี่ยวกับศาลยุติธรรม

judicious, *adj.* rɔ̂ɔp-kɔ̂ɔp รอบคอบ; sù-kǔm สุขุม

judo, *n.* gii-laa-yuu-doo กีฬายูโด

jug, *n.* yʉ̀ak เหยือก

juice, *n.* náam-pǒn-la-máai น้ำผลไม้

juicy, *adj.* mii-náam มีน้ำ; chàm ฉ่ำ

July, *n.* gà-rák-gà-daa-kom กรกฎาคม

jumble, *v.* bpon-bpee ปนเป

jump, *v.* grà-dòot กระโดด

jumpy, *adj.* lôot-dtên โลดเต้น

junction, *n.* chum-taang ชุมทาง; gaan-bprà-sǎan การประสาน

juncture, *n.* jùt-chʉ̂am จุดเชื่อม; wí-grìt-dtà-gaan วิกฤตการณ์

June, *n.* mí-tù-naa-yon มิถุนายน

jungle, *n.* bpàa-túp ป่าทึบ

junior, *n.* ɔ̀ɔn-aa-wú-sŏo
อ่อนอาวุโส; aa-yú-nɔ́ɔi-gwàa
อายุน้อยกว่า

junk, *n.* kà-yà ขยะ

jurisdiction, *n.* am-nâat-sǎan
อำนาจศาล

juror, *n.* lûuk-kǔn ลูกขุน

jury, *n.* ka-ná-lûuk-kǔn คณะลูกขุน

just, *adj., adv.,* yú-dtì-tam ยุติธรรม
(fair); tâo-nán เท่านั้น (only)

justice, *n.* kwaam-yú-dtì-tam
ความยุติธรรม

justification, *n.* gaan-pi-sùut-wâa-
tùuk-dtɔ̂ng การพิสูจน์ว่าถูกต้อง

justify, *v.* pi-sùut-wâa-tùuk-dtɔ̂ng
พิสูจน์ว่าถูกต้อง

juvenile, *adj.* gìao-gàp-dèk-lé-yao-
wa-chon เกี่ยวกับเด็กและเยาวชน

juxtapose, *v.* waang-kâang-kâang
วางข้างๆ

K

kangaroo, *n.* jing-jôo จิงโจ้

karate, *n.* kaa-raa-dtêe คาราเต้

Karen, *n.* gà-rìang กะเหรี่ยง (a hill
tribe)

keen, *adj.* kom คม (sharp); lɛ̌ɛm
แหลม (pointed); wai-mâak ไวมาก
(very quick)

keep, *v.* gèp เก็บ; rák-sǎa รักษา

keepsake, *n.* sìng-dtʉan-jai

สิ่งเตือนใจ

keg, *n.* tǎng-lék ถังเล็ก

kennel, *n.* kɔ̂ɔk-sù-nák คอกสุนัข

kept woman, *n.* mia-gèp เมียเก็บ

kerchief, *n.* pâa-pôok-hǔa
ผ้าโพกหัว

kernel, *n.* nʉ́a-nai-pǒn-la-máai-
bplʉ̀ak-kɛ̌ng เนื้อในผลไม้เปลือกแข็ง
(of a nut); gèn แก่น (core)

kerosene, *n.* náam-man-gáat
น้ำมันก๊าซ

ketchup, *n.* sɔ́ɔt-má-kʉ̌a-têet
ซอสมะเขือเทศ

kettle, *n.* gaa-dtôm-náam กาต้มน้ำ

key, *n.* gun-jɛɛ กุญแจ

key, *adj.* sǎm-kan สำคัญ

keyboard, *n.* kii-bɔ̀ɔt คีย์บอร์ด;
bpɛn-pim แป้นพิมพ์

key ring, *n.* puang-gun-jɛɛ
พวงกุญแจ

kick, *v.* dtè เตะ; tìip ถีบ

kid, *n.* dèk เด็ก; lûuk ลูก

kidnap, *v.* lák-paa-dtua ลักพาตัว

kidnapper, *n.* joon-lák-paa-dtua
โจรลักพาตัว

kidnapping, *n.* gaan-lák-paa-dtua
การลักพาตัว

kidney, *n.* dtai ไต

kill, *v.* kâa ฆ่า; sǎng-hǎan สังหาร

killer, *n.* nák-kâa นักฆ่า

killing, *n.* gaan-kâa การฆ่า

kill-joy, *n.* pûu-tam-laai-kwaam-
sùk-kon-ʉ̀ʉn ผู้ทำลายความสุขคนอื่น

English · Phonetic · Thai

kilogram, n. gì-loo-gram กิโลกรัม

kilohertz, n. gì-loo-hə́ət กิโลเฮิร์ซ

kilometer, n. gì-loo-méet กิโลเมตร

kilowatt, n. gì-loo-wàt กิโลวัตต์

kin, n. yâat ญาติ

kind, adj. jai-dii ใจดี

kindergarten, n. roong-rian-à-nú-baan โรงเรียนอนุบาล

kindle, v. gɔ̀ɔ-fai ก่อไฟ (make a fire); ráo-aa-rom เร้าอารมณ์ (arouse)

kindly, adv. yàang-gà-ru-naa อย่างกรุณา; yàang-ɔ̀ɔn-yoon อย่างอ่อนโยน

kindness, n kwaam-gà-ru-naa ความกรุณา; kwaam-mêet-dtaa ความเมตตา

kindred, adj. gìao-gàp-yâat-pîi-nɔ́ɔng เกี่ยวกับญาติพี่น้อง

king, n. gà-sàt กษัตริย์; prá-raa-chaa พระราชา

kingdom, n. râat-chá-aa-naa-jàk ราชอาณาจักร

king-size, adj. kà-nàat-yài ขนาดใหญ่

kinship, n. kwaam-bpen-yâat-mít ความเป็นญาติมิตร

kiosk, n. pɛ̌ɛng-kǎai-nǎng-sǔu-pim แผงขายหนังสือพิมพ์

kiss, n., v. jùup จูบ

kit, n. chút-krûang-muu ชุดเครื่องมือ

kitchen, n. hɔ̂ng-krua ห้องครัว

kite, n. wâo ว่าว

kitten, n. lûuk-mɛɛo ลูกแมว

knapsack, n. bpêe เป้

knead, v. nûat นวด; bpân ปั้น

knee, n. hǔa-kào หัวเข่า

kneecap, v. sà-bâa-kào สะบ้าเข่า

kneel, v. kúk-kào-long คุกเข่าลง

knickknack, n. ngang-lék-lék-nɔ́ɔi-nɔ́ɔi เรื่องเล็กๆน้อยๆ

knife, n. mîit มีด

knight, n. àt-sà-win อัศวิน

knit, v. tàk ถัก

knitting, n. gaan-tàk การถัก

knob, n. lûuk-bìt ลูกบิด; bpùm ปุ่ม

knock, v. kɔ́ เคาะ

knock, n. gaan-kɔ́ การเคาะ (act of knocking); sǐang-kɔ́ เสียงเคาะ (sound of knocking)

knot, n. bpom ปม; nguan เงื่อน

know, v. rúu รู้; sâap ทราบ

know-how, n. kwaam-cham-naan ความชำนาญ

know-it-all, n. kon-tîi-rúu-bpai-mòt คนที่รู้ไปหมด

knowledge, n. kwaam-rúu ความรู้

knuckle, n. kɔ̂ɔ-níu-muu ข้อนิ้วมือ

Korea, n. bprà-têet-gao-lǐi ประเทศเกาหลี

Korean, n., adj., chaao-gao-lǐi ชาวเกาหลี (people); paa-sǎa-gao-lǐi ภาษาเกาหลี (language); gìao-gàp-gao-lǐi เกี่ยวกับเกาหลี (relating to Korea)

English · Phonetic · Thai

L

label, *n.* chà-làak ฉลาก; bpâai ป้าย

labor, *v.* tam-ngaan ทำงาน (work); klɔ̂ɔt-lûuk คลอดลูก (deliver a baby)

laboratory, *n.* hɔ̂ng-tót-lɔɔng ห้องทดลอง

laborer, *n.* gam-ma-gɔɔn กรรมกร

laborious, *adj.* chái-rɛɛng-mâak ใช้แรงมาก

labor union, *n.* sà-hà-pâap-rɛɛng-ngaan สหภาพแรงงาน

labyrinth, *n.* kǎo-wong-gòt เขาวงกต

lace, *n.* sǎai-tàk สายถัก; laai-chà-lù ลายฉลุ

lacerate, *v.* chìik ฉีก (rip, tear)

laceration, *n.* gaan-chìik-kàat การฉีกขาด

lack, *v.* kàat-klɛɛn ขาดแคลน

lack, *n.* gaan-kàat-klɛɛn การขาดแคลน

lacquer, *n.* náam-yaa-lék-gɔ̂ɔ น้ำยาแลคเกอร์

lad, *n.* dèk-nùm เด็กหนุ่ม

ladder, *n.* ban-dai บันได

ladle, *n.* táp-pii ทัพพี

lady, *n.* sù-pâap-sà-dtrii สุภาพสตรี; kun-pûu-yǐng คุณผู้หญิง

ladybug, *n.* má-lɛɛng-dtào-tɔɔng แมลงเต่าทอง

lag, *v.* láa ล้า (weaken); yùu-lǎng อยู่หลัง (fall behind)

Lahu, *n.* muu-sɔɔ มูเซอ (hill tribe)

lake, *n.* tá-lee-sàap ทะเลสาบ

lamb, *n.* gɛ̀ แกะ

lame, *adj.* pí-gaan พิการ (disabled); chái-mâi-dâai ใช้ไม่ได้ (not usable)

lament, *n.* kwaam-sòok-sǎo ความโศกเศร้า

lamp, *n.* koom-fai โคมไฟ; dtà-giang ตะเกียง

lance, *n.* hɔ̀ɔk หอก; lǎao หลาว

land, *n.* tîi-din ที่ดิน (property); pèn-din แผ่นดิน (solid ground of the earth, nation, country)

land, *v.* long-sùu-pɯ́ɯn-din ลงสู่พื้นดิน (e.g. an airplane); kɯ̂n-bòk ขึ้นบก (disembark)

landing, *n.* gaan-long-sùu-pɯ́ɯn-din การลงสู่พื้นดิน; gaan-kɯ̂n-bòk การขึ้นบก

landlady, *n.* jâo-kɔɔng-tîi-din-yǐng เจ้าของที่ดินหญิง

landlord, *n.* jâo-kɔɔng-tîi-din-chaai เจ้าของที่ดินชาย

landmark, *n.* làk-kèet-tîi-din หลักเขตที่ดิน; krɯ̂ang-mǎai-chíi-bòng เครื่องหมายชี้บ่ง

landscape, *n.* puum-mí-tát ภูมิทัศน์

landslide, *n.* din-tà-lòm ดินถล่ม

lane, *n.* sɔɔi ซอย; dtrɔ̀ɔk ตรอก

language, *n.* paa-sǎa ภาษา

lantern, *n.* koom-fai โคมไฟ; bpó โป๊ะ

English · Phonetic · Thai

lap, *n.* dtàk ตัก

lapel, *n.* bpòk-kɔɔ-bɛ̀-kɔ̌ɔng-sûa ปกคอแบะของเสื้อ

lapse, *n.* gaan-plâat-pláng การพลาดพลั้ง (a slip, failure); gaan-lá-ləəi การละเลย (neglect); rá-yá-wee-laa-tîi-pàan-bpai ระยะเวลาที่ผ่านไป (period of time)

laptop, *n.* kon-píu-dtə̂ə-bɛ̀ɛp-hîu คอมพิวเตอร์แบบหิ้ว

lard, *n.* náam-man-mǔu น้ำมันหมู

large, *adj.* yài ใหญ่; gwâang-kwǎang กว้างขวาง

large-scale, *adj.* yàang-mâak อย่างมาก; sùan-yài ส่วนใหญ่

lark, *n.* gaan-lên-sà-nùk การเล่นสนุก (carefree play)

larva, *n.* dàk-dɛ̂ɛ ดักแด้; dtua-nɔ̌ɔn ตัวหนอน

larynx, *n.* glɔ̀ng-sǐang กล่องเสียง

lascivious, *adj.* dtan-hǎa-jàt ตัณหาจัด; laa-mók ลามก

laser, *n.* sɛɛng-lee-sɔ̂ɔ แสงเลเซอร์

lash, *n.* gaan-kîan การเฆี่ยน; bplaai-sɛ̂ɛ ปลายแส้

lass, *n.* yǐng-sǎao หญิงสาว

last, *v.* chái-dâai ใช้ได้ (remain in good or usable condition); mii-chii-wít-yùu มีชีวิตอยู่ (survive)

last, *adj.* sùt-táai สุดท้าย

lasting, *adj.* ton ทน; ton-naan ทนนาน

last name, *n.* naam-sà-gun นามสกุล

latch, *n.* glɔɔn กลอน; sà-làk-bprà-dtuu สลักประตู

lately, *adv.* mûa-reo-reo-níi เมื่อเร็วๆนี้

latent, *adj.* fɛɛng-yùu แฝงอยู่; sɔ̂n-rén ซ่อนเร้น

lateral, *adj.* dâan-kâang ด้านข้าง

Latin, *n.* paa-sǎa-laa-dtin ภาษาลาติน

Latin America, *n.* tá-wîip-à-mee-ri-gaa-glaang ทวีปอเมริกากลาง

latitude, *n.* sên-lá-dtì-jùut เส้นละติจูด; sên-rúng เส้นรุ้ง

latter, *adj.* an-lǎng อันหลัง; sùan-tîi-sɔ̌ɔng ส่วนที่สอง

laud, *v.* sǎn-sɔ̌ɔn สรรเสริญ; yók-yɔ̂ng ยกย่อง

laudable, *adj.* nâa-yók-yɔ̂ng น่ายกย่อง

laugh, *v.* hǔa-rɔ́ หัวเราะ

laugh, *n.* sǐang-hǔa-rɔ́ เสียงหัวเราะ

launch, *v.* bplɔ̀i ปล่อย (release); ying ยิง (shoot); rə̂əm เริ่ม (begin)

launder, *v.* sák-rîit ซักรีด (e.g. clothes); sák-fɔ̂ɔk ซักฟอก (e.g. money)

Laundromat, *n.* ráan-sák-pâa ร้านซักผ้า

laundry, *n.* gaan-sák-rîit การซักรีด; gaan-sák-fɔ̂ɔk การซักฟอก

laurel, *n.* dtôn-lɔɔ-ren ต้นลอเรล (tree); gìat-dtì-yót เกียรติยศ (honor)

lava, n. laa-waa ลาวา; hǐn-lá-laai หินละลาย

lavatory, n. hɔ̂ng-náam ห้องน้ำ

lavender, n. sǐi-mûang-ɔ̀ɔn สีม่วงอ่อน (light purple); laa-wen-dɔ̂ɔ ลาเวนเดอร์ (plant)

lavish, adj. fûm-fuai ฟุ่มเฟือย

law, n. gòt-mǎai กฎหมาย

lawful, adj. tùuk-dtɔ̂ng-dtaam-gòt-mǎai ถูกต้องตามกฎหมาย

lawless, adj. mâi-mii-gòt-mǎai ไม่มีกฎหมาย

lawn, n. sà-nǎam-yâa สนามหญ้า

lawsuit, n. gaan-fɔ́ɔng-rɔ́ɔng-ka-dii การฟ้องร้องคดี

lawyer, n. tá-naai-kwaam ทนายความ; nák-gòt-mǎai นักกฎหมาย

lax, adj. yɔ̀n หย่อน

laxative, n. yaa-tàai ยาถ่าย; yaa-ra-baai ยาระบาย

lay, v. waang วาง; bpuu ปู

layer, n. chán ชั้น

layman, n. bùk-kon-tam-ma-daa บุคคลธรรมดา

layout, n. bpleɛn-ngaan แปลนงาน; sà-pâap สภาพ

lazy, adj. kîi-gìat ขี้เกียจ

lead, n. tâat-dtà-gùa ธาตุตะกั่ว

lead, v. nam นำ; chák-juung ชักจูง; bpen-hǔa-nâa เป็นหัวหน้า

leader, n. hǔa-nâa หัวหน้า; pûu-nam ผู้นำ

leadership, n. gaan-bpen-pûu-nam การเป็นผู้นำ

leaf, n. bai-máai ใบไม้; bai ใบ

leaflet, n. bai-bpliu ใบปลิว

league, n. sǎn-ní-bàat สันนิบาต (alliance); sà-maa-kom สมาคม (association); bprà-pêet ประเภท (class or level of competition)

leak, v. rûa รั่ว

leak, n. ruu-rûa รูรั่ว; rɔ́ɔi-rûa รอยรั่ว

lean, v. iang เอียง; een เอน

lean, adj. sùan-tûi-mâi-kɔ̂i-mii-núa ส่วนที่ไม่ค่อยมีเนื้อ (meat)

leap, v. grà-dòot กระโดด; kâam ข้าม

leap year, n. bpii-tîi-mii-sǎam-rɔ́ɔi-hòk-sìp-hòk-wan ปีที่มี ๓๖๖ วัน

learn, v. rian เรียน; rian-rúu เรียนรู้; sùk-sǎa ศึกษา

learned, adj. mii-kwaam-rúu มีความรู้

learning, n. gaan-rian-rúu การเรียนรู้

lease, v. hâi-châo ให้เช่า

lease, n. sǎn-yaa-châo สัญญาเช่า; gaan-châo การเช่า

leash, n. sǎai-juung สายจูง (animal strap); gaan-kûap-kum การควบคุม (control)

least, n. jam-nuan-tûi-nɔ́ɔi-tûi-sùt จำนวนน้อยที่สุด

leather, n. nǎng หนัง

leave, v. ɔ̀ɔk-jàak ออกจาก

English • Phonetic • Thai

(depart); jàak-bpai จากไป (go away); tíng-wái ทิ้งไว้ (something)

lecture, n. gaan-ban-yaai การบรรยาย; bpaa-tà-gà-tǎa ปาฐกถา

lecturer, n. pûu-ban-yaai ผู้บรรยาย

leech, n. bpling ปลิง; tâak ทาก

leek, n. pûut-kláai-hɔ̌ɔm พืชคล้ายหอม

leer, v. chaai-dtaa-mɔɔng ชายตา มอง (look with a sidelong glance)

left, adj. sáai ซ้าย

left, n. daan-sáai ด้านซ้าย (the left side); pûak-iang-sáai พวกเอียงซ้าย (radical people)

left-handed, adj. tà-nàt-sáai ถนัดซ้าย

leftovers, n. kɔ̌ɔng-lʉ̌a ของเหลือ

leg, n. kǎa ขา

legacy, n. mɔɔ-ra-dòk-dtòk-tɔ̌ɔt มรดกตกทอด

legal, adj. tùuk-gòt-mǎai ถูกกฎหมาย

legalize, v. tam-hâi-tùuk-gòt-mǎai ทำให้ถูกกฎหมาย

legation, n. tûut ทูต; ka-ná-tûut คณะทูต

legend, n. dtam-naan ตำนาน

legendary, adj. gìao-gàp-dtam-naan เกี่ยวกับตำนาน

legible, adj. àan-ɔ̀ɔk อ่านออก

legislate, v. ban-yàt-gòt-mǎai บัญญัติกฎหมาย

legislative, adj. gìao-gàp-gòt-mǎai เกี่ยวกับกฎหมาย

legislator, n. pûu-ban-yàt-gòt-mǎai ผู้บัญญัติกฎหมาย

legislature, n. sà-paa-ní-dtì-ban-yàt สภานิติบัญญัติ

legitimate, adj. tùuk-dtɔ̂ng-dtaam-gòt-mǎai ถูกต้องตามกำหมาย

legitimize, v. tam-hâi-tùuk-gòt-mǎai ทำให้ถูกกฎหมาย

leisure, n. wee-laa-wâang เวลาว่าง

lemon, n. má-naao มะนาว

lemonade, n. náam-má-naao น้ำมะนาว

lend, v. hâi-yʉʉm ให้ยืม

length, n. kwaam-yaao ความยาว

lengthen, v. tam-hâi-yaao ทำให้ยาว; dtɔ̀ɔ ต่อ

lengthwise, adv. dtaam-yaao ตามยาว

lengthy, adj. yaao-mâak ยาวมาก

lenient, adj. pɔ̀n-pǎn ผ่อนผัน (inclined not to be harsh or strict); mii-mêet-dtaa มีเมตตา (merciful)

lens, n. len เลนส์

leopard, n. sʉ̌a-daao เสือดาว

leprosy, n. rôok-rʉan โรคเรื้อน

lesbian, n. lét-sa-bîan เลสเบี้ยน

less, adj. nɔ́ɔi-gwàa น้อยกว่า (than); mâi-mâak-nák ไม่มากนัก (not a lot)

lessen, v. tam-hâi-nɔ́ɔi-long ทำให้น้อยลง

lesser, adj. nɔ́ɔi-gwàa น้อยกว่า

English • Phonetic • Thai

lesson, *n.* bòt-rian บทเรียน

lessor, *n.* pûu-hâi-châo ผู้ให้เช่า

lest, *conj.* pûa-mâi-hâi เพื่อไม่ให้; mí-chà-nán มิฉะนั้น

let, *v.* hâi hâi (allow, give); à-nú-yâat อนุญาต (permit, allow); kɔ̌ɔ-hâi ขอให้ (express a request, or proposal)

lethal, *adj.* tǔng-dtaai ถึงตาย; ráai-rɛɛng ร้ายแรง

let's ..., *v.* ... gan-tɤ̀ ...กันเถอะ

letter, *n.* jòt-mǎai จดหมาย (mail); àk-sɔ̌ɔn อักษร (of an alphabet)

lettuce, *n.* pàk-gàat-hɔ̌ɔm ผักกาดหอม

leukemia, *n.* rôok-luu-kii-mia โรคลูคีเมีย; má-reng-nai-mét-lûat-kǎao มะเร็งในเม็ดเลือดขาว

level, *n.* rá-dàp ระดับ

lever, *n.* chá-lɛɛng ชะแลง (a device); wí-tii-gaan วิธีการ (a means of doing something)

levity, *n.* kwaam-ká-nɔɔng ความคะนอง

levy, *v.* jàt-gèp จัดเก็บ (e.g. tax); geen-tá-hǎan เกณฑ์ทหาร (draft into military service); yʉ́t-sàp ยึดทรัพย์ (confiscate property)

lewd, *adj.* laa-mók ลามก (obscene)

lexicon, *n.* pót-jà-naa-nú-grom-sàp-chà-pɔ́ พจนานุกรมศัพท์เฉพาะ

liability, *n.* paa-rá-nâa-tîi ภาระหน้าที่ (duty); nîi หนี้ (debt);

kwaam-ráp-pìt-chɔ̂ɔp ความรับผิดชอบ (responsibility)

liable, *adj.* dtɔ̂ng-ráp-pìt-chɔ̂ɔp ต้องรับผิดชอบ

liaison, *n.* gaan-dtìt-dtɔ̀ɔ การติดต่อ (connection, communication); pûu-tam-gaan-dtìt-dtɔ̀ɔ ผู้ทำการติดต่อ (one that maintains communication)

liar, *n.* kon-goo-hòk คนโกหก

liberal, *adj.* jai-gwâang ใจกว้าง; sěe-rii-taang-kwaam-kít เสรีทางความคิด; bpen-ìt-sà-rà เป็นอิสระ

liberate, *v.* hâi-bpen-ìt-sà-rà ให้เป็นอิสระ

liberation, *n.* ìt-sà-rà อิสระ

liberty, *n.* ìt-sà-rà-pâap อิสรภาพ

libido, *n.* dtan-hǎa ตัณหา; kwaam-krâi ความใคร่

librarian, *n.* ban-naa-rák บรรณารักษ์

library, *n.* hɔ̂ng-sà-mùt ห้องสมุด

license, *n.* bai-à-nú-yâat ใบอนุญาต; tá-bian ทะเบียน

lick, *v.* lia เลีย

lid, *n.* fǎa-bpìt ฝาปิด

lie, *v.* goo-hòk โกหก

lie, *n.* gaan-goo-hòk การโกหก; kam-goo-hòk คำโกหก

lieu, *n.* gaan-tɛɛn-tîi การแทนที่

lieutenant, *n.* rɔ́ɔi-too ร้อยโท; rua-too เรือโท

life, *n.* chii-wít ชีวิต

English • Phonetic • Thai

lifeboat, *n.* rʉa-chuu-chîip เรือชูชีพ

life expectancy, *n.* chûang-aa-yú ช่วงอายุ

lifeguard, *n.* jâo-nâa-tîi-chûai-chii-wít เจ้าหน้าที่ช่วยชีวิต

life insurance, *n.* gaan-bprà-gan-chii-wít การประกันชีวิต

lifeless, *adj.* mâi-mii-chii-wít ไม่มีชีวิต; jùut-chûut จืดชืด

lifelong, *adj.* dtà-lɔ̀ɔt-chii-wít ตลอดชีวิต

lifestyle, *n.* wí-tii-dam-nəən-chii-wít วิถีดำเนินชีวิต

lift, *v.* yók ยก

lift, *n.* gaan-yók การยก; líp ลิฟต์ (elevator)

ligament, *n.* en เอ็น

light, *n.* jùt-fai จุดไฟ

light, *n.* sɛ̌ɛng แสง (radiation of any wavelength); fai ไฟ (source of light, e.g. lamp); glaang-wan กลางวัน (daytime)

light bulb, *n.* lɔ̀ɔt-fai หลอดไฟ

lighten, *v.* tam-hâi-sà-wàang ทำให้สว่าง; tam-hâi-bao ทำให้เบา

lighter, *n.* fai-chék ไฟแช็ก

lighthouse, *n.* bprà-paa-kaan ประภาคาร

lighting, *n.* gaan-jùt-fai การจุดไฟ; kwaam-sà-wàang ความสว่าง

lightning, *n.* fáa-lɛ̂p ฟ้าแลบ

light-year, *n.* bpii-sɛ̌ɛng ปีแสง

likable, *n.* nâa-chʉ̂ʉn-chɔ̂ɔp น่าชื่นชอบ

like, *v.* chɔ̂ɔp ชอบ

likelihood, *n.* kwaam-bpen-bpai-dâai ความเป็นไปได้

likely, *adj.* nâa-jà น่าจะ; kɔ̂n-kâang-jà ค่อนข้างจะ

liken, *v.* bprìap-sà-mǔan เปรียบเสมือน

likeness, *n.* kwaam-mǔan ความเหมือน

lily, *n.* dɔ̀ɔk-lin-líi ดอกลิลลี่

limb, *n.* kɛ̌ɛn-kǎa แขนขา (arm or leg); gìng-gâan กิ่งก้าน (branch)

limber, *adj.* ngɔɔ-dâai งอได้ (bending readily); yʉ̂ʉt-yùn ยืดหยุ่น (flexible)

lime, *n.* má-naao มะนาว (citrus fruit); bpuun-kǎao ปูนขาว (mineral)

limestone, *n.* hǐn-bpuun หินปูน

limit, *v.* jam-gàt จำกัด

limit, *n.* kɔ̀ɔp-kèet ขอบเขต; kìt-jam-gàt ขีดจำกัด

limitation, *n.* gaan-jam-gàt การจำกัด; kɔ̀ɔp-kèet ขอบเขต

limousine, *n.* rót-li-muu-siin รถลิมูซีน

limp, *adj.* bpùak-bpìak ปวกเปียก (lacking rigidity); ɔ̀ɔn-ɛɛ อ่อนแอ (weak)

line, *v.* tam-hâi-dtrong ทำให้ตรง

line, *n.* sên เส้น; sǎai สาย

lineage, *n.* chʉ́a-sǎai เชื้อสาย;

wong-dtrà-guun วงศ์ตระกูล

linear, *adj.* bpen-nɛɛo-dtrong
เป็นแนวตรง; dtaam-nɛɛo-yaao
ตามแนวยาว

linen, *n.* pâa-li-nin ผ้าลินิน

linger, *v.* ɔ̂i-ìng อ้อยอิ่ง; ɔ̀ɔ-rá-hɔ̌ɔi
เอ้อระเหย

lingerie, *n.* chút-chán-nai-sà-dtrii
ชุดชั้นในสตรี

linguistic, *adj.* gìao-gàp-paa-sǎa-
sàat เกี่ยวกับภาษาศาสตร์

linguistics, *n.* paa-sǎa-sàat
ภาษาศาสตร์

lining, *n.* sáp-nai ซับใน (of a piece
of cloth)

link, *v.* chûam เชื่อม; dtɔ̀ɔ ต่อ

link, *n.* gaan-chûam-dtɔ̀ɔ
การเชื่อมต่อ (a connected series of
units); kwaam-sǎm-pan
ความสัมพันธ์ (association; a relationship)

linkage, *n.* gaan-chûam การเชื่อม;
gaan-dtɔ̀ɔ การต่อ

linoleum, *n.* pèn-àap-náam-man
แผ่นอาบน้ำมัน

lint, *n.* pâa-sǎm-lii ผ้าสำลี; pâa-
pan-plɛɛ ผ้าพันแผล

lion, *n.* sǐng-dtoo สิงโต; râat-cha-sǐi
ราชสีห์

lioness, *n.* sǐng-dtoo-dtua-mia
สิงโตตัวเมีย

lip, *n.* rim-fǐi-bpàak ริมฝีปาก; rim
ริม

lipstick, *n.* líp-sà-dùk ลิปสติก

liqueur, *n.* lâo เหล้า; sù-raa สุรา

liquid, *n.* kɔ̌ɔng-lǎeo ของเหลว

liquor, *n.* lâo เหล้า; bà-ràn-dii
บรั่นดี; wít-sà-gîi วิสกี้

list, *n.* raai-gaan รายการ

listen (to), *v.* fang ฟัง

listener, *n.* pûu-fang ผู้ฟัง

Lisu, *n.* sǐi-sɔɔ ลีซอ (hill tribe)

liter, *n.* lít ลิตร

literacy, *n.* gaan-àan-ɔ̀ɔk-kǐan-dâai
การอ่านออกเขียนได้

literal, *adj.* dtaam-dtua-àk-sɔ̌ɔn
ตามตัวอักษร; tɛ́ɛ-jing แท้จริง

literally, *adv.* dtaam-dtua-àk-sɔ̌ɔn
ตามตัวอักษร

literary, *adj.* gìao-gàp-wan-ná-ka-
dii เกี่ยวกับวรรณคดี

literate, *adj.* mii-gaan-sùk-sǎa
มีการศึกษา

literature, *n.* wan-ná-ka-dii
วรรณคดี; àk-sɔ̌ɔn-sàat อักษร
ศาสตร์

litigation, *n.* gaan-fɔ́ɔng-rɔ́ɔng
การฟ้องร้อง

litter, *n.* kà-yà ขยะ; bplee-hǎam
เปลหาม

little, *adj.* lék เล็ก; nɔ́ɔi น้อย

live, *v.* yùu อยู่; aa-sǎi อาศัย

live, *adj.* mii-chii-wít มีชีวิต; sòt สด

livelihood, *n.* gaan-dam-rong-chii-
wít การดำรงชีวิต

lively, *adj.* mii-chii-wít-chii-waa

มีชีวิตชีวา

liver, n. dtàp ตับ

living, n. gaan-dam-rong-chîip
การดำรงชีพ; gaan-krɔɔng-chîip
การครองชีพ

living room, n. hɔ̂ng-nâng-lên
ห้องนังเล่น

lizard, n. gîng-gàa กิ้งก่า (wild);
jîng-jòk จิ้งจก (home)

load, v. ban-túk บรรทุก; kŏn ขน

load, n. kɔ̌ɔng-ban-túk ของบรรทุก
(something that is carried); bpɔɔ-rí-
maan-ngaan ปริมาณงาน (of work)

loaf, n. gɔ̂ɔn ก้อน; tɛ̂ɛo แถว

loan, v. hâi-gûu ให้กู้; hâi-yɯɯm
ให้ยืม

loan, n. ngən-gûu เงินกู้; gaan-hâi-
gûu การให้กู้

loath, adj. mâi-dtem-jai ไม่เต็มใจ;
lang lee ลังเล

loathe, v. rang-gìat รังเกียจ; mâi-
chɔ̂ɔp ไม่ชอบ

lobby, n. hɔ̂ng-lɔ́p-bîi ห้องล็อบบี้;
glùm-pûu-ron-na-rong กลุ่มผู้รณรงค์

lobbyist, n. pûu-ron-na-rong
ผู้รณรงค์

lobe, n. dtìng ติ่ง

lobster, n. gûng-gâam-graam
กุ้งก้ามกราม

local, n. kon-tɔ́ɔng-tìn คนท้องถิ่น;
tɔ́ɔng-tîi ท้องที่

locate, v. gam-nòt-tîi-dtâng
กำหนดที่ตั้ง; dtâng-yùu ตั้งอยู่

location, n. tîi-dtâng ที่ตั้ง; tîi-yùu
ที่อยู่

lock, v. lɔ́k ล็อก; bpìt ปิด (close)

lock, n. gun-jɛɛ กุญแจ (key); grà-
jùk-pŏm กระจุกผม (curl of hair)

locker, n. dtûu ตู้ (small storage);
lín-chák ลิ้นชัก (drawer)

locket, n. dtà-làp ตลับ; lɔ́k-gèt
ล็อกเก็ต

locksmith, n. châng-tam-gun-jɛɛ
ช่างทำกุญแจ

locomotive, n. hŭa-rót-jàk
หัวรถจักร

locust, n. dták-gà-dtɛɛn ตั๊กแตน
(grasshopper); dtôn-loo-kát
ต้นโลคัส (locust tree)

lodge, n. bâan-lék-lék บ้านเล็กๆ
(small house); roong-rɛɛm โรงแรม
(hotel)

lodging, n. gaan-pák การพัก (stay-
ing temporarily); hɔ̂ng-hâi-châo
ห้องให้เช่า (room for rent)

loft, n. hɔ̂ng-pee-daan ห้องเพดาน

lofty, adj. sŭung-dtrà-ngâan สูงตระ
หง่าน (of imposing height); ùat-dii
อวดดี (haughty)

log, n. tɔ̂n-máai ท่อนไม้; sung ซุง

logger, n. kon-dtàt-máai คนตัดไม้

logic, n. dtàk-gà-wít-ta-yaa
ตรรกวิทยา; hèet-pŏn เหตุผล

logical, adj. mii-hèet-pŏn มีเหตุผล

logistics, n. gam-lang-tá-hăan
กำลังทางทหาร; pá-laa-ti-gaan-

taang-tá-hǎan พลาธิการทางทหาร

loin, *n.* néa-dtà-pôok เนื้อตะโพก

loiter, *v.* dəən-dtrèe เดินเตร่; tà-lěe-tà-lǎi เถลไถล

lollipop, *n.* om-yím อมยิ้ม

lone, *adj.* dòot-dìao โดดเดี่ยว

loneliness, *n.* kwaam-diao-daai ความเดียวดาย

lonely, lonesome, *adj.* dòot-dìao โดดเดี่ยว; diao-daai เดียวดาย; ngǎo เหงา

long, *adj.* yaao ยาว

long-distance, *adj.* taang-glai ทางไกล

longevity, *n.* chûang-chii-wít ช่วงชีวิต

longing, *n.* kwaam-dtôŋ-gaan ความต้องการ

longitude, *n.* sên-waang เส้นแวง

long-term, *adj.* rá-yá-yaao ระยะยาว

look, *v.* duu ดู; mɔɔng มอง; hěn เห็น

loom, *n.* krûang-tɔɔ-pâa เครื่องทอผ้า

loop, *n.* hùang ห่วง; bùang บ่วง

loose, *adj.* lǔam หลวม

loosen, *v.* tam-hâi-lǔam ทำให้หลวม

loot, *v.* kà-mooi ขโมย

lord, *n.* kǔn-naang ขุนนาง (duke or marquis); jâao เจ้า (high rank in a feudal society); prá-pûu-bpen-jâao พระผู้เป็นเจ้า (god)

lose, *v.* sǐa เสีย (e.g. loved one); pée แพ้ (defeated); kàat-tun ขาดทุน (e.g. money)

loser, *n.* pûu-pée ผู้แพ้; pûu-sǔun-sǐa ผู้สูญเสีย

loss, *n.* gaan-sǔun-sǐa การสูญเสีย; gaan-pâai-pée การพ่ายแพ้

lost, *adj.* hǎai หาย (gone); pée แพ้ (defeated); lǒng-taang หลงทาง (to get lost)

lot, *n.* bɔɔ-ri-ween บริเวณ

lotion, *n.* loo-chân โลชั่น; kriim-bam-rung-pǐu ครีมบำรุงผิว

lottery, *n.* lɔ́t-dtəə-rîi ลอตเตอรี่

loud, *adj.* dang ดัง; ùk-gà-túk อึกทึก

loudspeaker, *n.* lam-poong ลำโพง

lounge, *n.* hɔ̂ng-ráp-rɔɔng ห้องรับรอง; hɔ̂ng-dùum-kɔ́k-teo ห้องดื่มค็อกเทล

louse, *n.* hǎo เหา

lousy, *adj.* nâa-rang-gìat น่ารังเกียจ; mii-hǎo มีเหา (having lice)

love, *v.* rák รัก

love, *n.* kwaam-rák ความรัก

lovely, *adj.* nâa-rák น่ารัก

lover, *n.* kon-rák คนรัก; chúu-rák ชู้รัก

low, *adj.* dtàm ต่ำ; dtîa เตี้ย

lower, *v.* lót-long ลดลง

loyal, *adj.* jong-rák-pák-dii จงรักภักดี; sûu-sàt ซื่อสัตย์

loyalty, *n.* kwaam-jong-rák-pák-dii

ความจงรักภักดี

lubricant, *n.* săan-lɔ̀ɔ-lʉ̂ʉn สารหล่อลื่น

lubricate, *v.* lɔ̀ɔ-lʉ̂ʉn หล่อลื่น

luck, *n.* chôok โชค

lucky, *adj.* chôok-dii โชคดี

luckily, *adv.* chôok-dii โชคดี

luggage, *n.* grà-bpǎo-dəən-taang กระเป๋าเดินทาง

lukewarm, *adj.* ùn ùn อุ่น ๆ

lull, *v.* glɔ̀m กล่อม

lullaby, *n.* pleeng-glɔ̀m-dèk เพลงกล่อมเด็ก

lumber, *n.* chín-máai ชิ้นไม้

luminous, *adj.* bplèng-sɛ̌ɛng เปล่งแสง

lump, *n.* gɔ̂ɔn ก้อน; jam-nuan-mâak จำนวนมาก

lunar, *adj.* gìao-gàp-prá-jan เกี่ยวกับพระจันทร์

lunatic, *n.* wí-gon-jà-rìt วิกลจริต; bâa บ้า

lunch, *n.* aa-hǎan-glaang-wan อาหารกลางวัน

luncheon, *n.* aa-hǎan-glaang-wan อาหารกลางวัน

lung, *n.* bpɔ̀ɔt ปอด

lunge, *n.* gaan-tîm การทิ่ม; gaan-tɛɛng การแทง

lure, *v.* lɔ̂ɔ ล่อ

lure, *n.* sìng lɔ̂ɔ สิ่งล่อ; krʉ̂ang lɔ̂ɔ เครื่องล่อ

lurk, *v.* sûm-sɔ̂ɔn ซุ่มซ่อน; dàk ดัก

luscious, *adj.* hɔ̌ɔm-wǎan หอมหวาน; mii-sà-nèe มีเสน่ห์

lust, *n.* raa-ká ราคะ; dtan-hǎa ตัณหา

luster, *n.* pûu-mii-dtan-hǎa ผู้มีตัณหา

lustful, *adj.* dtan-hǎa-jàt ตัณหาจัด

lusty, *adj.* mii-gam-lang-wang-chaa มีกำลังวังชา

luxurious, *adj.* rǔu-rǎa หรูหรา

luxury, *n.* kwaam-rǔu-rǎa ความหรูหรา

lyre, *n.* pin-dtâng พิณตั้ง

lyric, *n.* bòt-gà-wii บทกวี (poem); nʉ́a-pleeng เนื้อเพลง (words of a song)

M

macaroni, *n.* mák-gà-roo-nii มักกะโรนี

machine, *n.* krʉ̂ang เครื่อง; krʉ̂ang-jàk เครื่องจักร

machine gun, *n.* bpʉʉn-gon ปืนกล

machinery, *n.* rá-bòp-gaan-tam-ngaan ระบบการทำงาน; krʉ̂ang-jàk เครื่องจักร

mackerel, *n.* bplaa-mék-kəə-reo ปลาแม็คเคอเรล

mad, *adj.* moo-hǒo โมโห (angry); bâa บ้า (crazy)

madam, *n.* kun-pûu-yǐng คุณผู้หญิง

madness, *n.* kwaam-bâa ความบ้า;

kwaam-klúm-klâng ความคลุ้มคลั่ง

magazine, n. nít-dtà-ya-sǎan
นิตยสาร

magic, n. wêet-mon เวทมนตร์

magician, n. nák-maa-yaa-gon
นักมายากล

magistrate, n. pûu-pí-pâak-sǎa
ผู้พิพากษา (judge); fàai-bpòk-
krɔɔng ฝ่ายปกครอง (administer
and enforce law)

magnesium, n. mèk-nii-sìam
แมกนีเซียม

magnet, n. mêɛ-lèk แม่เหล็ก

magnetic, adj. gìao-gàp-mêɛ-lèk
เกี่ยวกับแม่เหล็ก

magnify, v. pɔ̀ɔm-kà-nàat
เพิ่มขนาด; kà-yǎai ขยาย

magnifying glass, n. wɛ̂n-kà-yǎai
แว่นขยาย

mahogany, n. dtôn-ma-hɔ́k-gaa-nii
ต้นมะฮ้อกกานี

maid, n. kon-ráp-chái-yǐng
คนรับใช้หญิง (female servant);
mêɛ-bâan แม่บ้าน (housekeeper)

maiden, n. yǐng-sǎao หญิงสาว

mail, n. jòt-mǎai จดหมาย; bprai-
sà-nii ไปรษณีย์

mailbox, n. dtûu-bprai-sà-nii
ตู้ไปรษณีย์

mailman, n. bù-rùt-bprai-sà-nii
บุรุษไปรษณีย์

mail order, n. gaan-sàng-sɯ́ɯ-
taang-bprai-sà-nii การสั่งซื้อทาง

ไปรษณีย์

main, n. sùan-yài ส่วนใหญ่ (majority); sǎm-kan สำคัญ (important)

mainland, n. pèn-din-yài
แผ่นดินใหญ่

mainstream, n. kwaam-kít-tîi-dòot-
dèn ความคิดที่โดดเด่น (prevailing
current of thought)

main street, n. tà-nǒn-sǎai-sǎm-kan
ถนนสายสำคัญ; tà-nǒn-làk ถนนหลัก

maintain, v. dam-rong-wái ดำรงไว้
(preserve); kong-yùu คงอยู่ (carry
on, continue); bam-rung-rák-sǎa
บำรุงรักษา (e.g. machine or vehicle)

maintenance, n. gaan-dam-rong-
wái การดำรงไว้; gaan-bam-rung-
rák-sǎa การบำรุงรักษา

majestic, adj. sǔung-sòng สูงส่ง;
sà-ngàa สง่า

majesty, n. kwaam-sǔung-sòng
ความสูงส่ง

major, n. pan-dtrii พันตรี (rank);
wí-chaa-èek วิชาเอก (subject)

majority, n. kon-sùan-mâak
คนส่วนมาก; sìang-sùan-mâak
เสียงส่วนมาก

make, v. tam ทำ; sâang สร้าง

maker, n. kon-tam คนทำ (one that
makes); pûu-sâang ผู้สร้าง
(builder); krɯ̂ang เครื่อง (machine)

make-up, n. gaan-dtɛ̀ng-nâa
การแต่งหน้า (the act of wearing
make-up); krɯ̂ang-sǎm-aang

English • Phonetic • Thai

เครื่องสำอาง (cosmetics)

malaria, *n.* kâi-maa-lee-ria
ไข้มาเลเรีย

male, *n.* pûu-chaai ผู้ชาย (for men);
dtua-pûu ตัวผู้ (for animals); pêet-
chaai เพศชาย (male gender)

mall, *n.* hâang-sàp-pa-sǐn-káa
ห้างสรรพสินค้า; moon มอลล์

malnutrition, *n.* paa-wá-kàat-sǎan-
aa-hǎan ภาวะขาดสารอาหาร

malt, *n.* kâao-màk ข้าวหมัก

mammal, *n.* sat-líang-lûuk-dûai-
nom สัตว์เลี้ยงลูกด้วยนม

mammoth, *n.* cháang-mɛm-móot
ช้างแมมมอธ

man, *n.* pûu-chaai ผู้ชาย; kon คน

manage, *v.* jàt-gaan จัดการ

management, *n.* gaan-jàt-gaan
การจัดการ

manager, *n.* pûu-jàt-gaan ผู้จัดการ

mandarin, *n.* sôm-jiin ส้มจีน
(orange)

Mandarin, *n.* paa-sǎa-jiin-glaang
ภาษาจีนกลาง (language)

mane, *n.* pɛ̌ɛng-kɔɔ-sàt แผงคอสัตว์

maneuver, *n.* gon-la-yút-taang-tá-
hǎan กลยุทธ์ทางทหาร (strategic
military); kân-dtɔɔn ขั้นตอน (procedure)

manganese, *n.* mɛng-gaa-níit
แมงกานีส

mango, *n.* má-mûang มะม่วง

manicure, *n.* gaan-dtòk-dtɛ̀ng-lép-

muu การตกแต่งเล็บมือ

manifesto, *n.* gaan-tà-lɛ̌ɛng-gaan
การแถลงการณ์ (public declaration);
ná-yoo-baai นโยบาย (policy)

manipulate, *v.* jàt-gaan จัดการ
(arrange); chái ใช้ (operate)

mankind, *n.* má-nút-sà-ya-châat
มนุษยชาติ

manly, *adj.* mii-kwaam-bpen-lûuk-
pûu-chaai มีความเป็นลูกผู้ชาย

mannequin, *n.* hùn-sà-dɛɛng-bɛ̀ɛp
หุ่นแสดงแบบ

manner, *n.* gì-ri-yaa กิริยา (way of
acting); lák-sà-nà-tâa-taang
ลักษณะท่าทาง (behavior); maa-ra-
yâat มารยาท (etiquette)

mannerism, *n.* tam-niam
ธรรมเนียม; gaan-tǔu-dtaam-tam-
niam การถือตามธรรมเนียม

manor, *n.* kà-rú-hàat คฤหาสน์

manpower, *n.* rɛɛng-ngaan แรงงาน

mansion, *n.* bâan-yài บ้านใหญ่

mantel, *n.* hǐng-bon-dtao-pǐng
หิ้งบนเตาผิง

manual, *n.* kûu-muu คู่มือ

manufacture, *v.* pà-lìt ผลิต

manufacture, *n.* gaan-pà-lìt
การผลิต

manufacturer, *n.* pûu-pà-lìt ผู้ผลิต

manuscript, *n.* dtôn-chà-bàp-
ngaan-kǐan ต้นฉบับงานเขียน

many, *adj.* mâak มาก

map, *v.* tam-pɛ̌ɛn-tîi ทำแผนที่

map 206 mask

(make a map of); săm-rùat สำรวจ
(survey)

map, n. pĕɛn-tîi แผนที่

maple, n. dtôn-mee-bpə̂n ต้นเมเปิ้ล

marathon, n. gaan-kèng-maa-raa-toon การแข่งมาราธอน

marble, n. hĭn-ɔ̀ɔn หินย่อน

march, v. dəən-tɛ̌ɛo เดินแถว

march, n. gaan-dəən-tɛ̌ɛo
การเดินแถว; gaan-dəən-kà-buan
การเดินขบวน

March, n. duan-ii-naa-kom
เดือนมีนาคม (month)

mare, n. máa-dtua-mia ม้าตัวเมีย

margarine, n. nəəi-tiam เนยเทียม;
maa-gaa-riin มากาารีน

margin, n. kɔ̀ɔp ขอบ; rim ริม

marijuana, n. gan-chaa กัญชา

marina, n. tîi-jɔ̀ɔt-rua-lék
ที่จอดเรือเล็ก

marine, adj. gìao-gàp-tá-lee
เกี่ยวกับทะเล

mariner, n. gà-laa-sǐi-rua กลาสีเรือ

marital, adj. gìao-gàp-gaan-sŏm-rót
เกี่ยวกับการสมรส

maritime, n. rua-sà-mùt เรือสมุทร

mark, v. hâi-ká-nɛɛn ให้คะแนน
(score); tam-krûang-mǎai ทำเครื่อง
หมาย (make a mark)

mark, n. ká-nɛɛn คะแนน (score);
krûang-mǎai เครื่องหมาย (written
symbol)

marketing, n. gaan-dtà-làat
การตลาด

marmalade, n. yɛɛm-bplùak-sôm
แยมเปลือกส้ม

marriage, n. gaan-dtɛ̀ng-ngaan
การแต่งงาน; gaan-sŏm-rót
การสมรส

married, adj. dtɛ̀ng-ngaan-lɛ́ɛo
แต่งงานแล้ว

marrow, n. kǎi-grà-dùuk ไขกระดูก

marry, v. dtɛ̀ng-ngaan แต่งงาน

Mars, n. daao-ang-kaan ดาวอังคาร

marsh, n. tîi-lûm ที่ลุ่ม

marshal, n. jɔɔm-pon จอมพล;
naai-am-pəə นายอำเภอ

martial, adj. gìao-gàp-gaan-róp
เกี่ยวกับการรบ; glâa กล้า

martyr, n. pûu-sǐa-sà-là-chii-wít-
pûa-sàat-sà-nǎa ผู้เสียสละชีวิตเพื่อ
ศาสนา

marvelous, adj. nâa-pít-sà-wŏng
น่าพิศวง; dtùn-dtaa-dtùn-jai
ตื่นตาตื่นใจ

Marxism, n. lát-tí-máak-sít
ลัทธิมาร์กซิส

mascara, n. máat-sà-gaa-râa
มาสการ่า

mascot, n. dtua-nam-chôok
ตัวนำโชค

masculine, adj. kêm-kĕng-sŏm-
chaai เข้มแข็งสมชาย

mash, v. tam-hâi-lé ทำให้เละ; lé-té
เละเทะ

mask, n. nâa-gàak หน้ากาก

masochism, *n.* gaam-wít-dtà-tǎan-tíi-chɔ̂ɔp-hâi-tùuk-tam-ráai กามวิตถารที่ชอบให้ถูกทำร้าย

masochist, *n.* maa-soo-kìt มาโซคิสท์

mason, *n.* châng-gɔ̀ɔ-dtùk ช่างก่อตึก

masquerade, *n.* ngaan-dtên-ram-sùam-nâa-gàak งานเต้นรำสวม หน้ากาก

mass, *n.* muan มวล; gɔ̂ɔn ก้อน; jam-nuan-mâak จำนวนมาก

massacre, *n.* gaan-kâa-dtà-gam-mùu การฆาตกรรมหมู่

massage, *v.* nûat นวด

massage, *n.* gaan-nûat การนวด

massive, *adj.* jam-nuan-mâak จำนวนมาก; bpen-gɔ̂ɔn-yài เป็นก้อนใหญ่

mast, *n.* sǎo เสา

master, *v.* tam-dâai-dii ทำได้ดี

master, *n.* naai นาย (owner, boss, employer); pûu-chîao-chaan ผู้เชี่ยวชาญ (expert); kruu/aa-jaan ครู/อาจารย์ (teacher, schoolmaster)

master of ceremony, *n.* pí-tii-gɔɔn พิธีกร; koo-sòk โฆษก

masterpiece, *n.* ngaan-chín-èek งานชิ้นเอก

master's degree, *n.* bpa-rin-yaa-má-hǎa-ban-dìt ปริญญามหาบัณฑิต

mat, *n.* prom-chét-táao พรมเช็ดเท้า (for wiping one's shoes or feet); sùa เสื่อ (to sit on)

match, *v.* sûu สู้ (place in competition); kèng แข่ง (fight, compete); mǔan-gan เหมือนกัน (resemble); dtrong-gan ตรงกัน (correspond exactly)

match, *n.* gaan-kèng-kǎn การแข่งขัน (tournament); máai-kìit-fai ไม้ขีดไฟ (for lighting fire)

matchmaker, *n.* mɛ̂ɛ-sʉ̀ʉ แม่สื่อ

mate, *n.* pʉ̂an เพื่อน (friend); kûu คู่ (pair of animals or human beings); sǎa-mii-rʉ̌u-pan-rá-yaa สามีหรือ ภรรยา (husband or wife)

material, *n.* wát-tù วัตถุ (substance); sùan-bprà-gɔ̀ɔp อุปกรณ์ (tools or apparatus)

materialism, *n.* wát-tù-ní-yom วัตถุนิยม

maternity, *n.* chûang-dtâng-kan ช่วงตั้งครรภ์ (period of pregnancy); kwaam-bpen-mɛ̂ɛ ความเป็นแม่ (motherhood)

mathematical, *adj.* gìao-gàp-kà-nít-dtà-sàat เกี่ยวกับคณิตศาสตร์

mathematics, *n.* kà-nít-dtà-sàat คณิตศาสตร์

matinee, *n.* má-hǒɔ-ra-sòp-dtɔɔn-glaang-wan มหรสพตอนกลางวัน

matrimony, *n.* pí-tii-sǒm-rót พิธีสมรส; gaan-mii-rʉan การมีเรือน

matter, *n.* wát-tù วัตถุ (substance); sà-sǎan สสาร (something that occupies space); rʉ̂ang เรื่อง (subject of concern, feeling, or action)

mattress, n. fûuk ฟูก

mature, adj. jà-rəən-dtəəp-dtoo-dtem-tîi เจริญเติบโตเต็มที่ (having reached full natural growth); bpen-pûu-yài เป็นผู้ใหญ่ (as an adult); sùk สุก (ripe)

maturity, n. kwaam-jà-rəən-dtəəp-dtoo-dtem-tîi ความเจริญเติบโตเต็มที่; kwaam-bpen-pûu-yài ความเป็นผู้ใหญ่

maximize, v. kà-yǎai ขยาย (expand, increase); pəəm/tamhâi-mâak-tîi-sùt เพิ่ม/ทำให้มากที่สุด (increase or make as great as possible)

maximum, n. jam-nuan-mâak-tîi-sùt จำนวนมากที่สุด (greatest possible quantity); kâa-sǔung-sùt ค่าสูงสุด (highest degree)

may, aux. v. àat-jà อาจจะ

May, n. dʉan-prʉt-sà-paa-kom เดือนพฤษภาคม

maybe, adv. baang-tii บางที; àat-jà อาจจะ

mayonnaise, n. maa-yɔɔng-néet มายองเนส

mayor, n. naa-yók-têet-sà-mon-dtrii นายกเทศมนตรี

maze, n. taang-kót-kíao ทางคด-เคี้ยว (labyrinth); kwaam-yûng-yɔ̌ɔng ความยุ่งเหยิง (confusion)

me, pron. chǎn ฉัน (female

speaker); pǒm ผม (male speaker)

meadow, n. tûng-yâa ทุ่งหญ้า

meal, n. mʉʉ-aa-hǎan มื้ออาหาร

mean, v. mǎai-kwaam-wâa หมายความว่า

mean, n. kâa-chà-lìa ค่าเฉลี่ย

meaning, n. kwaam-mǎai ความหมาย

meaningful, adj. mii-kwaam-mǎai มีความหมาย (having meaning); sǎm-kan สำคัญ (significant)

means, n. wí-tii-gaan วิธีการ (way of doing); krʉ̂ang-mʉʉ เครื่องมือ (device)

meantime, adv. nai-rá-wàang-nán ในระหว่างนั้น

meanwhile, adv. nai-kà-nà-diao-gan ในขณะเดียวกัน

measles, n. rôok-hàt โรคหัด

measure, v. wát วัด

measure, n. gaan-wát การวัด (the act of measuring); krʉ̂ang-wát เครื่องวัด (device)

measurement, n. gaan-wát การวัด

meat, n. nʉ́a-sàt เนื้อสัตว์

meatball, n. lûuk-chín ลูกชิ้น

mechanic, n. châng ช่าง

mechanical, adj. gìao-gàp-krʉ̂ang-jàk-gon เกี่ยวกับเครื่องจักรกล

mechanics, n. gon-lá-sàat กลศาสตร์; rá-bòp-krʉ̂ang-gon ระบบเครื่องกล

mechanism, n. rá-bòp-krʉ̂ang-gon

ระบบเครื่องกล

medal, *n.* rĭan-bprà-dàp
เหรียญประดับ

media, *n.* sùu sĕu สื่อ

mediate, *v.* glài-glìa ไกล่เกลี่ย

mediation, *v.* gaan-glài-glìa
การไกล่เกลี่ย

mediator, *n.* pûu-glài-glìa
ผู้ไกล่เกลี่ย

medical, *adj.* taang-gaan-pêet
ทางการแพทย์

medication, *n.* gaan-chái-yaa
การใช้ยา

medicine, *n.* gaan-pêet การแพทย์
(the science of); yaa ยา (drug)

medieval, *adj.* gìao-gàp-sà-măi-
glaang เกี่ยวกับสมัยกลาง

meditate, *v.* tam-sà-maa-tí
ทำสมาธิ; kâo-chaan เข้าฌาณ

meditation, *n.* gaan-tam-sà-maa-tí
การทำสมาธิ

Mediterranean, *n.* tá-lee-mee-dì-
dtəə-ree-nîan ทะเลเมดิเตอเรเนียน

medium, *adj.* glaang กลาง

medium, *n.* wí-tii-gaan วิธีการ
(means); krûang-muu เครื่องมือ
(device)

meek, *adj.* wâa-ngâai ว่าง่าย;
chûang เชื่อง

meet, *v.* póp พบ; jəə เจอ; bprà-
chum ประชุม

meeting, *n.* gaan-póp-gan
การพบกัน; gaan-bprà-chum

การประชุม; gaan-chum-num
การชุมนุม

megahertz, *n.* mék-gà-hóot
เมกกะเฮิร์ช

megaphone, *n.* krûang-grà-jaai-
sĭang เครื่องกระจายเสียง

mellow, *adj.* glom-glòm กลมกล่อม
(as of wine); râa-rəəng ร่าเริง
(easygoing); ɔ̀ɔn-nûm อ่อนนุ่ม
(mild)

melody, *n.* tam-nɔɔng ทำนอง

melon, *n.* dtɛɛng แตง; dtɛɛng-moo
แตงโม

melt, *v.* lá-laai ละลาย

member, *n.* sà-maa-chík สมาชิก

membership, *n.* gaan-bpen-sà-
maa-chík การเป็นสมาชิก

memorable, *adj.* kuan-jam ควรจำ;
nâa-jòt-jam น่าจดจำ

memorandum, *n.* ban-túk บันทึก

memorial, *n.* à-nú-sɔ̌ɔn อนุสรณ์

memorize, *v.* jam จำ

memory, *n.* kwaam-jam ความจำ;
kwaam-song-jam ความทรงจำ

menace, *n.* an-dtà-raai อันตราย;
sìng-tîi-kúk-kaam สิ่งที่คุกคาม

mend, *v.* sɔ̀m-sɛɛm ซ่อมแซม; gɛ̂ɛ-
kăi แก้ไข

menial, *adj.* dtàm-dtɔ̂i ต่ำต้อย

menopause, *n.* chûang-bprà-jam-
duan-mòt ช่วงประจำเดือนหมด

menstruation, *n.* bprà-jam-duan
ประจำเดือน

mental, *adj.* gìao-gàp-jìt-jai เกี่ยวกับจิตใจ

mention, *v.* glàao-tǔng กล่าวถึง; âang-tǔng อ้างถึง

mentor, *n.* tîi-bprùk-sǎa ที่ปรึกษา

menu, *n.* mee-nuu เมนู; raai-gaan-aa-hǎan รายการอาหาร

meow, *n.* sǐang-mɛɛo-rɔ́ɔng เสียงแมวร้อง

merchandise, *n.* sǐn-káa สินค้า

merchant, *n.* pɔ̂ɔ-káa พ่อค้า (male); mɛ̂ɛ-káa แม่ค้า (female); kon-kǎai คนขาย (vendor)

merciful, *adj.* bpraa-nii ปรานี; mii-mêet-dtaa มีเมตตา

merciless, *adj.* mâi-mii-kwaam-sǒng-sǎan ไม่มีความสงสาร; mâi-mii-kwaam-hěn-jai ไม่มีความเห็นใจ

mercury, *n.* bpà-rɔ̀ɔt ปรอท

mercy, *n.* kwaam-mêet-dtaa-gà-ru-naa ความเมตตากรุณา

merge, *v.* ruam-dtua รวมตัว

merger, *n.* gaan-ruam-dtua-rá-wàang-bɔɔ-rí-sàt การรวมตัวระหว่างบริษัท

meridian, *n.* sên-mɚ-ri-dîan เส้นเมอริเดียน; wong-glom-sǒm-mút วงกลมสมมุติ

meringue, *n.* kà-nǒm-sài-kài-kǎao-pà-sǒm-náam-dtaan ขนมใส่ไข่ขาวผสมน้ำตาล (dessert, pastry)

merit, *n.* kwaam-dii-lɚt ความดีเลิศ; kɔ̂ɔ-dii ข้อดี

mermaid, *n.* naang-ngʉ̂ak นางเงือก

merry, *adj.* rʉ̂ʉn-rɚɚng รื่นเริง; sà-nùk-sà-nǎan สนุกสนาน

merry-go-round, *n.* máa-mǔn ม้าหมุน

mess, *n.* kwaam-yûng-yɚ̌ɚng ความยุ่งเหยิง

message, *n.* kɔ̂ɔ-kwaam ข้อความ; kàao-sǎan ข่าวสาร

messenger, *n.* pʉ̂u-sòng-kàao ผู้ส่งข่าว

messy, *adj.* mâi-bpen-rá-bìap ไม่เป็นระเบียบ (not neat); yûng-yɚ̌ɚng ยุ่งเหยิง (disorderly; difficult to settle)

metabolism, *n.* gaan-pǎo-plǎan การเผาผลาญ; gaan-sǎn-dàap การสันดาป

metal, *n.* loo-hà โลหะ

metaphor, *n.* kam-ùp-bpà-maa คำอุปมา

metaphysics, *n.* à-pí-bpràt-cha-yaa อภิปรัชญา

meteor, meteorite, *n.* daao-dtòk ดาวตก; pǐi-pûng-dtâai ผีพุ่งใต้

meter, *n.* nùai-wát หน่วยวัด

method, *n.* wí-tii-gaan วิธีการ

metric, *adj.* gìao-gàp-rá-bòp-mét-dtrìk เกี่ยวกับระบบเมตริก

metropolitan, *n.* ná-kɔɔn-lǔang นครหลวง

Mexico, *n.* bprà-têet-mék-si-goo ประเทศเม็กซิโก

mezzanine, *n.* chán-lɔɔi ชั้นลอย (a

partial story between two main sto-
ries); tîi-nâng-dtàm-sùt ที่นั่งต่ำสุด
(the lowest balcony in a theater)

microbe, *n.* jù-lin-sii จุลินทรีย์

microcosm, *n.* jun-la-pâak จุลภาค

microfilm, *n.* mai-kroo-fiim
ไมโครฟิล์ม

microphone, *n.* mai-kroo-foon
ไมโครโฟน

microscopic, *adj.* mɔɔng-dûai-
dtaa-bplàao-mâi-hěn
มองด้วยตาเปล่าไม่เห็น

microwave, *n.* mai-kroo-wéep
ไมโครเวฟ

middle, *adj.* dtrong-glaang
ตรงกลาง; pɔɔ-bpra-maan
พอประมาณ

middle-aged, *adj.* wai-glaang-kon
วัยกลางคน

Middle Ages, *n.* sà-mǎi-glaang
สมัยกลาง

middle-class, *n.* chon-chán-glaang
ชนชั้นกลาง

Middle East, *n.* dtà-wan-ɔ̀ɔk-
glaang ตะวันออกกลาง

middleman, *n.* pɔ̂ɔ-káa-kon-glaang
พ่อค้าคนกลาง

middle school, *n.* roong-rian-mát-
ta-yom โรงเรียนมัธยม

midnight, *n.* tîang-kʉʉn เที่ยงคืน

midwife, *n.* mɔ̌ɔ-dtam-yɛɛ
หมอตำแย

Mien, *n.* yáo เย้า

might, *n.* am-nâat อำนาจ; kwaam-

sǎa-mâat ความสามารถ

mighty, *adj.* mii-am-nâat มีอำนาจ
(having power); mii-kwaam-sǎa-
mâat มีความสามารถ (having ability)

migraine, *n.* mai-green ไมเกรน;
rôok-bpùat-hǔa-kâang-diao โรคปวด
หัวข้างเดียว

migration, *n.* gaan-òp-pa-yóp
การอพยพ; gaan-yáai-tìn การย้าย
ถิ่น

mild, *adj.* ɔ̀ɔn-yoon อ่อนโยน (gentle); bao เบา (soft); mai-pèt
ไม่เผ็ด (not spicy)

mildew, *n.* chúa-raa เชื้อรา

mile, *n.* mai ไมล์

milestone, *n.* làk หลัก (stone
marker); hèet-gaan-sǎm-kan
เหตุการณ์สำคัญ (important event)

military, *n.* gam-lang-tá-hǎan
กำลังทหาร

milk, *n.* nom นม

milkshake, *n.* nom-yen-pà-sǒm-ai-
sà-kriim นมเย็นผสมไอศครีม; míu-
chéek มิ๊ลค์เชค

milky, *adj.* kláai-nom คล้ายนม (like
milk); mii-sǐi-kǎao มีสีขาว (having
white color)

Milky Way, *n.* taang-cháang-pùak
ทางช้างเผือก

mill, *n.* roong-sǐi โรงสี (building);
krûang-sǐi เครื่องสี (machine)

miller, *n.* jâo-kɔ̌ɔng-roong-sǐi

English · Phonetic · Thai

เจ้าของโรงสี

milligram, *n.* min-li-gram มิลลิกรัม

millimeter, *n.* min-li-méɛt มิลลิเมตร

million, *n.* nùng-láan หนึ่งล้าน

millionaire, *n.* sèɛt-tǐi-ngən-láan เศรษฐีเงินล้าน

mime, *n.* lá-kɔɔn-bâi ละครใบ้

mimic, *v.* lɔɔ-lian ล้อเลียน (mock, imitate); jam-lɔɔng จำลอง (copy)

mind, *n.* jìt-jai จิตใจ; kwaam-kít ความคิด; jai ใจ

mine, *pron.* kɔɔng-chǎn ของฉัน

mine, *n.* mǔang-rɛ̂ɛ เหมืองแร่

miner, *n.* kon-ngaan-nai-mǔang คนงานในเหมือง

mineral, *n.* rɛ̂ɛ-tâat แร่ธาตุ

mingle, *v.* pà-sǒm ผสม; ruam-gan รวมกัน

miniature, *n.* kà-nàat-tîi-yɔ̂ɔ-sùan ขนาดที่ย่อส่วน

minimal, *adj.* nɔ́ɔi-tîi-sùt น้อยที่สุด

minimum, *n.* jam-nuan-tîi-nɔ́ɔi-tîi-sùt จำนวนที่น้อยที่สุด

mining, *n.* gaan-tam-mǔang-rɛ̂ɛ การทำเหมืองแร่

minister, *n.* prá พระ; rát-tà-mon-dtrii รัฐมนตรี

ministry, *n.* grà-suang กระทรวง; ká-ná-rát-tà-mon-dtrii คณะรัฐมนตรี

mink, *n.* dtua-míng ตัวมิ้งค์

minor, *n.* pûu-yao ผู้เยาว์ (juvenile); wí-chaa-rɔɔng วิชารอง (subject)

minority, *n.* chon-glùm-nɔ́ɔi ชนกลุ่มน้อย

mint, *n.* sà-ra-nɛ̀ɛ สะระแหน่ (plant); glìn-mín กลิ่นมิ้นท์ (smell)

minus, *prep.* lóp-ɔ̀ɔk ลบออก; bpràat-sà-jàak ปราศจาก

minute, *n.* naa-tii นาที

minute, *adj.* lék-mâak เล็กมาก

miracle, *n.* à-pí-ní-hǎan อภินิหาร; rûang-àt-sà-jan เรื่องอัศจรรย์

mirage, *n.* pâap-luang-dtaa ภาพลวงตา

mirror, *n.* grà-jòk กระจก

misbehave, *v.* bprà-prút-mâi-dii ประพฤติไม่ดี

miscarriage, *n.* gaan-tɛ́ng-lûuk การแท้งลูก

miscellaneous, *adj.* bpà-gin-ná-gà ปกิณกะ; bèt-dtà-lèt เบ็ดเตล็ด

mischief, *n.* kwaam-súk-son ความซุกซน (behavior); kwaam-sǐa-hǎai ความเสียหาย (damage)

mischievous, *adj.* bpen-pai เป็นภัย (causing harm or damage); súk-son ซุกซน (naughty)

misconduct, *n.* gaan-tam-pìt การทำผิด

misdemeanor, *n.* lá-hù-tôot ลหุโทษ (offense less serious than a felony)

miser, *n.* kon-kîi-nǐao คนขี้เหนียว

miserable, *adj.* túk-yâak ทุกข์ยาก; nâa-sǎng-wêet น่าสังเวช

misery, *n.* kwaam-túk-yâak ความทุกข์ยาก

ความทุกข์ยาก

misfortune, *n.* chôok-mâi-dii
โชคไม่ดี

mishap, *n.* ù-bàt-dtì-hèet อุบัติเหตุ

mislead, *v.* chák-nam-bpai-nai-
taang-tîi-pìt ชักนำไปในทางที่ผิด
(lead in the wrong direction); tam-
hâi-kâo-jai-pìt ทำให้เข้าใจผิด
(cause misunderstanding)

miss, *v.* plâat พลาด; kìt-tǔng คิดถึง
(think about, be wistful)

miss, *n.* gaan-tam-plâat การทำ
พลาด (failure); naang-sǎao
นางสาว (a title)

missile, *n.* kǐi-bpà-naa-wút-nam-wí-
tii ขีปนาวุธนำวิถี

missing, *adj.* mâi-póp ไม่พบ (cannot be found); hǎai-bai หายไป
(lost, disappeared); kàat-kleen
ขาดแคลน (lacking)

mission, *n.* ká-ná-pûu-teen
คณะผู้แทน (body of persons sent as
representative); paa-rá-nâa-tîi
ภาระหน้าที่ (duty)

missionary, *n.* mít-chan-naa-rîi
มิชชันนารี; nák-pòoi-prêe-sàat-sà-
nǎa นักเผยแพร่ศาสนา

mist, *n.* mòok หมอก (fog, haze);
kwaam-prâa-mua ความพร่ามัว
(dimness or obscurity)

mistake, *n.* kwaam-pìt-plâat
ความผิดพลาด

Mister, *n.* naai นาย

mistress, *n.* à-nú-pan-ra-yaa
อนุภรรยา; mia-nóoi เมียน้อย

misty, *adj.* mii-mòok มีหมอก; prâa-
mua พร่ามัว

misunderstand, *v.* kâo-jai-pìt
เข้าใจผิด

misunderstanding, *n.* gaan-kâo-
jai-pìt การเข้าใจผิด

misuse, *v.* chái-nai-taang-tîi-pìt
ใช้ในทางที่ผิด

mite, *n.* dtua-rai ตัวไร

mitten, *n.* tǔng-mɯɯ ถุงมือ

mix, *v.* pà-sǒm ผสม; ruam-gan
รวมกัน

mixture, *n.* sùan-pà-sǒm ส่วนผสม;
gaan-pà-sǒm การผสม

moan, *v.* kruan-kraang ครวญคราง

moat, *n.* kuu-mɯang คูเมือง

mob, *n.* fǔung-chon ฝูงชน; móp
ม็อบ

mobile, *adj.* klɯ̂an-tîi-dâai
เคลื่อนที่ได้

mock, *v.* yó-yóəi เยาะเย้ย (treat
with ridicule or contempt); lóo-lian
ล้อเลียน (mimic)

mockery, *n.* gaan-lóo-lian
การล้อเลียน

model, *n.* bèep แบบ (style or
design); sìng-jam-loong สิ่งจำลอง
(preliminary work or construction);
dtua-yàanq ตัวอย่าง (sample, example); pûu-sà-deeng-bèep ผู้แสดง
แบบ (person employed to display

English • Phonetic • Thai

merchandise)

moderate, *adj.* bpaan-glaang
ปานกลาง; pɔɔ-sǒm-kuan
พอสมควร

moderation, *n.* kwaam-pɔɔ-sǒm-
kuan ความพอสมควร; gaan-rúu-jàk-
bprà-maan การรู้จักประมาณ

moderator, *n.* sǎan-lót-kwaam-reo-
kǒong-niu-dtrɔn สารลดความเร็วของ
นิวตรอน (of neutron); pí-tii-gɔɔn-
gaan-bpraa-sǎi พิธีกรการปราศรัย
(M.C. of a panel discussion)

modern, *adj.* sà-mǎi-mài สมัยใหม่
(relating to a recently developed or
advanced style, etc.); bpàt-jù-ban
ปัจจุบัน (of the present)

modernize, *v.* tam-hâi-tan-sà-mǎi
ทำให้ทันสมัย

modest, *adj.* tɔm-dtua ถ่อมตัว
(humble); sù-pâap สุภาพ (polite)

modify, *v.* gɛ̂ɛ-kǎi แก้ไข (correct);
bpràp-bprung ปรับปรุง (improve)

moist, *adj.* chúun ชื้น

moisture, *n.* kwaam-chúun
ความชื้น

moisturize, *n.* hâi-kwaam-chúun
ให้ความชื้น

moisturizer, *n.* kriim-tà-nɔ̌ɔm-pǐu
ครีมถนอมผิว (cosmetics)

molar, *n.* fan-graam ฟันกราม

mold, *n.* chúa-raa เชื้อรา

mole, *n.* dtua-dtùn ตัวตุ่น (animal);
fǎi ไฝ (on the skin)

molecule, *n.* moo-lee-gun โมเลกุล

molest, *v.* róp-guan รบกวน

moment, *n.* kà-nà-nán ขณะนั้น (a
specific point in time); chûa-krûu
ชั่วครู่ (a brief period of time)

momentary, *adj.* chûa-bprà-dǐao
ชั่วประเดี๋ยว

momentum, *n.* rɛɛng-gaan-klûan-
tii แรงการเคลื่อนที่; moo-men-dtâm
โมเมนตัม

monarch, *n.* gà-sàt กษัตริย์

monarchy, *n.* rá-bòp-gà-sàt
ระบอบกษัตริย์

monastery, *n.* wát วัด

Monday, *n.* wan-jan วันจันทร์

monetary, *n.* gìao-gàp-ngən
เกี่ยวกับเงิน

money, *n.* ngən เงิน

money order, *n.* tá-naa-nát ธนาณัติ

mongrel, *n.* sàt-pan-pà-sǒm
สัตว์พันธุ์ผสม (animal); pûut-pan-
pà-sǒm พืชพันธุ์ผสม (plant)

monitor, *n.* jɔɔ-pâap จอภาพ
(screen); krûang-dtuan เครื่องเตือน
(machine or program)

monk, *n.* prá พระ

monkey, *n.* ling ลิง

monopolize, *v.* tǔu-èek-gà-sìt
ถือเอกสิทธิ์

monopoly, *n.* èek-gà-sìt เอกสิทธิ์

monotonous, *adj.* sám-sâak ซ้ำซาก
(lacking in variety)

monsoon, *n.* lom-mɔɔ-ra-sǔm

ลมมรสุม; lom-fǒn ลมฝน

monster, *n.* sàt-bprà-làat
สัตว์ประหลาด; à-sù-rá-gaai
อสุรกาย

month, *n.* dʉan เดือน

monthly, *n.* raai-dʉan รายเดือน;
túk-dʉan ทุกเดือน

monument, *n.* à-nú-sǎa-wa-rii
อนุสาวรีย์

moo, *v.* wua-rɔ́ɔng วัวร้อง

moo, *n.* sǐang-wua เสียงวัว

mood, *n.* aa-rom อารมณ์

moody, *adj.* aa-rom-sǐa อารมณ์เสีย
(having a bad mood); jâo-aa-rom
เจ้าอารมณ์ (temperamental)

moon, *n.* prá-jan พระจันทร์

moonlight, *n.* sěeng-jan แสงจันทร์

moose, *n.* gwaang-yài กวางใหญ่

mop, *n.* máai-tǔu-pʉ́ʉn ไม้ถูพื้น

moral, *n.* sǐin-la-tam ศีลธรรม

morale, *n.* kwǎn ขวัญ

more, *adj.* mâak-gwàa มากกว่า

moreover, *adv.* yîng-gwàa-nán
ยิ่งกว่านั้น; nɔ̂ɔk-nʉ̌a-jàak-nán
นอกเหนือจากนั้น

morgue, *n.* sà-tǎan-tîi-gèp-sòp
สถานที่เก็บศพ

morning, *n.* dtɔɔn-cháao ตอนเช้า

moron, *n.* kon-ngôo คนโง่; kon-tʉ̂m คนทึ่ม

morphine, *n.* mɔɔ-fiin มอร์ฟีน

mortal, *adj.* mâi-am-ma-dtà ไม่อมตะ

mortality, *n.* kwaam-bpen-am-má-

dtà ความไม่เป็นอมตะ

mortar, *n.* krók ครก

mortgage, *n.* gaan-jam-nɔɔng
การจำนอง

mortuary, *n.* sà-tǎan-tîi-gèp-sòp
สถานที่เก็บศพ

Moslem, *n.* mút-sà-lim มุสลิม

mosque, *n.* sù-rào สุเหร่า

mosquito, *n.* yung ยุง

moss, *n.* mɔ́ɔt มอส; dtà-krâi-náam
ตะไคร่น้ำ

most, *adj.* mâak-tîi-sùt มากที่สุด;
tîi-sùt ที่สุด

motel, *n.* roong-rɛɛm โรงแรม

moth, *n.* pǐi-sʉ̂a-glaang-kʉʉn
ผีเสื้อกลางคืน

mothball, *n.* lûuk-měn ลูกเหม็น

mother, *n.* mɛ̂ɛ แม่; maan-daa
มารดา

mother-in-law, *n.* mɛ̂ɛ yaai แม่ยาย
(wife's mother); mɛ̂ɛ-yâa แม่ย่า
(husband's mother)

mother-of-pearl, *n.* hɔ̌i-múk
หอยมุก

motivate, *v.* grà-dtûn กระตุ้น; don-jai คลใจ

motive, *n.* sìng-grà-dtûn สิ่งกระตุ้น;
sìng-don-jai สิ่งคลใจ

motor, *n.* krʉ̂ang-yon เครื่องยนต์

motorcycle, *n.* jàk-grà-yaan-yon
จักรยานยนต์; mɔɔ-dtɚɚ-sai
มอเตอร์ไซค์

motorist, *n.* nák-kèng-rót นักแข่งรถ

(car racer); pûu-kàp-kìi ผู้ขับขี่
(driver)

motto, *n.* ká-dtì-pót คติพจน์; kam-
kwǎn คำขวัญ

mount, *v.* kûn ขึ้น

mount, *n.* nɔɔn-kǎo เนินเขา (hill);
puu-kǎo ภูเขา (mountain); gaan-
kûn การขึ้น (act of climbing or
ascending)

mountain, *n.* puu-kǎo ภูเขา

mountaineer, *n.* nák-dtài-kǎo
นักไต่เขา

mourn, *n.* wái-túk ไว้ทุกข์; aa-lai
อาลัย

mouse, *n.* nǔu หนู

mousetrap, *n.* gàp-dàk-nǔu
กับดักหนู

mouth, *n.* bpàak ปาก

mouthful, *n.* dtem-bpàak เต็มปาก

move, *v.* klûan-tîi เคลื่อนที่; klûan-
wǎi เคลื่อนไหว

movement, *n.* gaan-klûan-wǎi
การเคลื่อนไหว; gaan-klûan-tîi
การเคลื่อนที่

movie, *n.* pâap-pa-yon ภาพยนตร์;
nǎng หนัง

moving, *adj.* sûng-klûan-tîi
ซึ่งเคลื่อนที่ (changing position); sà-
tɯan-jai สะเทือนใจ (arousing deep
emotion)

mow, *v.* dtàt-yâa ตัดหญ้า; daai-yâa
ดายหญ้า

Mr., *n.* naai นาย; kun คุณ

Mrs., *n.* naang นาง

much, *adj.* mâak มาก

mud, *n.* kloon โคลน; dtom ตม

muddy, *adj.* bpen-kloon เป็นโคลน
(full of or covered with mud); kûn
ขุ่น (dull, cloudy)

muffin, *n.* kà-nǒm-máp-fin
ขนมมัฟฟิน

muffler, *n.* pâa-pan-kɔɔ-yàang-nǎa
ผ้าพันคออย่างหนา (heavy scarf);
krûang-gèp-sǐang เครื่องเก็บเสียง
(device that absorbs noise)

mug, *n.* yɯ̀ak เหยือก

muggy, *adj.* àp-chɯ́un อับชื้น

multiple, *adj.* lǎai-tâo หลายเท่า

multiply, *v.* kuun คูณ (in math);
pɔ̂m-jam-nuan เพิ่มจำนวน
(increase, grow in amount)

mummy, *n.* mam-mîi มัมมี่

mumps, *n.* rôok-kaang-tuum
โรคคางทูม

municipal, *adj.* gìao-gàp-têet-sà-
baan เกี่ยวกับเทศบาล

murder, *v.* kâa ฆ่า

murder, *n.* kâat-dtà-gam ฆาตกรรม

murmur, *v.* pɯm-pam พึมพำ; bòn-
pɯm-pam บ่นพึมพำ

murmur, *n.* sǐang-pɯm-pam
เสียงพึมพำ; gaan-bòn การบ่น

muscle, *n.* glâam-nɯ́a กล้ามเนื้อ

museum, *n.* pí-pít-ta-pan
พิพิธภัณฑ์

mushroom, *n.* hèt เห็ด

musical, *adj.* gìao-gàp-don-dtrii
เกี่ยวกับดนตรี (relating to music)

musical, *n.* lá-kɔɔn-pleeng
ละครเพลง (musical play or movie)

musical instrument, *n.* krûang-
don-dtrii เครื่องดนตรี

musician, *n.* nák-don-drii นักดนตรี

musket, *n.* bpuun-kâap-sì-laa
ปืนคาบศิลา; bpuun-yài ปืนใหญ่

must, *v.* dtɔ̂ng ต้อง

must, *n.* sìng-tîi-dtɔ̂ng-tam
สิ่งที่ต้องทำ; kwaam-jam-bpen
ความจำเป็น

mustache, *n.* nùat หนวด

mustard, *n.* mát-sa-dtàat มัสตาร์ด

mutant, *n.* sìng-mii-chii-wít-pan-
mài สิ่งมีชีวิตพันธุ์ใหม่

mutation, *n.* gaan-bplìan-lák-sà-nà-
kɔ̌ɔng-yiin การเปลี่ยนลักษณะของยีน

mute, *adj.* bâi ใบ้ (unable to speak);
ngîap เงียบ (no sound); mâi-ɔ̀ɔk-
sǐang ไม่ออกเสียง (no sound made)

mutilate, *v.* tam-hâi-pí-gaan
ทำให้พิการ; tam-hâi-sǐa-chǒom
ทำให้เสียโฉม

mutter, *v.* pum-pam พึมพำ

mutton, *n.* nʉ́a-gɛ̀ เนื้อแกะ

mutual, *adj.* táng-sɔ̌ɔng-fàai
ทั้งสองฝ่าย; mii-rûam-gan มีร่วมกัน

my, *adj.* kɔ̌ɔng-chǎn ของฉัน

myopia, *n.* paa-wá-sǎai-dtaa-sân
ภาวะสายตาสั้น (nearsightedness);
gaan-mɔɔng-gaan-glai การมอง
การณ์ไกล (in thinking or planning)

myself, *pron.* dtua-chǎn-eeng
ตัวฉันเอง

mysterious, *adj.* lʉ́k-láp ลึกลับ

mystery, *n.* kwaam-lʉ́i-láp
ความลี้ลับ; kwaam-lʉ́k-láp
ความลึกลับ

mystify, *v.* tam-hâi-lʉ́k-láp ทำให้
ลึกลับ; tam-hâi-bprà-làat-jai ทำให้
ประหลาดใจ

myth, *n.* rûang-lâo-dtaam-dtam-
naan เรื่องเล่าตามตำนาน

mythology, *n.* gaan-sùk-sǎa-rûang-
kwaam-chʉ̂a-dtaam-dtam-naan
การศึกษาเรื่องความเชื่อตามตำนาน

N

nab, *v.* jàp จับ; yʉ́t ยึด

nag, *v.* kɔ̂n-ké คอนแคะ; pûut-hâi-
ram-kaan พูดให้รำคาญ

nail, *n.* lép เล็บ (finger or toe);
dtà-bpuu ตะปู (for carpentry)

nail polish, *n.* yaa-taa-lép
ยาทาเล็บ

naïve, *adj.* rái-bprà-sòp-gaan
ไร้ประสบการณ์ (lacking
experience); mâi-mii-maan-yaa
ไม่มีมารยา (artless; e.g. a baby)

naked, *adj.* bplʉ̄ai เปลือย (nude);
bplàao เปล่า (no covering, e.g. eye)

nap, *v.* ngîip-làp งีบหลับ

nap, *n.* gaan-ngîip-làp การงีบหลับ

nape, *n.* lǎng-kɔɔ หลังคอ

napkin, *n.* pâa-chét-bpàak

ผ้าเช็ดปาก (table); pâa-à-naa-mai
ผ้าอนามัย (sanitary feminine napkin)

narcotic, *n.* yaa-sèep-dùt ยาเสพติด

narrate, *v.* lâo-rûang เล่าเรื่อง

narrator, *n.* pûu-lâo-rûang
ผู้เล่าเรื่อง

narrow, *adj.* kêep แคบ

narrow-minded, *adj.* jai-kêep
ใจแคบ

nasal, *adj.* gìao-gàp-jà-mùuk
เกี่ยวกับจมูก (relating to the nose);
sĭang-naa-sìk เสียงนาสิก (sound)

nasty, *adj.* nâa-chang น่าชัง; ráai
ร้าย

nation, *n.* châat ชาติ

national, *adj.* hèng-châat แห่งชาติ

native, *adj.* dtèe-gam-nòot แต่กำเนิด
(being such by birth); tɔ́ɔng-tìn
ท้องถิ่น (local); púun-muang
พื้นเมือง (indigenous)

natural, *adj.* bpen-tam-ma-châat
เป็นธรรมชาติ; tam-ma-daa ธรรมดา

naturalize, *v.* tam-hâi-bpen-tam-
ma-châat ทำให้เป็นธรรมชาติ

nature, *n.* tam-ma-châat ธรรมชาติ

naughty, *adj.* son ซน; mâi-chûa-
fang ไม่เชื่อฟัง

nausea, *n.* aa-gaan-klûun-hĭan
อาการคลื่นเหียน

nauseous, *adj.* tam-hâi-klûun-hĭan
ทำให้คลื่นเหียน (causing nausea)

nautical, *adj.* gìao-gàp-gaan-dəən-
rua เกี่ยวกับการเดินเรือ

naval, *adj.* gìao-gàp-rua เกี่ยวกับเรือ

navel, *n.* sà-duu สะดือ

navigate, *v.* dəən-rua เดินเรือ
(ship); nam-taang นำทาง (an area;
to guide)

navigation, *n.* gaan-dəən-rua
การเดินเรือ

navigator, *n.* pûu-dəən-rua
ผู้เดินเรือ (ship); pûu-kàp-krûang-
bin ผู้ขับเครื่องบิน (airplane)

navy, *n.* gɔɔng-táp-rua กองทัพเรือ;
râat-cha-naa-wii ราชนาวี

near, *adj.* glâi ใกล้

nearby, *adj.* glâi-kiang ใกล้เคียง;
tɛ̌o-níi แถวนี้

nearly, *adv.* gùap-jà เกือบจะ

near-sighted, *adj.* sǎai-dtaa-sân
สายตาสั้น

neat, *adj.* rîap-rɔ́ɔi เรียบร้อย; bpen-
rá-bìap เป็นระเบียบ

necessary, *adj.* jam-bpen จำเป็น

necessity, *n.* kwaam-jam-bpen
ความจำเป็น (condition of being necessary); sìng-jam-bpen สิ่งจำเป็น
(something necessary)

neck, *n.* kɔɔ คอ

necklace, *n.* sɔ̂i-kɔɔ สร้อยคอ

neckline, *n.* kɔ̀ɔp-sûa-chûang-kɔɔ
ขอบเสื้อช่วงคอ

necktie, *n.* nék-tái เนคไท

need, *n.* kwaam-jam-bpen
ความจำเป็น

needle, *n.* kěm เข็ม

needless, *adj.* mâi-jam-bpen
ไม่จำเป็น

needy, *adj.* jam-bpen จำเป็น; kàt-sǒn ขัดสน

negative, *adj.* bpen-lóp เป็นลบ

neglect, *v.* mâi-sǒn-jai ไม่สนใจ; lá-ləəi ละเลย

negotiate, *v.* jee-ra-jaa เจรจา

negotiation, *n.* gaan-jee-ra-jaa การเจรจา

neigh, *v.* máa-rɔ́ɔng ม้าร้อง

neigh, *n.* sǐang-máa เสียงม้า

neighbor, *n.* pʉ̂an-bâan เพื่อนบ้าน

neighborhood, *n.* bɔɔ-ri-ween-glâi-kiang บริเวณใกล้เคียง

neither, *pron., v.* mâi-châi-táng-sɔ̌ɔng ไม่ใช่ทั้งสอง

neon, *n.* fai-nii-ɔɔn ไฟนีออน

nephew, *n.* lǎan-chaai หลานชาย

nerve, *n.* sên-bprà-sàat เส้นประสาท

nervous, *adj.* dtʉ̀ʉn-glua ตื่นกลัว;
bpen-bprà-sàat เป็นประสาท;
taang-bprà-sàat ทางประสาท

nest, *n.* rang รัง

net, *n.* dtaa-kàai ตาข่าย (snare;
mesh; made of openwork fabric);
nét เน็ท (used in sports, e.g. basketball net, tennis net, etc.); raai-dâai-
sùt-tí รายได้สุทธิ (income)

net, *adj.* sùt-tí สุทธิ (e.g. profit after
expense)

Netherlands, *n.* bprà-têet-nee-tɔ̂ɔ-
lɛɛn ประเทศเนเธอร์แลนด์

network, *n.* rá-bòp-nùai-ngaan
ระบบหน่วยงาน

neurology, *n.* bprà-sàat-wít-ta-yaa
ประสาทวิทยา

neurotic, *adj.* gìao-gàp-rá-bòp-bprà-
sàat เกี่ยวกับระบบประสาท

neuter, *adj.* mâi-mii-pêet ไม่มีเพศ

neutral, *adj.* bpen-glaang เป็นกลาง

neutron, *n.* niu-dtrɔɔn นิวตรอน

never, *adv.* mâi-kəəi ไม่เคย

nevertheless, *adv.* mɛ́ɛ-grà-nán
แม้กระนั้น

new, *adj.* mài ใหม่

newlywed, *n.* kon-tʉ̂ʉ-pɔ̂ng-dtɛ̀ng-
ngaan คนที่เพิ่งแต่งงาน

news, *n.* kàao ข่าว

newscast, *n.* gaan-tàai-tɔ̂ɔt-kàao
การถ่ายทอดข่าว

newscaster, *n.* pûu-àan-kàao
ผู้อ่านข่าว

newsletter, *n.* waa-rá-sǎan-kàao
วารสารข่าว

newspaper, *n.* nǎng-sʉ̌ʉ-pim
หนังสือพิมพ์

newsstand, *n.* tîi-kǎai-nǎng-sʉ̌ʉ-
pim ที่ขายหนังสือพิมพ์

New Year, *n.* bpii-mài ปีใหม่

next, *adj.* tàt-bpai ถัดไป; dtɔ̀ɔ-bpai
ต่อไป

nibble, *v.* té แทะ; dtɔ̀ɔt ตอด

nice, *adj.* dii ดี (good); nâa-rák
น่ารัก (cute, good-mannered, polite);
sǔai สวย (pretty, beautiful)

nickname, *n.* chʉ̂ʉ-lên ชื่อเล่น

niece, *n.* lǎan-sǎao หลานสาว

night, *n.* glaang-kɯɯn กลางคืน

night club, *n.* nái-klàp ในท์คลับ

nightgown, *n.* chút-nɔɔn ชุดนอน

nightingale, *n.* nók-nai-dîng-geo นกในติงเกล

nightmare, *n.* fǎn-ráai ฝันร้าย

nimble, *adj.* wɔ̂ng-wai ว่องไว; chà-làat ฉลาด

nine, *n.* gâao เก้า

nine hundred, *n.* gâao-rɔ́ɔi เก้าร้อย

nineteen, *nm.* sìp-gâao สิบเก้า

ninety, *nm.* gâao-sìp เก้าสิบ

nip, *v.* nìip หนีบ (pinch); dèt เด็ด (remove by snipping)

nipple, *n.* hǔa-nom หัวนม

nitrogen, *n.* nai-dtroo-jèn ไนโตรเจน

no, *adv.* mâi ไม่; mâi-dâai ไม่ได้; mâi-châi ไม่ใช่

nobility, *n.* pûak-pûu-dii พวกผู้ดี (high class people); kǔn-naang ขุนนาง (a class of persons distinguished by high birth or rank)

noble, *adj.* chán-sǔung ชั้นสูง; mii-sàk มีศักดิ์; bpen-pûu-dii เป็นผู้ดี

nobleman, -woman, *n.* pûu-dii-mii-dtrà-guun ผู้ดีมีตระกูล; chon-chán-sǔung ชนชั้นสูง

nobody, *n., pron.* mâi-mii-krai ไม่มีใคร (not anyone); kon-mâi-sǎm-kan คนไม่สำคัญ (unimportant person)

nocturnal, *adj.* gìao-gàp-glaang-

kɯɯn เกี่ยวกับกลางคืน (of the night); hǎa-gin-dtɔɔn-glaang-kɯɯn หากิน ตอนกลางคืน (active at night)

nod, *v.* pa-yák-nâa พยักหน้า

noise, *n.* sǐang เสียง

noisy, *adj.* sǐang-dang เสียงดัง

nominate, *v.* sà-nɔ̌ɔ-chɯ̂ɯ เสนอชื่อ

nomination, *n.* gaan-sà-nɔ̌ɔ-chɯ̂ɯ การเสนอชื่อ

nominee, *n.* pûu-dâai-ráp-gaan-sà-nɔ̌ɔ-chɯ̂ɯ ผู้ได้รับการเสนอชื่อ

none, *pron., adv., adj.* mâi-mii ไม่มี

nonexistent, *adj.* mâi-mii-yùu ไม่มีอยู่

nonetheless, *adv.* tǔng-grà-nán ถึงกระนั้น; mɛ́ɛ-grà-nán-gɔ̂ɔ-dii แม้กระนั้นก็ดี

nonfiction, *n.* wan-na-gam-tîi-mâi-châi-ni-yaai วรรณกรรมที่ไม่ใช่นิยาย

nonsense, *n.* rɯ̂ang-ráis-sǎa-rá เรื่องไร้สาระ

nonsmoking, *adj.* hâam-sùup-bù-rìi ห้ามสูบบุหรี่

nonstop, *adj.* mâi-mii-gaan-yùt ไม่มีการหยุด; mâi-yùt ไม่หยุด

noodle, *n.* gǔai-dtǐao ก๋วยเตี๋ยว (rice); bà-mìi บะหมี่ (egg)

nook, *n.* mum มุม; sɔ̂ɔk ซอก

noon, *n.* tîang-wan เที่ยงวัน

no one, *pron.* mâi-mii-krai ไม่มีใคร

norm, *n.* mâat-dtaa-tǎan มาตรฐาน; bɛ̀ɛp-pɛ̌ɛn แบบแผน

normal, *adj.* bpòk-gà-dtì ปกติ; tam-ma-daa ธรรมดา

north, *n.* nŭa เหนือ

North America, *n.* tá-wíip-à-mee-ri-gaa-nŭa ทวีปอเมริกาเหนือ

northeast, *n.* dtà-wan-ɔ̀ɔk-chǐiang-nŭa ตะวันออกเฉียงเหนือ

northern, *adj.* taang-nŭa ทางเหนือ

North Pole, *n.* kûa-lôok-nŭa ขั้วโลกเหนือ

northwest, *n.* dtà-wan-dtòk-chǐiang-nŭa ตะวันตกเฉียงเหนือ

nose, *n.* jà-mùuk จมูก

nostril, *n.* ruu-jà-mùuk รูจมูก

nosy, *adj.* sɔ̀ɔt-rúu-sɔ̀ɔt-hĕn สอดรู้สอดเห็น; yûng-rûuang-kon-ùun ยุ่งเรื่องคนอื่น

not, *adv.* mâi ไม่

notable, *adj.* dèn เด่น; sà-dùt-dtaa สะดุดตา

notary, *n.* pá-nák-ngaan-tá-bian พนักงานทะเบียน

notary public, *n.* pûu-ráp-rɔɔng-laai-sen ผู้รับรองลายเซ็น

notch, *n.* rɔɔi-bàak รอยบาก

note, *v.* ban-túk บันทึก; jòt จด

note, *n.* ban-túk บันทึก (record); mǎai-hèet หมายเหตุ (remark)

notebook, *n.* sà-mùt สมุด

nothing, *adv.* mâi-mii-à-rai ไม่มีอะไร

notice, *v.* sǎng-gèet สังเกต

notice, *n.* kɔ̂ɔ-sǎng-gèet ข้อสังเกต (remark); gaan-dtuan การเตือน

observing); bprà-gàat ประกาศ

noticeable, *adj.* nâa-sŏn-jai น่าสนใจ

notification, *n.* gaan-jɛ̂ɛng การแจ้ง; gaan-bprà-gàat การประกาศ

notify, *v.* jɛ̂ɛng แจ้ง (inform); bprà-gàat ประกาศ (make known)

notion, *n.* kwaam-kít-hĕn ความคิดเห็น

notorious, *adj.* rúu-gan-tûa รู้กันทั่ว

noun, *n.* kam-naam คำนาม

nourish, *v.* bam-rung บำรุง; lɔ̀ɔ-líang หล่อเลี้ยง

nourishment, *n.* gaan-bam-rung การบำรุง

novel, *n.* ná-wá-ní-yaai นวนิยาย

novelist, *n.* nák-kian-ná-wá-ní-yaai นักเขียนนวนิยาย

novelty, *n.* kwaam-mài ความใหม่ (newness); sìng-bplɛ̀ɛk-mài สิ่งแปลกใหม่ (innovation)

November, *n.* prút-sà-jì-gaa-yon พฤศจิกายน

novice, *n.* neen เณร (young monk); pûu-rə̂əm-hàt ผู้เริ่มหัด (beginner)

now, *adv.* dǐao-níi เดี๋ยวนี้; dtɔɔn-níi ตอนนี้

nowadays, *adv.* bpàt-jù-ban-níi ปัจจุบันนี้

nowhere, *adv.* mâi-mii-tîi-nǎi ไม่มีที่ไหน

nozzle, *n.* hŭa-chìit หัวฉีด

nuance, *n*. kwaam-dtèek-dtàang-tîi-mâi-hěn-chát-jeen ความแตกต่างที่ไม่เห็นชัดเจน

nuclear, *n*. niu-klia นิวเคลียร์

nucleus, *n*. niu-klíat, niu-klías นิวเคลียส

nude, *adj*. bplʉai เปลือย

nudge, *v*. tɔ̌ɔng ถอง; dun ดุน; dan ดัน

nugget, *n*. gɔ̂ɔn ก้อน

nuisance, *n*. sìng-róp-guan สิ่งรบกวน; sìng-nâa-ram-kaan สิ่งน่ารำคาญ

null, *adj*. mâi-mii-à-rai ไม่มีอะไร

nullify, *v*. tam-hâi-rái-pǒn ทำให้ไร้ผล (invalidate); tam-hâi-mâi-mii-pǒn-bang-káp ทำให้ไม่มีผลบังคับ (counteract the force or effectiveness of); yók-lôək ยกเลิก (cancel)

numb, *adj*. chaa ชา

number, *n*. dtua-lêek ตัวเลข; jam-nuan จำนวน

numerical, *adj*. gìao-gàp-dtua-lêek เกี่ยวกับตัวเลข

numerous, *adj*. mâak-maai มากมาย

nun, *n*. mêe-chii แม่ชี

nuptial, *adj*. gìao-gàp-gaan-sǒm-rót เกี่ยวกับการสมรส

nurse, *n*. naang-pá-yaa-baan นางพยาบาล

nursing home, *n*. bâan-pák-kon-cha-raa บ้านพักคนชรา

nut, *n*. pǒn-la-máai-bplʉak-kěng ผลไม้เปลือกแข็ง

nutrient, *v*. bam-rung-líang บำรุงเลี้ยง

nutrition, *n*. pôot-cha-naa-gaan โภชนาการ

nutritious, *adj*. mii-kun-kâa-taang-aa-hǎan มีคุณค่าทางอาหาร

nylon, *n*. nai-lɔ̂n ไนล่อน

O

oaf, *n*. kon-ngôo คนโง่

oak, *n*. dtôn-óok ต้นโอ๊ก

oar, *v*. paai พาย

oar, *n*. máai-paai ไม้พาย

oasis, *n*. bɔɔ-ri-ween-ù-don-sǒm-buun-nai-tá-lee-saai บริเวณอุดมสมบูรณ์ในทะเลทราย; oo-ee-sít โอเอซิส

oat, *n*. kâao-óok ข้าวโอ๊ต

oath, *n*. kam-sǎa-baan คำสาบาน; sàt-jà สัจจะ

oatmeal, *n*. kâao-óot ข้าวโอ๊ต

obedient, *adj*. chʉa-fang เชื่อฟัง; yùu-nai-oo-wâat อยู่ในโอวาท

obese, *adj*. ûan-mâak-gəən-bpai อ้วนมากเกินไป

obey, *v*. chʉa-fang เชื่อฟัง

obituary, *n*. kàao-mɔɔ-ra-ná-gam ข่าวมรณกรรม

object, *v*. kát-káan คัดค้าน

object, *n*. sìng-kɔ̌ɔng สิ่งของ; wát-tù วัตถุ

objection, n. gaan-kát-káan การคัดค้าน; gaan-dtôo-yéeng การโต้แย้ง

objective, n. wát-tù-bprà-sŏng วัตถุประสงค์ (goal)

objective, adj. mâi-lam-iang ไม่ลำเอียง

obligate, v. hâi-kam-mân-săn-yaa ให้คำมั่นสัญญา (commit, promise); bpen-geen เป็นเกณฑ์ (restrict); mii-pan-tá มีพันธะ (bind or firmly hold to an act)

obligation, n. pan-tá พันธะ; paa-rá-nâa-ûi ภาระหน้าที่

oblige, v. bang-káp บังคับ (constrain); bpen-nîi-bun-kun เป็นหนี้ บุญคุณ (indebted or grateful)

obscene, adj. laa-mók ลามก

obscure, adj. klum-krua คลุมเครือ (vague); mûut-mon มืดมน (dark)

observant, adj. châng-săng-gèet ช่างสังเกต; sài-jai ใส่ใจ

observation, n. gaan-săng-gèet การสังเกต

observe, v. săng-gèet สังเกต

obsess, v. krôop-ngam-jìt-jai ครอบงำจิตใจ

obsession, n. gaan-krôop-ngam-jìt-jai การครอบงำจิตใจ

obsolete, adj. láa-sà-măi ล้าสมัย (outmoded in style); lôək-chái-léeo เลิกใช้แล้ว (no longer in use)

obstacle, n. ùp-bpà-sàk อุปสรรค

obstinate, adj. dan-tú-rang ดันทุรัง; hŭa-kĕng หัวแข็ง

obstruct, v. kàt-kwăang ขัดขวาง; gìit-kwăang กีดขวาง

obstruction, n. sìng-gìit-kwăang สิ่งกีดขวาง (something that obstructs); ùp-bpà-sàk อุปสรรค (obstacle)

obtain, v. dâai-maa ได้มา

obvious, adj. chát-jeen ชัดเจน; chát-jɛɛng ชัดแจ้ง

occasion, n. oo-gàat โอกาส; waa-rá วาระ

occasional, adj. dtaam-oo-gàat ตามโอกาส; bpen-kráng-kraao เป็นครั้งคราว

occasionally, adv. baang-oo-gàat บางโอกาส

occupant, n. pûu-krôop-krɔɔng ผู้ครอบครอง (one who occupies, or takes possession); pûu-aa-săi ผู้อาศัย (tenant)

occupation, n. aa-chîip อาชีพ (career); gaan-krɔ̂ɔp-krɔɔng การครอบครอง (taking and keeping possession)

occupied, adj. mâi-wâang ไม่ว่าง (not vacant); kít-yùu-dtà-lɔ̀ɔt-wee-laa คิดอยู่ตลอดเวลา (mind)

occupy, v. krɔ̂ɔp-krɔɔng ครอบครอง

occur, v. bpraa-gòt ปรากฏ (appear); mii-kûn มีขึ้น (happen)

English • Phonetic • Thai

English · Phonetic · Thai

occurrence, *n.* gaan-gòɔt-kʉ̂n การเกิดขึ้น

ocean, *n.* má-hǎa-sà-mùt มหาสมุทร

October, *n.* dtù-laa-kom ตุลาคม

octopus, *n.* bplaa-mʉ̀k-yák ปลาหมึกยักษ์

odd, *adj.* bplὲɛk แปลก (strange); kîi คี่ (not even)

odds, *n.* kwaam-bpen-bpai-dâai ความเป็นไปได้ (probability or chance)

ode, *n.* bòt-gà-wii-sǎn-ra-sɵ̌ɔn บทกวีสรรเสริญ

odor, *n.* glìn กลิ่น

of, *prep.* kɔ̌ɔng ของ; hὲng แห่ง

off, *adj., adv.* ɔ̀ɔk ออก (distant or removed); yὲɛk-ɔ̀ɔk แยกออก (separated); yùt-ngaan หยุดงาน (be away from work); lùt หลุด (not connected); bpìt ปิด (e.g. T.V., radio)

offend, *v.* tam-hâi-mâi-pɔɔ-jai ทำให้ไม่พอใจ (cause displeasure); lá-mɵ̂ɵt ละเมิด (violate)

offense, *n.* gaan-tam-hâi-mâi-pɔɔ-jai การทำให้ไม่พอใจ; gaan-lá-mɵ̂ɵt การละเมิด

offensive, *adj.* kùn-kʉang ขุ่นเคือง; nâa-rang-gìat น่ารังเกียจ

offer, *v.* sà-nɵ̌ɔ เสนอ; hâi ให้

offering, *n.* sìng-tîi-sà-nɵ̌ɔ-hâi สิ่งที่เสนอให้ (something being offered); kɔ̌ɔng-kwǎn ของขวัญ (gift)

office, *n.* sǎm-nák-ngaan สำนักงาน

officer, *n.* jâo-nâa-tîi เจ้าหน้าที่

official, *adj.* bpen-taang-gaan เป็นทางการ

offspring, *n.* pà-lìt-dtà-pǒn ผลิตผล (a product); lûuk-lǎan ลูกหลาน (descendant)

often, *adv.* bɔ̀i บ่อย

oil, *n.* náam-man น้ำมัน

oily, *adj.* bpen-man เป็นมัน

ointment, *n.* kriim ครีม; yaa-kîi-pʉ̂ng ยาขี้ผึ้ง

okay, O.K., *adj., v.* dtòk-long ตกลง (yes, agree); sà-baai-dii สบายดี (be well)

okra, *n.* grà-jíap กระเจี๊ยบ

old, *adj.* gào เก่า (objects); gὲɛ แก่ (living things)

older, *adj.* gào-gwàa เก่ากว่า; gὲɛ-gwàa แก่กว่า

old-fashioned, *adj.* láa-sà-mǎi ล้าสมัย

old maid, *n.* sǎao-gὲɛ สาวแก่

olive, *n.* dtôn-má-gɔ̀ɔk ต้นมะกอก

olive oil, *n.* náam-man-má-gɔ̀ɔk น้ำมันมะกอก

Olympics, *n.* gii-laa-oo-lim-bpìk กีฬาโอลิมปิก

omelet, *n.* kài-jiao ไข่เจียว

omen, *n.* laang-bɔ̀ɔk-hèet ลางบอกเหตุ

omission, *n.* gaan-lá-wén การละเว้น

omit, *v.* wén เว้น; dtàt-ɔɔk ตัดออก

omnipotent, *adj.* mii-am-nâat-túk-yàang มีอำนาจทุกอย่าง

on, *prep.* bon บน (opposite of under); tîi ที่ (at); dtaam ตาม (along); ná ณ; nai-wee-laa-tîi ในเวลาที่ (at the time); bpèət เปิด (e.g. T.V., radio)

once, *adv.* kráng-nùng ครั้งหนึ่ง

one, *nm.* nùng หนึ่ง

oneself, *pron.* dtua-eeng ตัวเอง

one-way, *adj.* taang-diao ทางเดียว

ongoing, *adj.* dtɔ̀ɔ-nûang ต่อเนื่อง

onion, *n.* hǔa-hɔ̌ɔm หัวหอม; hɔ̌ɔm หอม

only, *adj.* tâo-nán เท่านั้น; kêe-nán แค่นั้น

opal, *n.* múk-daa มุกดา; plɔɔi-sǐi-lǔap-lǔang พลอยสีเหลือบเหลือง

opaque, *adj.* túp ทึบ; túp-sɛɛŋ ทึบแสง

open, *adj.* bpə̀ət เปิด; bpə̀ət-gwâaŋ เปิดกว้าง

opening, *n.* gaan-bpə̀ət การเปิด (act of opening); chɔ̂ŋ ช่อง (slot, gap); pí-tii-bpə̀ət พิธีเปิด (an event)

opera, *n.* oo-bpee-râa โอเปร่า; ùp-bpà-raa-gɔɔn อุปรากร

operate, *v.* tam-ngaan ทำงาน; bpà-dtì-bàt-gaan ปฏิบัติการ

operation, *n.* gaan-tam-ngaan การทำงาน (way in which something

works; working); gaan-pàa-dtàt การผ่าตัด (surgery)

operator, *n.* pûu-bpà-dtì-bàt-ngaan ผู้ปฏิบัติงาน (one that operates); pa-nák-ngaan-ráp-too-rá-sàp พนักงานรับโทรศัพท์ (telephone operator)

opinion, *n.* kwaam-kít-hěn ความคิดเห็น; tát-sà-ná ทัศนะ

opinionated, *adj.* dûu-duŋ ดื้อดึง

oppose, *v.* dtɔ̀ɔ-dtâan ต่อต้าน; kát-káan คัดค้าน

opposite, *adj.* dtroŋ-kâam ตรงข้าม

opposition, *n.* gaan-kát-káan การคัดค้าน (opposing); gaan-dtɔ̀ɔ-sûu การต่อสู้ (fighting, conflict)

oppress, *v.* gòt-kìi กดขี่; bìip-baŋ-káp บีบบังคับ

optic, -al, *adj.* gìao-gàp-sǎai-dtaa เกี่ยวกับสายตา; gìao-gàp-dtaa เกี่ยวกับตา

optician, *n.* châŋ-tam-wên-dtaa ช่างทำแว่นตา

optics, *n.* wít-ta-yaa-sàat-taaŋ-sɛɛŋ-lɛ́-sǎai-dtaa วิทยาศาสตร์ทางแสงและสายตา

optimism, *n.* gaan-mɔɔŋ-nai-ŋɛ̂ɛ dii การมองในแง่ดี

optimistic, *adj.* mɔɔŋ-lôok-nai-ŋɛ̂ɛ-dii มองโลกในแง่ดี

option, *n.* gaan-lûak การเลือก; taaŋ-lûak ทางเลือก

optional, *adj.* hâi-lûak-dâai ให้เลือกได้; mii-taaŋ-lûak

มีทางเลือก

optometrist, *n.* pûu-chîao-chaan-dâan-sǎai-dtaa ผู้เชี่ยวชาญด้านสายตา

opulent, *adj.* mâng-kâng มั่งคั่ง

or, *conj.* rǔe หรือ; rú รึ

oracle, *n.* kam-pá-yaa-gɔɔn คำพยากรณ์

oral, *adj.* dûai-bpàak ด้วยปาก; bpàak-bplàao ปากเปล่า

orange, *adj.* sǐi-sôm สีส้ม

orange, *n.* sôm ส้ม

orange juice, *n.* náam-sôm น้ำส้ม

orator, *n.* pûu-glàao-woo-hǎan ผู้กล่าวโวหาร; kon-glàao-kam-bpraa-sǎi คนกล่าวคำปราศรัย

oratory, *n.* gaan-sà-dɛɛng-woo-hǎan การแสดงโวหาร; kam-bpraa-sǎi คำปราศรัย

orbit, *n.* wong-koo-jɔɔn วงโคจร

orchard, *n.* sǔan-pǒn-la-máai สวนผลไม้

orchestra, *n.* wong-ɔɔ-két-sa-dtrâa วงออเคสตร้า

orchid, *n.* glûai-máai กล้วยไม้

ordain, *v.* bùat บวช (as a monk or priest); gam-nòt-cha-dtaa กำหนดชะตา (predestine)

ordeal, *n.* gaan-tót-sɔ̀ɔp-kwaam-òt-ton การทดสอบความอดทน; kwaam-tɔɔ-ra-hòt ความทรหด

order, *v.* sàng สั่ง

order, *n.* kam-sàng คำสั่ง (command); gaan-sàng-súa ใบสั่งซื้อ

(merchandise)

ordinal, *adj.* gìao-gàp-lam-dàp เกี่ยวกับลำดับ; dtaam-lam-dàp ตามลำดับ

ordinary, *adj.* tam-ma-daa ธรรมดา; sǎa-man สามัญ

ore, *n.* rɛ̂ɛ แร่; sǐn-rɛ̂ɛ สินแร่

organ, *n.* à-wai-ya-wá อวัยวะ

organic, *adj.* gìao-gàp-in-sii เกี่ยวกับอินทรีย์

organization, *n.* ong-gɔɔn องค์กร (e.g. association, company); ká-ná คณะ (group); rá-bòp ระบบ (system)

organize, *v.* jàt-rá-bòp จัดระบบ (arrange into a system); jà-dtâng จัดตั้ง (establish); jàt-hâi-rîap-rɔ́ɔi จัดให้เรียบร้อย (make neat)

orgasm, *n.* jùt-sùt-yɔ̂ɔt จุดสุดยอด

orgy, *n.* sék-mùu เซ็กซ์หมู่

orient, *n.* bprà-têet-nai-tɛ̀ɛp-dtà-wan-ɔ̀ɔk ประเทศในแถบตะวันออก

Oriental, *n.* chaao-dtà-wan-ɔ̀ɔk ชาวตะวันออก

orientation, *n.* bpà-tòm-ní-têet ปฐมนิเทศน์ (introductory instruction); gaan-bpràp-dtua การปรับตัว (adjustment); tít-taang ทิศทาง (direction); kwaam-sǒn-jai-taang-pêet ความสนใจทางเพศ (sexual orientation)

origin, *n.* lɛ̀ng-gam-nɔ̀ɔt แหล่งกำเนิด; tîi-maa ที่มา

original, *n.* dtôn-chà-bàp ต้นฉบับ (the source from which a copy is made); kɔ̌ɔng-tɛ́ɛ ของแท้ (authentic)

originate, *v.* rí-rə̂əm ริเริ่ม; rə̂əm เริ่ม

ornament, *n.* krûang-bprà-dàp เครื่องประดับ

orphan, *n.* dèk-gam-práa เด็กกำพร้า

orphanage, *n.* sà-tǎan-líang-dèk-gam-práa สถานเลี้ยงเด็กกำพร้า

orthodox, *adj.* dâng-dəəm ดั้งเดิม; dtaam-bɛ̀ɛp-boo-raan ตามแบบโบราณ

orthopedic, *adj.* gìao-gàp-grà-dùuk เกี่ยวกับกระดูก

ostrich, *n.* nók-grà-jɔ̀ɔk-têet นกกระจอกเทศ

other, *adj.* ùun-ùun อื่นๆ; ùun อื่น

otherwise, *conj.* mâi-chên-nán ไม่เช่นนั้น (if not)

otherwise, *adv.* bpen-yàang-ùun เป็นอย่างอื่น (in another way)

otter, *n.* dtua-nâak ตัวนาก

ought, *aux. v.* dtɔ̂ng ต้อง

ounce, *n.* ɔɔn ออนซ์

our, *adj.* kɔ̌ɔng-rao ของเรา; kɔ̌ɔng-pûak-rao ของพวกเรา

ours, *pron.* kɔ̌ɔng-rao ของเรา; kɔ̌ɔng-pûak-rao ของพวกเรา

ourselves, *pron.* dtua-rao-eeng ตัวเราเอง; dtua-pûak-rao-eeng

ตัวพวกเราเอง

out, *adv.* ɔ̀ɔk ออก (used with other words, e.g. take out, come out, go out); kâang-ngɔ̂ɔk ข้างนอก (outside, exterior, external)

outbreak, *v.* rá-bàat ระบาด (sudden increase); rá-bə̀ət ระเบิด (outburst)

outbreak, *n.* gaan-rá-bàat การระบาด; gaan-rá-bə̀ət การระเบิด

outburst, *v.* rá-bə̀ət ระเบิด (of activity or emotion); dùat-plâan เดือดพล่าน (of emotion)

outburst, *n.* gaan-rá-bə̀ət การระเบิด; gaan-dùat-plâan การเดือดพล่าน

outcast, *n.* kon-jɔɔn-jàt คนจรจัด (vagabond); kon-nɔ̂ɔk-sǎng-kom คนนอกสังคม (one that has been excluded from a society); jan-taan จัณฑาล (of the Indian caste system)

outcome, *n.* pǒn-láp ผลลัพธ์; pǒn-tíi-dtaam-maa ผลที่ตามมา

outdated, *adj.* láa-sà-mǎi ล้าสมัย

outdo, *v.* ao-chá-ná เอาชนะ

outdoor, *adj.* nɔ̂ɔk-bâan นอกบ้าน; glaang-jɛ̂ɛng กลางแจ้ง

outer, *adj.* chán-nɔ̂ɔk ชั้นนอก

outfit, *n.* chút ชุด; sûa-pâa เสื้อผ้า

outgoing, *adj.* chɔ̂ɔp-ɔ̀ɔk-sǎng-kom ชอบออกสังคม

outgrow, *v.* dtoo-reo โตเร็ว

English · Phonetic · Thai

outing, *n.* gaan-ɔ̀ɔk-nɔ̂ɔk-bâan การออกนอกบ้าน

outlaw, *n.* kon-nɔ̂ɔk-gòt-mǎai คนนอกกฎหมาย

outlet, *n.* taang-ɔ̀ɔk ทางออก (exit, vent); ráan-káa ร้านค้า (store)

outline, *v.* râang ร่าง

outline, *n.* káo-kroong เค้าโครง; kroong-râang โครงร่าง

outlive, *v.* aa-yú-yɯɯn-gwàa อายุยืนกว่า

outlook, *n.* pâap ภาพ (view); tát-sà-ná ทัศนะ (attitude)

out-of-date, *adj.* láa-sà-mǎi ล้าสมัย

outpatient, *n.* pûu-bpùai-nɔ̂ɔk ผู้ป่วยนอก

output, *n.* pà-lìt-dtà-pǒn ผลิตผล (amount produced); kɔ̂ɔ-muun-tîi-sòng-ɔ̀ɔk-maa ข้อมูลที่ส่งออกมา (information)

outrage, *v.* gròot-jàt โกรธจัด

outrage, *n.* gaan-tam-laai การทำลาย (destruction); kwaam-hòot-ráai ความโหดร้าย (extreme violence)

outrageous, *adj.* run-rɛɛng รุนแรง (violent); ráp-mâi-dâai รับไม่ได้ (unacceptable, very bad, e.g. outrageous behavior); pìt-bpòk-gà-dtì ผิดปกติ (very unusual)

outside, *adj.* kâang-nɔ̂ɔk ข้างนอก; dâan-nɔ̂ɔk ด้านนอก

outsider, *n.* kon-nɔ̂ɔk คนนอก

outskirts, *n.* chaan-mɯang ชานเมือง

outsmart, *v.* chà-làat-gwàa ฉลาดกว่า

outspoken, *adj.* pûut-pǒong-pǎang พูดโผงผาง (frank)

outstanding, *adj.* dèn เด่น (prominent, distinguished); yang-kong-mii-yùu ยังคงมีอยู่ (still in existence)

outward, *adv.* paai-nɔ̂ɔk ภายนอก; dâan-nɔ̂ɔk ด้านนอก

oval, *n.* rûup-kài รูปไข่; wong-rii วงรี

ovary, *n.* rang-kài รังไข่

oven, *n.* dtao-òp เตาอบ

over, *adv.* nǔa เหนือ (above); sǔung-gwàa สูงกว่า (higher); mâak-gwàa มากกว่า (more); gɔɔn เกิน (too much); jòp จบ (finished)

overall, *adj.*, *adv.* táng-mòt ทั้งหมด (the whole, everything); tûa-túk-dâan ทั่วทุกด้าน (every aspect)

overbearing, *adj.* krɔ̂ɔp-ngam ครอบงำ; yîng-yá-sǒo หยิ่งยโส

overboard, *v.*, *adv.* tam-gɔɔn-bpai ทำเกินไป (to go overboard = go to extremes); dtòk-rɯa ตกเรือ (fall overboard); long-náam ลงน้ำ (fall or go into the water)

overcast, *adj.* mii-mêek-mâak มีเมฆมาก (having a lot of clouds); krúm ครึ้ม (cloudy, gloomy)

overcoat, *n.* sɯ̂a-klum เสื้อคลุม

overcome, *v.* ao-cha-ná เอาชนะ;

pi-chít พิชิต

overdo, v. tam-gəən ทำเกิน

overdose, v. gin-mâak-gəən-bpɔɔ-ri-maan กินมากเกินปริมาณ

overdose, n. mâak-gəən-bpɔɔ-ri-maan มากเกินปริมาณ

overdue, adj. pón-gam-nòt พ้นกำหนด; ləəi-wee-laa เลยเวลา

overflow, v. lón ล้น

overhead, adj. nŭa-hŭa เหนือหัว; nŭa-sĭi-sà เหนือศีรษะ

overhead, n. kâa-chái-jàai ค่าใช้จ่าย (expenses)

overlap, v. kâap-gìao คาบเกี่ยว (have an area or range in common with); táp ทับ (lie over)

overload, v. ban-túk-gəən-pi-gàt บรรทุกเกินพิกัด

overlook, v. mɔɔng-kâam มองข้าม (fail to notice or consider, look over or at from a higher place); məən-chɔ̌əi เมินเฉย (ignore, disregard)

overnight, adv., adj. káang-kʉʉn ค้างคืน; dtà-lɔ̀ɔt-kʉʉn ตลอดคืน

overpopulation, n. bprà-chaa-gɔɔn-lón ประชากรล้น

overpower, v. ao-cha-ná เอา เชนะ

overrule, v. lóp-láang ลบล้าง (prevail over); dtii-glàp ตีกลับ (reverse)

overseas, adj. póon-ta-lee โพ้นทะเล; nɔ̂ɔk-bprà-têet นอกประเทศ

oversee, v. kum-ngaan คุมงาน (supervise); dtrùat-dtraa ตรวจตรา (examine or inspect)

oversight, n. gaan-sǎng-gèet-pìt-plâat การสังเกตผิดพลาด

overstay, v. yùu-gəən-gam-nòt อยู่เกินกำหนด

overtake, v. dtaam-tan ตามทัน (catch up with); joom-dtii โจมตี (attack); tam-hâi-bprà-làat-jai ทำให้ประหลาดใจ (take by surprise); ao-chá-ná เอาชนะ (conquer, defeat)

overthrow, v. kôon โค่น; lóm-láang ล้มล้าง

overtime, n. ngaan-nɔ̂ɔk-wee-laa งานนอกเวลา; oo-tii โอที

overturn, v. lóm-láang ล้มล้าง (overthrow); plìk พลิก (turn over)

overweight, adj. náam-nàk-gəən น้ำหนักเกิน

overwhelm, v. tûam-tón ท่วมท้น

overwork, v. tam-ngaan-mâak-gəən-bpai ทำงานมากเกินไป

owe, v. bpen-nîi เป็นหนี้

owl, n. nók-hûuk นกฮูก

own, adj., pron. dtua-eeng ตัวเอง; dûai-dtua-eeng ด้วยตนเอง

owner, n. jâo-kɔ̌ɔng เจ้าของ

ox, n. wua วัว

oxygen, n. ɔ́k-si-jên ย็อกซิเจน

oyster, n. hɔ̌i naang rom หอยนางรม

ozone, n. oo-soon โอโซน

P

English · Phonetic · Thai

pace, *v.* gâao ก้าว

pace, *n.* gâao ก้าว; r̆ii-táao ฝีเท้า

pacifier, *n.* jùk-nom จุกนม

pacify, *v.* bplɔ̀ɔp ปลอบ (calm); tam-hâi-sà-ngòp ทำให้สงบ (establish peace)

pack, *v.* hɔ̀ɔ ห่อ

pack, *n.* hɔ̀ɔ ห่อ (small package); bpêe เป้ (backpack)

package, *n.* hɔ̀ɔ ห่อ (something wrapped); mát มัด (something tied)

pact, *n.* săn-yaa สัญญา (contract); kɔ̂ɔ-dtòk-long ข้อตกลง (agreement)

pad, *n.* bɔ̀ เบาะ (thick piece of soft material); sà-nàp-kɛ̂ng สนับแข้ง (padded material to protect the legs)

padding, *n.* wát-sà-dù-rɔɔng วัสดุรอง; krûang-rɔɔng เครื่องรอง

paddle, *n.* máai-paai ไม้พาย (oar); máai-guan ไม้กวน (for stirring food)

paddock, *n.* kɔ̂ɔk-máa-kâang-sà-năam-kɛ̀ng คอกม้าข้างสนามแข่ง

page, *v.* r̆ak เรียก

page, *n.* nâa หน้า; nâa-năng-s̆u̇u หน้าหนังสือ

pageant, *n.* gaan-hɛ̀ɛ การแห่ (procession); gaan-sà-dɛɛng-glaang-jɛ̂ɛng การแสดงกลางแจ้ง (outdoor performance)

pager, *n.* pèet-jɔ̂ɔ เพจเจอร์; pèet เพจ

pagoda, *n.* jee-dii เจดีย์

pain, *n.* kwaam-jèp-bpùat ความเจ็บปวด

painful, *adj.* jèp-bpùat เจ็บปวด; bpùat ปวด

painkiller, *n.* yaa-gɛ̂ɛ-bpùat ยาแก้ปวด

paint, *v.* taa-s̆ii ทาสี

paint, *n.* s̆ii สี; s̆ii-taa สีทา

paintbrush, *n.* pûu-gan พู่กัน; bprɛɛng-taa-s̆ii แปรงทาสี

painter, *n.* châng-taa-s̆ii ช่างทาสี; châng-k̆ian-pâap ช่างเขียนภาพ

painting, *n.* gaan-taa-s̆ii การทาสี; pâap-k̆ian ภาพเขียน

pair, *n.* kûu คู่

pajamas, *n.* chút-nɔɔn ชุดนอน

pal, *n.* pûan เพื่อน

palace, *n.* wang วัง

palate, *n.* pee-daan-bpàak เพดานปาก

pale, *adj.* s̆iit ซีด; ɔ̀ɔn-gam-lang อ่อนกำลัง

palette, *n.* jaan-s̆ii จานสี; gaan-pà-s̆ŏm-s̆ii การผสมสี

palm, *n.* fàa-mʉʉ ฝ่ามือ (hand); dtôn-bpaam ต้นปาล์ม (tree)

pamper, *v.* ao-jai เอาใจ; dtaam-jai ตามใจ

pamphlet, *n.* jun-lá-s̆ăan จุลสาร

pan, *v.* rɔ̂n ร่อน (e.g. for gold)

pan, *n*. grà-tá กระทะ; gà-tá กะทะ

panacea, *n*. yaa-gɛ̂ɛ-sǎa-ra-pát-rôok ยาแก้สารพัดโรค

pancake, *n*. pɛɛn-kéek แพนเค้ก; kà-nǒm-bûang ขนมเบื้อง

panda, *n*. mǐi-pɛɛn-dâa หมีแพนด้า

pane, *n*. kɔ̀ɔp-nâa-dtàang ขอบหน้าต่าง (for window)

panel, *n*. raai-chûu รายชื่อ; ka-ná คณะ; gaan-à-pí-bpraai-glùm การอภิปรายกลุ่ม

panic, *v*. dtòk-jai-glua ตกใจกลัว

panic, *n*. kwaam-dtòk-jai-glua ความตกใจกลัว

panorama, *n*. pâap-kà-nàat-gwâang ภาพขนาดกว้าง; tát-sà-nii-ya-pâap-ruam ทัศนียภาพรวม

pant, *v*. hǎai-jai-lúk-lé-reo หายใจถี่และเร็ว; hɔ̀ɔp หอบ

panther, *n*. sǔa-dam เสือดำ; sǔa-daao-dam เสือดาวดำ

panties, *n*. gaan-geeng-chán-nai-sà-dtrii กางเกงชั้นในสตรี

pantomime, *n*. lá-kɔɔn-bâi ละครใบ้

pantry, *n*. hɔ̂ng-gèp-aa-hǎan ห้องเก็บอาหาร

pants, *n*. gaang-geeng กางเกง

pantyhose, *n*. tǔng-nɔ̂ng ถุงน่อง

paper, *n*. grà-dàat กระดาษ; èek-gà-sǎan เอกสาร; nǎng-sǔu-pim หนังสือพิมพ์

paperback, *n*. nǎng-sǔu-bpòk-ɔ̀ɔn หนังสือปกอ่อน

paper clip, *n*. tîi-nìip-grà-dàat ที่หนีบกระดาษ

par, *n*. raa-kaa-dəəm ราคาเดิม (face value); paa พาร์ (golf)

parade, *n*. kà-buan-paa-rêet ขบวนพาเหรด

paradise, *n*. sà-wǎn สวรรค์

paradox, *n*. sìng-tîi-kàt-yɛ́ɛng-gan สิ่งที่ขัดแย้งกัน

paragon, *n*. dtua-yàang-yɔ̂ɔt-yîam ตัวอย่างยอดเยี่ยม (perfect example); kon-tîi-sǒm-buun-bɛ̀ɛp คนที่สมบูรณ์แบบ (perfect person)

paragraph, *n*. yɔ̂ɔ-nâa ย่อหน้า; wák วรรค; dtɔɔn ตอน

parallel, *adj*. kà-nǎan-gan ขนานกัน

parallel, *n*. sên-kà-nǎan เส้นขนาน; sìng-tîi-kà-nǎan-gan สิ่งที่ขนานกัน

paralysis, *n*. am-ma-pâat อัมพาต

paralyze, *v*. bpen-am-ma-pâat เป็นอัมพาต

paramedic, *n*. bpà-tǒm-pá-yaa-baan ปฐมพยาบาล

parameter, *n*. kɔ̂ɔ-jam-gàt ข้อจำกัด

paranoid, *adj*. wí-dtòk-gang-won วิตกกังวล

paraphrase *n*. pûut-ìik-nɛɛo-nùng พูดอีกแนวหนึ่ง

parasite, *n*. pá-yâat พยาธิ

parcel, *n*. pát-sà-dù พัสดุ; hɔ̀ɔ ห่อ

parch, *v*. tam-hâi-griam ทำให้เกรียม; tam-hâi-hɛ̂ng ทำให้แห้ง

pardon, *v*. kɔ̌ɔ-tôot ขอโทษ

pardon, *n*. gaan-hâi-à-pai

การให้อภัย; gaan-lá-wén-tôot
การละเว้นโทษ

parent, n. pɔ̂ɔ-rǔu-mɛ̂ɛ พ่อหรือแม่

parentage, n. tɤ̌ak-tǎo-lào-gɔɔ
เทือกเถาเหล่ากอ

parenthesis, n. wong-lép วงเล็บ

park, v. jɔ̀ɔt จอด

park, n. sǔan-sǎa-taa-ra-ná
สวนสาธารณะ; sǔan สวน

parking, n. gaan-jɔ̀ɔt-rót
การจอดรถ; tîi-jɔ̀ɔt-rót ที่จอดรถ

parliament, n. sà-paa สภา; rát-tà-
sà-paa รัฐสภา

parlor, n. hɔ̂ng-ráp-kɛ̀ɛk ห้องรับ
แขก (for guests); hɔ̂ng-nâng-lên
ห้องนั่งเล่น (living room)

parody, n. gaan-lɔ́ɔ-lian
การล้อเลียน

parole, n. tan-bon ทัณฑ์บน

parrot, n. nók-gɛ̂ɛo นกแก้ว

parsley, n. pàk-chii ผักชี

part, n. sùan ส่วน; sùan-bprà-gɔ̀ɔp
ส่วนประกอบ

partial, adj. baang-sùan บางส่วน;
sùan-nùng ส่วนหนึ่ง

participant, n. pûu-kâo-rûam
ผู้เข้าร่วม

participate, v. kâo-rûam เข้าร่วม;
rûam ร่วม

participation, n. gaan-kâo-rûam
การเข้าร่วม; gaan-mii-sùan-rûam
การมีส่วนร่วม

particle, n. à-nú-pâak อนุภาค; tú-

lii ธุลี

particular, adj. dooi-chà-pɔ́
โดยเฉพาะ

partly, adv. baang-sùan บางส่วน;
bpen-sùan เป็นส่วน

partner, n. hûn-sùan หุ้นส่วน (in
business); pûu-rûam-mɯɯ ผู้ร่วมมือ
(who works together or cooperates);
kûu คู่ (pair); pûu-rûam-ngaan
ผู้ร่วมงาน (co-worker)

partnership, n. kwaam-bpen-hûn-
sùan ความเป็นหุ้นส่วน

party, n. ngaan-bpaa-dtîi งานปาร์ตี้
(e.g. birthday party); ngaan-sǎng-
sǎn งานสังสรรค์ (social gathering);
pák พรรค (political); glùm กลุ่ม
(group)

pass, v. pàan ผ่าน (a location, the
exam); sòng ส่ง (e.g. the ball)

pass, n. sên-taang เส้นทาง (passage); taang ทาง (e.g. mountain
pass); bàt-pàan บัตรผ่าน (ticket
for transportation or admission);
gaan-sòng-lûuk การส่งลูก (e.g. the
ball)

passage, n. kɔ̂ɔ-kian ข้อเขียน
(written article); gaan-kâam
การข้าม (act of passing); taang-
pàan ทางผ่าน (way)

passenger, n. pûu-dooi-sǎan
ผู้โดยสาร

passer-by, n. kon-dɤɤn-pàan
คนเดินผ่าน; kon-sǎn-jɔɔn คนสัญจร

passion, *n.* aa-rom อารมณ์
(mood); kwaam-krâi ความใคร่
(desire)

passionate, *adj.* mii-kwaam-rúu-
sùk-run-rɛɛng มีความรู้สึกรุนแรง

passive, *adj.* mâi-dtòo-dtɔ̀ɔp
ไม่โต้ตอบ (subjected to an action
without responding); tùuk-grà-tam
ถูกกระทำ (passive voice); chùai
เฉื่อย (not active)

passport, *n.* nǎng-sǔu-dəən-taang
หนังสือเดินทาง; bai-pàan-dɛɛn
ใบผ่านแดน

past, *n.* à-dìit อดีต; sà-mǎi-gɔ̀ɔn
สมัยก่อน

pasta, *n.* páat-sa-dtâa พาสต้า; aa-
hǎan-kláai-sa-bpaa-gét-dtîi
อาหารคล้ายสปาเก็ตตี้

paste, *v.* bpà ปะ

paste, *n.* sìng-tîi nǐao-kôn
สิ่งที่เหนียวข้น

pasteurize, *v.* kâa-chúa ฆ่าเชื้อ

pastime, *n.* gaan-kâa-wee-laa
การฆ่าเวลา

pastry, *n.* kà-nǒm-bpang-wǎan
ขนมปังหวาน

pasture, *n.* tûng-lîang-sàt
ทุ่งเลี้ยงสัตว์

pat, *v.* dtòp-bao-bao ตบเบาๆ

pat, *n.* gaan-dtòp-bao-bao
การตบเบาๆ

patch, *v.* bpà ปะ

patch, *n.* pèn-bpà แผ่นปะ; pèn-

sə̌əm แผ่นเสริม

patent, *n.* sìt-tì-bàt สิทธิบัตร

paternal, *adj.* gìao-gàp-pɔ̂ɔ
เกี่ยวกับพ่อ

paternity, *n.* kwaam-bpen-pɔ̂ɔ
ความเป็นพ่อ

path, *n.* taang ทาง; nɛɛo-taang
แนวทาง

pathetic, *adj.* nâa-wêet-ta-naa
น่าเวทนา; nâa-sǒng-sǎan น่าสงสาร

pathology, *n.* pá-yâat-wít-ta-yaa
พยาธิวิทยา

patience, *n.* kwaam-òt-ton
ความอดทน

patient, *n.* kon-kâi คนไข้; pûu-
bpùai ผู้ป่วย

patient, *adj.* òt-ton อดทน

patio, *n.* laan-bâan ลานบ้าน

patriot, *n.* pûu-rák-châat ผู้รักชาติ

patriotic, *adj.* rák-châat รักชาติ

patriotism, *n.* châat-ní-yom
ชาตินิยม

patrol, *n.* gaan-lâat-dtrà-ween
การลาดตระเวน

patron, *n.* pûu-ùp-bpà-gaa-rá
ผู้อุปการะ

patronize, *v.* ùp-hpà-gaa-rá
อุปการะ; sà-nàp-sà-nǔn สนับสนุน

pattern, *n.* bèɛp-yàang แบบอย่าง
(model); bèɛp-pɛɛn แบบแผน
(plan, diagram or model to be followed); lûat-laai ลวดลาย (style)

pause, *n.* gaan-yùt-chûa-kraao

การหยุดชั่วคราว

pave, *v.* bpuu-taang ปูทาง; bpuu-púɛn ปูพื้น

pavement, *n.* taang-dɔɔn-táao ทางเดินเท้า (sidewalk); taang-lâat-yaang ทางลาดยาง (paved road)

pavilion, *n.* grà-joom กระโจม (light building); hɔ̌ɔ-sà-dɛɛng-sǐn-káa หอแสดงสินค้า (for exhibition)

paw, *n.* ûng-táao อุ้งเท้า (feet); ûng-mɯɯ อุ้งมือ (hands or front feet)

pawn, *v.* jam-nam จำนำ

pawnshop, *n.* roong-ráp-jam-nam โรงรับจำนำ

pay, *v.* jàai จ่าย

pay, *n.* kâa-jâang ค่าจ้าง

payday, *n.* wan-jàai-ngən วันจ่ายเงิน

payment, *n.* gaan-jàai-ngən การจ่ายเงิน; gaan-cham-rá-ngən การชำระเงิน

pay phone, *n.* dtûu-too-ra-sàp-sǎa-taa-ra-ná ตู้โทรศัพท์สาธารณะ

payroll, *n.* ban-chii-ngən-dɯan บัญชีเงินเดือน

pea, *n.* tùa ถั่ว

peace, *n.* kwaam-sà-ngòp ความสงบ; sǎn-dtì-pâap สันติภาพ

peaceful, *adj.* sà-ngòp-sùk สงบสุข

peach, *n.* lûuk-tɔ́ɔ ลูกท้อ

peacock, *n.* nók-yuung นกยูง

peak, *n.* yɔ̂ɔt ยอด; jùt-sǔung-sùt จุดสูงสุด

peal, *n.* sǐang-rua-rá-kang เสียงรัวระฆัง (loud ringing of a bell)

peanut, *n.* tùa-lí-sǒng ถั่วลิสง

pear, *n.* lûuk-pɛɛ ลูกแพร์

pearl, *n.* kài-múk ไข่มุก

peasant, *n.* chaao-râi-chaao-naa ชาวไร่ชาวนา

pebble, *n.* grùat-hǐn กรวดหิน

peck, *v.* jìk จิก; tàak-tǎang ถากถาง

peculiar, *adj.* bprà-làat ประหลาด; bplɛ̀ɛk แปลก

pedal, *n.* tîi-yìap ที่เหยียบ; kan-rêng คันเร่ง

pedantic, *adj.* chɔ̂ɔp-ùat-rúu ชอบอวดรู้

peddle, *v.* rêe-kǎai เร่ขาย; pɔ̌əi-prɛ̂ɛ เผยแพร่

peddler, *n.* pá-nák-ngaan-rêe-kǎai พนักงานเร่ขาย

pedestal, *n.* tên แท่น; tǎan ฐาน

pedestrian, *n.* kon-dɔɔn-táao คนเดินเท้า

pediatrician, *n.* mɔ̌ɔ-dèk หมอเด็ก; gù-maan-ra-pɛ̂ɛt กุมารแพทย์

pedigree, *n.* sǎai-lɯ̂at สายเลือด; tîi-maa ที่มา

peek, *v.* ɛ̀ɛp-mɔɔng แอบมอง

peek, *n.* gaan-ɛ̀ɛp-mɔɔng การแอบมอง

peel, *n.* bpɔ̀ɔk-bplɯ̀ak ปอกเปลือก; lɔ̀ɔk-bplɯ̀ak ลอกเปลือก; gè แกะ

peep, *v.* ɛ̀ɛp-mɔɔng แอบมอง

peer, *n.* pɯ̂an เพื่อน

peg, *n.* mùt หมุด; dtà-bpuu ตะปู

Peking, *n.* bpàk-gìng ปักกิ่ง

pelican, *n.* nók-grà-tung นกกระทุง

pelvis, *n.* grà-dùuk-chəəng-graan กระดูกเชิงกราน

pen, *n.* bpàak-gaa ปากกา (for writing); kɔ̂ɔk คอก (animal enclosure)

penal, *adj.* gìao-gàp-aa-yaa เกี่ยวกับอาญา

penalize, *v.* long-tôot ลงโทษ

penalty, *n.* gaan-long-tôot การลงโทษ

pencil, *n.* din-sɔ̌ɔ ดินสอ

pendant, *n.* jîi-sɔ̂i-kɔɔ จี้สร้อยคอ

pending, *adj.* yùu-nai-rá-wàang อยู่ในระหว่าง; káang-yùu ค้างอยู่; kaa-raa-kaa-sang คาราคาซัง

penetrate, *v.* pàan-ta-lú ผ่านทะลุ; tɛɛng แทง

penguin, *n.* nók-pen-gwîn นกเพนกวิน

penicillin, *n.* yaa-pen-ní-si-lin ยาเพนนิซิลิน

peninsula, *n.* kâap-sà-mùt คาบสมุทร

penis, *n.* à-wai ya-wá-pêet-chaai อวัยวะเพศชาย; kuai ควย (very vulgar)

pen name, *n.* naam-bpàak-gaa นามปากกา

penniless, *adj.* mâi-mii-ngən ไม่มีเงิน; mòt-dtua หมดตัว

penny, *n.* nùng-sen หนึ่งเซนต์

pension, *n.* ngən-bam-naan เงินบำนาญ

pensive, *adj.* krûn-kit ครุ่นคิด

penthouse, *n.* pəəng เพิง (sloping roof); chán-sǔung-sùt ชั้นสูงสุด (highest floor)

people, *n.* kon คน (person); bprà-chaa-chon ประชาชน (populace)

pep, *n.* gam-lang-wang-chaa กำลังวังชา

pepper, *n.* prík-tai พริกไทย

peppermint, *n.* sà-ra-nɛ̀ɛ สะระแหน่

perceive, *v.* mɔɔng มอง; kâo-jai เข้าใจ

percent, *n.* bpəə-sen เปอร์เซ็นต์; rɔ́ɔi-lá ร้อยละ

percentage, *n.* àt-dtraa-rɔ́ɔi-lá อัตราร้อยละ

perception, *n.* gaan-kâo-jai การเข้าใจ; gaan-mɔɔng-hĕn การมองเห็น

perceptive, *adj.* gìao-gàp-gaan-kâo-jai เกี่ยวกับการเข้าใจ

percussion, *n.* krûang-dtii เครื่องตี; gaan-kɔ́ การเคาะ

perfect, *adj.* sŏm-buun-bɛ̀ɛp สมบูรณ์แบบ

perfection, *n.* kwaam-sŏm-buun-bɛ̀ɛp ความสมบูรณ์แบบ

perform, *v.* sà-dɛɛng แสดง (act or show), tam ngaan ทำงาน (work or function); dam-nəən-gaan ดำเนินการ (act in an official way)

performance, *n.* gaan-sà-dɛɛng

English • Phonetic • Thai

การแสดง; gaan-dam-nəən-gaan
การดำเนินการ

performer, *n.* pûu-sà-dɛɛng
ผู้แสดง; pûu-dam-nəən-gaan
ผู้ดำเนินการ

perfume, *n.* náam-hɔ̌ɔm น้ำหอม

perhaps, *adv.* baang-tii บางที

perimeter, *n.* sên-rɔ̂ɔp-wong
เส้นรอบวง (geometry); bpà-rí-mon-
ton ปริมณฑล (boundary)

period, *n.* wee-laa เวลา (length of
time); ra-yá ระยะ (interval of
time); sà-mǎi สมัย (era); chûa-
moong-rian ชั่วโมงเรียน (lesson)

periodic, *adj.* bpen-chûang-chûang
เป็นช่วงๆ; bpen-wee-laa เป็นเวลา

periodical, *n.* nít-dtà-ya-sǎan
นิตยสาร; waa-rá-sǎan วารสาร

peripheral, *adj.* yùu-rɔ̂ɔp-nɔ̂ɔk
อยู่รอบนอก

periphery, *n.* sên-rɔ̂ɔp-wong
เส้นรอบวง; sùan-nɔ̂ɔk ส่วนนอก

perishable, *adj.* nâo-bpùai-dâai
เน่าเปื่อยได้

perjury, *n.* gaan-hâi-gaan-tét
การให้การเท็จ

permanent, *adj.* tǎa-wɔɔn ถาวร

permeate, *v.* sɛ̂ɛk-sum แทรกซึม

permission, *n.* gaan-à-nú-yâat
การอนุญาต

permit, *v.* à-nú-yâat อนุญาต

permit, *n.* bai-à-nú-yâat ใบอนุญาต

perpendicular, *adj.* dtâng-chàak

ตั้งฉาก

perpetual, *adj.* dtà-lɔ̀ɔt-gaan
ตลอดกาล

perseverance, *n.* kwaam-pâak-
pian ความพากเพียร

persevere, *v.* pâak-pian พากเพียร

persimmon, *n.* dtôn-plam ต้นพลัม;
lûuk-plam ลูกพลัม

persist, *v.* yɯɯn-graan ยืนกราน

persistent, *adj.* dûu-rán ดื้อรั้น;
yɯɯn-graan ยืนกราน

person, *n.* bùk-kon บุคคล; kon คน

personality, *n.* bùk-kà-lík-gà-pâap
บุคลิกภาพ

personnel, *n.* bùk-kà-laa-gɔɔn
บุคลากร

perspective, *n.* tát-sà-ná-wí-sǎi
ทัศนวิสัย; mum-mɔɔng มุมมอง

perspiration, *n.* ngùa เหงื่อ; gaan-
kàp-ngùa การขับเหงื่อ

perspire, *v.* ngùa-ɔ̀ɔk เหงื่อออก

persuade, *v.* chák-juung ชักจูง

persuasion, *n.* gaan-chák-juung
การชักจูง

pertain, *v.* gìao-gàp เกี่ยวกับ;
bpen-rɯ̂ang-gìao-gàp
เป็นเรื่องเกี่ยวกับ

pertinent, *adj.* kao-rɯ̂ang เข้าเรื่อง;
gìao-kɔ̂ng เกี่ยวข้อง

pervert, *n.* ɔ̀ɔk-nɔ̂ɔk-lûu-nɔ̂ɔk-taang
ออกนอกลู่นอกทาง; pûak-gaam-wí-
bpà-rìt พวกกามวิปริต

pessimism, *n.* gaan-mɔɔng-lôok-nai-ngêe-ráai การมองโลกในแง่ร้าย

pessimistic, *adj.* mɔɔng-lôok-nai-ngêe-ráai มองโลกในแง่ร้าย

pest, *n.* sàt-ûii-róp-guan สัตว์ที่รบกวน

pester, *n.* gaan-gɔ̀ɔ-guan การก่อกวน

pesticide, *n.* yaa-kâa-má-lɛɛng ยาฆ่าแมลง

pet, *n.* sàt-líang สัตว์เลี้ยง

petal, *n.* glìip-dɔ̀ɔk กลีบดอก

petition, *n.* gaan-rɔ́ɔng-rian การร้องเรียน; gaan-yûun-kam-rɔ́ɔng การยื่นคำร้อง

petroleum, *n.* bpì-dtoo-lîam ปิโตรเลียม

petty, *adj.* lék เล็ก; jai-kɛ̂ɛp ใจแคบ

phantom, *n.* bpii-sàat ปีศาจ

pharmacist, *n.* pee-sàt-cha-gɔɔn เภสัชกร

pharmacy, *n.* ráan-kǎai-yaa ร้านขายยา (drug store); pee-sàt-cha-sàat เภสัชศาสตร์ (subject)

phase, *n.* rá-yá ระยะ; kân ขั้น

pheasant, *n.* gài-fáa ไก่ฟ้า

phenomenal, *adj.* yɔ̂ɔt-yîam ยอดเยี่ยม; má-hàt-sà-jan มหัศจรรย์

phenomenon, *n.* bpraa-gòt-dtà-gaan ปรากฏการณ์

philanthropist, *n.* kon-jai-bun คนใจบุญ

philanthropy, *n.* gaan-chûai-lǔa-

pǔan-ma-nút การช่วยเหลือเพื่อนมนุษย์

Philippines, *n.* bprà-têet-fi-líp-bpin ประเทศฟิลิปปินส์

philosopher, *n.* nák-bpràt-cha-yaa นักปรัชญา

philosophical, *adj.* taang-bpràt-cha-yaa ทางปรัชญา

philosophy, *n.* bpràt-cha-yaa ปรัชญา

phlegm, *n.* sěem-hà เสมหะ; sà-lèet เสลด

phobia, *n.* rôok-glua โรคกลัว

phoenix, *n.* nók-fii-nìk-nai-dtam-naam นกฟีนิกซ์ในตำนาน

phone, *n.* too-ra-sàp โทรศัพท์

phonetic, *adj.* gìao-gàp-rá-bòp-sǐang เกี่ยวกับระบบเสียง

phonetics, *n.* gaan-sùk-sǎa-rá-bòp-gaan-ɔ̀ɔk-sǐang การศึกษาระบบการออกเสียง

phony, *adj.* bplɔɔm ปลอม; gée เก๊

phosphorus, *n.* fɔ́ɔt-fɔɔ-rát ฟอสฟอรัส

photo, *n.* pâap-tàai ภาพถ่าย

photocopy, *n.* sǎm-nao-èek-gà-sǎan สำเนาเอกสาร

photogenic, *adj.* tàai-rûup-kun ถ่ายรูปขึ้น

photograph, *v.* tàai-pâap ถ่ายภาพ

photograph, *n.* pâap-tàai ภาพถ่าย

photographer, *n.* châng-tàai-pâap ช่างถ่ายภาพ

English • Phonetic • Thai

photography, *n.* gaan-tàai-pâap การถ่ายภาพ

phrase, *n.* wá-lii วลี; tôi-kam ถ้อยคำ

physical, *adj.* taang-râang-gaai ทางร่างกาย; taang-gaai-ya-pâap ทางกายภาพ

physician, *n.* pɛ̂ɛt แพทย์; mɔ̌ɔ หมอ

physicist, *n.* nák-fí-sìk นักฟิสิกส์

physics, *n.* wí-chaa-fí-sìk วิชาฟิสิกส์

physiology, *n.* sà-rii-rá-wít-ta-yaa สรีระวิทยา

pianist, *n.* nák-bpai-noo นักเปียโน

piano, *n.* bpia-noo เปียโน

pick, *v.* lɨ̂ak เลือก

pickle, *n.* kɔ̌ɔŋ-dɔɔŋ ของดอง

pickpocket, *v.* lúaŋ-grà-bpǎo ล้วงกระเป๋า

picnic, *n.* bpìk-ník ปิกนิก

picture, *n.* pâap ภาพ; rûup-pâap รูปภาพ

pie, *n.* kà-nǒm-paai ขนมพาย

piece, *n.* chín ชิ้น; an อัน

pier, *n.* tâa-rɨa ท่าเรือ (wharf)

pierce, *v.* jɔ̀ เจาะ; tɛɛŋ แทง

pig, *n.* mǔu หมู

pigeon, *n.* nók-pí-râap นกพิราบ

pigment, *n.* sǐi-pǐu สีผิว; sǐi สี

pile, *n., v.* gɔɔŋ กอง

pilgrim, *n.* pûu-sà-wɛɛŋ-bun ผู้แสวงบุญ

pill, *n.* yaa-mét ยาเม็ด; yaa ยา

pillar, *n.* sǎo-hǐn เสาหิน; sǎo-làk เสาหลัก

pillow, *n.* mɔ̌ɔn หมอน

pilot, *n.* nák-bin นักบิน

pimento, *n.* prík-mét-yài พริกเม็ดใหญ่

pimp, *n.* mɛɛŋ-daa แมงดา

pimple, *n.* sǐu สิว

pin, *n.* kěm เข็ม (sharp object used for fastening); kěm-glàt เข็มกลัด (safety pin, brooch); mùt หมุด (peg)

pinch, *v.* yìk หยิก; nèp เหน็บ; dèt เด็ด

pine, *n.* dtôn-sǒn ต้นสน

pineapple, *n.* sàp-bpà-rót สับปะรด

Ping-Pong, *n.* bpiŋ-bpɔɔŋ ปิงปอง

pink, *n., adj.* sǐi-chom-puu สีชมพู

pioneer, *n.* pûu-bùk-bə̀ək ผู้บุกเบิก

pipe, *n.* tɔ̂ɔ ท่อ; glɔ̂ŋ-yaa-sùup กล้องยาสูบ (for smoking)

piracy, *n.* gaan-bplôn การปล้น; gaan-lá-mə̂ət การละเมิด

pirate, *n.* joon-sà-làt โจรสลัด (who robs at sea); gaan-lá-mə̂ət-lík-kà-sìt ผู้ละเมิดลิขสิทธิ์ (who violates copyright)

pistol, *n.* bpɨɨn-pók ปืนพก

piston, *n.* lûuk-sùup ลูกสูบ

pit, *n.* lǔm หลุม (hole); bɔ̀ɔ บ่อ (pond); má-lét-pǒn-la-náai เมล็ดผลไม้ (central kernel or stone of certain fruits)

pitch, v. kwâang ขว้าง

pitch, n. rá-dàp-sĭang ระดับเสียง (sound)

pitcher, n. yùak-náam เหยือกน้ำ (jug); pûu-kwâang ผู้ขว้าง (thrower)

pitch-dark, n. dam-mûut ดำมืด

pitfall, n. lŭm-praang หลุมพราง; gàp-dàk กับดัก

pith, n. yûa-máai เยื่อไม้ (soft tissue of certain plants); săa-rá-săm-kan สาระสำคัญ (essence)

pitiful, adj. nâa-sŏng-săan น่าสงสาร

pity, n. sŏng-săan สงสาร

pivot, n. gɛɛn-mŭn แกนหมุน; làk หลัก

place, n. sà-tăan-tîi สถานที่ (location); bɔɔ-ri-ween บริเวณ (area)

plague, n. rôok-rá-bàat โรคระบาด

plain, n. tîi-râap ที่ราบ

plaintiff, n. jòot โจทก์

plaintive, adj. sĭa-jai เสียใจ; sâo เศร้า

plan, n. pĕɛn-gaan แผนการ; kroong-gaan โครงการ

plane, v. sài máai ไสไม้ (in carpentry)

plane, n. krûang-bin เครื่องบิน (airplane); nɛɛo-râap แนวราบ (flat); gòp-sài-máai กบไสไม้ (in carpentry)

planet, n. daao-krɔ́ ดาวเคราะห์

plank, n. máai-grà-daan ไม้กระดาน

planner, n. pûu-waang-pĕɛn

ผู้วางแผน (one that plans); sà-mùt-ban-túk-we-laa-nát สมุดบันทึกเวลานัด (appointment book)

plant, v. bplùuk ปลูก

plant, n. pûut พืช; dtôn-máai ต้นไม้

plaque, n. pèn-bpâai แผ่นป้าย (a sign); hĭn-bpuun หินปูน (on teeth)

plasma, n. kɔɔ̌ng-lĕeo-nai-lûat ของเหลวในเลือด; bplàat-sa-mâa ปลาสมา

plaster, n. bpuun-bplàat-sa-dtɔ̀ɔ ปูนปลาสเตอร์

plastic, n. pláat-sa-dtìk พลาสติก

plastic bag, n. tŭng-pláat-sa-dtìk ถุงพลาสติก

plastic surgery, n. săn-ya-gam-pláat-sa-dtìk ศัลยกรรมพลาสติก

plate, n. jaan จาน (dish); klûap-loo-hà เคลือบโลหะ (coating metal)

plateau, n. tîi-râap-sŭung ที่ราบสูง

platform, n. chaan-chaa-laa ชานชาลา; tên แท่น

platinum, n. tɔɔng-kam-kăao ทองคำขาว

platitude, n. kwaam-sám-sâak ความซ้ำซาก

platter, n. pèn-sĭang แผ่นเสียง

play, v. lên เล่น

play, n. lá-kɔɔn ละคร

player, n. pûu-lên ผู้เล่น (any player); pûu-ban-leeng ผู้บรรเลง (music)

playboy, *n.* plee-bɔɔi เพลบอย; chaai-jâo-chúu ชายเจ้าชู้

playful, *adj.* kîi-lên ขี้เล่น; chɔ̂ɔp-sà-nùk ชอบสนุก

playground, *n.* sà-nǎam-dèk-lên สนามเด็กเล่น

playmate, *n.* pûan-lên เพื่อนเล่น

playwright, *n.* nák-kian-bòt-lá-kɔɔn นักเขียนบทละคร

plaza, *n.* laan-gwâang ลานกว้าง (spacious area); hâang-ráan ห้างร้าน (shops); sǔun-gaan-káa ศูนย์การค้า (shopping center)

plea, *n.* kam-kɔ̌ɔ-rɔ́ɔng คำขอร้อง (request or appeal); kam-gɛ̂ɛ-dtua คำแก้ตัว (excuses)

plead, *v.* dtɔ̀ɔp-kɔ̂ɔ-glàao-hǎa ตอบข้อกล่าวหา (answer to charges)

plead, *v.* wing-wɔɔn วิงวอน (implore); gɛ̂ɛ-dtua แก้ตัว (make excuses)

pleasant, *adj.* sà-baai-jai สบายใจ

please, *v.* tam-hâi-pɔɔ-jai ทำให้พอใจ

pleased, *adj.* dii-jai ดีใจ; pɔɔ-jai พอใจ

pleasure, *n.* kwaam-sùk ความสุข

pleat, *n.* rɔɔi-páp รอยพับ; rɔɔi-jìip รอยจีบ

pleat, *adj.* bpen-jìip เป็นจีบ

pledge, *v.* bpà-dtì-yaan ปฏิญาณ

(vow; e.g. pledge allegiance); sǎa-baan สาบาน (swear)

pledge, *n.* kam-bpà-dtì-yaan คำปฏิญาณ; kam-sǎa-baan คำสาบาน

plentiful, *adj.* mâak-maai มากมาย

plenty, *n.* kwaam-mâng-kâng ความมั่งคั่ง

pliers, *n.* kiim คีม

plod, *v.* kɔ̂i-kɔ̂i-dəən ค่อยๆเดิน

plot, *n.* bplɛɛng-tîi-din แปลงที่ดิน (land); kroong-rûang โครงเรื่อง (story)

plow, *v.* tǎi ไถ

pluck, *v.* dɯng ดึง; tɔ̌ɔn ถอน

plum, *n.* dtôn-plam ต้นพลัม

plumber, *n.* châng-bprà-bpaa ช่างประปา; châng-bàt-grii ช่างบัดกรี

plumbing, *n.* gaan-tam-tɔ̂ɔ-náam การทำท่อน้ำ

plume, *n.* kǒn-nók ขนนก

plump, *adj.* ìm-ɔ̀əp อิ่มเอิบ

plunge, *v.* jùm จุ่ม (dip in); jûang จ้วง (thrust); pǒo โผ (move suddenly forward)

plunge, *n.* gaan-jùm การจุ่ม; gaan-jûang การจ้วง; gaan-pǒo การโผ

plural, *n.* pá-hǔu-pót พหูพจน์; jam-nuan-mâak จำนวนมาก

plus, *prep.* bùak บวก; pɔ̂əm เพิ่ม

plutonium, *n.* sǎan-pluu-dtoo-nîam สารพลูโตเนียม

plywood, *n.* máai-àt ไม้อัด

p.m., v. lǎng-tîang หลังเที่ยง

pneumonia, n. rôok-bpɔ̀ɔt-buam โรคปอดบวม

pocket, n. grà-bpǎo กระเป๋า; tǔng-lék-lék ถุงเล็กๆ

pod, n. fàk-tùa ฝักถั่ว (pea); rang-mǎi รังไหม (silk)

podium, n. tên-yuun แท่นยืน

poem, n. bòt-gà-wii บทกวี

poet, n. gà-wii กวี

poetry, n. gà-wii-ní-pon กวีนิพนธ์

point, n. jùt จุด; bprà-den ประเด็น

pointed, adj. lɛ̌ɛm แหลม

pointless, adj. rái-kwaam-mǎai ไร้ความหมาย; mâi-dâai-ká-nɛɛn ไม่ได้คะแนน

poise, n. gaan-song-dtua การทรงตัว (balance); kwaam-sà-ngàa-ngaam ความสง่างาม (grace)

poison, n. pít พิษ; yaa-pít ยาพิษ

poisonous, adj. mii-pít มีพิษ

poke, v. yɛ̀ɛ แหย่; grà-túng กระทุ้ง; grà-tɛ̀ɛk กระแทก

poker, n. pûu-yɛ̀ɛ ผู้แหย่ (one that pokes); pâi-bpóok-gɔ̂ɔ ไพ่โป๊กเกอร์ (card game); mái-yɛ̀ɛ-dtao-pǐng ไม้แหย่เตาผิง (metal fireplace stick)

polar, adj. yùu-dtrong-kâam อยู่ตรงข้าม

pole, n. mái-yaao ไม้ยาว (long stick); sǎo-fai เสาไฟ (electric pole); kûa-lôok ขั้วโลก (e.g. North Pole)

police officer, n. dtam-rùat ตำรวจ

policy, n. ná-yoo-baai นโยบาย

polio, n. rôok-bpoo-li-oo โรคโปลิโอ

polish, v. kàt ขัด

polite, adj. sù-pâap สุภาพ

politeness, n. kwaam-sù-pâap ความสุภาพ

political, adj. taang-gaan-muang ทางการเมือง

politician, n. nák-gaan-muang นักการเมือง

politics, n. gaan-muang การเมือง

poll, n. gaan-sǎm-rùat-kwaam-kít-hěn การสำรวจความคิดเห็น

pollen, n. gee-sɔ̌ɔn-dɔ̀ɔk-máai เกสรดอกไม้

pollute, v. tam-hâi-sòk-gà-bpròk ทำให้สกปรก

pollution, n. mon-la-pít มลพิษ

pomegranate, n. táp-tim ทับทิม

pomp, n. gaan-waang-tâa-oo การวางท่าโอ่

pompous, adj. kîi-òo ขี้โอ่ (exaggerated dignity); tá-nong-dtua ทนงตัว (bombastic)

pond, n. bɔ̀ɔ-náam บ่อน้ำ; sà-náam สระน้ำ

ponder, v. krûn-kít ครุ่นคิด; kam-nung คำนึง

pony, n. máa-pan-lék ม้าพันธุ์เล็ก

pool, n. ὲng náam แอ่งน้ำ (small body of still water); sà-náam สระน้ำ (pond); sà-wâai-náam สระว่ายน้ำ

English · Phonetic · Thai

สระว่ายน้ำ (swimming pool)

poor, *adj.* yâak-jon ยากจน; mâi-dii ไม่ดี; nâa-sǒng-sǎan น่าสงสาร

pop, *v.* plòo โผล่ (appear abruptly); tam-sǐang-dang-bpɔ́k ทำเสียงดัง ป๊อก (make sharp, explosive sound)

pop, *n.* gaan-bprà-tú การปะทุ (hit or strike); sǐang-dang-bpɔ́k เสียงดัง ป๊อก (short, explosive sound)

popcorn, *n.* kâao-pôot-kûa ข้าวโพดคั่ว

poppy, *n.* dɔ̀ɔk-fìn ดอกฝิ่น

popular, *adj.* bpen-tîi-ni-yom เป็นที่นิยม

popularity, *n.* kwaam-ní-yom ความนิยม

populated, *adj.* mii-bprà-chaa-gɔɔn-mâak มีประชากรมาก

population, *n.* bprà-chaa-gɔɔn ประชากร

porcelain, *n.* krûang-laai-kraam เครื่องลายคราม

porch, *n.* rá-biang ระเบียง; chà-lǐang เฉลียง

porcupine, *n.* mên เม่น

pore, *n.* ruu-kǔm-kǒn รูขุมขน

pork, *n.* núa-mǔu เนื้อหมู

pornography, *n.* pâap-bpóo ภาพโป๊

port, *n.* tâa-rua ท่าเรือ

portable, *adj.* hîu-dâai หิ้วได้

porter, *n.* pà-nák-ngaan-tǔu-grà-bpǎo พนักงานถือกระเป๋า

portfolio, *n.* grà-bpǎo-èek-gà-sǎan กระเป๋าเอกสาร (briefcase); gaan-rûap-ruam-gaan-long-tun การรวบ รวมการลงทุน (collections of invest-ments); gaan-rûap-ruam-pǒn-ngaan การรวบรวมผลงาน (collection of work)

portion, *n.* sùan ส่วน; sùan-bèng ส่วนแบ่ง

portly, *adj.* kôn-kâang-ûan ค่อนข้างอ้วน; gam-yam กำยำ

portrait, *n.* rûup-mǔan-bùk-kon รูปเหมือนบุคคล

portray, *v.* wâat วาด (draw); kǐan เขียน (write); sà-dɛɛng แสดง (show)

portrayal, *n.* gaan-sà-dɛɛng การแสดง; pâap ภาพ

pose, *v.* tam-tâa ทำท่า; dtâng-tâa ตั้งท่า

position, *n.* dtam-nèng ตำแหน่ง; tǎa-ná ฐานะ

positive, *adj.* dâan-bùak ด้านบวก; dâan-dii ด้านดี

possess, *v.* krɔ̂ɔp-krɔɔng ครอบครอง; mii มี

possession, *n.* gaan-krɔ̂ɔp-krɔɔng การครอบครอง; sìng-tîi-krɔ̂ɔp-krɔɔng สิ่งที่ครอบครอง

possibility, *n.* kwaam-bpen-bpai-dâai ความเป็นไปได้

possible, *adj.* bpen-bpai-dâai เป็นไปได้

post, *n.* sǎo เสา (mast); làk หลัก (point; e.g. in racing); gaan-bprai-

(point; e.g. in racing); gaan-bprai-sà-nii การไปรษณีย์ (mail)

postage, n. sà-dtem แสตมป์

postal, adj. gìao-gàp-bprai-sà-nii เกี่ยวกับไปรษณีย์

postbox, n. dtûu-bprai-sà-nii ตู้ไปรษณีย์

postcard, n. bprai-sà-nii-ya-bàt ไปรษณียบัตร

poster, n. bpóot-sa-dtɔ̂ɔ โปสเตอร์; bai-bprà-gàat ใบประกาศ

posterity, n. chon-rún-lǎng ชนรุ่นหลัง

posthumous, adj. lǎng-gaan-dtaai หลังการตาย

postman, n. bù-rùt-bprai-sà-nii บุรุษไปรษณีย์

postmark, n. dtraa-bprà-táp-kɔ̌ɔng-bprai-sà-nii ตราประทับของไปรษณีย์

post office, n. tîi-tam-gaan-bprai-sà-nii ที่ทำการไปรษณีย์

postpone, v. lɯ̂an เลื่อน

postscript, n. bpàt-chìm-li-kìt ปัจฉิมลิขิต; bpɔɔ-lɔɔ ป.ล. (p.s.)

posture, n. tâa-taang ท่าทาง; dtam-nɛ̀ng ตำแหน่ง

pot, n. mɔ̂ɔ หม้อ (container); grà-bpùk กระปุก (round vessel); grà-tǎang กระถาง (flowerpot)

potato, n. man-fa-ràng มันฝรั่ง

potbelly, n. pung-dtoo พุงโต

potent, adj. mii-gam-lang มีกำลัง (powerful.); mii-sà-mát-dtà-pâap-

taang-pêet มีสมรรถภาพทางเพศ (able to perform sexual intercourse)

potential, n. bpen-bpai-dâai เป็นไปได้; mii-kwaam-sǎa-mâat มีความสามารถ

potion, n. yaa-bprung ยาปรุง (liquid mixture); yaa-pít ยาพิษ (poison)

potter, n. châng-bpân-mɔ̂ɔ ช่างปั้นหม้อ

pottery, n. krûang-bpân-din-pǎo เครื่องปั้นดินเผา

pouch, n. grà-bpǎo กระเป๋า (bag); tǔng ถุง (sack)

poultry, n. sàt-bpìik สัตว์ปีก

pounce, v. joom-dtii โจมตี (attack suddenly); chǔai ฉวย (seize something swiftly and eagerly)

pound, v. dtii ตี (hit, strike)

pound, n. bpɔɔn ปอนด์ (unit of weight); bɔ̀ɔ-bplaa บ่อปลา (fish pond)

pour, v. tee เท; rin ริน; râat ราด

pout, v. tam-nâa-bûng ทำหน้าบึ้ง; bûi-bpàak บุ้ยปาก

poverty, n. kwaam-yâak-jon ความยากจน

powder, n. bpɛ̂ɛng แป้ง (for cosmetics or cooking); fùn ฝุ่น (small particle); pǒng ผง (dust)

power, n. pá lang พลัง; am-nâat อำนาจ

powerful, adj. mii-am-nâat

มีอำนาจ; mii-gam-lang มีกำลัง;
kɛ̌ng-rɛɛng แข็งแรง

practical, *adj.* chái-dâai-dii ใช้ได้ดี;
nam-bpai-bpà-dtì-bàt-dâai
นำไปปฏิบัติได้; mii-bprà-yòot
มีประโยชน์

practice, *v.* fùk ฝึก; hàt หัด; fùk-
hàt ฝึกหัด

practice, *n.* gaan-fùk การฝึก (act
of practice); bɛ̀ɛp-fùk-hàt
แบบฝึกหัด (exercise)

practitioner, *n.* pɛ̂ɛt แพทย์ (doctor); pûu-bpà-dtì-bàt-gaan
ผู้ปฏิบัติการ (one that practices)

pragmatic, *adj.* gìao-gàp-kwaam-
bpen-jing เกี่ยวกับความเป็นจริง

prairie, *n.* tûng-yâa ทุ่งหญ้า

praise, *v.* sǎn-sɔ̌ɔn สรรเสริญ;
chom-chəəi ชมเชย

prawn, *n.* gûng-naang กุ้งนาง

pray, *v.* sùat-mon สวดมนต์; à-tí-
tǎan อธิษฐาน

prayer, *n.* pûu-sùat-mon ผู้สวดมนต์;
bòt-sùat-mon บทสวดมนต์

preach, *v.* têet เทศน์; sà-dɛɛng-
tam แสดงธรรม

preacher, *n.* nák-têet นักเทศน์;
pûu-sàng-sɔ̌ɔn ผู้สั่งสอน

preamble, *n.* bòt-nam บทนำ; grə̀n
เกริ่น

precarious, *adj.* mâi-bplɔ̀ɔt-pai
ไม่ปลอดภัย; lɔ̂ɔ-lɛ̌ɛm ล่อแหลม

precaution, *n.* gaan-rá-mát-rá-

wang การระมัดระวัง

precede, *v.* nam นำ; maa-gɔ̀ɔn
มาก่อน

precedent, *n.* rûang-raao-dtɛ̀ɛ-gɔ̀ɔn
เรื่องราวแต่ก่อน

preceding, *adj.* nam-nâa นำหน้า
(come before in order); maa-gɔ̀ɔn
มาก่อน (come, exist, or occur before
in time)

precept, *n.* gaan-òp-rom การอบรม;
sǐin ศีล; ká-dtì-pót คติพจน์

precinct, *n.* kɔ̀ɔp-kèet ขอบเขต;
kèet-bɛ̀ng เขตแบ่ง

precious, *adj.* mii-kâa มีค่า; bpen-
tîi-rák เป็นที่รัก

predecessor, *n.* ban-pá-bù-rùt
บรรพบุรุษ

predicament, *n.* sà-tǎa-ná-gaan
สถานการณ์

predict, *v.* tam-naai ทำนาย

prediction, *n.* gaan-tam-naai
การทำนาย

preface, *n.* kam-nam คำนำ

prefer, *v.* chɔ̂ɔp-mâak-gwàa
ชอบมากกว่า

preferable, *adj.* tîi-chɔ̂ɔp ที่ชอบ;
bpen-tîi-dtɔ̂ng-gaan เป็นที่ต้องการ

preference, *n.* gaan-chɔ̂ɔp
การชอบ; sìng-tîi-chɔ̂ɔp สิ่งที่ชอบ

prefix, *n.* kam-sɔ̌ɔm-nâa
คำเสริมหน้า (as opposed to suffix)

pregnancy, *n.* gaan-dtâng-kan
การตั้งครรภ์

tɔ́ɔng มีท้อง; dtáng-kan ตั้งครรภ์

prejudice, *n.* kwaam-mii-à-ká-dtì ความมีอคติ

preliminary, *adj.* bûang-dtôn เบื้องต้น

premature, *adj.* yang-mâi-dtoo-dtem-tîi ยังโตไม่เต็มที่ (immature); yang-mâi-króp-gam-nòt ยังไม่ครบกำหนด (arriving, existing, or performed before the proper or usual time); yang-reo-gəən-bpai ยังเร็วเกินไป (too soon)

premise, *n.* làk-tǎan หลักฐาน; som-mút-dtì-tǎan สมมติฐาน

premium, *n.* bîa-bprà-gan เบี้ยประกัน (in insurance); ngən-pí-sèet เงินพิเศษ (money or bonus paid in addition)

preoccupied, *adj.* krɔ̂ɔp-ngam ครอบงำ (absorbed in thought)

preparation, *n.* gaan-dtriam-(dtua) การเตรียม(ตัว)

prepare, *v.* dtriam เตรียม

preposition, *n.* bùp-pà-bòt บุพบท

prescribe, *v.* sàng สั่ง (e.g. doctor); gam-nòt กำหนด (set as a rule); nέ แนะ (advice)

prescription, *n.* bai-sàng-yaa ใบสั่งยา

presence, *n.* gaan-mii-yùu การมีอยู่; gaan-bpraa gòt การปรากฏ

presentation, *n.* gaan-sà-nəə

การเสนอ; gaan-sà-dɛɛng-pǒn-ngaan การแสดงผลงาน

present, *v.* sà-nəə เสนอ; hâi ให้; sà-dɛɛng-hâi-hěn แสดงให้เห็น

preservation, *n.* gaan-gèp-rák-sǎa การเก็บรักษา; gaan-sà-ngǔan การสงวน

preservative, *n.* yaa-gan-bùut ยากันบูด

preserve, *v.* gèp-rák-sǎa เก็บรักษา (keep or maintain); dɔɔng ดอง (pickle); màk หมัก (ferment)

preside, *v.* bpen-bprà-taan เป็นประธาน (act as chairperson); kûap-kum ควบคุม (control)

presidency, *n.* dtam-nèng-bprà-taan ตำแหน่งประธาน

president, *n.* bprà-taan ประธาน (of an organization); bprà-taa-naa-típ-bɔɔ-dii ประธานาธิบดี (of a country)

press, *v.* gòt กด; bìip บีบ

pressing, *adj.* dùan ด่วน (urgent)

pressure, *n.* kwaam-dan ความดัน; kwaam-gòt-dan ความกดดัน

prestige, *n.* chûu-sǐang ชื่อเสียง (fame); gìat-dtì-kun เกียรติคุณ (honor)

prestigious, *adj.* mii-gìat มีเกียรติ

presume, *v.* sǎn-ní-tǎan สันนิษฐาน

presumption, *n.* gaan-sǎn-ní-tǎan การสันนิษฐาน

pretend, *v.* sɛ̌e-sɛ̂ɛng เสแสร้ง;

glêeng-tam แกล้งทำ

pretentious, *adj.* sêe-sêeng เสแสร้ง

pretext, *n.* kôo-gêe-dtua ข้อแก้ตัว

pretty, *adj.* sǔai สวย; ngót-ngaam งดงาม

prevail, *v.* mii-chai มีชัย (triumph); bpen-dtòo เป็นต่อ (be greater in strength or influence)

prevent, *v.* bpôong-gan ป้องกัน

prevention, *n.* gaan-bpôong-gan การป้องกัน

preventive, *adj.* gìao-gàp-gaan-bpôong-gan เกี่ยวกับการป้องกัน

preview, *n.* gaan-duu-gòon การดูก่อน; pâap-dtua-yàang ภาพตัวอย่าง

previous, *adj.* gòon ก่อน; dtèe-gòon แต่ก่อน

prey, *n.* yùa เหยื่อ

price, *n.* raa-kaa ราคา (amount as of money, cost); raang-wan รางวัล (reward)

priceless, *adj.* raa-kaa-sǔung ราคาสูง

prick, *v.* teeng แทง

prick, *n.* gaan-teeng การแทง (act of piercing)

pride, *n.* kwaam-puum-jai ความภูมิใจ (pleasure or satisfaction); tì-tì ทิฐิ (self-respect, haughtiness)

priest, *n.* prá พระ

primary, *adj.* sǎm-kan-tîi-sùt สำคัญที่สุด (most important); an-

dàp-rêek อันดับแรก (first); bprà-tom ประถม (elementary)

primary school, *n.* roong-rian-bprà-tǒm โรงเรียนประถม

prime, *n.* chûang-tîi-dii-tîi-sùt ช่วงที่ดีที่สุด (peak condition); rá-yá-rêek-rôəm ระยะแรกเริ่ม (beginning period)

primitive, *adj.* dùk-dam-ban ดึกดำบรรพ์

prince, *n.* jâo-chaai เจ้าชาย

princess, *n.* jâo-yǐng เจ้าหญิง

principal (school), *n.* kruu-yài ครูใหญ่

principle, *n.* làk-gaan หลักการ

print, *v.* pim พิมพ์

print, *n.* gaan-pim การพิมพ์; pâap-pim ภาพพิมพ์

printer, *n.* pûu-pim ผู้พิมพ์; krûang-pim เครื่องพิมพ์

printing, *n.* gaan-pim การพิมพ์

prior, *adj.* gòon ก่อน; yùu-gòon อยู่ก่อน

priority, *n.* gaan-maa-gòon การมาก่อน; gaan-mii-sìt-gòon การมีสิทธิ์ก่อน

prism, *n.* bprì-sum ปริซึม

prison, *n.* kúk คุก; rʉan-jam เรือนจำ

prisoner, *n.* nák-tôot นักโทษ

privacy, *n.* kwaam-bpen-sùan-dtua ความเป็นส่วนตัว

private, *adj.* sùan-dtua ส่วนตัว;

sùan-bùk-kon ส่วนบุคคล
privilege, n. sìt-ti-pi-sèet สิทธิพิเศษ
privileged, adj. mii-sìt-ti-pi-sèet
มีสิทธิพิเศษ
privy, adj. sùan-dtua ส่วนตัว; láp
ลับ
prize, n. raang-wan รางวัล
probability, n. kwaam-bpen-bpai-
dâai ความเป็นไปได้
probable, adj. bpen-bpai-dâai
เป็นไปได้
probably, adv. sûng-bpen-bpai-dâai
ซึ่งเป็นไปได้
probate, n. gaan-pi-sùut-dtaam-gòt-
mǎai การพิสูจน์ตามกฎหมาย
probation, n. pâak-tan ภาคทัณฑ์
problem, n. bpan-hǎa ปัญหา
procedure, n. wí-tii-gaan วิธีการ
(manner of proceeding); kân-dtɔɔn
ขั้นตอน (series of steps)
proceed, v. dam-nɔɔn-gaan
ดำเนินการ
proceeds, n. raai-dâai รายได้
(income); gam-rai กำไร (profit)
procession, n. kà-buan-hὲɛ
ขบวนแห่
proclaim, v. bprà-gàat ประกาศ;
tà-lὲɛng แสดง
proclamation, n. kam-bprà-gàat
คำประกาศ
procrastinate, v. lûan-wee-laa
เลื่อนเวลา (put off); plàt-wan-bprà-
gan-prûng ผลัดวันประกันพรุ่ง (post-

pone or delay needlessly)
prodigy, n. àt-chà-ri-yá อัจฉริยะ
produce, v. pà-lìt ผลิต
producer, n. pûu-pà-lìt ผู้ผลิต
product, n. pà-lìt-dtà-pan
ผลิตภัณฑ์; pà-lìt-dtà-pǒn ผลิตผล
production, n. gaan-pà-lìt การผลิต
(act of production); pǒn-ngaan
ผลงาน (result of productivity)
productive, adj. ù-dom-sǒm-buun
อุดมสมบูรณ์
productivity, n. gaan-pà-lìt
การผลิต
profane, adj. yàap-kaai หยาบคาย
profanity, n. kwaam-yàap-kaai
ความหยาบคาย
profession, n. aa-chîip อาชีพ
professional, n. muu-aa-chîip
มืออาชีพ; pûu-chîao-chaan
ผู้เชี่ยวชาญ
professor, n. sàat-dtraa-jaan
ศาสตราจารย์
proficient, adj. cham-naan ชำนาญ;
klɔ̂ng-klὲɛo คล่องแคล่ว
profile, n. kroong-râang โครงร่าง
(outline of an object); bprà-wàt-yɔ̂ɔ
ประวัติย่อ (formal summary); dâan-
kâang ด้านข้าง
profit, n. gam-rai กำไร
profitable, adj. hâi-pǒn-gam-rai
ให้ผลกำไร
profound, adj. lúk-súng ลึกซึ้ง;
nɛ̂n-fɛ́ɛn แน่นแฟ้น

prognosis, *n.* gaan-kâat-ka-nee การคาดคะเน

program, *n.* bproo-grɛɛm โปรแกรม; kroong-gaan โครงการ

progress, *n.* kwaam-gâao-nâa ความก้าวหน้า

prohibit, *v.* hâam ห้าม

prohibition, *n.* kɔ̂ɔ-hâam ข้อห้าม; gaan-hâam การห้าม

project, *n.* kroong-gaan โครงการ

projectile, *n.* kĭi-bpà-naa-wút ขีปนาวุธ

projector, *n.* krûang-chǎai-pâap เครื่องฉายภาพ

prolong, *v.* dtɔ̀ɔ ต่อ (lengthen in extent); yûut-yúa ยืดเยื้อ (lengthen in duration)

promenade, *n.* gaan-dəən-lên การเดินเล่น

prominent, *adj.* dèn-chát เด่นชัด; dang ดัง

promiscuous, *adj.* sǎm-sòn สำส่อน

promise, *n., v.* sǎn-yaa สัญญา

promote, *v.* sòng-sǒəm ส่งเสริม (contribute to the progress or growth); lûan-dtam-nèng เลื่อนตำแหน่ง (advance to higher position)

promotion, *n.* gaan-sòng-sǒəm การส่งเสริม; gaan-lûan-dtam-nèng การเลื่อนตำแหน่ง

prompt, *adj.* rûat-reo รวดเร็ว; tan-tii ทันที

prone, *adj., adv.* kwâm คว่ำ; mɔ̂ɔp

หมอบ; een-iang เอนเอียง

prong, *n.* ngâam ง่าม; krâat คราด

pronoun, *n.* sàp-pa-naam สรรพนาม

pronounce, *v.* ɔ̀ɔk-sǐang ออกเสียง

pronouncement, *n.* gaan-bprà-gàat การประกาศ

pronunciation, *n.* gaan-ɔ̀ɔk-sǐang การออกเสียง

proof, *n.* gaan-pí-sùut การพิสูจน์

proofread, *v.* pí-sùut-àk-sɔ̌ɔn พิสูจน์อักษร; àan-tuan อ่านทวน

propaganda, *n.* gaan-koo-sà-naa-chuan-chûa การโฆษณาชวนเชื่อ

propeller, *n.* bai-pát ใบพัด

proper, *adj.* mɔ̀-sǒm เหมาะสม

property, *n.* sàp-sǐn ทรัพย์สิน

prophecy, *n.* gaan-pá-yaa-gɔɔn การพยากรณ์

prophet, *n.* pûu-pá-yaa-gɔɔn ผู้พยากรณ์

proponent, *n.* pûu-sà-nɔ̌ɔ ผู้เสนอ; pûu-sà-nàp-sà-nǔn ผู้สนับสนุน

proportion, *n.* sàt-sùan สัดส่วน

proportionate, *adj.* dâai-sàt-sùan ได้สัดส่วน

proposal, *n.* kɔ̂ɔ-sà-nɔ̌ɔ ข้อเสนอ; pɛɛn-ngaan แผนงาน

propose, *v.* sà-nɔ̌ɔ-ngaan เสนองาน (work); kɔ̌ɔ-dtɛ̀ng-ngaan ขอแต่งงาน (marriage)

proposition, *n.* gaan-sà-nɔ̌ɔ การเสนอ

proprietor, *n.* jâo-kɔ̌ɔng เจ้าของ

English · Phonetic · Thai

propriety, *n.* gam-ma-sìt กรรมสิทธิ์

proscribe, *v.* lâi-ɔ̀ɔk ไล่ออก
(expel); nee-rá-têet เนรเทศ (ban-
ish)

prose, *n.* rɔ́ɔi-gɛ̂ɛo ร้อยแก้ว

prosecute, *v.* fɔ́ɔng-rɔ́ɔng ฟ้องร้อง

prosecution, *n.* gaan-fɔ́ɔng-rɔ́ɔng
การฟ้องร้อง; gaan-dam-nəən-ka-dii
การดำเนินคดี

prospect, *n.* oo-gàat โอกาส;
kwaam-wǎng ความหวัง

prosper, *v.* jà-rəən เจริญ; rûng-
ruang รุ่งเรือง

prosperity, *n.* kwaam-jà-rəən-rûng-
ruang ความเจริญรุ่งเรือง

prosperous, *adj.* jà-rəən เจริญ;
mâng-kâng มั่งคั่ง

prostate, *n.* dtɔ̀m-lûuk-màak
ต่อมลูกหมาก

prostitute, *n.* sǒo-pee-nii โสเภณี

prostitution, *n.* gaan-káa-bprà-
wee-nii การค้าประเวณี

prostrate, *adj.* nɔɔn-râap นอนราบ
(lie flat); mòt-gam-lang หมดกำลัง
(reduce to extreme weakness);
mɔ̂ɔp-râap หมอบราบ (face down)

protagonist, *n.* dtuua-èek-kɔ̌ɔng-
rûang ตัวเอกของเรื่อง

protect, *v.* bpòk-bpɔ̂ng ปกป้อง;
kúm-krɔɔng คุ้มครอง

protection, *n.* gaan-bpòk-bpɔ̂ng
การปกป้อง; gaan-kúm-krɔɔng
การคุ้มครอง

protein, *n.* bproo-dtiin โปรตีน

protest, *v.* bprà-túang ประท้วง

protest, *n.* gaan-bprà-túang
การประท้วง

Protestant, *n.* krít-ní-gaai-bproo-
dtét-dtɛn คริสต์นิกายโปรเตสแตนท์

protocol, *n.* dtôn-râang ต้นร่าง;
bproo-dtoo-kɔɔ โปรโตคอล

protract, *v.* yûut ยืด (prolong); kà-
yǎai ขยาย (extend)

protrude, *v.* yûun ยื่น (stick out);
tà-lòn ถลน (thrust outward)

proud, *adj.* puum-jai ภูมิใจ

prove, *v.* pí-sùut พิสูจน์

proverb, *n.* sù-paa-sìt สุภาษิต

provide, *v.* jàt-hâi จัดให้; hâi ให้

provided, providing, *conj.* mii-
kɔ̂ɔ-mɛ́ɛ-wâa มีข้อแม้ว่า

providence, *n.* kwaam-sù-kǔm
ความสุขุม

province, *n.* jang-wàt จังหวัด

provincial, *adj.* dtàang-jang-wàt
ต่างจังหวัด; gìao-gàp-jang-wàt
เกี่ยวกับจังหวัด

provision, *n.* gaan-jàt-hǎa
การจัดหา (act of supplying); kɔ̂ɔ-
gam-nòt ข้อกำหนด (stipulation or
qualification)

provoke, *v.* yú ยุ; grà-dtûn กระตุ้น

proximity, *n.* kwaam-glâi-kiang
ความใกล้เคียง

prudence, *n.* kwaam-rɔ̂ɔp-kɔ̂ɔp
ความรอบคอบ

English • Phonetic • Thai

prudent, *adj.* rɔ̂ɔp-kɔ̂ɔp รอบคอบ

prune, *n.* lûuk-plam-hɛ̂ɛng
ลูกพลัมแห้ง

pry, *v.* lɔ́ɔt-mɔɔng ลอดมอง; ngát
งัด

pseudonym, *n.* naam-fɛ̌ɛng
นามแฝง

psyche, *n.* jìt-jai จิตใจ

psychiatrist, *n.* jìt-dtà-pɛ̂ɛt
จิตแพทย์

psychiatry, *n.* jìt-dtà-wêet จิตเวช

psychological, *adj.* gìao-gàp-jìt-
dtà-wít-ta-yaa เกี่ยวกับจิตวิทยา

psychology, *n.* jìt-dtà-wít-ta-yaa
จิตวิทยา

puberty, *n.* wai-jà-rəən-pan
วัยเจริญพันธุ์

public, *adj.* sǎa-taa-ra-ná สาธารณะ

public, *n.* sǎa-taa-ra-ná สาธารณะ
(community of people); bprà-chaa-
chon ประชาชน (the people)

publication, *n.* gaan-pim การพิมพ์

publicity, *n.* gaan-bprà-chaa-sǎm-
pan การประชาสัมพันธ์

publicize, *v.* pə̀əi-prɛ̂ɛ เผยแพร่;
bprà-chaa-sǎm-pan ประชาสัมพันธ์

publish, *v.* jàt-pim จัดพิมพ์; pim-
pə̀əi-prɛ̂ɛ พิมพ์เผยแพร่

publisher, *n.* sǎm-nák-pim
สำนักพิมพ์

pudding, *n.* kà-nǒm-pút-dîng
ขนมพุดดิ้ง

puddle, *n.* ɛ̀ng-náam แอ่งน้ำ

puff, *n.* gaan-pôn การพ่น (emission); glùm-kwan กลุ่มควัน
(smoke)

pull, *v.* dung ดึง; lâak ลาก

pulp, *n.* núa-pǒn-la-máai เนื้อผลไม้

pulse, *n.* chîip-pa-jɔɔn ชีพจร

pump, *n.* krûang-sùup เครื่องสูบ

pumpkin, *n.* fák-tɔɔng ฟักทอง

punch, *n.* náam-pǒn-la-máai-ruam
น้ำผลไม้รวม

punctual, *adj.* dtrong-wee-laa
ตรงเวลา

punctuation mark, *n.* krûang-
mǎai-wák-dtɔɔn เครื่องหมาย
วรรคตอน

punish, *v.* long-tôot ลงโทษ

punishment, *n.* gaan-long-tôot
การลงโทษ

punitive, *adj.* bpen-gaan-long-tôot
เป็นการลงโทษ

pupil, *n.* nák-rian นักเรียน

puppet, *n.* hùn หุ่น; hùn-chə̂ət
หุ่นเชิด

puppeteer, *n.* kon-chə̂ət-hùn
คนเชิดหุ่น

puppy, *n.* lûuk-sù-nák ลูกสุนัข;
lûuk-mǎa ลูกหมา

purchase, *v.* súu ซื้อ

purchase, *n.* gaan-súu การซื้อ (act
of buying); sìng-tîi-súu-maa
สิ่งที่ซื้อมา (something bought)

pure, *adj.* bɔɔ-ri-sùt บริสุทธิ์

purge, *v.* cham-rá-láang ชำระล้าง;

láang-bpàap ล้างบาป

purify, v. tam-hâi-bɔɔ-ri-sùt
ทำให้บริสุทธิ์

purity, n. kwaam-bɔɔ-ri-sùt
ความบริสุทธิ์

purple, adj. sǐi-mûang สีม่วง

purpose, n. wát-tù-bprà-sǒng
วัตถุประสงค์ (objective); bpâo-
mǎai เป้าหมาย (goal)

purse, n. grà-bpǎo-ngən กระเป๋าเงิน

pursue, v. dam-nəən-dtaam
ดำเนินตาม (proceed along the
course); dtìt-dtaam ติดตาม (follow)

pursuit, n. gaan-dtìt-dtaam
การติดตาม; gaan-dam-nəən-dtɔ̀ɔ
การดำเนินต่อ

pus, n. nɔ̌ɔng หนอง

push, v. plàk ผลัก; dan ดัน

put, v. waang วาง; sài ใส่; jàt จัด

puzzle, n. bprìt-sà-nǎa ปริศนา

pyramid, n. bpì-raa-mít ปีรามิด

Q

quack, v. bpèt-rɔ́ɔng เป็ดร้อง

quack, n. siang-bpèt เสียงเป็ด

quadruple, v. sìi-tâo สี่เท่า

quail, n. nòk-grà-taa นกกระทา

quaint, adj. bplèɛk แปลก

quake, v. sàn สั่น

quake, n. gaan-sàn การสั่น (act of
shaking); pèn-din-wǎi แผ่นดินไหว

(earthquake)

qualification, n. kun-na-sǒm-bàt
คุณสมบัติ

qualified, adj. mii-kun-na-sǒm-bàt
มีคุณสมบัติ

qualify, v. tam-hâi-mɔ̀-sǒm ทำให้
เหมาะสม

quality, n. kun-na-pâap คุณภาพ

quandary, n. kwaam-ùt-àt-jai
ความอึดอัดใจ

quantity, n. bpà-ri-maan ปริมาณ

quarantine, n. gaan-gàk-gan
การกักกัน

quarrel, v. tá-lɔ́ ทะเลาะ

quarrel, n. gaan-tá-lɔ́-wí-wâat
การทะเลาะวิวาท

quarry, n. mʉang-hǐn เหมืองหิน
(for stone); gaan-lâa-kɔ̂ɔ-muun
การล่าข้อมูล (search for information)

quart, n. kwɔ́ɔt ควอร์ท; nʉ̀ng-jùt-
nʉ̀ng-sìi-lít 1.14 ลิตร

quarter, n. sìao เสี้ยว; nʉ̀ng-nai-sìi
หนึ่งในสี่

quarterly, adj. túk-sǎam-dʉan
ทุกสามเดือน

quartet, n. glùm-sìi-kon กลุ่มสี่คน

quartz, n. hǐn-kǐao-hà-nú-maan
หินเขี้ยวหนุมาน

quay, n. tâa-rʉa ท่าเรือ

queasy, adj. klʉ̂ʉn-hǐan คลื่นเหียน;
yàak-aa-jian อยากอาเจียน

queen, n. raa-chi-nii ราชินี

queer, adj. bprà-làat ประหลาด; pí-
lʉ́k พิลึก

English • Phonetic • Thai

quench, *v.* ra-ngáp ระงับ (put an end to); dàp-grà-hǎai ดับกระหาย (satisfy by drinking)

quest, *v.* kón-hǎa ค้นหา

quest, *n.* gaan-kón-hǎa การค้นหา

question, *v.* tǎam ถาม

question, *n.* kam-tǎam คำถาม

questionnaire, *n.* bpèep-sòop-tǎam แบบสอบถาม

queue, *n.* kiu คิว

quick, *adj.* reo เร็ว; rûat-reo รวดเร็ว

quicken, *v.* tam-hâi-reo ทำให้เร็ว

quiet, *adj.* ngîap เงียบ

quilt, *v.* dtòo-pâa ต่อผ้า

quilt, *n.* pâa-hòm-laai-dtòo ผ้าห่มลายต่อ (blanket)

quintet, *n.* glùm-tîi-bprà-gòop-dûai-hâa กลุ่มที่ประกอบด้วยห้า

quip, *n.* kam-kom คำคม (witty remark)

quit, *v.* lôok เลิก (finish); yùt หยุด (stop); laa-òok ลาออก (resign)

quite, *adv.* kôn-kâang ค่อนข้าง

quiver, *v.* sàn-tao สั่นเทา

quiz, *n.* gaan-tót-sòop การทดสอบ

quota, *n.* koo-dtâa โควต้า

quotation, *n.* an-yá-bprà-gàat อัญประกาศ

quote, *v.* âang-kam-pûut อ้างคำพูด (cite or refer to he words of another); dtii-raa-kaa ตีราคา (a price)

R

rabbit, *n.* grà-dtàai กระต่าย

rabies, *n.* rôok-glua-náam โรคกลัวน้ำ

race, *v.* kèng-kǎn แข่งขัน

race, *n.* chúa-châat เชื้อชาติ (human race); chon-châat ชนชาติ (nationality); gaan-kèng-kǎn-kwaam-reo การแข่งขันความเร็ว (contest of speed)

race track, *n.* lûu-kèng ลู่แข่ง

racial, *adj.* gìao-gàp-chúa-châat เกี่ยวกับเชื้อชาติ

racism, *n.* lát-tí-yìat-pǐu ลัทธิเหยียดผิว

racist, *n.* kon-tîi-yìat-pǐu คนที่เหยียดผิว

rack, *n.* chán ชั้น (shelf); raao ราว (for hanging things on); kroong โครง (framework)

racket, *n.* máai-dtii-lûuk ไม้ตีลูก

radar, *n.* ree-dâa เรดาร์

radiant, *adj.* bplèng-bplàng เปล่งปลั่ง

radiation, *n.* gaan-pèe-rang-sǐi การแผ่รังสี; gaam-man-dtà-rang-sǐi กัมมันตรังสี

radical, *n.* hǔa-run-reeng หัวรุนแรง; fàai-sáai ฝ่ายซ้าย

radio, *n.* wít-ta-yú วิทยุ

radioactive, *adj.* gìao-gàp-gam-man-dtà-rang-sǐi เกี่ยวกับกัมมันตรังสี

radish, *n.* hŭa-pàk-gàat หัวผักกาด

radium, *n.* tâat-ree-dîam
ธาตุเรเดียม

radius, *n.* sên-rát-sà-mĭi เส้นรัศมี

raffle, *n.* gaan-jàp-chà-làak-ching-
chôok การจับฉลากชิงโชค (prize
drawing)

raft, *n.* pɛɛ แพ

rafter, *n.* kon-tɔ̂ɔ-pɛɛ คนถ่อแพ
(one that operates a raft); kaan-kám-
lǎng-kaa คานค้ำหลังคา (sloping
beams)

rag, *n.* sèet-pâa เศษผ้า (scrap of
cloth); pâa-kîi-ríu ผ้าขี้ริ้ว (piece of
cloth used for cleaning, washing, or
dusting)

rage, *n.* kwaam-dùat-daan
ความเดือดดาล; kwaam-klâng
ความคลั่ง

ragged, *adj.* rûng-rîng รุ่งริ่ง

raid, *v.* jùu-joom จู่โจม; joom-dtii
โจมตี

raid, *n.* gaan-jùu-joom การจู่โจม;
gaan-joom-dtii การโจมตี

rail, *n.* raao ราว (e.g. handrail);
raang ราง (track)

railroad, *n.* tang-rót-fai ทางรถไฟ

rain, *v.* fŏn dtòk ฝนตก

rain, *n.* fŏn ฝน

rainbow, *n.* rúng-gin-náam รุ้งกินน้ำ

raincoat, *n.* sûa-gan-fŏn เสื้อกันฝน

rainfall, *n.* bpà-ri-maan-fŏn-tîi-dtòk
ปริมาณฝนที่ตก; fŏn ฝน

rainy, *adj.* mii-fŏn-dtòk มีฝนตก

raise, *v.* yók ยก (lift, elevate); kɯ̂n
ขึ้น (increase, grow, rise); líang-duu
เลี้ยงดู (bring up)

raise, *n.* gaan-yók-kɯ̂n การยกขึ้น;
gaan-lɯ̂an-kɯ̂n การเลื่อนขึ้น

raisin, *n.* lûuk-gèet ลูกเกด

rake, *n.* krâat คราด (a tool)

rally, *n.* gaan-kèng-kăn การแข่งขัน

ram, *n.* gè-dtua-pûu แกะตัวผู้

ramble, *v.* dəən-tîao เดินเที่ยว
(walk for pleasure); kui-rûai-bpùai
คุยเรื่อยเปื่อย (wander in one's
speech)

ramp, *n.* taang-lâat ทางลาด
(slope); gaan-kùu-kĕn การขู่เข็ญ
(extort)

rampage, *v.* tam-run-rɛɛng
ทำรุนแรง

rampart, *n.* bpɔ̂m ป้อม

ranch, *n.* faam-bpà-sù-sàt
ฟาร์มปศุสัตว์

rancher, *n.* kon-tam-ngaan-nai-
faam คนทำงานในฟาร์ม

random, *adj.* dooi-gaan-sùm
โดยการสุ่ม; mâi-lûak ไม่เลือก

range, *n.* rá-dàp ระดับ (level);
kɔ̀ɔp-kèet ขอบเขต (area or sphere);
sà-năam-ying-bpɯɯn สนามยิงปืน
(shooting)

rank, *n.* dtam-nèng ตำแหน่ง (position in a scale of responsibility); yót
ยศ (position for government offi-

English · Phonetic · Thai

cials); chán ชั้น (grade)

ransom, *n.* kâa-tài ค่าไถ่

rap, *v.* kɔ́ เคาะ (knock); dtii-reo ตีเร็ว (strike quickly)

rape, *v.* kòm-kʉ̌ʉn ข่มขืน

rape, *n.* gaan-kòm-kʉ̌ʉn การข่มขืน

rapid, *adj.* reo เร็ว; wɔ̌ɔng-wai ว่องไว

rapport, *n.* sǎai-sǎm-pan สายสัมพันธ์

rare, *adj.* nɔ́ɔi น้อย; hǎa-yâak หายาก

rascal, *n.* an-ta-paan อันธพาล

rash, *n.* pʉ̀ʉn ผื่น (on the skin); gaan-ra-bàat การระบาด (something that is widespread, outbreak)

rat, *n.* nǔu หนู

rate, *v.* jàt-an-dàp จัดอันดับ

rate, *n.* àt-dtraa อัตรา (proportion); raa-kaa ราคา (price); rá-dàp ระดับ (level)

rather, *adv.* kɔ̂n-kâang ค่อนข้าง

rating, *n.* gaan-jàt-an-dàp การจัดอันดับ (placing in rank); kân ขั้น (level)

ratio, *n.* àt-dtraa-sùan อัตราส่วน

ration, *n.* gaan-bpan-sùan การปันส่วน

rational, *adj.* mii-hèet-pǒn มีเหตุผล

rationale, *n.* kɔ̂ɔ-kwaam-hɛ̀ng-hèet-pǒn ข้อความแห่งเหตุผล

rattle, *n.* sǐang-rua เสียงรัว (short, sharp sound)

rattlesnake, *n.* nguu-hǎang-grà-dìng งูหางกระดิ่ง

rave, *v.* pûut-pɔ́ɔ-jɔ̂ɔ พูดเพ้อเจ้อ

raven, *n.* nók-gaa นกกา

ravine, *n.* hùp-kǎo-lʉ́k หุบเขาลึก

raw, *adj.* dìp ดิบ (unripe, uncooked); yàap หยาบ (rough)

ray, *n.* rang-sǐi รังสี (light beam)

rayon, *n.* pâa-ree-yɔɔng ผ้าเรยอง

raze, *v.* rʉ́ʉn-tɔ̌ɔn รื้อถอน (demolish, scrape or shave off); tam-laai ทำลาย (destroy); kà-jàt ขจัด (get rid of)

razor, *n.* mîit-goon มีดโกน

re-, *pfx.* iik อีก; gɛ̂ɛ แก้; dtɔ̀ɔp ตอบ

reach, *v.* maa-tʉ̌ng มาถึง (at a location); bpai-tʉ̌ng ไปถึง (at a location - further); ʉ̂am เอื้อม (for something)

react, *v.* dtɔ̀ɔp-dtôo ตอบโต้; dtɔ̀ɔp-sà-nɔ̌ɔng ตอบสนอง

reaction, *n.* bpà-dtì-gì-ri-yaa ปฏิกิริยา; gaan-dtôo-dtɔ̀ɔp การโต้ตอบ

reactionary, *n.* fàai-kwǎa ฝ่ายขวา

reactor, *n.* pûu-dtôo-dtɔ̀ɔp ผู้โต้ตอบ (one that reacts); krʉ̂ang-kûap-kum-pa-lang-niu-klia เครื่องควบคุมพลังนิวเคลียร์ (machine that controls the nuclear reaction)

read, *v.* àan อ่าน

reader, *n.* pûu-àan ผู้อ่าน

readily, *adv.* yàang-rûat-reo

อย่างรวดเร็ว

reading, *n.* gaan-àan การอ่าน

ready, *adj.* prɔ́ɔm พร้อม (prepared
or available); sèt เสร็จ (finish)

real, *adj.* jing จริง; tɛ́ɛ-jing แท้จริง

real estate, *n.* bâan-lɛ́-ûii-din
บ้านและที่ดิน (house and land); à-
sǎng-hǎa-rim-ma-sáp อสังหา
ริมทรัพย์ (immovable property)

realistic, *adj.* mǔan-jing เหมือนจริง

reality, *n.* kwaam-bpen-jing
ความเป็นจริง

realize, *v.* dtrà-nàk ตระหนัก (com-
prehend completely); tam-hâi-bpen-
jing ทำให้เป็นจริง (make real); rúu
รู้ (know)

really, *adv.* jing-jing จริงๆ

realm, *n.* aa-naa-jàk อาณาจักร;
bɔɔ-ri-ween บริเวณ

realtor, *n.* naai-nâa-kǎai-bâan-lɛ́-ûii-
din นายหน้าขายบ้านและที่ดิน

reap, *v.* gèp-gìao เก็บเกี่ยว; gìao
เกี่ยว

rear, *n.* kâang-lǎng ข้างหลัง (the
back part, behind); sùan-lǎng
ส่วนหลัง (the back part); gôn ก้น
(bottom)

reason, *n.* hèet-pǒn เหตุผล

reasonable, *adj.* mii-hèet-pǒn
มีเหตุผล

reassure, *v.* tam-hâi-nɛ̂ɛ-jai-kʉ̂n
ทำให้แน่ใจขึ้น (assure again); ráp-
rɔɔng รับรอง (affirm, restore confi-

dence to)

rebate, *n.* ngən-kʉʉn เงินคืน
(returned money); sùan-lót ส่วนลด
(discount)

rebel, *n.* gà-bòt กบฏ

rebound, *v.* dêng-glàp เด้งกลับ
(bounce back); hǔan-glàp หวนกลับ
(return)

rebound, *n.* gaan-dêng-glàp
การเด้งกลับ; gaan-hǔan-glàp
การหวนกลับ

rebuff, *v.* bɔ̀ɔk-bpàt บอกปัด

rebuke, *v.* dù-dàa ดุด่า; dàa-wâa
ด่าว่า

rebut, *v.* dtôo-yɛ́ɛng โต้แย้ง

recall, *v.* jam-dâai จำได้ (remember); rá-lʉ́k-dâai ระลึกได้ (summon back to awareness); rîak-glàp
เรียกกลับคืน (call back)

recede, *v.* wʉ́ʉi ถอย

receipt, *n.* bai-sèt-ráp-ngən
ใบเสร็จรับเงิน

receive, *v.* dâai-ráp ได้รับ

receiver, *n.* pûu-ráp ผู้รับ (human);
krûang-ráp-sǎn-yaan เครื่องรับ
สัญญาณ (machine)

recent, *adj.* rɛo-rɛo-níi เร็วๆนี้ (not
long ago); bpàt-jù-ban ปัจจุบัน
(the present time)

reception, *n.* gaan-ráp-rɔɔng
การรับรอง; gaan-dtɔ̂ɔn-ráp
การต้อนรับ

receptionist, *n.* pá-nák-ngaan-dtɔ̂ɔn-ráp พนักงานต้อนรับ

recess, *n.* gaan-yùt-pák การหยุดพัก

recession, *n.* gaan-tɔ̌ɔi การถอย
(act of going back); gaan-tɔ̌ɔn
การถอน (act of withdrawing); sèet-
tà-gìt-cha-lɔɔ-dtua เศรษฐกิจซลอตัว
(slow economy)

recipe, *n.* sùut สูตร; dtam-ràp
ตำรับ

recipient, *n.* pûu-ráp ผู้รับ

reciprocal, *adj.* sʉ̂ng-gan-lé-gan
ซึ่งกันและกัน

recital, *n.* gaan-dìao-krʉ̂ang-don-
dtrii การเดี่ยวเครื่องดนตรี (in
music); gaan-àan-ɔ̀ɔk-sǐang
การอ่านออกเสียง (reading)

recite, *v.* tɔ̂ng ท่อง (repeat, rehearse
in order to memorize); àan-ɔ̀ɔk-
sǐang อ่านออกเสียง (read aloud)

reckless, *adj.* bprà-màat ประมาท

recline, *v.* een เอน (lie back or
down); pîng พิง (lean against)

recluse, *adj.* sǎn-dòot สันโดษ

recluse, *n.* rʉ̄ʉ-sǐi ฤาษี

recognition, *n.* gaan-rá-lʉ́k-dâai
การระลึกได้; gaan-jam-dâai
การจำได้

recognize, *v.* jam-dâai จำได้
(recall, remember); rúu-jàk รู้จัก
(know something perceived before)

recollect, *v.* jam-dâai จำได้
(remember); rá-lʉ́k-dâai ระลึกได้
(recall to mind)

recollection, *n.* kwaam-song-jam
ความทรงจำ

recommend, *v.* né-nam แนะนำ
(advise, praise or commend); fàak-
fǎng ฝากฝัง (entrust)

recommendation, *n.* gaan-né-nam
การแนะนำ (the act of); jòt-mǎai-
né-nam จดหมายแนะนำ (letter)

reconcile, *v.* glài-glìa ไกล่เกลี่ย
(settle or resolve); tam-hâi-kʉʉn-dii-
gan ทำให้คืนดีกัน (reestablish a
relationship)

record, *v.* ban-tʉ́k บันทึก

record, *n.* ban-tʉ́k บันทึก (something recorded); bprà-wàt ประวัติ
(history)

record a sound, *v.* ban-tʉ́k-sǐang
บันทึกเสียง; àt-sǐang อัดเสียง

record player, *n.* krʉ̂ang-lên-jaan-
sǐang เครื่องเล่นจานเสียง

recover, *v.* hǎa-jəə หาเจอ (find);
kʉʉn-sà-pâap คืนสภาพ (return to a
normal state); hǎai-bpen-bpòk-gà-
dtì หายเป็นปกติ (from sickness)

recovery, *n.* gaan-hǎai-bpen-bpòk-
gà-dtì การหายเป็นปกติ; gaan-glàp-
sùu-sà-pâap-dəəm
การกลับสู่สภาพเดิม

re-create, *v.* sâang-mài สร้างใหม่;
tam-mài ทำใหม่

recreation, *n.* gaan-sâang-mài
การสร้างใหม่

recruit, *n.* sà-maa-chík-mài
สมาชิกใหม่ (new member); gaan-

jâang การจ้าง (employment)

rectangle, *n.* sìi-lìam-pʉ̌ʉn-pâa สี่เหลี่ยมผืนผ้า

recycle, *v.* nam-glàp-maa-chái-ìik นำกลับมาใช้อีก

red, *adj.* sǐi-dɛɛng สีแดง

Red Cross, *n.* gaa-châat กาชาด

redeem, *v.* sʉ́ʉ-kʉʉn ซื้อคืน (buy back); tài ไถ่ (obtain the freedom of somebody by payment); bplòt-nîi ปลดหนี้ (pay off)

reduce, *v.* lót-long ลดลง (bring down, lower); lót ลด (decrease); yɔ̂ɔ ย่อ (diminish)

reduction, *n.* gaan-lót การลด; gaan-yɔ̂ɔ การย่อ

redundant, *adj.* chái-kam-fûm-fuai ใช้คำฟุ่มเฟือย (needlessly wordy); mâak-gəən-bpai มากเกินไป (excessive)

reed, *n.* dtôn-gòk ต้นกก

reef, *n.* hǐn-sǒo-krôok หินโสโครก

reek, *n.* glìn-měn กลิ่นเหม็น (bad smell); kwan-túp ควันทึบ (thick smoke)

reel, *n.* lɔ̀ɔt-dâai หลอดด้าย (thread); lɔ̀ɔt หลอด (any cyllinder or roller)

refer, *v.* âang-ing อ้างอิง (e.g. to a dictionary); gìao-gàp เกี่ยวกับ (concern, pertain to); né-nam-lâi-bpai-hǎa แนะนำให้ไปหา (e.g. to a specialist)

referee, *n.* pûu-dtàt-sǐn ผู้ตัดสิน

reference, *n.* gaan-âang-ing การอ้างอิง

refill, *v.* dtəəm เติม

refill, *n.* sìng-tîi-dtəəm สิ่งที่เติม

refine, *v.* glàn กลั่น (purify); kàt-glao ขัดเกลา (improve by removing defects)

refinement, *n.* kwaam-bprà-nîit ความประณีต

refinery, *n.* roong-glàn โรงกลั่น

reflect, *v.* sà-tɔ́ɔn สะท้อน

reflection, *n.* gaan-sà-tɔ́ɔn การสะท้อน

reflector, *n.* krʉ̂ang-sà-tɔ́ɔn เครื่องสะท้อน; sìng-sà-tɔ́ɔn สิ่งสะท้อน

reflex, *n.* pâap-sà-tɔ́ɔn ภาพสะท้อน

reform, *v.* bpà-dtì-rûup ปฏิรูป (abolish or change; e.g. the government); bpràp-bprung ปรับปรุง (improve)

refrain, *n.* bòt-sám บทซ้ำ (e.g. song or poem)

refrain, *v.* ngót งด (from doing something)

refresh, *v.* dtəəm-pá-lang เติมพลัง (give strength or energy); tam-hâi-sòt-sǎi ทำให้สดใส (revive); dtʉan-kwaam-jam เตือนความจำ (memory)

refreshment, *n.* krʉ̂ang-dʉ̀ʉm-rʉ̌ʉ-aa-hǎan เครื่องดื่มหรืออาหาร

refrigerate, *v.* chɛ̂ɛ-yen แช่เย็น

refrigerator, *n.* dtûu-yen ตู้เย็น

refuge, *v.* lòp-pai หลบภัย; lîi-pai ลี้ภัย

refugee, *n.* pûu-lîi-pai ผู้ลี้ภัย

refund, *v.* kɯɯn-ngən คืนเงิน

refusal, *n.* gaan-bpà-dtì-sèet การปฏิเสธ

refuse, *v.* bpà-dtì-sèet ปฏิเสธ

refute, *v.* hàk-láang หักล้าง (prove to be false); dtôo-yéeng โต้แย้ง (overthrow by argument)

regain, *v.* ao-kɯɯn เอาคืน (get something back); fɯɯn-kɯɯn-sà-dtì ฟื้นคืนสติ (consciousness)

regal, *adj.* gìao-gàp-gà-sàt เกี่ยวกับกษัตริย์

regard, *v.* gìao-gàp เกี่ยวกับ

regarding, *prep.* gìao-gàp เกี่ยวกับ

regards, *n.* gaan-ták-taai การทักทาย (greetings)

regardless, *adv.* dooi-mâi-kam-nɯng-tɯ̌ng โดยไม่คำนึงถึง

regime, *n.* rá-bòp-gaan-bpòk-krɔɔng ระบบการปกครอง

region, *n.* din-dɛɛn ดินแดน

regional, *adj.* gìao-gàp-din-dɛɛn เกี่ยวกับดินแดน

register, *v.* long-tá-bian ลงทะเบียน

register, *n.* gaan-long-tá-bian การลงทะเบียน (formal or official recording); krɯ̂ang-ráp-jàai-ngən-sòt เครื่องรับจ่ายเงินสด (cash)

registered, *adj.* long-tá-bian-lɛ́ɛo

ลงทะเบียนแล้ว; ban-tɯ́k-wái-lɛ́ɛo บันทึกไว้แล้ว

registrar, *n.* naai-tá-bian นายทะเบียน

registration, *n.* gaan-long-tá-bian การลงทะเบียน; gaan-jòt-tá-bian การจดทะเบียน

regret, *v.* sǐa-jai เสียใจ

regular, *adj.* bpòk-gà-dtì ปกติ; tam-ma-daa ธรรมดา

regulate, *v.* kûap-kum-duu-lɛɛ ควบคุมดูแล (control or direct); waang-rá-bìap วางระเบียบ (set rules)

rehabilitate, *v.* pák-fɯɯn พักฟื้น; bam-bàt บำบัด

rehabilitation, *n.* gaai-ya-pâap-bam-bàt กายภาพบำบัด

rehearsal, *n.* gaan-sɔ́ɔm การซ้อม

rehearse, *v.* sɔ́ɔm ซ้อม

reign, *n.* am-nâat-gaan-bpòk-krɔɔng อำนาจการปกครอง

reimburse, *v.* cham-rá-ngən-kɯɯn ชำระเงินคืน

rein, *n.* bang-hǐan บังเหียน

reincarnate, *v.* gə̀ət-mài เกิดใหม่

reincarnation, *n.* gaan-gə̀ət-mài การเกิดใหม่

reinforce, *v.* sɔ̌əm-gam-lang เสริมกำลัง (make stronger); sà-nàp-sà-nǔn สนับสนุน (give support)

reiterate, *v.* glàao-sám กล่าวซ้ำ; tam-sám ทำซ้ำ

reject, *v.* bpà-dtì-sèet ปฏิเสธ

rejoice, *v.* dii-jai ดีใจ; yin-dii ยินดี

rejuvenate, *v.* tam-hâi-duu-ɔ̀ɔn-wai ทำให้ดูอ่อนวัย

relate, *v.* gìao-kɔ̂ɔng-gàp เกี่ยวข้องกับ (something to/with something); bpen-yâat เป็นญาติ (as relatives)

relation, *n.* gaan-gìao-kɔ̂ɔng-gan การเกี่ยวข้องกัน

relationship, *n.* kwaam-sǎm-pan ความสัมพันธ์

relative, *n.* yâat ญาติ

relatively, *adj.* kɔ̂n-kâang ค่อนข้าง

relax, *v.* pɔ̀n ผ่อน; pɔ̀n-klaai ผ่อนคลาย

relaxation, *n.* gaan-pɔ̀n-klaai การผ่อนคลาย

relay, *v.* tàai-tɔ̂ɔt ถ่ายทอด (broadcast); pàt-bplìan ผลัดเปลี่ยน (receive and pass on)

release, *n.* bplɔ̀i ปล่อย

relevant, *adj.* sǎm-pan-gan สัมพันธ์กัน

reliability, *n.* kwaam-nâa-chûa-tǔu ความน่าเชื่อถือ

reliable, *adj.* nâa-chûa-tǔu น่าเชื่อถือ (trustworthy); wái-jai-dâai ไว้ใจได้ (dependable)

relic, *n.* sìng-dtòk-tɔ̂ɔt สิ่งตกทอด

relief, *n.* gaan-ban-tao การบรรเทา; kwaam-pɔ̀n-klaai ความผ่อนคลาย

relieve, *v.* ban-tao บรรเทา (allevi-

ate); pɔ̀n-klaai ผ่อนคลาย (free from pain, anxiety, or distress)

religion, *n.* sàat-sà-nǎa ศาสนา

religious, *adj.* krêng-sàat-sà-nǎa เคร่งศาสนา

relinquish, *v.* yók-lɤ̂ɤk ยกเลิก (give up, cancel); sà-là สละ (renounce); bplòt ปลด (release)

relish, *n.* rót-châat รสชาติ

reluctant, *adj.* lang-lee ลังเล (hesitant); mâi-dtem-jai ไม่เต็มใจ (unwilling)

rely on, *v.* wái-waang-jai ไว้วางใจ; chûa-jai เชื่อใจ

remain, *v.* lǔa-yùu เหลืออยู่

remain, *n.* sìng-tîi-lǔa-yùu สิ่งที่เหลืออยู่; sèet เศษ

remainder, *n.* sìng-tîi-lǔa-yùu สิ่งที่เหลืออยู่

remark, *n.* kwaam-hěn ความเห็น

remarkable, *adj.* pí-sèet พิเศษ (extraordinary); nâa-tʉ̂ng น่าทึ่ง (worthy of notice, incredible)

remedy, *n.* gaan-yiao-yaa การเยียวยา

remember, *v.* jam จำ; jam-dâai จำได้

remind, *v.* dtuan-kwaam-jam เตือนความจำ

reminder, *n.* sìng-dtuan-kwaam-jam สิ่งเตือนความจำ

remorse, *n.* kwaam-sǎm-núk-pìt ความสำนึกผิด

remote, *adj.* glai ไกล; yaao-naan ยาวนาน

remote control, *n.* rii-mòot-kon-troon รีโมทคอนโทรล

remove, *v.* ao-ɔ̀ɔk เอาออก (take away from one place to another); yáai ย้าย (move)

remunerate, *v.* jàai-ngən จ่ายเงิน (pay); hâi-raang-wan ให้รางวัล (reward)

Renaissance, *n.* yúk-fʉ́ʉn-fuu-sǐn-lá-bpà ยุคฟื้นฟูศิลปะ

rend, *v.* chìik ฉีก (tear); yɛ̂ɛk แยก (separate); pàa ผ่า (split by cutting)

render, *v.* jàt-hâi จัดให้ (provide); yɔɔm-hâi ยอมให้ (yield); sà-nə̌ə เสนอ (submit or present)

rendezvous, *n.* gaan-nát-póp การนัดพบ

rendition, *n.* gaan-sà-dɛɛng การแสดง (performance); gaan-tɔ̀ɔt-kwaam การถอดความ (interpretation)

renew, *v.* rə̂əm-mài เริ่มใหม่ (begin); tam-mài ทำใหม่ (redo); dtɔ̀ɔ-aa-yú ต่ออายุ (e.g. expired card)

renewal, *n.* gaan-rə̂əm-mài การเริ่มใหม่

renounce, *v.* sà-là สละ; tíng ทิ้ง

renovate, *v.* tam-mài ทำใหม่; bpràp-bprung ปรับปรุง

renown, *n.* chʉ̂ʉ-sǐang ชื่อเสียง; gìt-dì-sàp กิตติศัพท์

renowned, *adj.* mii-chʉ̂ʉ-sǐang มีชื่อเสียง

rent, *v.* châo เช่า

rent, *n.* kâa-châo ค่าเช่า (cost of renting); gaan-châo การเช่า (act of renting)

rental, *n.* gaan-hâi-châo การให้เช่า

rental car, *n.* rót-châo รถเช่า

repair, *v.* sɔ̂m ซ่อม; gɛ̂ɛ แก้; rák-sǎa รักษา

reparation, *n.* gaan-sɔ̂m-sɛɛm การซ่อมแซม; gaan-bpràp-bprung การปรับปรุง

repay, *v.* jàai-kʉʉn จ่ายคืน (pay back); chót-chəəi ชดเชย (compensate)

repeat, *v.* pûut-sám พูดซ้ำ (speech); tam-sám ทำซ้ำ (action)

repent, *v.* sǎm-nʉ́k-pìt สำนึกผิด; sǐa-jai เสียใจ

repetition, *n.* gaan-tam-sám การทำซ้ำ

replace, *v.* tɛɛn-tîi แทนที่ (put back in its place); tam-tɛɛn ทำแทน (take the place of somebody)

replacement, *n.* gaan-tɛɛn-tîi การแทนที่

replenish, *v.* dtəəm เติม; sə̀əm เสริม

replete, *adj.* dtem-bpìam เต็มเปี่ยม (full of); nɛ̂n แน่น (packed)

replica, n. sìng-jam-lɔɔng สิ่งจำลอง

reply, v. dtɔ̀ɔp ตอบ

reply, n. kam-dtɔ̀ɔp คำตอบ; gaan-dtɔ̀ɔp การตอบ

report, n., v. raai-ngaan รายงาน

reporter, n. pûu-raai-ngaan ผู้รายงาน

represent, v. sà-dɛɛng-hâi-hěn แสดงให้เห็น (make an image or show); bpen-dtua-tɛɛn เป็นตัวแทน (act as a substitute); bpen-dtua-yàang เป็นตัวอย่าง (symbolize)

representation, n. dtua-yàang ตัวอย่าง (example); dtua-tɛɛn ตัวแทน (something that represents)

representative, n. dtua-tɛɛn ตัวแทน

repress, v. òt-glân อดกลั้น (restrain or suppress); rá-ngáp ระงับ (prevent from breaking out)

reproach, n. dtɔ̀ɔ-wâa ต่อว่า; dtam-nì ตำหนิ

reproduce, v. lɔ́ɔk ลอก (make copy); tam-sám ทำซ้ำ (do or make again); ɔ̀ɔk-lûuk ออกลูก (produce offspring)

reproduction, n. gaan-tam-sám การทำซ้ำ (act of reproducing); gaan-kát-lɔ́ɔk การคัดลอก (copying, imitating); gaan-ɔ̀ɔk-lûuk การออกลูก (procreation)

reptile, n. sàt-lúai-klaan สัตว์เลื้อยคลาน

republic, n. sǎa-taa-rá-ná-rát สาธารณรัฐ

republican, adj. gìao-gàp-pák-rii-páp-li-gan เกี่ยวกับพรรครีพับลิกัน

repugnant, adj. dtɔ̀ɔ-dtâan ต่อต้าน; káan ค้าน

repulse, v. kàp-lâi ขับไล่

reputable, adj. nâa-náp-tǔu น่านับถือ

repute, n. chûu-sǐang ชื่อเสียง

request, v. kɔ̌ɔ-rɔ́ɔng ขอร้อง

request, n. gaan-kɔ̌ɔ-rɔ́ɔng การขอร้อง

require, v. dtɔ̂ng-gaan ต้องการ

request, n. gaan-kɔ̌ɔ-rɔ́ɔng การขอร้อง; kwaam-dtɔ̂ng-gaan ความต้องการ; rîak-rɔ́ɔng เรียกร้อง

requirement, n. sìng-tîi-dtɔ̂ng-gaan สิ่งที่ต้องการ (something wanted); sìng-tîi-jam-bpen สิ่งที่จำเป็น (something necessary); kɔ̂ɔ-gam-nòt ข้อกำหนด (rules, regulations)

requisite, adj. jam-bpen จำเป็น (essential); gam-nòt-wái กำหนดไว้ (required)

requisition, n. gaan-rîak-rɔ́ɔng การเรียกร้อง (demand); kwaam-jam-bpen ความจำเป็น (necessity); kam-rɔ́ɔng-yàang-bpen-taang-gaan คำร้องอย่างเป็นทางการ (written request)

rescue, v. chûai-chii-wít ช่วยชีวิต

rescue, n. gaan-chûai-chii-wít การช่วยชีวิต

research, v. kón-kwáa ค้นคว้า; wi-jai วิจัย

research, n. gaan-kón-kwáa การค้นคว้า; gaan-wi-jai การวิจัย

researcher, n. pûu-kón-kwáa ผู้ค้นคว้า; nák-wi-jai นักวิจัย

resemblance, n. kwaam-kláai-gan ความคล้ายกัน

resemble, v. kláai คล้าย; kláai-gàp คล้ายกับ

resent, v. mâi-pɔɔ-jai ไม่พอใจ

resentful, adj. kùn-kuang ขุ่นเคือง

resentment, n. kwaam-mâi-pɔɔ-jai ความไม่พอใจ

reservation, n. gaan-sǎm-rɔɔng การสำรอง; gaan-sà-ngǔan-rák-sǎa การสงวนรักษา

reserve, v. sǎm-rɔɔng สำรอง (e.g. hotel, air ticket); sà-ngǔan สงวน (e.g. energy)

reserved, adj. sǎm-rɔɔng-wái สำรองไว้; sà-ngǔan-wái สงวนไว้; rák-sǎa-tâa-tii รักษาท่าที (manner)

reservoir, n. àang-gèp-náam อ่างเก็บน้ำ

reside, v. yùu อยู่; aa-sǎi อาศัย

residence, n. tîi-yùu-aa-sǎi ที่อยู่อาศัย; gaan-yùu-aa-sǎi การอยู่อาศัย

resident, n. pûu-aa-sǎi ผู้อาศัย

residential, adj. gìao-gàp-gaan-yùu-aa-sǎi เกี่ยวกับการอยู่อาศัย

residue, n. tîi-lǔa ที่เหลือ; sùan-tîi-lǔa ส่วนที่เหลือ

resign, v. laa-ɔɔk ลาออก

resignation, n. gaan-laa-ɔɔk การลาออก

resilient, adj. glàp-sùu-sà-pâap-dəəm กลับสู่สภาพเดิม

resin, n. yaang-máai ยางไม้

resist, v. dtâan ต้าน; dtɔɔ-dtâan ต่อต้าน

resistance, n. gaan-dtɔɔ-dtâan การต่อต้าน; gaan-dtâan-taan การต้านทาน

resistant, adj. ton-dtɔɔ ทนต่อ; dtɔɔ-dtâan ต่อต้าน

resolute, adj. nɛ̂ɛ-nɛ̂ɛ แน่วแน่; dèt-dìao เด็ดเดี่ยว

resolution, n. gaan-gɛ̂ɛ-bpan-hǎa การแก้ปัญหา

resolve, v. dtòk-long-jai ตกลงใจ (determine); mii-má-dtì มีมติ (of a committee or assembly); gɛ̂ɛ-bpan-hǎa แก้ปัญหา (a problem)

resonant, adj. gɔ̂ng ก้อง; gang-waan กังวาน

resort, n. rii-sɔ̀ɔt รีสอร์ท

resound, v. dang-gɔ̂ng ดังก้อง; sà-tɔ́ɔn-glàp สะท้อนกลับ

resource, n. lɛ̀ng-tîi-maa แหล่งที่มา (origin); sáp-pa-yaa-gɔɔn ทรัพยากร (supplies of raw materials)

respect, v. kao-róp เคารพ

respectable, adj. nâa-kao-róp

น่าเคารพ

respectful, *adj.* mii-kwaam-kao-róp
มีความเคารพ

respective, *adj.* dooi-cha-pó
โดยเฉพาะ

respectively, *adv.* dtaam-lam-dàp
ตามลำดับ

respiration, *n.* gaan-hǎai-jai
การหายใจ

respite, *n.* gaan-pák-pòn
การพักผ่อน (rest); gaan-tú-lao
การทุเลา (relief)

respond, *v.* dtɔ̀ɔp ตอบ; dtôo-dtɔ̀ɔp
โต้ตอบ

response, *n.* gaan-dtɔ̀ɔp การตอบ;
gaan-dtɔ̀ɔp-sà-nɔ̌ɔng การตอบสนอง

responsibility, *n.* kwaam-ráp-pìt-
chɔ̂ɔp ความรับผิดชอบ

responsible, *adj.* mii-kwaam-ráp-
pìt-chɔ̂ɔp มีความรับผิดชอบ

responsive, *adj.* dtôo-dtɔ̀ɔp
โต้ตอบ; dtɔ̀ɔp-sà-nɔ̌ɔng ตอบสนอง

rest, *v.* pák-pòn พักผ่อน (relax);
yùt-pák หยุดพัก (stop to rest)

restaurant, *n.* ráan-aa-hǎan
ร้านอาหาร; pát-dtaa-kaan ภัตตาคาร

restitution, *n.* gaan-sɔ̂m-sɛɛm
การซ่อมแซม (restoration to its original state); kâa-sǐa-hǎai ค่าเสียหาย
(reparation in the form of money)

restless, *adj.* grà-sap-grà-sàai
กระสับกระส่าย

restoration, *n.* gaan-bpà-dtì-sǎng-

kɔ̌ɔn การปฏิสังขรณ์

restore, *v.* sɔ̂m-sɛɛm ซ่อมแซม;
sâang-mài สร้างใหม่

restrain, *v.* yáp-yáng ยับยั้ง (hold
back from action); hâam-bpraam
ห้ามปราม (restrict, control)

restraint, *n.* gaan-hâam การห้าม;
gaan-yùt-yáng การหยุดยั้ง

restrict, *v.* jam-gàt จำกัด

restriction, *n.* kɔ̂ɔ-jam-gàt
ข้อจำกัด; gaan-bang-káp การบังคับ

restroom, *n.* hɔ̂ng-náam ห้องน้ำ

result, *v.* mii-pǒn มีผล

result, *n.* pǒn ผล; ma-dtì มติ

resume, *v.* rɔ̂ɔm-mài เริ่มใหม่
(begin); tam-dtɔ̀ɔ ทำต่อ (continue)

résumé, *n.* bprà-wàt-yɔ̂ɔ ประวัติย่อ

retail, *n., v.* kǎai-bplìik ขายปลีก

retailer, *n.* pûu-kǎai-bplìik
ผู้ขายปลีก

retain, *v.* rák-sǎa-wái รักษาไว้

retaliate, *v.* dtɔ̀ɔp-dtôo ตอบโต้;
gɛ̂ɛ-pèt แก้เผ็ด

retard, *v.* tam-hâi-cháa ทำให้ช้า

retarded, *adj.* bpan-yaa-ɔ̀ɔn
ปัญญาอ่อน

retina, *n.* ree dtì nâa เรตินา

retire, *v.* bplòt-gà-sǐan ปลดเกษียณ
(from work); tɔ̌ɔn-dtua ถอนตัว
(withdraw voluntarily)

retirement, *n.* gaan-gà-sǐan
การเกษียณ

retort, *v.* dtôo-dtɔ̀ɔp โต้ตอบ; yɛ́ɛng

แย้ง

retract, v. เริ่ว_น-kam-pûut ถอนคำพูด
(take back what has been said); tɔ̌ɔi-
glàp ถอยกลับ (draw back)

retreat, v. เริ่ว_น-dtua ถอนตัว (withdraw); tɔ̌ɔi ถอย (draw back)

retribution, n. gam กรรม (punishment or reward, karma); gaan-tót-
tɛɛn การทดแทน (recompense)

retrieve, v. ao-kɯɯn-maa เอาคืนมา
(get back); gûu กู้ (rescue or save)

return, v. glàp-maa กลับมา; yɔ́ɔn-
glàp ย้อนกลับ; glàp กลับ

reunite, v. glàp-maa-jəə-gan-iik
กลับมาเจอกันอีก

reveal, v. bpə̀ət-pə̌əi เปิดเผย (make
known); sà-dɛɛng-hâi-hěn
แสดงให้เห็น (show)

revel, v. chà-lɔ̌ɔng-yàang-nàk
ฉลองอย่างหนัก (celebrate enthusias-
tically)

revelation, n. gaan-bpə̀ət-pə̌əi
การเปิดเผย

revenge, v. gɛ̂ɛ-kéɛn แก้แค้น

revenue, n. paa-sǐi ภาษี (tax);
raai-dâai-rát รายได้รัฐ (government
income); raai-dâai-ruam-gɔ̀ɔn-hàk-
paa-sǐi รายได้รวมก่อนหักภาษี (gross
income)

revere, v. kao-róp เคารพ (respect);
buu-chaa บูชา (regard with awe,
deference, and devotion)

reverie, n. kwaam-pə̌ə-fǎn

ความเพ้อฝัน

reverse, v. glàp-dâan กลับด้าน

reverse, n. dâan-glàp ด้านกลับ

revert, v. glàp-sùu กลับสู่; kɯɯn-
glàp คืนกลับ

review, v. tóp-tuan ทบทวน (look
over or examine again); pí-jaa-ra-
naa พิจารณา (consider)

revise, v. gɛ̂ɛ-kǎi แก้ไข; bpràp-
bprung ปรับปรุง

revision, n. gaan-bpràp-bprung-
gɛ̂ɛ-kǎi การปรับปรุงแก้ไข

revival, n. gaan-fúɯn-fuu การฟื้นฟู

revive, v. fúɯn-fuu ฟื้นฟู

revoke, v. yók-lə̂ək ยกเลิก; pə̀ək-
tɔ̌ɔn เพิกถอน

revolt, n. bpà-dtì-wàt ปฏิวัติ; jà-
raa-jon จราจล

revolution, n. gaan-bpà-dtì-wát
การปฏิวัติ

revolutionary, adj. gìao-gàp-gaan-
bpà-dtì-wát เกี่ยวกับการปฏิวัติ

revolutionize, v. bpà-dtì-wát
ปฏิวัติ; bpràp-bprung-ka-nǎan-yài
ปรับปรุงขนาดใหญ่

revolve, v. mǔn-rɔ̂ɔp หมุนรอบ;
koo-jɔɔn โคจร

revolver, n. bpɯɯn-pók ปืนพก

revolving, adj. mǔn-rɔ̂ɔp หมุนรอบ

reward, n. raang-wan รางวัล

rhetoric, n. gaan-chái-sǎm-nuan
การใช้สำนวน

rheumatism, n. rôok-bpùat-dtaamkɔɔ̂ โรคปวดตามข้อ

rhyme, v. săm-pàt สัมผัส

rhyme, n. sĭang-săm-pàt เสียงสัมผัส

rhythm, n. jang-wà จังหวะ

rib, n. sîi-kroong ซี่โครง

ribbon, n. rîp-bîn ริบบิ้น

rice, n. kâao ข้าว

rich, adj. ruai รวย (wealthy); kêm-kôn เข้มข้น (containing large amount)

riches, n. kwaam-râm-ruai ความร่ำรวย

rid, v. kà-jàt ขจัด; gam-jàt กำจัด

riddle, n. bprìt-sà-năa ปริศนา

ride, v. kàp ขับ (drive a vehicle), kìi ขี่ (bicycle, motorcycle, horse); nâng นั่ง (sit in or on a vehicle)

ride, n. gaan-kàp-rót การขับรถ (car); gaan-kìi-máa การขี่ม้า (horse)

rider, n. pûu-kìi ผู้ขี่ (one that rides); paa-hà-ná พาหนะ (vehicle)

ridge, n. săn-kăo สันเขา (of a mountain); sùan-tîi-nuun ส่วนที่นูน (raised line or part)

ridicule, v. hŭa-rɔ́-yɔ́ หัวเราะเยาะ; yɔ́-yə́əi เยาะเย้ย

ridiculous, adj. nâa-hŭa-rɔ́ น่าหัวเราะ; nâa-kăn น่าขัน

rife, adj. mii-tûa-bpai มีทั่วไป (common); prɛ̂ɛ-lăai แพร่หลาย (widespread)

rifle, n. bpʉʉn-yaao ปืนยาว

rift, n. rɔɔi-yɛ́ɛk รอยแยก (e.g. in the earth); gaan-dtɛ̀ɛk-ráao การแตกร้าว (break in friendly relations)

right, n. sìt, sìt-ti สิทธิ์, สิทธิ (e.g. legal right)

right, adj. tùuk-dtɔ̂ng ถูกต้อง (correct); kwăa ขวา (opposite of left)

righteous, adj. tùuk-dtɔ̂ng ถูกต้อง; chɔ̂ɔp-tam ชอบธรรม

right-handed, adj. tà-nàt-kwăa ถนัดขวา

rightist, n. pûak-a-nú-rák-ní-yom พวกอนุรักษ์นิยม; pûak-iang-kwăa พวกเอียงขวา

rim, n. kɔ̀ɔp ขอบ; rim ริม

rind, n. bplʉ̀ak-pŏn-la-máai เปลือกผลไม้ (fruit); năng-sàt หนังสัตว์ (animal skin)

ring, n. wɛ̆ɛn แหวน (for fingers); wong-wɛ̆ɛn วงแหวน (circle, circular band of any kind of material); sà-năam-kɛ̀ng สนามแข่ง (for fighting or racing)

rink, n. laan-sà-gét-náam-kɛ̀ng ลานสเก็ตน้ำแข็ง

rinse, v. láang ล้าง

riot, n. jà-raa-jon จราจล; kwaam-on-la-màan ความอลหม่าน

rip, v. chìik ฉีก; pàa ผ่า

ripe, adj. sùk สุก

ripen, v. tam-hâi-sùk ทำให้สุก; tam-hâi-dtoo-dtem-tîi ทำให้โตเต็มที่

ripple, n. rá-lôok-klûen ระลอกคลื่น

rise, v. lúk ลุก (from bed, stand up, etc.); kûn ขึ้น (e.g. the sun)

rise, n. gaan-lúk-kûn การลุกขึ้น; gaan-dtùun-kûn การตื่นขึ้น

risk, v. sìang เสี่ยง

risk, n. gaan-sìang การเสี่ยง (act of being risky); pai ภัย (danger)

risky, adj. sìang เสี่ยง; bpen-an-dtà-raai เป็นอันตราย

rite, n. pí-tii-gaan-taang-sàat-sà-nǎa พิธีการทางศาสนา

ritual, n. pí-tii พิธี; pí-tii-gaan พิธีการ

rival, n. kûu-kèng คู่แข่ง; kûu-bpràp คู่ปรับ

rivalry, n. gaan-kèng-kǎn การแข่งขัน; kûu-bpràp คู่ปรับ

river, n. mɛ̂ɛ-náam แม่น้ำ

roach, n. má-lɛɛng-sàap แมลงสาบ

road, n. tà-nǒn ถนน

roam, v. tông-tîao ท่องเที่ยว; dəən-dtrèe เดินเตร่

roar, v. kam-raam คำราม; pèet-sǐang แผดเสียง

roast, v. òp อบ

roast beef, n. núa-òp เนื้ออบ

rob, v. bplôn ปล้น

robber, n. joon โจร

robbery, n. gaan-bplôn การปล้น

robe, n. sûa-klum-yaao เสื้อคลุมยาว; sûa-chút-pí-tii เสื้อชุดพิธี (for ceremony)

robot, n. hùn-yon หุ่นยนต์

robust, adj. kɛ̌ng-rɛɛng-dii แข็งแรงดี (full of health and strength); gam-yam กำยำ (sturdy)

rock, v. yôok โยก; gwèng แกว่ง

rock, n. gɔ̂ɔn-hǐn ก้อนหิน; hǐn หิน

rocker, n. gâo-îi-yôok เก้าอี้โยก

rocket, n. jà-rùat จรวด

rocky, adj. mii-hǐn-mâak มีหินมาก

rod, n. tôn-máai ท่อนไม้ (piece of wood); kan-bèt คันเบ็ด (fishing)

role, n. bòt-bàat บทบาท

roll, v. múan ม้วน

roll, n. lûuk-glîng ลูกกลิ้ง

roll call, n. gaan-kǎan-chûu การขานชื่อ

roller, n. lûuk-glîng ลูกกลิ้ง

roller skate, v. lên-sa-gét-náam-kěng เล่นสเก็ตน้ำแข็ง

roller skate, n. sa-gét-náam-kěng สเก็ตน้ำแข็ง

romance, n. rûang-rák-rák-krâi-krâi เรื่องรักๆใคร่ๆ

romantic, adj. roo-mɛɛn-dtìk โรแมนติก

roof, n. lǎng-kaa หลังคา

room, n. hông ห้อง

roommate, n. pûan-rûam-hông เพื่อนร่วมห้อง

roomy, adj. gwâang กว้าง

rooster, n. gài-dtua-pûu ไก่ตัวผู้

root, n. râak ราก

rope, n. chûak เชือก

rose, *n.* dɔ̀ɔk-gù-làap ดอกกุหลาบ

rosy, *adj.* sǐi-gù-làap สีกุหลาบ

rot, *v.* nâo-bpʉ̀ai เน่าเปื่อย

rotary, *adj.* mǔn-rɔ̂ɔp หมุนรอบ;
wian เวียน

rotate, *v.* mǔn-rɔ̂ɔp หมุนรอบ

rotation, *n.* gaan-mǔn-rɔ̂ɔp
การหมุนรอบ

rotten, *adj.* nâo เน่า (having a foul
odor); bpʉ̀ai เปื่อย (decomposed);
pù ผุ (decayed, e.g. tooth)

rouge, *n.* tîi-taa-gɛ̂ɛm ที่ทาแก้ม

rough, *adj.* krù-krà ขรุขระ; yàap
หยาบ

round, *adj.* glom กลม

round, *n.* sìng-tîi-bpen-wong-glom
สิ่งที่เป็นวงกลม

roundabout, *adj.* ɔ̂ɔm อ้อม

rouse, *v.* bplùk ปลุก; yú-yong ยุยง

route, *n.* taang ทาง; sên-taang
เส้นทาง

routine, *n.* gìt-jà-wát กิจวัตร

rove, *v.* rêe-rɔ̂n เร่ร่อน

row, *n.* tɛ̌o แถว

row, *v.* paai-rʉa พายเรือ

rowdy, *adj.* hee-haa เฮฮา

royal, *adj.* gìao-gàp-râat-chá-wong
เกี่ยวกับราชวงศ์ (relating to a
monarch)

royalty, *n.* râat-chá-dtrà-guun
ราชตระกูล

rub, *v.* tǔu ถู; kàt ขัด

rubber, *n.* yaang ยาง (elastic sub-

stance); tǔng-yaang ถุงยาง (condom)

ruby, *n.* táp-tim ทับทิม

rude, *adj.* yàap-kaai หยาบคาย

ruffle, *v.* grà-pʉam กระเพื่อม

rug, *n.* prom พรม

ruin, *v.* tam-hâi-pí-nâat ทำให้พินาศ

ruin, *n.* kwaam-pí-nâat ความพินาศ
(destruction); sâak-bpà-ràk-hàk-
pang ซากปรักหักพัง (remains)

rule, *v.* bpòk-krɔɔng ปกครอง

rule, *n.* gòt กฎ (used in sports,
etc.); làk หลัก (principle); kɔ̂ɔ-
bang-káp ข้อบังคับ (regulation)

ruler, *n.* pûu-bpòk-krɔɔng
ผู้ปกครอง; máai-ban-tát ไม้บรรทัด

ruling, *n.* gaan-kûap-klum
การควบคุม (controlling); gaan-
chíi-kàat การชี้ขาด (judging); gaan-
dtàt-sǐn การตัดสิน (court judgment)

rum, *n.* lâo-ram เหล้ารัม

rumble, *v.* dang-gɔ̂ng ดังก้อง

rumor, *n.* kàao-lʉʉ ข่าวลือ; rʉ̂ang-
nin-taa เรื่องนินทา

rump, *n.* núa-sà-pôok เนื้อสะโพก

run, *v.* wîng วิ่ง; rîip-rɔ́ɔn รีบร้อน
(hurry)

runner, *n.* nák-wîng นักวิ่ง

runway, *n.* laan-wîng ลานวิ่ง

rural, *adj.* chon-na-bòt ชนบท;
bâan-nɔ̂ɔk บ้านนอก

ruse, *n.* ù-baai อุบาย; lêe-gon
เล่ห์กล

rush, v. rêng-rîip เร่งรีบ

rush, n. kwaam-rêng-rîip
ความเร่งรีบ

rush hour, n. chûa-moong-rêng-rîip
ชั่วโมงเร่งรีบ

Russian, n. chaao-rát-sia
ชาวรัสเซีย (people); paa-sǎa-rát-sia
ภาษารัสเซีย (language); gìao-gàp-
rát-sia เกี่ยวกับรัสเซีย (relating to
Russia)

rust, v. bpen-sà-nǐm เป็นสนิม

rust, n. sà-nǐm สนิม

rustic, adj. bâan-nɔ̂ɔk บ้านนอก

rusty, adj. bpen-sà-nǐm เป็นสนิม

rye, n. kâao-rai ข้าวไรย์

S

sabotage, n. wí-nâat-sà-gam
วินาศกรรม

sack, n. grà-sɔ̀ɔp กระสอบ (e.g.
rice); tǔng ถุง (bag)

sacred, adj. sàk-sìt ศักดิ์สิทธิ์

sacrifice, v. sǐa-sà-là เสียสละ

sacrifice, n. gaan-sǐa-sà-là
การเสียสละ; gaan-plii การพลี;
gaan-buang-sǔang การบวงสรวง

sad, adj. sâo เศร้า; sǐa-jai เสียใจ

sadden, v. tam-hâi-sǐa-jai
ทำให้เสียใจ

saddle, n. aan-máa อานม้า

saddlebag, n. tǔng-krûang-mʉʉ

sadistic, adj. gaam-wí-bpà-rìt
กามวิปริต; saa-dìt ซาดิสต์

sadness, n. kwaam-sâo ความเศร้า

safe, n. dtûu-ní-rá-pai ตู้นิรภัย

safe, adj. bplɔ̀ɔt-pai ปลอดภัย

safeguard, n. krûang-bpɔ̂ng-gan
เครื่องป้องกัน

safety, n. kwaam-bplɔ̀ɔt-pai
ความปลอดภัย

safety belt, n. kěm-kàt-ní-rá-pai
เข็มขัดนิรภัย

safety pin, n. kem-glàt เข็มกลัด

sag, v. jom-long จมลง; yɔ́ɔi-long
ย้อยลง

saga, n. dtam-naan ตำนาน

sage, n. nák-bpràat นักปราชญ์

sail, v. lên-rʉa แล่นเรือ

sail, n. bai-rʉa ใบเรือ; gaan-lên-rʉa
การแล่นเรือ

sailboat, n. rʉa-bai เรือใบ

sailing, n. gaan-dəən-rʉa
การเดินเรือ

sailor, n. gà-laa-sǐi-rʉa กลาสีเรือ

saint, n. nák-bun นักบุญ

sake, n. pǒn-bprà-yòot ผลประโยชน์
(benefit); kwaam-hěn-gèɛ... ความ
เห็นแก่... (for the sake of...)

salad, n. sà-làt สลัด

salary, n. ngən-dʉan เงินเดือน

sale, n. gaan-kǎai การขาย

sales tax, n. paa-sǐi-gaan-káa
ภาษีการค้า

English · Phonetic · Thai

saliva, n. náam-laai น้ำลาย

salmon, n. bplaa-sɛɛn-mɔ̂n ปลาแชลมอน

salon, n. hɔ̂ng-tǒong ห้องโถง; ráan-sɔ̌ɔm-sǔai ร้านเสริมสวย

salt, n. glua เกลือ

salty, adj. kem เค็ม

salute, v. kam-náp คำนับ (show honor); sà-dɛɛng-kaa-ra-wá แสดงคารวะ (pay respect)

salvation, n. gaan-chûai-lɯ̌a การช่วยเหลือ

same, adj. mɯ̌an-gan เหมือนกัน; mɯ̌an-dɔɔm เหมือนเดิม

sample, n. dtua-yàang ตัวอย่าง

sanctify, v. tam-hâi-sàk-sìt ทำให้ศักดิ์สิทธิ์

sanction, v. à-nú-yâat-bpen-taang-gaan อนุญาตเป็นทางการ (authorize, approve formally); long-tôot ลงโทษ (punish)

sand, n. saai ทราย

sandal, n. rɔɔng-táao-dtè รองเท้าแตะ

sandpaper, n. grà-dàat-saai กระดาษทราย

sandwich, n. sɛɛn-wít แซนด์วิช

sandy, adj. mii-saai mâak มีทรายมาก

sane, adj. mii-sà-dtì มีสติ (sensible); sùk-kà-pâap-jìt-dii สุขภาพจิตดี (having a healthy mind)

sanitary, adj. tùuk-sùk-kà-lák-sà-nà ถูกสุขลักษณะ

sanitation, n. sùk-kà-à-naa-mai สุขอนามัย

sanity, n. sùk-kà-pâap-jìt-bpòk-gà-dtì สุขภาพจิตปกติ

sap, v. gam-lang-wang-chaa กำลังวังชา (strength); kon-ngôo คนโง่ (stupid person)

sapphire, n. nin-sǐi-kaam นิลสีคราม

sarcastic, adj. nèp-nɛɛm เหน็บแนม; sìat-sǐi เสียดสี; tàak-tǎang ถากถาง

sardine, n. bplaa-saa-diin ปลาซาร์ดีน

sash, n. sǎai-kâat สายคาด (long strip of cloth worn around the waist or shoulder); wong-gòp วงกบ (of window frames)

Satan, n. saa-dtaan ซาตาน

satellite, n. daao-tiam ดาวเทียม

satin, n. pâa-prɛɛ-dtùan ผ้าแพรต่วน

satire, n. gaan-sìat-sǐi การเสียดสี; gaan-tàak-tǎang การถากถาง

satisfaction, n. kwaam-pɔɔ-jai ความพอใจ

satisfactory, adj. pɔɔ-jai พอใจ

satisfied, adj. pɔɔ-jai พอใจ

satisfy, v. tam-hâi-pɔɔ-jai ทำให้พอใจ

saturate, v. tam-hâi-ìm-dtua ทำให้อิ่มตัว (fill completely); tam-hâi-chôok ทำให้โชก (make wet)

saturated, adj. ìm-dtua อิ่มตัว

Saturday, n. wan-sǎo วันเสาร์

sauce, n. sɔ́ɔt ซอส; náam-bprung-rót น้ำปรุงรส

saucer, n. tûai-rɔɔng ถ้วยรอง

saucy, adj. ta-lûng ทะลึ่ง

sausage, n. sâi-grɔ̀ɔk ไส้กรอก

sauté, n. pàt-fai-dɛɛng ผัดไฟแดง

savage, n. dù-ráai ดุร้าย; bpàa-tùan ป่าเถื่อน

save, v. chûai-lǔa ช่วยเหลือ (help); chûai-chii-wít ช่วยชีวิต (life); gèp-ngən เก็บเงิน (money)

savings, n. ngən-sà-sǒm เงินสะสม

savior, n. pûu-chûai-chii-wit ผู้ช่วยชีวิต

savor, v. rót-châat รสชาติ (taste); glìn กลิ่น (smell)

saw, n. lûai เลื่อย

sawdust, n. kîi-lûai ขี้เลื่อย

sawmill, n. roong-lûai โรงเลื่อย

saxophone, n. sɛ́k-soo-foon แซกโซโฟน

say, v. pûut พูด; glàao กล่าว; bɔ̀ɔk บอก

saying, n. kam-pûut คำพูด

scab, n. sà-gèt-plɛ̌e สะเก็ดแผล

scale, n. dtaa-châng ตาชั่ง (weighing instrument); mâat-dtraa-sùan มาตราส่วน (proportion)

scallop, n. hɔ̌i-krɛɛng หอยแครง

scalp, n. nǎng-sǐi-sà หนังศีรษะ; nǎng-hǔa หนังหัว

scan, v. duu-pǝ̀ən-pǝ̀ən ดูเผินๆ (glance at quickly); sa-gɛɛn สแกน (machine)

scandal, n. rûang-ǔu-chǎao เรื่องอื้อฉาว

scanner, n. krûang-sà-gɛɛn เครื่องสแกน

scapegoat, n. pɛ́-ráp-bàap แพะรับบาป

scar, n. plɛ̌e-bpen แผลเป็น

scarce, adj. kàat-klɛɛn ขาดแคลน

scare, v. tam-hâi-dtòk-jai ทำให้ตกใจ

scarecrow, n. hùn-lâi-gaa หุ่นไล่กา

scared, adj. glua กลัว

scarf, n. pâa-pan-kɔɔ ผ้าพันคอ

scarlet, adj. sǐi-dɛɛng-sòt สีแดงสด

scary, adj. nâa-glua น่ากลัว; sà-yɔ̌ɔng-kwǎn สยองขวัญ

scatter, v. tam-hâi-grà-jaai ทำให้กระจาย; tam-hâi-dtɛ̀ɛk ทำให้แตก

scenario, n. bòt-pâap-pá-yon บทภาพยนตร์; hèet-gaan-jam-lɔɔng เหตุการณ์จำลอง

scene, n. chàak ฉาก; pâap ภาพ

scenery, n. tiu-tát ทิวทัศน์; puum-mí-bprà-têet ภูมิประเทศ

scent, n. glìn กลิ่น (odor); náam-hɔ̌ɔm น้ำหอม (perfume)

schedule, n. gam-nòt-gaan กำหนดการ; raai-gaan รายการ; dtaa-raang-wee-laa ตารางเวลา

scheme, v. pɛ̌ɛn-gaan แผนการ

(plan); kroong-gaan โครงการ (program)

schizophrenia, n. rôok-jìt-chá-nít-nùng โรคจิตชนิดหนึ่ง

scholar, n. nák-wí-chaa-gaan นักวิชาการ

scholarship, n. tun-gaan-sùk-săa ทุนการศึกษา

scholastic, adj. gìao-gàp-gaan-sùk-săa เกี่ยวกับการศึกษา

school, n. roong-rian โรงเรียน

science, n. wìt-ta-yaa-sàat วิทยาศาสตร์

scientific, adj. gìao-gàp-wìt-ta-yaa-sàat เกี่ยวกับวิทยาศาสตร์

scientist, n. nák-wìt-ta-yaa-sàat นักวิทยาศาสตร์

scissors, n. gan-grai กรรไกร

scold, v. dàa ด่า; dtɔ̀ɔ-wâa ต่อว่า

scoop, n. grà-buai กระบวย (a tool); kàao-dùan ข่าวด่วน (latest news)

scooter, n. rót-jàk-grà-yaan-yon-lék รถจักรยานยนต์เล็ก

scope, n. kɔ̀ɔp-kèet ขอบเขต

score, v. tam-ká-nɛɛn ทำคะแนน

score, n. ká-nɛɛn คะแนน (point); nóot-pleeng โน้ตเพลง (music)

scorn, n. gaan-duu-mìn การดูหมิ่น

scorpion, n. mɛɛng-bpɔ̀ng แมงป่อง

scotch, n. rɔɔi-dtàt รอยตัด

Scotch tape, n. téep-dtìt-grà-dàat เทปติดกระดาษ; sa-gɔ́t-téep

สก็อตเทป

scout, n. tá-hăan-sɔ̀ɔt-nɛɛm ทหารสอดแนม; lûuk-sŭa ลูกเสือ

scramble, n. bpiin ปีน (climb)

scrap, n. chín ชิ้น; sèet เศษ

scrape, v. kùut ขูด

scratch, v. kùan ข่วน (with the nail); kìit ขีด (make marks)

scratch, n. rɔɔi-kùan รอยข่วน; rɔɔi-kìit รอยขีด

scrawl, v. kĭan-wàt เขียนหวัด

scream, v. wĭit-rɔ́ɔng หวีดร้อง; rɔ́ɔng-grìit ร้องกรี๊ด

screen, n. jɔɔ จอ (monitor)

screw, n. dtà-hpuu-kuang ตะปูควง; ruu-gliao รูเกลียว

screwdriver, n. kăi-kuang ไขควง

scribble, n. laai-muu-wàt ลายมือหวัด

script, n. dtôn-râang ต้นร่าง

scrub, v. tŭu ถู; kàt ขัด

scrutinize, v. dtrùat-yàang-lá-ìat ตรวจอย่างละเอียด

sculptor, n. châng-gè-sà-làk ช่างแกะสลัก (in carving); châng-bpân ช่างปั้น (in shaping clay); châng-lɔ̀ɔ ช่างหล่อ (in molding); bprà-dtì-maa-qɔɔn ประติมากร (such artists)

sculpture, n. bprà-dtì-maa-gam ประติมากรรม

sea, n. tá-lee ทะเล

seafood, n. aa-hăan-tá-lee

อาหารทะเล

seal, *v.* bprà-táp-dtraa ประทับตรา

seal, *n.* dtraa-bprà-táp ตราประทับ
(stamp); mɛɛo-náam แมวน้ำ (animal)

seam, *n.* dtà-kèp ตะเข็บ

seamstress, *n.* yĭng-yép-pâa
หญิงเย็บผ้า

seaport, *n.* tâa-rua ท่าเรือ

search, *v.* kón-hăa ค้นหา

search, *n.* gaan-kón-hăa การค้นหา

seashore, *n.* chaai-tá-lee ชายทะเล

seasickness, *n.* gaan-mao-rua
การเมาเรือ

season, *n.* rú-duu-gaan ฤดูกาล;
nâa หน้า

seasonal, *adj.* dtaam-rú-duu-gaan
ตามฤดูกาล

seat, *n.* tîi-nâng ที่นั่ง

seat belt, *n.* kĕm-kàt-ní-rá-pai
เข็มขัดนิรภัย

seaweed, *n.* săa-ràai-tá-lee
สาหร่ายทะเล

secluded, *adj.* yɛ̂ɛk-dtua แยกตัว;
gèp-dtua เก็บตัว

second, *n.* wí-naa-tii วินาที

secondary, *adj.* rɔɔng รอง; tîi-
sɔ̆ɔng ที่สอง

second-hand, *adj.* muu-sɔ̆ɔng
มือสอง

secret, *n.* kwaam-láp ความลับ

secretary, *n.* lee-kăa-nú-gaan
เลขานุการ

sect, *n.* săm-nák สำนัก; ní-gaai
นิกาย

section, *n.* glùm กลุ่ม; mùat
หมวด; sùan ส่วน

sector, *n.* rûup-dtàt รูปตัด

secular, *adj.* taang-lôok ทางโลก

secure, *adj.* bplɔ̀ɔt-pai ปลอดภัย
(safe); mân-kong มั่นคง (firm)

security, *n.* kwaam-bplɔ̀ɔt-pai
ความปลอดภัย

sediment, *n.* dtà-gɔɔn ตะกอน

see, *v.* hĕn เห็น (with the eye);
kâo-jai เข้าใจ (understand); póp
พบ (meet)

seed, *n.* má-lét เมล็ด

seek, *v.* kón-hăa ค้นหา; sùup-hăa
สืบหา

seem, *v.* duu-mŭan ดูเหมือน; raao-
gàp-wâa ราวกับว่า

seeming, *adj.* dtaam-tîi-bpraa-gòt
ตามที่ปรากฏ

seesaw, *n.* grà-daan-hòk
กระดานหก

segment, *n.* sùan ส่วน; dtɔɔn ตอน

segregate, *v.* yɛ̂ɛk-ɔ̀ɔk แยกออก;
bèng-yɛ̂ɛk แบ่งแยก

seismic, *adj.* gìao-gàp-pèn-din-wăi
เกี่ยวกับแผ่นดินไหว

seize, *v.* jàp-gum จับกุม; yút ยึด;
chûai ฉวย

seizure, *n.* gaan-jàp-gum
การจับกุม; gaan-yút-krɔɔng
การยึดครอง

select, *v.* lûak เลือก

selection, *n.* gaan-lûak การเลือก

selective, *adj.* gìao-gàp-gaan-lûak เกี่ยวกับการเลือก

self, *n.* dton ตน; dton-eeng ตนเอง

self-centered, *adj.* kam-nung-tǔng-dton-eeng คำนึงถึงตนเอง

self-control, *n.* gaan-kûap-kum-dton-eeng การควบคุมตนเอง

self-defense, *n.* gaan-bpông-gan-dtua การป้องกันตัว

self-employed, *adj.* tam-ngaan-ìt-sà-rà ทำงานอิสระ

self-esteem, *n.* kwaam-yîng-nai-sàk-sǐi ความหยิ่งในศักดิ์ศรี

selfish, *adj.* hěn-gèe-dtua เห็นแก่ตัว

self-service, *n.* bɔɔ-ri-gaan-dtua-eeng บริการตัวเอง

sell, *v.* kǎai ขาย

seller, *n.* kon-kǎai คนขาย

semen, *n.* náam-gaam น้ำกาม

semester, *n.* pâak-rian ภาคเรียน

semi-, *v.* krûng ครึ่ง; gùng กึ่ง

semicolon, *n.* àt-ta-pâak อัฒภาค

seminar, *n.* gaan-sǎm-má-naa การสัมมนา

seminary, *n.* roong-rian-sàat-sà-nǎa โรงเรียนศาสนา

senate, *n.* sà-paa-sǔung สภาสูง

senator, *n.* sà-maa-chík-wút-tì-sà-paa สมาชิกวุฒิสภา

send, *v.* sòng ส่ง

sender, *n.* pûu-sòng ผู้ส่ง

senile, *adj.* chá-raa ชรา; sǔung-aa-yú สูงอายุ

senior, *n.* pûu-sǔung-aa-yú ผู้สูงอายุ

seniority, *n.* kwaam-mii-aa-wú-sǒo ความมีอาวุโส

sensation, *n.* bprà-sàat-sǎm-pàt ประสาทสัมผัส

sensational, *adj.* gìao-gàp-bprà-sàat-sǎm-pàt เกี่ยวกับประสาทสัมผัส

sense, *n.* kwaam-rúu-sùk ความรู้สึก (feeling); sǎm-pàt สัมผัส (i.e. sight, touch, taste, sound, smell); hèet-pǒn เหตุผล (reason)

sensible, *adj.* mii-hèet-pǒn มีเหตุผล

sensitive, *adj.* rúu-sùk-wai รู้สึกไว

sensual, *adj.* mòk-mûn-nai-raa-ká หมกมุ่นในราคะ

sensuous, *adj.* gìao-gàp-kwaam-rúu-sùk เกี่ยวกับความรู้สึก

sentence, *n.* bprà-yòok ประโยค (grammar); gaan-dtàt-sǐn การตัดสิน (ruling)

sentiment, *n.* kwaam-rúu-sùk ความรู้สึก; aa-rom อารมณ์

separate, *adj.* yêek-ɔ̀ɔk แยกออก; bèng แบ่ง

separation, *n.* gaan-yêek-ɔ̀ɔk การแยกออก; gaan-bèng การแบ่ง

September, *n.* gan-yaa-yon กันยายน

septic, *adj.* dtìt-chúa ติดเชื้อ

sequence, *n.* lam-dàp ลำดับ; gaan-dtɔ̀ɔ-nûang การต่อเนื่อง

serene, *adj.* sà-ngòp สงบ

sergeant, *n.* naai-sìp นายสิบ; jàa
จ่า

serial, *n.* sìng-tîi-dtɔ̀ɔ-nûang-gan
สิ่งที่ต่อเนื่องกัน

series, *n.* chút ชุด; lam-dàp ลำดับ

serious, *adj.* krîat เครียด; jing-jang
จริงจัง

sermon, *n.* gaan-sɔ̌ɔn การสอน;
gaan-têet-sà-nǎa การเทศนา

serpent, *n.* nguu-yài งูใหญ่

serum, *n.* see-rûm เซรุ่ม

servant, *n.* kon-ráp-cháai คนรับใช้

serve, *v.* ráp-cháai รับใช้; hâi-bɔɔ-
ri-gaan ให้บริการ

serve, *n.* gaan-ráp-cháai การรับใช้;
gaan-bɔɔ-rí-gaan การบริการ

service, *n.* bɔɔ-rí-gaan บริการ

sesame, *n.* ngaa งา

session, *n.* rá-yá ระยะ; pâak ภาค

set, *v.* dtìt-dtâng ติดตั้ง (install);
dtâng ตั้ง (place, put in place); tam-
hâi-dtìt-nên ทำให้ติดแน่น (fix firmly)

set, *n.* chút ชุด (set of things);
glùm กลุ่ม (group)

settle, *v.* jàt จัด; dtâng-rók-râak
ตั้งรกราก

settlement, *n.* gaan-dtâng-rók-râak
การตั้งรกราก

settler, *n.* pûu-dtâng-tìn-tǎan
ผู้ตั้งถิ่นฐาน

setup, *n.* gaan-dtìt-dtâng การติดตั้ง

seven, *nm.* jèt เจ็ด

seventeen, *nm.* sìp-jèt สิบเจ็ด

seventeenth, *adj.* tîi-sìp-jèt
ที่สิบเจ็ด

seventy, *nm* jèt-sìp เจ็ดสิบ

sever, *v.* dtàt-kàat ตัดขาด

several, *adj.* mâak-maai มากมาย

severe, *adj.* rung-rɛɛng รุนแรง;
krêng เคร่ง

sew, *v.* yép เย็บ

sewage, *n.* sìng-sǒo-krôok
สิ่งโสโครก (liquid or solid waste);
náam-sǐa น้ำเสีย (waste water)

sewer, *n.* pûu-yép ผู้เย็บ (one that
sews); krûang-yép เครื่องเย็บ
(machine); kɔ̌ɔng-sǐa ของเสีย
(waste)

sewing, *n.* gaan-yép-pâa การเย็บผ้า

sex, *n.* pêet เพศ

sexism, *n.* gaan-gìit-gan-taang-pêet
การกีดกันทางเพศ

sexist, *n.* pûu-bɛ̀ng-yɛ̂ɛk-pêet
ผู้แบ่งแยกเพศ

sexual, *adj.* gìao-gàp-pêet
เกี่ยวกับเพศ

sexy, *adj.* sèk-sîi เซ็กซี่

shackle, *n.* sôo-dtruan โซ่ตรวน;
gun-jɛɛ-mɯɯ กุญแจมือ

shade, *n.* tîi-rôm ที่ร่ม; rôm-ngao
ร่มเงา

shadow, *n.* ngao เงา

shady, *adj.* bpen-ngao เป็นเงา;
hâi-rôm-ngao ให้ร่มเงา; mii-rôm
มีร่ม

English · Phonetic · Thai

shaft, n. dâam ด้าม; kan คัน; gâan ก้าน

shake, v. sàn สั่น (quiver); kà-yào เขย่า (move to and fro with jerky movements); yôok โยก (rock)

shaky, adj. sàn สั่น; yôok โยก

shall, aux. v. jà-dtôŋ จะต้อง; nâa-jà น่าจะ

shallow, adj. dtûun ตื้น

sham, n. gaan-lòok-luang การหลอกลวง

shame, n. kwaam-àp-aai ความอับอาย

shameful, adj. nâa-àp-aai น่าอับอาย; nâa-lá-aai น่าละอาย

shampoo, n. chɛm-puu แชมพู; yaa-sà-pǒm ยาสระผม

shape, n. rûup-râaŋ รูปร่าง; sǎn-tǎan สัณฐาน

share, v. bèŋ แบ่ง

share, n. sùan ส่วน; sùan-bèŋ ส่วนแบ่ง

shareholder, n. pûu-tǔu-hûn ผู้ถือหุ้น

shark, n. chà-lǎam ฉลาม

sharp, adj. kom คม (not dull); chát-jeen ชัดเจน (clear); chìap-lɛ̌ɛm เฉียบแหลม (clever)

sharpen, v. tam-hâi-kom ทำให้คม; fǒn ฝน

sharpener, n. gòp-lǎo-din-sɔ̌ɔ กบเหลาดินสอ (pencil); hǐn-láp-mîit หินลับมีด (knife)

shatter, v. tam-hâi-dtɛ̀ɛk-la-ìat ทำให้แตกละเอียด

shave, v. goon โกน

shaver, n. mîit-goon มีดโกน (razor with blade); krûaŋ-goon เครื่องโกน (machine or electric)

shawl, n. pâa-klum-lài ผ้าคลุมไหล่

she, pron. kǎo เขา; tɘɘ เธอ

shear, v. dtàt ตัด; klìp ขลิบ

shears, n. gan-grai กรรไกร

sheath, n. fàk-dàap ฝักดาบ (for swords); bplɔ̀ɔk-mîit ปลอกมีด (for knives)

shed, n. pɤɤŋ-gèp-kɔ̌ɔŋ เพิงเก็บของ (storage); rooŋ-rót โรงรถ (garage)

sheen, n. kwaam-sà-wàaŋ-sòt-sǎi ความสว่างสดใส

sheep, n. gὲ แกะ

sheepish, adj. nîam-aai เหนียมอาย

sheer, adj. baaŋ-sǎi บางใส (transparent); mâi-jua-bpon ไม่เจือปน (unmixed)

sheet, n. pâa-bpuu-tîi-nɔɔn ผ้าปูที่นอน (for bed); pὲn แผ่น (broad, thin, rectangular mass or piece of material, such as paper)

shelf, n. hîŋ หิ้ง; chán ชั้น

shelf-life, n. aa-yú-kwaam-ton-bon-hîŋ อายุความทนบนหิ้ง

shell, n. bplùak-hɔ̌i เปลือกหอย; bplùak เปลือก; bplɔ̀ɔk ปลอก

shellfish, n. hɔ̌i-rǔu-gûŋ หอยหรือกุ้ง

shelter, *n.* tîi-lòp-pai ที่หลบภัย

shepherd, *n.* kon-líang-gè คนเลี้ยงแกะ

sherbet, *n.* náam-pǒn-la-máai-sài-náam-kěng น้ำผลไม้ใส่น้ำแข็ง

sheriff, *n.* naai-am-pəə นายอำเภอ

shield, *n.* lôo โล่ (piece of armor); ùp-bpà-gɔɔn-bpɔ̂ng-gan อุปกรณ์ป้องกัน (protective device)

shift, *v.* yáai ย้าย; bplìan เปลี่ยน

shiftless, *adj.* kîi-gìat ขี้เกียจ (lazy)

shilling, *n.* chin-lîng ชิลลิง

shin, *n.* nâa-kêng หน้าแข้ง

shine, *v.* sɔ̀ng-sěeng ส่องแสง

shiny, *adj.* sà-wàang สว่าง; bplèng-bplàng เปล่งปลั่ง

ship, *n.* rua เรือ

shirt, *n.* sûa-chóɔt เสื้อเชิ้ต

shiver, *v.* dtua-sàn ตัวสั่น

shock, *n.* aa-gaan-chɔ́k อาการช็อก

shock, *v.* chɔ́k ช็อก

shoe, *n.* rɔɔng-táao รองเท้า

shoehorn, *n.* chɔ́ɔn-sài-rɔɔng-táao ช้อนใส่รองเท้า

shoemaker, *n.* châng-tam-rɔɔng-táao ช่างทำรองเท้า

shoe polish, *n.* yaa-kàt-ngao-rɔɔng-táao ยาขัดเงารองเท้า

shoestring, *n.* chûak-pùuk-rɔɔng-táao เชือกผูกรองเท้า

shoot, *v.* ying ยิง

shoot, *n.* gaan-ying การยิง

shop, *n.* ráan ร้าน (store); roong-

fùk-ngaan โรงฝึกงาน (factory)

shop, *v.* sɯ́ɯ-kɔ̌ɔng ซื้อของ

shopkeeper, *n.* jâo-kɔ̌ɔng-ráan เจ้าของร้าน

shoplifting, *n.* gaan-kà-mooi-kɔ̌ɔng-nai-ráan การขโมยของในร้าน

shopper, *n.* kon-sɯ́ɯ คนซื้อ

shopping, *n.* gaan-sɯ́ɯ-kɔ̌ɔng การซื้อของ

shore, *n.* chaai-fàng ชายฝั่ง

short, *adj.* dtîa เตี้ย (not tall - used with people); sân สั้น (length); mâi-naan ไม่นาน (duration)

short circuit, *n.* lát-wong-jɔɔn ลัดวงจร

shortcut, *n.* taang-lát ทางลัด

shorten, *v.* tam-hâi-sân ทำให้สั้น; lót-kà-nàat ลดขนาด

shorts, *n.* gaang-geeng-kǎa-sân กางเกงขาสั้น

short story, *n.* rûang-sân เรื่องสั้น

short-tempered, *adj.* jai-rɔ́ɔn ใจร้อน

shortwave, *n.* klɯ̂ɯn-sân คลื่นสั้น

shot, *n.* gaan-ying การยิง (shooting); gaan-chìit-yaa การฉีดยา (injection)

shotgun, *n.* bpɯɯn-sân ปืนสั้น

should, *aux. v.* kuan ควร

shoulder, *n.* lài ไหล่

shout, *v.* dtà-goon ตะโกน

shove, *v.* dan ดัน

shovel, *n.* plûa พลั่ว; sìam เสียม

English · Phonetic · Thai

show, n. gaan-sà-dɛɛng การแสดง

showcase, n. dtûu-sà-dɛɛng-sĭn-káa ตู้แสดงสินค้า (for display)

shower, n. fŏn-dtòk-bprɔɔi-bprɔɔi ฝนตกปรอยๆ (rain); fàk-bua ฝักบัว (in the bathroom)

show-off, v. ôo-ùat โอ้อวด

showroom, n. choo-ruum โชว์รูม; hɔ̂ng-choo ห้องโชว์

shred, n. sèet เศษ; chín-lék-chín-nɔ́ɔi ชิ้นเล็กชิ้นน้อย

shrew, n. yĭng-bpàak-ráai หญิงปากร้าย

shrewd, adj. làk-lɛ̌ɛm หลักแหลม

shriek, n. sĭang-grìit-rɔ́ɔng เสียงกรีดร้อง

shrimp, n. gûng กุ้ง

shrine, n. hĭng-buu-chaa หิ้งบูชา; sǎan-jâao ศาลเจ้า

shrink, v. hòt-dtua หดตัว; yôn ย่น

shroud, n. pâa-hɔ̀ɔ-sòp ผ้าห่อศพ

shrub, n. pûm-máai พุ่มไม้

shrug, v. yák-lài ยักไหล่

shuffle, v. sàp-pâi สับไพ่

shun, v. lìik-lìang หลีกเลี่ยง

shut, v. bpìt ปิด; yùt หยุด

shutter, n. nâa-dtàang-baan-glèt หน้าต่างบานเกล็ด; chát-dtɔ̂ɔ-glɔ̂ng ชัตเตอร์กล้อง

shuttle, n. grà-sǔai กระสวย; rót-nam-sòng รถนำส่ง

shy, adj. aai อาย; kîi-aai ขี้อาย

sibling, n. pîi-nɔ́ɔng พี่น้อง

sick, adj. bpùai ป่วย; mâi-sà-baai ไม่สบาย

sickness, n. rôok โรค; aa-gaan-mâi-sà-baai อาการไม่สบาย

side, n. dâan-kâang ด้านข้าง; kâang ข้าง

sideburns, n. jɔɔn จอน

side effect, n. pŏn-kâang-kiang ผลข้างเคียง

sidewalk, n. taang-dəən ทางเดิน

siege, v. ɔ̀op-lɔ́ɔm โอบล้อม; lɔ́ɔm-joom-dtii ล้อมโจมตี

siege, n. gaan-ɔ̀op-lɔ́ɔm การโอบล้อม; gaan-lɔ́ɔm-joom-dtii การล้อมโจมตี

sigh, v. tɔ̌ɔn-hǎai-jai ถอนหายใจ

sigh, n. gaan-tɔ̌ɔn-hǎai-jai การถอนหายใจ

sight, n. sǎai-dtaa สายตา

sightseeing, v. bpai-tîao ไปเที่ยว; tát-sà-naa-jɔɔn ทัศนาจร

sightseeing, n. gaan-bpai-tîao การไปเที่ยว; gaan-tát-sà-naa-jɔɔn การทัศนาจร

sign, n. bpâai ป้าย; sǎn-ya-lák สัญลักษณ์

signal, n. sǎn-yaan สัญญาณ

signature, n. laai-sen ลายเซ็น

significance, n. kwaam-sǎm-kan ความสำคัญ

significant, adj. sǎm-kan สำคัญ

silence, n. kwaam-ngîap ความเงียบ

silent, adj. ngîap เงียบ

silicon, *n.* si-li-kɔn ซิลิคอน

silk, *n.* măi ไหม; pâa-măi ผ้าไหม

silky, *adj.* mŭan-măi เหมือนไหม
(silk-like); lûen ลื่น (smooth); nîm
นิ่ม (soft)

sill, *n.* tăan ฐาน; kaan คาน

silliness, *n.* kwaam-ngôo-klăo
ความโง่เขลา

silly, *adj.* ngôo โง่; ngîi-ngâo งี่เง่า

silver, *n.* ngən เงิน

silverware, *n.* krûang-ngən
เครื่องเงิน

similar, *adj.* kláai คล้าย; mŭan-gan
เหมือนกัน

similarity, *n.* kwaam-mŭan-gan
ความเหมือนกัน

simile, *n.* ù-bpà-maa-ù-bpà-mai
อุปมาอุปไมย

simmer, *v.* kîao เคี่ยว; dtŭn ตุ๋น

simple, *adj.* tam-ma-daa ธรรมดา;
ngâp-ngâai เรียบง่าย

simplify, *v.* tam-hâi-ngâai ทำให้ง่าย

simulate, *v.* lɔ́ɔk-lian ลอกเลียน

simultaneous, *adj.* nai-wee-laa-
diao-gan ในเวลาเดียวกัน

sin, *n.* bàap บาป

since, *prep.* dtâng-dtɛ̀ɛ ตั้งแต่

sincere, *adj.* jing-jai จริงใจ

sincerely, *adv.* dûai-kwaam-jing-jai
ด้วยความจริงใจ

sincerity, *n.* kwaam-jing-jai
ความจริงใจ

sinful, *adj.* mii-bàap มีบาป; bpen-

bàap เป็นบาป

sing, *v.* rɔ́ɔng-pleeng ร้องเพลง

singer, *n.* nák-rɔ́ɔng นักร้อง

singing, *n.* gaan-rɔ́ɔng-pleeng
การร้องเพลง

single, *adj.* sòot โสด (not married);
dìao เดี่ยว (not in a pair)

singular, *adj.* èek-gà-pót เอกพจน์

sink, *n.* àang อ่าง; àang-lék
อ่างเล็ก

sinner, *n.* pûu-mii-bàap ผู้มีบาป;
kon-bàap คนบาป

sinus, *n.* proong-sai-nát โพรงไซนัส

sip, *v.* jìp จิบ

sir, *n.* kun คุณ; tân ท่าน

siren, *n.* sĭang-wɔ̌ɔ เสียงหวอ

sister, *n.* pîi-săao พี่สาว; nɔ́ɔng-
săao น้องสาว

sister-in-law, *n.* nɔ́ɔng-sà-pái
น้องสะใภ้; pîi-sà-pái พี่สะใภ้

sit, *v.* nâng นั่ง; dtâng-yùu ตั้งอยู่

site, *n.* dtam-nɛ̀ng ตำแหน่ง; tîi-
dtâng ที่ตั้ง

sitting, *n.* gaan-nâng การนั่ง

situation, *n.* sà-tăa-ná-gaan
สถานการณ์

six, *nm.* hòk หก

six hundred, *nm.* hòk-rɔ́ɔi หกร้อย

sixteen, *nm.* sìp-hòk สิบหก

sixty, *nm.* hòk-sìp หกสิบ

size, *n.* kà-nàat ขนาด

sizzle, *n.* sĭang-tɔ̂ɔt เสียงทอด

skate, *n.* rɔɔng-táao-sà-gét

รองเท้าสเก็ต

skate board, *n.* grà-daan-sa-gét
กระดานสเก็ต

skeleton, *n.* kroong-grà-dùuk
โครงกระดูก

skeptical, *adj.* kîi-sŏng-săi ขี้สงสัย

sketch, *v.* râang-pâap ร่างภาพ;
wâat-krâao-krâao วาดคร่าวๆ

sketch, *n.* pâap-râang ภาพร่าง

ski, *n., v.* sà-gii สกี

skid, *v.* lʉ̂ʉn-tà-lǎi ลื่นไถล

skid, *n.* rɔɔi-lʉ̂ʉn-tà-lǎi รอยลื่นไถล

skier, *n.* nák-lên-sà-gii นักเล่นสกี

skiing, *n.* gaan-lên-sà-gii การเล่นสกี

skill, *n.* ták-sà ทักษะ

skillful, *adj.* mii-ták-sà มีทักษะ;
cham-naan ชำนาญ

skim, *v.* dtàk-sùan-pĭu-ɔ̀ɔk
ตักส่วนผิวออก

skim milk, *n.* nom-tîi-sà-gàt-kǎi-
man-ɔ̀ɔk นมที่สกัดไขมันออก

skin, *n.* pĭu-nǎng ผิวหนัง; bplʉ̀ak
เปลือก (crust)

skinny, *adj.* pɔ̌ɔm-mâak ผอมมาก

skip, *v.* grà-dòot กระโดด (hop,
jump); kâam ข้าม (bounce over)

skip, *n.* gaan-grà-dòot การกระโดด;
gaan-kâam การเว้นข้าม

skirt, *n.* grà-bproong กระโปรง

skit, *n.* là-kɔɔn-sân ละครสั้น

skull, *n.* gà-lòok กะโหลก

skunk, *n.* sà-gáng สกั๊ง; dtua-měn
ตัวเหม็น

sky, *n.* tɔ́ɔng-fáa ท้องฟ้า

skylight, *n.* sɛ̌ɛng-jàak-tɔ́ɔng-fáa
แสงจากท้องฟ้า

skyrocket, *v.* kʉ̂n-yàang-rûat-reo
ขึ้นอย่างรวดเร็ว

skyrocket, *n.* bâng-fai บั้งไฟ

skyscraper, *n.* dtʉ̀k-sǔung ตึกสูง

slack, *adj.* yɔ̀n หย่อน (lacking firmness; loose); nʉai เนือย (lacking in
activity); chʉ̀ai เฉื่อย (sluggish)

slacks, *n.* gaang-geeng-lam-lɔɔng
กางเกงลำลอง

slam, *v.* bpìt-sĭang-dang ปิดเสียงดัง;
grà-tɛ̂ɛk กระแทก

slang, *n.* paa-sǎa-sà-lɛɛng
ภาษาสแลง

slant, *adj.* lâat ลาด; iang เอียง

slap, *v.* dtòp ตบ; dtòp-nâa ตบหน้า

slap, *n.* gaan-dtòp-nâa การตบหน้า

slapstick, *n.* dtà-lòk-bpɛ̀ɛp-ngîi-
ngâo ตลกแบบงี่เง่า

slash, *v.* chʉ̌an เฉือน (lash); dtàt
ตัด (cut); kîan เฆี่ยน (whip)

slash, *n.* gaan-dtàt การตัด; krʉ̂ang-
mǎai-táp เครื่องหมายทับ (/)

slate, *n.* grà-daan-chá-nuan
กระดานชนวน

slaughter, *v.* kâa ฆ่า; sǎng-hǎan
สังหาร

slaughterhouse, *n.* roong-kâa-sàt
โรงฆ่าสัตว์

slave, *n.* tâat ทาส

slavery, *n.* kwaam-bpen-tâat

ความเป็นทาส

slay, v. kâa ฆ่า; sǎng-hǎan สังหาร

sleep, v. nɔɔn นอน; nɔɔn-làp
นอนหลับ

sleeping bag, n. tǔng-nɔɔn ถุงนอน

sleeping pill, n. yaa-nɔɔn-làp
ยานอนหลับ

sleepy, adj. ngûang-nɔɔn ง่วงนอน

sleet, n. hì-má-fǒn หิมะฝน

sleeve, n. kɛ̌ɛn-sûa แขนเสื้อ

sleigh, n. rót-lûan-bon-hì-má
รถเลื่อนบนหิมะ

slender, adj. yaao-riao ยาวเรียว;
ɔɔ-ra-chɔɔn อรชร

slice, n. chín ชิ้น; pèn-baang
แผ่นบาง

slide, v. lûan เลื่อน; lûun ลื่น

slider, n. grà-daan-lûan
กระดานเลื่อน

slight, adj. lék-nɔ́ɔi เล็กน้อย (small
amount); bao-baang เบาบาง
(frail)

slim, adj. yaao-riao ยาวเรียว
(objects); pɔ̌ɔm-baang ผอมบาง
(human beings or animals)

slimy, adj. lěeo-nǐao เหลวเหนียว
(sticky and slippery); lûun-lǎi
ลื่นไหล (slippery); leeo-saam
เลวทราม (viscious)

sling, n. sǎai-yoong สายโยง

slingshot, n. nǎng-sà-dtìk หนังสติ๊ก

slip, v. lûun ลื่น; lǎi ไหล

slip, n. gaan-lûun การลื่น (sliding);

kwaam-pìt-plâat ความผิดพลาด
(mistake); grà-bproong-chán-nai
กระโปรงชั้นใน (petite coat)

slipper, n. rɔɔng-táao-dtè
รองเท้าแตะ

slippery, adj. lûun ลื่น; lùt-ngâai
หลุดง่าย

slit, n. rɔɔi-pàa รอยผ่า; rɔɔi-yɛ̂ɛk
รอยแยก

sliver, n. sèet-máai เศษไม้; sîan-
máai เสี้ยนไม้

slob, n. kon-ngá-ngá คนเงอะงะ

slogan, n. kam-kwǎn คำขวัญ

slope, n. taang-lâat-iang
ทางลาดเอียง

sloppy, adj. mâi-bpen-rá-bìap
ไม่เป็นระเบียบ; sà-prâo สะเพร่า

slot, n. chɔ̂ng ช่อง; chɔ̂ng-lék
ช่องเล็ก

slow, adj. cháa ช้า

slowly, adv. cháa-cháa ช้าๆ

slug, n. dtua-tâak ตัวทาก

sluggish, adj. chûang-cháa เชื่องช้า

slum, n. sà-lam สลัม; lèng-sùam-
soom แหล่งเสื่อมโทรม

sly, adj. jâo-lêe เจ้าเล่ห์

smack, v. dtii ตี (hit); jùup-sǐang-
dang จูบเสียงดัง (kiss loudly)

small, adj. lék เล็ก; nɔ́ɔi น้อย

small change, n. ngən-tɔɔn
เงินทอน

smallpox, n. fǐi-dàat ฝีดาษ; kâi-
tɔɔ-ra-pít ไข้ทรพิษ

smart, *adj.* chà-làat ฉลาด; gèng เก่ง

smash, *v.* tam-laai ทำลาย

smear, *v.* taa ทา (put on, e.g. color); tam-ló ทำเลอะ (make a mess); bpaai-sǐi ป้ายสี (paint)

smell, *v.* dom ดม

smell, *n.* glìn กลิ่น

smile, *n., v.* yím ยิ้ม

smith, *n.* châng-lèk ช่างเหล็ก (iron, steel); châng-loo-hà ช่างโลหะ (metal)

smoke, *n.* kwan ควัน; kwan-fai ควันไฟ

smoke, *v.* sùup สูบ

smoker, *n.* kon-sùup-bù-rìi คนสูบบุหรี่

smoky, *adj.* mii-kwan มีควัน; mii-kwan-mâak มีควันมาก

smooth, *adj.* rîap เรียบ (flat); râap-rûun ราบรื่น (free from difficulties, problems, etc.)

smuggle, *v.* lák-lɔ́ɔp ลักลอบ

smuggler, *n.* kon-lák-lɔ́ɔp คนลักลอบ

snack, *n.* aa-hǎan-wâang อาหารว่าง

snail, *n.* hɔ̌ɔi-tâak หอยทาก

snake, *n.* nguu งู

snap, *v.* tàai-rûup-dùan ถ่ายรูปด่วน (a picture); hùat-sɛ̌ɛ หวดแส้ (whip); dìt-níu ดีดนิ้ว (the fingers)

snapshot, *n.* gaan-tàai-rûup-dùan การถ่ายรูปด่วน

snare, *n.* gàp-dàk กับดัก

snarl, *v.* hào เห่า; kam-raam คำราม

snatch, *v.* chòk ฉก; chǔai ฉวย; yɛ̂ɛng-ching แย่งชิง

sneak, *v.* ɛ̀ep แอบ; lòp หลบ; tam-láp-láp-lɔ́ɔ-lɔ́ɔ ทำลับๆล่อๆ

sneakers, *n.* rɔɔng-táao-pâa-bai รองเท้าผ้าใบ

sneer, *v.* hǔa-rɔ́-yɔ́ หัวเราะเยาะ; yɔ́-yɔ́ɔi เยาะเย้ย

sneeze, *v., n.* jaam จาม

sniff, *v.* sùut-glìn สูดกลิ่น; dom ดม

snip, *v.* dtàt-lem ตัดเล็ม

snob, *n.* kon-yàak-bpen-pûu-dii คนอยากเป็นผู้ดี

snobbish, *adj.* ùat-dii อวดดี; yìng หยิ่ง

snoop, *v.* sɔ̀ɔt-nɛɛm สอดแนม (pry into); sùup สืบ (investigate)

snoopy, *adj.* sɔ̀ɔt-rúu-sɔ̀ɔt-hěn สอดรู้สอดเห็น; sɔ̀ɔt-nɛɛm สอดแนม

snooze, *v.* ngîip-làp งีบหลับ; sàp-bpà-ngòk สัปหงก

snore, *v.* gron กรน

snore, *n.* sǐang gron เสียงกรน

snort, *v.* hǎai-jai-run-rɛɛng หายใจรุนแรง (breathe harshly); pôn-lom-taang-jà-mùuk พ่นลมทางจมูก (blow air from the nose)

snow, *n.* hì-má หิมะ

snowy, *adj.* mii-hì-má-mâak

มีหิมะมาก (full of snow); kǎao-mǔan-hì-má ขาวเหมือนหิมะ (white as snow)

so, *adv.* dang-nán ดังนั้น; chà-nán ฉะนั้น

soak, *v.* chêɛ แช่

soap, *n.* sà-bùu สบู่

soap opera, *n.* lá-kɔɔn-too-ra-tát ละครโทรทัศน์

soar, *v.* bin-tà-lǎa บินถลา (fly up high quickly); ta-yaan ทะยาน (move upwards); bin-sǔung บินสูง (fly high); lɔɔi ลอย (float)

sob, *v.* rám-hâi ร่ำไห้; sà-ɯ̂ɯn สะอื้น

sober, *adj.* mii-sà-dtì มีสติ (conscious); yɯ̂ak-yen เยือกเย็น (solemn); sàang-mao สร่างเมา (from alcohol)

soccer, *n.* fút-bɔɔn ฟุตบอล

sociable, *adj.* chɔ̂ɔp-sǎng-kom ชอบสังคม

social, *adj.* gìao-gap-sǎng-kom เกี่ยวกับสังคม

socialism, *n.* rá-bòp-sǎng-kom-ní-yom ระบบสังคมนิยม

socialist, *n.* nák-sang-kom-ní-yom นักสังคมนิยม

socialize, *v.* kóp-hǎa-sà-maa-kom คบหาสมาคม (with others); òp-rom-sàng-sɔ̌ɔn อบรมสั่งสอน (e.g. young children)

social science, *n.* sǎng-kom-sàat สังคมศาสตร์

social security, *n.* sà-wàt-dì-gaan-sǎng-kom สวัสดิการสังคม; bprà-gan-sǎng-kom ประกันสังคม

social work, *n.* ngaan-sǎng-kom-sǒng-krɔ́ งานสังคมสงเคราะห์

society, *n.* sǎng-kom สังคม; sà-maa-kom สมาคม (association); chum-chon ชุมชน (community)

sociology, *n.* sǎng-kom-wít-ta-yaa สังคมวิทยา

sock, *n.* tǔng-táao ถุงเท้า

socket, *n.* bâo เบ้า; proong โพรง

soda, *n.* soo-daa โซดา; náam-àt-lom น้ำอัดลม

sodium, *n.* tâat-soo-diam ธาตุโซเดียม

sofa, *n.* gâo-ʔîi-nuam เก้าอี้นวม; soo-faa โซฟา

soft, *adj.* ɔ̀ɔn อ่อน; nîm นิ่ม; ɔ̀ɔn-yoon อ่อนโยน

soften, *v.* tam-hâi-nîm ทำให้นิ่ม; tam-hâi-ɔ̀ɔn-long ทำให้อ่อนลง

softness, *n.* kwaam-nîm ความนิ่ม; kwaam-ɔ̀ɔn-nûm ความอ่อนนุ่ม

soil, *n.* din ดิน; pɯ́ɯn-din พื้นดิน

solar, *adj.* gìao-gàp-duang-aa-tít เกี่ยวกับดวงอาทิตย์

soldier, *n.* tá-hǎan ทหาร

sole, *adj.* an-diao อันเดียว (being the only one); dtɛ̀ɛ-piang-pûu-diao แต่เพียงผู้เดียว (exclusive)

sole, *n.* pɯ́ɯn-rɔɔng-táao พื้นรองเท้า

(bottom of a shoe); fàa-táao ฝ่าเท้า
(underside of the foot)

solemn, *adj.* krêng-krǔm เคร่งขรึม;
kǔng-kàng ขึงขัง; ao-jing-ao-jang
เอาจริงเอาจัง

solicit, *v.* rîak-róong เรียกร้อง;
chák-chuan ชักชวน; kɔ̌ɔ-róong
ขอร้อง

solid, *adj.* kɔ̌ɔng-kěng ของแข็ง (not
liquid); àt-nɛ̂n อัดแน่น (not hollow); kɛ̌ng-rɛɛng แข็งแรง (strong);
mân-kong มั่นคง (firm)

solidarity, *n.* kwaam-sǎm-pan-gan
ความสัมพันธ์กัน

solitary, *adj.* dòot-dìao โดดเดี่ยว;
kon-diao คนเดียว; sǎn-dòot
สันโดษ

solitude, *n.* kwaam-sǎn-dòot
ความสันโดษ

solo, *n.* gaan-sà-dɛɛng-dìao
การแสดงเดี่ยว

soloist, *n.* pûu-sà-dɛɛng-dìao
ผู้แสดงเดี่ยว

soluble, *adj.* lá-laai-dâai ละลายได้

solution, *n.* taang-ɔ̀ɔk ทางออก
(way out); gaan-gɛ̂ɛ-bpan-hǎa
การแก้ปัญหา (problem solving)

solve, *v.* gɛ̂ɛ-bpan-hǎa แก้ปัญหา;
hǎa-kam-dtɔ̀ɔp หาคำตอบ

solvent, *adj.* lá-laai-dâai ละลายได้

somber, *adj.* mûɨt-sà-lǔa มืดสลัว
(dark); mua-sua มัวซัว (dim);
sòok-sâo โศกเศร้า (sad)

some, *pron., adj.* baang บาง;
baang-yàang บางอย่าง

somebody, someone, *pron.*
baang-kon บางคน

someday, *adv.* baang-wan บางวัน;
wan-dai-wan-nɨ̀ng วันใดวันหนึ่ง

somehow, *adv.* dûai-hèet-pǒn-
baang-bprà-gaan
ด้วยเหตุผลบางประการ

somersault, *v.* dtii-lang-gaa
ตีลังกา; plìk-glàp พลิกกลับ

something, *pron.* baang-sìng
บางสิ่ง; baang-yàang บางอย่าง

sometime, *adv.* baang-kráng
บางครั้ง; baang-kraao บางคราว

sometimes, *adv.* baang-kráng
บางครั้ง; baang-oo-gàat บางโอกาส

somewhat, *adv.* kɔ̂n-kâang
ค่อนข้าง; bâang บ้าง; baang-sùan
บางส่วน

somewhere, *adv.* baang-hɛ̀ng
บางแห่ง; tîi-dai-tîi-nɨ̀ng ที่ใดที่หนึ่ง

son, *n.* lûuk-chaai ลูกชาย; bùt-
chaai บุตรชาย

song, *n.* pleeng เพลง

sonic, *adj.* gìao-gàp-sìang
เกี่ยวกับเสียง

son-in-law, *n.* lûuk-kǒei ลูกเขย

soon, *adv.* nai-mâi-cháa ในไม่ช้า;
mâi-naan ไม่นาน

soot, *n.* kà mào เขม่า

soothe, *v.* bplɔ̀ɔp-yoon ปลอบโยน;
ban-tao บรรเทา

English • Phonetic • Thai

sophisticated, *adj.* châm-chɔɔng-lôok ช่ำชองโลก (worldly experienced); gèɛ-dèɛt แก่แดด (knowing or acting more than one's age); sáp-sɔɔn ซับซ้อน (complicated)

sophomore, *n.* nák-sùk-sǎa-bpii-sɔɔng นักศึกษาปีสอง

soprano, *n.* sǐang-rɔɔng-rá-dàp-sǔung เสียงร้องระดับสูง

sorcerer, -ess, *n.* pɔɔ-mót พ่อมด (male wizard); mɛ̂ɛ-mót แม่มด (female wizard); mɔɔ-pǐi หมอผี (any wizard); pûu-wí-sèet ผู้วิเศษ (magician)

sore, *adj.* bpùat ปวด; jèp-sɛ̀ɛp เจ็บแสบ

sorrow, *n.* kwaam-sǐa-jai ความเสียใจ; kwaam-sâo-jai ความเศร้าใจ

sorry, *adj.* sǐa-jai เสียใจ; sâo-jai เศร้าใจ

sort, *v.* yɛ̂ɛk แยก; yɛ̂ɛk-hâi-bpen-rá-bìap แยกให้เป็นระเบียบ

sort, *n.* chá-nít ชนิด; bprà-pêet ประเภท; jam-pûak จำพวก

so-so, *adj.* chɔ̌ɔi-chɔ̌ɔi เฉยๆ; mâi-dii-lé-mâi-leeo ไม่ดีและไม่เลว; tam-ma-daa ธรรมดา

soul, *n.* win-yaan วิญญาณ; jìt-jai จิตใจ

sound, *n.* sǐang เสียง

soundtrack, *n.* sǐang-nai-fiim เสียงในฟิล์ม

soup, *n.* súp ซุป; náam-gɛɛng น้ำแกง

sour, *adj.* bprîao เปรี้ยว

source, *n.* lɛ̀ng-tîi-maa แหล่งที่มา (origin); lɛ̀ng-kɔ̂ɔ-muun แหล่งข้อมูล (data)

south, *n.* tít-dtâai ทิศใต้; taang-dtâai ทางใต้

South Africa, *n.* ép-fa-rí-gaa-dtâai แอฟริกาใต้

South America, *n.* tá-wîip-à-mee-rí-gaa-dtâai ทวีปอเมริกาใต้

southeast, *n.* tít-dtà-wan-ɔ̀ɔk-chǐang-dtâai ทิศตะวันออกเฉียงใต้

southeast Asia, *n.* ee-chia-dtà-wan-ɔ̀ɔk-chǐang-dtâai เอเชียตะวันออกเฉียงใต้

South Pole, *n.* kûa-lôok-dtâai ขั้วโลกใต้

southwest, *n.* tít-dtà-wan-dtòk-chǐang-dtâai ทิศตะวันตกเฉียงใต้

souvenir, *n.* kɔ̌ɔng-tîi-rá-rúk ของที่ระลึก

Soviet Union, *n.* sà-hà-pâap-soo-wìat สหภาพโซเวียต

sow, *v.* wàan หว่าน

soy, *n.* tùa-lǔang ถั่วเหลือง

soy sauce, *n.* sɔ́ɔt-tùa-lǔang ซอสถั่วเหลือง

spa, *n.* bɔ̀ɔ-náam-rɛ̂ɛ บ่อน้ำแร่

space, *n.* a-wa-gàat อวกาศ (astronomical); chɔ̂ng-wâang ช่องว่าง (empty space); tîi-wâang-bplàao ที่ว่างเปล่า (blank area)

spaceship, *n.* yaan-a-wa-gàat
ยานอวกาศ

spacious, *adj.* mii-núa-tîi-mâak
มีเนื้อที่มาก; gwâang-kwǎang
กว้างขวาง

spade, *n.* sîam เสียม; plûa พลั่ว;
jɔ̀ɔp จอบ; poo-dam โพธิ์ดำ (in
playing cards)

spaghetti, *n.* sà-bpaa-gét-dtîi
สปาเก็ตตี้

Spain, *n.* bprà-têet-sà-bpeen
ประเทศสเปน

span, *n.* chûang-hàang ช่วงห่าง;
rá-yá-gwâang ระยะกว้าง

Spanish, *n.* gìao-gàp-sà-bpeen
เกี่ยวกับสเปน (relating to Spain);
paa-sǎa-sà-bpeen ภาษาสเปน (language)

spank, *v.* dtii-gôn ตีก้น

spare, *v.* bpraa-nii ปรานี (treat
mercifully)

spare, *adj.* sà-ngûan สงวน (conserve); mii-lǔa-bâang มีเหลือบ้าง
(not much left); bprà-yàt ประหยัด
(frugal)

spare time, *n.* wee-laa-wâang
เวลาว่าง

spare tire, *n.* lɔ́ɔ-à-lài ล้ออะหลั่ย
(e.g. for cars); pung พุง (stomach)

spark, *n.* bprà-gaai-fai ประกายไฟ;
bprà-gaai-wɛɛo-waao
ประกายแววาว

sparkle, *v.* bpen-bprà-gaai-fai
เป็นประกายไฟ; sɔ̀ng-sɛ́ɛng-wɛɛo-

waao ส่องแสงแววาว

sparrow, *n.* nók-grà-jɔ̀ɔk
นกกระจอก

spasm, *n.* gâam-núa-grà-dtùk
กล้ามเนื้อกระตุก

spatula, *n.* chɔ́ɔn-bpàak-bɛɛn
ช้อนปากแบน

speak, *v.* pûut พูด; kui คุย

speaker, *n.* pûu-pûut ผู้พูด (one
that speaks); krûang-kà-yǎai-sǐang
เครื่องขยายเสียง (loud speaker)

spear, *n.* hɔ̀ɔk หอก; lǎao หลาว

special, *adj.* pi-sèet พิเศษ

specialist, *n.* pûu-chîao-chaan
ผู้เชี่ยวชาญ

specialize, *v.* bpen-pûu-chîao-
chaan เป็นผู้เชี่ยวชาญ

specialty, *n.* kwaam-cham-naan-pi-
sèet ความชำนาญพิเศษ

species, *n.* chá-nít ชนิด (type,
kind); jam-pûak จำพวก (category)

specific, *adj.* dooi-cha-pɔ́
โดยเฉพาะ; jɔ̀-jong เจาะจง

specification, *n.* gaan-jɔ̀-jong
การเจาะจง (the act of); raai-lá-ìat
รายละเอียด (details)

specify, *v.* qam-nòt กำหนด; rá-bù
ระบุ

specimen, *n.* dtua-yàang ตัวอย่าง

speck, *n.* jùt-dàang จุดด่าง; rɔɔi-
bpûan รอยเปื้อน

spectacle, *n.* gaan-sà-dɛɛng
การแสดง; bpraa-gòt-dtà-gaan

ปรากฏการณ์
spectacular, *adj.* nâa-dtùun-dtên
น่าตื่นเต้น; bprà-táp-jai ประทับใจ
spectator, *n.* pûu-chom ผู้ชม; pûu-duu ผู้ดู
speech, *n.* sǔn-cɔɔ-ra-pót
สุนทรพจน์; kam-ban-yaai
คำบรรยาย; kam-pûut คำพูด
speed, *n.* kwaam-reo ความเร็ว
speeding, *adj.* reo เร็ว
speed limit, *n.* kwaam-reo-jam-gàt
ความเร็วจำกัด
speedometer, *n.* krûang-wát-kwaam-reo เครื่องวัดความเร็ว
speedy, *adj.* rûat-reo รวดเร็ว;
chàp-plan ฉับพลัน
spell, *v.* sà-gòt สะกด (both words
and magic)
spell, *n.* wêet-mon เวทมนตร์; kaa-tǎa คาถา; mon-sà-gòt มนต์สะกด
spelling, *n.* gaan-sà-gòt-kam
การสะกดคำ (word)
spend, *v.* chái-jàai ใช้จ่าย; chái ใช้
spendthrift, *n., v.* kon-sù-rûi-sù-râai
คนสุรุ่ยสุร่าย; cháai-jàai-fûm-fuai
ใช้จ่ายฟุ่มเฟือย
sperm, *n.* náam-à-sù-jì น้ำอสุจิ
sphere, *n.* rûup-song-glom
รูปทรงกลม
spice, *n.* krûang-têet เครื่องเทศ;
rót-châat รสชาติ
spicy, *adj.* pèt เผ็ด; rót-jàt รสจัด
spider, *n.* mɛɛng-mum แมงมุม

spike, *n.* lèk-lɛ̌ɛm เหล็กแหลม
spill, *v.* hòk หก
spin, *v.* bpàn ปั่น; mǔn หมุน
spinach, *n.* pàk-kǒm ผักขม
spine, *n.* grà-dùuk-sǎn-lǎng
กระดูกสันหลัง
spinster, *n.* sǎao-tun-túk สาวทึนทึก
spiny, *adj.* mii-nǎam มีหนาม (full
of spines); krù-krà ขรุขระ (rough)
spiral, *n.* kòt ขด; bpen-gliao
เป็นเกลียว
spire, *n.* yɔ̂ɔt-lɛ̌ɛm ยอดแหลม;
song-gruai ทรงกรวย
spirit, *n.* jìt-jai จิตใจ (of the mind);
win-yaan วิญญาณ (soul); kwaam-mûng-mân ความมุ่งมั่น (dedication)
spiritual, *adj.* gìao-gàp-jìt-jai
เกี่ยวกับจิตใจ
spit, *v.* tòm-náam-laai ถ่มน้ำลาย
spite, *n.* jèet-dtà-naa-ráai
เจตนาร้าย; kwaam-mûng-ráai
ความมุ่งร้าย
splash, *v.* sàat สาด
splash, *n.* gaan-sàat การสาด;
gaan-grà-den การกระเด็น; rɔɔi-sàat
รอยสาด
spleen, *n.* máam ม้าม
splendid, *adj.* yɔ̂ɔt-yîam ยอดเยี่ยม;
wí-sèet วิเศษ
split, *v.* pàa ผ่า (divide or break by
a sharp blow); yɛ̂ɛk แยก (separate)
split, *n.* gaan-pàa การผ่า; rɔɔi-yɛ̂ɛk รอยแยก; gaan-dtɛ̀ɛk-yɛ̂ɛk

การแตกแยก

spoil, v. tam-hâi-sĭa ทำให้เสีย (e.g. food); dtaam-jai ตามใจ (someone)

spokesman, n. koo-sòk โฆษก; pûu-tà-lĕeng-kàao ผู้แถลงข่าว

sponge, n. fɔɔng-náam ฟองน้ำ

sponsor, n. pûu-ù-bpà-tăm ผู้อุปถัมภ์ (one that supports); pûu-sa-bpon-sɔ̂ɔ ผู้สปอนเซอร์ (e.g. in advertising)

spontaneous, adj. prɔ́ɔm-gan พร้อมกัน; bpen-bpai-eeng เป็นไปเอง

spoof, n. gaan-dtòp-dtaa การตบตา; qaan-lɔ̀ɔk-luang การหลอกลวง

spook, n. pûut-pĭi ภูติผี (ghost); nák-sùup นักสืบ (spy)

spoon, n. chɔ́ɔn ช้อน

spoonful, n. dtem-chɔ́ɔn เต็มช้อน

sporadic, adj. bpen-pák-pák เป็นพักๆ; bpen-rá-yá เป็นระยะ

spore, n. chúa-rôok เชื้อโรค; sà-pɔɔ สปอร์

sport, n. gii-laa กีฬา; gaan-lên การเล่น

spot, n. jùt จุด; mon-tin มลทิน

spotlight, n. sà-hpɔ̀t-lái สปอตไลท์

spouse, n. kûu-sŏm-rót คู่สมรส

spout, n. puai-gaa พวยกา (for releasing liquid); tɔ̂ɔ-pôn ท่อพ่น (blowhole)

sprain, n. gaan-bìt การบิด; gaan-klét การเคลื่ด

spray, v. chìit ฉีด

spray, n. lá-ɔɔng-náam ละอองน้ำ; náam-grà-sen น้ำกระเซ็น

spread, v. pɛ̀ɛ แผ่; grà-jaai กระจาย; kà-yáai ขยาย

spring, v. grà-dòot กระโดด (jump); dêng-kûn เด้งขึ้น (bounce forward)

spring, n. sà-bpring สปริง (elastic device); gaan-grà-dòot การกระโดด (act of jumping); rɯ-duu-bai-máai-plì ฤดูใบไม้ผลิ (the season)

sprinkle, v. prom พรม; bprooi โปรย; wàan หว่าน

sprint, n. gaan-wîng-kèng การวิ่งแข่ง

sprite, n. pĭi-săang ผีสาง (spirit); têep เทพ (angel)

sprout, v. dtɛ̀ɛk-nɔ̀ɔ แตกหน่อ

sprout, n. nɔ̀ɔ หน่อ

spruce, adj. rîap-rɔ́ɔi เรียบร้อย (neat); duu-tee ดูเท่ (good-looking)

spy, n. nák-sùup นักสืบ; săai-láp สายลับ

squad, n. mùu หมู่; ká-ná คณะ

square, n. sìi-lìam-jà-dtù-ràt สี่เหลี่ยมจตุรัส

square root, n. râak-tîi-sɔ̌ɔng รากที่สอง

squash, n. pûut-jam-pûak-dtɛɛng พืชจำพวกแตง

squat, v. nâng-yɔɔng-yɔɔng นั่งยองๆ (sit in a crouching position)

squat, adj. ûan-nǎa อ้วนหนา (short

and thick); mɔ̂ɔ-dtɔ̂ɔ ม่อต้อ (low and broad)

squeeze, v. bìip-kán บีบคั้น; rát วัด; ríit รีด

squid, n. bplaa-mùk ปลาหมึก

squirrel, n. grà-rɔ̂ɔk กระรอก

squirt, v. pôn พ่น; chìit ฉีด

stab, v. tɛɛng แทง

stable, adj. mân-kong มั่นคง

stack, n. gɔɔng-yâa กองหญ้า; gɔɔng-faang กองฟาง

stadium, n. sà-nǎam-gii-laa สนามกีฬา

staff, n. pá-nák-ngaan พนักงาน

stag, n. gwaang-dtua-pûu กวางตัวผู้

stage, n. wee-tii เวที; wee-tii-sà-dɛɛng เวทีแสดง

stagger, v. dəən-soo-see เดินโซเซ; sàai ส่าย

stagnant, adj. yùt-nîng หยุดนิ่ง; yùu-chɔ̀əi-chɔ̀əi อยู่เฉยๆ

stagnate, v. yùt-nîng หยุดนิ่ง (still); yùt-lǎi หยุดไหล (stop flowing); yùu-chɔ̀əi-chɔ̀əi อยู่เฉยๆ (be motionless); sóp-sao ซบเซา (cease to be brisk or active)

stain, v. tam-hâi-bpûan ทำให้เปื้อน

stain, n. rɔɔi-bpûan รอยเปื้อน

stainless, adj. mâi-bpûan ไม่เปื้อน

stairs, staircase, n. ban-dai บันได; kân-ban-dai ขั้นบันได

stake, n. sǎo-làk เสาหลัก (pole); ngən-dəəm-pan เงินเดิมพัน (bet,

wager); sùan-dâai-sǐa ส่วนได้เสีย (money or property risked)

stale, adj. mâi-sòt ไม่สด; měn-àp เหม็นอับ; nâo-bpùai เน่าเปื่อย

stalk, n. lam-dtôn ลำต้น; gɛɛn แกน; gâan ก้าน

stall, n. kɔ̂ɔk คอก (animal shed); pɛ̂ɛng-lɔɔi แผงลอย (booth)

stamina, n. kwaam-kɛ̌ng-rɛɛng ความแข็งแรง; kwaam-tɔɔ-ra-hòt ความทรหด

stamp, n. sà-dtɛm สแตมป์ (postage); dtraa-bprà-táp ตราประทับ (seal)

stampede, n. gaan-wîng-on-la-mâan การวิ่งอลหม่าน; gaan-dtɛ̀ɛk-dtùun การแตกตื่น

stand, v. yuun ยืน (rise to an upright position on the feet); dtâng-yùu ตั้งอยู่ (locate)

standard, n. mâat-dtà-tǎan มาตรฐาน; geen เกณฑ์

standardize, v. tam-hâi-dâai-mâat-dtà-tǎan ทำให้ได้มาตรฐาน

stand-in, n. dtua-tɛɛn ตัวแทน

standing, n. dtam-nɛ̀ng ตำแหน่ง (position); tǎa-ná ฐานะ (position, base); jùt-yuun จุดยืน (standing point)

staple, n. sǐn-káa-làk สินค้าหลัก (main goods); wát-tù-dìp วัตถุดิบ (raw material); aa-hǎan-làk อาหารหลัก (e.g. rice, bread)

stapler, *n.* sà-dtép-bpân สแต็ปเปิ้ล; krûang-yép-nǎng-sǔu เครื่องเย็บ หนังสือ

star, *n.* daao ดาว (in the sky); duang-chá-dtaa ดวงชะตา (astrology); daa-raa คารา (in a movie)

start, *v.* rɔ̂ɔm เริ่ม; rɔ̂ɔm-dtôn เริ่มต้น

starch, *n.* bpɛ̂ɛng แป้ง

stare, *v.* jɔ̂ng-mɔɔng จ้องมอง

starfish, *n.* bplaa-daao ปลาดาว

startle, *v.* tam-hâi-dtòk-jai ทำให้ตกใจ

starve, *v.* òt-aa-hǎan อดอาหาร; òt-yàak อดอยาก

starving, *adj.* hǐu หิว; òt-yàak อดอยาก

state, *n.* sà-pâap สภาพ (condition e.g. mental or physical); sà-paa-wá สภาวะ (condition or mode of being with regard to circumstances); rát รัฐ (e.g. California)

stately, *adj.* yîng-yài ยิ่งใหญ่

statement, *n.* kam-tà-lɛ̌ɛng คำแถลง; kam-hâi-gaan คำให้การ

static, *adj.* kong-tîi คงที่

station, *n.* sà-tǎa-nii สถานี

stationary, *adj.* mâi-klûan-tîi ไม่เคลื่อนที่; kong-tîi คงที่

stationery, *n.* krûang-kian เครื่องเขียน

station wagon, *n.* rót-yon-tîi-mâi-mii-tǎai รถยนต์ที่ไม่มีท้าย

statistics, *n.* sà-tì-dtì สถิติ; kɔ̂ɔ-muun ข้อมูล

statue, *n.* rûup-bpân รูปปั้น; à-nú-sǎo-wa-rii อนุสาวรีย์

status, *n.* tǎa-ná ฐานะ; sà-tǎa-ná-pâap สถานะภาพ

status symbol, *n.* krûang-wát-tǎa-ná เครื่องวัดฐานะ

stay, *v.* yùu อยู่; pák-yùu พักอยู่

steadfast, *adj.* nɛɔ-nɛ̂ɛ แน่วแน่; yút-mân ยึดมั่น

steady, *adj.* mân-kong มั่นคง (firm); sà-màm-sà-mɔ̌ɔ สม่ำเสมอ (constant)

steak, *n.* núa-hàn เนื้อหั่น; núa-sa-dték เนื้อสเต็ค

steal, *v.* kà-mooi ขโมย; lák-lɔ̂ɔp ลักลอบ

steam, *v.* òp-ai-náam อบไอน้ำ

steam, *n.* ai-náam ไอน้ำ

steamboat, steamship, steamer, *n.* rua-gon-fai เรียเลไฟ

steed, *n.* máa-chán-dii ม้าชั้นดี

steel, *n.* lèk-glâa เหล็กกล้า

steep, *adj.* sǔung-chan สูงชัน

steer, *v.* tǔu-puang-maa-lai ถือพวงมาลัย (hold the steering wheel); nam-taang นำทาง (guide)

steering wheel, *n.* puang-maa-lai พวงมาลัย

stem, *n.* lam-dtôn ลำต้น

step, *n.* gâao ก้าว (footstep); kân ขั้น (stairs); rá-dàp ระดับ (level)

stepbrother, *n.* pîi-líang (chaai) พี่เลี้ยง (ชาย)

stepfather, *n.* pɔ̂ɔ-líang พ่อเลี้ยง

stepsister, *n.* pîi-líang (yǐng)
พี่เลี้ยง (หญิง)

stepson, -daughter, *n.* lûuk-líang
ลูกเลี้ยง

stereo, *n.* krûang-sǐang เครื่องเสียง

stereotype, *n.* tát-sa-ná-ká-dì-tûa-
bpai ทัศนคติทั่วไป

sterilize, *v.* kâa-chúa ฆ่าเชื้อ (kill
germ); tam-hâi-bpen-măn
ทำให้เป็นหมัน (make unable to produce children)

sterling silver, *n.* loo-hà-ngen-bɔɔ-
ri-sùt โลหะเงินบริสุทธิ์

stethoscope, *n.* krûang-dtrùat-fang
เครื่องตรวจฟัง

stew, *n.* aa-hǎan-dtǔn อาหารตุ๋น

steward, *n.* pá-nák-ngaan-dtɔ̂ɔn-
ráp พนักงานต้อนรับ

stewardess, *n.* pá-nák-ngaan-
dtɔ̂ɔn-ráp-yǐng พนักงานต้อนรับหญิง

stick, *n.* máai-táao ไม้เท้า; tɔ̂n-
máai ท่อนไม้

stick, *v.* dtìt ติด

sticker, *n.* chà-làak-dtìt ฉลากติด;
sa-dtík-gɔ̂ɔ สติ๊กเกอร์

sticky, *adj.* nǐao เหนียว; dtìt-nɛ̂n
ติดแน่น

stiff, *adj.* kɛ̌ng แข็ง; kɛ̌ng-tûu
แข็งทื่อ; kêm-ngûat เข้มงวด

still, *adj.* ngîap-sà-ngòp เงียบสงบ

still, *adv.* yang-kong ยังคง

stimulant, *n.* dtua-grà-dtûn
ตัวกระตุ้น

stimulate, *v.* grà-dtûn กระตุ้น; ráo
เร้า

sting, *v.* dtɔ̀i ต่อย (e.g. bee); gàt
กัด (e.g. insect); bpùat-sɛ̀ɛp
ปวดแสบ (feel stinging pain)

stingy, *adj.* kîi-nǐao ขี้เหนียว

stink, *v.* mii-glìn-měn มีกลิ่นเหม็น

stinking, *adj.* měn เหม็น

stipulate, *v.* rá-bu ระบุ (specify);
waang-ngûan-kǎi วางเงื่อนไข (set
conditions)

stipulation, *n.* ngûan-kǎi-nai-sǎn-
yaa เงื่อนไขในสัญญา (a term or condition in an agreement); kɔ̂ɔ-dtòk-
long-rá-wàang-tá-naai ข้อตกลง
ระหว่างทนาย (agreement between
lawyers)

stir, *v.* guan กวน; kon คน

stitch, *v.* yép-bpàk เย็บปัก; yép-
dtà-kèp เย็บตะเข็บ

stock, *n.* sà-dtók สต๊อก (inventory);
klang-sǐn-káa คลังสินค้า (where
stock is kept); hûn หุ้น (share)

stockbroker, *n.* naai-nâa-súu-kǎai-
hûn นายหน้าซื้อขายหุ้น

stock exchange, *n.* dtà-làat-hûn
ตลาดหุ้น; dtà-làat-làk-sáp
ตลาดหลักทรัพย์

stockholder, *n.* pûu-tǔu-hûn
ผู้ถือหุ้น

stocking, *n.* tǔng-nɔ̂ng ถุงน่อง

stocky, *adj.* lâm-sǎn ล่ำสัน; gam-yam กำย้ำ

stomach, *n.* grà-pó-aa-hǎan กระเพาะอาหาร (organs of digestion); tɔ́ɔng tʰɔ́ɔng ท้อง (belly); chɔ̂ng-tɔ́ɔng ช่องท้อง (abdomen)

stomachache, *n.* aa-gaan-bpùat-tɔ́ɔng อาการปวดท้อง

stone, *n.* hǐn หิน

stop, *v.* yùt หยุด (cease); hâam ห้าม (prevent, prohibit); yú-dtì ยุติ (discontinue)

stopover, *n.* tîi-pák-káang ที่พักค้าง

storage, *n.* gaan-gèp-rák-sǎa การเก็บรักษา; sà-tǎan-tîi-gèp สถานที่เก็บ

store, *v.* gèp เก็บ; gèp-rák-sǎa เก็บรักษา

store, *n.* ráan-(káa) ร้าน(ค้า)

storm, *n.* paa-yú พายุ

stormy, *adj.* mii-lom-paa-yú มีลมพายุ (having strong wind); goo-laa-hǒn โกลาหล (full of strong outbursts)

story, *n.* rɯ̂ang เรื่อง; ní-yaai นิยาย; ní-taan นิทาน

stove, *n.* dtao เตา; dtûu-òp ตู้อบ

stow, *v.* gèp เก็บ (keep); ban-jù บรรจุ (pack carefully)

stowaway, *n.* lòp-sɔ̂n-dtua หลบซ่อนตัว

straight, *adj.* dtrong ตรง

straighten, *v.* tam-hâi-dtrong ทำให้ตรง

straightforward, *adj.* sɯ̂ɯ-dtrong ซื่อตรง (honest); kâo-jai-ngâai เข้าใจง่าย (easy to understand)

strain, *v.* tam-hâi-dtɯng ทำให้ตึง (stretch tightly); tam-hâi-dtɯng-krîat ทำให้ตึงเครียด (cause tension); tam-hâi-ɔ̀ɔn-gam-lang ทำให้อ่อนกำลัง (weaken)

strainer, *n.* tîi-grɔɔng ที่กรอง; krɯ̂ang-grɔɔng เครื่องกรอง

straits, *n.* chɔ̂ng-kɛ̂ɛp ช่องแคบ

strand, *n.* gliao-chɯ̂ak เกลียวเชือก; sǎai-chɯ̂ak สายเชือก

strange, *adj.* bplɛ̀ɛk แปลก; bprà-làat ประหลาด

stranger, *n.* kon-bplɛ̀ɛk-nâa คนแปลกหน้า

strangle, *v.* bìip-kɔɔ บีบคอ (the neck); bìip-bang-káp บีบบังคับ (restrict, force)

strap, *n.* sǎai-rát สายรัด

stratosphere, *n.* ban-yaa-gàat-chán-bon บรรยากาศชั้นบน

stratum, *n.* chán ชั้น

straw, *n.* faang ฟาง (hay); lɔ̀ɔt-dùut หลอดดูด (for drinks)

strawberry, *n.* sà-dtrɔɔ-bəə-rîi สตรอเบอรี่

stray, *adj.* lǒng-taang หลงทาง; plát-prâak พลัดพราก

stream, *n.* lam-taan ลำธาร

street, *n.* tà-nǒn ถนน

strength, *n.* gam-lang กำลัง; pá-lang พลัง

English · Phonetic · Thai

strengthen, v. tam-hâi-kĕng-rɛɛng ทำให้แข็งแรง

strenuous, adj. kĕng-rɛɛng แข็งแรง; mii-pá-lang มีพลัง

stress, v. dtung-krîat ดึงเครียด

stretch, v. kŭng ขึง (tighten); dung ดึง (pull); yûut ยืด (lengthen); yûut-sên-yûut-săai ยืดเส้นยืดสาย (oneself or one's limbs)

stretcher, n. dtiang-hăam เตียงหาม (a litter for transporting ill or dead people); tîi-kŭng ที่ขึง (e.g. the wooden framework)

strew, v. bprooi โปรย; wàan หว่าน

strict, adj. kêm-ngûat เข้มงวด; krêng-krát เคร่งครัด

stride, v. dɔɔn-gâao-yaao เดินก้าวยาว

stride, n. gâao-yaao ก้าวยาว (long step)

strike, v. dtii ตี; bpà-tá ปะทะ; joom-dtii โจมตี

striking, adj. bprà-táp-jai ประทับใจ (impressive)

string, n. chûak เชือก; dâai ด้าย

strip, v. lɔ̀ɔk ลอก (remove, e.g. leaves; exterior coating); bplʉ̀ang-pâa เปลื้องผ้า (remove clothing)

stripe, n. rîu ริ้ว; laai ลาย; tɛ̀ɛp แถบ

strive, v. mûng-mân มุ่งมั่น; dtɔ̀ɔ-sûu ต่อสู้

stroke, n. gaan-dtii การตี (act of striking); sên-sà-mɔ̌ɔng-dùip-dtan เส้นสมองตีบตัน (of the brain)

stroll, v. dɔɔn-lên เดินเล่น

strong, adj. kĕng-rɛɛng แข็งแรง (person); rɛɛng แรง (e.g. drinks, medicine, etc.)

structure, n. kroong-sâang โครงสร้าง; kroong โครง

struggle, v. dîn-ron ดิ้นรน; dtɔ̀ɔ-sûu ต่อสู้

stub, n. dtɔɔ-máai ตอไม้ (of a tree); hăang หาง (e.g. ticket, check)

stubborn, adj. dûʉ-dung ดื้อดึง; dûʉ-rán ดื้อรั้น

student, n. nák-rian นักเรียน; nák-sùk-săa นักศึกษา

studio, n. hɔ̂ng-dìao ห้องเดี่ยว; hɔ̂ng-tam-ngaan ห้องทำงาน

studious, adj. kà-yăn-rian ขยันเรียน (in learning); grà-dtʉʉ-rʉʉ-rón กระตือรือร้น (enthusiastic)

study, v. rian เรียน; sùk-săa ศึกษา

study, n. gaan-rian การเรียน; gaan-sùk-săa การศึกษา

stuff, n. sìng-kɔ̌ɔng สิ่งของ

stuffy, adj. òp-âao อบอ้าว; ùt-ûu อุดอู้

stumble, v. sà-dùt สะดุด; tam-plâat ทำพลาด

stun, v. tam-hâi-bprà-làat-jai ทำให้ประหลาดใจ

stunning, adj. nâa-bprà-làat-jai น่าประหลาดใจ; yɔ̂ɔt-yîam ยอดเยี่ยม

Desperate
search

AP

French soldiers yesterday approach a piece of debris believed to be part of Air France flight 447 that crashed into the Atlantic Ocean with 228 passengers. A hectic search is on to find the aircraft's flight-data recorders to determine the cause of the crash.

Blind wife pours hot congee on cheating hubby

A blind Hong Kong woman who suspected her husband was cheating on her poured boiling hot congee on his groin as he slept naked.

Taxi driver Leung Yiu-yuen, 56, suffered second-degree burns to his genitals after his wife attacked him with the congee, a form of Chinese porridge served hot for breakfast.

Earlier, Miu Tsui-fun, 58, laced his drinks with female hormones in an attempt to make him impotent when she became convinced he was having an affair, the *Hong Kong Standard* newspaper reported.

After the congee attack last September, Leung was taken to hospital with burns that required three weeks of treatment and still left an unhealed wound, Hong Kong's High Court heard on Tuesday.

Miu, who is totally blind and married Leung in 2002, pleaded guilty to wounding with intent and will be sentenced on September 4, the *Standard* reported. The couple have separated.

DPA

ALEC BALDWIN, ON STRESS CAUSED BY A LEAKED, VULGAR VOICEMAIL TWO YEARS AGO AND A CHILD-CUSTODY BATTLE WITH EX-WIFE KIM BASINGER.

"I [was] very serious. I spoke to a lot of professionals, who helped me. If I committed suicide, [Basinger's lawyers] would have considered that a victory. Destroying me was their avowed goal."

"

ONE THING I CAN'T STAND ABOUT HOLLYWOOD IS WASTE.

Michael Bay

English · Phonetic · Thai

stunt, *n.* gaan-sà-dɛɛng-lôot-pǒon
การแสดงโลดโผน

stupid, *adj.* ngôo โง่

stutter, *v.* pûut-dtìt-àang พูดติดอ่าง

sty, *n.* kɔ̂ɔk-mǔu คอกหมู (for pig);
rôok-gûng-ying โรคกุ้งยิง (of an eyelid)

style, *n.* chá-nít ชนิด (type); lák-
sà-nà ลักษณะ (feature); tâa-taang
ท่าทาง (manner); lii-laa ลีลา
(mode of doing something)

stylish, *adj.* tan-sà-mǎi ทันสมัย
(modish); gěe เก๋ (elegant)

stylist, *n.* nák-ɔ̀ɔk-bɛ̀ɛp นักออกแบบ

subconscious, *n.* jìt-dtâai-sǎm-núk
จิตใต้สำนึก

subject, *n.* rûang เรื่อง (e.g. of an
article or story); bprà-den ประเด็น
(e.g. of a discussion); hǔa-kɔ̂ɔ
หัวข้อ (theme)

subjective, *adj.* sùan-dtua ส่วนตัว
(personal); dtɛ̀ɛ-lá-bùk-kon
แต่ละบุคคล (particular to a given
person)

subjunctive, *adj.* tîi-sà-dɛɛng-
ngûan-kǎi ที่แสดงเงื่อนไข

sublet, *v.* bɛng-hâi-châo แบ่งให้เช่า

sublime, *adj.* sǔung sùt สูงสุด
(highest); lɔ̂ɔt เลิศ (supreme)

submarine, *n.* rɯa-dam-náam
เรือดำน้ำ

submerge, *v.* dam-náam ดำน้ำ
(dive; go under water); jùm จุ่ม (dip
into water); chɛ̂ɛ แช่ (place under
water)

submissive, *adj.* yɔɔm ยอม; wâa-
ngâai ว่าง่าย

submit, *v.* yɔɔm ยอม (yield); sà-
nɔ̌ɔ-pûa-pí-jaa-ra-naa เสนอเพื่อ
พิจารณา (give in to authority)

subordinate, *n.* rɔɔng รอง; sìng-
tîi-bpen-rɔɔng สิ่งที่เป็นรอง

subpoena, *n.* mǎai-sǎan หมายศาล;
mǎai-rîak หมายเรียก

subscribe, *v.* bpen-sà-maa-chík
เป็นสมาชิก (e.g. to a magazine)

subscriber, *n.* pûu-sàng-sɯ́ɯ
ผู้สั่งซื้อ; sà-maa-chík สมาชิก

subsequent, *adj.* paai-lǎng
ภายหลัง; dtɔ̀ɔ-maa ต่อมา

subside, *v.* jom-long จมลง (sink);
sút ทรุด (sink to a lower level);
ban-tao บรรเทา (e.g. pain - getting
better)

subsidiary, *adj.* sòng-sǒɛm ส่งเสริม
(serving to supplement); chûai-lɯ̌a
ช่วยเหลือ (serving to assist); sǎng-
gàt สังกัด (subordinate)

subsidiary company *n.* bɔɔ-ri-sàt-
rɔɔng บริษัทรอง

subsidize, *v.* chûai sǒng-krɔ́
ช่วยสงเคราะห์ (grant a subsidy);
ùt-nǔn อุดหนุน (support)

subsidy, *n.* ngən-sǒng-krɔ́
เงินสงเคราะห์; ngən-chûai-lɯ̌a
เงินช่วยเหลือ; ngən-ùt-nǔn
เงินอุดหนุน

English • Phonetic • Thai

substance, *n.* sǎan สาร (that which has mass); gèn-sǎan แก่นสาร (essence, gist); núa-hǎa เนื้อหา (matter, essence)

substantial, *adj.* mii-núa-hǎa มีเนื้อหา (having substance); sǎa-rá-sǎm-kan สาระสำคัญ (considerable in importance)

substitute, *n.* dtua-tɛɛn ตัวแทน (person); sìng-tɛɛn สิ่งแทน (thing)

subtitle, *n.* hǔa-kàao-rɔɔng หัวข่าวรอง (news); hǔa-kɔ̂ɔ-yɔ̂i หัวข้อย่อย (literary work); kam-bplɛɛ-nǎng คำแปลหนัง (movie)

subtle, *adj.* kâo-jai-yâak เข้าใจยาก (difficult to understand); lúk-láp ลึกลับ (insidious)

subtract, *v.* tɔ̀ɔn-ɔ̀ɔk ถอนออก; lóp-ɔ̀ɔk ลบออก

suburb, *n.* chaan-muang ชานเมือง

subway, *n.* rót-fai-fáa-dtâai-din รถไฟฟ้าใต้ดิน

succeed, *v.* sǎm-rèt สำเร็จ; ban-lú-pòn บรรลุผล

success, *n.* kwaam-sǎm-rèt ความสำเร็จ (achievement); chai-cha-ná ชัยชนะ (victory)

successful, *adj.* bpen-pòn-sǎm-rèt เป็นผลสำเร็จ; mii-chai-cha-ná มีชัยชนะ

succession, *n.* gaan-sùup-mɔɔ-ra-dòk การสืบมรดก (succeed to an estate; will); gaan-ráp-chûang การรับช่วง (act or process of following in order; succeed to a title, throne, etc.)

such, *pron., adj.* chên-níi เช่นนี้; sìng-níi สิ่งนี้; sìng-nán สิ่งนั้น

suck, *v.* dùut ดูด

suction, *n.* gaan-dùut การดูด

sudden, *adj.* tan-tii ทันที; chàp-plan ฉับพลัน; gà-tan-hǎn กะทันหัน

suddenly, *adv.* yaang-chàp-plan อย่างฉับพลัน; dooi-kâat-mâi-tǔng โดยคาดไม่ถึง

suds, *n.* fɔɔng-sà-bùu ฟองสบู่

sue, *v.* fɔ́ɔng ฟ้อง; fɔ́ɔng-rɔ́ɔng ฟ้องร้อง; yʉʉn-fɔ́ɔng ยื่นฟ้อง

suede, *n.* nǎng-nîm หนังนิ่ม

suffer, *v.* ton-túk ทนทุกข์; òt-ton อดทน

sufferer, *n.* pûu-ton-túk ผู้ทนทุกข์

suffering, *n.* túk ทุกข์

sufficient, *adj.* pɔɔ พอ; pɔɔ-piang พอเพียง

suffix, *n.* kam-dtɔ̀ɔ-táai คำต่อท้าย; bpàt-jai ปัจจัย

suffocate, *v.* hǎai-jai-mâi-ɔ̀ɔk หายใจไม่ออก; sǎm-lák สำลัก

sugar, *n.* náam-dtaan น้ำตาล

sugar cane, *n.* dtôn-ɔ̂ɔi ต้นอ้อย

suggest, *v.* né-nam แนะนำ; sà-nɔ̌ɔ-né เสนอแนะ

suggestion, *n.* gaan-né-nam การแนะนำ; gaan-sà-nɔ̌ɔ-né การเสนอแนะ

suicidal, *adj.* àat-kâa-dtua-dtaai-dâai อาจฆ่าตัวตายได้

suicide, *v.* kâa-dtua-dtaai ฆ่าตัวตาย

suicide, *n.* gaan-kâa-dtua-dtaai การฆ่าตัวตาย

suit, *n.* gaan-fɔ́ɔng-rɔ́ɔng การฟ้องร้อง (law suit); chút-sùut ชุดสุท (for wearing)

suitable, *adj.* mɔ̀-sǒm เหมาะสม; sǒm-kuan สมควร

suitcase, *n.* grà-bpǎo-dəən-taang กระเป๋าเดินทาง

suite, *n.* chút ชุด (group of products, things); glùm กลุ่ม (group); hɔ̂ng-chút ห้องชุด (rooms)

sulfur, *n.* gam-ma-tǎn กำมะถัน

sulk, *v.* gròot-kuang โกรธเคือง

sulky, *adj.* bùut-bûng บูดบึ้ง

sum, *n.* pǒn-bùak ผลบวก; yɔ̂ɔt ยอด

summarize, *v.* sà-rùp สรุป

summary, *n.* sà-rùp สรุป; bòt-kwaam-yɔ̂ɔ บทความย่อ

summer, *n.* rú-duu-rɔ́ɔn ฤดูร้อน

summit, *n.* sùt-yɔ̂ɔt สุดยอด

summon, *v.* rîak-dtua เรียกตัว; ɔ̀ɔk-mǎai-rîak ออกหมายเรียก

summons, *n.* gaan-rîak-dtua การเรียกตัว; mǎai-sǎan หมายศาล (of the court)

sun, *n.* duang-aa-tít ดวงอาทิตย์; prá-aa-tít พระอาทิตย์

sunburn, *n.* pǐu-tîi-pɛ́ɛ-dèet ผิวที่แพ้แดด

Sunday, *n.* wan-aa-tít วันอาทิตย์

sundial, *n.* naa-lí-gaa-dèet นาฬิกาแดด

sundry, *adj.* dtàang-dtàang-naa-naa ต่างๆนานา; làak-lǎai หลากหลาย

sunflower, *n.* dtôn-taan-dtà-wan ต้นทานตะวัน

sunglasses, *n.* wên-dtaa-gan-dèet แว่นตากันแดด

sunlight, *n.* sɛ̌ɛng-dèet แสงแดด

sunny, *adj.* mii-sɛ̌ɛng-dèet มีแสงแดด; dèet-glâa แดดกล้า

sunny side-up, *adj.* kài-daao ไข่ดาว (for egg)

sunrise, *n.* prá-aa-tít-kʉ̂n พระอาทิตย์ขึ้น

sunset, *n.* prá-aa-tít-dtòk พระอาทิตย์ตก

sunshine, *n.* sɛ̌ɛng-dèet แสงแดด

sunstroke, *n.* rôok-lom-dèet โรคลมแดด

suntan, *n.* pǐu-tîi-tùuk-dèet ผิวที่ถูกแดด

superb, *adj.* dii-lɛ̂ɔt ดีเลิศ; yɔ̂ɔt-yîam ยอดเยี่ยม

superficial, *adj.* pǐu-pɔ̌ɔn ผิวเผิน (being on or near the surface); mâi-sǎm-kan ไม่สำคัญ (insignificant)

superintendent, *n.* puu-kûap-kum ผู้ควบคุม (one that directs); pûu-am-nuai-gaan ผู้อำนวยการ (director)

superior, *n.* sìng-tîi-nʉ̌a-gwàa

สิ่งที่เหนือกว่า (something superior);
pûu-bang-káp-ban-chaa
ผู้บังคับบัญชา (one that is higher
than another in rank or authority)

superiority complex, *n.* bpom-dèn
ปมเด่น

superlative, *adj.* sǔung-sùt สูงสุด;
sùt-yɔ̂ɔt สุดยอด

supermarket, *n.* súp-bpɔ̂ɔ-maa-gét
ซูเปอร์มาร์เก็ต

supernatural, *adj.* nǔa-tam-ma-
châat เหนือธรรมชาติ; à-pi-ní-hǎan
อภินิหาร

superpower, *n.* má-hǎa-am-nâat
มหาอำนาจ

supersede, *v.* tɛɛn-tîi แทนที่;
yêng-tîi แย่งที่

supersonic, *adj.* reo-nǔa-sǐang
เร็วเหนือเสียง

superstition, *n.* kwaam-chûa-
chôok-laang ความเชื่อโชคลาง

superstitious, *adj.* chûa-chôok-
laang เชื่อโชคลาง

supervise, *v.* duu-lɛɛ ดูแล; kûap-
kum ควบคุม

supervisor, *n.* pûu-kûap-kum
ผู้ควบคุม; hǔa-nâa-ngaan
หัวหน้างาน

supper, *n.* aa-hǎan-yen อาหารเย็น

supplier, *n.* pûu-jàt-hǎa ผู้จัดหา;
pûu-jàt-sòng ผู้จัดส่ง

supply, *n.* gaan-jàt-hǎa การจัดหา;
sà-biang เสบียง

support, *v.* sà-nàp-sà-nǔn
สนับสนุน; chûai-lǔa ช่วยเหลือ

supporter, *n.* pûu-sà-nàp-sà-nǔn
ผู้สนับสนุน; pûu-chûai-lǔa
ผู้ช่วยเหลือ

suppose, *v.* sǒm-mút สมมุติ
(assume); núk-ao นึกเอา (guess)

suppress, *v.* bpràap-bpraam
ปราบปราม (subdue); yùt-yáng
หยุดยั้ง (prohibit; inhibit the expression of); rá-ngáp ระงับ (keep
from); kà-jàt ขจัด (get rid of)

supreme, *adj.* sùt-yɔ̂ɔt สุดยอด
(highest); mii-am-nâat-sǔung-sùt
มีอำนาจสูงสุด (most powerful)

sure, *adj.* nɛ̂ɛ-nɔɔn แน่นอน; mân-
jai มั่นใจ; nɛ̂ɛ-jai แน่ใจ

surf, *v.* lên-grà-daan-dtôo-klûun
เล่นกระดานโต้คลื่น

surf, *n.* klûun-sát-fàng คลื่นซัดฝั่ง

surface, *n.* pǐu-nâa ผิวหน้า; dâan-
nâa ด้านหน้า

surfer, *n.* nák-lên-grà-daan-dtôo-
klûun นักเล่นกระดานโต้คลื่น

surfing, *n.* gii-laa-dtôo-klûun
กีฬาโต้คลื่น

surge, *v.* grà-pûam กระเพื่อม

surge, *n.* klûun-rɛɛng คลื่นแรง

surgeon, *n.* sǎn-ya-pɛ̂ɛt ศัลยแพทย์

surgery, *n.* sǎn-ya-gam ศัลยกรรม;
gaan-pàa-dtàt การผ่าตัด

surgical, *adj.* gìao-gàp-gaan-pàa-
dtàt เกี่ยวกับการผ่าตัด; sǎn-ya-gam
ศัลยกรรม

surname, *n.* naam-sà-gun นามสกุล

surpass, *v.* gəən เกิน; ləəi-təət
เลยเถิด; nǔa-gwàa เหนือกว่า; dii-
gwàa ดีกว่า

surplus, *n.* sùan-gəən ส่วนเกิน;
jam-nuan-gəən จำนวนเกิน; ngən-
tii-lǔa เงินที่เหลือ

surprise, *v.* tam-hâi-bprà-làat-jai
ทำให้ประหลาดใจ

surprised, *adj.* bprà-làat-jai
ประหลาดใจ

surprising, *adj.* tam-hâi-bprà-làat-
jai ทำให้ประหลาดใจ

surrender, *v.* yɔɔm-pɛ́ɛ ยอมแพ้;
yɔɔm-jam-non ยอมจำนน; dtaam-jai
ตามใจ

surround, *v.* lɔ́ɔm-rɔ̂ɔp ล้อมรอบ;
ɔ̀ɔp-lɔ́ɔm โอบล้อม

surrounding, *adj.* lɔ́ɔm-rɔ̂ɔp
ล้อมรอบ; wɛ̂ɛt-lɔ́ɔm แวดล้อม

surroundings, *n.* sà-pâap-wɛ̂ɛt-
lɔ́ɔm สภาพแวดล้อม

surveillance, *n.* gaan-sǎng-gèet-
gaan การสังเกตการณ์ (act of
observing); gaam-sà-gòt-rɔɔi
การสะกดรอย (close observation)

survey, *v.* sam-rùat สำรวจ (examine or look at comprehensively);
rang-wát รังวัด (e.g. land); dtrùat-
dtraa ตรวจตรา (inspect)

survival, *n.* gaan-yùu-rɔ̂ɔt
การอยู่รอด; gaan-rɔ̂ɔt-dtaai
การรอดตาย

survive, *v.* yùu-rɔ̂ɔt อยู่รอด; rɔ̂ɔt-
dtaai รอดตาย; dam-rong-yùu
ดำรงอยู่

survivor, *n.* pûu-rɔ̂ɔt-dtaai
ผู้รอดตาย; pûu-tîi-lǔa-yùu
ผู้ที่เหลืออยู่

susceptible, *adj.* rúu-sùk-wai
รู้สึกไว; wàn-wǎi-ngâai หวั่นไหวง่าย

suspect, *v.* sǒng-sǎi สงสัย; rá-
wɛɛng ระแวง

suspend, *v.* yùt-chûa-kraao
หยุดชั่วคราว (stop temporarily);
lɔɔi-dtua ลอยตัว (hang so as to
allow free movement); dtàt-sìt-chûa-
kraao ตัดสิทธิ์ชั่วคราว (from a privilege); hâi-yùt-pák ให้หยุดพัก (from
school or job)

suspender, *n.* saai-kwɛɛn
สายแขวน; sìng-kwɛɛn สิ่งแขวน

suspense, *n.* bprìt-sà-nǎa ปริศนา

suspension bridge, *n.* sà-paan-
kɛ́ɛn สะพานแขวน

suspicion, *n.* kwaam-sǒng-sǎi
ความสงสัย; kwaam-rá-wɛɛng
ความระแวง

suspicious, *adj.* nâa-sǒng-sǎi
น่าสงสัย (something suspicious);
kîi-rá-wɛɛng ขี้ระแวง (of something)

sustain, *v.* sà-nàp-sà-nǔn สนับสนุน;
kám-jun ค้ำจุน

swab, *v.* tǔu ถู (wipe)

swab, *n.* pâa-sáp ผ้าซับ

swallow, v. gluun กลืน

swallow, n. nók-naang-ɛ̀n นกนางแอ่น

swamp, n. nɔ́ɔng-náam หนองน้ำ; buŋ บึง

swan, n. hǒŋ หงส์

swap, n. gaan-lɛ̂ɛk-bplìan การแลกเปลี่ยน

swarm, n. fǔuŋ-pʉ̂ŋ ฝูงผึ้ง (of bees); glùm-yài กลุ่มใหญ่ (big group)

sway, v. gwɛ̀ɛŋ แกว่ง; gwai ไกว

swear, v. sǎa-baan สาบาน (vow); sà-bòt สบถ (make a solemn declaration, invoking a deity); sàap-chɛ̂ŋ สาปแช่ง (curse)

sweat, v. ngʉ̀a-ɔ̀ɔk เหงื่อออก

sweat, n. ngʉ̀a เหงื่อ (perspiration); kwaam-nʉ̀ai-yâak ความเหนื่อยยาก (difficulty)

sweater, n. sʉ̂a-kǒn-sàt เสื้อขนสัตว์

sweep, v. gwàat กวาด; gwàat-láaŋ กวาดล้าง

sweet, adj. wǎan หวาน (having the taste of sugar); pai-rɔ́ ไพเราะ (sounding sweet); nâa-rák น่ารัก (lovable)

sweetheart, n. tîi-rák ที่รัก

sweet potato, n. man-têet มันเทศ

swell, v. buam บวม (e.g. skin); kà-yǎai-dtua ขยายตัว (expand); pɔɔŋ-dtua พองตัว (increase in size)

swelling, n. gaan-buam การบวม;

gaan-kà-yǎai-dtua การขยายตัว

swerve, v. hàk-lîao หักเลี้ยว

swim, v. wâai-náam ว่ายน้ำ

swimmer, n. nák-wâai-náam นักว่ายน้ำ

swimming, n. gaan-wâai-náam การว่ายน้ำ

swimming pool, n. sà-wâai-náam สระว่ายน้ำ

swimsuit, n. chút-wâai-náam ชุดว่ายน้ำ

swing, n. chin-cháa ชิงช้า

swing, v. gwɛ̀ɛŋ แกว่ง (move back and forth); kwɛ̌ɛn แขวน (hang, suspend)

swipe, v. dtii-yàaŋ-rɛɛŋ ตีอย่างแรง (hit hard); rûut-bàt รูดบัตร (a credit card)

swirl, v. mǔn หมุน (turn); won-wian วนเวียน (move with a twisting motion)

switch, n. tîi-bpə̀ət-bpìt ที่เปิดปิด (to turn on and off); tîi-sàp-bplìan ที่สับเปลี่ยน (an exchange)

sword, n. dàap ดาบ

syllable, n. pá-yaang พยางค์

syllabus, n. làk-sùut หลักสูตร; sǎa-rá-sǎm-kan สาระสำคัญ

symbol, n. krʉ̂ang-mǎai เครื่องหมาย; sǎn-yá-lák สัญลักษณ์

symbolic, adj. bpen-krʉ̂ang-mǎai เป็นเครื่องหมาย; bpen-sǎn-yá-lák เป็นสัญลักษณ์

symbolize, v. bpen-săn-yá-lák เป็นสัญลักษณ์; bpen-krûang-sà-dɛɛng เป็นเครื่องแสดง

sympathetic, adj. hěn-òk-hěn-jai เห็นอกเห็นใจ

sympathize, v. hěn-òk-hěn-jai เห็นอกเห็นใจ

sympathy, n. kwaam-hěn-òk-hěn-jai ความเห็นอกเห็นใจ

symphony, n. don-dtrii-bprà-săan-sĭang ดนตรีประสานเสียง

symposium, n. gaan-bprà-chum-săm-ma-naa การประชุมสัมนา

symptom, n. aa-gaan อาการ; aa-gaan-rôok อาการโรค

synagogue, n. bòot-yiu โบสถ์ยิว

synchronize, v. tam-hâi-sòot-klóong-gan ทำให้สอดคล้องกัน

syndrome, n. aa-gaan-rôok อาการโรค

synonym, n. kam-pÓong คำพ้อง

synopsis, n. sà-rùp-kwaam สรุปความ; kôo-sà-rùp ข้อสรุป

syntax, n. gaan-sâang-bprà-yòok การสร้างประโยค

synthesis, n. gaan-săng-kró การสังเคราะห์

synthesize, v. săng-kró สังเคราะห์

syphilis, n. rôok-sí-fi-lít โรคซิฟิลิส

syringe, n. qrà-bòok-chìit-yaa กระบอกฉีดยา

syrup, n. náam-chûam น้ำเชื่อม

system, n. rá-bòp ระบบ

T

tab, n. tép แท็บ (a key on a computer keyboard); tèep แถบ (flap, or short strip attached to an object)

table, n. dtó โต๊ะ (furniture); dtaa-raang ตาราง (chart)

tablecloth, n. pâa-bpuu-dtó ผ้าปูโต๊ะ

tablespoon, n. chóon-dtó ช้อนโต๊ะ

tablet, n. yaa-mét ยาเม็ด (pill); sà-mùt-ban-túk สมุดบันทึก (notebook)

taboo, n. kôo-hâam ข้อห้าม

tack, n. nɛɛo-taang แนวทาง

tactic, n. rá-bòp ระบบ

tadpole, n. lûuk-gòp ลูกกบ

tag, n. bpâai ป้าย; săai-yoong สายโยง

tail, n. hăang หาง

tailor, n. châng-dtàt-sûa ช่างตัดเสื้อ

take, v. ao เอา (get into one's possession); yìp หยิบ (with the hand); cháai-wee-laa ใช้เวลา (take time); paa พา (convey; take someone from one place to another)

take off, v. tòot ถอด (e.g. clothes, shoes); yùt-pák-pòon หยุดพักผ่อน (have a vacation); òok-dəən-taang ออกเดินทาง (for a trip)

take out, n. ao-òok เอาออก

talc, n. bpɛ̂ɛng-taa-dtua แป้งทาตัว

tale, n. ní-taan นิทาน; rûang-lâo

English • Phonetic • Thai

เรื่องเล่า

talent, *n.* pɔɔn-sà-wǎn พรสวรรค์

talented, *adj.* mii-pɔɔn-sà-wǎn มีพรสวรรค์

talk, *v.* pûut พูด (speak); sǒn-ta-naa สนทนา (converse); kui คุย (chat)

talkative, *adj.* châng-kui ช่างคุย

tall, *adj.* sǔung สูง

tame, *adj.* chûang เชื่อง

tamper, *v.* gâao-gàai ก้าวก่าย (interfere); hâi-sǐn-bon ให้สินบน (use bribery)

tampon, *n.* pâa-à-naa-mai-bɛ̀ɛp-sɔ̀ɔt ผ้าอนามัยแบบสอด

tan, *n.* sǐi-náam-dtaan สีน้ำตาล

tangerine, *n.* sôm-jiin ส้มจีน

tangible, *adj.* sǎm-pàt-dâai สัมผัสได้; jàp-dtɔ̂ng-dâai จับต้องได้

tangle, *v.* yûng-yɔ̌ɔng ยุ่งเหยิง; pua-pan พัวพัน

tank, *n.* tǎng ถัง (container); rót-tǎng รถถัง (combat vehicle)

tanker, *n.* rót-ban-túk-náam-man รถบรรทุกน้ำมัน

tap, *v.* dtɛ̀-bao-bao แตะเบาๆ; dtɔ̀p-bao-bao ตบเบาๆ

tap, *n.* hǔa-gɔ́k-náam หัวก๊อกน้ำ

tape, *n.* sǎai-téep สายเทป; téep เทป

taper, *v.* riao-long เรียวลง (become thin); lót-long ลดลง (reduce)

tape recorder, *n.* téep เทป; krûang-ban-túk-sǐang เครื่องบันทึกเสียง

tapestry, *n.* sìng-tɔɔ สิ่งทอ (woven material); pâa-bprà-dàp ผ้าประดับ (for decoration)

tar, *n.* náam-man-din น้ำมันดิน

tardy, *adj.* cháa ช้า; láa-lǎng ล่าหลัง; chùai-chaa เฉื่อยชา

target, *n.* bpâo เป้า (e.g. for shooting); bpâo-mǎai เป้าหมาย (aim); jùt-mûng-mǎai จุดมุ่งหมาย (objective)

tariff, *n.* paa-sǐi-sǔn-lá-gaa-gɔɔn ภาษีศุลกากร

tarnish, *v.* tam-hâi-mua-mɔ̌ɔng ทำให้มัวหมอง

tart, *n.* kà-nǒm-tâat ขนมทาร์ท

task, *n.* ngaan งาน; paa-rá-nâa-tii ภาระหน้าที่

taste, *n.* rót-sà-ní-yom รสนิยม; rót-châat รสชาติ

tasty, *adj.* à-rɔ̀i อร่อย; mii-rót-dii มีรสดี

tattoo, *n.* rɔɔi-sàk รอยสัก; laai-sàk ลายสัก

tavern, *n.* roong-rɛɛm-lék-lék โรงแรมเล็กๆ (inn); roong-kǎai-lâo โรงขายเหล้า (where liquor is sold)

tawdry, *adj.* púun-púun พื้นๆ; rîap-rîap เรียบๆ

tax, *n.* paa-sǐi ภาษี

tax-free, *adj.* bplɔ̀ɔt-paa-sǐi ปลอดภาษี

taxi, *n.* rót-tɛ́k-sîi รถแท็กซี่

taxpayer, *n.* pûu-sǐa-paa-sǐi ผู้เสียภาษี

tax rate, *n.* àt-dtraa-paa-sǐi อัตราภาษี

tea, *n.* náam-chaa น้ำชา

teach, *v.* sɔ̌ɔn สอน; òp-rom อบรม

teacher, *n.* kruu ครู; aa-jaan อาจารย์

teaching, *n.* gaan-sɔ̌ɔn การสอน

team, *n.* tiim ทีม; ká-ná คณะ

tear, *v.* chìik ฉีก

tear, *n.* náam-dtaa น้ำตา

tease, *v.* yûa ยั่ว; yɛ̂ɛ แหย่; lɔ́ɔ-lian ล้อเลียน

teaspoon, *n.* chɔ́ɔn chaa ช้อนชา

teat, *n.* hǔa-nom หัวนม

technical, *adj.* taang-ték-nìk ทางเทคนิค

technician, *n.* châng-ték-nìk ช่างเทคนิค

technique, *n.* ték-nìk เทคนิค; gon-lá-wí-tii กลวิธี

technology, *n.* ték-noo-loo-yîi เทคโนโลยี

teenage, *adj.* rûn-nùm-sǎao รุ่นหนุ่มสาว

teenager, *n.* wai-rûn วัยรุ่น

telegram, *n.* too ra-lêek โทรเลข

telegraph, *n.* krɨ̂ang-sòng-too-ra-lêek เครื่องส่งโทรเลข

telepathy, *n.* too-ra-jìt โทรจิต

telephone, *n.* too-ra-sàp โทรศัพท์

telephone booth, *n.* dtûu-too-ra-sàp ตู้โทรศัพท์

telephone number, *n.* bɜɜ-too-ra-sàp เบอร์โทรศัพท์

telescope, *n.* glɔ̂ng-sɔ̀ng-taang-glai กล้องส่องทางไกล

televise, *v.* tàai-tɔ̂ɔt-too-ra-tát ถ่ายทอดโทรทัศน์

television, *n.* too-ra-tát โทรทัศน์

tell, *v.* bɔ̀ɔk บอก; lâo เล่า; pûut พูด

teller, *n.* pûu-bɔ̀ɔk ผู้บอก (one that informs); pûu-lâo ผู้เล่า (one that tells a story); jâo-nâa-tîi-ráp-jàai-ngən เจ้าหน้าที่รับจ่ายเงิน (e.g. in a bank)

temper, *n.* aa-rom อารมณ์; ní-sǎi นิสัย

temperament, *n.* aa-rom อารมณ์ (mood); ní-sǎi นิสัย (behavior, habit); paa-wá-jìt-jai ภาวะจิตใจ (state of mind)

temperamental, *adj.* jâo-aa-rom เจ้าอารมณ์ (moody); mii-kwaam-rúu-sùk-wai มีความรู้สึกไว (sensitive)

temperature, *n.* un-ná-hà-puum อุณหภูมิ

template, *n.* pɛ̀n-lɔ̂ɔk-bɛ̀ɛp แผ่นลอกแบบ (for pattern or gauge); pɛ̀n-máai-rɔɔng แผ่นไม้รอง (as in woodworking or carving); tem-plèet เทมเพลท (in computer science)

temple, *n.* wát วัด

tempo, *n.* jang-wà จังหวะ (rhythm); kwaam-reo ความเร็ว

(speed)

temporary, *adj.* chûa-kraao ชั่วคราว

tempt, *v.* lôo ล่อ; yûa-jai ยั่วใจ; yûa-yuan ยั่วยวน

ten, *nm.* sìp สิบ

tenant, *n.* pûu-châo ผู้เช่า

tend, *v.* duu-lɛɛ ดูแล

tendency, *n.* kwaam-nóom-iang ความโน้มเอียง; ní-sǎi นิสัย

tender, *adj.* ɔ̀ɔn-yoon อ่อนโยน; nîm-nuan นิ่มนวล

tenderness, *n.* kwaam-ɔ̀ɔn-yoon ความอ่อนโยน; kwaam-nîm-nuan ความนิ่มนวล

tendon, *n.* en เอ็น; sên-en เส้นเอ็น

tennis, *n.* gii-laa-ten-nít กีฬาเทนนิส

tense, *n.* gà-rí-yaa-sà-dɛɛng-wee-laa กริยาแสดงเวลา

tension, *n.* kwaam-dtung-krîat ความตึงเครียด

tent, *n.* grà-joom กระโจม; dtént เต็นท์

tenth, *adj.* tîi-sìp ที่สิบ

tenure, *n.* gaan-krɔ̂ɔp-krɔɔng การครอบครอง

term, *n.* kraao คราว; rá-yá-wee-laa ระยะเวลา

terminal, *n.* sùan-táai ส่วนท้าย (ending part); bplaai-taang ปลายทาง (destination)

terminate, *v.* sîn-sùt สิ้นสุด (end); yú-dtì ยุติ (finish); long-ɵ̀ɵi ยกเลิก (cancel)

termination, *n.* gaan-sîn-sùt การสิ้นสุด; gaan-yú-dtì การยุติ; gaan-yók-lɵ̂ɵk การยกเลิก

terminology, *n.* kam-sàp คำศัพท์; rá-bòp-kam-sàp ระบบคำศัพท์

termite, *n.* bplùak ปลวก

terrace, *n.* rá-biang ระเบียง (balcony, deck); dàat-fáa ดาดฟ้า (on the roof)

terrain, *n.* pʉʉn-din ผืนดิน

terrible, *adj.* nâa-glua น่ากลัว; ráai-rɛɛng ร้ายแรง

terrific, *adj.* yîng-yài ยิ่งใหญ่ (grand); dii-yîam ดีเยี่ยม (very good; great)

terrify, *v.* tam-hâi-nâa-glua ทำให้น่ากลัว; tam-hâi-wàat-glua ทำให้หวาดกลัว

territory, *n.* aa-naa-kèet อาณาเขต; din-dɛɛn ดินแดน

terror, *n.* kwaam-nâa-glua ความน่ากลัว; kwaam-sà-yɔ̌ɔng-kwǎn ความสยองขวัญ

terrorism, *n.* lát-tí-gɔ̀ɔ-gaan-ráai ลัทธิก่อการร้าย

terrorist, *n.* pûu-gɔ̀ɔ-gaan-ráai ผู้ก่อการร้าย

test, *v.* tót-sɔ̀ɔp ทดสอบ; tót-lɔɔng ทดลอง

testament, *n.* prá-kam-pii พระคัมภีร์

testicle, *n.* lûuk-an-tá ลูกอัณฑะ

testify, *v.* bpen-pá-yaan เป็นพยาน (ascertain as a witness); yʉʉn-yan

ยืนยัน (confirm)

testimony, *n.* làk-tǎan หลักฐาน;
kam-hâi-gaan คำให้การ

text, *n.* kɔ̂ɔ-kwaam ข้อความ (words
of a speech appearing in print); jai-
kwaam ใจความ (of a printed work)

textbook, *n.* dtam-raa ตำรา; bɛ̀ɛp-
rian แบบเรียน

textile, *n.* wát-tù-sìng-tɔɔ วัตถุสิ่งทอ

texture, *n.* núa-pâa เนื้อผ้า; sìng-
tɔɔ สิ่งทอ

Thai, *n., adj.* kon-tai คนไทย (Thai
people); gìao-gàp-muang-tai เกี่ยว
กับเมืองไทย (relating to Thailand)

Thailand, *n.* bprà-têet-tai
ประเทศไทย; muang-tai เมืองไทย

than, *conj.* gwàa กว่า

thank, *v.* kɔ̀ɔp-kun ขอบคุณ; kɔ̀ɔp-
jai ขอบใจ

thankful, *adj.* rúu-sùk-kɔ̀ɔp-kun
รู้สึกขอบคุณ

Thanksgiving Day, *n.* wan-kɔ̀ɔp-
kun-prá-jâao วันขอบคุณพระเจ้า

that, *pron., adj., adv.* nân นั้น; nôon
โน่น; nán นั้น

thaw, *v.* lá-laai ละลาย

the, *art.* kam-nam-nâa-kam-naam
คำนำหน้าคำนาม

theater, *n.* roong-pâap-pa-yon
โรงภาพยนตร์ (movie); roong-lá-
kɔɔn โรงละคร (play)

theft, *n.* gaan-kà-mooi การขโมย

their, *adj.* kɔ̌ɔng-pûak-kǎo

ของพวกเขา

theirs, *pron.* kɔ̌ɔng-pûak-kǎo
ของพวกเขา

them, *adj.* lao-nán เหล่านั้น

theme, *n.* sǎa-rá-sǎm-kan
สาระสำคัญ (essential matter); hǔa-
kɔ̂ɔ หัวข้อ (topic of discussion)

themselves, *pron.* pûak-kǎo
พวกเขา

then, *adv.* dang-nán ดังนั้น (therefore, so); nai-kà-nà-nán ในขณะนั้น
(at that time)

theology, *n.* sàat-sà-ná-sàat
ศาสนศาสตร์; tee-wá-wít-ta-yaa
เทววิทยา

theory, *n.* tít-sà-dii ทฤษฎี; làk-
gaan หลักการ

therapeutic, *adj.* gìao-gàp-gaan-
rák-sǎa-rôok เกี่ยวกับการรักษาโรค

therapy, *n.* gaan-bam-bàt-rôok
การบำบัดโรค; aa-yú-ra-wêet
อายุรเวท

there, *adv.* tîi-nân ที่นั่น; dtrong-nán
ตรงนั้น

therefore, *adv.* prɔ́-chà-nán
เพราะฉะนั้น

thermometer, *n.* krûang wát un-ná-
hà-puum เครื่องวัดอุณหภูมิ

thermos, *n.* grà-dtìk-náam-rɔ́ɔn
กระติกน้ำร้อน

thesaurus, *n.* pót jà naa-nú-grom-
kam-mǔan พจนานุกรมคำเหมือน

these, *pron.* lào-níi เหล่านี้

thesis, *n.* wít-ta-yaa-ní-pon

English · Phonetic · Thai

วิทยานิพนธ์

they, *pron.* pûak-kǎo พวกเขา

thick, *adj.* nǎa หนา (not thin); túp ทึบ (dense); nǐao เหนียว (sticky)

thicken, *v.* tam-hâi-nǎa-kɛ̂n ทำให้หนาขึ้น

thickness, *n.* kwaam-nǎa ความหนา; sùan-nǎa ส่วนหนา

thief, *n.* kà-mooi ขโมย

thigh, *n.* dtôn-kǎa ต้นขา; kǎa-ɔ̀ɔn ขาอ่อน

thin, *adj.* baang บาง (for things); pɔ̌ɔm ผอม (for people or animals)

thing, *n.* sìng-kɔ̌ɔng สิ่งของ; sìng สิ่ง

think, *v.* kít คิด; núk นึก

third, *adj.* tîi-sǎam ที่สาม

third party, *n.* bùk-kon-tîi-sǎam บุคคลที่สาม; fàai-tîi-sǎam ฝ่ายที่สาม

third person, *n.* bùk-kon-tîi-sǎam บุคคลที่สาม; bùk-kon-paai-nɔ̂ɔk บุคคลภายนอก

thirst, *n.* kwaam-grà-hǎai-náam ความกระหายน้ำ

thirsty, *adj.* hǐu-náam หิวน้ำ; grà-hǎai-náam กระหายน้ำ

this, *pron., adj, adv.* níi นี้; nîi นี่

thorn, *n.* nǎam หนาม

thorny, *adj.* mii-nǎam-mâak มีหนามมาก

thorough, *adj.* dooi-dtà-lɔ̀ɔt โดยตลอด; tûa-bpai-mòt ทั่วไปหมด

those, *pron., adj.* lào-nán เหล่านั้น

though, *adv.* yàang-rai-gɔ̂ɔ-dtaam อย่างไรก็ตาม

thought, *n.* kwaam-kít ความคิด

thoughtful, *adj.* krûn-kít ครุ่นคิด (careful thought); dtrài-dtrɔɔng-dii ไตร่ตรองดี (contemplative)

thousand, *n.* nùng-pan หนึ่งพัน

thread, *n.* sên-dâai เส้นด้าย

threat, *n.* gaan-kúk-kaam การคุกคาม; gaan-kùu-kěn การขู่เข็ญ

threaten, *v.* kùu ขู่; kùu-kěn ขู่เข็ญ

three, *nm.* sǎam สาม

three dimensional, *adj.* sǎam-mí-dtì สามมิติ

three hundred, *nm.* sǎam-rɔ́ɔi สามร้อย

threshold, *n.* bprà-dtuu-taang-kâo ประตูทางเข้า

thrift, *n.* kwaam-bprà-yàt ความประหยัด

thrifty, *adj.* bprà-yàt ประหยัด; dtrà-nìi ตระหนี่

thrill, *n.* sìng-ráo-jai สิ่งเร้าใจ

thrilling, *adj.* ráo-jai เร้าใจ

thrive, *v.* dtɔ̀ɔp-dtuu เติบโต (prosper, flourish); gâao-nâa ก้าวหน้า (make steady progress)

throat, *n.* kɔɔ คอ; lam-kɔɔ ลำคอ

throne, *n.* ban-lang บัลลังก์; râat-cha-ban-lang ราชบัลลังก์

through, *prep.* pàan ผ่าน; tá-lú ทะลุ

ทะลุ; dtà-lɔ̀ɔt ตลอด

throughout, *prep.* dooi-dtà-lɔ̀ɔt
โดยตลอด

throw, *v.* kwâang ขว้าง; bpaa ปา;
yoon โยน

thrust, *v.* dan-yàang-reeng
ดันอย่างแรง

thumb, *n.* níu-hǔa-mɛ̂ɛ-muu
นิ้วหัวแม่มือ

thunder, *n.* fáa-rɔ́ɔng ฟ้าร้อง

Thursday, *n.* wan-pá-rú-hàt-sà-bɔɔ-
dii วันพฤหัสบดี

thus, *adv.* dang-níi ดังนี้; dûai-hèet-
níi ด้วยเหตุนี้

tic, *n.* aa-gaan-glâam-núa-grà-dtùk
อาการกล้ามเนื้อกระตุก

tick, *v.* kìit ขีด (make a line); tam-
krûeang-mǎai ทำเครื่องหมาย (make
a mark); sǐang-dang-dtík-dtík
เสียงดังติ๊กๆ (make a tick sound)

tick, *n.* sǐang-dang-dtík-dtík
เสียงดังติ๊กๆ (sound); krûeang-mǎai
เครื่องหมาย (mark)

ticket, *n.* dtǔa ตั๋ว (e.g. movie,
train); bai-sàng ใบสั่ง (written summons, e.g. for speeding)

tickle, *v.* tam-hâi-ják-gà-jîi
ทำให้จั๊กจี้

ticklish, *adj.* ják-gà-jîi จั๊กจี้; bâa-jîi
บ้าจี้

tidal wave, *n.* klʉ̂ʉn-yák คลื่นยักษ์

tide, *n.* grà-sɛ̌ɛ-náam กระแสน้ำ

tidy, *adj.* rîap-rɔ́ɔi เรียบร้อย

tie, *v.* pùuk ผูก; mát มัด; rát รัด

tier, *n.* tɛ̌ɛo-tîi-nâng แถวที่นั่ง (as of
seats); chán ชั้น (layer); rá-dàp
ระดับ (level)

tiger, *n.* sʉ̌a เสือ

tight, *adj.* nɛ̂n แน่น (fixed firmly);
káp-kɛ̂ɛp คับแคบ (not spacious)

tighten, *v.* tam-hâi-nɛ̂n-nǎa
ทำให้แน่นหนา; tam-hâi-rát-gum
ทำให้รัดกุม

tile, *n.* pɛ̀n-grà-bûang แผ่นกระเบื้อง

till, *n.* lín-chák-gèp-ngən ลิ้นชัก
เก็บเงิน (money till)

till, *conj.* jon-grà-tâng จนกระทั่ง

tilt, *v.* iang เอียง

tilt, *n.* gaan-iang การเอียง; pâa-
klum-rót ผ้าคลุมรถ

timber, *n.* tɔ̂n-máai ท่อนไม้

time, *n.* wee-laa เวลา (the passing
of minutes, days, etc.); sà-mǎi สมัย
(era); kráng ครั้ง (number of occurrence); chûang ช่วง (during the
period of)

time, *v.* jàp-wee-laa จับเวลา;
dtâng-wee-laa ตั้งเวลา

time-consuming, *adj.* chái-wee-
laa-mâak ใช้เวลามาก

timely, *adj.* tùuk-gaa-lá-tee-sà
ถูกกาลเทศะ; dâai-wee-laa ได้เวลา

timer, *n.* pûu-jàp-wee-laa ผู้จับเวลา
(person), krûeang jàp-wee-laa
เครื่องจับเวลา (machine)

times, *prep.* kuun-dûai คูณด้วย

timetable, *n.* dtaa-raang-wee-laa ตารางเวลา

timid, *adj.* kîi-aai ขี้อาย (shy); kîi-klàat ขี้ขลาด (cowardly)

tin, *n.* dii-bùk ดีบุก (mineral); grà-bpɔ̌ng กระป๋อง (can)

tingle, *v.* rúu-sùk-sǐao รู้สึกเสียว; rúu-sùk-bpùat-sǐao รู้สึกปวดเสียว

tinkle, *v.* gɔ̀ɔt-sǐang-dtíng-dtíng เกิดเสียงติ๋งๆ

tint, *n.* sǐi-yɔ́ɔm-pǒm สีย้อมผม (for the hair); sǐi-púun สีพื้น (basic color)

tiny, *adj.* lék-mâak เล็กมาก; jǐu จิ๋ว

tip, *n.* sùan-bplaai ส่วนปลาย (end part); yɔ̂ɔt ยอด (top); ngən-típ เงินทิป (gratuity); kɔ̂ɔ-né-nam ข้อแนะนำ (suggestion)

tirade, *n.* gaan-bpraa-sǎi-tîi-dù-dùat การปราศรัยที่ดุเดือด (long angry or violent speech)

tire, *n.* yaang-rót ยางรถ

tired, *adj.* nùai เหนื่อย; bùa-nàai เบื่อหน่าย

tireless, *n.* mâi-nèt-nùai ไม่เหน็ดเหนื่อย; mâi-bùa-nàai ไม่เบื่อหน่าย

tiresome, *adj.* nâa-bùa-nàai น่าเบื่อหน่าย; nâa-ram-kaan น่ารำคาญ

tissue, *n.* nɯ́a-yɯ̂a เนื้อเยื่อ (cells); grà-dàat-tít-chúu กระดาษทิชชู (paper)

title, *n.* chɯ̂u-rɯ̂ang ชื่อเรื่อง (of a story; heading); dtam-nɛ̀ng ตำแหน่ง (position)

toad, *n.* kaang-kók คางคก

toast, *n.* kà-nǒm-bpang-bpîng ขนมปังปิ้ง

toaster, *n.* krɯ̂ang-bpîng-kà-nǒm-bpang เครื่องปิ้งขนมปัง

tobacco, *n.* bai-yaa-sùup ใบยาสูบ; yaa-sùup ยาสูบ

today, *n.* wan-níi วันนี้

toe, *n.* níu-táao นิ้วเท้า

together, *adv.* dûai-gan ด้วยกัน; prɔ́ɔm-gan พร้อมกัน; ruam-gam รวมกัน

toil, *n.* ngaan-nàk งานหนัก (hard work); kwaam-nèt-nùai ความเหน็ดเหนื่อย (exhausting labor)

toilet, *n.* hɔ̂ng-náam ห้องน้ำ

token, *n.* krɯ̂ang-mǎai เครื่องหมาย (mark); sǎn-yá-lák สัญลักษณ์ (symbol); rǐan เหรียญ (coin)

tolerate, *n.* ɔ̀t-ton อดทน

tolerance, *n.* kwaam-ɔ̀t-ton ความอดทน; kwaam-ton-taan ความทนทาน

tolerant, *adj.* ɔ̀t-ton อดทน (forbearing); ton-taan ทนทาน (able to withstand)

toll, *n.* kâa-pàan-taang ค่าผ่านทาง

tomato, *n.* má-kɯ̌a-têet มะเขือเทศ

tomb, *n.* sùu-sǎan สุสาน; lǔm-fǎng-sòp หลุมฝังศพ

tombstone, *n.* hǐn-jaa-rúk-nâa-lǔm-fǎng-sòp หินจารึกหน้าหลุมฝังศพ

tomorrow, *n.* prûng-níi พรุ่งนี้

tone, *v.* tam-hâi-kěng-rɛɛng ทำให้แข็งแรง (e.g. tone up the body)

tone, *n.* sǐang-sǔung-dtàm เสียงสูงต่ำ (pitch)

toner, *n.* loo-chân-sà-mǎan-pǐu โลชันสมานผิว (cosmetics); mùk หมึก (ink)

tongue, *n.* lín ลิ้น; sǎm-nuan-paa-sǎa สำนวนภาษา

tonic, *n.* yaa-bam-rung-gam-lang ยาบำรุงกำลัง

tonight, *n.* kʉʉn-níi คืนนี้

tonsil, *n.* dtɔ̀m-tɔɔn-sin ต่อมทอนซิล

too, *adv.* dûai ด้วย (also); mʉ̌an-gan เหมือนกัน (either, neither); gə-ən-bpai เกินไป (excessively)

tool, *n.* krʉ̂ang-mʉʉ เครื่องมือ; ù-bpà-gɔɔn อุปกรณ์

toot, *v.* bpào-dtrɛɛ เป่าแตร (blow a horn)

tooth, *n.* fan ฟัน

toothache, *n.* aa-gaan-bpùat-fan อาการปวดฟัน

toothbrush, *n.* bprɛɛng-sǐi-fan แปรงสีฟัน

toothpaste, *n.* yaa-sǐi-fan ยาสีฟัน

toothpick, *n.* máai-jîm-fan ไม้จิ้มฟัน

tootsie, *n.* gà-təəi กะเทย

top, *v.* dtàt-sùan-bon-ɔ̀ɔk ตัดส่วนบนออก (cut off the top); sài-kâang-bon ใส่ข้างบน (put on top)

top, *n.* sùan-bon ส่วนบน; sùan-yɔ̂ɔt ส่วนยอด; kâang-bon ข้างบน; dtam-nɛ̀ng-sǔung-sùt ตำแหน่งสูงสุด

topic, *n.* hǔa-kɔ̂ɔ หัวข้อ

topping, *n.* sùan-tîi-yùu-kâang-bon ส่วนที่อยู่ข้างบน

topple, *v.* lóm-long ล้มลง (fall); kwâm-long คว่ำลง (turn upside down); kôon-lóm โค่นล้ม (fell, defeat)

torch, *n.* kóp-fai คบไฟ; fai-chǎai ไฟฉาย

tornado, *n.* paa-yú-mǔn พายุหมุน

torso, *n.* lam-dtua ลำตัว

tortoise, *n.* dtào เต่า

torture, *v.* tɔɔ-rá-maan ทรมาน

toss, *v.* yoon โยน; kwâang ขว้าง; wîang เหวี่ยง

tot, *n.* dèk-lék เด็กเล็ก

total, *n.* ruam-táng-mòt รวมทั้งหมด

totality, *n.* jam-nuan-táng-mòt จำนวนทั้งหมด

totem, *n.* rûup-sà-làk-bon-sǎo-in-dia-dɛɛng รูปสลักบนเสาอินเดียแดง

touch, *v.* sǎm-pàt สัมผัส; dtè-dtɔ̂ng แตะต้อง; jàp จับ

touch, *n.* gaan-sǎm-pàt การสัมผัส; gaan-jàp-dtɔ̂ng การจับต้อง

touching, *adj.* sà-tʉan-jai สะเทือนใจ (causing strong emotion); bprà-táp-jai ประทับใจ (impressive)

touchy, *adj.* kîi-moo-hǒo ขี้โมโห (irritable); dtɔ̂ng-rá-mát-rá-wang-

English • Phonetic • Thai

mâak ต้องระมัดระวังมาก (requiring
caution)

tough, *adj.* nĭao เหนียว (not
tender); ton-taan ทนทาน
(durable); kĕng-rɛɛng แข็งแรง
(strong)

toughen, *v.* tam-hâi-nĭao
ทำให้เหนียว; tam-hâi-ton-taan
ทำให้ทนทาน

toupee, *n.* pŏm-bplɔɔm-pûu-chaai
ผมปลอมผู้ชาย

tour, *v.* tɔ̂ng-tîao ท่องเที่ยว

tourism, *n.* gaan-tɔ̂ng-tîao
การท่องเที่ยว

tourist, *n.* nák-tɔ̂ng-tîao
นักท่องเที่ยว

tournament, *n.* gaan-kèng-kǎn
การแข่งขัน

tout, *v.* rîak-lûuk-káa เรียกลูกค้า
(solicit customers)

tout, *n.* kon-rîak-lûuk-káa
คนเรียกลูกค้า

tow, *v.* lâak ลาก; juung จูง; pûang
พ่วง; dung ดึง

toward, *prep.* bpai-yang ไปยัง;
bpai-tǔng ไปถึง; gìao-gàp เกี่ยวกับ

towel, *n.* pâa-chét-dtua ผ้าเช็ดตัว

tower, *n.* hɔ̌ɔ-sǔung หอสูง; hɔ̌ɔ-
kɔɔi หอคอย

town, *n.* muang เมือง (city); kèet-
chum-chon เขตชุมชน (population
center)

toxic, *adj.* bpen-pít เป็นพิษ

toxin, *n.* pít พิษ

toy, *n.* kɔ̌ɔng-lên ของเล่น

trace, *v.* dtaam-rɔɔi ตามรอย

trace, *n.* rɔ̂ng-rɔɔi ร่องรอย

track, *v.* dùt-dtaam ติดตาม (follow)

track, *n.* rɔɔi-táao รอยท้าว (footprint); taang-dəən ทางเดิน (course
for walking); sên-taang เส้นทาง
(way, rail, road); lûu-kèng ลู่แข่ง
(course for racing)

tractor, *n.* krûang-trɛ́ɛk-dtəə
เครื่องแทรกเตอร์; krûang-lâak
เครื่องลาก

trade, *v.* káa-kǎai ค้าขาย (buy and
sell; do business); lɛ̂ɛk-bplìan
แลกเปลี่ยน (exchange)

trade, *n.* gaan-káa การค้า; gaan-
lɛ̂ɛk-bplìan การแลกเปลี่ยน

trademark, *n.* krûang-mǎai-gaan-
káa เครื่องหมายการค้า

tradition, *n.* tam-niam ธรรมเนียม;
bprà-pee-nii ประเพณี

traditional, *adj.* gìao-gàp-bprà-pee-
nii เกี่ยวกับประเพณี

traffic, *n.* gaan-jà-raa-jɔɔn
การจราจร

tragedy, *n.* lá-kɔɔn-sòok ละครโศก
(play); rûang-sòok เรื่องโศก (sad
story); pai-pí-bàt ภัยพิบัติ (calamity)

tragic, *adj.* gìao-gàp-rûang-sòok
เกี่ยวกับเรื่องโศก; gìao-gàp-pai-pí-
bàt เกี่ยวกับภัยพิบัติ

trail, *n.* rɔɔi รอย; rɔɔi-taang

รอยทาง; sùan-hǎang ส่วนหาง

trailer, *n.* pûu-lâak ผู้ลาก; rót-pûang รถพ่วง; krûang-pûang เครื่องพ่วง

train, *v.* fùk ฝึก (coach); òp-rom อบรม (give specialized instructions)

train, *n.* rót-fai รถไฟ

training, *n.* gaan-fùk-hàt การฝึกหัด; gaan-òp-rom การอบรม

traitor, *n.* pûu-tɔɔ-ra-yót ผู้ทรยศ; pûu-hàk-lǎng ผู้หักหลัง

tram, *n.* rót-raang รถราง

tramp, *n.* kon-jɔɔn-jàt คนจรจัด (vagrant); gaan-dəən-taang-dûai-táao การเดินทางด้วยเท้า (walking trip)

trance, *n.* kwaam-mun-ngong ความมึนงง

tranquilize, *v.* tam-hâi-sà-ngòp ทำให้สงบ; glòm-bprà-sàat กล่อมประสาท

tranquilizer, *n.* yaa-glòm-bprà-sàat ยากล่อมประสาท

tranquility, *n.* kwaam-sà-ngòp ความสงบ; kwaam-ngîap ความเงียบ

transact, *v.* dùt-dtɔɔ ติดต่อ (contact), jàt-gaan จัดการ (manage); tam-gaan-káa ทำการค้า (in business)

transaction, *n.* gaan-dùt-dtɔɔ การติดต่อ; gaan jàt-gaan การจัดการ; gaan-káa-tú-rá-gìt การค้าธุรกิจ

transcend, *v.* yùu-nǔa อยู่เหนือ; mii-chai มีชัย

transcribe, *v.* kát คัด (write); tɔɔt-kwaam ถอดความ (make a full written copy of); bplɛɛ แปล (translate or transliterate)

transcript, *n.* sǎm-nao สำเนา (printed copy); bai-ráp-rɔɔng-pǒn-gaan-sùk-sǎa ใบรับรองผลการศึกษา (school record)

transfer, *v.* yáai ย้าย (move); klûan-yáai เคลื่อนย้าย (convey, move); bplìan เปลี่ยน (change); oon โอน (e.g. money, ownership)

transform, *v.* bplìan-rûup เปลี่ยนรูป (change the nature or condition of); bplɛɛng-râang แปลงร่าง (change the appearance)

transfuse, *v.* tàai-lûat ถ่ายเลือด; tàai-tee ถ่ายเท; yôok-yáai โยกย้าย

transistor, *n.* wít-ta-yú-tran-sìt-sa-dtɔɔ วิทยุทรานซิสเตอร์

transit, *v.* pàan-taang ผ่านทาง

transit, *n.* gaan-pàan-taang การผ่านทาง

transition, *n.* gaan-pàan การผ่าน (passing); gaan-plìan-bplɛɛng การเปลี่ยนแปลง (change)

transitory, *adj.* mâi-tǎa-wɔɔn ไม่ถาวร; mâi-yâng-yuun ไม่ยั่งยืน; chûa-kraao ชั่วคราว

translate, *v.* bplɛɛ แปล

translation, *n.* gaan-bplɛɛ การแปล

translator, *n.* pûu-bplɛɛ ผู้แปล; nák-bplɛɛ นักแปล

transmission, *n.* gaan-sòng-pàan การส่งผ่าน; gaan-prêe-chúa การแพร่เชื้อ; gaan-grà-jaai การกระจาย

transmit, *v.* sòng-pàan ส่งผ่าน (send through); prêe-chúa แพร่เชื้อ (pass on, e.g. germ); grà-jaai กระจาย (spread); tàai-tɔ̂ɔt ถ่ายทอด (broadcast); sòng-sǎn-yaan ส่งสัญญาณ (send signal)

transparent, *adj.* bpròong-sɛ̌ɛng โปร่งแสง; chát-jêeng ชัดแจ้ง

transplant, *v.* yáai-tîi-bplùuk ย้ายที่ปลูก; yáai-tîi ย้ายที่

transport, *v.* kǒn-sòng ขนส่ง; nam-sòng นำส่ง; kǒn-yáai ขนย้าย

transportation, *n.* gaan-kǒn-sòng การขนส่ง

transvestite, *n.* gà-təəi กะเทย

trap, *v.* dàk ดัก

trap, *n.* gàp-dàk กับดัก

trash, *n.* kà-yà ขยะ; kɔ̌ɔng-sǐa ของเสีย

trauma, *n.* gaan-jèp-bpùat การเจ็บปวด; kwaam-chɔ̂ɔk-chám ความชอกช้ำ

travel, *v.* dəən-taang เดินทาง

travel, *n.* gaan-dəən-taang การเดินทาง; gaan-tôong-tîao การท่องเที่ยว

traveler, *n.* nák-dəən-taang นักเดินทาง

tray, *n.* tàat ถาด; jaan-rɔɔng จานรอง

treachery, *n.* gaan-tɔɔ-ra-yót การทรยศ; gaan-hàk-lǎng การหักหลัง

tread, *v.* yâm ย่ำ; yìap เหยียบ

treason, *n.* gaan-gà-bòt การกบฏ; gaan-tɔɔ-ra-yót การทรยศ

treasure, *n.* sáp-sǒm-bàt ทรัพย์สมบัติ

treasurer, *n.* hěe-ran-yík เหรัญญิก; pûu-rák-sǎa-sáp-sǒm-bàt ผู้รักษาทรัพย์สมบัติ

treasury, *n.* klang-sǒm-bàt คลังสมบัติ; sáp-sǒm-bàt ทรัพย์สมบัติ

treat, *v.* grà-tam-gàp กระทำกับ (act, behave); rák-sǎa รักษา (care, cure); jàt-gaan จัดการ (provide); líang เลี้ยง (e.g. somebody a meal)

treatment, *n.* gaan-rák-sǎa การรักษา

treaty, *n.* sǒn-tì-sǎn-yaa สนธิสัญญา; kɔ̂ɔ-dtòk-long ข้อตกลง

tree, *n.* dtôn-máai ต้นไม้; wát-sà-dù-máai วัสดุไม้

trek, *n.* gaan-dəən-taang-tîi-lam-bàak การเดินทางที่ลำบาก

tremble, *v.* sàn-wǎi สั่นไหว

tremendous, *adj.* yài-dtoo-mâak ใหญ่โตมาก; má-hù-maa มหึมา; dii-yîam ดีเยี่ยม

tremor, *n.* gaan-sàn-tao-kɔ̌ɔng-

râang-gaai การสั่นเทาของร่างกาย;
gaan-sàn-sà-tuan การสั่นสะเทือน

trench, n. kuu-rá-baai คูระบาย; sà-nǎam-plɔ̂ สนามเพลาะ

trend, n. nɛɛo-nóom แนวโน้ม (tendency); tít-taang ทิศทาง (direction); bɛ̀ɛp-sà-mǎi-ní-yom แบบสมัยนิยม (current style)

trespass, v. bùk-rúk บุกรุก; lûang-lám ล่วงล้ำ

trial, n. gaan-tót-lɔɔng การทดลอง (testing); gaan-pí-jaa-rá-naa-ká-dii การพิจารณาคดี (in a court of law)

triangle, n. sǎm-lìam สามเหลี่ยม

tribe, n. pào เผ่า

tribunal, n. sǎan-yú-dtì-tam ศาลยุติธรรม

tribute, n. kɔ̌ɔng-kwǎn ของขวัญ (gift); sùai ส่วย (by one ruler or nation to another); gaan-sǎn-sɔ̌ɔn การสรรเสริญ (acknowledgment of respect, or admiration)

trick, v. lɔ̂ɔk-lɔ̂ɔ หลอกล่อ

trick, n. ù-baai อุบาย; gon-ù-baai กลอุบาย; lêe-lìam เล่ห์เหลี่ยม

tricky, adj. mii-lêe-lìam มีเล่ห์เหลี่ยม; mii-lûuk-maai มีลูกไม้

trifle, n. rûang-jùk-jìk เรื่องจุกจิก; rûang-lék-nɔ́ɔi เรื่องเล็กน้อย

trigger, n. gai-bpuun ไกปืน

trill, n. sǐang-sàn เสียงสั่น; sǐang-rua เสียงรัว

trim, v. dtàt ตัด (remove by cutting)

trim, adj. pɔ̌ɔm-baang ผอมบาง (slim); rîap-rɔ́ɔi เรียบร้อย (neat)

trio, n. glùm-sǎam-kon กลุ่มสามคน

trip, n. gaan-dəən-taang การเดินทาง

tripe, n. krûang-nai เครื่องใน; sìng-lěeo-lǎi สิ่งเหลวไหล

triple, adj. sǎam-tâo สามเท่า

triplet, n. fɛ̀ɛt-sǎam-kon แฝดสามคน

tripod, n. tîi-dtâng-sǎam-kǎa ที่ตั้งสามขา

trite, adj. sám-sâak ซ้ำซาก; nâa-bùa-nàai น่าเบื่อหน่าย

triumph, n. chai-chá-ná ชัยชนะ

trivial, adj. mâi-sǎm-kan ไม่สำคัญ; yúm-yîm หยุมหยิม

trolley, n. rót-kěn รถเข็น; rót-lâak รถลาก

troop, n. gɔɔng-tá-hǎan กองทหาร; gɔɔng-gam-lang กองกำลัง

trophy, n. kɔ̌ɔng-raang-wan ของรางวัล; kɔ̌ɔng-tîi-rá-lúk ของที่ระลึก

tropical, adj. gìao-gàp-kèet-rɔ́ɔn เกี่ยวกับเขตร้อน

tropic, n. kèet-rɔ́ɔn เขตร้อน

tropics, n. bɔɔ-rí-ween kèet rɔ́ɔn บริเวณเขตร้อน

trot, v. wîng-yɔ̂-yɔ̂ วิ่งเหยาะๆ; wîng-chá-chá วิ่งช้าๆ

trouble, n. kwaam yûng-yâak ความยุ่งยาก; kwaam-lam-bàak ความลำบาก; gaan-róp-guan

การรบกวน

troublesome, *adj.* tam-hâi-yûng-yâak ทำให้ยุ่งยาก; nâa-ram-kaan น่ารำคาญ

trough, *n.* raang-náam-dùùm รางน้ำดื่ม (for drinking); lǔm-bɔ̀ɔ หลุมบ่อ (low spot)

trousers, *n.* gaang-geeng กางเกง; gaang-geeng-kǎa-yaao กางเกงขายาว

trout, *n.* bplaa-tráo ปลาเทราท์

truce, *n.* gaan-yùt-pák การหยุดพัก (temporary cessation)

truck, *n.* rót-ban-túk รถบรรทุก

true, *adj.* jing จริง (real); mâi-bplɔɔm ไม่ปลอม (not fake); nɛ̂ɛ-nɔɔn แน่นอน (certain); tùuk ถูก (not false)

truly, *adv.* yàang-tɛ́ɛ-jing อย่างแท้จริง; yàang-tùuk-dtɔ̂ng อย่างถูกต้อง; dooi-jai-jing โดยใจจริง

trumpet, *n.* dtrɛɛ แตร; sǐang-dtrɛɛ เสียงแตร

trunk, *n.* lam-dtôn ลำต้น (of a tree); lam-dtua ลำตัว (body); tîi-gèp-kɔ̌ɔng-táai-rót ที่เก็บของท้ายรถ (of a car); nguang-cháang งวงช้าง (of an elephant)

trust, *v.* chûa-tùu เชื่อถือ (expect with assurance); wái-jai ไว้ใจ (grant discretion)

trust, *n.* kwaam-chûa-tùu ความเชื่อถือ; kwaam-wái-waang-jai

ความไว้วางใจ; sǐn-chûa สินเชื่อ (credit); trát, trás ทรัสต์ (legal entity for holding assets)

trustworthy, *adj.* nâa-wái-waang-jai น่าไว้วางใจ; chûa-tùu-dâai เชื่อถือได้

truth, *n.* kwaam-jing ความจริง; kwaam-tùuk-dtɔ̂ng ความถูกต้อง

try, *v.* pá-yaa-yaam พยายาม (endeavor); tót-lɔɔng ทดลอง (test); lɔɔng ลอง (e.g. try something on)

trying, *adj.* dûu ดื้อ (troubling, e.g. child); lǔa-ton เหลือทน (difficult to bear)

tub, *n.* àang อ่าง

tube, *n.* lɔ̀ɔt หลอด (container, e.g. for toothpaste); tɔ̂ɔ ท่อ (hollow cylinder); sǎai-yaang สายยาง (plastic tube, e.g. for medical use)

tuberculosis, *n.* wan-na-rôok วัณโรค

tuck, *v.* páp พับ (fold); sài-kâang-nai ใส่ข้างใน (put inside)

Tuesday, *n.* wan-ang-kaan วันอังคาร

tuft, *n.* bpɔɔi ปอย; bpui ปุย

tug, *v.* dung ดึง; lâak ลาก; yoong โยง; pûang พ่วง

tugboat, *n.* rua-lâak เรือลาก; rua-pûang เรือพ่วง

tuition, *n.* kâa-rian ค่าเรียน; kâa-sɔ̌ɔn ค่าสอน

tulip, *n.* dtôn-tiu-lìp ต้นทิวลิป

tummy, *n.* tɔ́ɔng ท้อง; chɔ̂ng-tɔ́ɔng ช่องท้อง

tumor, *n.* núa-ngɔ̂ɔk เนื้องอก; gɔ̂ɔn-buam ก้อนบวม

tuna, *n.* bplaa-tuu-nâa ปลาทูน่า

tune, *v.* bpràp ปรับ (adjust)

tune, *n.* tam-nɔɔng-pleeng ทำนองเพลง (melody); kwaam-sɔ̀ɔt-klɔ́ɔng ความสอดคล้อง (harmony)

tunnel, *n.* ù-moong อุโมงค์

turbulence, *n.* kwaam-wûn-waai ความวุ่นวาย (disorder); kwaam-goo-laa-hǒn ความโกลาหล (confusion); lom-rɛɛng-jàt ลมแรงจัด (strong wind)

turbulent, *adj.* wûn-waai วุ่นวาย; goo-laa-hǒn โกลาหล

turf, *n.* sà-nǎam-yâa สนามหญ้า (natural); yâa-tiam หญ้าเทียม (artificial)

turkey, *n.* gài-nguang ไก่งวง

turmoil, *n.* kwaam-yûng-yâak ความยุ่งยาก; kwaam-yûng-yǝ̌ǝng ความยุ่งเหยิง

turn, *v.* mǔn หมุน (spin); hǎn หัน (look back); líao เลี้ยว (e.g. a car while driving); bplìan เปลี่ยน (change)

turn, *n.* dtaa ตา (e.g. my turn)

turnip, *n.* hǔa pàk gàat หัวผักกาด

turnover, *n.* gaan-plík-glàp การพลิกกลับ; gaan-kwâm การคว่ำ

turntable, *n.* jaan-mǔn จานหมุน

turquoise, *n.* rɛ̂ɛ-sǐi-nám-ngǝn แร่สีน้ำเงิน

turtle, *n.* dtào เต่า

tusk, *n.* ngaa-cháang งาช้าง (elephant); kǐao-yaao เขี้ยวยาว (long tooth)

tutor, *n.* kruu-sɔ̌ɔn ครูสอน; kruu-pí-sèet ครูพิเศษ

tuxedo, *n.* chút-ták-si-dôo ชุดทักซิโด้

tweezers, *n.* kiim-nìip คีมหนีบ; nɛ̀ɛp แหนบ

twelve, *nm.* sìp-sɔ̌ɔng สิบสอง

twenty, *nm.* yîi-sìp ยี่สิบ

twice, *adv.* sɔ̌ɔng-kráng สองครั้ง; sɔ̌ɔng-tâo สองเท่า

twig, *n.* gìng-máai กิ่งไม้; kà-nɛ̌ɛng แขนง

twilight, *n.* sɛ̌ɛng aa-tít-dtɔɔn-yen แสงอาทิตย์ตอนเย็น

twin, *n.* fǎa-fɛ̀ɛt ฝาแฝด

twin bed, *n.* dtiang-dìao-lék เตียงเดี่ยวเล็ก

twine, *v.* fan-bpen-gliao พันเป็นเกลียว (intertwine); bìt บิด (twist); kɔ̀t ขด (coil)

twinkle, *v.* sòng-sɛ̌ɛng-wɛɛo-wáp ส่องแสงแวววับ (shine); grà-príp-dtaa กระพริบตา (blink); kà-yìp-dtaa ขยิบตา (wink)

twist, *v.* bìt บิด (turn so as to face another direction); bìt-bpen-gliao

บิดเป็นเกลียว (wind together; coil); ngɔɔ งอ (bend); bìt-buan บิดเบือน (distort)

two, nm. sɔ̌ɔng สอง

two-handed, adj. tà-nàt-táng-sɔ̌ɔng-muu ถนัดทั้งสองมือ (ambidextrous)

two hundred, nm. sɔ̌ɔng-rɔ́ɔi สองร้อย

tycoon, n. nák-tú-rá-gìt-tîi-râm-ruai นักธุรกิจที่ร่ำรวย

type, v. pim พิมพ์

type, n. rûup-bèɛp รูปแบบ (traits or characteristics); chá-nít ชนิด (kind); bprà-pêet ประเภท (class)

typewriter, n. krûang-pim-dìit เครื่องพิมพ์ดีด; kon-pim-dìit คนพิมพ์ดีด

typhoon, n. paa-yú-dtâi-fùn พายุใต้ฝุ่น

typical, adj. bpen-dtua-yàang เป็นตัวอย่าง; bpen-bèɛp-chà-bàp เป็นแบบฉบับ

typing, n. gaan-pim การพิมพ์

typist, n. pá-nák-ngaan-pim-dìit พนักงานพิมพ์ดีด; pûu-pim-dìit ผู้พิมพ์ดีด

tyranny, n. gaan-bpòk-krɔɔng-bèɛp-pà-dèt-gaan การปกครองแบบเผด็จการ

tyrant, n. pûu-bpòk-krɔɔng-bèɛp-pà-dèt-gaan ผู้ปกครองแบบเผด็จการ

U

ugly, adj. nâa-glìat น่าเกลียด

ulcer, n. plɛ̌ɛ-bpùai แผลเปื่อย (as on the skin); plɛ̌ɛ-pú-pɔɔng แผลพุพอง (with inflammation or pus); plɛ̌ɛ-nai-grà-pɔ́ แผลใน กระเพาะ (stomach ulcer)

ultimate, adj. sùt-táai สุดท้าย (the last); tîi-sùt ที่สุด (most extreme); táng-mòt ทั้งหมด (total)

ultraviolet rays, n. rang-sǐi-wai-oo-lét รังสีอุลตราไวโอเลต

unable, adj. mâi-sǎa-mâat ไม่สามารถ; rái-kwaam-sǎa-mâat ไร้ความสามารถ

unabridged, adj. mâi-dtàt-dtɔɔn ไม่ตัดตอน

unanimous, adj. bpen-èek-gà-chǎn เป็นเอกฉันท์

unarmed, adj. mâi-mii-aa-wút ไม่มีอาวุธ

unavoidable, adj. lìik-lîang-mâi-dâai หลีกเลี่ยงไม่ได้

unaware, adj. mâi-rúu-dtua ไม่รู้ตัว (not aware); mâi-rúu ไม่รู้ (not knowing); mâi-kâat-kít-maa-gɔ̀ɔn ไม่คาดคิดมาก่อน (not expected)

unbalanced, adj. mâi-sǒm-dun ไม่สมดุล

unbearable, adj. ton-mâi-dâai ทนไม่ได้

unbelievable, adj. mâi-nâa-chûa

ไม่น่าเชื่อ

uncertain, *adj.* mâi-nɛ̂ɛ-nɔɔn
ไม่แน่นอน (not certain); mâi-nɛ̂ɛ-
jai ไม่แน่ใจ (not sure)

unchanged, *adj.* mâi-bpl̀ian-
bpleeng ไม่เปลี่ยนแปลง

uncivilized, *adj.* bpàa-tùan ป่าเถื่อน
(barbarous); mâi-jà-rəən ไม่เจริญ
(not civilized)

uncle, *n.* lung ลุง (father or mother's older brother); aa อา (father's
younger brother or sister); náa น้า
(mother's younger brother or sister)

uncomfortable, *adj.* mâi-sà-baai
ไม่สบาย (not comfortable); mâi-sà-
baai-jai ไม่สบายใจ (worried); rá-
kaai-kuang ระคายเคือง (irritated);
ùt-àt อึดอัด (uneasy)

uncommon, *adj.* mâi-bpòk-gà-dtì
ไม่ปกติ; mâi-tam-má-daa
ไม่ธรรมดา

unconditional, *adj.* mâi-mii-ngûan-
kǎi ไม่มีเงื่อนไข

unconscious, *adj.* mâi-dâai-sà-dtì
ไม่ได้สติ; sà-lòp สลบ

unconstitutional, *adj.* mâi-bpen-
bpai-dtaam-rát-tà-tam-ma-nuun
ไม่เป็นไปตามรัฐธรรมนูญ

uncontrollable, *adj.* kûap-kum-
mâi-dâai ควบคุมไม่ได้

uncover, *v.* bpə̀ət-pə̌əi เปิดเผย,
bpə̀ət-bpoong เปิดโปง

undamaged, *adj.* mâi-dâai-ráp-

kwaam-sǐa-hǎai ไม่ได้รับความ
เสียหาย

undecided, *adj.* yang-mâi-dtàt-sǐn-
jai ยังไม่ตัดสินใจ

undefeatable, *adj.* ao-chá-ná-mâi-
dâai เอาชนะไม่ได้

under, *prep.* dtâai ใต้; paai-dtâai
ภายใต้; kâang-lâang ข้างล่าง

undercover, *adj.* sǎai-láp สายลับ;
dtam-rùat-nɔ̂ɔk-krûang-bὲɛp
ตำรวจนอกเครื่องแบบ

undercut, *v.* dtàt-raa-kaa ตัดราคา;
dtàt-sùan-lâang ตัดส่วนล่าง; rɔ̂
เซาะ

underdeveloped, *n.* dɔ̂ɔi-pát-tá-
naa ด้อยพัฒนา

underdog, *n.* pûu-tîi-bpen-bîa-
lâang ผู้ที่เป็นเบี้ยล่าง

underestimate, *v.* bprà-məən-kâa-
dtàm-bpai ประเมินค่าต่ำไป

undergo, *v.* bprà-sòp ประสบ
(experience); bpàan ผ่าน (put
through); òt-ton อดทน (endure)

undergraduate, *n.* nák-sùk-sǎa-
bpà-rin-yaa-dtrii นักศึกษาปริญญาตรี

underground, *adv.* dtâai-din ใต้ดิน
(beneath the ground); mâi-bprə̀ət-
pə̌əi ไม่เปิดเผย (not openly)

underline, *v.* kìit-sên-dtâai
ขีดเส้นใต้

underlying, *adj.* yùu-kâang-dtâai
อยู่ข้างใต้ (lying beneath something
else); bpen-râak-tǎan เป็นรากฐาน

(basic, fundamental); fěɛng-yùu แฝงอยู่ (hidden)

undermine, v. ɛ̀ɛp-joom-dtii แอบโจมตี (attack by hidden means); tam-hâi-ɔ̀ɔn-long ทำให้อ่อนลง (weaken)

underneath, adv., prep. kâang-dtâai ข้างใต้; kâang-lâang ข้างล่าง

underpants, n. gaang-geeng-chán-nai กางเกงชั้นใน

underpay, v. jàai-nɔ́ɔi-gwàa-tîi-kuan จ่ายน้อยกว่าที่ควร

underprivileged, adj. mâi-dâai-sìt-tíi-sǒm-kuan-dâai ไม่ได้สิทธิที่สมควรได้

undersea, adj. dtâai-tá-lee ใต้ทะเล

undershirt, n. sɯ̂a-glâam เสื้อกล้าม

understand, v. kâo-jai เข้าใจ

understandable, adj. sǎa-mâat-kâo-jai-dâai สามารถเข้าใจได้

undertake, v. pá-yaa-yaam-tam พยายามทำ (attempt); dam-nəən-gaan ดำเนินการ (perform); ráp-rɔɔng รับรอง (guarantee); sǎn-yaa สัญญา (promise); ráp-pìt-chɔ̂ɔp รับผิดชอบ (take charge or responsibility)

undertaking, n. gaan-ngaan การงาน (task); kwaam-ráp-pìt-chɔ̂ɔp ความรับผิดชอบ (responsibility)

underwear, n. chút-chán-nai ชุดชั้นใน

underworld, n. yom-má-lôok ยมโลก (world of the dead); ná-rók นรก (hell)

underwrite, v. long-chɯ̂u-kâang-dtâai ลงชื่อข้างใต้ (write one's name at the end); ráp-bprà-gan รับประกัน (insure)

undeveloped, adj. dɔ̂ɔi-pát-ta-naa ด้อยพัฒนา; mâi-jà-rəən ไม่เจริญ

undo, v. bplìan-glàp เปลี่ยนกลับ (reverse); lóp ลบ (erase); kà-jàt ขจัด (get rid of); yók-lə̂ək ยกเลิก (cancel); bplòt ปลด (untie, loosen)

undone, adj. mâi-dâai-grà-tam ไม่ได้กระทำ (not done); mâi-sǒm-buun ไม่สมบูรณ์ (not complete)

undress, v. tɔ̀ɔt-sɯ̂a-pâa ถอดเสื้อผ้า; bplɯ̂ang-pâa เปลื้องผ้า

uneasy, adj. grà-sàp-grà-sàai กระสับกระส่าย; mâi-sà-baai ไม่สบาย

unemployed, adj. dtòk-ngaan ตกงาน; mâi-mii-ngaan-tam ไม่มีงานทำ

unemployment, n. gaan-dtòk-ngaan การตกงาน; gaan-mâi-mii-ngaan-tam การไม่มีงานทำ

unequal, adj. mâi-tâo-tiam ไม่เท่าเทียม; mâi-tâo-gan ไม่เท่ากัน

uneven, adj. mâi-rîap ไม่เรียบ; krù-krà ขรุขระ

unexpected, adj. nɯ́k-mâi-tǔng นึกไม่ถึง; bprà-làat-jai ประหลาดใจ; mâi-kâat-kít ไม่คาดคิด

unfair, *adj.* mâi-yú-dtì-tam
ไม่ยุติธรรม

unfit, *adj.* mâi-mɔ̀-sǒm ไม่เหมาะสม
(not suitable); mâi-mii-kun-ná-sǒm-
bàt ไม่มีคุณสมบัติ (not qualified)

unfold, *v.* klîi คลี่ (open out); pɛ̀ɛ
แผ่ (spread); gaang กาง (open);
bpɔ̀ɔt-bpoong เปิดโปง (reveal)

unforgettable, *adj.* mâi-àat-luum-
dâai ไม่อาจลืมได้; luum-mâi-dâai
ลืมไม่ได้

unforgivable, *adj.* hâi-à-pai-mâi-
dâai ให้อภัยไม่ได้

unfortunate, *adj.* chôok-mâi-dii
โชคไม่ดี

unfortunately, *adv.* chôok-mâi-dii
โชคไม่ดี

unfurnished, *adj.* mâi-mii-krûang-
ruan ไม่มีเครื่องเรือน

unhappy, *adj.* mâi-mii-kwaam-sùk
ไม่มีความสุข; sâo เศร้า

unharmed, *adj.* mâi-bpen-an-dtà-
raai ไม่เป็นอันตราย

unhealthy, *adj.* sùk-kà-pâap-mâi-dii
สุขภาพไม่ดี

uniform, *n.* krûang-bɛ̀ɛp เครื่องแบบ

unify, *v.* ruam-gan รวมกัน

unimportant, *adj.* mâi-sǎm-kan
ไม่สำคัญ

unintelligible, *adj.* mâi-chà-làat
ไม่ฉลาด

uninteresting, *adj.* mâi-nâa-sǒn-jai
ไม่น่าสนใจ (not interesting); nâa-
bùa-nàai น่าเบื่อหน่าย (boring)

union, *n.* gaan-ruam-gan
การรวมกัน (being united); kwaam-
sǎa-mák-kii ความสามัคคี
(harmony); sà-hà-pâap สหภาพ
(e.g. labor union)

unique, *adj.* mii-èek-gà-lák
มีเอกลักษณ์

unisex, *adj.* mâi-bɛ̀ng-pêet
ไม่แบ่งเพศ

unit, *n.* nùai หน่วย (individual
regarded as a constituent of a
whole); glùm กลุ่ม (group);
gɔɔng-gam-lang กองกำลัง (e.g. in
military); nùai-gìt หน่วยกิต (academic course)

unite, *v.* ruam-gan รวมกัน

United Nations, *n.* sà-hà-bprà-
chaa-châat สหประชาชาติ

United States of America, *n.* sà-
hà-rát-a-mee-ri-gaa สหรัฐอเมริกา

unity, *n.* kwaam-sǎa-mák-kii
ความสามัคคี; gaan-ruam-gan
การรวมกัน

universal, *adj.* sǎa-gon สากล;
gìao-gàp-jàk-grà-waan เกี่ยวกับ
จักรวาล (of the universe); tûa-bpai
ทั่วไป (general, broad)

universe, *n.* jàk-grà-waan จักรวาล

university, *n.* ma-hǎa-wít-ta-yaa-
lai มหาวิทยาลัย

unjust, *adj.* mâi-yú-dtì-tam
ไม่ยุติธรรม

unkind, *adj.* mâi-bpraa-nii ไม่ปรานี;
mâi-mêet-dtaa ไม่เมตตา

English • Phonetic • Thai

unknown, *adj.* mâi-rúu ไม่รู้; mâi-rúu-jàk ไม่รู้จัก; mâi-mii-chûu-sĭang ไม่มีชื่อเสียง; mâi-kâo-jai ไม่เข้าใจ; lúk-láp ลึกลับ

unlawful, *adj.* pìt-gòt-măai ผิดกฎหมาย

unless, *conj.* nɔ́ɔk-jàak นอกจาก; yók-wén ยกเว้น; jon-gwàa จนกว่า; wén-sĭa-dtɛ̀ɛ-wâa เว้นเสียแต่ว่า

unlike, *adj.* mâi-mŭan-gan ไม่เหมือนกัน; dtɛ̀ɛk-dtàang แตกต่าง

unlikely, *adj.* mâi-nâa-bpen-bpai-dâai ไม่น่าเป็นไปได้; mâi-nâa ไม่น่า

unlimited, *adj.* mâi-jam-gàt ไม่จำกัด

unload, *v.* ao-long เอาลง; kŏn-long ขนลง

unlock, *v.* kăi-gun-jee ไขกุญแจ (undo a lock); bplɔ̀i-ɔ̀ɔk ปล่อยออก (set free, release); bpə̀ət-ɔ̀ɔk เปิดออก (open)

unlucky, *adj.* chôok-ráai โชคร้าย; chôok-mâi-dii โชคไม่ดี

unnatural, *adj.* mâi-bpen-bpai-dtaam-tam-ma-châat ไม่เป็นธรรมชาติ (not natural); tiam เทียม (not real)

unnecessary, *adj.* mâi-jam-bpen ไม่จำเป็น

unpack, *v.* gɛ̀ɛ-hɔ̀ɔ แก้ห่อ

unpaid, *adj.* mâi-dâai-cham-rá ไม่ได้ชำระ; mâi-dâai-ráp-kâa-dtɔ̀ɔp-tɛɛn ไม่ได้รับค่าตอบแทน

unpopular, *adj.* mâi-ní-yom-gan ไม่นิยมกัน; mâi-prɛ̂ɛ-lăai ไม่แพร่หลาย

unravel, *v.* gɛ̀ɛ แก้; bplòt ปลด; bplɔ̀i ปล่อย

unreal, *adj.* mâi-jing ไม่จริง

unrealistic, *adj.* mâi-sŏm-jing ไม่สมจริง; mâi-tɛ́ɛ-jing ไม่แท้จริง

unreasonable, *adj.* rái-hèet-pŏn ไร้เหตุผล (not governed by reason); gəən-bpai เกินไป (exceeding limits)

unrest, *n.* kwaam-mâi-sà-ngòp ความไม่สงบ; kwaam-wûn-waai ความวุ่นวาย

unruly, *adj.* dûu-rán ดื้อรั้น

unsafe, *adj.* mâi-bplɔ̀ɔt-pai ไม่ปลอดภัย; an-dtà-raai อันตราย

unselfish, *adj.* mâi-hěn-gɛ̀ɛ-dtua ไม่เห็นแก่ตัว

unstable, *adj.* mâi-mân-kong ไม่มั่นคง; mâi-nɛ̂ɛ-nɔɔn ไม่แน่นอน

untie, *v.* gɛ̀ɛ-mát แก้มัด (undo or loosen); bplɔ̀i ปล่อย (free, release)

until, *prep.* jon-grà-tâng จนกระทั่ง; jon-tǔng จนถึง

untrue, *adj.* mâi-jing ไม่จริง; mâi-sûu-sàt ไม่ซื่อสัตย์

unusual, *adj.* pìt-tam-ma-daa ผิดธรรมดา

unwilling, *adj.* mâi-dtem-jai ไม่เต็มใจ (not willing, reluctant); dtɔ̀ɔ-dtâan ต่อต้าน (resistant)

unworthy, *adj.* mâi-kúu-kuan ไม่คู่ควร; mâi-sŏm-kuan ไม่สมควร;

mâi-mii-kun-kâa ไม่มีคุณค่า

up, *adv.* kŭn ขึ้น; yùu-nŭa อยู่เหนือ; dtâng-dtrong ตั้งตรง; lúk-kŭn ลุกขึ้น

upbringing, *n.* gaan-líang-duu การเลี้ยงดู; gaan-òp-rom-sàng-sɔ̌ɔn การอบรมสั่งสอน

update, *v.* tam-hâi-tan-sà-mǎi ทำให้ทันสมัย (make modern); sài-kɔ̂ɔ-muun-mài-mài ใส่ข้อมูลใหม่ๆ (the data)

update, *n.* kɔ̂ɔ-muun-mài ข้อมูลใหม่

upgrade, *v.* yôk-rá-dàp ยกระดับ; lɯ̂an-kŭn เลื่อนขึ้น

upheaval, *n.* gaan-yôk-kŭn การยกขึ้น; gaan-yôk-rá-dàp-kŭn การกระดับขึ้น

uphold, *v.* yôk-kŭn ยกขึ้น (raise); sà-nàp-sà-nǔn สนับสนุน (support); yɯɯn-yàt ยืนหยัด (affirm); bpɔ̂ng-gan ป้องกัน (prevent)

upon, *prep.* bon บน (on); nǔa เหนือ (above); nai-oo-gàat ในโอกาส (in the occasion); nai-wee-laa ในเวลา (at the time)

upper, *adj.* nǔa-gwàa เหนือกว่า; sǔung-gwàa สูงกว่า

upper-class, *n.* sǎng-kom-chán-sǔung สังคมชั้นสูง

upright, *adj.* dtâng-dtrong ตั้งตรง (vertical); sɯ̂ɯ-dtrong ซื่อตรง (sincere); yú-dtì-tam ยุติธรรม (righteous)

uprising, *n.* gaan-jà-laa-jon การจลาจล

uproar, *n.* kwaam-wûn-waai ความวุ่นวาย; kwaam-goo-laa-hǒn ความโกลาหล

upset, *v.* kwâm คว่ำ (turn over); tam-hâi-sĭa-jai ทำให้เสียใจ (distress); gɔ̀ɔ-guan ก่อกวน (disturb)

upside down, *adv.* kwâm-long คว่ำลง (turn over); plík-glàp พลิกกลับ (reverse)

upstairs, *adv.* chán-bon ชั้นบน

up-to-date, *adj.* tan-sà-mǎi ทันสมัย; bpàt-jù-ban ปัจจุบัน

upward, *adv.* kŭn ขึ้น; nǔa-kŭn-bpai เหนือขึ้นไป

uranium, *n.* tâat-yuu-ree-niam ธาตุยูเรเนียม

urban, *adj.* gìao-gàp-mɯang เกี่ยวกับเมือง

urchin, *n.* dèk-kâang-tà-nǒn เด็กข้างถนน (street kid); mên-tá-lee เม่นทะเล (sea urchin)

urge, *v.* rêng เร่ง; grà-dtûn กระตุ้น; plàk-dan ผลักดัน

urgent, *adj.* rêng-dùan เร่งด่วน; chùk-chǒən ฉุกเฉิน

urinal, *n.* tîi-bpàt-sa-wá ที่ปัสสาวะ

urinate, *v.* kàp-bpàt-sa-wá ขับปัสสาวะ; chìi ฉี่ (collq.)

urine, *n.* bpàt-sa-wá ปัสสาวะ

urn, *n.* yɯ̀ak เหยือก (jug); gòot โกศ (for ashes)

us, *pron.* pûak-rao พวกเรา

use, *v.* chái ใช้

used, *adj.* chái-léeo ใช้แล้ว (has been used); kəəi-chin เคยชิน (be used to)

useful, *adj.* mii-bprà-yòot มีประโยชน์

usefulness, *n.* bpen-bprà-yòot เป็นประโยชน์

useless, *adj.* mâi-mii-bprà-yòot ไม่มีประโยชน์; mâi-dâai-pǒn ไม่ได้ผล

user, *n.* pûu-chái ผู้ใช้

usher, *n.* jâo-nâa-tîi-dtɔɔn-ráp เจ้าหน้าที่ต้อนรับ

usual, *adj.* bpen-bpòk-gà-dtì เป็นปกติ; bpen-tam-ma-daa เป็นธรรมดา

utensil, *n.* krûang-krua เครื่องครัว

uterus, *n.* mót-lûuk มดลูก

utility, *n.* bprà-yòot ประโยชน์ (usefulness); bɔɔ-ri-gaan-sǎa-taa-ra-ná บริการสาธารณะ (public utility); náam-fai น้ำไฟ (water and electricity)

utilize, *v.* chái-bpen-bprà-yòot ใช้เป็นประโยชน์

utmost, *adj.* sùt-kìit สุดขีด; tîi-sùt ที่สุด; sùt-wîang สุดเหวี่ยง

utter, *v.* bplèng-sǐang เปล่งเสียง (send forth with the voice, e.g. a cry); pûut พูด (speak)

V

vacancy, *n.* kwaam-wâang ความว่าง; dtam-nèng-wâang ตำแหน่งว่าง

vacant, *adj.* wâang ว่าง; wâang-bplào ว่างเปล่า

vacate, *v.* tam-hâi-wâang ทำให้ว่าง (empty); ɔ̀ɔk-jàak-ngaan ออกจากงาน (leave a job); tɔ̌ɔn-ɔ̀ɔk ถอนออก (remove); yáai ย้าย (move)

vacation, *n.* rá-yá-yùt-ngaan ระยะหยุดงาน (period of not working); wan-yùt วันหยุด (holiday)

vaccinate, *v.* chìit-wák-siin ฉีดวัคซีน

vaccine, *n.* wák-siin วัคซีน

vacuum, *n.* sǔun-yaa-gàat สุญญากาศ

vacuum cleaner, *n.* krûang-dùut-fùn เครื่องดูดฝุ่น

vagabond, *n.* kon-pá-nee-jɔɔn คนพเนจร; kon-rôn-rêe คนร่อนเร่

vagina, *n.* chɔ̂ng-klɔ̂ɔt ช่องคลอด

vague, *adj.* klum-kluua คลุมเคลือ; mâi-chát-jeeng ไม่ชัดแจ้ง

vain, *adj.* rái-bprà-yòot ไร้ประโยชน์; mâi-mii-sǎa-rá ไม่มีสาระ; tǔu-dtua ถือตัว

valet, *n.* kon-chái-chaai คนใช้ชาย; hîng-sûua-pâa หิ้งเสื้อผ้า

valid, *adj.* mii-hèet-pǒn มีเหตุผล (reasonable); bpen-taang-gaan

เป็นทางการ (official); chái-dâai
ใช้ได้ (useable)

valley, *n.* hùp-kǎo หุบเขา

valuable, *adj.* mii-kâa มีค่า (having
value); mii-raa-kaa มีราคา (having
a price); mii-bprà-yòot มีประโยชน์
(useful)

value, *n.* muun-kâa มูลค่า; raa-kaa
ราคา; kâa ค่า

valve, *n.* lín-bpìt-bpə̀ət ลิ้นปิดเปิด

vampire, *n.* pǐi-dùut-lûat ผีดูดเลือด

van, *n.* rót-dtûu รถตู้

vanguard, *n.* gɔɔng-nâa กองหน้า;
nɛɛo-nâa แนวหน้า

vanish, *v.* lǎai-bpai หายไป

vanity, *n.* kwaam-yìng-yá-sǒo
ความหยิ่งยโส; kwaam-wâang-bplào
ความว่างเปล่า; kwaam-rái-sǎa-rá
ความไร้สาระ

vapor, *n.* ai-mɔ̀ɔk ไอหมอก; ai-
náam ไอน้ำ

variable, *adj.* bplìan-bpleɛng-dâai
เปลี่ยนแปลงได้; mâi-nɛ̂ɛ-nɔɔn
ไม่แน่นอน; bpree-bpruan แปรปรวน

variant, *n.* dtua-bpree ตัวแปร
(something variable); sìng-tîi-mâi-
muan-gan สิ่งที่ไม่เหมือนกัน (something different)

variation, *n.* gaan-bplìan-bpleɛng
การเปลี่ยนแปลง; gaan-pǎn-bpree
การผันแปร

variety, *n.* kwaam-làak-lǎai
ความหลากหลาย; kwaam-dtɛ̀ɛk-

dtàang ความแตกต่าง

various, *adj.* dtàang-dtàang-gan
ต่างๆกัน; làak-lǎai หลากหลาย;
dtàang-chá-nít ต่างชนิด

vary, *v.* bplìan-bpleɛng
เปลี่ยนแปลง; bpree-bpruan
แปรปรวน; pǎn-bpree ผันแปร

vase, *n.* jɛɛ-gan แจกัน; tǒo โถ;
grà-tǎang กระถาง

vast, *adj.* yài-dtoo-mâak
ใหญ่โตมาก; gwâang-kwǎang
กว้างขวาง; mâak-maai มากมาย

vat, *n.* tǎng-yài ถังใหญ่ (big
bucket); mɔ̂ɔ-yài หม้อใหญ่ (big
pot)

vault, *n.* lǎng-kaa-kóong หลังคาโค้ง
(an arched roof); hɔ̂ng-dtâi-din
ห้องใต้ดิน (underground room)

veal, *n.* núa-lûuk-wua เนื้อลูกวัว

vegetable, *n.* pàk ผัก

vegetarian, *n.* kon-gin-jee
คนกินเจ; kon-gin-mang-sà-wí-rát
คนกินมังสวิรัติ

vegetation, *n.* gaan-jà-rəən-dtə̀p-
dtoo-kɔ̌ɔng-pûut การเจริญเติบโต
ของพืช

vehicle, *n.* paa hà ná พาหนะ;
yuat-yaan ยวดยาน

veil, *n.* pâa-klum-nâa ผ้าคลุมหน้า
(face cover); sìng-bpòk-klum
สิ่งปกคลุม (something used for covering)

vein, *n.* sên-lûat เส้นเลือด; sên-loo-hìt เส้นโลหิต

velvet, *n.* gam-má-yìi กำมะหยี่

velocity, *n.* kwaam-reo ความเร็ว; àt-dtraa-kwaam-reo อัตราความเร็ว

vendor, *n.* pûu-kǎai ผู้ขาย; pûu-jam-nàai ผู้จำหน่าย

venerate, *v.* kao-róp เคารพ; náp-tʉ̌ʉ นับถือ

venereal, *adj.* gìao-gàp-gaam-ma-rôok เกี่ยวกับกามโรค

venereal disease, *n.* gaam-ma-rôok กามโรค

vengeance, *n.* gaan-gɛ̂ɛ-kɛ́ɛn การแก้แค้น

venom, *n.* pìt พิษ; sìng-tîi-mii-pìt สิ่งที่มีพิษ

vent, *n.* ruu-bpə̀ət รูเปิด (outlet); chɔ̂ng ช่อง (slot); taang-ɔ̀ɔk ทางออก (exit)

ventilate, *v.* rá-baai-lom ระบายลม; rá-baai-aa-gàat ระบายอากาศ

venture, *n.* gaan-sìang การเสี่ยง

veranda, *n.* rá-biang ระเบียง (balcony); chà-liang เฉลียง (porch)

verb, *n.* kam-gà-rí-yaa คำกริยา

verbal, *adj.* gìao-gàp-kam เกี่ยวกับคำ; bpen-waa-jaa เป็นวาจา

verdict, *n.* kam-dtàt-sǐn คำตัดสิน

verify, *v.* pí-sùut-kwaam-jing พิสูจน์ความจริง; kón-hǎa-kwaam-jing ค้นหาความจริง

versatile, *adj.* mii-bprà-yòot-lǎai-yàang มีประโยชน์หลายอย่าง (serv-

ing many functions); à-nèek-bprà-sǒng อเนกประสงค์ (can be used for several purposes); mii-kwaam-sǎa-mâat-lǎai-yàang มีความสามารถหลายอย่าง (capable of doing many things)

verse, *n.* kloong-gloon โคลงกลอน; bòt-gà-wii บทกวี

version, *n.* rûang-raao เรื่องราว (literary work); bòt-bplɛɛ บทแปล (translated version); wəə-chân เวอร์ชั่น (in computer science)

versus, *prep.* dtɔ̀ɔ ต่อ; dtrong-gan-kâam ตรงกันข้ามกับ; gàp กับ

vertical, *adj.* nai-nɛɛo-dìng ในแนวดิ่ง; dtrong-dìng ตรงดิ่ง

very, *adv.* mâak มาก

vessel, *n.* rʉa เรือ (airship); lɔ̀ɔt หลอด (tube); tɔ̂ tɔ̀ ท่อ (pipe)

vest, *n.* sʉ̂a-yʉ̂ʉt เสื้อยืด (shirt); sʉ̂a-gák เสื้อกั๊ก (a waist-length, sleeveless garment)

veteran, *n.* tá-hǎan-gào ทหารเก่า; tá-hǎan-pàan-sùk ทหารผ่านศึก

veterinarian, *n.* sàt-dtà-wa-pɛ̂ɛt สัตวแพทย์

veto, *v.* kát-káan คัดค้าน; yáp-yáng ยับยั้ง; sìt-tí-yáp-yáng สิทธิยับยั้ง; tòk-tiang ถกเถียง (debate or discuss)

vex, *v.* tam-hâi-túk ทำให้ทุกข์ (bring distress or suffering to); róp-guan รบกวน (annoy)

via, *prep.* dooi-taang โดยทาง;

taang ทาง

vibrate, v. sàn-sà-tɯan สั่นสะเทือน; sàn-wǎi สั่นไหว

vibration, n. gaan-sàn การสั่น; gaan-sàn-sà-tɯan การสั่นสะเทือน; gaan-sàn-rá-rua การสั่นระรัว

vice, n. kwaam-chûa ความชั่ว (evil); bpom-dɔ̂i ปมด้อย (physical defect or weakness); kɔ̂ɔ-bòk-prɔ̂ng ข้อบกพร่อง (defect)

vice, pfx. rɔɔng รอง

vice-president, n. rɔɔng-bprà-taan รองประธาน; rɔɔng-bprà-taa-naa-típ-bɔɔ-dii รองประธานาธิบดี

vicinity, n. bɔɔ-rí-ween-glâi-kiang บริเวณใกล้เคียง

vicious, adj. chûa-ráai ชั่วร้าย; leeo-saam เลวทราม

victim, n. yùa เหยื่อ; pûu-krɔ́-ráai ผู้เคราะห์ร้าย

victor, n. pûu-mii-chai ผู้มีชัย

victorious, adj. mii-chai-cha-ná มีชัยชนะ; dâai-chai-cha-ná ได้ชัยชนะ

victory, n. chai-cha-ná ชัยชนะ

video, n. wii-dii-oo วีดีโอ

videocassette, n. téep-wii-dii-oo เทปวีดีโอ

videodisc, n. pèn-wii-dii-oo แผ่นวีดีโอ

video game, n. wii-dii-oo-geem วีดีโอเกม

videotape, n. téep-wii-dii-oo

เทปวีดีโอ; téep-too-ra-tát เทปโทรทัศน์

Vietnam, n. bprà-têet-wîat-naam ประเทศเวียดนาม

Vietnamese, n. chaao-wîat-naam ชาวเวียดนาม (person); paa-sǎa-wîat-naam ภาษาเวียดนาม (language)

view, n. pâap ภาพ (picture); tiu-tát ทิวทัศน์ (picture of a landscape); kɔ̂ɔ-kít-hěn ข้อคิดเห็น (opinion)

viewer, n. pûu-duu ผู้ดู; pûu-chom ผู้ชม

viewpoint, n. tát-sa-ná-ká-dti ทัศนคติ; kɔ̂ɔ-kít-hěn ข้อคิดเห็น

vigil, n. kwaam-rá-mát-rá-wang ความระมัดระวัง; gaan-fâo-rɔɔ การเฝ้ารอ

vigorous, adj. kěng-reeng แข็งแรง; mii-pá-lang มีพลัง; mii-am-nâat มีอำนาจ

villa, n. bâan-pák บ้านพัก; bâan-dtàak-aa-gàat บ้านตากอากาศ

village, n. mùu-bâan หมู่บ้าน

villager, n. chaao-bâan ชาวบ้าน

villain, n. pûu-ráai ผู้ร้าย (scoundrel, as opposed to hero); kon-chûa-ráai คนชั่วร้าย (evil person)

vindicate, v. gêe-dtua แก้ตัว; gêe-dtàang แก้ต่าง; bpɔ̂ng-gan ป้องกัน

vindictive, adj. gêe-kéen แก้แค้น; pá-yaa-bàat พยาบาท; aa-kâat

อามาด

vine, n. dtôn-à-ngùn ต้นองุ่น; pùut-à-ngùn พืชองุ่น

vinegar, n. náam-sôm-săai-chuu น้ำส้มสายชู

vineyard, n. râi-à-ngùn ไร่องุ่น

vinyl, n. săan-ree-sîn สารเรซิน

violent, adj. rung-rɛɛng รุนแรง; dù-dùat ดุเดือด

violet, n. sĭi-mûang สีม่วง (color); dtôn-wai-oo-lèt ต้นไวโอเล็ต (tree)

violin, n. krûang-wai-oo-lin เครื่องไวโอลิน

viper, n. nguu-pít งูพิษ

virgin, adj., n. bɔɔ-ri-sùt บริสุทธิ์ (pure); săao-bɔɔ-ri-sùt สาวบริสุทธิ์ (a chaste woman)

virtual, adj. gên-săan แก่นแท้; dooi-tée-jing โดยแท้จริง

virtue, n. kun-kwaam-dii คุณความดี

virtuous, adj. mii-sĭin-lá-tam มีศีลธรรม (having virtue); bɔɔ-ri-sùt บริสุทธิ์ (pure)

virus, n. chúa-wai-rát เชื้อไวรัส

visa, n. wii-sâa วีซ่า

visible, adj. hĕn-dâai เห็นได้; hĕn-dâai-chát เห็นได้ชัด

vision, n. săai-dtaa สายตา (eyesight); wí-săi-tát วิสัยทัศน์ (foresight); jin-dtà-naa-gaan จินตนาการ (perception)

visit, v. yîam เยี่ยม; bpai-yîam ไปเยี่ยม; maa-yîam มาเยี่ยม

visitor, n. pûu-yîam-yian ผู้เยี่ยมเยียน; pûu-maa-yîam ผู้มาเยียม; kɛ̀ɛk แขก

visual, adj. gìao-gàp-săai-dtaa เกี่ยวกับสายตา

vital, adj. gìao-gàp-chii-wít เกี่ยวกับชีวิต (relating to life); mii-chii-wít-chii-waa มีชีวิตชีวา (full of life); săm-kan สำคัญ (essential); mii-gam-lang มีกำลัง (full of strength)

vitamin, n. wai-dtaa-min ไวตามิน; wí-dtaa-min วิตามิน

vocabulary, n. kam-sàp คำศัพท์

vocal, adj. gìao-gàp-sĭang-pûut เกี่ยวกับเสียงพูด

vocation, n. aa-chîip อาชีพ

voice, n. sĭang เสียง (vocal sound); sĭang-rɔ́ɔng เสียงร้อง (a cry); kwaam-kít-hĕn ความคิดเห็น (opinion)

voiced, adj. sĭang-gɔ̂ɔng เสียงก้อง

voice less, adj. mâi-ɔ̀ɔk-sĭang ไม่ออกเสียง

void, n. moo-ká โมฆะ (null); mâi-dâai-pŏn ไม่ได้ผล (ineffective); wâang ว่าง (empty)

volatile, adj. rá-hɔ̌ɔi-bpen-ai ระเหยเป็นไอ (evaporating); bpà-tú-dâai-ngâai ปะทุได้ง่าย (explosive); chûa-kraao ชั่วคราว (ephemeral)

volcano, n. puu-kăo-fai ภูเขาไฟ

volleyball, n. gii-laa-wɔn-lêe-bɔɔn กีฬาวอลเลย์บอล

volt, *n.* vóon โวลต์

volume, *n.* chà-bàp ฉบับ (of a book); bpà-ri-maan ปริมาณ (amount); rá-dàp-sĭang ระดับเสียง (loudness)

volunteer, *v.* bpen-aa-săa-sà-màk เป็นอาสาสมัคร

volunteer, *n., v.* aa-săa-sà-màk อาสาสมัคร

vomit, *v.* aa-jian อาเจียน; ûak อ้วก (collq.)

vote, *v.* ɔ̀ɔk-sĭang ออกเสียง

vote, *n.* gaan-ɔ̀ɔk-sĭang การออกเสียง (act of voting); gaan-lûak-dtâng การเลือกตั้ง (election); ká-nɛɛn-sĭang คะแนนเสียง (number of votes cast)

vow, *v.* săa-baan สาบาน

vow, *n.* gaan-săa-baan การสาบาน; kam-saa-baan คำสาบาน; kam-mân คำมั่น

vowel, *n.* sà-rà สระ

voyage, *n.* gaan-dəən-taang การเดินทาง

voyager, *n.* gaan-dəən-taang การเดินทาง

vulgar, *adj.* yàap หยาบ; yàap-kaai หยาบคาย

vulnerable, *adj.* bàat-jèp-dâai-ngâai บาดเจ็บได้ง่าย; mâi-kong-grà-pan ไม่คงกระพัน

vulture, *n.* ii-rɛ́ɛng อีแร้ง

W

wade, *v.* lui ลุย; lui-náam ลุยน้ำ

waffle, *n.* kà-nŏm-wɔ́ɔp-fən ขนมวอฟเฟิล

wag, *v.* gwèng แกว่ง; grà-dìk กระดิก

wage, *n.* kâa-jâang ค่าจ้าง; kâa-dtɔ̀ɔp-tɛɛn ค่าตอบแทน

wager, *v.* sìang เสี่ยง

wager, *n.* gaan-waang-dəəm-pan การวางเดิมพัน (a gamble)

wagon, *n.* dtûu-ban-túk-kɔ̌ɔng-rót-fai ตู้บรรทุกของรถไฟ (of a train); rót máa รถม้า (horse-drawn vehicle); rót-ban-túk-sĭi-lɔ́ɔ รถบรรทุกสี่ล้อ (four-wheeled transport vehicle)

wail, *v.* krâm-kruan คร่ำครวญ; rɔ́ɔng-hŏoi-hŭan ร้องโหยหวน

waist, *n.* eeo เอว

wait, *v.* kɔɔi คอย; rɔɔ รอ; bɔɔ-ri-gaan บริการ (serve)

waiter, *n.* pá-nák-ngaan-sə̀əp พนักงานเสิร์ฟ (in a restaurant)

waitress, *n.* pá-nák-ngaan-sə̀əp-yĭng พนักงานเสิร์ฟหญิง

waive, *v.* sà-là สละ (give up, relinquish); lá-wén ละเว้น (refrain from); lûan เลื่อน (postpone)

wake, *v.* dtɯ̀ɯn ตื่น; dtɯ̀ɯn-nɔɔn ตื่นนอน; dtɯ̀ɯn-dtua ตื่นตัว

walk, *v.* dəən เดิน

walk, *n.* gaan-dəən-lên การเดินเล่น

wall, *n.* gam-pɛɛng กำแพง (exterior siding of a building); pà-nǎng ผนัง (in a house, of a room)

wallet, *n.* grà-bpǎo-sà-dtaang กระเป๋าสตางค์

wallpaper, *n.* grà-dàat-bù-pà-nǎng กระดาษบุผนัง

walnut, *n.* pǒn-wɔɔn-nát ผลวอลนัท

walrus, *n.* sǐng-dtoo-tá-lee สิงโตทะเล

waltz, *n.* jang-wà-wɔɔn จังหวะวอลทซ์

wan, *adj.* sìit ซีด

wand, *n.* máai-riao ไม้เรียว; ka-taa คทา

wander, *v.* tɔ̂ng-tîao ท่องเที่ยว

wanderer, *n.* pûu-tɔ̂ng-tîao ผู้ท่องเที่ยว

wane, *v.* lót ลด (decline); kɔ̂i-kɔ̂i-sà-lǎai ค่อยๆสลาย (decrease gradually)

waning moon, *n.* prá-jan-kâang-rɛɛm พระจันทร์ข้างแรม

want, *v.* yàak อยาก; dtɔ̂ng-gaan ต้องการ; yàak-dâai อยากได้

wanton, *n.* gíao เกี๊ยว (a Chinese food)

war, *n.* sǒng-kraam สงคราม

ward, *n.* dtùk-kon-kâi ตึกคนไข้ (in the hospital)

warden, *n.* yaam ยาม; pûu-klum ผู้คุม

wardrobe, *n.* dtûu-sûa-pâa ตู้เสื้อผ้า

ware, *n.* sǐn-káa สินค้า (article of commerce); paa-cha-ná ภาชนะ (container, e.g. food ware)

warehouse, *n.* goo-dang โกดัง; klang-sǐn-káa คลังสินค้า

warfare, *n.* gaan-sǒng-kraam การสงคราม; gaan-sûu-róp การสู้รบ

warm, *adj.* òp-ùn อบอุ่น; ùn อุ่น

warmth, *n.* kwaam-òp-ùn ความอบอุ่น

warn, *v.* dtuan เตือน

warning, *n.* kam-dtuan คำเตือน; gaan-jɛɛng-hâi-sâap การแจ้งให้ทราบ

warp, *v.* ngɔɔ งอ; kóong โค้ง; bìt บิด

warrant, *v.* bprà-gan ประกัน

warrant, *n.* krûang-bprà-gan เครื่องประกัน (a guarantee); gaan-ráp-rɔɔng การรับรอง (assurance or confirmation)

warranty, *n.* gaan-ráp-rɔɔng การรับรอง; gaan-kám-bprà-gan การค้ำประกัน

warrior, *n.* nák-róp นักรบ

warship, *n.* rʉa-róp เรือรบ

wart, *n.* hùut หูด; bpùm ปุ่ม

wary, *adj.* rá-mát-rá-wang ระมัดระวัง; kɔɔi-fâo-duu คอยเฝ้าดู; rɔ̂ɔp-kɔ̂ɔp รอบคอบ

wash, *v.* láang ล้าง; sák ซัก (clothes)

washing, *n.* gaan-sák การซัก;

gaan-láang การล้าง

wasp, *n.* dtua-dtɔ̀ɔ ตัวต่อ

waste, *v.* sǐa เสีย (lose, e.g. energy, time); bplàao-bprà-yòot เปล่า ประโยชน์ (no benefits) ; mòt-bplʉang หมดเปลือง (exhaust)

wasteful, *adj.* sîn-bplʉang สิ้นเปลือง; bplào-bprà-yòot เปล่าประโยชน์

watch, *v.* duu ดู (look); fâo เฝ้า (wait expectantly); rá-wang ระวัง (be careful)

watchdog, *n.* sù-nák-fâo-bâan สุนัขเฝ้าบ้าน (guarding dog); yaam ยาม (guard)

water, *n.* náam น้ำ

watercolor, *n.* sǐi-náam สีน้ำ

waterfall, *n.* náam-dtòk น้ำตก

watering can, *n.* grà-bpɔ̌ng-rót-dtôn-máai กระป๋องรดต้นไม้

watermelon, *n.* dtɛɛng-moo แตงโม

waterproof, *adj.* gan-náam กันน้ำ

watt, *n.* wàt วัตต์; nùai-gam-lang-fai-fáa หน่วยกำลังไฟฟ้า

wave, *n.* klʉ̂ʉn คลื่น (in the ocean)

waver, *v.* gwɛ̀ng-bpai-maa แกว่งไปมา (move back and forth), pǎn-bprɛɛ ผันแปร (be unsteady); bòok-mʉʉ โบกมือ (the hand, e.g. to say good-bye)

wavy, *adj.* bpen-klʉ̂ʉn เป็นคลื่น, bpen-lɔɔn เป็นลอน; mii-klʉ̂ʉn-mâak มีคลื่นมาก

wax, *n.* kîi-pʉ̂ng ขี้ผึ้ง; yaang-nǐao ยางเหนียว

waxing moon, *n.* prá-jan-kâang-kʉ̂n พระจันทร์ข้างขึ้น

way, *n.* taang ทาง; hǒn-taang หนทาง; sên-taang เส้นทาง; tít-taang ทิศทาง; wí-tii-gaan วิธีการ

we, *pron.* rao เรา; pûak-rao พวกเรา

weak, *adj.* ɔ̀ɔn-ɛɛ อ่อนแอ

weaken, *v.* tam-hâi-ɔ̀ɔn-ɛɛ ทำให้อ่อนแอ

weakness, *n.* kwaam-ɔ̀ɔn-ɛɛ ความอ่อนแอ

wealth, *n.* kwaam-mâng-kâng ความมั่งคั่ง; kwaam-mâng-mii ความมั่งมี; sáp-sǐn ทรัพย์สิน

wealthy, *adj.* mâng-kâng มั่งคั่ง; râm-ruai ร่ำรวย; ruai รวย

wean, *v.* ɔ̀ɔk-hàang ออกห่าง

weapon, *n.* aa-wút อาวุธ

wear, *v.* sǔam สวม; sài ใส่

weary, *adj.* nèt-nùai เหน็ดเหนื่อย; mʉ̂ai-láa เมื่อยล้า; ìt-rooi อิดโรย

weasel, *n.* dtua-wii-sôn ตัววีเซิล

weather, *n.* aa-gàat อากาศ

weave, *v.* tɔɔ ทอ; sǎan สาน; ràk ถัก

weaver, *n.* pûu-tɔɔ ผู้ทอ; châng-tɔɔ-pâa ช่างทอผ้า

web, *n.* yai-mɛɛng-mum ใยแมงมุม; yai ใย

wed, *v.* sǒm-rót สมรส

wedding, *n.* pí-tii-sŏm-rót พิธีสมรส; ngaan-dtèng-ngaan งานแต่งงาน

wedge, *n.* lîm ลิ่ม; lèk-ngát เหล็กงัด

Wednesday, *n.* wan-pút วันพุธ

weed, *n.* wát-cha-pûut วัชพืช (unwanted plant); dtôn-gan-chaa ต้นกัญชา (marijuana)

week, *n.* sàp-daa สัปดาห์; aa-tít อาทิตย์

weekday, *n.* wan-tam-má-daa วันธรรมดา; wan-tam-ngaan วันทำงาน

weekend, *n.* wan-sùt-sàp-daa วันสุดสัปดาห์

weekly, *n.* dtɔɔ-sàp-daa ต่อสัปดาห์; raai-sàp-daa รายสัปดาห์

weep, *v.* rɔ́ɔng-hâi ร้องไห้; râm-hâi ร่ำไห้

weigh, *v.* châng ชั่ง

weight, *n.* náam-nàk น้ำหนัก

weird, *adj.* bprà-làat ประหลาด

welcome, *v.* dtɔ̂ɔn-ráp ต้อนรับ

Welcome!, yin-dii-dtɔ̂ɔn-ráp ยินดีต้อนรับ

weld, *v.* chûam เชื่อม; bprà-sǎan ประสาน

welder, *n.* châng-chûam ช่างเชื่อม

welfare, *n.* sà-wàt-dì-gaan สวัสดิการ

well, *n.* bɔ̀ɔ บ่อ; bɔ̀ɔ-náam บ่อน้ำ

well-being, *n.* sà-pâap-tîi-dii สภาพที่ดี; kwaam-pǎa-sùk ความผาสุข

well-done, *adj.* sùk สุก (cooked)

well-to-do, *adj.* râm-ruai ร่ำรวย

werewolf, *n.* má-nút-mǎa-bpàa มนุษย์หมาป่า

west, *n.* dtà-wan-dtòk ตะวันตก; tít-dtà-wan-dtòk ทิศตะวันตก

western, *adj.* yùu-taang-tít-dtà-wan-dtòk อยู่ทางทิศตะวันตก

wet, *adj.* bpìak เปียก

whale, *n.* bplaa-waan ปลาวาฬ

wharf, *n.* tâa-rɯa-yài ท่าเรือใหญ่

what, *pron.* à-rai อะไร

whatever, *adj.* à-rai-gɔ̂ɔ-dtaam อะไรก็ตาม

wheat, *n.* kâao-sǎa-lii ข้าวสาลี

wheel, *n.* lɔ́ɔ ล้อ

when, *adv.* mɯ̂a-rài เมื่อไหร่; dtɔɔn-nǎi ตอนไหน

whenever, *conj.* mɯ̂a-rai-gɔ̂ɔ-dtaam เมื่อไรก็ตาม

where, *adv.* tîi-nǎi ที่ไหน; dtrong-nǎi ตรงไหน

whereabouts, *n.* sà-tǎan-tîi สถานที่; dtam-nèng-tîi-yùu ตำแหน่งที่อยู่

wherever, *conj.* tîi-nǎi-gɔ̂ɔ-dtaam ที่ไหนก็ตาม; mâi-wâa-tîi-dai ไม่ว่าที่ใด

whet, *v.* fǒn ฝน (hone); láp-hâi-kom ลับให้คม (sharpen); grà-dtûn กระตุ้น (stimulate)

whether, *conj.* rɯ̌u-mâi หรือไม่

which, *adj.* an-nǎi อันไหน; sùannǎi ส่วนไหน

whichever, *adj.* an-nǎi-gɔ̂ɔ-dtaam
อันไหนก็ตาม

while, *n.* chûa-kà-nà ชั่วขณะ; pák-
nùng พักหนึ่ง

whimsical, *adj.* pí-gon พิกล (queer,
strange)

whine, *v.* kraang คราง (make a
moaning sound): bòn-pɯm-pam
บ่นพึมพำ (complain); ɔ́ɔn ย้อน (in
a childish fashion)

whip, *v.* hùat หวด; dtii ตี; kîan
เฆี่ยน

whipping cream, *n.* wíp-kriim
วิปครีม

whirl, *v.* mǔn หมุน

whirlpool, *n.* náam-won น้ำวน

whirlwind, *n.* lom-won ลมวน;
lom-bâa-mǔu ลมบ้าหมู

whiskers, *n.* nùat krao หนวดเครา

whiskey, *n.* lâo-wít-sà-gîi เหล้าวิสกี้

whisper, *v.* grà-síp กระซิบ

whistle, *n.* nók-wìit นกหวีด

white, *adj.* kǎao ขาว

white-collar, *adj.* nák-wí-chaa-gaan
นักวิชาการ

White House, *n.* tam-nîap-kǎao
ทำเนียบขาว

whiten, *v.* tam-hâi-kǎao ทำให้ขาว

whittle, *v.* lâo-máai เหลา (shape
wood); chǐan เฉือน (cut small bits)

who, *pron.* krai ใคร; pûu-tîi ผู้ที่

whoever, *pron.* krai-gɔ̂ɔ-dtaam

ใครก็ตาม

whole, *adj.* táng-mòt ทั้งหมด

wholesale, *n.* gaan-kǎai-sòng
การขายส่ง

wholesome, *adj.* dii-dtɔ̀ɔ-sù-kà-
pâap ดีต่อสุขภาพ (good for health);
bpen-bprà-yòot เป็นประโยชน์ (useful)

whom, *pron.* krai ใคร; pûu-tîi ผู้ที่

whore, *n.* sǒo-pee-nii โสเภณี

whose, *pron.* kɔ̌ɔng-krai ของใคร

why, *adv.* tam-mai ทำไม

wicked, *adj.* ráai-gàat ร้ายกาจ;
hòot-ráai โหดร้าย

wicker, *n.* gìng-máai กิ่งไม้ (bough
of a tree); krûang-jàk-sǎan
เครื่องจักสาน (wickerwork)

wide, *adj.* gwâang กว้าง; gwâang-
kwaang กว้างขวาง

widen, *v.* tam-hâi-gwâang
ทำให้กว้าง; kà-yǎai-gwâang
ขยายกว้าง

widespread, *adj.* prɛ̂ɛ-lǎai
แพร่หลาย; grà-jaai กระจาย

widow, *n.* mɛ̂ɛ-mâai แม่ม่าย

widower, *n.* pɔ̂ɔ-mâai พ่อม่าย

width, *n.* kwaam-qwâang
ความกว้าง

wife, *n.* pan-ra-yaa ภรรยา

wig, *n.* pǒm-bplɔɔm ผมปลอม

wild, *adj.* bpàa-tùan ป่าเถื่อน (barbarous); dù-ráai ดุร้าย (savage)

wilderness, *n.* bɔɔ-ri-ween-

gwâang-yài บริเวณกว้างใหญ่; jam-
nuan-má-hǎa-sǎan จำนวนมหาศาล

wildlife, n. sàt-bpàa สัตว์ป่า

wile, n. ù-baai อุบาย; pĕen-ráai
แผนร้าย

will, aux. v. jà จะ

will, n. kwaam-dtâng-jai ความตั้งใจ
(determination); pí-nai-gam
พินัยกรรม (legal document)

willful, adj. dtâng-jai ตั้งใจ (said or
done on purpose); dûu-rán ดื้อรั้น
(obstinate)

willing, adj. dtem-jai เต็มใจ (act
gladly); sà-màk-jai สมัครใจ (done
voluntarily)

willingly, adv. yàang-dtem-jai
อย่างเต็มใจ; sà-màk-jai สมัครใจ

willow, n. dtôn-lǐu ต้นหลิว

willpower, n. am-nâat อำนาจ;
gam-lang-jai กำลังใจ

win, v. cha-ná ชนะ; mii-chai มีชัย

wind, n. lom ลม

windfall, n. lâap-looi ลาภลอย
(unexpected piece of good fortune);
sìng-tîi-lom-pát-dtòk-long-maa
สิ่งที่ลมพัดตกลงมา (something
blown down by the wind)

windmill, n. gang-hǎn-lom กังหันลม

window, n. nâa-dtàang หน้าต่าง

windshield, n. grà-jòk-nâa-rót
กระจกหน้ารถ

windy, adj. lom-reeng ลมแรง; mii-
lom-mâak มีลมมาก

wine, n. lâo-à-ngùn เหล้าองุ่น

wing, n. bpìik ปีก; bpìik-nók ปีกนก
(for birds)

wink, v. grà-príp กระพริบ; kà-yìp-
dtaa ขยิบตา

winner, n. pûu-cha-ná ผู้ชนะ

winter, n. rú-duu-nǎao ฤดูหนาว

wipe, v. chét เช็ด; tǔu ถู; kà-jàt
ขจัด

wire, n. lûat ลวด; sǎai-fai สายไฟ;
sùu-sǎan สื่อสาร

wisdom, n. bpan-yaa ปัญญา; sà-
dtì-bpan-yaa สติปัญญา; kwaam-
chà-làat ความฉลาด

wise, adj. chà-làat ฉลาด; rɔ̂ɔp-rúu
รอบรู้

wish, v. dtɔ̂ng-gaan ต้องการ
(desire); yàak อยาก (want);
bpràat-tà-nǎa ปรารถนา (long for);
kɔ̌ɔ-hâi ขอให้ (express a wish)

wish, n. kwaam-bpràat-tà-nǎa
ความปรารถนา

wit, n. bpan-yaa ปัญญา

witch, n. mɛ̂ɛ-mót แม่มด

witchcraft, n. gaan-chái-wêet-mon
การใช้เวทมนตร์

with, prep. gàp กับ; dûai ด้วย

withdraw, v. tɔ̌ɔn ถอน

withdrawal, n. gaan-tɔ̌ɔn การถอน

wither, v. hìao-hɛ̂ng เหี่ยวแห้ง;
rûang-rooi ร่วงโรย

withhold, v. rá-ngáp ระงับ; yáp-
yáng ยับยั้ง

without, *prep.* bpràat-sà-jàak
ปราศจาก; mâi-mii ไม่มี

withstand, *v.* ton-dtɔ̀ɔ ทนต่อ
(endure); dtɔ̀ɔ-dtâan ต่อต้าน
(resist)

witness, *n.* pá-yaan พยาน

witty, *adj.* mii-wǎi-príp มีไหวพริบ

wizard, *n.* pɔ̂ɔ-mót พ่อมด; pûu-wi-
sèet ผู้วิเศษ

wobble, *v.* soo-see โซเซ; kloong-
kleeng โคลงเคลง

woe, *n.* kwaam-sâo-sòok
ความเศร้าโศก; kwaam-túk
ความทุกข์

wolf, *n.* su-nak-bpàa สุนัขป่า

woman, *n.* pûu-yǐng ผู้หญิง

womanhood, *n.* kwaam-bpen-pûu-
yǐng ความเป็นผู้หญิง

womanizer, *n.* pûu-chaai-jào-chúu
ผู้ชายเจ้าชู้

womanly, *adj.* klaai-pûu-yǐng
คล้ายผู้หญิง

womb, *n.* mót-lûuk มดลูก; kan
ครรภ์

wonder, *v.* bprà-làat-jai
ประหลาดใจ (have a feeling of surprise); sǒng-sǎi สงสัย (be filled
with curiosity or doubt)

wonderful, *adj.* má-hàt-sà-jan
มหัศจรรย์; yɔ̂ɔt-yîam ยอดเยี่ยม

woo, *v.* jìip จีบ (court)

wood, *n.* máai ไม้

woodcutter, *n.* kon-dtàt-máai
คนตัดไม้

wooden, *adj.* tam-dûai-máai
ทำด้วยไม้

woodpecker, *n.* nók-hǔa-kwǎan
นกหัวขวาน

woodwind, *n.* krûang-don-dtrii-
bprà-pêet-bpào-lom เครื่องดนตรี
ประเภทเป่าลม

woodwork, *n.* pà-lìt-dtà-pan-máai
ผลิตภัณฑ์ไม้

wool, *n.* kǒn-gè ขนแกะ; dâai-kǒn-
ge ด้ายขนแกะ

word, *n.* kam คำ; kam-pûut คำพูด;
kam-sàp คำศัพท์

wording, *n.* gaan-chái-kam
การใช้คำ

word processor, *n.* kɔm-piu-dtɔ̂ɔ
คอมพิวเตอร์

wordy, *adj.* chái-kam-mâak-gɔɔn-
bpai ใช้คำมากเกินไป

work, *v.* tam-ngaan ทำงาน

work, *n.* ngaan งาน

workaholic, *n.* kon-bâa-ngaan
คนบ้างาน

workbook, *n.* kûu-mʉʉ คู่มือ (manual); sà-mùt-ban-tʉ́k สมุดบันทึก
(record book)

workday, *n.* wan-tam-ngaan
วันทำงาน

worker, *n.* kon-ngaan คนงาน

workout, *v.* ɔ̀ɔk-gam-lang-gaai
ออกกำลังกาย

workout, *n.* gaan-ɔ̀ɔk-gam-lang-
gaai การออกกำลังกาย

workshop, *n.* hɔ̂ɔng-bpà-dtì-bàt-ngaan ห้องปฏิบัติงาน (where work is done); gaan-òp-rom การอบรม (educational seminar)

world, n. lôok โลก

worldly, adj. gìao-gàp-lôok เกี่ยวกับโลก

worldwide, adj. tûa-lôok ทั่วโลก

worm, n. nɔ̌ɔn หนอน (any of various crawling insect larvae, e.g. caterpillar); sâi-dɯan ไส้เดือน (earthworm); pá-yâat พยาธิ (parasite)

worn, adj. chái-jon-gào ใช้จนเก่า

worn-out, adj. gào-mâak เก่ามาก (very old); chái-jon-sǐa ใช้จนเสีย (no longer usable); mòt-rɛɛng หมดแรง (exhausted)

worried, adj. gang-won กังวล; glûm-jai กลุ้มใจ

worry, v. bpen-hùang เป็นห่วง (about someone); glûm-jai กลุ้มใจ (feel distressed); gang-won กังวล (feel anxious, be troubled)

worse, adj. leeo-long เลวลง; yɛ̂ɛ-long แย่ลง

worsen, v. tam-hâi-leeo-long ทำให้เลวลง; tam-hâi-yɛ̂ɛ-long ทำให้แย่ลง

worship, v. buu-chaa บูชา; gaan-náp-tɯ̌ɯ นับถือ

worship, n. gaan-buu-chaa การบูชา; gaan-náp-tɯ̌ɯ การนับถือ

worshipper, n. pûu-buu-chaa ผู้บูชา; pûu-náp-tɯ̌ɯ ผู้นับถือ

worst, adj. leeo-tîi-sùt เลวที่สุด; yɛ̂ɛ-tîi-sùt แย่ที่สุด

worth, n. kun-kâa คุณค่า; bprà-yòot ประโยชน์

worthless, adj. rái-kâa ไร้ค่า

worthwhile, adj. kúm-kâa คุ้มค่า

worthy, adj. mii-kâa มีค่า (valuable); kúm-kâa คุ้มค่า (worthwhile)

would, aux.v. jà จะ

wound, n. bàat-plɛ̌ɛ บาดแผล

wrath, n. kwaam-gròot-kɯang ความโกรธเคือง; kwaam-moo-hǒo ความโมโห

wrathful, adj. gròot โกรธ; moo-hǒo โมโห

wreath, n. puang-rìit พวงหรีด

wreck, v. tam-pang ทำพัง

wreck, n. sâak ซาก

wrench, n. bprà-jɛɛ ประแจ; kiim คีม

wrest, v. bìt บิด; kǎn ขัน

wrestle, v. bplâm ปล้ำ

wrestling, n. gii-laa-muai-bplâm กีฬามวยปล้ำ

wring, v. bìip บีบ (compress, extract liquid); rát รัด (clasp firmly); kán คั้น (squeeze)

wrinkle, n. rɔɔi-yôn รอยย่น (on face or skin); rɔɔi-yáp รอยยับ (on paper or cloth)

wrist, n. kɔ̂ɔ-mɯɯ ข้อมือ

wristwatch, n. naa-lí-gaa-kɔ̂ɔ-mɯɯ

นาฬิกาข้อมือ

write, *v.* kǐan เขียน; dtèng แต่ง
(compose)

writer, *n.* nák-kǐan นักเขียน

writhe, *v.* bìt บิด; bìt-ngɔɔ บิดงอ;
bìt-bîao บิดเบี้ยว

writing, *n.* gaan-kǐan การเขียน

writing desk, *n.* dtó-kǐan-nǎng-sǔu
โต๊ะเขียนหนังสือ

wrong, *adj.* pìt ผิด (incorrect); pìt-
plâat ผิดพลาด (erroneous); mâi-
tùuk-dtɔ̂ng ไม่ถูกต้อง (unjust,
immoral)

X

xenophobia, *adj.* kwaam-glìat-
glua-kɔ̌ɔng-dtàang-tìn
ความเกลียดกลัวของต่างถิ่น;
kwaam-glìat-glua-pûu-tîi-mâi-mǔan-
dton ความเกลียดกลัวผู้ที่ไม่เหมือนคน

xebec, *n.* sǎo-grà-doong-rʉa-boo-
raan เสากระโดงเรือโบราณ

Xerox, *n.* krʉ̂ang-tàai-èek-ga-sǎan
เครื่องถ่ายเอกสาร

xiphoid, *n.* grà-dùuk-lín-bpìi
กระดูกลิ้นปี่

x-ray, *v.* tàai-ék-sa-ree ถ่ายเอกซเรย์

x-ray, *n.* rang-sǐi-ék-sa-ree
รังสีเอกซเรย์

xylograph, *n.* gaan-gè-sà-làk-máai
การแกะสลักไม้

xylophone, *n.* rá-nâat ระนาด

Y

yacht, *n.* rʉa-yɔ́ɔt เรือยอชท์

yard, *n.* lǎa หลา (unit of length);
sà-nǎam สนาม (ground, field)

yarn, *n.* sên-dâai เส้นด้าย

yawn, *v.* hǎao หาว; hǎao-nɔɔn
หาวนอน

year, *n.* bpii ปี

yearly, *adj.* bprà-jam-bpii ประจำปี

yearn, *v.* bpràat-tà-nǎa ปรารถนา;
dtɔ̂ng-gaan-mâak ต้องการมาก

yeast, *n.* chʉ́a-yíit เชื้อยีสต์

yell, *v.* dtà-goon ตะโกน

yellow, *adj., n.* sǐi-lʉ̌ang สีเหลือง

yen, *n.* ngən-yeen เงินเยน

yes, *adv.* châi ใช่; .kráp ครับ; kâ
ค่ะ

yesterday, *adv.* mʉ̂a-waan-níi
เมื่อวานนี้

yet, *adv.* yang ยัง; yang-kong
ยังคง; grà-nán กระนั้น

yield, *v.* yɔɔm ยอม (surrender);
hâi-taang ให้ทาง (give way, i.e. in
driving); ɔ̀ɔk-pǒn ออกผล (fruit)

yield, *n.* pǒn-tîi-dâai ผลที่ได้; pǒn-
pà-lìt ผลผลิต

yoga, *n.* yoo ká โยคะ

yogurt, *n.* nom-bprîao นมเปรี้ยว;
yoo-gòət โยเกิร์ต

yolk, *n.* kài-dɛɛng ไข่แดง

you, *pron.* kun คุณ; tân ท่าน; təə
เธอ

young, *adj.* nùm หนุ่ม (used with men); săao สาว (used with women); aa-yú-nɔ́ɔi อายุน้อย (youthful)

youngster, *n.* kon-nùm-săao คนหนุ่มสาว

your, *adj.* kɔ̌ɔng-kun ของคุณ; kɔ̌ɔng-tân ของท่าน

yours, *adv.* kɔ̌ɔng-kun ของคุณ; kɔ̌ɔng-tân ของท่าน

yourself, -selves, *pron.* dtua-kun-eeng ตัวคุณเอง; dtua-tân-eeng ตัวท่านเอง; kun-eeng คุณเอง

youth, *n.* kon-nùm-săao คนหนุ่มสาว (young person; adolescence); kwaam-yao-wai ความเยาว์วัย (condition or quality of being young)

youthful, *adj.* yao-wai เยาว์วัย

Z

zany, *adj.* dtà-lòk-bpɔ̀n-bpɔ̀n ตลกเป็นๆ

zeal, *n.* gaan-mii-jai-jòt-jɔɔ การมีใจจดจ่อ

zealot, *n.* pûu-klâng-klái ผู้คลั่งไคล้

zealous, *adj.* grà-dtɯɯ-rɯɯ-rón กระตือรือร้น

zebra, *n.* máa-laai ม้าลาย

Zen, *n.* ní-gaai-sen นิกายเซน

zenith, *n.* jùt-sùt-yɔ̂ɔt จุดสุดยอด

zero, *nm.* sǔun ศูนย์

zero in, *v.* leng เล็ง

zest, *n.* kwaam-nâa-dtɯ̀ɯn-dtên ความน่าตื่นเต้น (excitement); kwaam-grà-dtɯɯ-rɯɯ-rón ความกระตือรือร้น (enthusiasm)

zibet, *n.* dtua-chá-mót ตัวชะมด (animal)

zigzag, *v.* sík-sék ซิกแซก

zigzag, *n.* rûup-sík-sék รูปซิกแซก; rûup-fan-lûai รูปฟันเลื่อย

zinc, *n.* săng-gà-sǐi สังกะสี

zip, *v.* rûut-síp รูดซิป

zip, *n.* sǐang-wǔɯ เสียงหวือ (brief sharp hissing sound); pa-lang-ngaan พลังงาน (energy)

zip code, *n.* ra-hàt-bprai-sà-nii รหัสไปรษณีย์

zipper, *n.* síp ซิป

zodiac, *n.* jàk-raa-sǐi จักรราศี

zone, *v.* bèng-kèet แบ่งเขต

zone, *n.* kèet เขต

zoning, *n.* gaan-bèng-kèet การแบ่งเขต

zoo, *n.* sǔan-sàt สวนสัตว์

zooid, *adj.* kláai-sàt คล้ายสัตว์

zoology, *n.* sàt-dtà-wá-wít-ta-yaa สัตววิทยา

zoom, *v.* bpràp-pâap ปรับภาพ

zoom, *n.* leen-suum เลนส์ซูม

zoon, *n.* sìng-tîi-gə̀ət-jàak-kài สิ่งที่เกิดจากไข่

SECTION 2 PHONETIC-THAI-ENGLISH

a (อ)

aa อา uncle (father's younger brother or sister), *n.*

âa อ้า open wide, *v.*

aa-bàt อาบัติ violation, *n.*

aa-chîip อาชีพ occupation, *n.*

áa-frí-gaa อาฟริกา Africa, *n.*

aa-gaan อาการ symptom, *n.*

aa-gàat อากาศ air, *n.*

aa-gɔɔn อากร tax, revenue *n.*

aa-hǎan อาหาร food, *n.*

aa-hǎan-cháao อาหารเช้า breakfast, *n.*

aa-hǎan-glaang-wan อาหารกลางวัน lunch, *n.*

aa-hǎan-kâm อาหารค่ำ supper, *n.*

aa-hǎan-tá-lee อาหารทะเล seafood, *n.*

aa-hǎan-tîang อาหารเที่ยง lunch, *n.*

aa-hǎan-wâang อาหารว่าง snack, *n.*

aa-hǎan-yen อาหารเย็น dinner, *n.*

aai อาย shy, *adj.*

âai อ้าย eldest son, elder brother, *n.*

aa-jaan อาจารย์ teacher, professor *n.*

aa-jian อาเจียน vomit, *n., v.*

aa-jin อาจิณ regular, *adj.*

aa-kaan อาคาร building, *n.*

aa-kâat อาฆาต seek revenge, *v.*

aa-kom อาคม magical incantation, *n.*

aa-lai อาลัย miss, think about, deplore the loss of, *v.*

aa-la-wâat อาละวาด disturb, *v.*

aan อาน saddle, *n.*

àan อ่าน read, *v.*

aa-naa-kèet อาณาเขต boundary, *n.*

aa-naa-ní-kom อาณานิคม colony, *n.*

àang อ่าง basin, *n.*

âang, âang-ing อ้าง, อ้างอิง assert, claim, cite, refer to, *v.*

àang-àap-náam อ่างอาบน้ำ bathtub, *n.*

âang-wâa อ้างว่า allege, assert, *v.*

âang-wáang อ้างว้าง lonely, *adj.*

aa-ní-sǒng อานิสงส์ good result, *n.*

àan-nǎng-sǔɯ อ่านหนังสือ read, *v.*

aa-nú-pâap อานุภาพ power, *n.*

àao อ่าว gulf, bay, *n.*

àap อาบ bathe, *v.*

aa-pâat อาพาธ illness, suffering, *n.*

aa-páp อาภัพ unfortunate, *adj.*

aa-pêet อาเพศ abnormal, *adj.*

àap-náam อาบน้ำ take a bath or shower, v.

aa-pɔɔn อาภรณ์ adornments, n.

aa-raam อาราม temple, n.

aa-râat-ta-naa อาราธนา request, v.

aa-raam อาราม temple, n.

aa-ràp อาหรับ Arab, n.

aa-rák-kǎa อารักขา care, protect, v.

aa-ra-yá-chon อารยชน civilized people, n.

aa-rii อารี generous, adj.

aa-rom อารมณ์ mood, feeling n.

aa-rom-kǎn อารมณ์ขัน humor n.

aa-sǎa, aa-sǎa-sà-màk อาสา, อาสาสมัคร volunteer, n., v.

aa-sǎi อาศัย live, inhabit, v.

aa-sǎn อาสัญ die, v.

aa-sǒm อาศรม hermitage, n.

àat, àat-jà อาจ, อาจจะ maybe, perhaps, adv.

àat-cha-yaa-gam อาชญากรรม crime, n.

àat-cha-yaa-gɔɔn อาชญากร criminal, n.

àat-dtà-maa อาตมา (for monks) I, me, myself, pron.

aa-tí อาทิ example, instance, n.

aa-tít อาทิตย์ sun, week, n.

aa-tɔɔn อาทร care, v.

àat-sà-ná อาสนะ seat, n.

aa-wâat อาวาส temple, monastery, n.

aa-wɔɔn อาวรณ์ long for, v.

aa-wú-sǒo อาวุโส seniority, n.

aa-wút อาวุธ arms, weapon, n.

aa-yát อายัด attach (property), consign to custody, deactivate, v.

aa-yú อายุ age, n.

aa-yú-kwaam อายุความ statute of limitations, n.

à-baai-ya-múk อบายมุข path of ruining one's self, n.

à-dìit อดีต past, n

à-dì-rèek อดิเรก hobby, n.

à-gà-dtan-yuu อกตัญญู ungrateful, adj.

à-gù-sǒn อกุศล evil, harmful, inauspicious, adj.

à-hǎng-gaan อหังการ proud, adj.

à-hǐng-sǎa อหิงสา nonviolence, n.

à-hì-waa อหิวาต์ cholera, n.

à-hǒo-sì อโหสิ forgive, v.

ai ไอ cough, n., v.

ai ไอ vapor, n.

âi ไอ้ a derogatory title used with first

names of men and also for insult, *n.*

ai-náam ไอน้ำ steam, vapor, *n.*

ai-oo-diin ไอโอดีน iodine, *n.*

ai-sa-griim ไอศกรีม ice cream, *n.*

ai-sa-kriim, ai-dtim ไอศรีม, ไอติม ice cream, *n.*

ai-sĭa ไอเสีย exhaust fumes, *n.*

ai-ya-gaan อัยการ public prosecutor, district attorney, *n.*

à-ka-dtì อคติ prejudice, *n.*

àk-kà-rà อักขระ letter of the alphabet, character, *n.*

àk-kii อัคคี fire, *n.*

àk-kii-pai อัคคีภัย disaster caused by fire, *n.*

àk-sèep อักเสบ infected, inflamed, *adj.*

àk-sɔ̆ɔn อักษร alphabet, *n.*

àk-sɔ̆ɔn-(ra)-sàat อักษรศาสตร์ liberal arts, *n.*

à-lài อะไหล่, อะหลัย spare parts (cars, etc.), *n.*

à-làang-chàang อล่างฉ่าง vivid, *adj.*

à-lang-gaan อลังการ decoration, adornment, *n.*

à-loo-hà อโลหะ non-material, *n.*

à-lúm-à-lùai อะลุ่มอล่วย conciliato-

ry, meet half-way, *v.*

am อำ hide, conceal, *v.*

à-ma-nút อมนุษย์ non-human being, *n.*

à-mee-ri-gaa อเมริกา America, *n.*

am-laa อำลา take one's leave, *n.*

am-màat อำมาตย์ king's minister, *n.*

am-ma-dtà อมตะ immortal, *adj.*

am-nâat อำนาจ power, influence, authority, *n.*

am-nuai อำนวย give, produce, *v.*

am-ma-hìt อำมหิต cruel, savage, *adj.*

à-mɔɔn อมร immortal, *n.*

am-pan อำพัน amber, *n.*

am-pəə อำเภอ district, registration office *n.*

an อัน clf. used for small or long objects, *n.*

à-naa-jaan อนาจาร obscene, *adj.*

à-naa-kót อนาคต future, *n.*

à-naa-mai อนามัย hygiene, *n.*

à-naa-ra-yá อนารยะ uncivilized, *adj.*

à-nàat อนาถ feel pity, *v.*

à-naa-tǎa อนาถา having no support, pitiful *adj.*

à-naa-típ-bpà-dtai อนาธิปไตย

Phonetic · Thai · English

a b bp ch d dt e ɛ ə f g h i j k l m n ŋ ng ɔ o p r s t u ʉ w y

Phonetic · Thai · English

anarchy, *n.*

à-naa-tɔɔn อนาทร worry about, *v.*

à-nát-dtaa อนัตตา soulless self, *n.*

an-chəən อัญเชิญ invite, *v.*

an-dàp อันดับ series, order, rank, *n.*

an-dtà-raai อันตราย dangerous, *adj.*

an-dtra-taan อันตรธาน disappear, *v.*

à-nèek อเนก several, *adj.*

à-nèek-bprà-sŏng อเนกประสงค์ versatile, *adj.*

ang-grìt อังกฤษ English, England, *n.*

ang-kaan อังคาร Tuesday, *n.*

âng-pao อั้งเปา red envelope, *n.*

à-ngùn องุ่น grape, *n.*

an-năi อันไหน Which one?

à-nin-sii อนินทรีย์ inorganic, *adj.*

à-nít-jaa อนิจจา Alas, *interj.*

à-nít-jang อนิจจัง uncertain, *adj.*

an-tá อัณฑะ testicles, *n.*

an-ta-paan อันธพาล gangster, *n.*

à-nú-baan อนุบาล kindergarten, *n.*

à-nú-baan อนุบาล take care of, *v.*

à-nú-bpà-rin-yaa อนุปริญญา junior college, diploma, *n.*

à-nú-bprà-yòok อนุประโยค subordinate clause, *n.*

à-nú-chaa อนุชา one born after, (royal) brother, *n.*

à-nú-chon อนุชน younger generation, *n.*

à-nú-gaa-châat อนุกาชาด junior Red Cross, *n.*

à-nú-grom อนุกรม series, order, *n.*

à-nú-guun อนุกูล support, *v.*

à-nú-krɔ́ อนุเคราะห์ help, assist, *v.*

à-nú-loom อนุโลม compromise, yield, follow suit, *v.*

à-nú-mát อนุมัติ approve, *v.*

à-nú-moo-ta-naa อนุโมทนา express gratitude, *v.*

à-nú-pâak อนุภาค particle, *n.*

à-nú-pâap อนุภาพ knowledge, influence, *n.*

à-nú-pan-ra-yaa อนุภรรยา minor wife, *n.*

à-nú-rák อนุรักษ์ conserve, *v.*

à-nú-săo-wa-rii อนุสาวรีย์ monument, statue, *n.*

à-nú-sɔ̆ɔn อนุสรณ์ memorial, *n.*

à-nuu อณู atom, *n.*

à-nú-yâat อนุญาต permit, *v.*

à-nùng อนึ่ง besides, in addition to, *prep.*

an-yá-ma-nii อัญมณี precious

stones, *n.*

ao เอา take or get something, want, *v.*

ao-bpai เอาไป take away, *v.*

ao-bprìap เอาเปรียบ take advantage of, *v.*

ao-jai-sài เอาใจใส่ concentrate, pay attention, *v.*

ao-maa เอามา bring, *v.*

àp อับ stale, musty, *adj.*

à-pai อภัย forgive, pardon, *v.*

àp-aai อับอาย shameful, *adj.*

á-pai-ya-tôot อภัยโทษ amnesty, *n.*

à-pí-baan อภิบาล look after, *v.*

àp-bpaang อับปาง wrecked, *adj.*

àp-bpà-mong-kon อับปมงคล inauspicious, *adj.*

à-pí-bpraai อภิปราย discuss, *v.*

à-pí-nan-ta-naa-gaan อภินันทนาการ compliments, *n.*

à-pí-nì-hǎan อภินิหาร supernatural power, *n.*

à-pí-sèek อภิเษก royal wedding, *n.*

à-pí-sìt อภิสิทธิ์ privilege, *n.*

à-pí-tam อภิธรรม higher doctrine, *n.*

à-ràam อร่าม lustrous, *adj.*

à-rai อะไร what, *pron.*

à-rai-ná อะไรนะ What did you say?

à-rì อริ foe, *n.*

à-ri-yá อริยะ converted person, *n.*

à-ròi อร่อย delicious, *adj.*

à-run อรุณ red, dawn, *n.*

à-sǎng-hǎa-rim-ma-sáp อสังหาริมทรัพย์ immovable property, *n.*

à-sǎn-yii อสัญญี unconscious, *adj.*

à-sǎn-yii-pêet อสัญญีแพทย์ anesthetist, *n.*

à-sòok อโศก not causing sorrow, *adj.*

à-sɔ̌ɔ-ra-pít อสรพิษ creatures with poisonous fangs, *n.*

à-sù-jì อสุจิ sperm, semen, *n.*

à-sǔun อสูร giant, demon, *n.*

àt อัด record (voice), compress, make copies, *v.*

àt อัฐ an obsolete unit of Thai currency, money, *n.*

à-tam อธรรม evil, unrighteous, *n.*

àt-chà-ri-yá อัจฉริยะ genius, *n.*

àt-dtà-kát อัตคัด poor, needy, *adj.*

àt-dtà-noo-mát อัตโนมัติ automatic, *adv.*

àt-dtraa อัตรา rate, *n.*

àt-ta-yaa-sǎi อัธยาศัย temperament, *n.*

à-tí-baai อธิบาย explain, *v.*

à-tí-gaan อธิการ abbot, superior, *n.*

a b bp ch d dt e ɛ ə f g h i j k l m n ng o ɔ p r s t u ɯ w y

à-tí-gaan-bɔɔ-dii อธิการบดี director, *n.*

à-típ-bpà-dtai อธิปไตย sovereignty, *n.*

à-típ-bɔɔ-dii อธิบดี director general, head of a department, *n.*

à-tít-tǎan อธิษฐาน pray, make a wish, *v.*

àt-rûup อัครูป print a photograph, *v.*

àt-sà-jan อัศจรรย์ miraculous, *adj.*

àt-sà-jee-rii อัศเจรีย์ an exclamation mark, *n.*

àt-sà-win อัศวิน knight, *n.*

a-wa-dtaan อวตาร descend from heaven, reincarnated, *v., adj.*

à-wa-gàat อวกาศ space, vacuum, *n.*

à-wai-ya-wá อวัยวะ organ (of the body), *n.*

à-wai-ya-wá-pêet, à-wai-ya-wá-sùup-pan อวัยวะเพศ, อวัยวะสืบพันธุ์ genitals, *n.*

à-wá-mong-kon อวมงคล inauspiciousness, *n.*

a-wa-sǎan อวสาน end, finish, *v.*

à-wee-jii อเวจี hell, *n.*

à-wít-chaa อวิชชา nascence, ignorance, *n.*

b (บ)

baa บาร์ bar, *n.*

bàa บ่า shoulder, *n.*

bâa บ้า crazy, mad, insane, *adj.*

bâa-bâa-bɔɔ-bɔɔ บ้าๆบอๆ odd, crazy (colloq.), *adj.*

baa-bii-kiu บาร์บีคิว barbeque, *n.*

baa-daan บาดาล underground region, *n.*

bâa-gaam บ้ากาม crave sex, *v.*

bàai บ่าย afternoon, *n.*

bàai-bìang บ่ายเบี่ยง avoid, deviate, *v.*

baa-lêe บาร์เลย์ barley, *n.*

baa-lii บาลี Pali language, *n.*

bâa-mǔu บ้าหมู epilepsy, *n.*

baan บาน bloom, *v.*

baan บาน clf. for doors, windows, mirrors, *n.*

baan บาล guard, *v.*

bâan บ้าน house, home, *n.*

baang บาง thin (layer), *adv.*

baang, bâang บาง, บ้าง some, *adj.*

bâan-gə̀ət บ้านเกิด hometown, *n.*

baang-kráng บางครั้ง sometime,

sometimes, *adv.*

baang-kon บางคน some people, *n.*

baang-tii บางที sometimes, *adv.*

bâan-lêek-tîi บ้านเลขที่ address, *n.*

bâan-nɔ̂ɔk บ้านนอก rural area, countryside, *n.*

bâan-pák บ้านพัก residence (house), *n.*

bàao บ่าว servant, slave, *n.*

bàap บาป sin, *n.*

baa-ra-mii บารมี merit, *n.*

bàat บาท baht, *n.*

bàat บาด cut, wound, *v.*

bàat บาตร Buddhist monk's round alms-bowl, *n.*

bàat บาศก์ dice, *n.*

bàat-jai บาดใจ hurt one's feelings, *v.*

bàat-jèp บาดเจ็บ injured, *adj.*

bàat-lǔang บาทหลวง Christian priest, *n.*

bàat-mǎang บาดหมาง have a rift, have dissension, *v.*

bàat-plɛ̌ɛ บาดแผล wound, *n.*

bàat-sà-gét-bɔn บาสเก็ตบอล basketball, *n.*

bàat-ta-yak บาดทะยัก tetanus, *n.*

bai, bai-máai ใบ, ใบไม้ leaf, *n.*

bai ใบ clf. for round and hollow objects, e.g. fruit, eggs, *n.*

bâi ใบ้ dumb (unable to speak), *n.*

bai-à-nú-yâat ใบอนุญาต license, *n.*

bai-bɔ̂n ไบเบิ้ล the Bible, *n.*

bai-bpliu ใบปลิว leaflet, *n.*

bai-gə̀ət ใบเกิด birth certificate, *n.*

bai-kàp-kìi ใบขับขี่ driver license, *n.*

bai-ráp-ngən ใบรับเงิน receipt, *n.*

bai-ráp-rɔɔng ใบรับรอง testimonial, certificate, *n.*

bai-sà-màk ใบสมัคร application form, *n.*

bai-sèt ใบเสร็จ receipt, *n.*

bai-yàa ใบหย่า divorce certificate, *n.*

bàk บัก a form of address applied to a man of equal status, or to show familiarity or contempt, *n.*

bàk-dtee-rii บักเตรี bacteria, *n.*

bam-bàt บำบัด cure, treat, *v.*

bà-mìi บะหมี่ egg noodle, *n.*

bam-naan บำนาญ pension, *n.*

bam-nèt บำเหน็จ reward, remuneration, *n.*

bam-pen บำเพ็ญ do, perform, *v.*

bam-rəə บำเรอ serve, tend, wait on, *v.*

bam-rung บำรุง improve, maintain, *v.*

ban บรรณ wing, leaf, *n.*

bàn บั่น cut, cut into pieces, *v.*

bân บั้น half, part, *n.*

ban-chaa บัญชา order, *v.*

ban-chii บัญชี account, *n.*

ban-daa บรรดา all, all of, *adv., adj.*

ban-daan บันดาล produce, cause, create (esp. by supernatural means), *v.*

ban-dai บันได ladder, stairs, *n.*

ban-dai-lûan บันไดเลื่อน escalator, *n.*

ban-dìt บัณฑิต university graduate, scholar, *n.*

bang บัง block (the view), *v.*

bâng บั้ง insignia of rank, *n.*

bang-àat บังอาจ dare, *v.*

bang-ga-loo บังกาโล bungalow, *n.*

bang-gòɛt บังเกิด born, *adj.*

bang-ɛɛn บังเอิญ by chance, *n.*

bang-hĭan บังเหียน bridle, rein, *n.*

bang-káp บังคับ force, command, *v.*

bang-kom บังคม pay respect before a monarch, *v.*

bang-ɔɔn บังอร woman, girl, *n.*

bang-sù-kun บังสุกุล yellow robe drawn by a Buddhist monk from a coffin, *n.*

ban-jòɛt บรรเจิด make pretty, *v.*

ban-jong บรรจง perform with care, do nicely, *v.*

ban-jòp บรรจบ connected, *adj.*

ban-jù บรรจุ pack, *v.*

ban-jùap บรรจวบ meet, join, *v.*

ban-lai บรรลัย collapse, go to destruction, *v.*

ban-lang บัลลังก์ throne, *n.*

ban-lêe บัลเล่ต์ ballet, *n.*

ban-leeng บรรเลง sing, play (music), *v.*

ban-lú บรรลุ succeed, *v.*

ban-luun บัลลูน balloon, *n.*

ban-lɯɯ บันลือ echo, *v.*

ban-naa-gaan บรรณาการ gift, offering, *n.*

ban-naa-tí-gaan บรรณาธิการ editor, *n.*

ban-na-sǎan บรรณสาร official letter, *n.*

ban-pá-bù-rùt บรรพบุรุษ ancestor, *n.*

ban-pót บรรพต mountain, *n.*

ban-tao บรรเทา alleviate, *v.*

ban-tát บรรทัด ruler, *n.*

ban-tát-tǎan บรรทัดฐาน standard, convention, *n.*

ban-tɛɛng บันเทิง joyful, entertained, *adj.*

ban-tom บรรทม sleep (royal), *v.*

ban-túk บรรทุก load on (truck, ship), pack on, *v.*

ban-túk บันทึก memo, note, record, write down *n.*, *v.*

ban-yaa-gàat บรรยากาศ atmosphere, *n.*

ban-yaai บรรยาย describe, *v.*

ban-yàt บัญญัติ regulate, *v.*

bao เบา light, quiet, *adj.*

bâo เบ้า crucible, socket, *n.*

bâo-dtaa เบ้าตา eye-socket, *n.*

bao-wǎan เบาหวาน diabetes, *n.*

bàt บัตร card, *n.*

bàt บัด time, occasion, period, *n.*

bàt-bprà-chaa-chon บัตรประชาชน identity card, *n.*

bàt-chəən บัตรเชิญ invitation card, *n.*

bàt-grii บัดกรี solder, weld, *v.*

bàt-kree-dìt บัตรเครดิต credit card, *n.*

bàt-sǐi บัดสี shameful, *adj.*

bàt-sóp บัดซบ very stupid, *adj.*

bèng เบ่ง swell, expand, *v.*

ben-jà-sǐin เบญจศีล the five basic Buddhist precepts of morality, *n.*

bèt เบ็ด hook, *n.*

bèt-dtà-lèt เบ็ดเตล็ด miscellaneous, *adj.*

bèt-sèt เบ็ดเสร็จ entirely, in total, *adv.*

bè แบะ spread open, *adj.*

bɛɛ แบ spread, *v.*

bɛ̀ɛk แบก carry (heavy object), *v.*

bɛɛn แบน flat, *adj.*

bɛ̀ɛp แบบ pattern, style, type, model, form, *n.*

bɛ̀ɛp-fɔɔm แบบฟอร์ม form, *n.*

bɛ̀ɛp-fùk-hàt แบบฝึกหัด exercise (school work), *n.*

bèng แบ่ง divide, *v.*

béng แบ็งค์ banknote, *n.*

bèt-dtəə-rîi แบตเตอรี่ battery, *n.*

bèt-min-dtân แบดมินตัน badminton, *n.*

bəə เบอร์ number, *n.*

bə̀ək เบิก open, widen, expand, *v.*

bə̀ək-baan เบิกบาน cheerful, *adj.*

bə̀ək-pa-yaan เบิกพยาน call in witnesses, *v.*

bə̀ək-ngən เบิกเงิน withdraw money, *v.*

bə̀ng เบิ่ง stare, look, *v.*

bia เบียร์ beer, *n.*

bìa เบี้ย cowrie shell, *n.*

bìat เบียด squeeze in, *v.*

bìang เบียง turn, turn aside, *v.*

bìao เบี้ยว crooked, deformed, *adj.*

bì-daa บิดา father (formal), *n.*

bìip บีบ squeeze, compress, *v.*

bìip-dtrɛɛ บีบแตร honk, *v.*

bìip-kɔɔ บีบคอ strangle, *v.*

bin บิน fly, *v.*

bìn บิ่น chip, chipped, *v., adj.*

bin-ta-bàat บิณฑบาต go about with an alms bowl to receive food, *v.*

bìt บิด twist, *v.*

bìt บิด dysentery, *n.*

bìt-bɨan บิดเบือน distort, *v.*

bòk บก land (as supposed to sea), terrestrial, *n.*

bòk-prɔ̂ng บกพร่อง deficient, defective, *adj.*

bòm บ่ม cure (tobacco), ripen, *v.*

bon บน on, *prep.*

bon บน vow, *v.*

bòn บ่น complain, *v.*

bòng บ่ง indicate, *v.*

bong-gaan บงการ dictate, *v.*

boo โบว์ bow (ribbon), *n.*

bǒo โบ๋ containing holes, *adj.*

booi โบย beat, whip, *v.*

bòok โบก wave, beckon, *v.*

boo-lîng โบลิ่ง bowling, *n.*

boo-nát โบนัส bonus, *n.*

boo-raan โบราณ ancient, old, antique, *n., adj.*

bòot โบสถ์ church, chapel in a temple compound, *n.*

bòt บด grind, *v.*

bòt, bòt-rian บท, บทเรียน lesson, *n.*

bòt-glɔɔn บทกลอน poem, *n.*

bòt-kwaam บทความ article, *n.*

bòt-tîi บทที่ chapter, *n.*

bɔ เบาะ cushion, *n.*

bɔ̀i บ่อย often, *adv.*

bɔ̌i บ๋อย waiter, bellboy, *n.*

bɔ̀n บ่อน casino, *n.*

bɔ̂ng บ้อง hollow cylindrical piece of wood, *n.*

bɔ̂ng-fai บ้องไฟ bamboo rocket, *n.*

bɔ̂ng-gan-chaa บ้องกัญชา pipe for smoking marijuana, *n.*

bɔɔ บ่ (Lao) no, not, never, *adj.*

bɔ̀ɔ บ่อ pond, well, *n.*

bɔ̀ɔ-gə̀ət บ่อเกิด source, *n.*

bɔ̀ɔk บอก tell, *v.*

bɔ̀ɔk-bâi บอกใบ้ tell by making signs, giving some clues, *v.*

bɔɔ-kɔ̌ɔ-sɔ̌ɔ บ.ข.ส. bus terminal, n.

bɔ̀ɔ-náam บ่อน้ำ water well, n.

bɔ̀ɔp บอบ worn out, weakened, adj.

bɔ̀ɔp-baang บอบบาง frail, thin, breakable, fragile, adj.

bɔ̀ɔp-chám บอบช้ำ badly injured, adj.

bɔɔ-ra-pét บอระเพ็ด a species of climber, n.

bɔɔ-ri-baan บริบาล guard, v.

bɔɔ-ri-buun บริบูรณ์ complete, ontiro, adj.

bɔɔ-ri-gaan บริการ service, serve, n., v.

bɔɔ-ri-gam บริกรรม adorn, v.

bɔɔ-ri-hǎan บริหาร manage, v.

bɔɔ-ri-jàak บริจาค donate, v.

bɔɔ-ri-kǎan บริขาร the eight necessary requisites of the Buddhist monk, n.

bɔɔ-ri-pâat บริภาษ reprimand, v.

bɔɔ-ri-pan บริภัณฑ์ belt, girdle, n.

bɔɔ-ri-pát บริพัตร change, v.

bɔɔ-ri-pôok บริโภค consume, v.

bɔɔ-ri-sàt บริษัท company, firm, n.

bɔɔ-ri-sùt บริสุทธิ์ pure, virgin, adj.

bɔɔ-ri-waan บริวาร followers, satellites, n.

bɔɔ-ri-ween บริเวณ area, region, vicinity, zone, compound, sector, n.

bɔ̀ɔt บอด blind, darkened, adj.

brèek เบรค brake (car), n., v.

brèek เบรก break, rest, n., v.

bua บัว lotus, n.

búai บ๊วย the last, a kind of fruit, n.

bùak บวก add, sum, plus, n., v.

buam บวม inflamed, swollen, adj.

bûan บ้วน spit out, v.

bùang บ่วง loop, snare, trap, n.

buang-sǔang บวงสรวง propitiate, v.

buap บวบ dishrag gourd, a kind of squash, n.

bua-rót-náam บัวรดน้ำ watering can, n.

bùat บวช ordained, adj.

bùat-chii บวชชี become a nun, v.

bùat-neen บวชเณร become a Buddhist novice, v.

bùat-prá บวชพระ become a monk, v.

bûi บุ้ย protrude the lips, pout, v.

bùk บุก invade, v.

bùk-ka-laa-gɔɔn บุคลากร personnel, n.

bùk-ka-lík บุคลิก personally, personality, adv., n.

bùk-ka-lík-gà-pâap บุคลิกภาพ personality, characteristic, *n.*

bùk-kon บุคคล person, individual *n.*

bǔm บุ๋ม dented, dimpled, *adj.*

bùm-bàam บุ่มบ่าม uncouth, *adj.*

bun บุญ merit, virtue, good deeds, *n.*

bûng บุ้ง caterpillar, *n.*

bù-ngǎa บุหงา flower, *n.*

bùp บุบ pound lightly, *v.*

bùp-pa-bòt บุรพบท preposition, *n.*

bù-rìi บุหรี่ cigarette, *n.*

bù-rùt บุรุษ man, person, *n.*

bù-rùt-bprai-sà-nii บุรุษไปรษณีย์ postman, *n.*

bùt บุตร child, son (formal), *n.*

bùt-dtrii บุตรี daughter (formal), *n.*

bùt-sà-raa-kam บุษราคัม topaz, *n.*

buu-chaa บูชา worship (sacred objects), *v.*

buum บูม boom, *n.*

buum-məə-rɛɛng บูมเมอแรง boomerang, *n.*

buu-ra-ná บูรณะ repair, *v.*

buu-ra-paa บูรพา the east, *n.*

bùut บูด rotten, decayed, *adj.*

bùa เบื่อ bored, *adj.*

buan เบือน turn, turn away, twist, deviate, *v.*

bûang เบื้อง side, part, *n.*

bung บึง large swamp, *n.*

bùng บึ่ง go very fast, speed, *v.*

bûng บึ้ง serious, solemn, *adj.*

bûng-dtung บึ้งตึง sullen, frowning, sulky, *adj.*

bp (ป)

bpà ปะ patch, mend (clothing), *v.*

bpaa ปา throw, *v.*

bpàa ป่า forest, *n.*

bpâa ป้า aunt (father or mother's older sister), *n.*

bpǎa ป๋า father (Chinese Thai), *n.*

bpàa-cháa ป่าช้า cemetery, *n.*

bpâai ป้าย brush or wipe with a sweeping motion, smear, *v.*

bpâai ป้าย sign, billboard, label, tag, *n.*

bpàak ปาก mouth, *n.*

bpàak-gaa ปากกา pen, *n.*

bpaan ปาน birthmark, *n.*

bpaan-glaang ปานกลาง moderate, *adv.*

bpàat ปาด smooth or level off, *v.*

bpà-bpon ปะปน mix, mingle, *v.*

bpà-dtì-sèet ปฏิเสธ deny, refuse, v.

bpà-dtì-tin ปฏิทิน calendar, n.

bpà-gaa-rang ปะการัง coral, n.

bpai ไป go, v.

bpai-glàp ไปกลับ round trip, v.

bpai-hǎa ไปหา go see someone, v.

bpai-hâi-pón ไปให้พ้น Go away!

bpai-maa ไปมา back and forth, adv.

bpai-nǎi ไปไหน Where are you going?

bpai-nɔ̂ɔk ไปนอก go abroad, v.

bpai-nɔɔn ไปนอน go to bed, v.

bpai-tîao ไปเที่ยว go out, take a trip, v.

bpai-tʉ̌ng ไปถึง arrive, reach, v.

bpai-yîam ไปเยี่ยม visit, v.

bpàk ปัก stick in, insert, embroider, v.

bpám ปั๊ม gas station, n.

bpan ปัน share, divide, v.

bpàn ปั่น spin, become confused, v.

bpân ปั้น mold, n.

bpan-hǎa ปัญหา problem, n.

bpân-jàn ปั้นจั่น crane, n.

bpan-yaa ปัญญา intelligence, n.

bpan-yaa-ɔ̀ɔn ปัญญาอ่อน mentally handicapped, feeble-minded, adj.

bpào เป่า blow, v.

bpâo เป้า target, n.

bpà-ra-maa-nuu ปรมาณู atom, n.

bpà-rɔ̀ɔt ปรอท mercury, thermometer, n.

bpàt ปัด brush away, wipe, dust off, v.

bpàt-jù-ban ปัจจุบัน nowadays, present (time), adv., n.

bpà-tá ปะทะ collide, v.

bpà-tú ปะทุ burst, v.

bpen เป็น be, v.

bpen-bpai-dâai เป็นไปได้ possible, adj.

bpen-bpai-mâi-dâai เป็นไปไม่ได้ impossible, adj.

bpen-dtôn เป็นต้น etcetera, v.

bpen-hùang เป็นห่วง worry, concern v.

bpen-lom เป็นลม faint, v.

bpen-nîi เป็นหนี้ be in debt, v.

bpen-wàt เป็นหวัด have a cold, v.

bpèt เป็ด duck, n.

bpɛ̂ɛng แป้ง powder, n.

bpɛ̀ɛt แปด eight, n.

bpên แป้น keyboard, n.

bpên แป้น round and flat, adj.

bpə̀ət เปิด open, v.

bpìak เปียก wet, adj.

bpia-noo เปียโน piano, n.

bpii ปี year, n.

bpìi ปี่ wind instrument (general term), *n.*

bpìik ปีก wing, *n.*

bpii-mài ปีใหม่ new year, *n.*

bpiin ปีน climb, *v.*

bpii-sɛ̌ɛng ปีแสง light year, *n.*

bping-bpong ปิงปอง ping pong, *n.*

bpìt ปิด close, switch off, *v.*

bpìt ปิด closed, *adj.*

bplaa ปลา fish, *n.*

bplaai ปลาย edge, end, *n.*

bplaai-bpii ปลายปี end of the year, *n.*

bplaai-duan ปลายเดือน end of the month, *n.*

bplaai-níu ปลายนิ้ว fingertip, *n.*

bplaa-lǎi ปลาไหล eel, *n.*

bplaa-loo-maa ปลาโลมา dolphin, *n.*

bplaa-mùk ปลาหมึก squid, cuttlefish, *n.*

bplàao เปล่า empty, *adj.*

bplàao-bprà-yòot เปล่าประโยชน์ useless, vain, in vain, *adj., adv.*

bplaa-waan ปลาวาฬ whale, *n.*

bplàk ปลัก swamp, *n.*

bplák ปลั๊ก socket, *n.*

bplâm ปล้ำ struggle with, wrestle

with, force, rape, *v.*

bplee เปล cradle, *n.*

bpleeo เปลว flame, *n.*

bplɛɛ แปล translate, *v.*

bplɛ̀ɛk แปลก strange, *adj.*

bplɛ̀ɛk-jai แปลกใจ surprised, *adj.*

bplìan เปลี่ยน change, exchange, *v.*

bplìan-bplɛɛng เปลี่ยนแปลง change, correct, modify, restore, transform, *v.*

bplìao เปลี่ยว isolated, *adj.*

bplii ปลี spathe, spadix or flower cluster (of the banana tree) *n.*

bplìik ปลีก break up, separate, *v.*

bpling ปลิง leech, *n.*

bplìt ปลิด pick off, *v.*

bpliu ปลิว blow, flow, float, *v.*

bplôn ปล้น rob, *v.*

bplɔ̀i ปล่อย release, *v.*

bplɔ̀ng ปล่อง hole, chimney, *n.*

bplɔ̀ɔk ปลอก collar, pillow slip, case, slip-cover, *n.*

bplɔ̀ɔk-kɛ̌ɛn ปลอกแขน armband, *n.*

bplɔ̀ɔk-kɔɔ ปลอกคอ collar, *n.*

bplɔ̀ɔk-mɔ̌ɔn ปลอกหมอน pillowcase, *n.*

bplɔ̀ɔk-níu ปลอกนิ้ว thimble, *n.*

bplɔɔm ปลอม fake, *v.*, *adj.*

bplɔ̀ɔp, bplɔ̀ɔp-jai ปลอบ, ปลอบใจ comfort, console, *v.*

bplɔ̀ɔp-yoon ปลอบโยน comfort, calm, *v.*

bplɔ̀ɔt-pai ปลอดภัย safe, *adj.*

bplùak ปลวก termite, *n.*

bplùk ปลุก wake someone up, *v.*

bplùuk ปลูก cultivate, plant, *v.*

bplùuk-fǐi ปลูกฝี vaccinate, *v.*

bplɯai เปลือย bare, naked, *adj.*

bplɯ̀ak เปลือก skin, rind, shell, *n.*

bplɯ̂ang เปลื้อง undress, get rid off, *v.*

bpòk ปก cover, *n.*

bpòk-bpìt ปกปิด cover, conceal, *v.*

bpòk-bpɔ̂ng ปกป้อง protect, *v.*

bpòk-kěng ปกแข็ง hard cover, *n.*

bpòk-klum ปกคลุม cover, *v.*

bpòk-krɔɔng ปกครอง rule, govern, *v.*

bpom ปม knot, complex, *n.*

bpom-dèn ปมเด่น superiority complex, *n.*

bpom-dɔ̂i ปมด้อย inferiority complex, *n.*

bpon ปน mix, mingle, *v.*

bpɔ́-bpía เปาะเปี๊ยะ spring roll, *n.*

bpɔ̂ng-gan ป้องกัน prevent, protect, *v.*

bpɔɔ ปอ hemp, *n.*

bpɔ̀ɔk ปอก peel, *v.*

bpɔɔn ปอนด์ pound, *n.*

bpɔ̂ɔn ป้อน feed, *v.*

bpɔ̀ɔt ปอด lung, *n.*

bpɔ̀ɔt-buam ปอดบวม pneumonia, *n.*

bpraa-chai ปราชัย defeated, *adj.*

bpraa-gòt ปรากฏ appear, *v.*

bpraa-gòt-dtà-gaan ปรากฏการณ์ phenomenon, *n.*

bpraa-nii ปรานี have mercy, *v.*

bpràap ปราบ conquer, overcome, *v.*

bpraa-sàat ปราสาท castle, *n.*

bpràat-sà-jàak ปราศจาก without, free from, *adv.*, *prep.*

bpràat-tà-nǎa ปรารถนา desire, wish, dream of, want, *v.*

bprà-chaa-châat ประชาชาติ nation, *n.*

bprà-chaa-chon ประชาชน people, population, *n.*

bprà-chaa-gɔɔn ประชากร people, populace, *n.*

bprà-chaa-sǎm-pan ประชา สัมพันธ์ public relations, *n.*

bprà-chaa-sǒng-krɔ́ ประชา สงเคราะห์ public welfare, *n.*

bprà-chaa-típ-bpà-dtai ประชาธิปไตย democracy, *n.*

bprà-chum ประชุม meeting, *n.*

bprà-chum ประชุม hold a meeting, assemble, *v.*

bprà-daa-náam ประดาน้ำ diver, skilled diver, *n.*

bprà-dàp ประดับ decorate, *v.*

bprà-den ประเด็น issue, point or matter in question, *n.*

bprà-dəəm ประเดิม begin, start, *v.*

bprà-dìt ประดิษฐ์ invent, *v.*

bprà-dtuu ประตู door, *n.*

bprà-gaai ประกาย spark, sparkle, *n., adj.*

bprà-gaa-sà-nii-ya-bàt ประกาศ นียบัตร certificate, diploma, *n.*

bprà-gàat ประกาศ announce, *v.*

bprà-gan ประกัน assurance, *v.*

bprà-gan-chii-wít ประกันชีวิต life insurance, *n., v.*

bprà-gan-pai ประกันภัย insurance, *n., v.*

bprà-gùat ประกวด compete, contest, *v.*

bprà-hǎan ประหาร kill, destroy *v.*

bprà-hǎan-chii-wít ประหารชีวิต execute, *v.*

bprai-sà-nii ไปรษณีย์ mail, *n.*

bprai-sà-nii-aa-gàat ไปรษณีย์อากาศ airmail, *n.*

bprai-sà-nii-yá-bàt ไปรษณียบัตร postcard, *n.*

bprai-sà-nii-yaa-gɔɔn ไปรษณี ยากร stamp, *n.*

bprà-jam ประจำ regular, steady, staple, permanent, stationed at, on duty, assigned to, *adj.*

bprà-jam-bpii ประจำปี annually, *adv.*

bprà-jam-dɯan ประจำเดือน monthly, menstruation, *adv., n.*

bprà-jam-sàp-daa ประจำสัปดาห์ weekly, *adv.*

bprà-jam-wan ประจำวัน daily, *adv.*

bprà-làat ประหลาด strange, unusual, *n.*

bprà-làat-jai ประหลาดใจ wonder, surprise, surprised, *v., adj.*

bprà-maan ประมาณ about, approximately, *adj.*

bprà-màat ประมาท careless, overconfident, belittle, disparage, *v.*

bprà-mong ประมง fish, *v.*

bprà-muan ประมวล compile, *v.*

bprà-múk ประมุข head, chief, *n.*

bprà-muun ประมูล bid, *v.*

bprà-paa-kaan ประภาคาร lighthouse, *n.*

bprà-pan ประพันธ์ compose, *v.*

bprà-pee-nii ประเพณี custom, tradition, *n.*

bprà-prút ประพฤติ behave, *v.*

bprà-sǎan ประสาน link, join, *v.*

bprà-sàat ประสาท nerve, *n.*

bprà-sǒng ประสงค์ desire, *v.*

bprà-sòp ประสพ encounter, *v.*

bprà-sòp-gaan ประสบการณ์ experience, *n.*

bprà-taan ประธาน president, *n.*

bprà-taa-naa-típ-bɔɔ-dii ประธานาธิบดี president (of a country), *n.*

bprà-táp-jai ประทับใจ impress, impressed, *v., adj.*

bprà-tát ประทัด firecracker, *n.*

bpràt-cha-yaa ปรัชญา philosophy, *n.*

bprà-têet ประเทศ country, *n.*

bprà-tǒm ประถม first, primary, elementary, *adj.*

bpràt-sà-nii ปรัศนี question, *n.*

bprà-túang ประท้วง protest, *v.*

bprà-yàt ประหยัด frugal, *adj.*

bprà-yòok ประโยค sentence, *n.*

bprà-yòot ประโยชน์ advantage, usefulness, benefit, *n.*

bprà-yúk ประยุกต์ apply, utilize, *v.*

bprɛɛng แปรง brush, *n., v.*

bprɛɛng-fan แปรงฟัน brush the teeth, *v.*

bprîao เปรี้ยว sour, *adj.*

bprîao-wǎan เปรี้ยวหวาน sweet and sour, *adj.*

bprìt-sà-nǎa ปริศนา puzzle, riddle, *n.*

bproo-dtiin โปรตีน protein, *n.*

bprooi โปรย sprinkle, *v.*

bprɔ̀ เปราะ fragile, *adj.*

bprɔɔng-dɔɔng ปรองดอง compromise, *v.*

bpùai ป่วย sick, ill, *n.*

bpùat ปวด ache, be in pain, *v.*

bpùat-fan ปวดฟัน have a toothache, *v.*

bpùat-hǔa ปวดหัว have a headache, *v.*

bpùat-mûai, ปวดเมื่อย have a muscle ache, *v.*

bpùat-sǐi-sà ปวดศีรษะ have a

headache, *v.*

bpùat-tɔ́ɔng ปวดท้อง have a stomach ache, *v.*

bpui ปุย fluff, fluffy, *n., adj.*

bpŭi ปุ๋ย fertilizer, *n.*

bpuu ปู crab, *n.*

bpùu ปู่ grandfather (paternal), *n.*

bpùu-tûat ปู่ทวด great-grandfather (paternal), *n.*

bpuun ปูน lime, mortar, cement *n.*

bpʉ̂an เปื้อน get dirty, *n.*

bpʉʉn ปืน gun, *n.*

bpʉʉn-yài ปืนใหญ่ cannon, *n.*

ch (ช, ฉ, ฌ)

chà ฉะ hit, attack, strike (with a sword or knife), fight, quarrel (of people), *v.*

chaa ชา tea, *n.*

chaa ชา numb, *v., adj.*

cháa ช้า slow, *adj.*

chaa-bpà-ná-gìt ฌาปนกิจ cremation, cremate, *n., v.*

chaa-bpà-ná-sà-tăan ฌาปนสถาน crematory, *n.*

chaai ชาย masculine, man, *adj., n.*

chaai ชาย edge, rim, border, *n.*

chăai ฉาย shine, project (on a screen), reflect, *v.*

chaai-dɛɛn ชายแดน border, frontier, *n.*

chăai-năng ฉายหนัง show a movie, *v.*

chăai-tá-lee ชายทะเล seashore, *n.*

chàak ฉาก curtain, scene, scenery, act (of a show or play), screen for dividing rooms, partition, *n.*

chàak ฉาก carpenter's or draftsman's square (L- or T-shaped), *n.*

chàak-dtaa ฉากตา retina, *n.*

chaam ชาม bowl, dish, *n.*

chaan ชาน platform, porch (without roof), *n.*

chăan ฉาน scatter, *v.*

chaan-chaa-laa ชานชาลา platform (at station), *n.*

chàang ฉ่าง the sound of clanking of metal objects, *n.*

cháang ช้าง elephant, *n.*

chăang ฉาง barn, storehouse (for rice), storage bin, Thai silo, *n.*

cháang-náam ช้างน้ำ hippopotamus, walrus *n.*

cháang-pùak ช้างเผือก albino elephant, *n.*

cháan-mʉang ชานเมือง outskirts,

environs of a city, *n.*

chaao ชาว people, person, *n.*

cháao เช้า morning, *n.*

chaao-bprà-mong ชาวประมง fisherman, *n.*

cháao-chôo ฉาวโฉ่ widely and unfavorably (of being talked about), notoriously, *adv.*

cháao-dtrùu เช้าตรู่ early morning, dawn, *n.*

cháao-mûut เช้ามืด dawn, *n.*

chaao-naa ชาวนา farmer (mainly rice farming), *n.*

chaao-râi ชาวไร่ farmer, *n.*

chaao-sŭan ชาวสวน gardener, *n.*

chaao-tai ชาวไทย Thai people, *n.*

chàap ฉาบ large type of cymbal, *n.*

chàap ฉาบ paint, coat, whitewash, *v.*

chàap-chŭai ฉาบฉวย cursory, cursorily, *adj., adv.*

chàat ฉาด the sound of slapping, clapping, of striking together, *n.*

châat ชาติ nation, *n.*

chàat-chǎan ฉาดฉาน distinctly, clearly, fluently (of speech), *adv.*

chǎa-yaa ฉายา shade, shadow, image, projection, photographic portrait, the Pali name of a priest, *n.*

chá-baa ชบา hibiscus (the flower), *n.*

chà-bàp ฉบับ clf. for an issue, edition (of books or newspapers), letters, lottery tickets, documents, *n.*

chà-chǎan ฉะฉาน clear, distinct (of speech), clearly, distinctly, *adj., adv.*

chá-daa ชฎา theatrical high-pinnacled headdress or crown, *n.*

chá-dtaa ชะตา destiny, fate, *n.*

chà-gàat ฉกาจ bold, brave, daring, fierce, *adj.*

chà-gan ฉกรรจ์ strong, severe, grave, extreme, fierce, cruel, able-bodied, adult (of a man 18-30 yrs. old), *adj., n.*

chai ไช bore, pierce, bore through, *v.*

châi ใช่ yes, That's right!, *adv.*

chái ใช้ use, *v.*

chai, chai-cha-ná ชัย, ชัยชนะ victory, *n.*

chái-dâai ใช้ได้ valid, usable, *adj.*

chái-jàai ใช้จ่าย spend, *v.*

chái-mâi-dâai ใช้ไม่ได้ useless, *adj.*

chái-mòt ใช้หมด use up, *v.*

chái-wee-laa ใช้เวลา spend time, *v.*

chai-yá-puum ชัยภูมิ victorious place, strategically favorable position, *n.*

chai-yoo ไชโย Bravo!, Hurrah!,

Cheers!, *interj.*

chák ชัก pull, draw up, have spasms or convulsions, be inclined to, *v.*

chák-cháa ชักช้า hesitate, *v.*

chák-juung ชักจูง persuade, *v.*

chák-nam ชักนำ lead, *v.*

chák-wâao ชักว่าว fly a kite, masturbate (collq.) *v.*

chà-lǎam ฉลาม shark, *n.*

chà-làak ฉลาก label, lot (as a ticket in a lottery), *n.*

chà-làat ฉลาด intelligent, wise, clever, talented, *adj.*

chà-lâm แฉลั่ม beautiful, pretty, attractive, lovely, *adj.*

chà-làp แฉลบ move, slide, fly, *v.*

chá-lɛɛng ชะแลง crowbar, *n.*

chá-lǝǝi เชลย prisoner (of war), *n.*

chà-lǝ̌ǝi เฉลย solve (a problem or puzzle), give an answer, *v.*

chà-lǝ̌ǝm เฉลิม commemorate, celebrate, *v.*

chà-lǝ̌ǝm เฉลิม add to, increase, extend, *v.*

chà-lǝ̌ǝm-prá-chon-pan-sǎa เฉลิมพระชนม์พรรษา celebrate the king's birthday, *v.*

chà-lìa เฉลี่ย average, distribute even-

ly, divide equally, *v.*

chà-lǐang เฉลียง veranda, *n.*

chà-lǐao เฉลียว have a flash of realization, have an inkling, *v.*

chà-lǐao-chà-làat เฉลียวฉลาด clever, bright, smart, intelligent, *adj.*

chà-lòok โฉลก luck, fortune, *n.*

chá-lɔɔ ชลอ slow down, *v.*

chá-lɔɔm ชะลอม a kind of bamboo basket used for fruit, *n.*

chà-lɔ̌ɔng ฉลอง celebrate, *v.*

chà-lù ฉลุ perforate, make an intricate pattern on a scroll, *v.*

chà-lǔu ฉลู Year of the Ox, *n.*

chàm ฉ่ำ juicy, wet, damp, moist, humid, *adj.*

chám ช้ำ bruised, *adj.*

chǎm-chǎa ฉำฉา deal, wood of pine and other conifers, *n.*

cham-naan ชำนาญ skillful, expert, experienced, *adj.*

chá-mót ชะมด civet cat, *n.*

cham-rá ชำระ pay, *v.*

cham-rao ชำเรา rape, *v.*

cham-rút ชำรุด damaged, out of order, defective, *adj.*

chà-mùak ฉมวก a three-pronged fish spear, trident, *n.*

Phonetic • Thai • English

chan ชัน steep, *adj.*

chán ชั้น class, floor, shelf, level, layer, rank, grade, story, clf. for same, *n.*

chăn ฉัน I, me, *pron.*

chăn ฉัน eat (for monk), *v.*

chăn ฉันท์ a kind of Thai poem, *n.*

chá-ná ชนะ win, *v.*

chà-nàak ฉนาก sawfish, *n.*

chà-năi ไฉน how, why, for what reason, *adv.*

chà-nán ฉะนั้น therefore, like that, *adv.*

chán-bon ชั้นบน upstairs, upper story, upper layer, upper shelf, *n.*

chán-bprà-tŏm ชั้นประถม elementary grades, grade school level, *n.*

chán-chəəng ชั้นเชิง tactic, trick, strategy, *n.*

chán-dtôn ชั้นต้น beginning level, *n.*

châng ชั่ง weigh, *v.*

châng ช่าง master, expert, mechanic, specialist, artisan, *n.*

chà-ngák ชะงัก stop abruptly, *v.*

chà-ngát ชะงัด effective, sure, certain, *adj.*

châng-bprà-bpaa ช่างประปา plumber, *n.*

châng-dàt-pŏm ช่างตัดผม hair-dresser, *n.*

châng-dtàt-pŏm ช่างตัดผม barber, *n.*

châng-dtàt-sûa ช่างตัดเสื้อ tailor, dressmaker, *n.*

châng-fai-fáa ช่างไฟฟ้า electrician, *n.*

châng-gon ช่างกล mechanic, *n.*

chà-ngəə ชะเง้อ stretch one's neck out to see, *v.*

châng-krûang ช่างเครื่อง mechanic, engineer (operator of an engine), *n.*

châng-máai ช่างไม้ carpenter, *n.*

chán-mát-tà-yom ชั้นมัธยม secondary grades, junior/high school, *n.*

châng-náam-nàk ชั่งน้ำหนัก weigh, *v.*

chà-ngŏn ฉงน be puzzled, be perplexed, be confused, uncertain, skeptical, *v., adj.*

chà-ngôok ชะโงก poke (one's head) out, lean out, *v.*

chá-ngôn ชะง่อน overhanging rock, *n.*

châng-pâap ช่างภาพ photographer, camera man, *n.*

chà-níi ฉะนี้ like this, such as this, *adv.*

chá-nii ชะนี gibbon, *n.*

chá-nít ชนิด kind, type, sort, *n.*

chán-lâang ชั้นล่าง downstairs, lower story, lower layer, lower shelf, *n.*

chán-mát-ta-yom ชั้นมัธยม secondary school level, *n.*

chán-nai ชั้นใน the inside, the inner layer, *n.*

chán-nam ชั้นนำ leading, outstanding, *adj.*

chà-nòot โฉนด title deed for a piece of land, *n.*

chá-nuan ชนวน slate, fuse, primer, *n.*

chà-nŭan ฉนวน insulator, *n.*

chán-yîam ชั้นเยี่ยม top grade, first class, best, *n.*

chao เชาวน์ intelligence, quick wit, *n.*

châo เช่า rent, hire, *n.*

chǎo เฉา wilt, wither, shrivel up, *v.*

châo-chûang เช่าช่วง take a sublease, *v.*

chàp ฉับ quickly, instantly, *adv.*

chàp ฉับ an abrupt sound, *n.*

chà-pɔ́ เฉพาะ be specific, peculiar to, particularly, especially, exclusively, *v., adv.*

chà-pɔ́-gaan เฉพาะกาล temporary, seasonal, *adj.*

chà-pɔ́-nâa เฉพาะหน้า confronting, immediate, *adj.*

chàp-plan ฉับพลัน suddenly, *adv.*

chàp-wai ฉับไว quickly, promptly, *adv.*

chá-raa ชรา old, aged (of people), *adj.*

chàt ฉัตร tiered umbrella (emblem of royalty), *n.*

chát ชัด obvious, clear, distinct, sharp (picture), *n.*

chàt-mong-kon ฉัตรมงคล celebration of Coronation Day, *n.*

chá-waa ชวา Java, *n.*

chá-waa-laa ชวาลา (oil) lamp, torch, *n.*

chá-wá-lêek ชวเลข shorthand, *n.*

chà-wàt-chà-wĭan ฉวัดเวียน swoop or dart about (in the air), fly rapidly and haphazardly about with turning or wheeling motion, dash around (of a person or vehicle), *v.*

chà-wĭi ฉวี skin, complexion, *n.*

chĕe เฉ slant, not straight, deviated, diverged, out of line, *adj.*

chèet เฉด drive off, expel, *v.*

chék เช็ค cheque, check, *n.*

chên เช่น such as, for instance, like (for example), *adv.*

chèng เฉ่ง pay, settle up (an account), *v., slang.*

chét เช็ด wipe, *n.*

chè แฉะ swampy, wet, *adj.*

chɛ̀ɛ แช่ soak, immerse, *n.*

chɛ̌ɛ, chɛ̌ɛ-pooi แฉ, แฉโพย reveal, disclose (a secret), *v.*

chêek แฉก jagged, shred, stripped, *adj.*

chɛm-bpeen แชมเปญ champagne, *n.*

chêng แช่ง curse, *v.*

chɔ̌ɔi เชย old-fashioned, *adj.*

chɔ̌ɔi เฉย impassive, indifferent, quiet, still, calm, *adj.*

chɔ̌ɔi-mɔɔi เฉยเมย impassive, indifferent, quiet, still, calm, *adj.*

chəən เชิญ invite, *v.*

chəəng เชิง base, foot, foundation, *n.*

chəəng-kǎo เชิงเขา foothills, *n.*

chəəng-tian เชิงเทียน candlestick, *n.*

chəə-rîi เชอรี่ cherry, *n.*

chə̀ət-chǎai เฉิดฉาย radiant, bright, attractive, *adj.*

chə̀ət-chǎn เฉิดฉัน pretty, elegant,

beautiful, *adj.*

chia เชียร์ cheer, *v.*

chǐang เฉียง oblique, aslant, deflected, inclined, diagonal, *adj.*

chǐao เฉียว swoop down upon, snatch, snatch away suddenly, pass swiftly, *v.*

chîao เชี่ยว strong, swift, rapid (of current of water), *adj.*

chìap-kàat เฉียบขาด resolute (of a person), irrevocable (of an order), absolute, *adj.*

chìap-lǎam เฉียบแหลม keen, sharp, shrewd (of people), *adj.*

chìat เฉียด pass too close, very close, just miss, almost graze, *v.*

chii ชี nun, *n.*

chìi ฉี่ pee, urinate, *v.*

chíi ชี้ point, *v.*

chíi-dtua ชี้ตัว identify, point at (a person), *v.*

chíi-jɛɛng ชี้แจง explain, *v.*

chìik ฉีก tear, rip, *v.*

chîip-pa-jɔɔn ชีพจร pulse, *n.*

chìit ฉีด inject, spray, squirt *v.*

chìit-yaa ฉีดยา inject medicine, *v.*

chii-wá-bprà-wàt ชีวประวัติ biography, *n.*

chii-wá-wít-ta-yaa ชีววิทยา biology, *n.*

chii-wít ชีวิต life, *n.*

chim ชิม taste, *v.*

chin ชิน be used to, get used to, *v.*

chín ชิ้น piece, slice, *n.*

chìng ฉิ่ง cymbal, *n.*

ching-cháa ชิงช้า swing, *n.*

ching-chang ชิงชัง hate, abhor, *v.*

chìp-hǎai ฉิบหาย destroyed, ruined, perished, *adj.*

chít ชิด close, near, nearby, *adj.*

chǐu ฉิว angry, indignant, peeved, *adj.*

chòk ฉก snatch, grab, strike (as a snake), *v.*

chók, chók-muai ชก, ชกมวย box, *v.*

chom ชม admire, look at with pleasure, praise, look at, view, *v.*

chom, chom-chəəi ชม, ชมเชย admire, praise, compliment, *v.*

chom-puu ชมพู pink, *adj.*

chom-pûu ชมพู่ rose apple, *n.*

chom-rom ชมรม gathering, meeting, club, *n.*

chon ชน collide, run into, hit, *v.*

chon ชล water, *n.*

chon-bprà-taan ชลประทาน irriga-

tion, *n.*

chon-châat-tai ชนชาติไทย people of Thai nationality, *n.*

chon-gài ชนไก่ cockfight, *n.*

chon-la-mâak ชลมารค water-course, *n.*

chon-na-bòt ชนบท the country, rural area, *n.*

chooi โชย blow gently (of the wind), *v.*

chôok โชก soaking wet, *adj.*

chôok โชค luck, *n.*

chôok-choon โชกโชน extensively, *adv.*

chôok-dii โชคดี lucky, good luck, *adj.*

chôok-mâi-dii โชคไม่ดี unlucky, *adj.*

chǒom โฉม appearance, look, figure, shape, *n.*

chǒom-nâa โฉมหน้า face, facial features, countenance, *n.*

chǒom-ngaam โฉมงาม beautiful girl, a beauty, *n.*

chòop โฉบ swoop down on, swoop down on and snatch away, *v.*

chòot-klǎo โฉดเขลา foolish, stupid, *adj.*

chót-chái ชดใช้ reimburse, repay, compensate, *v.*

chót-chəəi ชดเชย replace what is

lost, compensate, v.

chɔ̀ เฉาะ chop, break open (as a coconut), v.

chɔ́k ชอล์ก chalk, n.

chɔ́k ช็อค shock, adj.

chɔ́k-goo-lét ช็อคโกแลต chocolate, n.

chɔ̂ng ช่อง opening, hole, cavity, space, gap, n.

chɔ̂ng-kǎo ช่องเขา mountain pass, n.

chɔ̂ng-kɛ̂ɛp ช่องแคบ strait, channel, n.

chɔ̂ng-klɔ̂ɔt ช่องคลอด vagina, n.

chɔ̂ng-taang ช่องทาง way, means, chance, opportunity, n.

chɔ̂ng-tɔ́ɔng ช่องท้อง abdominal cavity, n.

chɔ̂ng-wâang ช่องว่าง blank space, gap, n.

chɔ̂ɔ ช่อ cluster, bunch (as of fruit, flowers), n.

chɔ̂ɔ-dɔ̀ɔk-máai ช่อดอกไม้ bouquet, n.

chɔ̂ɔ-goong ฉ้อโกง cheat, v.

chɔ̂ɔ-lɔ́ ฉอเลาะ coo, talk fondly, amorously, speak cajolingly, v.

chɔ́ɔn ช้อน spoon, n.

chɔ́ɔn-chaa ช้อนชา teaspoon, n.

chɔ́ɔn-dtó ช้อนโต๊ะ tablespoon, n.

chɔ̂ɔp ชอบ like, v.

chɔ̂ɔp-gon ชอบกล funny, strange, peculiar, adj.

chɔ̂ɔp-jai ชอบใจ pleased with, happy, amused, v.

chɔ̂ɔp-mâak-gwàa ชอบมากกว่า prefer, v.

chɔ̂ɔp-pɔɔ ชอบพอ be fond of, love, v.

chɔ̂ɔp-tam ชอบธรรม righteous, just, honest, adj.

chɔ́p-bpîng ช้อปปิ้ง shopping, shop, n., v.

chù จุ fat, flabby, adj.

chûa ชั่ว bad, vile, wicked, adj.

chûai ช่วย help, assist, v.

chûai ฉวย snatch, grab, seize (suddenly or with a quick motion), v.

chûai-chii-wít ช่วยชีวิต rescue, v.

chûai-dtua-eeng ช่วยตัวเอง help oneself, masturbate, v.

chûai-dûai ช่วยด้วย Help!, interj.

chûai-oo-gàat ฉวยโอกาส seize the opportunity, v.

chûa-kraao, chûa-kà-nà ชั่วคราว, ชั่วขณะ for a while, tempo-

362

rary, adv., adj.

chûa-moong ชั่วโมง hour, n.

chuan ชวน urge, persuade, ask, invite (to do something), v.

chûang ช่วง span, extent, interval, n.

chûa-ráai ชั่วร้าย mean, disgusting, wicked, adj.

chûat ชวด Year of the Rat, n.

chûat ชวด great-grandparent (on either side), n.

chûi ฉุ่ย carelessly, haphazardly, sloppily, untidily, adv.

chǔi ฉุย be wafted quickly in large quantity (of smoke and odor only), v.

chǔi-chǎai ฉุยฉาย a posture of the Thai classical dance, n.

chǔi-chǎai ฉุยฉาย ostentatious (in manner), foppish, adj.

chùk ฉุก happen unexpectedly, v.

chùk-chǝ̌ǝn ฉุกเฉิน exigent, of an emergency nature, in a state of critical disorder, v.

chùk-lá-hùk ฉุกละหุก be in confusion, disorder (because of haste, unpreparedness), v.

chum ชุม abundant, plentiful, adj.

chum-chon ชุมชน assemblage of people, community, n.

chûm-chûun ชุ่มชื่น happy, joyful, adj.

chûm-chúun ชุ่มชื้น wet, soaked, adj.

chum-num ชุมนุม gather together, congregate, v.

chǔn ฉุน angry, furious, enraged, strong (of odors), pungent, adj.

chǔn-chǐao ฉุนเฉียว hot-tempered, quick-tempered, adj.

chun-la-mun ชุลมุน in confusion or commotion, adj.

chúp ชุบ dip, dipped in, v., adj.

chúp-líang ชุบเลี้ยง foster, raise, v.

chùt ฉุด drag, pull, haul, abduct, v.

chút ชุด suit, costume, set, n.

chùt-grà-chàak ฉุดกระชาก drag, drag off by force, v.

chút-nɔɔn ชุดนอน pajamas, n.

chút-raa-dtrii ชุดราตรี evening dress, n.

chút-wâai-náam ชุดว่ายน้ำ swimsuit, n.

chuu ชู raise, lift, elevate, boost, v.

chúu ชู้ adulterer, lover (usually refer to extra-marital relations), n.

chùut-chàat ฉูดฉาด vivid, loud, flashy (of colors, of clothing), adj.

chûa เชื่อ believe, v.

chúa เชื้อ germ, bacteria, enzyme, ferment, leaven, *n.*

chúa เชื้อ family line, *n.*

chúa-châat เชื้อชาติ race, nationality, *n.*

chúa-fang เชื้อฟัง obey, *v.*

chúa-jai เชื้อใจ trust, *v.*

chûak เชือก rope, cord, clf. for elephants, *n.*

chùai เฉื่อย slow, steadily but gently, lazily (of a breeze blowing), *adj., adv.*

chùai-chaa เฉื่อยชา inert, inactive, *adj.*

chùai-cháa เฉื่อยช้า slow, *adj.*

chûam เชื่อม join, solder, weld, cook in thick syrup, *v.*

chúa-mân เชื่อมั่น believe firmly, *v.*

chûan เฉือน cut off, slice off, edge out (in a contest), *v., slang.*

chûang เชื่อง tame, docile, *adj.*

chúa-plɔɔng เชื้อเพลิง fuel, *n.*

chúa-rôok เชื้อโรค germ, microbe, bacteria, *n.*

chûat เชือด cut forcefully, slit, *v.*

chúa-tǔu เชื่อถือ have trust, *v.*

chúa-wai-rát เชื้อไวรัส virus, *n.*

chûu ชื่อ name, *n.*

chûu-dang ชื่อดัง famous, *adj.*

chûu-dtua ชื่อตัว first name, *n.*

chûu-lên ชื่อเล่น nick name, *n.*

chúun ชื้น be damp, moist, humid, *v.*

chúun-jai ชื่นใจ delightful, refreshing, *adj.*

chûu-sà-gun ชื่อสกุล family name, *n.*

chûu-sǐang ชื่อเสียง fame, reputation, *n.*

chûut ชืด tasteless, *adj.*

d (ด, ฎ)

dàa ด่า curse, scold, *v.*

daai ดาย mow, cut (grass), *v.*

dâai ได้ get, obtain, able to, can, could, might, may, *v.*

dâai ได้ All right! O.K.!

dâai-bprìap ได้เปรียบ have an advantage, *v.*

dâai-gam-rai ได้กำไร profit, *v.*

dâai-gɛ̀ɛ ได้แก่ consist of, include, *v.*

dâai-ráp ได้รับ receive, *v.*

dâai-yin ได้ยิน hear, *v.*

dàak ดาก anus (very vulgar), *n.*

daam ดาม brace, strengthen, *v.*

dâam ด้าม handle, clf. for pens, *n.*

dàan ด่าน official station or post, customs house, port of entry, *n.*

dâan ด้าน side, sector, aspect, *n.*

dâan ด้าน dull, shameless, *adj.*

dàang ด่าง alkali, *n.*

dâan-glàp ด้านกลับ reverse, *n.*

dàang-prɔɔi ด่างพร้อย blemish, spotted, *adj.*

dàang-táp-tim ด่างทับทิม potassium permanganate, *n.*

dâan-kâo-muang ด่านเข้าเมือง immigration office, *n.*

dâan-sáai ด้านซ้าย left side, *n.*

daao ดาว star, *n.*

daao-dtòk ดาวตก shooting star, meteor, *n.*

daao-hǎang ดาวหาง comet, *n.*

daao-krɔ́ ดาวเคราะห์ planet, *n.*

daao-má-rú-dtà-yuu ดาวมฤตยู Uranus, *n.*

daao-nǔa ดาวเหนือ Pole Star, *n.*

daao-pá-rú-hàt ดาวพฤหัส Jupiter, *n.*

daao-pluu-dtoo ดาวพลูโต Pluto, *n.*

daao-prá-gèet ดาวพระเกตุ Venus, *n.*

daao-prá-krɔ́, daao-krɔ́ ดาวพระเคราะห์, ดาวเคราะห์ planet, *n.*

daao-prá-pút, daao-pút ดาวพระ

พุธ, ดาวพุธ Venus, *n.*

daao-prá-sùk, daao-sùk ดาวพระศุกร์, ดาวศุกร์ Venus, *n.*

daao-rɔ̂ək ดาวฤกษ์ fixed star, *n.*

daao-tiam ดาวเทียม satellite, *n.*

dàap ดาบ sword, *n.*

daa-raa ดารา movie star, star, *n.*

daa-raa-sàat ดาราศาสตร์ astronomy, *n.*

dàat ดาด pave, spread out, *v.*

dàat ดาษ widely distributed, *adj.*

dàat-fáa ดาดฟ้า deck, *n.*

dàa-wâa ด่าว่า scold at, speak abusively, *v.*

dɔ̀ เดาะ bat up, *v.*

dai ใด which, whichever, who, whoever, what, whatever, any, *pron., adj., adv.*

dai ใด any, a, an, *adj.*

dai-dai ใดๆ whatsoever, anyone, *adv.*

dai-noo-sǎo ไดโนเสาร์ dinosaur, *n.*

dàk ดัก trap, snare, *n., v.*

dàk-dɛɛ ดักแด้ cocoon, larva, *n.*

dam ดำ black, *adj.*

dam, dam-náam ดำ, ดำน้ำ dive, *v.*

dam-nəən ดำเนิน proceed, go on, *v.*

dam-ràt ดำรัส say (royal), *v.*

dam-rì ดำริ think, *v.*

dam-rong ดำรง uphold, sustain, *v.*

dan ดัน push, *v.*

dang ดัง loud, famous, *adj.*

dàng ดั่ง like, just as, *adj.*

dâng-dəəm ดั้งเดิม original, *adj.*, *adv.*

dang-glàao ดังกล่าว as mentioned, *adv.*

dâng-jà-mùuk ดั้งจมูก bridge of the nose, *n.*

dang-nán ดังนั้น therefore, *adv.*

dao เดา guess, reckon, *v.*

dàp ดับ extinguish, abolish, abate, *v.*

dàp-fai, dàp-pləəng ดับไฟ, ดับเพลิง put out fire, *v.*

dàt ดัด bend, adjust, change, *v.*

dàt-cha-nii ดัชนี index finger, *n.*

dàt-jà-rìt ดัดจริต pretend in manner, *v.*

deen เดน residues, *n.*

dee-rát-chǎan เดรัจฉาน beast, *n.*

dèet เดช power, might, *n.*

dèk เด็ก child, *n.*

dèk-chaai เด็กชาย boy, *n.*

dèk-gam-práa เด็กกำพร้า orphan, *n.*

dèk-ɔ̀ɔn เด็กอ่อน infant, *n.*

dèk-yǐng เด็กหญิง girl, *n.*

dèn เด่น prominent, conspicuous, *adj.*

dêng เด้ง bounce, *v.*

dèt เด็ด pluck, snap apart, *v.*

dèt-kàat เด็ดขาด decisive, absolute, firm, *adj.*

dɛ̀ɛ แด่ to, for, *prep.*

dɛ̀ɛk แดก eat, devour, *v., vulg.*

dɛɛn แดน border, *n.*

dɛɛng แดง red, *adj.*

dɛ̀ɛt แดด sunlight, *n.*

dɛ̀ɛt-ɔ̀ɔk แดดออก sunny, *adj.*

dəəm เดิม start, origin, *n.*

dəəm-pan เดิมพัน bet, *v.*

dəəm-tii เดิมที at first, from the beginning, *adv.*

dəən เดิน walk, *v.*

dəən-kà-buan เดินขบวน demonstrate, parade, *v.*

dəən-lên เดินเล่น go for a walk, *v.*

dəən-taang เดินทาง travel, *v.*

dəən-tɛ̌ɛo เดินแถว march, *v.*

diang-sǎa เดียงสา lack worldly wisdom, *v.*

diao เดียว sole, single, one, same, solely, alone, individual, exclusive, *adj.*, *adv.*

dìao เดี๋ยว alone, *adj.*

dĭao เดี๋ยว moment, in a moment, suddenly, *n., adv.*

dĭao-diao เดี๋ยวเดียว just a moment, *adv.*

dĭao-níi เดี๋ยวนี้ now, nowadays, *adv.*

dìat-chǎn เดียดฉันท์ dislike, *v.*

dì-chǎn, dì-chán ดิฉัน, ดิชั้น I, me (female speaker), *pron.*

dii ดี good, *adj.*

dii ดี gall bladder, *n.*

dii-bùk ดีบุก tin, *n.*

dii-gaa ฎีกา petition, *n.*

   sǎan-dii-gaa ศาลฎีกา supreme court, *n.*

dii-gan ดีกัน reconcile, make up, *v.*

dii-gwàa ดีกว่า better, *adj.*

dii-jai ดีใจ glad, happy, *adj.*

dii-kʉ̂n ดีขึ้น improve, *v.*

dii-mâak ดีมาก very good, *n.*

dii-sâan ดีซ่าน jaundice, *n.*

dìit ดีด flick, pluck, flip, *v.*

dìk ดิก (short for) dictionary, *n.*

din ดิน soil, ground, earth, *n.*

dîn ดิ้น struggle, wriggle, *v.*

din-bpʉʉn ดินปืน gunpowder, *n.*

din-dɛɛn ดินแดน land, territory, *n.*

dìng ดิ่ง vertical, righteous, *n.*

din-pǎo ดินเผา porcelain, china, *n.*

din-rá-bə̀ət ดินระเบิด dynamite, *n.*

dîn-ron ดิ้นรน struggle, *v.*

din-sɔ̆ɔ ดินสอ pencil, *n.*

dìp ดิบ raw, unripe *adj.*

dòk ดก prolific, *adj.*

dom ดม smell, sniff, *v.*

dôn ด้น penetrate, run a seam by hand, *v.*

don-dtrii ดนตรี music, *n.*

dòo โด่ pointed, *adj.*

dooi โดย by, through, by way of, *prep.*

dooi-chà-pɔ́ โดยเฉพาะ especially, *adv.*

dooi-dtrong โดยตรง directly, *adv.*

dooi-lá-ìat โดยละเอียด thoroughly, *adv.*

doon โดน hit, strike, *v.*

dòong โด่ง high up in the air, elevated, *adj.*

dòong-dang โด่งดัง famous, renowned, *adj.*

dòot โดด jump, leap, spring, bound, *v.*

dòot-dìao โดดเดี่ยว solitary, alone, *adj.*

dɔ̀i ด้อย inferior, undeveloped, *adj.*

dɔ̂m ด้อม snoop, *v.*

dɔɔi ดอย hill, mountain, peak, *n.*

dɔ̀ɔk ดอก flower, clf. for flowers,

incense, arrows, *n.*

dɔɔk-bîa ดอกเบี้ย interest (money), *n.*

dɔɔk-bua ดอกบัว lotus, *n.*

dɔɔk-dtuum ดอกตูม bud, *n.*

dɔɔk-fìn ดอกฝิ่น poppy, *n.*

dɔɔk-gà-làm ดอกกะหล่ำ cauliflower, *n.*

dɔɔk-jìk ดอกจิก club (in the deck of cards), *n.*

dɔɔk-máai ดอกไม้ flower, *n.*

dɔɔk-máai-fai ดอกไม้ไฟ fireworks, *n.*

dɔɔk-má-lí ดอกมะลิ jasmine, *n.*

dɔɔn ดอน highland, *n.*

dɔɔng ดอง pickle, pickled, *v., adj.*

dù ดุ scold, reproach, *v.*

dûai ด้วย with, by means of, also, as well, *prep.*

dûai-dtua-eeng ด้วยตัวเอง by oneself, *adv.*

dûai-gan ด้วยกัน mutual, together, *adj, adv.*

duan ดวล compete, *v.*

dùan ด่วน urgent, hasty, *adj.*

dûan ด้วน cut, cut off, be cut off, amputated, cut short, *v.*

duang ดวง clf. for some round objects

or shapes such as stamps, seals, stars, the sun, the moon, *n.*

duang, duang-chá-dtaa ดวง, ดวงชะตา fortune, luck, *n.*

duang-aa-tít ดวงอาทิตย์ sun, *n.*

duang-jan ดวงจันทร์ moon, *n.*

dù-dan ดุดัน fierce, *adj.*

dùk-dìk ดุกดิก move about, *v.*

dum ดุม button, *n.*

dun ดุน push, poke, *v.*

dun ดุล balance, *n.*

dûn ดุ้น stick, *n.*

dun-gaan-káa ดุลการค้า trade balance, *n.*

dun-la-páap ดุลภาพ equality, *n.*

dùt ดุจ as if, as, as though, *adj., adv., prep.*

dùt-sà-dii-ban-dìt ดุษฎีบัณฑิต doctorate degree, *n.*

dùt-sà-dii-ní-pon ดุษฎีนิพนธ์ dissertation, *n.*

duu ดู watch, look, look at, *v.*

duu-lɛɛ ดูแล take care of, keep an eye on, *v.*

duu-ngaan ดูงาน observe, *v.*

dùut ดูด suck, *v.*

dɯai เดือย spur (of a cock), *n.*

dɯan เดือน month, *n.*

dùat เดือด boil, *v.*

dùat เดือด furious, *adj.*

dùk ดึก late at night, *adv.*

dung ดึง pull, *v.*

dung-dùut ดึงดูด attract, *v.*

dûu ดื้อ stubborn, naughty, *adj.*

dûu-dung ดื้อดึง obstinate, disobedient, *adj.*

dùum ดื่ม drink, *v.*

dt (ด, ฎ)

dtaa ตา grandfather (maternal), *n.*

dtaa ตา eye, *n.*

dtaa-bɔ̀ɔt ตาบอด blind, *adj.*

dtaa-châng ตาชั่ง scale, *n.*

dtaa-dtùm ตาตุ่ม anklebone, *n.*

dtàak ตาก spread (in the sun), expose (to light, air, etc.), be exposed, be dried, *v.*

dtàak-aa-gàat ตากอากาศ take an airing, get out in the open, *v.*

dtaa-kàai ตาข่าย net, *n.*

dtaa-kǎao ตาขาว the white of the eye, cowardly, *n., adj.*

dtàak-dèet ตากแดด expose to the sun, spread out in the sun, *v.*

dtaa-kěe ตาเข slightly cross-eyed, squint-eyed, *adj.*

dtaai ตาย die, cease, stop, be dead, be fixed or motionless, *v.*

dtâai ใต้ below, under, *prep.*

dtâai ไต้ torch, *n.*

dtâai-din ใต้ดิน underground, *adj.*

dtâai-fùn ใต้ฝุ่น typhoon, *n.*

dtaai-jai ตายใจ have implicit faith in, trust implicitly, *v.*

dtaam ตาม follow, *v.*

dtaam ตาม along, *prep.*

dtaam-dəəm ตามเดิม as before, *adv.*

dtaam-gan ตามกัน follow each other, *v.*

dtaam-gòt-mǎai ตามกฎหมาย according to the law, legal, legally, *adj., adv.*

dtaam-jai ตามใจ please, yield to the wishes of, do as one pleases, *v.*

dtaam-lam-pang ตามลำพัง alone, *adv.*

dtàang ต่าง be different, separate, *v.*

dtàang-bprà-têet ต่างประเทศ overseas, foreign country, *n.*

dtàang-châat ต่างชาติ foreign, of another nationality, *n.*

dtàang-dâao ต่างด้าว alien, *n.*

dtàang-dtàang ต่างๆ various, varied, *adj.*

dtàang-hǔu ต่างหู earring, *n.*

dtàang-jang-wàt ต่างจังหวัด out of town, provincial, *n., adj.*

dtaa-raang ตาราง table (tabulation), square (e.g. square kilometer), *n.*

dtà-bai ตะไบ file (e.g. nail), *n., v.*

dtà-bai-lép ตะไบเล็บ nail file, *n.*

dtà-bɔɔng-pét ตะบองเพชร cactus, *n.*

dtà-bpuu ตะปู nail, *n.*

dtà-gaai ตะกาย climb, scramble up, *v.*

dtà-giang ตะเกียง lamp, *n.*

dtà-gìap ตะเกียบ chopsticks, *n.*

dtà-goon ตะโกน yell, *v.*

dtà-gɔɔn ตะกอน sediment, silt, *n.*

dtà-gráa ตะกร้า basket, *n.*

dtà-grai ตะไกร scissors, *n.*

dtà-greenq ตะแกรง shallow basket used as a sieve or strainer, sieve, *n., v.*

dtà-grɔɔ ตะกร้อ rattan ball, kind of a Thai ball game, *n.*

dtà-gùa ตะกั่ว lead, *n.*

dtà-gùat ตะกวด large brown lizard, the monitor, *n.*

dtai ไต kidney, *n.*

dtài ไต่ climb, *v.*

dtài-sǔan ไต่สวน investigate, *v.*

dtàk ตัก lap, *n.*

dták-gà-dtɛɛn ตั๊กแตน grasshopper, locust, *n.*

dtà-kàai ตะข่าย net, *n.*

dtà-kàap ตะขาบ centipede, *n.*

dtà-kɔ̌ɔ ตะขอ hook, *n.*

dtà-krai ตะไคร่ moss, *n.*

dtà-krái ตะไคร้ lemon grass, *n.*

dtà-kriu ตะคริว cramp, *n.*

dtà-làat ตลาด market, *n.*

dtà-làat-hûn ตลาดหุ้น stock market, *n.*

dtà-làat-mûut ตลาดมืด black market, *n.*

dtà-làat-sòt ตลาดสด food market, market in which raw or perishable foodstuffs are sold, *n.*

dtà-lìng ตลิ่ง bank (of a river), *n.*

dtà-lòk ตลก funny, joke, *adj., n.*

dtà-lòp ตลบ fold back, pull back, *v.*

dtà-lɔ̀ɔt ตลอด round the clock, all the time, through, throughout, *adv.*

dtà-lɔ̀ɔt-bpai ตลอดไป forever, all the time, on and on, *adv.*

dtà-lɔ̀ɔt-chii-wít ตลอดชีวิต for life,

Phonetic · Thai · English

lifelong, *adv.*

dtà-lɔɔt-taang ตลอดทาง all the way, *adv.*

dtàm ต่ำ low, *adj.*

dtam-bon ตำบล subdivision of a Thai district, *n.*

dtam-lʉng ตำลึง old Thai monetary unit, a kind of Thai plant, *n.*

dtam-naan ตำนาน legend, *n.*

dtam-nàk ตำหนัก palace, *n.*

dtam-nèng ตำแหน่ง location, *n.*

dtam-nì ตำหนิ reproach, blame, *v.*

dtam-raa ตำรา textbook, reference book, manual, formula, prescription, *n.*

dtam-ràp ตำรับ formula, prescription, *n.*

dtam-rùat ตำรวจ police, *n.*

dtan ตัน ton, *n.*

dtan ตัน clogged up, solid (not hollow), stopped up, *adj.*

dtâng ตั้ง set, place, set up, erect, establish, settle, locate, appoint, form, *v.*

dtâng ตั้ง as many as, as much as, *adv.*

dtâng-chʉ̂ʉ ตั้งชื่อ name, *v.*

dtâng-dtɛ̀ɛ ตั้งแต่ since, from, *prep.*

dtâng-jai ตั้งใจ intend, intend to, pay attention *v.*

dtâng-kan, dtâng-tɔ́ɔng ตั้งครรภ์, ตั้งท้อง pregnant, *adj.*

dtang-mee ตังเม caramel, *n.*

dtâng-sà-dtì ตั้งสติ concentrate, *v.*

dtao เตา stove, *n.*

dtào เต่า turtle, *n.*

dtâo เต้า breast, *n.*

dtao-bpîng เตาปิ้ง toaster, *n.*

dtao-fai เตาไฟ stove, *n.*

dtao-gɛ́ɛt เตาแก๊ส gas stove, *n.*

dtâo-hûu เต้าหู้ tofu, bean curd, *n.*

dtâo-jîao เต้าเจี้ยว bean paste, *n.*

dtao-òp เตาอบ oven, *n.*

dtao-pǐng เตาผิง fireplace, *n.*

dtao-rîit เตารีด iron, *n.*

dtàp ตับ liver, row, *n.*

dtà-pôok ตะโพก hip (body part), *n.*

dtàp-ɔ̀ɔn ตับอ่อน pancreas, *n.*

dtàt ตัด cut, sever, *v.*

dtàt-dtɔɔn ตัดตอน cut off, *v.*

dtàt-hǔa ตัดหัว behead, *v.*

dtàt-pǒm ตัดผม cut hair, *v.*

dtàt-pǒm ตัดผม hair cut, *n.*

dtàt-sǐn ตัดสิน judge, sentence, *v.*

dtàt-sǐn-jai ตัดสินใจ decide, *v.*

dtàt-tà-nǒn ตัดถนน build a road, *v.*

dtà-wan ตะวัน sun, *n.*

dtà-wan-dtòk ตะวันตก west, *n.*

dtà-wan-ɔ̀ɔk ตะวันออก east, *n.*

dtè เตะ kick, *v.*

dtem เต็ม full, *adj.*

dtem-jai เต็มใจ willing, *adj.*

dtên, dtên-ram เต้น, เต้นรำ dance, *v.*

dtè แตะ touch, *v.*

dtɛ̀ɛ, dtɛ̀ɛ-wâa แต่, แต่ว่า but, *conj.*

dtɛ̀ɛ-gɔ̀ɔn แต่ก่อน formerly, previously, *adv.*

dtɛ̀ɛk แตก break, *v.*

dtɛ̀ɛk-ngâai แตกง่าย breakable, *adj.*

dtɛ̀ɛ-lá แต่ละ each, *adj.*

dtɛ́ɛm แต้ม smear, *v.*

dtɛɛn แตน hornet, *n.*

dtɛɛng แตง squash, melon, *n.*

dtɛɛng-gwaa แตงกวา cucumber, *n.*

dtɛɛng-moo แตงโม watermelon, *n.*

dtɛ̀ɛt แตด clitoris (vulg.), *n.*

dtɛ̀ng แต่ง decorate, beautify, *v.*

dtɛ̀ng-dtâng แต่งตั้ง appoint, *v.*

dtɛ̀ng-dtua แต่งตัว get dressed, *n.*

dtɛ̀ng-nâa แต่งหน้า make-up, *v.*

dtɛ̀ng-ngaan แต่งงาน marry, *v.*

dtɛ̀ng-pleeng แต่งเพลง write a song, *v.*

dtəəm เติม fill, add on, add to, *v.*

dtəəm-náam-man เติมน้ำมัน refuel (gasoline), *v.*

dtì ติ criticize, blame, *v.*

dtîa เตี้ย short (height), *adj.*

dtiang เตียง bed, *n.*

dtiang-dìao เตียงเดี่ยว single bed, *n.*

dtiang-kûu เตียงคู่ double bed, *n.*

dtì-chom ติชม find fault with, find both good and bad points, *v.*

dtì-dtian ติเตียน reprove, criticize, express disapproval, *v.*

dtii ตี hit, beat, strike, *v.*

dtii-dtraa ตีตรา stamp (as with a seal), *v.*

dtii-dtŭa ตีตั๋ว buy a tick (collq.), *v.*

dtii-glɔɔng ตีกลอง drum, *v.*

dtii-kwaam ตีความ explain, interpret, *v.*

dtiin ตีน foot, paw (sometimes considered vulgar), *n.*

dtii-nâa ตีหน้า put on an expression feigning (e.g. ignorance), *v.*

dtiin-gòp ตีนกบ diving fins, *n.*

dtii-pim ตีพิมพ์ print, publish, *v.*

dtii-raa-kaa ตีราคา name the price, *v.*

dtii-sà-nìt ตีสนิท pretend to be acquainted, behave like a close friend in order to obtain favor, *v.*

dtìng ติ่ง outgrowth, appendage, *n.*

   sâi-dting ไส้ติ่ง appendix (body part), *n.*

dtìt ติด connect, attach, stick, adhere, be addicted to, get stuck, ignite, *v.*

dtìt-àang ติดอ่าง stutter, stammer, *v.*

dtìt-dtaam ติดตาม follow, *v.*

dtìt-dtâng ติดตั้ง install, *v.*

dtìt-dtɔ̀ɔ ติดต่อ contact, *v.*

dtìt-jai ติดใจ like, be fond of, be attracted or impressed *v.*

dtìt-kúk, dtìt-dtà-raang ติดคุก, ติดตะราง be in jail, imprisoned, *v.*

dtìt-lâo ติดเหล้า alcohol addicted, *adj.*

dtìt-lòm ติดหล่ม get stuck in the mud, *v.*

dtìt-pan ติดพัน engage, occupy, concern, involve, be engaged, be occupied, be in love, *v.*

dtìt-rôok ติดโรค catch a disease, *v.*

dtó โต๊ะ table, *n.*

dtòk ตก fall, *v.*

dtòk-bplaa ตกปลา fish, *v.*

dtòk-jai ตกใจ frightened, *adj.*

dtòk-long ตกลง agree, O.K., *v.*

dtom ตม bog, mud, *n.*

dtôm ต้ม boil, *v.*

dton ตน self, one's own self, *n.*

dtôn ต้น beginning, source, *n.*

dtôn ต้น clf. for trees or plants, *n.*

dtôn-chà-bàp ต้นฉบับ script, manuscript, *n.*

dtôn-kǎa ต้นขา thigh, *n.*

dtôn-kɔɔ ต้นคอ neck, *n.*

dtôn-máai ต้นไม้ tree, *n.*

dtôn-náam ต้นน้ำ spring (river), *n.*

dtoo โต big, *adj.*

dtôo โต้ oppose, *v.*

dtòp ตบ clap, slap, *v.*

dtòp-dtèng ตบแต่ง decorate, *v.*

dtòp-muu ตบมือ clap hands, *v.*

dtòt ตด fart, *v.*

dtɔ̀m ต่อม gland, *n.*

dtɔ̀m-kǎi-man ต่อมไขมัน sebaceous gland, *n.*

dtɔ̀m-náam-laai ต่อมน้ำลาย salivary gland, *n.*

dtɔ̀m-náam-lǔang ต่อมน้ำเหลือง lymph gland, *n.*

dtɔ̂ng ต้อง must, *v.*

dtɔ̂ng-gaan ต้องการ want, need, desire, wish, would like *v.*

dtông-hǎa ต้องหา accused, *adj.*

dtɔɔ ตอ stump (of a tree), *n.*

dtɔ̀ɔ ต่อ kind of wasp, *n.*

dtɔ̀ɔ ต่อ join, connect, put together, construct, continue, extend, add on, bargain, haggle, decoy (animal), *v., n.*

dtɔ̀ɔ ต่อ per, *prep.*

dtɔ̀ɔ-bpai ต่อไป continue, *v.*

dtɔ̀ɔk ตอก hammer, nail, *v.*

dtɔɔ-lɛ̌ɛ ตอแหล lie, talk a lot, babble, chatter (collq.), *v.*

dtɔɔm ตอม fly around, swamp around (e.g. flies or insects), *v.*

dtɔɔn ตอน at (time), *prep.*

dtɔ̂ɔn ต้อน herd (along), round up, trap, *v.*

dtɔɔn-bàai ตอนบ่าย in the afternoon

dtɔɔn-cháao ตอนเช้า in the morning

dtɔɔn-dùk ตอนดึก late at night

dtɔɔn-kâm ตอนค่ำ at night

dtɔɔn-glaang-kɯɯn ตอนกลางคืน night time

dtɔɔn-glaang-wan ตอนกลางวัน day time

dtɔɔn-nǎi ตอนไหน When?, What time?

dtɔɔn-níi ตอนนี้ now, *adv.*

dtɔ̂ɔn-ráp ต้อนรับ welcome, greet, receive (guests), *v.*

dtɔɔn-sǎai ตอนสาย late morning

dtɔɔn-tîang ตอนเที่ยง at noon

dtɔɔn-tîi ตอนที่ as, *prep.*

dtɔɔn-yen ตอนเย็น in the evening

dtɔ̀ɔp ตอบ answer, *v.*

dtraa ตรา mark, sign, symbol, stamp, brand, trademark, seal, *n.*

dtraa-châng ตราชั่ง scale, *n.*

dtrai ไตร three, *nm.*

dtrài, drài-dtrɔɔng ไตร่, ไตร่ตรอง consider, think carefully, *v.*

dtrɛɛ แตร horn, trumpet, bugle, *n.*

dtriam เตรียม prepare, *v.*

dtriam-dtua เตรียมตัว prepare oneself, prepare for, *v.*

dtriam-prɔ́ɔm เตรียมพร้อม prepare for, get ready, *v.*

dtrong ตรง straight, direct, honest, upright, accurate, *adj.*

dtrong-bpai ตรงไป straight ahead, go straight on, *adj.*

dtrong-gan ตรงกัน correspond, coincide, *v.*

dtrong-gan-kâam ตรงกันข้าม reverse, opposite, *v., adj.*

dtrong-kâam ตรงข้าม opposite, *adj.*

dtrong-wee-laa ตรงเวลา punctual, *adj.*

dtrɔ̀ɔk ตรอก lane, alley, *n.*

dtrɔɔng, dtrɔɔng-duu ตรอง, ตรองดู consider, think over, *v.*

dtrùat ตรวจ examine, check, *v.*

dtrùat-dtraa ตรวจตรา inspect, check, examine, *v.*

dtrùat-duu ตรวจดู go over (something) carefully, examine for, *v.*

dtrùat-kón ตรวจค้น search, *v.*

dtrùat-sɔ̀ɔp ตรวจสอบ check, verify, review, *v.*

dtrùt ตรุษ new year observances, *n.*

dtrɯng ตรึง fasten, fix, nail down, pin down, be held in place *v.*

dtrɯng-krîat ตรึงเครียด strenuous, stressful, *adj.*

dtua ตัว self, body, clf. for animals, chairs, tables, clothing, letters of the alphabet, digits, *n.*

dtŭa ตั๋ว ticket, *n.*

dtua-bprà-gan ตัวประกัน hostage, *n.*

dtua-dtà-lòk ตัวตลก clown, comedian, funny person, *n.*

dtua-dtɔ̀ɔ ตัวต่อ wasp, *n.*

dtua-eeng ตัวเอง oneself, *pron.*

dtua-gaan ตัวการ the culprit, *n.*

dtua-lá-kɔɔn ตัวละคร character (in a play), *n.*

dtua-lêek ตัวเลข number, *n.*

dtua-măi ตัวไหม silkworm, *n.*

dtua-mia ตัวเมีย female (animal), *n.*

dtua-năng-sɯ̌ɯ ตัวหนังสือ letter, character (of the alphabet), *n.*

dtua-nóot ตัวโน๊ต musical note, *n.*

dtua-nɔ̌ɔn ตัวหนอน maggot, *n.*

dtua-pim ตัวพิมพ์ block letter, *n.*

dtua-pûu ตัวผู้ male (animal), *n.*

dtua-rɔ́ɔn ตัวร้อน have a high temperature, *v.*

dtua-sàn ตัวสั่น shake, tremble, *v.*

dtua-tɛɛn ตัวแทน agent, representative, *n.*

dtua-yàang ตัวอย่าง sample, example, specimen, *n.*

dtua-yɔ̂ɔ ตัวย่อ abbreviation, *n.*

dtúk-gà-dtaa ตุ๊กตา doll, *n.*

dtù-laa-gaan ตุลาการ judge, *n.*

dtù-laa-kom ตุลาคม October, *n.*

dtùm ตุ่ม jar, *n.*

dtûm-hŭu ตุ้มหู earring, *n.*

dtun ตุน stock up, *v.*

dtùn ตุ่น bamboo rat, mole, *n.*

dtûu ตู้ cabinet, cupboard, *n.*

dtûu-bprai-sà-nii ตู้ไปรษณีย์ letter box, *n.*

dtùut ตูด ass, bottom, anus (vul.), *n.*

dtûu-too-rá-sàp ตู้โทรศัพท์ telephone box, *n.*

dtûu-yen ตู้เย็น refrigerator, *n.*

dtʉan เตือน warn, *v.*

dtʉk ตึก building, *n.*

dtʉk-rá-fáa ตึกระฟ้า skyscraper, *n.*

dtʉng ตึง tight, *adj.*

dtʉ̀ʉn ตื่น awake, *adj.*

dtʉ̂ʉn ตื้น shallow, *adj.*

dtʉ̀ʉn-dtên ตื่นเต้น excited, *adj.*

dtʉ̀ʉn-nɔɔn ตื่นนอน get up (from sleeping), *v.*

dtʉ̀ʉt ตืด tapeworm, *n.*

dtʉ̀ʉt ตืด stingy (collq.), *adj.*

e (เอ)

èek เอก one, prime, first, highest, leading, *n., adj.*

èek-àk-ka-râat-cha-tûut เอกอัครราชทูต ambassador, *n.*

èek-gà-chǎn เอกฉันท์ unanimity, unanimous, *n., adj.*

èek-gà-chon เอกชน private (not public), *n., adj.*

èek-gà-pâap เอกภาพ unity, *n.*

èek-gà-pót เอกพจน์ singular, *n.*

èek-gà-râat เอกราช independence (political), *n.*

èek-ga-sǎan เอกสาร document, *n.*

èek-gà-sìt เอกสิทธิ์ monopoly, *n.*

èek-gà-têet เอกเทศ independent, *adj.*

een เอน lean, recline, *v.*

een-iang เอนเอียง lean forward, *v.*

eeng เอง oneself, *pron.*

een-lǎng เอนหลัง lean back, *v.*

ee-sia, ee-chia เอเชีย, เอเชีย Asia, *n.*

èet เอดส์ AIDS, *n.*

ee-yên เอเย่นต์ agent, agency, *n.*

ék-sà-ree เอ็กซ์เรย์ X-ray, *v., n.*

en เอ็น tendon, sinew, gut, *n.*

en-duu เอ็นดู be tender toward, have compassion and affection for, *v.*

eng เอ็ง you (vulg.), *pron.*

èt เอ็ด scold, *v.*

èt เอ็ด one (used after tens, hundreds, etc.), *nm.*

èt-dtà-roo เอ็ดตะโร scold loudly, shout, *v.*

ɛ (แอ)

ɛɛ แอร์ air-conditioner, *n.*

ɛɛ-àt แออัด crowded, *adj.*

ɛɛ-hóot-sà-dtèet แอร์โฮสเตส์ stewardess, *n.*

ɛ̀ek แอก yoke, *n.*

ɛɛm-bpɛɛ แอมแปร์ ampere, *n.*

ɛ̀ɛp แอบ hide, *v.*

ɛ̀ɛp-jìt แอบจิด in the closet, *v., n.*

ɛ́ɛs-pai-rin แอสไพริน aspirin, *n.*

ɛ̀n แอ่น curve, bend out, *v.*

ɛ̀ng แอ่ง basin, *n.*

ɛ́p-bpɔ̂n แอ็ปเปิ้ล apple, *n.*

ɛ́p-frí-gaa แอฟริกา Africa, *n.*

ə (เออ)

əə เออ expressing agreement, assent, concurrence, approval, *excl.*

ə̀ə เอ่อ overflow, well up, *v.*

ə̀əi เอ่ย mention, utter, *v.*

ə̀ək-gà-rə̀ək เอิกเกริก clamorous, uproarious, hilarious, *adj.*

ə̂ə-rá-hə̌əi เอ้อระเหย dally, waste time, be without any care, at leisure, *v.*

f (ฟ, ฝ)

fàa ฝ่า go through, walk through, brave (hardship, danger), *v.*

fâa ฝ้า foggy, cloudy, dim, *adj.*

fáa ฟ้า sky, *n.*

fǎa ฝา lid, cover, wall *n.*

fǎa-chii ฝาชี cover placed over a dish of food, *n.*

fǎa-fɛ̀ɛt ฝาแฝด twins, *n.*

fàak ฝาก deposit, entrust, leave (something with someone), put (something) in the care of, enroll (a child in a school), *v.*

fàak ฟาก side (of street, waterway), shore, bank (of waterway), *n.*

fàak-ngən ฝากเงิน deposit money (in the bank), *v.*

fáa-lɛ̂p ฟ้าแลบ lightning, *n.*

faam ฟาร์ม farm, *n.*

fǎan ฝาน slice, cut thin, *v.*

faang ฟาง straw, *n.*

fǎa-pà-nǎng ฝาผนัง wall, *n.*

fáa-rɔ́ɔng ฟ้าร้อง thunder, *n., v.*

fàat ฝาด astringent (in taste), *adj.*

fàat ฝาด have an illusion, *v.*

fâat ฟาด strike, slap, hit hard, *v.*

fàa-táao ฝ่าเท้า sole (of the foot), *n.*

fai ไฟ fire, flame, light, *n.*

fài ใฝ have an interest, *v.*

fǎi ไฝ mole (on the skin), *n.*

fai-chǎai ไฟฉาย flashlight, torch, *n.*

fai-chék ไฟแช็ค lighter, *n.*

fai-fáa ไฟฟ้า electricity, *n.*

fài-fǎn ใฝ่ฝัน dream, *v.*

fai-nâa ไฟหน้า headlight, *n.*

fai-táai ไฟท้าย taillight, *n.*

fàk ฝัก pod, hull, case, sheath, scabbard, clf. for same, *n.*

fák ฟัก hatch, *v.*

fák ฟัก vegetable of the squash or melon family, *n.*

fàk-bua ฝักบัว shower (head), *n.*

fák-tɔɔng ฟักทอง pumpkin, *n.*

fan ฟัน tooth, *n.*

fǎn ฝัน dream, *n., v.*

fan-dàap ฟันดาบ fence, slash, cut, chop, sever, fencing, *v., n.*

fang ฟัง listen, *v.*

fàng ฝั่ง shore, coast, *n.*

fǎng ฝัง bury, *v.*

fâo เฝ้า guard, watch over, take care of, have an audience with, *v.*

fa-ràng ฝรั่ง Caucasian, *n.*

fa-ràng ฝรั่ง guava, *n.*

fɛɛ-chân แฟชั่น fashion, *n.*

fɛ̀ɛk แฝก elephant grass (used for roofing), *n.*

fɛɛn แฟน loved one, fan, boyfriend, girlfriend, fiancé (e), husband, wife, *n.*

fɛ̌ɛng แฝง hide, conceal, *v.*

fém แฟ้ม file, folder, *n.*

fəə-ní-jəə เฟอนิเจอร์ furniture, *n.*

fǐi ฝี pustule, boil, *n.*

fǐi-bpàak ฝีปาก verbal skill, *n.*

fǐi-dàat ฝีดาษ smallpox, *n.*

fǐi-mɯɯ ฝีมือ manual skill, craftsmanship, *n.*

fǐi-táao ฝีเท้า speed of foot, *n.*

fìn ฝิ่น opium, *n.*

flɛ̀t แฟล็ต flat, apartment, *n.*

flɛ̀t แฟลช flash (camera), *n.*

flúk ฟลุ๊ค fluke, a lucky chance, *n.*

fók, fók-chám ฟก, ฟกช้ำ bruised, swollen, *adj.*

fǒn ฝน rain, *n., v.*

fǒn ฝน sharpen, rub against, *v.*

fǒn-dtòk ฝนตก rain, *v.*

fǒn-lɛ́ɛng ฝนแล้ง drought, *n.*

fɔ̀ɔ ฝ่อ wither, dry out, abortive, *adj.*

fɔ̌ɔi ฝอย shreds, fibers, droplets, trivial details, *n.*

fɔ̌ɔi ฝอย brag (collq.), *v.*

fɔɔng ฟอง bubble, foam, *n.*

fɔ́ɔng ฟ้อง accuse, sue, prosecute, take to court, charge, *v.*

fɔɔng-náam ฟองน้ำ sponge, *n.*

fɔ́ɔng-rɔ́ɔng ฟ้องร้อง sue, bring charges against, *v.*

frii ฟรี free, *adj.*

fùn ฝุ่น dust, *n.*

fúng-fə́ə ฟุ้งเฟ้อ extravagant, *adj.*

fút-bɔɔn ฟุตบอล football, soccer, *n.*

fuu ฟู become fluffy, *v.*

fûuk ฟูก mattress (collq.), *n.*

fǔung ฝูง flock, herd, swamp, group, crowd, party, clf. for same, *n.*

fùak เฝือก plaster, cast, splint (for setting bones), *n.*

fuang เฟือง gearwheel, *n.*

fùk, fùk-hàt, fùk-fǒn ฝึก, ฝึกหัด, ฝึกฝน, practice, *v.*

fùk-sɔ́ɔm ฝึกซ้อม train, *v.*

fuun ฟืน firewood, *n.*

fúun ฟื้น recover, revive, bring back, restore, *n.*

fǔun ฝืน do against, act against, *v.*

fùut ฝืด tight, stuck, difficult to move, *adj.*

---

g (ก)

gà กะ estimate, guess, calculate, *v.*

gà กะ and (variant of กับ), *conj.*

gaa กา crow, kettle, pot, *n.*

gaa กา check, make a mark, *v.*

gaa-fɛɛ กาแฟ coffee, *n.*

gaa-gà-bàat กากบาท the plus or multiplication sign (+, x), *n.*

gaa-gii กากี khaki (color), *adj.*

gaai กาย body, *n.*

gàai ก่าย lean on, rest on, *v.*

gaai-bɔɔ-ri-hǎan กายบริหาร exercise, *n., v.*

gaai-ya-gam กายกรรม gymnastics, *n.*

gàak กาก refuse, residue, *n.*

gaam กาม sexual desire, *n.*

gâam ก้าม claw, pincer (of crab), *n.*

gaa-maa-rom กามารมณ์ sex, *n.*

gaam-ma-rôok กามโรค venereal disease, *n.*

gaan การ work, affair(s), matter(s), *n.*

gaan การ bound element placed before nouns or active verbs to form noun derivatives meaning "affairs of..., matters of...", *pfx.*

---

gâan ก้าน stem, stalk, *n*.

gaan-bâan การบ้าน homework, housework, household affairs, *n*.

gaan-ban-chii การบัญชี bookkeeping, *n*.

gaan-bin การบิน aviation, *n*.

gaan-bprà-chum การประชุม meeting, conference, *n*.

gaan-chûai-lɐ̌a การช่วยเหลือ aid, assistance, *n*.

gaang กาง spread out, stretch out, hang out, *v*.

gâang ก้าง bone (fish), *n*.

gaang-geeng กางเกง pants, trousers, *n*.

gaang-geeng-ling กางเกงลิง slip, underpants, *n*.

gaang-geeng-nai กางเกงใน underpants, panties, *n*.

gaang-kɐ̌en กางเขน cross, *n*.

gaan-líang การเลี้ยง feast, banquet, feeding, *n*.

gaan-mɐang การเมือง political affairs, *n*.

gaan-rák-sɐ̌a การรักษา care, maintenance, remedy, *n*

gaan-tûut การทูต diplomacy, *n*.

gaao กาว glue, *n*.

gâao ก้าว nine, *nm*.

gâao ก้าว step, pace, *v*.

gâao-nâa ก้าวหน้า step ahead, go forward, progress, advance, *v*.

gâao-ráao ก้าวร้าว aggressive, disrespectful, *adj*.

gàap กาบ bract, spathe, fragment of the clove tree, *n*.

gà-baan กบาล head, *n*.

gà-bòt กบฏ rebel, rebellion, *v*., *n*.

gá-bpì กะปิ shrimp paste, *n*.

gà-dtan-yuu กตัญญู grateful, *adj*.

gà-dti-gaa กติกา rule (in sports), *n*.

gài ไก่ chicken, cock, *n*.

gái ไก๊ด์ tour guide, *n*.

gài-nguang ไก่งวง turkey, *n*.

gàk กัก confine, restrict, detain, *v*.

gák กั๊ก waistcoat, waist jacket, *n*.

gàk-kɐ̌ng กักขัง confine, restrict, detain, *v*.

gàk-gan กักกัน confine, restrict, detain, *v*.

gà-laa กะลา hard shell coconut, *n*.

gà-laa-sɐ̌i กะลาสี sailor, seaman, *n*.

ga-la-mang กะละมัง enameled bowl or basin, *n*.

gà-làm-bplii กะหล่ำปลี cabbage, *n*.

gà-làm-dɔ̀ɔk กะหล่ำดอก cauli-

Phonetic · Thai · English

flower, *n.*

ga-la-mɛɛ กะละแม caramel, *n.*

gà-lòok กะโหลก skull, hard shell of the coconut, *n.*

gam-bpân กำปั้น fist, *n.*

gam-dao กำเดา nosebleed, *n.*

gam-guam กำกวม ambiguous, *adj.*

gam-lai กำไล bracelet, bangle, *n.*

gam-lang กำลัง power, strength, *n.*

gam-lang กำลัง progressive adverb-auxiliary indicating action going or the present time, *pfx.*

gam-ma-gaan กรรมการ committee, judge (competition), *n.*

gam-man-dtà-pâap กัมมันตภาพ radioactivity, *n.*

gam-man-dtà-pâap-rang-sǐi กัมมันตภาพรังสี radioactive, *n.*

gam-ma-tǎn กำมะถัน sulfur, *n.*

gam-ma-yìi กำมะหยี่ velvet, *n.*

gam-nàt กำหนัด joy, excitement, *n.*

gam-nòt กำหนด limit, set, stipulate, fix, *v.*

gam-nòt-gaan กำหนดการ schedule, program, *n.*

gam-pɛɛng กำแพง wall, *n.*

gam-puu-chaa กัมพูชา Cambodia, *n.*

gam-rai กำไร profit, *n.*

gan กัน each other, one another, mutually, together, severally (imparting a distributive sense to the verb, not usually rendered in English), *adv.*

gan กัน prevent, protect from, bar, shield, cut off, obstruct, *v.*

gan กัน shave, remove hair, *v.*

gân กั้น cut off, shut off, bar, *v.*

gan-chaa กัญชา marijuana, *n.*

gan-chon กันชน bumper, *n.*

gan-daan กันดาร barren, arid, lacking, *adj.*

gang-hǎn กังหัน windmill, *n.*

gang-kǎa กังขา doubt, have doubts, be skeptical, *v.*

gan-grai กรรไกร scissors, *n.*

gang-won กังวล worry, *n.*

gan-yaa-yon กันยายน September, *n.*

gao เกา scratch, *v.*

gào เก่า old (thing), *adj.*

gâo-ìi เก้าอี้ chair, *n.*

gàp กับ with, *prep.*

gàp-dàk กับดัก trap, snare, *n.*

gàp-dtan กัปตัน captain, *n.*

gàp-kâao กับข้าว food to eat with rice, *n.*

gà-prao กะเพรา basil, *n.*

gà-rá-gà-daa-kom กรกฎาคม July, *n.*

gà-ràt กะรัต carat, *n.*

gà-rìang กะเหรี่ยง Karen tribe, *n.*

gà-rìi กะหรี่ curry, female prostitute (collq.), *n.*

gà-rú-naa กรุณา please (do such and such), *v.*

gà-rú-naa กรุณา kind, merciful, *adj.*

gà-sàt กษัตริย์ king, *n.*

gà-sì-gam กสิกรรม agriculture, *n.*

gà-sì-gɔɔn กสิกร farmer, *n.*

gàt กัด bite, corrode, eat away, *v.*

gàt-fan กัดฟัน gnash one's teeth, *v.*

gàt-grɔ̀n กัดกร่อน corrosive, *adj.*

gà-tá กะทะ frying pan, skillet, *n.*

gà-təəi กะเทย transvestite, transsexual, *n.*

gà-tí กะทิ coconut cream, *n.*

gà-wii กวี poet, *n.*

gee เกย์ gay man, *n.*

gèng เก่ง good at, intelligent, smart, efficient, clever, competent, *adj.*

gèp เก็บ keep, collect, pick, pick up, *v.*

gèp-kɔ̌ɔng เก็บของ pack, clean up, clear the area, *v.*

gèp-ngən เก็บเงิน save money,

check the bill, *v.*

gè แกะ sheep, *n.*

gè แกะ carve, pick out, remove, *v.*

gɛ̂ɛ แก่ old, *adj.*

gɛ̀ɛ แก่ to, *prep.*

gɛ̂ɛ แก้ untie, undo, take off (clothes), mend, repair, solve, relieve, correct, make an excuse, *v.*

gɛ̂ɛ-bpan-hǎa แก้ปัญหา solve a problem, solve a puzzle, *v.*

gɛ̂ɛ-dtua แก้ตัว make false excuse, make up for one's losses or errors, *v.*

gɛ̂ɛ-kǎi แก้ไข correct, mend, revise, resolve *v.*

gɛ̂ɛ-kéen แก้แค้น take revenge, *v.*

gɛ̂ɛm แก้ม cheek, *n.*

gɛɛn แกน axis, *n.*

gɛɛng แกง curry, soup, *n.*

gɛɛng-jùut แกงจืด mild curry, *n.*

gɛɛng-pèt แกงเผ็ด hot curry, *n.*

gɛ̂ɛo แก้ว glass, *n.*

gɛ̂ɛo-dtaa แก้วตา pupil (of the eye), *n.*

gɛ̂ɛo-hǔu แก้วหู eardrum, *n.*

gɛ̂ɛ-pâa แก้ผ้า undress, *v.*

gɛ́ɛt แก๊ส gas, *n.*

gəən เกิน too (much), over, *adv.*

gəən-bpai เกินไป too (much), *adv.*

a b bp ch d dt e ɛ ə f **g** h i j k l m n ng o ɔ p r s t u ʉ w y

gə̀ət เกิด be born, arise, occur, happen, take place, originate, give rise to, take birth, bring about, start up, *v.*

gə̀ət เกิด happen, occur, *v.*

gia เกียร์ gear, *n.*

gìao เกี่ยว hook, hitch, *n.*

gìao เกี่ยว cut (with a sickle), harvest, reap, concern, be related to, *v.*

gìao-gàp เกี่ยวกับ about, *prep.*

gìat เกียรติ honor, *n.*

gìat-dtì-yót เกียรติยศ honor, prestige, *n.*

gìi กี่ how much, how many

gii-dtâa กีต้าร์ guitar, *n.*

gii-laa กีฬา sport, *n.*

gìi-moong กี่โมง What time?

gìit-kwǎang กีดขวาง impede, hinder, obstruct *v.*

gì-loo กิโล kilo, *n.*

gì-loo-gram กิโลกรัม kilogram, *n.*

gì-loo-méet กิโลเมตร kilometer, *n.*

gin กิน eat, *v.*

gìng กิ่ง bough (of a tree), *n.*

gìng-gàa กิ้งก่า tree lizard, *n.*

gìng-gɯɯ กิ้งกือ millipede, *n.*

gin-kâao กินข้าว have a meal, *v.*

gíp กิ๊บ hairclip, *n.*

glâa กล้า brave, bold, *adj.*

glâa-hǎan กล้าหาญ brave, courageous *adj.*

glaai, glaai-bpen กลาย, กลายเป็น change, transform, turn into, convert, become, *v.*

glâam กล้าม muscle, *n.*

glaang กลาง center, middle, *n.*

glàao กล่าว make a statement, say, declare, mention, *v.*

glàao-hǎa กล่าวหา accuse, allege, charge, *v.*

glai ไกล far, *adj.*

glâi ใกล้ near, *adj.*

glàn กลั่น distill, extract, *v.*

glân กลั้น suppress, hold back, restrain, inhibit, refrain from, *v.*

glàp กลับ return, turn back, turn over, turn upside down, turn inside out, *v.*

glèt เกล็ด scale, flake, tuck, dart, *n.*

glɛ̂ɛng แกล้ง make a pretence, do on purpose, tease, annoy, *v.*

glìat เกลียด hate, detest, *v.*

glìn กลิ่น odor, smell, *n., v.*

glîng กลิ้ง roll, slide, *v.*

glom กลม round, *adj.*

glɔ̀ng กล่อง box, case, *n.*

glɔ̂ng, glɔ̂ng-tàai-rûup กล้อง, กล้องถ่ายรูป camera, *n.*

glɔ̂ng-jun-la-tát กล้องจุลทรรศน์ microscope, *n.*

glɔ̂ng-sɔ̀ng-taang-glai กล้องส่องทางไกล binoculars, *n.*

glɔɔn กลอน bolt, latch, a kind of Thai verse form, *n.*

glɔɔng กลอง drum, *n.*

glua กลัว afraid, scared, fear, *adj., v.*

glûai กล้วย banana, *n.*

glûai-máai กล้วยไม้ orchid, *n.*

glùm กลุ่ม group, *n.*

glûm, glûm-jai กลุ้ม, กลุ้มใจ worry, worried, gloomy, *v., adj.*

glɯa เกลือ salt, *n.*

glɯng กลึง lathe, *v.*

glɯɯn กลืน swallow, *v.*

gòk กก hatch, *v.*

gôm ก้ม bend, bow, *v.*

gôn ก้น bottom, *n.*

gong-sǔn กงสุล consul, *n.*

gôo โก้ elegant, grand, all dressed up, beautiful, *adj.*

goo-dang โกดัง warehouse, *n.*

goo-gôo โกโก้ cocoa, *n.*

goo-hòk โกหก lie, *n., v.*

goo-laa-hǒn โกลาหล tumult, disturbance, confusion, *n.*

goo-meen โกเมน garnet, *n.*

goon โกน shave, *v.*

goong โกง cheat, deceive, defraud, bent, crooked, *v., adj.*

gòong โก่ง arch, bend upward, *v.*

gòot โกศ urn, *n.*

gòp กบ frog, *n.*

gòt กด press, dial, *v.*

gòt-mǎai กฎหมาย law, *n.*

gɔ̀ เกาะ island, *n.*

gɔ̀ เกาะ cling to, *v.*

gɔ́k, gɔ́k-náam ก๊อก, ก๊อกน้ำ tap, faucet, *n.*

gɔɔ กอ clump (of trees), *n.*

gɔ̀ɔ ก่อ build, construct *v.*

gɔ̂ɔ ก็ also, too, then, *adv.*

gɔ̀ɔn ก่อน before, previous, first, *adv., prep., conj.*

gɔɔng กอง troop, force, pile, heap, *n.*

gɔɔng-ban-chaa-gaan กองบัญชาการ headquarters, *n.*

gɔɔng-táp กองทัพ armed forces, *n.*

gɔɔng-táp-aa-qàat กองทัพอากาศ air force, *n.*

gɔɔng-táp-bòk กองทัพบก army, military land forces, *n.*

gɔɔng-táp-rɯa กองทัพเรือ navy, naval forces, *n.*

gɔ́ɔp กอล์ฟ golf, *n.*

gɔɔ-ra-nii กรณี case, incident, *n.*

gɔ̀ɔ-sâang ก่อสร้าง construct, *v.*

gɔ̀ɔt กอด embrace, hug, *v.*

graam กราม jaw, *n.*

grà-bìi กระบี่ sword, *n.*

grà-bɔ̀ɔk กระบอก cylinder, *n.*

grà-bpǎo กระเป๋า bag, pocket, *n.*

grà-bpǎo-dəən-taang กระเป๋า เดินทาง suitcase, *n.*

grà-bpǎo-ngən, grà-bpǎo-sà-dtaang กระเป๋าเงิน, กระเป๋าสตางค์ purse, wallet, *n.*

grà-bpǎo-tʉ̌ʉ กระเป๋าถือ handbag, *n.*

grà-bpɔ̌ng กระป๋อง can, tin, *n.*

grà-bproong กระโปรง skirt, *n.*

grà-buan กระบวน procession, line, train, clf. for processions, lines, trains, in the matter of, procedure, method, strategy, technique, *n.*

grà-bʉ̂ang กระเบื้อง tile *n.*

grà-cháo กระเช้า bamboo basket, *n.*

grà-daan กระดาน board, *n.*

grà-dàat กระดาษ paper, *n.*

grà-dàat-cham-rá กระดาษชำระ tissue paper, toilet paper, *n.*

grà-dàat-saai กระดาษทราย sandpaper, *n.*

grà-dìng กระดิ่ง bell, doorbell, *n.*

grà-dòot กระโดด jump, *v.*

grà-dɔɔng กระดอง shell (of crustaceans), carapace, *n.*

grà-dtàai กระต่าย rabbit, hare, *n.*

grà-dtìk กระติก canteen, *n.*

grà-dtìk-náam-rɔ́ɔn กระติกน้ำ ร้อน thermos bottle, *n.*

grà-dtùk กระตุก jerk, *v.*

grà-dtûn กระตุ้น encourage, stimulate, *v.*

grà-dum กระดุม button, *n.*

grà-dùuk กระดูก bone, *n.*

grà-jòk กระจก mirror, *n.*

grà-joom กระโจม tent, *n.*

gram กรัม gram, *n.*

grà-pǒm กระผม I, me, *pron.*

grà-pɔ́ กระเพาะ stomach, *n.*

grà-pɔ́-bpàt-sa-wá กระเพาะ ปัสสาวะ urinary bladder, *n.*

grà-príp, grà-príp-dtaa กระพริบ, กระพริบตา blink, twinkle, *v.*

grà-rɔ̂ɔk กระรอก squirrel, *n.*

grà-sɛ̌ɛ กระแส current, *n.*

grà-sɛ̌ɛ-fai-fáa กระแสไฟฟ้า electric current, *n.*

grà-sɛ̌ɛ-náam กระแสน้ำ current of water, *n.*

grà-sɛ̌ɛ-ngən กระแสเงิน monetary currency, circulation of money, *n.*

grà-sɔ̀ɔp กระสอบ sack, bag, *n.*

grà-suang กระทรวง ministry, *n.*

grà-suang-gaan-dtàang-bprà-têet กระทรวงการต่างประเทศ Ministry of Foreign Affairs, *n.*

grà-suang-gaan-klang กระทรวงการคลัง Ministry of Finance, *n.*

grà-suang-gà-laa-hŏom กระทรวงกลาโหม Ministry of Defense, *n.*

grà-suang-gà-sèet กระทรวงเกษตร Ministry of Agriculture, *n.*

grà-suang-má-hàat-tai กระทรวงมหาดไทย Ministry of the Interior, *n.*

grà-suang-paa-nít กระทรวงพาณิชย์ Ministry of Commerce, *n.*

grà-suang-sǎa-taa-ra-ná-sùk กระทรวงสาธารณสุข Ministry of Public Health, *n.*

grà-suang-sùk-sǎa-tí-qaan กระทรวงศึกษาธิการ Ministry of Education, *n.*

grà-suang-ùt-sǎa-hà-gam กระทรวงอุตสาหกรรม Ministry of Industry, *n.*

grà-suang-yút-dtì-tam กระทรวง ยุติธรรม Ministry of Justice, *n.*

grà-tǎang กระถาง flowerpot, *n.*

grà-tiam กระเทียม garlic, *n.*

grà-tə̀p กระเถิบ move over, *v.*

grà-tŏon กระโถน spittoon, *n.*

grìt กริช dagger, *n.*

grom กรม department, *n.*

grom-ma-tan กรมธรรม์ contract, *n.*

grom-ma-tan-bprà-gan-pai กรมธรรม์ประกันภัย insurance policy, *n.*

gron กรน snore, *v.*

grong กรง cage, jail, *n.*

gròot โกรธ angry, *adj.*

gròt กรด acid, *n.*

grɔ̀ɔk กรอก fill with, pour into, fill in (a form, an application), *v.*

grɔɔng กรอง filter, strain, *v.*

grɔ̀ɔp กรอบ frame, *n.*

grùat กรวด pebble, *n.*

grung กรุง city, metropolis, *n.*

grung-têep กรุงเทพฯ Bangkok, *n.*

guan กวน stir, trouble, bother, *v.*

guan-jai กวนใจ disturb, bother, agitate, *v.*

gùat กวด chase, pursue, *v.*

gùat-wí-chaa กวดวิชา tutor, coach, teach, *v.*

a b bp ch d dt e ɛ ə f **g** h i j k l m n ŋ o ɔ p r s t u ʉ w y

gù-làap กุหลาบ rose, *n.*

gum-paa-pan กุมภาพันธ์ February, *n.*

gûng กุ้ง shrimp, prawn, *n.*

gûng-gâam-graam กุ้งก้ามกราม lobster, *n.*

gun-jɛɛ กุญแจ key, *n.*

gun-jɛɛ-bpàak-dtaai กุญแจปาก ตาย spanner, wrench, *n.*

guu กู I, me (impolite), *pron.*

gùak เกือก (horse) shoe, *n.*

gùap เกือบ almost, nearly *adv.*

gwàa กว่า more (to a greater degree), more than, *adj.*

gwàa กว่า remainder (collq.), small fraction, *n.*

gwâan กว้าน haul in, take great quantities of, *n.*

gwaang กวาง dear, *n.*

gwâang กว้าง broad, wide, *adj.*

gwàat กวาด sweep, *v.*

gwai ไกว rock, swing, sway, *v.*

gwàk กวัก beckon, summon, *v.*

gwàt กวัด swing, sway, *v.*

gwèng แกว่ง swing, *v.*

gwǔai-dtĭao ก๋วยเตี๋ยว rice noodle, *n.*

h (ห, ฮ)

há ฮะ yes, variant of kráp (ครับ) or ká (คะ), *adv.*

haa ฮา the sound of a laugh, *n.*

hàa ห่า clf. for a heavy rainfall, *n.*

hàa ห่า a spirit believed to be responsible for plague, cholera, anthrax, *n.*

hâa ห้า five, *nm.*

hǎa หา look for, search for, seek, *v.*

hǎai หาย disappear, vanish, lose, be missing, be lost from sight, get well, recover, be healed or cured, *v.*

hǎai-jai หายใจ breathe, *v.*

hǎai-jai-kâo หายใจเข้า inhale, *v.*

hǎai-jai-ɔ̀ɔk หายใจออก exhale, *v.*

hàak หาก if, in case, *conj.*

hàam ห่าม almost ripe (fruit), *adj.*

hâam ห้าม ban, forbid, prohibit, *v.*

hǎam หาม carry, bear, *v.*

hàan ห่าน goose, *n.*

hǎan หาร divide (math), *v.*

hàang ห่าง far apart, distant, *adj.*

hâang ห้าง scaffold, firm, commercial establishment, department store, *n.*

hǎang หาง tail, *n.*

hǎang-bpia หางเปีย pigtail, *n.*

hâang-sàp-pa-sǐn-káa ห้างสรรพสินค้า department store, *n.*

hǎao หาว yawn, *v.*

hàap หาบ carry at both ends of a pole on one's shoulder, *v.*

hǎa-ruu หารือ consult, *v.*

hàat หาด beach, *n.*

hǎa-ya-ná หายนะ disaster, calamity, destruction, *n.*

hâi ให้ give, let, allow, *v.*

hâi ให้ to, so that, for, in order to, *prep., conj.*

hâi-à-pai ให้อภัย forgive, *v.*

hâi-châo ให้เช่า rent out, rent, for rent, *v., adj.*

hai-droo-jên ไฮโดรเจน hydrogen, *n.*

hâi-sǎn-yaa ให้สัญญา promise, *v.*

hâi-tâa ให้ท่า encourage a man to make advances, *v.*

hâi-taan ให้ทาน give alms, *v.*

hâi-yuum ให้ยืม lend, *v.*

hàk หัก break, *v.*

hàk-lǎng หักหลัง betray, *v.*

hǎn หัน turn, *v.*

han-lang หันหลัง turn around, *v.*

han-lǒo ฮัลโหล Hello! (on the phone)

hào เห่า bark, *v.*

hǎo เหา louse, *n.*

hàt หัด practice, tame (animal), *v.*

hěe เห deviate, deflect, *v.*

hee-lí-kôp-dtəə เฮลิคอปเตอร์ helicopter, *n.*

hěeo เหว gorge, chasm, abyss, *n.*

hee-roo-iin เฮโรอีน heroin, *n.*

hèet เหตุ cause, reason, *n.*

hèet-chùk-chəən เหตุฉุกเฉิน emergency, *n.*

hèet-gaan เหตุการณ์ incident, event, situation, circumstances, *n.*

hèet-pǒn เหตุผล reason, *n.*

hěn เห็น see, *v.*

hěn-dûai เห็นด้วย agree, *v.*

hěn-gèe-dtua เห็นแก่ตัว selfish, *adj.*

hěn-jai เห็นใจ sympathize, *v.*

hèp เห็บ tick, wood tick, hail, *n.*

hèt เห็ด mushroom, *n.*

hěe แห fishing net *n.*

hem แฮม ham, *n.*

hêng แห้ง dry, *adj.*

hǐi หี vagina (vulg.), vulva, *n.*

hìip หีบ box, *n.*

hìip-sòp หีบศพ coffin, *n.*

hì-má หิมะ snow, *n.*

hì-má-dtòk หิมะตก snow, *v.*

Phonetic · Thai · English

hǐn หิน rock, stone, pebble, *n.*

hǐn-bpuun หินปูน limestone, tartar, *n.*

hin-duu ฮินดู Hindu, *n.*

hǐng หิ้ง shelf, *n.*

hǐng-hɔ̂i หิ้งห้อย firefly, *n.*

hǐn-ná-yaan หินยาน Hinayana, Theravada Buddhism, *n.*

hǐn-ngɔ̂ɔk หินงอก stalagmite, *n.*

hǐn-ɔ̀ɔn หินอ่อน marble, *n.*

hǐn-yɔ́ɔi หินย้อย stalactite, *n.*

hîu หิ้ว hold, carry, *v.*

hǐu หิว hungry, *adj.*

hǐu-kâao หิวข้าว hungry, *adj.*

hǐu-náam หิวน้ำ thirsty, *adj.*

hòk หก six, *nm.*

hòk หก spill, spilled, *v., adj.*

hòk-lóm หกล้ม stumble and fall, *v.*

hǒng หงส์ swan, *n.*

hǒn-taang หนทาง way, route, *n.*

hoo โฮ the sound imitating crying, *n.*

hǒom โหม push (one's strength) to the limit, *v.*

hǒon โหน hang, swing from by the hands, *n.*

hǒon โหร astrologer, *n.*

hòot, hòot-ráai โหด, โหดร้าย cruel, wild, brutal, ruthless, *n.*

hòt หด shrink, *v.*

hɔ̂ng ห้อง room, *n.*

hɔ̂ng-dtâai-din ห้องใต้ดิน basement, *n.*

hɔ̂ng-gèp-kɔ̌ɔng ห้องเก็บของ storeroom, *n.*

hɔ̂ng-krua ห้องครัว kitchen, *n.*

hɔ̂ng-náam ห้องน้ำ bathroom, lavatory, toilet, *n.*

hɔ̂ng-nɔɔn ห้องนอน bedroom, *n.*

hɔ̂ng-ráp-kɛ̀ɛk ห้องรับแขก living room, *n.*

hɔ̂ng-rian ห้องเรียน classroom, *n.*

hɔ̂ng-sà-mùt ห้องสมุด library, *n.*

hɔ̂ng-tǒong ห้องโถง hall, *n.*

hɔ̀ɔ ห่อ wrap, *v.*

hɔ̌ɔ หอ tower, dormitory, *n.*

hɔ̌ɔ-duu-daao หอดูดาว observatory, *n.*

hɔ̌ɔi หอย shell, oyster, snail, *n.*

hɔ̌ɔi-kòong หอยโข่ง snail, *n.*

hɔ̌ɔi-naang-rom หอยนางรม oyster, *n.*

hɔ̌ɔ-kɔɔi หอคอย tower, *n.*

hɔ̌ɔm หอม onion, *n.*

hɔ̌ɔm หอม smell, sniff kiss, *v.*

hɔɔ-moon ฮอร์โมน hormone, *n.*

hɔ̀ɔp หอบ gasp, *v.*

hǔa หัว head, *n.*

hǔa-dɯɯ หัวดื้อ stubborn, *adj.*

hǔa-gào หัวเก่า conservative, old-fashioned, *adj.*

hǔa-gà-lòok หัวกะโหลก skull, *n.*

hùai ห่วย no good (slang), *adj.*

hûai ห้วย creek, brook, stream, *n.*

hǔai หวย lottery, gambling game, *n.*

hǔa-jai หัวใจ heart, *n.*

hǔa-jai-waai หัวใจวาย heart attack, *n.*

hǔa-kào หัวเข่า knee, *n.*

hǔa-kěng หัวแข็ง stubborn, *adj.*

hǔa-kɔ̂ɔ หัวข้อ topic, heading, *n.*

hǔa-láan หัวล้าน bald, bald head, *adj., n.*

hǔa-mɛ̂ɛ-mɯɯ หัวแม่มือ thumb, *n.*

hǔan หวน turn back, *v.*

hǔa-nâa หัวหน้า leader, chief, *n.*

hùang ห่วง worry, *v.*

hûang ห้วง vastness, depth, *n.*

hǔang หวง refuse to share or give away, *v.*

hǔa-nom หัวนม nipple, teat, *n.*

hǔa-rɔ́ หัวเราะ laugh, *v.*

hǔa-sà-mɔ̌ɔng หัวสมอง brain concussion, *n.*

hǔa-sùup หัวสูบ valve, *n.*

hùat หวด whip, lash, *v.*

hùat หวด an earthenware steamer, *n.*

hǔa-tian หัวเทียน spark plug, *n.*

hûm หุ้ม cover, wrap around, *v.*

hûm-grɔ̀ หุ้มเกราะ armored, *adj.*

hùn หุ่น model, puppet, shape, *n.*

hûn หุ้น share, stock, *n.*

hǔng หุง cook, *v.*

hùn-grà-bɔ̀ɔk หุ่นกระบอก puppet, marionette, *n.*

hûn-sùan หุ้นส่วน partnership, *n.*

hùn-yon หุ่นยนต์ robot, *n.*

hùp หุบ shut, close, space (between mountains and hills), *v., n.*

húp ฮุบ strike, snatch at, snap up, swallow up, *v.*

hùp-kào หุบเขา valley, *n.*

hùu หู่ shrunken, wrinkled, *adj.*

hǔu หู ear, *n.*

hǔu-bao หูเบา credulous, *adj.*

hǔu-dtɯng หูตึง hard of hearing, *adj.*

hǔu-fang หูฟัง headset, headphone, earphone, *n.*

hûuk หูก loom, *n.*

húuk ฮูก owl, *n..*

hǔu-nùak หูหนวก deaf, *adj.*

hùut หูด wart, *n.*

hǔu-too-ra-sàp หูโทรศัพท์ telephone receiver, *n.*

hǔng หึง jealous (lovers), *adj.*

húk-hə̌əm ฮึกเหิม bold, daring, *adj.*

hút-hát ฮึดฮัด grunt or expel the breath with exasperation, *v.*

huu ฮือ a crying or groaning sound, *n.*

huu ฮือ suddenly burst into flame, *v.*

hùut หืด asthma, *n.*

hùut-hɔ̀ɔp หืดหอบ asthma attack, *n.*

i (อิ)

iang เอียง bend, slant, incline, *v.*

îang เอี้ยง singing myna, *n.*

iang-aai เอียงอาย shy, bashful, *adj.*

îao เอี้ยว twist, swerve, *n.*

ii อี (derogatory) title used with first names of women, bound element in names of birds and animals, *n.*

ii-gaa อีกา crow, *n.*

ii-gêeng อีเก้ง barking deer, *n.*

îik อีก more, in addition, again, another, the other, *adv.*

ii-sùk-ii-sǎi อีสุกอีใส chicken pox, *n.*

ii-sǎan อีสาน the Northeast, *n.*

ìm อิ่ม full (from eating), *adj.*

ìm-dtua อิ่มตัว saturated, *adj.*

ìm-ə̀əp อิ่มเอิบ pleased, contented, satisfied, *adj.*

ing อิง lean, rest against, refer to, *v.*

in-sii อินทรี eagle, *n.*

in-sii อินทรีย์ organic compound, *n.*

in-ta-pǎa-lam อินทผาลัม date (fruit), *n.*

ì-sǎan อิสาน the Northeast, *n.*

ìt อิฐ brick, *n.*

ìt-chǎa อิจฉา envious, jealous, *adj.*

ìt-sà-laam อิสลาม Islam, *n.*

ìt-sà-rà อิสระ independent, free, *adj.*

ìt-sà-ra-pâap อิสรภาพ independence, freedom, *n.*

ìt-tí-pon อิทธิพล influence, *n.*

ìt-tí-rìt อิทธิฤทธิ์ power, force, *n.*

j (จ)

jà จะ will, shall, *aux. v.*

jâ จ๊ะ a final particle of statements

já จ๊ะ a final particle of questions

jàa จ่า leader, head, chief, *n.*

jàa, jàa-nâa จ่า, จ่าหน้า address, provide with a heading, *v.*

jâa จ้า bright, strong (light), *adj.*

jǎa จ๋า particle placed after name or kin term to call the attention of someone in an intimate way

jàai จ่าย pay, disburse, spend, *v.*

jàai-dtà-làat จ่ายตลาด buy the groceries, go to shop at the market, *v.*

jàai-yaa จ่ายยา give medicine, *v.*

jàak จาก leave, depart, go away, *v.*

jàak จาก from, *prep.*

jàak จาก nipa palm, *n.*

jaam จาม sneeze, *v.*

jaan จาน plate, dish, *n.*

jaang จาง fade, faded, dilute, *v., adj.*

jâang จ้าง hire, employ, *v.*

jâao, jâo เจ้า prince, ruler, holy being, *n.*

jà-dtù-bàat จตุบาท quadruped, *n.*

jà-dtù-ràt จตุรัส square, *n.*

jai ใจ heart, mind, spirit, *n.*

jai-bàap ใจบาป sinful, *adj.*

jai-bun ใจบุญ pious, charitable, *adj.*

jai-chúun ใจชื้น cheerful, carefree, relieved, *adj.*

jai-dam ใจดำ merciless, mean, *adj.*

jai-diao ใจเดียว faithful, *adj.*

jai-dii ใจดี kind-hearted, good-natured, *adj.*

jai-dtɛ̀ɛk ใจแตก opoiled, colf indulgent and unrestrained, *adj.*

jai-glâa ใจกล้า brave, bold, *adj.*

jai-gwâang ใจกว้าง generous, *adj.*

jai-hǎai ใจหาย shocked, stunned with fear, *adj.*

jai-kɛ̂ɛp ใจแคบ selfish, narrow-minded, *adj.*

jai-kěng ใจแข็ง unyielding, *adj.*

jai-kwaam ใจความ gist, essence, *n.*

jai-lɔɔi ใจลอย absent-minded, *adj.*

jai-ngâai ใจง่าย cheap (women), easy to get, *adj.*

jai-ɔ̀ɔn ใจอ่อน yielding, soft-hearted, easily influenced, easily touched, *adj.*

jai-ráai ใจร้าย malicious, *adj.*

jai-rɔ́ɔn ใจร้อน impatient, impetuous, hasty, *adj.*

jai-sàn ใจสั่น frightened, *adj.*

jai-yen ใจเย็น calm, cool-hearted, steady, imperturbable, *adj.*

jàk จักร wheel, machine, engine, *n.*

ják-gà-jàn จักจั่น cicada, *n.*

jàk-grà-pát จักรพรรดิ emperor, *n.*

jàk-grà-póp จักรภพ empire, *n.*

jàk-grà-waan จักรวาล universe, *n.*

jàk-grà-yaan จักรยาน bicycle, *n.*

jàk-grà-yaan-yon จักรยานยนต์ motorcycle, *n.*

jàk-grii จักรี king, monarch, the Chakri Dynasty, *n.*

jàk-yép-pâa จักรเย็บผ้า sewing machine, *n.*

jam จำ remember, memorize, *v.*

jam-dâai จำได้ recall, remember, *v.*

jam-gàt จำกัด limit, define, *v.*

jam-jai จำใจ force or be forced to do something, *v.*

jam-jee จำเจ tiresome, monotonous, repetitious, *adj.*

jam-lɛɛng จำแลง transform, *v.*

jam-ləəi จำเลย defendant, *n.*

jam-lɔɔng จำลอง imitate, copy, reproduce, model, *v.*

jam-nàai จำหน่าย sell, be sold, distribute, *v.*

jam-nam จำนำ pawn, mortgage, *v.*

jam-nɛ̂ɛk จำแนก divide, *v.*

jam-nong จำนง desire, wish, *v.*

jam-nɔɔng จำนอง mortgage, *v.*

jam-nuan จำนวน number, quantity, amount, *n.*

jam-pûak จำพวก group, type, *n.*

jà-mùuk จมูก nose, *n.*

jan จันทร์ the moon, *n.*

jang จัง very much, a great deal (collq.), *adv.*

jang-wà จังหวะ rhythm, *n.*

jang-wàt จังหวัด province, *n.*

jan-rai จัญไร evil, wicked, *adj.*

jâo-bàao เจ้าบ่าว groom, *n.*

jâo-chaai เจ้าชาย prince, *n.*

jâo-chúu เจ้าชู้ philanderer, *n.*

jao-dtua เจ้าตัว the person in question, *n.*

jâo-kɔ̌ɔng เจ้าของ owner, *n.*

jâo-naai เจ้านาย master, *n.*

jâo-nâa-tîi เจ้าหน้าที่ official, staff, *n.*

jâo-nîi เจ้าหนี้ creditor, *n.*

jâo-pâap เจ้าภาพ host, *n.*

jâo-sǎao เจ้าสาว bride, *n.*

jâo-sàp เจ้าทรัพย์ owner, *n.*

jâo-ying เจ้าหญิง princess, *n.*

jàp จับ catch, grab, hold, catch, *v.*

jà-raa-jɔɔn จราจร traffic, *n.*

jà-rùat จรวด rocket, *n.*

jàt จัด arrange, prepare, manage, *v.*

jàt จัด hard, strong, *n.*

jàt-jeen จัดเจน experienced, skilled, well-versed, *adj.*

jèp เจ็บ ache, pain, *v.*

jèt เจ็ด seven, *nm.*

jɛɛ-gan แจกัน vase, *n.*

jɛ̀ɛk แจก distribute, share, hand out *v.*

jɛ̂ɛng แจ้ง notify, tell, inform, report, make known, clear, unobscured, *v., adj.*

jɛ̂ɛng-kwaam แจ้งความ give information, report (to the police), *v.*

jêm, jêm-jêeng แจ่ม, แจ่มแจ้ง clear, bright, unobscured, *adj.*

jəə เจอ meet, encounter, find, *v.*

jiam-dtua เจียมตัว modest, *adj.*

jii จี้ poke, tickle, point at, point out, prod, exhort, *v.*

jii จี้ pendant of a necklace, *n.*

jiin จีน Chinese, China, *n.*

jìip จีบ pleat, *n.*

jìip จีบ pleat, gather in folds, woo, *v.*

jii-rang จีรัง endure, last long, *v.*

jii-wɔɔn จีวร the robe of a Buddhist monk, *n.*

jìk จิก peck, *v.*

jîm จิ้ม dip in, pick, *v.*

jîm จิ๋ม vagina, *n.*

jing จริง real, true, *adj.*

jing-jai จริงใจ sincere, honest, *adj.*

jing-jang จริงจัง serious, *adj.*

jing-jing จริงๆ really, *adv.*

jîng-jòk จิ้งจก lizard, *n*

jîng-jôo จิ้งโจ้ kangaroo, *n.*

jîng-jɔ̀ɔk จิ้งขยก fox, *n.*

jîng-rìit จิ้งหรีด cricket (insect), *n.*

jìp จิบ sip, *v.*

jìt จิต spirit, soul, *n.*

jom จม sink, *v.*

jom-náam จมน้ำ drown, sink, *v.*

jon จน poor, *adj.*

jong-jai จงใจ intend, *v.*

jôok โจ๊ก joke, rice porridge, *n.*

joom-dtii โจมตี attack, *v.*

joon โจร robber, *n.*

joon-sà-làt โจรสลัด pirate, *n.*

jòot โจทก์ plaintiff, *n.*

jòot โจทย์ arithmetical problem, *n.*

jòp จบ end, close, graduate, *v.*

jot จด note, *v.*

jot-jam จดจำ memorize, *v.*

jot-màai จดหมาย letter, *n.*

jɔ̀ เจาะ drill, make a hole, *v.*

jɔɔ จอ screen, Year of the Dog, *n.*

jɔ̀ɔk จอก small cup or glass, *n.*

jɔɔm จอม highest, supreme, *n.*

jɔɔm-bpluak จอมปลวก termite hill, ant hill, *n.*

jɔɔn จอน sideburns, *n.*

jɔɔn-jàt จรจัด homeless wanderer, vagabond, *n.*

jɔɔng จอง reserve, make a reservation, *v.*

jɔ̂ɔng จ้อง gaze at, stare, *v.*

jɔɔng-hɔ̌ɔng จองหอง unduly proud, haughty, *adj.*

jɔ̀ɔt จอด stop, park, *v.*

jɔ̀-ruu เจาะรู make a hole, v.

jùk จุก topknot, stopper (of bottle), cork, n.

jun-chii-wan จุลชีวัน microbe, n.

jùt จุด point, dot, period, spot, n.

jùt จุด light, set on fire, v.

jùt-mǎai จุดหมาย destination, n.

jûu-jîi จู้จี้ fussy, adj.

jùu-joom จู่โจม attack, rush, v.

juung จูง tow, drag, v.

jùup จูบ kiss, n., v.

jʉng จึง therefore, so, adv.

jʉ̀ʉt จืด insipid, flat in taste, adj.

k (ข, ค, ฆ)

kaa คา remain stuck, be left unfinished, v.

kàa ข่า galanga, n.

kâa ข้า slave, servant, attendant, n.

kâa ฆ่า kill, murder, execute, v.

kâa ค่า fee, cost, price, value, n.

káa ค้า trade, sell, do business, v.

kǎa ขา leg, n.

kǎa-bpai ขาไป the outgoing trip, n.

kâa-bpìt-bpàak ค่าปิดปาก hush money, n.

kâa-chái-jàai ค่าใช้จ่าย expense, n.

kâa-châo ค่าเช่า rent, rental fee, n.

kâa-chʉ́a-rôok, kâa-chʉ́a, ฆ่าเชื้อโรค, ฆ่าเชื้อ disinfect, v.

kâa-dooi-sǎan ค่าโดยสาร fare, n.

kâa-dtua ค่าตัว price for one's service, n.

kâa-dtua-dtaai ฆ่าตัวตาย commit suicide, v.

kaa-fee-iin คาเฟอีน caffeine, n.

kǎa-glàp ขากลับ return trip, n.

kaai คาย spit out, give out, v.

kàai ข่าย net, network, limit, scope, n.

kâai ค่าย camp, n.

kǎai ขาย sell, v.

kǎai-nâa ขายหน้า lose face, be ashamed, v.

kǎai-òp-pa-yóp ค่ายอพยพ refugee camp, n.

kǎai-sòng ขายส่ง wholesale, v., n.

kâa-jâang ค่าจ้าง wage, n.

kàak ขาก spit, spit out, spit mucus, v.

káa-kǎai ค้าขาย trade, do business, v.

kǎa-kâo ขาเข้า incoming, adj.

kâa-krɔɔng-chîip ค่าครองชีพ cost of living, n.

kâam ข้าม cross, v.

kaan คาน block, clog, impede, support, counter-balance, *v.*

kaan คาน pole, beam, lever, *n.*

kâan ค้าน oppose, object, contradict, reject *v.*

kǎan ขาน answer, call in reply, *v.*

kaang คาง chin, *n.*

kàang ข่าง spinning top, *n.*

kâang ข้าง side, *n.*

kâang-bon ข้างบน above, upstairs, *prep., adv.*

kâang-diao ข้างเดียว one-sided, *adj.*

kâang-kâang ข้างๆ beside, next to, *prep.*

káang-kaao ค้างคาว bat (mammal), *n.*

kâang-kiang-gan ข้างเคียงกัน side by side, *prep.*

kaang-kók คางคก toad (animal), *n.*

kâang-kûn ข้างขึ้น waxing (moon), *adj.*

káang-kuun ค้างคืน stay overnight, spend the night, *v.*

kâang-lâang ข้างล่าง below, downstairs, *prep., adv.*

kâang-lǎng ข้างหลัง behind, *prep., adv.*

kâang-nâa ข้างหน้า ahead, in front of, *prep., adv.*

kâang-nai ข้างใน inside, *prep., adv.*

kâang-nǎi ข้างไหน Which way?

kâang-nɔ̂ɔk ข้างนอก outside, *prep., adv.*

kâang-reem ข้างแรม waning (moon), *adj.*

káang-reem ค้างแรม stay overnight, spend the night, *v.*

kǎa-nìip ขาหนีบ knock-knees, *n.*

kaao คาว fishy (in smell), *adj.*

kàao ข่าว news, *n.*

kâao ข้าว rice, *n.*

kǎao ขาว white, *adj.*

kâao-bplùak ข้าวเปลือก unhusked rice, paddy, *n.*

kâao-cháao ข้าวเช้า breakfast, *n.*

kâao-dtôm ข้าวต้ม rice porridge, *n.*

kâao-gɛɛng ข้าวแกง rice with curry (eaten as complete meal), *n.*

kâao-jâao ข้าวเจ้า non-glutinous rice, *n.*

kâao-lǎam ข้าวหลาม rice in bamboo, *n.*

kâao-lǎam-dtàt ข้าวหลามตัด diamonds (in playing cards), *n.*

kàao-luu ข้าวลือ rumor, *n.*

kâao-nǐao ข้าวเหนียว sticky rice, *n.*

kâao-óot ข้าวโอ๊ต oats, *n.*

kâao-pàt ข้าวผัด fried rice, *n.*

kâao-pôot ข้าวโพด corn, *n.*

kâao-sǎa-lii ข้าวสาลี wheat, *n.*

kàao-sǎan ข่าวสาร news, information, *n.*

kâao-sǎan ข้าวสาร husked rice, *n.*

kâao-sǔai ข้าวสวย cooked non-glutinous rice, cooked white rice, *n.*

kâao-sùk ข้าวสุก cooked rice, *n.*

kâao-tîang ข้าวเที่ยง lunch, *n.*

kâao-yen ข้าวเย็น dinner, *n.*

kǎa-ɔ̀ɔk ขาออก outgoing, *adj.*

kǎa-ɔ̀ɔn ขาอ่อน thigh, *n.*

kâap คาบ retrieve, hold, seize, clamp (in the teeth or beak) *v.*

kâa-pàan-bprà-dtuu ค่าผ่านประตู admission fee, *n.*

kâa-pa-jâao ข้าพเจ้า I, me, myself, *pron. (formal)*

kâap-gìao คาบเกี่ยว overlap, *v.*

kâap-sà-mùt คาบสมุทร peninsula, *n.*

kâap-sên คาบเส้น be situated on the border line, *v.*

kaa-ra-wâat ฆราวาส layman, *n.*

kâa-râat-cha-gaan ข้าราชการ government official, *n.*

kâa-sǐa-hǎai ค่าเสียหาย the damages, the amount of the loss, *n.*

kâa-sùk ข้าศึก enemy, *n.*

kàat ขาด missing, incomplete, torn, worn out, broken, severed from, *adj.*

kàat ขาด lack, miss (e.g. school), *v.*

kâat คาด anticipate, guess, speculate, expect, *v.*

kâat คาด put around, tie around, belt, strap, *v.*

kâa-tài ค่าไถ่ ransom, *n.*

kâa-tam-kǔan ค่าทำขวัญ consolation money, *n.*

kâa-tam-niam ค่าธรรมเนียม fee, fees, *n.*

kâat-dtà-gam ฆาตกรรม murder, killing, *n.*

kâat-dtà-gɔɔn ฆาตกร murderer, killer, *n.*

kǎa-tiam ขาเทียม prosthesis (for the leg), *n.*

kâat-ká-nee คาดคะเน speculate, guess, estimate, *v.*

kâat-mǎai คาดหมาย anticipate, expect, *v.*

kaa-tɔɔ-lìk คาธอลิก Catholic, *n.*

kâat-wǎng คาดหวัง anticipate,

expect, *v.*

ká-dii คดี case, charge (legal), *n.*

ká-dii-aa-yaa คดีอาญา criminal case, *n.*

ká-dii-pêng คดีแพ่ง civil case, *n.*

ká-dtì คดี moral precept, ethical teaching, *n.*

kài ไข่ egg, *n.*

kâi ไข้ fever, illness, *n.*

kǎi ไข fat, grease, marrow, *n.*

kâi-bpàa ไข้ป่า malaria, *n.*

kài-daao ไข่ดาว fried egg, sunny side-up, *n.*

kài-dɛɛng ไข่แดง egg yolk, *n.*

kài-jiao ไข่เจียว omelet, *n.*

kài-kǎao ไข่ขาว egg white, albumen *n.*

kǎi-kuang ไขควง screwdriver, *n.*

kài-man ไขมัน fat, grease, *n.*

kài-múk ไข่มุก pearl, *n.*

kâi-wàt ไข้หวัด common cold, *n.*

kâi-wàt-yài ไข้หวัดใหญ่ influenza, *n.*

kam คำ word, mouthful bite, *n., clf.*

kâm ค่ำ night, *n.*

kǎm ขำ funny, *adj.*

kà-màp ขมับ temple (of the head), *n.*

kam-bplɛɛ คำแปล translation, *n.*

kam-bpraa-sǎi คำปราศรัย speech, *n.*

kam-bùp-pa-bòt คำบุพบท preposition, *n.*

kam-chíi-jɛɛng คำชี้แจง explanation, *n.*

kam-dàa คำด่า cursing, *n.*

kam-dtàt-sǐn คำตัดสิน judgment, *n.*

kam-dtɔ̀ɔp คำตอบ answer, *n.*

kà-mɛ̌ɛn เขมร Cambodia, *n.*

kam-gà-rí-yaa คำกริยา verb, *n.*

kam-glàao คำกล่าว a saying, *n.*

kam-hâi-gaan คำให้การ questioning, interrogation, *n.*

kà-mîn ขมิ้น turmeric, *n.*

kam-káan คำค้าน objection, *n.*

kam-kàat คำขาด ultimatum, *n.*

kam-kun-na-sàp คำคุณศัพท์ adjective, *n.*

kam-naam คำนาม noun, *n.*

kam-nam คำนำ preface, *n.*

kam-né-nam คำแนะนำ advice, *n.*

kam-nuan คำนวณ calculate, *v.*

kà-mooi ขโมย thief, *n.*

kà-mooi ขโมย steal, *v.*

kam-pii คัมภีร์ Bible, sacred book, *n.*

kam-pí-pâak-sǎa คำพิพากษา verdict, decision, *n.*

kam-pûut คำพูด spoken word, *n.*

kam-raam คำราม growl, *v.*

kam-rɔ́ɔng คำร้อง petition, request, *n.*

kam-sǎa-baan คำสาบาน oath, *n.*

kam-sàap คำสาป curse, *n.*

kam-sàng คำสั่ง order, command, *n.*

kam-sàng-sǎan คำสั่งศาล judgment, *n.*

kam-sǎn-taan คำสันธาน conjunction, *n.*

kam-sǎn-yaa คำสัญญา promise, *n.*

kam-sàp คำศัพท์ vocabulary, *n.*

kam-sàp-pa-naam คำสรรพนาม pronoun, *n.*

kam-sɔ̌ɔn คำสอน teaching, *n.*

kam-tǎam คำถาม question, *n.*

kam-tà-lɛ̌ɛng คำแถลง declaration, statement, *n.*

kam-ù-taan คำอุทาน interjection, *n.*

kam-wing-wɔɔn คำวิงวอน plea, supplication, *n.*

kam-wí-sèet คำวิเศษณ์ adverb, *n.*

kam-yin-yɔɔm คำยินยอม consent, *n.*

kam-yɔ̂ɔ คำย่อ abbreviation, *n.*

kan คัน itch, *v.*

kan คัน itchy, *adj.*

kan ครรภ์ womb, pregnancy, *n.*

kan คัน clf. for long-handled objects (e.g. spoons, forks, umbrellas), clf. for vehicles, *n.*

kân คั่น separate, divide, *v.*

kân ขั้น step, stage, *n.*

kán คั้น squeeze, press, *v.*

kǎn ขัน bowl, *n.*

kǎn ขัน tighten by turning or twisting, *v.*

kà-nà ขณะ while, during, *conj.*

ká-ná คณะ group, team, party, *n.*

kà-nǎan ขนาน parallel, *adj.*

kà-nǎan ขนาน dose (of medicine), *n.*

kân-ban-dai ขั้นบันได stair, *n.*

kan-bèt คันเบ็ด fishing rod, *n.*

ká-nɛɛn คะแนน score, mark, *n.*

kǎng ขัง shut up, confine, jail, *v.*

ká-nít-sàat คณิตศาสตร์ mathematics, *n.*

kà-nǒm ขนม sweet, dessert, *n.*

kà-nǒm-bpang ขนมปัง bread, *n.*

kà-nǒm-bpang-bpîng ขนมปังปิ้ง toast, *n.*

kà-nǒm-bpang-grɔ̀ɔp ขนมปังกรอบ biscuit, *n.*

kà-nǒm-kéek ขนมเค้ก cake, *n.*

kà-nòp-tam-niam ขนบธรรมเนียม

custom, tradition, *n.*

kan-rêng คันเร่ง accelerator, *n.*

kan-tǎi คันไถ plough, *n.*

kâo เข้า enter, insert, join, come into contact with, in, into, *v., prep.*

káo, kǎo เค้า, เขา he, she, her, him, they, them (used mostly with people), *pron.*

kǎo เขา horn, hill, small mountain, *n.*

kâo-jai เข้าใจ understand, *v.*

kâo-jai-pìt เข้าใจผิด misunderstand, *v.*

kâo-tii เข้าที sound all right, *v.*

kǎo-wong-gòt เขาวงกต labyrinth, *n.*

kàp ขับ drive, *v.*

káp คับ tight, jammed, crowded, *adj.*

káp-kǎn คับขัน of a critical or an emergency nature, *adj.*

kàp-lâi ขับไล่ expel, *v.*

kàt ขัด obstruct, hinder, interrupt, interfere, oppose, resist, disagree, conflict, cross, feel sore or broken or uncomfortable, polish, scrub, *v.*

kàt-jang-wà, kàt-kɔɔ, kàt-kwǎang ขัดจังหวะ, ขัดคอ, ขัดขวาง interrupt, object, *v.*

kàt-yɔ̀ɔk ขัดยอก muscle ache, *v.*

kà-yà ขยะ garbage, rubbish, *n.*

kà-yǎai ขยาย enlarge, expand, *v.*

kà-yà-kà-yɛ̌ɛng ขยะแขยง be disgusted, revolted, repelled, *v.*

kà-yǎm ขยำ squeeze with the hand, knead, *v.*

kà-yǎn ขยัน diligent, industrious, *adj.*

kà-yǎn-kǎn-kɛ̌ng ขยันขันแข็ง diligent, industrious, *adj.*

kà-yào เขย่า shake, *v.*

kà-yàp ขยับ move slightly, *v.*

kà-yèek เขยก limp, *v.*

kà-yǐi ขยี้ rub hard with the hands, *v.*

kà-yìp ขยิบ wink, *v.*

kee-mii เคมี chemistry, *n.*

kèet เขต district, limit, boundary, border, area, zone, territory, *n.*

kèet-dɛɛn เขตแดน frontier, territory, boundary, *n.*

kem เค็ม salty, *adj.*

kêm เข้ม strong, concentrated, dark (in color) *adj.*

kěm เข็ม needle, pin, *n.*

kěm-chìit-yaa เข็มฉีดยา injection needle, *n.*

kěm-glàt เข็มกลัด brooch, *n.*

kěm-kàt เข็มขัด belt, *n.*

kěm-kàt-ní-ra-pai เข็มขัดนิรภัย

safety belt, *n.*

kêm-kĕng เข้มแข็ง strong, powerful, *adj.*

kĕm-mùt เข็มหมุด pin, *n.*

kêm-nguât เข้มงวด strict, rigid, *adj.*

kĕm-tít เข็มทิศ compass, *n.*

kĕn เข็น push, move forward by pushing, *v.*

kəəi เคย used to, *v.*

kèɛk แขก visitor, guest, person from India, Pakistan, the Middle East, Malaya, Java, *n.*

kɛɛ-lɔɔ-rîi แคลอรี่ calorie, *n.*

kĕɛn แขน arm (body part), sleeve, *n.*

kêɛp แคบ narrow, *adj.*

kɛɛ-rɔ̀t แครอท carrot, *n.*

kèng แข่ง compete, *v.*

kèng แข่ง racing, *adj.*

kêng แข้ง shin, *n.*

kĕng แข็ง hard, *adj.*

kèng-kăn แข่งขัน compete, *v.*

kĕng-rɛɛng แข็งแรง strong, *adj.*

ken-sìam แคลเซี่ยม calcium, *n.*

kép-suun แคปซูล capsule, *n.*

két-dtaa-lɔ́k แคตตาลอก catalog, *n.*

kîan เฆี่ยน whip, beat, *v.*

kĭan เขียน write, *v.*

kiao เคียว sickle, *n.*

kiao เขี้ยว fang, *n.*

kíao เคี้ยว chew, *v.*

kĭao เขียว green, *adj.*

kìi ขี่ ride (e.g. a horse, bicycle), *v.*

kîi คี่ odd, uneven, *adj.*

kîi ขี้ excrement, dung, shit, dirt, ashes, residue, *n.*

kîi ขี้ defecate, *v.*

kîi ขี้ a prefix meaning "characterized by, given to, having tendency to", *pfx.*

kîi-aai ขี้อาย shy, *adj.*

kîi-gìat ขี้เกียจ lazy, *adj.*

kîi-goong ขี้โกง cheating, *adj.*

kîi-hŭu ขี้หู earwax, *n.*

kîi-hĕng ขี้หึง jealous (between lovers), *adj.*

kîi-kâa ขี้ข้า slave, servant, *n.*

kîi-klàat ขี้ขลาด cowardly, timid, *adj.*

kîi-klai ขี้ไคล scurf, *n.*

kîi-kloon ขี้โคลน mud, sludge, *n.*

kîi-luum ขี้ลืม forgetful, *adj.*

kiim คีม tongs (tool), *n.*

kîi-mûuk ขี้มูก nose mucus, booger, *n.*

kîi-nĭao ขี้เหนียว stingy, *adj.*

kîi-pûng ขี้ผึ้ง wax, beeswax, *n.*

kîi-rang-kɛɛ ขี้รังแค dandruff, *n.*

kîi-rôok ขี้โรค sickly, unhealthy, *adj.*

kìit ขีด draw, scratch, mark, *v.*

kìit-sên-dtâai ขีดเส้นใต้ underline, *v.*

kìi-tâo ขี้เถ้า ash, *n.*

kìit-kâa ขีดฆ่า cross out, strike out, *v.*

kìi-yaa ขี้ยา drug addict, cigarette addict, *n.*

kĭng ขิง ginger, *n.*

kít คิด think, *v.*

kít-tŭng คิดถึง miss, think about, *v.*

kít-wâa คิดว่า think that..., *v.*

kíu คิ้ว eyebrow, *n.*

klà คละ mixed, assorted, *adj.*

klaai คลาย loosen, diminish, lessen, unravel, unroll, *v.*

kláai คล้าย resemble, look like, *v.*

kláai-klŭng คล้ายคลึง resemble, similar, *v., adj.*

klaan คลาน crawl, *v.*

kláat-sìk คลาสสิก classic, *adj.*

klam คลำ feel, probe (as doctor), caress, fondle, *v.*

klám คล้ำ dark, swarthy, *adj.*

klang คลัง treasury, *n.*

klâng คลั่ง delirious, crazy, *adj.*

klâng-klâi คลั่งไคล้ crazy, mad about, *adj.*

klăo เขลา stupid, foolish, *adj.*

klîi คลี่ unfold, unroll, *v.*

kloon โคลน mud, mush, *n.*

kloong โคลง a kind of Thai poem, *n.*

klôŋ คล่อง active, fluent, *adj.*

klôŋ-klêo คล่องแคล่ว skillful, nimble, agile, adroit, *adj.*

klɔɔŋ คลอง canal, *n.*

klɔɔn-kleen คลอนแคลน wobble, *v.*

klɔɔ-riin คลอรีน chlorine, *n.*

klɔ̂ɔt คลอด give birth to, be born, *v.*

klŭan เคลื่อน move, glide, *v.*

klŭan-wǎi เคลื่อนไหว move, *v.*

klŭap เคลือบ glaze, enamel, coat, *v.*

klŭun คลื่น wave, *n.*

klŭun-sâi คลื่นไส้ feel nauseated, *v.*

kom คม sharp (e.g. knife), *adj.*

kòm ข่ม oppress, suppress, *v.*

kŏm ขม bitter, *adj.*

kòm-hĕeng ข่มเหง bully, abuse, *v.*

kom-kaai คมคาย attractive, *n.*

kòm-kìi ข่มขี่ oppress, tyrannize, *v.*

kòm-kùu ข่มขู่ threaten, *v.*

kòm-kŭun ข่มขืน rape, *v.*

kom-ma-naa-kom คมนาคม communication, *n.*

kon คน person, human being, people, *n., clf.*

kôn ข้น thick, concentrated, *adj.*

Phonetic · Thai · English

kón ค้น search, *v.*

kǒn ขน fur, hair (except of the head), feather, *n.*

kǒn ขน carry, transfer, *v.*

kon-dəən คนเดิน pedestrian, *n.*

kon-diao คนเดียว alone, *adv.*

kǒn-dtaa ขนตา eyelash, *n.*

kon-duu คนดู spectator, watcher, viewer, *n.*

kǒn-gè ขนแกะ lamb's wool, *n.*

kong-grà-pan คงกระพัน invulnerable, *adj.*

kong-jà คงจะ perhaps, possibly, *adv.*

kong-tîi คงที่ remain, stay put, *v.*

kong-yùu คงอยู่ remain, stay, *v.*

kon-kâi คนไข้ patient, *n.*

kon-krέ คนแคระ dwarf, *n.*

kǒn-lúk ขนลุก have the hair standing on end, *v.*

kon-nǎi คนไหน which person?, who?, *pron.*

kon-ngaan คนงาน worker, *n.*

kǒn-nók ขนนก feather, *n.*

kón-póp ค้นพบ discover, *v.*

kon-ráp-chái คนรับใช้ servant, *n.*

kon-rúu-jàk คนรู้จัก acquaintance, *n.*

kǒn-sàt ขนสัตว์ fur, *n.*

kon-tai คนไทย Thai person, Thai people, *n.*

kǒn-yáai ขนย้าย remove, clear, *v.*

koo โค cow, ox, *n.*

koo-keen โคเคน cocaine, *n.*

koom-fai โคมไฟ lantern, lamp, *n.*

kôon โค่น fell (tree), *v.*

koo-sà-naa โฆษณา advertise, advertisement, *v., n.*

koo-sòk โฆษก announcer, spokesperson, master of ceremony, *n.*

kòp ขบ crack with the teeth, *v.*

kóp คบ torch, *n.*

kóp คบ associate with, be friends with, *v.*

kòt ขด coil, roll into a coil, *v.*

kòt-lûat ขดลวด coil of wire, *n.*

kɔ̀ เคาะ knock, *v.*

kɔ̀i ค่อย quiet, gentle, *adj.*

kɔ̀i-kɔ̀i ค่อยๆ quietly, gently, softly, gradually, *adv.*

kɔm-píu-dtəə คอมพิวเตอร์ computer, *n.*

kɔn-grìit คอนกรีต concrete, *n.*

kɔn-tὲk-leen คอนแทคเลนส์ contact lens, *n.*

kɔɔ คอ neck, *n.*

kɔ̂ɔ ข้อ joint (of the body), item, *n.*

kɔ̌ɔ ขอ hook, clasp, *n.*

kɔ̌ɔ ขอ ask for, beg, request, *v.*

kɔ̂ɔ-âang ข้ออ้าง pretext, justification, supporting statement, excuse, *n.*

kɔ̂ɔ-à-pai ขออภัย excuse, apologize, ask for pardon, *v.*

kɔ̂ɔ-bang-káp ข้อบังคับ rule, regulation, *n.*

kɔ̂ɔ-bòk-prông ข้อบกพร่อง mistake, fault, , *n.*

kɔ̂ɔ-dtɔ̀ɔ ข้อต่อ joint, connection, *n.*

kɔ̂ɔ-dtua ขอตัว excuse oneself, *v.*

kɔ̂ɔ-glàao-hǎa ข้อกล่าวหา accusation, charge, *n.*

kɔ̂ɔ-hǎa ข้อหา accusation, charge, *n.*

kɔ̂ɔ-hɔ̌i คอหอย larynx, throat, *n.*

kɔɔi คอย wait, *v.*

kɔ̂ɔk คอก animal pen, *n.*

kɔ̂ɔ-kǐan ข้อเขียน written exam, *n.*

kɔ̂ɔ-kít ข้อคิด idea, opinion, *n.*

kɔ̂ɔ-klét ข้อเคล็ด dislocated joint, *n.*

kɔ̂ɔk-pá-yaan คอกพยาน witness stand, *n.*

kɔ̂ɔ-kwaam ข้อความ statement, passage, text, *n.*

kɔ̂ɔ-mɛ́ɛ ข้อแม้ condition, *n.*

kɔ̂ɔ-muu ข้อมือ wrist, *n.*

kɔ́ɔn ค้อน hammer, *n.*

kɔ̌ɔn ขอน log, *n.*

kɔ́ɔng ฆ้อง gong, *n.*

kɔ̌ɔng ของ thing, article, goods, stuff, substance, belonging, *n.*

kɔ̌ɔng ของ of, *prep.*

kɔ̌ɔng-chǎn, kɔ̌ɔng-chán ของฉัน, ของชั้น my, mine, *adj., adv.*

kɔ̌ɔng-gào ของเก่า antique, *n.*

kɔ̌ɔng-kaao ของคาว dish of the main course, *n.*

kɔ̌ɔng-kɛ̌ng ของแข็ง solid, *n.*

kɔ̌ɔng-krai ของใคร whose, *pron.*

kɔ̌ɔng-kun ของคุณ your, yours, *adj, adv.*

kɔ̌ɔng-kwǎn ของขวัญ gift, present, *n.*

kɔ̌ɔng-láp ของลับ private parts, *n.*

kɔ̌ɔng-lěeo ของเหลว liquid, *n.*

kɔ̌ɔng-lên ของเล่น toy, *n.*

kɔ̌ɔng-tùan ของเถื่อน smuggled goods, bootleg goods, *n.*

kɔ̌ɔng-rao ของเรา our, ours, *adj., adv.*

kɔ̌ɔng-wǎan ของหวาน dessert, sweets, candy, *n.*

kɔ̀ɔp ขอบ edge, rim, margin, *n.*

kɔ̀ɔp-fáa ขอบฟ้า horizon, *n.*

kɔ̂ɔ-pí-sùut ข้อพิสูจน์ proof, *n.*

kɔ̀ɔp-kèet ขอบเขต scope, limit, *n.*

kɔ̀ɔp-kun ขอบคุณ thank, *v.*

kɔ̂ɔ-rîak-rɔ́ɔng ข้อเรียกร้อง demand, request, *n.*

kɔ̂ɔ-rɔ́ɔng ขอร้อง request, implore, beseech, *v.*

kɔ̂ɔ-sà-nə̌ə ข้อเสนอ proposal, offer, proposition, *n.*

kɔ̂ɔ-sǒng-sǎi ข้อสงสัย doubtful point, point of doubt, *n.*

kɔ̂ɔ-sɔ̀ɔk ข้อศอก elbow, *n.*

kɔ̂ɔ-sɔ̀ɔp ข้อสอบ exam question, *n.*

kɔ̀ɔt ขอด scrape off, knot, *v.*

kɔ̂ɔ-taan ขอทาน beggar, *n.*

kɔ̂ɔ-taan ขอทาน beg for alms, *v.*

kɔ̂ɔ-táao ข้อเท้า ankle, *n.*

kɔ̂ɔ-tôot ขอโทษ excuse, apologize, ask for pardon, *v.*

kɔ̂ɔ-yɯɯm ขอยืม borrow, *v.*

kraam คราม indigo, *adj.*

kraang คราง moan, groan, *v.*

kraao คราว time, occasion, *n.*

krâat คราด rake, *n.*

krai ใคร who, whom, *pron.*

krâi ใคร่ which, desire, *v.*

kram คร่ำ refuse water, *n.*

kráng ครั้ง time, instance, classifier for an event or occurrence, *n., clf.*

kráng-nɯ̀ng ครั้งหนึ่ง once, *n.*

krao เครา beard, *n.*

krêng, krêng-krát เคร่ง, เคร่งครัด strict, devout, *adj.*

krêng-krîat เคร่งเครียด serious, grave, gloomy, *adj.*

krîat เครียด tense, strained, *adj.*

kriim ครีม cream, *n.*

kriim-gan-dèet ครีมกันแดด sun screen cream, *n.*

krîip ครีบ fin, *n.*

krít, krís คริสต์ Jesus Christ, *n.*

krít-sa-dtian, krít-sa-dtang, คริสเตียน, คริสตัง Christian, *n.*

krít-sa-mâat, krít-sa-mâas คริสต์มาส Christmas, *n.*

kroong โครง frame, skeleton, *n.*

kroong-gaan โครงการ plan, plot, scheme, *n.*

kroong-grà-dùuk โครงกระดูก skeleton, *n.*

kroong-rɯ̂ang โครงเรื่อง plot, outline (of a story), *n.*

kroong-sâang โครงสร้าง structure, framework, *n.*

króp ครบ complete, *adj.*

króp-gam-nòt ครบกำหนด due, *adj.*

króp-kran ครบครัน complete, *adj.*

krɔ́ เคราะห์ fortune, fate, *n.*

krɔ̂ɔp-krua ครอบครัว family, *n.*

kruan, kruan-kraang, ครวญ,
ครวญคราง groan, moan, *v.*

krù-krà ขรุขระ rough, bumpy, *adj.*

krûn-kít ครุ่นคิด contemplate, *v.*

krút ครุฑ the Garuda, *n.*

kruu ครู teacher, *n.*

krûu ครู่ moment, *n.*

kruu-yài ครูใหญ่ school principal, *n.*

krua เครือ bunch (of fruit), family, lineage, *n.*

krûang เครื่อง apparatus, machine,
device, engine, *n.*

krûang-bèep เครื่องแบบ uniform,
n.

krûang-bin เครื่องบิน airplane, *n.*

krûang-bprà-dàp เครื่องประดับ
jewelry, accessory, *n.*

krûang-dàp-pləəng เครื่องดับ
เพลิง fire extinguisher, *n.*

krûang-dtɛ̀ng-gaai เครื่องแต่งกาย
dress, clothing, *n.*

krûang-dtòk-dtɛ̀ng เครื่องตกแต่ง
decorations, ornaments, *n.*

krûang-dùut-fùn เครื่องดูดฝุ่น vacuum cleaner, *n.*

krûang-dùum เครื่องดื่ม drinks,
beverage, *n.*

krûang-gɛɛng เครื่องแกง curry
spices, *n.*

krûang-grɔɔng เครื่องกรอง filter,
n.

krûang-jàk, krûang-jàk-gon
เครื่องจักร, เครื่องจักรกล machine,
machinery, *n.*

krûang-kà-yǎai-sǐang เครื่อง
ขยายเสียง amplifier, microphone, *n.*

krûang-kǐan เครื่องเขียน stationary,
writing supplies, *n.*

krûang-kít-lêek เครื่องคิดเลข calculator, *n.*

krûang-láang-jaan เครื่องล้างจาน
dishwasher, *n.*

krûang-mǎai เครื่องหมาย mark,
sign, *n.*

krûang-muu เครื่องมือ tool, instrument, equipment, *n.*

krûang-pim-dìit เครื่องพิมพ์ดีด
typewriter, *n.*

krûang-têet เครื่องเทศ spice, *n.*

krûang-wát เครื่องวัด measuring
device, *n.*

krûang-yon เครื่องยนต์ engine, *n.*

krŭm ขรึม solemn, grave, sober, *adj.*

krúm ครึ้ม cloudy, overcast, *adj.*

krûng ครึ่ง half, *n.*, *nm.*

kûa ขั้ว pole, connecting point, *n.*

kûa-fai-fáa ขั้วไฟฟ้า electrode, *n.*

kûa-lôok-dtâai ขั้วโลกใต้ south pole, *n.*

kûa-lôok-nŭa ขั้วโลกเหนือ north pole, *n.*

kuan ควร should, *v.*

kùan ขว่น scratch, *v.*

kuang ควง twirl, go on a date, *v.*

kûap ควบ gallop, combine, blend, *v.*

kûap-kum ควบคุม control, *v.*

kùat ขวด bottle, *n.*

kui คุย chat, talk, *n.*

kúk คุก jail, prison, *n.*

kum คุม take care of, watch over, take charge of, *v.*

kúm คุ้ม protect, worthwhile, *v.*, *adj.*

kúm-kâa คุ้มค่า worthwhile, *adj.*

kum-kăng คุมขัง lock up, *v.*

kŭm-kŏn ขุมขน pore (of the skin), *n.*

kúm-krɔɔng คุ้มครอง protect, *v.*

kun คุณ you, *pron.*

kun คุณ virtue, value, *n.*

kùn ขุ่น cloudy, muddy, turbid, unclear, *adj.*

kun-kâa คุณค่า virtue, value, *n.*

kun-kruu คุณครู teacher, *n.*

kun-naai คุณนาย you, she, her (woman of higher class), title placed before the first name of such lady, *pron.*, *n.*

kun-na-lák-sà-nà คุณลักษณะ qualities, attributes, *n.*

kun-na-pâap คุณภาพ quality, *n.*

kun-na-sàp คุณศัพท์ adjective, *n.*

kun-na-sŏm-bàt คุณสมบัติ quality, property, *n.*

kun-na-tam คุณธรรม moral principles, virtue, goodness, *n.*

kun-na-wút(tí) คุณวุฒิ qualification, competence, *n.*

kun-nŭu คุณหนู you, he, him, she, her (to or of a child; used by servants of the household), *pron.*

kun-yĭng คุณหญิง you, she, her (woman of higher class), title placed before the first name of such lady, *pron.*, *n.*

kùt ขุด dig, dig up, turn over, *v.*

kuu คู ditch, *n.*

kùu ขู่ threaten, *v.*

kûu คู่ pair, couple, *n.*

kûu-bàao-săao คู่บ่าวสาว bride and bridegroom, *n.*

kuu-bpɔɔng คูปอง coupon, voucher, *n.*

kûu-chii-wít คู่ชีวิต spouse, *n.*

kuu-hǎa คูหา building unit, *n.*

kûu-kǎa คู่ขา partner, *n.*

kûu-mân คู่หมั้น fiancé (e), *n.*

kuun คูณ multiply, *v.*

kûu-rák คู่รัก lover, *n.*

kùut ขูด scrape, grate, *v.*

kùan เขื่อน dam, embankment, *n.*

kuang เคือง annoy, annoyed, *v., adj.*

kûn ขึ้น get on, get in, rise, go up, *v.*

kǔng ขึง stretch, *v.*

kuun คืน night, *n.*

kuun คืน return, *v.*

kuun-chîip คืนชีพ resurrect, *v.*

kuun-nîi คืนนี้ tonight, this evening, *adj.*

kwáa คว้า snatch, grab, reach for, *v.*

kwǎa ขวา right (hand side), *n.*

kwaai ควาย buffalo, water buffalo, *n.*

kwaam ความ the sense, the substance, the gist (of a matter), case, lawsuit, a prefix to form a noun, *n.*

kwaam-bpràat-ta-nǎa ความปรารถนา wish, *n.*

kwaam-bprà-prút ความประพฤติ behavior, *n.*

kwaam-bùa-nàai ความเบื่อหน่าย boredom, *n.*

kwaam-dan-loo-hìt ความดันโลหิต blood pressure, *n.*

kwaam-dii ความดี virtue, *n.*

kwaam-glâa-hǎan ความกล้าหาญ bravery, *n.*

kwaam-gòt-dan ความกดดัน pressure, *n.*

kwaam-gròot ความโกรธ anger, *n.*

kwaam-jing ความจริง truth, *n.*

kwaam-kít ความคิด thought, *n.*

kwaam-kít-hěn ความคิดเห็น opinion, idea, *n.*

kwaam-láp ความลับ secret, *n.*

kwaam-pɔɔ-jai ความพอใจ satisfaction, *n.*

kwaam-rá-mát-rá-wang ความระมัดระวัง caution, *n.*

kwaam-reo ความเร็ว speed, *n.*

kwaam-rúu ความรู้ knowledge, *n.*

kwaam-sǎa-mâat ความสามารถ ability, *n.*

kwaam-sǎm-kan ความสำคัญ importance, significance, *n.*

kwaam-sǎm-rèt ความสำเร็จ success, *n.*

kwaam-sà-ngòp ความสงบ peace,

serenity, *n.*

kwaam-sĭa-hăai ความเสียหาย
damage, *n.*

kwaam-sìang ความเสี่ยง risk, *n.*

kwaam-sŏm-dun ความสมดุล balance, *n.*

kwaam-song-jam ความทรงจำ
memory, *n.*

kwaam-sùk ความสุข happiness, *n.*

kwaam-sŭung ความสูง height, altitude, tallness, *n.*

kwaam-sûu-sàt ความซื่อสัตย์ honesty, *n.*

kwaam-tìi ความถี่ frequency, *n.*

kwaam-tùang ความถ่วง force of gravity, *n.*

kwaam-wăng ความหวัง hope, *n.*

kwaam-yâak-jon ความยากจน
poverty, *n.*

kwáan คว้าน take out from the inside, core, pit, *v.*

kwăan ขวาน ax, axe, hatchet, *n.*

kwâang ขว้าง throw, hurl, cast, *v.*

kwáang คว้าง adrift, aimless, floating aimlessly, *adj.*

kwăang ขวาง lie across, obstruct, thwart, bar (the way), *v.*

kwâm คว่ำ turn over, *v.*

kwan ควัน smoke, *n.*

kwăn ขวัญ guardian spirit, morale, the whorl of hair on top of the head, *n.*

kwan-rót ควันรถ car exhaust fume, *n.*

kwàp ขวับ abruptly, *adv.*

kwĕen แขวน hang, *v.*

kwĭ-nin ควินิน quinine, *n.*

kwìt ขวิด attack with the horns, *v.*

l (ล, หล)

lá ละ leave, desert, *v.*

lá ละ per, *prep.*

lá ละ particle used often with mildly corroborative force, *part.*

laa ลา donkey, *n.*

laa ลา say good by, request to take leave, *v.*

lâa ล่า hunt, *v.*

lâa ล่า late, *adj.*

láa ล้า lag, be tired, *v.*

lăa หลา yard, *n.*

laa-gòɔn ลาก่อน good-bye, *v.*

laai ลาย design, pattern, *n.*

lăai หลาย many, several, *nm.*

lá-aai ละอาย ashamed, shy, bashful, *adj.*

laai-muu ลายมือ hand writing, finger print, *n.*

làak หลาก abundant, *adj.*

lâak ลาก pull, draw, drag, haul, tow, *v.*

laam ลาม spread all over, *v.*

lâam ล่าม chain, put a rope around, tie up, *v.*

lâam ล่าม interpreter, *n.*

laan ลาน an open, wide, level area, *n.*

láan ล้าน bald, *adj.*

lǎan หลาน grandchild, nephew or niece, *n.*

lǎan-chaai หลานชาย grandson, nephew, *n.*

laang ลาง omen, *n.*

láang ล้าง wash, wash off, *v.*

laang-sàat ลางสาด langsa, a kind of fruit, *n.*

lǎan-kə̌əi หลานเขย the husband of one's niece or granddaughter, *n.*

lǎan-sǎao หลานสาว granddaughter, niece, *n.*

lǎan-sà-pái หลานสะใภ้ the wife of one's nephew or grandson, *n.*

laao ลาว Lao, Laos, *n.*

laao หลาว spear, *n.*

làap หลาบ have learned one's lesson, dread (to do something), *v.*

lâap ลาภ unexpected piece of good fortune, *n.*

láa-sà-mǎi ล้าสมัย out-of-date, *adj.*

lâat ลาด cover, spread over, pave, *v.*

lâat ลาด slant, incline, slope, *v.*

lâat-dtrà-ween ลาดตระเวณ patrol, *v.*

lâat-yaang ลาดยาง paved with asphalt, *v.*

lá-gɔ̂ɔ ละก็ particle sometimes used at the end of a conditional clause, particle used at the end of the subject of a predication in a corroborative sense, *part.*

lá-hɔ̂i ละห้อย mournful, sad, *adj.*

lá-hù-tôot ลหุโทษ minor offense, misdemeanor, *n.*

lâi ไหล tip of the shoulder, *n.*

lâi ไล่ chase, recite, *v.*

lǎi ไหล flow, run, *v.*

lá-ìat ละเอียด fine, delicate, detailed, *adj.*

lâi-fîa ไล่เลี่ย equal, about the same, *adj.*

làk หลัก pole, pillar, *n.*

làk ลัก steal, *v.*

làk-bprà-gan หลักประกัน security, *n.*

làk-chai หลักชัย goal, destination, *n.*

làk-gaan หลักการ principle, *n.*

làk-geen หลักเกณฑ์ rules, *n.*

lá-koon ละคร drama, play, *n.*

lá-koon-sàt ละครสัตว์ circus, *n.*

làk-lèng หลักแหล่ง the place where one settles down to live, *n.*

làk-lɔ̀ɔp ลักลอบ act under cover, in secret, *v.*

làk-sà-nà ลักษณะ characteristics, appearance, *n.*

làk-sáp หลักทรัพย์ property, *n.*

làk-sùut หลักสูตร curriculum, *n.*

làk-tǎan หลักฐาน basis, foundation, evidence, testimony, proof, *n.*

làk-yím ลักยิ้ม dimple, *n.*

lá-laai ละลาย dissolve, melt, *v.*

lá-ləəi ละเลย neglect, *v.*

lá-lɔ̀ɔk ละลอก ripple, wave, *n.*

là-lǔam หละหลวม careless, *adj.*

lam ลำ clf. for boats, ships, airplanes; for long objects, *clf.*

lám ล้ำ go beyond, exceed, pass, *v.*

lam-bàak ลำบาก hard, difficult, troublesome, *adj.*

lam-dàp ลำดับ order, *n.*

lam-iang ลำเอียง partial, *adj.*

lam-ken ลำเค็ญ poor, *adj.*

lam-kɔɔ ลำคอ throat, *n.*

lam-liang ลำเลียง transport, *v.*

lá-mâng ละมั่ง deer, *n.*

lá-məə ละเมอ talk in one's sleep, *v.*

lá-mêət ละเมิด violate, *v.*

lá-môop ละโมบ greedy, *adj.*

lá-mɔ́ ละเมาะ grove, *n.*

lám-nâa ล้ำหน้า offside, *adj., adv.*

lam-pang ลำพัง by oneself, alone, *adv.*

lam-poong ลำโพง loudspeaker, *n.*

lam-sâi ลำไส้ bowel, intestine, *n.*

lam-taan ลำธาร stream, *n.*

lá-mút ละมุด sapota, *n.*

lam-yai ลำไย longan (a fruit), *n.*

lân ลั่น fire, shoot, *v.*

lang ลัง crate, wooden box, *n.*

làng หลั่ง let flow, pour, sprinkle, *v.*

lǎng หลัง back (body-part), back, hind, rear, for house, mosquito-nets, tents, *n., clf.*

lǎng-goong หลังโก่ง have a crooked back, *v.*

lǎng-jàak หลังจาก after, *adv.*

lǎng-kaa หลังคา roof, *n.*

lang-lee ลังเล hesitate, *v.*

lào เหล่า group, *n.*

lâo เล่า tell, *v.*

lâo เหล้า liquor, intoxicating beverage, *n.*

lâo เล้า pen, coop, enclosure (for animals), *n.*

lǎo เหลา sharpen, *v.*

láo-loom เล้าโลม console, soothe, appease, *v.*

lâo-ni-taan เล่านิทาน tell a story, *v.*

lá-ɔɔng ละออง fine particle, dust, powder, *n.*

làp หลับ close (the eyes), sleep, fall asleep, *v.*

láp ลับ secret, hidden, *adj.*

láp ลับ sharpen, *v.*

làp-nai หลับใน daydream, *v.*

lát ลัด take a short cut, cut across, *v.*

lát-tì ลัทธิ doctrine, creed, *n.*

lá-wén ละเว้น abstain from, *v.*

lá-wêɛk ละแวก vicinity, *n.*

lé เละ mushy, *adj.*

lêe เล่ห์ trick, *n.*

lêe-gon เล่ห์กล trick, *n.*

lêek เลข numeral, number, figure, *n.*

lee-kǎa เลขา secretary, *n.*

lee-kǎa-nú-gaan เลขานุการ secretary, *n.*

lee-kǎa-tí-gaan เลขาธิการ secretary of a large organization, *n.*

lêek-kà-nít เลขคณิต arithmetic, *n.*

lêek-kîi เลขคี่ odd number, *n.*

lêek-kûu เลขคู่ even number, *n.*

lee-lǎng เลหลัง auction, *v.*

leen เลน very wet mud, *n.*

lěen เหลน great-grandchild, *n.*

leeo เลว bad, poor (in quality), *adj.*

lěeo เหลว liquid, *adj.*

lèk เหล็ก iron (the metal), *n.*

lék เล็ก small, little, *adj.*

lék-nɔ́ɔi เล็กน้อย a little bit, *adv.*

lem เล็ม graze (of cattle), nibble, cut a little, *v.*

lêm เล่ม for sharp-pointed objects, *clf.*

len เลนส์ lens, *n.*

lên เล่น play, *v.*

leng เล็ง take aim, *v.*

lên-ngaan เล่นงาน hit, strike, attack, hurt, *v.*

lép เล็บ nail, *n.*

lép-muu เล็บมือ fingernail, *n.*

lép-táao เล็บเท้า toenail, *n.*

lé-té เละเทะ messed up, disorderly, *adj.*

lét-lɔ́ɔt เล็ดลอด slip or sneak, *v.*

lé และ and, *conj.*

lɛɛ แล see, watch, look, *v.*

lɛ̂ɛk แลก exchange, swap, *v.*

lêɛk-bplìan แลกเปลี่ยน trade, swap, barrier, exchange, *v.*

léɛng แล้ง dry, arid, *adj.*

léɛo แล้ว finished, already, *adj., adv.*

léɛo-dtèɛ แล้วแต่ depends on, is up to, *v.*

lêp แลบ flash, *v.*

lên แล่น run, move, *v.*

lə́ เลอะ dirty, messy, *adj.*

ləəi เลย beyond, at all, onward, further, *adj, adv.*

lə̂ək เลิก quit, finish, discontinue, *v.*

lə̂ək เลิก lift, lift up, raise, *v.*

lə̂ək-gan เลิกกัน break off friendship or relationship, *v.*

lə̌əng เหลิง forget oneself, be spoiled, carry too far beyond a proper limit (of behavior), *v.*

lə̂ət เลิศ excellent, *adj.*

lə́-tə́ เลอะเทอะ messy, *adj.*

lia เลีย lick, seek favors by flattering, *v.*

lìam เหลี่ยม edge, side (as of a triangle, rectangle), *n.*

lîam เลี่ยม plate, cover, be plated, covered with a thin sheet of metal, enflame, *v., adj.*

lian เลียน imitate, *v.*

lîan เลี่ยน be cleared away until noth-

ing is left, *v.*

lîan เลี่ยน greasy, *adj.*

lîang เลี่ยง sneak away, evade, avoid, *v.*

líang เลี้ยง feed, nourish, take care of, look after, keep, tame, domesticate, *v.*

líao เลี้ยว turn, *v.*

lǐao เหลียว turn (one's face), *v.*

lǐao-lǎng เหลียวหลัง to look back, *v.*

lǐao-lɛɛ เหลียวแล pay attention to, *v.*

lîap เลียบ go along the edge of, *v.*

lí-gee ลิเก musical folk dramas, *n.*

líi ลี้ escape, hide, *v.*

lìik หลีก evade, avoid, get away from, step aside, move aside, *v.*

lii-laa ลีลา graceful poise, *n.*

lii-lâat ลีลาศ dance (ballroom), *n.*

lík-ka-sìt ลิขสิทธิ์ copyright, *n.*

lí-kìt ลิขิต write, *v.*

lí-lít ลิลิต mixed form of Thai versification, *n.*

lîm ลิ่ม wedge, *n.*

lím-rót ลิ้มรส taste, *v.*

lín ลิ้น tongue, *n.*

lín-chák ลิ้นชัก drawer, *n.*

ling ลิง monkey, *n.*

lín-gài ลิ้นไก่ uvula, *n.*

lín-jìi ลิ้นจี่ litchi (a fruit), *n.*

líp ลิบ far apart, *adv.*

líp-sa-dtìk ลิบสติก lipstick, *n.*

ló โละ discard, *v.*

lom ลม wind, breeze, air, *n.*

lòm หล่ม mud, muddy place, *n.*

lôm ล่ม sink, capsize, overturn, *v.*

lóm ล้ม fall, topple, fell, kill, cancel, abandon, *v.*

lom-bâa-mǔu ลมบ้าหมู whirlwind, epilepsy, *n.*

lom-hǎai-jai ลมหายใจ breath, *n.*

lóm-láang ล้มล้าง overthrow, abolish, *v.*

lóm-lá-laai ล้มละลาย go bankrupt, *v.*

lóm-lěeo ล้มเหลว fall, *v.*

lóm-lə̂ək ล้มเลิก abandon, quit, give up, abolish, *v.*

lom-paa-yú ลมพายุ windstorm, *n.*

lon ลน excited, flustered, *adj.*

lòn หล่น drop, fall, *v.*

lón ล้น filled to overflowing, *adj.*

lon หลน a kind of shrimp sauce served with raw vegetables, *n.*

lon-fai ลนไฟ singe, hold over a flame, *v.*

long ลง descend, get out of, get off, (a car, train, etc.), put (something) down,

release, drop, down, *v.*

lǒng หลง get lost, forget, *v.*

long-chûu ลงชื่อ sign, sign one's name, *v.*

long-əəi ลงเอย end up, *v.*

lǒng-lǎi หลงใหล crazy about, *adj.*

long-muu ลงมือ start, begin, undertake, *v.*

long-naam ลงนาม sign, *v.*

lǒng-pìt หลงผิด err, *v.*

long-pung ลงพุง have a big belly, *v.*

lǒng-rák หลงรัก be passionately in love, *v.*

long-rɔɔi ลงรอย in good harmony, in agreement, *adj.*

lǒng-sà-nèe หลงเสน่ห์ fall for someone's charms, *v.*

long-táai ลงท้าย be at the end, *adj.*

lǒng-taang หลงทาง lose one's way, *v.*

long-tá-bian ลงทะเบียน register, to be registered, *v.*

long-tan ลงทัณฑ์ punish, *v.*

long-tôot ลงโทษ punish, *v.*

long-tun ลงทุน invest, *v.*

lǒo โหล last, behind, *adj.*

lôo โล่ shield, *n.*

lóo โล้ rock, swing, row, *v.*

lŏo โหล dozen, *n.*

lŏo โหล jar (usually of glass and with a wide mouth), *n.*

lŏo โหล hollow, sunken, *adj.*

loo-hà โลหะ metal, *n.*

loo-hìt โลหิต blood, *n.*

lôok โลก the world, the earth, *n.*

loo-lee โลเล ever-changing, unreliable, *adj.*

loo-maa โลมา dolphin, *n.*

loong โลง coffin, *n.*

lôong โล่ง open, empty, clear, *adj.*

lôong-jai โล่งใจ feel relieved, free, at ease, *v.*

lôong-òk โล่งอก feel relieved, free, at ease, *v.*

lôop โลภ greedy, covetous, *adj.*

lôot โลด jump, *v.*

lòp หลบ duck in order to escape, slip or sneak away, hide, avoid, *v.*

lóp ลบ erase, subtract, *v.*

lóp-láang ลบล้าง wipe out, eradicate, *v.*

lót ลด lower, reduce, decrease, discount, *v.*

lót-long ลดลง subside, become lower, *v.*

lɔ́ เลาะ skirt, go along the edge of,

remove stitches, take the hem out, *v.*

lɔ́-lè เหลาะแหละ nonsense (of speech), unreliable, undependable, unsettled, *adj.*

lɔɔn ลอน wave, undulation, *n.*

lɔ̀n หล่อน she, her, *pron.*

lɔɔng ลอย float, cause to float along, *v.*

lɔɔng-hŏn ลอยหน move about invisibly, *v.*

lɔɔng-lɔɔi ล่องลอย wander, drift, *v.*

lɔ̂n-jɔ̂n ล่อนจ้อน nude, naked, *adj.*

lɔ̀ɔ หล่อ cast (in a mold), *v.*

lɔ̀ɔ หล่อ handsome, *adj.*

lɔɔ ล่อ mule, *n.*

lɔɔ ล่อ lure, tempt, allure, seduce, *v.*

lɔ́ɔ ล้อ wheel, *n.*

lɔ́ɔ ล้อ tease, mock, *v.*

lɔɔ หลอ hollowed out, *adj.*

lɔɔi ลอย float, drift, *v.*

lɔ̀ɔk หลอก trick, deceive, fool, *v.*

lɔ̀ɔk ลอก copy, make a copy, skin peel, *v.*

lɔ́ɔ-lian ล้อเลียน mock, ridicule, *v.*

lɔ̀ɔ-luang ล่อลวง deceive, *v.*

lɔ́ɔm ล้อม surround, encircle, besiege, *v.*

lɔ̌ɔm หลอม melt, fuse (metal), *v.*

lɔ́ɔm-rúa ล้อมรั้ว fence, *v.*

lɔ̌ɔn หลอน scare, spook, haunt, v.

lɔɔng ลอง try, try out, try on, v.

lɔɔng-jai ลองใจ test one's feelings, v.

lɔ̀ɔp ลอบ sneak, do (something) secretly, v.

lɔ̀ɔt หลอด tube, n.

lɔ̂ɔt ลอด pass through or under, v.

lɔ̀ɔt-fai หลอดไฟ light bulb, n.

lûak ลวก scald, burn, or scorch superficially, cook briefly, v.

lǔam หลวม loose, too large, baggy, n.

lúan ล้วน entirely, purely, completely, adv.

luang ลวง deceive, v.

lûang ล่วง pass (of time), go beyond (a certain limit), v.

lúang ล้วง reach into, reach in for, v.

lǔang หลวง government, royal, element used to address rank, n.

lûang-bprà-wee-nii ล่วงประเวณี commit adultery, v.

lûang-gəən ล่วงเกิน trespass against, offend, show disrespect to (someone), v.

lûang-lám ล่วงล้ำ intrude, v.

lûang-láp ล่วงลับ pass away, v.

luang-nâa ล่วงหน้า go before, in advance, v., adv.

luan-laam ลวนลาม overstep the rules of propriety, v.

lûat ลวด wire, n.

lûat-laai ลวดลาย pattern, decorative design, special talents, skills or abilities of a person, n.

lûat-nǎam ลวดหนาม barbed wire, n.

lui ลุย wade, go through, v.

lúk ลุก get up, rise, arise, v.

lú-lûang ลุล่วง done, finished, completed, adj.

lûm ลุ่ม lowland, n.

lǔm หลุม hole, n.

lûm-lǒng ลุ่มหลง crazy (about), infatuated (with), adj.

lung ลุง elder uncle (older brother of father or mother), n.

lùp หลุบ droop, hang down, v.

lùt หลุด slip loose, v.

lûuk ลูก child, offspring, fruit, n.

lûuk-bàat ลูกบาศก์ cube, n.

lûuk-bìt ลูกบิด doorknob, n.

lûuk-bpàt ลูกปัด bead, n.

lûuk-bpòong ลูกโป่ง toy balloon, n.

lûuk-bpɯɯn ลูกปืน bullet, n.

lûuk-chaai ลูกชาย son, *n.*

lûuk-dtǎo ลูกเต๋า die, dice, *n.*

lûuk-dtûm ลูกตุ้ม pendulum, *n.*

lûuk-fɛ̀ɛt ลูกแฝด twin, *n.*

lûuk-gài ลูกไก่ chick, *n.*

lûuk-grà-sǔn ลูกกระสุน bullet, *n.*

lûuk-gèet ลูกเกด raisin, *n.*

lûuk-gè ลูกแกะ lamb, *n.*

lûuk-gɛ̂ɛo ลูกแก้ว (glass) marble, *n.*

lûuk-glîng ลูกกลิ้ง roller, *n.*

lûuk-grong ลูกกรง balustrade, railing, the sides of a cage or pen, *n.*

lûuk-gun-jɛɛ ลูกกุญแจ key, *n.*

lûuk-hèp ลูกเห็บ hail, *n.*

lûuk-jâang ลูกจ้าง employee, *n.*

lûuk-káa ลูกค้า customer, *n.*

lûuk-kàang ลูกข่าง top, *n.*

lûuk-kə̌əi ลูกเขย son-in-law, *n.*

lûuk-kít ลูกคิด abacus, *n.*

lûuk-kǔn ลูกขุน juror, *n.*

lûuk-kwaam ลูกความ litigant, client, *n.*

lûuk-líang ลูกเลี้ยง step-child, adopted child, *n.*

lûuk-lôok ลูกโลก globe, *n.*

lûuk-máai ลูกไม้ fruit, lace, *n.*

lûuk-mên ลูกเหม็น moth ball, *n.*

lûuk-náam ลูกน้ำ mosquito larva, *n.*

lûuk-nîi ลูกหนี้ debtor, *n.*

lûuk-nɔ́ɔng ลูกน้อง subordinate, *n.*

lûuk-om ลูกอม candy, *n.*

lûuk-rá-bə̀ət ลูกระเบิด bomb, *n.*

lûuk-rɔ̂ɔk ลูกรอก pulley, *n.*

lûuk-rʉa ลูกเรือ crew, *n.*

lûuk-sǎao ลูกสาว daughter, *n.*

lûuk-sà-pái ลูกสะใภ้ daughter-in-law, *n.*

lûuk-sìt ลูกศิษย์ student, follower, disciple, *n.*

lûuk-sôo ลูกโซ่ link (of a chain), *n.*

lûuk-sɔ̌ɔn ลูกศร arrow, *n.*

lûuk-sùt-tʰɔ́ɔng ลูกสุดท้อง the last-born child, youngest child, *n.*

lûuk-sʉ̌a ลูกเสือ boy scout, tiger cub, *n.*

lûuk-tôot ลูกโทษ penalty kick, *n.*

lûup ลูบ stroke, pat, *v.*

lûup-klam ลูบคลำ caress, fondle, *v.*

lûup-lái ลูบไล้ stroke, rub lightly, *v.*

lʉ̌a เหลือ left over, remaining, be surplus, *v.*

lʉ̌a-chʉ̂a เหลือเชื่อ unbelievable, *adj.*

lʉ̌a-fʉ̌a เหลือเฟือ plentiful, *adj.*

lʉ̌a-gəən เหลือเกิน very, extremely, *adv.*

lʉ̂ai เลื่อย saw, *n.*

lûai เลื้อย crawl, creep, v.

lûak เหลือก roll the eyes up, v.

lûak เลือก choose, pick out, select, elect, v.

lûak-dtâng เลือกตั้ง elect, v.

lǔa-lǎai เหลือหลาย abundant, adj.

lûam เหลื่อม overlap, v.

lûam-sǎi เลื่อมใส believe whole-heartedly, v.

luan เลือน fade away, blur, v.

lûan เลื่อน move, move along, slide, change position, be promoted, post-pone, v.

lǔang เหลือง yellow, adj.

lûang-luu เลื่องลือ spread far and wide, widely known, adj.

lûap เหลือบ horsefly, gadfly, n.

lûap เหลือบ glance, look sideways, v.

lûat เลือด blood, n.

lûat-lǎi, lûat-ɔ̀ɔk เลือดไหล, เลือดออก bleed, v.

lúk ลึก deep, adj.

lúk-láp ลึกลับ mysterious, adj.

lúk-súng ลึกซึ้ง profound, adj.

luu ลือ rumor, be rumored, v.

luum ลืม forget, v.

lûun ลื่น slippery, smooth, adj.

lûup หลืบ narrow space, n.

m (ม, หม)

maa มา come, coming, hitherward, v., adv.

máa ม้า horse, bench, n.

mǎa หมา dog, n.

mǎa-bâa หมาบ้า mad dog, n.

mǎa-bpàa หมาป่า wolf, n.

maa-hǎa มาหา come to see, come to visit, v.

mâai ม่าย a window, n.

máai ไม้ wood, stick, n.

mǎai หมาย indicate, mark, aim at, expect, v.

máai-ban-tát ไม้บรรทัด ruler, n.

máai-dtaai ไม้ตาย boxing decisive blow, decisive trick, n.

máai-dtrii ไม้ตรี the third tone mark, n.

máai-èek ไม้เอก the first tone mark, n.

máai-gwàat ไม้กวาด broom, n.

máai-jàp หมายจับ arrest warrant, n.

máai-jàt-dtà-waa ไม้จัตวา the fourth tone mark, n.

máai-jîm-fan ไม้จิ้มฟัน toothpick, n.

máai-kaan ไม้คาน bamboo pole, n.

máai-kìit-fai ไม้ขีดไฟ match, *n.*

mǎai-kón หมายค้น search warrant, *v.*

mǎai-kwaam-wâa หมายความว่า mean that, *v.*

máai-kwɛɛn-sûa ไม้แขวนเสื้อ coat hanger, *n.*

máai-paai ไม้พาย paddle, *n.*

máai-pài ไม้ไผ่ bamboo, *n.*

máai-riao ไม้เรียว rod, *n.*

máai-táao ไม้เท้า walking stick, *n.*

máai-too ไม้โท the second tone mark, *n.*

mǎai-tǔng หมายถึง mean, imply, refer to, *v.*

mǎa-jîng-jɔ̀ɔk หมาจิ้งจอก fox, jackal, *n.*

màak หมาก areca nut, betel nut, *n.*

mâak มาก much, many, a lot of, *adj.*

màak-fa-ràng หมากฝรั่ง chewing gum, *n.*

mâak-gəən-bpai มากเกินไป too much, *adv.*

mâak-gwàa มากกว่า more, more than, *adj., adv.*

mâak-maai มากมาย much, a lot, many, a great many, *adv.*

màak-rúk หมากรุก chess, *n.*

máam ม้าม spleen, *n.*

maan มาร devil, demon, *n.*

mâan ม่าน curtain, drape, *n.*

maa-nâng ม้านั่ง bench, stool, *n.*

maan-daa มารดา mother, *n.*

mâan-dtaa ม่านตา iris of the eye, *n.*

maan-yaa มารยา trick, artifice, *n.*

maa-ráp มารับ come to meet, get, or receive, *v.*

maa-ra-yâat มารยาท manners, etiquette, *n.*

mâat-dtraa มาตรา system of measurement, standard, *n.*

mâat-dtraa-sùan มาตราส่วน scale, *n.*

mâat-dtra-tǎan มาตรฐาน standard, *n.*

maa-tǔng มาถึง arrive, *v.*

má-dtì มติ resolution, decision, opinion, *n.*

má-fɨang มะเฟือง carambola (fruit), *n.*

má-gɔ̀ɔk มะกอก olive, *n.*

má-grùut มะกรูด Kaffir lime, *n.*

má-hǎa มหา great, *adj.*

má-hǎa-chon มหาชน the public, *n.*

má-hǎa-sèet-tǐi มหาเศรษฐี multi-millionaire, *n.*

má-hàat-tai มหาดไทย Department of the Interior, *n.*

má-hǎa-wít-ta-yaa-lai มหาวิทยาลัย university, *n.*

má-hǎa-yaan มหายาน Mahayana Buddhism, *n.*

má-hàt-sà-jan มหัศจรรย์ miraculous, *adj.*

má-hěe-sǐi มเหสี queen, *n.*

má-hǒo-raan มโหฬาร splendid, magnificent, grand, *adj.*

má-hǒo-rii มโหรี Thai orchestra, *n.*

má-hɔ̌ɔ-ra-sòp มหรสพ entertainment, *n.*

mài ใหม่ new, *adj.*

mâi ไม่ not, *adv.*

mǎi ไหม silk, *n.*

mǎi ไหม fine, *v.*

mǎi ไหม used to convert a statement into a yes-or-no question, *part.*

mâi-bpen-rai ไม่เป็นไร your welcome, it doesn't matter, that's all right, not at all, it's nothing, never mind!, forget it!, *v.*, *adv.*

mâi-châi ไม่ใช่ is not, are not, am not, No, it's not!, No!, *adv.*

mâi-dâai ไม่ได้ not get, gain, obtain, procure, didn't, not get to, didn't get to,

can't, cannot, unable to, No!, *v.*

mâi-dtɔ̂ng ไม่ต้อง not to have to, *v.*

mai-dtrii ไมตรี friendship, *n.*

mâi-hâi ไม่ให้ not to give, not to let, not to, without, *v.*

mâi-hěn-dûai ไม่เห็นด้วย disagree, *v.*

mâi-kəəi ไม่เคย never, *adv.*

mâi-kɔ̂i ไม่ค่อย scarcely, hardly, not quite, not very, *adv.*

mâi-tan ไม่ทัน not in time, late, *adj.*

mâi-wǎi ไม่ไหว unable to, cannot, is incapable of, How impossible!, *adj.*, *adv.*

màk หมัก leave (something) to ferment, *v.*

má-kǎam มะขาม tamarind, *n.*

màk-dɔɔng หมักดอง preserve or pickle by slow fermentation, *v.*

mák-ngâai มักง่าย careless, sloppy, *adj.*

má-kǔa มะเขือ eggplant, *n.*

má-kǔa-têet มะเขือเทศ tomato, *n.*

má-lá-gɔɔ มะละกอ papaya, *n.*

má-lét เมล็ด seed, *n.*

má-lɛɛng แมลง insect, *n.*

má-lɛɛng-bpɔ̀ng แมลงป่อง scorpion, *n.*

má-lɛɛng-bpɔɔ แมลงปอ dragonfly, n.

má-lɛɛng-mum แมลงมุม spider, n.

má-lɛɛng-pûu แมลงภู่ carpenter bee, n.

má-lɛɛng-sàap แมลงสาบ cockroach, n.

má-lɛɛng-wan แมลงวัน fly, n.

má-lɛɛng-wìi แมลงหวี่ fruit fly, n.

má-lí มะลิ jasmine, n.

má-mɛɛ มะแม Year of the Goat, n.

má-mia มะเมีย Year of the Horse, n.

má-mûang มะม่วง mango, n.

man มัน oil, fat, grease, n.

man มัน potato, yam, n.

man มัน it, they, them, pron.

màn หมั่น diligent, industrious, adj.

mân มั่น firm, adj.

mân หมั้น be engaged, v.

măn หมัน sterile, useless, fruitless, futile, adj.

má-naao มะนาว lime, lemon, n.

man-fa-ràng มันฝรั่ง potato, n.

mang-gɔɔn มังกร dragon, n.

mâng-kâng มั่งคั่ง wealthy, adj.

mang-kút มังคุด mangosteen (a fruit), n.

mâng-mii มั่งมี wealthy, adj.

má-nii มณี precious stones, gems, n.

mân-jai มั่นใจ confident, certain, adj.

mân-kong มั่นคง stable, firm, secure, adj.

man-sǎm-bpà-lǎng มันสำปะหลัง cassava, n.

má-nút มนุษย์ man, human being, n.

man-yâat มรรยาท manners, etiquette, n.

mao เมา drunk, intoxicated, affected with motion sickness, adj.

mǎo เหมา contract for work, buy or sell as a whole, deduce, v.

má-práao มะพร้าว coconut, n.

má-rá มะระ bitter melon, n.

má-reng มะเร็ง cancer, n.

má-roong มะโรง Year of the Dragon, n.

má-ruɯn มะรืน the day after tomorrow, n.

má-sɛ̌ng มะเส็ง Year of the Snake, n.

màt หมัด flea n.

màt หมัด fist, punch n.

mát มัด tie, bind, v.

mát-jù-râat มัจจุราช god of death, n.

mát-ta-yát มัธยัสถ์ thrifty, economical, *adj.*

mát-ta-yom มัธยม secondary educational level, *n.*

mee-sǎa-yon เมษายน April, *n.*

méet เมตร meter, *n.*

méet-dtaa เมตตา kindness, mercifulness, *n.*

mêk เมฆ cloud, *n.*

mém เม้ม fold the edge or border in, *v.*

mên เม่น porcupine, *n.*

měn เหม็น smell bad, stink, *adj.*

mét เม็ด seed, grain, *n.*

mêε แม่ mother, *n.*

mέε แม้ even though, even if, *conj.*

mἔε แหม Say!, Well!, *excl.*

mêε-bâan แม่บ้าน housewife, *n.*

mέε-dtὲε แม้แต่ even, *conj.*

mêε-kǒong แม่โขง the Mekong River, *n.*

mêε-káa แม่ค้า vendor, market woman, *n.*

mêε-krua แม่ครัว (female) cook, *n.*

mêε-lèk แม่เหล็ก magnet, *n.*

mêε-lîang แม่เลี้ยง stepmother, foster mother, *n.*

mêε-mâai แม่หม้าย window, *n.*

mêε-mót แม่มด witch, *n.*

mêε-náam แม่น้ำ river, *n.*

mεεng แมง insect, *n.*

mεεng-bpòng แมงป่อง scorpion, *n.*

mεεng-bpɔɔ แมงปอ dragonfly, *n.*

mεεng-mum แมงมุม spider, *n.*

mεεng-wan แมงวัน fly, *n.*

mεεng-wìi แมงหวี่ fruit fly, *n.*

mεεo แมว cat, *n.*

mêε-sὺὺ แม่สื่อ female go-between, *n.*

mêε-táp แม่ทัพ general, *n.*

mêε-yaai แม่ยาย (man's) mother-in-law, *n.*

mὲm แหม่ม an occidental woman, *n.*

mên แม่น accurate, correct, exact, precise, *n.*

mên-yam แม่นยำ accurately, clearly, vividly, *adv.*

méo แม้ว Hmong, a tribe of hill people in North Thailand, *n.*

mɔ̀ɔ เหม่อ inattentive, *adj.*

mɔ̀ɔ-lɔɔi เหม่อลอย wandering, aimlessly (of eyes and mind), *adj., adv.*

mɔɔn เมิน turn away, *v.*

mí มิ not, *adv.*

mia เมีย wife, *n.*

mîang เมี่ยง fermented leaves of wild

Phonetic • Thai • English

tea plants, *n.*

mǐao เหมียว meow, *v.*, *n.*

mii มี have, possess, *v.*

mìi หมี่ egg noodles, *n.*

mǐi หมี bear, *n.*

mii-naa-kom มีนาคม March, *n.*

mîit มีด knife, *n.*

mîit-goon มีดโกน razor, *n.*

mii-tɔ́ɔng มีท้อง pregnant, *adj.*

mìn หมิ่น insult, look down upon, despise, *v.*

mít มิด entirely, completely, *adv.*

mít มิตร friend, *n.*

mít-chǎa มิจฉา wrong, improper, *n.*

mít-chǎa-chîip มิจฉาชีพ illegal or wrong means of making a living, *n.*

mít-dtà-pâap มิตรภาพ friendship, *n.*

mí-tù-naa-yon มิถุนายน June, *n.*

mòk หมก bury, place underneath, cover over, *v.*

mók-gà-raa-kom มกราคม January, *n.*

mòk-mûn หมกมุ่น be engrossed (in), preoccupied (with), *v.*

mon มนต์, มนตร์ sacred words, prayer, sacrificial formula, magic spell, *n.*

mǒn หม่น dull, gray, *adj.*

mon-dtrii มนตรี councilor, councilman, *n.*

mong-gùt มงกุฎ crown, *n.*

mong-kon มงคล auspicious sign, cotton band worn on the head, *n.*

mon-tin มลทิน blemish, impurity, *n.*

mon-ton มณฑล province, *n.*

môo โม่ grind, mill, *v.*

móo โม้ boast, brag, *v.*

moo-hǒo โมโห angry, *adj.*

moo-ká โมฆะ void, invalid, useless, *adj.*

moong โมง o' clock, time, *adv.*, *n.*

môong โม่ง oversized, hooded, *adj.*

mòt หมด used up, exhausted (in supply), *adj.*

mót มด ant, *n.*

mòt-aa-yú หมดอายุ expire, terminate, *v.*

mòt-dtua หมดตัว have nothing left, be broke, *v.*

mɔ̀ เหมาะ suitable, appropriate, fitting, *adj.*

mɔɔm มอม dirty, smeared, *adj.*

mɔ̀n หม่อน white mulberry, *n.*

mɔ̂ɔ หม้อ cooking pot, *n.*

mɔ̌ɔ หมอ doctor, fellow, guy, *n.*

mɔ̌ɔ-dtam-yɛɛ หมอตำแย midwife, *n.*

mɔ̌ɔ-duu หมอดู fortuneteller, *n.*

mɔ̌ɔ-fan หมอฟัน dentist, *n.*

mɔ̀ɔk หมอก fog, mist, *n.*

mɔɔn หมอน pillow, *n.*

mɔɔng มอง look, look at, *v.*

mɔ̌ɔng หมอง sad, depressed, *adj.*

mɔ̌ɔ-nûat หมอนวด masseur, masseuse, *n.*

mɔ̂ɔp หมอบ crouch, prostrate oneself, *v.*

mɔ̂ɔp มอบ delegate, commit, entrust, *v.*

mɔɔ-ra-dòk มรดก inheritance, *n.*

mɔɔ-ra-gòt มรกต emerald, *n.*

mɔɔ-ra-ná มรณะ death, to die, *n.*, *v.*

mɔɔ-ra-sǔm มรสุม monsoon, *n.*

mɔ̌ɔ-sàt หมอสัตว์ veterinarian, *n.*

mɔ̌ɔ-sɔ̌ɔn-sàat-sà-nǎa หมอสอนศาสนา missionary, *n.*

mɔ̂ɔt มอด weevil, *n.*

mɔ̂ɔt มอด die down, die out, *v.*

mua มัว dim, obscure, cloudy, *adj.*

mûa มั้ว assemble, congregate, *v.*

muai มวย boxing, *n.*

muai มวย chignon, bun, *n.*

mùak หมวก hat, cap, *n.*

muan มวน clf. for cigars, cigarettes, to roll, *n. v.*

muan มวล mass, *n.*

múan ม้วน roll, roll up, reel, *v.*

mûang ม่วง purple, *adj.*

muat หมวด section, group, category, *n.*

múk มุก pearl oyster, *n.*

múk มุข front porch, *n.*

mum มุม corner, *n.*

mǔn หมุน turn, rotate, spin, *v.*

mung มุง roof, be roofed with, crowd around, *v.*

mûng มุ่ง aim for, *v.*

múng มุ้ง mosquito net, *n.*

mûng-mǎai มุ่งหมาย have a definite purpose, *v.*

mûng-nâa มุ่งหน้า head toward determinedly, *v.*

mûng-ráai มุ่งร้าย intend to do harm, *v.*

mǔn-wian หมุนเวียน rotate, circulate, *v.*

mú-sǎa มุสา lie, *v.*

mùt หมุด tack, peg, small screw, *n.*

mút มุด crawl under, go underneath, *v.*

mùu หมู่ group, *n.*

mǔu หมู pig, hog, pork, *n.*

mùu-bâan หมู่บ้าน village, *n.*

mùu-gɔ̀ หมู่เกาะ archipelago, *n.*

mûuk มูก mucus, *n.*

mûu-lǐi มู่ลี่ bamboo blind, *n.*

muum-maam มูมมาม sloppy, messy, uncouth in manner, *adj.*

muun มูน knoll, mound, *n.*

muun มูน stir coconut cream into, *v.*

muun มูล excrement, dung, *n.*

muun มูล base, origin, source, root, *n.*

mûa เมื่อ for a time, times, *clf.*

mûa-dai เมื่อใด when, whenever, *adv.*

mûa-gíi เมื่อกี้ a moment ago, just now, *adv.*

mûai เมื่อย tired, stiff (of muscles), *adj.*

mûak เมือก slime, *n.*

mûa-kuun-níi เมื่อคืนนี้ last night, *adv.*

mǔan เหมือน be the same as, resemble, *v.*

muang เมือง town, city, country, *n.*

mǔang เหมือง mine (of ore), *n.*

mǔan-gan เหมือนกัน similar, alike, also, too, likewise, *adj., adv.*

muang-kûn เมืองขึ้น colony, *n.*

muang-lǔang เมืองหลวง capital, *n.*

muang-nɔ̂ɔk เมืองนอก foreign country, abroad, *n.*

muang-tâa เมืองท่า seaport town, *n.*

muang-tai เมืองไทย Thailand, *n.*

mùk หมึก ink, *n.*

mun มึน tipsy, groggy, *adj.*

mung มึง you (rude), *pron.*

muu มือ hand, *n.*

múu มื้อ for meals, *clf.*

mùun หมื่น ten thousand, *nm.*

mûut มืด dark, *adj.*

n (น, ณ, หน)

nà นะ particle used to express urging, insisting, importuning, particle indicating qualified or equivocal acceptance or agreement, *part.*

ná นะ particle used to make an utterance gentler, milder, particle indicating a mild question, *part.*

naa นา paddy field, rice field, *n.*

nâa น่า bound stem placed in front of verbs to make new verb derivatives, ought to, might like to, worthy of, *v., adj.*

nâa หน้า face, front, fore, in front of, ahead, in front, *n., adj., adv.*

nâa หน้า season (of the year), *n.*

náa น้า younger maternal uncle or ant, *n.*

nǎa หนา thick, *adj.*

nâa-àan น่าอ่าน worth reading, *adj.*

nâa-baan หน้าบาน beam (with pleasure), delighted, *adj.*

nâa-bâan หน้าบ้าน the area in front of a house, facade of a house, in front of the house, *n.*

nâa-bpàt หน้าปัด dial, face (of a clock), *n.*

nâa-bpòk หน้าปก the front of the cover, *n.*

nâa-chom น่าชม admirable, *adj.*

nâa-chûa น่าเชื่อ believable, *adj.*

nâa-dâan หน้าด้าน brazen, shameless, *adj.*

nâa-dtaa หน้าตา countenance, look, *n.*

nǎa-dtaa หนาตา get thick (in number, as of crowd), *v.*

nâa-dtàang หน้าต่าง window, *n.*

nâa-dtua-mai หน้าตัวเมีย sissy, effeminate, Sissy!, *adj.*

nâa-duu น่าดู worth seeing, *adj.*

nâa-fang น่าฟัง pleasant to listen to, *adj.*

nâa-fǒn หน้าฝน rainy season, *n.*

nâa-gàak หน้ากาก mask, hood, cover, *n.*

nâa-gin น่ากิน tasty-looking, *adj.*

nâa-glìat น่าเกลียด ugly, *adj.*

nâa-glua น่ากลัว frightening, scary, *adj.*

nâa-grà-daan หน้ากระดาน rank, line, *adj.*

nâa-grà-dàat หน้ากระดาษ page (of a book, newspaper, letter), *n.*

naai นาย master, employer, boss, element placed before verbs or nouns to form agent nouns, *n.*

naai-am-pəə นายอำเภอ head official of a district, *n.*

naai-châang นายช่าง craftsman, artisan, *n.*

naai-jâang นายจ้าง employer, *n.*

naai-nâa นายหน้า broker, *n.*

naai-pêet นายแพทย์ physician, doctor, *n.*

naai-pon นายพล general, *n.*

naai-praan นายพราน hunter, *n.*

naai-tá-bian นายทะเบียน registrar, *n.*

naai-tá-hǎan นายทหาร officer (of the army, navy, air force), *n.*

naai-tun นายทุน capitalist, *n.*

nâa-jà น่าจะ ought to, might like to, *v.*

nâak นาก alloy of gold and copper, *n.*

nâak นาก otter, *n.*

nâak นาค man entering priesthood, Naga, a legendary serpent, *n.*

nâa-kǎn น่าขัน funny, *adj.*

nâa-kěng หน้าแข้ง shin, *n.*

nâa-kǐao น่าเขียว look sick, turn pale (as when sick or exhausted), *v.*

nâa-kít น่าคิด worth thinking about, *adj.*

nâa-lǎng หน้าหลัง the last page, the back page (of a newspaper), the reverse side (of a single sheet), *n.*

nâa-léeng หน้าแล้ง dry season, *n.*

naa-lí-gaa นาฬิกา clock, watch, *n.*

naam นาม name, *n.*

náam น้ำ water, liquid, fluid, *n.*

nǎam หนาม thorn, barb of wire, *n.*

nâa-máa หน้าม้า decoy (of people only), *n.*

nâa-máai หน้าไม้ crossbow, *n.*

nâa-mài หน้าใหม่ new face, newcomer, new one, stranger, *n.*

náam-baa-daan น้ำบาดาล underground water, *n.*

naam-bàt นามบัตร business card, name card, *n.*

naam-bpàak-gaa นามปากกา pen name, *n.*

náam-bplaa น้ำปลา fish sauce, *n.*

náam-bpà-bpaa น้ำประปา city water, *n.*

náam-bɔ̀ɔ น้ำบ่อ well water, *n.*

náam-chaa น้ำชา tea, *n.*

náam-chûam น้ำเชื่อม syrup, *n.*

náam-dii น้ำดี bile, *n.*

náam-dtaa น้ำตา tears, teardrops, *n.*

náam-dtaan น้ำตาล sugar, brown, *n., adj.*

náam-dtòk น้ำตก waterfall, falls, *n.*

naam-fɛ̌ɛng นามแฝง pseudonym, pen name, *n.*

náam-fǒn น้ำฝน rain water, *n.*

náam-gaam น้ำกาม semen, *n.*

náam-gà-tí น้ำกะทิ coconut cream, *n.*

náam-glàn น้ำกลั่น distilled water, *n.*

náam-gròt น้ำกรด acid, *n.*

náam-hɔ̌ɔm น้ำหอม perfume, *n.*

náam-jai น้ำใจ good will, thoughtfulness, *n.*

náam-jîm น้ำจิ้ม sauce, dip, *n.*

náam-jùut น้ำจืด fresh water, *n.*

náam-káang น้ำค้าง dew, *n.*

náam-kem น้ำเค็ม salt water, *n.*

náam-kɛ̌ng น้ำแข็ง ice, *n.*

náam-má-gɔ̀ɔk น้ำมะกอก olive oil, *n.*

náam-laai น้ำลาย saliva, *n.*

náam-man น้ำมัน oil, fuel oil, *n.*

náam-má-naao น้ำมะนาว lemonade, *n.*

náam-man-din น้ำมันดิน tar, *n.*

náam-man-dìp น้ำมันดิบ crude oil, *n.*

náam-man-gáat น้ำมันก๊าส kerosene, *n.*

náam-man-krûang น้ำมันเครื่อง motor oil, *n.*

náam-man-mǔu น้ำมันหมู lard, *n.*

náam-man-pûut น้ำมันพืช vegetable, *n.*

náam-man-sǒn น้ำมันสน turpentine, *n.*

náam-mao น้ำเมา intoxicating beverage, *n.*

náam-má-práao น้ำมะพร้าว coconut milk, *n.*

náam-mom น้ำมนต์ holy water, *n.*

náam-mûuk น้ำมูก nasal mucus, nasal discharge, *n.*

náam-mɯɯ น้ำมือ (one's own) deed, act, action, *n.*

náam-nàk น้ำหนัก weight, *n.*

náam-ngən น้ำเงิน blue, the color blue, *adj.*

náam-nom น้ำนม milk, *n.*

nâa-mɔɔ-ra-sǔm หน้ามรสุม monsoon season, *n.*

náam-pǒn-la-máai น้ำผลไม้ fruit juice, *n.*

náam-prík น้ำพริก hot chili paste sauce, *n.*

náam-pú น้ำพุ fountain, spring, water spout, *n.*

náam-pɯ̂ng น้ำผึ้ง honey, *n.*

naam-sà-gun นามสกุล family name, last name, *n.*

náam-sôm น้ำส้ม vinegar, orange juice, *n.*

náam-tá-lee น้ำทะเล seawater, *n.*

nâa-múk หน้ามุข front balcony, front porch, portico, *n.*

náam-tûam น้ำท่วม flood, *n.*

nâa-mɯ̂ɯt หน้ามืด black out, have a dizzy spell, lose control of oneself, be blind with passion, *v.*

náam-wǎan น้ำหวาน soft drink, flavored syrup, *n.*

náam-won น้ำวน whirlpool, *n.*

náam-yaa น้ำยา chemical solution, a kind of sauce made of fish, coconut cream and other ingredients and served with vermicelli, *n.*

náam-yɔ̂i น้ำย่อย gastric juice, *n.*

naan นาน long (of time), *adj.*

naa-naa นานา various, different, all, *adj.*

nâa-naa หน้านา rice-planting season, *n.*

nâa-nǎa หน้าหนา brazen, shameless, *adj.*

nâa-nǎao หน้าหนาว winter, the cold season, *n.*

nâa-náp-tʉ̌ʉ น่านับถือ worthy of respect, *adj.*

nǎa-nɛ̂n หนาแน่น crowded, congested, densely populated, *adj.*

naang นาง lady, woman, element placed before nouns or verbs to form female agent nouns, *n.*

naang-èek นางเอก leading lady, heroine, *n.*

naang-fáa นางฟ้า angel, fairy, *n.*

naang-máai นางไม้ wood fairy, *n.*

naang-pá-yaa-baan นางพยาบาล nurse, *n.*

naang-sǎao นางสาว young lady, miss, *n.*

nâa-ngɔɔ หน้างอ have an angry face, look sullen, *v.*

nǎao หนาว be cold (weather or personal sensation), *v.*

nâa-òk หน้าอก chest, *n.*

nâa-pǎa หน้าผา cliff, *n.*

nâa-pàak หน้าผาก forehead, *n.*

nâa-rák น่ารัก lovely, attractive, cute, *adj.*

nâa-ram-kaan น่ารำคาญ annoying, *adj.*

nâa-rang-gìat น่ารังเกียจ objectionable, repugnant, offensive, *adj.*

nâa-rɔ́ɔn หน้าร้อน summer, the hot season, *n.*

nâa-sâo หน้าเศร้า look sad, *v.*

nâa-sǐa-daai น่าเสียดาย regrettable, What a pity!, What a shame!, It's too bad!, *adj.*

nâa-sǐa-jai น่าเสียใจ regrettable, *adj.*

nâa-siit หน้าซีด pale (of face), *adj.*

nâa-sǒng-sǎan น่าสงสาร pitiful, What a pity!, *adj.*

nâa-sǒng-sǎi น่าสงสัย doubtful, suspicious, questionable, *adj.*

nâa-sǒn-jai น่าสนใจ interesting, *adj.*

naa-tii นาที minute, *n.*

nâa-tîi หน้าที่ duty, function, *n.*

naa-waa นาวา boat, vessel, *n.*

naa-yók นายก prime official, chairman, *n.*

naa-yók-rát-tà-mon-dtrii
นายกรัฐมนตรี prime minister, *n.*

naa-yók-têet-sà-mon-dtrii
นายกเทศมนตรี president of the city council, mayor, *n.*

nai นัย hint, intimation, *n.*

nai ใน inner, internal, in, at, on, *adv.*, *prep.*

nai-dtɔɔn-níi ในตอนนี้ at this time, *adv.*

nai-jai ในใจ in one's head, in one's mind, *adj.*, *adv.*

nai-kà-nà-níi ในขณะนี้ at this time, *adv.*

nai-lǔang ในหลวง the king (short form), *n.*

nai-mâi-cháa ในไม่ช้า shortly, soon, *adv.*

nai-oo-gàat ในโอกาส on the occasion of, *adv.*

nai-paai-lǎng ในภายหลัง afterward, later, in the future, *adv.*

nai-rá-wàang ในระหว่าง between,

among, *prep.*

nai-reo-reo-níi ในเร็วๆนี้ soon, *adv.*

nai-rôm ในร่ม in the shade, indoors, *adj.*

nai-tîi-sùt ในที่สุด in the end, at last, finally, *adv.*

nàk หนัก heavy, hard, heavily, severely, very, extremely, *adj.*, *adv.*

nák นัก person, doer, *n.*

nák-bin นักบิน aviator, pilot, *n.*

nák-boo-raan-ka-dii นักโบราณ คดี archeologist, *n.*

nák-bpràat นักปราชญ์ learned man, philosopher, sage, *n.*

nák-bprà-pan นักประพันธ์ poet, writer, author, *n.*

nák-bùat นักบวช ascetic, priest, hermit, *n.*

nák-bun นักบุญ saint, *n.*

nák-don-dtrii นักดนตรี musician, *n.*

nák-gaan-mɯang นักการเมือง politician, *n.*

nák-gaan-tûut นักการทูต diplomat, *n.*

nák-gii-laa นักกีฬา athlete, *n.*

nák-gòt-mǎai นักกฎหมาย legal

authority, lawyer, *n.*

nàk-jai หนักใจ depressed, heavy-hearted, anxious, *adj.*

nák-kǐan นักเขียน writer, author, *n.*

nák-leeng นักเลง rascal, bold person, *n.*

nák-muai นักมวย boxer, *n.*

nàk-nǎa หนักหนา very much, extremely, *adv.*

nák-nǎa นักหนา so very much, extremely, *adv.*

nák-nǎng-sǔu-pim นักหนังสือพิมพ์ journalist, *n.*

nàk-nên หนักแน่น steady, firm (as in character, conviction, decision), *adj.*

nàk-nùang หนักหน่วง strong, steady, unflinching, *adj.*

ná-kɔɔn นคร city, town, *n.*

ná-kɔɔn-lǔang นครหลวง capital, *n.*

nák-pà-jon-pai นักผจญภัย adventurer, *n.*

nák-pûut นักพูด orator, expert speaker, *n.*

nák-rian นักเรียน student, *n.*

nák-róp นักรบ warrior, *n.*

nák-rɔ́ɔng นักร้อง singer, *n.*

nák-sùk-sǎa นักศึกษา student, *n.*

nák-sùup นักสืบ detective, *n.*

nák-tɔ̂ng-tîao นักท่องเที่ยว tourist, traveler, *n.*

nák-tôot นักโทษ prisoner, convict, *n.*

nák-wí-jaan นักวิจารณ์ critic, *n.*

nák-wìt-ta-yaa-sàat นักวิทยาศาสตร์ scientist, *n.*

nam นำ lead, conduct, guide, *v.*

nân นั่น that, there, *pron., adv.*

nán นั้น that, those (is usually preceded by a *clf*), *adj.*

nâng นั่ง sit, ride, *v.*

nǎng หนัง skin, hide, leather, movie, *n., collq.*

nǎng-dtà-lung หนังตะลุง shadow play, *n.*

nǎng-pleeng หนังเพลง musical film, *n.*

nǎng-sǔu หนังสือ book, *n.*

nǎng-sǔu-dəən-taang หนังสือเดินทาง passport, *n.*

nǎng-sǔu-pim หนังสือพิมพ์ newspaper, *n.*

nǎng-sǔu-rian หนังสือเรียน schoolbook, textbook, *n.*

nǎng-sǔu-wian หนังสือเวียน circular, *n.*

nâo เน่า rotten, decayed, *adj.*

nâo-bp̀uai เน่าเปื่อย decomposed, *adj.*

náp นับ count, regard, consider, *v.*

náp-dtâng-dtèɛ นับตั้งแต่ starting from, since, *adv.*

náp-mâi-tûan นับไม่ถ้วน countless, innumerable, *adj.*

náp-tǔu นับถือ respect, *v.*

ná-rók นรก hell, *n.*

nát นัด make an appointment, set a date, set the time, *v.*

ná-wá-ní-yaai นวนิยาย novel, *n.*

ná-yoo-baai นโยบาย policy, *n.*

nee-dtì-ban-dìt เนติบัณฑิต attorney, *n.*

neen เณร one who enters the priesthood while under the age of twenty, a novice, *n.*

nee-ra-kun เนรคุณ ungraceful, *adj.*

nee-ra-têet เนรเทศ exile, depart, *v.*

nén เน้น stress, emphasize, *v.*

nɛ̀p เหน็บ insert, numbness, *v.*, *n.*

nɛ̂ɛ แน่ sure, certain, firm, stable, *adj.*

nɛ̂ɛ-chát แน่ชัด definite, sure, *adj.*

nɛ̂ɛ-jai แน่ใจ sure, certain, *adj.*

nɛ̂ɛn แน่น tight, compact, *v.*, *adj.*

nɛ̂ɛn-nâa แน่นหนา strong, tightly constructed, *adj.*

nɛɛo แนว line, row, strip, *n.*

nɛɛo-lǎng แนวหลัง the rear, rear echelon, *n.*

nɛɛo-nâa แนวหน้า the front, front line, *n.*

nɛɛo-róp แนวรบ battle line, *n.*

nɛɛo-taang แนวทาง way, direction, *n.*

nɛ̂ɛ-nɔɔn แน่นอน certain, definite, *adj.*

nɛ̂ɛp แนบ close to, flat against, *v.*

nɛ̂ɛp-dtìt แนบติด attached to, *v.*

nɛ̂ɛp-nian แนบเนียน well-fitted, well-jointed, *adj.*

né แนะ advise, guide, hint, suggest, *v.*

né-nam แนะนำ advise, guide, introduce, *v.*

nɛ̂o-nɛ̂ɛ แน่วแน่ resolute, determined, *adj.*

nǝǝi เนย butter, cheese, *n.*

nǝǝi-kěng เนยแข็ง cheese, *n.*

nǝǝi-tiam เนยเทียม margarine, *n.*

nǝǝn เนิน knoll, mound, *n.*

nɔ̀ɔn เนิ่น early, earlier, *adv.*

nɔ̂ɔp-nâap เนิ่นนาบ slow, sluggish, *adj.*

nǝ̀-nà เหนอะหนะ sticky (collq.), *adj.*

nìao เหนียว hold back, pull, *v.*

nǐao เหนียว sticky, adj.

ní-dtì-ban-yàt นิติบัญญัติ legislation, n.

ní-dtì-bùk-kon นิติบุคคล justice entity, n.

ní-dtì-gam นิติกรรม justice act, legal act, n.

ní-dtì-nai นิตินัย legal sense, n.

ní-dtì-paa-wá นิติภาวะ legal competency, n.

ní-dtì-sàat นิติศาสตร์ law (as a subject of study), n.

ní-gaai นิกาย sect, n.

nîi นี่ this, here, adj., adv., pron.

nîi หนี้ debt, n.

níi นี้ this, these (is usually preceded by a clf.), adj.

nǐi หนี flee, escape, v.

nìip หนีบ nip, grip, pinch, seize with pincers or the like, v.

nîi-sǐn หนี้สิน debt, liabilities, n.

ní-kom นิคม settlement, colony, n.

nîm นิ่ม soft, yielding, adj.

ní-mít นิมิต sign, omen, adj.

ní-mon นิมนต์ invite (a priest), v.

nîm-nuan นิ่มนวล gentle, tender, gracious, adj.

nin นิล jet (stone), black or dark precious stone, n.

nîng นิ่ง still, quiet, motionless, adj.

nin-taa นินทา gossip about, v.

nip-paan นิพพาน Nirvana, n.

ní-pon นิพนธ์ write, compose, v.

ní-sǎi นิสัย habit, characteristic trait, n.

ní-sìt นิสิต university student, college student, n.

nít นิด tiny, little, small, adj.

ní-taan นิทาน fable, tale, story, n.

nít-nòi นิดหน่อย tiny, little, small, a little bit, adj.

ní-ran-doon นิรันดร forever, adv.

ní-rá-pai นิรภัย safe, not dangerous, adj.

níu นิ่ว gallstone, n.

níu นิ้ว digit, finger, toe, n.

níu-bpôo, níu-bpôong นิ้วโป้, นิ้วโป้ง thumb, n.

níu-chíi นิ้วชี้ index finger, n.

níu-dtiin นิ้วตีน toe, n.

níu-glaang นิ้วกลาง middle finger, n.

níu-gôi นิ้วก้อย little finger, n.

níu-hǔa-mɛɛ-mʉʉ นิ้วหัวแม่มือ thumb, n.

níu-mʉʉ นิ้วมือ finger, n.

níu-naang นิ้วนาง ring finger, *n.*

níu-táao นิ้วเท้า toe, *n.*

ní-yaai นิยาย legend, tale, fable, story, *n.*

ní-yom นิยม prefer, favor, like, *v.*

nók นก bird, *n.*

nók-gɛ̂ɛo นกแก้ว parrot, *n.*

nók-grà-jɔ̀ɔk นกกระจอก sparrow, *n.*

nók-grà-jɔ̀ɔk-têet นกกระจอกเทศ ostrich, *n.*

nók-hûuk นกฮูก owl, *n.*

nók-îang นกเอี้ยง singing mynả, *n.*

nók-in-sii นกอินทรี eagle, *n.*

nók-káo-mɛɛo นกเค้าแมว a kind of owl, *n.*

nók-pî-râap นกพิราบ pigeon, *n.*

nók-wìit นกหวีด whistle, *n.*

nók-yuung นกยูง peacock, *n.*

nom นม breast, milk, *n.*

nom-kôn นมข้น condensed milk, *n.*

nom-pǒng นมผง powdered milk, *n.*

noo โน get a swelling, raise a lump, *v.*

nóom โน้ม bend down, bend over, *v.*

nôon โน่น that (one) over there, *adv.*, *adj.*

nóon โน้น that (one) over there, *adv.*, *adj.*

nóot โน้ต note, *v.*

nóp-nɔ̂ɔp นบนอบ pay respect by pressing the palms together, *v.*

nɔ̀i หน่อย a little, a little bit, *adj.*

nɔ̂ng น่อง calf, *n.*

nɔɔ นอ horn, *n.*

nɔ̀ɔ หน่อ offshoot, sprout, *n.*

nɔ́ɔi น้อย little, less, small, slight, *adj.*

nɔ́ɔi-gwàa น้อยกว่า less than, *adj.*

nɔ́ɔi-jai น้อยใจ feel slighted, feel inferior, feel neglected, *v.*

nɔ́ɔi-long น้อยลง decrease, diminish, *v.*

nɔ́ɔi-nàa น้อยหน่า custard apple, *n.*

nɔ̂ɔk นอก outer external, outside, *adv.*

nɔ̂ɔk-jàak นอกจาก besides, outside of, aside from, except, other than, excluding, beyond, *adj., adv.*

nɔ̂ɔk-jai นอกใจ unfaithful, *adj.*

nɔ̀ɔ-máai หน่อไม้ young bamboo shoot, *n.*

nɔɔn นอน recline, sleep, *v.*

nɔ̌ɔn หนอน worm, caterpillar (any hairless variety), *n.*

nɔɔng นอง flood, *v.*

nɔ́ɔng น้อง younger sibling, title used before the first name, *n.*

nɔ̌ɔng หนอง swamp, lagoon, large pool, pus, *n.*

nɔ́ɔng-chaai น้องชาย younger brother, *n.*

nɔ́ɔng-kə̌əi น้องเขย brother-in-law, *n.*

nɔ́ɔng-mài น้องใหม่ newborn brother or sister, freshman in a college or university, new member, *n.*

nɔ̌ɔng-nai หนองใน gonorrhea, *n.*

nɔ́ɔng-sǎao น้องสาว younger sister, *n.*

nɔ́ɔng-sà-pái น้องสะใภ้ sister-in-law, *n.*

nɔɔn-jai นอนใจ nonchalant, unconcerned, *adj.*

nɔɔn-làp นอนหลับ sleep, be asleep, *v.*

nɔɔn-mâi-làp นอนไม่หลับ unable to sleep, *adj.*

nɔ́ɔp-nɔ́ɔm นอบน้อม show respect, *v.*

nùai หน่วย unit, *nm.*

nùai-dàp-pləəng หน่วยดับเพลิง fire department, fire-fighting unit, *n.*

nùai-róp หน่วยรบ fighting unit, *n.*

nùak-hǔu หนวกหู noisy, deafening, *adj.*

nuam นวม padding, boxing gloves, quilt, comforter, *n.*

nûam นิ่ม soft, lacking firmness, *adj.*

nuan นวล soft-colored, cream-colored, *adj.*

nùang หน่วง delay, hold back, *v.*

nùang-nìao หน่วงเหนี่ยว delay, *v.*

nùat หนวด mustache, beard, whiskers, antennae (of insect), *n.*

nûat นวด thresh, massage, knead, *v.*

nùat-krao หนวดเครา beard (including the mustache), *n.*

nùm หนุ่ม young man, adolescent boy, be young, be adolescent (of men and boys), *n., v.*

nûm นุ่ม soft, spongy, yielding, *adj.*

nûm-nuan นุ่มนวล soft, gentle, smooth, graceful, *adj.*

nûm-nîm นุ่มนิ่ม soft, yielding, gentle, *adj.*

nùm-sǎao หนุ่มสาว young people, teenagers (of both sexes), young couple, *n.*

nûn นุ่น kapok, *n.*

nǔn หนุน support, prop up, encourage, *v.*

nûng นุ่ง dress, put on, wear, *v.*

nǔn-lǎng หนุนหลัง support, back, *v.*

nŭn-nûang หนุนเนื่อง bring up reinforcements (troops) in a continuous stream, *v.*

nŭu หนู mouse, rat, I, me (used by children), you, *n., pron.*

nŭu-bâan หนูบ้าน house rat, *n.*

nŭu-dtà-pao หนูตะเภา guinea pig, *n.*

nuun นูน bulge out, curve out, be convex, swell, *v.*

nûun, núun นูน, นู้น that, that (one) over there, *adv.*

nŭu-nɔ́ɔi หนูน้อย baby, little child, little one, *n.*

nŭu-púk หนูพุก field rat, *n.*

núa เนื้อ meat, flesh, beef, gist, substance, *n.*

nŭa เหนือ above, north, *prep., adv.*

núa-hǎa เนื้อหา text, gist, substance, *n.*

nùai เหนื่อย tired, weary, *adj.*

núa-kwaam เนื้อความ essence of a matter, *n.*

núa-mǔu เนื้อหมู pork, *n.*

nûang เนื่อง due to, connected (with), related (to), *adj.*

nûang-jàak เนื่องจาก owing to, on account of, due to, owing to the fact

that, because of the fact that, since, *adj., adv., conj.*

núa-pâa เนื้อผ้า texture of cloth, *n.*

núa-pleeng เนื้อเพลง the words of a song, lyrics, *n.*

núa-rûang เนื้อเรื่อง subject matter, essential part of a story, *n.*

núa-sàt เนื้อสัตว์ meat, flesh, *n.*

núa-tîi เนื้อที่ area, room (space), *n.*

núa-wua เนื้อวัว beef, *n.*

núk นึก think, *v.*

núk-fǎn นึกฝัน imagine, dream, *v.*

nùng หนึ่ง one, *nm.*

nûng นึ่ง steam (food), *v.*

nùut หนืด viscous, sticky, *adj.*

ng (ง)

ngaa งา sesame, tusk (of the elephant), ivory, *n.*

ngaa-cháang งาช้าง ivory, elephant tusk, *n.*

ngâai ง่าย simple, easy, convenient, *adj.*

ngâai-daai ง่ายดาย very easy, very simple, *adj.*

ngaam งาม flourish, beautiful, pretty, attractive, graceful, charming, *v., adj.*

ngaan งาน work, task, job, ceremony, festival, affair, duty, fair, *n.*

ngaan-à-dì-rèek งานอดิเรก hobby, *n.*

ngaan-bâan งานบ้าน housework, household chores, *n.*

ngaan-bpii-mài งานปีใหม่ New Year festival, *n.*

ngaan-chà-lɔ̌ɔng งานฉลอง festival, celebration, *n.*

ngáang ง้าง pull out, pull back, *v.*

ngaan-gaan งานการ work (in general), *n.*

ngaan-gɔ̀ɔ-sâang งานก่อสร้าง construction work, *n.*

ngaan-lii-lâat งานลีลาศ dancing party, *n.*

ngaan-sòp งานศพ funeral, *n.*

ngaan-wát งานวัด a fair held within the Buddhist temple grounds, *n.*

ngaan-wí-jai งานวิจัย research work, *n.*

ngáao ง้าว a pike with curved blade, *n.*

ngâng งั่ง stupid, foolish, dull, *adj.*

ngao เงา image, reflection, shadow, *n.*

ngǎo เหงา lonely, *adj.*

ngáp งับ snap, snap at, nip, clamp,

close, shut, *v.*

ngát งัด pry out, force up, raise with a lever, *v.*

ngé แงะ pry, pry open, *v.*

ngɛ́ɛm แง้ม open slightly, be ajar, *v.*

ngəəi-nâa เงยหน้า look up, raise one's head, lift up one's face, *v.*

ngən เงิน silver, money, *n.*

ngən-dtraa เงินตรา minted currency, *n.*

ngən-dʉan เงินเดือน monthly salary, *n.*

ngən-fàak เงินฝาก deposit, *n.*

ngən-gûu เงินกู้ loan, *n.*

ngən-mát-jam เงินมัดจำ deposit (down payment), *n.*

ngən-pɔ̀n เงินผ่อน installment, *n.*

ngən-sòt เงินสด cash, *n.*

ngən-tɔɔn เงินทอน change (money returned), *n.*

ngən-tun เงินทุน capital (money in an investment), *n.*

ngîan เงี่ยน lust for, desirous (sexually), have a craving for, *adj., v.*

ngîang เงี่ยง hook, barb, *n.*

ngîap เงียบ silent, quiet, *adj.*

ngîap-grìp เงียบกริบ completely soundless, *adj.*

ngîap-ngǎo เงียบเหงา silent and lonely, *adj.*

ngòk งก greedy, gluttonous, avaricious, stingy, mean, *adj.*

ngom งม grope in the water for, dive for, fumble, *v.*

ngom-ngaai งมงาย foolish, stupid, mentally sluggish, beyond reason, *adj.*

ngong งง dizzy, dazed, stunned, puzzled, *adj.*

ngong-nguai งงงวย dazed, stunned, puzzled, *adj.*

ngôo โง่ stupid, foolish, dull, silly, *adj.*

ngôo-klǎo โง่เขลา stupid, foolish, dull, silly, *adj.*

ngóp-ban-chii งบบัญชี close an account, calculate the balance in an account, *v.*

ngóp-bprà-maan งบประมาณ budget, *n.*

ngóp-dun งบดุล balance sheet, the balance, *n.*

ngòt งด stop, halt, cancel, dissolve, *v.*

ngòt-ngaam งดงาม pretty, beautiful, attractive. good-looking, *adj.*

ngòt-wén งดเว้น refrain (from), abstain (from), *v.*

ngôi ง่อย lame, paralyzed, crippled,

withered, motionless, *adj.*

ngó เงาะ rambutan (a fruit), *n.*

ngɔɔ งอ bend, fold, curl, *v.*

ngɔ́ɔ ง้อ humble oneself in order to conciliate, reconcile, *v.*

ngɔ̂ɔk งอก sprout, bud, grow, increase, multiply (esp. for plants), *v.*

ngɔ̂ɔk-ngaam งอกงาม grow, develop, thrive (of plants), *v.*

ngɔɔm งอม overripe, very ripe, severe, serious, extreme, very old, very tired, *adj.*

ngɔɔn งอน bend, curve upward, *v.*

ngɔɔn งอน pout, show displeasure (esp. women, children), feign displeasure, *v.*

ngɔɔ-ngɛɛ งอแง fussy, childish, crying like a baby, clumsy, *adj.*

ngɔ̂ɔp งอบ a kind of hat made of palm leaves and bamboo worn by farmers, *n.*

nguang งวง trunk, proboscis, *n.*

ngûang ง่วง sleepy, drowsy, *adj.*

nguang-cháang งวงช้าง trunk of the elephant, *n.*

ngûat งวด occasion, time, period, installment, fixed period of time for payment, *n.*

ngûat งวด dry out, dry up, *n.*

ngûm-ngâam งุ่มง่าม clumsy, awkward, *adj.*

ngun-ngong งุนงง be dazed, be bewildered, be perplexed, *v.*

nguu งู snake, *n.*

nguu-hào งูเห่า cobra, *n.*

nguu-jong-aang งูจงอาง king cobra, *n.*

nguu-kǐao งูเขียว a common green snake, *n.*

nguu-lǔam งูเหลือม python, *n.*

ngùa เหงื่อ sweat, *n.*

ngúa เงื้อ raise (the hand, a weapon) in a threatening gesture, *v.*

ngùak เหงือก gum (of teeth), *n.*

ngúak เงือก mermaid, *n.*

ngùa-ɔ̀ɔk เหงื่อออก sweat, *v.*

ngúam-ngam งึมงำ murmur, mutter, *v.*

ngûan เงื่อน knot, joint, hint, clue, *n.*

ngûan-kǎi เงื่อนไข condition, stipulation, proviso, *n.*

ngûan-ngam เงื่อนงำ clue, key to a solution, hidden point, catch, *n.*

O (โอ)

òo โอ่ boast, *v.*

ŏo โอ๋ console, express solace (especially to small children), *v.*

ôo-êe โอ้เอ้ linger, delay, loiter, *v.*

oo-gàat โอกาส chance, occasion, opportunity, *n.*

oo-hǎng โอหัง arrogant, haughty, disdainful, proud, daring, *adj.*

ôo-hǒo โอ้โห Wow! Gosh, Oh!, *excl.*

oo-laan โอฬาร great, spacious, *adj.*

ooi, ôoi โอย, โอ๊ย Ouch! Oh!, *excl.*

oon โอน transfer (ownership, control, etc.), *v.*

oon โอน bend, incline, *v.*

oon-een โอนเอน swaying, unsteady, *adj.*

òong โอ่ง large water jar, *n.*

oon-sǎn-châat โอนสัญชาติ become naturalized, change one's citizenship, *v.*

òop โอบ embrace, encircle, *v.*

oo-sòt โอสถ medicine, drug, *n.*

ôo-tǒong โอ่โถง splendid, magnificent, luxurious, *adj.*

ôo-ùat โอ้อวด boast, brag, *v.*

oo-wâat โอวาท teaching, advice, *n.*

ɔ (ออ)

ɔ̀i อ๋อย soft and slow, *adj.*

ɔ́k-si-jên ออกซิเจน oxygen, *n.*

ɔ̂ɔ อ้อ reed, *n.*

ɔ̌ɔ อ๋อ Oh (I see, I get it), *excl.*

ɔ̂ɔi อ้อย sugarcane, *n.*

ɔ̂ɔi-ìng อ้อยอิ่ง linger, delay, *n.*

ɔ̀ɔk ออก leave, be out, *v.*

ɔ̀ɔk-aa-gàat ออกอากาศ broadcast, be on the air, *v.*

ɔ̀ɔk-bɛ̀ɛp ออกแบบ design, *v*

ɔ̀ɔk-bpai ออกไป go out, *v.*

ɔ̀ɔk-dəən-taang ออกเดินทาง start out, set out on a journey, *v.*

ɔ̀ɔk-dɔ̀ɔk ออกดอก blossom, flourish, blossom out, *v.*

ɔ̀ɔk-gam-lang, ɔ̀ɔk-gam-lang-gaai ออกกำลัง, ออกกำลังกาย exercise, *v.*

ɔ̀ɔk-gòt-mǎai ออกกฎหมาย make law, pass a bill, *v.*

ɔ̀ɔk-hàang ออกห่าง turn away (from), stay away (from), break (relations with), *v.*

ɔ̀ɔk-hàt ออกหัด break out with measles, *v.*

ɔ̀ɔk-kài ออกไข่ lay eggs, *v.*

ɔ̀ɔk-kam-sàng ออกคำสั่ง issue an order, give a command, *v.*

ɔ̀ɔk-lûuk ออกลูก bear a child, give birth, *v.*

ɔ̀ɔk-maa ออกมา come out, *v.*

ɔ̀ɔk-pan-sǎa ออกพรรษา come out of Lent (the Buddhist Lent), *v.*

ɔ̀ɔk-pǒn ออกผล yield fruit, *v.*

ɔ̀ɔk-sǐang ออกเสียง vote, *v.*

ɔɔm ออม save, reserve, put away, *v.*

ɔ̂ɔm อ้อม detour, wrap around, *v.*

ɔ̂ɔm-kɔ́ɔm อ้อมค้อม indirect, roundabout, *adj.*

ɔɔn ออนซ์ ounce, *n.*

ɔ̀ɔn อ่อน soft, tender, young, pale, weak, light (of colors), *adj.*

ɔ̂ɔn อ้อน whine, *v.*

ɔ̀ɔn-ɛɛ อ่อนแอ weak, feeble, *adj.*

ɔ̀ɔn-plia อ่อนเพลีย weak, exhausted, *adj.*

ɔ̂ɔn-wɔɔn อ้อนวอน implore, *v.*

ɔ́ɔp-fít ออฟฟิส office, *n.*

ɔ̀ɔt-sa-dtee-lia ออสเตรเลีย Australia, *n.*

ɔ̀ɔt-sa-dtria ออสเตรีย Austria, *n.*

p (ผ, พ, ภ)

paa พา lead, bring along, *v.*

pàa ผ่า split, *v.*

pâa ผ้า cloth, *n.*

pǎa ผา cliff, *n.*

paa-cha-ná ภาชนะ vessel, *n.*

paa-hà พาหะ carrier, *n.*

paa-hà-ná พาหนะ vehicle, *n.*

paai พาย paddle, *v., n.*

paai ภาย side, part, place, *n.*

pâai พ่าย flee, defeated, *v., adj.*

paai-nai ภายใน inside, interior, *adj., adv.*

paai-nɔ̀ɔk ภายนอก outside, exterior, *adj., adv.*

pâak พากย์ word, speech, language, speech of a theatrical performance, *n.*

pâak ภาค section, division, side, *n.*

pâak-pian พากเพียร diligent, industrious, *adj.*

pâak-pian พากเพียร persevere, *v.*

paan พาน tray with pedestal, *n.*

paan พาน meet, encounter, *v.*

paan พาล bad, wicked, troublesome, *adj.*

pàan ผ่าน pass, *v.*

paa-nít พาณิชย์ commerce, *n.*

paao-wa-naa ภาวนา pray, *v.*

pâap ภาพ image, picture, drawing, gesture, *n.*

paa-rá ภาระ burden, task, duty, *n.*

paa-sǎa ภาษา language, speech, *n.*

paa-sǎa-bâi ภาษาใบ้ sign language, *n.*

paa-sǐi ภาษี tax, duty, toll, *n.*

paa-sìt ภาษิต proverb, maxim, *n.*

pǎa-sùk ผาสุข happiness, *n.*

pâat พาด lean against, *v.*

paa-wá ภาวะ condition, state, status, *n.*

paa-yáp พายัพ northwest, *n.*

paa-yú พายุ storm, *n.*

pà-chəən เผชิญ confront, *v.*

pá-hùu-sùut พหูสูต all knowing, omniscient, a learned man, *adj., n.*

pai ภัย fear, dread, danger, calamity, accident, *n.*

pâi ไพ่ playing card, *n.*

pai-buun ไพบูลย์ fullness, completeness, abundance, prosperity, *n.*

pai-lin ไพลิน amethyst, *n.*

pai-rii ไพรี enemy, *n.*

pai-rôot ไพโรจน์ prosperous, bright, *adj.*

pai-rɔ́ ไพเราะ melodious, tuneful, *adj.*

pai-săan ไพศาล large, expansive, *adj.*

pai-tuun ไพฑูรย์ lapis, lazuli, *n.*

pà-jon-pai ผจญภัย adventure, *v.*

pàk ผัก vegetable, *n.*

pák พรรค group, party, *n.*

pák พัก rest, stop temporarily, *v.*

pák-dii ภักดี loyal, have faith, *adj., v.*

pák-fúun พักฟื้น convalesce, *v.*

pák-pɔ̀n พักผ่อน take a rest, relax, *v.*

pá-lá พละ strength, power, *n.*

pá-lang พลัง energy, strength, *n.*

pá-mâa พม่า Burma, *n.*

pam-nák พำนัก stay, reside, *v.*

pá-mɔɔn ภมร bee, *n.*

pan พัน bind, tie, wrap, *v.*

pan พันธุ์ relatives, kinsman, relationship, lineage, *n.*

pan ภัณฑ์ goods, *n.*

păn ผัน change, conjugate, *v.*

pá-nák พนัก the back of a chair, *n.*

pá-nák-ngaan พนักงาน officer, employee, staff, *n.*

pá-nan พนัน bet, gamble, *v.*

pá-náo-pá-nɔɔ พะเน้าพะนอ please, coax, *n.*

pá-nee-jɔɔn พเนจร wander, *v.*

pá-nɛɛng พะแนง a thick curry with large pieces of chicken or meat, *n.*

pá-nəən พะเนิน large hammer, large pile, *n.*

pang พัง tumble down, collapse, crumble, destroy, tear down, *v.*

pà-ngòk ผงก nod, *v.*

pang-pâap พังพาบ lie face down, lie prone, *v.*

pang-pəəi พังเพย adage, saying, proverb, axiom, *n.*

pang-pɔɔn พังพอน mongoose, *n.*

pang-pùut พังผืด fascia, *n.*

pan-la-wan พัลวัน tangles, *adj.*

pá-nom พนม clasp palms together in the attitude of salutation, *n.*

pan-pua พันพัว involved, connected, related, *adj.*

pan-ra-naa พรรณนา explain, depict, *v.*

pan-ra-yaa ภรรยา wife, *n.*

pan-săa พรรษา rain, rainy season, *n.*

pan-tá พันธะ bind, *v.*

pào เผ่า race, tribe, *n.*

păo เผา burn, burn up, cremate, *v.*

páp พับ fold, dismiss as lost, *v.*

páp-plap พับเพียบ sit with both legs tucked back to one side, *v.*

pá-rung-pá-rang พะรุงพะรัง disheveled, *adj.*

pá-rú-hàt-sà-bɔɔ-dii พฤหัสบดี Thursday, *n.*

pà-sǒm ผสม mix, *v.*

pàt ผัด fry, fried, *v., adj.*

pát พัด fan, blow, *v.*

pát-sà-dù พัสดุ article, object, parcel, *n.*

pát-ta-naa พัฒนา develop, progress, *v.*

pá-tuu พธู bride, wife, *n.*

pá-ùut-pá-om พะอืดพะอม feel nauseated, *v.*

pà-wǎa ผวา scared, *adj.*

pá-wong พะวง worried, *adj.*

pá-yaa พญา king, lord, *n.*

pá-yaa-baan พยาบาล nurse, treat, care for the sick, *v.*

pá-yaa-bàat พยาบาท revenge, *n.*

pá-yaa-gɔɔn พยากรณ์ forecast, prediction, prophecy, *n.*

pá-yaan พยาน witness, evidence, *n.*

pá-yâat พยาธิ sickness, illness, malady, ailment, *n.*

pá-yâat พยาธิ parasite, *n.*

pá-yaa-yaam พยายาม persevere, endeavor, attempt, make an effort, *v.*

pá-yák พยัก nod, *v.*

pá-yák พยัคฆ์ tiger, *n.*

pá-yan-cha-ná พยัญชนะ consonant, *n.*

pá-yót พยศ refractory, *adj.*

pá-yung พยุง support, *v.*

pee เพ crumble, collapse, *v.*

pee-daan เพดาน ceiling, palate, mouth, *n.*

pee-laa เพลา time, period, *n.*

pee-sàt เภสัช pharmacy, drug, *n.*

pee-sàt-cha-gɔɔn เภสัชกร pharmacist, chemist, *n.*

pee-sàt-cha-pan เภสัชภัณฑ์ pharmaceuticals, *n.*

pêet เพศ sex, gender, kind, form, shape, sort, apparel, *n.*

pee-taai เพทาย zircon, *n.*

pêng เพ่ง stare at, gaze, *v.*

pèt เผ็ด hot, spicy, *adj.*

pét เพชร diamond, *n.*

pét-cha-kâat เพชฌฆาต executioner, *n.*

pét-plɔɔi เพชรพลอย gems, precious stones, *n.*

Phonetic • Thai • English

pé แพะ goat, *n.*

pɛɛ แพ raft, house-boat, *n.*

pɛ́ɛ แพ้ defeated, beaten, overcome, *adj.*

pɛ̌ɛn แผน plan, *n.*

pɛɛng แพง expensive, dear, *adj.*

pɛ̌ɛn-păng แผนผัง chart, *n.*

pɛ̂ɛt แพทย์ physician, doctor, *n.*

pɛ̂ɛt-sà-yăa แพทยา prostitute, whore, adulteress, *n.*

pɛ̀n แผ่น piece, slice, *n.*

pɛ̂ng แพ่ง strength, civil case, *n.*

pé-ráp-bàap แพะรับบาป scape-goat, *n.*

pə́ə เพ้อ delirious, *adj.*

pə̀ək-chə̌əi เพิกเฉย inattentive, *adj.*

pə̀ək-tɔ̌ɔn เพิกถอน withdraw, *v.*

pə̂əm เพิ่ม increase, add, *v.*

pə̂ng เพิ่ง just, just now, *adv.*

pian เพียร diligent, *adj.*

pian เพี้ยน differing just a little, *adj.*

piang เพียง until, merely, only, equal to, comparable to, as far as, *adv., adj.*

piang-pɔɔ เพียงพอ just enough, just sufficient, *adv.*

pí-gaan พิการ deformed, disabled, *adj.*

pí-gàt พิกัด standard, limit, fix, *n.*

pí-gàt พิกัด coordinate, *n.*

pí-gon พิกล odd, abnormal, *adj.*

pîi พี่ elder brother or sister, a polite prefix to the name of an older sibling, you, he, she, him, her, *n.*

pǐi ผี ghost, *n.*

pîi-kə̌əi พี่เขย brother-in-law, *n.*

pîi-líang พี่เลี้ยง nurse maid, step-brother, step-sister, nanny, *n.*

pîi-nɔ́ɔng พี่น้อง brothers, *n.*

pîi-sà-pái พี่สะใภ้ sister-in-law, *n.*

pîi-sʉ̂a ผีเสื้อ butterfly, *n.*

pí-jaa-ra-naa พิจารณา examine, investigate, consider, *v.*

pí-kâat พิฆาต kill, *v.*

pík-sù ภิกษุ Buddhist monk, *n.*

pí-lai พิไล pretty, *adj.*

pí-lʉ́k พิลึก strange, odd, queer, *adj.*

pim พิมพ์ print, type, *v.*

pin พิณ lute, a Thai instrument, *n.*

pí-nâat พินาศ ruin, destruction, *n.*

pí-nai-gam พินัยกรรม will, *n.*

ping พิง lean against, *v.*

pí-nít พินิจ examine, investigate, consider attentively, *v.*

pí-nɔ́ɔp-pí-tao พินอบพิเทา make obeisance, *v.*

pí-pâak-săa พิพากษา judge,

decide, sentence, *v.*

pi-pâat พิพาท dispute, *v.*

pi-pit-ta-pan พิพิธภัณฑ์ museum, *n.*

pi-póp พิภพ the earth, the world, *n.*

pi-reen พิเรน pervert, unusual, *adj.*

pi-rôot พิโรธ angry (royal), *adj.*

pi-sǎan พิศาล broad, wide, *adj.*

pi-sǎi พิสัย district, region, *n.*

pi-sèet พิเศษ special, particular, *adj.*

pi-sùut พิสูจน์ prove, verify, *v.*

pìt ผิด wrong, *adj.*

pìt พิษ poison, *n.*

pi-ták พิทักษ์ take care, protect, *v.*

pi-tii พิธี ceremony, ritual, rite, *n.*

pi-tii-pi-tǎn พิธีพิถัน fussy, meticulous, *adj.*

pìt-sa-daan พิสดาร strange, extraordinary, *adj.*

pìt-sa-mǎi พิสมัย love, joy, *adj.*

pìt-sa-wàat พิศวาส intimacy, love, delight, affectionate, regard, *adj.*

pìt-sa-wǒng พิศวง puzzled about, bewildered, *adj.*

pìt-ta-yaa พิทยา knowledge, *n.*

pǐu ผิว skin, *n.*

plâa พล่า dish of slice of seasoned raw meats or prawns, *n.*

plaai พลาย (elephant) male, *n.*

plâan พล่าน confused, disordered, *adj., adv.*

plaang พลาง simultaneously, *adv.*

plâat พลาด miss, slip, *v.*

plàk ผลัก push, *v.*

plam พลัม plum, *n.*

plan พลัน at once, urgently, *adv.*

pláng พลั้ง make a slip, slip, to err, *v.*

plao เพลา axle, axis, shaft, boom, *n.*

plao เพลา lap, thigh, leg, *n.*

pláp-plaa พลับพลา pavilion, *n.*

plàt ผลัด take turns, *v.*

plát พลัด fall, trip and fall, *v.*

pleen เพล midday meal-time for Buddhist monks, *n.*

pleeng เพลง song, music, *n.*

pleeng-châat เพลงชาติ national anthem, *n.*

plɛɛng แพลง sprained, twisted, *adj.*

pləəng เพลิง fire, blaze, flame, *n.*

plə̂ət-pləən เพลิดเพลิน enjoying, amused, entertained, *adj.*

plia เพลีย tired, exhausted, worn out, *adj.*

plía เพลี้ย aphid, plant louse, *n.*

plîang เพลี่ยง slip, avoid, *v.*

plii พลี offering, sacrifice, *n.*

plii พลี powerful, *adj.*

plii พลี sacrifice, *v.*

plík พลิก turn over, *v.*

plíu พลิ้ว wrong, mistaken, *adj.*

plòo โผล่ emerge, come up, *v.*

plóo-plée โพล้เพล้ dusk, twilight, *n.*

plóp พลบ dusk, twilight, *n.*

plɔɔi พลอย gem, precious stone, *n.*

plɔ̀ɔi พล่อย simply, flippantly, *adv.*

plɔ̀ɔt พลอด talk volubly, court, *v.*

plú พลุ firework, cannon cracker, *n.*

plûa พลั่ว shovel, spade, *n.*

plûi พลุ้ย obese, *adj.*

plùk ผลึก crystal, *n.*

pók พก carry or hide on the body, put into the pouch pocket, *v.*

pŏm ผม hair, *n.*

pŏm ผม I, *pron.*

pon พล strength, power, force, *n.*

pôn พ่น blow, spray, spout, *v.*

pón พ้น pass beyond, go beyond, go past, *v.*

pŏn ผล result, effect, fruit, *n.*

pong พง thicket, brush, *n.*

pŏng ผง dust, *n.*

pŏn-grà-tóp ผลกระทบ impact, *n.*

pŏn-la múai ผลไม้ fruit, *n.*

pŏn-láp ผลลัพธ์ final result, *n.*

poo โพธิ์ intelligence, *n.*

poo-chá-naa โภชนา nutrition, *n.*

poo-chá-naa-gaan โภชนาการ nutrition, dietetics, *n.*

pooi โพย thrash, beat, whip, *v.*

pôok โพก wrap a piece of cloth around the head, *v.*

pôok โภค property, goods, *n.*

póon โพ้น there, beyond, *adj., adv.*

poo-sòp โพสพ Goddess of rice, *n.*

poo-tí-sàt โพธิสัตว์ one who will become the Buddha, *n.*

póp พบ meet, find, encounter, *v.*

póp ภพ world, earth, land, *n.*

pót พจน์ word, speech,, *n.*

pòt ผด rash, *n.*

pót พด bent, coiled, *n.*

pót-jà-naa-nú-grom พจนานุกรม dictionary, *n.*

pɔ́ เพาะ plant, *v.*

pɔɔ พอ enough, sufficient, *adj.*

pɔ̂ɔ พ่อ father, male, a polite form of addressing a boy or younger man, *n*

pɔ́ɔ พ้อ complain, *v.*

pɔ̂ɔ-bâan พ่อบ้าน head of the family, husband, *n.*

pɔ̂ɔ-dtaa พ่อตา father-in-law, *n.*

pɔɔ-jai พอใจ pleased, satisfied, contented with, *adj.*

pɔ̀ɔk พอก   put on in layer, cover, plaster, v.

pɔ̂ɔ-káa พ่อค้า   merchant, n.

pɔ̂ɔ-krua พ่อครัว   cook, n.

pɔ̂ɔ-líang พ่อเลี้ยง   stepfather, n.

pɔ̌ɔm ผอม   thin, adj.

pɔ̂ɔ-mâai พ่อหม้าย   widower, n.

pɔ̂ɔ-mɛ̂ɛ พ่อแม่   parents, n.

pɔ̂ɔ-mót พ่อมด   wizard, sorcerer, n.

pɔɔn พร   boon, choice, blessing, n.

pɔɔng พอง   swell, get a swelling, v.

pɔɔng พอง   swollen, inflated, adj.

pɔ́ɔng พ้อง   sound alike, coincide, v.

pɔɔn-sà-wǎn พรสวรรค์   gift, natural gift, n.

pɔɔ-sǒm-kuan พอสมควร   reasonable, moderate, adj.

prá พระ   priest, monk, Buddha image, n.

prâa พร่า   destroy, ruin, v.

práa พร้า   large knife, sickle, n.

praai พราย   spirit, ghost, n.

prâak พราก   leave, part, separate, deprive, v.

praam พราหมณ์   Brahmin, n.

praan พราน   hunter, trapper, n.

praang พราง   camouflage, disguise, v.

prâang พร่าง   blurred, adv.

praao พราว   dazzling, adj.

prai ไพร   forest, wood, n.

prâi ไพร่   commoner, subjects of a king, low-class citizen, n.

prá-jâao พระเจ้า   god, n.

prá-jâao-pèn-din พระเจ้าแผ่นดิน the king, n.

pram พรม   (rain) drizzling, adj.

prâm พร่ำ   repeatedly, adv.

prá-pút-ta-jâao พระพุทธเจ้า the Buddha, n.

prá-raa-chaa พระราชา the king, n.

prɛɛ แพร   silk cloth, n.

prɛ̂ɛ แพร่   spread, scatter, v.

prɛɛo แพรว   shining, adj.

prɛ̂ng แพร่ง   spread out, v.

priao เพรียว   slender, slim, adj.

prík พริก   chili, pepper, n.

prím พริ้ม   smiling, adj.

príng พริ้ง   pretty, beautiful, adj.

príp พริบ   blink the eyes, v.

prom พรม   carpet, rug, n.

prom พรหม   the god Brahma, n.

prom-dɛɛn พรมแดน   frontier, border, n.

proong โพรง   cavity, space, hollow, n.

pró เพราะ melodious, tuneful, *adj.*

pró-cha-nán เพราะฉะนั้น therefore, consequently, *adv.*

próom พร้อม ready, set, together, *adj.*

pró-wâa เพราะว่า reason for, due to, because, because of, on account of, *adv., conj.*

pruan-din พรวนดิน loosen the soil, *v.*

prun พรุน holed, *adj.*

prûng-nii พรุ่งนี้ tomorrow, *adv.*

pruu พรู go in crowds, flock, *v.*

prút-dtì-gam พฤติกรรม behavior, conduct, *n.*

prút-dtì-nai พฤตินัย in practice, in fact, *adv.*

prút-sà-jì-gaa-yon พฤศจิกายน November, *n.*

prûut พรืด abundantly, in great numbers, *adv.*

pù ผุ rotten, decayed, *adj.*

pú พุ break out, erupt, *v.*

pua ผัว husband, *n.*

puai พวย spout, nozzle, *n.*

pûak พวก community, party, group, *n.*

puang พวง garland, bunch, *n.*

puang พ่วง tow, connect, *v.*

puang-maa-lai พวงมาลัย garland, steering, wheel, *n.*

pûm พุ่ม bush, shrub, *n.*

pung พุง abdomen, belly, stomach, *n.*

pûng พุ่ง throw, thrust, *v.*

pút พุทธ Buddha, Buddhist, *n.*

pút พุธ the planet Mercury, Wednesday, *n.*

pút-tá-jâao พุทธเจ้า Buddha, *n.*

pút-tá-paa-sìt พุทธภาษิต The Buddhist proverbs, *n.*

pút-tá-sàk-gà-ràat พุทธศักราช Buddhist Era, *n.*

puu ภู earth, land, ground, soil, *n.*

pûu พู่ tassel, tuft, pendant, *n.*

pûu ผู้ male, *adj.*

pûu ผู้ doer, person, *n.*

pûu-dii ผู้ดี refined person, *n.*

pùuk ผูก tie, *v.*

puu-kǎo ภูเขา mountain, *n.*

puu-kǎo-fai ภูเขาไฟ volcano, *n*

puu-kǎo-náam-kěng ภูเขาน้ำแข็ง iceberg, *n.*

puum ภูมิ soil, *n.*

puum-bpan-yaa ภูมิปัญญา intelligence, knowledge, *n.*

puum-jai ภูมิใจ proud, *adj.*

puum-kúm-gan ภูมิคุ้มกัน immunity, *n.*

puum-lam-nao ภูมิลำเนา habitat, native habitat, *n.*

puum-mí-bprà-têet ภูมิประเทศ landscape, scenery, *n.*

puum-mí-pâak ภูมิภาค provinces, region, *n.*

puum-péɛ ภูมิแพ้ allergy, *n.*

puum-tăan ภูมิฐาน grand, dignified, *adj.*

puu-păa ภูผา precipice, cliff, *n.*

pûu-ráai ผู้ร้าย wrongdoer, *n.*

pûut พูด speak, talk, say, *v.*

pûut ภูติ ghost, evil spirit, demon, *n.*

pûa เพื่อ for, for the sake of, behalf of, in order to, *prep., conj..*

pùak เผือก taro, *n.*

pûan เพื่อน friend, comrade, companion, company, colleague, fellow, associate, pal, *n.*

pûng พึ่ง just now, *adv.*

pûng ผึ้ง bee, *n.*

púun พื้น floor, surface, foundation, base, *n.*

pûut พืช plant, fauna, vegetation, *n.*

pûut พืด range, line, row, *n.*

r (ร, หร, ฤ)

raa รา mould, mold, fungus, *n.*

raa-chaa ราชา king, ruler, *n.*

raa-chí-nii ราชินี queen, *n.*

raa-dtrii ราตรี night, *n.*

raa-hŭu ราหู mythological monster, *n.*

râai ร่าย a kind of Thai verse, *n.*

ráai ร้าย severe, bad, fierce, evil, wicked, *adj.*

raai-dâai รายได้ income, *n.*

râak ราก root, foundation, source, origin, *n.*

raa-ká ราคะ lust, sexual desire, *n.*

raa-kaa ราคา price, cost, value, *n.*

râak-gɛ̂ɛo รากแก้ว tap root, *n.*

raa-kii ราคี flaw, blemish, stain, *n.*

râak-sàat-nɔ́ɔi รากสาดน้อย typhoid, *n.*

râak-sàp รากศัพท์ vocabulary root, *n.*

râak-tăan รากฐาน foundation, base, *n.*

raa-maa รามา bully, disturb, *v.*

raam-ma-gian รามเกียรติ์ Ramayana, *n.*

rân̂an ร้าน lustful, eager, *adj.*

rán̂an ร้าน store, stall, shop, market shop, *n.*

rán̂an-aa-hǎan ร้านอาหาร restaurant, *n.*

raang ราง groove, rail, track, *n.*

rân̂ang ร่าง shape, figure, structure, *n.*

rán̂ang ร้าง deserted, abandoned, *adj.*

raang-ná̂am รางน้ำ gutter, *n.*

raang-raang รางๆ in distinctly, blurredly, *adv.*

raang-wan รางวัล reward, prize, *n.*

raao ราว hand-rail, rail, *n.*

rán̂ao ร้าว cracked, *adj.*

raao-raao ราวๆ about, approximately, *adv.*

rân̂ap ราบ smooth, even, flat, level, *adj.*

rân̂a-rəəng ร่าเริง cheerful, *adj.*

raa-sǐi ราศี zodiacal sign, *n.*

raa-sǐi-dtun ราศีตุล Libra, Balance, *n.*

raa-sǐi-gan ราศีกันย์ Virgo, Virgin, *n.*

raa-sǐi-gɔɔ-ra-gòt ราศีกรกฎ Cancer, Crab, *n.*

raa-sǐi-gum ราศีกุมภ์ Aquarius, Water bearer, *n.*

raa-sǐi-mang-gɔɔn ราศีมังกร Capricorn, Horn goat, *n.*

raa-sǐi-mêet ราศีเมษ Aries, Ram, *n.*

raa-sǐi-mee-tǔn ราศีเมถุน Gemini, Twins, *n.*

raa-sǐi-miin ราศีมีน Pisces, Fish, *n.*

raa-sǐi-pí-jìk ราศีพิจิก Scorpio, Scorpion, *n.*

raa-sǐi-prút ราศีพฤษภ Taurus, Bull, *n.*

raa-sǐi-sǐng ราศีสิงห์ Leo, Lion, *n.*

raa-sǐi-tá-nuu ราศีธนู Sagittarius, Archer, *n.*

râat ราด pour, spill, top, *v.*

râat ราช king, monarch, *n.*

râat-cha-aa-naa-jàk ราชอาณาจักร kingdom, *n.*

râat-cha-gaan ราชการ government service, *n.*

râat-cha-sǐi ราชสีห์ lion, king-lion, *n.*

râat-cha-tûut ราชทูต ambassador, *n.*

râat-sà-dɔɔn ราษฎร citizens, population, *n.*

a b bp ch d dt e ɛ ə f g h i j k l m n ng o ɔ **p r** s t u ɯ w y

rá-bian ระเบียน record, pattern, registration, *n.*

rá-biang ระเบียง veranda, balcony, porch, *n.*

rá-bìap ระเบียบ order, rule, regulation, *n.*

rá-bə̀ət ระเบิด explode, burst, *v.*

rá-bom ระบม feel stiff and sore, *v.*

rá-bòp ระบบ system, *n.*

rá-bù ระบุ mention, specify, *v.*

rá-dàp ระดับ level, altitude, *n.*

rá-dom ระดม call up, *v.*

rá-duu ระดู menses, menstruation, *n.*

rá-gaa ระกา Year of the Cock, *n.*

rá-gam ระกำ sorrow, grief, *n.*

rá-hàt รหัส code, *n.*

rá-hə̀əi ระเหย evaporate, *v.*

rá-hǒng ระหง tall and slender, *adj.*

rá-hǒoi ระโหย tired, *adj.*

rai ไร species of insect, *n.*

rai ไร what, which, dimly, *adv.*

râi ไร่ farm, field, *n.*

rái ไร้ poor, lacking, needy, *adj.*

rái ไร้ without, *adv.*

rái-kâa ไร้ค่า worthless, *adj.*

rái-kwaam-sǎa-mâat ไร้ความสามารถ incapable, incapacitated, *adj.*

rái-sǎa-rá ไร้สาระ nonsensical, *adj.*

rák รัก love, cherish, fond of, *v.*

rá-kaai ระคาย irritated, itchy, *adj.*, *v.*

rá-kang ระฆัง bell, *n.*

rá-ké ระแคะ trick, mystery, *n.*

rák-rέε รักแร้ armpit, *n.*

rák-sǎa รักษา take care of, treat, watch over, *v.*

rák-sà-nùk รักสนุก playful, *adj.*

ram รำ dance, *v.*

rá-mát-rá-wang ระมัดระวัง cautious, *adj.*

ram-kaan รำคาญ annoyed, *adj.*

ram-pan รำพัน bemoan, *v.*

ram-pʉng รำพึง think of, *v.*

ram-wong รำวง perform Thai folkdance, *v.*

ran รัน beat, hit, *v.*

rán รั้น stubborn, obstinate, *adj.*

rá-nâap ระนาบ lie flat, *v.*

rá-nâat ระนาด xylophone, *n.*

rá-nɛɛng ระแนง stand in a row, *v.*

rang รัง nest, home, *n.*

ráng รั้ง stop, wait, *v.*

rá-ngáp ระงับ stop, halt, cease, *v.*

rang-gɛɛ รังแก bully, molest, *v.*

rang-kɛɛ รังแค dandruff, *n.*

ra-ngom ระงม loud, noisy, *adj.*

rao เรา we, I, us, me, *pron.*

ráo เร้า rouse, stimulate, *v.*

ráo-jai เร้าใจ encourage, arouse, *v.*

ráp รับ receive, get, *v.*

ráp-bàap รับบาป be a scapegoat, *v.*

ráp-cháai รับใช้ serve, *v.*

ráp-jâang รับจ้าง take employment, *v.*

ráp-krɔ́ รับเคราะห์ have misfortunes, *v.*

rá-raan ระราน cause trouble, *v.*

rá-rəəng ระเริง rejoice, *v.*

rá-rík ระริก giggle mirthfully, beat fast (e.g. heart), *v.*

rá-sàm-rá-săai ระส่ำระสาย disordered, *adj.*

rát รัด squeeze, bind, *v.*

rát รัฐ state, country, nation, territory, *n.*

rát-tà-baan รัฐบาล government, *n.*

rát-dtà-ná รัตนะ jewel, precious stone, gem, *n.*

rát-dtà-naa รัตนา glass, jewel, *n.*

rát-dtì-gaan รัตติกาล night, *n.*

rá-tom-túk ระทมทุกข์ suffer from excessive anguish or sorrow, *v.*

rá-tót ระทด sad, sorrowful, oppressed, *adj.*

rát-sà-mĭi รัศมี ray, radius, halo, *n.*

rát-tà-bù-rùt รัฐบุรุษ statesman, *n.*

rá-tuai ระทวย languid, weak, *adj.*

rá-túk ระทึก (of the heart) beat fast from fear, *v.*

rá-wàang ระหว่าง middle, middle section, space, interval, period, *n.*

rá-wàang-châat ระหว่างชาติ international, *adj.*

rá-wɛɛng ระแวง doubt, *v.*

rá-yá ระยะ distance, period, range, *n.*

rá-yam ระยำ accursed, mean, *adj.*

rá-yáp ระยับ brilliant, glittering, dazzling, *adj.*

rá-yá-taang ระยะทาง distance, *n.*

rêe เร่ wander about, *v.*

ree-kăa เรขา drawing, graphic, *n.*

ree-kăa-kà-nít เรขาคณิต geometry, *n.*

réen เร้น hide, *v.*

ree-nuu เรณู pollen, *n.*

ree-rai เรไร a kind of cicada, *n.*

ree-ruan เรรวน hesitate, *v.*

rêng เร่ง accelerate, hurry, *v.*

rêng-krûang เร่งเครื่อง speed up

the engine, v.

rêng-rát เร่งรัด urge, v.

reo เร็ว quick, fast, rapid, hasty, swift, adj.

rêε แร่ mineral, n.

rêek แรก initial, original, primary, first, adj.

rêek แรก before, at first, adv.

rεεm แรม spend (the night), stay (overnight), v.

rεεng แรง strength, force, power, n.

réeng แร้ง vulture, n.

rεεng-ngaan แรงงาน labor, n.

réen-kéen แร้นแค้น poor, penniless, adj.

réεo แร้ว snare, trap, n.

rêεt แรด rhinoceros, n.

rəə เรอ belch, v.

rəəm เริม nettle, rash, hives, n.

rə̂əm เริ่ม begin, start, commence, lead, v.

rə̂əm-dtôn เริ่มต้น begin, start, v.

rəəng เริง joyful, cheerful, merry, adj.

rəəng-sà-wàat เริงสวาท enjoy sexual intercourse, v.

rə̂ət เริด suspended, overly dressed, adj.

rí ริ initiate, v.

rîak เรียก call, call out, v.

rîak-wâa เรียกว่า called, adj.

rian เรียน study, learn, report or inform, v.

riang เรียง place in a row, v.

riang-kiu เรียงคิว in sequence, adv.

riang-kwaam เรียงความ essay, n.

rian-năng-sŭu เรียนหนังสือ study, v.

riao เรียว tapering, slender, adj.

rîao-rεεng เรียวแรง strength, energy, power, n.

rîap เรียบ even, adj.

rîa-raai เรี่ยราย scattered, adj.

rìi หรี่ lower, lessen the light, v.

rîi รี่ rush, v.

riim ริม ream, n.

rîip รีบ hurry, hasten, v.

rii-rɔɔ รีรอ wait for, hesitate, v.

rîit รีด squeeze, press, v.

rîit รีด custom, religious sect, n.

rim ริม edge, rim, n.

rin ริน pour slowly, v.

rín ริ้น gnat, n.

ríp ริบ confiscate, v.

rîp-rìi ริบหรี่ dim, twinkling, dusky, adj.

rìt-rɔɔn ริดรอน take away, cut, *v.*

rìt-sà-yǎa ริษยา jealousy, envy, *n.*

rìt-sǐi-duang ริดสีดวง a group of chronic maladies, *n.*

rìt-sǐi-duang-dtaa ริดสีดวงตา trachoma, *n.*

rìt-sǐi-duang-jà-mùuk ริดสีดวงจมูก rhinitis, *n.*

rìt-sǐi-duang-ta-waan-nàk ริดสีดวงทวารหนัก hemorrhoids, *n.*

rìu ริ้ว strip, stripe, wrinkle, *n.*

rìu-rɔɔi ริ้วรอย wrinkle, blemish, *n.*

rók รก placenta, afterbirth, *n.*

rók รก littered, untidy, *adj.*

rom รม smoke, expose to vapor, *v.*

rôm ร่ม shade, sunshade, umbrella, shade, *n.*

rôm-chuu-chîip ร่มชูชีพ parachute, *n.*

rôm-yen ร่มเย็น secure and peaceful, *adj.*

rôn ร่น move closer, retreat, *v.*

roo-dtii โรตี a kind of Indian food made of flour, *n.*

rooi โรย sprinkle, *v.*

rôok โรค disease, sickness, malady, *n.*

roo-ká โรคะ disease, ailment, *n.*

roong โรง hall, shed, house, *n.*

roong-glàn โรงกลั่น refinery, *n.*

roong-jam-nam โรงจำนำ pawnshop, *n.*

roong-nǎng โรงหนัง movie, cinema, *n.*

roong-ngaan โรงงาน factory, *n.*

roong-pâap-pa-yon โรงภาพยนตร์ cinema, *n.*

roong-pá-yaa-baan โรงพยาบาล hospital, *n.*

roong-pim โรงพิมพ์ printing office, *n.*

rǒong-rěeng โหรงเหรง sparse, few, thin, *adj.*

roong-reem โรงแรม hotel, *n.*

roong-rian โรงเรียน school, *n.*

roong-sǐi โรงสี rice-mill, *n.*

rôot โรจน์ prosperous, bright, *adj.*

róp รบ fight, make war, *v.*

rót รด sprinkle, water, pour water on, *v.*

rót รถ vehicle, wheeled vehicle, carriage, car, cart, bus, van, wagon, truck, automobile, tricycle, bicycle, *n.*

rót รส taste, flavor, relish, *n.*

rót-ban-túk รถบรรทุก truck, *n.*

rót-châat รสชาติ taste, flavor, *n.*

rót-chǎo รถเช่า rented car, *n.*

rót-dtûu รถตู้ van, *n.*

rót-dùan รถด่วน express, *n.*

rót-fai รถไฟ train, *n.*

rót-fai-fáa รถไฟฟ้า sky train, electric train, *n.*

rót-gěng รถเก๋ง sedan, car, *n.*

rót-sà-nì-yom รสนิยม liking, preference, *n.*

rɔ́-dtà-kèp เราะตะเข็บ cut out a seam, *v.*

rɔ̂n ร่อน sift, pan, winnow, *v.*

rɔ̂ng ร่อง furrow, channel, ditch, path, way, *n.*

rɔ̂ng-rêng ร่องแร่ง hanging, swaying, precarious, *adj.*

rɔɔ รอ wait, stay, *v.*

rɔ̌ɔ หรอ worn off, *v.*

rɔɔi รอย trace, mark, sign, path, *n.*

rɔɔ-kɔɔi รอคอย wait, wait for, *v.*

rɔɔm-rɔ́ɔ รอมร่อ nearly, almost, *adv.*

rɔɔn รอน cut, cut down, reduce, *v.*

rɔ̂ɔk รอก pulley, *v.*

rɔ́ɔn ร้อน hot, very warm, torrid, *adj.*

rɔ́ɔn-dtua ร้อนตัว afraid of being involved or incriminated, *adj.*

rɔɔng รอง place something under,

support, *v.*

rɔ́ɔng ร้อง cry, scream, exclaim, *v.*

rɔ́ɔng-kɔ̌ɔ ร้องขอ beg for, request, *v.*

rɔ́ɔng-hâi ร้องไห้ cry, *v.*

rɔ́ɔng-pleeng ร้องเพลง sing, *v.*

rɔ́ɔng-rian ร้องเรียน complain, *v.*

rɔɔng-táao รองเท้า shoe, *n.*

rɔ́ɔng-tɔ́ɔng ร้องท้อง eat just enough not to be hungry, *v.*

rɔ́ɔng-túk ร้องทุกข์ complain, *v.*

rɔ́ɔn-jai ร้อนใจ anxious, perturbed, in trouble, *adj.*

rɔ́ɔn-ngən ร้อนเงิน desperately in need of money, in urgent need of money, *adj.*

rɔ́ɔn-ron ร้อนรน impatient, anxious, zealous, *adj.*

rɔ̂ɔp รอบ cycle, round, turn, *n.*

rɔ̂ɔ-rɛ̂ɛ ร่อนแร่ near death, *adj.*

rɔ̂ɔt รอด safe, saved, *adj.*

rɔ̂ɔt รอด escape, survive, *v.*

rua รัว vibrate, roll, *v.*

rûa รั่ว leak, leak out, *v.*

rúa รั้ว fence, hedge, *n.*

ruai รวย rich, wealthy, affluent, *adj.*

rûa-lǎi รั่วไหล leak out, *v.*

ruam รวม combine, add, include,

incorporate, assemble, *v.*

rûam ร่วม share, participate, join, *v.*

ruam-táng-mòt รวมทั้งหมด altogether, *adj.*

ruan รวน roast, fry, *v.*

rûan ร่วน crumbling, *adj.*

rûang ร่วง fall off, drop, *v.*

ruan-ree รวนเร doubtful, uncertain, *adj.*

rûap รวบ gather, compile, *v.*

rûat รวด round, time (one time, two times, etc.), *n.*

rûat-diao รวดเดียว all at once, *adv.*

rûat-reo รวดเร็ว quickly, *adv.*

rûi รุ่ย loose, brittle, *adj.*

rúk รุก push forward, *v.*

rum รุม crowd around, mob, *v.*

rûm รุ่ม strike or hit repeatedly, *v.*

rûm-râam รุ่มร่าม shabbily dressed, *adj.*

run รุน push, urge, *v.*

rûn รุ่น time, age, period, era, generation, *n.*

rûng รุ่ง dawn, *n.*

rúng รุ้ง rainbow, prismatic colors, *n.*

rúng-yin-náam รุ้งกินน้ำ rainbow, *n.*

rung-rang รุงรัง untidy, *adj.*

run-reeng รุนแรง violent, *adj.*

rút รุด hurry, *v.*

ruu รู hole, *n.*

rúu รู้ know, aware of, *v., adj.*

rǔu หรู beautiful, *adj.*

rúu-jàk รู้จัก acquainted with, *adj.*

rûup รูป picture, form, shape, *n.*

rǔu-rǎa หรูหรา elegant, grand, *adj.*

rúut รูด slip, slide smoothly, pull, draw, *v.*

rý รี either...or, or, *conj.*

rɯa เรือ boat, ship, *n.*

rɯa-bin เรือบิน airplane, *n.*

rɯan เรือน house, dwelling place, *n.*

rɯ́an เรื้อน leprosy, *n.*

rɯang เรือง shining, *adj.*

rɯ̂ang เรื่อง story, subject, *n.*

rɯan-hɔ̌ɔ เรือนหอ bridal house, *n.*

rɯan-jam เรือนจำ prison, *n.*

rɯan-pɛɛ เรือนแพ houseboat, *n.*

rɯ̂ai เรื่อย continuous, continual, *adj.*

rɯ́a-rang เรื้อรัง chronic, *adj.*

rɯ̂at เรือด bedbug, *n.*

rɯ́ɯ รื้อ tear down, *v.*

rɯ̌ɯ หรือ either...or, or, *conj.*

rɯ̂ɯn รื่น joyful, *adj.*

rɯ̂ɯn-rəəng รื่นเริง delightful, *adj.*

Phonetic · Thai · English

S

(ส, ศ, ษ, ซ, ทร)

sà สระ pool, pond, *n.*

saa ซา diminish, subside, lessen, *v.*

sàa ส่า yeast, rash, *n.*

sà-àat สะอาด clean, *adj.*

sǎa-baan สาบาน swear, *v.*

sǎa-gon สากล universal, all, *adj., adv.*

sǎa-hàt สาหัส severe, extreme, cruel, *adj.*

sǎa-hèet สาเหตุ cause, motive, *n.*

saai ทราย sand, *n.*

sàai ส่าย swing, sway, swerve, *v.*

sáai ซ้าย left, *adj., adv.*

sǎai สาย line, string, wire, rope, road, stream, steak, lineage, *n.*

sǎai-chá-nuan สายชนวน fuse, *n.*

sǎai-chuu สายชู vinegar, *n.*

sǎai-dtaa สายตา eyesight, *n.*

sǎai-gaan-bin สายการบิน airline, *n.*

sàak สาก pestle, *n.*

sàak สาก rough, *adj.*

sâak ซาก dead body, remains, *n.*

sǎa-kǎa สาขา branch, chain, *n.*

sǎa-kuu สาคู sago, *n.*

sǎa-laa ศาลา rest-house, public rest-house, *n.*

sǎa-laa-glaang ศาลากลาง city hall, *n.*

saam ทราม low, mean, *adj.*

sǎam สาม three, *nm.*

sǎa-mâat สามารถ able, efficient, can, *adj., v.*

sǎa-mák-kii สามัคคี unity, harmony, concord, *n.*

sǎa-man สามัญ common, ordinary, *adj.*

sǎa-man-chon สามัญชน lay people, commoner, *n.*

sǎa-mii สามี husband, *n.*

sǎam-lɔ́ɔ สามล้อ tricycle, *n.*

sǎam-ma-neen สามเณร novice, *n.*

sâan ซ่าน diffuse, permeate, *v.*

sǎan ศาล court, court of justice, *n.*

sǎan สาน weave, *v.*

sǎan สาร letter, document, message, large elephant, *n.*

sǎan สาส์น letter, document, *n.*

sâang ส้าง recover, *v.*

sàang สาง disappear, *v.*

sâang สร้าง build, create, make, *v.*

sǎang สาง ghost, demon, *n.*

sàang-mao สร่างเมา become

sober, v.

săan-kee-mii สารเคมี chemical substances, n.

săa-nú-sìt สานุศิษย์ disciple, n.

săao สาว girl, young woman, n.

săao สาว pull in, haul, v.

săao-cháai สาวใช้ maid, n.

săao-gèe สาวแก่ old maid, n.

sàap สาบ pungent odor, n.

sàap สาป curse, put a curse, v.

sàap-chêng สาปแช่ง curse, v.

sàap-sŭun สาปสูญ disappear, v.

săa-rá สาระ essence, substance, n.

săa-ràai สาหร่าย seaweeds, n.

săa-raa-nú-grom สารานุกรม encyclopedia, n.

săa-rá-ka-dii สารคดี article, n.

săa-rá-leeo สารเลว despicable, adj.

săa-rá-nɛɛ สาระแน impudent, adj.

săa-ra-ní-têet สารนิเทศ information, n.

săa-ra-pan สารพัน everything, all, all kinds, adj., adv., n.

săa-ra-pát สารพัด every, all things, adj., n.

săa-ra-tii สารถี driver, guide, n.

săa-ra-wát สารวัตร inspector,

headman, n.

săa-rii-rík-ga-tâat สารีริกธาตุ Buddha's relic, n.

sàat ศาสตร์ science, n.

sàat สาด splash, toss out, v.

sàat สารท autumn festival, n.

săa-taa-ra-ná สาธารณะ public, general, common, adj.

săa-taa-ra-ná-rát สาธารณรัฐ republic, n.

săa-taa-ra-ná-sùk สาธารณสุข public health, n.

săa-taa-ra-nuu-bpà-pook สาธารณูปโภค public utility, n.

săa-ta-yaai สาธยาย explain, v.

sàat-dtraa-jaan ศาสตราจารย์ professor, n.

săa-tít สาธิต finished, accomplished, demonstrated, adj.

săa-tít สาธิต demonstrate, v.

sàat-sà-daa ศาสดา religious founder, n.

sàat-sà-năa ศาสนา religion, n.

sàat-sà-năa-ìt-sa-laam ศาสนาอิสลาม Islam, n.

sàat-sà-năa-krít, sàat-sà-năa-krís ศาสนาคริสต์ Christianity, n.

sàat-sà-năa-praam ศาสนา

พราหมณ์ Brahmanism, n.

sàat-sà-nǎa-pút ศาสนาพุทธ
Buddhism, n.

sǎa-tú สาธุ (Buddhist) amen, interj.

sǎa-wók สาวก disciple, n.

sǎa-yan สายัณห์ evening, n.

sà-baai สบาย comfortable, adj.

sà-bâa-hǔa-kào สะบ้าหัวเข่า
kneecap, n.

sà-baai-jai สบายใจ contented, adj.

sà-bai สไบ shawl, wrap, n.

sà-ban สะบั้น broken off, adj.

sà-bàt สะบัด shake, flip, v.

sà-biang เสบียง provisions, n.

sà-bong สบง a piece of cloth worn
by Buddhist monks, n.

sà-bòt สบถ swear, v.

sà-bùu สบู่ soap, n.

sà-dàp สดับ listen, hear, v.

sà-dèt สะเด็ด dried, adj.

sà-dèt เสด็จ go (for royalty), v.

sà-dɛɛng แสดง show, demonstrate, v.

sà-dîng สะดิ้ง feigning, adj.

sà-dɔ̀ สะเดาะ perform deeds by
magic power, v.

sà-dtà ศต hundred, n.

sà-dtaai สไตล์ style, n.

sà-dtaang สตางค์ money, a copper

Thai coin equal to one hundredth of a
baht, n.

sà-dtɛm แสตมป์ stamp, n.

sà-dtì สติ consciousness, mind,
thought, n.

sà-dtì-pan-yaa สติปัญญา wisdom,
intelligence, n.

sà-dtrii สตรี woman, female, n.

sà-dùak สะดวก convenient, adj.

sà-dûng สะดุ้ง startled, adj.

sà-dùt สะดุด stumble, v.

sà-dɯɯ สะดือ navel, n.

sà-gaao สกาว white, clean, adj.

sà-gàt สกัด obstruct, intercept, v.

sà-gèt สะเก็ด fragment, flake, scab, n.

sà-gìt สะกิด tap, nudge gently, v.

sà-gon สกล full, complete, adj.

sà-gòt สะกด suppress, control, spell
(words), put to sleep by magic, v.

sà-gòt-jìt สะกดจิต hypnotize, v.

sà-gòt-rɔɔi สะกดรอย follow tracks, v.

sà-gruu สกรู screw, n.

sà-gun สกุล family, lineage, n.

sà-hà สห with, together with, prep.

sà-hǎai สหาย friend, companion, n.

sà-hà-bprà-chaa-châat
สหประชาชาติ United Nations, n.

sà-hà-gɔɔn สหกรณ์ cooperative, n.

sà-hà-pan สหพันธ์ federation, *n.*

sà-hà-rát-à-mee-ri-gaa

สหรัฐอเมริกา the United States of
America, *n.*

sài ใส่ put into, wear, fill, contain, load,
enclose, insert, *v.*

sâi ไส้ intestines, bowels, *n.*

sái ใช้ dig for food with the beak (e.g.
chicken), *v.*

săi ใช what, which, whatsoever, *adj.*

săi ใส clear, transparent, pure, *adj.*

săi ไส push forward, *v.*

sâi-dtìng ไส้ติ่ง appendix, *n.*

sâi-duan ไส้เดือน earthworm, *n.*

sài-jai ใส่ใจ pay attention, *v.*

sài-kwaam ใส่ความ blame, *v.*

sâi-lʉan ไส้เลื่อน hernia, *n.*

sà-ìng สะอิ้ง belt, girdle, *n.*

sài-sùk ไส้ศึก spy, *n.*

sà-ìt-sà-ian สะอิดสะเอียน disgusted, *adj.*

săi-ya-sàat ไสยศาสตร์ magic, *n.*

sà-jai สะใจ satisfied, *v.*

sàk ศักย์ potential, *n.*

sàk สัก teak, teak tree, *n.*

sàk สัก tattoo, *v.*

sák ซัก wash, launder, inquire, *v.*

sàk-daa ศักดา power, might, *n.*

sàk-gaa-rá สักการะ worship, *v.*

sàk-gà-làat สักหลาด flannel, *n.*

sàk-gà-ràat ศักราช era, *n.*

sàk-gà-waa สักวา a form of Thai
poetry, *n.*

sàk-kìi สักขี witness, *n.*

sák-sɔ́ɔm ซักซ้อม rehearse, *v.*

sà-là สละ renounce, relinquish, *v.*

sà-lăai สลาย disintegrate, decompose, *v.*

sà-làak สลาก label, *n.*

sà-làak-gin-bèng สลากกินแบ่ง
lottery ticket, *n.*

sà-làk สลัก carve, *v.*

sà-lam สลัม slum, *n.*

sà-làp สลับ alternate, *v.*

sà-làt สลัด throw off, shake, *v.*

sà-làt สลัด salad, *n.*

sà-lèet เสลด phlegm, *n.*

sà-lɛ̌ɛng แสลง harmful, *adj.*

sà-lòp สลบ unconscious, *adj.*

sà-lòt สลด sorrowful, *adj.*

sà-lɔ̌ɔn สลอน many, abundant, *adj.*

sà-lǔa สลัว dim, *adj.*

sà-lǔai สลวย beautiful, pretty, *adj.*

sà-lʉ̌ng สลึง small Thai coin equal to
one fourth of a baht, *n.*

sám ซ้ำ repeat, recur, *v.*

sà-maa ษมา beg pardon, v.

sà-maa-chík สมาชิก member, n.

sà-maa-kom สมาคม society, association, n.

sà-măan สมาน connect, assimilate, v.

săm-aang สำอาง cosmetics, n.

sà-măan-plɛ̌ɛ สมานแผล heal a wound, v.

sà-maa-pan สมาพันธ์ confederation, n.

sà-maa-tì สมาธิ concentration, n.

sà-maa-tôot ษมาโทษ ask for pardon for sin or wrong-doings, v.

sa-ma-gaan สมการ equation, n.

sà-măi สมัย era, period, age, time, n.

sà-màk สมัคร volunteer, join willingly, apply (e.g. for a job), v.

sà-màk-jai สมัครใจ willing, adj.

sà-màm-sà-mɤ̌ɤ สม่ำเสมอ regular, consistent, adj.

sà-ma-ná สมณะ religious mendicant, priest, monk, n.

sà-ma-ná-pêet สมณเพศ ascetics, n.

sà-ma-tà สมตะ peace of mind, n.

sà-mát-chaa สมัชชา assembly, n.

sà-màt-tà-pâap สมรรถภาพ efficiency, ability, n.

săm-bpà-chan-yá สัมปชัญญะ

conscience, n.

săm-bpà-taan สัมปทาน concession, n.

săm-dɛɛng สำแดง exhibit, manifest, v.

sà-mɤ̌ɤ เสมอ even, level, equal, adj.

sà-mɤ̌ɤ เสมอ always, adv.

sà-mɤ̌ɤ-bplaai เสมอปลาย consistently, adv.

sà-mɤ̌ɤ-gan เสมอกัน equal, adj.

sà-mɤ̌ɤ-pâak เสมอภาค equal, adj.

sà-mĭan เสมียน clerk, secretary, n.

săm-kan สำคัญ important, significant, essential, adj.

săm-lák สำลัก choke, v.

săm-lii สำลี cotton, n.

săm-maa สัมมา right, correct, honest, virtuous, adj.

săm-má-naa สัมนา meet, v.

săm-má-naa สัมมนา seminar, n.

săm-má-noo-krʉa สำมะโนครัว census, n.

săm-nák สำนัก office, bureau, institution, n.

săm-nák-ngaan สำนักงาน office, n.

săm-nao สำเนา copy, n.

săm-niang สำเนียง tone of voice, accent, n.

sǎm-nuan สำนวน style of writing or speaking, *n.*

sǎm-núk สำนึก aware, *adj.*

sà-moo-sɔɔn สโมสร club, association, *n.*

sà-mɔɔ สมอ anchor, stone, *n.*

sǎm-ɔɔi สำออย implore, wheedle, *v.*

sà-mɔɔng สมอง brain, head, *n.*

sà-mɔɔ-ra-puum สมรภูมิ battle field, *n.*

sà-mɔɔ-rua สมอเรือ anchor, *n.*

sǎm-paa-rá สัมภาระ supplies, *n.*

sǎm-pâat สัมภาษณ์ interview, *v.*

sǎm-pan สัมพันธ์ related, connected, *adj.*

sǎm-pan-ta-mai-dtrii สัมพันธไมตรี friendship, *n.*

sǎm-pan-ta-mít สัมพันธมิตร ally, *n.*

sǎm-pan-ta-pâap สัมพันธภาพ relation, *n.*

sǎm-pàt สัมผัส touch, feel, contact, *v.*

sǎm-pát สัมพัทธ์ relative, *adj.*

sǎm-pát-ta-pâap สัมพัทธภาพ relativity, *n.*

sǎm-raan สำราญ cheerful, *adj.*

sǎm-ràp สำหรับ in order that, for, in favor of, *prep.*

sǎm-ráp สำรับ set, suit, tray con-

taining plates and bowls of food, *n.*

sǎm-rèt สำเร็จ succeed, accomplish, *v.*

sǎm-rèt-kwaam-krâi สำเร็จความใคร่ have one's sexual gratification, *v.*

sǎm-rèt-rûup สำเร็จรูป ready-made, *adj.*

sǎm-rít สัมฤทธิ์ alloy, *n.*

sǎm-rít-pǒn สัมฤทธิ์ผล successful, *adj.*

sǎm-rɔɔng สำรอง preserve, *v.*

sǎm-ruai สำเริง pleasure-loving, *adj.*

sǎm-ruam สำรวม careful, *adj.*

sǎm-rùat สำรวจ explore, *v.*

sǎm-sɔ̀n สำส่อน promiscuous, *adj.*

sà-mù-hà-ban-chii สมุหบัญชี accountant general, *n.*

sà-mǔn สมุน attendant, follower, *n.*

sà-mǔn-prai สมุนไพร medicinal herbs, *n.*

sà-mùt สมุด notebook, *n.*

sà-mùt สมุทร ocean, *n.*

sà-mù-tai สมุทัย cause, *n.*

sà-mǔan เสมือน like, similar to, *adv.*

sàn สั่น tremble, vibrate, shake, *v.*

sân สั้น short, brief, *adj.*

săn สัน ridge, back, *n.*

săn สรร choose, *v.*

sà-năam สนาม field, ground, lawn, yard, *n.*

sà-năam-bin สนามบิน airport, *n.*

sà-năam-gii-laa สนามกีฬา stadium, *n.*

sà-năam-góɔp สนามกอล์ฟ golf course, *n.*

sà-năam-róp สนามรบ battle, *n.*

sà-nàn สนั่น very loud, *adj.*

sà-nàp สนับ glove, covering for protection, *n.*

sà-nàp-sà-nŭn สนับสนุน support, *v.*

săn-châat สัญชาติ nationality, citizenship, place of birth, *n.*

săn-châat-dtà-yaan สัญชาติญาณ instinct, *n.*

săn-daan สันดาน in-born traits, *n.*

săn-dàap สันดาป combustion, *n.*

săn-dòot สันโดษ seclusion, *n.*

săn-dtà-bpa-bpa สันตะปาปา Pope, *n.*

săn-dtì สันติ calmness, tranquility, peacefulness, *n.*

săn-dtì-pâap สันติภาพ peace, *n.*

sà-nèe-hăa เสน่หา love, *v.*

sà-nə̌ə เสนอ propose, present a proposal, submit, *v.*

sàng สั่ง order, command, instruct, give orders, *v.*

săng สังข์ shell, conch, *n.*

sà-ngàa สง่า dignified, grand, *adj.*

sà-ngàt สงัด calm, *adj.*

săng-gà-sĭi สังกะสี zinc, *n.*

săng-gàt สังกัด belong, *v.*

săng-gèet สังเกต observe, notice, note, *v.*

săng-hăan สังหาร kill, execute, *v.*

săng-hăa-rim-ma-sáp สังหาริมทรัพย์ movable property, *n.*

săng-hɔ̌ɔn สังหรณ์ have a foreboding, have a bad feeling, *v.*

săng-hɔ̌ɔn-jai สังหรณ์ใจ have a premonition, *v.*

sà-ngìam เสงี่ยม careful, modest, tactful, *adj.*

săng-ká สังฆะ monk, *n.*

săng-kăan สังขาร body and mind, *n.*

săng-ká-lôok สังคโลก a type of famous pottery, *n.*

săng-ká-naa-yók สังฆนายก chief of all the Buddhist, *n.*

săng-ká-râat สังฆราช pontiff, *n.*

săng-ká-taan สังฆทาน alms, *n.*

sǎng-kà-yǎa สังขยา a kind of Thai
pudding, *n.*

sǎng-kèep สังเขป summary, *n.*

sǎng-kom สังคม society, association, *n.*

sǎng-krɔ́ สังเคราะห์ synthesize, *v.*

sà-ngòp สงบ become quiet, *v.*

sǎng-sǎn สังสรรค์ converse, have
an informal conversation, *v.*

sà-ngǔan สงวน keep, preserve,
reserve, *v.*

sǎng-waan สังวาล chain, *n.*

sǎng-wâat สังวาส copulate, have
sexual intercourse, *v.*

sǎng-wêet สังเวช pity, *v.*

sǎng-wəəi สังเวย sacrifice, *v.*

sǎng-wian สังเวียน arena, fighting
ring, *n.*

sǎng-wɔɔn สังวร caution, constraint, *n.*

sǎng-wɔɔn สังวรณ์ closure, protection, *n.*

sà-nìat เสนียด evil, misfortune, *n.*

sà-nǐm สนิม rust, *n.*

sà-nìt สนิท fitting closely, close, tight,
adj.

sǎn-jɔɔn สัญจร way, path, *n.*

sǎn-ní-bàat สันนิบาต league, congress, *n.*

sǎn-ní-tǎan สันนิษฐาน assume, *v.*

sǎn-ní-wâat สันนิวาส dwelling
place, *n.*

sà-nǒm สนม lady of the court, royal
concubine, *n.*

sà-nɔ̀ เสนาะ melodious, *adj.*

sà-nɔ̌ɔng สนอง reply, respond, *v.*

sǎn-sà-grìt สันสกฤต Sanskrit, *n.*

sǎn-sɔ̌ɔn, sǎn-ra-sɔ̌ɔn สรรเสริญ
praise, laud, *v.*

sǎn-taan สันธาร conjunction, *n.*

sǎn-tǎan สันถาร act of spreading
down to cover the floor, *n.*

sǎn-tát สันทัด proficient, skillful, *adj.*

sà-nùk สนุก entertaining, amusing,
cheerful, enjoyable, agreeable, *adj.*

sǎn-yaa สัญญา promise, pledge,
agree, contract, *v.*

sǎn-yaa สัญญา promise, agreement,
contract, *n.*

sǎn-yaan สัญญาณ signal, *n.*

sǎn-ya-gam ศัลยกรรม surgery, *n.*

sǎn-ya-lák สัญลักษณ์ symbol, *n.*

sao เซา stop, cease, *v.*

sâo เศร้า sad, sorrowful, *adj.*

sâo เต้า cane, walking stick, *n.*

sǎo เสา post, pole, pillar, *n.*

săo เสาร์ Saturn, Saturday, *n.*

sàp ศัพท์ vocabulary, *n.*

sàp ศัพท์ voice, speech, *n.*

sàp สรรพ whole, all, *adj.*

sàp สับ chop, mince, *v.*

sáp ซับ absorb, *v.*

sáp ทรัพย์ wealth, property, *n.*

sà-paa สภา council, assembly, *n.*

sà-paa-gaa-châat สภากาชาด Red Cross, *n.*

sà-paai สะพาย carry (on the shoulder), *v.*

sà-paan สะพาน bridge, *n.*

sà-pâap สภาพ nature, status, natural state, *n.*

sà-paa-wá สภาวะ nature, status, *n.*

sà-pái สะใภ้ female relative by marriage, *n.*

sàp-daa สัปดาห์ week, *n.*

sàp-bpà-don สัปดน obscene, lewd, *adj.*

sàp-bpà-ngòk สัปหงก sleepy, nodding, *adj.*

sàp-bpà-rɔ̀ɔ สัปเหร่อ undertaker, *n.*

sàp-bpà-rót สับปะรด pineapple, *n.*

sáp-nai ซับใน lining, underwear, *n.*

sáp-pa-yaa-gɔɔn ทรัพยากร natural resources, *n.*

sà-prâng สะพรั่ง ready, total, *adj.*

sà-prâo สะเพร่า careless, negligent, *adj.*

sáp-sǐn ทรัพย์สิน assets, *n.*

sàp-sǒn สับสน confused, *adj.*

sáp-sɔ́ɔn ซับซ้อน complicated, intricate, *adj.*

sà-ra-ná สรณะ protection, place of refuge, *n.*

sà-rá-nɛɛ สะระแหน่ mint, *n.*

sà-rii-rá สรีระ body, *n.*

sà-rii-rá-wít-ta-yaa สรีรวิทยา physiology, *r.*

sà-rong สโร่ง sarong, a garment worn by Thai woman, *n.*

sà-rùp สรุป conclude, sum up, *v.*

sà-săang สะสาง clear up, solve, *v.*

sà-sǒm สะสม accumulate, collect, *v.*

sàt สัตย์ oath, honesty, truth, *n.*

sàt สัตว์ animal, beast, *n.*

sát ซัด throw, hurl, filing, cast, dash, *v.*

sà-tăa-ban สถาบัน institution, *n.*

sà-tăa-bpà-naa สถาปนา construct, *v.*

sà-tăa-bpà-ník สถาปนิก architect, *n.*

sà-tăa-bpàt สถาปัตย์ architecture, *n.*

sà-táan สะท้าน tremble, *v.*

sà-tǎan สถาน place, site, *n.*

sà-tǎa-ná สถานะ status, state, rank, situation, *n.*

sà-tǎa-nii สถานี station, shipping station, *n.*

sà-tǎa-nii-dàp-pləəng สถานีดับเพลิง fire station, *n.*

sà-tǎa-nii-dtam-rùat สถานีตำรวจ police station, *n.*

sà-tǎa-nii-rót-fai สถานีรถไฟ railway station, *n.*

sà-tǎa-pɔɔn สถาพร permanent, *adj.*

sàt-dtà-yaa-ban สัตยาบัน ratify, *v.*

sàt-dtruu ศัตรู enemy, foe, opponent, adversary, *n.*

sà-təən สะเทิน half, half-way, *adj.*

sà-tian เสถียร strong, *adj.*

sà-tì-dtì สถิติ statistics record, *n.*

sà-tìt สถิต stay, remain, dwell, *v.*

sàt-ja สัจจะ truth, *n.*

sà-tɔ́ɔn สะท้อน rebound, *v.*

sà-tɔ́ɔn สะท้อน reflected, *adj.*

sà-tɔ́ɔn-jai สะท้อนใจ disheartened, *adj.*

sàt-sà-dii สัสดี recruiting officer, conscription registrar, *n.*

sàt-sùu สัตย์ซื่อ loyal, *adj.*

sàt-taa ศรัทธา faith, trust, *n.*

sà-tùup สถูป stupa, *n.*

sà-tɯan สะเทือน tremble, *v.*

sà-ùk สะอึก hiccup, *v.*

sà-wǎi ไสว plentiful, numerous, *adj.*

sà-wàan สว่าน drill, *n.*

sà-wàang สว่าง bright, clear, glowing, shining, light, *adj.*

sà-wàat สวาท lovable, *adj.*

sà-wǎn สวรรค์ heaven, *n.*

sà-wǎn-na-kót สวรรคต (royal) die, *v.*

sà-wàt-dì-gaan สวัสดิการ welfare, *n.*

sà-wàt-dii สวัสดี word of greeting, good day, *n.*

sà-wèet เศวต white color, *n.*

sà-wɛ̌ɛng แสวง search, *v.*

sà-wɔ̌əi เสวย eat, *v.*

sà-wǐng สวิง hand-net, *n.*

sà-yǎai สยาย spread, untangle, *v.*

sà-yǎam สยาม Siam, former name for Thailand, *n.*

sà-yǎam-rát สยามรัฐ Siam, *n.*

sà-yè แสยะ grin broadly, *v.*

sà-yɛ̌ɛng แสยง frightful, *adj.*

sà-yǐu สยิว feel a sense of thrill, *v.*

Phonetic · Thai · English

sà-yòp สยบ bend the head down, n.

sà-yòt-sà-yɔ̌ɔng สยดสยอง horrible, dreadful, adj.

sà-yɔ̌ɔng สยอง dreadful, horrified, adj.

see เซ stagger, v., adj.

sèek เสก pronounce religious or magical formula, v.

sěem-hà เสมหะ phlegm, n.

sěe-naa เสนา troops, soldiers, n.

sěe-naa-tí-gaan เสนาธิการ chief of military staff, n.

sèep เสพย์ eat, consume, v.

sěe-paa เสภา a kind of Thai song recital, solo, n.

sěe-plee เสเพล ill-behaved, adj.

sèep-mee-tǔn เสพเมถุน have sexual intercourse, v.

sěe-rii เสรี free, independent, adj.

sěe-rii-ní-yom เสรีนิยม liberalism, n.

sěe-rii-pâap เสรีภาพ freedom, n.

sěe-sɛ̂ɛng เสแสร้ง disguise, pretend, v.

sèet เศษ remainder, remnants, fraction, n.

sèet-grà-dàat เศษกระดาษ scrap of paper, waste paper, n.

sèet-máai เศษไม้ splinter, n.

sèet-sùan เศษส่วน fraction, n.

sèet-tà-gìt เศรษฐกิจ economy, n.

sèet-tǐi เศรษฐี millionaire, n.

sen เซ็น sign, v.

sên เซ่น make offering or sacrifice to the spirit, v.

sên เส้น thread, line, string, strand, rope, cord, n.

seng เซ็ง dull, insipid, tasteless, adj.

séng เซ้ง sell out, v.

sèt เสร็จ finished, ready, adj.

sɛ̌ɛ แส่ provoke, v.

sɛ̂ɛ แซ่ family name, n.

sɛ̂ɛ แส้ whip, n.

sɛ̀ɛk แสก barn owl, n.

sɛ̂ɛk แทรก mix, insert, intervene, v.

sɛ̂ɛk-glaang แสกกลาง parted in the middle, adj.

sɛ̌ɛn แสน one hundred thousand, n.

sɛ̌ɛn แสน extremely, very, adv.

sɛɛng แซง interfere, intervene, v.

sɛ̌ɛng แสง light, n.

sɛ̂ɛng แสร้ง pretend, feign, v.

sɛ̂ɛp, sɛ̂p แซ่บ delicious, adj.

sèɛp แสบ sting, feel pain, v.

sèɛp แสบ stinging, piercing (pain), burning (pain), adj.

sɛ̀ɛt แสด red orange, orange yellow, *n.*

sɔ̀ɔ เซ่อ stupid, silly, foolish, *adj.*

sɔ̌ɔi เสย scoop up, *v.*

sɔ̌ɔm เสริม supplement, add, reinforce, *v.*

sɔ̀ɔp เสิร์ฟ serve, *v.*

sǐa เสีย lose, waste, get out of order, *v.*

sìa เสีย wealthy Chinese man, *n.*

sǐa-chii-wít เสียชีวิต die, *v.*

sǐa-dtua เสียตัว lose one's virginity, *v.*

sǐam เสี้ยม taper, grind down, *v.*

sìam เสียม spade, *n.*

sìan เสี้ยน splinter, *n.*

sìang เสี่ยง fractions, fragments, *n.*

sìang เสี่ยง risk, gamble, *v.*

sǐang เสียง sound, voice, noise, *n.*

sìao เซียว withered, wrinkled, *adj.*

sìao เสี่ยว friend (Lao), *n.*

sìao เสี่ยว quarter, *n.*

sìao เสี่ยว feel a sudden pain, feel a thrill of fear, feel a thrill of lust, *v.*

sìap เสียบ pierce, penetrate, *v.*

sìat เสียด pierce, thrust, penetrate, *v.*

sìi สี่ four, *nm.*

sǐi ซี่ rib, bar, tooth, classifier for rib, bar, tooth, *n.*

sǐi ศรี good fortune, dignity, *n.*

sǐi สี color, *n.*

sǐi-daa สีดา furrow, Rama's wife, *n.*

sǐi-gaa สีกา female layman, *n.*

sǐi-íu ซีอิ๊ว soy bean sauce, *n.*

sìik ซีก part, piece, *n.*

sìik-máai ซีกไม้ splinter, *n.*

sǐi-maa สีมา border, *n.*

sǐin ศีล moral precepts, *n.*

sǐin-lá-tam ศีลธรรม morality, *n.*

sǐi-sà ศีรษะ head, top, *n.*

sìit ซีด pale, faded, *adj.*

sì-kǎa ศิขา lock of hair on the head, peak, summit, *n.*

sìk-kǎa สิกขา education, *n.*

sìk-kǎa-bòt สิกขาบท religious precepts, *n.*

sì-laa ศิลา rock, stone, *n.*

sîn สิ้น end, terminate, *v.*

sǐn สิน property, wealth, *n.*

sǐn-bon สินบน bribe, *n.*

sìng สิ่ง things, articles, objects, *n.*

sǐng สิง haunted, *adj.*

sǐng สิงห์ lion, *n.*

sǐng-dtoo สิงโต lion, *n.*

sǐng-hǎa-kom สิงหาคม August, *n.*

sìng-kɔ̌ɔng สิ่งของ articles, objects, things, goods, *n.*

sìng-wɛ̂ɛt-lɔ́ɔm สิ่งแวดล้อม surrounding, environment, *n.*

sǐn-káa สินค้า goods, *n.*

sǐn-lá-bpà ศิลป art, *n.*

sǐn-lá-bpà-gam ศิลปกรรม art work, *n.*

sǐn-lá-bpà-gɔɔn ศิลปกร artist, *n.*

sǐn-lá-bpin ศิลปิน artist, *n.*

sǐn-sɔ̀ɔt สินสอด dowry, *n.*

sǐn-tao สินเธาว์ rock salt, *n.*

sìp สิบ ten, *nm.*

sì-rì-mong-kon สิริมงคล luck, prosperity, *n.*

sìt ศิษย์ pupil, student, disciple, *n.*

sìt-tǐ สิทธิ right, privilege, *n.*

sìt-tǐ-bàt สิทธิบัตร patent, *n.*

sǐu สิว chisel, *n.*

sǐu สิว pimple, acne, *n.*

sì-wá ศิวะ the god of construction, *n.*

sì-wí-lai ศิวิไลซ์ civilization, *n.*

sòk ศก hair, *n.*

sòk ศก year, years, era, *n.*

sòk-gà-pròk สกปรก dirty, filthy, *adj.*

sôm ส้ม orange, *n.*

sǒm สม suitable, appropriate, *adj.*

sǒm-bàt สมบัติ property, wealth, possession, *n.*

sǒm-bùk-sǒm-ban สมบุกสมบัน confront difficulties, *v.*

sǒm-buun สมบูรณ์ perfect, complete, absolute, full, *adj.*

sǒm-buu-ra-naa-yaa-sìt-tì-râat สมบูรณาญาสิทธิราช absolute monarchy, *n.*

sǒm-dèt สมเด็จ abbot, great one, a title of high rank of a Buddhist monk, *n.*

sòm-dtam ส้มตำ a kind of Thai salad made of sliced green papaya, *n.*

sǒm-jing สมจริง truthful, *adj.*

sôm-kǐao-wǎan ส้มเขียวหวาน tangerine, *n.*

sǒm-mâat สมมาตร symmetry, *n.*

sǒm-má-naa สมนา repay, *v.*

sǒm-má-naa-kun สมนาคุณ return thanks, *v.*

sǒm-mút สมมติ suppose, *v.*

sǒm-mút สมมติ hypothesis, *n.*

sǒm-mút-dtì-tǎan สมมติฐาน hypothesis, *n.*

sǒm-mút-dtì-têep สมมติเทพ supposed deity, *n.*

sǒm-náam-nâa สมน้ำหน้า serve (somebody) right, *v.*

sôm-oo ส้มโอ pomelo, *n.*

sǒm-paan สมภาร abbot, *n.*

sŏm-pôot สมโภช celebration, *n.*

sŏm-póp สมภพ birth, *n.*

sŏm-rúu-rûam-kìt สมรู้ร่วมคิด conspire, *v.*

sŏm-sùu สมสู่ have sexual intercourse, *v.*

sŏm-wai สมวัย suitable for the age, *adj.*

sŏm-yaa สมญา fame, renown, *n.*

son ซน mischievous, naughty, *adj.*

sôn ส้น heel, *n.*

sŏn สน pine, pine tree, *n.*

song ทรง form, figure, *n.*

sòng ส่ง pass, hand, send, deliver, ship, *v.*

sŏng สงฆ์ priest, monk, *n.*

sŏng-graan สงกรานต์ Thai New Year, Songkran Day, *n.*

sŏng-kraam สงคราม war, battle, *n.*

sŏng-krɔ́ สงเคราะห์ help, assist, *v.*

sŏng-náam สรงน้ำ bathe, *v.*

sŏng-săan สงสาร pity, have pity on, sympathize with, *v.*

sŏng-săi สงสัย doubt, doubtful, *v.*, *adj.*

sŏn-jai สนใจ pay attention, *v.*

sôn-sǔung ส้นสูง high heels, *n.*

sôn-táao ส้นเท้า heel, *n.*

sŏn-tá-naa สนทนา converse, *v.*

sŏn-tá-yaa สนธยา twilight, *n.*

sŏn-têe สนเท่ห์ doubtful, *adj.*

sŏn-têet สนเทศ news, information, *n.*

sŏn-tí สนธิ junction, connection, union, joint, intercourse, *n.*

soo โซ needy, poor, penniless, *adj.*

sôo โซ่ chain, *n.*

sôo-daa โสดา listener, *n.*

sôo-gaa โศกา cry, weep, *v.*

sòok โศก sorrow, grief, *n.*

sòo-krôok โสโครก dirty, filthy, *adj.*

soom โทรม ruined, destroyed, *adj.*

sŏom โสม ginseng, *n.*

sŏom-ma-nát โสมนัส glad, *adj.*

sŏo-mom โสมม dirty, filthy, *adj.*

sŏo-paa โสภา beautiful, *adj.*

sòot โสด single, unmarried, *adj.*

sòot โสต organ of hearing, *n.*

sòp ศพ corpse, *n.*

sóp ซบ rest (one's face on), *v.*

sòp-bprà-màat สบประมาท insult, *v.*

sòp-dtaa สบตา meet the eyes of, *v.*

sóp-sao ซบเซา depressed, dull, *adj.*

sòt สด fresh, green, *adj.*

sót ซด sip, *v.*

sòt-chûun สดชื่น fresh, joyful, *adj.*

sòt-săi สดใส bright, *adj.*

a b bp ch d dt e ɛ ə f g h i j k l m n ng o ɔ p r s t u ʉ w y

sɔ̀ เสาะ seek, search for, v.

sɔ̂i สร้อย necklace, n.

mɔ̂m ซ่อม renovate, repair, mend, restore, v.

mɔ̂m ส้อม fork, n.

sɔm-sɔ̂ ซอมซ่อ shabby, adj.

sɔ̂n ซ่อน hide, conceal, v.

sɔ̀ng ส่อง shine, throw light upon, look in a mirror, v.

sɔ̌ng ซ่อง brothel, whore house, n.

sɔ̂n-hǎa ซ่อนหา hide-and-seek, n.

sɔ̂n-rén ซ่อนเร้น conceal, hide, v.

sɔɔ ซอ fiddle (musical instrument), n.

sɔ̀ɔ ส่อ indicate, reveal, v.

sɔɔi ซอย divide into pieces, v.

sɔɔi ซอย lane, Soi, n.

sɔ̌ɔi สอย hem, stitch, v.

sɔ̀ɔk ศอก elbow, n.

sɔ̂ɔk ซอก lane, alley, n.

sɔ́ɔm ซ้อม exercise, practice, train, drill, v.

sɔ́ɔn ซ้อน overlap, v.

sɔ̌ɔn ศร arrow, n.

sɔ̌ɔn สอน teach, instruct, train, v.

sɔɔng ซอง envelope, case, sheath, n.

sɔ̌ɔng สอง two, twin, adj.

sɔ̀ɔp สอบ examine, test, v.

sɔ̌ɔ-plɔɔ สอพลอ flatter, v.

sɔ̀ɔ-sìat ส่อเสียด stimulate, v.

sɔ̀ɔt สอด insert, v.

suai ซวย unlucky, adj.

sǔai ส่วย tribute, n.

sǔai สวย beautiful, pretty, lovely, attractive, adj.

sûam ส้วม water closet, toilet, n.

sǔam สวม put on, wear, v.

sùan ส่วน part, share, portion, n.

sǔan สรวล laugh, smile, v.

sǔan สวน garden, n.

sǔan สวน encounter, pass in opposite positions, v.

sùan-bprà-gɔ̀ɔp ส่วนประกอบ component, n.

suang ทรวง breast, n.

suang-òk ทรวงอก bosom, n.

sǔan-sàt สวนสัตว์ zoo, n.

sùat สวด chant, v.

sù-bpà-dtì-bpan-noo สุปฏิบันโน well-behaved person, Buddhist monk, n.

sù-jà-rìt สุจริต honest, adj.

sùk ศุกร์ planet Venus, Friday, n.

sùk สุก ripe, adj.

sùk สุข well, happy, content, adj.

sùk สุข happiness, pleasure, n.

súk ซุก hide, conceal, v.

sù-kǎa สุขา water closet, *n.*

sù-kǎa-pí-baan สุขาภิบาล sanitation, *n.*

sù-kà-dtì สุคติ happiness, bliss heaven, *n.*

sù-kǐi สุขี happy, *adj.*

sùk-kà-pâap สุขภาพ health, *n.*

sùk-kà-sùk-sǎa สุขศึกษา health education, *n.*

sùk-sǎi สุกใส bright, *adj.*

súk-son ซุกซน mischievous, naughty, *adj.*

súk-sôn ซุกซ่อน hide, conceal, *adj.*

sù-kǔm สุขุม prudent, thoughtful, *adj.*

sùm สุ่ม chicken coop, *n.*

sùm สุ่ม make a wild guess, *v.*

sûm ซุ่ม lie in ambush, *v.*

súm ซุ้ม archway, *n.*

sǔm สุม pile up, *v.*

súm-bprà-dtuu ซุ้มประตู porch, window facade, *n.*

sǔm-sâam ซุ่มซ่าม careless, *adj.*

sûm-sôn ซุ่มซ่อน hide, *v.*

sù-nák สุนัข dog, *n.*

sung ซุง log, lumber, timber, *n.*

sung-sǐng สูงสิ่ง associate, *v.*

sǔn-lá-gaa-gɔɔn ศุลกากร customs, *n.*

sǔn-ta-rii สุนทรี beautiful, *adj.*

sǔn-tɔɔn สุนทร words, *n.*

sǔn-tɔɔ-ra-pót สุนทรพจน์ speech, *n.*

sù-pâap สุภาพ polite, gentle, *adj.*

sù-paa-sìt สุภาษิต proverb, *n.*

súp-síp ซุบซิบ whisper, *v.*

sù-raa สุรา liquors, spirits, *n.*

sù-rào สุเหร่า mosque, *n.*

sù-ri-yá สุริยะ the sun, *n.*

sù-ri-yá-jàk-grà-waan สุริยจักรวาล the Solar system, *n.*

sù-ri-yú-bpà-raa-kaa สุริยุปราคา solar eclipse, *n.*

sù-rûi-sù-râai สุรุ่ยสุร่าย extravagant, *adj.*

sùt สุด extreme, last, highest, *adj.*

sút ทรุด get worse, *v.*

sù-têep สุเทพ good deity, *n.*

sùt-tì สุทธิ purity, total, *n.*

sùt-yɔɔt สุดยอด top, *n.*

sùu สู่ get to, reach, arrive at, *v.*

sûu สู้ fight, struggle, *v.*

sǔu-dtì-bàt สูติบัตร birth certificate, *n.*

sǔu-dtì-wêet สูติเวช obstetrics, *n.*

sǔu-jì-bàt สูจิบัตร program, *n.*

sùu-kɔ̌ɔ สู่ขอ ask a girl to marry, *v.*

sǔun สูญ vanish, *v.*

sǔun ศูนย์ center, zero, *n.*

sǔun-bplàao สูญเปล่า wasteful, *adj.*

sǔung สูง high, tall, *adj.*

sǔun-sǐa สูญเสีย lost, *adj.*

sùup สูบ pump, inflate, *v.*

sûup ซูบ pale, *adj.*

sùup-bù-rìi สูบบุหรี่ smoke cigarette, *v.*

sûup-pɔɔm ซูบผอม pale and skinny, *adj.*

sûup-sìit ซูบซีด emaciated and pale, *adj.*

sùu-rúu สู่รู้ know conjointly, *v.*

sùut สูด inhale, *v.*

sùut สูตร formula, *n.*

sùut สูติ birth, *n.*

sù-wan สุวรรณ gold, *n.*

sɯ̀a เสื่อ mat, *n.*

sɯ̂a เสื้อ coat, cloak, jacket, shirt, upper garment, *n.*

sɯ̌a เสือ tiger, *n.*

sɯ̂a-chán-nai เสื้อชั้นใน undergarment, *n.*

sɯ̀ak เสือก push, intrude, butt in, *v.*

sɯ̀am เสื่อม deteriorate, *v.*

sɯ̀am-saam เสื่อมทราม get worse, deteriorate, *v.*

sɯ̂ang-sɯm เซื่องซึม inactive and drowsy, *adj.*

sɯ̂a-nɔɔk เสื้อนอก overcoat, jacket, *n.*

sɯ̂a-pâa เสื้อผ้า clothes, *n.*

sɯ̀k ศึก battle, war, *n.*

sɯ̀k สึก disrobe, *v.*

sɯ̀k-sǎa ศึกษา study, *v.*

sɯm ซึม permeate, drowsy, sluggish, *v., adj.*

sɯm-sâap ซึมซาบ permeate, *v.*

sɯm-sao ซึมเซา drowsy, dull, *adj.*

sɯ̂ng ซึ่ง which, that, who, whose, whom, *pron.*

sɯ́ng ซึ้ง deep, profound, *adj.*

sɯ́ng-jai ซึ้งใจ impressive, *adj.*

sɯ̀ɯ สื่อ go-between, liaison, *n.*

sɯ̂ɯ ซื่อ honest, truthful, *adj.*

sɯ́ɯ ซื้อ buy, purchase, *n.*

sɯ̂ɯ-dtrong ซื่อตรง honest, faithful, *adj.*

sɯ́ɯ-kǎai ซื้อขาย trade, *v.*

sɯ̀ɯ-muan-chon สื่อมวลชน mass media, *n.*

sɯ̀ɯp สืบ succeed, search for the facts, examine, *v.*

sɯ̀ɯp-sǔan สืบสวน investigate, *v.*

sɯ̀ɯ-sǎan สื่อสาร communicate, *v.*

t

(ฐ, ฑ, ฒ, ถ, ท, ธ)

taa ทา apply, smear on, paint, *v.*

tâa ท่า posture, gesture, manner, *n.*

tâa ถ้า if, in case, *conj.*

táa ท้า dare, challenge, *v.*

taai ทาย foretell, *n.*

tàai ถ่าย excrete, transfer, *v.*

táai ท้าย rear, end, *n.*

tàai-èek-gà-sǎan ถ่ายเอกสาร make a copy, *v.*

tàai-pâap ถ่ายภาพ take a picture, *v.*

táai-rʉa ท้ายเรือ stern of a ship or boat, *n.*

tàak ถาก cut in pieces, *v.*

tâak ทาก leech, land leech, *n.*

tàak-tǎang ถากถาง speak ironically, *v.*

tǎam ถาม ask, question, *v.*

tâam-glaang ท่ามกลาง center, *n.*

taan ทาน alms, donation, gift, *n.*

taan ทาน bear, resist, *v.*

taan ธาร stream, *n.*

tàan ถ่าน charcoal, *n.*

tǎan ฐาน base, foot, pedestal, ground, platform, reason, basis, foundation, *n.*

tǎa-ná ฐานะ position, status, *n.*

tǎa-naa-nú-grom ฐานานุกรม ecclesiastical orders, *n.*

tǎa-nan-dɔɔn ฐานันดร rank, title, *n.*

taan-dtà-wan ทานตะวัน sunflower, *n.*

taang ทาง way, path, road, route, means, course, direction, pass, trail, *n.*

tàang ถ่าง spread apart, *v.*

tǎang ถาง clear (a forest), cut away, mow, *v.*

taang-dəən ทางเดิน foot-path, *n.*

taang-gaai ทางกาย physical, bodily, *adj., adv.*

taang-gaan ทางการ official, governmental, *adj.*

taang-glai ทางไกล long distance, *n.*

taang-jai ทางใจ mental, *adj.*

taang-kâo ทางเข้า entrance, *n.*

taang-lôok ทางโลก mundane, worldly, *adj.*

taang-lǔang ทางหลวง public highway, *n.*

taang-nai ทางใน transcendental meditation, *n.*

taang-rót-fai ทางรถไฟ railway, *n.*

taang-tam ทางธรรม religious, *adj.*

taan-kâao ทานข้าว have food, eat, *v.*

taa-nii ธานี city, *n.*

tǎan-táp ฐานทัพ military base, *n.*

táao ท้าว king, ruler, sovereign, *n.*

táao เท้า rest on, prop up, *v.*

táao เท้า foot, feet, *n.*

tâap ทาบ place over, *v.*

taa-rók ทารก infant, *n.*

taa-run ทารุณ torture, ill-treat, *v.*

taa-sǐi ทาสี paint, *v.*

tàat ถาด tray, *n.*

tâat ทาส slave, *n.*

tâat ธาตุ element, chemical element, *n.*

táa-taai ท้าทาย challenge, *v.*

tâat-téɛ ธาตุแท้ real characteristics, *n.*

tǎa-wɔɔn ถาวร permanent, stable, *adj.*

taa-yâat ทายาท heir, heiress, *n.*

tá-bian ทะเบียน record, register, *n.*

tá-bian-bâan ทะเบียนบ้าน census registration, *n.*

tá-buang ทบวง bureau, *n.*

tá-hǎan ทหาร soldier, *n.*

tá-hǎan-aa-gàat ทหารอากาศ air force officer, *n.*

tá-hǎan-bòk ทหารบก army officer, *n.*

tá-hǎan-geen ทหารเกณฑ์ conscript, *n.*

tá-hǎan-rɯa ทหารเรือ naval officer, *n.*

tai ไท freedom, *n.*

tài ไถ่ redeem, purchase back, *v.*

tǎi ไถ plough, *v.*

tàk ถัก braid, knit, *v.*

ták ทัก greet, *v.*

ták-sà ทักษะ capability, skill, *n.*

ták-sǐn ทักษิณ south, *n.*

tà-lǎa ถลา lean to on side, *v.*

tá-laai ทลาย collapse, *v.*

tá-laai ทะลาย tumble down, *v.*

tà-lǎi ไถล slide, skid, *v.*

tá-lák ทะลัก protrude, *v.*

tà-lǎm ถลำ blunder, slip, *v.*

tá-lee ทะเล sea, *n.*

tá-lee-saai ทะเลทราย desert, *n.*

tá-lee-sàap ทะเลสาป lake, *n.*

tà-lěe-tà-lǎi เถลไถล truant, *adj.*

tá-lén ทะเล้น protrude, giggly, *v.*, *adj.*

tà-lɛ̌ɛng แถลง express, *v.*

tà-lə̀əng เถลิง   rise, ascend, *v.*

tà-lòk ถลก   roll up, *v.*

tà-lòm ถล่ม   collapse, subside, *v.*

tá-lɔ̌n ถลน   protrude, *v.*

tá-lɔ́ ทะเลาะ   quarrel, dispute, *v.*

tá-lɔ̀ɔk ถลอก   scraped, *adj.*

tá-lú ทะลุ   pierced through, *adj.*

tá-luaŋ ทะลวง   hollow out, *v.*

tà-lǔŋ ถลุง   smelt (ore), spend extravagantly, *v.*

tá-lɯ̂ŋ ทะลึ่ง   soar, intrude, *v.*

tà-lɯ̌ŋ ถลึง   stare fiercely, *v.*

tam ธรรม   Buddhist teaching, Dharma, *n.*

tam ทำ   do, perform, commit, act, *v.*

tâm ถ้ำ   cave, tunnel, *n.*

tá-mát-tá-mɛɛŋ ทะมัดทะแมง   energetic, serious, *adj.*

tam-bàap ทำบาป   sin, *v.*

tam-bun ทำบุญ   make merit, *v.*

tam-dtaam ทำตาม   imitate, *v.*

tam-gàp-kâao ทำกับข้าว   cook, *v.*

tá-min ทมิฬ   Tamil (from India or Ori Lanka), *n.*

tá-min ทมิฬ   vicious, *adj.*

tam-kwǎn ทำขวัญ   make compensation, perform ceremony for strength and encouragement, *v.*

tam-laai ทำลาย   destroy, *v.*

tam-laai-sà-tì-dtì ทำลายสถิต   break a record, *v.*

tam-lee ทำเล   location, *n.*

tam-mai ทำไม   why, *adv.*

tam-naa ทำนา   grow rice, *v.*

tam-naai ทำนาย   predict, foretell, *v.*

tam-nâa-tîi ทำหน้าที่   do duty, *v.*

tam-nao ทำเนา   slacken, relieve, *v.*

tam-ŋaan ทำงาน   work, *v.*

tam-nîap ทำเนียบ   official residence of a high-ranking official, *n.*

tam-nîap-kaao ทำเนียบขาว   White House, *n.*

tam-nîap-rát-tà-baan ทำเนียบรัฐบาล   prime minister's residence, *n.*

tam-nóp ทำนบ   dam, dike, *n.*

tam-nɔɔŋ ทำนอง   manner, way, melody, *n.*

tam-nú-bam-ruŋ ทำนุบำรุง   nourish, maintain, *v.*

ta-moon ทโมน   big monkey, mischievous child, *n.*

ta-moon ทะโมน   high and large, *adj.*

tam-tâa ทำท่า   strike a pose, *v.*

tam-tôot ทำโทษ   punish, *v.*

ta-mɯɯn ทมึน   black, *adj.*

a b bp ch d dt e ɛ ə f g h i j k l m n ŋ o ɔ p r s t u ɯ w y

tà-mǔng ถมึง scowling, *adj.*

tan ทัณฑ์ penalty, *n.*

tan ทัน overtake, catch up, *v.*

tân ท่าน the second and third pronoun, you, he, him, she, her, they, them, *pron.*

tǎn ถัน breast, *n.*

tá-naai ทนาย lawyer, *n.*

tà-nàt ถนัด skilled, dexterous, *adj.*

tan-dai ทันใด promptly, quickly, *adv.*

tan-dtà-pêet ทันตแพทย์ dentist, *n.*

táng ทั้ง whole, entire, *adj., adv., prep.*

tǎng ถัง pail, tank, bucket, *n.*

táng-kûu ทั้งคู่ both, *prep., adv.*

táng-kuun ทั้งคืน all night, *adv.*

táng-nán ทั้งนั้น all the same, *adv.*

táng-sîn ทั้งสิ้น altogether, *adv.*

táng-wan ทั้งวัน the whole day, *adv.*

tan-jai ทันใจ as quickly as desired, *adv.*

tà-nǒn ถนน street, road, *n.*

tá-nong ทะนง arrogant, *adj.*

tà-nɔ̌ɔm ถนอม cherish, conserve, *v.*

tá-nuu ธนู bow, arrow, *n.*

tan-sà-mǎi ทันสมัย modern, *adj.*

tan-waa-kom ธันวาคม December, *n.*

tan-ya-pûut ธัญญพืช cereals, grains, *n.*

tao เทา (color) gray, *adj.*

tâo เท่า equal, equivalent, *adj.*

tâo เฒ่า very old person, chief, person of age, *n.*

tâo เฒ่า aged, very old, *adj.*

tâo เถ้า ashes, *n.*

tǎo เถา vine, creeping plant, *n.*

tâo-gɛ̀ɛ เฒ่าแก่ match-maker, *n.*

táp ทัพ army, fighting forces, *n.*

táp-aa-gàat ทัพอากาศ air force, *n.*

táp-bòk ทัพบก army, *n.*

táp-pii ทัพพี ladle, *n.*

táp-rʉa ทัพเรือ navy, *n.*

táp-tim ทับทิม ruby, pomegranate, *n.*

tàt ถัด next to, *prep., adv.*

tát ทัศน์ vision, view, *n.*

tát-sà-naa ทัศนา look, view, *v.*

tát-sà-ná ทรรศนะ opinion, vision, *n.*

tát-sà-ná-sùk-sǎa ทัศนศึกษา visual education, *n.*

tát-tiam ทัดเทียม equal, *adj.*

ta-wǎai ถวาย present, offer, *v.*

ta-waan ทวาร door, opening, *n.*

ta-wii ทวี two, twice, *adj.*

ta-wii-kuun ทวีคูณ double, two-fold, *adj.*

ta-wîip ทวีป continent, *n.*

tà-wĭn ถวิล long for, *v.*

tá-yaan ทะยาน thrust forward, *v.*

tá-yɛɛng ทแยง oblique, *adj.*

tá-yəə-tá-yaan ทะเยอทะยาน
ambitious, *adj.*

tá-yɔɔi ทยอย come or go in succession, *v.*

tá-yɔɔi ทะยอย follow gradually, *v.*

tee เท pour off, *v.*

têe เท้ elegant, *adj.*

tĕen เถร Buddhist priest, *n.*

têep เทพ god, divine being, *n.*

tee-pii เทพี beautiful lady, *n.*

tee-poo เทโพ a species of catfish, *n.*

têep-pa-bùt เทพบุตร male god, *n.*

têep-pa-nom เทพนม figure of a
deity clasping hands in token of worship, *n.*

têep-tí-daa เทพธิดา goddess, *n.*

têet เทศ foreigner, country, *n.*

têet เทศน์ preach, teach, *v.*

teet-sà-naa เทศนา preach, give a
sermon, *v.*

tee wa daa เทวดา group of gods,
divinity, *n.*

ték-noo-loo-yîi เทคโนโลยี technol-

ogy, *n.*

tem-bpù-rá เทมปุระ a kind of
Japanese food, *n.*

ten-nís, ten-nít เทนนิส tennis, *n.*

tét เท็จ deceptive, untrue, false, *adj.*

té แทะ gnaw on, *v.*

tɛ́ɛ แท้ real, genuine, *adj.*

tɛ̌ɛm แถม add on, *v.*

tɛɛn แทน substitute, replace, represent, *v.*

tɛɛng แทง stab, pierce, *v.*

tɛ̌ɛo แถว row, line, *n.*

tɛ̀ɛp แถบ strip, area, *n.*

tɛ̀ɛp แทบ almost, nearly, *adv.*

ték-sîi แท็กซี่ taxi, *n.*

tên แท่น altar, *n.*

têng แท่ง bar, chunk, *n.*

téng แท้ง have a miscarriage, have
an abortion, *v.*

tə̀ เถอะ an ending particle indicating
suggestion, *part.*

təə เธอ you, he, him, she, her, they,
them, *pron.*

tə̀ək เถิก exposed, rolled up, *adj.*

tə̀ət เถิด a word used to mark a
request or command, *part.*, *adv.*

tə̂ət เทิด hold up, honor, *v.*

tə̀-tá เทอะทะ bulky, *adj.*

tiam เทียม   harness, team up, *v.*

tian เทียน   candle, *n.*

tîang เที่ยง   noon, midday, *n.*

tîang เที่ยง   accurate, precise, exact, *adj.*

tîang เถียง   argue, *v.*

tîang-dtrong เที่ยงตรง   exact, accurate, *adj.*

tîang-kʉʉn เที่ยงคืน   midnight, *n.*

tîang-téɛ เที่ยงแท้   certain, sure, *adj.*

tîang-wan เที่ยงวัน   noon, *n.*

tiao เทียว   go back and forth, *v.*

tiao เที่ยว   promenade, wonder, roam, stroll about, make a pleasure tour, *v.*

tîap เทียบ   compare, *v.*

tí-daa ธิดา   daughter, *n.*

tí-dtì ธิติ   retention, *n.*

tí-dtì ฐิติ   maintenance, existence, status, perpetuity, *n.*

tii ที   time, turn, chance, *n.*

tìi ถี่   frequent, *adj.*

tîi-din ที่ดิน   lot, piece of land, *n.*

tîi-dtâng ที่ตั้ง   location, *n.*

tîi-gəət ที่เกิด   birth-place, *n.*

tîi-jɔ̀ɔt-rót ที่จอดรถ   parking lot, *n.*

tîi-kìa-bù-rìi ที่เขี่ยบุหรี่   ashtray, *n.*

tîi-láang-nâa ที่ล้างหน้า   wash basin, sink, *n.*

tîi-lûm ที่ลุ่ม   basin, *n.*

tîi-maa ที่มา   origin, source, *n.*

tìip ถีบ   kick, pedal, *v.*

tîi-râap-lûm ที่ราบลุ่ม   low plain, basin, *n.*

tîi-râap-sǔung ที่ราบสูง   plateau, *n.*

tîi-râi-tîi-naa ที่ไร่ที่นา   farm, field, rice field *n.*

tîi-rák ที่รัก   darling, dear, *n.*

tîi-sùt ที่สุด   to the end, *adv.*

tîi-tam-ngaan ที่ทำงาน   office, *n.*

tîi-yùu ที่อยู่   address, *n.*

tîm ทิ่ม   prick, thrust, poke, *v.*

tìn ถิ่น   home, locality, town, *n.*

tíng ทิ้ง   throw away, *v.*

típ ทิพย์   supernatural, *adj.*

tít ทิด   one who has just left the Buddhist monkhood, *n.*

tít ทิศ   direction, *n.*

tít-sà-dii ทฤษฎี   theory, *n.*

tiu ทิว   row, line, order, *n.*

tòk ถก   pull, roll up, *v.*

tòm ถ่ม   spit, spout, *v.*

tǒm ถม   fill up, fill in, *v.*

ton ทน   endure, *v.*

tón ท้น   flooded, *adj.*

tong ธง   flag, banner, *n.*

ton-taan ทนทาน   durable, *adj.*

too โท second, two, *adj.*

tôo โธ่ Alas! What a pity!, *interj.*

tǒo โถ water globet, jug, *n.*

tǒom โถม swoop down, *v.*

tǒong โถง spacious, *adj.*

toon-tôo โทนโท่ clear, obvious, apparent, *adj.*

too-rá-ka-ma-naa-kom โทรคมนาคม telecommunications, *n.*

too-ra-sǎan โทรสาร fax, *n.*

too-ra-sàp โทรศัพท์ telephone, *n.*

too-ra-tát โทรทัศน์ television, *n.*

too-sà โทษะ anger, *n.*

tôot โทษ offence, punishment, guilt, *n.*

tóp ทบ fold up, *v.*

tóp-tuan ทบทวน review, *v.*

tòt ถด retreat, move back, *v.*

tót ทศ ten, *n.*

tót-lɔɔng ทดลอง test, *v.*

tɔ̀ เถาะ rabbit, *n.*

tɔ̀m ถ่อม humble, *adj.*

tɔn ท่อน section, part, *n.*

tɔ̀ng ถ่อง clear, vivid, *adj.*

tɔ̂ng ท่อง recite, *v.*

tɔ̂ng-jam ท่องจำ learn by rote, *v.*

tɔn-sin ท่อนซิล tonsil, *n.*

tɔɔ ทอ weave, emit rays, *v.*

tɔ̀ɔ ถ่อ punt, *v.*

tɔ̂ɔ ท่อ duct, tube pipe, *n.*

tɔ́ɔ ท้อ discouraged, *adj.*

tɔ̂ɔ-ai-náam ท่อไอน้ำ steam pipe, *n.*

tɔ̂ɔ-ai-sǐa ท่อไอเสีย exhaust pipe, *n.*

tɔɔi ทอย pitch, *v.*

tɔ̀ɔi ถ่อย mean, *adj.*

tɔ̂ɔi ถ้อย words, *n.*

tɔ̌ɔi ถอย retreat, *v.*

tɔ̀ɔk ถอก draw back, *v.*

tɔɔn ทอน cut, give change, *v.*

tɔ̌ɔn ถอน pull, draw, *v.*

tɔɔng ทอง gold, *n.*

tɔ́ɔng ท้อง stomach, abdomen, *n.*

tɔ́ɔng ท้อง pregnant, *adj.*

tɔ̌ɔng ถอง strike or nudge with the elbow, *v.*

tɔ́ɔng-fáa ท้องฟ้า sky, heavens, *n.*

tɔɔng-kam ทองคำ gold, pure gold, *n.*

tɔ́ɔng-sǐa ท้องเสีย diarrhea, *n.*

tɔ́ɔng-tii ท้องที่ district, locality, *n.*

tɔ́ɔng-tìn ท้องถิ่น district, area, *n.*

tɔ́ɔng-ùut ท้องอืด constipation, *n.*

tɔ̂ɔ-rá-baai-náam ท่อระบายน้ำ drain pipe, *n.*

tɔɔ-ra-chon ทรชน outlaw, *n.*

Phonetic · Thai · English

tɔɔ-ra-hòt ทรหด enduring, *adj.*

tɔɔ-ra-maan ทรมาน torture, *v.*

tɔɔ-ra-nii ธรณี earth, soil, *n.*

tɔɔ-ra-pii ทรัพย์ coconut-shell spoon, ungrateful son or daughter, *n.*

tɔɔ-ra-pít ทรพิษ small-pox, *n.*

tɔɔ-ra-yót ทรยศ betray, *v.*

tɔ̀ɔt ถอด remove, undo, *v.*

tɔ̂ɔt ทอด fry, deep fry, *v.*

tɔ̂ɔt-tíng ทอดทิ้ง discard, abandon, *v.*

tɔ́p-fíi ท็อปฟี่ toffee, *n.*

tùa ถั่ว peas, beans, *n.*

tua ทัวร์ tour, *n.*

tûa ทั่ว total, all, *adj.*

tǔa ถัว average, *v.*

tûa-bpai ทั่วไป all over, in general, *adv.*

tûa-bprà-têet ทั่วประเทศ all over the country, *adv.*

tûai ถ้วย cup, small bowl, *n.*

tûa-lôok ทั่วโลก all over the world, *adv.*

tûam ท่วม flood, overflow, *v.*

tuan ทวน lance, *n.*

tûan ถ้วน complete, entire, *adj.*

tuang ทวง solicit the return of a borrowed article, *v.*

tùang ถ่วง weight, load, *v.*

túang ท้วง protest, *v.*

tûang-tii ท่วงที attitude, manner, *n.*

tuan-lom ทวนลม go against the wind, *v.*

tuan-náam ทวนน้ำ move against the tide, *v.*

tûat ทวด great-grandfather, great-grandmother, *n.*

tûa-tǔng ทั่วถึง all, all over, *adv.*

tú-dong ธุดงค์ pilgrimage, *n.*

tú-dtì-yá ทุติย second class, *n.*

tú-dtì-yá ทุติย second, doubled, *adj.*

tui ทุย oval, irregularly shaped, *adj.*

tǔi ถุย spit, *v.*

tú-jà-rìt ทุจริต dishonesty, *n.*

túk ทุก every, each, all, complete, entire, *adj.*

túk ทุกข์ difficulty, suffering, pain, distress, sorrow, poverty, *n.*

túk-kon ทุกคน everybody, *adv.*

túk-kráng ทุกครั้ง every time, *adv.*

túk-kɯɯn ทุกคืน every night, *adv.*

túk-mɯ̂a ทุกเมื่อ always, *adv.*

túk-tii ทุกที every time, *adv.*

tú-lák-tú-lee ทุลักทุเล difficult, tangled, struggling, *adj., adv.*

tú-lao ทุเลา relieve, alleviate, *v.*

tú-lii ธุลี dust, powder, *n.*

tûm ทุ่ม throw down, *v.*

túm ทุ้ม bass, lowest tone of an instrument, *n.*

tun ทุน capital, fund, *n.*

tûn ทุ่น buoy, float, *n.*

tûn ถุน take just enough of opium or drug, *v.*

tûng ทุ่ง field, plain, *n.*

tǔng ถุง bag, purse, *n.*

tun-gaan-sùk-sǎa ทุนการศึกษา scholarship, *n.*

tûn-gam-lang ทุ่นกำลัง save labor, *v.*

tǔng-muu ถุงมือ glove, *n.*

tǔng-táao ถุงเท้า socks, hose, *n.*

tǔng-yaang-à-naa-mai ถุงยางอนามัย condom, *n.*

tun-na-sáp ทุนทรัพย์ capital, fund, *n.*

tûn-ngən ทุ่นเงิน save money, *v.*

tûn-rɛɛng ทุ่นแรง save labor, save energy, *v.*

tûn-wee-laa ทุ่นเวลา save time, *v.*

túp ทุบ pound, smash, *v.*

túp-pon-la-pâap ทุพพลภาพ disabled, crippled, incapacitated, *adj.*

tú-rá ธุระ business, duty, affair, *n.*

tú-rá-chon ทุรชน villain, *n.*

tú-rá-gan-daan ทุรกันดาร barren, *adj.*

tú-rêet ทุเรศ pitiable, piteous, shameful, obscene, *adj.*

tú-rian ทุเรียน durian, *n.*

tú-ron-tú-raai ทุรนทุราย restless, *adj.*

tûu ทู่ blunt, *v.*

tǔu ถู rub, scrub, *v.*

tùuk ถูก hit, touch, *v.*

tùuk ถูก correct, right, inexpensive, cheap, *adj.*

tùuk-chá-dtaa ถูกชะตา compatible, *adj.*

tùuk-jai ถูกใจ please, *v.*

tùuk-dtɔ̂ng ถูกต้อง correct, right, *adj.*

tuun ทูน hold over the head, *v.*

tûup ธูป incense, joss-stick, *n.*

tûut ทูต ambassador, diplomatic agent, *n.*

tʉak เทือก line, range, *n.*

tʉan เถื่อน illegal, savage, *adj.*

tʉk-ták ทึกทัก presume, take for granted, *v.*

tʉ̂m ทึ่ม dull, stupid, *adj.*

tʉ̂ng ทึ่ง amazed, *adj.*

tǔng ถึง arrive, reach, v.

tǔng-gὲε-gam ถึงแก่กรรม die, v.

tǔng-grà-nán ถึงกระนั้น although, adv., conj.

tǔng-jai ถึงใจ satisfactorily, adv.

tun-túk ทึนทึก old maid, spinster, adj.

túp ทึบ dense, opaque, adj.

tûu ทื่อ blunt, dull, adj.

tǔu ถือ hold, carry, v.

tǔu-dtua ถือตัว conceited, adj.

u (อุ)

ù-baai อุบาย trick, n.

ù-baa-sì-gaa อุบาสิกา devout lay-woman, n.

ù-baa-sòk อุบาสก devout layman, n.

ù-bàat อุบาทว์ wicked, evil, adj.

ù-bàt อุบัติ happen, occur, v.

ù-bàt-dtì-hèet อุบัติเหตุ accident, n.

ù-bèek-kǎa อุเบกขา equanimity, impartiality, n.

ù-bon อุบล lotus, n.

ù-boo-sòt อุโบสถ Buddhist building, n.

ù-bpà-gaa-rá อุปการะ patronize, assist, v.

ù-bpà-gaa-rii อุปการี benefactor, n.

ù-bpà-gɔɔn อุปกรณ์ equipment, apparatus, n.

ù-bpà-maa อุปมา analogy, n.

ù-bpà-naa-yók อุปนายก Vice President, n.

ù-bpà-ní-sǎi อุปนิสัย character, virtue, n.

ù-bpà-pôok อุปโภค consume, v.

ù-bpà-raa-kaa อุปราคา eclipse, n.

ù-bpà-sàk อุปสรรค barrier, obstacle, n.

ù-bpà-sǒm-bòt อุปสมบท ordained as a Buddhist monk, adj.

ù-bpa-taan อุปาทาน bias, prejudice, adhere(nce) to wrong beliefs, n., v.

ù-bpà-tǎm อุปถัมภ์ support, v.

ù-bpàt-chaa อุปัชฌาย์ spiritual teacher, n.

ù-bpà-tûut อุปทูต chargé d'affaires, n.

ù-dom อุดม abundant, plentiful, adj.

ù-dom-ka-dtì อุดมคติ ideal, n.

ù-dom-sùk-sǎa อุดมศึกษา higher education, n.

ù-dɔɔn อุดร the north, n.

ù-dtà-ri อุตริ unconventional, unusual, weird, adj.

ù-jàat อุจาด shameless, lewd, *adj.*

ûm อุ้ม carry in one's arms, *v.*

ù-moong อุโมงค์ tunnel, *n.*

ûm-tɔ́ɔng อุ้มท้อง pregnant, *adj.*

ùn อุ่น warm, *adj.*

un-ná-hà-puum อุณหภูมิ temperature, *n.*

ù-raa อุรา chest, breast, *n.*

ùt อุด plug, *v.*

ùt-dtà-lùt อุตลุด hurried, tumultuous, *adj.*

ù-dtù-ní-yom-wít-ta-yaa อุตุนิยม วิทยา meteorology, *n.*

ùn อุ่น warm, *adj.*

ù-taan อุทาน exclaim, cry out, *v.*

ù-taa-hɔ̌ɔn อุทาหรณ์ example, *n.*

ù-tít อุทิศ dedicate, donate, *v.*

ùt-jaa-rá อุจจาระ feces, *n.*

ùt-nǔn อุดหนุน support, *v.*

ùt-sàa อุตส่าห์ attempt, *v.*

ùt-sǎa-hà อุตสาหะ industry, endeavor, *n.*

ùt-sǎa-hà-gam อุตสาหกรรม industry, *n.*

ù-tai อุทัย rioing oun, *n.*

ù-taa-hɔ̌ɔn อุทาหรณ์ illustration, *n.*

ù-taan อุทาน interjection, exclamation, *n.*

ùt-ta-yaan อุทยาน garden, park, national park, *n.*

ù-tít อุทิศ dedicate, devote, *v.*

ùt-tɔɔn อุทธรณ์ appeal, *v.*

ùt-ûu อุดอู้ stuffy, *adj.*

ùu อู่ dock, harbor, cradle, garage, *n.*

uum อูม swelling, *adj.*

ûu-ngaan อู้งาน work with unnecessary delay, *v.*

ùu-rʉa อู่เรือ dock, *n.*

ùu-rót อู่รถ garage, *n.*

ùut อูฐ camel, *n.*

ʉ (อือ)

ʉ̀a เอื้อ thoughtful, *adj.*

ʉ̂a-fʉ́a เอื้อเฟื้อ help, assist, *v.*

ʉ̂a-fʉ́a-pʉ̀a-pɛ̀ɛ เอื้อเฟื้อเผื่อแผ่ generous, *adj.*

ʉ̀ai เอื่อย slowly, *adv.*

ʉ̂ai เอื้อย eldest sister, eldest child, *n.*

ʉ̀am เอือม fed up, *adj.*

ʉ̂am เอื้อม reach for, *v.*

ʉ̀am-rá-aa เอือมระอา fed up with, *adj.*

ʉ̂an เอื้อน draw out the voice or sounds, *v.*

W (ว, หว)

waa วา Thai measure of length equal to two meters (about 80 inches), *n.*

waa วา stretch both arms fully, *v.*

wâa ว่า say, speak, remark, criticize, scold, *v.*

wâa-dtà-pai วาตภัย disaster from a wind storm, *n.*

wâai ไหว้ salute by placing the hands palm against palm and raising them to the face, *v.*

wǎai หวาย rattan, *n.*

wâai-náam ว่ายน้ำ swim, *v.*

waa-jaa วาจา words, speech, *n.*

waan วาน ask, request, *v.*

wàan หว่าน sow, cast, *v.*

wǎan หวาน sweet, sugary, *adj.*

waang วาง lay, lay down, *v.*

wâang ว่าง empty, unoccupied, vacant, open, *adj.*

wâang-bplàao ว่างเปล่า empty, *adj.*

waang-jai วางใจ confident, *adj.*

wâang-ngaan ว่างงาน unemployed, *adj.*

waang-pləəng วางเพลิง commit arson, *v.*

waan-suun วานซืน the day before yesterday, *n., adv.*

wâap วาบ flashing, glittering, *adj.*

waa-rá วาระ period, time, *n.*

wâat วาด draw, sketch, *v.*

wâat-sà-nǎa วาสนา fate, fortune, *n.*

wáa-wèe ว้าเหว่ lonely, *adj, v.*

wai วัย age, years, *n.*

wai ไว swift, quick, fast, *adj.*

wái ไว้ keep, preserve, conserve, *v.*

wǎi ไหว shake, tremble, *v.*

wai-dtaa-min ไวตามิน vitamin, *n.*

wǎi-dtua ไหวตัว aware, *adj.*

wái-jai ไว้ใจ trust, *v.*

wǎi-príp ไหวพริบ adroitness, *n.*

wá-jii วจี words, speech, language, *n.*

wák วรรค paragraph, space, *n.*

wák-siin วัคซีน vaccine, *n.*

wá-lii วลี phrase, *n.*

wan วรรณ color, *n.*

wan วัน day, day of the week, daytime, date, *n.*

wàn หวั่น fear, shaken, *v., adj.*

wang วัง palace, *n.*

wǎng หวัง hope for, *v.*

wǎng-dii หวังดี have good wishes, *v.*

wá-ni-pók วณิพก beggar, *n.*

wan-na-rôok วัณโรค tuberculosis, *n.*

wáo เว้า speak, talk, (Lao) *v.*

wáo เว้า concave, *adj.*

wáp วับ flashingly, *adv.*

wá-run วรุณ god of rain, *n.*

wàt หวัด cold, *n.*

wát วัด temple, monastery, *n.*

wát วัด measure, *v.*

wát วัตร duty, practice, custom, *n.*

wát-sà-dù วัสดุ material, objects, *n.*

wát-ta-naa วัฒนา grow, proper, *v.*

wát-tù วัตถุ matter, object, *n.*

wa-sǎn วสันต์ spring, *n.*

wee-laa เวลา time, period, *n.*

ween เวร turn, shift, fate, *n.*

wéet-cha-pan เวชภัณฑ์ medical
supplies, *n.*

wéet-cha-sàat เวชศาสตร์ medicine, *n.*

wee-tii เวที stage, *n.*

wéet-mon เวทมนตร์ magic spell, *n.*

wéet-ta-naa เวทนา pity, *v.*

wén เว้น exclude, except, *v.*

wè แหวะ rip open, *v.*

wé แวะ drop in, stop in, *v.*

wèek แหวก penetrate, make one's
way, *v.*

wèek-nɛɛo แหวกแนว abnormal,
adj.

wɛɛn แหวน ring, *n.*

wɛɛng แวง longitude, *n.*

wéeng แว้ง turn back, *v.*

wɛɛo-dtaa แววตา expression of
the eye, *n.*

wɛɛo แวว light, look, sign, *n.*

wêet แวด surround, *v.*

wên แว่น glasses, *n.*

wên-dtaa แว่นตา glasses, *n.*

wèng แหว่ง chipped, partly broken,
adj.

wên-gan-dèet แว่นกันแดด sun
glasses, *n.*

wên-kà-yǎai แว่นขยาย magnifying
glass, *n.*

wɛ̂o แว่ว hear vaguely, *v.*

wian เวียน revolve, circle, *v.*

wìang เหวี่ยง hurl, *v.*

wian-hǔa เวียนหัว dizzy, *adj.*

wian-sǐi-sà เวียนศีรษะ dizzy, *adj.*

wîat-naam เวียดนาม Vietnam, *n.*

wí-bàak วิบาก hardship, obstacle,
obstruction, *n.*

wí-bàt วิบัติ destruction, ruin, calamity, catastrophe, *n.*

wí-bpà-rìt วิปริต change, alternate,

deviate, *v.*

wî-bpàt-sà-naa วิปัสสนา meditation, *n.*

wî-chaa วิชา knowledge, subject, *n.*

wî-dtòk วิตก worry, mediate, *v.*

wî-gaan วิกาล improper time, night time, *n.*

wî-gon วิกล deformed, disfigured, *adj.*

wî-grìt วิกฤต critical, *adj.*

wî-hǎan วิหาร temple, *n.*

wî-hòk วิหค bird, *n.*

wìi หวี่ gnat, *n.*

wǐi หวี comb, *v.*, *n.*

wii-rá-bù-rùt วีรบุรุษ hero, *n.*

wii-rá-sà-dtrii วีรสตรี heroine, *n.*

wǐi-wɛɛɔ วี่แวว trace, clue, *n.*

wî-jaan วิจารณ์ criticize, *v.*

wî-jai วิจัย research, *n.*

wî-krɔ́ วิเคราะห์ analyze, *v.*

wî-lai วิไล beautiful, *adj.*

wî-nâat วินาศ ruined, *adj.*

wî-naa-tii วินาที second, *n.*

wî-nai วินัย discipline, rule, *n.*

wîng วิ่ง run, get busy, *v.*

wing-wian วิงเวียน dizzy, *adj.*

wî-nít-chǎi วินิจฉัย investigate, examine, diagnose, *v.*

win-yaan วิญญาณ soul, mind, *n.*

wî-pâak วิพากษ์ criticize, *v.*

wî-rí-yá วิริยะ diligence, industry, *n.*

wî-run วิรุฬห์ prosperous, *adj.*

wî-sǎa-hà-gìt วิสาหกิจ enterprise, *n.*

wî-sǎa-man วิสามัญ special, extraordinary, *adj.*

wî-sǎa-sà วิสาสะ familiarity, intimacy, *n.*

wî-sǎi วิสัย object of the senses, *n.*

wî-sǎi-tát วิสัยทรรศน์ vision, *n.*

wî-sa-nú วิษณุ protector, Vishnu, *n.*

wî-sǎn-yii-pêet วิสัญญีแพทย์ anesthetist, *n.*

wî-sà-wá-gam วิศวกรรม engineering, *n.*

wî-sà-wá-gɔɔn วิศวกร engineer, *n.*

wî-sèet วิเศษ excellent, *adj.*

wî-sèet วิเศษณ์ predicate, qualifier, adjective, *n.*

wìt หวิด passing near by, nearly, almost, *adj.*

wít-(dtà)-tǎan วิตถาร abnormal, peculiar, queer, strange, *adj.*

wî-tii วิธี way, method, means, *n.*

wî-tǐi วิถี path, route, *n.*

wít-náam วิดน้ำ draw off water, *v.*

wít-ta-yaa วิทยา knowledge, *n.*

wît-ta-yaa-lai วิทยาลัย college, *n.*

wît-ta-yaa-sàat วิทยาศาสตร์ science, *n.*

wît-ta-yú วิทยุ radio, wireless, *n.*

wîu หวิว dizzy, giddy, *adj.*

wí-waa วิวาห์ marriage, wedding, *n.*

wí-wâat วิวาท dispute, *v.*

wí-wêek วิเวก desolation, *n.*

wók วก turn, turn back, *v.*

wók-glàp วกกลับ turn back, return to the starting point, *v.*

won วน whirl, *v.*

wong วง circle, sphere, ring, *n.*

wong วงศ์ lineage, family, dynasty, clan, *n.*

wong-gaan วงการ circle, field, sources, *n.*

wong-gaan-pêet วงการแพทย์ medical circles, *n.*

wong-gòt วงกด maze, *n.*

wong-joon วงจร circuit, *n.*

wong-lép วงเล็บ parenthesis, bracket, *n.*

wong-sǎa-ká-naa-yâat
วงศาคณาญาติ family, lineage, relatives, *n.*

wong-wian วงเวียน circular place, circle, *n.*

won-wian วนเวียน circle, *v.*

woo โว boastful, *adj.*

wòo โหว่ hollowed out, *adj.*

woo-hǎan โวหาร eloquence, *n.*

wooi โวย boisterous, *adj.*

wooi-waai โวยวาย shout, scream, *v.*

wôn ว่อน great herds, *adj.*

wông ว่อง quick, *adj.*

wǒo หวอ open, exposed, *adj.*

wôok วอก Year of the Monkey, *n.*

woon วอน implore, plead, *v.*

woon-kǒo วอนขอ beg for, *v.*

wôot วอด exhausted, ruined, *adj.*

wua วัว cow, cattle, bull, ox, *n.*

wua-kwaai วัวควาย cattle, *n.*

wûn วุ่น confused, busy, *adj.*

wún วุ้น jelly, *n.*

wún-sên วุ้นเส้น vermicelli, *n.*

wút-tì วุฒิ elderly, senior, *adj.*

wút-tì-sà-maa-chík วุฒิสมาชิก senator, *n.*

wút-tì-sà-paa วุฒิสภา senate, *n.*

wùt-wìt หวุดหวิด almost, nearly, narrowly, *adj.*

wûup วูบ disappear instantly, *v.*

wûup-wâap วูบวาบ flashing, *adj.*

wûu-waam วู่วาม act hastily, *v.*

y (ย, ญ, หย, หญ)

yaa ยา medicine, drug, remedy, tobacco, cigarette, *n.*

yàa หย่า divorce, wean, withdraw, *v.*

yâa ย่า paternal grandmother, *n.*

yâa หญ้า grass, *n.*

yaa-fèet ยาแฝด love potion, *n.*

yaa-gan-yung ยากันยุง mosquito repellent, *n.*

yaa-gin ยากิน oral drug, *n.*

yaai ยาย maternal grandmother, old woman, a form of addressing an old woman, *n.*

yáai ย้าย transfer, move, *v.*

yaa-jòk ยาจก beggar, poor person, *n.*

yâak ยาก difficulty, hardness, *n.*

yâak ยาก difficult, *adj.*

yàak-yâi หยากไย่ cobweb, *n.*

yaam ยาม time, hour, occasion, period, watchman, *n.*

yâam ย่าม satchel, sack, bag, *n.*

yǎam หยาม insult, *v.*

yaan ยาน vehicle, carriage, carrier, *n.*

yâan ย่าน region, district, area, *n.*

yaang ยาง resin, rubber, *n.*

yâang ย่าง tread, stride, roast, bake, grill, barbecue, *v.*

yaang-dtèek ยางแตก blow-out, puncture, *n.*

yâang-gâao ย่างก้าว stride, take a slow step, *v.*

yâang-graai ย่างกราย approach, *v.*

yaang-paa-raa ยางพารา rubber tree, *n.*

yaang-tiam ยางเทียม artificial rubber, *n.*

yaang-yùut ยางยืด elastic band, *n.*

yaao ยาว long, stretched, extended, *adj.*

yàap หยาบ rough, rude, *adj.*

yàap-kaai หยาบคาย rude, *adj.*

yàap-yǎam หยาบหยาม contemptuous, scornful, *adj.*

yàat หยาด drop, drip, *n., v.*

yá-hoo-waa ยะโฮวา Jehovah, God, *n.*

yai ใย fiber, web, cobweb, *n.*

yài ใหญ่ big, large, great, *adj.*

yai-dii ใยดี care for, *v.*

yài-dtoo ใหญ่โต huge, enormous, *adj.*

yàk หยัก notch, indent, *v.*

yák ยัก move up and down, *v.*

yák ยักษ์ giant, ogre, demon, *n.*

yák-lài ยักไหล่ shrug, *v.*

yák-yɔ́ɔk ยักยอก embezzle, *v.*

yam ยำ Thai salad, *n.*

yâm ย่ำ tramp upon, *v.*

yám ย้ำ repeat, reaffirm, confirm, emphasize, *v.*

yam-greeng ยำเกรง afraid of, respect, *adj., v.*

ya-mók ยมก the Thai repeat symbol (ๆ), *n.*

yan ยัน support, sustain, *v.*

yan ยันต์ magic design or letters placed or inscribed on a piece of cloth or metal plate, *n.*

yân ยั้น (slang) fear, afraid of, *v., adj.*

yang ยัง remain still, maintain, have, exist, *v.*

yang ยัง yet, still, *adv.*

yang ยัง till, until, as far as, *prep.*

yàng หยั่ง fathom, measure, *v.*

yáng ยั้ง stop, cease, withhold, halt, restrain, *v.*

yao เยา little, weak, light, low, *adj.*

yao เยาว์ young, adolescent, *adj.*

yâo เหย้า dwelling place, *n.*

yáp ยับ creased, crumpled, *adj.*

yáp-yəən ยับเยิน utterly destroyed, completely crushed, *adv.*

yá-sǒo ยโส arrogant, conceited, *adj.*

yée เย้ leaning, *adj.*

yeen เยน yen, *n.*

yee-suu เยซู Jesus Christ, *n.*

yen เย็น evening, dusk, *n.*

yen เย็น cool, cold, *adj.*

yen-chûut เย็นชืด cold, tasteless, *adj.*

yen-jai เย็นใจ calm, *adj.*

yen-wan-níi เย็นวันนี้ this evening, *n.*

yép เย็บ sew, stitch, *v.*

yét เย็ด (very vulgar) fuck, have sexual intercourse, *v.*

yɛ̌ɛ แหย่ insert, poke, tease, provoke, disturb, *v.*

yɛ̂ɛ แย่ in trouble, *adj.*

yɛ́ɛ แย้ a kind of ground lizard, *n.*

yɛ̂ɛk แยก separate, part, divide up, distinguish, *v.*

yɛ́ɛm แย้ม open slightly, *v.*

yɛɛng แยง insert, poke, *v.*

yɛ́ɛng แย้ง oppose, contradict, object, argue, dispute, protest, *v.*

yɛ̂ɛp-yon แยบยล trick, trickery, *n.*

yɛɛ-sɛ̌ɛ แยแส pay attention to, *v.*

yêng แย่ง snatch, grab, seize, *v.*

yə́ เยอะ many, much, abundant, *adj.*

yə́əi เย้ย ridicule, mock, *v.*

yə́əm เยิ้ม oozing, flowing gradually, *adj.*

yəən-yɔɔ เยินยอ praise, flatter, *v.*

yə̀ə-yîng เย่อหยิ่ง proud, arrogant, *adj.*

yôn เยิ่น long, lengthy, *adj.*

yîam เยี่ยม visit, pay a visit, *v.*

yîam-yɔ̂ɔt เยี่ยมยอด excellent, *adj.*

yîam-yuan เยี่ยมเยือน pay a visit, *v.*

yian เยียน visit, *v.*

yîang เยี่ยง model, pattern, *n.*

yìao เหยี่ยว hawk, *n.*

yìao เยี่ยว urine, *n.*

yiao-yaa เยียวยา treat, give medication, *v.*

yìap เหยียบ step on, condemn, *v.*

yìat เหยียด stretch out, despise, *v.*

yǐi ยี two, *adj.*

yǐi หยี squinting, narrow, *adj.*

yǐi-hɔ̂ɔ ยี่ห้อ trade mark, brand, *n.*

yǐi-rà ยี่หระ care about, *v.*

yǐi-ráap ยีราฟ giraffe, *n.*

yǐi-sìp ยี่สิบ twenty, *nm.*

yìk หยิก pinch, nip, *v.*

yìk หยิก curled, wavy, *adj.*

yím ยิ้ม smile, beam, *v.*

yin ยิน hear, *v.*

ying ยิง shoot, fire, *v.*

yìng หยิ่ง proud, haughty, *adj.*

yîng ยิ่ง excessive, profuse, many, much, extreme, *adj.*

yǐng หญิง female, *n.*

yìp หยิบ take hold of, seize, *v.*

yíp ยิบ closely packed, closely woven, *adj.*

yiu ยิว Jew, thrifty, *n.*, *adj.*

yòk หยก jade, *n.*

yók ยก raise, lift, elevate, *v.*

yók-dtua-yàang ยกตัวอย่าง give an example, *v.*

yók-tong-kǎao ยกธงขาว surrender, *v.*

yók-tôot ยกโทษ forgive, *v.*

yom-ma-baan ยมบาล God of Hell, *n.*

yom-ma-lôok ยมโลก world of the dead, *n.*

yom-ma-tûut ยมทูต messenger of death, *n.*

yon ยนต์ machine, engine, *n.*

yôn ย่น shorten, abbreviate, wrinkled, *v.*, *adj.*

yôok โยก rock, shake from side to

side, *v.*

yoo-ká โยคะ yoga, *n.*

yôok-yêek โยกเยก unsteady, *adj.*

yoom โยม Buddhist monk's form of
addressing laymen, *n.*

yoon โยน throw, cast, toss, *v.*

yoong โยง tie to a post, link, connect,
v.

yôong โย่ง lanky, tall and thin, *adj.*

yŏong โหยง nimble, *adj.*

yoo-taa โยธา troop, soldier, construction work, *n.*

yoo-tin โยธิน warrior, winner, *n.*

yóo-yée โย้เย้ leaning, not straight,
adj.

yòt หยด drop, *v.*

yót ยศ rank, dignity, *n.*

yôi ย่อย digest, crush, dissolve, *v.*

yôi ย่อย minor, small, unimportant,
insignificant, subordinate, *adj.*

yôi ย่อย enzyme, digestive juice, *n.*

yôi-aa-hǎan ย่อยอาหาร digest, *v.*

yôi-yáp ย่อยยับ crushed, *adj.*

yôm หย่อม cluster, *n.*

yôm-yém หยอมแหยม sparse, *adj.*

yòn หย่อน decrease, lower, *v.*

yông ย่อง walk quietly, creep up,
walk on tiptoes, *v.*

yòn-jai หย่อนใจ relax, *adj.*

yɔɔ ยอ praise, extol, *v.*

yɔ̂ɔ ย่อ abridge, shorten, abbreviate, *v.*

yɔ̂ɔ-dtua ย่อตัว lower oneself, *v.*

yɔ́ɔi ย้อย drop, hang down, *v.*

yɔ̀ɔk หยอก jest, joke, *v.*

yɔ̀ɔk-lɔ́ɔ หยอกล้อ tease, *v.*

yɔ̂ɔ-kwaam ย่อความ abbreviate,
summarize, *v.*

yɔɔm ยอม allow, let, agree, permit, *v.*

yɔ́ɔm ย้อม dye, *v.*

yɔ́ɔm-jai ย้อมใจ comfort, console, *v.*

yɔɔm-kwaam ยอมความ compromise in a legal case, *v.*

yɔɔm-ráp ยอมรับ admit, agree, *v.*

yɔ́ɔn ย้อน return, come back, retrace
one's steps, *v.*

yɔ̀ɔt หยอด drop, *v.*

yɔ̂ɔt ยอด top, peak, summit, total, *n.*

yɔ̂ɔt-kǎo ยอดเขา mountain top, *n.*

yɔ̂ɔ-tɔ́ɔ ย่อท้อ discouraged, *adj.*

yɔ̂ɔt-yîam ยอดเยี่ยม excellent, *adj.*

yɔ́-yə́əi เยาะเย้ย ridicule, *v*

yú ยุ stimulate, provoke, *v.*

yûa ยั่ว tease, provoke, tempt, excite,
irritate, *v.*

yúa ยั้วะ hot tempered, *adj.*

yûa-jai ยั่วใจ arouse desire, tempt, *v.*

yùak หยวก soft herbaceous stalk, *n.*

yuan ยวน stimulate, arouse, *v.*

yûap ยวบ sink deeper, *v.*

yûa-too-sà ยั่วโทสะ provoke anger, irritate, *v.*

yûat-yaan ยวดยาน vehicle, *n.*

yûa-yuan ยั่วยวน tempt, provoke, allure, entice, *v.*

yú-dtì ยุติ terminate, end, *v.*

yú-dtì-tam ยุติธรรม justice, fairness, *n.*

yûi ยุ่ย tender, fragile, *adj.*

yúi ยุ้ย plump, inflated, *adj.*

yúk ยุค era, time, age, period, *n.*

yûm-yâam ยุ่มย่าม disorderly, tangled, *adj.*

yǔm-yǐm หยุมหยิม petty, trivial, *adj.*

yung ยุง mosquito, *n.*

yûng ยุ่ง entangled, confusing, busy, *adj.*

yúng ยุ้ง barn, *n.*

yûng-yâak ยุ่งยาก very difficult, very complicated, *adj.*

yú-ròop ยุโรป Europe, *n.*

yúp ยุบ sink, diminish in size, *v.*

yúp-sa-paa ยุบสภา dissolve parliament, *v.*

yúp-yíp ยุบยิบ fussy, too detailed,

fastidious, *adj.*

yùt หยุด stop, cease, *v.*

yút ยุทธ battle, war, *n.*

yùt-pák หยุดพัก rest, *v.*

yút-ta-puum ยุทธภูมิ battlefield, *n.*

yút-ta-sàat ยุทธศาสตร์ strategy, *n.*

yút-too-bpà-gɔɔn ยุทโธปกรณ์ war material, *n.*

yuung ยูง peacock, *n.*

yûu-yîi ยู่ยี่ shrunkened, wrinkled, *adj.*

yú-wá ยุว young man, lad, *n.*

yʉ̀a เหยื่อ prey, bait, victim, *n.*

yʉ̂a เยื่อ tissue, fiber, film, *n.*

yʉ̀ak เหยือก pitcher, jug, *n.*

yʉ̂ak เยือก piercingly cold, *adv.*

yʉʉan เยือน visit, pay a visit, *v.*

yʉ́ang เยื้อง deviate from, walk slowly with an air, *v.*

yʉ́t ยึด hold, seize, *v.*

yʉ́ʉ ยื้อ take by force, *v.*

yʉʉm ยืม borrow, *v.*

yʉʉn ยืน stand, insist, *n.*

yʉ̂ʉn ยื่น extend, hand out, *v.*

yʉʉn-yan ยืนยัน confirm, *v.*

yʉ̂ʉt ยืด stretch, extend, *v.*

yʉ̂ʉt-yʉ́a ยืดเยื้อ prolong, prolonged, *v., adj.*

SECTION 3 THAI-PHONETIC-ENGLISH

THAI DICTIONARY ORDER

When you look up words in a Thai dictionary, every syllable begins with a consonant or consonant cluster followed by a vowel. The final consonant, if there is one, comes last. In multi-syllabic words this dictionary order is repeated with each following syllable. Since every syllable must start with a consonant, the silent consonant อ is used as a marker for syllables that begin with a vowel sound. Some vowels are written in front of the initial consonant. This, however, does not change the dictionary order of consonant first, vowel next. In the case of initial consonant clusters, both consonants come before the vowel in dictionary order. ฤ and ฦๅ are commonly classified as vowels, but for the purpose of dictionary order they are considered consonants. When words are spelled the same except for tone marks, the word with no tone marks will come first, followed by mái èek (˘), mái too (˘), mái dtrii (˘) and mái jàt-dtà-waa (˘) respectively. For the order of the vowels, please see the section "Thai Writing System" in the front of the dictionary.

ก

ก gɔɔ the first consonant of the Thai alphabet (mid consonant), *n.*

ก็ gɔ̂ɔ also, too, *adv.*

ก็ดี gɔ̂ɔ-dii quite good, good enough, *adv.*

ก็ได้ gɔ̂ɔ-dâai possibly, can also, may, *adv.*

กก gòk cuddle, sit or lie on (so as to cover), throw an arm over, *n.*

กงสุล gong-sǔn consul., *n.*

ก้น gôn the bottom (of anything), *n.*

กบ gòp frog, carpenter's plane, *n.*

ก้ม gôm bend (over), stoop, bow (the head) *v.*

กรกฎาคม gà-rák-gà-daa-kom, gɔɔ-rák-gà-daa-kom July, *n.*

กรง grong cage, (prison) cell, *n.*

กรณี gɔɔ-ra-nii, ga-ra-nii case, incident, circumstances, causes, *n.*

กรด gròt acid, *n.*

กรน gron snore, *v.*

กรรไกร gan-grai scissors, *n.*

กรวด grùat pebbles, gravel, *n.*

กรอก grɔ̀ɔk fill with, pour into, fill, fill in (a blank form, an application), *v.*

กรอง grɔɔng filter, strain, sort, *v.*

กรอบ grɔ̀ɔp frame, border, edge, *n.*

กรอบ grɔ̀ɔp crispy, fragile, *adj.*

กระจก grà-jòk mirror, glass, *n.*

กระจาด grà-jàat a deep tray or basket, *n.*

กระจาย grà-jaai scatter, spread, broadcast, be dispersed, *v.*

กระฉอก grà-chɔ̀ɔk spill over, shake, splash out, *v.*

กระชับ grà-cháp tight, fastened firmly, *adj.*,

กระซิบ grà-síp whisper, *v.*

กระดาน grà-daan board, *n.*

กระดานดำ grà-daan-dam blackboard, *n.*

กระดาษ grà-dàat paper, *n.*

กระดาษชำระ grà-dàat-cham-rá toilet paper, *n.*

กระดุม grà-dum button, *n.*

กระดูก grà-dùuk bone (of person, animal, but not fish), *n.*

กระดูก grà-dùuk tough, stingy, *adj.*

กระโดด grà-dòot jump, leap, hop, *v.*

กระได grà-dai stairs, ladder, *n*

กระต่าย grà-dtàai rabbit, hare, *n.*

กระต่าย grà-dtàai a coconut grater, *n.*

ก ข ฃ ค ฅ ฆ ง จ ฉ ช ซ ฌ ญ ฎ ฏ ฐ ฑ ฒ ณ ด ต ถ ท

กระติก grà-dtìk water flask, canteen, thermos bottle, *n.*

กระตุ้น grà-dtûn stimulate, encourage, urge, push, *v.*

กระถาง grà-tǎang pitcher, earthen flower-pot, metal pot, *n.*

กระโถน grà-tǒon spittoon, *n.*

กระทง grà-tong count (in an indictment), a section, clause (of a text), *n.*

กระทง grà-tong a small tray made of banana leaves, paper, etc., *n.*

กระทบ grà-tóp strike, strike against, collide with, hit, effect, *v.*

กระท่อม grà-tôm hut, cottage, *n.*

กระทันหัน grà-tan-hǎn sudden, abrupt, *adj.*

กระทำ grà-tam perform, do, make, act, bring about, *v.*

กระเทียม grà-tiam garlic, *n.*

กระเทือน grà-tuan shake, effect, *v.*

กระแทก grà-têɛk hit, collide with, hit against, dash violently against, *v.*

กระบอก grà-bɔ̀ɔk cylinder, *n.*

กระบอง grà-bɔɔng club, baton, staff, stick, *n.*

กระบะ grà-bà small wooden tray, *n.*

กระเบื้อง grà-bûang tile, roof-tile, *n.*

กระป๋อง grà-bpɔ̌ng tin, can, *n.*

กระโปรง grà-bproong skirt, hood, *n.*

กระรอก grà-rɔ̂ɔk squirrel, *n.*

กระสุน grà-sǔn bullet, *n.*

กรัม gram gram, *n.*

กริ่ง grìng bell, buzzer, *n.*

กลม glom round, circular, *adj.*

กล้วย glûai banana, *n.*

กลอง glɔɔng drum, *n.*

กล่อง glòng box, case, *n.*, *clf.*

กล้อง glông pipe, camera, binoculars, opera glass, *n.*

กลอน glɔɔn bolt, latch, *n.*

กลอน glɔɔn a Thai verse form, *n.*

กลั่น glàn distill, extract, *v.*

กลับ glàp turn back, change back to, return, turn around, reverse, turn over, turn upside down, turn inside out, *v.*

กลัว glua fear, afraid of, dread, apprehensive, *v.*, *adj.*

กล้า glâa brave, bold, dare, venturous, strong, powerful, *adj.*

กลาง glaang center, medium, middle, *n.*

กลาง glaang central, middle, moderate, intermediate, mean, *adj.*

กล้าม glâam muscle, *n.*

กลิ้ง glîng roll, v.

กลิ่น glìn odor, scent, smell, n.

กลืน gluun swallow, devour, match in color, v.

กลุ่ม glùm cluster, aggregation, group, crowd, bundle, collection, assemblage, body, n.

กลุ้ม glûm worried, depressed, mentally confused, vexed, darkened, gloomy, adj.

กวน guan stir, stir up, trouble, bother, disturb, v.

ก๋วยเตี๋ยว gǔai-dtiao rice noodles, n.

กว่า gwàa more (to a greater degree), more than, adv.

กวาง gwaang deer, n.

กว้าง gwâang wide, broad, expansive, roomy, spacious, large, ample, adj.

กวาด gwàat sweep, remove, v.

กอ gɔɔ clump, crowd, group, pack, stalks, n.

ก่อ gɔ̀ɔ start, create, originate, instigate, incite, v.

ก่อสร้าง gɔ̀ɔ-sâang build, construct, v.

ก๊อก gɔ́k faucet, tap, cock, n.

กอง gɔɔng troop, force, pile, heap, n.

กอด gɔ̀ɔt embrace, hug, caress, v.

ก่อน gɔ̀ɔn previous, first (before doing something else), formerly, previously, last, past, ahead, adj, adv.

ก่อนหน้า gɔ̀ɔn-nâa prior to, before, prep.

ก้อน gɔ̂ɔn lump, mass, piece, round, chunk, morsel, rock, sum(s), n.

ก้อนหิน gɔ̂ɔn-hǐn stone, rock, n.

กะทะ gà-tá frying pan, skillet, n.

กะเทย gà-tɔɔi hermaphrodite, transvestite, gay man, n.

กะทิ gà-tí coconut milk, n.

กะเพรา gà-prao basil, n.

กะละมัง gà-la-mang enameled bowl or basin, n.

กะลา gà-laa hard shell of the coconut, half of a coconut shell, n.

กะโหลก gà-lòok skull, cranium, hard shell of the coconut, n.

กังวล gang-won worry, v.

กัด gàt bite, corrode, nibble, nip, eat away (by chemical action), erode, attack, betray, v.

กัน gan prevent, v.

กัน gan each other, mutual, adv., adj.

กั้น gân cut off (by coming in between), shut off, bar, block, shelter, cover, v.

กันยายน gan-yaa-yon September, *n.*

กับ gàp with (in the sense of "accompanying"), together with, accompanied by, and, *conj., prep.*

กับ gàp food, dishes on condiments eaten with rice, *n.*

กา gaa crow, *n.*

กา gaa teapot, kettle, *n.*

กา gaa mark with +, x, or a check *v.*

กาก gàak refuse, leavings, residue, *n.*

กาง gaang spread out, hang out, expand, open, spreading, apart, *v., adj.*

กางเกง gaang-geeng pants, trousers, shorts, *n.*

ก้าง gâang fish-bone, *n.*

ก้าน gâan stem, stalk, twig, *n.*

กาแฟ gaa-fɛɛ coffee, coffee tree, *n.*

กาม gaam sexual desire, lust, karma, sensuality, *n.*

กามโรค gaam-ma-rôok venereal disease, *n.*

ก้าม gâam claw, pincer (of lobster or crab), *n.*

กาย gaai body, physical form, *n.*

การ gaan work, affair(s), matter(s), act, action, task, employment, doer, maker, business bureau, office, *n.*

การขาย gaan-kǎai selling, *n.*

การต่อสู้ gaan-dtɔ̀ɔ-sûu fight, struggle, *n.*

การทดลอง gaan-tót-lɔɔng experiment, *n.*

การทะเลาะ gaan-tá-lɔ́ quarrel, *n.*

การบรรยาย gaan-ban-yaai lecture, *n.*

การบิน gaan-bin aviation, flying, *n.*

การประชุม gaan-bprà-chum meeting, conference, session, *n.*

การ์ด gáat card, *n.*

กาว gaao glue, *n.*

ก้าว gâao step, pace, *n.*

ก้าว gâao step, take a step, *v.*

ก๊าส gáat, gáas kerosene, *n.*

กำ gam hold tightly in the hand, grasp, clinch the fingers or the fist, *v.*

กำ gam handful, bunch (as of vegetables), package, bundle, *n.*

กำมือ gam-muu clench the hand, *v.*

กำมือ gam-muu grip, clutch, *n.*

กำกับ gam-gàp direct, control, supervise, accompany, go with, *v.*

กำจัด gam-jàt expel, drive away, eliminate, get rid of, extinguish, *v.*

กำนัน gam-nan village elder, sub-district headman, *n.*

กำนัล gam-nan give a present, *v.*

กำเนิด gam-nòət birth, origin, race, *n.*

กำเนิด gam-nòət be born, bring forth, *v.*

กำบัง gam-bang obstruct, shield, cover, shelter, veil, *v.*

กำบัง gam-bang shelter, *n.*

กำพร้า gam-práa epidermis, cuticle, the outer layer of skin, *n.*

กำพร้า gam-práa be bereaved of (one's parent or parents), *v.*

กำแพง gam-pɛɛng wall (surrounding a town, a temple), *n.*

กำมะถัน gam-ma-tǎn sulfur, *n.*

กำยำ gam-yam large, big and strong, muscular, well-built, massive, *adj.*

กำไร gam-rai profit, gain, benefit, advantage, fruits, profitable, remunerative, accruing, *n., adj.*

กำลัง gam-lang strength, force, power, energy, vigor, capacity, *n.*

กำลัง gam-lang progressive adverb indicating action going on or state prevailing at a given time, *adv.*

กำไล gam-lai bracelet, anklet, *n.*

กำหนด gam-nòt limit (of time), schedule, act, law, rule, *n.*

กำหนด gam-nòt limit, set, stipulate, fix, appoint, assign, degree, estimate, schedule, *v.*

กิ่ง gìng branch, twig, branch (as a knowledge), *n.*

กิน gin eat, consume, take (food, drink, medicine), denude, be eaten, take up space, use up, win (a game), be worn away, *v.*

กิน gin corruption, corrupt, *n., v., colltq.*

กินข้าว gin-kâao eat (esp. with reference to eating one's meal), *v.*

กินยา gin-yaa take a medicine, *v.*

กิโล gì-loo kilo (i.e. kilogram, kilometer), *n., clf.*

กิโลกรัม gì-loo-gram kilogram, *n., clf.*

กิโลเมตร gì-loo-méet kilometer, *n., clf.*

กี่ gìi how many, how many? (must be followed by a classifier except in a few special expression), *adj.*

กีฬา gⁱⁱ-laa sport, game, *n.*

กึ่งกลาง gừng-glaang center, middle, *n.*

กุ้ง gûng shrimp, prawn, lobster, *n.*

กุญแจ gun-jɛɛ lock, key, wrench, *n.*

กุญแจมือ gun-jɛɛ-muu handcuffs, *n.*

ธ น บ ป ผ ฝ พ ฟ ภ ม ย ร ฤ ฦ ล ว ศ ษ ส ห ฬ อ ฮ

กุมภาพันธ์ gum-paa-pan February, *n.*

กุหลาบ gù-làap rose, *n.*

กู guu (vulgar) I, me, *pron.*

กู้ gûu redeem, salvage (a ship), borrow (money at interest), save (the situation or face), lift, retrieve what has been lost, rescue, *v.*

เก gee twisted, distorted, slanted, lame, crippled, irregular, disfigured, *adj.*

เก๊ gée fake, false, counterfeit, not genuine, *adj., collq.*

เก่ง gèng bold, able, adept, skillful, proficient, daring, courageous, *adj.*

เก่ง gèng be expert (in doing something), be good at (doing something), *v.*

เก็บ gèp pick up, collect, gather, keep, store, confine, preserve, put away, kill, put into jail, imprison, *v.*

เกย์ gee gay man, *n.*

เกม geem game, *n.*

เกรง greeng fear, respect with fear, be in awe of, revere, be afraid of, *v.*

เกรงใจ greeng-jai have consideration for, be reluctant to impose (upon), be disinclined to disturb or offending, be afraid of offending, *v.*

เกร็ง greng contract, rigid, *v., adj.*

เกราะ grɔ̀ armor, suit of armor, defensive covering, *n.*

เกล็ด glèt scale (as of fish), flake, *n.*

เกลี้ยง glîang smooth, clean, level, even, finished, used up, cleaned out, all gone, exhausted, *adj.*

เกลียด glìat hate, abhor, detest, loathe, despise, *v.*

เกลียว gliao be twisted, entwine, stand, ply, twisted string, thread, whorl, coil, spiral, twisted, *v., n., adj.*

เกลือ glɯa salt, *n.*

เกลื้อน glɯ̂an a chloasma, skin disease characterized by yellowish-brown spots, *n.*

เกวียน gwian cart, bullock cart, cartload, wagon, *n.*

เกา gao scratch, *v.*

เก่า gào old, ancient, former, *adj.*

เก้า gâao nine, the number nine, *nm.*

เกาหลี gao-lǐi Korea, *n.*

เก้าอี้ gâo-ʔîi chair, *n.*

เกาะ gɔ̀ island, *n.*

เกาะ gɔ̀ cling, perch, cling to, *v.*

เกิด gɜ̀ɜt be born, arise, occur, happen, take place, originate, give rise to, take birth, bring about, start up, *v.*

เกิน gəən exceed, be in excess of, go beyond, surpass, v.

เกิน gəən too much, too far, beyond, excessively, over, adv.

เกียร์ gia gear, n.

เกี่ยว gìao hook, hitch, reap, cut, mow, harvest, link, be caught in, v.

เกี๊ยว gíao wonton, n.

เกี๊ยะ gía Chinese wooden slippers, n.

เกือก gùak shoes, n., collq.

เกือบ gùap almost, soon, nearly, shortly, about, approximately, on the verge of, on the point of, adv.

แก gɛɛ you, he, him, she, her, they, them, pron.

แก่ gɛ̀ɛ old, aged, ripe, mature, grown-up, proficient, concentrated, dark, of long duration, vigorous, adj.

แก้ gɛ̂ɛ untie, undo, unwrap, take off (clothes), loosen, solve, remedy, mend, repair, cure, answer, correct, revise, strip, counteract, rectify, alter, v.

แก้ไข gɛ̂ɛ-kǎi correct, amend, improve, revise, resolve, v.

แก้แค้น gɛ̂ɛ-kéɛn take revenge, v.

แก้ตัว gɛ̂ɛ-dtua find an excuse, make false excuse, make up for one's losses

or errors, v.

แกง gɛɛng curry, curried food, n.

แกน gɛɛn axis, spindle, n.

แกน gɛɛn stunt, undeveloped, unripe, half, hard-pressed, dreary, adj.

แก้ม gɛ̂ɛm cheek, n.

แกล้ง glɛ̂ɛng do on purpose, tease, annoy, do out of spite, do with malice, feign, pretend, pull another's leg, v.

แก้ว gɛ̂ɛo crystal, glass, transparent or translucent objects, n.

แก้ว gɛ̂ɛo precious thing, n.

แก้วน้ำ gɛ̂ɛo-náam water glass, n.

แก๊ส géet, géɛs gas, gaseous substance, n.

แกะ gè sheep, n.

แกะ gè carve, etch, engrave, v.

โกโก้ goo-gôo cocoa, chocolate, n.

โกง goong cheat, swindle, embezzle, defraud, deceive, chisel, v.

โกง goong bent, curved, dishonest, fraudulent, corrupt, crooked, adj.

โกน goon shave, n.

โกรธ gròot be angry, get angry, v.

โกหก goo-hòk tell a lie, v.

ใกล้ glâi near, close by, neighboring, adjacent, adjoining, adj.

ไก gai trigger, n.

ไก่ gài chicken, n.

ไกล glai far, distant, off away, remote, lengthy, long, adj.

ไกว gwai rock, swing, sway, v.

ข

ข kɔ̌ɔ the second consonant of the Thai alphabet (high consonant), n.

ขณะ kà-nà time, moment, instant, a short time, in the mean time, meanwhile, adv., conj.

ขด kòt roll into a coil, coil, bend, curled up, v.

ขด kòt coil, ring, circle, n.

ขน kǒn fur, hair (except of the head), n.

ขน kǒn transport, take away, remove, carry off, v.

ขนตา kǒn-dtaa eyelashes, n.

ขนนก kǒn-nók feathers, n.

ข้น kôn concentrated, strong, thick, dense, semi fluid, viscid, condensed, adj.

ขนม kà-nǒm general term for sweets, candied foods, snack, etc., n.

ขนมเค้ก kà-nǒm-kéek cake, n.

ขนมปัง kà-nǒm-bpang bread, n.

ขนาด kà-nàat size, dimension, measure, extent, degree, rate, n.

ขนาน kà-nǎan be parallel to, lie parallel, designate, name, give a name, v.

ขนาน kà-nǎan dose (of medicine), n.

ขนาบ kà-nàap brace, sandwich, compress on two opposite side, reprimand, scold, go on, continuous, v., adj.

ขบ kòp bite on, crack with the teeth, v.

ขบ kòp decide (an issue), solve, crack (a riddle), v.

ขบวน kà-buan process, line, procession, caravan, train, n., clf.

ขม kǒm bitter, adj.

ข่ม kòm press down, oppress, suppress, intimidate, v.

ข่มขู่ kòm-kùu threaten, intimidate, v.

ข่มขืน kòm-kǔun rape, coerce, v.

ข่มเหง kòm-hěeng bully, abuse, mistreat, v.

ขโมย kà-mooi thief, n.

ขโมย kà-mooi steal, thieve, pilfer, v.

ขยะ kà-yà waste, garbage, refuse, trash, litter, n.

ขยัน kà-yǎn diligent, industrious, adj.

ขยับ kà-yàp move slightly, shift, adjust,

change position, v.

ขยาย kà-yăai expand, enlarge, magnify, dilate, amplify, extend, inflate, v.

ขยำ kà-yăm squeeze with the hand, knead or mix with the hands, v.

ขยี้ kà-yîi rub hard with the hands, scrub, squeeze, crush (by rubbing), v.

ขรึม krǔm be solemn, be grave, v.

ขรุขระ krù-krà tough, rough, rugged, uneven, bumpy, jagged, uncomfortable, untrimmed, adj.

ขลาด klàat timid, fearful, coward, adj.

ขลุ่ย klùi flute, n.

ขวด kùat bottle, flask (generally made of glass), for thing in bottles, n., clf.

ข่วน kùan scratch on (with claws, nails, thorns, etc.), v.

ขวบ kùap years of age, n., clf.

ขวัญ kwǎn the whorl of hair on top of the head, n.

ขวัญ kwǎn spirits, morale, courage, n.

ขวา kwǎa right (hand), to the right, adj.

ขวาง kwǎang lie across, obstruct, thwart, oppose, impede, v.

ขวางทาง kwǎang-taang block the way, bar the way, v.

ขว้าง kwâang throw, hurl, cast, fling, toss, hitch, v.

ขวาน kwǎan axe, hatchet, n.

ขวิด kwìt attack with the horns, v.

ขอ kɔ̌ɔ ask for, beg for, request, plead with, v.

ขอ kɔ̌ɔ crook, hook, n.

ขอทาน kɔ̌ɔ-taan beg, ask for alms, v.

ขอทาน kɔ̌ɔ-taan beggar, n.

ขอโทษ kɔ̌ɔ-tôot apologize, ask for forgiveness, Excuse me! Pardon me!, v., excl.

ขอร้อง kɔ̌ɔ-rɔ́ɔng request, implore, entreat, beseech, v.

ข้อ kɔ̂ɔ joint, node, n., clf.

ข้อ kɔ̂ɔ items, section, n., clf.

ข้อกล่าวหา kɔ̂ɔ-glàao-hǎa accusation, charge, n.

ข้อเขียน kɔ̂ɔ-kǐan written examination (as opposed to oral), n.

ข้อความ kɔ̂ɔ-kwaam item, point (of discourse, inquiry), passage (article), text (of speech, letter), statement, n.

ข้อเท้า kɔ̂ɔ-táao ankle, n.

ข้อบกพร่อง kɔ̂ɔ-bòk-prɔ̂ng weakness, fault, defect, flaw, n.

ข้ออ้าง kɔ̂ɔ-âang justification, supporting statement, citation, reference (to an authority), n.

ธ น บ ป ผ ฝ พ ฟ ภ ม ย ร ฤ ฦ ล ว ศ ษ ส ห ฬ อ ฮ

ขับรถ kàp-rót drive a car, *v.*

ขับไล่ kàp-lâi drive away, chase away, repel, *v.*

ขั้ว kûa pole (of the earth, of a magnet), connecting point, e.g. point where stem is attached to fruit, *n.*

ขา kǎa leg (of the body, of a piece of furniture, of journey), *n.*

ขากลับ kǎa-glàp the return trip, (on) the way back, *prep.*

ขาเข้า kǎa-kâo (on) the way in, incoming, *prep.*

ขาประจำ kǎa-bprà-jam steady customer, regular customer, *n.*

ขาหัก kǎa-hàk have a broken leg, *v.*

ข่า kàa galanga, an aromatic rhizome used in cookery and medicine, *n.*

ข้า kâa servant, attendant, slave, I, me, *n., pron.*

ข้าราชการ kâa-râat-cha-gaan government official, *n.*

ข้าง kâang side, lateral part, boundary, group, faction, clique, *n.*

ข้าง kâang side, near, neighboring, *adj.*

ข้าง kâang towards, *prep.*

ข้างขึ้น kâang-kûn (period of) the waxing moon, *n.*

ข้างเคียง kâang-kiang near by, by the side of, adjacent, close, *adj.*

ข้างนอก kâang-nɔ̂ɔk outside, the outside, *n.*

ข้างใน kâang-nai inside, the inside, *n.*

ข้างบน kâang-bon upper part, on top, upstairs, above, *adv., prep.*

ข้างแรม kâang-rɛɛm (period of) the waning moon, *n.*

ข้างหลัง kâang-lǎng in back, behind, *adv., prep.*

ข้างหน้า kâang-nâa in front, ahead, in front of, in the future, *adv., prep.*

ขาด kàat be torn, be worn out (of clothing), be broken, be missing (from), be absent, *v.*

ขาดแคลน kàat-klɛɛn lack, be short of, have a shortage of, *v.*

ขาดใจ kàat-jai die, expire, *v.*

ขาดตัว kàat-dtua fix-priced, constant, fixed, definite, *adj.*

ขาดตลาด kàat-dtà-làat scarce, out of stock, *adj., v.*

ขาดทุน kàat-tun lose money, sustain loose (in business), disadvantage, *v., n.*

ขาดมือ kàat-mɯɯ be wanting, in short supply, out of stock, run out, *v.*

ของ kɔ̌ɔng thing, something, article, goods, stuff, material, substance, possession, belonging, property, effects, *n.*

ของขวัญ kɔ̌ɔng-kwǎn gift, present (given on the occasion of a birthday, anniversary, etc.), *n.*

ของแข็ง kɔ̌ɔng-kěng solid, *n.*

ของใช้ kɔ̌ɔng-chái useful articles, things to use, *n.*

ของว่าง kɔ̌ɔng-wâang snack, *n.*

ของสด kɔ̌ɔng-sòt fresh, raw foods (of any kind), *n.*

ของหวาน kɔ̌ɔng-wǎan dessert, sweet stuff, *n.*

ขอนไม้ kɔ̌ɔn-máai log, section of unhewn timber, *n.*

ขอบ kɔ̀ɔp edge, rim, margin, *n.*

ขอบเขต kɔ̀ɔp-kèet limit, boundary, confines, perimeter, *n.*

ขอบถนน kɔ̀ɔp-tà-nǒn curb (along the edge of a street), *n.*

ขอบคุณ kɔ̀ɔp-kun Thank you, *v.*

ขอบใจ kɔ̀ɔp-jai Thank you (to the younger), *v.*

ขัง kǎng chut up, pon up, confine detain, cage, jail, *v.*

ขัด kàt obstruct, interrupt, hinder, inter-

fere, oppose, resist, object, refuse, disagree (with), conflict (with), *v.*

ขัด kàt fasten, latch, *v.*

ขัดขวาง kàt-kwǎang interfere, get into the way, block, restrain, *v.*

ขัดข้อง kàt-kɔ̂ng object, have objections, dissent, *v.*

ขัดคอ kàt-kɔɔ interrupt, break in repeatedly (as while someone is speaking), *v.*

ขัดจังหวะ kàt-jang-wà intervene, break into in the middle of, *v.*

ขัดใจ kàt-jai annoy, get in the way, be contrary, *v.*

ขัดแย้ง kàt-yéɛng conflict, contradict (one another), *v.*

ขัดสน kàt-sǒn lack, be short of, be in need of, be poor, needy, *v., adj.*

ขัน kǎn tighten by turning or twisting, *v.*

ขัน kǎn bowl, basin, *n.*

ขัน kǎn crow, coo, *v.*

ขัน kǎn funny, amusing, laughable, ludicrous, absurd, *adj.*

ขั้น kân step (of ladder, stairs), step (in a procedure), rank, level, stage (of development), *n.*

ขับ kàp drive, operate (a vehicle), drive (a herd), drive away, chase away, *v.*

Thai • Phonetic • English

ธ น บ ป ผ ฝ พ ฟ ภ ม ย ร ฤ ฦ ล ว ศ ษ ส ห อ ฮ

ขาน kǎan call out, call (the roll), v.

ขานรับ kǎan-ráp answer (the call), call in reply, v.

ข้าม kâam cross, cross over, step over, skip, v.

ข้ามถนน kâam-tà-nǒn cross the street, v.

ขาย kǎai sell, betray, v.

ขายของ kǎai-kɔ̌ɔng sell (things), v.

ขายปลีก kǎai-bplìik retail, n., adj.

ขายส่ง kǎai-sòng wholesale, n., adj.

ข่าย kàai net, limit, scope, range, sphere, category, n.

ขาว kǎao white, clear, pure, pale, lucid, innocent, free from blame, adj.

ข่าว kàao news, n.

ข่าวคราว kàao-kraao news (especially one's personal news), tidings, n.

ข่าวล่า kàao-lâa late news, n.

ข่าวล่าสุด kàao-lâa-sùt latest news, n.

ข่าวลือ kàao-lɯɯ rumor, n.

ข่าวสาร kàao-sǎan news, information, report, n.

ข้าว kâao rice, cereals, grain, food, n.

ข้าวแกง kâao-gɛɛng rice with curry, n.

ข้าวเจ้า kâao-jâao non-glutinous rice, n.

ข้าวต้ม kâao-dtôm rice porridge, n.

ข้าวตอก kâao-dtɔ̀ɔk popped rice, n.

ข้าวตัง kâao-dtang crispy cooked rice crust that sticks to the bottom of the pot (eaten like crackers when fried), n.

ข้าวเปลือก kâao-bplɯ̀ak paddy, unhusked rice, n.

ข้าวผัด kâao-pàt fried rice, n.

ข้าวโพด kâao-pôot corn, n.

ข้าวสวย kâao-sǔai boiled or steamed rice, n.

ข้าวสาร kâao-sǎan uncooked rice, n.

ข้าวสาลี kâao-sǎa-lii wheat, n.

ข้าวสุก kâao-sùk cooked rice, n.

ข้าวเหนียว kâao-nǐao glutinous rice, n.

ขิง kǐng ginger, n.

ขี่ kìi ride, drive, v.

ขี่จักรยาน kìi-jàk-gra-yaan ride a bicycle, v.

ขี้ kîi excrement, dung, droppings, excretion, feces, fecal matter, stool, dregs, refuse, filings, sweepings, impurity, residue, n., vulg.

ขี้ kîi defecate, v., vulg.

ขี้เกียจ kîi-gìat lazy, adj.

ขี้โกง kîi-goong cheating, adj.

ขี้ขลาด kîi-klàat cowardly, timid, timorous, *adj.*

ขี้ข้า kîi-kâa slave, servant, menial person, *n.*

ขี้โคลน kîi-kloon mud, *n., collq.*

ขี้ตา kîi-dtaa matter (in the eye), *n.*

ขี้เถ้า kîi-tâo ashes, *n.*

ขี้บุหรี่ kîi-bù-rìi cigarette ashes, *n.*

ขี้บ่น kîi-bòn complaining, grumbling, *adj.*

ขี้ผึ้ง kîi-pûng wax, beeswax, *n.*

ขี้ฟัน kîi-fan decaying food particles between the teeth, *n.*

ขี้มูก kîi-mûuk snot, nose mucus, *n., collq.*

ขี้ยา kii-yaa addict, drug addict, *n.*

ขี้ร้อน kîi-rɔ́ɔn sensitive to hot weather, *adj.*

ขี้โรค kîi-rôok sickly, unhealthy, *adj.*

ขี้ลืม kîi-luum forgetful, *adj.*

ขี้สงสัย kîi-sŏng-săi skeptical, suspicous, doubtful, *adj.*

ขี้สงสาร kîi-sŏng-săan overly sympathetic, compassionate, *adj.*

ขี้รังแค kîi-rang-kɛɛ dandruff, *n., collq.*

ขี้หนาว kîi-năao be sensitive to cold

weather, *v.*

ขี้หึง kîi-hǔng jealous (of husband and wife; of lovers), *adj.*

ขี้หู kîi-hǔu earwax, *n.*

ขี้เหนียว kîi-nĭao stingy, cheap, *adj., collq.*

ขี้อวด kîi-ùat boastful, braggy, *adj.*

ขี้อาย kîi-aai shy, bashful, *adj.*

ขีด kìit line, dash (typographical symbol), limit, *n.*

ขีด kìit draw, scratch (lines), mark, score (with lines), *v.*

ขีดเขียน kìit-kĭan write, *v.*

ขีดฆ่า kìit-kâa scratch out, cross out, strike out, *v.*

ขึง kŭng stretch, stretch taut, stretch out, *v.*

ขึงขัง kŭng-kăng vigorous, serious, energetic, *adj.*

ขึ้น kûn go up, rise, ascend (a throne), enter upon (a new reign, a new year), grow, climb, increase, progress, *v.*

ขึ้นเงา kûn-ngao glossy, lustrous, *adj.*

ขึ้นเงิน kûn-ngən redeem for cash, *v.*

ขึ้นใจ kûn-jai remember vividly, learn by heart, *v.*

ขึ้นชื่อ kûn-chûu famous, well-known, popular, *adj.*

ธ น บ ป ผ ฝ พ ฟ ภ ม ย ร ฤ ฦ ล ว ศ ษ ส ห ฬ อ ฮ

ขึ้นบก kûn-bòk land, go ashore, v.

ขึ้นปีใหม่ kûn-bpii-mài start a new year, v.

ขึ้นไป kûn-bpai go up, up, upward, v.

ขึ้นมา kûn-maa come up, rise, grow, increase, v.

ขึ้นรถ kûn-rót take, board, get on a train or bus; to take, get in a car, v.

ขึ้นรา kûn-raa get mildew, moldy, v., adj.

ขึ้นลง kûn-long rise and fall, v.

ขึ้นศาล kûn-sǎan appear in court, go to court, v.

ขึ้นสนิม kûn-sà-nǐm rust, get rusty, v.

ขึ้นเสียง kûn-sǐang rise one's voice, v.

ขืน kǔun oppose, counteract, v.

ขื่อ kʉ̂ʉ tie beam, stocks, horizontal piece of supporting wood of a roof, n.

ขุด kùt dig, dig up, v.

ขุน kǔn feed, nourish, big, large, gigantic, great, v., adj.

ขุนเขา kǔn-kǎo great mountain, n.

ขุนนาง kǔn-naang noble, honored person (often in government service), the nobility, with conferred rank, n.

ขุนพล kǔn-pon military commander; war lord, n.

ขุนศึก kǔn-sʉ̀k a powerful military leader, war lord, n.

ขุ่น kùn cloudy, muddy, turbid, unclear, adj.

ขุ่นเคือง kùn-kuang irritated, displeased, adj.

ขุ่นมัว kùn-mua murky, unclear, adj.

ขุม kǔm cavity, abyss, pit, n.

ขุมขน kǔm-kǒn hair follicle; pore, n.

ขุมทรัพย์ kǔm-sáp treasure (often buried), n.

ขุย kǔi flaky crust, scaly or powdery residue, n.

ขู่ kùu threaten, menace, scare, v.

ขู่เข็ญ kùu-kěn intimidate, coerce by intimidation, v.

ขู่ขวัญ kùu-kwǎn terrorize, threaten, v.

ขูด kùut scrape, grate, v.

เขก kèek hit with the knuckles, v.

เข่ง kèng a kind of bamboo basket, n.

เข็ด kèt skein, n.

เข็ด kèt dread (to do something), be afraid (esp. because of a previous bad experience), v.

เขต kèet limit, boundary, area, zone, territory, n.

เขตคุ้มครอง kèet-kúm-krɔɔng protectorate, *n.*

เขตแดน kèet-dɛɛn border, frontier, boundary, *n.*

เขตเทศบาล kèet-têet-sà-baan the city limits, municipal boundary, municipal area, *n.*

เขตปลอดภัย kèet-bplɔ̀ɔt-pai safety zone, *n.*

เข็น kĕn push, move forward by pushing and pulling, *v.*

เข็ม kĕm needle, pin, hand (of a clock), *n.*

เข็มกลัด kĕm-glàt safety pin, pin, brooch, *n.*

เข็มขัด kĕm-kàt belt, *n.*

เข็มทิศ kĕm-tít compass, *n.*

เข็มเย็บผ้า kĕm-yép-pâa sewing needle, *n.*

เข็มหมุด kĕm-mùt pin, *n.*

เข้ม kêm intense, strong, concentrated, deep, dark (of colors), *adj.*

เข้มข้น kêm-kôn concentrated, thick, *adj.*

เข้มแข็ง kêm-kĕng strong, powerful, *adj.*

เข้มงวด kêm-ngûat strict, rigid, harsh, *adj.*

เขม่น kà-mèn (muscles) twitch, *v.*

เขม่น kà-mèn find irritating, get on someone's nerve, *v., slang*

เขมร kà-mĕen Cambodia, Cambodian, Khmer, *n.*

เขม่า kà-mào soot, carbon, lampblack, carbon deposit (as in car engine), *n.*

เขย kə̌əi a male relative by marriage, the term designates a man as an in-law of his wife's blood relatives, *n.*

เขย่ง kà-yèng tiptoe, stand on tiptoe, hop on one leg, *v.*

เขย่า kà-yào shake, *v.*

เขว kwĕe go awry, be off the right track, misunderstand, distortedly, obliquely, astray, *v., adv.*

เขา kăo mountain, hill, *n.*

เขา kăo horn (of an animal), horn (for blowing signals), *n.*

เขา kăo he, him, she, her, they, them, *pron.*

เขากวาง kăo-gwaang antlers, *n.*

เข่า kào knee, *n.*

เข้า kâo enter, insert, put on, join, come into contact (with), *v.*

เข้าเกียร์ kâo-gia put in gear, engage the gears, *v.*

เข้าใกล้ kâo-glâi come near, get

close, *v.*

เข้าใจ kâo-jai understand, *v.*

เข้าใจผิด kâo-jai-pìt misunderstand, *v.*

เข้านอน kâo-nɔɔn go to bed, *v.*

เข้าไป kâo-bpai go in, join, enter (an organization), *v.*

เข้าพบ kâo-póp call on, make a (formal) call, visit with, *v.*

เข้ามา kâo-maa come in, *v.*

เข้าเมือง kâo-muang immigrate, enter a country or town, *v.*

เข้าร่วม kâo-rûam join, participate, *v.*

เข้ารูป kâo-rûup fit in (with), conform (to), *v.*

เข้าหน้า kâo-nâa face, confront, arrange pages in proper order, insert pages, *v.*

เข้าหา kâo-hǎa go see (someone about something), give oneself up, turn oneself in, *v.*

เข้าหุ้น kâo-hûn go into partnership, team up, *v.*

เขี่ย kìa flick, flick off (e.g. ashes from cigarette), remove, dislodge, scratch (as a chicken), scrape away, *v.*

เขียง kiang chopping block, cutting board, *n.*

เขียด kìat small green frog, *n.*

เขียน kian write, draw, *v.*

เขียนหนังสือ kian-nǎng-sǔu write, *v.*

เขียว kǐao green, *adj.*

เขี้ยว kîao fang, canine tooth, *n.*

เขื่อน kùan dam, dike, embankment, levee, barrage, breakwater, *n.*

แขก kὲɛk guest, visitor, Indian, dark skinned foreinger (esp. those from India, Pakistan, the Middle East, Indonesia, Java), *n.*

แข็ง kěng hard, firm, strong, stiff, *adj.*

แข็งขัน kěng-kǎn diligent, *adj.*

แข็งขึ้น kěng-kûn harder, firmer, *adj.*

แข็งใจ kěng-jai summon up one's courage, steel oneself (to do something), *v.*

แข็งตัว kěng-dtua harden, solidify, set, freeze (of itself), *v.*

แข็งแรง kěng-rɛɛng strong, powerful, solid, *adj.*

แข่ง kὲng compete, *v.*

แข้ง kɛ̂ng shin, *n.*

แขน kɛ̌ɛn arm, sleeve, *n.*

แขวง kwɛ̌ɛng district, region, subdivision of a province, *n.*

แขวน kwɛ̌ɛn hang, suspend, *v.*

ก ข ฃ ค ฅ ฆ ง จ ฉ ช ซ ฌ ญ ฎ ฏ ฐ ฑ ฒ ณ ด ต ถ ท

แขวนนวม kwɛ̌ɛn-nuam to quit boxing, v., idiom.

โขก kòok knock, rap, poke at, v.

โขลก klòok pound, crush to a pulp, v.

ไข kǎi fat, grease, n.

ไข kǎi unlock, open, turn, explain, tell,
expand, v.

ไขควง kǎi-kuang screwdriver, n.

ไขมัน kǎi-man fat, n.

ไข่ kài egg, testicles, n., collq.

ไข่ kài lay eggs, produce eggs, v.

ไข่ขาว kài-kǎao egg white, n.

ไข่ดาว kài-daao sunny side-up, n.

ไข่แดง kài-dɛɛng egg yolk, n.

ไข่ต้ม kài-dtôm hard-boiled egg, n.

ไข่ลวก kài-lûak soft-boiled egg, n.

ไข้ kâi fever, illness, n.

ไขว้ kwâi cross, be twisted, v.

ไขว้เขว kwâi-kwěe be confused,
mixed up, disorganized, v.

ฃ

ฃ kɔ̌ɔ the third consonant of the Thai
alphabet (high consonant) (obsolete), n.

ค

ค kɔɔ the fourth consonant of the Thai
alphabet (low consonant), n.

คง kong likely to, probably, surely, sure
to, may be, adv.

คง kong endure, last, stand, enduring,
durable, constant, solid, permanent, v.,
adj.

คงกระพัน kong-grà-pan invulnerable,
adj.

คงทน kong-ton resistant, durable, adj.

คงที่ kong-tîi constant, invariable, adj.

คณะ kà-ná group, body, organization,
team, party, n.

คณะกรรมการ kà-ná gam-ma-gaan
committee, commission, n.

คณะรัฐมนตรี kà-ná-rát-ta-mon-dtrii
cabinet, council of ministers, n.

คด kót bent, not straight-forward,
curved, crooked, dishonored, dishonest,
adj.

คดเคี้ยว kót-kíao winding, adj.

คดี kà-dii case, charge (legal), n.

คดีแพ่ง kà-dii-pêng civil case, n.

คดีอาญา kà-dii-aa-yaa criminal case,
n.

คติ kà-dtì moral precept, ethical teaching, maxim, *n.*

คน kon person, human, *n., clf.*

คน kon stir (a liquid), stir up (ingredients), *v.*

คนกลาง kon-glaang the middle man (in the group), middleman, mediator, arbitrator, *n.*

คนไข้ kon-kâi sick person, patient, *n.*

คนใช้ kon-chái servant, the user, *n.*

คนต่างชาติ kon-dtàang-châat foreigner, *n.*

คนตาย kon-dtaai deaths (i.e. cases of death, dead person), *n.*

คนทั่วไป kon-tûa-bpai people in general, the public, *n.*

คนไทย kon-tai Thai person, *n.*

คนนอก kon-nɔ̂ɔk an outsider, *n.*

คนใน kon-nai an insider, *n.*

คบ kóp associate or be friend with, *v.*

คบ, คบเพลิง kóp, kóp-plɤɤng torch, *n.*

คม kom edge of blade, sharp point, sharp border, sharp, razor-sharp, *n., adj.*

คมคาย kom-kaai witty, sharp, sagacious, sarcastic, *adj.*

ครก krók mortar, grinding bowl, *n.*

ครบ króp complete, perfect, whole, entire, every, ready, due, *adj.*

ครบถ้วน króp-tûan complete, full, entire, *adj.*

ครรภ์ kan womb, pregnancy, *n.*

ครอก krɔ̂ɔk litter, brood, *n.*

ครอง krɔɔng rule, govern, wield, maintain, wear, put on, *v.*

ครอบ krɔ̂ɔp cover up, dominate, *v.*

ครอบครอง krɔ̂ɔp-krɔɔng govern, control, posses, *v.*

ครอบครัว krɔ̂ɔp-krua family, *n.*

ครอบงำ krɔ̂ɔp-ngam overwhelm, overpower (of emotion, temptation, etc.), *v.*

ครั่ง krâng sealing wax; lacquer, *n.*

ครั้ง kráng time, instance, for an event, incident, occurrence, *n., clf.*

ครั้งก่อน kráng-gɔ̀ɔn last time, the time before, previously, formerly, *adv., prep.*

ครั้งแรก kráng-rɛ̂ɛk the first time, *prep.*

ครับ kráp particle used as the final element of statements and questions (for male speakers), *part.*

ครัว krua kitchen, n.

ครัวเรือน krua-ruan family, household, n.

คราว kraao time, occasion, n., clf.

คราวก่อน kraao-gɔ̀ɔn the time before, on the last occasion, prep.

คราวละ kraao-lá each time, prep.

คราวหน้า kraao-nâa next time, on the next occasion, prep.

คริสต์ krít, krís Christ, n.

คริสต์มาส krít-sa-máat, krít-sa-máas Christmas, n.

คริสตัง, คริสเตียน krít-sa-dtang, krít-sa-dtian Christian, n.

ครีบ krîip fin, n.

ครีม kriim cream, n.

ครึ่ง krûng half, midway, mid, adj., nm.

ครู kruu teacher, instructor, tutor, master, n.

ครูใหญ่ kruu-yài headmaster, headmistress, school principal, n.

คลอง klɔɔng canal, watercourse, n.

คล่อง klɔ̂ng nimble, fluent, facile, skillful smooth, proficient, adj.

คล้อง klɔ́ɔng rope, lasso, put around, rhyme, be compatible with, v.

คลอด klɔ̂ɔt bear, give birth, deliver (a baby), v.

คลัง klang treasury, storehouse, n.

คลั่ง klâng delirious, crazy, insane, adj.

คลั่งไคล้ klâng-klái be crazed, be mad about, be infatuated with, v.

คลาด klâat miss, fail to join, deviate, escape, v.

คลาดเคลื่อน klâat-klɨ̂an deviate, be off, be different (from the original), v.

คลาน klaan crawl, creep, v.

คลาย klaai lessen, diminish, abate, unravel, unroll, v.

คล้าย kláai resemble, look like, v.

คลำ klam grope, probe (as a doctor), look for something by touching, v.

คล้ำ klám dark (in color), swarthy (of complexion), adj.

คลี่ klîi unfold, unroll, v.

คลื่น klɨ̂ɨn wave, curl, ripple, surge, swell, n.

คลื่นเสียง klɨ̂ɨn-sǐang sound wave, n.

คลื่นไส้ klɨ̂ɨn-sâi be nauseated, be squeamish, v.

คลื่นไส้ klɨ̂ɨn-sâi loathing, disgust, adj.

คลุก klúk mix together, stir in, turn over, v.

คลุม klum cover up, spread over, v.

ธ น บ ป ผ ฝ พ ฟ ภ ม ย ร ฤ ฦ ล ว ศ ษ ส ห ฬ อ ฮ

คลุมเครือ klum-krɰa ambiguous, unclear, indistinct, *adj.*

ควง kuang twirl, date, go on a date (with a friend or the opposite sex), *v.*

ควบ kûap combine, blend, merge, twist together, join, link, *v.*

ควบ kûap ride fast, gallop, *v.*

ควบคุม kûap-kum control, supervise, detain, *v.*

ควบม้า kûap-máa gallop a horse, *v.*

ควย kuai penis, *n., vulg.*

ควร kuan ought to, should, appropriate, fitting, suitable, proper, deserving, *v., adj.*

ควัน kwan smoke, fumes, *n.*

คว้า kwáa snatch, grab, reach for, *v.*

ความ kwaam the sense, the substance, the gist (of a matter, an account, etc.), legal case, lawsuit, *n.*

ความกดดัน kwaam-gòt-dan pressure, *n.*

ความกล้าหาญ kwaam-glâa-hǎan bravery, *n.*

ความคิด kwaam-kít thought, thinking, idea, *n.*

ความพอใจ kwaam-pɔɔ-jai satisfaction, *n.*

ความรู้ kwaam-rúu knowledge, *n.*

ความสามารถ kwaam-sǎa-mâat ability, *n.*

ความสูง kwaam-sǔung altitude, height, tallness, *n.*

ความหวัง kwaam-wǎng hope, *n.*

ควาย kwaai water buffalo, *n.*

คว่ำ kwâm turn over, turn upside down, *v.*

คอ kɔɔ neck, *n.*

คอเสื้อ kɔɔ-sɰ̂a collar (of a shirt, coat, etc.), neck (of a garment), *n.*

คอหอย kɔɔ-hɔ̌i throat, *n., collq.*

คอเหล้า kɔɔ-lâo heavy drinker, *n.*

คอก kɔ̂ɔk enclosure, pen, sty (for animal), stable, cow barn, *n.*

คอด kɔ̂ɔt narrow, constricted, worn away, *adj.*

ค้อน kɔ́ɔn hammer, gavel, *n.*

ค้อน kɔ́ɔn glance sidewise, *v.*

คอนกรีต kɔn-grìit concrete, *n.*

คอนแทกเลนส์ kɔn-tɛ̀k-leen contact lens, *n.*

คอมพิวเตอร์ kɔm-piu-dtɤɤ computer, *n.*

ค่อม kɔ̂m hunchbacked, round shouldered, *adj.*

คอย kɔɔi wait, wait for, linger, *v.*

ค่อย kɔ̂i gradually, slowly, gently, little by little, softly, low (of sound), *adv., adj.*

คะ ká particle used as the final element in questions or after other particles at the end of statements (for female speakers), *part.*

ค่ะ kâ particle used at the end of statements and commands, yes (in answer to a question) (for female speakers), *part.*

คะเน ká-nee estimate, guess, *v.*

คะแนน ká-nɛɛn mark(s), point(s), grade, score, vote, *n.*

คัด kát choose, select, pick out, copy, excerpt, *v.*

คัด kát stuffed, clogged, congested, *adj.*

คัดค้าน kát-káan object, oppose, *v.*

คัดลอก kát-lɔ̂ɔk copy, imitate, *v.*

คัดเลือก kát-lɨ̂ak select, sort out, pick out, *v.*

คัน kan classifier for long-handled objects (spoons, forks, umbrellas, fishing rods), *n., clf.*

คัน kan classifier for vehicles, *n., clf.*

คันเบ็ด kan-bèt fishing rod, *n.*

คั่น kân separate, interpose, divide, *v.*

คั้น kán squeeze, press (so as to extract, e.g. juice), *v.*

คับ káp tight, tight-fitting, tightly packed, confined, crowded, *adj.*

คับขัน káp-kǎn critical, crucial in tight situation; emergency mature, *adj.*

คับคั่ง káp-kâng crowded, dense, thick (of population), *adj.*

ค่า kâa fee, cost, price, value, *n.*

ค่าจ้าง kâa-jâang wage, pay, *n.*

ค่าเช่า kâa-châo the rent, rental fee, *n.*

ค่าใช้จ่าย kâa-chái-jàai expense, *n.*

ค่าโดยสาร kâa-dooi-sǎan fare, cost of passage, *n.*

ค่าผ่านประตู kâa-pàan-bprà-dtuu admission fee, charge, *n.*

ค่ารถ kâa-rót fare, carfare, *n.*

ค่าเสียหาย kâa-sǐa-hǎai the damage, the amount of loss, *n.*

ค้า káa do business (in), trade (in), sell, engage in trade, *v.*

ค้าขาย káa-kǎai engage in trade, buy and sell, *v.*

คาง kaang chin, jaw, *n.*

ค้าง káang stay over night, *v.*

ค้าง káang unfinished, lodged, stuck,

dangling, incomplete, pending, *adj.*

คางคก kaang-kók toad, *n.*

ค้างคาว káang-kaao bat (mammal), *n.*

คาด kâat put around, tie around, belt, strap, anticipate, expect, guess, *v.*

คาดคั้น kâat-kán press for, *v.*

คาดคะเน kâat-ka-nee speculate, guess, *v.*

คาดหมาย kâat-mǎai expect, anticipate, *v.*

คาน kaan horizontal beam, lever, beam (of a balance), *n.*

ค้าน káan oppose, contradict, *v.*

คาบ kâap period, cycle (of time), *n.*

คาบ kâap hold, seize, clamp (in the teeth, in the beak), *v.*

คาบเกี่ยว kâap-gìao overlap, be overlapping, extend over (into), *v.*

คาย kaai spit out, give off (e.g. steam), secrete, *v.*

คาย kaai rough, rugged, *adj.*

ค่าย kâai camp, stockade, *n.*

คาว kaao fishy (in smell), stigma, *n.*

คำ kam word, (oral) speech, mouthful, bite, classifier for an utterance, a word, *n., clf.*

คำขาด kam-kàat ultimatum, *n.*

คำตอบ kam-dtɔ̀ɔp answer, reply, *n.*

คำเชิญ kam-chəən invitation, request, *n.*

คำถาม kam-tǎam question, *n.*

คำนำ kam-nam preface, foreword, *n.*

คำแนะนำ kam-né-nam advise, suggestion, instruction, *n.*

คำแปล kam-bplɛɛ translation, meaning, *n.*

คำพิพากษา kam-pi-pâak-sǎa verdict, decision judgment, *n.*

คำพูด kam-pûut spoken word, utterance, *n.*

คำมั่นสัญญา kam-mân-sǎn-yaa promise, pledge, *n.*

คำย่อ kam-yɔ̂ɔ abbreviation, *n.*

คำยินยอม kam-yin-yɔɔm consent, *n.*

คำร้อง kam-rɔ́ɔng petition, *n.*

คำสอน kam-sɔ̌ɔn teaching, *n.*

คำสั่ง kam-sàng order, command, instruction(s), *n.*

คำหยาบ kam-yàap vulgar word(s), vulglar speech, *n.*

คำให้การ kam-hâi-gaan testimony, *n.*

คำอธิบาย kam-à-tí-baai explanation, *n.*

ค่ำ kâm dusk, nightfall, *n.*

ค้ำ kám support, hold up, prop up, *v.*

คำนวณ kam-nuan calculate, estimate, v.

คำนับ kam-náp salute, v.

คำราม kam-raam roar, growl, v.

คิด kít think, figure, calculate, v.

คิดถึง kít-tŭng think of, miss, v.

คิดร้าย kít-ráai intend to do harm, plot against, v.

คิดออก kít-ɔ̀ɔk figure out, solve, v.

คิว kiu queue, line, queue up, n., v.

คิ้ว kíu eyebrow, n.

คีบ kîip grip, take up (with forceps, chopsticks, etc.), v.

คีม kiim pincers, tongs, pliers, n.

คืน kʉʉn return, go back, restore, get back, recover, v.

คืน kʉʉn night, n.

คืนคำ kʉʉn-kam retract, revoke one's promise, v.

คืนดี kʉʉn-dii be reconciled, v.

คืนนี้ kʉʉn-níi tonight, n.

คืนวาน kʉʉn-waan last night, n.

คือ kʉʉ be (as follows, as defined), equal, namely, v., adv.

คุก kúk prison, jail, n

คุกเข่า kúk-kào kneel, v.

คุกคาม kúk-kaam threaten, loom

menacingly, v.

คุณ kun good, virtue, value, quality, n.

คุณ kun you, title used before the first name of both men and women, pron.

คุณครู kun-kruu teacher, title placed before the first name of a teacher, pron.

คุณค่า kun-kâa value, n.

คุณธรรม kun-na-tam moral principles, virtue, good, n.

คุณพ่อ kun-pɔ̂ɔ father, n.

คุณภาพ kun-na-pâap quality, n.

คุณแม่ kun-mɛ̂ɛ mother, n.

คุ้น kún get used (to), be accustomed (to), be intimate, familiar (with), be tame, v.

คุ้นหู kún-hŭu sound familiar, v.

คุม kum take care of, watch over, take charge of, v.

คุมขัง kum-kăng jail, imprison, detain in custody, v.

คุ้ม kúm protect, escort for protection, cover, v.

คุ้มกัน kúm-gan protect, guard against, v.

คุ้มครอง kúm-krɔɔng give protection to, watch over, v.

คุ้มค่า kúm-kâa be worth-while, worth the expense, v.

คุ้มคลั่ง kúm-klâng lose one's temper, be mad, be insane, *v.*

คุย kui chat, talk, converse, *v.*

คุยโต kui-dtoo brag, boast, talk big, *v.*

คุ้ย kúi dig (with claws, as a dog), scratch the ground (as a chicken), *v.*

คู kuu small canal, ditch, moat, *n.*

คูปอง kuu-bpɔɔng coupon, *n.*

คู่ kûu classifier for pairs (of anything), couples, even, *n., adj., clf.*

คู่แข่ง kûu-kɛ̀ng competitor, rival, *n.*

คู่ครอง kûu-krɔɔng spouse, mate, *n.*

คู่ความ kûu-kwaam one or both of the parties to a legal case, i.e., the plaintiff and/or the defendant, *n.*

คู่คี่ kûu-kîi odd or even, be about even, equal, *v., adj.*

คู่ใจ kûu-jai faithful, trusted, *adj.*

คู่ต่อสู้ kûu-dtɔ̀ɔ-sûu opponent, antagonist, *n.*

คู่บ่าวสาว kûu-bàao-sǎao the bride and groom, *n.*

คู่มือ kûu-muu handbook, manual, always at hand, *n.*

คู่รัก kûu-rák lovers, sweethearts, (one's) sweetheart, *n.*

คู่หมั้น kûu-mân fiancé(e), *n.*

คู่หู kûu-hǔu (an) intimate, (one's) trusted companion, *n.*

คูณ kuun multiply, *v.*

คูหา kuu-hǎa cave, cavern, booth, space between pillars (in a building), *n.*

เค็ม kem salty, cunning, canny, *adj.*

เคมี kee-mii chemistry, *n.*

เคย kəəi be familiar, be accustomed, ever, at some (one) time, used to, *v.*

เคยตัว kəəi-dtua be in the habit of, get into the habit of, act by habit, *v.*

เคร่ง krêng strict, serious, *adj.*

เคร่งเครียด krêng-krîat serious, grave, gloomy, stressed, *adj.*

เครดิต kree-dìt credit, *n.*

เครา krao beard, whiskers, *n.*

เครียด krîat tensed, strained, serious, *adj.*

เครื่อง krûang gear, apparatus, complex machinery, engine, *n.*

เครื่องจักร krûang-jàk engine, machine, *n.*

เครื่องใน krûang-nai internal body organs, giblets, *n.*

เครื่องมือ krûang-muu tool, device, instrument, equipment, *n.*

เครื่องสำอาง krûang-sǎm-aang cosmetics, *n.*

เครื่องหมาย krûang-măai sign, mark, symbol, signal, *n.*

เคล็ด klét trick, tactic, technique, *n.*

เคล็ด klét be sprained, get sprained, *v.*

เคล็ดลับ klét-láp trick, tactic, technique, secret *n.*

เคลื่อน klûan move, shift, displace, be vary, be inaccurate, *v.*

เคลื่อนที่ klûan-tîi be mobile, be out of place, be dislocated, *v.*

เคลื่อนไหว klûan-wăi move, move about, *v.*

เคลือบ klûap enamel, glaze, plate, coat, *v.*

เคาะ kó knock, tap, *v.*

เคียว kiao sickle, *n.*

เคี้ยว kíao chew, masticate, grind, *v.*

แค่ kêe to the extent of, as far as, as long, as long as, as far as, up to, about, only, almost, *adv., prep.*

แคน kɛɛn mouth organ used by people in N and NE Thailand, *n.*

แค้น kéen harbor feelings of anger, feel resentful, *v.*

แคบ kɛ̂ɛp narrow, cramped, small, selfish, narrow-minded, *adj.*

แคระ kré diminutive, stunted, dwarfed,

under-sized, *adj.*

แคะ ké pick out, pry out, take out, *v.*

โคเคน koo-keen cocaine, *n.*

โคจร koo-joon travel (of celestial bodies), *v.*

โค้ง kóong bend over, bow, curve, arch, *v.*

โคน koon base (as of tree), *n.*

โค่น kôon cut down, fell, over throw, fall down, *v.*

โครง kroong frame (as of window, kite), *n.*

โครงกระดูก kroong-grà-dùuk skeleton, *n.*

โครงการ kroong-gaan plan, project, program, *n.*

โครงเรื่อง kroong-rûang plot, outline, structure (of a story), *n.*

โครงสร้าง kroong-sâang structure, arrangement of constituents, *n.*

โคราช koo-râat Khorat, colloquial name of Nakhon Ratchasima, *n.*

โคลน kloon mud, *n.*

ใคร krai who, someone, anyone, *pron.*

ใคร่ครวญ krâi-kruan contemplate, consider carefully, *v.*

ธ น บ ป ผ ฝ พ ฟ ภ ม ย ร ฤ ฦ ล ว ศ ษ ส ห ฬ อ ฮ

ค

ค kɔɔ the fifth consonant of the Thai
alphabet (low consonant) (obsolete), *n.*

ฆ

ฆ kɔɔ the sixth consonant of the Thai
alphabet (low consonant) , *n.*
ฆ้อง kɔ́ɔng gong, *n.*
ฆ่า kâa kill, execute, destroy, cross out,
strike out, *v.*
ฆ่าฟัน kâa-fan kill, slay, *v.*
ฆาตกร kâat-dtà-gɔɔn murderer, *n.*
ฆาตกรรม kâat-dtà-gam murder, *n.*
เฆี่ยน kian beat, whip, *v.*
โฆษก koo-sòk announcer, spokesperson, *n.*
โฆษณา koo-sa-naa advertise, publicize, advertisement, *v., n.*

ง

ง ngɔɔ the seventh consonant of the
Thai alphabet (low consonant), *n.*
งก ngók greedy, gluttonous, avaricious,
stingy, mean, *adj.*

งง ngong dizzy, dazed, stunned, puzzled, confused, *adj.*
งด ngót stop, halt, cancel dissolve, *v.*
งดงาม ngót-ngaam pretty, beautiful,
attractive. good-looking, *adj.*
งดเว้น ngót-wén refrain (from),
abstain (from), *v.*
งบดุล ngóp-dun balance sheet, the
balance, *n.*
งบบัญชี ngóp-ban-chii close an
account, calculate the balance in an
account, *v.*
งบประมาณ ngóp-bprà-maan budget,
n.
งม ngom grope in the water for, dive
for, fumble, *v.*
งมงาย ngom-ngaai foolish, stupid,
mentally sluggish, absorb in beyond
reason, *adj.*
งวง nguang trunk, proboscis, *n.*
งวงช้าง nguang-cháang trunk of the
elephant, *n.*
ง่วง ngûang sleepy, drowsy, *adj.*
งวด ngûat occasion, time, period,
installment, fixed period of time for payment, *n.*
งวด ngûat dry out, dry up, *adj.*

งอ ngɔɔ bend, fold, curl, v.

งอแง ngɔɔ-ngɛɛ fussy, childish, crying like a baby, clumsy, adj.

ง้อ ngɔ́ɔ humble oneself in order to conciliate, reconcile, v.

งอก ngɔ̂ɔk sprout, bud, grow, increase, multiply (esp. for plants), v.

งอกงาม ngɔ̂ɔk-ngaam grow, develop, thrive (of plants), v.

งอน ngɔɔn bend, curve upward, v.

งอน ngɔɔn pout, show displeasure (esp. women, children), feign displeasure, v.

งอบ ngɔ̂ɔp a kind of hat made of palm leaves and bamboo worn by farmers, n.

งอม ngɔɔm overripe, very ripe, severe, serious, very old, very tired, adj.

ง่อย ngɔ̂i lame, paralyzed, crippled, withered, motionless, adj.

งั่ง ngâng stupid, foolish, dull, adj.

งัด ngát pry out, force up, raise with a lever, v.

งับ ngáp snap, snap at, nip, clamp, close, shut, v.

งา ngaa sesame, tusk (of the elephant), ivory, n.

งาช้าง ngaa-cháang ivory, elephant tusk, n.

ง้าง ngáang pull out, pull back, v.

งาน ngaan work, task, job, ceremony, festival, affair, duty, fair, n.

งานก่อสร้าง ngaan-gɔ̀ɔ-sâang construction work, n.

งานการ ngaan-gaan work (in general), n.

งานขึ้นปีใหม่ ngaan-kûn-bpii-mài New Year festival, n.

งานฉลอง ngaan-chà-lɔɔng festival, celebration, n.

งานบ้าน ngaan-bâan housework, household chores, n.

งานวัด ngaan wát a fair held within the Buddhist temple grounds, n.

งานศพ ngaan-sòp funeral, n.

งานอดิเรก ngaan-à-dì-rèek hobby, n.

งาม ngaam flourish, beautiful, pretty, attractive, graceful, charming, v., adj.

ง่าย ngâai simple, easy, convenient, adj.

ง่ายดาย ngâai-daai very easy, very simple, adj.

ง้าว ngáao a pike with curved blade, n.

งุนงง ngun-ngong be dazed, be bewildered, be perplexed, *v.*

งุ่มง่าม ngûm-ngâam clumsy, awkward, *adj.*

งู nguu snake, *n.*

งูเขียว nguu-kǐao a common green snake, *n.*

งูเหลือม nguu-lǔam python, *n.*

งูเห่า nguu-hào cobra, *n.*

เงยหน้า ngəəi-nâa look up, raise one's head, lift up one's face, *v.*

เงา ngao image, reflection, shadow, *n.*

เงาะ ngɔ́ rambutan, *n.*

เงิน ngən silver, money, *n.*

เงินกู้ ngən-gûu loan, *n.*

เงินเดือน ngən-dɯan monthly salary, *n.*

เงินทอน ngən-tɔɔn change (money returned), *n.*

เงินทุน ngən-tun capital (money in an investment), *n.*

เงินผ่อน ngən-pɔ̀n installment, *n.*

เงินฝาก ngən-fàak deposit, *n.*

เงินมัดจำ ngən-mát-jam deposit (down payment), *n.*

เงินสด ngən-sòt cash, *n.*

เงียบ ngîap silent, quiet, *adj.*

เงียบกริบ ngîap-grìp completely soundless, *adj.*

เงียบเหงา ngîap-ngǎo silent and lonely, *adj.*

เงื้อ ngúa raise (the hand, a weapon) in a threatening gesture, *v.*

เงือก ngûak mermaid, *n.*

เงื่อน ngûan knot, joint, hint, clue, *n.*

เงื่อนไข ngûan-kǎi condition, stipulation, proviso, *n.*

เงื่อนงำ ngûan-ngam clue, key to a solution, hidden point, catch, *n.*

แง้ม ngɛ́ɛm open slightly, be ajar, *v.*

แงะ ngɛ́ pry, pry open, *v.*

โง่ ngôo stupid, foolish, dull, silly, *adj.*

โง่เขลา ngôo-klǎo stupid, foolish, dull, silly, *adj.*

จ

จ jɔɔ the eighth consonant of the Thai alphabet (mid consonant), *n.*

จง jong intend, must, have to, *v.*

จด jòt take note, *v.*

จน jon poor, penniless, *adj.*

จนกระทั่ง jon-grà-tâng until, *conj.*

จนใจ jon-jai at the end of one's wit, *adj.*

จบ jòp finish, end, *v.*

จม jom sink, *v.*

จมน้ำตาย jom-náam-dtaai drown, *v.*

จมูก jà-mùuk nose, *n.*

จร jɔɔn wander, *v.*

จรจัด jɔɔn-jàt vagrant, *adj.*

จรด jà-ròt place against, *v.*

จรรยาบรรณ jan-yaa-ban ethics, *n.*

จรวด jà-rùat rocket, missile, *n.*

จระเข้ jɔɔ-ra-kêe crocodile, alligator, *n.*

จราจร jà-raa-jɔɔn traffic, *n.*

จริง jing real, true, genuine, *adj.*

จริงจัง jing-jang sincere, serious, truthful, *adj.*

จริงใจ jing-jai sincere, truthful, *adj.*

จริต jà-rìt conduct, behavior, *n.*

จริต ja-rìt mental basis, psychic control, *n.*

จริยธรรม jà-rí-ya-tam ethics, *n.*

จริยา jà-rí-yaa conduct, morals, *n.*

จลาจล jà-laa-jon riot, *n.*

จ้วง jûang stab with full force, *v.*

จวน juan residence of a provincial governor, *n.*

จวน juan almost, narrowly, very near, *adv.*

จวนจะ juan-jà almost, nearly, *adv.*

จวบ jùap meet, reach, *v.*

จวบเหมาะ jùap-mò timing, *adj.*

จอ jɔɔ Year of the Dog, *n.*

จอแก้ว jɔɔ-gɛ̂ɛɔ television, *n.*

จอเงิน jɔɔ-ngən movie screen, *n.*

จอแจ jɔɔ-jɛɛ crowded, noisy, clamorous, *adj.*

จ่อ jɔ̀ɔ place against, *v.*

จ้อ jɔ́ɔ garrulously, talkative, *adv.*

จอก jɔ̀ɔk small cup, *n.*

จอง jɔɔng reserve, make a reservation, engage, *v.*

จองจำ jɔɔng-jam incarcerate, *v.*

จ้อง jɔ̂ng stare at, *v.*

จองหอง jɔɔng-hɔ̌ɔng arrogant, haughty, unduly proud, *adj.*

จอด jɔ̀ɔt stop, park, *v.*

จอน jɔɔn sideburn, *n.*

จอม jɔɔm highest, head, chief, *n.*

จ้อย jɔ̂i small, petite, *adj.*

จ๋อย jɔ̌i distinct, clear, *adj.*

จะ jà the final particle in questions, used to urge or suggest, *n.*

จักสาน jàk-sǎan wickerwork, *n.*

จั๊กจี้ ják-ga-jîi tickle, feel ticklish, *v.*

จักร jàk wheel, circle, *n.*

จักรพรรดิ์ jàk-gra-pát emperor, *n.*

จักรี jàk-grii the god Krishna, the Chakri Dynasty, *n.*

จัง jang greatly, quite, *adv.*

จังกอบ jang-gɔɔp tax, *n.*

จังหวะ jang-wà rhythm, time, *n.*

จังหวัด jang-wàt province, *n.*

จัญไร jan-rai accursed, damned, *adj.*

จัณฑาล jan-taan outcast, *n.*

จัด jàt prepare, adjust, arrange, manage, *v.*

จัด jàt strong, severe, violent, *adj.*

จัดการ jàt-gaan manage, arrange, *v.*

จัตวา jàt-dtà-waa four, fourth, *adj.*

จัตุบาท jàt-dtù-bàat four-footed animal, *n.*

จันทร์ jan moon, Monday, *n.*

จันทรุปราคา jan-ta-rúp-bprà-raa-kaa eclipse of the moon, *n.*

จับ jàp catch, hold, arrest, grasp, *v.*

จับกัง jàp-gang coolie, *n.*

จั่ว jùa gable, *n.*

จ่า jàa head, chief, leader, master, *n.*

จ้า jáa intense, strong, brilliant, *adj.*

จาก jàak separated from, away from, *adj.*

จาง jaang faded, *adj.*

จ้าง jâang hire, employ, *v.*

จาน jaan plate, dish, *n.*

จานรอง jaan-rɔɔng saucer, *n.*

จานบิน jaan-bin flying saucer, UFO, *n.*

จานเสียง jaan-sǐang record, *n.*

จ่าย jàai spend, pay, disburse, *v.*

จาระบี jaa-ra-bii lubricating grease, *n.*

จารึก jaa-rúk engrave, *v.*

จารีต jaa-rîit custom, *n.*

จ้าละหวั่น jâa-la-wàn confusion, chaos, *n.*

จำ jam remember, recollect, recall, memorize, recognize, *v.*

จำกัด jam-gàt limit, confine, *v.*

จำคุก jam-kúk imprison, *v.*

จ้ำ jâm hasten, stab, *v.*

จิก jìk peck, *v.*

จิ้งจก jîng-jòk house lizard, *n.*

จิ้งจอก jîng-jɔ̀ɔk fox, *n.*

จิงโจ้ jing-jôo kangaroo, *n.*

จิ้งหรีด jîng-rîit cricket, *n.*

จิ้งเหลน jîng-lěen skink, *n.*

จิต jìt mind, thought, heart, *n.*

จิตใจ jìt-jai mind, thought, *n.*

จิตแพทย์ jìt-dtà-pɛ̂ɛt psychiatrist, *n.*

จิตรกรรม jìt-dtà-gam painting, *n.*

จินดา jin-daa precious gem, *n.*

จินตนาการ jin-dtà-naa-gaan thought, imagination, *n.*

จิบ jìp sip, taste, *v.*

จิ้ม jîm dip into, pick, *v.*

จิ้มลิ้ม jîm-lím lovely, *adj.*

จี้ jîi poke with a finger, rob, *v.*

จี้ jîi locket pendant, *n.*

จี๋ jǐi extremely, *adv.*

จีน jiin Chinese, *n.*

จีบ jìip gather in folds, woo, court, *v.*

จีวร jii-wɔɔn robe of a Buddhist monk, *n.*

จืด jùut tasteless, dull, flat, *adj.*

จุ jù contain, hold, *v.*

จุก jùk cork, topknot, *n.*

จุกจิก jùk-jìk fussy, fastidious, *adj.*

จุด jùt spot, dot, mark, *n.*

จุด jùt dot, mark, ignite, light, *v.*

จุดจบ jùt-jòp end-point, *n.*

จุดหมาย jùt-mǎai aim, purpose, destination, *n.*

จุนเจือ jun-jʉa support, *v.*

จุ่ม jùm immerse, *v.*

จุมพิต jum-pít kiss, *v.*

จุลภาค jun-la-pâak the comma, *n.*

จุลินทรีย์ jù-lín-sii microbe, *n.*

จูง juung lead by the hand, lead,

induce, *v.*

จูงใจ juung-jai persuade, *v.*

จูบ jùup kiss, *v.*

เจ็ด jèt seven, *n.*

เจดีย์ jee-dii pagoda, *n.*

เจตนา jèet-dta-naa intention, determination, *n.*

เจนจัด jeen-jàt experienced, skillful, *adj.*

เจ็บ jèp sick, painful, hurt, *adj.*

เจ็บไข้ jèp-kâi get sick, *v.*

เจ็บใจ jèp-jai suffer mental pain, *v.*

เจ็บป่วย jèp-bpùai sick, ill, *adj.*

เจรจา jee-ra-jaa discuss, negotiate, converse, *v.*

เจริญ ja-rəən progress, grow, prosper, *v.*

เจอ jəə meet, encounter, find, discover, *v.*

เจ้า jâao prince, ruler, lord, master, holy being, guy, fellow, *n.*

เจ้าของ jâo-kɔ̌ɔng owner, *n.*

เจ้าชู้ jâo-chúu flirtatious, *adj.*

เจ้าชู้ jâo-chúu flirt, butterfly, philanderer, *n.*

เจ้าบ่าว jâo-bàao groom, *n.*

เจ้าสาว jâo-sǎao bride, *n.*

เจ้านาย jâo-naai master, boss, *n.*

เจ้าหน้าที่ jâo-nâa-ñi authority, n.

เจาะ jɔ̀ puncture, make a hole, pierce, punch a hole, v.

เจาะจง jɔ̀-jong specific, specify, adj., v.

เฉิดฉาย jɔ̀ət-jǎa gorgeous, shining, adj.

เจิม jəəm bless, v.

เจียน jian trim, cut, v.

เจียมตัว jiam-dtua moderate, humble, adj.

เจียว jiao fry, v.

เจียวไข่ jiao-kài make an omelet, v.

เจี๊ยวจ๊าว ñiao-jáao noisy, adj.

เจือ jʉa mix, v.

เจือจาง jʉa-jaang dilute, v.

แจ้ jêɛ bantam rooster, hen, n.

แจ้ jɛ̂ɛ small, dwarfed, adj.

แจก jèɛk distribute, v.

แจกแจง jèɛk-jɛɛng explain thoroughly, v.

แจกัน jɛɛ-gan vase, n.

แจ้ง jɛ̂ɛng clear, bright, vivid, adj.

แจ้งความ jɛ̂ɛng-kwaam inform, notify, v.

แจ่ม jɛ̀m clear, bright, distinct, adj.

แจวเรือ jɛɛo-rʉa row a boat, v.

แจ่ว jɛ̀o condiment composed of chili sauce and pickled fish, n.

แจ้ว jɛ̂o talkative, melodious, adj.

แจ๋ว jɛ̌o clear, distinct, bright, transparent, adj.

โจก jòok leader, chief, n.

โจ๊ก jóok joke, rice porridge, n.

โจ่งแจ้ง jòong-jɛ̂ɛng obvious, clear, opened, adj.

โจทก์ jòot prosecutor, plaintiff, n.

โจทย์ jòot arithmetical problem, n.

โจน joon jump, leap, plunge, v.

โจม joom tent, canopy, n.

โจมตี joom-dtii attack, assault, v.

โจร joon robber, thief, bandit, n.

โจรกรรม joo-ra-gam robbery, theft, n.

โจษ jòot spread about a rumor, v.

ใจ jai mind, heart, spirit, n.

ใจกล้า jai-glâa brave, adj.

ใจกลาง jai-glaang center, n.

ใจกว้าง jai-gwâang generous, adj.

ใจความ jai-kwaam substance, n.

ใจดี jai-dii kind, adj.

ใจดำ jai-dam cruel, mean, adj.

ใจเย็น jai-yen calm, adj.

ใจร้าย jai-ráai cruel, mean, adj.

ใจสั่น jai-sàn frightened, adj.

ฉ

ฉ chɔ̌ɔ the ninth consonant in the Thai alphabet (high consonant), *n.*

ฉก chòk snatch and run, *v.*

ฉกฉวย chòk-chǔai snatch, clutch, *v.*

ฉกรรจ์ chà-gan severe, *adj.*

ฉกาจ chà-gàat brave, *adj.*

ฉนวน chà-nǔan insulator, *n.*

ฉบับ chà-bàp issue, *n.*

ฉมวก chà-mùak harpoon, *n.*

ฉลาก chà-làak lottery ticket, raffle, tag, *n.*

ฉลากกินแบ่ง chà-làak-gin-bèng lottery, *n.*

ฉลาด chà-làat smart, clever, *adj.*

เฉลียวฉลาด chà-lǐao-chà-làat very clever, *adj.*

ฉลาม chà-lǎam shark, *n.*

ฉลุ chà-lù crave, engrave, *v.*

ฉลู chà-lǔu ox, cow, Year of the Ox, *n.*

ฉวย chǔai snatch, *v.*

ฉ้อโกง chɔ̂ɔ-goong defraud, cheat, *v.*

ฉะ chà cut, slash, fight, scold, *v.*

ฉะฉาน chà-chǎan clearly, *adj.*

ฉะนั้น chà-nán therefore, *adv.*

ฉะนี้ chà-níi for this reason, *adv.*

ฉัตร chàt parasol, royal umbrella, *n.*

ฉัน chǎn I, me, eat (used only Buddhist monks), *pron., v.*

ฉันใด chǎn-dai how, however, likewise, *adv.*

ฉันเพล chǎn-peen have food before noon (used for Buddhist monks), *v.*

ฉันท์ chǎn a Thai verse form, *n.*

ฉันทะ chǎn-tá approval, willingness, representation, *n.*

ฉาก chàak curtain, screen, *n.*

ฉาง chǎang barn, *n.*

ฉาบ chàap cymbals, *n.*

ฉาบฉวย chàap-chǔai snatch away, *v.*

ฉาย chǎai project, shine, reflect, *v.*

ฉายา chǎa-yaa reflection, name, *n.*

ฉาว chǎao widespread, *adj.*

ฉ่ำ chàm juicy, watery, *adj.*

ฉี่ chìi urine, urinate, *n., v.*

ฉีก chìik tear, lacerate, *v.*

ฉีด chìit inject, inoculate, squirt, spray, *v.*

ฉุกเฉิน chùk chɔ̌ɔn exigent, critical, of an emergency, immediately, *adj.*

ฉุด chùt pull, haul, drag, abduct, *v.*

ฉุน chǔn pungent, acrid, *adj.*

ฉุนเฉียว chǔn-chǐao furious, *adj.*

เฉพาะ chà-pɔ́ specific, particular, *adj.*

เฉย chɤ̌ɤi indifferent, apathetic, impartial, *v.*

เฉยเมย chɤ̌ɤi-mɤɤi indifferent, uninteresting, *adj.*

เฉลย chà-lɤ̌ɤi give an answer, *v.*

เฉลิมฉลอง chà-lɤ̌ɤm-cha-lɔ̌ɔng celebrate, commemorate, *v.*

เฉลี่ย chà-lìa average, share equally, *v.*

เฉลียง chà-lǐang balcony, porch, *n.*

เฉลียว chà-lǐao truly wise or clever, *adj.*

เฉา chǎo wither, *v.*

เฉาะ chɔ̀ split open, *v.*

เฉิ่ม chɤ̀m old-fashioned, *adj.*

เฉียด chìat pass near, just miss, *v.*

เฉียบ chìap very acute, severe, *adj.*

เฉียว chǐao strong, severe, *adj.*

เฉี่ยว chìao swoop, pass swiftly, *v.*

เฉือน chǔan carve, cut into pieces, *v.*

เฉื่อย chùai sluggish, *adj.*

แฉ chɛ̌ɛ reveal, disclose, *v.*

แฉก chɛ̌ɛk forked, notched, jagged, *adj.*

แฉะ chɛ̀ wet, damp, muddy, *v.*

โฉนด chà-nòot title-deed, *n.*

โฉบฉวย chòop-chǔai swoop down upon, *v.*

โฉม chǒom figure, shape, appearance, profile, look, shape, *n.*

โฉมงาม chǒom-ngaam beautiful, *adj.*

โฉลก chà-lòok luck, chance, fortune, treatise of fortune-telling, *n.*

ไฉน chà-nǎi why, how, for what reason, *adv.*

ไฉไล chǎi-lai pretty, shining, *adj.*

ช

ช chɔɔ the tenth consonant of the Thai alphabet (low consonant), *n.*

ชก chók punch, box, fight, *v.*

ชง chong make an infusion, soak in a liquid, *v.*

ชฎา chá-daa pointed head decoration, *n.*

ชดเชย chót-chɤ̌ɤi compensate, reimburse, *v.*

ชน chon collide with, bump against, hit, run into, *v.*

ชนบท chon-na-bòt rural area, *n.*

ชนวน chá-nuan fuse, *n.*

ชนะ chá-ná win, beat, *v.*

ชม chom admire, praise, *v.*

ชมพู chom-puu pink, *adj.*

ชมพู่ chom-pûu rose apple, *n.*

ชมรม chom-rom assembly, group, party, *n.*

ชรา chá-raa old age, senility, *n.*

ชล chon water, *n.*

ชโลม chá-loom smear, bathe, *v.*

ช่วง chûang section, interval, span *n.*

ช่วงชิง chûang-ching snatch, *v.*

ช่วงโชติ chûang-chôot brilliant, *adj.*

ช่วงเวลา chûang-wee-laa period of time, *n.*

ชวด chûat great grandfather, great grandmother, Year of the Rat, *n.*

ช่วย chûai help, assist, support, *v.*

ช่อ chôɔ cluster, bunch, bouquet, *n.*

ช่อง chɔ̂ɔng hole, gap, channel, *n.*

ช่องแคบ chɔ̂ɔng-kɛ̂ɛp straits, channel, *n.*

ช่องท้อง chɔ̂ɔng-tɔ́ɔng abdomen, *n.*

ช้อน chóɔn dig up, scoop up, *v.*

ช้อน chóɔn spoon, *n.*

ช้อนชา chóɔn-chaa tea-spoon, *n.*

ชอบ chɔ̂ɔp like, admire, *v.*

ชอบกัน chɔ̂ɔp-gan fond of each other, *adj.*

ชะ chá cleanse, purify, *v.*

ชะล้าง chá-láang rinse, *v.*

ชะงัก chá-ngák stop abruptly, stop short, *v.*

ชะเง้อ chá-ngɤ̂ɤ stretch the neck, *v.*

ชะโงก chá-ngôok peer out, poke one's head, *v.*

ชะตา chá-dtaa fate, destiny, fortune, *n.*

ชะนี chá-nii gibbon, *n.*

ชะมด chá-mót civet cat, *n.*

ชะลอ chá-lɔɔ slow down, move with care, *v.*

ชะลอม chá-lɔɔm a kind of bamboo basket, *n.*

ชัก chák pull, draw, haul, *v.*

ชักเย่อ chák-ga-yɤ̂ɤ tug-of-war, *n.*

ชักโครก chák-krôok flush toilet, flush, *n., v.*

ชักชวน chák-chuan persuade, *v.*

ชัง chang hate, abhor, dislike, detest, *v.*

ชั่ง châng weigh, *v.*

ชั่งใจ châng-jai weigh the pros and cons, consider, *v.*

ชัด chát clear, distinct, legible, *adj.*

ชัดเจน chát-jeen clear, distinct, *adj.*

ชัน chan steep, *adj.*

ชั้น chán grade, layer, level, shelf, floor, *n.*

ชันสูตร chan-na-sùut verify, prove, *v.*

ชันสูตรศพ chan-na-sùut-sòp perform an autopsy, *v.*

ชัยชนะ chai-cha-ná victory, triumph, *n.*

ชั่ว chûa bad, wicked, evil, *adj.*

ชั่วช้า chûa-cháa vicious, wicked, *adj.*

ชา chaa feel numb, numb, tea, *v., adj., n.*

ช้า cháa slow, long, tardy, *adj.*

ช่าง châng engineer, mechanic, maker, artisan, *n.*

ช่างกล châng-gon mechanic, *n.*

ช่างก่อสร้าง châng-gɔ̀ɔ-sâang builder, *n.*

ช่างเขียน châng-kǐan artist, *n.*

ช้าง cháang elephant, *n.*

ชาญ chaan skilled, *adj.*

ชาดก chaa-dòk existence of the Lord Buddha, *n.*

ชาตรี chaa-dtrii warrior, artist, *n.*

ชาตะ chaa-dtà born, *adj.*

ชาติ châat nation, nationality, race, *n.*

ชาติ châat life, *n.*

ชาติก่อน châat-gɔ̀ɔn previous life, *n.*

ชาน chaan platform, porch, outskirt, *n.*

ชาม chaam dish, bowl, *n.*

ชาย chaai male, man, *n.*

ชายคา chaai-kaa eaves, *n.*

ชายแดน chaai-dɛɛn border, *n.*

ชายทะเล chaai-ta-lee seaside, beach, *n.*

ชาว chaao people, tribe, race, *n.*

ชาวเขา chaao-kǎo tribesman, mountaineer, *n.*

ชาวนา chaao-naa farmers, *n.*

ชำ cham soak a cutting, *v.*

ชื่ม châm rejoicing, *adj.*

ช้ำ chám bruised, *adj.*

ช้ำใจ chám-jai hurt, *adj.*

ชำนาญ cham-naan skilled, experienced, *adj.*

ชำร่วย cham-rûai little gift, little present, *n.*

ชำระ cham-rá wash, purify, pay off, *v.*

ชำรุด cham-rút damaged, *adj.*

ชำเรา cham-rao rape, ravish, *v.*

ชำเลือง cham-lɯang look askance, *v.*

ชำแหละ cham-lè cut open, *v.*

ชิง ching snatch, *v.*

ชิงชัง ching-chang hate, *v.*

ชิงชัย ching-chai compete, v.

ชิงช้า ching-cháa swing, n.

ชิด chít close, near, adj., adv.

ชิน chin accustomed to, used to, adj.

ชิ้น chín piece, part, fragment, slice, n.

ชิม chim taste, sample by tasting, v.

ชี chii nun, ascetic, n.

ชี้ chíi point, indicate, v.

ชีพจร chîip-pa-jɔɔn pulse, n.

ชีพจรลงเท้า chîip-pa-jɔɔn-long-táao
unsettling, traveling all the time, adj.

ชีวประวัติ chii-wá-bprà-wàt biography, n.

ชีวิต chii-wít life, livelihood, n.

ชื่นใจ chûun-jai delightful, adj.

ชื้น chúun damp, moist, humid, adj.

ชื่อ chûu name, n.

ชื่อดัง chûu-dang famous, adj.

ชื่อเสียง chûu-sǐang fame, n.

ชุก chúk abundant, adj.

ชุด chút suit, n.

ชุน chun repair, make embroidery, v.

ชุบ chúp dip, immerse, v.

ชุบชีวิต chúp-chii-wít revive, rejuvenate, v.

ชุม chum assemble, collect, v.

ชุมชน chum-chon community, n.

ชุ่ม chûm moist, damp, soaked, adj.

ชุมนุม chum-num gather, assemble,
v.

ชุมนุมชน chum-num-chon community, congregation, n.

ชุลมุน chun-la-mun disorderly, confused, tumultuous, adj.

ชู chuu raise up high, lift, uphold,
boost, elevate, v.

ชูรส chuu-rót enhance the flavor, v.

ชู้ chúu lover, adulterer, n.

เช็ด chét wipe, rub, scrub, clean, v.

เช่น chên example, instance, n.

เช่น chên similar to, like, as if, adj.

เช่นเคย chên-kəəi as usual, adv.

เช่นเดียวกัน chên-diao-gan the same
as, adv.

เช่นว่า chên-wâa as mentioned, prep.

เชย chəəi silly, rustic, rural, adj.

เชลย chá-ləəi captive, hostage, prisoner of war, n.

เช่า châo rent, lease, let, v.

เช้า cháao morning, n.

เช้าตรู่ cháao-dtrùu early morning, n.

เชิง chəəng pedestal, stand, n.

เชิงอรรถ chəəng-àt footnote, n.

เชิญ chəən invite, v.

เชิด chə̂ət elevate, increase, *v.*

เชิดชู chə̂ət-chuu lift up, *v.*

เชิดหุ่น chə̂ət-hùn perform puppet dance, *v.*

เชี่ยว chîao rapid, swift, *adj.*

เชื่อ chûa believe, trust, rely on, *v.*

เชื่อใจ chûa-jai trust, *v.*

เชื่อมั่น chûa-mân confident, *adj.*

เชื้อ chúa origin, lineage, offspring, race, grim, microbe, bacteria, *n.*

เชือก chûak rope, cord, string, *n.*

เชื่อง chûang tame, docile, gentle, *adj.*

เชือด chûat slice, *v.*

เชื่อม chûam join, solder, cement, *v.*

แช่ chɛ̂ɛ soak, steep, saturate, *v.*

แช่ง chɛ̂ng curse, revile, vilify, *v.*

โชค chôok fortune, luck, fate, *n.*

โชคดี chôok-dii good luck, *n.*

โชติ chôot prosperity, *n.*

โชติช่วง chôot-chûang brilliant, *adj.*

โชย chooi blow gently, *v.*

ใช่ châi yes, indeed, *adv.*

ใช้ cháai employ, send to, order someone, use, spend, *v.*

ไช chai form by drilling or digging, make a hole, *v.*

ไชโย chai-yoo bravo, cheers, *interj.*

ซ

ซ sɔɔ the eleventh consonant of the Thai alphabet (low consonant), *n.*

ซด sót sip, *v.*

ซน son mischievous, naughty, *adj.*

ซบ sóp rest (one's face on), *v.*

ซบเซา sóp-sao depressed, dull, *adj.*

ซวย suai unlucky, *adj.*

ซอ sɔɔ fiddle (musical instrument), *n.*

ซอก sɔ̂ɔk lane, alley, *n.*

ซอง sɔɔng envelope, case, sheath, *n.*

ซ่อง sɔ̂ng brothel, whore house, *n.*

ซ่อน sɔ̂n hide, conceal, *v.*

ซ่อนเร้น sɔ̂n-rén conceal, hide, *v.*

ซ่อนหา sɔ̂n-hǎa hide-and-seek, *n.*

ซ้อน sɔ́ɔn overlap, *v.*

ซ่อม sɔ̂m renovate, repair, mend, restore, *v.*

ซ้อม sɔ́ɔm exercise, practice, train, drill, *v.*

ซอมซ่อ sɔm-sɔ̂ɔ shabby, *adj.*

ซอย sɔɔi divide into pieces, *v.*

ซอย sɔɔi lane, Soi, *n.*

ซัก sák wash, launder, inquire, *v.*

ซักซ้อม sák-sɔ́ɔm rehearse, *v.*

ซัด sát throw, hurl, filing, cast, dash, *v.*

ก ข ฃ ค ฅ ฆ ง จ ฉ ช ซ ฌ ญ ฎ ฏ ฐ ฑ ฒ ณ ด ต ถ ท

ซับ sáp absorb, *v.*

ซับซ้อน sáp-sɔ́ɔn complicated, intricate, *adj.*

ซับใน sáp-nai lining, underwear, *n.*

ซา saa diminish, subside, lessen, *v.*

ซาก sâak dead body, remains, *n.*

ซ่าน sâan diffuse, permeate, *v.*

ซ้าย sáai left, *adj., adv.*

ซ้ำ sám repeat, recur, *v.*

ซีอิ๊ว sii-íu soy bean sauce, *n.*

ซี่ sîi rib, bar, tooth, classifier for rib, bar, tooth, *n.*

ซีก sîik part, piece, *n.*

ซีกไม้ sîik-máai splinter, *n.*

ซีด sîit pale, faded, *adj.*

ซึ่ง sûng which, that, who, whose, whom, *pron.*

ซึ้ง súng deep, profound, *adj.*

ซึ้งใจ súng-jai impressive, *adj.*

ซึม sɯm permeate, drowsy, sluggish, *v., adj.*

ซึมเซา sɯm-sao drowsy, dull, *adj.*

ซึมซาบ sɯm-sâap permeate, *v.*

ซื่อ sɯ̂ɯ honest, truthful, *adj.*

ซื่อตรง sɯ̂ɯ-dtrong honest, faithful, *adj.*

ซื้อ sɯ́ɯ buy, purchase, *n.*

ซื้อขาย sɯ́ɯ-kǎai trade, *v.*

ซุกซน súk-son mischievous, naughty, *adj.*

ซุกซ่อน súk-sɔ̂n hide, conceal, *adj.*

ซุง sung log, lumber, timber, *n.*

ซุบซิบ súp-síp whisper, *v.*

ซุ่ม sûm lie in ambush, *v.*

ซุ้ม súm archway, *n.*

ซุ้มประตู súm-bprà-dtuu porch, window facade, *n.*

ซุ่มซ่าม sûm-sâam careless, *adj.*

ซูบ sûup pale, *adj.*

ซูบซีด sûup-sîit emaciated and pale, *adj.*

ซูบผอม sûup-pɔ̌ɔm pale and skinny, *adj.*

เซ see stagger, *v., adj.*

เซ็ง seng dull, insipid, tasteless, *adj.*

เซ้ง séng sell out, *v.*

เซ่น sên make offering or sacrifice to the spirit, *v.*

เซ็น sen sign, *v.*

เซ่อ sɔ̂ɔ stupid, silly, foolish, *adj.*

เซียว siao withered, wrinkled, *adj.*

เซื่องซึม sɯ̂ang-sɯm inactive and drowsy, *adj.*

แซ่ sɛ̂ɛ family name, *n.*

แซง sɛɛng interfere, intervene, v.
แซ่บ sɛ̂ɛp, sɛ̂p delicious, adj.
โซ soo needy, poor, penniless, adj.
โซ่ sôo chain, n.
ไซ้ sái dig for food with the beak, v.

ฌ

ฌ chɔɔ the twelfth consonant of the
Thai alphabet (low consonant), n.
ฌาน chaan meditative, transcendent
insight, vision, n.
ฌาน chaan a sect in Buddhism, n.
ฌาปนกิจ chaa-bpa-ná-gìt cremation,
n.
ฌาปนสถาน chaa-bpa-na-sà-tăan
crematorium, n.

ญ

ญ yɔɔ the thirteenth consonant of the
Thai alphabet (low consonant), n.
ญวน yuan Vietnamese, n.
ญัตติ yát-dtì motion, resolution, proposition, n.
ญาณ yaan transcendent insight, perception vision, n.

ญาณี yaa-nii intelligent person, n.
ญาติ yâat relative, kinsman, n.
ญี่ปุ่น yîi-bpùn Japan, Japanese, n.

ฎ

ฎ dɔɔ the fourteenth consonant of the
Thai alphabet (mid consonant), n.
ฎีกา dii-gaa petition or appeal to the
Supreme Court, subscription for
Buddhist monk, n.

ฏ

ฏ dtɔɔ the fifteenth consonant of the
Thai alphabet (mid consonant), n.

ฐ

ฐ tɔ̌ɔ the sixteenth consonant of the
Thai alphabet (high consonant), n.
ฐาน tăan base, foot, pedestal, ground,
platform, reason, basis, foundation, n.
ฐานทัพ tăan-táp military base, n.
ฐานะ tăa-ná position, status, n.
ฐานันดร tăa-nan-dɔɔn rank, title, n.
ฐานานุกรม tăa-naa-nú-grom ecclesi-

astical orders, *n.*

ฐิติ tĭ-dtì maintenance, existence, status, perpetuity, *n.*

ฑ

ฑ tɔɔ the seventeenth consonant of the Thai alphabet (low consonant), *n.*

ฒ

ฒ tɔɔ the eighteenth consonant of the Thai alphabet (low consonant), *n.*

เฒ่า tâo very old person, chief, person of age, *n.*

เฒ่า tâo aged, very old, *adj.*

เฒ่าแก่ tâo-gèè a go between who arranges a marriage, *n.*

ณ

ณ nɔɔ the nineteenth consonant of the Thai alphabet (low consonant), *n.*

ณ ná at, by, on, upon, in, near, *prep.*

ณรงค์ na-rong fighting, campaign, competition, *n.*

เณร neen Buddhist novice, *n.*

ด

ด dɔɔ the twentieth consonant of the Thai alphabet (mid consonant)

ดก dòk prolific, *adj.*

ด้น dôn penetrate, run a seam by hand, *v.*

ดนตรี don-dtrii music, *n.*

ดม dom smell, sniff, *v.*

ดล don inspire, motivate, *v.*

ดวง duang round object, sphere, classifier for things circular in shape, *n.*

ดวงจันทร์ duang-jan the moon, *n.*

ดวงชะตา duang-cha-dtaa fate, luck, *n.*

ด่วน dùan urgent, pressing, express, hasty, *adj.*

ด้วน dûan cut off, *adj.*

ด้วย dûai also, too, together, *adv.*

ดวล duan compete, *v.*

ดอก dɔ̀ɔk flower, *n., clf.*

ดอง dɔɔng pickle, *v.*

ดอน dɔɔn highland, *n.*

ด้อม dɔ̂m snoop, *v.*

ดอย dɔɔi hill, mountain, peak, *n.*

ด้อย dɔ̂i inferior, undeveloped, *adj.*

ดัก dàk trap, set a trap, *v.*

ดัง dang loud, boisterous, *adj., adv.*

ดังกล่าว dang-glàao as mentioned, *adv.*

ดั่ง dàng like, just as, *adj.*

ดั้งจมูก dâng-jà-mùuk bridge of the nose, *n.*

ดั้งเดิม dâng-dəəm original, *adj., adv.*

ดัชนี dàt-cha-nii index finger, *n.*

ดัด dàt bend, alter, *v.*

ดัดจริต dàt-jà-rìt pretend in manner, *v.*

ดัน dan push, *v.*

ดับ dàp extinguish, *v.*

ด่า dàa curse, *v.*

ดาก dàak anus (very vulgar), *n.*

ด่าง dàang alkaline salt, *n.*

ด่างพร้อย dàang-prɔ́ɔi blemish, spotted, *adj.*

ดาด dàat pave, spread out, *v.*

ด่าน dàan customs house, *n.*

ด่านเข้าเมือง dàan-kâo-mʉang immigration office, *n.*

ด้าน dâan side, face, direction, *n.*

ด้านกลับ dâan-glàp reverse, *n.*

ด้านซ้าย dâan-sáai left side, *n.*

ดาบ dàap sword, *n.*

ดาม daam brace, strengthen, *v.*

ด้าม dâam handle, *n.*

ดาย daai trim, *v.*

ด้าย dâai cotton thread, *n.*

ดารา daa-raa star, *n.*

ดาราศาสตร์ daa-raa-sàat astronomy, *n.*

ดาว daao star, celestial body, *n.*

ดาวเคราะห์ daao-krɔ́ planet, *n.*

ดาวตก daao-dtòk shooting star, *n.*

ดาษ dàat widely distributed, *adj.*

ดำ dam dive, submerge, *v.*

ดำเนิน dam-nəən proceed, go on, *v.*

ดำรง dam-rong uphold, sustain, *v.*

ดำรัส dam-ràt say, *v.*, *royal.*

ดำริ dam-rì think, *v.*

ดิค dìk (short for) dictionary, *n.*

ดิ่ง dìng vertical, righteous, *n.*

ดิฉัน dì-chǎn, dì-chán, I, me, *n.*

ดิน din earth, soil, ground, *n.*

ดิ้น dîn struggle, wriggle, *v.*

ดิบ dìp raw, unripe, *adj.*

ดี dii gall, gallbladder, *n.*

ดี dii good, fine, well, *adj.*

ดีกัน dii-gan reconciled, *adj.*

ดีซ่าน dii-sâan jaundice, *n.*

ดีใจ dii-jai glad, pleased, *adj.*

ดีด dìit flick, pluck, flip, *v.*

ดีบุก dii-bùk tin, *n.*

ดึก dùk late at night, *n.*

ดึง dung stretch out, pull, draw, *v.*

ดื่ม dùum drink, *v.*

ดื้อ dûu stubborn, headstrong, *adj.*

ดื้อดึง dûu-dung obstinate, disobedient, *adj.*

ดุ dù scold, reproach, *v.*

ดุดัน dù-dan fierce, *adj.*

ดุกดิก dùk-dìk move about, *v.*

ดุจ dùt as if, as, as though, *adj., adv.,
prep.*

ดุน dun push, poke, *v.*

ดุ้น dûn stick, *n.*

ดุม dum button, *n.*

ดุล dun balance, *n.*

ดุลการค้า dun-qaan-káa trade balance, *n.*

ดุลภาพ dun-la-pâap equality, *n.*

ดุษฎีนิพนธ์ dùt-sà-dii-ní-pon dissertation, *n.*

ดุษฎีบัณฑิต dùt-sà-dii-ban-dìt doctorate degree, *n.*

ดู duu look, look at, watch, stare, *v.*

ดูงาน duu-ngaan observe, *v.*

ดูด dùut suck, absorb, *v.*

ดึงดูด dung-dùut attract, *v.*

เด็ก dèk child, infant, baby, *n.*

เด็กชาย dèk-chaai boy, *n.*

เด็กหญิง dèk-yǐng girl, *n.*

เด้ง dêng bounce, *v.*

เดช dèet force, might, *n.*

เด็ด dèt pick, pluck, *v.*

เด็ดขาด dèt-kàat decisive, *adj.*

เดน deen residues, *n.*

เด่น dèn prominent, conspicuous, *adj.*

เดรัจฉาน dee-rát-chǎan beast, *n.*

เดา dao guess, reckon, *v.*

เดาะ dɔ̀ bat up, *v.*

เดิน dəən walk, *v.*

เดินขบวน dəən-kà-buan demonstrate, parade, *v.*

เดินแถว dəən-tɛ̌ɛo march, *v.*

เดินทาง dəən-taang take a trip, travel,
v.

เดิม dəəm start, origin, *n.*

เดิมที dəəm-tii at first, from the beginning, *adv.*

เดิมพัน dəəm-pan bet, *n.*

เดียงสา diang-sǎa laok worldly wisdom, *v.*

เดียดฉันท์ dìat-chǎn dislike, *v.*

เดียว diao single, one, alone, *adj.*

เดี่ยว dìao single, alone, sole, *adj.*

เดี๋ยว dǐao moment, *n.*

เดี่ยวเดียว dǐao-diao just a moment, *adv.*

เดือด dùat boil, *v.*

เดือด dùat furious, *adj.*

เดือน dɯan moon, month, *n.*

เดือย dɯai spur, cock's spur, *n.*

แด่ dɛ̀ɛ to, for, *prep.*

แดก dɛ̀ɛk eat, devour, *v., vulg.*

แดง dɛɛng red, *n.*

แดด dɛ̀ɛt sunlight, sunshine, *n.*

แดน dɛɛn border, *n.*

โด่ dòo pointed, *adj.*

โด่ง dòong high up in the air, elevated, *adj.*

โด่งดัง dòong-dang famous, renowned, *adj.*

โดด dòot jump, leap, spring, bound, *v.*

โดดเดี่ยว dòot-dìao solitary, alone, *adj.*

โดน doon hit, strike, *v.*

โดย dooi by, by means of, with, through, following, *prep.*

โดยตรง dooi-dtrong directly, *adv.*

ใด dai which, whichever, who, whoever, what, whatever, any, *pron., adj., adv.*

ใด dai any, a, an, *adj.*

ใดๆ dai-dai whatsoever, anyone, *adv.*

ได้ dâai get, can, obtain, acquire, attain, receive, *v.*

ไดโนเสาร์ dai-noo-sǎo dinosaur, *n.*

ต

ต dtɔɔ the twenty-first consonant of the Thai alphabet (mid consonant), *n.*

ตก dtòk fall, drop, miss, *v.*

ตกกระ dtòk-grà have freckles, *v.*

ตกกล้า dtòk-glâa transplant seedling rice, *v.*

ตกค้าง dtòk-káang left over, *adj.*

ตกงาน dtòk-ngaan unemployed, *adj.*

ตกต่ำ dtòk-dtàm decline, *v.*

ตกแต่ง dtòk-dtèng decorate, *v.*

ตกผลึก dtòk-plùk crystallize, *v.*

ตด dtòt fart, *v., n.*

ตน dton self, oneself, body, *n.*

ต้น dtôn trunk, stalk, origin, source, beginning, *n.*

ต้นคอ dtôn-kɔɔ nape of neck, *n.*

ต้นตอ dtôn-dtɔɔ source, *n.*

ตบ dtòp slap, clap, pat, *v.*

ตะบะ dtà-bà religious meditation, *n.*

ต้ม dtôm boil, *v.*

ตรง dtrong straight, upright, true, direct, adj.

ตรรกศาสตร์ dtàk-gà-sàat logic, n.

ตรวจ dtrùat examine, survey, check, inspect, v.

ตรวน dtruan ankle chains, n.

ตรอก dtrɔ̀ɔk lane, alley, n.

ตรอง dtrɔɔng think carefully, v.

ตรอมใจ dtrɔɔm-jai sorrowful, adj.

ตระการตา dtrà-gaan-dtaa pleasing to the eye, adj.

ตระกูล dtrà-guun family, n.

ตระเวน dtrà-ween roam, v.

ตระหง่าน dtrà-ngàan high, prominent, adj.

ตระหนก dtrà-nòk frightened, adj.

ตระหนัก dtrà-nàk realize, become aware, v.

ตระหนี่ dtrà-nìi stingy, adj.

ตรัย dtrai three, adj.

ตรัส dtràt (royal) tell, speak, v.

ตรา dtraa seal, stamp, brand, n.

ตรากตรำ dtràak-dtram endure, v.

ตราบเท่า dtràap-tâo so long as, until, prep., conj.

ตรี dtrii three, adj.

ตรึกตรอง dtrùk-dtrɔɔng think carefully, v.

ly, v.

ตรึง dtrung fasten, tie up, v.

ตรุษ dtrùt the New Year, n.

ตรู่ dtrùu dawn, n.

ตลก dtà-lòk joker, comedian, funny man, n.

ตลก dtà-lòk funny, adj.

ตลบ dtà-lòp fold back, v.

ตลอด dtà-lɔ̀ɔt through, all over, through out, adj., adv.

ตลอดเวลา dtà-lɔ̀ɔt-wee-laa always, all the time, adv.

ตลับ dtà-làp junction box, n.

ตลาด dtà-làat market, n.

ตลิ่ง dtà-lìng bank, n.

ตลึง dtà-lung stunned, adj.

ตวัด dtà-wàt strike with the arm bent, v.

ตวาด dtà-wàat scold harshly, shout threateningly, v.

ตอ dtɔɔ stump, n.

ต่อ dtɔ̀ɔ connect, join, link, unite, v.

ต่อจากนั้น dtɔ̀ɔ-jàak-nán then, adv.

ต่อต้าน dtɔ̀ɔ-dtâan resist, v.

ต้อกระจก dtɔ̂ɔ-grà-jòk cataract, n.

ต้อหิน dtɔ̂ɔ-hǐn glaucoma, n.

ตอก dtɔ̀ɔk pound down, nail, v.

ต้อง dtɔ̂ng must, v.

ต้องการ dtɔ̂ŋ-gaan want, need, v.

ตอด dtɔ̀ɔt nibble, bite, v.

ตอน dtɔɔn section, period, time, n.

ต้อน dtɔ̂ɔn herd, v.

ต้อนรับ dtɔ̂ɔn-ráp welcome, v.

ตอบ dtɔ̀ɔp reply, answer, respond, v.

ตอม dtɔɔm fly around, v.

ต่อม dtɔ̀m gland, n.

ต่อย dtɔ̀i box, punch, v.

ต้อยต่ำ dtɔ̂i-dtàm low, low-classed, adj.

ตอแย dtɔɔ-yɛɛ annoy, v.

ตอแหล dtɔɔ-lɛ̌ɛ fib, lie, v.

ตะกร้อ dtà-grɔ̂ɔ a Thai ball game, n.

ตะกร้า dtà-grâa basket, n.

ตะกละ dtà-glà greedy, adj.

ตะกอน dtà-gɔɔn sediment, n.

ตะกั่ว dtà-gùa lead, n.

ตะกาย dtà-gaai crawl, v.

ตะกุกตะกัก dtà-gùk-dtà-gàk rough, uneven, adj.

ตะกุย dtà-gui scratch, n.

ตะเกียง dtà-giang lamp, n.

ตะเกียบ dtà-gìap chopsticks, n.

ตะแกรง dtà-grɛɛŋ sieve, n.

ตะโก dtà-goo ebony, n.

ตะโก้ dtà-gôo Thai coconut pudding, n.

ตะโกน dtà-goon shout, v.

ตะขาบ dtà-kàap centipede, n.

ตะเข็บ dtà-kèp seam, n.

ตะคริว dtà-kriu cramp, n.

ตะครุบ dtà-krúp pound upon and seize, v.

ตะคอก dtà-kɔ̂ɔk shout threateningly, v.

ตะแคง dtà-kɛɛŋ tilt on one side, v.

ตะไคร่ dtà-krâi moss, n.

ตะไคร้ dtà-krái lemon grass, n.

ตะไบ dtà-bai file, v., n.

ตะปู dtà-bpuu nail, n.

ตะพาบ dtà-pâap snapping turtle, n.

ตะเพิด dtà-pə̂ət drive off, v.

ตะโพก dtà-pôok buttock, hips, n.

ตะราง dtà-raang prison, n.

ตะล่อม dtà-lɔ̂m approach, v.

ตะลีตะลาน dtà-lii-dtà-laan hurried, adj.

ตะลึง dtà-lʉŋ frightened, stunned, adj.

ตะลุง dtà-luŋ shadow play, n.

ตะลุย dtà-lui break through, v.

ตะแลงแกง dtà-lɛɛŋ-gɛɛŋ scaffold, n.

ตะวัน dtà-wan the sun, n.

ตะเวน dtà-ween patrol, v.

ตะหลิว dtà-lǐu ladle, *n.*

ตัก dtàk dip up, *v.*

ตักบาตร dtàk-bàat present food to a Buddhist monk, *v.*

ตักเตือน dtàk-dtuan warn, *v.*

ตั๊กแตน dták-gà-dtɛɛn grasshopper, *n.*

ตั่ง dtàng stool, *n.*

ตั้ง dtâng set up, establish, appoint, *v.*

ตั้งแต่ dtâng-dtɛ̀ɛ since, from, *adv.*

ตั้งท้อง dtâng-tɔ́ɔng become pregnant, *v.*

ตั้งมั่น dtâng-mân establish firmly, *v.*

ตัณหา dtan-hǎa lust, desire, *n.*

ตัด dtàt cut, sever, *v.*

ตัดชีวิต dtàt-chii-wít kill, *v.*

ตัดถนน dtàt-tà-nǒn build a road, *v.*

ตัดสิน dtàt-sǐn decide, judge, *v.*

ตัดสินใจ dtàt-sǐn-jai determine, make up one's mind, *v.*

ตัน dtan solid, *n.*

ตัน dtan ton, *n.*

ตับ dtàp liver, *n.*

ตัว dtua body, person, self, substance, classifier for animals, insects, desks, chairs, tables, cigarettes, characters, figures, *n.*

ตัวประกัน dtua-bprà-gan hostage, *n.*

ตัวตลก dtua-dtà-lòk clown, *n.*

ตัวละคร dtua-lá-kɔɔn character, *n.*

ตัวเลข dtua-lêek numeral, *n.*

ตัวหนังสือ dtua-nǎng-sǔu letter, character, alphabet, *n.*

ตัวอย่าง dtua-yàang example, *n.*

ตั๋ว dtǔa ticket, *n.*

ตา dtaa maternal grandfather, old man, eye, *n.*

ตาขาว dtaa-kǎao cowardly, *adj.*

ตาขาว dtaa-kǎao white of the eye, *n.*

ตาเข dtaa-kěe cross-eyed, squint-eyed, *adj.*

ตาชั่ง dtaa-châng scales, *n.*

ตาตุ่ม dtaa-dtùm anklebone, *n.*

ตาบอด dtaa-bɔ̀ɔt blind, *n.*

ตาราง dtaa-raang square, *n.*

ตารางวา dtaa-raang-waa square-yard (Thai measurement), *n.*

ตารางเวลา dtaa-raang-wee-laa time table, *n.*

ตาก dtàak sun dried, *adj.*

ต่าง dtàang different, various, *adj.*

ต่างๆ dtàang-dtàang various, diverse, miscellaneous, *adv.*, *adj.*

ต่างๆนานา dtàang-dtàang-naa-naa

in various ways, *adv.*

ต่างกัน dtàang-gan different, *adj.*

ต่างกับ dtàang-gàp different from, *adj.*

ต่างจังหวัด dtàang-jang-wàt provincial, *adj.*

ต่างชาติ dtàang-châat foreign, *adj.*

ต่างด้าว dtàang-dâao alien, *n.*

ต่างประเทศ dtàang-bprà-têet foreign country, *n., adj.*

ต้าน dtâan resist, oppose, *v.*

ตาม dtaam follow, pursue, *v.*

ตามใจ dtaam-jai yield to the wishes of, *v.*

ตามเดิม dtaam-dəəm as before, *adv.*

ตามทาง dtaam-taang along the way, *adv.*

ตามลำดับ dtaam-lam-dàp respectively, *adv.*

ตามลำพัง dtaam-lam-pang alone, *adj.*

ตามสมัย dtaam-sà-măi fashionable, *adj.*

ตามสบาย dtaam-sà-baai at ease, *adv.*

ตาย dtaai die, *v.*

ตายด้าน dtaai-dâan insensitive, *adj.*

ตายตัว dtaai-dtua stable, *adj.*

ตาล dtaan sugar palm, *n.*

ตำ dtam pierce, puncture, pound, *v.*

ต่ำ dtàm low, short, *adj.*

ต่ำช้า dtàm-cháa degraded, *adj.*

ตำนาน dtam-naan legend, *n.*

ตำรวจ dtam-rùat police, *n.*

ตำรับ dtam-ràp formula, *n.*

ตำรา dtam-raa textbook, *n.*

ตำลึง dtam-lɯng an old Thai monetary unit of four ticals, *n.*

ตำหนัก dtam-nàk house or residence of royalty, *n.*

ตำหนิ dtam-nì defect, flaw, blame, *n.*

ตำแหน่ง dtam-nèng position, *n.*

ติ dtì censure, reproach, criticize, *v.*

ติ๊ก dtík mark, *v.*

ติง dting move, *v.*

ติ่ง dtìng outgrowth, appendix, *n.*

ติ่งหู dtìng-hŭu lowest tip to the earlobe, *n.*

ติด dtìt adhere, connect, adjoin, stick, attach, *v.*

ติดค้าง dtìt-káang in debt, *adj.*

ติดคุก dtìt-kúk imprisoned, *adj.*

ติดใจ dtìt-jai impressed by, *adj.*

ติดต่อ dtìt-dtɔɔ connect, *v.*

ติดตั้ง dtìt-dtâng install, *v.*

ติดยา dtìt-yaa addicted to drugs, *adj.*

ติดสินบน dtìt-sĭn-bon bribe, v.

ติดอ่าง dtìt-àang stutter, v.

ตี dtii beat, strike, hit, whip, v.

ตีความ dtii-kwaam interpret, v.

ตีตั๋ว dtii-dtŭa buy tickets, v.

ตีน dtiin foot, pedestal, stand, n.

ตีบ dtìip constricted, narrow, adj.

ตึก dtùk building, n.

ตึกระฟ้า dtùk-rá-fáa skyscraper, n.

ตึง dtung tense, tight, adj.

ตืด dtùut stingy, adj.

ตื่น dtùun awake, adj.

ตื่นตัว dtùun-dtua become alert, v.

ตื้น dtûun shallow, adj.

ตื้อ dtûu persist, v.

ตุ๊กๆ dtúk-dtúk small motor tricycle or boat, n.

ตุ๊กแก dtúk-gɛɛ gecko, large house-lizard, n.

ตุ๊กตา dtúk-gà-dtaa doll, n.

ตุกติก dtùk-dtìk tricky, adj.

ตุ่น dtùn mole (animal), n.

ตุ๋น dtǔn cook by steaming, v.

ตุ่ม dtùm large water jar, n.

ตุ้ม dtûm pendant, suspend object, n.

ตุ้มหู dtûm-hǔu earring, n.

ตุลาการ dtù-laa-gaan judge, n.

ตุลาคม dtù-laa-kom October, n.

ตู่ dtùu claim falsely, v.

ตู้ dtûu cupboard, wardrobe, chest, n.

ตูด dtùut buttock, bottom, anus, n.

ตูม dtuum budding, adj.

เต่งตึง dtèng-dtung elevated and firm, adj.

เต้น dtên jump, skip, v.

เต้นรำ dtên-ram dance, n.

เต็ม dtem full, adj.

เต็มใจ dtem-jai willingly, adv.

เต็มที่ dtem-tîi to the utmost, adv.

เต็มไปด้วย dtem-bpai-dûai full of, adj.

เตร่ dtrèe wander about, v.

เตรียม dtriam prepare, make ready, v.

เตะ dtè kick, v.

เตา dtao stove, fireplace, oven, n.

เต่า dtào turtle, tortoise, n.

เต้า dtâo water bottle, n.

เต้าเจี้ยว dtâo-jîao bean paste, n.

เต้านม dtâo-nom breast, n.

เต๋า dtǎo Taoism, dice, n.

เติบโต dtə̀əp-dtoo grow, v.

เติม dtəəm add, increase, v.

เตียง dtiang low, short, bed, adj., n.

เตียน dtian cleared, flat, adj.

ธ น บ ป ผ ฝ พ ฟ ภ ม ย ร ฤ ฦ ล ว ศ ษ ส ห ฬ อ ฮ

เตือน dtɯan warn, *v.*

เตือนใจ dtɯan-jai remind, *v.*

แต่ dtɛ̀ɛ only, *adv., adj., conj.*

แต่ก่อน dtɛ̀ɛ-gɔ̀ɔn before, *adv.*

แต่แรก dtɛ̀ɛ-rɛ̂ɛk at first, *adv.*

แต่ละ dtɛ̀ɛ-lá each, *adv., adj.*

แต่ว่า dtɛ̀ɛ-wâa but, however, *conj.*

แต่วัน dtɛ̀ɛ-wan early, *adv.*

แตก dtɛ̀ɛk break, split, *v.*

แตกฉาน dtɛ̀ɛk-chǎan vividly, clearly, *adv.*

แตกต่าง dtɛ̀ɛk-dtàang differ, *v.*

แตกพวก dtɛ̀ɛk-pûak separated from, *adj.*

แตง dtɛɛng climbing plants, *n.*

แต่ง dtɛ̀ng decorate, adorn, *v.*

แต่งงาน dtɛ̀ng-ngaan marry, *v.*

แต่งตั้ง dtɛ̀ng-dtâng assign, *v.*

แต่งตัว dtɛ̀ng-dtua get dressed, *v.*

แต้จิ๋ว dtɛ̂ɛ-jiu Taechew, *n.*

แตน dtɛɛn wasp, hornet, *n.*

แต้ม dtɛ̂ɛm smear, *v.*

แต้มสี dtɛ̂ɛm-sǐi paint, *v.*

แตะ dtɛ̀ touch, *v.*

แตะต้อง dtɛ̀-dtɔ̂ng touch, contact, *v.*

โต dtoo big, large, great, *adj.*

โตขึ้น dtoo-kɯ̂n grow up, *v.*

โต้ dtôo refuse, oppose, *v.*

โต้เถียง dtôo-tiang argue, *v.*

โต้รุ่ง dtôo-rûng till the morning, *adv.*

โต้วาที dtôo-waa-tii debate, *v.*

โตงเตง dtoong-dteeng swaying, *adj.*

โตน dtoon skip, *v.*

โต๊ะ dtó table, desk, *n.*

ใต้ dtâai low, south, below, under, beneath, *adv., prep.*

ไต dtai kidney, *n.*

ไต่ dtài climb, creep, *v.*

ไต่ถาม dtài-tǎam question, *v.*

ไต่สวน dtài-sǔan investigate, *v.*

ไต้ dtâi torch, *n.*

ไต๋ dtǎi real purpose, secret, *n.*

ไต้ฝุ่น dtâi-fùn typhoon, *n.*

ไตร dtrai three, great, *adj.*

ไตร่ตรอง dtrài-dtrɔɔng think over, *v.*

ถ

ถ tɔ̌ɔ the twenty-second consonant in the Thai alphabet (high consonant), *n.*

ถก tòk pull, roll up, *v.*

ถด tòt retreat, move back, *v.*

ถนน tà-nǒn street, road, *n.*

ถนอม tà-nɔɔm cherish, conserve, *v.*

ถนัด tà-nàt skilled, dexterous, *adj.*

ถม tǒm fill up, fill in, *v.*

ถ่ม tòm spit, spout, *v.*

ถมึง tà-mǔng scowling, *adj.*

ถลก tà-lòk roll up, *v.*

ถลน tà-lǒn protrude, *v.*

ถล่ม tà-lòm collapse, subside, *v.*

ถลอก tà-lɔ̀ɔk scraped, *adj.*

ถลา tà-lǎa lean to on side, *v.*

ถลำ tà-lǎm blunder, slip, *v.*

ถลึง tà-lǔng stare fiercely, *v.*

ถลุง tà-lǔng smelt (ore), spend extravagantly, *v.*

ถ่วง tùang weight, load, *v.*

ถ้วน tûan complete, entire, *adj.*

ถ้วย tûai cup, small bowl, *n.*

ถวาย tà-wǎai present, offer, *v.*

ถวิล tà-wǐn long for, *v.*

ถ่อ tɔ̀ɔ punt, *v.*

ถอก tɔ̀ɔk draw back, *v.*

ถอง tɔ̌ɔng strike or nudge with the elbow, *v.*

ถ่อง tɔ̀ng clear, vivid, *adj.*

ถอด tɔ̀ɔt remove, undo, take off, *v.*

ถอน tɔ̌ɔn pull, draw, *v.*

ถ่อม tɔ̀m humble, *adj.*

ถอย tɔ̌ɔi retreat, *v.*

ถ่อย tɔ̀i mean, *adj.*

ถ้อยคำ tɔ̂i-kam words, *n.*

ถัก tàk braid, knit, *v.*

ถัง tǎng pail, tank, bucket, *n.*

ถัด tàt next to, next, *prep., adj., adv.*

ถัน tǎn breast, *n.*

ถัว tǔa average, *v.*

ถั่ว tùa peas, beans, *n.*

ถ้า tâa if, in case, *conj.*

ถาก tàak cut in pieces, *v.*

ถากถาง tàak-tǎang speak ironically, *v.*

ถาง tǎang clear (a forest), cut away, mow, *v.*

ถ่าง tàang spread apart, *v.*

ถาด tàat tray, *n.*

ถ่าน tàan charcoal, *n.*

ถาม tǎam ask, question, *v.*

ถ่าย tàai excrete, transfer, *v.*

ถ่ายภาพ tàai-pâap take a picture, *v.*

ถ่ายเอกสาร tàai-èek-gà-sǎan make a copy, *v.*

ถาวร tǎa-wɔɔn permanent, stable, *adj.*

ถ้ำ tâm cave, tunnel, *n.*

ถิ่น tìn home, locality, town, *n.*

ถี่ tìi frequent, *adj.*

ถีบ tìip kick, pedal, *v.*

ถึง tǔng arrive, reach, *v.*

ธ น บ ป ผ ฝ พ ฟ ภ ม ย ร ฤ ฦ ล ว ศ ษ ส ห ฬ อ ฮ

ถึงกระนั้น tǔng-grà-nán although, *adv., conj.*

ถึงแก่กรรม tǔng-gὲε-gam die, *v.*

ถึงใจ tǔng-jai satisfactorily, *adv.*

ถือ tǔu hold, carry, *v.*

ถือตัว tǔu-dtua conceited, *adj.*

ถุง tǔng bag, purse, *n.*

ถุงเท้า tǔng-táao socks, hose, *n.*

ถุงมือ tǔng-mɯɯ glove, *n.*

ถุงยางอนามัย tǔng-yaang-à-naa-mai condom, *n.*

ถุน tǔn take just enough of opium or drug, *v.*

ถุย tǔi spit, *v.*

ถู tǔu rub, scrub, *v.*

ถูก tùuk hit, touch, *v.*

ถูก tùuk correct, right, inexpensive, cheap, *adj.*

ถูกใจ tùuk-jai please, *v.*

ถูกชะตา tùuk-chá-taa compatible, *adj.*

ถูกต้อง tùuk-dtɔ̂ng correct, right, *adj.*

เถร tĕen Buddhist priest, *n.*

เถลไถล tà-lĕe-tà-lǎi truant, *adj.*

เถลิง tà-lɤ̆ɤng rise, ascend, *v.*

เถอะ tὲ an ending particle indicating suggestion, *part.*

เถา tǎo vine, creeping plant, *n.*

เถ้า tâo ashes, *n.*

เถาะ tɔ̀ The year of Rabbit, *n.*

เถิก tɤ̀ɤk exposed, rolled up, *adj.*

เถิด tɤ̀ɤt a word used to make a request or command, *part., adv.*

เถียง tǐang argue, *v.*

เถื่อน tɤ̀an illegal, savage, *adj.*

แถบ tὲεp strip, area, *n.*

แถม tĕεm add on, *v.*

แถลง tà-lĕεng express, *v.*

แถว tĕεo row, line, *n.*

โถ tǒo water globet, jug, *n.*

โถง tǒong spacious, *adj.*

โถม tôom swoop down, *v.*

ไถ tǎi plough, *v.*

ไถ่ tài redeem, purchase back, *v.*

ไถล tà-lǎi slide, skid, *v.*

ท

ท tɔɔ the twenty-third consonant of the Thai alphabet (low consonant), *n.*

ทดลอง tót-lɔɔng test, *v.*

ทน ton endure, *v.*

ทนทาน ton-taan durable, *adj.*

ท้น tón flooded, *adj.*

ทนาย tà-naai lawyer, *n.*

ทบ tóp fold up, *v.*

ทบทวน tóp-tuan review, *v.*

ทบวง tà-buang bureau, *n.*

ทมิฬ tà-min Tamil (from India or Sri Lanka) India, *n.*

ทมิฬ tà-min vicious, *adj.*

ทมื่น tà-mʉn black, *adj.*

ทโมน tà-moon big monkey, mischievous child, *n.*

ทยอย tà-yɔɔi come or go in succession, *v.*

ทแยง tà-yɛɛng oblique, *adj.*

ทรชน tɔɔ-ra-chon outlaw, *n.*

ทรพิษ tɔɔ-ra-pít small-pox, *n.*

ทรพี tɔɔ-ra-pii coconut-shell spoon, ungrateful son or daughter, *n.*

ทรมาน tɔɔ-ra-maan torture, *v.*

ทรยศ tɔɔ-ra-yót betray, *v.*

ทรง song form, figure, *n.*

ทรรศนะ tát-sa-ná opinion, vision, *n.*

ทรวง suang breast, *n.*

ทรวงอก suang-òk bosom, *n.*

ทรหด tɔɔ-ra-hòt enduring, *adj.*

ทรัพย์ sáp wealth, property, *n.*

ทรัพย์สิน sáp-sǐn assets, *n.*

ทรัพยากร sáp-pa-yaa-gɔɔn natural resources, *n.*

ทราม saam low, mean, *adj.*

ทราย saai sand, *n.*

ทรุด sút get worse, *v.*

ทฤษฎี tít-sa-dii theory, *n.*

ทลาย tà-laai collapse, *v.*

ทวง tuang solicit the return of a borrowed article, *v.*

ท้วง túang protest, *v.*

ท่วงที tûang-tii attitude, manner, *n.*

ทวด tûat great-grandfather, great-grandmother, *n.*

ทวน tuan lance, *n.*

ทวนน้ำ tuan-náam move against the tide, *v.*

ทวนลม tuan-lom go against the wind, *v.*

ท่วม tûam flood, overflow, *v.*

ทวาร tà-waan door, opening, *n.*

ทวี tá-wii two, twice, *adj.*

ทวีคูณ tá-wii-kuun double, two-fold, *adj.*

ทวีป tá-wîip continent, *n.*

ทศ tót ten, *n.*

ทหาร tá-hǎan soldier, *n.*

ทหารเกณฑ์ tá-hǎan-geen conscript, *n.*

ทหารบก tá-hǎan-bòk army officer, *n.*

ทหารเรือ tá-hǎan-rɯa naval officer, n.

ทหารอากาศ tá-hǎan-aa-gàat air force officer, n.

ทอ tɔɔ weave, emit rays, v.

ท่อ tɔ̂ɔ duct, tube pipe, n.

ท่อระบายน้ำ tɔ̂ɔ-ra-baai-náam drain pipe, n.

ท่อไอน้ำ tɔ̂ɔ-ai-náam steam pipe, n.

ท่อไอเสีย tɔ̂ɔ-ai-sǐa exhaust pipe, n.

ท้อ tɔ́ɔ discouraged, adj.

ทอง tɔɔng gold, n.

ทองคำ tɔɔng-kam gold, pure gold, n.

ท่อง tɔ̂ng recite, v.

ท่องจำ tɔ̂ng-jam learn by rote, v.

ท้อง tɔ́ɔng stomach, n.

ท้อง tɔ́ɔng pregnant, adj.

ท้องถิ่น tɔ́ɔng-tìn district, area, n.

ท้องที่ tɔ́ɔng-tîi district, locality, n.

ท้องฟ้า tɔ́ɔng-fáa sky, heavens, n.

ท้องเสีย tɔ́ɔng-sǐa diarrhea, n.

ท้องอืด tɔ́ɔng-ùɯt constipation, n.

ทอด tɔ̂ɔt fry, deep fry, v.

ทอดทิ้ง tɔ̂ɔt-tíng discard, abandon, v.

ทอน tɔɔn cut, give change, v.

ท่อน tɔ̂n section, part, n.

ทอนซิล tɔɔn-sin tonsil, n.

ท็อฟฟี่ tɔ́p-fîi toffee, n.

ทอย tɔɔi pitch, v.

ทะนง tá-nong arrogant, adj.

ทะเบียน tá-bian record, register, n.

ทะเบียนบ้าน tá-bian-bâan census registration, n.

ทะมัดทะแมง tá-mát-tá-mɛɛng energetic, serious, adj.

ทะโมน tá-moon high and large, adj.

ทะยอย tá-yɔɔi follow gradually, v.

ทะยาน tá-yaan thrust forward, v.

ทะเยอทะยาน tá-yəə-tá-yaan ambitious, adj.

ทะลวง tá-luang hollow out, v.

ทะลัก tá-lák protrude, v.

ทะลาย tá-laai tumble down, v.

ทะลิ่ง tá-lîng soar, intrude, v.

ทะลุ tá-lú pierced through, adj.

ทะเล tá-lee sea, n.

ทะเลทราย tá-lee-saai desert, n.

ทะเลสาป tá-lee-sàap lake, n.

ทะเล้น tá-lén protrude, giggly, v., adj.

ทะเลาะ tá-lɔ́ quarrel, dispute, v.

ทัก ták greet, v.

ทักษะ ták-sà capability, skill, n.

ทักษิณ ták-sǐn south, n.

ทั้ง táng whole, entire, adj., adv., prep.

ทั้งคืน táng-kɯɯn all night, adv.

ทั้งคู่ táng-kûu both, *prep., adv.*

ทั้งนั้น táng-nán all the same, *adv.*

ทั้งวัน táng-wan the whole day, *adv.*

ทั้งสิ้น táng-sîn altogether, *adv.*

ทัณฑ์ tan penalty, *n.*

ทัด tát equal, *adj.*

ทัน tan overtake, catch up, *v.*

ทันใจ tan-jai as quickly as desired, *adv.*

ทันใด tan-dai promptly, quickly, *adv.*

ทันสมัย tan-sa-mǎi modern, *adj.*

ทันตแพทย์ tan-dta-pêet dentist, *n.*

ทับทิม táp-tim ruby, pomegranate, *n.*

ทัพ táp army, fighting forces, *n.*

ทัพบก táp-bòk army, *n.*

ทัพเรือ táp rua navy, *n.*

ทัพอากาศ táp-aa-gàat air force, *n.*

ทัพพี táp-pii ladle, *n.*

ทั่ว tûa total, all, *adj.*

ทั่วถึง tûa-tǔng all, all over, *adv.*

ทั่วประเทศ tûa-bprà-têet all over the country, *adv.*

ทั่วไป tûa-bpai all over, in general, *adv.*

ทั่วโลก tûa-lôok all over the world, *adv.*

ทัวร์ tua tour, *n.*

ทัศน์ tát vision, view, *n.*

ทัศนศึกษา tát-sa-na-sùk-sǎa visual education, *n.*

ทัศนา tát-sa-naa look, view, *v.*

ทา taa apply on, smear on, paint, *v.*

ท่า tâa posture, gesture, manner, *n.*

ท้า táa dare, challenge, *v.*

ท้าทาย táa-taai challenge, *v.*

ทาก tâak leech, land leech, *n.*

ทาง taang way, path, road, route, means, course, direction, pass, walk, trail, *n.*

ทางกาย taang-gaai physical, bodily, *adj., adv.*

ทางการ taang-gaan official, governmental, *adj.*

ทางไกล taang-glai long distance, *n.*

ทางเข้า taang-kâo entrance, *n.*

ทางใจ taang-jai mental, *adj.*

ทางเดิน taang-dəən foot-path, *n.*

ทางธรรม taang-tam religious, *adj.*

ทางใน taang-nai transcendental meditation, *n.*

ทางรถไฟ taang-rót-fai railway, *n.*

ทางโลก taang-lôok mundane, worldly, *adj.*

ทางหลวง taang-lǔang public highway,

freeway, *n.*

ทาน taan alms giving, donation, gift, *n.*

ทาน taan bear, resist, *v.*

ทานข้าว taan-kâao have food, eat, *v.*

ทานตะวัน taan-dtà-wan the sun-flower, *n.*

ท่าน tân the second and third pronoun, you, he, him, she, her, they, them, *pron.*

ทาบ tâap place over, *v.*

ท่ามกลาง tâam-glaang center, *n.*

ทาย taai foretell, *n.*

ท้าย táai rear, end, *n.*

ท้ายเรือ táai-rɯa stern of a ship or boat, *n.*

ทายาท taa-yâat heir, heiress, *n.*

ทารก taa-rók infant, *n.*

ทารุณ taa-run torture, ill-treat, *v.*

ท้าว táao king, ruler, sovereign, *n.*

ทาส tâat slave, *n.*

ทาสี taa-sǐi paint, *v.*

ทำ tam do, perform, commit, act, *v.*

ทำกับข้าว tam-gàp-kâao cook, *v.*

ทำขวัญ tam-kwǎn make compensation, perform ceremony for strength and encouragement, *v.*

ทำงาน tam-ngaan work, *v.*

ทำตาม tam-dtaam imitate, *v.*

ทำท่า tam-tâa strike a pose, *v.*

ทำโทษ tam-tôot punish, *v.*

ทำนา tam-naa grow rice, *v.*

ทำบาป tam-bàap sin, *v.*

ทำบุญ tam-bun make merit, *v.*

ทำหน้าที่ tam-nâa-tîi do duty, *v.*

ทำนบ tam-nóp dam, dike, *n.*

ทำนอง tam-nɔɔng manner, way, melody, *n.*

ทำนาย tam-naai predict, foretell, *v.*

ทำนุบำรุง tam-nú-bam-rung nourish, maintain, *v.*

ทำเนา tam-nao slacken, relieve, *v.*

ทำเนียบ tam-nîap official residence of a high-ranking official, *n.*

ทำเนียบขาว tam-nîap-kaao White House, *n.*

ทำเนียบรัฐบาล tam-nîap-rát-ta-baan prime minister's residence, *n.*

ทำไม tam-mai why, *adv.*

ทำลาย tam-laai destroy, *v.*

ทำลายสถิติ tam-laai-sà-tì-dtì break a record, *v.*

ทำเล tam-lee location, *n.*

ทิ้ง tíng throw away, *v.*

ทิด tít one who has just left the Buddhist monkhood, *n.*

ทิพย์ típ supernatural, *adj.*

ทิ่ม tîm prick, thrust, poke, v.

ทิศ tít direction, n.

ที tii time, turn, chance, n.

ที่ tîi place, site, location, spot, land, real estate n.

ที่ tîi at, to, in, for, on, as, prep., adv.

ที่เกิด tîi-gə̀ət birth-place, n.

ที่เขี่ยบุหรี่ tîi-kìa-bù-rìi ashtray, n.

ที่จอดรถ tîi-jɔ̀ɔt-rót parking lot, n.

ที่ดิน tîi-din lot, piece of land, n.

ที่ตั้ง tîi-dtâng location, n.

ที่ทำงาน tîi tam ngaan office, n.

ที่มา tîi-maa origin, source, n.

ที่ราบลุ่ม tîi-râap-lûm basin, n.

ที่ราบสูง tîi-râap-sǔung plateau, n.

ที่ไร่ที่นา tîi-râi-tîi-naa farm, field, n.

ที่รัก tîi-rák darling, dear, n.

ที่ล้างหน้า tîi-láang-nâa wash basin, sink, n.

ที่ลุ่ม tîi-lûm basin, n.

ที่สุด tîi-sùt to the end, adv.

ที่อยู่ tîi-yùu address, n.

ทึกทัก túk-ták presume, take for granted, v.

ทึ่ง tûng amazed, adj.

ทึนทึก tun-túk old maid, spinster, adj.

ทึบ túp dense, opaque, adj.

ที่ม tûm dull, stupid, adj.

ทื่อ tûu blunt, dull, adj.

ทุก túk every, each, all, entire, adj.

ทุกคน túk-kon everybody, adv.

ทุกครั้ง túk-kráng every time, adv.

ทุกคืน túk-kuun every night, adv.

ทุกที túk-tii every time, adv.

ทุกเมื่อ túk-mûa always, adv.

ทุกข์ túk difficulty, suffering, pain, distress, sorrow, poverty, n.

ทุ่ง tûng field, plain, n.

ทุจริต tú-jà-rìt dishonesty, n.

ทุติย tú-dtì-yá second, doubled, adj.

ทุน tun capital, fund, n.

ทุนการศึกษา tun-gaan-sùk-sǎa scholarship, n.

ทุนทรัพย์ tun-na-sáp capital, fund, n.

ทุ่น tûn buoy, float, n.

ทุ่นกำลัง tûn-gam-lang save labor, v.

ทุ่นเงิน tûn-ngən save money, v.

ทุ่นเวลา tûn-wee-laa save time, v.

ทุ่นแรง tûn-reeng save labor, save energy, v.

ทุบ túp pound, smash, v.

ทุพพลภาพ túp-pon-lá-pâap disabled, crippled, weak, incapacitated, adj.

ทุ่ม tûm throw down, v.

ทุ้ม túm bass, lowest tone of an instrument, *n.*

ทุรกันดาร tú-rá-gan-daan barren, *adj.*

ทุรชน tú-rá-chon villain, *n.*

ทุรนทุราย tú-ron-tú-raai restless, *adj.*

ทุเรศ tú-rêet pitiable, piteous, shameful, obscene, *adj.*

ทุเรียน tú-rian the durian, *n.*

ทุลักทุเล tú-lák-tú-lee difficult, tangled, struggling, *adj., adv.*

ทุเลา tú-lao relieve, alleviate, *v.*

ทู่ tûu blunt, *v.*

ทูต tûut ambassador, diplomatic agent, *n.*

ทูน tuun hold over the head, *v.*

เท tee pour off, *v.*

เท่ têe elegant, *adj.*

เทคโนโลยี ték-noo-loo-yîi technology, *n.*

เท็จ tét deceptive, untrue, false, *adj.*

เทนนิส ten-nís, ten-nít tennis, *n.*

เทพ têep god, divine being, *n.*

เทพธิดา têep-tí-daa goddess, *n.*

เทพนม têep-pa-nom figure of a deity clasping hands in token of worship, *n.*

เทพบุตร têep-pa-bùt male god, *n.*

เทพี tee-pii beautiful lady, *n.*

เทโพ tee-poo a species of catfish, *n.*

เทมปุระ tem-bpu-rá a kind of Japanese food, *n.*

เทวดา tee-wa-daa group of gods, divinity, *n.*

เทศ têet foreigner, country, *n.*

เทศน์ têet preach, teach, *v.*

เทศนา têet-sà-nǎa preach, give a sermon, *v.*

เทอะทะ tɔ́-tá bulky, *adj.*

เทา tao (color) gray, *adj.*

เท่า tâo equal, equivalent, *adj.*

เท้า táao rest on, prop up, *v.*

เท้า táao foot, feet, *n.*

เทิด tɔ̂ət hold up, honor, *v.*

เที่ยง tîang noon, midday, *n.*

เที่ยง tîang accurate, precise, exact, *adj.*

เที่ยงคืน tîang-kuun midnight, *n.*

เที่ยงแท้ tîang-téɛ certain, sure, *adj.*

เที่ยงตรง tîang-dtrong exact, accurate, *adj.*

เที่ยงวัน tîang-wan noon, *n.*

เทียน tian candle, *n.*

เทียบ tîap compare, *v.*

เทียม tiam harness, team up, *v.*

เที่ยว tiao go back and forth, *v.*

เที่ยว tîao promenade, wonder, roam, stroll about, make a pleasure tour, v.

เทือก tûak line, range, n.

แท้ tέε real, genuine, adj.

แท็กซี่ ték-sîi taxi, n.

แทง tεεng stab, pierce, v.

แท่ง tε̂ng bar, chunk, n.

แท้ง tέng have a miscarriage, have an abortion, v.

แทน tεεn substitute, replace, represent, v.

แท่น tε̂n altar, n.

แทบ tε̂ερ almost, nearly, adv.

แทรก sε̂εk mix, insert, intervene, v.

แทะ tέ gnaw on, v.

โท too second, two, adj.

โทนโท่ toon-tôo clear, obvious, apparent, adj.

โทรคมนาคม too-rá-ká-má-naa-kom telecommunication, n.

โทรทัศน์ too-ra-tát television, n.

โทรศัพท์ too-ra-sàp telephone, n.

โทรสาร too-ra-sǎan fax, n.

โทรม soom ruined, destroyed, adj.

โทษ tôot offence, punishment, guilt, n.

ไท tai freedom, n.

ธ

ธ tɔɔ the twenty-fourth consonant of the Thai alphabet (low consonant), n.

ธง tong flag, banner, n.

ธนู tá-nuu bow, arrow, n.

ธรณี tɔɔ-ra-nii earth, soil, n.

ธรรม tam Buddhist teaching, Dharma, n.

ธัญญพืช tan-ya-pûut cereals, grains, n.

ธันวาคม tan-waa-kom December, n.

ธาตุ tâat element, chemical element, n.

ธาตุแท้ tâat-tέε real characteristics, n.

ธานี taa-nii city, n.

ธาร taan stream, n.

ธิดา tí-daa daughter, n.

ธิติ tí-dtì retention, n.

ธุดงค์ tú-dong pilgrimage, n.

ธุระ tú-rá business, duty, affair, n.

ธุลี tú-lii dust, powder, n.

ธูป tûup incense, joss-stick, n.

เธอ tɘɘ you, he, him, she, her, they, them, pron.

โธ่ tôo Alas! What a pity, interj.

น

น nɔɔ the twenty-fifth consonant of the Thai alphabet (low consonant), *n.*

นก nók bird, *n.*

นคร ná-kɔɔn city, *n.*

นง nong woman, *n.*

นที ná-tii river, *n.*

นบ nóp pay respect by clasping, *v.*

นพ nóp nine, *adj.*

นภา ná-paa sky, *n.*

นม nom breasts, *n.*

นมัสการ ná-mát-sà-gaan the act of showing respect, *n.*

นโยบาย ná-yoo-baai policy, *n.*

นรก ná-rók hell, *n.*

นวด nûat massage, thrash, knead, *v.*

นวนิยาย ná-wá-ní-yaai novel, fiction, *n.*

นวม nuam padding, quilt, cushion, *n.*

น่วม nûam soft, pliable, *adj.*

นวยนาด nuai-nâat walk gracefully, *v.*

นวล nuan creamy white, *adj.*

นอ nɔɔ horn, *n.*

นอก nɔ̂ɔk outside, external, *adj., adv.*

นอกจาก nɔ̂ɔk-jàak besides, except, *adv., prep.*

น็อค nɔ́k knock, *v.*

นอง nɔɔng flooded, *adj.*

นองเลือด nɔɔng-lɨ̂at bloody, sanguinary, *adj.*

น่อง nɔ̂ng calf, *n.*

น้อง nɔ́ɔng younger brother, younger sister, *n.*

น้องเขย nɔ́ɔng-kɨ̌ɨi brother-in-law, *n.*

น็อต nɔ́t knot, *n.*

นอน nɔɔn lie down, sleep, *v.*

นอบ nɔ̂ɔp bow in respect, *v.*

น้อม nɔ́ɔm bow down, *v.*

น้อย nɔ́ɔi little, small, scarce, *adj.*

น้อยกว่า nɔ́ɔi-gwàa less than, *adv.*

น้อยใจ nɔ́ɔi-jai easily irritated, touchy, *adj.*

น้อยหน่า nɔ́ɔi-nàa sugar apple, *n.*

นัก nák person, man, expert, *n.*

นักกวี nák-gà-wii poet, *n.*

นักกีฬา nák-gii-laa athlete, *n.*

นักเขียน nák-kĩan author, *n.*

นักดนตรี nák-don-dtrii musician, *n.*

นักโทษ nák-tôot prisoner, *n.*

นักเรียน nák-rian student, *n.*

นัก nák so, so much, *adv.*

นักหนา nák-năa intensely, so much, *adv.*

นักขัตฤกษ์ nák-kàt-dta-lòɔk seasonal festival, annual holiday, n.

นั่ง nâng sit, squat, v.

นัด nát make an appointment, date, arrange to meet, v.

นั่น nân that, there, prep., pron.

นั้น nán that, there, adj., pron.

นับ náp count, v.

นัมเบอร์ nam-bəə number, n.

นา naa rice field, n.

น่า nâa a prefix for verbs or nouns to intensify their meanings, prefix., adj.

น่ากิน nâa-gin tasty-looking, adj.

น่ากลัว nâa-glua horrible, frightening, scary, adj.

น่าฟัง nâa-fang pleasant to listen to, adj.

น้า náa uncle, aunt, mother's younger brother or sister, n.

นาก nâak otter, n.

นาค nâak snake, Naga, person about to be ordained as a Buddhist priest, n.

นาง naang married woman, title placed before the first name of a married woman, n.

นาที naa-tii minute, n.

นาน naan long, adj.

นาบ nâap press down flat, v.

นาม naam name, n.

นาย naai master, owner, boss, n.

นายก naa-yók president, chief leader, n.

นายกรัฐมนตรี naa-yók-rát-tà-mon-dtrii Prime Minister, n.

นารายณ์ naa-raai name of a Brahmin god, Rama, the god Vishnu, n.

นารี naa-rii woman, girl, female, n.

น้าว náao bend, v.

นาวา naa-waa boat, ship, n.

นาวิกโยธิน naa-wík-gà-yoo-tin marine, n.

นาวี naa-wii navy, boat, ship, n.

นาฬิกา naa-lí-gaa clock, watch, n.

นำ nam lead, guide, v.

น้ำ náam water, liquid, fluid, n.

น้ำเกลือ náam-glua saline solution, n.

น้ำกาม náam-gaam semen, n.

น้ำแข็ง náam-kěng ice, n.

น้ำเงิน náam-ngən blue, n.

น้ำใจ náam-jai spirit, good will, n.

น้ำดี náam-dii bile, n.

น้ำตก náam-dtòk waterfall, n.

น้ำตาล náam-dtaan sugar, n.

น้ำท่วม náam-tûam flood, n.

น้ำมัน náam-man oil, *n.*

น้ำมันดิบ náam-man-dìp crude oil, *n.*

น้ำเสียง náam-sĭang tone of voice, *n.*

น้ำหนัก náam-nàk weight, *n.*

นิกาย ní-gaai sect, denomination, *n.*

นิคม ní-kom community, *n.*

นิ่ง nîng still, quiet, *adj.*

นิจ nít continued, regular, *adj.*

นิด nít very small, very little, *adj.*

นิติ ní-dtì law, administrative method, *n.*

นิทรา nít-traa sleep, drowsiness, *n.*

นิทัศน์ ní-tát example, sample, *n.*

นิเทศ ní-têet demonstration, exhibition, *n.*

นินทา nin-taa blame, gossip about, *v.*

นิบาต ní-bàat agreement, *n.*

นิพนธ์ ní-pon compose, *v.*

นิพพาน níp-paan Nirvana, *n.*

นิ่ม nîm soft, gentle, *adj.*

นิมนต์ ní-mon invite a Buddhist monk, *v.*

นิมิต ní-mít token, sign, dream, *n.*

นิยม ní-yom admire, favor, *v.*

นิยาม ní-yaam definition, *n.*

นิยาย ní-yaai tale, fable, *n.*

นิรันดร์ ní-ran connected, perpetual, permanent, *adj.*

นิราศ ní-râat depart, a kind of long lyric Thai poem on departure, *v., n.*

นิโรธ ní-rôot death, *n.*

นิล nin black, *adj.*

นิ่ว nîu calculus, gall stone, *n.*

นิ้ว níu finger, toe, *n.*

นิสัย ní-săi habit, *n.*

นิสิต ní-sìt undergraduate, *n.*

นี่ nîi this, these, *pron., adv.*

นี้ níi this, these, *adj.*

นึก núk think, consider, *v.*

นึ่ง nûng cook by stream, *v.*

นุ่ง nûng dress, put on, *v.*

นุช nút junior, younger, *adj.*

นุ่น nûn kapok, white cotton, *n.*

นุ่ม nûm soft, tender, *adj.*

นุ้ย núi plump, fat, *adj.*

นูน nuun convexed, elevated, *adj.*

เน้น nén stress, emphasize, *v.*

เนย nəəi butter, cheese, *n.*

เนรคุณ nee-ra-kun ungrateful, *adj.*

เนรเทศ nee-ra-têet deport, exile, *v.*

เนรมิต nee-ra-mít build, *v.*

เน่า nâo rotten, *adj.*

เนิน nəən mound, *n.*

เนิ่น nən slow, tardy, *adj.*

เนิบ nə̂əp slow, tardy, *adj.*

เนื้อ núa meat, flesh, *n.*

เนื้อคู่ núa-kûu soul mate, *n.*

เนื้องอก núa-ngɔ̂ɔk tumor, *n.*

เนื้อที่ núa-tîi area, space, *n.*

เนื้อเพลง núa-pleeng words of a
song, *n.*

เนือง nuang frequent, constant, regular, *adj.*

เนื่อง nûang due to, related to, *adj.*

เนือย nuai sluggish, slow, *adj.*

แน่ nêɛ certain, sure, firm, *adj.*

แน่น nên feel tight, *v.*

แนบ nêɛp close to, *adj.*

แนว nɛɛo line, row, *n.*

แน่ว nêo straight, *adj.*

แนะ né direct, advise, *v.*

โน้ต nóot note, *v.*

โน่น nôon there, *pron., adv.*

โน้น nóon there, *adv.*

โน้ม nóom bend down, *v.*

โน้มถ่วง nóom-tùang gravitate, *v.*

ใน nai inside, in, into, *prep.*

ในตัว nai-dtua internal, *adj.*

ในไส้ nai-sâi of the same parents, *adj.*

ในหลวง nai-lŭang the king, His
Majesty the king, *pron.*

บ

บ bɔɔ the twenty-sixth consonant of
the Thai alphabet (mid consonant), *n.*

บ่ bɔɔ (Lao) no, not, never, *adj.*

บก bòk land, dry land, *n.*

บกพร่อง bòk-prɔ̂ng deficient, defective, *adj.*

บ่ง bòng indicate, *v.*

บงการ bong-gaan dictate, *v.*

บด bòt crush, grind, *v.*

บท bòt stanza, paragraph of verse,
subject, chapter, *n.*

บทกลอน bòt-glɔɔn poem, *n.*

บทความ bòt-kwaam article, *n.*

บทเรียน bòt-rian lesson, *n.*

บน bon vow, *v.*

บน bon above, overhead, *adv.*

บ่น bòn complain, *v.*

บ่ม bòm cure (tobacco), ripen, *v.*

บรรจง ban-jong perform with care, do
nicely, *v.*

บรรจบ ban-jòp connected, *adj.*

บรรจวบ ban-jùap meet, join, *v.*

บรรเจิด ban-jə̀ət make pretty, *v.*

บรรณ ban wing, leaf, *n.*

บรรณสาร ban-na-sǎan official letter,

n.

บรรณาการ ban-naa-gaan gift, offering, *n.*

บรรณาธิการ ban-naa-tí-gaan editor, *n.*

บรรดา ban-daa whole, entire, all, *adj.*, *n.*

บรรทม ban-tom sleep, *v.*

บรรทัด ban-tát line, ruler, ruled line, *n.*

บรรทัดฐาน ban-tát-tǎan standard, convention, *n.*

บรรทุก ban-túk load up with, *v.*

บรรเทา ban-tao relieve, give relief, *v.*

บรรพต ban-pót mountain, *n.*

บรรยากาศ ban-yaa-gàat atmosphere, *n.*

บรรยาย ban-yaai teach, lecture, *v.*

บรรลัย ban-lai collapse, go to destruction, *v.*

บรรลุ ban-lú attain, *v.*

บรรเลง ban-leeng sing, play (music), *v.*

บริกร bɔɔ-ri-gɔɔn waiter, *n.*

บริกรรม bɔɔ-ri-gam adorn, *v.*

บริขาร bɔɔ-ri-kǎan the eight necessary requisites of the Buddhist monk, *n.*

บริจาค bɔɔ-ri-jàak donate, *v.*

บริบาล bɔɔ-ri-baan guard, *v.*

บริบูรณ์ bɔɔ-ri-buun complete, entire, *adj.*

บริพัตร bɔɔ-ri-pát change, *v.*

บริภัณฑ์ bɔɔ-ri-pan belt, girdle, *n.*

บริภาษ bɔɔ-ri-pâat reprimand, *v.*

บริโภค bɔɔ-ri-pôok consume, *v.*

บริวาร bɔɔ-ri-waan followers, satellites, *n.*

บริเวณ bɔɔ-ri-ween surroundings, neighborhood, *n.*

บริษัท bɔɔ-ri-sàt company, firm, *n.*

บริสุทธิ์ bɔɔ-ri-sùt pure, *adj.*

บริหาร bɔɔ-ri-hǎan administer, manage, *v.*

บวก bùak add, add together, *v.*

บวงสรวง buang-sǔang propitiate, *v.*

บ่วง bùang loop, snare, trap, *n.*

บวช bùat ordained, *adj.*

บวชชี bùat-chii go into nunhood, *v.*

บวชเณร bùat-neen become a Buddhist novice, *v.*

บวชพระ bùat-prá go into the monkhood, *v.*

บ้วน bûan spit, *v.*

บวบ bùap dishrag gourd, a kind of squash, *n.*

บวม buam swollen, inflamed, *adj.*

บ๊วย búai the last, a kind of fruit, *n.*

บ่อ bɔ̀ɔ pond, well, *n.*

บ่อเกิด bɔ̀ɔ-gə̀ət origin, source, *n.*

บอก bɔ̀ɔk tell, say, *v.*

บอกใบ้ bɔ̀ɔk-bâi tell by making signs, giving some clues, *v.*

บ้อง bɔ̂ng hollow cylindrical piece of wood, *n.*

บ้องกัญชา bɔ̂ng-gan-chaa pipe for smoking marijuana, *n.*

บ้องไฟ bɔ̂ng-fai bamboo rocket, *n.*

บอด bɔ̀ɔt blinded, darkened, *adj.*

บ่อน bɔ̀n gambling den, casino, *n.*

บอบ bɔ̀ɔp worn out, weakened, *adj.*

บอบช้ำ bɔ̀ɔp-chám badly injured, *adj.*

บอบบาง bɔ̀ɔp-baang frail, thin, breakable, fragile, *adj.*

บ่อย bɔ̀i frequently, often, *adv.*

บอระเพ็ด bɔɔ-ra-pét a species of climber, *n.*

บะหมี่ bà-mìi egg noodles, *n.*

บ๊ะ bàk a form of address applied to a man of equal status, or to show familiarity or contempt, *n.*

บักเตรี bàk-dtee-rii bacteria, *n.*

บัง bang hide, conceal, *v.*

บั้ง bâng insignia of rank, *n.*

บังกาโล bang-gaa-loo bungalow, *n.*

บังเกิด bang-gə̀ət born, *adj.*

บังคม bang-kom pay respect before a monarch, *v.*

บังคับ bang-káp force, compel, *v.*

บังสุกุล bang-sù-kun yellow robe drawn by a Buddhist monk from a coffin, *n.*

บังเหียน bang-hǐan bridle, bit, rein, *n.*

บังอร bang-ɔɔn woman, girl, *n.*

บังเอิญ bang-əən by chance, *adv.*

บัญชา ban-chaa command, order, *v.*

บัญชี ban-chii list, account, *n.*

บัญญัติ ban-yàt prescribe, provide, *v.*

บัณฑิต ban-dìt graduate, *n.*

บัด bàt time, occasion, period, *n.*

บัดกรี bàt-grii solder, *v.*

บัดซบ bàt-sóp very stupid, *adj.*

บัดสี bàt-sǐi shameful, *adj.*

บัตร bàt card, ticket, coupon, *n.*

บั่น bàn cut, cut into pieces, *v.*

บั้น bân half, part, *n.*

บันดาล ban-daan cause, happen, *v.*

บันได ban-dai stairs, steps, *n.*

บันทึก ban-túk record, register, *v.*

บันเทิง ban-təəng joyful, entertained, *adj.*

บันลือ ban-lɯɯ echo, v.

บัลลังก์ ban-lang throne, n.

บัลลูน ban-luun balloon, n.

บัลเล่ต์ ban-lêe ballet, n.

บัว bua water-lily, lotus, n.

บ่า bàa shoulder, n.

บ้า bâa mad, insane, crazy, adj.

บาง baang thin, rare, adj.

บางคน baang-kon some people, n.

บางที baang-tii sometimes, adv.

บ้าง bâang some, any, somewhat, adj., adv.

บาด bàat cut, make a cut, v.

บาดใจ bàat-jai hurt one's feelings, v.

บาดทะยัก bàat-ta-yák tetanus, n.

บาดหมาง bàat-mǎang have a rift, have dissension, v.

บาดาล baa-daan underground region, n.

บาตร bàat Buddhist monk's round alms-bowl, n.

บาท bàat baht, n.

บาทหลวง bàat-lǔang Christian priest, n.

บาน baan open, bloom, blossom, v.

บ้าน bâan house, home, n.

บาป bàap sin, n.

บ่าย bàai afternoon, n.

บ่ายเบี่ยง bàai-bìang avoid, deviate, v.

บาร์ baa bar, n.

บาร์บีคิว baa-bii-kiu barbeque, n.

บาร์เลย์ baa-lêe barley, n.

บารมี baa-ra-mii merit, n.

บาล baan guard, v.

บาลี baa-lii Pali, n.

บ่าว bàao servant, slave, n.

บาศก์ bàat dice, n.

บำนาญ bam-naan pension, n.

บำบัด bam-bàt cure, treat, v.

บำเพ็ญ bam-pen do, perform, v.

บำรุง bam-rung maintain, nurture, v.

บำเรอ bam-rəə serve, tend, wait on, v.

บำเหน็จ bam-nèt reward, remuneration, n.

บิณฑบาต bin-ta-bàat go about with an alms bowl to receive food, v.

บิด bìt twist, v.

บิดเบือน bìt-bɯan distort, v.

บิด bìt dysentery, n.

บิดา bì-daa father, n.

บิน bin fly, v.

บิ่น bìn chip, chipped, v., adj.

บีบ biip squeeze, compress, press, v.

บึง bɯng large swamp, n.

ปิ่ง bìng go very fast, speed, v.

ปิ้ง bîng serious, solemn, adj.

ปิ้งตึง bîng-dtʉng sullen, frowning, sulky, adj.

บุก bùk invade, v.

บุคคล bùk-kon person, individual, n.

บุคลากร bùk-ka-laa-gɔɔn personnel, n.

บุคลิก bùk-ka-lík personally, personality, adv., n.

บุคลิกภาพ bùk-ka-lík-gà-pâap personality, characteristic, n.

บุ้ง bûng caterpillar, n.

บุญ bun merit, good deeds, n.

บุตร bùt son, child, n.

บุตรี bùt-dtrii daughter, n.

บุบ bùp pound lightly, v.

บุ๋ม bǔm dented, dimpled, adj.

บุ่มบ่าม bùm-bàam uncouth, adj.

บุ้ย bûi protrude the lips, pout, v.

บุรพบท bùp-pa-bòt preposition, n.

บุรุษ bù-rùt man, person, n.

บุษราคัม bùt-sa-raa-kam topaz, n.

บุษหงา bù-ngàa flower, n.

บุหรี่ bù-rìi cigarette, n.

บูชา buu-chaa worship, v.

บูด bùut rotten, decayed, adj.

บูม buum boom, n.

บูมเมอแรง buum-mɚɚ-rɛɛng boomerang, n.

บูรณะ buu-ra-ná repair, v.

บูรพา buu-ra-paa the east, n.

เบ่ง bèng swell, expand, v.

เบญจศีล ben-jà-sǐin The five basic Buddhist precepts of morality, n.

เบ็ด bèt hook, fish hook, n.

เบ็ดเตล็ด bèt-dtà-lèt miscellaneous, adj.

เบ็ดเสร็จ bèt-sèt entirely, in total, adv.

เบน been turn the bow, v.

เบรค brèek brake (car), n., v.

เบา bao urine, light, n., adj.

เบ้า bâo crucible, socket, n.

เบ้าตา bâo-dtaa eye-socket, n.

เบาะ bɔ̀ cushion, n.

เบิก bɚ̀ɚk open, widen, expand, v.

เบิกเงิน bɚ̀ɚk-ngɚn withdraw money, v.

เบิกบาน bɚ̀ɚk-baan cheerful, adj.

เบิกพยาน bɚ̀ɚk-pá-yaan call in witnesses, v.

เบิ่ง bɚ̀ng stare, look, v.

เบี้ย bîa cowrie shell, n.

เบี่ยง bìang turn, turn aside, v.

เบียด bìat squeeze in, v.

ธ น บ ป ผ ฝ พ ฟ ภ ม ย ร ฤ ฦ ล ว ศ ษ ส ห ฬ อ ฮ

เบี้ยว bîao distorted, *adj.*

เบื่อ bùa tired of, bored, *adj.*

เบื้อง bûang side, partion, *n.*

เบือน buan turn, turn away, twist, deviate, *v.*

แบ bɛɛ spread, *v.*

แบก bɛ̀ɛk carry on the shoulder, *v.*

แบ่ง bɛ̀ng divide, share with, allot, *v.*

แบตเตอรี่ bɛ̀t-dtəə-rîi battery, *n.*

แบน bɛɛn flat, level, *adj.*

แบบ bɛ̀ɛp model, pattern, example, style, design, form, mould, copy, *n.*

แบะ bɛ̀ spread open, *adj.*

โบ๋ bǒo containing holes, *adj.*

โบก bòok wave, *v.*

โบนัส boo-nát bonus, *n.*

โบย booi whip, *v.*

ใบ้ bâi dumb, mute, *adj.*

ไบเบิ้ล bai-bə̂n the Bible, *n.*

ป

ป bpɔɔ the twenty-seventh consonant of the Thai alphabet (mid consonant), *n.*

ปก bpòk cover, flap, *n.*

ปกติ bpòk-gà-dtì, bpà-ga-dtì normal, natural, usual, *adj.*

ปกิณกะ bpà-gin-na-gà miscellaneous, *adj.*

ปฏิกิริยา bpà-dtì-gì-ri-yaa reaction, *n.*

ปฏิกูล bpà-dtì-guun excretion, refuse, *n.*

ปฏิคม bpà-dtì-kom host, *n.*

ปฏิชีวนะ bpà-dtì-chii-wa-ná antibiotic, *n.*

ปฏิทิน bpà-dtì-tin calendar, almanac, *n.*

ปฏิบัติ bpà-dtì-bàt do, perform, *v.*

ปฏิปักษ์ bpà-dtì-bpàk enemy, *n.*

ปฏิพจน์ bpà-dtì-pót answer, *n.*

ปฏิพัทธ์ bpà-dtì-pát connect, *v.*

ปฏิภาณ bpà-dtì-paan quickness of mind, intelligence, *n.*

ปฏิมากรรม bpà-dtì-maa-gam sculpture, *n.*

ปฏิรูป bpà-dtì-rûup reform, *v.*

ปฏิวัติ bpà-dtì-wát revolution, *n.*

ปฏิสนธิ bpà-dtì-sǒn-tí conception, birth, *n.*

ปฏิสังขรณ์ bpà-dtì-sǎng-kɔ̌ɔn restoration, repairs, *n.*

ปฏิสันถาร bpà-dtì-sǎn-tǎan welcome, greeting, *n.*

ปฏิเสธ bpà-dtì-sèet deny, refuse, *v.*

ปฐพี bpà-tà-pii earth, land, *n.*

ปฐม bpà-tŏm first, initial, primary, original, *adj.*

ปทานุกรม bpà-taa-nú-grom dictionary, *n.*

ปทุม bpà-tum lotus, *n.*

ปน bpon combine, mix, *v.*

ป่น bpòn grind, *v.*

ปม bpom knot, complex, knob, *n.*

ปมเด่น bpom-dèn superiority complex, *n.*

ปมด้อย bpom-dɔ̂i inferiority complex, *n.*

ปรนเปรอ bpron-bprəə minister to the wants of, *v.*

ปรนนิบัติ bpron-ni-bàt serve, take care of, *v.*

ปรนัย bpɔɔ-ra-nai objective education, *n.*

ปรบมือ bpròp-mɯɯ applaud, *v.*

ปรมาจารย์ bpà-ra-maa-jaan first teacher, *n.*

ปรมาณู bpà-ra-maa-nuu atom, *n.*

ปรมินทร์ bpà-ra-min the supreme, *n.*

ปรวนแปร bpruan-bprɛɛ change, vary, *v.*

ปร๋อ bprɔ̌ɔ speedily, rapidly, *adv.*

ปรองดอง bprɔɔng-dɔɔng harmonious, *adj.*

ปรอท bpa-rɔ̀ɔt mercury, quicksilver, *n.*

ปรอย bprɔɔi drizzle, drop, *v.*

ประ bprà sprinkle, add, affix, *v.*

ประกบ bprà-gòp put together, join, *adj., v.*

ประกวด bprà-gùat contest, *v.*

ประกอบ bprà-gɔ̀ɔp assemble, put together, *v.*

ประกอบด้วย bprà-gɔ̀ɔp-dûai composed of, consist of, *adj.*

ประกอบอาชีพ bprà-gɔ̀ɔp-aa-chîip earn a living, *v.*

ประกัน bprà-gan guarantee, insure, assure, bail out, *v.*

ประกันชีวิต bprà-gan-chii-wít insure one's life, *v.*

ประกันชีวิ bprà-gan-chii-wít life insurance, *n.*

ประกาย bprà-gaai flash, spark, *n.*

ประการ bprà-gaan kind, type, sort, *n.*

ประกาศ bprà-gàat announce, make known, *v.*

ประกาศนียบัตร bprà-gaa-sa-nii-ya-bàt certificate, *n.*

ประกาศิต bprà-gaa-sìt exposition,

decree, *n*.

ประคบ bprà-kóp massage, massage with hot press, *v*.

ประคอง bprà-kɔɔng support carefully, handle gently, *v*.

ประคับประคอง bprà-káp-bprà-kɔɔng hold very carefully, *v*.

ประคำ bprà-kam rosary, string of beads, *n*.

ประเคน bprà-keen offer an offering or gift to a Buddhist monk with both hands, *v*.

ประโคม bprà-koom blow, sound, *v*.

ประจบ bprà-jòp flatter, curry favor, *v*.

ประจวบ bprà-jùap meet, collide, *v*.

ประจักษ์ bprà-jàk evident, obvious, *adj*.

ประจักษ์พยาน bprà-jàk-pa-yaan eyewitness, *n*.

ประจัญ bprà-jan combat, fight, confront, *v*.

ประจัน bprà-jan partition off, *v*.

ประจาน bprà-jaan condemn, *v*.

ประจำ bprà-jam stationed, *adj*.

ประจำเดือน bprà-jam-duan monthly, menses, menstrual period, *n*.

ประจิม bprà-jim west, *n*.

ประจุ bprà-jù load, charge, *v*.

ประเจิดประเจ้อ bprà-jə̀ət-bprà-jɔ̂ɔ unconcealed, shameless, unduly exposed, *adj*.

ประแจ bprà-jɛɛ key wrench, padlock, *n*.

ประชด bprà-chót sarcastic, *adj*.

ประชวร bprà-chuan royal to be sick, *v*.

ประชัน bprà-chan compete, rival, *v*.

ประชา bprà-chaa people, citizens, *n*.

ประชากร bprà-chaa-gɔɔn population, people, populace, *n*.

ประชาชน bprà-chaa-chon people, population, *n*.

ประชาทัณฑ์ bprà-chaa-tan punishment by the people, *n*.

ประชาธิปไตย bprà-chaa-típ-bpa-dtai democracy, *n*.

ประชิด bprà-chít approach, *v*.

ประชุม bprà-chum meet, *v*.

ประณาม bprà-naam condemn, criticize, *v*.

ประณีต bprà-nîit fine, delicate, intricate, meticulous, *adj*.

ประดัง bprà-dang crowded, overwhelming, *adj*.

ประดับ bprà-dàp decorate, adorn, *v*.

ประดา bprà-daa march abreast, throng, dive and remain submerged, v.

ประดาน้ำ bprà-daa-náam diver, skilled diver, scuba diver, n.

ประดิษฐ์ bprà-dìt invent, v.

ประดุจ bprà-dùt as if, as, like, such as, for example, adv., conj.

ประเด็น bprà-den important question, issue, n.

ประเดิม bprà-dəəm begin, start, v.

ประเดี๋ยว bprà-dĭao shortly, just a moment, adv.

ประถม bprà-tŏm primary, preliminary, prime, elementary, first, adj.

ประถมศึกษา bprà-tŏm-sùk-săa elementary education, n.

ประท้วง bprà-túang protest, v.

ประทัง bprà-tang maintain, prolong for a while, v.

ประทัด bprà-tát firecrackers, n.

ประทับ bprà-táp royal to stop, sit, stand, imprint, affix, v.

ประทับใจ bprà-táp-jai impressive, adj.

ประทาน bprà-taan royal to give, bestow, v.

ประทิน bprà-tin tend, take care of, v.

ประทีป bprà-tîip lamp, light, n.

ประทุน bprà-tun cover, roof, hood, n.

ประทุษ bprà-tút harm, v.

ประเทศ bprà-têet country, nation, n.

ประธาน bprà-taan chairman, president, chief, leader, n.

ประธานาธิบดี bprà-taa-naa-típ-bɔɔ-dii president, n.

ประนม bprà-nom bring both hands together in obeisance or respect, raise both hands up palm against palm, v.

ประนาม bprà-naam insult, v.

ประนีประนอม bprà-nii-bprà-nɔɔm compromise, v.

ประปราย bprà-bpraai sparse, slight, light, adj.

ประปา bprà-bpaa water supply, city water-supply, n.

ประพฤติ bprà-prút behave, conduct oneself, v.

ประพันธ์ bprà-pan compose, v.

ประพาส bprà pâat travel for pleasure, v.

ประเพณี bprà-pee-nii custom, tradition, n.

ประภาส bprà-pâat light, n.

ประภาส bprà-pâat shine, illumine, v.

ประเภท bprà-pêet kind, type, sort, species, class, category, subdivision, variety, n.

ประมง bprà-mong fish, fishery, v., n.

ประมวล bprà-muan compile, v.

ประมวลกฎหมาย bprà-muan-gòt-mǎai law code, n.

ประมาณ bprà-maan approximate, estimate, v.

ประมาท bprà-màat careless, negligent, imprudent, adj.

ประมุข bprà-múk leader, chief, head of state, n.

ประมูล bprà-muun bid, v.

ประเมิน bprà-məən estimate, v.

ประยุกต์ bprà-yúk applied, make useful, adj.

ประโยค bprà-yòok sentence (grammar), n.

ประโยชน์ bprà-yòot use, usage, advantage, n.

ประลอง bprà-lɔɔng test, experiment, n.

ประลัย bprà-lai death, calamity, n.

ประวัติ bprà-wàt history, story, n.

ประวัติศาสตร์ bprà-wàt-dtì-sàat history, n.

ประเวณี bprà-wee-nii custom, tradition, sexual intercourse, n.

ประสงค์ bprà-sǒng purpose, aim, wish, n.

ประสบ bprà-sòp meet, encounter, find, n.

ประสบการณ์ bprà-sòp-gaan experience, n.

ประสพ bprà-sòp success, n.

ประสม bprà-sǒm meet, add, v.

ประสา bprà-sǎa manner, way, conduct, n.

ประสาท bprà-sàat nerve, n.

ประสาน bprà-sǎan join, connect, v.

ประสิทธิ์ bprà-sìt success, n.

ประสิทธิภาพ bprà-sìt-ti-pâap efficiency, n.

ประสูติ bprà-sùut born, adj.

ประเสริฐ bprà-sə̀ət excellent, esteemed, precious, adj.

ประหนึ่ง bprà-nùng as if, conj.

ประหม่า bprà-màa timid, abashed, adj.

ประหยัด bprà-yàt saving, frugal, adj.

ประหลาด bprà-làat strange, odd, adj.

ประหวั่น bprà-wàn apprehend, fear, v.

ประหาร bprà-hǎan kill, execute, *v.*

ปรักปรำ bpràk-bpram incriminate, blame, *v.*

ปรัชญา bpràt-cha-yaa philosophy, *n.*

ปรับ bpràp fine, impose a fine on, *v.*

ปรับความเข้าใจ bpràp-kwaam-kâo-jai negotiate for mutual understanding, *v.*

ปรับเครื่อง bpràp-krûang tune a motor, *v.*

ปรับทุกข์ bpràp-túk tell one's troubles, *v.*

ปรัมปรา bpà-ram-bpà-raa legendary, *adj.*

ปรัศนี bpràt-sà-nii question mark, *n.*

ปรากฏ bpraa-gòt happen, appear, *v.*

ปรากฏการณ์ bpraa-gòt-dtà-gaan phenomenon, *n.*

ปราการ bpraa-gaan wall, fort, *n.*

ปรางค์ bpraang stupa, pagoda, *n.*

ปราจีน bpraa-jiin eastern, *adj.*

ปราชญ์ bpraat scholar, *n.*

ปราชัย bpraa-chai defeated, *n.*

ปราณ bpraan inspiration, breath, *n.*

ปรานี bpraa-nii show pity of, *v.*

ปราด bpràat swiftly, quickly, *adv.*

ปรานี bpraa-nii show compassion, *v.*

ปราบ bpràap subdue, conquer, *v.*

ปราบปราม bpràap-bpraam suppress, *v.*

ปราม bpraam prohibit, *v.*

ปราโมทย์ bpraa-móot joy, *n.*

ปราย bpraai sow, *v.*

ปรารถนา bpràat-tà-nǎa desire, wish, *v.*

ปรารภ bpraa-róp ask about, *v.*

ปราศจาก bpràat-sà-jàak without, *adj.*

ปราศรัย bpraa-sǎi address, *v.*

ปราสาท bpraa-sàat palace, *n.*

ปริญญา bpà-rin-yaa academic degree, *n.*

ปริทัศน์ bpà-ri-tát periscope, *n.*

ปรินิพพาน bprà-rí-ní-paan the Buddha's death, *n.*

ปริมณฑล bprà-rí-mon-ton perimeter, surroundings, *n.*

ปริมาณ bprà-ri-maan quantity, *n.*

ปริมาตร bprà-ri-máat volume, *v.*

ปริยาย bprà-ri-yaai way, course, *n.*

ปริศนา bprìt-sà-nǎa puzzle, *n.*

ปรีชา bprii-chaa knowledge, *n.*

ปรีดา bprii-daa delighted, *adj.*

ปรึกษา bpruk-sǎa consult, *v.*

ปรุง bprung mix, prepare, cook, *v.*

ธ น บ **ป** ผ ฝ พ ฟ ภ ม ย ร ฤ ฦ ล ว ศ ษ ส ห ฬ อ ฮ

ปลง bplong put down, *v.*

ปลด bplòt take out, release, *v.*

ปล้น bplôn rob, *v.*

ปลวก bplùak termite, *n.*

ปลอก bplòɔk collar, pillow slip, sheath, case, *n.*

ปล่อง bplòng tube, shaft, chimney, *n.*

ปล้อง bplông section, segment, *n.*

ปลอด bplòɔt free from, safe from, *adj.*

ปลอบ bplòɔp pacify, comfort, *v.*

ปลอม bplɔɔm imitate, falsify, *v.*

ปล่อย bplòi release, let go, *v.*

ปลัก bplàk mud hole, *n.*

ปลั๊ก bplák plug, *n.*

ปลั่ง bplàng shining, glowing, *adj.*

ปลัด bpà-làt deputy, administrative assistant, deputy governor, *n.*

ปลา bplaa fish, *n.*

ปลาย bplaai tip, end, point, *n.*

ปลายข้าว bplaai-kâao broken milled rice, *n.*

ปลายทาง bplaai-taang destination, *n.*

ปลาโลมา bplaa-loo-maa dolphin, *n.*

ปลาวาฬ bplaa-waan whale, *n.*

ปลาสติก bplàat-sa-dtìk plastic, *n.*

ปลาสเตอร์ bpláat-sa-dtɔ̀ɔ plaster, *n.*

ปลาสมา bpláat-sa-mâa plasma, *n.*

ปลาหมึก bplaa-mùk cuttlefish, squid, *n.*

ปล้ำ bplâm struggle with, wrestle with, force, rape, *v.*

ปลิง bpling leech, *n.*

ปลิด bplìt pick, *v.*

ปลิ้น bplîn turn inside out, *v.*

ปลิว bpliu blown, carried by wind, *adj.*

ปลี bplii blossom of the banana tree, *n.*

ปลีก bplìik separate, *v.*

ปลิ้ม bplûm pleased, *adj.*

ปลุก bplùk awaken, arouse, *v.*

ปลูก bplùuk plant, *v.*

ปวกเปียก bpùak-bpìak weak, limp, *adj.*

ปวง bpuang entire, all, *adj.*

ปวด bpùat ache, suffer from pain, *v.*

ป่วน bpùan confused, *adj.*

ป่วย bpùai sick, ill, *adj.*

ปศุสัตว์ bpà-sù-sàt domesticated animals, *n.*

ปอ bpɔɔ hemp, *n.*

ปอก bpɔ̀ɔk peel, skin, flay, *v.*

ปอง bpɔɔng aim, *v.*

ป้อง bpɔ̀ng scorpion, *n.*

ป้อง bpɔ̂ng protect, *v.*

ป้องกัน bpɔ̂ng-gan prevent, guard, defend, protect, v.

ปอด bpɔ̀ɔt lung, n.

ปอดบวม bpɔ̀ɔt-buam pneumonia, n.

ปอดแหก bpɔ̀ɔt-hɛ̀ɛk scared, adj.

ปอน bpɔɔn shabby, adj.

ป้อน bpɔɔn feed, v.

ปอนด์ bpɔɔn pound, n.

ปอบ bpɔ̀ɔp ogre, a kind of ghost, n.

ป้อม bpɔ̂m fortress, fort, n.

ปอย bpɔɔi tuft, n.

ปะ bpà patch up, repair, meet, v.

ปะการัง bpà-gaa-rang coral, n.

ปะทะ bpà-tá contact with, collide, clash, v.

ปะทัง bpà-tang sustain, support, v.

ปะทุ bpà-tú explode, v.

ปะปน bpà-bpon mix, v.

ปะรำ bpà-ram pavilion, n.

ปัก bpàk pitch, embroider, braid, v.

ปักเป้า bpàk-bpâo globe fish, n.

ปักษ์ bpàk wing, fortnight, quarter, n.

ปักษิน bpàk sǐn winged animal, n.

ปัจจัย bpàt-jai cause, motive, factor, means, ground, requisite, necessary thing, n.

ปัจจุบัน bpàt-jù-ban present time, n.

ปัจฉิม bpàt-chǐm west, n.

ปัญญา bpan-yaa intellect, wisdom, knowledge, intelligence wit, n.

ปัญหา bpan-hǎa problem, question, riddle, n.

ปัด bpàt wipe, wipe off, v.

ปัน bpan divide, share, v.

ปั่น bpàn spin, turn on an axis, rotate, agitate, v.

ปั้น bpân mold, mould, v.

ปั้นจั่น bpân-jàn crane, n.

ปั๊ม bpám pump, v.

ปัสสาวะ bpàt-saa-wá urine, n.

ป่า bpàa forest, woods, jungle, n.

ป้า bpâa elder sister of the mother or father, n.

ป้าสะใภ้ bpâa-sà-pái elder aunt-in-law, n.

ป๋า bpǎa father, n.

ปาก bpàak mouth, beak, lips, entrance, opening, n.

ปากกา bpàak gaa pen, n.

ปาง bpaang epoch, era, the time when, episode, n.

ปาฏิหาริย์ bpaa-dti-hǎan miracle, n.

ปาฐกถา bpaa-tà-gà-tǎa lecture, n.

ปาด bpàat slice, shave, level off, v.

ปาติโมกข์ bpaa-dtì-môok the code of 227 Buddhist precepts, *n.*

ป่าท่องโก๋ bpaa-tông-gŏo a kind of Chinese flour sweetmeat, *n.*

ปาน bpaan birth mark, *n.*

ปาน bpaan comparable to, like, similar, as if, almost, *adv.*

ป่าน bpàan hemp, *n.*

ป้าน bpâan blunt, obtuse, *adj.*

ป่าย bpàai climb, scale, *v.*

ป้าย bpâai poster, sign, notice board, placard, tag, label, name plate, *n.*

ป่าว bpàao proclaim, broadcast, *v.*

ปิ้ง bpíng bake, roast, toast, *v.*

ปิงปอง bping-bpong ping pong, *n.*

ปิฎก bpì-dòk collection of writings, *n.*

ปิด bpìt close, shut, cover, hide, *v.*

ปิโตรเลียม bpì-dtroo-liam petroleum, *n.*

ปิ่น bpìn hairpin, *n.*

ปิ่นโต bpìn-dtoo tiffin-carrier, food carrier, *n.*

ปิยมหาราช bpì-yá-ma-hǎa-râat the beloved king, Kind Rama V of Thailand, *n.*

ปีศาจ bpii-sàat ogre, ghost, spirit, devil, sprite, *n.*

ปี bpii year, *n.*

ปี่ bpìi pipe, flute, oboe, *n.*

ปีก bpìik wing, side, *n.*

ปีน bpiin climb, mount, *v.*

ปึก bpùk pack, stack, *n.*

ปืน bpuun gun, firearm, *n.*

ปุ่ม bpùm knot, knob, *n.*

ปุย bpui fluff, *n.*

ปุ๋ย bpǔi manure, fertilizer, *n.*

ปู bpuu spread out, pave, crab, *v., n.*

ปู่ bpùu grandfather, paternal grandfather, *n.*

ปูชนียบุคคล bpuu-cha-nii-yá-bùk-kon venerable person, *n.*

ปูชนียวัตถุ bpuu-cha-nii-yá-wát-tù object worthy of worship, *n.*

ปูชนียสถาน bpuu-cha-nii-yá-sà-tǎan place worthy of worship, *n.*

ปูน bpuun lime, calcium oxide, *n.*

ปู้ยี่ปู้ยำ bpûu-yìi-bpûu-yam damaged, ruined, *adj.*

เป้ bpêe knapsack, *n.*

เป๋ bpěe twisted, slanted, *adj.*

เป็ด bpèt duck, *n.*

เป็น bpen happen, occur, live, be, exist, be alive, continue, become to know how to, *v.*

เปรด bprèet demon, ghost, *n.*

เปรย bprəəi speak insinuatingly, *v.*

เปรียบ bprìap compare, *v.*

เปรียว bpriao active, wild, *adj.*

เปรี้ยว bprîao sour, *adj.*

เปรื่อง bprùang smart, brilliant, *adj.*

เปล bplee stretch, *n.*

เปลญวน bplee-yuan hammock, *n.*

เปล่ง bplèng emit, radiate, *v.*

เปลว bpleeo flame, *n.*

เปล่า bplàao empty, void, bare, naked, *adj.*

เปลี่ยน bplìan change, convert, *v.*

เปลี่ยว bplìao wild, untamed, *adj.*

เปลือก bplùak bark, rind, husk, shell, skin, *n.*

เปลือง bplùang consume, waste, *v.*

เปลื้อง bplûang strip off, take off, undress, *v.*

เปลือย bplùai naked, undressed, *adj.*

เป่า bpào blow, play by blowing, *v.*

เป้า bpâo target, mark, purpose, aim, shooting butt, *n.*

เปิด bpə̀ət open, reveal, *v.*

เปิ่น bpə̀n awkward, embarrassed, *adj.*

เปีย bpia pigtail, queue, tassel, *n.*

เปียก bpìak wet, soaked, damp, *adj.*

เปี่ยม bpìam completely filled, *adj.*

เปื้อน bpûan dirty, soiled, filthy, *adj.*

เปื่อย bpùai tender, softened, *adj.*

แป้ง bpɛ̂ɛng flour, powder, *n.*

แปด bpὲɛt eight, *nm.*

แปร bprɛɛ change, alter, vary, *v.*

แปรง bpreeng brush, bristles, *n.*

แปร่ง bprὲng discordant, *adj.*

แปล bplɛɛ translate, interpret, *v.*

แปล้ bplɛ̂ɛ loaded, *adj.*

แปลก bplὲɛk strange, odd, queer, *adj.*

แปลง bplɛɛng plot of land, *n.*

แปลง bplɛɛng modify, adapt, *v.*

แปลงกาย bplɛɛng-gaai transfigure, *v.*

แปลน bplɛɛn plan, *n.*

แปะ bpὲ pat gently, *v.*

แป๊ะ bpέ Chinese old man, *n.*

โป๊ bpóo repair, mend, patch, *v.*

โป๊ bpóo pornographic, sex-stimulating, naked, *adj.*

โป่ง bpòong swollen, inflated, *adj.*

โป้ง bpôong boastful, *adj.*

โปน bpoon swollen, *adj.*

โปรแกรม bproo-grɛɛm program, *n.*

โปร่ง bpròong airy, clear, *adj.*

โปรด bpròot favor, like, *v.*

โปรดปราน bpròot-bpraan love for, *v.*

โปรตีน bproo-dtiin protein, *n.*

โปลิโอ bpoo-li-oo polio, *n.*

โปสการ์ด bpóot-sa-gáat postcard, *n.*

โปสเตอร์ bpóot-sa-dtəə poster, *n.*

ไป bpai go, proceed, depart, *v.*

ไปรษณีย์ bprai-sà-nii post, postage, mail, *n.*

ไปรษณีย์บัตร bprai-sà-nii-ya-bàt postcard, *n.*

ไปรษณีย์โทรเลข bprai-sà-nii-too-ra-lêek posts and telegraph, *n.*

ผ

ผ pɔ̌ɔ the twenty-eighth consonant of the Thai alphabet (high consonant), *n.*

ผกผัน pòk-pǎn turn round, *v.*

ผง pǒng powder, dust, *n.*

ผงขาว pǒng-kǎao heroin, *n.*

ผงซักฟอก pǒng-sák-fɔ̂ɔk powdered detergent, *n.*

ผงะ pà-ngà draw back, *v.*

ผจญภัย pà-jon-pai fight danger, *v.*

ผด pòt prickly heat, rash, *n.*

ผนวช pà-nùat add, enter the Buddhist monkhood, *v.*

ผนัง pà-nǎng wall, *n.*

ผนึก pà-nùk seal, *v.*

ผม pǒm hair, *n.*

ผยอง pà-yɔ̌ɔng arrogant, *adj.*

ผรุสวาท pà-rú-sa-wâat obscene words, *n.*

ผล pǒn fruit, effect, consequence, product, *n.*

ผละ plà leave, *v.*

ผลัก plàk push, *v.*

ผลัด plàt take turns, *v.*

ผลาญ plǎan destroy, *v.*

ผลิ plì bud, sprout, *v.*

ผลิต pà-lìt produce, *v.*

ผลีผลาม plǐi-plǎam too fast, rash, hasty, *adj.*

ผลึก pà-lùk crystal, *n.*

ผลุด plùt slip in, *v.*

ผลุน plǔn go quickly, *v.*

ผลุบ plùp dive down, *v., adv.*

ผวน pǔan turn back, *v.*

ผวา pà-wǎa scared, *adj.*

ผสม pà-sǒm mix, blend, *v.*

ผอง pɔ̌ɔng complete, total, all, *adj.*

ผ่อง pɔ̀ng clean, pure, *adj.*

ผ่อน pɔ̀n slacken, relax, *v.*

ผอม pɔ̌ɔm thin, slim, lean, *adj.*

ผะอบ pà-òp chrismatory cup, *n.*

ผัก pàk vegetable, *n.*

ผัง pǎng chart, diagram, *n.*

ผัด pàt fry, *v.*

ผัน pǎn alter, deviate, *v.*

ผับ pàp hastily, *adv.*

ผัว pǔa husband, *n.*

ผา pǎa stone, rock, cliff, *n.*

ผ่า pàa slit, split, *v.*

ผ้า pâa cloth, *n.*

ผ้ากันเปื้อน pâa-gan-bpûan apron, *n.*

ผ้าขาวม้า pâa-kǎao-máa a loincloth

used by men for various purpose, *n.*

ผ้าไหม pâa-mǎi silk cloth, *n.*

ผาก pàak brow, forehead, *n.*

ผาด pàat pass by quickly, *v.*

ผาดๆ pàat-pàat briefly, *adj.*

ผาดโผน pàat-pǒon spring forth, *v.*

ผ่าน pàan pass, walk pass, bypass,

cross, *v.*

ผายปอด pǎai-bpɔ̀ɔt administer artifi-

cial respiration, perform CPR, *v.*

ผ่ายผอม pàai-pɔ̌ɔm thin, *adj.*

ผ่าว pàao hot, *adj.*

ผาสุก pǎa-sùk happiness, comfort,

peace, *n.*

ผิง pǐng bake, *v.*

ผิด pìt wrong, *adj.*

ผิว pǐu surface, *n.*

ผี pǐi spirit, evil spirit, ghost, corpse,

dead body, devil, demon, *n.*

ผึ่ง pùng dry, spread out, *v.*

ผึ้ง pûng bee, *n.*

ผื่น pùun rash, *n.*

ผุ pù decayed, *adj.*

ผุด pùt pop up, *v.*

ผุยผง pǔi-pǒng dust, *n.*

ผู้ pûu person, who, one who, *n.*

ผู้จัดการ pûu-jàt-gaan manager, *n.*

ผูก pùuk hind, tie, *v.*

เผชิญ pà-chəən confront, *v.*

เผชิญหน้า pà-chəən-nâa face, *v.*

เผ็ด pèt peppery, hot, *adj.*

เผด็จ pà-dèt cut, suppress, *v.*

เผ่น pèn leap, spring, *v.*

เผย pəəi open, disclose, *v.*

เผยอ pà-yəə open slightly, *v.*

เผลอ plǒə forgetful, *adj.*

เผลอเรอ plǒə-rəə careless, *adj.*

เผอิญ pà-əən by chance, *adv.*

เผา pǎo burn, *v.*

เผ่า pào tribe, race, group, *n.*

เผื่อ pùa reserved, *adj.*

เผือก pùak taro, albino, *n.*

เผือด pùat faded, pale, *adj.*

แผ่ pὲε expand, v.

แผง pἕεng woven bamboo shelter, mat, booth, n.

แผด pὲεt shout, v.

แผน pἕεn plan, scheme, n.

แผ่น pὲn sheet, plate, n.

แผ่นดิน pὲn-din earth surface, n.

แผนก pà-nὲεk division, section, department, n.

แผล plἕε wound, cut, sore, n.

แผลง plἕεng manifest, display, v.

แผลงฤทธิ์ plἕεng-rít manifest one's power, n.

แผล็บ plὲp very rapidly, adj., adv.

แผ่ว pὲo slightly, adv.

โผ pŏo dash, dart, v.

โผน pŏon leap, v.

โผล่ plòo pop up, emerge, v.

โผลกเผลก plòok-plèek limp, adj.

ไผ่ pài bamboo, n.

ฝ

ฝ fɔ̌ɔ the twenty-ninth consonant of the Thai alphabet (high consonant), n.

ฝน fŏn rain, rub, n., v.

ฝนตก fŏn-dtòk rain, v.

ฝรั่ง fa-ràng white race, Europeans, guava, n.

ฝรั่งเศส fa-ràng-sὲεt French, n.

ฝ่อ fɔ̀ɔ withered, adj.

ฝอย fɔ̌ɔi fibers, spray, shower, particles, minute drops, droplets, trivial details, n.

ฝอย fɔ̌ɔi brag, chat, v.

ฝอยทอง fɔ̌ɔi-tɔɔng Thai dessert made of egg yolk and sugar, n.

ฝัก fàk sheath, case, n.

ฝักใฝ่ fàk-fài pay attention to, v.

ฝัง fǎng bury, v.

ฝังเข็ม fǎng-kěm perform acupuncture to, v.

ฝังใจ fǎng-jai impress, impressed, v., adj.

ฝั่ง fàng bank, side, shore, n.

ฝัด fàt winnow (grain), sift, v.

ฝัน fǎn dream, fancy, v.

ฝันร้าย fǎn-ráai have a bad dream, v.

ฝา fǎa cover, wall, lid, shell, crust, n.

ฝ่า fàa go through, go against, v.

ฝ่าฝืน fàa-fǔun violate, disobey, v.

ฝ้า fâa scum, film, membrane, blemish, n.

ฝ้า fâa dim, misty, foggy, adj.

ฝาก fàak entrust, deposit, leave, consign, v.

ฝากเงิน fàak-ngən deposit money in a bank, v.

ฝากฝัง fàak-fǎng put into the care of, v.

ฝาด fàat astringent, acidulous, adj.

ฝาน fǎan slice, cut into pieces, v.

ฝาแฝด fǎa-fɛ̀ɛt twins, n., adj.

ฝาย fàai dike dam, n.

ฝ่าย fàai side, party, faction, group, n.

ฝ่ายค้าน fàai-káan opposition, n

ฝ้าย fàai cotton, n.

ฝิ่น fìn opium, n.

ฝี fǐi boil, pustule, n.

ฝีดาษ fǐi-dàat small pox, n.

ฝีมือ fǐi-muu ability to perform, n.

ฝึก fùk drill, train, practice, exercise, teach, v.

ฝืด fùut difficult to move, stuck, tight, adj.

ฝืน fǔun resist, oppose, v.

ฝุ่น fùn dust, powder, n.

ฝูง fǔung flock (of sheep), n.

ฝูงชน fǔung-chon crowd, group, n.

เฝ้า fâo watch over, guard, v.

เฝือ fǔua rice-field, n.

เฝือก fùak splint, plaster caster, n.

เฝื่อน fùan abashed, adj.

แฝก fɛ̀ɛk elephant grass, n.

แฝง fɛ̌ɛng hide, conceal, v.

แฝด fɛ̀ɛt twins, doubles, n.

ใฝ่ fài intend, hope, v.

ใฝ่ใจ fài-jai keenly interested in, adj.

ใฝ่ฝัน fài-fǎn dream of, v.

ไฝ fǎi mole, n.

พ

พ pɔɔ the thirtieth consonant of the Thai alphabet (low consonant), n.

พก pók carry or hide on the body, put into the pouch pocket, v.

พง pong thicket, bush, n.

พงศ์ pong kinship, n.

พจน์ pót word, speech,, n.

พจนานุกรม pót-ja-naa-nú-grom dictionary, n.

พญา pá-yaa king, lord, n.

พด pót bent, coiled, n.

พฐู pá-tuu bride, wife, n.

พ่น pôn blow, spurt, spray, spout, blabber, v.

พ้น pón pass beyond, go beyond, go

ธ น บ ป ผ ฝ พ ฟ ภ ม ย ร ฤ ฦ ล ว ศ ษ ส ห ฬ อ ฮ

past, v.

พนม pá-nom clasp hands together palm in the attitude of salutation, n.

พนัก pá-nák the back of a chair, n.

พนักงาน pá-nák-ngaan officer, employee, staff, n.

พนัน pá-nan bet, gamble, v.

พเนจร pá-nee-joon wander, v.

พบ póp meet, find, encounter, v.

พม่า pá-mâa Burma, n.

พยศ pá-yót fling and throw, kick against, v.

พยศ pá-yót recalcitrant, refractory, adj.

พยัก pá-yák nod, v.

พยัคฆ์ pá-yák tiger, n.

พยัญชนะ pá-yan-cha-ná consonant, n.

พยากรณ์ pá-yaa-goon forecast, prediction, prophecy, n.

พยาธิ pá-yaa-tí sickness, illness, malady, ailment, n.

พยาธิ์ pá-yâat parasite, n.

พยาน pá-yaan witness, evidence, n.

พยาบาท pá-yaa-bàat revenge, n.

พยาบาล pá-yaa-baan nurse, treat, care for the sick, v.

พยายาม pá-yaa-yaam persevere, endeavor, attempt, make an effort, v.

พยุง pá-yung support, v.

พร poon boon, blessing, n.

พรสวรรค์ poon-sà-wǎn gift, natural gift, n.

พรม prom carpet, rug, n.

พรมแดน prom-dɛɛn frontier, border, n.

พรรค pák group, party, n.

พรรณนา pan-ra-naa explain, depict, v.

พรรษา pan-sǎa rain, rainy season, n.

พรวด prûat quickly, adv.

พรวนดิน pruan-din loosen the soil, v.

พรหม prom the god Brahma, n.

พร้อม próom ready, set, together, adj.

พระ prá priest, monk, Buddha image, n.

พระเจ้า prá-jâao god, n.

พระเจ้าแผ่นดิน prá-jâao-pèn-din the king, n.

พระเจ้าอยู่หัว prá-jâao-yùu-hǔa the king, n.

พระพุทธเจ้า prá-pút-ta-jâao the Buddha, n.

พระราชา prá-raa-chaa the king, n.

พร่ำ prâa destroy, ruin, v.

พร้า práa large knife, sickle, n.

พราก prâak leave, part, separate,

deprive, v.

พราง praang camouflage, disguise, v.

พร่าง prâang blurred, adv.

พราน praan hunter, trapper, n.

พราย praai spirit, ghost, n.

พราว praao dazzling, adj.

พราหมณ์ praam Brahmin, n.

พรำ pram (of rain) falling or drizzling, adj.

พร่ำ prâm repeatedly, adv.

พริก prík chili, pepper, n.

พริ้ง príng pretty, beautiful, adj.

พริบ príp blink the eyes, v.

พริ้ม prím smiling, adj.

พรืด prûut abundantly, in great numbers, adv.

พรุ่งนี้ prûng-níi tomorrow, adv.

พรุน prun holed, adj.

พรู pruu go in crowds, flock, v.

พฤติกรรม prút-dtì-gam behavior, conduct, n.

พฤตินัย prút-dtì-nai in fact, adv.

พฤศจิกายน prút-sà-jì-gaa-yon November, n.

พฤหัสบดี pá-rú-hàt-sà-bɔɔ-dii Thursday, n.

พล pon strength, power, force, n.

พลบ plóp dusk, twilight, n.

พลอด plɔ̂ɔt talk volubly, court, v.

พลอย plɔɔi gem, precious stone, n.

พล่อย plɔ̀i simply, flippantly, adv.

พละ pa-lá strength, power, n.

พลัง pa-lang energy, strength, n.

พลั้ง pláng make a slip, slip, to err, v.

พลัด plát fall, trip and fall, v.

พลัน plan at once, urgently, adv.

พลับพลา pláp-plaa pavilion, n.

พลัม plam plum, n.

พลั่ว plûa shovel, spade, n.

พล่า plâa dish of slice of seasoned raw meats or prawns, n.

พลาง plaang simultaneously, adv.

พลาด plâat miss, slip, v.

พล่าน plâan confused, disordered, adj., adv.

พลาย plaai (elephant) male, n.

พลิก plík turn over, v.

พลิ้ว plíu wrong, mistaken, adj.

พลี plii tribute, offering, sacrifice, n.

พลี plii powerful, adj.

พลี plii sacrifice, v.

พลุ plú firework, cannon cracker, n.

พลุ้ย plúi obese, adj.

พวก pûak community, party, group, n.

พวง puang garland, cluster, bunch, n.

ธ น บ ป ผ ฝ พ ฟ ภ ม ย ร ฤ ฦ ล ว ศ ษ ส ห ฬ อ

พวงมาลัย puang-maa-lai garland, *n.*

พ่วง pûang tow, connect, *v.*

พ่วง pûang appended, *adj.*

พวย puai spout, nozzle, *n.*

พหูสูต pá-hǔu-sùut one who has many children, one who has a lot of knowledge, *n.*

พอ pɔɔ enough, adequate, sufficient, *adj.*

พอใจ pɔɔ-jai pleased, satisfied, contented with, *adj.*

พ่อ pɔ̂ɔ father, male, a polite form of addressing a boy or younger man, *n.*

พ่อครัว pɔ̂ɔ-krua cook, *n.*

พ่อค้า pɔ̂ɔ-káa merchant, *n.*

พ่อตา pɔ̂ɔ-dtaa father-in-law, *n.*

พ้อ pɔ́ɔ complain, *v.*

พอก pɔ̂ɔk put on in layer, cover, plaster, *v.*

พอง pɔɔng swell, get a swelling, *v.*

พอง pɔɔng swollen, inflated, blistered, *adj.*

พ้อง pɔ́ɔng sound alike, coincide, *v.*

พะเน้าพะนอ pá-náo-pá-nɔɔ please, coax, cajole, *n.*

พะเนิน pá-nəən large hammer, large pile, *n.*

พะแนง pá-nɛɛng a thick curry with large pieces of roast chicken or meat, *n.*

พะรุงพะรัง pá-rung-pá-rang disheveled, *adj.*

พะวง pá-wong anxious for, worried, *adj.*

พะอืดพะอม pa-ùut-pa-om feel nauseated, *v.*

พัก pák rest, stop temporarily, *v.*

พักผ่อน pák-pɔ̀n take a rest, relax, *v.*

พักฟื้น pák-fúɯn convalesce, *v.*

พัง pang tumble down, collapse, crumble, destroy, tear down, *v.*

พังผืด pang-pùɯt fascia, *n.*

พังพอน pang-pɔɔn mongoose, *n.*

พังพาบ pang-pâap lie face down, lie prone, *v.*

พังเพย pang-pəəi adage, saying, proverb, axiom, *n.*

พัฒนา pát-ta-naa develop, progress, *v.*

พัด pát fan, blow, *v.*

พัน pan bind, tie, wrap, *v.*

พันพัว pan-pua involved, connected, related, *adj.*

พันธะ pan-tá bind, *v.*

พันธุ์ pan relatives, kinsman, relationship, lineage, *n.*

พับ páp fold, get rid, dismiss as lost, *v.*

พับเพียบ páp-piap sit with both legs tucked back to one side, *v.*

พัลวัน pan-la-wan tangles, *adj.*

พัสดุ pát-sa-dù article, object, parcel, *n.*

พา paa lead, guide, conduct, bring along, *v.*

พากเพียร pâak-pian diligent, industrious, *adj.*

พากเพียร pâak-pian persevere, *v.*

พากย์ pâak word, speech, language, speech of a theatrical performance, *n.*

พาณิชย์ paa-nit commerce, trading, *n.*

พาด pâat lean against, *v.*

พาน paan tray with pedestal, *n.*

พาน paan meet, encounter, *v.*

พาย paai paddle, *v., n.*

พ่าย pâai flee, defeated, *v., adj.*

พายัพ paa-yap northwest, *n.*

พายุ paa-yú storm, *n.*

พาล paan mischievous, bad, wicked, *adj.*

พาหนะ paa-hà-ná carrier, vehicle, *n.*

พาหะ paa-hà carrier, *n.*

พำนัก pam-nák stay, reside, *v.*

พิกล pì-gon odd, abnormal, *adj.*

พิกัด pì-gàt standard, limit, fix, *n.*

พิกัด pì-gàt coordinate, *n.*

พิการ pì-gaan deformed, disabled, *adj.*

พิฆาต pì-kâat kill, *v.*

พิง ping lean against, *v.*

พิจารณา pì-jaa-ra-naa examine, investigate, consider, *v.*

พิณ pin lute, a Thai orchestra instrument, *n.*

พิถีพิถัน pì tǐi pì-tǎn fussy, meticulous, *adj.*

พิทยา pìt-ta-yaa knowledge, *n.*

พิทักษ์ pì-ták take care, protect, *v.*

พิธี pì-tii ceremony, ritual, rite, *n.*

พินอบพิเทา pì-nɔ̀ɔp-pì-tao make obeisance, *v.*

พินัยกรรม pì-nai-gam will, *n.*

พินาศ pì-nâat ruin, destruction, *n.*

พินิจ pì-nít examine, investigate, consider attentively, *v.*

พิพากษา pì-pâak-sǎa judge, decide, sentence, *v.*

พิพาท pì-pâat dispute, *v.*

พิพิธภัณฑ์ pì-pít-ta-pan museum, *n.*

พิภพ pì-póp the earth, the world, *n.*

พิมพ์ pim print, type, v.

พิเรน pi-reen pervert, unusual, adj.

พิโรธ pi-root angry, adj.

พิโรธ pi-root rage, v.

พิลึก pi-lúk strange, odd, queer, adj.

พิไล pi-lai pretty, adj.

พิศวง pit-sà-wŏng puzzled about, bewildered, adj.

พิศวาส pit-sà-wàat intimacy, love, delight, affectionate regard, n.

พิศาล pi-săan broad, wide, adj.

พิเศษ pi-sèet special, particular, adj.

พิษ pít poison, n.

พิสดาร pít-sà-daan detailed, n.

พิสมัย pít-sà-măi love, joy, n.

พิสัย pi-săi district, region, n.

พิสูจน์ pí-sùut prove, verify, v.

พี่ pîi elder brother or sister, a polite prefix to the name of an older sibling, you, he, she, him, her, n.

พี่เขย pîi-kŏoi brother-in-law, n.

พี่สะใภ้ pîi-sà-pái sister-in-law, n.

พี่น้อง pîi-nóong brothers, n.

พี่เลี้ยง pîi-líang nurse maid, step-brother, step-sister, nanny, n.

พึ่ง pûng just now, must, a moment ago, adv.

พืช pûut plant, fauna, vegetation, n.

พืด pûut range, line, row, n.

พื้น púun floor, surface, foundation, base, n.

พุ pú break out, erupt, v.

พุง pung abdomen, belly, stomach, n.

พุ่ง pûng throw, thrust, v.

พุทธ pút Buddha, Buddhist, n.

พุทธเจ้า pút-ta-jâao Buddha, n.

พุทธภาษิต pút-ta-paa-sìt The Buddhist proverbs, n.

พุทธศักราช pút-ta-sàk-gà-ràat Buddhist Era, n.

พุธ pút the planet Mercury, Wednesday, n.

พุ่ม pûm bush, shrub, n.

พุ้ย púi paddle, push rice into the mouth, v.

พู puu the segmental divisions of fruit, n.

พู่ pûu tassel, tuft, pendant, n.

พูด pûut speak, talk, say, v.

พูน puun heap up, pile up, v.

เพ pee crumble, collapse, v.

เพ่ง pêng stare at, gaze, v.

เพชฌฆาต pét-cha-kâat executioner, n.

เพชร pét diamond, *n.*

เพชรพลอย pét-plɔɔi gems, precious stones, *n.*

เพดาน pee-daan ceiling, palate, mouth, *n.*

เพทาย pee-taai zircon, *n.*

เพราะ prɔ́ melodious, tuneful, *adj.*

เพราะว่า prɔ́-wâa reason for, due to, because, because of, on account of, *adv., conj.*

เพราะฉะนั้น prɔ́-cha-nán therefore, consequently, *adv.*

เพรียว priao slender, slim, *adj.*

เพล peen midday meal-time for Buddhist monk, *n.*

เพลง pleeng song, melody, music, *n.*

เพลงชาติ pleeng-châat national anthem, *n.*

เพลา pee-laa time, period, *n.*

เพลา plao axle, axis, shaft, boom, *n.*

เพลา plao lap, thigh, leg, *n.*

เพลิง plɔɔng fire, blaze, flame, *n.*

เพลิดเพลิน plɔ́ɔt-plɔɔn enjoying, amused, entertained, *adj.*

เพลีย plia tired, exhausted, worn out, *adj.*

เพลี้ย plía aphid, plant louse, *n.*

เพลี่ยง plîang slip, avoid, *v.*

เพศ pêet sex, gender, kind, form, shape, sort, apparel, *n.*

เพ้อ pɔ́ə delirious, *adj.*

เพาะ pɔ́ plant, *v.*

เพิกเฉย pɔ̂ək-chɔ̌əi inattentive, *adj.*

เพิกถอน pɔ̂ək-tɔ̌ɔn withdraw, *v.*

เพิ่ง pɔ̂ng just, just now, *adv.*

เพิ่ม pɔ̂əm increase, add, *v.*

เพียง piang until, merely, only, equal to, comparable to, as far as, *adv., adj.*

เพียงพอ piang-pɔɔ just enough, just sufficient, *adv.*

เพี้ยน pían deviating, differing just a little, *adj.*

เพียบ pîap heavily loaded, extremely full, *adj.*

เพียร pian diligent, *adj.*

เพื่อ pûa for, for the purpose of, for the sake of, behalf of, in order to, *prep., conj..*

เพื่อน pûan friend, comrade, companion, company, colleague, fellow, associate, pal, *n.*

แพ pɛɛ raft, house-boat, *n.*

แพ้ pɛ́ɛ defeated, beaten, overcome, *adj.*

ธ น บ ป ผ ฝ พ ฟ ภ ม ย ร ฤ ฦ ล ว ศ ษ ส ห ฬ อ

แพง pɛɛng expensive, dear, *adj.*

แพ่ง pɛ̂ng strength, civil case, *n.*

แพทย์ pɛ̂ɛt physician, doctor, *n.*

แพร prɛɛ silk cloth, *n.*

แพร่ prɛ̂ɛ spread, scatter, *v.*

แพร่ง prɛ̂ng spread out, *v.*

แพรว prɛɛo shining, *adj.*

แพลง plɛɛng sprained, twisted, *adj.*

แพศยา pɛ̂ɛt-sà-yǎa prostitute, whore, adulteress, *n.*

แพะ pé goat, *n.*

แพะรับบาป pé-ráp-bàap scapegoat, *n.*

โพก pôok wrap a piece of cloth around the head, *v.*

โพธิ์ poo intelligence, bo tree, *n.*

โพธิสัตว์ poo-tí-sàt one who will become the Buddha, *n.*

โพ้น póon there, beyond, *adj., adv.*

โพย pooi thrash, beat, whip, *v.*

โพรง proong cavity, space, hollow, *n.*

โพล้เพล้ plóo-plée dusk, twilight, *n.*

โพสพ poo-sòp the Goddess of rice, *n.*

ไพ่ pâi gambling card, playing card, *n.*

ไพทูรย์ pai-tuun lapis, *n.*

ไพบูลย์ pai-buun fullness, completeness, abundance, prosperity, *n.*

ไพร prai forest, wood, *n.*

ไพร่ prâi commoner, subjects of a king, low-class citizen, *n.*

ไพรี pai-rii enemy, *n.*

ไพเราะ pai-rɔ́ melodious, tuneful, *adj.*

ไพโรจน์ pai-rôot prosperous, bright, *adj.*

ไพลิน pai-lin amethyst, *n.*

ไพศาล pai-sǎan large, expansive, *adj.*

ฟ

ฟ fɔɔ the thirty-first consonant of the Thai alphabet (low consonant), *n.*

ฟก fók bruised, *adj.*

ฟกช้ำดำเขียว fók-chám-dam-kǐao bruised black and blue, *adj.*

ฟรี frii free, independent, *adj.*

ฟลุค flúk fluke, *n.*

ฟอก fɔ̂ɔk cleanse, purify, wash, bleach, *v.*

ฟอกเลือด fɔ̂ɔk-lɨ̂at purify blood, *v.*

ฟอกสบู่ fɔ̂ɔk-sà-bùu wash with soap, *v.*

ฟอง fɔɔng foam, bubbles, *n.*

ฟองน้ำ fɔɔng-náam sponge, foam, *n.*

ฟองสบู่ fɔɔng-sà-bùu soap suds, *n.*

ฟ้อง fɔ́ɔng accuse, prosecute, sue, take into court, charge, allege, v.

ฟ่อน fɔ̂n sheaf, bundle, v.

ฟ้อน fɔ́ɔn dance, v.

ฟอร์ม fɔɔm form, uniform, shape, n.

ฟัก fák incubate, broad, hatch, v.

ฟัก fák a gourd like plant, n.

ฟักทอง fák-tɔɔng pumpkin, n.

ฟัง fang listen to, pay attention to, hear, v.

ฟัด fát wrestle, shake or pull about, v.

ฟัน fan cut. slash, chop. sever. hit. v.

ฟัน fan tooth, n.

ฟ้า fáa sky, heaven, n.

ฟ้าผ่า fáa-pàa thunderbolt, n.

ฟ้าร้อง fáa-rɔ́ɔng thunder, n.

ฟ้าแลบ fáa-lɛ̂p lightning, n.

ฟาก fâak shore, bank, n.

ฟาง faang straw, n.

ฟาด fâat slash, strike, v.

ฟาดเคราะห์ fâat-krɔ́ give away something to dispel misfortune, v.

ฟิต fít fit, feet, n.

ฟิล์ม fiim film, n.

ฟิวส์ fiu fuse, n.

ฟิสิกส์ fí-sìk physics, n.

ฟืน fʉʉn wood fuel, firewood, n.

ฟื้น fʉ́ʉn recover from, regain consciousness, revive, v.

ฟื้นฟู fʉ́ʉn-fuu restore, v.

ฟุ้ง fúng disseminate, spread, v.

ฟุ้งซ่าน fúng-sâan confused, full of fancies, adj.

ฟุต fút foot, n.

ฟุบ fúp crouch, stoop, fall face down, v.

ฟุ่มเฟือย fûm-fʉai extravagant, adj.

ฟู fuu swell, rise and swell, v.

ฟูก fûuk mattress. n.

เฟ้อ fɤ́ɔ overabundant, adj.

เฟอร์นิเจอร์ fɤɤ-ni-jɤ̀ɔ furniture, n.

เฟอะ fɤ́ dirty, muddy, rotten, adj.

เฟิร์น fɤɤn fern, n.

เฟือง fʉang lobe, cog, n.

เฟื่อง fʉ̂ang diffused, adj.

แฟน fɛɛn fan, lover, husband or wife, boyfriend, girlfriend, fiancé(e), n.

แฟนซี fɛɛn-sii fancy, adj.

แฟบ fɛ̂ɛp deflated, flattened, flat, adj.

แฟ้บ fɛ́p detergent, n.

โฟกัส foo-gát focus, v.

ไฟ fai fire, n.

ไฟฉาย fai-chǎai search light, flash light, n.

ไฟแช็ก fai-chék cigarette lighter, *n.*

ไฟท้าย fai-táai tail light, *n.*

ไฟฟ้า fai-fáa electricity, *n.*

ไฟพะเนียง fai-pa-niang fireworks, *n.*

ไฟสัญญาณ fai-săn-yaan signal, *n.*

ภ

ภ pɔɔ the thirty-second consonant of the Thai alphabet (low consonant), *n.*

ภพ póp world, earth, land, *n.*

ภมร pà-mɔɔn bee, *n.*

ภรรยา pan-ra-yaa wife, *n.*

ภักดี pák-dii loyal to, *adj.*

ภัณฑ์ pan goods, *n.*

ภัย pai fear, dread, danger, calamity, accident, *n.*

ภาค pâak section, division, side, region, *n.*

ภาชนะ paa-cha-ná vessel, *n.*

ภาพ pâap image, picture, drawing, gesture, *n.*

ภาย paai side, part, place, *n.*

ภายนอก paai-nɔ̂ɔk outside, exterior, *adj., adv.*

ภายใน paai-nai inside, interior, *adj., adv.*

ภาระ paa-rá burden, task, duty, *n.*

ภาวนา paa-wa-naa meditate, pray, *v.*

ภาวะ paa-wá condition, state, status, *n.*

ภาษา paa-săa language, speech, *n.*

ภาษาใบ้ paa-săa-bâi sign language, *n.*

ภาษิต paa-sìt proverb, maxim, adage, *n.*

ภาษี paa-sĭi tax, duty, toll, *n.*

ภิกษุ pík-sù Buddhist monk, *n.*

ภู puu earth, land, ground, soil, *n.*

ภูเขา puu-kăo mountain, *n.*

ภูเขาน้ำแข็ง puu-kăo-náam-kĕng iceberg, *n.*

ภูเขาไฟ puu-kăo-fai volcano, *n.*

ภูผา puu-păa precipice, cliff, *n.*

ภูติ pùut ghost, genii, evil spirit, demon, *n.*

ภูมิ puum land, floor, site, place, ground, soil, earth, *n.*

ภูมิประเทศ puum-mí-bprà-têet landscape, scenery, *n.*

ภูมิภาค puum-mí-pâak provinces, region, *n.*

ภูมิลำเนา puum-mí-lam-nao habitat, native habitat, *n.*

ภูมิคุ้มกัน puum-kúm-gan immunity, *n.*

ภูมิใจ puum-jai proud, *adj.*

ภูมิฐาน puum-tǎan grand, dignified, *adj.*

ภูมิปัญญา puum-bpan-yaa intelligence, knowledge, *n.*

ภูมิแพ้ puum-péɛ allergy, *n.*

เภสัช pee-sàt pharmacy, drug, *n.*

เภสัชกร pee-sàt-cha-gɔɔn pharmacist, chemist, *n.*

เภสัชภัณฑ์ pee-sàt-cha-pan pharmaceuticals, *n.*

เภสัชวิทยา pee-sàt-cha-wít-ta-yaa pharmacologist, *n.*

โภค pôok property, goods, *n.*

โภชนา poo-cha-naa nutrition, *n.*

โภชนาการ poo-cha-naa-gaan nutrition, dietetics, *n.*

โภชนาหาร poo-cha-naa-hǎan nutrient, food, *n.*

ม

ม mɔɔ the thirty-third consonant of the Thai alphabet (low consonant), *n.*

มกราคม mók-ga-raa-kom January, *n.*

มงกุฎ mong-gùt crown, *n.*

มงคล mong-kon garland worn over the head, luck, auspicious sign, *n.*

มณฑล mon-ton precinct, county, province, district, *n.*

มณเฑียร mon-tian royal residence, palace, *n.*

มณี má-nii precious stone, jewel, gem, *n.*

มด mót ant, *n.*

มดลูก mót-lûuk uterus, *n.*

มติ má-dtì thought, opinion, view, conclusion, knowledge, understanding, intelligence, thought, opinion, mind, *n.*

มนต์, มนตร์ mon prayer, *n.*

มนตรี mon-dtrii advisor, councilman, *n.*

มนัส má-nát mind, heart, *n.*

มนุษย์ má-nút human being, man, *n.*

มนุษยชาติ má-nút-sà-ya-châat human race, mankind, *n.*

มนุษยศาสตร์ má-nút-sà-ya-sàat humanities, *n.*

มโนกรรม má-noo-gam mental work, *n.*

มโนคติ má-noo-ká-dtì thought, idea, *n.*

มโนราห์ má-noo-raa fabulous nymph in Thai folklore, *n.*

มรกต mɔɔ-ra-gòt emerald, *n.*

มรณะ mɔɔ-ra-ná death, the act of dying, *n.*

มรณภาพ mɔɔ-ra-ná-pâap die (used only for monks), *v.*

มรดก mɔɔ-ra-dòk legacy, heritage, bequest, inheritance, *n.*

มรรคา mák-kaa way, reason, path, *n.*

มรรยาท maa-ra-yâat etiquette, behaviour, *n.*

มรสุม mɔɔ-ra-sǔm monsoon, storm, *n.*

มรสุมชีวิต mɔɔ-ra-sǔm-chii-wít the confusion and obstacles in one's life-time, *n.*

มฤตยู ma-rʉ́-dtà-yuu death, god of Death, the planet Uranus, *n.*

มลรัฐ mon-la-rát state, *n.*

มลาย má-laai break, die, *v.*

มลายู má-laa-yuu Malay, *n.*

มวน muan roll, reel, *v.*

ม่วน mûan sonorous, having fun, *adj.*

ม้วน múan roll, wind, coil, curl, *v.*

มวย muai boxing, *n.*

มวยไทย muai-tai Thai boxing, *n.*

ม้วย múai die, expire, *v.*

มวล muan total, whole, entire, *adj.*

มวลชน muan-chon the multitude, the masses, *n.*

มวลสาร muan-sǎan mass, *n.*

มหรสพ má-hɔ̌ɔ-ra-sòp entertainment, great festival, *n.*

มหัศจรรย์ má-hàt-sà-jan marvelous, extraordinary, miraculous, *adj.*

มหา mà-hǎa great, large, many, much, *adj.*

มหากษัตริย์ mà-hǎa-gà-sàt great king, *n.*

มหาชน mà-hǎa-chon the public, *n.*

มหาชาติ mà-hǎa-châat the story of the last earthly existence of the Lord Buddha, *n.*

มหายาน mà-hǎa-yaan name of a major denomination in Buddhism, *n.*

มหาดไทย má-hàat-tai Ministry of the Interior, *n.*

มหิดล má-hì-don earth, ground, *n.*

มหึมา má-hʉ̌-maa great, *adj.*

มเหสี má-hěe-sǐi king's wife, *n.*

มโหรี má-hǒo-rii grand orchestra, *n.*

มโหฬาร má-hǒo-raan enormous, *adj.*

มอ mɔɔ the moo of a cow, *n.*

มอซอ mɔɔ-sɔɔ drab, livid, shabby, dowdy, adj.

มอง mɔɔng look, look at, glance, v.

มอญ mɔɔn Peguans, living in Pegu, in the southern part of Burma, n.

มอญซ่อนผ้า mɔɔn-sɔ̂n-pâa a kind of children's game, n.

มอด mɔ̂ɔt wood mite, n.

มอม mɔɔm stain, smear, tar, make dirty, v.

มอมเมา mɔɔm-mao lead astray, v.

มอมแมม mɔɔm-mɛɛm dirty, stained, adj.

ม่อย mɔ̂i half asleep, adj.

ม่อฮ่อม mɔ̂ɔ-hɔ̂m a kind of shirt in northern Thailand, n.

มะกรูด má-grùut kaffir, n.

มะกอก má-gɔ̀ɔk olive, n.

มะขาม má-kǎam tamarind, n.

มะเขือ má-kʉ̌a egg plant, n.

มะเขือเทศ má-kʉ̌a-têet tomato, n.

มะนาว má-naao lemon, n.

มะพร้าว má-práao coconut, n.

มะม่วง má-mûang mango, n.

มะเมีย má-mia Year of the Horse, n.

มะแม má-mɛɛ Year of the Goat, n.

มะยม má-yom country gooseberry, n.

มะระ má-rá charantia, n.

มะเร็ง má-reng cancer, n.

มะโรง má-roong Year of the Dragon, n.

มะละกอ má-lá-gɔɔ papaya, n.

มะลิ má-lí jasmine, n.

มะเส็ง má-sěng Year of the Snake, n.

มัก mák love, like, v.

มัก mák satisfied, prone, liable, adj.

มัก mák often, likely, usually, habitually, generally, commonly, adv.

มักง่าย mák-ngâai careless, thoughtless, negligent, adj.

มักจะ mák-jà usually likely, adv.

มักได้ mák-dâai covetous, adj.

มักน้อย mák-nɔ́ɔi contented, adj.

มักใหญ่ใฝ่สูง mák-yài-fài-sǔung over ambitious, adj.

มัคคุเทศน์ mák-ku-têet guide, conductor, n.

มังกร mang-gɔɔn dragon, n.

มังคุด mang-kút mangosteen, n.

มั่งคั่ง mâng-kâng rich, wealthy, adj.

มั่งมี mâng-mii rich, wealthy, adj.

มังสวิรัติ mang-sa-wi-rát vegetarianism, n.

มัจฉะ, มัจฉา mát-chǎa fish, n.

มัด mát bind, wrap, tie, v.

มัธยม mát-ta-yom secondary education, middle school, high school, n.

มัธยัสถ์ mát-ta-yát frugal, thrifty, adj.

มันฝรั่ง man-fa-ràng potato, n.

มัน man fat, oil, grease oil, n.

มั่น mân secure, certain, adj.

มั่นคง mân-kong stable, secure, adj.

มั่นใจ mân-jai confident, adj.

มั่นหมาย mân-mǎai intend to, mean to, v.

มัว mua gloomy, blurred, cloudy, dim, adj.

มัวเมา mua-mao intoxicated, infatuated, adj.

มัวหมอง mua-mɔ̌ɔng blemished, tarnished, adj.

มั่ว mûa gather, conspire, v.

มั่วสุม mûa-sǔm meet for unlawful purpose, v.

มัสมั่น mát-sa-màn a kind of highly seasoned curry, n.

มา maa come, approach, v.

ม่า mâa Chinese mother, n.

ม้า máa horse, n.

ม้าน้ำ máa-náam seahorse, n.

ม้ามืด máa-mûut black horse, one who wins the race or competition unexpectedly, n.

มาก mâak much, many, ample, plentiful, abundant, several, very, very much, adj.

มาตร mâat measure, quality, n.

มาตรฐาน mâat-dtà-tǎan measure, standard, n.

มาตรา mâat-dtraa system of measurement, n.

ม่าน mâan screen, curtain, blind, n.

มานะ maa-ná diligence, n.

ม้าม máam spleen, n.

มายา maa-yaa illusion, delusion, n.

มาร maan the Devil, wicked angel, the evil one, n.

มารค mâak path, way, course, n.

มาร์ค máak German Mark, n.

มารดา maan-daa mother, n.

มารยา maan-yaa illusion, n.

มารยาท maa-ra-yâat manners, etiquette, n.

มาลา maa-laa flower, hat, wreath, garland, n.

มาลี maa-lii florist, n.

มิ่ง mîng good luck, n.

มิ่งขวัญ mîng-kwǎn something bringing good luck, n.

มิจฉา mìt-chǎa wrong, false, immoral, *adj.*

มิจฉาชีพ mìt-chǎa-chîip gangsters, desperadoes, criminals, *n.*

มิด mít submerged completely, hidden entirely, *adj., adv.*

มิตร mít friend, companion, *n.*

มิตรภาพ mít-dtà-pâap friendship, *n.*

มิติ mí-dtì measurement, dimension, *n.*

มิถุน mí-tǔn Gemini, *n.*

มิถุนายน mí-tù-naa-yon June, *n.*

มิน่า mí-nâa That's why!, *interj.*

มี mii have, posses, own, exist, *v.*

มีครรภ์ mii-kan pregnant, *adj.*

มีชื่อเสียง mii-chûu-sǐang known, famous, *adj.*

มีด mîit knife, *n.*

มีดโกน mîit-goon razor, *n.*

มีนาคม mii-naa-kom March, *n.*

มึง mʉng you (impolite), *pron.*

มึน mʉn dazed, stunned, *adj.*

มึนหัว mʉn-hǔa dizzy, *adj.*

มืด mʉ̂ut dark, *adj.*

มืดครึ้ม mʉ̂ut-krúm cloudy, *adj.*

มืดมน mʉ̂ut-mon obscure, *adj.*

มือ mʉʉ hand, *n.*

มื้อ mʉ́ʉ meal, time, occasion, *n.*

มุก múk pearl oyster, *n.*

มุกดาหาร múk-daa-hǎan pearl, *n.*

มุข múk face, mouth, chairman, president, chief, front porch, *n.*

มุง mung put on a roof, roof, *v.*

มุ่ง mûng intend, aim at, expect, *v.*

มุ่งร้าย mûng-ráai intend to do harm, *v.*

มุ้ง múng mosquito net, *n.*

มุ้งลวด múng-lûat mosquito wire screen, *n.*

มุด mút crawl underneath, *v.*

มุทิตา mú-tì-dtaa kindness, *n.*

มุนี mú-nii sage, priest, monk, *n.*

มุม mum angle, corner, *n.*

มุมฉาก mum-chàak right angle, *n.*

มุสลิม mút-sà-lim Muslim, *n.*

มุสา mú-sǎa wrong, false, untruthful, lying, *adj.*

มูก mûuk mucus form the nose, *n.*

มูก mûuk dumb, mute, silent, *adj.*

มูเซอ muu-sǝǝ Lahu, *n.*

มูน muun mound, heap, *n.*

มูมมาม muum-maam filthy, greedy, *adj.*

มูล muun cost, dung, excrement, waste matter, *n.*

ธ น บ ป ผ ฝ พ ฟ ภ ม ย ร ฤ ฦ ล ว ศ ษ ส ห ฬ อ ฮ

มูลค่า muun-la-kâa price, value, *n.*

มูลฐาน muun-tǎan original cause, *n.*

มูลฝอย muun-fɔ̌ɔi rubbish, waste matter, *n.*

มูลนิธิ muun-la-ní-tí foundation, *n.*

มูลเหตุ muun-hèet cause, origin, *n.*

มู่ลี่ mûu-lîi blind, bamboo blind, sun-blind, *n.*

เมฆ mêek cloud, *n.*

เม็ด mét seed, *n.*

เมตตา mêet-dtaa goodwill, kindness, mercy, clemency, *n.*

เมตร méet metre, meter, *n.*

เมถุน mee-tǔn sexual intercourse, *n.*

เม่น mên porcupine, *n.*

เมรุ mee-rú cremation tower, *n.*

เมษายน mee-sǎa-yon April, *n.*

เมา mao drunk, intoxicated, *adj.*

เมาคลื่น mao-klʉ̂ʉn seasick, *adj.*

เมามัว mao-mua addicted, *adj.*

เม่า mâo a species of insect or rice, *n.*

เมิน məən turn the face away from, *v.*

เมีย mia wife, spouse, *n.*

เมียน้อย mia-nɔ́ɔi minor wife, *n.*

เมียหลวง mia-lǔang legal wife, *n.*

เมียงมอง miang-mɔɔng look at from the corner of the eye, *v.*

เมี่ยง mîang fermented leaves of tea-plants, a kind of Thai appetizer, *n.*

เมื่อ mʉ̂a time, moment, *n.*

เมื่อก่อน mʉ̂a-gɔ̀ɔn previously, before, *adv.*

เมื่อครั้ง mʉ̂a-kráng at the time when, *adv.*

เมือก mʉ̂ak mucus, stick and slimy liquid, *n.*

เมือง mʉang city, town, country, province, *n.*

เมืองกรุง mʉang-grung capital, *n.*

เมืองขึ้น mʉang-kʉ̂n colony, *n.*

เมืองไทย mʉang-tai Thailand, *n.*

เมื่อย mʉ̂ai fatigued, tired, *adj.*

แม่ mɛ̂ɛ mother, the female of an animal, prefix for referring to certain relationship, term for endearment, *n.*

แม่ไก่ mɛ̂ɛ-gài hen, *n.*

แม่โขง mɛ̂ɛ-kǒong the Mekong River, a kind of Thai whiskey, *n.*

แม่ครัว mɛ̂ɛ-krua cook, *n.*

แม่ค้า mɛ̂ɛ-káa female street vendor, female shopkeeper, *n.*

แม่งาน mɛ̂ɛ-ngaan party organizer, *n.*

แม่น้ำ mɛ̂ɛ-náam river, *n.*

แม่แบบ mɛ̂ɛ-bὲɛp pattern, model, *n.*

แม่ย่านาง mɛ̂ɛ-yâa-naang guardian spirit of a ship or boat, *n.*

แม้ mɛ́ɛ though, even though, if, *conj.*

แมง mɛɛng prefix to the names of certain animals, *n.*

แมงดา mɛɛng-daa pimp, gigolo, *n.*

แมงมุม mɛɛng-mum spider, *n.*

แมงป่อง mɛɛng-pɔ̀ng scorpion, *n.*

แม่น mɛ̂n accurate, correct, exact, precise, sure, *adj.*

แมลง má-lɛɛng insect, bug, beetle, *n.*

แมว mɛɛo cat, *n.*

แม้ว mɛ́ɛo hill tribe people in northern Thailand, Hmong, *n.*

โม่ môo grind with a mill, *v.*

โม้ móo brag, boast, *v.*

โมฆะ moo-ká null and void, vain, *adj.*

โมเต็ล moo-dten motel, *n.*

โมทนา moo-ta-naa pleased, rejoice, *adj., v.*

โมโห moo-hǒo angry, *adj.*

ไม่ mâi no, not, do not, *adv.*

ไม่ได้ mâi-dâai fail, not gain, not got, cannot, *v.*

ไม้ máai wood, timber, tree, plant, *n.*

ไมตรี mai-dtrii friendliness, *n.*

ไมล์ maai mile, *n.*

ย

ย yɔɔ the thirty-fourth consonant of the Thai alphabet (low consonant), *n.*

ยก yók raise, lift, elevate, *v.*

ยกตัวอย่าง yók-dtua-yàang give an example, *v.*

ยกโทษ yók-tôot forgive, *v.*

ยกธงขาว yók-tong-kǎao surrender, *v.*

ย่น yôn shorten, abbreviate, wrinkled, *v., adj.*

ยนต์ yon machine, engine, *n.*

ยมทูต yom-ma-tûut messenger of death, *n.*

ยมบาล yom-ma-baan God of Hell, *n.*

ยมโลก yom-ma-lôok world of the dead, *n.*

ยมก ya-mók the Thai repeat symbol (ๆ), *n.*

ยวดยาน yûat-yaan vehicle, *n.*

ยวน yuan stimulate, arouse, *v.*

ยวบ yûap sink deeper, *v.*

ยศ yót rank, dignity, *n.*

ยโส yá-sǒo arrogant, conceited, *adj.*

ยอ yɔɔ praise, extol, *v.*

ย่อ yɔ̂ɔ abridge, shorten, abbreviate, *v.*

ย่อตัว yɔ̂ɔ-dtua lower oneself, *v.*

ธ น บ ป ผ ฝ พ ฟ ภ ม **ย** ร ฤ ฦ ล ว ศ ษ ส ห ฬ อ ฮ

ย่อท้อ yɔ̂ɔ-tɔ́ɔ discouraged, *adj.*

ย่อความ yɔ̂ɔ-kwaam abbreviate, summarize, *v.*

ยอก yɔ̂ɔk prick, string, *v.*

ย่อง yɔ̂ng walk quietly, creep up, walk on tiptoe, *v.*

ยอด yɔ̂ɔt top, peak, summit, total, *n.*

ยอดเขา yɔ̂ɔt-kǎo mountain top, *n.*

ยอดเยี่ยม yɔ̂ɔt-yîam excellent, *adj.*

ย้อน yɔ́ɔn return, come back, retrace one's steps, *v.*

ยอม yɔɔm allow, let, agree, permit, *v.*

ยอมความ yɔɔm-kwaam compromise in a legal case, *v.*

ยอมรับ yɔɔm-ráp admit, agree, *v.*

ย้อม yɔ́ɔm dye, *v.*

ย้อมใจ yɔ́ɔm-jai comfort, console, *v.*

ย่อย yɔ̂i digest, crush, dissolve, *v.*

ย่อย yɔ̂i minor, small, unimportant, insignificant, subordinate, *adj.*

ย่อย yɔ̂i enzyme, digestive juice, *n.*

ย่อยยับ yɔ̂i-yáp crushed, *adj.*

ย่อยอาหาร yɔ̂i-aa-hǎan digest, *v.*

ย้อย yɔ́ɔi drop, hang down, *v.*

ยะโฮวา yá-hoo-waa Jehovah, God, *n.*

ยัก yák move up and down, *v.*

ยักยอก yák-yɔ̂ɔk embezzle, *v.*

ยักไหล่ yák-lài shrug, *v.*

ยักษ์ yák giant, ogre, demon, *n.*

ยัง yang remain still, maintain, have, exist, *v.*

ยัง yang yet, still, *adv.*

ยัง yang till, until, as far as, *prep.*

ยั้ง yáng stop, cease, withhold, halt, restrain, *v.*

ยัน yan support, sustain, *v.*

ยั่น yân (slang) fear, afraid of, *v., adj.*

ยันต์ yan magic design or letters placed or inscribed on a piece of cloth or metal plate, *n.*

ยับ yáp creased, crumpled, *adj.*

ยับเยิน yáp-yəən utterly destroyed, completely crushed, *adv.*

ยั่ว yûa tease, provoke, tempt, excite, irritate, *v.*

ยั่วใจ yûa-jai arouse desire, tempt, *v.*

ยั่วโทสะ yûa-too-sà provoke anger, irritate, *v.*

ยั่วยวน yûa-yuan tempt, provoke, allure, entice, *v.*

ยัวะ yúa hot tempered, *adj.*

ยา yaa medicine, drug, remedy, tobacco, cigarette, *n.*

ยากิน yaa-gin oral drug, *n.*

ยากันยุง yaa-gan-yung mosquito repellent, *n.*

ยาแฝด yaa-fὲὲt love potion, *n.*

ย่า yâa paternal grandmother, *n.*

ยาก yâak difficulty, hardness, *n.*

ยาก yâak difficult, *adj.*

ยาง yaang resin, rubber, *n.*

ยางแตก yaang-dtὲὲk blow-out, puncture, *n.*

ยางเทียม yaang-tiam artificial rubber, *n.*

ยางพารา yaang-paa-raa rubber tree, *n.*

ยางยืด yaang-yʉ̂ʉt elastic band, *n.*

ย่าง yâang tread, stride, roast, bake, grill, barbecue, *v.*

ย่างกราย yâang-graai approach, *v.*

ย่างก้าว yâang-gâao stride, take a slow step, *v.*

ยาจก yaa-jòk beggar, poor person, *n.*

ยาน yaan vehicle, carriage, carrier, *n.*

ย่าน yâan region, district, area, *n.*

ยาม yaam time, hour, occasion, period, watchman, *n.*

ย่าม yâam satchel, sack, bag, *n.*

ยาย yaai maternal grandmother, old woman, a form of addressing an old woman, *n.*

ย้าย yáai transfer, move, *v.*

ยาว yaao long, stretched, extended, *adj.*

ยำ yam Thai salad, *n.*

ยำเกรง yam-greeng afraid of, respect, *adj., v.*

ย่ำ yâm tramp upon, *v.*

ย้ำ yám repeat, reaffirm, confirm, emphasize, *v.*

ยิง ying shoot, fire, *v.*

ยิ่ง yîng excessive, profuse, many, much, extreme, *adj.*

ยิน yin hear, *v.*

ยิบ yíp closely packed, closely woven, *adj.*

ยิ้ม yím smile, beam, *v.*

ยิว yiu Jew., thrifty, *n., adj.*

ยีราฟ yii-ráap giraffe, *n.*

ยี่ yîi two, *adj.*

ยี่สิบ yîi-sìp twenty, *nm.*

ยี่หระ yîi-rà care about, *v.*

ยี่ห้อ yîi-hɔ̂ɔ trade mark, brand, *n.*

ยึด yʉ́t hold, seize, *v.*

ยืด yʉ̂ʉt stretch, extend, *v.*

ยืน yʉʉn stand, insist, *n.*

ยืน yʉʉn lasting, *adj.*

ยืนยัน yʉʉn-yan confirm, *v.*

ยื่น yนิ̂un extend, hand out, v.

ยืม yนยม borrow, v.

ยื้อ yนิ́u take by force, v.

ยุ yú stimulate, provoke, v.

ยุค yúk era, time, age, period, n.

ยุง yung mosquito, n.

ยุ่ง yûng entangled, confusing, busy, adj.

ยุ่งยาก yûng-yâak very difficult, very complicated, adj.

ยุ้ง yúng barn, n.

ยุติ yú-dtì terminate, end, v.

ยุติธรรม yú-dtì-tam justice, fairness, n.

ยุทธ yút battle, war, n.

ยุทธภูมิ yút-ta-puum battlefield, n.

ยุทธศาสตร์ yút-ta-sàat strategy, n.

ยุทโธปกรณ์ yút-too-bpà-goon war material, n.

ยุบ yúp sink, diminish in size, v.

ยุบยิบ yúp-yíp fussy, too detailed, adj.

ยุบสภา yúp-sà-paa dissolve parliament, v.

ยุ่มย่าม yûm-yâam disorderly, tangled, adj.

ยุ่ย yûi tender, fragile, adj.

ยุ้ย yúi plump, inflated, adj.

ยุโรป yú-rôop Europe, n.

ยุวา yú-wá young man, lad, n.

ยู่ยี่ yûu-yîi shrunken, wrinkled, adj.

ยูง yuung peacock, n.

เย้ yée leaning, adj.

เยซู yee-suu Jesus Christ, n.

เย็ด yét (very vulgar) fuck, have sexual intercourse, v.

เยน yeen yen, n.

เย็น yen evening, dusk, n.

เย็น yen cool, cold, adj.

เย็นใจ yen-jai calm, adj.

เย็นชืด yen-chûut cold, tasteless, adj.

เย็นวันนี้ yen-wan-níi this evening, n.

เย็บ yép sew, stitch, v.

เย้ย yóəi ridicule, mock, v.

เย่อหยิ่ง yôə-yìng proud, arrogant, adj.

เยอะ yó many, much, abundant, adj.

เยา yao little, weak, light, low, adj.

เยาว์ yao young, adolescent, adj.

เยาะเย้ย yó-yóəi ridicule, v.

เยินยอ yəən-yɔɔ praise, flatter, v.

เยิ่น yə̂n long, lengthy, adj.

เยิ้ม yóəm oozing, flowing gradually, adj.

เยี่ยง yîang model, pattern, n.

เยี่ยน yian visit, v.

เยี่ยม yîam visit, pay a visit, v.

เยี่ยมยอด yîam-yɔ̂ɔt excellent, adj.

เยี่ยมเยือน yîam-yʉan pay a visit, v.

เยี่ยว yîao urine, n.

เยียวยา yiao-yaa treat, give medication, v.

เยื่อ yʉ̂a tissue, fiber, film, n.

เยื้อ yʉ́a endure, v.

เยือก yʉ̂ak piercingly cold, adv.

เยื้อง yʉ́ang deviate from, walk slowly with an air, v.

เยือน yuan visit, pay a visit, v.

แย่ yɛ̂ɛ in trouble, adj.

แย้ yɛ́ɛ a kind of ground lizard, n.

แยก yɛ̂ɛk separate, part, divide up, distinguish, v.

แยง yɛɛng insert, poke, v.

แย่ง yɛ̂ng snatch, grab, seize, v.

แย้ง yɛɛng oppose, contradict, object, argue, dispute, protest, v.

แยบยล yɛ̂ɛp-yon trick, trickery, n.

แย้ม yɛ́ɛm open slightly, v.

แยแส yɛɛ-sɛ̌ɛ pay attention to, v.

โย้เย้ yóo-yée leaning, not straight, adj.

โยก yôok rock, shake from side to side, v.

โยคะ yoo-ká yoga, n.

โยง yoong tie to a post, link, connect, v.

โย่ง yôong lanky, tall and thin, adj.

โยธา yoo-taa troop, soldier, construction work, n.

โยธิน yoo-tin warrior, winner, n.

โยน yoon throw, cast, toss, v.

โยม yoom Buddhist monk's form of addressing laymen, n.

ใย yai fiber, web, cobweb, n.

ใยดี yai-dii care for, v.

ร

ร rɔɔ the thirty-fifth consonant of the Thai alphabet (low consonant), n.

รก rók placenta, afterbirth, n.

รก rók littered, untidy, adj.

รด rót sprinkle, water, pour water on, v.

รถ rót vehicle, wheeled vehicle, carriage, car, cart, bus, van, wagon, truck, automobile, tricycle, bicycle, n.

รถเช่า rót châo rented car, n.

รถด่วน rót-dùan express, n.

รถไฟ rót-fai train, n.

ร่น rôn move closer, retreat, v.

รบ róp fight, make war, v.

รม rom smoke, expose to vapor, v.

ร่ม rôm shade, sunshade, umbrella, *n.*

ร่มชูชีพ rôm-chuu-chîip parachute, *n.*

ร่มเย็น rôm-yen secure and peaceful, *adj.*

ร่วง rûang fall off, drop, *v.*

ร่วงโรย rûang-rooi wane, *v.*

รวด rûat round, time, an instance, *n.*

รวดเดียว rûat-diao all at once, *adv.*

รวดเร็ว rûat-reo quickly, speedily, *adv.*

รวน ruan roast, fry, *v.*

รวนเร ruan-ree doubtful, uncertain, *adj.*

ร่วน rûan crumbling, *adj.*

รวบ rûap gather, together, compile, *v.*

รวม ruam combine, add, include, incorporate, assemble, *v.*

รวมทั้งหมด ruam-táng-mòt altogether, *adj.*

ร่วม rûam share, participate, join in, *v.*

รวย ruai rich, wealthy, affluent, *adj.*

รส rót taste, flavor, relish, *n.*

รสชาติ rót-châat taste, flavor, *n.*

รสนิยม rót-sà-ni-yom liking, preference, *n.*

รหัส rá-hàt code, *n.*

รอ rɔɔ wait, stay, *v.*

รอคอย rɔɔ-kɔɔi wait, wait for, *v.*

ร่อ rɔ̂ɔ place adjoining, *v.*

ร่อแร่ rɔ̂ɔ-rɛ̂ɛ near death, *adj.*

รอก rɔ̂ɔk pulley, *v.*

รอง rɔɔng place something under, support, *v.*

ร่อง rɔ̂ng furrow, channel, ditch, path, way, *n.*

ร้อง rɔ́ɔng cry, scream, exclaim, *v.*

ร้องขอ rɔ́ɔng-kɔ̌ɔ beg for, request, *v.*

รองท้อง rɔɔng-tɔ́ɔng eat just enough not to be hungry, *v.*

ร้องทุกข์ rɔ́ɔng-túk complain, *v.*

รองเท้า rɔɔng-táao shoe, *n.*

ร้องเพลง rɔ́ɔng-pleeng sing, *v.*

ร้องเรียน rɔ́ɔng-rian complain, *v.*

ร่องแร่ง rɔ̂ng-rɛ̂ng hanging, swaying, precarious, *adj.*

รอด rɔ̂ɔt safe, saved, *adj.*

รอด rɔ̂ɔt escape, survive, *v.*

รอน rɔɔn cut, cut down, reduce, *v.*

ร่อน rɔ̂n sift, pan, winnow, *v.*

ร้อน rɔ́ɔn hot, very warm, torrid, *adj.*

ร้อนเงิน rɔ́ɔn-ngən desperately in need of money, in urgent need of money, *adj.*

ร้อนใจ rɔ́ɔn-jai anxious, perturbed, in trouble, *adj.*

ร้อนตัว rɔ́ɔn-dtua afraid of being involved or incriminated, *adj.*

ร้อนรน rɔ́ɔn-ron impatient, anxious, zealous, *adj.*

รอบ rɔ̂ɔp cycle, round, circuit, turn, *n.*

รอม rɔɔm curved, bent around, *adj.*

รอมร่อ rɔɔm-rɔ̂ɔ nearly, almost, *adv.*

รอย rɔɔi trace, mark, sign, path, *n.*

ระกา rá-gaa Year of the Cock, *n.*

ระกำ rá-gam sorrow, grief, *n.*

ระคาย rá-kaai irritated, itchy, cause itching, *adj.*, *v.*

ระแคะ rá-ké trick, mystery, *n.*

ระฆัง rá-kang bell, *n.*

ระงม rá-ngom loud, noisy, *adj.*

ระงับ rá-ngáp stop, halt, cease, *v.*

ระดม rá-dom call up, *v.*

ระดับ rá-dàp level, altitude, surface, *n.*

ระดู rá-duu menses, menstruation, *n.*

ระทด rá-tót sad, sorrowful, oppressed, *adj.*

ระทมทุกข์ rá-tom-túk suffer from excessive anguish or sorrow, *v.*

ระทวย rá-tuai languid, weak, *adj.*

ระทึก rá-túk (of the heart) beating fast from fear, *adj.*

ระนาด rá-nâat xylophone, *n.*

ระนาบ rá-nâap lie flat, *v.*

ระแนง rá-nɛɛng stand in a row, *v.*

ระบบ rá-bòp system, *n.*

ระบม rá-bom feel stiff and sore, *v.*

ระบุ rá-bù mention, specify, *v.*

ระเบิด rá-bə̀ət explode, burst, *v.*

ระเบียง rá-biang verandah, veranda, balcony, porch, *n.*

ระเบียน rá-bian record, pattern, registration, *n.*

ระเบียบ rá-bìap order, regulation, *n.*

ระมัดระวัง rá-mát-rá-wang cautious, *adj.*

ระยะ rá-yá distance, period, range, *n.*

ระยะทาง rá-yá-taang distance, *n.*

ระยับ rá-yáp brilliant, glittering, dazzling, *adj.*

ระย้า rá-yáa festoons, pendent, *n.*

ระยำ rá-yam accursed, mean, *adj.*

ระราน rá-raan trouble, *v.*

ระริก rá-rík giggle, beat fast, *v.*

ระเริง rá-rəəng rejoice, *v.*

ระแวง rá-wɛɛng doubt, *v.*

ระส่ำระสาย rá-sàm-rá-sǎai disordered, *adj.*

ระหง rá-hǒng tall and slender, *adj.*

ระหว่าง rá-wàang middle, middle section, space, interval, period, *n.*

ระหว่างชาติ rá-wàang-châat international, *adj.*

ระเหย rá-hǒoi evaporate, *v.*

ระโหย rá-hǒoi tired, *adj.*

รัก rák love, cherish, fond of, *v.*

รักสนุก rák-sà-nùk playful, *adj.*

รักษา rák-sǎa take care of, treat, watch over, *v.*

รักแร้ rák-réε armpit, *n.*

รัง rang nest, home, *n.*

รังแก rang-gεε bully, molest, *v.*

รังแค rang-kεε dandruff, *n.*

รั้ง ráng stop, wait, *v.*

รัฐ rát state, country, nation, territory, *n.*

รัฐบาล rát-tà-baan government, *n.*

รัฐบุรุษ rát-tà-bù-rùt statesman, *n.*

รัด rát squeeze, bind, *v.*

รัตติกาล rát-dtì-gaan night, *n.*

รัตนะ rát-dtà-ná jewel, precious stone, gem, *n.*

รัตนา rát-dtà-naa glass, jewel, *n.*

รั้น rán stubborn, obstinate, *adj.*

รับ ráp receive, get, *v.*

รับเคราะห์ ráp-krɔ́ have or receive misfortunes, *v.*

รับจ้าง ráp-jâang take employment, *v.*

รับใช้ ráp-chái serve, *v.*

รับบาป ráp-bàap undergo sufferings, be a scapegoat, *v.*

ริว rua vibrate, roll, *v.*

รั่ว rûa leak, leak out, *v.*

รั่วไหล rûa-lǎi leak out, *v.*

รั้ว rúa fence, hedge, *n.*

รัศมี rát-sà-mǐi ray, radius, halo, *n.*

รา raa mould, mold, fungus, *n.*

ร่าเริง râa-rɔɔng cheerful, *adj.*

ราก râak root, foundation, source, origin, *n.*

รากแก้ว râak-gêεo tap root, *n.*

รากฐาน râak-tǎan foundation, base, *n.*

รากศัพท์ râak-sàp vocabulary root, *n.*

รากสาดน้อย râak-sàat-nɔ́ɔi typhoid, *n.*

ราคะ raa-ká lust, sexual desire, *n.*

ราคา raa-kaa price, cost, value, *n.*

ราคี raa-kii flaw, blemish, stain, *n.*

ราง raang groove, rail, track, *n.*

รางน้ำ raang-náam gutter, *n.*

รางวัล raang-wan reward, prize, *n.*

รางๆ raang-raang in distinctly, blurredly, *adv.*

ร่าง râang shape, figure, structure, *n.*

ร้าง ráang deserted, abandoned, *adj.*

ราช râat king, monarch, *n.*

ราชการ râat-cha-gaan government service, *n.*

ราชทูต râat-cha-tûut ambassador, *n.*

ราชสีห์ râat-cha-sîi lion, king-lion, *n.*

ราชา raa-chaa king, ruler, *n.*

ราชินี raa-chi-nii queen, *n.*

ราด râat pour, spill, top, *v.*

ราตรี raa-dtrii night, *n.*

ร่าน râan lustful, eager, *adj.*

ร้าน ráan store, stall, shop, market shop, *n.*

ราบ râap smooth, even, flat, level, *adj.*

รามเกียรติ์ raam-ma-gian Ramayana, *n.*

รามา raa-maa bully, disturb, *v.*

รายได้ raai-dâai income, *n.*

ร่าย râai a kind of Thai verse, *n.*

ร้าย ráai severe, bad, fierce, evil, wicked, *adj.*

ราว raao hand-rail, rail, *n.*

ราวๆ raao-raao about, approximately, *adv.*

ร้าว ráao cracked, *adj.*

ราศี raa-sîi zodiacal sign, *n.*

ราศีเมษ raa-sîi-mêet Aries, Ram, *n.*

ราศีพฤษภ raa-sîi-prút Taurus, Bull, *n.*

ราศีมิถุน raa-sîi-mí-tǔn Gemini, Twins, *n.*

ราศีกรกฎ raa-sîi-gɔɔ-ra-gòt Cancer, Crab, *n.*

ราศีสิงห์ raa-sîi-sǐng Leo, Lion, *n.*

ราศีกันย์ raa-sîi-gan Virgo, Virgin, *n.*

ราศีตุล raa-sîi-dtun Libra, Balance, *n.*

ราศีพิจิก raa-sîi-pí-jìk Scorpio, Scorpion, *n.*

ราศีธนู raa-sîi-ta-nuu Sagittarius, Archer, *n.*

ราศีมังกร raa-sîi-mang-gɔɔn Capricornus, Horn goat, *n.*

ราศีกุมภ์ raa-sîi-gum Aquarius, Water bearer, *n.*

ราศีมีน raa-sîi miin Pisces, Fish, *n.*

ราษฎร râat-sà-dɔɔn citizens, population, *n.*

ราหู raa-hǔu mythological monster, *n.*

รำ ram dance (traditionally), *v.*

รำวง ram-wong perform Thai folkdance, *v.*

รำคาญ ram-kaan annoyed, *adj.*

รำพัน ram-pan bemoan, *v.*

รำพึง ram-pung think of, *v.*

ริ rí initiate, *v.*

ริดรอน rít-rɔɔn take away, cut, *v.*

ริดสีดวง rít-sǐi-duang a group of chronic maladies, n.

ริดสีดวงจมูก rít-sǐi-duang-jà-mùuk rhinitis, n.

ริดสีดวงตา rít-sǐi-duang-dtaa trachoma, n.

ริดสีดวงทวารหนัก rít-sǐi-duang-ta-waan-nàk hemorrhoids, n.

ริน rin pour slowly, v.

ริ้น rín gnat, n.

ริบ ríp confiscate, v.

ริบหรี่ ríp-rìi dim, twinkling, dusky, adj.

ริม rim edge, rim, n.

ริ้ว ríu strip, stripe, wrinkle, n.

ริษยา rít-sà-yǎa jealousy, envy, n.

รีรอ rii-rɔɔ wait for, hesitate, v.

รี่ rîi rush, v.

รีด rîit squeeze, press, iron, v.

รีต rîit custom, religious sect, n.

รีบ rîip hurry, hasten, v.

รีม riim ream, n.

รื่น rûun joyful, adj.

รื่นเริง rûun-rəəng delightful, adj.

รื้อ rúu tear down, v.

รุก rúk push forward, v.

รุ่ง rûng dawn, n.

รุ้ง rúng rainbow, luster, prismatic colors, n.

รุ้งกินน้ำ rúng-gin-náam rainbow, n.

รุงรัง rung-rang untidy, adj.

รุด rút hurry, v.

รุน run push, urge, v.

รุนแรง run-rɛɛng violent, adj.

รุ่น rûn time, age, period, era, generation, n.

รุม rum crowd around, mob, v.

รุ่ม rûm strike or hit repeatedly, v.

รุ่มร่าม rûm-râam shabbily dressed, adj.

รุ่ย rûi loose, brittle, adj.

รู ruu hole, n.

รู้ rúu know, aware of, v., adj.

รู้จัก rúu-jàk acquainted with, adj.

รูด rûut slip, slide smoothly, pull, draw, v.

รูป rûup picture, form, shape, n.

เร่ rêe wander about, v.

เรขา ree-kǎa drawing, graphic, adj.

เรขาคณิต ree-kǎa-ka-nít geometry, n.

เร่ง rêng accelerate, hurry, v.

เร่งเครื่อง rêng-krûang speed up the engine, v.

เร่งรัด rêng-rát urge, v.

เรณู ree-nuu pollen, n.

เร้น rén hide, v.

เรรวน ree-ruan hesitate, *v.*

เรไร ree-rai a kind of cicada, *n.*

เร็ว reo quick, rapid, hasty, swift, *adj.*

เรอ rəə belch, *v.*

เรา rao we, I, us, me, *pron.*

เร้า ráo rouse, stimulate, *v.*

เร้าใจ ráo-jai encourage, arouse, *v.*

เราะตะเข็บ ró-dtà-kèp cut out a

seam, *v.*

เริง rəəng joyful, cheerful, merry, *adj.*

เริงสวาท rəəng-sà-wàat enjoy sexual

intercourse, *v.*

เริด rəət suspended, overly dressed,

adj.

เริม rəəm nettle rash, uticaria, hives, *n.*

เริ่ม rə̂əm begin, start, commence,

lead, *v.*

เริ่มต้น rə̂əm-dtôn begin, start, *v.*

เรี่ยราย rîa-raai scattered, *adj.*

เรียก rîak call, call out, *v.*

เรียกว่า rîak-wâa called, *adj.*

เรียง riang place in a row, *v.*

เรียงความ riang-kwaam essay, *n.*

เรียงคิว riang-kiu in sequence, *adv.*

เรียน rian study, learn, report or

inform, *v.*

เรียนหนังสือ rian-nǎng-sǔu study, *v.*

เรียบ rîap even, *adj.*

เรียว riao tapering, slender, *adj.*

เรี่ยวแรง rîao-rɛɛng strength, energy,

power, *n.*

เรือ rua boat, ship, *n.*

เรือบิน rua-bin airplane, *n.*

เรื้อรัง rúa-rang chronic, *adj.*

เรือง ruang shining, *adj.*

เรื่อง rûang story, subject, *n.*

เรือด rûat bedbug, *n.*

เรือน ruan house, dwelling place, *n.*

เรือนจำ ruan-jam prison, *n,*

เรือนแพ ruan-pɛɛ houseboat, *n.*

เรือนหอ ruan-hɔ̌ɔ bridal house, *n.*

เรื้อน rúan leprosy, *n.*

เรื่อย rûai continuous, continual, *adj.*

แร่ rɛ̂ɛ mineral, *n.*

แรก rɛ̂ɛk initial, original, primary, first,

adj.

แรก rɛ̂ɛk before, at first, *adv.*

แรง rɛɛng strength, force, power, *n.*

แรงงาน rɛɛng ngaan labor, *n*

แร้ง rɛ́ɛng vulture, *n.*

แรด rɛ̂t rhinoceros, *n.*

แร้นแค้น rɛ́ɛn-kɛ́ɛn poor, penniless,

adj.

แรม rɛɛm spend (the night), stay

(overnight), *v.*

แร้ว rέεo snare, trap, *n.*

โรค rôok disease, sickness, malady, *n.*

โรคะ roo-ká disease, ailment, *n.*

โรคหวัด rôok-wàt cold, *n.*

โรคปอดบวม rôok-bpɔ̀ɔt-buam pneu-mococcal, *n.*

โรง roong hall, shed, house, *n.*

โรงกลั่น roong-glàn refinery, *n.*

โรงงาน roong-ngaan factory, *n.*

โรงจำนำ roong-jam-nam pawnshop, *n.*

โรงพยาบาล roong-pá-yaa-baan hospital, *n.*

โรงพิมพ์ roong-pim printing office, *n.*

โรงภาพยนตร์ roong-pâap-pa-yon cinema, *n.*

โรงรถ roong-rót garage, *n.*

โรงเรียน roong-rian school, *n.*

โรงแรม roong-rεεm hotel, *n.*

โรงสี roong-sǐi rice-mill, *n.*

โรงหนัง roong-nǎng movie, cinema, *n.*

โรจน์ rôot prosperous, bright, *adj.*

โรตี roo-dtii a kind of Indian food made of flour, *n.*

โรย rooi sprinkle, *v.*

ไร rai species of insect, *n.*

ไร rai what, which, dimly, *adv., pron.*

ไร่ rài farm, field, *n.*

ไร้ rái poor, lacking, needy, *adj.*

ไร้ rái without, *prep.*

ไร้ค่า rái-kâa worthless, *adj.*

ไร้ความสามารถ rái-kwaam-sǎa-mâat incapable, incapacitated, *adj.*

ไร้สาระ rái-sǎa-rá nonsensical, *adj.*

ฤ

ฤกษ์ rɔ̂ɔk auspicious occasion, *n.*

ฤดู rɯ́-duu season, period, *n.*

ฤดูกาล rɯ́-duu-gaan season, time, *n.*

ฤดูวางไข่ rɯ́-duu-waang-kàai spawning season, *n.*

ฤทธิ์ rít increasing, prosperous, abundant, *adj.*

ฤทธิ์ rít effect, supernatural power, might, power, energy, force, *n.*

ฤทัย rɯ́-tai heart, mind, soul, *n.*

ฤษี rɯ́-sǐi ascetic, hermit, *n.*

ฤา

ฤาษี rɯɯ-sǐi hermit, ascetic, *n.*

ล

ล lɔɔ the thirty-sixth consonant of the Thai alphabet (low consonant), *n.*

ลง long descend, go down, diminish, decrease, *v.*

ลงคะแนน long-ka-nɛɛn cast a ballot, *v.*

ลงชื่อ long-chŵu sign one's name, *v.*

ลงทะเบียน long-ta-bian register, *v.*

ลงทุน long-tun invest, *v.*

ลงโทษ long-tôot punish, *v.*

ลงนาม long-naam sign, *v.*

ลงพุง long-pung potbellied, *adj.*

ลงมติ long-ma-dtì decide by a vote, *v.*

ลงรอย long-rɔɔi get along well, *v.*

ลงแรง long-rɛɛng expend energy, *v.*

ลงเอย long-ǝǝi settled, *adj.*

ลด lót decrease, reduce, *v.*

ลน lon hold over a flame, *v.*

ลบ lóp erase, *v.*

ลบล้าง lóp-láang wipe out, *v.*

ลม lom air, wind, *n.*

ลมบ้าหมู lom-bâa-mǔu epilepsy, *n.*

ลมหายใจ lom-hǎai-jai breath, *n.*

ล่ม lôm overturn, sink, *v.*

ล่มจม lôm-jom go bankrupt, *v.*

ล้ม lóm fall, topple, *v.*

ล้มละลาย lóm-lá-laai go bankrupt, *v.*

ลวก lûak scald, cook briefly, *v.*

ลวง luang deceive, *v.*

ล่วง lûang go beyond, *v.*

ล้วง lúang withdraw, pick, *v.*

ล้วงกระเป๋า lúang-grà-pǎo pickpocket, *v.*

ลวด lûat wire, strand, *n.*

ล้วน lúan pure, sole, complete, *adj.*

ล้วนแต่ lúan-dtɛ̀ɛ completely, entirely, all, *adv.*

ล้วนๆ lúan-lúan purely, completely, *adv.*

ลวนลาม luan-laam harass, *v.*

ลหุ lá-hù light, minor, *adj.*

ลหุโทษ lá-hù-tôot misdemeanor, *n.*

ล่อ lɔ̂ɔ tempt, entice, seduce, *v.*

ล้อ lɔ́ɔ wheel, *n.*

ล้อเลียน lɔ́ɔ-lian tease, mock, *v.*

ลอก lɔ̂ɔk peel off, skin, *v.*

ลอง lɔɔng toot, attempt, try, *v.*

ล่อง lɔ̂ng descend, come down, *v.*

ลอด lɔ̂ɔt pass through, sneak, *v.*

ลอดช่อง lɔ̂ɔt-chɔ̂ng a kind of Thai sweetmeat made of short noodles and coconut milk, *n.*

ล็อตเตอรี่ lɔ́t-dtəə-rîi lottery, *n.*

ลอน lɔɔn wave, curl, wavy ridge, *n.*

ล่อน lɔ̂n peel off, scale off, *v.*

ลอบ lɔ̂p do something secretly, *v.*

ลอบทำร้าย lɔ̂p-tam-ráai ambush, attack by surprise, *v.*

ล้อม lɔ́m surround, *v.*

ลอย lɔɔi float, *v.*

ลอยกระทง lɔɔi-grà-tong a Thai annual floating festival, *n.*

ลออ lá-ɔɔ beautiful, *adj.*

ละ lá abandon, *v.*

ละคร lá-kɔɔn play, drama, stage performance, *n.*

ละม้าย lá-máai similar, *adj.*

ละมุด lá-mút sapota, *n.*

ละมุน lá-mun gentle, tender, soft, *adj.*

ละเมอ lá-məə talk in one's sleep, *v.*

ละเมิด lá-mə̂ət violate, *v.*

ละเมียด lá-mîat well-mannered, *adj.*

ละโมบ lá-môop greedy, *adj.*

ละลอก lá-lɔ̂ɔk ripples, *n.*

ละลาบละล้วง lá-lâap-lá-lúang intrude, trespass, *v.*

ละลาย lá-laai melt, dissolve, *v.*

ละเลง lá-leeng mix, smear, *v.*

ละแวก lá-wɛ̂ɛk vicinity, outskirt, *n.*

ละห้อย lá-hɔ̂i moan, woe, *v.*

ละหุ่ง lá-hùng castor-oil, *n.*

ละเหี่ย lá-hìa feel weary, *v.*

ละออง lá-ɔɔng dust, *n.*

ละอาย lá-aai ashamed, *adj.*

ละเอียด lá-ìat delicate, fine, powdered, *adj.*

ลัก lák steal, *v.*

ลักปิดลักเปิด lák-gà-bpìt-lák-gà-bpə̀ɔt scurvy, *n.*

ลักยิ้ม lák-yím dimple, *n.*

ลักษณะ lák-sà-nà character, characteristic, *n.*

ลักษณนาม lák-sà-nà-naam qualitative noun, classifier, *n.*

ลักษมี lák-sà-mǐi sign, symbol, *n.*

ลัคนา lák-ka-naa auspicious moment, *n.*

ลังเล lang-lee hesitate, *v.*

ลัด lát make short cut, snap, *v.*

ลัดวงจร lát-wong-jɔɔn have an electric short-circuit, *v.*

ลัทธิ lát-tí doctrine, cult, ideology, creed, faith, belief, *n.*

ลั่น lân explode, burst, *v.*

ลันเตา lan-dtao the Holland bean, *n.*

ลั่นทม lân-tom temple tree, pagoda

tree, *n.*

ลับ láp sharpen, hone, *v.*

ลัพธ์ láp resulting, *n.*

ลา laa say good-bye, *v.*

ลา laa ass, donkey, *n.*

ล่า lâa hunt, *v.*

ล้า láa exhausted, fatigued, *adj.*

ล้าสมัย láa-sà-mǎi old fashioned, out of date, *adj.*

ลาก lâak drag, pull, haul, *v.*

ลาง laang omen, prophetic sign, *n.*

ล่าง lâang below, beneath, underneath, *adj.*

ล้าง láang wash, clean, rinse, *v.*

ล้างแค้น láang-kɛ́ɛn take revenge, *v.*

ลาด lâat spread, *v.*

ลาด lâat sloping, inclining, *adj.*

ลาดยาง lâat-yaang paved with asphalt, *v.*

ลาติน laa-dtin Latin, *n.*

ลาน laan yard, lawn, court, court yard, *n.*

ลาบ lâap minced meat, *n.*

ลาภ lâap unexpected gain, piece of luck, *n.*

ลาม laam advance, spread, *v.*

ล่าม lâam tie up, interpreter, *v., n.*

ล่ามโซ่ lâam-sôo chain, *v.*

ลามก laa-mók obscene, lewd, *adj.*

ลาย laai line, mark, stripe, design, pattern, *n.*

ลายเซ็น laai-sen signature, *n.*

ลายนิ้วมือ laai-níu-muu finger-print, *n.*

ลาว laao Laos, Lao, Laotian, *n.*

ลำ lam body, trunk, stalk, *n.*

ล่ำ lâm stout, sturdy, muscular, *adj.*

ล่ำซำ lâm-sam rich, wealthy, *adj.*

ล้ำ lám trespass, invade, *v.*

ล้ำค่า lám-kâa very precious, *adj.*

ล้ำหน้า lám-nâa surpass, *v.*

ลำเค็ญ lam-ken poor, suffering hardship, *adj.*

ลำดับ lam-dàp order, series, sequence, *n.*

ลำเนา lam-nao domain, row, line, *n.*

ลำบาก lam-bàak difficult, hard, *adj.*

ลำพัง lam-pang individual, lonely, solely, *adj.*

ลำโพง lam-poong loud speaker, *n.*

ลำไย lam-yai longan, *n.*

ลำเลียง lam-liang transport, *v.*

ลำเอียง lam-iang partial, biased, *adj.*

ลิเก lí-gee a kind of Thai song and dance, *n.*

ธ น บ ป ผ ฝ พ ฟ ภ ม ย ร ฤ ฦ **ล** ว ศ ษ ส ห ฬ อ

ลิขิต lí-kìt scrape, write, engrave, v.

ลิง ling monkey, ape, n.

ลิงโลด ling-lôot joyful, adj.

ลิตร lít litre, liter, n.

ลิ้น lín tongue, n.

ลิ้นไก่ lín-gài uvula, n.

ลิ้นปี่ lín-bpìi xiphoid cartilage, n.

ลิบ líp distant, far, remote, adj.

ลิ่ม lîm wedge, n.

ลิ้ม lím taste, v.

ลิลิต lí-lít a kind of Thai stanza, n.

ลี้ líi hide, flee, slip away, v.

ลีซอ lii-sɔɔ Lisu, n.

ลีบ lîip withered, dry, parched, adj.

ลีลา lii-laa attitudes, gestures, grace, n.

ลีลาศ lii-lâat ballroom dance, n.

ลึก lúk profound, deep, adj.

ลึกซึ้ง lúk-súng deeply felt, adj.

ลื่น lûun slippery, smooth, adj.

ลืม luum forget, v.

ลืมตา luum-dtaa open the eyes, v.

ลือ luu spread as a rumor, v.

ลุล่วง lú-lûang completed, adj.

ลุก lúk rise, get up, v.

ลุง lung uncle (father or mother's older brother), a term for addressing a mid-dle-aged man, n.

ลุ่ม lûm low, adj.

ลุ่มๆดอนๆ lûm-lûm-dɔɔn-dɔɔn uncertain, uneven, adj.

ลุ่มหลง lûm-lǒng infatuated, adj.

ลุย lui wade, v.

ลู่ lûu track, course, route, n.

ลูก lûuk child, offspring, n.

ลูกกรง lûuk-grong bar of a cage, n.

ลูกกรอก lûuk-grɔɔk stillborn fetus, n.

ลูกกลิ้ง lûuk-glîng roller, n.

ลูกกวาด lûuk-gwàat candy, n.

ลูกเกด lûuk-gèet raisin, n.

ลูกแก้ว lûuk-gɛ̂ɛo glass ball, n.

ลูกไก่ lûuk-gài chick, n.

ลูกขนไก่ lûuk-kǒn-gài shuttlecock, n.

ลูกข่าง lûuk-kàang top (the toy), n.

ลูกขุน lûuk-kǔn jury, n.

ลูกเขย lûuk-kǒəi son-in-law, n.

ลูกครึ่ง lûuk-krûng half-breed, n.

ลูกความ lûuk-kwaam lawyer's client, n.

ลูกค้า lûuk-káa customer, client, n.

ลูกคิด lûuk-kít abacus, n.

ลูกจ้าง lûuk-jâang employee, n.

ลูกดอก lûuk-dɔ̀ɔk dart, n.

ลูกเต๋า lûuk-dtǎo dice, n.

ลูกโทษ lûuk-tôot free kick, n.

ลูกบิด lûuk-bìt door-knob, *n.*

ลูกไม้ lûuk-máai fruit, trick, lace, *n.*

ลูกโลก lûuk-lôok globe, *n.*

ลูบ lûup stroke, pat, *v.*

เล็ก lék small, little, *adj.*

เลข lêek number, numeral, figure, *n.*

เลขา lee-kǎa writing, letter, *n.*

เลขานุการ lee-kǎa-nú-gaan secretary, *n.*

เล็ด lét seed, pit, stone, *n.*

เลน leen mud, *n.*

เล่น lên play, amuse oneself, sport, gamble, bet, *v.*

เล่นงาน lên-ngaan assault, *v.*

เล่นชู้ lên-chúu commit adultery, *v.*

เล่นตัว lên-dtua play hard to get, *v.*

เล่นพวก lên-pûak give way to favoritism, *v.*

เล่นเพื่อน lên-pûan be a lesbian, *v.*

เล่นไพ่ lên-pâi play cards, *v.*

เล่นแร่แปรธาตุ lên-rɛ̂ɛ-bpree-tâat perform alchemy, *v.*

เล่นละคร lên-lá-kɔɔn play, put on an act, *v.*

เล็บ lép nail, claw, *n.*

เล็ม lem hem the edge, trim, *v.*

เล่ม lêm classifier for books, knives, scissors, swords, spears, oars, sickles, etc., *n.*

เลย lɔɔi beyond, further, farther, past, more, too, *adv.*

เลย lɔɔi pass, surpass, *v.*

เลว leeo inferior, bad, poor, base, mean, evil, *adj.*

เลวที่สุด leeo-tîi-sùt worse, *adj.*

เลศนัย lêet-sà-nai hint, ruse, *adj.*

เลสเบี้ยน léet-sa-bîan lesbian, *n.*

เลหลัง lee-lǎng auction, *n.*

เลอเลิศ lɔɔ-lɔ̂ɔt excellent, *adj.*

เลอะ lɔ́ stained, soiled, *adj.*

เลอะเทอะ lé-té messed up, *adj.*

เล่า lâo tell, narrate, *v.*

เล่านิทาน lâo-ní-taan tell a story, *v.*

เล่าเรียน lâo-rian learn, study, *v.*

เล้า láo pen, sty, coop, *n.*

เลาะ lɔ́ skirt, remove stitches, *v.*

เลิก lɔ̂ɔk discontinue, quit, stop, *v.*

เลิกทาส lɔ̂ɔk-tâat abolish slavery, *v.*

เลิกร้าง lɔ̂ɔk-ráang divorced, *adj.*

เลินเล่อ lɔɔn-lɔ̂ careless, *adj.*

เลิศ lɔ̂ɔt excellent, *adj.*

เลีย lia lick, *v.*

เลียง liang a kind of mild vegetable curry, *n.*

เลี่ยง liang evade, avoid, *v.*

เลี้ยง líang feed, nourish, *v.*

เลี้ยงชีพ líang-chîip make a living, *v.*

เลี้ยงส่ง líang-sòng give a farewell party, *v.*

เลี่ยน lîan level, smooth, oily, glossy, *adj.*

เลียบเคียง líap-kiang sound, speak indirectly about another, *v.*

เลี่ยม lîam follow the edge, cap, garnish, *v.*

เลี้ยว líao turn, *v.*

เลือก lûak select, choose, pick, *v.*

เลือกตั้ง lûak-dtâng elect, *v.*

เลือด lûat blood, *n.*

เลือดจาง lûat-jaang anemic, *adj.*

เลือดเย็น lûat-yen cold-blooded, *adj.*

เลือน luan dim, blurred, *adj.*

เลื่อน lûan slide, slip, *v.*

เลื่อนขึ้น lûan-kûn move up, *v.*

เลื่อนตำแหน่ง lûan-dtam-nèng promoted, *adj.*

ล้อเลื่อน lɔ́ɔ-lûan wheeled vehicle, *n.*

เลื่อม lûam smooth, polished, *adj.*

เลื่อย lûai saw, *v., n.*

เลื้อย lúai crawl, creep, *v.*

แล lɛɛ look at, watch, *v.*

แลก lɛ̂ɛk exchange, *v.*

แลกเงิน lɛ̂ɛk-ngən change money, *v.*

แลกเปลี่ยน lɛ̂ɛk-bplìan exchange, *v.*

แล้ง lɛ́ɛng dry, arid, *adj.*

แล้ง lɛ́ɛng drought, *n.*

แล้งน้ำใจ lɛ́ɛng-náam-jai kindless, *adj.*

แล่น lɛ̂n move, run, sail, *v.*

แลบ lɛ̂p stick out, *v.*

แล้ว lɛ́ɛo already, afterwards, then, later, *adv.*

แล้ว lɛ́ɛo finished, ready, completed in itself, *adj.*

แล้วก็ lɛ́ɛo-gɔ̂ɔ then, *adv.*

แล้วกัน lɛ́ɛo-gan indicating surprise, *interj.*

แล้วแต่ lɛ́ɛo-dtɛ̀ɛ depends on, *adv.*

แล้วเสร็จ lɛ́ɛo-sèt completed, done, finished, *adj.*

และ lɛ́ with, also, likewise, *adv.*

โล่ lôo shield, *n.*

โล้ lóo swing, *v.*

โลก lôok earth, world, *n.*

โลกีย์ loo-gii worldly matter, lust, *n.*

โลง loong coffin, *n.*

โล่ง lôong open, vacant, *adj.*

โล่งใจ lôong-jai feel relieved, *v.*

โลด lôot jump, spring, *v.*

โล้น lóon bald, *adj.*

โลภ lôop greed, *n.*

โลม loom caress, *v.*

โลมา loo-maa dolphin, *n.*

โลเล loo-lee unsteady, unpredictable, *adj.*

โลหะ loo-hà metal, *n.*

โลหะผสม loo-hà-pà-sŏm alloy, *n.*

โลหิต loo-hìt blood, *n.*

โลหิตจาง loo-hìt-jaang anemia, *n.*

โละ ló put down, throw away, *v.*

ไล่ lâi chase, pursue, hunt, *v.*

ไล่ทัน lâi-tan catch up with, *v.*

ไล่เลี่ย lâi-lîa equal, *adj.*

ไล่ออก lâi-ɔ̀ɔk dismiss, expel, *v.*

ว

ว wɔɔ the thirty-seventh consonant of the Thai alphabet (low consonant), *n.*

วก wók turn, turn back, *v.*

วกกลับ wók-glàp turn back, return to the starting point, *v.*

วง wong circle, sphere, ring, *n.*

วงการ wong-gaan circle, field, sources, *n.*

วงการแพทย์ wong-gaan-pɛ̂ɛt med-ical circles, *n.*

วงจร wong-jɔɔn circuit, *n.*

วงเล็บ wong-lép parenthesis, bracket, *n.*

วงเวียน wong-wian circular place, *n.*

วงกต wong-gòt maze, *n.*

วงศ์ wong lineage, family, dynasty, clan, *n.*

วงศาคณาญาติ wong-sǎa-ka-naa-yâat family, lineage, relatives, *n.*

วจี wá-jii words, speech, language, *n.*

วณิพก wá-ní-pók beggar, *n.*

วน won whirl, *v.*

วนเวียน won-wian circle, *v.*

วรรค wák paragraph, space, *n.*

วรรณ wan color, *n.*

วรุณ wá-run god of rain, *n.*

วลี wá-lii phrase, *n.*

วสันต์ wá-sǎn spring, *n.*

วอก wɔ̂ɔk Year of the Monkey, *n.*

ว่อง wɔ̂ng quick, *adj.*

วอด wɔ̂ɔt exhausted, ruined, *adj.*

วอน wɔɔn implore, plead, *v.*

วอนขอ wɔɔn-kɔ̌ɔ beg for, *v.*

ว่อน wɔ̂n great herds, *adj.*

วัคซีน wák-siin vaccine, *n.*

วัง wang palace, *n.*

วัฒนา wát-ta-naa grow, proper, *v.*

วัณโรค wan-na-rôok tuberculosis, *n.*

วัด wát temple, monastery, *n.*

วัตถุ wát-tù matter, object, *n.*

วัตร wát duty, practice, custom, *n.*

วัน wan day, day of the week, daytime, date, *n.*

วับ wáp flashingly, *adv.*

วัย wai age, years, *n.*

วัว wua cow, cattle, bull, ox, *n.*

วัวควาย wua-kwaai cattle, *n.*

วัสดุ wát-sà-dù material, objects, *n.*

วา waa Thai measure of length equal to two meters (about 80 inches), *n.*

วา waa stretch both arms fully, *v.*

ว่า wâa say, speak, remark, criticize, scold, *v.*

ว้าเหว่ wáa-wèe lonely, *adj., v.*

วาง waang lay, lay down, put down, *v.*

วางใจ waang-jai confident, *adj.*

วางเพลิง waang-pləəng commit arson, *v.*

ว่าง wâang empty, unoccupied, vacant, open, *adj.*

ว่างงาน wâang-ngaan unemployed, *adj.*

ว่างเปล่า wâang-bplàao empty, *adj.*

วาจา waa-jaa words, speech, *n.*

วาด wâat draw, sketch, *v.*

วาตภัย wâat-dtà-pai disaster from a wind storm, *n.*

วาน waan ask, request, *v.*

วานซืน waan-suun the day before yesterday, *n., adv.*

วาบ wâap flashing, glittering, *adj.*

ว่ายน้ำ wâai-náam swim, *v.*

วาระ waa-rá period, time, *n.*

วาสนา wâat-sà-nǎa fate, fortune, *n.*

วิกฤต wí-grìt critical, *adj.*

วิกล wí-gon deformed, disfigured, *adj.*

วิกาล wí-gaan improper time, night-time, *n.*

วิเคราะห์ wí-krɔ́ analyze, *v.*

วิ่ง wîng run, get busy, *v.*

วิจัย wí-jai research, *n.*

วิจารณ์ wí-jaan criticize, *v.*

วิชา wí-chaa knowledge, subject, *n.*

วิญญาณ win-yaan soul, mind, *n.*

วิดน้ำ wít-náam draw off water, *v.*

วิตก wí-dtòk worry, mediate, *v.*

วิตถาร wít-(dtà)-tǎan abnormal, peculiar, queer, strange, *adj.*

วิถี wí-tǐi path, route, *n.*

วิทยา wít-ta-yaa knowledge, *n.*

วิทยาลัย wít-ta-yaa-lai college, *n.*

วิทยาศาสตร์ wít-ta-yaa-sàat science, *n.*

วิทยุ wít-ta-yú radio, wireless, *n.*

วิธี wí-tii way, method, means, *n.*

วินัย wí-nai discipline, rule, *n.*

วินาที wí-naa-tii second, *n.*

วินาศ wí-nâat ruined, *adj.*

วินิจฉัย wí-nít-chǎi investigate, examine, diagnose, *v.*

วิบัติ wí-bàt destruction, ruin, calamity, catastrophe, *n.*

วิบาก wí-bàak hardship, obstacle, obstruction, *n.*

วิปริต wí-bpà-rìt change, alternate, deviate, *v.*

วิปัสสนา wí-bpàt-sà-naa meditation, *n.*

วิพากษ์ wí-pâak criticize, *v.*

วิริยะ wí-rí-yá diligence, industry, *n.*

วิรุฬห์ wí-run prosperous, *adj.*

วิไล wí-lai beautiful, *adj.*

วิวาท wí-wâat dispute, *v.*

วิวาห์ wí-waa marriage, wedding, *n.*

วิเวก wí-wêek desolation, *n.*

วิเศษ wí-sèet excellent, *adj.*

วิเศษณ์ wí-sèet predicate, qualifier, adjective, *n.*

วิษณุ wí-sà-nú protector, Vishnu, *n.*

วิสัญญีแพทย์ wí-sǎn-yii-pêet anesthetist, *n.*

วิสัย wí-sǎi object of the senses, *n.*

วิสามัญ wí-sǎa-man special, extraordinary, *adj.*

วิสาสะ wí-sǎa-sà familiarity, intimacy, *n.*

วิสาหกิจ wí-sǎa-hà-gìt enterprise, *n.*

วิหค wí-hòk bird, *n.*

วิหาร wí-hǎan temple, *n.*

วีรบุรุษ wii rá-bù-rùt hero, *n.*

วี่แวว wîi-wɛɛɛ trace, clue, *n.*

วุฒิ wút-tí elderly, senior, *adj.*

วุฒิสภา wút-tí-sà-paa senate, *n.*

วุฒิสมาชิก wút-tí-sà-maa-chík senator, *n.*

วุ่น wûn confused, busy, *adj.*

วุ้น wún jelly, *n.*

วุ้นเส้น wún-sên vermicelli, *n.*

วูบ wûup disappear instantly, *v.*

วูบวาบ wûup-wâap flashing, *adj.*

ว่าวาม wûu-waam act hastily, *v.*

เวชภัณฑ์ wêet-cha-pan medical supplies, *n.*

เวชศาสตร์ wêet-cha-sàat medicine, *n.*

เวทนา wéet-ta-naa pity, *v.*

เวที wee-tii stage, *n.*

เว้น wén exclude, except, *v.*

เวร ween turn, shift, fate, *n.*

เวลา wee-laa time, period, *n.*

เว้า wáo speak, talk, *v.*

เวียดนาม wîat-naam Vietnam, *n.*

เวียน wian revolve, circle, *v.*

เวียนศีรษะ wian-sii-sà dizzy, *adj.*

เวียนหัว wian-hǔa dizzy, *adj.*

แวง wεεng longitude, *n.*

แวด wêεt surround, *v.*

แว่น wên glasses, *n.*

แว่นกันแดด wên-gan-dèεt sun glasses, *n.*

แว่นขยาย wên-ka-yǎai magnifying glass, *n.*

แว่นตา wên-dtaa glasses, *n.*

แวว wεεo light, *n.*

แว่ว wêo hear vaguely, *v.*

แวะ wé drop in, *v.*

โวย wooi boisterous, *v.*

โวหาร woo-hǎan eloquence, *n.*

ไว wai swift, quick, fast, *adj.*

ไว้ wái keep, preserve, conserve, *v.*

ไว้ใจ wái-jai trust, *v.*

ไวตามิน wai-dtaa-min vitamin, *n.*

ศ

ศ sɔ̌ɔ the thirty-eighth consonant of the Thai alphabet (high consonant), *n.*

ศก sòk hair, *n.*

ศก sòk year, years, era, *n.*

ศต sà-dtà hundred, *n.*

ศพ sòp corpse, *n.*

ศร sɔ̌ɔn arrow, *n.*

ศรัทธา sàt-taa faith, trust, *n.*

ศรี sǐi good fortune, dignity, *n.*

ศอก sɔ̀ɔk elbow, *n.*

ศักดา sàk-daa power, might, effect, *n.*

ศักดิ์ sàk rank, authority, status, *n.*

ศักย์ sàk potential, *n.*

ศักราช sàk-gà-ràat era, *n.*

ศัตรู sàt-dtruu enemy, foe, opponent, adversary, *n.*

ศัพท์ sàp vocabulary, *n.*

ศัพท์ sàp voice, speech, *n.*

ศัลยกรรม sǎn-ya-gam surgery, *n.*

ศาล sǎan court, court of justice, *n.*

ศาลแขวง sǎan-kwěεng district court, *n.*

ศาลฎีกา sǎan-dii-gaa supreme court, *n.*

ศาลา sǎa-laa rest-house, public rest-house, *n.*

ศาลากลาง săa-laa-glaang city hall, *n.*

ศาสดา sàat-sà-daa religious founder, *n.*

ศาสตร์ sàat science, *n.*

ศาสตราจารย์ sàat-sà-dtraa-jaan professor, *n.*

ศาสนา sàat-sà-năa religion, *n.*

ศาสนาคริสต์ sàat-sà-năa-krít, sàat-sà-năa-krís Christianity, *n.*

ศาสนาพราหมณ์ sàat-sà-năa-praam Brahmanism, *n.*

ศาสนาพุทธ saat-sà-năa-pút Buddhism, *n.*

ศาสนาอิสลาม sàat-sà-năa-ìt-sà-laam Islam, *n.*

ศิขา sì-kăa lock of hair on the head, peak, summit, *n.*

ศิลป sĭn-lá-bpà art, *n.*

ศิลปกร sĭn-lá-bpà-goon artist, *n.*

ศิลปกรรม sĭn-la-bpà-gam art work, *n.*

ศิลปิน sĭn-lá-bpin artist, *n.*

ศิลา sì-laa rock, stone, *n.*

ศิวะ sì-wá the god of construction, *n.*

ศิวิไลซ์ sì-wi-lai civilization, *n.*

ศิษย์ sìt pupil, student, disciple, *n.*

ศีรษะ sĭi-sà head, top, *n.*

ศีล sĭin moral precepts, *n.*

ศีลธรรม sĭin-la-tam morality, *n.*

ศึก sùk battle, war, *n.*

ศึกษา sùk-săa study, *v.*

ศุกร์ sùk planet Venus, Friday, *n.*

ศุลกากร sŭn-lá-gaa-goon customs, *n.*

ศูนย์ sŭun center, zero, *n.*

เศรษฐกิจ sèet-tà-gìt economy, *n.*

เศรษฐี sèet-tĭi millionaire, *n.*

เศร้า sâo sad, sorrowful, *adj.*

เศวต sà-wèet white color, *n.*

เศษ sèet remainder, remnants, fraction, *n.*

เศษกระดาษ sèet-grà-dàat scrap of paper, waste paper, *n.*

เศษไม้ sèet-máai splinter, *n.*

เศษส่วน sèet-sùan fraction, *n.*

โศก sòok sorrow, grief, *n.*

โศกา sŏo-gaa cry, weep, *v.*

ษ

ษ sɔ̌ɔ the thirty-ninth consonant of the Thai alphabet (high consonant), *n.*

ยมา sà-maa beg pardon, *v.*

ยมาโทษ sà-maa-tôot ask for pardon for sin or wrong-doings, *v.*

ธ น บ ป ผ ฝ พ ฟ ภ ม ย ร ฤ ฎ ล ว ศ ษ ส ห ฬ อ

ส

ส sɔ̌ɔ the fortieth consonant of the Thai alphabet (high consonant), *n.*

สกรู sà-gruu screw, *n.*

สกล sà-gon full, complete, *adj.*

สกัด sà-gàt obstruct, intercept, *v.*

สกาว sà-gaao white, clean, *adj.*

สกุล sà-gun family, lineage, *n.*

สกปรก sòk-gà-bpròk dirty, filthy, *adj.*

ส่ง sòng pass, hand, send, deliver, ship, *v.*

สงกรานต์ sǒng-graan Thai New Year, Songkran Day, *n.*

สงคราม sǒng-kraam war, battle, *n.*

สงเคราะห์ sǒng-krɔ́ help, assist, *v.*

สงฆ์ sǒng priest, monk, *n.*

สงบ sà-ngòp become quiet, *v.*

สงวน sà-nguan keep, preserve, reserve, *v.*

สงสัย sǒng-sǎi doubt, doubtful, *v., adj.*

สงสาร sǒng-sǎan pity, have pity on, sympathize with, *v.*

สงัด sà-ngàt calm, *adj.*

สง่า sà-ngàa dignified, grand, *adj.*

สด sòt fresh, green, *adj.*

สดชื่น sòt-chʉ̂ʉn fresh, joyful, *adj.*

สดใส sòt-sǎi bright, *adj.*

สดับ sà-dàp listen, hear, *v.*

สตรี sà-dtrii woman, female, *n.*

สตางค์ sà-dtaang money, a copper Thai coin equal to one hundredth of a baht, *n.*

สติ sà-dtì consciousness, mind, thought, *n.*

สติปัญญา sà-dtì-bpan-yaa wisdom, intelligence, *n.*

สไตล์ sà-dtaai style, *n.*

สถาน sà-tǎan place, site, *n.*

สถานะ sà-tǎa-ná status, state, rank, situation, *n.*

สถานี sà-tǎa-nii station, shipping station, *n.*

สถานีดับเพลิง sà-tǎa-nii-dàp-plɤɤng fire station, *n.*

สถานีตำรวจ sà-tǎa-nii-dtam-rùat police station, *n.*

สถานีรถไฟ sà-tǎa-nii-rót-fai railway station, *n.*

สถาบัน sà-tǎa-ban institution, *n.*

สถาปนา sà-tǎa-bpà-naa construct, *v.*

สถาปนิก sà-tǎa-bpà-ník architect, *n.*

สถาปัตย์ sà-tǎa-bpàt architecture, *n.*

สถาพร sà-tǎa-pɔɔn permanent, *adj.*

สถิต sà-tìt stay, remain, dwell, v.

สถิติ sà-tì-dtì statistics record, n.

สถูป sà-tùup stupa, n.

สน sŏn pine, pine tree, n.

สนใจ sŏn-jai pay attention, v.

ส้น sôn heel, butt, n.

ส้นเท้า sôn-táao heel, n.

ส้นสูง sôn-sŭung high heels, n.

สนทนา sŏn-ta-naa converse, v.

สนเทศ sŏn-têet news, information, n.

สนเท่ห์ sŏn-têe doubtful, adj.

สนธยา sŏn-ta-yaa twilight, n.

สนธิ sŏn-tì junction, connection, union, joint, intercourse, n.

สนม sà-nŏm lady of the court, royal concubine, n.

สนอง sà-nɔ̌ɔng reply, respond, v.

สนั่น sà-nàn very loud, adj.

สนับ sà-nàp glove, covering for protection, n.

สนับสนุน sà-nàp-sà-nŭn support, v.

สนาม sà-nǎam field, ground. lawn, yard, n.

สนามกอล์ฟ sà-nǎam-gɔ́ɔp golf course, n.

สนามกีฬา sà-nǎam-gii-laa stadium, n.

สนามบิน sà-nǎam-bin airport, n.

สนามรบ sà-nǎam-róp battle, n.

สนิท sà-nìt fitting closely, close, tight, adj.

สนิม sà-nǐm rust, n.

สนุก sà-nùk entertaining, amusing, cheerful, enjoyable, agreeable, adj.

สบตา sòp-dtaa meet the eyes of, v.

สบประมาท sòp-bprà-màat insult, v.

สบง sà-bong a piece of cloth worn by Buddhist monks, n.

สบถ sà-bòt swear, v.

สบาย sà-baai well, happy, comfortable, adj.

สบายใจ sà-baai-jai contented, adj.

สบู่ sà-bùu soap, n.

สไบ sà-bai shawl, wrap, n.

สภา sà-paa council, assembly, n.

สภากาชาด sà-paa-gaa-châat Red Cross, n.

สภาพ sà-pâap nature, status, natural state, n

สภาวะ sà-paa-wá nature, status, condition, n.

สม sŏm suitable, appropriate, adj.

สมจริง sŏm-jing truthful, adj.

สมน้ำหน้า sŏm-náam-nâa serve

(somebody) right, *v.*

สมรู้ร่วมคิด sŏm-rúu-rûam-kít con-spire, *v.*

สมสู่ sŏm-sùu have sexual intercourse, *v.*

ส้ม sôm orange, *n.*

ส้มเขียวหวาน sôm-kĭao-wăan tangerine, *n.*

ส้มตำ sôm-dtam a kind of Thai salad made of sliced green papaya, *n.*

ส้มโอ sôm-oo pomelo, *n.*

สมการ sa-ma-gaan equation, *n.*

สมญา sŏm-yaa fame, renown, *n.*

สมณะ sà-ma-ná religious mendicant, priest, monk, *n.*

สมณเพศ sà-ma-ná-pêet ascetics, *n.*

สมเด็จ sŏm-dèt abbot, great one, a title of high rank of a Buddhist monk, *n.*

สมถะ sà-ma-tà peace of mind, *n.*

สมนา sŏm-ma-naa repay, *v.*

สมนาคุณ sŏm-ma-naa-kun return thanks, *v.*

สมบัติ sŏm-bàt property, wealth, possession, *n.*

สมบุกสมบัน sŏm-bùk-sŏm-ban confront difficulties, *v.*

สมบูรณ์ sŏm-buun perfect, complete, absolute, full, *adj.*

สมบูรณาญาสิทธิราช sŏm-buu-ra-naa-yaa-sìt-tí-râat absolute monarchy, *n.*

สมภพ sŏm-póp birth, *n.*

สมภาร sŏm-paan abbot, *n.*

สมโภช sŏm-pôot celebration, *n.*

สมมุติ sŏm-mút suppose, *v.*

สมมุติ sŏm-mút hypothesis, *n.*

สมมติเทพ sŏm-mút-dtì-têep supposed deity, *n.*

สมมาตร sŏm-mâat symmetry, *n.*

สมมติฐาน sŏm-mút-dtì-tăan hypothesis, *n.*

สมรภูมิ sà-mɔɔ-ra-puum battle field, *n.*

สมรรถภาพ sà-màt-tà-pâap efficiency, ability, *n.*

สมวัย sŏm-wai suitable for the age, *adj.*

สมอ sà-mɔɔ anchor, stone, *n.*

สมอเรือ sà-mɔɔ-rʉa anchor, *n.*

สมอง sà-mɔɔng brain, head, *n.*

สมัคร sà-màk volunteer, join willingly, apply (e.g. for a job), *v.*

สมัครใจ sà-màk-jai willing, *adj.*

สมัชชา sà-mát-chaa assembly, *n.*

สมัย sà-măi era, period, age, time, *n.*

สมาคม sà-maa-kom society, association, n.

สมาชิก sà-maa-chík member, n.

สมาธิ sà-maa-tí concentration, n.

สมาน sà-mǎan connect, assimilate, v.

สมานแผล sà-mǎan-plɛ̌ɛ heal the wound, v.

สมาพันธ์ sà-maa-pan confederation, n.

สม่ำเสมอ sà-màm-sà-mɤ̌ɤ regular, consistent, adj.

สมุด sà-mùt notebook, n.

สมุทร sà-mùt ocean, n.

สมุทัย sà-mù-tai cause, n.

สมุน sà-mǔn attendant, follower, n.

สมุนไพร sà-mǔn-prai medicinal herbs, n.

สมุหบัญชี sà-mù-ban-chii accountant general, n.

สโมสร sà-moo-sɔ̌ɔn club, association, n.

สยดสยอง sà-yòt-sà-yɔ̌ɔng horrible, dreadful, adj.

สยบ sà-yòp bend the head down, n.

สยอง sà-yɔ̌ɔng dreadful, horrified, adj.

สยาม sà-yǎam Siam, former name for Thailand, n.

สยามรัฐ sà-yǎam-rát Siam, n.

สยาย sà-yǎai spread, untangle, v.

สยิว sà-yiu feel a sense of thrill, v.

สรงน้ำ sòng-náam bathe, v.

สรณะ sà-ra-ná protection, place of refuge, n.

สรร sǎn choose, v.

สรรพ sàp whole, all, adj.

สรรเสริญ sǎn-sɤ̌ɤn, sǎn-ra-sɤ̌ɤn praise, laud, v.

สรวล sǔan laugh, smile, v.

สร้อย sɔ̂i necklace, n.

สระ sà pool, pond, n.

สระ sà wash, v.

สร่าง sàang recover, v.

สร่างเมา sàang-mao become sober, v.

สร้าง sâang build, create, make, v.

สรีระ sà-rii-rá body, n.

สรีรวิทยา sà-rii-rá-wít-ta-yaa physiology, n.

สรุป sà-rùp conclude, sum up, v.

สลด sà-lòt sorrowful, adj.

สลบ sà-lòp unconscious, adj.

สลวย sà-lǔai beautiful, pretty, adj.

สลอน sà-lɔ̌ɔn many, abundant, adj.

สละ sà-là renounce, relinquish, v.

สลัก sà-làk carve, v.

สลัด sà-làt throw off, shake, *v.*

สลัด sà-làt salad, *n.*

สลับ sà-làp alternate, *v.*

สลัม sà-lam slum, *n.*

สลัว sà-lǔa dim, *adj.*

สลาก sà-làak label, *n.*

สลากกินแบ่ง sà-làak-gin-bèng lottery ticket, *n.*

สลาย sà-lǎai disintegrate, decompose, *v.*

สลึง sà-lǔng small Thai coin equal to the fourth of a baht, *n.*

สวด sùat chant, *v.*

สวน sǔan garden, *n.*

สวน sǔan encounter, pass in opposite positions, *v.*

สวนสัตว์ sǔan-sàt zoo, *n.*

ส่วน sùan part, share, portion, *n.*

ส่วนประกอบ sùan-bprà-gɔ̀ɔp component, *n.*

สวม sǔam put on, wear, *v.*

ส้วม sûam water closet, toilet, *n.*

สวย sǔai beautiful, pretty, lovely, attractive, *adj.*

ส่วย sùai tribute, *n.*

สวรรค์ sà-wǎn heaven, *n.*

สวรรคต sà-wǎn-(na)-kót royal to die, *v.*

สวัสดิการ sà-wàt-dì-gaan welfare, *n.*

สวัสดี sà-wàt-dii word of greeting, *n.*

สว่าง sà-wàang bright, clear, glowing, shining, light, *adj.*

สวาท sà-wàat lovable, *adj.*

สว่าน sà-wàan drill, *n.*

สวิง sà-wǐng hand-net, *n.*

สห sà-hà with, together with, *prep.*

สหกรณ์ sà-hà-gɔɔn cooperative, *n.*

สหประชาชาติ sà-hà-bprà-chaa-châat United Nations, *n.*

สหพันธ์ sà-hà-pan federation, *n.*

สหรัฐอเมริกา sà-hà-rát-a-mee-ri-gaa the United States of America, *n.*

สหัส sà-hàt power, *n.*

สหาย sà-hǎai friend, companion, *n.*

ส่อ sɔ̀ɔ indicate, reveal, *v.*

สอง sɔ̌ɔng two, twin, *adj.*

ส่อง sɔ̀ng shine, throw light upon, look in a mirror, *v.*

สอด sɔ̀ɔt insert, *v.*

สอน sɔ̌ɔn teach, instruct, train, *v.*

สอบ sɔ̀ɔp examine, test, *v.*

สอพลอ sɔ̌ɔ-plɔɔ flatter, *v.*

ส้อม sɔ̂m fork, *n.*

สอย sɔ̌ɔi hem, stitch, *v.*

ส่อเสียด sɔ̀ɔ-sìat stimulate, *v.*

สะสม sà-sŏm accumulate, collect, v.

สะกด sà-gòt suppress, control, spell (words), put to sleep by magic, v.

สะกดจิต sà-gòt-jìt hypnotize, v.

สะกดรอย sà-gòt-rɔɔi follow, follow tracks, v.

สะกิด sà-gìt tap, nudge gently, v.

สะเก็ด sà-gèt fragment, flake, scab, pieces, n.

สะใจ sà-jai satisfied, v.

สะดวก sà-dùak convenient, adj.

สะดิ้ง sà-dîng feigning, adj.

สะดือ sà-duu navel, n.

สะดุ้ง sà-dûng startled, adj.

สะดุด sà-dùt stumble, v.

สะเด็ด sà-dèt dried, adj.

สะเดาะ sà-dɔ̀ perform deeds by magic power, v.

สะท้อน sà-tɔ́ɔn rebound, v.

สะท้อน sà-tɔ́ɔn reflected, adj.

สะท้อนใจ sà-tɔ́ɔn-jai disheartened, adj.

สะท้าน sà-táan tremble, v.

สะเทิน sà-təən half, half-way, adj.

สะเทือน sà-tuan tremble, v.

สะบัด sà-bàt shake, flip, v.

สะบั้น sà-bân broken off, adj.

สะบ้าหัวเข่า sà-bâa-hǔa-kào kneecap, n.

สะพรั่ง sà-prâng ready, total, adj.

สะพาน sà-paan bridge, n.

สะพาย sà-paai carry (on the shoulder), v.

สะเพร่า sà-prâo careless, negligent, adj.

สะใภ้ sà-pái female relative by marriage, n.

สะระแหน่ sà-ra-nὲɛ mint, n.

สะสาง sà-sǎang clear up, solve, v.

สะอาด sà-àat clean, adj.

สะอิ้ง sà-îng belt, girdle, n.

สะอิดสะเอียน sà-ìt-sà-ian disgusted, adj.

สะอึก sà-ùk hiccup, v.

สัก sàk teak, teak tree, n.

สัก sàk tattoo, v.

สักการะ sàk-gaa-rá worship, v.

สักขี sàk-kǐi witness, n.

สักวา sàk-gà-waa a form of poetry, n.

สักหลาด sàk-gà-làat flannel, n.

สั่ง sàng order, command, instruct, give orders, n.

สังกะสี sǎng-gà-sǐi zinc, n.

สังกัด sǎng-gàt belong, v.

สังเกต sǎng-gèet observe, notice, note, v.

สังข์ sǎng shell, conch, n.

สังขยา sǎng-kà-yǎa a kind of Thai pudding, n.

สังขาร sǎng-kǎan body and mind, n.

สังเขป sǎng-kèep summary, n.

สังคม sǎng-kom society, association, n.

สังคโลก sǎng-ka-lôok a kind of Thai famous pottery, n.

สังเคราะห์ sǎng-krɔ́ synthesize, v.

สังฆะ sǎng-ká monk, n.

สังฆทาน sǎng-ka-taan alms, n.

สังฆนายก sǎng-ka-naa-yók chief of all the Buddhist, n.

สังฆราช sǎng-ká-râat pontiff, n.

สังวร sǎng-wɔɔn caution, constraint, n.

สังวรณ์ sǎng-wɔɔn closure, n.

สังวาล sǎng-waan chain, n.

สังวาส sǎng-wâat copulate, have sexual intercourse, v.

สังเวช sǎng-wêet pity, v.

สังเวย sǎng-wǝǝi propitiate by offering or sacrifice, v.

สังเวียน sǎng-wian arena, fighting ring, n.

สังสรรค์ sǎng-sǎn converse, have an informal conversation, v.

สังหรณ์ sǎng-hɔ̌ɔn have a foreboding, have a bad feeling, v.

สังหรณ์ใจ sǎng-hɔ̌ɔn-jai have a premonition, v.

สังหาร sǎng-hǎan kill, execute, v.

สังหาริมทรัพย์ sǎng-hǎa-rim-ma-sáp movable property, n.

สัจจะ sàt-jà truth, n.

สัญจร sǎn-jɔɔn way, path, n.

สัญชาติญาณ sǎn-châat-dtà-yaan instinct, n.

สัญชาติ sǎn-châat nationality, citizenship, place of birth, n.

สัญญลักษณ์ sǎn-ya-lák symbol, n.

สัญญา sǎn-yaa promise, pledge, agree, contract, v.

สัญญา sǎn-yaa promise, agreement, contract, n.

สัญญาณ sǎn-yaan signal, n.

สัตย์ sàt oath, honesty, truth, n.

สัตย์ซื่อ sàt-sɨɨ loyal, adj.

สัตยาบัน sàt-dtà-yaa-ban ratify, v.

สัตว์ sàt animal, beast, n.

สัน sǎn ridge, back, n.

สั่น sàn tremble, vibrate, shake, v.

ก ข ฃ ค ฅ ฆ ง จ ฉ ช ซ ฌ ญ ฎ ฏ ฐ ฑ ฒ ณ ด ต ถ ท

สั้น săn short, brief, *adj.*

สันดาน săn-daan in-born traits, *n.*

สันดาป săn-dàap combustion, *n.*

สันโดษ săn-dòot seclusion, *n.*

สันตะปาปา săn-dtà-bpaa-bpaa Pope, *n.*

สันติ săn-dtì calmness, tranquility, peacefulness, *n.*

สันติภาพ săn-dtì-pâap peace, *n.*

สันถาร săn-tăan act of spreading down to cover the floor, *n.*

สันทัด săn tát proficient, skilful, *adj*

สันธาน săn-taan conjunction, *n.*

สันนิบาต săn-ní-bàat league, congress, *n.*

สันนิวาส săn-ní-wâat dwelling place, *n.*

สันนิษฐาน săn-nìt-tăan assume, *v.*

สันสกฤต săn-sà-grìt Sanskrit, *n.*

สับ sàp chop, mince, *v.*

สับสน sàp-sŏn confused, *adj.*

สับปะรด sàp-bpa-rót pineapple, *n.*

สับดน sàp-bpà don obscene, lewd, *adj.*

สับดาห์ sàp-daa week, *n.*

สับปหงก sàp-bpà-ngòk sleepy, nodding, *adj.*

สัปเหร่อ sàp-bpà-rəə undertaker, *n.*

สัมนา săm-ma-naa meet, *v.*

สัมปชัญญะ săm-bpà-chan-yá conscience, *n.*

สัมปทาน săm-bpà-taan concession, *n.*

สัมผัส săm-pàt touch, feel, contact, *v.*

สัมพัทธ์ săm-pát relative, *adj.*

สัมพัทธภาพ săm-pát-ta-pâap relativity, *n.*

สัมพันธ์ săm-pan related, connected, *adj.*

สัมพันธภาพ săm-pan-ta-pâap relation, *n.*

สัมพันธมิตร săm-pan-ta-mít ally, *n.*

สัมพันธไมตรี săm-pan-ta-mai-dtrii friendship, *n.*

สัมภาระ săm-paa-rá supplies, *n.*

สัมภาษณ์ săm-pâat interview, *n.*

สัมมนา săm-má-naa seminar, *n.*

สัมมา săm-maa right, correct, honest, virtuous, *adj.*

สังฤทธิ์ săm-rít alloy, *n.*

สัมฤทธิ์ผล săm-rít-pŏn successful, *adj.*

สัสดี sàt-sà-dii recruiting officer, conscription registrar, *n.*

ส่า sàa yeast, rash, *n.*

สาก sàak pestle, *n.*

สากล sǎa-gon universal, all, *adj., adv.*

สาขา sǎa-kǎa branch, chain, *n.*

สาคู sǎa-kuu sago, *n.*

สาง sǎang ghost, demon, *n.*

สาง sàang disappear, *v.*

สาด sàat splash, toss out, *v.*

สาธยาย sǎa-ta-yaai explain, *v.*

สาธารณะ sǎa-taa-ra-ná public, general, common, *adj.*

สาธารณรัฐ sǎa-taa-ra-ná-rát republic, *n.*

สาธารณสุข sǎa-taa-ra-ná-sùk public health, *n.*

สาธารณูปโภค sǎa-taa-ra-nuu-bpà-pôok public utility, *n.*

สาธิต sǎa-tít finished, accomplished, demonstrated, *adj.*

สาธิต sǎa-tít demonstrate, *v.*

สาธุ sǎa-tú (Buddhist) amen, *interj.*

สาน sǎan weave, *v.*

สานศิษย์ sǎa-nú-sìt disciple, *n.*

สาบ sàap pungent odor, *n.*

สาบาน sǎa-baan swear, *v.*

สาป sàap curse, put a curse, *v.*

สาปแช่ง sàap-chêng curse, *v.*

สาปสูญ sàap-sǔun disappear, *v.*

สาม sǎam three, *nm.*

สามล้อ sǎam-lɔ́ɔ tricycle, *n.*

สามเณร sǎam-ma-neen novice, *n.*

สามัคคี sǎa-mák-kii unity, harmony, concord, *n.*

สามัญ sǎa-man common, ordinary, *adj.*

สามัญชน sǎa-man-chon commoner, *n.*

สามารถ sǎa-mâat able, efficient, can, *adj., v.*

สามี sǎa-mii husband, *n.*

สาย sǎai line, string, wire, rope, road, stream, steak, lineage, *n.*

สายการบิน sǎai-gaan-bin airline, *n.*

สายชนวน sǎai-chá-nuan fuse, *n.*

สายตา sǎai-dtaa eyesight, *n.*

ส่าย sàai swing, sway, swerve, *v.*

สายชู sǎai-chuu vinegar, *n.*

สายัณห์ sǎa-yan evening, *n.*

สาร sǎan letter, document, message, large elephant, *n.*

สารคดี sǎa-rá-ka-dii article, documentary, *n.*

สารเคมี sǎan-kee-mii chemical substances, *n.*

สารถี sǎa-ra-tǐi driver, guide, *n.*

สารท sàat autumn festival, *n.*

สารนิเทศ sǎa-ra-ní-têet information, *n.*

สารพัด sǎa-ra-pát every, all things, *adj., n.*

สารพัน sǎa-ra-pan everything, all, all kinds, *adj., adv., n.*

สารเลว sǎa-ra-leeo despicable, *adj.*

สารวัตร sǎa-ra-wát inspector, headman, *n.*

สาระ sǎa-rá essence, substance, *n.*

สาระแน sǎa-ra-nɛɛ impudent, *adj.*

สารานุกรม sǎa-raa-nú-grom encyclopedia, *n.*

สารีริกธาตุ sǎa-rii- rík-gà-tâat Buddha's relic, *n.*

สาว sǎao girl, young woman, *n.*

สาว sǎao pull in, haul, *v.*

สาวแก่ sǎao-gɛ̀ɛ old maid, *n.*

สาวใช้ sǎao-chái maid, *n.*

สาวก sǎa-wók disciple, *n.*

สาส์น sǎan letter, document, *n.*

สาหร่าย sǎa rài seaweeds, *n*

สาหัส sǎa-hàt severe, extreme, cruel, *adj.*

สาเหตุ sǎa-hèet cause, motive, *n.*

สำคัญ sǎm-kan important, significant,

essential, *adj.*

สำแดง sǎm-dɛɛng exhibit, manifest, *v.*

สำนวน sǎm-nuan style of writing or speaking, *n.*

สำนัก sǎm-nák office, bureau, institution, *n.*

สำนักงาน sǎm-nák-ngaan office, *n.*

สำนึก sǎm-núk aware, *adj.*

สำเนา sǎm-nao copy, *n.*

สำเนียง sǎm-niang tone of voice, accent, *n.*

สำมะโนครัว sǎm-ma-noo-krua census, *n.*

สำรวจ sǎm-rùat explore, *v.*

สำรวม sǎm-ruam careful, *adj.*

สำราย sǎm-ruai pleasure-loving, *adj.*

สำรอง sǎm-rɔɔng preserve, *v.*

สำรับ sǎm-ráp set, suit, tray containing plates and bowls of food, *n.*

สำราญ sǎm-raan cheerful, *adj.*

สำเร็จ sǎm-rèt succeed, accomplish, *v.*

สำเร็จความใคร่ sǎm-rèt-kwaam-krâi have one's sexual gratification, *v.*

สำเร็จรูป sǎm-rèt-rûup ready-made, *adj.*

สำลัก sǎm-lák choke, *v.*

สำลี sǎm-lii cotton, *n.*

สำส่อน sǎm-sɔ̀n promiscuous, *adj.*

สำหรับ sǎm-ràp in order that, for, in favor of, *prep.*

สำออย sǎm-ɔɔi implore, wheedle, *v.*

สำอาง sǎm-aang cosmetics, *n.*

สิกขา sìk-kǎa education, *n.*

สิกขาบท sìk-kǎa-bòt religious precepts, *n.*

สิง sǐng haunted, *adj.*

สิ่ง sìng things, articles, objects, *n.*

สิ่งของ sìng-kɔ̌ɔng articles, objects, things, goods, *n.*

สิ่งแวดล้อม sìng-wɛ̂ɛt-lɔ́ɔm surrounding, environment, *n.*

สิงโต sǐng-dtoo lion, *n.*

สิงห์ sǐng lion, *n.*

สิงหาคม sǐng-hǎa-kom August, *n.*

สิทธิ sìt-tí, sìt right, privilege, *n.*

สิทธิบัตร sìt-tí-bàt patent, *n.*

สิน sǐn property, wealth, *n.*

สินค้า sǐn-káa goods, *n.*

สินบน sǐn-bon bribe, *n.*

สินสอด sǐn-sɔ̀ɔt dowry, *n.*

สิ้น sîn end, terminate, *v.*

สินเธาว์ sǐn-tao rock salt, *n.*

สิบ sìp ten, *nm.*

สิริมงคล sì-rì-mong-kon luck, prosperity, *n.*

สิว sǐu pimple, acne, *n.*

สิ่ว sìu chisel, *n.*

สี sǐi color, *n.*

สี่ sìi four, *nm.*

สีกา sǐi-gaa female layman, *n.*

สีดา sǐi-daa furrow, Rama's wife, *n.*

สีมา sǐi-maa border, *n.*

สึก sùk disrobe, *v.*

สืบ sùup succeed, search for the facts, examine, *v.*

สืบสวน sùup-sǔan investigate, *v.*

สื่อ sùu go-between, liaison, *n.*

สื่อมวลชน sùu-muan-chon mass media, *n.*

สื่อสาร sùu-sǎan communicate, *v.*

สุก sùk ripe, *adj.*

สุกใส sùk-sǎi bright, *adj.*

สุข sùk well, happy, content, *adj.*

สุข sùk happiness, pleasure, *n.*

สุขภาพ sùk-kà-pâap health, *n.*

สุขศึกษา sùk-kà-sùk-sǎa health education, *n.*

สุขา sù-kǎa water closet, *n.*

สุขาภิบาล sù-kǎa-pí-baan sanitation, *n.*

สุขี sù-kǐi happy, *adj.*

สุขุม sù-kǔm prudent, thoughtful, *adj.*

สุคติ sùk-ka-dtì happiness, bliss heaven, n.

สุงสิง sŭng-sĭng associate, v.

สุจริต sù-jà-rìt honest, adj.

สุด sùt extreme, last, highest, adj.

สุดยอด sùt-yɔ̂ɔt top, n.

สุทธิ sùt-tí purity, total, n.

สุเทพ sù-têep good deity, n.

สุนทร sŭn-tɔɔn words, n.

สุนทรพจน์ sŭn-tɔɔ-ra-pót speech, n.

สุนทรี sŭn-ta-rii beautiful, adj.

สุนัข sù-nák dog, n.

สุปฏิปันโน sù-bpà-dtì-bpan-noo well-behaved person, Buddhist monk, n.

สุภาพ sù-pâap polite, gentle, adj.

สุภาษิต sù-paa-sìt proverb, n.

สุ่ม sùm pile up, v.

สุ่ม sùm chicken coop, n.

สุ่ม sùm make a wild guess, v.

สุรา sù-raa liquors, spirits, n.

สุริยะ sù-ri-yá the sun, n.

สุริยจักรวาล sù-ri-yá-jàk-ga-waan the Solar system, n.

สุริยุปราคา sù-ri-yúp-bpà-raa-kaa solar eclipse, n.

สุรุ่ยสุร่าย sù-rûi-sù-râai extravagant, adj.

สุวรรณ sù-wan gold, n.

สุสาน sù-sǎan cemetery, n.

สุเหร่า sù-rào mosque, n.

สู่ sùu get to, reach, arrive at, v.

สู่ขอ sùu-kɔ̌ɔ ask a girl to marry, v.

สู่รู้ sùu-rúu know conjointly, v.

สู้ sûu fight, struggle, v.

สูง sǔung high, tall, adj.

สูจิบัตร sǔu-jì-bàt program, n.

สูญ sǔun vanish, v.

สูญเปล่า sǔun-bplàao wasteful, adj.

สูญเสีย sǔun-sǐa lost, adj.

สูด sùut inhale, v.

สูตร sùut formula, n.

สูติ sùut birth, n.

สูติบัตร sǔu-dtì-bàt birth certificate, n.

สูติเวช sǔu-dtì-wêet obstetrics, n.

สูบ sùup pump, inflate, v.

สูบบุหรี่ sùup-bù-rìi smoke cigarette, v.

เสแสร้ง sěe-sêeng disguise, pretend, v.

เสก sèek pronounce religious or magical formula, v.

เสงี่ยม sà-ngìam careful, modest, tactful, adj.

เสด็จ sà-dèt go (for royalty), v.

เสถียร sà-tĭan strong, *adj.*

เส้น sên thread, line, string, strand, rope, cord, *n.*

เสน่หา sà-nèe-hăa love, *v.*

เสนอ sà-nǒo propose, present a proposal, submit, *v.*

เสนา sĕe-naa troops, soldiers, *n.*

เสนาธิการ sĕe-naa-tí-gaan chief of military staff, *n.*

เสนาะ sà-nɔ́ melodious, *adj.*

เสนียด sà-nìat evil, misfortune, *n.*

เสบียง sà-biang provisions, *n.*

เสพย์ sèep eat, consume, *v.*

เสพเมถุน sèep-mee-tŭn have sexual intercourse, *v.*

เสเพล sĕe-plee ill-behaved, *adj.*

เสภา sĕe-paa a kind of Thai song recital, solo, *n.*

เสมหะ sĕem-hà phlegm, *n.*

เสมอ sà-mǒo even, level, equal, *adj.*

เสมอ sà-mǒo always, *adv.*

เสมอกัน sà-mǒo-gan equal, *adj.*

เสมอปลาย sà-mǒo-bplaai consistently, *adv.*

เสมอภาค sà-mǒo-pâak equal, *adj.*

เสมียน sà-mĭan clerk, secretary, *n.*

เสมือน sà-mŭan like, similar to, *adv.*

เสย sɔ̌oi scoop up, *v.*

เสร็จ sèt finished, ready, *adj.*

เสริม sɔ̌om supplement, add, reinforce, *v.*

เสรี sĕe-rii free, independent, *adj.*

เสรีนิยม sĕe-rii-ní-yom liberalism, *n.*

เสรีภาพ sĕe-rii-pâap freedom, *n.*

เสิร์ฟ sɔ̀op serve, *v.*

เสลด sà-lèet phlegm, *n.*

เสวย sà-wɔ̌oi eat, *v.*

เสา săo post, pole, pillar, *n.*

เส้า sâo cane, walking stick, *n.*

เสาร์ săo Saturn, Saturday, *n.*

เสาะ sɔ̀ seek, search for, *v.*

เสีย sĭa lose, waste, get out of order, *v.*

เสียชีวิต sĭa-chii-wít die, *v.*

เสียตัว sĭa-dtua lose one's virginity, *v.*

เสี่ย sìa wealthy Chinese, *n.*

เสียง sĭang sound, voice, noise, *n.*

เสี้ยง sìang fractions, fragments, *n.*

เสี่ยง sìang risk, gamble, *v.*

เสียด sìat pierce, thrust, penetrate, *v.*

เสี้ยน sîan splinter, *n.*

เสียบ sìap pierce, penetrate, *v.*

เสียม sĭam spade, *n.*

เสี้ยม sîam taper, grind down, *v.*

เสียว sĭao feel a sudden pain, feel a

thrill of fear, feel a thrill of lust, *v.*

เสี่ยว sìao friend (Lao), *n.*

เสี้ยว sìao quarter, *n.*

เสือ sǔa tiger, *n.*

เสื่อ sùa mat, *n.*

เสื้อ sûa coat, cloak, jacket, shirt, upper garment, *n.*

เสื้อชั้นใน sûa-chán-nai undergarment, *n.*

เสื้อนอก sûa-nɔ̂ɔk overcoat, jacket, *n.*

เสื้อผ้า sûa-pâa clothes, *n.*

เสือก sùak push, intrude, butt in, *v.*

เสื่อม sùam deteriorate, *v.*

เสื่อมทราม sùam-saam get worse, *v.*

แส่ sɛ̀ɛ provoke, *v.*

แส้ sɛ̂ɛ whip, *n.*

แสก sɛ̀ɛk the barn owl, *n.*

แสกกลาง sɛ̀ɛk-glaang parted in the middle, *adj.*

แสง sɛ̌ɛng light, *n.*

แสด sɛ̀ɛt red orange, orange yellow, *n.*

แสดง sà-dɛɛng show, demonstrate, *v.*

แสตมป์ sà-dtɛm stamp, *n.*

แสน sɛ̌ɛn one hundred thousand, *n.*

แสน sɛ̌ɛn extremely, very, *adv.*

แสบ sɛ̀ɛp sting, feel pain, *v.*

แสบ sɛ̀ɛp stinging, piercing (pain), burning (pain), *adj.*

แสยง sà-yɛ̌ɛng frightful, *adj.*

แสยะ sà-yɛ̀ grin broadly, *v.*

แสร้ง sɛ̂ɛng pretend, feign, *v.*

แสลง sà-lɛɛng harmful, *adj.*

แสวง sà-wɛ̌ɛng search, *v.*

โสโครก sǒo-krôok dirty, filthy, *adj.*

โสด sòot single, unmarried, *adj.*

โสต sòot organ of hearing, *n.*

โสน sà-nǒo a species of tall marsh, *n.*

โสภา sǒo-paa beautiful, *adj.*

โสม sǒom ginseng, *n.*

โสมม sǒo-mom dirty, filthy, *adj.*

โสร่ง sà-ròng sarong, a garment worn by Thai woman, *n.*

ใส sǎi clear, transparent, pure, *adj.*

ใส่ sài put into, wear, fill, contain, load, enclose, insert, *v.*

ใส่ความ sài-kwaam blame, *v.*

ใส่ใจ sài-jai pay attention, *v.*

ไส sǎi push forward, *v.*

ไส้ sâi intestines, bowels, *n.*

ไส้เดือน sâi-duan earthworm, *n.*

ไส้ติ่ง sâi-dtìng appendix, *n.*

ไส้เลื่อน sâi-lûan hernia, *n.*

ไส้ศึก sâi-sùk spy, *n.*

ไสยศาสตร์ sǎi-ya-sàat magic, *n.*

ไสว sà-wǎi plentiful, numerous, *adj.*

ห

ห hɔ̌ɔ the forty-first consonant of the Thai alphabet (high consonant), *n.*

หก hòk spill, splash over, six, *v., nm.*

หงส์ hǒng swan, *n.*

หงอ ngɔ̌ɔ timid, *adj.*

หงอก ngɔ̀ɔk gray, silver gray, *adj.*

หงอน ngɔ̌ɔn crest, cock's comb, *n.*

หงอย ngɔ̌ɔi low-spirit, *adj.*

หงอยเหงา ngɔ̌ɔi-ngǎo lonely, *adj.*

หงาย ngǎai turn up, turn face up, *v.*

หงิก ngìk wrinkled, distorted, crooked, *adj.*

หงิม ngǐm silent, *adj.*

หงุดหงิด ngùt-ngìt irritated, moody, *adj.*

หญ้า yâa grass, *n.*

หญิง yǐng female, *n.*

หด hòt shrink, *v.*

หทัย hà-tai heart, mind, soul, *n.*

หน hǒn direction, time, way, *n.*

หนวก nùak deaf, *adj.*

หนวกหู nùak-hǔu disturbed by the noise, *adj.*

หน่วง nùang delay, *v.*

หนวด nùat mustache, *n.*

หน่วย nùai unit, digit, *n.*

หน่อ nɔ̀ɔ sprout, offspring, *n.*

หน่อไม้ nɔ̀ɔ-máai young bamboo shoot, *n.*

หนอง nɔ̌ɔng marsh, swamp, bog, pus, *n.*

หนอน nɔ̌ɔn worm, maggot, *n.*

หน่อย nɔ̀i little, a small, tiny, *adj.*

หนัก nàk heavy, hard, *adj.*

หนักแน่น nàk-nɛ̂n firm, steady, *adj.*

หนัง nǎng skin, leather, movie, *n.*

หนังสือ nǎng-sɯ̌ɯ book, document, letters, alphabet, *n.*

หนา nǎa thick, dense, *adj.*

หนาแน่น nǎa-nɛ̂n condense, compact, *adj.*

หน้า nâa face, front, *n.*

หน้ากาก nâa-gàak mask, *n.*

หน้าแข้ง nâa-kɛ̂ng shin bone, *n.*

หน้าต่าง nâa-dtàang window, *n.*

หน้าที่ nâa-tîi duty, function, *n.*

หน้าฝน nâa-fǒn rainy season, *n.*

หน้าม้า nâa-máa decoy, *n.*

หนาม nǎam thorn, *n.*

หน่าย nàai tired of, *adj.*

หนาว nǎao cold, cool, chilly, *adj.*

หนี nǐi escape, flee, *v.*

ก ข ฃ ค ฅ ฆ ง จ ฉ ช ซ ฌ ญ ฎ ฏ ฐ ฑ ฒ ณ ด ต ถ ท

หนี้ nîi debt, *n.*

หนีบ nìip squeeze, pinch, *v.*

หนึ่ง nùng one, *adj.*

หนุน nǔn support, *v.*

หนุ่ม nùm young, juvenile, *adj.*

หนุมาน hà-nú-maan Hanuman, *n.*

หนู nǔu rat, mouse, *n.*

ห่ม hòm cover, clothe, enclose, *v.*

หมก mòk hide, bury, *v.*

หมกมุ่น mòk-mûn engrossed, *adj.*

หมด mòt finished, end, *adj., v.*

หมดกำลังใจ mòt-gam lang jai discouraged, *adj.*

หมดจด mòt-jòt spotless, clean, *adj.*

หมดตัว mòt-dtua penniless, broke, *adj.*

หมดเวลา mòt-wee-laa time is up, *v.*

หมดสติ mòt-sa-dtì unconscious, *adj.*

หม่น mòn dark, dull, *adj.*

หม่นหมอง mòn-mɔ̌ɔng gloomy, *adj.*

หมวก mùak hat, cap, *n.*

หมวด mùat section, division, group, *n.*

หมอ mɔ̌ɔ doctor, specialist, *n.*

หม้อ mɔ̂ɔ pot, *n.*

หม้อน้ำ mɔ̂ɔ-náam radiator, *n.*

หมอก mɔ̀ɔk fog, mist, *n.*

หมอก mɔ̀ɔk foggy, *adj.*

หมอง mɔ̌ɔng clouded, tarnished, dull, *adj.*

หมอน mɔ̌ɔn pillow, cushion, pad, *n.*

หม่อน mòn white mulberry, *n.*

หมอบ mɔ̀ɔp kneel, crouch, *v.*

หม่อม mòm commoner wife of a prince, *n.*

หมัก màk leaven, ferment, *v.*

หมัด màt fish, punch, a species of insect, flea, *n.*

หมัน mǎn sterile, fruitless, childless, *adj.*

หมั่น màn diligent, industrious, *adj.*

หมั่นไส้ màn-sâi cause disgust, *v.*

หมั้น mân engage, engaged, *v., adj.*

หมา mǎa dog, *n.*

หมาก màak betel palm, *n.*

หมากฝรั่ง màak-fa-ràng chewing gum, *n.*

หมากรุก màak-rúk chess, *n.*

หมาง mǎang estranged, *adj.*

หมางใจ mǎang-jai in dissension with, *adj.*

หมางเมิน mǎang-məən turn the face away, *v.*

หมาด màat half-dry, *adj.*

หมามุ่ย mǎa-mûi horse-eye cowitch,

bean, *n.*

หมาย mǎai warrant, notice, order, summons, *n.*

หมายค้น mǎai-kón search warrant, *n.*

หมายความ mǎai-kwaam mean, have the meaning of, indicate, *v.*

หมายจับ mǎai-jàp warrant of arrest, *n.*

หมายตา mǎai-dtaa take notice of, *v.*

หมายเหตุ mǎai-hèet footnote, remark, *n.*

หม้าย mâai widow, *n.*

หม่ำ màm eat, drink, *v.*

หมิ่น mìn insult, look down upon, *v.*

หมี mǐi bear, *n.*

หมี่ mìi vermicelli, fine noodles, egg noodles, *n.*

หมึก mùk ink, *n.*

หมื่น mùun ten thousand, *n.*

หมุด mùt peg, tack, pin, *n.*

หมุน mǔn turn, revolve, spin, rotate, *v.*

หมุนกลับ mǔn-glàp turn back, *v.*

หมุนเงิน mǔn-ngən circulate money, *v.*

หมุนตัว mǔn-dtua turn around, *v.*

หมู mǔu pig, *n.*

หมู่ mùu group, herd, flock, *n.*

หมู่เกาะ mùu-gɔ̀ archipelago, *n.*

หยก yòk jade, *n.*

หยด yòt drop, *v.*

หยวก yùak soft and fluffy herbaceous stalk, *n.*

หยอก yɔ̀ɔk jest, joke, *v.*

หยอกล้อ yɔ̀ɔk-lɔ́ɔ tease, *v.*

หยอด yɔ̀ɔt drop, *v.*

หย่อน yɔ̀n decrease, lower, *v.*

หย่อนใจ yɔ̀n-jai relax, *adj.*

หย่อม yɔ̀m cluster, *n.*

หยอมแหยม yɔ̌m-yɛ̌m sparse, *adj.*

หยัก yàk notch, indent, *v.*

หยั่ง yàng fathom, measure, *v.*

หย่า yàa divorce, wean, withdraw, *v.*

หยากไย่ yàak-yâi cobweb, *n.*

หยาด yàat drop, drip, *n.*, *v.*

หยาบ yàap rough, rude, *adj.*

หยาบคาย yàap-kaai rude, *adj.*

หยาบหยาม yàap-yǎam contemptuous, scornful, *adj.*

หยาม yǎam insult, *v.*

หยิก yìk pinch, nip, *v.*

หยิก yìk curled, wavy, *adj.*

หยิ่ง yìng proud, haughty, *adj.*

หยิบ yìp take hold of, seize, *v.*

หยี yǐi squinting, narrow, *adj.*

หยุด yùt stop, cease, *v.*

หยุดพัก yùt-pák rest, v.

หยุมหยิม yǔm-yǐm petty, trivial, adj.

หรรษา hǎn-sǎa joy, pleasure, n.

หรอ rɔ̌ɔ worn off, v.

หรี่ rìi lower, lessen the light, v.

หรือ rǔu either...or, ending particle used to form a question, conj., part.

หรู rǔu beautiful, luxurious, adj.

หฤโหด hà-rú-hòot cruel, brutal, adj.

หลง lǒng go astray, get lost, v.

หลงทาง lǒng-taang get lost, v.

หลน lǒn stew, simmer, v.

หล่น lòn drop, fall, v.

หลบ lòp avoid, v.

หล่ม lòm muddy place, n.

หลวง lǔang royal, adj.

หลวม lǔam not tight, loose, adj.

หลอ lɔ̌ɔ hollowed out, worn down, adj.

หล่อ lɔ̀ɔ cast molten metal, handsome, v., adj.

หลอก lɔ̀ɔk deceive, v.

หลอกหลอน lɔ̀ɔk-lɔ̌ɔn haunt, scare, spook, v.

หลอด lɔ̀ɔt pipe, tube, bulb, spool, n.

หลอดดูด lɔ̀ɔt-dùut straw, n.

หลอดไฟ lɔ̀ɔt-fai bulb, n.

หลอน lɔ̌ɔn scare, haunt, v.

หล่อน lɔ̀n she, her, you, pron.

หลอม lɔ̌ɔm fuse, melt, v.

หละหลวม là-lǔam careless, adj.

หลัก làk post, pillar, pole, n.

หลักการ làk-gaan principle, n.

หลักฐาน làk-tǎan proof, n.

หลักทรัพย์ làk-sáp property, n.

หลักประกัน làk-bprà-gan security, guaranty, n.

หลัง lǎng back, rear, n.

หลัง lǎng behind, after, classifier for house, etc, adv.

หลัง lǎng afterwards, back, latter, adj.

หลังคา lǎng-kaa roof, n.

หลั่ง làng pour, let flow, v.

หลับ làp sleep, be asleep, v.

หลา lǎa yard, n.

หล้า lâa world, earth, land, n.

หลาก làak various, different, adj.

หลาน lǎan nephew, niece, grandchild, n.

หลาบ làap fear, have learned one's lesson, v.

หลาม lǎam python, n.

หลาย lǎai many, several, numerous, much, adj.

หลายใจ lǎai-jai unfaithful, fickle, adj.

หลาว lǎao spear, *n.*

หลิ่วตา lìu-dtaa look with one eye closed, wink, *v.*

หลีก lìik avoid, evade, *v.*

หลีกทาง lìik-taang give way, *v.*

หลีกเลี่ยง lìik-lìang avoid, *v.*

หลืบ lùⱨp mountain pass, hidden spot, *n.*

หลุกหลิก lùk-lìk do hastily, *v.*

หลุด lùt come off, slip loose, *v.*

หลุดปาก lùt-bpàak utter, *v.*

หลุดมือ lùt-mⱨⱨ slip from the hand, *v.*

หลุดลุ่ย lùt-lûi detached, *adj.*

หลุม lǔm pit, ditch, *n.*

หลู่ lùu slight, scorn, *v.*

หวง hǔang jealous, possessive, *adj.*

หวงห้าม hǔang-hâam prohibit, *v.*

ห่วง hùang loop, ring, link, hoop, *n.*

ห่วง hùang worry about, worried, concerned about, *adj.*

ห่วงใย hùang-yai concerned about, *adj.*

ห้วง hûang vastness, *n.*

หวด hùat whip, lash, a kind of whisker, *v., n.*

หวน hǔan return, reverse, *v.*

หวนคิด hǔan-kít recall, think back, *v.*

ห้วน hûan short, brief, *adj.*

หวย hǔai lottery ticket, *n.*

หวยเถื่อน hǔai-tùan illegal lottery, *n.*

ห่วย hùai bad, no good, *adj.*

ห้วย hûai stream, brook, *n.*

หวอ wɔ̌ɔ open, exposed, *adj.*

หวัง wǎng hope for, *v.*

หวังดี wǎng-dii have good wishes, *v.*

หวัด wàt cold, *n.*

หวั่น wàn fear, shaken, *v., adj.*

หวาน wǎan sweet, sugary, *adj.*

หว่าน wàan sow, cast, *v.*

หวาย wǎai rattan, *n.*

หวิด wìt passing near by, nearly, almost, *adj.*

หวิว wǐu dizzy, giddy, *adj.*

หวี wǐi comb, *v., n.*

หวี่ wìi gnat, *n.*

หวุดหวิด wùt-wìt almost, nearly, narrowly, *adj.*

หอ hɔ̌ɔ tower, *n.*

หอการค้า hɔ̌ɔ-gaan-káa chamber of commerce, *n.*

หอประชุม hɔ̌ɔ-bprà-chum conference room, *n.*

หอสมุด hɔ̌ɔ-sà-mùt library, *n.*

ห่อ hɔ̀ɔ wrap, *v.*

ห้อ hɔ́ɔ gallop, run fast, *v.*

หอก hɔ̀ɔk lance, spear, spike, *n.*

ห้อง hɔ̂ng room, chamber, *n.*

หอน hɔ̌ɔn howl, *v.*

หอบ hɔ̀ɔp pant, gasp for breath, *v.*

หอม hɔ̌ɔm fragrant, aromatic, *adj.*

หอม hɔ̌ɔm kiss, sniff, *v.*

หอม hɔ̌ɔm onion, *n.*

ห้อมล้อม hɔ̂ɔm-lɔ́ɔm surround, *v.*

หอย hɔ̌i shells, *n.*

ห้อย hɔ̂i hang down, suspend, *v.*

หัก hàk break, *v.*

หักหลัง hàk-lǎng betray, *v.*

หักโหม hàk-hǒom overexert oneself, *v.*

หัด hàt train, practice, *n.*

หัน hǎn turn around, *v.*

หั่น hàn slice, chop, *v.*

หัว hǔa head, brain, *n.*

หัวกะโหลก hǔa-gà-lòok skull, *n.*

หัวใจ hǔa-jai heart, mind, *n.*

หัวเราะ hǔa-rɔ́ laugh, *v.*

ห่า hàa heavy fall of rain, evil spirit, *n.*

ห้า hâa five, *n.*

หาก hàak if, apart from, separated, *conj., adj.*

หาง hǎang tail, end, *n.*

ห่าง hàang far, far apart, distant, *adj.*

ห้าง hâang store, *n.*

หาญ hǎan brave, *adj.*

หาด hàat beach, *n.*

หาดทราย hàat-saai sandy beach, *n.*

ห่าน hàan goose, *n.*

หาบ hàap carry on the shoulder at both ends of a rod or pole, *v.*

หาม hǎam carry on the shoulder, *n.*

ห่าม hàam half-ripe, *adj.*

ห้าม hâam prohibit, forbid, *v.*

หาย hǎai lost, missing, *adj.*

หายนะ hǎa-ya-ná disaster, *n.*

หาร hǎan divide, *v.*

หาว hǎao yawn, *v.*

ห้าว hâao over-ripe, *adj.*

ห่ำ hàm (colloq.) testicles, *n.*

หิ้ง hîng shelf, *n.*

หิ่งห้อย hìng-hɔ̂i fireflies, *n.*

หิด hìt scabies, itch, *n.*

หิน hǐn stone, rock, *n.*

หินงอก hǐn-ngɔ̂ɔk stalagmite, *n.*

หินปูน hǐn-bpuun limestone, *n.*

หินยาน hǐn-na-yaan Hinayana, *n.*

หินย้อย hǐn-yɔ́ɔi stalactite, *n.*

หิมะ hì-má snow, *n.*

ธ น บ ป ผ ฝ พ ฟ ภ ม ย ร ฤ ฦ ล ว ศ ษ ส ห ฬ อ ฮ

หิว hǐu hungry, *adj.*

หิ้ว hîu hold, carry, *v.*

หีบ hìip box, *n.*

หึง hǔng jealous, envious, *adj.*

หืด hùut asthma, *n.*

หืน hǔun rancid, *adj.*

หื่น hùun crave, *v.*

หุงข้าว hǔng-kâao cook rice, *v.*

หุ่น hùn model, puppet, mannequin, *n.*

หุ่นกระบอก hùn-grà-bɔ̀ɔk puppet, *n.*

หุ่นยนต์ hùn-yon robot, *n.*

หุ้น hûn share, *n.*

หุนหัน hǔn-hǎn impetuous, *adj.*

หุบ hùp close, shut, *v.*

หุบเขา hùp-kǎo valley, ravine, *v.*

หุ้ม hûm cover, *v.*

หุ้มเกราะ hûm-grɔ̀ armored, *adj.*

หู hǔu ear, handle, *n.*

หูตึง hǔu-dtung hard of hearing, *adj.*

หูโทรศัพท์ hǔu-too-ra-sàp telephone receiver, *n.*

หูเบา hǔu-bao credulous, *adj.*

หู่ hùu shrink, shrivel, *v.*

หูก hùuk loom, *n.*

หูด hùut wart, *n.*

เหงา ngǎo lonely, lonesome, *adj.*

เหงื่อ ngùa sweat, *n.*

เหงือก ngùak gum, gill, *n.*

เห็ด hèt mushroom, fungus, *n.*

เหตุ hèet cause, reason, *n.*

เห็น hěn see, behold, *v.*

เห็นแก่ตัว hěn-gὲɛ-dtua selfish, *adj.*

เหน็ดเหนื่อย nèt-nùai exhausted, *adj.*

เหน็บ nèp attach, insert, *v.*

เหน็บชา nèp-chaa numb, *adj.*

เหนียว nǐao sticky, glutinous, *adj.*

เหนือ nǔa north, *n.*

เหนือ nǔa over, overhead, above, north, *adj.*

เหนือกว่า nǔa-gwàa superior to, *adj.*

เหนื่อย nùai tired, exhausted, *adj.*

เห็บ hèp dog ticks, hail, *n.*

เหม็น měn stink, foul odor, bad smell, *v.*, *n.*

เหม็น měn bad smelling, *adj.*

เหมา mǎo make an overall contract, *v.*

เหมาะ mɔ̀ suitable, appropriate, *adj.*

เหมาะสม mɔ̀-sǒm suitable, proper, appropriate, *adj.*

เหมือง mǔang mine, *n.*

เหมือน mǔan similar, like, same, *adj.*

เหมือนกัน mǔan-gan equal to, alike, *adj.*

เหย้า yâo dwelling place, *n.*

เหยียด yìat stretch out, despise, v.

เหยียบ yìap step on, condemn, v.

เหยี่ยว yìao hawk, n.

เหยื่อ yùa prey, bait, victim, n.

เหยือก yùak pitcher, jug, n.

เหรียญ rǐan medal, coin, n.

เหล่ lèe squint, adj.

เหลว lěeo fluid, liquid, melted, adj.

เหลา lǎo sharpen, v.

เหล่า lào group, class, species, n.

เหล้า lào liquor, alcohol, spirit, n.

เหลิง lǒong haughty, adj.

เหลี่ยม lìam edge, side, corner, n.

เหลียว lìao turn, look sideways, v.

เหลือ lǔa remain, to leave, v.

เหลือเกิน lǔa-qəən too excessive, adj.

เหลือเชื่อ lǔa-chûa unbelievable, adj.

เหลือง lǔang yellow, adj.

เหลือบ lùap glance, v.

เหลือม lǔam python, n.

เหลื่อม lùam overlapping, adj.

เหวี่ยง wìang hurl, v.

เห่อ hə̀ə lofty, too proud, adj.

เหา hǎo louse, n.

เห่า hào bark, v.

เหาะ hɔ̀ fly, soar into the air, v.

เหิน hə̌ən fly, v.

เหิม hǒəm become bold, v.

เหี้ย hîa water lizard, illomened person (vulgar), n.

เหี้ยน hîan stripped of all, adj.

เหี้ยม hîam ruthless, cruel, adj.

เหี่ยว hìao withered, adj.

เหิร hə̌ən fly, v.

เหือด hùat dry up, v.

แห hɛ̌ɛ cat-net, fishing net, n.

แห่ hɛ̀ɛ go in procession, parade, v.

แห่ง hɛ̀ng place, location, n.

แห้ง hɛ̂ng dry, dried, parched, adj.

แหงน ngɛ̌ɛn look up, v.

แหน nɛ̌ɛ duckweed, n.

แหนงหน่าย nɛ̌ɛng-nàai bored, adj.

แหนบ nɛ̀ɛp pinch, v.

แหนบ nɛ̀ɛp tweezers, nippers, n.

แหนม nɛ̌ɛm a kind of Thai condiment made from fermented pork, n.

แหบ hɛ̀ɛp hoarse, harsh, dry, adj.

แหม่ม mɛ̀m madam, n.

แหย่ yɛ̀ɛ insert, poke, tease, provoke, disturb, v.

แหลก lɛ̀ɛk crushed, adj.

แหล่ง lɛ̀ng place, location, n.

แหลม lɛ̌ɛm cape, peninsula, sharp, n.

แหวก wɛ̀ɛk penetrate, make one's

way, v.

แหวกแนว wèek-nɛɛo abnormal, adj.

แหว่ง wèng chipped, partly broken, adj.

แหวน wɛ̌ɛn ring, n.

แหวะ wɛ̀ rip open, v.

โห่ hòo hail, cheer, v.

โหง hǒong spirit, ghost, devil, n.

โหงวเฮ้ง ngǒo-héng predictions, characteristics, n.

โหด hòot ruthless, brutal, adj.

โหน hǒon hang, swing, v.

โหนก nòok protruding, adj.

โหนก nòok bump, lump, n.

โหม hǒom exert, v.

โหม่ง mòong hit, v.

โหย hǒoi groan for, moan for, v.

โหยหา hǒoi-hǎa yearn for, v.

โหยหิว hǒoi-hǐu fatigue with hunger, adj.

โหยกเหยก yòok-yèek fussy, adj.

โหยง yǒong nimble, adj.

โหร hǒon astrologer, n.

โหรงเหรง rǒong-rěeng sparse, few, thin, adj.

โหระพา hǒo-rá-paa basil, n.

โหล lǒo dozen, n.

โหล่ lòo last, adj.

โหว่ wòo hollowed out, adj.

ให้ hâi give, offer, v.

ให้การ hâi-gaan give evidence, testify, v.

ให้ท่า hâi-tâa encourage, v.

ให้ทาน hâi-taan give alms, v.

ให้ท้าย hâi-táai back, v.

ให้ร้าย hâi-ráai defame, v.

ใหญ่ yài big, large, great, adj.

ใหญ่โต yài-dtoo huge, enormous, adj.

ใหม่ mài new, fresh, adj.

ใหม่เอี่ยม mài-ìam brand new, adj.

ไห hǎi earthen jar, n.

ไห้ hâi cry, v.

ไหน nǎi which, where, adj., adv.

ไหม mǎi silk worm, n.

ไหม้ mâi burn, v.

ไหล lǎi flow, run, v.

ไหล lǎi eel, n.

ไหล่ lài shoulder, n.

ไหว wǎi shake, tremble, v.

ไหวตัว wǎi-dtua aware, adj.

ไหวพริบ wǎi-príp adroitness, n.

ไหว้ wâai salute by placing the hands palm against palm and raising them to the face, pay a respect, v.

พ

พ lɔɔ the forty-second consonant of the Thai alphabet (low consonant), *n.*

อ

อ ɔɔ the forty-third consonant of the Thai alphabet (mid consonant), *n.*

อก òk breast, chest, *n.*

อกหัก òk-hàk heart-broken, *adj.*

อกตัญญู a-gà-dtan-yuu ungrateful, *adj.*

อกุศล à-gù-sŏn evil, harmful, inauspicious, *adj.*

อคติ a-ká-dtì evil, deeds, partiality, *n.*

องค์ ong act, organ, part of the body, section, characteristic, *n.*

องค์การ ong-gaan organization, *n.*

องคชาต ong-ka-châat penis, *n.*

องค์ประกอบ ong-bprà-gɔ̀ɔp composition, *n.*

องศา ong-săa degree, *n.*

องอาจ ong-àat brave, *adj.*

องุ่น à-ngùn grape, *n.*

อณู à-nuu atom, *n.*

อด òt refrain, abstain from, fast, give up, *v.*

อดิเรก à-dì-rèek hobby, *n.*

อดีต à-dìit past, *adj.*

อธรรม à-tam evil, badness, *n.*

อธิการ à-tí-gaan abbot, superior, *n.*

อธิการบดี à-tí-gaan-bɔɔ-dii rector, *n.*

อธิบดี à-típ-bɔɔ-dii director general, head of a department, *n.*

อธิบาย à-tí-baai explain, *v.*

อธิปไตย à-típ-bpà-dtai sovereignty, *n.*

อธิษฐาน à-tìt-tăan pray, make a wish, *n.*

อนัตตา à-nát-dtaa soulless self, *n.*

อนาคต à-naa-kót future, *n.*

อนาจาร à-naa-jaan obscene, *adj.*

อนาถ à-nàat fool pity, *v.*

อนาถา à-naa-tăa having no support, *adj.*

อนาทร à-naa-tɔɔn worry about, *v.*

อนาธิปไตย à-naa-típ-bpà-dtai anarchy, *n.*

อนามัย à-naa-mai health, *n.*

อนารยะ à-naa-ra-yá uncivilized, *adj.*

อนิจจัง à-nít-jang uncertain, *adj.*

อนินทรีย์ à-nin-sii inorganic, *adj.*

อนึ่ง à-nùng besides, in addition to, *prep.*

ธ น บ ป ผ ฝ พ ฟ ภ ม ย ร ฤ ฦ ล ว ศ ษ ส ห ฬ อ ฮ

อนุกาชาด à-nú-gaa-châat junior Red Cross, *n.*

อนุประโยค à-nú-bprà-yòok subordinate clause, *n.*

อนุปริญญา à-nú-bpà-rin-yaa junior college, diploma, *n.*

อนุภรรยา à-nú-pan-ra-yaa minor wife, *n.*

อนุภาค à-nú-pâak particle, *n.*

อนุกรม à-nú-grom series, order, *n.*

อนุเคราะห์ à-nú-krɔ́ help, assist, *v.*

อนุชน à-nú-chon younger generation, *n.*

อนุชา à-nú-chaa one born after, *n.*

อนุญาต à-nú-yâat permit, *v.*

อนุบาล à-nú-baan kindergarten, *n.*

อนุภาพ à-nú-pâap knowledge, influence, *n.*

อนุมัติ à-nú-mát permit, approve, *v.*

อนุโมทนา à-nú-moo-ta-naa express gratitude, *v.*

อนุรักษ์ à-nú-rák conserve, *v.*

อนุโลม à-nú-loom compromise, *v.*

อนุสรณ์ à-nú-sɔ̌ɔn remembrance, *n.*

อนุสาวรีย์ à-nú-sǎo-wa-rii memorial, statue, monument, *n.*

อเนก à-nèek several, *adj.*

อบ òp perfume, *v.*

อบรม òp-rom instruct, *v.*

อบอ้าว òp-âao stuffy, *adj.*

อบอุ่น òp-ùn warm, *adj.*

อบเชย òp-chəəi cinnamon, *n.*

อบายมุข à-baai-ya-múk path of ruining one's self, *n.*

อพยพ òp-pa-yóp migrate, *v.*

อภัย à-pai forgive, pardon, *v.*

อภิธรรม à-pí-tam higher doctrine, *n.*

อภินันทนาการ à-pí-nan-ta-naa-gaan compliments, *n.*

อภินิหาร à-pí-ní-hǎan supernatural power, *n.*

อภิบาล à-pí-baan look after, *v.*

อภิปราย à-pí-bpraai debate, discuss, *v.*

อภิเษก à-pí-sèek royal wedding, *n.*

อภิสิทธิ์ à-pí-sìt privilege, *n.*

อม om keep in the mouth, *v.*

อมต am-ma-dtà immortal, *adj.*

อมนุษย์ à-ma-nút non-human being, ghost, *n.*

อมร à-mɔɔn immortal, *n.*

อเมริกา à-mee-ri-gaa America, *n.*

อย่า yàa forbid, prohibit, do not, *v.*

อยาก yàak want, desire, *v.*

อย่าง yàang kind, sort, *n.*

อยู่ yùu be, live, dwell, *v.*

อรหัง ɔɔ-ra-hǎng, a-ra-hǎng Buddha, *n.*

อรหันต์ ɔɔ ra-hǎn, a-ra-hǎn Buddha, *n.*

อร่อย à-rɔ̀i delicious, *adj.*

อร่าม à-ràam lustrous, *adj.*

อริ à-rì foe, enemy, *n.*

อริยะ à-rí-yá converted person, *n.*

อรุณ à-run red, dawn, *n.*

อลวน on-la-won confused, tumultuous, *adj.*

อดเวง on-la-weeng tumultuous, chaotic, *adj.*

อลหม่าน on-la-màan tumultuous, *adj.*

อลังการ à-lang-gaan decoration, adornment, *n.*

อล่างฉ่าง à-làang-chàang vivid, *adj.*

อโลหะ à-loo-hà non-metal matter, *n.*

อ้วก ûak vomit, *v.*

อวกาศ a-wa-gàat space, *n.*

อวด ùat boast, *v.*

อวดรู้ ùat-rúu think oneself smart, *v.*

อวตาร a-wa-dtaan descend from heaven, reincarnated, *v., adj.*

อวน uan purse net, *n.*

อ้วน ûan fat, plump, obese, *adj.*

อวบ ùap well-rounded, *adj.*

อ่วม ùam swelling, injured, *adj.*

อวมงคล à-wá-mong-kon inauspiciousness, *n.*

อวยชัย uai-chai wish (someone) success, *v.*

อวสาน a-wa-sǎan end, finish, *v.*

อวัยวะ à-wai-ya-wá organ, *n.*

อวิชชา à-wìt-chaa nascence, ignorance, *n.*

อเวจี à-wee-jii hell, *n.*

อโศก à-sòok not causing sorrow, *adj.*

อสรพิษ à-sɔ̌ɔ-ra-pít creatures with poisonous fangs, *n.*

อสังหาริมทรัพย์ à sǎng-hǎa-rim-ma-sáp immovable property, *n.*

อสัญญี à-sǎn-yii unconscious, *adj.*

อสัญญีแพทย์ à-sǎn-yii-pêɛt anesthetist, *n.*

อสุจิ à-sù-jì sperm, *n.*

อสูร à-sǔun giant, demon, *n.*

อหังการ à-hǎng-gaan proud, *adj.*

อหิงสา à-hǐng-sǎa nonviolence, *n.*

อโหสิ a-hǒo-sì forgive, *v.*

อ้อ ɔ̂ɔ reed, *n.*

Thai · Phonetic · English

ออก ɔ̀ɔk leave, go out, emit, *v.*

ออกกฎหมาย ɔ̀ɔk-gòt-mǎai legislate, make law, *v.*

ออกกำลังกาย ɔ̀ɔk-gam-lang-gaai exercise, *v.*

ออกไข่ ɔ̀ɔk-kài lay eggs, *v.*

ออกคำสั่ง ɔ̀ɔk-kam-sàng order, *v.*

อ่อเซาะ ɔɔ-rɔ́ impose on, wheedle, *v.*

อ่อน ɔ̀ɔn soft, feeble, tender, *adj.*

อ่อนเพลีย ɔ̀ɔn-plia weak, exhausted, *adj.*

อ่อนแอ ɔ̀ɔn-ɛɛ weak, *adj.*

อ้อน ɔ́ɔn whimper, implore, *v.*

ออม ɔɔm save, *v.*

อ้อม ɔ̂ɔm go by indirect, *v.*

อ้อมกอด ɔ̂ɔm-gɔ̀ɔt embrace, *n.*

อ่อย ɔ̀i lure, *v.*

อ้อย ɔ̂ɔi sugar cane, *n.*

อ๋อย ɔ̌i intense, bright, *adj.*

อะไร à-rai what, *adv.*

อะลุ้มอล่วย à-lúm-à-lùai conciliatory, meet half-way, *v.*

อักขระ àk-kà-rà letter of the alphabet, character, *n.*

อักษร àk-sɔ̌ɔn letter, *n.*

อักษรศาสตร์ àk-sɔ̌ɔn-sàat liberal arts, *n.*

อักเสบ àk-sèep inflamed, *adj.*

อัคคี àk-kii fire, *n.*

อัคคีภัย àk-kii-pai disaster caused by fire, *n.*

อังกฤษ ang-grìt English, England, *n.*

อังคาร ang-kaan Mars, Tuesday, *n.*

อั้งเปา âng-bpao red envelope, *n.*

อัจฉริยะ àt-cha-ri-yá prodigious, extraordinary, *adj.*

อัญเชิญ an-chəən invite, *v.*

อัญมณี an-yá-ma-nii precious stones, *n.*

อัฐ àt an obsolete unit of Thai currency, money, *n.*

อัณฑะ an-tá testicles, *n.*

อัด àt press, squeeze, compress, *v.*

อัดรูป àt-rûup print a photograph, *v.*

อัตโนมัติ àt-dtà-noo-mát automatic, *adj.*

อัตคัด àt-dtà-kát poor, needy, *adj.*

อัตรา àt-dtraa rate, *n.*

อัธยาศัย àt-ta-yaa-sǎi temperament, *n.*

อัน an piece, item, one, round, turn, classifier for various small things, *n.*

อันดับ an-dàp series, order, rank, *n.*

อันตรธาน an-dtrà-taan disappear, *v.*

อันตราย an-dtà-raai danger, harm, n.

อันธพาล an-ta-paan gangster, n.

อับ àp stale, musty, adj.

อับอาย àp-aai shameful, adj.

อับปาง àp-bpaang wrecked, adj.

อัปมงคล àp-bpà-mong-kon inauspicious, adj.

อัยการ ai-ya-gaan public prosecutor, district attorney, n.

อัศจรรย์ àt-sà-jan miraculous, adj.

อัศเจรีย์ àt-sà-jee-rii an exclamation mark, n.

อัศวิน àt-sà-win knight, n.

อา aa father's younger brother or sister, n.

อ้า âa open wide, expand, v.

อากร aa-gɔɔn revenue, tax, n.

อาการ aa-gaan symptom, sign, condition, n.

อากาศ aa-gàat air, n.

อาคม aa-kom magical incantation, n.

อาคาร aa-kaan building, n.

อาฆาต aa-kàat seek revenge, v.

อ่าง àang bowl, basin, tub, n.

อ้าง âang refer to, quote, v.

อ้างว่า âang-wâa allege, assert, v.

อ้างอิง âang-ing refer, v.

อาจ àat brave, bold, adj.

อาจารย์ aa-jaan teacher, instructor, professor, n.

อาจิณ aa-jin regular, adj.

อาเจียน aa-jian vomit, v.

อาชญา àat-cha-yaa crime, n.

อาชญากร àat-cha-yaa-gɔɔn criminal, n.

อาชญากรรม àat-cha-yaa-gam crime, n.

อาชีพ aa-chîip occupation, n.

อาณาเขต aa-naa-kèet boundary, n.

อาณานิคม aa-naa-ní-kom colony, n.

อาตมา àat-dtà-maa (for monks) I, me, myself, pron.

อาทร aa-tɔɔn care, v.

อาทิ aa-tí example, instance, n.

อาทิตย์ aa-tít sun, week, n.

อาน aan saddle, n.

อ่าน àan read, think, v.

อานิสงส์ aa-ní-sŏng good result, n.

อานุภาพ aa-nú-pâap power, n.

อาบ àap bathe, soak, v.

อาบัติ aa-bàt violation, n.

อาพาธ aa-pâat illness, suffering, n.

อาเพศ aa-pêet abnormal, adj.

อาภรณ์ aa-pɔɔn adornments, n.

อาภัพ aa-páp unfortunate, *adj.*

อาย aai ashamed, *adj.*

อ้าย âai eldest son, elder brother, *n.*

อายัด aa-yát attach (property), consign to custody, deactivate, *v.*

อายุ aa-yú age, lifetime, *n.*

อายุความ aa-yú-kwaam statute of limitations, *n.*

อารมณ์ aa-rom mood, feeling, temper, *n.*

อารยชน aa-ra-yá-chon civilized people, *n.*

อารักขา aa-rák-kǎa care, protect, *v.*

อาราธนา aa-râat-ta-naa request, *v.*

อาราม aa-raam temple, *n.*

อารี aa-rii generous, *adj.*

อาละวาด aa-la-wâat disturb, *v.*

อาลัย aa-lai miss, think about, deplore the loss of, *v.*

อ่าว àao bay, gulf, *n.*

อ้าว âao sultry, muggy, hot, *adj.*

อาวรณ์ aa-wɔɔn long for, *v.*

อาวาส aa-wâat temple, monastery, *n.*

อาวุธ aa-wút weapon, arms, *n.*

อาวุโส aa-wú-sǒo seniority, *n.*

อาศรม aa-sǒm hermitage, *n.*

อาศัย aa-sǎi dwell, live, reside, *v.*

อาสนะ àat-sà-ná seat, *n.*

อาสัญญ์ aa-sǎn die, *v.*

อาสา aa-sǎa volunteer, *v.*

อาหาร aa-hǎan food, nutrition, *n.*

อำ am hide, conceal, *v.*

อำนวย am-nuai give, produce, *v.*

อำนาจ am-nâat power, authority, right, force, *n.*

อำพัน am-pan amber, *n.*

อำเภอ am-pəə district, *n.*

อำมหิต am-ma-hìt cruel, savage, *adj.*

อิง ing lean on, *v.*

อิจฉา ìt-chǎa envious, jealous, *adj.*

อิฐ ìt brick, *n.*

อิดโรย ìt-rooi tired, *adj.*

อิทธิ ìt-tí power, *n.*

อินทรี in-sii eagle, *n.*

อินทรีย์ in-sii power, organism, *n.*

อิ่ม ìm fully satisfied, full, *adj.*

อิ่มตัว ìm-dtua saturated, *adj.*

อิริยาบท ì-rí-yaa-bòt bodily movement, *n.*

อิสระ ìt-sà-rà free, liberal, *adj.*

อิสรภาพ ìt-sà-ra-pâap freedom, *n.*

อิเหนา i-nǎo Indonesia(n), *n.*

อีก ìik again, more, *adj., adv.*

อีก้อ ii-gɔ̂ɔ name of a hil tribe in northern Thailand, Karen tribe, *n.*

อีกา ii-gaa crow, *n.*

อีเก้ง ii-gêeng barking deer, *n.*

อีตัว ii-dtua whore, prostitute, *n.*

อีโต้ ii-dtôo cleaver, *n.*

อีสาน ii-sǎan northeast, *n.*

อีสุกอีใส ii-sùk-ii-sǎi chicken-pox, *n.*

อี่ ì pass (collq.) fecal matter, feces, *v.,*
n.

อึกทึก ùk-gà-túk noisy, boisterous, *adj.*

อึกอัก ùk-àk hesitating, unable to
speak, *adj.*

อึ่ง ùng bull-fog, *n.*

อึ่งอ่าง ùng-àang bull-fog, *n.*

อึ้ง ûng silent, speechless, *adj.*

อึด ùt suppress, persist, persevere, *v.*

อึดอัด ùt-àt feel uncomfortable, *adj.*

อืด ùut swollen, sluggish, *adj.*

อืดอาด ùut-àat slow-moving, *adj.*

อื่น ùun other, different, opposite, *adj.*

อื้อ ûu noisy, loud, *adj.*

อุจจาระ ùt-jaa-rá feces, *n.*

อุจาด ù-jàat shameless, lewd, *adj.*

อุณหภูมิ un-na-hà-puum temperature,
n.

อุด ùt plug, *v.*

อุดหนุน ùt-nǔn support, *v.*

อุดอู้ ùt-ûu stuffy, *adj.*

อุดม ù-dom abundant, plentiful, *adj.*

อุดมคติ ù-dom-ká-dtì ideal, *n.*

อุดมศึกษา ù-dom-sùk-sǎa higher
education, *n.*

อุดร ù-dɔɔn the north, *n.*

อุตริ ù-dtà-rì unconventional, unusual,
weird, *adj.*

อุตลุด ùt-dtà-lùt hurried, tumultuous,
adj.

อุตสาหะ ùt-sǎa-hà industry, endeavor,
n.

อุตสาหกรรม ùt-sǎa-hà-gam industry,
n.

อุตส่าห์ ùt-sàa attempt, *v.*

อุตุนิยม ù-dtù-ní-yom meteorology, *n.*

อุทธรณ์ ùt-tɔɔn appeal, *v.*

อุทยาน ùt-ta-yaan garden, park,
national park, *n.*

อุทัย ù-tai rising sun, *n.*

อุทาน ù-taan interjection, exclamation,
n.

อุทาหรณ์ ù-taa-hɔ̌ɔn illustration, *n.*

อุทิศ ù-tít dedicate, devote, *v.*

อุ่น ùn warm, *v.*

อุบัติ ù-bàt happen, occur, *v.*

อุบาทว์ ù-bàat wicked, evil, *adj.*

อุบาย ù-baai trick, *n.*

Thai · Phonetic · English

อุบาสก ù-baa-sòk devout layman, *n.*

อุบาสิกา ù-baa-sì-gaa devout lay-
woman, *n.*

อุเบกขา ù-bèek-kǎa equanimity,
impartiality, *n.*

อุโบสถ ù-boo-sòt Buddhist building, *n.*

อุปกรณ์ ùp-bpà-gɔɔn equipment,
apparatus, *n.*

อุปการะ ùp-bpà-gaa-rá patronize,
assist, *v.*

อุปการี ùp-bpà-gaa-rii benefactor, *n.*

อุปถัมภ์ ùp-bpà-tǎm support, *v.*

อุปทูต ùp-bpa-tûut chargé d'affaires,
n.

อุปนายก ùp-bpà-naa-yók Vice
President, *n.*

อุปนิสัย ùp-bpà-ní-sǎi character,
virtue, *n.*

อุปโภค ùp-bpà-pôok eat, consume, *v.*

อุปมา ùp-bpà-maa analogy, *n.*

อุปราคา ùp-bpà-raa-kaa eclipse, *n.*

อุปสมบท ùp-bpà-sǒm-bòt ordained
as a Buddhist monk, *adj.*

อุปสรรค ùp-bpà-sàk barrier, obstacle,
n.

อุปัชฌาย์ ù-bpàt-chaa spiritual
teacher, *n.*

อุปาทาน ù-bpà-taan bias, prejudice,
adhere(nce) to wrong beliefs, *n., v.*

อุ้ม ûm carry in one's arms, *v.*

อุ้มท้อง ûm-tɔ́ɔng pregnant, *adj.*

อุโมงค์ ù-moong tunnel, *n.*

อุรา ù-raa chest, breast, *n.*

อู่ ùu dock, harbor, cradle, *n.*

อู่รถ ùu-rót garage, *n.*

อู่เรือ ùu-rɯa dock, *n.*

อู้งาน ûu-ngaan work with unnecessary delay, *v.*

อูฐ ùut camel, *n.*

อูม uum swelling, *adj.*

เอก èek sole, solitary, alone, chief,
first, prime, first-class, *adj.*

เอกฉันท์ èek-gà-chǎn unanimous,
adj.

เอกชน èek-gà-chon individual, *n.*

เอกพจน์ èek-gà-pót singular number,
n.

เอกราช èek-gà-râat independent, *adj.*

เอกสาร èek-gà-sǎan document, *n.*

เอง eeng alone, self, *adj.*

เอ็ง eng you, thou, *pron.*

เอ็ดตะโร èt-dtà-roo boisterous, *adj.*

เอน een lean, slant, recline, *v.*

เอ็น en tendon, sinew, *n.*

เอ็นดู en-duu have compassion for, care for, *v.*

เอ่ย ɔ̀əi utter, *v.*

เอ่ยถึง ɔ̀əi-tʉ̌ng refer to, speak of, *v.*

เอราวัณ ee-raa-wan three-headed elephant, *n.*

เอว eeo waist, *n.*

เออ əə particle expressing assent, agreement, *adj.*

เอ่อ ə̀ə flooded, *adj.*

เอะอะ è-à boisterous, *adj.*

เอา ao want, take, hold, bring, *v.*

เอาคืน ao-kʉʉn take back, *v.*

เอาจริง ao-jing serious, *adj.*

เอียง iang slant, *v.*

เอียน ian too sweet, sickishly sweet, too oily, *adj.*

เอี่ยม ìam fresh, *adj.*

เอี๊ยม íam a kind of apron, *n.*

เอี่ยว ìao ace, first, *adj.*

เอี้ยว îao twist, turn, *v.*

เอื้อเฟื้อ ʉ̂a-fʉ́a help, assist, *v.*

เอื้อน ʉ̂an draw out the voice or sounds, *v.*

เอือม ʉam fed up, *adj.*

เอือมระอา ʉam-rá-aa fed up with, *adj.*

เอื้อม ʉ̂am reach for, *v.*

เอื่อย ʉ̀ai slowly, *adv.*

เอื้อย ʉ̂ai eldest sister, eldest child, *n.*

แอก ɛ̀ɛk yoke, *n.*

แอ่ง ɛ̀ng basin, pool, pond, *n.*

แอ่น ɛ̀n bend the body backward, *v.*

แอบ ɛ̀ɛp hide, conceal, sneak, *v.*

แอ่ว ɛ̀o go wooing women, *v.*

โอ่ òo brag, boast, *v.*

โอ้โลม ôo-loom console, woo, *v.*

โอ้อวด ôo-ùat boast, brag, *v.*

โอ๋ ǒo console, soothe, comfort, *v.*

โอกาส oo-gàat opportunity, fortune, chance, *n.*

โอ๊ค óok oak tree, *n.*

โอ.เค oo-kee O.K., *adj., v.*

โอ่ง òong water-jar, *n.*

โอด òot cry, weep, *v.*

โอน oon transfer, incline, *v.*

โอนกรรมสิทธิ์ oon-gam-ma-sìt transfer ownership, *v.*

โอนสัญชาติ oon-sǎn-châat change one's nationality, *v.*

โอนเอน oon-een swaying, *adj.*

โอบ òop embrace, *v.*

โอย ooi ouch, *interj.*

โอรส oo-rót son (used only for royalty), *n.*

โอวาท oo-wâat advice, teaching, *n.*

โอสถ oo-sòt drugs, remedies, *n.*

โอหัง oo-hǎng arrogant, haughty, *adj.*

โอฬาร oo-laan enormous, *adj.*

โอ่อ่า òo-àa dignified and pretty, *adj.*

โอ้เอ้ ôo-êe linger, loiter, *v.*

ไอ ai vapor, gas, steam, *n.*

ไอ ai cough, *v.*

ไอ้ âi a derogatory title used with first names of men and also for insult, *n.*

ไอศกรีม ai-sà-griim ice-cream, *n.*

ไอสครีม ai-sà-kriim ice-cream, *n.*

ไอศวรรย์ ai-sǔan monarchy, *n.*

ไอโอดีน ai-oo-diin iodine, *n.*

ฮ

ฮ hɔɔ the forty-fourth consonant of the Thai alphabet (low consonant), *n.*

ฮวงซุ้ย huang-súi Chinese cemetery, *n.*

ฮวบ hûap collapse, *v.*

ฮ่วย hûai sound expressing surprise and upset, *interj.*

ฮ่อ hɔ̀ɔ gallop, *v.*

ฮ่องเต้ hɔ̂ng-dtêe Chinese emperor, *n.*

ฮอร์โมน hɔɔ-moon hormone, *n.*

ฮะ há a variant of "yes", *adv., part.*

ฮัก hák love, *v.*

ฮา haa laugh, *v.*

ฮินดู hin-duu Hindus, *n.*

ฮิปโป híp-bpoo hippopotamus, *n.*

ฮึด hút make up one's mind to fight, *v.*

ฮึม hʉm echoing, *adj.*

ฮือ hʉʉ burn violently, rush in, *v.*

ฮือฮา hʉʉ-haa hilarious, *adj.*

ฮุบ húp seize, *v.*

ฮูก hûuk a species of owl, *n.*

เฮ hee flock together, *v.*

เฮโล hee-loo flock in large numbers, *v.*

เฮง heng fortunate, lucky, *adj.*

เฮงซวย heng-suai fortunate and unfortunate, bad, *adj.*

เฮ่ย hôi onomatopoeia from the sound used to call attention, *interj.*

เฮโรอีน hee-roo-iin heroin, *n.*

แฮม hem ham, *n.*

โฮ hoo onomatopoeia from the sound produced by crying aloud, *interj.*

ไฮโดรเจน hai-droo-jên hydrogen, *n.*

ไฮโล hai-loo a kind of gambling played with dice, *n.*

APPENDIX

COMMON CLASSIFIERS

an	(อัน)	pieces of candy, ashtrays, round objects, objects with unknown classifiers
bai	(ใบ)	glasses, cups, fruits, plates, bottles, boxes, bags, eggs, sheets of paper, containers
baan	(บาน)	windows, mirrors, doors
bòt	(บท)	lessons, poems, stanzas, verses
chà-bàp	(ฉบับ)	newspapers, letters, documents
chán	(ชั้น)	floors of buildings, grades or classes in schools, classes of train or airplane seats
chín	(ชิ้น)	pieces of bread, pieces of meat, cookies etc.
chút	(ชุด)	sets of things, suits, dresses
chûak	(เชือก)	elephants
dâam	(ด้าม)	pens
dɔ̀ɔk	(ดอก)	flowers
dtôn	(ต้น)	trees
dtua	(ตัว)	animals, tables, chairs, shirts, costumes, letters of the alphabet, dolls, cigarettes, etc.
duang	(ดวง)	stamps, stars, suns, moons

fɔɔng	(ฟอง)	eggs
fǔung	(ฝูง)	flock of animals
gɛ̂ɛo	(แก้ว)	numbers of glasses of beer, water, etc.
glɔ̀ng	(กล่อง)	parcels, presents
gɔ̂ɔn	(ก้อน)	bars of soap, sugar cubes, pieces of candy, etc.
hɔ̂ng	(ห้อง)	rooms
hɔ̀ɔ	(ห่อ)	presents, bags of sweets, bags of snacks, wrapped things
jaan	(จาน)	numbers of plates of rice, food, etc.
kan	(คัน)	cars, motorcycles, bicycles, spoons, forks, umbrellas, fishing rods
kâang	(ข้าง)	each side, e.g. arm, leg, front, back
kon	(คน)	people
krûang	(เครื่อง)	radio, T.Vs., refrigerators, computers, electrical or mechanical machines
kráng	(ครั้ง)	times (numbers of occurrences).
kùat	(ขวด)	numbers of bottles of beer, water, etc.
kûu	(คู่)	pairs of things or people
lam	(ลำ)	ships, boats, airplanes
lǎng	(หลัง)	houses, buildings
lao	(เลา)	flutes

lêm	(เล่ม)	books, magazines, knives, candles, needles, carts
lûuk	(ลูก)	fruits, mountains, balls and other round things
muan	(มวน)	cigarettes
múan	(ม้วน)	rolls of film, casette tapes, video tapes
pèn	(แผ่น)	boards, pieces of paper
pleeng	(เพลง)	songs
pǒn	(ผล)	fruits
pǔun	(ผืน)	carpets, towels, pieces of cloth
rá lɔ̌ɔk	(ระลอก)	waves
rûup	(รูป)	pictures
rɯan	(เรือน)	clocks, watches
rɯ̂ang	(เรื่อง)	movies, plays, stories
sǎai	(สาย)	roads, rivers, canals, railways
sên	(เส้น)	threads, neckties, tires, necklaces, bracelets, roads, hairs
sɔɔng	(ซอง)	packages, packs, etc.
tɛ̂ng	(แท่ง)	pencils, pieces of chalk
tîi	(ที่)	numbers of dishes, cups, seats
tûai	(ถ้วย)	numbers of cups of tea, soup, coffee, etc.
wong	(วง)	rings, circles
yàang	(อย่าง)	kinds of things, numbers of things

COLORS

color	sǐi	สี
black	sǐi dam	สีดำ
brown	sǐi náam-dtaan	สีน้ำตาล
dark blue	sǐi náam-ngən	สีน้ำเงิน
gold	sǐi tɔɔng	สีทอง
green	sǐi kǐao	สีเขียว
grey	sǐi tao	สีเทา
indigo	sǐi kraam	สีคราม
khaki	sǐi gaa-gǐi	สีกากี
light blue	sǐi fáa	สีฟ้า
pink	sǐi chom-puu	สีชมพู
purple	sǐi mûang	สีม่วง
orange	sǐi sôm	สีส้ม
red	sǐi dɛɛng	สีแดง
silver	sǐi ngən	สีเงิน
white	sǐi kǎao	สีขาว
yellow	sǐi lǔang	สีเหลือง

NUMBERS

0	sǔun	ศูนย์
1	nùng	หนึ่ง
2	sɔ̌ɔng	สอง
3	sǎam	สาม
4	sìi	สี่
5	hâa	ห้า
6	hòk	หก
7	jèt	เจ็ด
8	bpὲεt	แปด
9	gâao	เก้า
10	sìp	สิบ
11	sìp-èt	สิบเอ็ด
12	sìp-sɔ̌ɔng	สิบสอง
13	sìp-sǎam	สิบสาม
20	yîi-sìp	ยี่สิบ
21	yîi-sìp-èt	ยี่สิบเอ็ด
22	yîi-sìp-sɔ̌ɔng	ยี่สิบสอง
30	sǎam-sìp	สามสิบ
31	sǎam-sìp-èt	สามสิบเอ็ด
32	sǎam-sìp-sɔ̌ɔng	สามสิบสอง

40	sìi-sìp	สี่สิบ
50	hâa-sìp	ห้าสิบ
60	hòk-sìp	หกสิบ
70	jèt-sìp	เจ็ดสิบ
80	bpèɛt-sìp	แปดสิบ
90	gâao-sìp	เก้าสิบ
100	(nùng) rɔ́ɔi	(หนึ่ง) ร้อย
200	sɔ̌ɔng-rɔ́ɔi	สองร้อย
300	sǎam-rɔ́ɔi	สามร้อย
1,000	(nùng) pan	(หนึ่ง) พัน
2,000	sɔ̌ɔng-pan	สองพัน
3,000	sǎam-pan	สามพัน
10,000	(nùng) mùun	(หนึ่ง) หมื่น
100,000	(nùng) sɛ̌ɛn	(หนึ่ง) แสน
1,000,000	(nùng) láan	(หนึ่ง) ล้าน
10,000,000	sìp-láan	สิบล้าน
100,000,000	(nùng) rɔ́ɔi-láan	(หนึ่ง) ร้อยล้าน
1,000,000,000	(nùng) pan-láan	(หนึ่ง) พันล้าน
10,000,000,000	(nùng) mùun-láan	(หนึ่ง) หมื่นล้าน
100,000,000,000	(nùng) sɛ̌ɛn-láan	(หนึ่ง) แสนล้าน
1,000,000,000,000	(nùng) láan-láan	(หนึ่ง) ล้านล้าน

DAYS OF THE WEEK

day	wan	วัน
Sunday	wan-aa-tít	วันอาทิตย์
Monday	wan-jan	วันจันทร์
Tuesday	wan-ang-kaan	วันอังคาร
Wednesday	wan-pút	วันพุธ
Thursday	wan-pá-rú-hàt	วันพฤหัส
Friday	wan-sùk	วันศุกร์
Saturday	wan-săo	วันเสาร์
holiday	wan-yùt	วันหยุด
weekend	săo-aa-tít	เสาร์อาทิตย์

MONTHS

month	dɰan	เดือน
January	má-gà-raa (kom)	มกรา (คม)
February	gum-paa (pan)	กุมภา (พันธ์)
March	mii-naa (kom)	มีนา (คม)
April	mee-sǎa (yon)	เมษา (ยน)
May	prút-sà-paa (kom)	พฤษภา (คม)
June	mí-tù-naa (yon)	มิถุนา (ยน)
July	gà-rá-gà-daa (kom)	กรกฎา (คม)
August	sǐng-hǎa (kom)	สิงหา (คม)
September	gan-yaa (yon)	กันยา (ยน)
October	dtù-laa (kom)	ตุลา (คม)
November	prút-sà-jì-gaa (yon)	พฤศจิกา (ยน)
December	tan-waa (kom)	ธันวา (คม)

THE TWELVE YEAR CYCLE

ปีชวด / ปีหนู	Year of the Rat	bpii-chûat/bpii-nŭu
ปีฉลู / ปีวัว	Year of the Ox	bpii-chà-lǔu/bpii-wua
ปีขาล / ปีเสือ	Year of the Tiger	bpii-kăan/bpii-sŭa
ปีเถาะ / ปีกระต่าย	Year of the Rabbit	bpii-tɔ̀/bpii-grà-dtàai
ปีมะโรง / ปีงูใหญ่	Year of the Dragon	bpii-má-roong/bpii-nguu-yài
ปีมะเส็ง / ปีงูเล็ก	Year of the Snake	bpii-má-sĕng/bpii-nguu-lék
ปีมะเมีย / ปีม้า	Year of the Horse	bpii-má-mia/bpii-máa
ปีมะแม / ปีแพะ	Year of the Goat	bpii-má-mɛɛ/bpii-pé
ปีวอก / ปีลิง	Year of the Monkey	bpii-wɔ̂ɔk/bpii-ling
ปีระกา / ปีไก่	Year of the Chicken	bpii-rá-gaa/bpii-gài
ปีจอ / ปีหมา	Year of the Dog	bpii-jɔɔ/bpii-măa
ปีกุน / ปีหมู	Year of the Pig	bpii-gun/bpii-mǔu

THE 76 PROVINCES OF THAILAND

1.	กรุงเทพ (มหานคร)	grung-têep (má-hǎa-ná-kɔɔn)
2.	กระบี่	grà-bìi
3.	กาญจนบุรี	gaan-jà-ná-bù-rii
4.	กาฬสินธุ์	gaa-lá-sǐn
5.	กำแพงเพชร	gam-pɛɛng-pét
6.	ขอนแก่น	kɔ̌n-gèn
7.	จันทบุรี	jan-tá-bù-rii
8.	ฉะเชิงเทรา	chà-chəəng-sao
9.	ชลบุรี	chon-bù-rii
10.	ชัยภูมิ	chai-yá-puum
11.	เชียงใหม่	chiang-mài
12.	เชียงราย	chiang-raai
13.	ชุมพร	chum-pɔɔn
14.	ชัยนาท	chai-nâat
15.	ตราด	dtràat
16.	ตาก	dtàak
17.	ตรัง	dtrang
18.	นครราชสีมา	ná-kɔɔn-râat-chá-sǐi-maa
19.	นครนายก	ná-kɔɔn-naa-yók
20.	นครพนม	ná-kɔɔn-pá-nom
21.	นครปฐม	ná-kɔɔn-bpà-tǒm
22.	นครศรีธรรมราช	ná-kɔɔn-sǐi-tammá-râat
23.	นครสวรรค์	ná-kɔɔn-sà-wǎn
24.	นนทบุรี	non-tá-bù-rii

25. นราธิวาส	ná-raa-tí-wâat
26. น่าน	nâan
27. บุรีรัมย์	bù-rii-ram
28. ปทุมธานี	bpà-tum-taa-nii
29. ปราจีนบุรี	bpraa-jiin-bù-rii
30. ประจวบคีรีขันธ์	bprà-jùap-kii-rii-kǎn
31. ปัตตานี	bpàt-dtaa-nii
32. พะเยา	pá-yao
33. แพร่	prɛ̂ɛ
34. พิจิตร	pí-jìt
35. พิษณุโลก	pít-sà-nú-lôok
36. เพชรบูรณ์	pét-chá-buun
37. เพชรบุรี	pét-chá-bù-rii, pét-bù-rii
38. พังงา	pang-ngaa
39. พัทลุง	pát-tá-lung
40. ภูเก็ต	puu-gèt
41. มุกดาหาร	múk-daa-hǎan
42. มหาสารคาม	má-hǎa-sǎa-rá-kaam
43. แม่ฮ่องสอน	mɛ̂ɛ-hông-sɔ̌ɔn
44. ยโสธร	yá-sǒo-tɔɔn
45. ยะลา	yá laa
46. ร้อยเอ็ด	rɔ́ɔi-èt
47. ระนอง	rá-nɔɔng
48. ระยอง	rá-yɔɔng
49. ราชบุรี	râat-chá-bù-rii, râat-bù-rii
50. ลพบุรี	lóp-bù-rii

51.	ลำปาง	lam-bpaang
52.	ลำพูน	lam-puun
53.	เลย	ləəi
54.	ศรีสะเกษ	sĭi-sà-gèet
55.	สกลนคร	sà-gonná-kɔɔn
56.	สงขลา	sŏng-klăa
57.	สตูล	sà-dtuun
58.	สมุทรปราการ	sà-mùt-bpraa-gaan
59.	สมุทรสงคราม	sà-mùt-sŏng-kraam
60.	สมุทรสาคร	sà-mùt-săa-kɔɔn
61.	สระแก้ว	sà-gɛ̂ɛo
62.	สระบุรี	sà-rà-bù-rii
63.	สิงห์บุรี	sĭng-bù-rii
64.	สุโขทัย	sù-kŏo-tai
65.	สุพรรณบุรี	sù-pan-bù-rii
66.	สุราษฎร์ธานี	sù-râat-taa-nii
67.	สุรินทร์	sù-rin
68.	หนองคาย	nɔ̆ɔng-kaai
69.	หนองบัวลำภู	nɔ̆ɔng-bua-lampuu
70.	อยุธยา	à-yút-tá-yaa
71.	อ่างทอง	àang-tɔɔng
72.	อุบลราชธานี	ù-bon-râat-chá-taa-nii
73.	อุทัยธานี	ù-tai-taa-nii
74.	อุดรธานี	ù-dɔɔn-taa-nii
75.	อุตรดิตถ์	ùt-dtà-rá-dìt
76.	อำนาจเจริญ	am-nâat-jà-rəən

THAI-ENGLISH ENGLISH-THAI DICTIONARY
FOR PALM OS® PDAS

-- WITH SEARCH-BY-SOUND™ --

Travelling to Thailand? Learning the Thai Language? Imagine having instant access to 21,000 English, Phonetic, and Thai words right on your Palm OS® PDA, with large, clear fonts and everyday vocabulary. If you're not familiar with the Thai alphabet, you can also look up Thai words by their sound. Perfect for the casual traveller or the dedicated Thai learner.

This Thai-English English-Thai Dictionary for Palm OS® PDAs...

☐ is software which runs on Palm OS® PDAs.
☐ has approximately 21,000 words
  (about 9,000 English, 6,000 phonetic and 6,000 Thai).
☐ has four crisp font sizes.
☐ is useful for people who know the Thai alphabet and
  those who don't.
☐ has three sections - just like the paper dictionary.
☐ can be used to look up a word by its "sound" without
  knowing the Thai alphabet.
☐ supports all Palm OS® devices with Palm OS® 3.5
  or greater, including devices from Palm, Inc.,
  Handspring, Sony, IBM, and Kyocera.
☐ has a convenient, optional on-screen keyboard for
  entering English, Phonetic, and Thai
☐ is completely standalone: does not require "Thai
  enablers" or any other third-party software.
☐ is fast for searching words: usually only need to tap in
  a few letters of your word.
☐ takes advantage of high-density Palm OS® devices by
  providing extra-crisp fonts.
☐ is very user-friendly.

Available by download or CD-ROM. Please check for
prices on our web site at www.paiboonpublishing.com.

Developed by Paiboon Publishing and Word in the Hand™ Inc.